U0934121

Codification Series of
Extraterritorial
Notarization Law

域外公证法
汇编系列

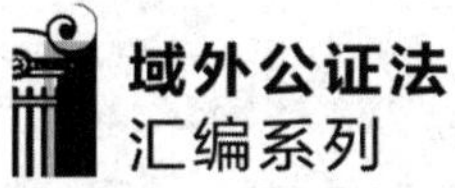

亚洲公证法汇编

COMPENDIUM OF ASIAN NOTARY LAWS

苏国强　汤庆发　刘志云 / 编

厦门大学出版社
XIAMEN UNIVERSITY PRESS
国家一级出版社
全国百佳图书出版单位

图书在版编目(CIP)数据

亚洲公证法汇编/苏国强,汤庆发,刘志云编.—厦门:厦门大学出版社，2020.7

(域外公证法汇编系列)

ISBN 978-7-5615-7482-9

Ⅰ.①亚… Ⅱ.①苏… ②汤… ③刘… Ⅲ.①公证法—汇编—亚洲 Ⅳ.①D930.66

中国版本图书馆 CIP 数据核字(2020)第 122480 号

出 版 人 郑文礼
责任编辑 李　宁
装帧设计 李夏凌
技术编辑 许克华

出版发行 厦门大学出版社
社　　址 厦门市软件园二期望海路 39 号
邮政编码 361008
总　　机 0592-2181111　0592-2181406(传真)
营销中心 0592-2184458　0592-2181365
网　　址 http://www.xmupress.com
邮　　箱 xmup@xmupress.com
印　　刷 厦门集大印刷厂

开本 787 mm×1 092 mm　1/16
印张 55
字数 2020 千字
版次 2020 年 7 月第 1 版
印次 2020 年 7 月第 1 次印刷
定价 388.00 元

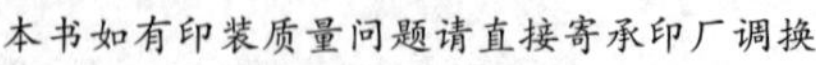

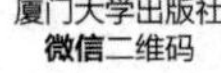
厦门大学出版社
微信二维码

厦门大学出版社
微博二维码

苏国强

一级公证员，现任福建省厦门市鹭江公证处党委书记、主任，厦门大学现代法律服务研究中心理事。主要社会职务有：福建省人大代表、厦门市人大代表、厦门市人大监察与司法委员会副主任、中国公证协会常务理事、中国公证协会信息化建设委员会主任委员、福建省公证协会监事长、厦门市公证协会会长、厦门市总商会副会长、厦门市政府立法咨询专家、厦门市仲裁委员会仲裁员。发表专业论文数十篇，共同主编《域外公证法汇编》《欧洲公证法汇编》《美洲公证法汇编》《公证信息化：理论前沿与技术规范》《“大家”之言——厦门市鹭江公证处成立十五周年名人传经讲座实录》《市场经济与公证立法》等。先后获得“全国优秀公证员”“福建省十佳公证员”“福建省公证行业文明公证员”“厦门市优秀社会主义事业建设者”“厦门市第四批、第五批、第九批拔尖人才”“厦门市直机关优秀共产党员”“2011—2015年厦门市法治宣传教育先进个人”“厦门市非公企业和社会组织党建领军人才”等荣誉。

汤庆发

一级公证员，现任福建省厦门市鹭江公证处党委副书记、副主任，厦门大学现代法律服务研究中心理事。主要社会职务有：福建省公证协会常务理事、福建省公证协会业务指导委员会主任委员、厦门仲裁委员会仲裁员。发表《公证机构“不以营利为目的”探析》《新型公证业务展望》《论公证权的性质》《论公证权的监督制约》《论公证程序的价值》《公证审查程序的证据规则》《商事财产在继承公证实务中的认定》《论赠与公证之存废》《论不动产登记中的“共同申请”之突破》等专业论文十余篇；共同主编《域外公证法汇编》《欧洲公证法汇编》《美洲公证法汇编》《“大家”之言——厦门市鹭江公证处成立十五周年名人传经讲座实录》等。先后获得“厦门市创建全国文明城市先进个人”“厦门市精神文明建设积极分子”“厦门市司法行政系统先进工作者”“厦门市直机关创先争优活动优秀党务工作者”“厦门市直机关优秀共产党员”“厦门市劳动模范”“全国优秀公证员”“新时代最美法律服务人特别提名奖”等荣誉。

刘志云

法学博士，现为厦门大学法学院教授、博士生导师，厦门大学现代法律服务研究中心执行主任，全国青联委员。至今已在《中国社会科学》等国内外杂志发表法学论文150余篇，出版个人专著5部，合著/译著10余部。先后入选“教育部新世纪优秀人才支持计划”、中组部“万人计划”。先后被评为“福建省优秀青年社会科学专家”“福建省优秀青年法学人才”“福建省法学英才”。

前言

随着社会经济、互联网技术，尤其是互联网金融的迅猛发展，公证业务，尤其是电子公证将有着广泛的应用空间。但对于这一新生事物，需要在法律、政策以及技术等问题上实现一系列的突破，并进行长期跟踪研究。由此，厦门大学、福建省厦门市鹭江公证处与法信公证云（厦门）科技有限公司在2014年6月达成共同发起成立“厦门大学公证法律与信息化研究中心”（以下简称研究中心）的共识。研究中心在2014年7月正式成立。研究中心是致力于公证法以及相关法律政策、电子公证以及信息化等相关领域的跨学科研究基地。2018年11月，为了更好地适应全面依法治国、深化司法改革的新要求，积极应对科技革命给法律服务行业带来的机遇和挑战，合作各方在总结实践经验的基础上，以更开阔的视野、更高的格局、面向未来的目标，调整研究中心的定位和发展方向，并决定将其更名为“厦门大学现代法律服务研究中心”。研究中心将在今后工作中始终坚持“产学研”一体化发展道路，充分凝聚合作各方力量，广泛借助政府、社会、教学科研资源，建立多领域、多层次的良性互动合作机制，聚力打造“服务高校、服务行业、服务社会”三位一体的功能格局。

长期以来，国内对公证领域的研究较少，尤其是缺乏一部比较全面与最新的域外公证法律汇编，供理论研究者与实务人员参考。鉴于此，在福建省厦门市鹭江公证处、法信公证云（厦门）科技有限公司的支持下，研究中心理事会原理事长、现理事苏国强先生，理事汤庆发先生，以及研究中心执行主任刘志云教授牵头成立了专门的“域外公证法律汇编系列”项目组。在2015年，项目组组织翻译与编写了《域外公证法律汇编》一书，并于2015年10月由法律出版社出版。该书出版后，引起公证行业的轰动，填补了公证理论研究与实务部门的一个空缺。短短两个月，该书就脱销，产生良好的学术价值与社会意义。在此基础上，研究中心与项目组计划在未来的几年，投入更多的人力物力，将更专门化的《欧洲公证法汇编》《美洲公证法汇编》《非洲公证法汇编》《亚洲公证法汇编》等逐一编译出版，为公证行业的发展贡献绵薄之力。呈现在读者面前的这本《亚洲公证法汇编》正是研究中心与项目组在2019年主要投入与产出的成果之一。

苏国强、汤庆发、刘志云等进行了本书的策划、组织、分工、讨论、协调、统稿、校对等工作。其中，各个部分翻译分工如下（排名不分先后）：厦门大学赵一旭负责翻译塞浦路斯、尼泊尔、阿曼、巴基斯坦、东帝汶、土库曼斯坦等国公证法律制度；厦门大学罗捷负责翻译阿联酋、柬埔寨、孟加拉国、哈萨克斯坦等国公证法律制度；厦门大学杨彦龙负责翻译印度尼西亚等国公证法律制度；厦门大学肖一负责翻译乌兹别克斯坦公证法律制度；厦门大学杨彦龙、杨皖宁、林钰钧合译了亚美尼亚公证法律制度；厦门大学黄真真负责翻译土耳其、塔吉克斯坦等国公证法律制度；厦门大学念伯涛负责翻译吉尔吉斯斯坦公证法律制度；厦门大学東嘉希翻译阿塞拜疆、斯里兰卡等国公证法律制度；厦门大学李素素负责翻译格鲁吉亚公证法律制度；厦门大学方海龙负责翻译日本公证法律制度；厦门大学曹振敏负责翻译韩国公证法律制度；厦门大学王倩负责翻译新加坡、马来西亚、印度、菲律宾等国公证法律制度；厦门大学李永隆负责翻译越南公证法。

同时，厦门大学王百济负责校对吉尔吉斯斯坦、哈萨克斯坦、塞浦路斯、科威特、东帝汶、塔吉克斯坦等国公证法律制度的译文；厦门大学刘博涵负责校对乌兹别克斯坦、朝鲜、柬埔寨、老挝、蒙古、斯里兰卡、土库曼斯坦等国公证法律制度的译文；厦门大学温长庆负责校对阿联酋、巴基斯坦、孟加拉国、尼泊尔、也门、以色列、印度尼西亚等国公证法律制度的译文；厦门大学杨彦龙负责校对格鲁吉亚、土耳其、阿曼、阿塞拜疆、巴林、亚美尼亚等国公证法律制度的译文；厦门大学杨皖宁负责校对整理以色列、也门、科威特、巴林、老挝等国公证法律制度的译文；厦门大学任宇、刘博涵负责整理中国内地（大陆）及港澳台地区公证法律制度。此外，厦门大学罗捷在课题组成员的联系、协调以及本书格式编排、校对整理、统稿等方面做出重要贡献。

无疑，搜集、整理以及翻译域外公证法律制度是一项费时费力的工作。翻译域外公证法律，尤其是涉及很多小语种的公证法律制度，对项目组来说是一个巨大的挑战。其不仅要求项目组成员必须谙熟域外语言的文字表达，还要懂得与了解相关公证法律制度的立法语境，才能准确翻译出相关法律条文。尽管项目组成员是来自各个单位的公证法专家、学者，也熟悉相关域外语言，多数成员都有在国外留学或访学交流的背景，但我们深知，要真正做到精准翻译是极其困难的，也超出了我们的能力范围。鉴于此，本书采取了中外文对照的方式，方便读者随时对照中外文条款，尽量避免被本书的中文译本可能存在的错译或疏漏所误导。同时，本书对亚洲公证法律制度的翻译纯粹是民间译本，并不是官方指定的标准译本，仅供公证领域理论研究者与实务人员参考使用。

此外，受人力、物力、智力的条件所限，本书所汇编的亚洲公证法律还是有限的，只是选取了亚洲的一些典型国家和地区。在条件成熟时，我们将推出本书的增补本，将更多的乃至全部亚洲公证法律制度汇编进去，以飨读者。

苏国强、汤庆发、刘志云

2019 年 11 月 11 日

目 录

CONTENTS

亚美尼亚

亚美尼亚共和国公证法

LAW OF THE REPUBLIC OF ARMENIA
of December 27, 2001 No. ZR-274
About notariate

(The last edition from 12-11-2016)

Accepted by National Assembly of the Republic of Armenia on December 4, 2001

亚美尼亚共和国法律
2001 年 12 月 27 日　编号 ZR–274
公证法

（2016 年 11 月 12 日最新修订版）

亚美尼亚共和国国民议会于 2001 年 12 月 4 日通过

Chapter 1. General provisions

第一章　一般规定

Article 1. Subject of regulation and coverage of the Law

1. This Law establishes the legal basis of activities of notaries in the Republic of Armenia, procedure of notarial activities and the main requirements imposed to notaries, procedure and the bases of appointment, discharge of notaries, legal protection of the notary, and also the relations connected with appeal of notarial actions and compensation of damage caused to persons by notarial activities.

第一条　法律适用对象和适用范围

1. 本法规定了亚美尼亚共和国公证员开展公证活动的法律依据、程序和对公证员开展业务的要求以及任命公证员的程序和依据，同时规定了公证员的职责、法律保护以及与公证活动相关的上诉程序和因公证活动造成损害后的赔偿。

Article 2. Legal basis of activities of the notary

1. The notary performs the activities on the basis of the Constitution of the Republic of Armenia, the Civil code of the Republic of Armenia (further the Civil code), this Law, other laws, legal acts and international treaties of the Republic of Armenia (further - the international agreements).

2. If international treaties establish the procedure for making of notarial actions other than this Law, then regulations of international treaties are applied.

第二条　公证活动的法律依据

1. 公证员依据《亚美尼亚共和国宪法》、《亚美尼亚共和国民法典》（即《民法典》）、本法、其他法律法规和亚美尼亚共和国签订的国际条约（即《国际协议》）开展公证活动。

2. 国际条约对公证程序另有规定的，适用国际条约的规定。

Chapter 2. Notarial activities

Article 3. Notary

1. The notary is person performing the public services promoting implementation of justice which on behalf of the Republic of Armenia, according to the Constitution and the laws of the Republic of Armenia makes notarial actions and renders the notarial services provided by this Law. Features of the status of the notary are established only by this Law.

2. The notary makes notarial actions by means of witnessing of documents or provision of attested documents or making of other actions provided by the law.

The notary, witnessing the document, confirms its legality and certifies full-fledged evidential force of the document. The notary has the right to render also services, that is to give legal assistance, to give consultation, explanation or the legal conclusion or to constitute drafts of transactions or other legal documents, to perform other legal services, and also other functions providing making of notarial actions.

3. The notarial act has the public importance and full-fledged evidential force provided by the law.

4. Notarial action is made without prejudice, on identical for all conditions.

5. Only the notaries appointed in the procedure established by this Law can use the word "notary" or its derivatives in the name or in the name of the offices.

Article 4. Independence of the notary

1. The notary is independent when making notarial action or implementing other notarial activities and submits only to the law.

When making notarial actions it is forbidden to interfere with activities of the notary or to influence it.

2. Activities of the notary can be suspended or stopped only in cases, procedure and on the bases which are provided by this Law.

3. The notary without its written consent cannot be transferred to other notarial territory. The notary from its consent can be transferred to work on other notarial territory only in the presence of vacant established post of the notary.

Established posts of the notaries performing notarial activities cannot be reduced.

Article 5. Notarial secret

1. The notary shall keep in secret data (the data

第二章　公证活动

第三条　公证员

1. 公证员是代表亚美尼亚共和国，根据亚美尼亚共和国宪法和法律的规定开展公证活动并提供本法规定的公证服务，从而促进司法公正运行的人员。公证员应具备的资质依据本法确定。

2. 公证员通过公证文件、出具公证书或者实施本法规定的其他行为开展公证活动。

公证员通过公证活动，确认文件的合法性和证明力，公证员有权提供以下服务：法律援助、咨询、解释或者作出具有法律效力的结论，公证员还可以通过起草交易文件或者其他法律文件等方式提供法律服务。

3. 公证行为具有法律赋予的公信力和充分的证明力。

4. 实施公证行为应当公正，出具的文书具有普遍适用性。

5. 只有依据本法任命的公证员才能在开展公证活动时或在其办事处名称中使用“公证员”一词或与其相关的术语。

第四条　公证员的独立性

1. 公证员独立开展公证活动，并只服从法律的规定。

任何人不得干涉或者影响公证员开展公证活动。

2. 公证活动只能依据本法规定的事由和程序被暂停或者终止。

3. 未经公证员书面同意，不得将其调任到其他公证机构。经公证员书面同意，且仅在公证机构常设职位有空缺时，方可调任。

公证机构常设岗位不能被减少。

第五条　公证中的保密义务

1. 公证员应当对公证活动中的文件内容及公证服

which are notarial secret) which became to it known of the documents certified or certified by it, and also about execution of notarial action or other services. This obligation is observed also after dismissal of the notary from work.

务的执行情况进行保密。公证员被解聘后，也应当继续遵守上述保密义务。

2. Person, from consent or concerning which notarial action is made and also his legal successor or the representative the written consent can exempt the notary from obligation to keep in secret making of notarial actions. The notary after death specified in this part of the face, in case of absence of his legal successor or impossibility to contact it, can be exempted from obligation of preserving notarial secret by the judgment. In the presence of other reasonable excuses the court can also exempt the notary from obligation of preserving notarial secret.

2. 经公证申请人或其法定继承人、代理人书面同意，可以免除公证员对职务的保密义务。公证员死亡后，若其没有法定继承人或难以与其法定继承人取得联系的，经裁定，可以免除其公证活动保密义务。在有其他合理理由的情况下，法院也可以免除公证员的保密义务。

3. The notary issues certificates of making of notarial actions only to physical persons, and also legal entities, state bodies or local self-government (further the organization) or to their representatives according to the statement, from consent or concerning which he made notarial actions.

3. 经公证机构同意，公证员可向自然人、法人、国家机关、地方自治机关（组织机构）及其代表出具公证书。

4. According to the written requirement of the prosecutor submitted according to the law, either the investigator, or body of inquiry the notary issues certificates of the notarial or other made by it actions, statements, copies or originals from notarial case only in connection with the criminal and civil cases which are in pretrial investigation or judicial proceedings.

4. 检察官、侦查机构或侦查人员依法提交的书面要求，询问公证员出具的公证机构证明、声明、原件或者复印件等经过公证的材料，应当与审前侦查或司法程序中的刑事和民事案件有关。

To the introduction of the court verdict in legal force the judge, the prosecutor, the investigator, body of inquiry or the lawyer is forbidden to provide information on notarial actions to other persons, including mass media, and also to disclose this information in the performances.

禁止法官、检察官、侦查人员、侦查机构或者律师向他人（包括媒体）提供与公证活动有关的信息，也禁止其在履职过程中披露相关信息。

With notarial actions within their competence have the right to get acquainted also the bodies performing according to the procedure and on the conditions established by the law, control of notarial actions or their officials.

依据法律规定的程序和事由，公证机构有权知悉公证员的工作情况，管理公证行为。

5. The notary in the procedure established by this Law can provide the information on the will or its content only after the death of the testator.

5. 依据本法规定的程序，公证员只有在遗嘱订立人去世后才能对外提供与遗嘱相关的信息。

The message of data on opening of inheritance to heirs, creditors is not considered violation of the procedure for provision of the data which are notarial secret established by this Law.

公证员向遗嘱继承人或遗嘱订立人的债权人公开有关遗嘱继承的资料信息，不视为违反本法规定的保密义务。

5.1. The message of data for the purpose of implementation of notarial action within notarial case to the notary, and also, in the cases which are directly provided by the law, to person specified in the law is not considered

5.1. 在与公证相关的诉讼案件执行的过程中，公证员提供有关资料信息，以及在法律有直接规定的情况下，公证员向法定主体提供资料信息不被视为违反提供本法规定的保密的义务。

violation of the procedure for provision of the data which are notarial secret established by this Law.

6. The rules about nondisclosure of notarial secret provided by this Article extend to persons participating in the procedure established by the law in notarial actions (the witness, the translator and other), and also to persons to whom these data became known in connection with execution of the labor and service duties by them.

6. 本条规定的保密规则也适用于依照法定程序参与公证活动的其他人员（见证人、翻译和其他人），以及在参与公证活动时知悉资料信息的人员。

7. Notaries store the data and documents containing the state or official secret in the procedure established by the law.

7. 公证员依照法律规定的程序，保存国家或官方机密的资料和文件。

8. In the cases provided by paragraph one of Item 4 of this Article, the notary within three days after issue of certificates of making of notarial actions, statements, copies or originals has the right to notify on it persons participating in this notarial action if the law does not provide other.

8. 依据本条第 4 款，在法律没有其他规定的情况下，公证员出具声明、复印件、原件公证书后的 3 日内通知本次公证活动的参与人。

9. Information provided by the Law of the Republic of Armenia"About anti-money laundering and terrorism financing" and being notarial secret is provided in case of representation to the authority established by this law, the report concerning the transaction which is subject to the obligatory notification in case of suspicion about money laundering or financing of terrorism or based on request of authorized body in the cases and procedure established by this law.

9. 依据《亚美尼亚共和国反洗钱和资助恐怖主义活动法》的相关规定和本法有关公证保密的规定，如果涉嫌洗钱或资助恐怖主义活动，根据有权机构的要求，必须予以报告。

Article 6. The right of the notary to use the image of the State Emblem of the Republic of Armenia and the words "Republic of Armenia"

第六条　使用亚美尼亚共和国国徽图案和“亚美尼亚共和国”字样的权利

1. The Ministry of Justice of the Republic of Armenia (further - the Ministry of Justice) issues to the notary seal with the image of the State Emblem of the Republic of Armenia, with the words "Republic of Armenia", with name, surname of the notary and with indication of the notarial territory.

1. 亚美尼亚共和国司法部制发公证员印章，印章图案由亚美尼亚共和国国徽、“亚美尼亚共和国”字样、公证员姓名和公证领域等标识组成。

The notary's seal is set everything certified, either the documents or reports witnessed, or issued by the notary, and also for their duplicates.

公证员印章可以用于公证文件或报告和由公证员出具的文件及其副本。

The notary has the right to have only one round stamp with the image of the State Emblem.

公证员拥有独一无二的刻有国徽图案的圆形印章。

2. The notary has the right to use the image of the State Emblem of the Republic of Armenia and the word "Republic of Armenia" on sign and forms of the office.

2. 公证员有权佩戴亚美尼亚共和国国徽，并在带有“亚美尼亚共和国”字样的办公室履行职务。

Article 7. Bank accounts of the notary

第七条　公证员的银行账户

1. The notary shall have in the bank determined by him bank and deposit accounts, including in foreign

1. 公证员应确定银行的存款账户和外币账户，公证员依照法律规定的方法独立管理其银行或存款账户。

currency. The notary in the procedure established by the legislation independently disposes of the means which are on its bank or deposit accounts.

2. On bank accounts of the notary collection judicially only in the cases provided by the law can be turned.

Article 8. Legal protection of the notary

1. During detention, the drive, arrest, search of the notary, attraction it to administrative or criminal liability judicially the Minister of Justice of the Republic of Armenia (further - the Minister of Justice) and notarial chamber is without delay informed of it.

2. The place of employment of the notary can be subjected to search only by a court decision with participation of the representative of notarial chamber.

3. The notarial acts which are stored at the notary can be withdrawn only in the cases and procedure provided by the law.

On property, including on money of the notary collection judicially only in the cases provided by the law can be turned.

The notarial acts which are stored at the notary can be withdrawn for the purpose of check only according to the procedure, established by the Minister of Justice.

4. The state competent authorities shall take the necessary measures for protection of the notary established by the law if it or members of his family in connection with execution of the obligations by it was threatened with physical violence, destruction of property or other illegal actions.

5. Criminal prosecution concerning the notary can be initiated only by the Attorney-General of the Republic of Armenia.

6. The notary is exempted from training sessions.

7. The notary has service weapon and (or) has the right to have and carry special means. The notary based on civil or employment contracts can perform protection of the notary office.

Article 9.

Voided

Article 10. Position assignment of the notary

1. According to the procedure, provided by this Law, any capable citizen of the Republic of Armenia having qualification of the bachelor of the lawyer or certified specialist of the lawyer to whom 25 years were performed, not having criminal record, last at least one year of notarial

2. 仅在法定情形下才能审查公证员的银行账户。

第八条　公证员的法律保护

1. 如需拘留、驱逐、逮捕、搜查公证员，追究其行政或刑事责任，应立即通知亚美尼亚共和国司法部部长和公证机构。

2. 仅在持有法院决定的情况下才可搜查公证员的办公地点，且搜查过程应当有公证机构代表参与。

3. 在法定情形下，公证申请人可以依据法定程序撤回公证申请。

公证服务收费应当遵循法定原则。

公证结果的撤销仅能依据司法部部长规定的程序方可作出。

4. 如果公证员或其家庭成员由于其履行公证义务而受到人身暴力、财产破坏或其他非法威胁时，国家主管当局应采取必要措施予以保护。

5. 对公证员的刑事起诉，仅能由亚美尼亚共和国总检察长提起。

6. 公证员免于课程培训。

7. 公证员有权持有公务专用武器，采取特殊手段。基于民事或雇佣合同的公证员有义务保护公证机构。

第九条

作废。

第十条　公证员的职位分配

1. 依照本法规定的程序，亚美尼亚共和国公民取得法学学士学位或经律师执业满 25 年、至少从事公证活动满 1 年、无犯罪记录，或有 3 年专业律师工作经验或律师学历，参加公证员培训至少 3 个月，并通过资格审查委员会的公证员资格考试，方可被任命为

activities, and in case of availability of 3-year working life of the professional lawyer or academic degree – minimum of 3-month training on notarial activities and passed qualification examination committee qualification examinations for position of the notary can be appointed to position of the notary.

The Minister of Justice can also appoint to position of the notary not past training on notarial activities and person who did not pass qualification examination who at least within three years performed in system of the Ministry of Justice of the Republic of Armenia or in notarial chamber within the last five years professional labor activity in the field of notariate.

In skill test of candidates for notaries can participate and be appointed to position of the notary also capable citizen of the Republic of Armenia having at least 5-year working life of the professional lawyer or academic degree irrespective of circumstance of training. The similar persons which underwent skill test are appointed to position of the notary after the end of the three-months occupations directed to training in skills of implementation of notarial activities according to the procedure, established by the Government.

2.The structure of qualification examination committee affirms the Minister of Justice. The commissions the equal number of persons employed of the Ministry and the notaries pushed by notarial chamber is included.

3. Position assignments of the notary are made by the Minister of Justice taking into account the conclusion of notarial chamber which shall be motivated and reasonable.

The Ministry of Justice grants to the notary the office certificate after appointment it to position.

Article 11. Procedure for test of qualification of candidates for notaries

1. Skill test of candidates for notaries is performed according to the qualification procedure for test approved by the Government.

2. The procedure for test of qualification establishes terms of carrying out skill test, the list of the documents necessary for participation in check, terms of their giving and quantity of the questions or tasks chosen for check, evaluation procedure, form of conducting check, time provided for conducting check, procedure for use of legal or other documents or technical means, the number of the points necessary for passing qualification examination, and procedure for protest of results of check, and also other

公证员。

司法部部长可以任命没有参与公证员培训和未通过资格考试的人员为公证员，但至少在最近5年从事公证领域专门工作，其中有3年以上在亚美尼亚共和国司法部系统或公证机构工作。

公证员的候选人参加技能考试方可成为公证员。根据政府制定的程序，经过技能考试的人员需进行为期3个月的职业培训，培训目的是使其具备提供公证服务的能力。

2. 司法部部长确定资格审查委员会的职权和架构。司法部有权确定公证机构雇佣人员的数量，其中包括公证机构推荐的公证员。

3. 公证员的职位分配由司法部部长根据公证机构的分布情况作出，应具有激励性和合理性。

司法部在任命公证员后，向公证员授予任职证书。

第十一条　公证员的候选人资格考试程序

1. 公证员候选人技能考试按照政府制定的考试资格程序开展。

2. 资格考试的有关规定包括以下内容：资格考试的要求、参加考试所需文件的清单、选择的问题、数量、评估程序、进行检查的形式、提供检查的时间或技术手段的使用步骤、资格审查合格的分数线、考试成绩的异议，以及其他有关公正开展资格考试的要求。其他问题由司法部规定。

provisions directed to proper carrying out skill test. The questions which are not subject to disclosure for check are prepared by the Ministry of Justice.

For all participants of skill test identical requirements shall be established.

If skill test is carried out by means of technical means, then the applicant shall get acquainted with procedure and conditions of use of technical means in advance.

3. To persons who passed qualification examination the certificate on qualification is granted.

Positive results of skill test of persons who are not appointed to position of the notary are valid within five years.

4. Legal acts about changes of procedure for qualification become effective in three months after their official publication if these acts do not establish later term.

5. About day, time and the venue of skill test the applicant is notified properly not later than seven days before check.

6. Skill test is carried out in Armenian.

7. Skill test is carried out in public. During conducting checks video filming, filming or sound recording can be made.

8. About results of checks the qualified person is notified properly, or they go to it not later than within five days after the end of checks.

9. For participation in skill test the state fee in the amount of and procedure, established by the law is collected.

10. Results of skill tests can be protested judicially within ten days after their obtaining.

Article 12. Quantity of established posts and site of work of the notary

1. The notary performs the activities in notary office which shall be in the notarial territory established for him. The notarial district (territory) is administrative and territorial unit within which the notary performs the activities. Notarial the district (territory), the minimum requirements imposed to notary offices and criteria of the location are established by the Minister of Justice. Notarial the district (territory) the minimum requirements imposed to notary offices and criteria of the location – by the principles of convenience to citizens, effective management of queues, safety, efficiency of time are established based on the principle of the territorial division based on activity of transactions, clients, and.

One or several notary offices can operate on one notarial territory. In one notary office one notary or more,

所有参考人员在资格考试中应遵守统一规定。

资格考试中需要借助技术手段时，申请人应事先熟悉技术使用程序和要求。

3. 通过资格考试的人员，可以获得资格证书。

未被任命为公证员的人员，其成绩在 5 年内有效。

4. 关于资格程序变更的法律行为，如果该行为没有确定生效期限，则在正式公布的 3 个月后生效。

5. 有关机构应在不少于资格考试日期的 7 日前，通知申请人具体的考试日期、时间和地点。

6. 资格考试在亚美尼亚进行。

7. 资格考试公开进行。在考试期间，由主管机关视频录像或录音。

8. 应当将考试结果及时通知合格人员，或者在考试结束后 5 日内送达合格人员。

9. 参加资格考试的人员应按照法律规定的数额和程序缴纳费用。

10. 在收到考试结果 10 日内，可依法提出异议。

第十二条　公证机构的常设职位和办公场所的数量

1. 公证员在其办公场所内开展公证活动。公证机构所在区域是公证员开展公证活动的行政单位和属地单位。司法部部长应根据公证机构所在区域、方便市民、有效管理、安全与时间效率、区域划分原则以及交易活动、客户数量等情况分配公证员。

一个或几个公证机构可以在同一公证区域运行。每个公证机构的一个或几个公证员，可以在同一公证

performing activities in the same notarial territory can work.

For making of notarial actions any person, irrespective of the place of residence or stay, except as specified, provided by this Law can address the notary.

2. The quantity of established posts of notaries is established by the Minister of Justice taking into account opinion of notarial chamber.

3.If because of the disease limiting possibility of movement or helpless condition implementation of notarial actions in notary office becomes impossible, then based on the statement of the interested person the notary shall in day of submission of the statement or the next working day to perform notarial operations outside notary office, in the notarial district (territory).

Notarial operations can be performed out of notary office also in the cases established by Articles 59, of 61, of 80, 82 these Articles.

In these cases the notary shall in text about assurance and the register to specify the place (address) of accomplishment of notarial action.

Article 13. The introduction of the notary in position

1. The notary starts execution of the job responsibilities not later than in two-month time after appointment. In case of failure to carry out of the obligations in two-month time the Minister of Justice declares invalid the order on appointment of person who received qualification as the notary, and the reappointed notary joins in the list not appointed, but having positive results on skill test.

2. The notary to assumption of office represents to the Minister of Justice and to notarial chamber the sample of the signature, the address of the office this about means of communication.

3. Prior to accomplishment of the obligations by the notary in the time established by part of 1 this Article, the notarial chamber provides it with possibility of access to electronic system of notariate.

Article 14. Restrictions in activities of the notary

The notary in parallel with the activities cannot hold other established post or perform other paid work, except pedagogical, scientific or creative.

Article 15. The paid nature of notarial actions and other services rendered by the notary

1. Making of notarial actions and rendering services

区域内开展公证活动。

依据本法规定，无论是居住地或暂住地的任何人，都可以就公证活动向公证员提出申诉，本法或其他法律另有规定的除外。

2. 司法部部长在考虑公证机构意见后确定公证机构的常设职位数量。

3. 公证员因疾病限制或者条件限制无法在公证机构开展公证活动时，依据终止公证员职务的规定，公证员应在提交声明当日或到公证机构（区域）以外的地方履行公证员职务下一个工作日之前完成既有的公证业务。

申请人可根据第 59 条、第 61 条、第 80 条、第 82 条规定的情形，向外地公证机构申请办理公证业务。

在此情况下，公证员应提供担保，并在登记簿上注明公证地点。

第十三条　公证员职位的介绍

1. 公证员应在接受聘任后的两个月内开始履行工作职责。若未能在两个月内开始履行职责，则司法部部长应宣布委任公证员的命令无效，被解除委任的公证员应当重新被委任，但其资格考试成绩仍然有效。

2. 在职的公证员向司法部部长和公证机构提供签字样本、办公地址以及通信方式。

3. 公证员在本条第 1 款规定的时间内履行公证员职务之前，公证机构应为其提供登录公证电子系统的账号。

第十四条　对公证活动的限制

除了教学、科研之外，公证员不能担任其他常设职务或从事其他有偿工作。

第十五条　公证活动和其他公证服务的有偿性

1. 公证服务是有偿的。公证申请人应当向公证员

by the notary are paid. The payment for making of notarial actions or for rendering services by the notary is paid to the notary. The notary disposes of the payments received for making of notarial actions or for rendering services by the notary.

支付公证或者提供其他公证服务的费用。公证员有权因提供公证服务而获得报酬。

2. For making of notarial actions the notary collects the state fee according to the procedure and the size, established by the Law of the Republic of Armenia "About the state fee".

2. 公证员根据《亚美尼亚共和国公共服务收费法》规定的程序和数额收取费用。

3. The notary has the right to receive compensation in the amount of the amount of the notarial actions of the transportation, postage, telephone, cable expenses connected with storage bank, payment and settlement documents or providing proofs, and also other expenses made or made by it in the course of making stipulated by the legislation.

3. 公证员有权获得在公证活动中产生的交通、邮资、电话、有线电视费用与银行储蓄、支付与结算文件或提供证据等产生的相应费用，其他费用由其他法律规定。

4. Rates for notarial actions affirm the Government.

4. 有关公证服务的费率由政府确认。

The amount of payment for the services rendered by the notary is established by the notary.

公证服务的具体价格由公证员确定。

The payment for notarial actions or the services rendered by the notary is levied according to the procedure and the terms established by the notary.

公证服务的其他费用，按照公证程序和公证条款收取。

5. The mode of business activity set by the Civil code is applied to notarial actions or paid services rendered by the notary.

5. 公证员提供的有偿服务，适用《民法典》有关经营活动的规定。

Income gained from committed notarial actions or or the services rendered by the notary and also income of the notary or the staff of notary office are assessed with tax in the amount of and procedure, established by the law.

公证活动所得或者公证员提供的服务所得，以及公证员或者公证机构工作人员的所得，依照法律规定的数额和程序计税。

Article 16. Suspension of operations of the notary

第十六条　公证活动暂停

1. Activities of the notary stop:

1. 出现以下情况应当暂停公证活动：

1) if he did not pay three months in a row the membership fees to notarial chamber;

（1）公证员连续 3 个月未向公证机构支付会费；

2) for up to 6 months in the cases provided by this Law;

（2）公证期间超过本法规定的 6 个月的最长期限；

3) in case of submission of the statement for recognition by the bankrupt, for all term of case on bankruptcy;

（3）若申请人提交确认破产的声明，则适用破产案件的期限；

4) in other cases, procedure and the terms provided by the law.

（4）在其他情况下，依照法律规定的程序和条款暂停公证活动。

2. The decision on suspension of notarial activities is passed by the Minister of Justice with indication of the term of suspension of operations. In the case provided by the subitem 1 of Item 1 of this Article, activities of the notary stop before payment of the membership fee.

2. 由司法部部长作出暂停公证活动的决定，并说明暂停的期限。在本条第 1 款第 1 项规定的情况下，公证活动在公证员支付会费之前应当暂停。

3. Activities of the notary are considered suspended from the next day after issue to him of the decision (order) on suspension of operations.

3. 司法部部长在作出暂停公证活动的决定后，从作出决定后的第二日开始生效。

4. The notary whose activities are stopped has no right to perform notarial operations and to provide other notarial services until the end of termination term.

5. The seal and stamp of the notary who suspended activities is stored in notarial chamber according to the procedure, established by the Minister of Justice.

6. The notary has the right to protest judicially the decision on suspension of its activities.

Article 17. Release of the notary from position or termination of its powers

1. The notary is dismissed if:

1) he submits the application for it;

2) to it 65 years were performed (reached age limit of continuance in office);

3) from its written consent he is chosen or appointed to other position or passed to other work not compatible to activities of the notary;

4) he owing to temporary disability more than did not come six months to work;

5) he more than without reasonable excuse did not come five days in a row to work;

6) he was appointed to position of the notary with violation of requirements of the law;

7) it is recognized as incapacitated, is limited by capable, is unknown absent or the dead based on the judgment which took legal effect;

8) the conviction of court about deprivation of its freedom took legal effect, or he in the procedure established by the law is recognized as person who committed crime of official;

9) it lost citizenship of the Republic of Armenia;

10) he is declared bankrupt judicially.

2. The notary can be dismissed if:

1) the transaction certified by it at the time of the certificate was insignificant;

2) No. ZR-180 voided according to the Law of the Republic of Armenia of 12.11.2016

3) within one year he three times certified transactions or approved documents which at the time of assurance or approval contradicted the obligatory rules established by the law,

4) he within one year was repeatedly brought to disciplinary responsibility for violation of the law;

5) it it is malicious evaded from execution of the tax liabilities;

6) the conviction pronounced concerning it which is

4. 暂停公证活动后，公证员不能开展公证业务，并在暂停期限结束前不能提供其他公证服务。

5. 依照司法部部长制定的程序，被暂停公证活动的公证员的印章应存放在公证机构。

6. 对暂停公证活动的决定，公证员有权依法提出异议。

第十七条 公证员职务的解除和公证员职权的终止

1. 公证员职务的解除应符合以下情况：

（1）本人提交申请；

（2）年满 65 周岁（达到工作年龄上限）；

（3）经其书面同意，本人被任命于其他职位，或被调任至与公证活动不相关的其他工作；

（4）因暂时伤残而在未来 6 个月不能工作；

（5）无正当理由连续旷工超过 5 日（包括 5 日）；

（6）公证员的任命程序违反法律规定；

（7）基于具有法律效力的裁定，公证员被认定为无行为能力、宣告失踪或死亡的；

（8）法院剥夺公证员人身自由的判决生效，或者依法律规定公证员被认定为犯罪的；

（9）公证员丧失亚美尼亚共和国公民身份；

（10）公证员被依法宣告破产。

2. 符合以下情况时，公证员的职位可以被解除：

（1）颁发的证书被认定无效；

（2）依据 2016 年 11 月 12 日亚美尼亚共和国法律而被认定为任命无效；

（3）在一年内，公证员提供的公证服务有 3 次及以上与法律的强制性规则相抵触的；

（4）一年内公证员多次因违法行为受到纪律处分的；

（5）公证员故意逃避纳税义务；

（6）因违反公证员职业道德规范，公证员被认定

not imprisoning him took legal effect or in the procedure established by the law he is recognized as person who intentionally committed crime if owing to making of these crimes requirements of rules of notarial ethics were also violated.

为故意犯罪的，或者依照法律规定被认定为故意犯罪的。

3. Recognition of the document certified or certified by the notary invalid or its change judicially in itself does not attract responsibility of the notary who certified or certified this document if when making notarial actions it was not changed or nullified because of violation by the notary of requirements of the law or other legal act.

3. 公证员开展公证活动时，因违反法律要求或其他法律规定，所制作的公证书不产生证明效力。

4. Powers of the notary stop with his death.

4. 公证员的职权因其死亡而终止。

5. On the bases provided by subitems 5-6 and 10 of Item 1 of this Article, and also Item 2 of this Article, the notary is dismissed by court. Concerning dismissal of the notary the Minister of Justice on the initiative or of the offer of notarial chamber has the right to take a legal action.

5. 若存在本条第 1 款第 5 项、第 6 项、第 10 项以及本条第 2 款规定的情形，法院可判决解除公证员职务。司法部部长或公证机构有权依法提请法院作出裁决，解除公证员职务。

The Minister of Justice before appeal to the court concerning release of the notary from position shall take written explanation from the notary. In the notification on capture of explanation, considering features of disciplinary production, the Minister of Justice establishes term for representation of explanation. The minimum term for representation of explanation is established the 3rd working day from the moment of receipt of the notification. In case of non-presentation of explanation in time, specified by the notary in the notification, the obligation of the Minister of Justice established by this part is considered executed.

司法部部长在向法院提出解除公证员职务的诉讼之前，应当获得公证员的书面陈述。在要求其作陈述的通知中，应包含纪律问责的内容，以及要求司法部部长解释相关术语的条款。要求解释的申请应在收到通知之日起第 3 个工作日内提出。通知中还应向公证员指明，如果公证员未及时要求解释，那么司法部部长的解释义务将视为已履行。

6. On the bases provided by subitems 1-4 and 7-9 of Item 1 of this Article, the notary is dismissed by the Minister of Justice.

6. 依据本条第 1 款第 1 项至第 4 项和第 7 项至第 9 项的规定，由司法部部长解除公证员职务。

7. According to the subitem 2 of Item 1 of this Article the notary is considered dismissed from the next day after achievement of age by it 65 years, and in the cases provided by subitems 4, 7-8 Items 1 of this Article, from the date of, specified in the decision (order). In case of release of the notary from position on other bases provided by this Article the notary is considered dismissed from the next day after issue to it of the decision (order) on dismissal.

7. 依据本条第 1 款第 2 项，公证员在年龄满 65 周岁的次日应当被解除公证员职务，若在本条第 1 款第 4 项、第 7 项至第 8 项规定的情形下，在规定（命令）的日期届满时视为公证员职务已被解除。若由于本条其他规定解除公证员职务，则解除决定（命令）作出后的次日视为公证员职务已被解除。

8. The notary discharged of position shall no later than in five-day time to hand over the seal and stamp in the Ministry of Justice, and notarial cases and other documents – in notarial chamber. In case of appointment of the replacement notary the notarial chamber submits the notarial cases and other documents to the replacement notary. The documents, seal and stamp which are stored at the notary exempted on the bases provided by subitems 4, 7-8

8. 被解除职务的公证员应在 5 日内向司法部交还印章以及证书和其他文件。若变更公证员，公证机构将证书和其他文件转交给变更的公证员。依据本条第 1 款第 4 项、第 7 项至第 8 项的规定，公证员因被免职提交的文件、印章均由委员会接收，该委员会由司法部部长组建，且其中应有公证机构的代表。

Items 1 of this Article or at the notary who stopped powers in case, stipulated in Item 4 these Articles are accepted by the commission created by the Minister of Justice which structure joins representatives of notarial chamber.

9. The trainee appointed the dismissed notary, and employees of the device of the notary are considered exempted from training and work from the date of release of the notary from position.

10. The notary has the right to protest judicially the order of the Minister of Justice on release it from position.

Article 18. Replacement and sending of the notary

1. In case of temporary absence of the notary in the notarial district or the terminations of its activities the Minister of Justice according to the offer of notarial chamber or on own initiative can assign accomplishment of notarial actions for this term to other notary.

2. The replacement notary has the right to perform notarial actions in the notary office or in notary office of the replaced notary.

3. The replacement notary acts on its own behalf and at own expense. The procedure for use of property of the replaced notary and compensation is established by the decision of notarial chamber.

4. The bases of replacement of the notary in case of temporary absence are:

1) stay in annual additional vacation,

2) maternity leave,

3) child care leave up to three years,

4) temporary disability,

5) disease of the child or family members (in case of need leaving),

6) business trips,

7) retrainings,

8) cases of the actual absence from work more than two working days.

5. The notary can be sent to other notarial district (territory) only from its consent according to the offer of notarial chamber by the order of the Minister of Justice.

Article 19. Control over activities of the notary

1. Control over notarial actions and provision of other services provided by this law, requirements of the Law of the Republic of Armenia "About anti-money laundering and terrorism financing" and the legal acts adopted on its basis, observance of rules of notarial ethics performs the Ministry of Justice, in the cases established by this Law and procedure.

9. 被解除的公证员正在接受培训的，从离职之日起免于培训和工作。

10. 公证员有权依法对司法部部长的解除决定提出申诉。

第十八条　公证员的变更和派遣

1. 在公证机构暂时没有公证员或其公证活动被终止时，司法部部长可根据公证机构的申请或主动将需要在一定限期内完成的公证业务转交给其他公证员。

2. 代班公证员有权在公证机构或被代班公证员的办公场所开展公证活动。

3. 代班公证员以自己的名义从事公证活动并支配经费。其资金使用和补偿由公证机构决定。

4. 变更公证员的情形包括：

（1）休假；

（2）产假；

（3）不超过 3 年的育儿假；

（4）暂时性感染疾病；

（5）儿童或家庭成员感染疾病（需要暂时离岗）；

（6）出差；

（7）培训；

（8）超过 2 个工作日的缺勤。

5. 按照司法部部长的要求，公证员可以根据公证机构的申请，到其他公证机构（区域）就职。

第十九条　公证活动的管理

1. 司法部在管理公证活动和提供其他公证服务时，应依据《亚美尼亚共和国反洗钱和资助恐怖主义活动法》以及在此基础上通过的其他法律规定，遵守相应的公证伦理规则。

2. Control is exercised by the Ministry of Justice by means of research of notarial actions and other services provided by the notary, based on the annual program which is confirmed by the Minister of Justice till December 20 of the year preceding research.

2. 司法部对公证员提供的公证活动以及其他公证服务的管理，依据司法部部长在上年度 12 月 20 日确定的年度计划执行。

The period and types of notarial actions and other services provided by the notary which are subject to research and also term and the venue of research are established by the order of the Minister of Justice on carrying out research.

公证员提供的公证服务和其他需要审查的服务的期限、种类、地点，由司法部部长有关命令确定。

The research is conducted with visit in notary office or without visit in notary office by means of the requirement at the notary of notarial cases and other documents, and also providing research by means of electronic system.

审查人员可以通过公证机构或者在未通过公证机构的情形下，对公证业务和有关文件进行审查，也可以通过电子网络系统进行审查。

During the researches person performing research has the right to require from the notary of explanation and the materials in writing relating to research which are subject to provision within one week from the moment of receipt of the notification.

在审查期间，审查人员有权要求公证员说明与审查有关的书面材料，公证员应在收到通知之日起一周内提供。

Person performing research has no right to be beyond the purpose specified in the order on carrying out research.

审查人员的审查活动不得超出审查令规定的范围。

In case of new circumstances and need during the research of the purpose and frame can change by order of the minister, according to reasons for person performing research. The notary is notified on change in writing, by means of submission of the copy of the new order.

依据司法部部长的要求，若出现新的情况和需要，审查人员可以改变审查目的和框架，从而满足审查的要求，但需以书面形式通知公证员更新材料。

3. The copy of the order of the Minister of Justice on carrying out research not earlier than in three working days prior to implementation of research goes to the notary specified in the order of the Minister of Justice and to notarial chamber for the purpose of ensuring participation in research of the representative of notarial chamber.

3. 司法部部长应在开展审查工作前的 3 个工作日内，依据有关法律规定的程序公布审查令，并指定公证员代表公证机构参与审查。

In case of ensuring participation in research of the representative of notarial chamber management of notarial chamber shall within one working day after receipt of the copy of the order of the Minister of Justice report about it in the Ministry of Justice, having provided the solution of management on appointment of the representative.

为确保公证机构派代表参加审查工作，公证机构应在收到司法部部长审查令副本的 1 个工作日内，提供指定代表的名单。

As a result of research person performing the research established by order of the Minister of Justice constitutes the conclusion.

审查人员应以执行司法部部长命令为目的，确定审查结论。

The representative of notarial chamber shall append the signature in the conclusion concerning the participation, and in case of objections about the conclusion, within one working day to provide them as separate documents which are attached to the conclusion.

公证机构代表应在审查结论上签字，公证员若对结论有异议，应在 1 个工作日内提出。

The copy of the conclusion is provided to the notary

审查人员应将结论的副本向公证员提供，该副本

for representation of the line item which is applied to the conclusion.

4. At the notary who underwent testing the next program research can be performed not earlier, than for the second year after the research.

5. The prosecutor's office, police, service of homeland security, and also other law enforcement agencies within one working day report about the criminal procedure actions performed in the attitude towards the notary to the Minister of Justice.

Data about being in the production the cases performed or performed further challenging actions of the notary, the court without delay sends to the Ministry of Justice, and also within three working days from the moment of acceptance sends copies of the made decisions or court decrees on the these cases.

6. Other state bodies can exercise control over other activities of the notary performed or performed further only in the cases and framework which is directly provided by the law. Other state bodies exercising control over activities of the notary before conducting checks at the notary shall report about it to the Minister of Justice. Also to the Minister of Justice copies of acts (protocols) on results of checks go.

Article 19.1. The rights and obligations of the notary who is subject to check

1. The notary who is subject to research has the right:

1) to forbid research if person performing research was beyond the purpose specified in the order on carrying out research;

2) to study the conclusion;

3) to furnish explanations, explanations, in the procedure established by the law to appeal actions of persons performing research;

4) not to fulfill the requirements which are beyond competences of persons performing research, and also not proceeding from the purpose and the program of research.

2. The notary who is subject to research shall:

1) not to interfere with the research course, to fulfill legal requirements of persons performing research;

2) upon the demand of person performing research to submit required documents, data.

Article 20. Protest of actions of the notary

1. Person whose interests are infringed by action of the notary or person to whom it is refused making of notarial action can protest in court committed notarial action

应与原本一致。

4. 若公证员正在接受审查，则下一个项目的审查可以在审查后的第二年进行。

5. 检察院、公安部门、国土安全部门以及其他执法机构对公证员采取刑事强制措施后，应在 1 个工作日内向司法部部长报告。

对在办案件所产生的或在执行公证活动中难以处理的数据信息，法院应立即向司法部提交这些数据，司法部应在收到之日起 3 个工作日内作出决定，确保法院能及时对案件作出裁判。

6. 其他国家机关仅能在法律有直接规定的情形和范围内，对公证员的其他活动进行管理或者进一步实施管控。其他国家机关对公证活动进行审查前，应当向司法部部长报告，并向司法部部长提交关于审查结果的文件副本。

第十九条之一　受审查的公证员的权利和义务

1. 受审查的公证员有权作以下行为：

（1）若审查人员的行为超出审查令范围，公证员可拒绝接受审查；

（2）对审查结论提出异议；

（3）依据法律规定的程序，要求审查人员作出说明，对审查人员的不正当行为提出申诉；

（4）对超出审查人员职权范围的，以及不符合审查目的和方案的审查行为，受审查的公证员可以提出异议。

2. 受审查的公证员应：

（1）不干涉审查工作的进行，积极配合审查人员合法的要求；

（2）按照审查人员的要求提供所需文件、数据及信息。

第二十条　公证申请人对公证结果的抗辩

1. 公证申请人的利益受到侵害或被拒绝公证的，可以在法庭上提出抗辩或者拒绝承认公证结果。

or refusal in making of notarial action.

2. In case of representation by the established part of 1 this Article of the claim in the Ministry of Justice and notarial chamber, it is considered in the stipulated in Clause 24 presents of the Law procedure.

Article 21. Making of notarial action by other officials

In the territory of other states notarial actions on behalf of the Republic of Armenia make diplomatic representations and consular establishments of the Republic of Armenia.

Chapter 3. Rights, obligations and responsibility of the notary

Article 22. Rights of the notary

1. For implementation of the competences the notary has the property and personal non-property rights and obligations, can hire and dismiss the staff of notary office, dispose of income gained for rendering other services to them, to appear in court as the claimant or the defendant, or the third party or to make other actions corresponding to the law.

2. The notary has the right to make the notarial actions provided by this Law or to render the services provided by this Law or other legal acts and also to make explanations concerning making of notarial actions.

3. For making of notarial actions the notary has the right to request the organizations, state or local government bodies from necessary data or documents. The corresponding data or documents shall be submitted within the term specified by the notary. This term cannot exceed fifteen days if submission of the relevant documents does not require longer term.

Violation of requirements of this Item attracts responsibility according to the procedure, established by the law for manifestation of the disrespectful relation to courts.

4. The notary has the right to annual leave lasting 30 working days.

In some cases, proceeding from personal, family or other circumstances, the Minister of Justice can permit the notary to use additional vacation lasting up to 30 calendar days in year.

5. The labor mode of the notary is set by the notary who is controlled by the Minister of Justice.

6. The notary in accordance with the established procedure has right to social insurance in old age, in case of

2. 依据本法第 1 条的规定，公证申请人可以向司法部或公证机构提出赔偿请求，司法部或公证机构应按本法第 24 条规定的程序处理。

第二十一条　其他官员作出的公证行为

在其他国家领土内，亚美尼亚共和国的外交代表和领事机构可以代表亚美尼亚共和国开展公证活动。

第三章　公证员的权利、义务和责任

第二十二条　公证员的权利

1. 为了让公证员更好地履行职责，公证员具有财产和非财产性权利和义务；可以雇用和解雇公证机构的工作人员；获取提供服务的酬劳；作为原告或被告或第三人出庭；或依法律规定采取其他行动。

2. 公证员有权依据本法的规定从事公证活动，或者提供本法或者其他法律规定的服务，并对公证活动作出说明。

3. 为了开展公证活动，公证员有权向其他机构、州或地方政府机构获取必要的数据信息或文件。相应的数据信息或文件应在公证员要求的期限内提供，该期限不得超过 15 日。

若公证员违反本法的规定，不尊重法院的司法程序，应依据法律规定的程序追究其责任。

4. 公证员有权享受 30 个工作日的年假。

在特定情形下，考虑个人、家庭或其他情况，司法部部长可以允许公证员额外享有不超过 30 日的休假。

5. 公证员的工作模式由公证机构确定，并由司法部部长最终决定。

6. 根据既定程序，公证员有权在年老、残疾、疾病、行为能力丧失以及法律规定的其他情形下享受社

disability, disease, loss of the supporter and in other cases provided by the law.

7. The notary has other provided by the law or legal acts of the right.

Article 23. Obligations of the notary

1. The notary shall:

1) to be impartial, to follow rules of notarial ethics when making notarial actions;

2) to keep the procedure established by this Law in secret data which became known to it in connection with its activities, except as specified, provided by the Law of the Republic of Armenia "About anti-money laundering and terrorism financing";

3) to refuse making of notarial action if it contradicts the laws or other legal acts or international treaties of the Republic of Armenia;

4) in case of absence from work more than five days due to illness or on other reasonable excuse to inform of it the Ministry of Justice and notarial chamber;

5) to approve address modification of notary office with the Ministry of Justice;

6) to provide fulfillment of requirements, established by the Law of the Republic of Armenia "About anti-money laundering and terrorism financing";

7) once a year to undergo the retraining organized by notarial chamber, in the procedures and conditions established by notarial chamber. Duration of rates of retraining - is at least 30, but no more than 60 class periods. Duration of class period - 40 minutes.

1.2. In stipulated in Item 5 parts of 1 this Article case, the Minister of Justice within one week refuses address modification of notary office if the new address of notary office to be outside the notarial district (territory), or the notary office does not conform to imposed minimum requirements or criteria of the location.

2. At the request of persons which brought the corresponding payment established for notarial actions and other services provided by the notary, the notary also shall:

1) for the purpose of assistance to persons when making notarial actions, implementation of their rights and legitimate interests to explain their rights and obligations, to warn about consequences of the made notarial actions legal lack of information of person could not be used to it to the detriment;

To explain 2) to the parties sense and value of the drafts of transactions provided by them and to check com-

会保险。

7. 公证员享有法律规定的其他权利。

第二十三条　公证员的义务

1. 公证员应：

（1）公正无私，在开展公证活动时遵守公证伦理规则；

（2）依照本法关于职务保密的规定以及《亚美尼亚共和国反洗钱和资助恐怖主义法》的规定，对职务行为保密；

（3）公证事项违反亚美尼亚共和国法律或国际条约的，公证员应拒绝公证；

（4）因疾病旷工超过5日或有其他正当理由，应告知司法部和公证机构；

（5）公证机构的地址变更须经司法部批准；

（6）不得违反《亚美尼亚共和国反洗钱和资助恐怖主义法》的规定；

（7）在公证机构规定的程序和条件下，每年接受1次公证机构组织的培训。每次培训的持续时间为30课时至60课时，每课时时长40分钟。

1.2. 依据本条第1款第5项的规定，公证机构变更的新地址不符合公证区域规划，或公证机构不符合法律规定的最低要求或标准，司法部部长应在1周内驳回公证机构地址变更的申请。

2. 应公证申请人的要求，公证员履行职务和提供其他公证服务时，还应：

（1）协助公证申请人办理公证手续，保障申请人的合法权益，并向申请人说明其权利和义务，提醒申请人公证的后果；

（解释2）明确公证申请人提供的公证方案对申请人的意义和价值，并审查其内容是否符合申请人的

pliance of their content to actual intent of the parties.

The paragraph of the second of Item 2) of part 2 of Article 23 voided according to the Law of the Republic of Armenia of 12.11.2016 No. ZR-180

3. If in the document submitted for the certificate or witnessing in notarial procedure the right of foreign state was applied or if the notary has doubts in the relation of application of the right of foreign state, then he reports about it to the addressed parties and does the corresponding mark in certifying text. In this case the notary shall not perform the obligations provided by the subitem 3 of Item 1 and Item 2 of this Article regarding rules of law of foreign state and does not bear any damage liability, caused thereof to the parties or the third parties.

4. The notary shall not verify authenticity of the statements or other documents issued by the organizations or the organizations provided to him which competence it enters, and also issued by physical persons according to the procedure, provided by the law or other legal acts, and does not bear any damage liability, caused thereof to the parties or the third parties if it is not provided by the law or if it is not proved that the notary knew or shall know that they are not true.

The notary shall not check in the certified transactions or the authenticity of data or the facts witnessed documents, specified by the parties or specified according to their offer, and does not bear any damage liability, caused thereof to the parties or the third parties if it is not provided by the law or if it is not proved that the notary knew or shall know that they are not true.

When making the notarial actions provided by subitems 6-7, 11-12, 14 of Item 1 of article 36 of this Law, the notary shall not check compliance of contents of the documents certified, witnessed or accepted for other notarial action to the laws or requirements of other legal acts and does not bear any damage liability, caused thereof to the parties or the third parties.

5. The obligations which are not provided by this Law cannot be assigned to the notary.

Article 24. Disciplinary responsibility of the notary

1. Concerning the notary can initiate disciplinary production:

1) Minister of Justice,

2) notarial chamber.

2. The Minister of Justice initiates disciplinary production as a result of research of the occasions established

真实意图。

（亚美尼亚共和国 2016 年 11 月 12 日第 ZR-180 号法令，第 23 条第 2 款第 2 项已被废止）

3. 依据外国法律提交的文件或通过的公证程序，公证员对外国国家法律的适用存有疑问时，应当向申请人指出，在证明文本中做相应的标记。在此情况下，公证员无须履行本条第 1 款第 3 项和第 2 款规定的有关外国法律规定的义务，并且不承担由此对申请人或第三方造成损害的赔偿责任。

4. 在法律未规定或无法证明公证员知道或应当知道公证材料虚假时，公证员无须核实法定组织向其提供的声明和文件的真实性，也无须核实自然人依据法律制作的文件的真实性，公证员不承担对申请人或第三方造成损害的赔偿责任。

在法律未规定或无法证明公证员知道或应当知道数据虚假的情形下，公证员无须核查已经被依法确认的数据的真实性，公证员不承担由此对申请人或第三方造成损害的赔偿责任。

公证员在履行本法第 36 条第 1 款第 6 项至第 7 项、第 11 项至第 12 项、第 14 项规定的职务时，无须核查证明、见证或者接受其他公证行为的文件内容是否符合法律的规定，不承担由此对申请人或第三方造成损害的赔偿责任。

5. 本法未规定的义务，公证员无须承担。

第二十四条　公证员的纪律责任

1. 对公证员的纪律问责主体包括：

（1）司法部部长；

（2）公证机构。

2. 司法部部长依据本法第 25 条第 1 款的规定，对本条第 5 款规定的情形进行审查，从而作出纪律处

by part 5 of this Article based on detection of signs of the disciplinary violation established by part 1 of article 25 of this Law.

分决定。

3. The research provided by part 2 of this Article is performed by means of studying of documents, and also the requirement by divisions of the Ministry of Justice or their officials of notarial cases and other documents with visit of notary office or without visit of notary office, and also providing research in electronic system. The operations provided by this part shall be performed within the questions considered in disciplinary production.

3. 本条第 2 款规定的审查内容包括有关文件，或司法部各司及其工作人员对公证案件审查提出的各项要求，以及公证机构提供的电子文件。对上述内容的审查应考虑纪律追责问题。

The notary provides the documents specified in this part, materials within two working days from the moment of receipt of the notification.

公证员应在收到通知之日起 2 个工作日内提供本款规定的文件材料。

4. The notarial chamber initiates disciplinary production on the basis, stipulated in Item 2 parts 1 of article 25 of this Law. In case of initiation of disciplinary productions by the Minister of Justice and notarial chamber on the same basis and the reason, the disciplinary production initiated by notarial chamber stops. The notarial chamber attaches the conclusion about the disciplinary basis to the decision on cessation of production.

4. 公证机构依据本法第 25 条第 1 款、第 2 款规定作出纪律问责决定。若司法部部长和公证机构依据相同条款作出纪律问责且原因一致，公证机构应停止纪律问责，并作出停止纪律问责的决定。

5. Reasons for initiation of disciplinary production are:

5. 作出纪律问责的原因是：

a) statement or claim;

（a）被控告或被要求赔偿；

b) message of state bodies and local government bodies, officials;

（b）泄露国家机构、地方政府机构或官员的信息；

c) the court resolution of court which took legal effect;

（c）违反已经生效的法院裁决；

d) the message of notarial chamber about submitted by it claims or applications for notarial actions or other services provided by the notary;

（d）泄漏申请人向公证机构申请公证的内容，或公证活动以及其他公证服务的信息；

e) independent detection of signs of violation of the Laws of the Republic of Armenia, others legal asset, and also rules of notarial ethics;

（e）经发现存在违反亚美尼亚共和国法律、其他法律规范和公证道德准则的行为；

f) detection of signs of violation as a result of generalization of notarial practice or program research.

（f）经发现在公证活动或对项目公证过程中存在违法行为。

6. Duration of disciplinary production cannot be more than six weeks, and can be prolonged only once – for a period of three weeks. The notary is notified on initiation of disciplinary production within one day.

6. 纪律问责的持续时间不得超过 6 周，并且只能延长一次，延长期间不得超过 3 周。应当在作出纪律问责决定后的 1 日内通知该公证员。

7. Person performing disciplinary production within the questions considered in disciplinary production, has the right:

7. 在纪律问责的范围内，执行纪律问责的人有权：

1) during disciplinary production to require from the notary necessary documents and information which shall be provided by the notary within two working days after

（1）在纪律问责过程中，要求公证员在收到通知后 2 个工作日内，提供必要的文件和资料；

receipt of the requirement;

2) to study necessary documents and materials in notary office;

3) to require from the notary of explanation in writing;

4) to address that face whose statement became the basis for initiation of disciplinary production, with the offer to submit additional documents and information.

8. The notary concerning whom disciplinary production was initiated shall represent explanations in writing to person which initiated disciplinary production.

In case of refusal to represent explanations in writing about it record which is signed by the notary is made, or record about refusal by the last to append the signature is made.

The notary concerning whom disciplinary production was initiated has the right not to provide the documents provided by part 3 of this Article if it does not enter framework of disciplinary production.

9. Before decision making by person who initiated disciplinary production, the notary concerning whom disciplinary production was initiated has the right to get acquainted with materials of disciplinary production. Materials are transferred to the notary not later than seven working days till deadline for decision making by person who initiated disciplinary production. Within seven working days after receipt of materials the notary has the right to represent additional explanations or to initiate the petition for carrying out additional research.

10. Person initiating production based on results of disciplinary production accepts one of the following decisions:

1) about the termination of disciplinary production;

2) o assignment of responsibility on the notary.

11. Person which initiated production after decision making about the termination of disciplinary production cannot initiate disciplinary production on the same basis again.

12. Person which initiated production, the witnesses and other persons participating in production shall observe privacy of disciplinary production.

13. The decisions made by notarial chamber as a result of disciplinary production within three working days from the moment of their acceptance go to the Ministry of Justice.

14. In case of initiation of disciplinary production, the terms established by part 3 of article 25 of this Law for

（2）在公证机构查阅必要的文件和材料；

（3）要求公证员以书面形式作出说明；

（4）处理作出纪律问责依据的事实声明，并要求提交相关文件和信息。

8. 受到纪律问责的公证员应向执行纪律问责的人员提供书面说明。

若拒绝提供书面说明，则由公证员签字备案，或者保留拒绝签名的记录。

对于接受纪律问责的公证员，若没有进入纪律问责程序，则有权不提供本条第 3 款规定的文件。

9. 在对公证员作出纪律问责决定前，公证员有权了解纪律问责的相关信息。执行纪律问责的人员在纪律问责决定作出后的 7 个工作日内将相关材料提供给公证员。公证员在收到材料后的 7 个工作日内，有权提出补充说明，并由有关人员进行补充审查。

10. 以纪律问责结果为前提的其他程序应等待有权主体作出以下决定：

（1）终止纪律问责；

（2）公证员承担责任。

11. 在作出终止纪律问责的决定后，审查人员不能基于相同事由再次启动纪律问责程序。

12. 启动纪律问责程序的人员、证人和其他参与人，应当遵守纪律问责的保密要求。

13. 公证机构在作出纪律问责决定的 3 个工作日内，应报司法部备案。

14. 在开始纪律问责的情形下，本法第 25 条第 3 款有关纪律问责的规定停止适用。

assignment of disciplinary responsibility, stop.

15. If during the terms established by part 3 of article 25 of this Law concerning the notary criminal case (prosecution) was brought or in court legitimacy of the action which is the basis for violation, then the course of term of initiation of disciplinary production is appealed, and in case of initiation of disciplinary production – process of the initiated disciplinary production stops. The term of initiation of disciplinary production or process of the initiated disciplinary production stop before the final decision on criminal case or acceptance of final court resolution by court. In case of variation of initiation of disciplinary production or the termination of criminal prosecution, and also after the introduction in legal force of the court resolution adopted by court, term of initiation of disciplinary production or the course of the initiated disciplinary production proceeds from the moment of the termination, in the procedure established by this Law.

15. 若纪律问责的事项是依据本法第 25 条第 3 款规定的刑事案件，或作为违法行为的合法诉讼，已经启动的纪律问责应当停止。在刑事案件的最终裁决或终审法院核准之前，即将启动或已经启动纪律问责程序的应当停止。以上依照本法规定，如果纪律问责事项变更或刑事诉讼终止，并且在法院作出生效判决后，即将启动或已经启动的纪律问责程序应立即终止。

16. If concerning the notary disciplinary production based on several facts was initiated, then more severe measure of authority punishment is applied to it.

16. 基于多种情形对公证员作出纪律问责的，则应对其采取更为严厉的处罚措施。

Article 24.1. Bases for the termination of disciplinary production

第二十四条之一　终止纪律问责的依据

1. Disciplinary production stops if:

1) the fact which is the basis for imposing of authority punishment on the notary is unreasonable;

2) the term provided for imposing of authority punishment on the notary expired;

3) its powers are stopped, or it is discharged of position;

4) in the case established by part 3 of article 24 of this Law.

1. 符合以下条件，应终止纪律问责：

（1）对公证员实施处罚所依据的理由是不合理的；

（2）对公证员实施处罚的条款已经停止适用；

（3）公证员职务已经被终止，或者已经被解除职务；

（4）出现本法第 24 条第 3 款规定的情形。

Article 25. The bases for imposing of authority punishment on the notary

第二十五条　对公证员实施处罚的依据

1. The bases for imposing of authority punishment on the notary are:

1) notorious violation of normative requirements of the law and other legal acts shown to implementation of activities of the notary, accomplishment, refusal, the termination, action delay;

2) notorious abuse of regulations of ethics;

3) absence is at least, than on 20 percent of occupations of rates of retraining without reasonable excuse.

1. 对公证员实施处罚的依据是：

（1）对公证活动的执行、完成、拒绝、终止、迟延等明显违反本法和其他法律的规范性要求；

（2）违背道德规范的；

（3）无正当理由缺席培训达到培训课程总量 20% 的。

2. Recognition invalid or its change judicially in itself does not result the document certified or approved by the notary in responsibility of the notary who assured or

2. 公证员违反法律，未使经过公证的文件的内容变更或无效的，之后公证申请人再次申请启动公证程序，且经过公证后的文件无效或被依法变更时，并不

approved this document if it was not changed or nullified for cause of infringement of requirements of the law made by the notary.

The notary cannot be made responsible if the certified or approved document was nullified, and the performed notarial operations were acknowledged illegal because of the false or illegal agreements or announcements provided to it, to check legality and which fidelity the notary could not or did not owe if it is not proved that the notary knew or owed know that content provided agreements, announcements or other documents are not true.

3. The notary cannot be made responsible if from the moment of making of the actions which caused the violations established by part 1 of article 25 of this Law there passed one year, except for the violations provided by subitems 1 and 3 of part 2 of article 17 of this Law for which disciplinary production cannot be initiated if from the date of accomplishment of actions there passed three years.

Article 26. The authority punishments applied to the notary

1. On the bases established by part 1 of article 25 of this Law, to the notary one of the following authority punishments can be appointed:

1) prevention;

2) reprimand;

3) serious reprimand;

4) the activities termination, for up to 6 months.

2. The Minister of Justice is competent to apply the penalties established by part of 1 this Article, and notarial chamber – the authority punishments established by Items 1 and 2 of part of 1 this Article.

3. The termination of activities of the notary as measure of authority punishment, can be applied in case of the violations of the notary provided by Items 1, 3 or 5 part 2 of article 17 of this Law.

4. The authority punishment applied to the notary shall be equivalent to committed violation. In case of application of authority punishment also violation consequences, degree of fault of the notary, the available penalties characterizing the notary other circumstances deserving attention are considered.

5. If within two years from the date of receipt of reprimand or serious reprimand or the termination of activities, and from the date of receipt of the prevention - within one year, the notary was not exposed to new authority punishment, then he is considered not having authority

导致此前公证员承担责任。

如果已经经过公证获批准的文件因合法性问题被认定无效，且公证结果因上述文件的无效而被认定为违法的，若没有证据表明公证员知道或应当知道这些文件不真实，则公证员对此不承担责任。

3. 依据本法第 25 条第 1 款的规定，违法行为自发生之日起已届 1 年，公证员不再承担责任。本法第 17 条第 2 款第 1 项和第 3 项规定的违法行为自行为发生之日起已届 3 年，不能对公证员进行纪律问责。

第二十六条　对公证员的惩罚

1. 依据本法第 25 条第 1 款的规定，可以对公证员作出下列形式之一的惩罚决定：

（1）警告；

（2）训诫；

（3）严重训诫；

（4）中止公证员职务活动，但不超过 6 个月。

2. 司法部部长有权依据本条第 1 款规定作出惩罚决定，公证机构有权依据本条第 1 款第 1 项和第 2 项作出惩罚决定。

3. 公证员若违反本法第 17 条第 2 款第 1 项、第 3 项、第 5 项的规定，则可以适用对公证员惩罚的规定，并终止其职务活动。

4. 对于公证员的惩罚应与其违法行为相对应。在实施惩罚时，可以同时考量违法后果、公证员的过错程度，以及其他可以考量的因素。

5. 在收到训诫、严重训诫或终止公证员职务的决定之日起 2 年内，或自收到警告之日起 1 年内，公证员未受到新的处罚，则视为公证员未被处罚。

punishment.

The notary can appeal purpose of authority punishment in court, within two months after receipt of the decision on collection application.

公证员在收到惩罚决定的 2 个月内，可以就惩罚决定向法院提起诉讼。

Article 27. Property responsibility of the notary

1. The notary bears the property damage liability established by the Civil code of the Republic of Armenia, put as a result of the violation made by it purposely or on imprudence.

In case of discharge of the notary from position, for contest of competence of the operations performed by the notary or other executed notarial services or refusal of their accomplishment, the notarial chamber, and according to requirements of compensation of damage, including, compensations of court costs – the notary discharged of position appears in court as the defendant.

2. The notary shall insure risk of the responsibility in double amount of the paid payment for the services provided during previous year, but at least 6 million dram of the Republic of Armenia.

3. In the case established by part 4 of article 35.1 of this Law damage caused by notaries is compensated from means of reserve fund.

第二十七条　公证员应承担的财产损害赔偿责任

1. 依据亚美尼亚共和国民法规定，公证员对因故意或过失而造成的财产损害承担赔偿责任。

公证员违反操作权限、违反其他服务的规范或拒绝履行公证职责而被解雇，被解雇的公证员作为被告出庭，公证机构可要求其赔偿损失，并承担法院诉讼费用。

2. 风险责任储备金应是公证员上一年度提供服务所收取费用数额的两倍，至少要达到 600 万德拉姆。

3. 在本法第 35.1 条第 4 款规定的情形下，公证员造成的损害由风险责任储备金支付。

Article 27.1. Responsibility of the notary for non-execution or improper execution of requirements of the Law of the Republic of Armenia "About anti-money laundering and terrorism financing" and the legal acts adopted on its basis

1. In case non-execution or improper execution of requirements of the Law of the Republic of Armenia "About anti-money laundering and terrorism financing" and the legal acts adopted on its basis, the notary is subject to responsibility according to the procedure, provided by part 5 of article 30 of that law.

第二十七条之一　公证员不遵守或不适当遵守《亚美尼亚共和国反洗钱和资助恐怖主义法》的规定，应对其做出的职务行为承担责任

1. 公证员不遵守或不适当遵守《亚美尼亚共和国反洗钱和资助恐怖主义法》的规定，对在此基础上实施的法律行为，公证员应依照该法第 30 条第 5 款的规定承担责任。

Article 28. Reporting of the notary

The notary shall represent quarterly to the Ministry of Justice and notarial chamber the report on notarial activities according to the procedure, established by the Minister of Justice.

The notary according to the procedure, the terms established by the legislation also represents the statistic, tax and other reports which are directly provided by the law to the bodies provided by the law.

第二十八条　公证员的汇报

公证员应当按照司法部部长规定的程序，每季度向司法部和公证机构提交公证活动报告。

公证员依据法律规定的条款向有关机构提供统计、税收和其他报告。

Article 29. Trainee and device of the notary

1. The notary can have the assistant or other workers

第二十九条　公证员助理及其培训

1. 公证员可以雇用和解雇公证员助理或其他工作

who are employed and discharged from office by the notary. The number of workers of the notary is determined by the notary.

人员。公证员助理的数量由公证机构决定。

The nominated person who does not have the higher legal education and also the notary dismissed according to of the 8th Item 1 of article 17 of this Law cannot be the assistant notary.

依据本法第 17 条第 1 款第 8 项的规定，未接受过高等法学教育的人员，或被解雇的公证员，不能成为公证员助理。

2. The notary can have the trainee whose training is performed according to the agreement signed between the notary and the trainee.

2. 公证机构可以对公证员和助理进行培训。

Any capable citizen of the Republic of Armenia having the higher or incomplete higher legal education and not having criminal record can be the trainee of the notary.

公证员助理应当具有民事行为能力，且为亚美尼亚共和国公民，接受过高等法学教育，并且没有犯罪记录。

3. The notary at the same time can have no more than two trainees.

3. 一名公证员的助理不能超过两名。

4. The assistant or the trainee of the notary has the right to make the following actions:

4. 公证员助理有权进行以下行为：

1) to accept citizens or to study the documents submitted by them;

2) to give consultation or to render other legal services;

3) to conduct notarial clerical work;

4) to constitute drafts of transactions and other documents of legal content;

5) to generalize notarial practice;

6) to work with archive;

7) to carry out other works established by the notary, except for making of notarial actions.

（1）接收公证申请人提交的文件，并开展审查工作；

（2）提供咨询或其他法律服务；

（3）从事公证文书工作；

（4）制订公证方案和制作其他文件；

（5）对公证活动进行整理总结；

（6）存档工作；

（7）公证员安排的公证活动以外的其他工作。

5. The rights and obligations of the assistant notary or other persons working for it are determined by the labor law of the Republic of Armenia and the employment contract signed between them and the notary.

5. 公证员助理或其他工作人员的权利和义务，由亚美尼亚共和国劳动法和他们与公证机构签订的劳动合同确定。

6. The assistant notary shall at least, than once a year undergo the retraining organized by notarial chamber, in the procedures and conditions established by notarial chamber.

6. 依照公证机构规定的程序和条件，公证员助理每年应至少接受一次公证机构组织的培训。

7. The procedure for acceptance of the notary as the trainee and passing of training is established by the Minister of Justice.

7. 由司法部部长规定公证员接收助理和培训的程序。

Chapter 4. To notarial chamber

第四章　公证机构

Article 30. Notarial chamber

1. The notarial chamber is the professional non-profit organization of notaries founded on the principles of self-government and obligatory membership of notaries. The notarial chamber performs the activities according

第三十条　公证机构

1. 公证机构是由公证员组成的非营利性专业组织，以自治原则和强制性原则为基础。公证机构依据亚美尼亚共和国宪法、本法、其他法律法规和章程开展活动。

to the Constitution of the Republic of Armenia, this Law, other laws, legal acts and the charter.

2. The charter of notarial chamber is accepted, changes, supplemented with notarial chamber, and is registered the Ministry of Justice.

The requirements established for the charter of public organizations extend to the charter of notarial chamber.

Registration of notarial chamber is performed according to the procedure, provided for registration of public organizations.

3. The notarial chamber represents and performs the interests of notaries, gives them help when implementing notarial activities, participates in holding qualification examinations, monitors advanced training of notaries, performs other powers provided by this Law.

4. The supreme body of notarial chamber is the meeting of members of notarial chamber, executive body - board of notarial chamber.

5. Activities of notarial chamber are financed by the membership fees of notaries and from other sources which are not forbidden by the law.

6. Control of observance by notarial chamber of this Law, other legal acts and authorized requirements of chamber performs the Ministry of Justice.

The chairman of notarial chamber shall send to three-day time to the copy of decisions of meeting, board of notarial chamber or decisions made by it in the Ministry of Justice. The last has the right to take a legal action for recognition by the invalid accepted notarial chamber or its officials and bodies of the decisions and other acts which are contradicting the law, legal acts and the charter of notarial chamber or not following from them.

Control of notarial chamber have the right to perform other state bodies which are directly provided by the law.

Article 31. Structure of notarial chamber

1. The notarial chamber consists of all notaries appointed in the procedure established by this Law.

2. The notary becomes the member of notarial chamber from the date of position assignment, and its membership stops from the date of dismissal.

Article 32. Methods of implementation by notarial chamber of the tasks

1. For implementation of the tasks notarial chamber:

1) establishes the relations with state bodies and local government bodies, the international organizations and associations of citizens;

2. 公证机构章程的制订、变更、补充，须向司法部登记。

公共机构章程的制订应符合公证机构的业务发展。

公证机构的登记按照公共组织登记程序进行。

3. 公证机构维护公证员的利益，在公证员进行公证活动时给予其帮助，组织公证员参加资格考试，监督公证员参与高级培训，履行本法规定的其他权力。

4. 公证机构的最高机构是公证机构成员大会，同时公证机构成员大会也是公证机构的执行机构。

5. 公证机构在活动中所支出的费用来自公证员的会费。

6. 公证机构应按照本法、其他法律的规定和大会的授权，执行司法部的要求。

公证机构主席应在 3 日内将公证机构成员大会决议的副本，或司法部作出决议的副本送达至有关主体。若决议内容与法律和公证机构章程的规定相抵触时，有关主体有权要求公证机构成员会议主席或其成员重新审查决议内容。

公证机构的管理机构有权依据法律规定行使职权。

第三十一条　公证机构的组织结构

1. 公证机构的人员组成包含依据本法规定的程序产生的所有公证员。

2. 公证员自被任命之日起成为公证机构成员，自解聘之日起不再承担公证员职务。

第三十二条　公证机构履行职责的方式

1. 公证机构履行的职责包括：

（1）与国家机关、地方政府部门、国际组织和社会团体建立联系；

Represents 2) to the Ministry of Justice of the offer about the notaries concerning activities the laws or other legal acts, and also about their change or amendment;

3) generalizes results of activities of notaries for the purpose of ensuring single practice of making of notarial actions;

4) will be organized by case of training and advanced training of notaries;

4. 1) will organize the works connected with replenishment, accounting, storage and use of notarial archive documents;

5) performs other powers provided by this Law.

2. The list of paid established posts of notarial chamber approves meeting of members of notarial chamber.

（2）向司法部提出公证员活动申请及其变更或修改的请求；

（3）对公证活动进行总结，保证公证员职务行为具有一致性；

（4）组织公证员培训和高级培训；

（4.1）负责组织公证档案文件的补充、核算、保管和使用工作；

（5）行使本法规定的其他职权。

2. 有关公证机构常设岗位的设置由公证机构成员会议批准。

Article 33. Meeting of members of notarial chamber

1. The meeting of members of notarial chamber is convened at least once a year.

2. The extraordinary meeting of members of notarial chamber is convened by the chairman of the board of notarial chamber on the initiative, according to the offer of board of notarial chamber or at least one heel from total number of members of notarial chamber. If the chairman of the board within 20 days does not convene extraordinary meeting, then offered have the right to convene extraordinary meeting.

3. The meeting of members of notarial chamber convokes and carries out board of notarial chamber which in two weeks notifies members of chamber on the place, time of carrying out and the agenda of meeting.

The chairman of the board of notarial chamber, and in its absence - his deputy presides over meeting of members of notarial chamber.

Notaries and the Ministry of Justice are notified on the place and time of meeting of members of notarial chamber not later than ten days prior to meeting. The representative of the Ministry of Justice shall be present at meeting.

4. The notary personally participates in meeting of members of notarial chamber.

5. The meeting of members of notarial chamber is competent if at it there are at least two thirds of members of chamber. Decisions of meeting of members of chamber are made by open or secret vote, by a majority vote the participants except for provided by this Law of cases.

6. The meeting of members of notarial chamber is competent to resolve any issue which is in competence of

第三十三条　公证机构成员会议

1. 公证机构成员会议每年至少召开一次。

2. 公证机构成员特别会议的召开由公证机构理事会主席根据公证机构理事会的提议或至少一名成员的提议召开。若在 20 日内未召开特别会议，则理事会主席有权决定召开特别会议。

3. 召开公证机构成员会议、公证机构理事会，须在两周前通知成员开会的时间、地点和会议议程。

公证机构理事会主席无法出席会议时，由副主席主持公证机构成员会议。

应在会议召开的 10 日前将会议的时间、地点通知公证员和司法部。司法部派代表出席会议。

4. 公证员应当亲自参加公证机构成员会议。

5. 公证机构成员会议，须有 2/3 以上的成员出席方才有效。成员会议的决议以公开表决或不记名表决的方式作出，以多数票通过，本法另有规定的除外。

6. 公证机构成员会议有权对职权范围内的任何问题作出处理决定。

notarial chamber.

Article 34. Competence of meeting of members of notarial chamber

1. The supreme body of notarial chamber is general meeting of her members which possesses the right of the solution of any question which is in competence of notarial chamber.

2. Are within the exclusive competence of meeting of members of notarial chamber:

1) adoption of the charter of notarial chamber, introduction in it of changes and amendments;

2) approval of the annual statement of notarial chamber;

3) election of the chairman, board members of notarial chamber and their release;

4) approval of balance of the income and expenses of notarial chamber;

5) approval according to the offer of board of the notarial House of Representatives of notarial chamber as a part of the qualification commission;

6) approval of the size of the membership fees of members of notarial chamber;

7) approval of the staff list and size of the salary of paid employees of notarial payment;

8) approval of rules of notarial ethics.

The solution of the questions which are in exclusive competence of notarial chamber cannot be transferred to competence of board of notarial chamber or its other body.

3. In case of reasonable excuse the meeting of members of notarial chamber is competent to permit board to make changes in balance of notarial chamber which are submitted for approval of the nearest meeting of members of notarial chamber.

Article 35. Board of notarial chamber

1. The meeting of members of notarial chamber elects board which consists of the chairman, his deputy and three members. The chairman of the board of notarial chamber at the same time is the chairman of notarial chamber. The chairman and board members of notarial chamber fulfill the duties on a voluntary basis without separation from the main work.

2. The chairman of notarial chamber and board are elected by meeting of members of notarial chamber secret vote, by a majority vote participants of the meeting.

Election of the chairman of notarial chamber, his deputy and board members is carried out separately.

第三十四条　公证机构成员会议的权限

1. 公证机构的最高机构是公证机构成员会议，会议有权处理公证机构职权范围内的任何问题。

2. 属于公证机构成员会议的专属职权的有：

（1）通过公证机构章程，修改章程的内容；

（2）批准公证机构年度报表；

（3）选举和任免公证机构成员会议的主席、理事；

（4）核定公证机构的收入与支出；

（5）根据公证机构理事会的提议，批准公证员加入资格评定委员会；

（6）核定公证机构成员会费数额；

（7）核定公证机构成员名单以及成员的工资；

（8）核准公证道德规范。

公证机构成员会议享有的解决问题的专有权，不能转移到公证机构理事会或者其他机构。

3. 在有正当理由的情况下，公证机构成员会议可允许理事会为了公证机构的利益而对公证事务作变更调整，并提交至公证机构成员会议批准。

第三十五条　公证机构理事会

1. 公证机构理事会由公证机构成员会议选举产生，理事会由主席、副主席和 3 名委员组成。理事会主席同时也是公证机构成员会议的主席。理事会主席、成员应自觉履行职责，不得无故脱离工作岗位。

2. 公证机构成员会议和理事会主席由公证机构成员会议以秘密投票方式选举产生，由参加会议人员的多数票通过。

公证机构理事会主席、副主席和委员的选举应分别进行。

If for election to position of the chairman of notarial chamber or his deputy more than two candidates are proposed and any of them did not receive necessary poll, then repeated vote in which two candidates who received the greatest poll participate is taken.

If two candidates stood and any of them was not elected, then new elections are held.

3. Term of office of board and chairman four years. Board members and the chairman cannot more than two be elected time in a row to the same positions.

4. The board convenes meetings at least once in three months.

The meeting convokes and the chairman of the board, and in its absence - the deputy conducts. The board can consider questions and pass decisions if more than a half of board members participates in its meeting. Board decisions are made by a majority vote. The voice of the chairman of the board in case of equality of votes is decisive.

5. Board of notarial chamber:

1) is provided by accomplishment of authorized tasks of notarial chamber and implementation of decisions of meeting of his members;

2) represents notarial chamber in the relations with the organizations, if necessary on behalf of notarial chamber represents offers and the conclusions;

3) presents candidacies of representatives of notarial chamber at meeting of members of notarial chamber;

4) to accomplishment of the tasks of other notaries who are not joining the board of notarial chamber;

5) constitutes forms of legal documents and provides the current consultation and informing notaries;

6) is recorded the income and expenses of notarial chamber and by accounting of fees of her members;

7) will organize rates on retraining of the notary, assistant notary.

6. The President of Chamber on position is notary.

President of Chamber:

1) convenes meetings and board meetings;

2) constitutes protocols of meetings of meeting and board;

3) acts on behalf of chamber without power of attorney, represents its interests;

4) disposes of property of chamber, on behalf of chamber signs contracts, including labor;

5) performs functions of the employer for hired employees of chamber;

若所提名的理事会主席或副主席有两名以上的候选人，若两名候选人票数相等，则需再次进行选举，由票数最多的候选人当选。

若有两名候选人参选，但没有任何一名当选，则应当重新选举。

3. 理事会成员和主席任期 4 年，理事会成员和主席连选连任不超过两届。

4. 理事会至少每 3 个月召开一次会议。

理事会会议由理事会主席或副主席主持，在主席无法主持时由副主席主持。理事会若需通过决议，须超过半数的理事会成员参加会议。理事会的决议由多数人投票通过。在赞成票数与反对票数相等的情况下，理事会主席有最终决定权。

5. 公证机构理事会应：

（1）完成公证机构授权的工作，并执行公证机构成员会议的决定；

（2）代表公证机构与有关机构开展联系，必要时代表公证机构提议并作出结论；

（3）在公证机构成员会议上提名公证员候选人；

（4）完成其他未参加公证机构理事会公证员的任务；

（5）起草法律文书，提供当面咨询、公证服务；

（6）对公证员的收入和费用进行核算；

（7）制定公证员、公证员助理的培训计划。

6. 公证机构理事会主席必须是公证员。

公证机构理事会主席有权：

（1）提议召开成员会议和理事会；

（2）主持制定理事会会议章程；

（3）出于公证机构利益的考虑，无须授权即可代表公证机构行使职权；

（4）处置公证机构财产，代表公证机构签订合同，其中包括劳动合同；

（5）履行对公证机构所聘员工的雇主职责；

6) performs other functions referred by this Law to competence of notarial chamber on which accomplishment it is authorized by meeting, except for special powers of general meeting.

7. The chairman of the board of notarial chamber, his deputy, other board members and the staff of chamber has no right to disclose data on notarial actions which became known to them in case of execution of the obligations by them in board. Such data are disclosed only with the permission of notarial chamber.

Specified persons shall keep notarial secret also after secession of board or dismissal from service.

8. Voided

Article 35.1. Reserve fund of notarial chamber

1. For guarantee of compensation of damage caused by notaries by means of capitalization at least ten percent of the membership fees of notaries on the bank account, the notarial chamber creates reserve fund (further - reserve fund).

2. Bank interests go for replenishment of reserve fund.

3. The meeting of members of notarial chamber can establish higher size of the percent paid to reserve fund.

4. From reserve fund losses caused by the notary are indemnified based on court resolution if the extent of damages exceeds the size of insurance sum of the notary, and it is impossible to indemnify completely due to personal property of the notary loss.

5. Means of reserve fund are used only for the purpose of compensation of damage caused by the notary.

6. Requirements of this Article are applicable also in cases of discharge of the notary from position or recognition by the bankrupt.

Chapter 5. Procedure for making of notarial actions and shown to them requirements

Article 36. The notarial actions made by the notary

1. The notary makes the following notarial actions:

1) certifies transactions (agreements, wills, powers of attorney, agreements and other);

2) takes measures to protection of heritable property;

3) grants certificates on the right to inheritance;

4) grants certificates on the property right to receivable share in the property which is in general joint or common ownership;

5) is witnessed by authenticity of copies of docu-

（6）履行本法规定的并由成员会议授权的公证机构职权范围内的其他职责，但成员特别会议规定的职权除外。

7. 公证机构理事会主席、副主席、其他理事会成员和工作人员，在履行其在理事会的职责时，无权披露其知悉的资料信息。相关资料信息须经公证机构许可方可披露。

离开理事会或者被辞退的人员，也应当保守职务秘密。

8. 已被废除。

第三十五条之一　公证机构的储备基金

1. 为保证有足够资金承担损害赔偿责任，公证机构应确保公证员在公共银行账户中存有 10% 的成员费，并以资本化的方式设立公证机构储备基金。

2. 银行利息用于补充公证机构储备基金。

3. 公证机构成员会议可以批准提高储备基金的缴纳比例。

4. 公证员造成储备基金损失，且损失数额超过公证员保险金数额的，公证员个人财产难以完全赔偿，则需根据法院判决赔偿。

5. 储备基金仅适用于公证员因造成损害而承担赔偿责任的情形。

6. 本条规定也适用于被解除职务的公证员或没有债务偿付能力的公证员。

第五章　公证程序及要求

第三十六条　公证员的公证活动

1. 公证员有权进行下列职务活动：

（1）对合同（协议、遗嘱、授权书、其他协议等）进行公证；

（2）采取措施保护继承财产；

（3）出具继承权公证书；

（4）在一般共有财产或者共同共有财产中，对共有人所占份额进行公证；

（5）对文件或副本的真实性作出公证；

ments or statements from them;

6) is witnessed by authenticity of the signature on documents;

7) is witnessed by fidelity of the translation of documents;

8) certifies the fact of finding of the citizen in live;

9) is certified by the fact of finding of the citizen in certain place;

10) is certified by identity of the citizen with person represented in the photo;

11) is certified by time of production of documents;

12) transfers statements, announcements or other documents of physical persons or organizations to other physical persons or the organizations;

13) Accepts the deposit on storage, transfers or returns sum of money or securities, precious metals, stones and issues the certificate;

14) accepts documents on storage;

15) provides proofs;

16) is certified by the protocol of general meeting of the organization or meeting of other collegiate organ;

17) is transferred by heritable property to trusteeship;

18) grants the certificates certifying powers of the testamentary executor;

19) in the consent of all heirs recognizes invalid earlier granted certificates on the right to inheritance;

20) is certified by authenticity of the signature of the confidential translator;

21) is issued by writ of execution for the signature;

22) issues copies of notarial acts;

23) performs other notarial actions provided by the law.

2. The officials who are directly provided by the Civil code can make the separate notarial actions provided by this Article.

3. For detection of heirs and possible creditors the notary publishes in the Internet the space intended for this purpose, the message on opening of heritage.

4. The notary, other performing notarial actions of person, when implementing notarial actions, can use electronic bases which conduct state bodies, for realization of the powers to obtain personal data, in the procedure established by the Government of the Republic of Armenia.

5. The notary, except the notarial services provided by this Article, provides the following services:

1) performs the functions directed to servicing of state registration of the rights arising from the transactions

（6）对文件中的签名的真实性作出公证；

（7）对文件翻译的准确性作出公证；

（8）对公民行为的真实性作出公证；

（9）对公民在特定地点的行为或事实作出公证；

（10）对公民与身份证件中照片是否一致作出公证；

（11）对文件制作的时间作出公证；

（12）将自然人或组织的报表、公告或其他文件转达给其他自然人或组织；

（13）接受存入的存款，转让、返还货币或者有价证券或保证金、贵金属、宝石的情况的公证；

（14）接受应储存的文件；

（15）提供证据；

（16）对其他合议机关会议的决议内容作出公证；

（17）对继承财产的委托管理情况进行公证；

（18）授予证明遗嘱执行人的公证书；

（19）经全体继承人同意，确认之前授予的继承权公证书无效；

（20）证明保密人员、翻译人员签名的真实性；

（21）出具执行令状；

（22）出具公证书副本；

（23）从事法律规定的其他公证活动。

2. 民法直接规定的公务员可以单独开展本条规定的公证活动。

3. 为了查明继承人和可能存在的债权人，公证员可在互联网上发布遗产信息。

4. 依照亚美尼亚共和国政府制定的程序，公证员或其他履行公证员职务的人员，在开展公证活动时，可使用国家机关的电子数据库，以获取个人资料信息。

5. 公证员除提供本条规定的公证服务外，还提供下列服务：

（1）提供国家登记服务，主要涉及财产的来源、变更、终止和转让所产生的权利；

directed to origin, change, the termination and assignment of rights on property;

2) in the cases provided by the law or the order of the Government of the Republic of Armenia, performs functions of office on servicing of state bodies;

3) for the purpose of providing the requirement of state registration of the rights proceeding from transactions notifies the bodies performing state registration of the rights to property about performing preliminary record about the right to property;

4) confirms the facts having legal value.

Article 36.1. Notarial act

1. The decision made as a result of the notarial actions performed by the notary, confirmation or assurance of the transaction or other document, the writ of execution for the signature are notarial acts.

2. The notarial act shall contain:

1) number of the notarial act, year, month, acceptance number;

2) notarial district (territory), name, surname of the notary,

3) the code confirming identification of the document;

4) sign and seal, stamp of the notary;

5) in the presence – the amount of the state tax and payment for the services provided by the notary;

6) other compulsory provisions established by the Law.

Article 37. Making of notarial actions

1. All notarial actions are made by any notary, except as specified, provided by this Law.

2. Any person for making of notarial action can address the notary (including, electronically), except as specified, provided by the law.

3. The application is electronically submitted to the notary with observance of the requirements established by the Law of the Republic of Armenia "About the electronic document and the digital signature".

Article 38. Restrictions in making of notarial actions

1. The notary or the official making the separate notarial actions having no right to make notarial actions on the name and on its own behalf addressed to and on behalf of the spouses, the or their parents, children, brothers, sisters, grandsons, the grandfather, the grandma and also addressed to and from employee name of this notary office.

（2）依据法律或亚美尼亚共和国政府的规定，履行国家机构的其他职责；

（3）根据国家财产权利登记的要求，告知有关主体财产权利，并对财产权利进行初步登记；

（4）确认具有法律价值的事实。

第三十六条之一　公证活动

1. 公证活动包括公证员履行公证员职务的活动、对交易或其他文件的公证以及对执行令状签字。

2. 公证书的内容应包括：

（1）公证书的编号、年、月及受理号；

（2）公证机构所在地及公证员姓名；

（3）公证文件的识别代码；

（4）公证员的签字盖章；

（5）提供公证服务的费用以及国家税收金额；

（6）法律规定的其他强制性内容。

第三十七条　公证员职务的履行

1. 除本法另有规定外，所有公证行为均由公证员作出。

2. 任何需要公证的人都可以向公证员提出公证申请，但法律另有规定的除外。

3. 公证申请人可以依据《亚美尼亚共和国电子文件和数字签名法》的规定，以电子方式提交公证申请。

第三十八条　公证活动的限制

1. 禁止公证员为其配偶、父母、子女、兄弟、姐妹、孙子女、祖父母作公证，禁止公证机构为其员工作公证。

2. The notary or the official making notarial actions and their relatives specified in Item 1 of this Article cannot act as intermediaries or witnesses of the transaction.

3. The restriction provided by Items 1 and 2 of this Article extends also to the notarial actions made by the organization:

a) which head is spouse (spouse) of the notary;

b) more than 50 percent of shares (shares, shares) of which belong to the notary or his spouse (spouse).

4. The restriction provided by this Article does not extend to the certificate of the transactions made through the public biddings.

5. If notarial actions concerning persons specified by this Article according to the law be made only by the notary specified by this Article, then the notary having power to make such notarial actions, the notarial chamber determines.

6. The notarial actions made with violation of requirements of this Article are insignificant.

Article 39. Language of making of notarial actions

1. Notarial actions are made in literary Armenian.

Only the documents constituted in literary Armenian are subject to the certificate or witnessing if the law does not provide other. The documents applied in the territory of the Republic of Armenia including the agreements requiring state registration of the rights following from transactions are constituted only in Armenian.

2. The bargains concluded with the foreign organizations, either foreign citizens, or stateless persons or between them, and also documents which shall be effective abroad can be at the same time certified or attested both on Armenian, and in foreign language (languages) if the notary sufficiently knows this language. If the notary and (or) the party sufficiently do not know document language, then the translator is invited. In this case the document is in accordance with the established procedure signed also by the translator. About service of the last in the text of the document the special mark becomes.

3. Texts of the documents which are at the same time certified or witnessed in the Armenian and foreign language (languages) can be stated one by one or near condition that in case of statement of texts one by one the text is located on Armenian in the upper part, and in case of statement with each other the text is located with row on Armenian in the left part.

4. The documents which are at the same time cer-

2. 本条第 1 款规定的公证机构、公证员及其亲属，不得作为公证的中间人或者见证人。

3. 本条第 1 款、第 2 款也适用于以下情形：

（a）负责人是该公证员的配偶；

（b）公证所涉企业超过 50% 的股份属于公证员或其配偶。

4. 本条规定不适用于对公开招标交易的公证。

5. 依据其他法律规定，若公证只能由本条中的公证员负责，须经公证机构批准后，该公证员方可开展公证活动。

6. 违反本条规定的公证活动无效。

第三十九条　公证活动的语言

1. 公证书以亚美尼亚文字作出。

若法律无其他规定，只有以亚美尼亚文字制作的公证书才对公证申请人或见证人产生约束力。在亚美尼亚共和国境内适用的公证书，包括需要进行官方登记的交易协议，只能用亚美尼亚文表述。

2. 公证事项涉及外国组织、外国公民、无国籍人，或需要对以外国文字作出的文件进行公证时，若公证员通晓此种语言，可同时以亚美尼亚语和外文版本制作公证书。若公证员和公证申请人不通晓该语言，应邀请翻译人员翻译。在此情况下，公证书需由翻译人员按照既定程序签署，且需在公证书末尾作翻译服务的特殊标记。

3. 以亚美尼亚语和外国文字分别制作公证书时，需对其文本进行翻译说明，并将外语文本置于亚美尼亚语版本的上方；若在同一公证书内同时使用两种文字，则应将外语置于亚美尼亚语左侧，以使其一一对应。

4. 使用亚美尼亚语或外语制作的两种版本的公证

tified or certified in the Armenian and foreign languages have identical legal force. In the presence of contradiction between the documents which are at the same time certified or certified in the Armenian and foreign languages preference is given certified or certified in Armenian.

5. Texts of the document certified or witnessed in different languages in the procedure established by this Law shall be signed and certified or attested separately.

6. If person does not know language in which the document is constituted, then it can sign it in language which knows.

7. Person who is not knowing Armenian can participate in notarial actions through the translator.

8. The document certified or certified with violation of requirements of this Article has no the evidential force provided by this Law.

Article 40. Identification of the notarial action of person which addressed for making, clarification of his legal capacity or capacity to act

1. When making notarial actions the notary shall identify the personality and check capacity to act of the notarial actions of physical persons, their representatives or representatives of the organization which addressed for making, and also to check legal capacity of the organizations, except as specified requests for consultations or rendering other notarial services which are not considered as notarial actions and also for making of the notarial actions provided by subitems 5-7 of Item 1 of article 36 of this Law.

When making notarial actions based on powers of attorney the notary shall check powers of the authorized parties.

2. The personality and capacity to act of physical person is determined by identification documents.

Legal capacity of the organization is determined proceeding from requirements of the legislation of the Republic of Armenia and the charter of the legal entity.

Legal capacity of the state or municipal authorities acting on behalf of the state or municipality are determined proceeding from requirements of the legislation of the Republic of Armenia and the charter of the bodies or organizations acting on behalf of the state or municipality.

Article 41. Obligation of the notary to request from documents for making of notarial actions

1. The notary requires from persons who addressed for notarial actions, to provide the necessary powers,

书具有相同的法律效力。当不同语言版本的公证书内容之间存在矛盾时，优先适用亚美尼亚语版本。

5. 依据本法规定，以不同语言作出的公证书，应当分别签署、确认。

6. 若签署人不通晓公证书的语言，可以使用其通晓的语言签署文件。

7. 不通晓亚美尼亚语的人，可以聘请翻译参加公证活动。

8. 违反本条规定的公证书，不具有本法规定的公证效力。

第四十条　确认参与公证活动的主体的行为能力

1. 公证员在公证活动中应当确定参与公证的主体、代理人或者法人代表的主体资格，审查自然人及法人是否具备完全的民事行为能力。但依据本法第 36 条第 1 款第 5 项至第 7 项的规定，若提供公证法律咨询或其他不被视为公证行为的服务时，无须确认相关主体的民事行为能力。

公证申请人委托代理人参与公证活动时，公证员应当审查代理人的权限。

2. 自然人的人格和行为能力通过身份证明文件确认。

法人的行为能力是根据亚美尼亚共和国的立法和法人实体法的要求确定的。

国家或市政当局代表的行为能力，根据亚美尼亚共和国立法和国家或市政当局组织章程的规定而确定。

第四十一条　公证员在公证时可以提出的要求

1. 公证员应依照法律和公证活动的实际情况，要求公证申请人提供必要的许可、协议或者其他文件。

permissions, agreements or documents, stipulated by the legislation for making of these notarial actions, following from the law and other legal acts.

For the certificate of transactions of acquisition, change or the termination of the rights to property the notary shall request from proofs of the rights to property, and also rights of the Party on acquisition, change or the termination of the rights to property except for provided by the law of cases.

2. The obligation of the proof of powers, the rights, obligations or privileges of persons who addressed for making of notarial actions is assigned to persons who addressed for making of notarial actions, and obligation of determination of compliance to the law or other legal acts of the transactions made by persons who addressed for making of notarial actions, or other operations performed for them - to the notary.

3. If the notary on single electronic information system can obtain information at other bodies or persons, presentation of information necessary for accomplishment of notarial action is not required from persons who addressed the notary.

Article 42. Requirements to the documents prepared for making of notarial actions

1. Are not subject to the certificate or witnessing, and also documents in which are not specified year, month, number of their creation are not accepted for the basis for making of notarial actions, or there are erasures or essential damages, either additions, or the crossed-out words, or other passed parts provided for further amendment, or other not stipulated corrections, and also the documents written by pencil.

Sheets in the document which amount exceeds one leaf shall be stitched, numbered.

2. Texts of the documents certified and witnessed in notarial procedure shall be written clearly, is accurate and legible, shall not contain abbreviations, and the numbers and terms relating to contents of the document in case of the first mentioning shall be written at least once by words, names of the organizations, their forms of business shall be written without reducings with indication of the place of their stay. In the certified or witnessed documents of surname, names and middle names of physical persons (in the identity document, - in case of its availability) shall be written completely, and names of the bodies acting on behalf of the state or municipality, their jurisdiction (with

对于公司收购、所有权变更或终止财产交易的公证事项，公证员应当要求有关主体提供财产权属证明，以及公证申请人取得、变更或终止财产权利的证明，但已经提供的和法律另有规定的情形除外。

2. 公证员在履行其基本权力、享受权利、承担义务或分配给其义务时，须严格遵守法律或其他人为进行公证行为或其他操作而向公证员提出的其他要求。

3. 若公证员能够从电子信息系统获取其他机构、个人的信息，则无须要求申请人提供。

第四十二条　对公证准备文件的要求

1. 若公证申请人提交的文件存在没有相关证据印证，并且未指明年、月信息，有删除或存在一定的毁损，或者刻意添加、修改、划掉部分内容，以及存在其他不合法的修改的情况，或存在铅笔书写的痕迹，则上述文件不得作为公证的依据。

对超过一页的文本需要编号排序。

2. 公证书的文字应清晰、准确、易读，在第一次提及的情况下不得缩写，与文件内容有关的编号和术语应至少用文字书写一次。组织的名称、业务形式应书写完整，并注明地点。公证书中的姓名和自然人名称应完整书写，国家或市政当局执行机构名称及其管辖权都应保持书写完整。

jurisdiction), the location shall be specified completely.

In the certified transactions the place of residence of physical persons, and also year, month, number of the birth of physical persons, shall be written completely.

3. If the witness or the translator participates in notarial action, then its surname, name and middle name (in the identity document, - shall be entered completely in case of its availability), year, month, number of the birth and the place of residence.

4. Upon the demand of the applicant in the document certified or witnessed by the notary also time of the certificate or witnessing is specified.

5. For making of notarial actions only the documents which are not conforming to requirements of the laws or other legal acts or containing the data discrediting honor and advantage of citizens are not accepted.

6. Sheets of the certified or witnessed documents are numbered in consecutive procedure.

7. The document certified or certified with violation of Items 1-3, 5-6 of this Article has no the evidential force provided by this Law.

8. The certified or notarized document is invalid if in it are not specified year, month and number of transaction, or year, month, number of the certificate or witnessing of the document, or name and middle name (name) of the party. The transactions or documents written by pencil specified in this Item, and also not signed by the participant are insignificant.

Article 43. Number of copies of the document certified by the notary

1. Number of copies of the document certified or witnessed by the notary is determined by persons who addressed for the certificate or witnessing, however it shall be constituted at least in duplicate, one of which is stored at the notary.

All certified or attested copies have equal legal force, however the original document, certified or certified by the notary, the copy which is stored at the notary, and in the presence of contradiction between the original and other copies is considered, it is preferred as the original.

2. For each heir the certificate on the right to inheritance is constituted separately.

Article 44. Procedure for signing of the documents certified or witnessed in notarial procedure

1. The documents certified or witnessed in notarial procedure are signed in the presence of the notary. If the

公证书应当完整记载自然人的住所，以及自然人的出生年、月信息。

3. 若见证人或者翻译人员参加公证活动的，公证书应注明这些人员的姓、名、中间名、年、月、出生地和居住地等信息。

4. 根据申请人在公证书中提出的请求，也应当明确公证的时间。

5. 审查公证申请时，若公证内容不符合法律或者其他规范要求，或者存在损害公民名誉和利益的内容，应不予受理。

6. 公证书的表格应连续编号。

7. 公证书违反本条第 1 款至第 3 款、第 5 款至第 6 款的规定，不具有本法规定的公证效力。

8. 公证书中未记录公证的年、月、日、证号、公证申请人姓名、中间名的，应认定为无效。使用铅笔书写的公证书，以及参与者未签名的公证书都应认定为无效。

第四十三条　公证书的副本数量

1. 公证员出具公证书副本时，应结合申请人或者见证人的人数确定副本数量，但至少一式两份，其中一份保存在公证员处。

所有经过核验的公证书副本具有同等法律效力，但公证书的副本与存放在公证员处的原件存在矛盾的情况下，以原件为准。

2. 公证员应当针对每位继承人单独制作遗产继承权公证书。

第四十四条　公证书的签字程序

1. 有关主体须在公证员在场的情况下签署公证书。若公证书或其他文件在没有公证员的情况下签署，

agreement or other document are signed in the absence of the notary, then signatory shall confirm that the document is signed by it with own hand. The notary has the right not to require from the face, signed the document not at its presence, the signature attestation at its presence if he officially received the specimen signature of person which signed the document.

2. The transactions made in the presence of witnesses become engrossed in reading of the notary completely.

3. If person owing to physical defect, disease or illiteracy cannot undersign, then according to its order, at its presence and in the presence of the notary the document can sign other person. The signature of the last shall be witnessed by the notary with indication of the reasons owing to which the document could not be signed by person who addressed for making of notarial action.

4. If person having hearing disorder which can read then the document participates in creation of the notarial act he reads and accurately declares that it was read by it aloud and expresses its will. The notary does in the document the corresponding mark about it.

If participant is person having hearing disorder, but which can read and write, then he reads the document and writes down at the end of the document, to the signature of the notary that the document is read to them personally and he approves it.

5. If persons having hearing disorder, speeches cannot read the document, the notary, except witnesses, invites the signer who can speak with specified persons. The signer shall speak with person having hearing disorder, speeches and to report to the notary that the document expresses its will and he approves it.

5.1. If the party of the transaction is the face having sight violation, then the notary reads aloud contents of the transaction, at presence it is at least, than two witnesses. Witnesses by means of the work of the signature on the transaction confirm the fact of announcement of contents of the transaction by the notary at their presence and explanations for the parties.

6. The document directly after its reading is signed by each of the parties. The transaction made in the presence of witnesses is signed by witnesses, and with the assistance of the translator - also the translator. The notary signs the transaction directly after them.

7. The document certified or certified with violation of requirements of this Article has no the evidential force provided by this Law.

则签字人应确认文件是亲笔签署的。若公证员已收到签字人的签字样本，则可不要求对方当场签名。

2. 对见证人当场作出的证词，公证员应仔细阅读。

3. 若由于身体缺陷、疾病或是文盲而不能签名的，依据相关程序，在有公证员在场的情况下，文件可以代为签名。公证员应当对该文件的签字作见证，并说明无法由公证申请人签名的原因。

4. 有听力障碍，但可以阅读的人参与公证时，应阅读并准确地表达其意愿。公证员应在文件中做相应的标记。

若参与者是有听力障碍但可以读写的人，在公证员面前阅读文件，并在文件的末尾处签名，表明文件是其亲自阅读并同意的。

5. 除见证人以外，有听力障碍、语言障碍的人不能阅读文件的，公证员应邀请签字人指定的人参加公证并向其说明情况。被邀请人应当与有听力障碍、语言障碍的人交谈，并向公证员陈述该文件表达的目的，以及签字人的意愿。

5.1. 若公证一方有视力障碍，则公证员应大声宣读公证书的内容，在场至少要有两名见证人。见证人应在公证书上签字，当场确认公证内容的真实性，并向双方作出解释。

6. 公证书应由各方签字。若见证人和翻译人员参与公证，则见证人和翻译人员应当签字，公证员在此后签字。

7. 公证书违反本条规定的，不具有公证效力。

Article 45. Amendment procedure in the documents certified or approved in notarial procedure

1. The notary corrects the linguistic or spelling errors which found the place in the documents certified or approved by it if they do not change essence and contents of the document. Amendments shall be made so that in the initial text it was possible to read all mistakes and amendments. Amendments are made on all copies of documents, except for case if all copies cannot be provided. Rules of this part extend also to the documents transferred to the notary certified or approved by other notary.

2. In case of availability of the passed number in figure or letters in the word in the certified or approved documents or the wrong writing of figure or the word, they are led round, and the right figure or the word completely is written. The notary shall annotate amendments.

3. In case of impossibility of the work of amendments to the certified or approved documents, the notary makes amendments to type of the separate document, annotates it and applies to the certified or approved document. The amendment made in the form of the separate document is integral part of the certified or approved document

4. In the summary it is specified that the amendment was made by the notary, and also day, month and year of her work. The summary is signed and certified seal by the notary.

5. Persons participating in notarial actions have no right to make amendments, changes or amendments in the certified or approved document.

6. Amendments, the changes or amendments made with violation of requirements of this Article or any other changes or amendments in the certified or approved documents are invalid.

Article 46. Translator

1. During notarial actions person having the certificate on qualification on ownership of the corresponding language to which the notary, the cases except for provided by this Law trusts can act as the translator. In case of the certificate of the transaction in foreign language or for explanation to the party which is not knowing Armenian, the choice of the translator will be approved by the parties. The procedure for issue of certificates of competency affirms the Government.

The translator also the translator of sign language is considered.

The certificate on qualification is terminated by the

第四十五条　公证书的修改程序

1. 公证员发现公证书中存在语言、拼写错误时，在不改变公证书真实意思和内容的情况下，可直接予以纠正。在最开始出现错误的文本处作出修正，以便申请人在公证书中能够阅读所有的错误和修正。除非不能提供副本，否则应对所有公证书副本同时进行修改。本部分规则也适用于其他形式的公证书。

2. 公证书中出现数字或文字书写错误，应圈出，将正确的数字或文字书写完整。公证员应当对修正作出注释。

3. 若难以在公证书中对错误之处作出修改的，应以单独文件的形式进行修改并注释，同时注明适用于该公证书。以单独文件形式作出的修改视为公证书的组成部分。

4. 需标明该修改部分是由公证员作出的，并同时标明修改的年、月、日等信息，由公证员签字盖章。

5. 除公证员以外的其他人员无权对公证书进行修改、变更。

6. 对违反本条规定所作的修改、变更，应被认定为无效。

第四十六条　翻译人员

1. 在公证中，持有公证员资格证书的人，除本法所规定的事项外，可以担任翻译人员。若公证是用外语进行的，或者是向不通晓亚美尼亚语一方作翻译解释，则翻译人员的选择须由双方同意。签发合格证书的程序由政府规定。

翻译人员也可以是手语翻译者。

亚美尼亚共和国政府委员会在下列情况下终止翻

commission established by the resolution the Government of the Republic of Armenia when:

1) The notary who issued the document on trust in writing reports about loss trust, and any other notary did not report about the trust;

2) the translator allowed obviously gross violation or made violation intentionally;

3) the translator for receipt of the certificate submitted false documents;

4) the translator did not store information which is notarial secret;

5) the translator submits the application for cancellation of the certificate on qualification;

6) the translator died, was recognized as incapacitated or is unknown absent;

7) results of retraining were negative.

Person having qualification undergoes retraining in the procedure established by the Minister of Justice of the Republic of Armenia at least, than time in three years.

2. The translator cannot be the participant or the witness of notarial action. Person working for the notary can be the translator.

3. The translator shall transfer in detail to the notary and the parties contents of the certified or witnessed document and to guarantee that the translation is made correctly, completely and it personally. About it the notary does the corresponding text.

4. Translation service is paid by the parties.

5. Before making of notarial action the notary shall warn the translator about need of preserving notarial secret.

6. The translator in the procedure established by the civil legislation bears property damage liability, caused owing to its incorrect or incomplete translations.

7. Cannot act as the translator:

a) the witness participating in notarial action;

b) person for benefit of whom notarial action is made.

8. In case of lack of the having certificate on qualification of the translator from sign language, person guaranteed by the specialized organization as the translator from sign language takes part in accomplishment of notarial action as the translator.

In case of absence of the translator from language of the ethnic minorities living in the Republic of Armenia having the certificate on qualification person guaranteed by the head of the public organization created for the purpose of protection of the rights of this ethnic minority, and

译人员资格：

（1）公证书的遗失仅能由出具公证书的公证员以书面形式报告，其他公证员不可进行报告；

（2）翻译人员严重或者故意违反本法的；

（3）翻译人员为领取资格证书而提交虚假文件的；

（4）翻译人员不保守公证秘密的；

（5）翻译人员提交了资格证书的注销申请的；

（6）翻译人员死亡、被认定为无行为能力或无故失踪的；

（7）培训成绩未通过的。

具有资格的人至少在三年以后才能接受再培训，该程序由亚美尼亚共和国司法部部长制定。

2. 翻译人员不得作为公证活动的见证人。公证员可以担任翻译。

3. 翻译人员应当向公证员和公证申请人详细转述有见证人在场见证的文件内容，并保证翻译内容正确、完整且亲自完成。公证员需进行相应的备案。

4. 翻译服务费用由公证申请人支付。

5. 公证作出前，公证员应当提醒翻译人员对公证信息保密。

6. 翻译人员承担因翻译不准确或不完整而造成的财产损害责任。

7. 不能作为翻译人员的主体包括：

（a）参与公证活动的见证人；

（b）与公证内容具有利益关联的人员。

8. 若无手语翻译资格证书，可由专业机构担保的手语翻译员参加公证活动。

在翻译人员知晓亚美尼亚共和国少数民族语言但没有获得翻译资格证书的情况下，若上述人员获得为保护此少数民族的权利而设立的公共组织的负责人的保荐资格，或获得该少数民族所在地区的市政负责人的保荐资格，则可以允许该翻译人员参与公证活动的

in the absence of such organization, person guaranteed by the head of municipality or the administrative district of accommodation of this ethnic minority takes part in accomplishment of notarial action as the translator.

翻译工作。

Article 47. Witness

1. During making of notarial actions presence of the witness is obligatory only in the cases provided by the law. According to the offer of the parties the notary performs notarial actions with the assistance of the witness (witnesses).

2. The witness shall be present at reading the notary of the document which is subject to the notarial certificate, signing of the document and during its certificate the notary if the law does not provide other.

3. The notary before making of notarial action shall warn the witness about need of preserving notarial secret about what the corresponding record is made.

4. Only sui juris persons can act as the witness.

5. Cannot act as the witness:

1) the notary, the other person making notarial action, their spouses, parents, children, brothers, sisters, grandsons, the grandfather or the grandma of their or their spouses;

2) the translator participating in notarial action;

3) person for benefit of whom notarial action is made;

4) the illiterate or other persons not capable to read the document which is subject to the notarial certificate or witnessing;

5) persons who are insufficiently knowing Armenian, except for case when the closed will is constituted.

6. Upon the demand of the notary the witness shall provide the announcement that he meets the requirements provided by this Article excluding performance as the witness. In this case the notary does not bear responsibility for consequences of the false announcement provided by the witness if it is not proved that the notary knew or owed know that contents of the announcement are not true.

第四十七条　见证人

1. 在进行公证活动时，见证人仅在法律规定的情况下才需要在场。根据公证申请人的申请，公证员在见证人的协助下开展公证活动。

2. 若法律无其他规定，见证人应当场阅读公证书，接收公证书的见证人应当按照公证书的要求，签署公证书。

3. 公证员在进行公证活动前，应当提醒见证人保守公证秘密。

4. 见证人须具有独立人格。

5. 不能作为见证人的情况包括：

（1）公证员、其他公证员及其配偶、父母、子女、兄弟姐妹、孙子女、祖父母；

（2）参与公证活动的翻译人员；

（3）与公证内容具有利益关联的人员；

（4）不认识文字或者不具备阅读能力的，或不具备见证证书能力的；

（5）不通晓亚美尼亚语言的人，但参与公证遗嘱时，有关主体的亲属可以作为见证人。

6. 经公证员要求，见证人应提供符合本条规定的证明文件。在这种情况下，若无法证明公证员知道或应该知道见证人提供的文件内容不真实，则公证员对见证人提供的虚假文件造成的后果不承担责任。

Article 48. Interpretation by the notary of the documents submitted for making of notarial actions

1. The notary has the right to interpret the documents submitted for making of the notarial actions, proceeding from literal value containing in them words and expressions. Only in case of ambiguity of literal value of separate conditions or provisions in them they are interpreted by the notary according to requirements of Articles 8 and 447 of the Civil code.

第四十八条　公证员对公证书的说明

1. 公证员有权对公证书进行说明，说明应从表述的文字含义出发。只有在个别情形或条款的文字含义不明确的情况下，公证员才能依据《民法典》第 8 条和第 447 条的规定作出说明。

2. The notary in case of determination of limit of powers of the authorized person shall proceed only from literal word meaning and expressions of the power of attorney. By proxy only the actions provided by it shall be made or make sure the transactions provided by it. The notary has no right to confer by interpretation of the power of attorney to person additional powers or to deprive of it powers.

Provisions of the powers of attorney which are containing powers on making of impersonal, senseless actions or not containing powers on the conclusion of transactions or containing multiple-valued powers are not accepted to the basis for transactions or other notarial actions.

If the power of attorney provides procedure, conditions, types of making of actions or the conclusion of transactions or other requirements (the place, term, the price and other), then notarial actions shall be made with strict observance of its requirements.

3. When making by the notary of notarial actions by interpretation of the document he shall fix content of interpretation which makes sure the signature and round stamp of the notary and joins the submitted document or its copy.

Article 49. Certifying text

1. When making of the notarial actions which are subject to the certificate the notary in the register makes the corresponding certifying text which, in particular, bears name, surname of the notary, the notarial territory, type of the made notarial action, year, month, number of its making (words), the corresponding registration number in the register, and also the announcement of the notary that the personalities of participants of notarial action are identified, their legal capacity or capacity to act is checked.

2. On the certified documents written in foreign language, certifying texts can be made in the corresponding language.

3. Approximate forms of certifying texts affirm the Minister of Justice on representation of notarial chamber.

4. Voided according to the Law of the Republic of Armenia of 12.11.2016 No. ZR-180

5. The document certified with violation of requirements of this Article has no the evidential force provided by this Law.

Article 50. Registration of notarial actions

1. All notarial actions made by the notary are registered in the notarial register.

2. Each notarial action is given separate number which without fail is specified in the documents issued by

2. 在确定受托方权限时，公证员仅依据授权书的字面意思和表达方式确定。受委托方仅对委托方要求的行为进行代理，或确认由委托方要求的代理。公证员无权解释委托书或否认其效力。

委托书中应明确所委托的内容，但若存在与个人无关的、无意义的内容，或者不包含代为行使公证权利，以及所授权限超出合理范围的授权书，不得作为公证的依据。

受委托方应当严格依照委托书中规定的程序、条件、权利类型或者履行公证约定达成的其他要求（地点、期限、价格等）参与公证活动。

3. 公证员对公证书进行说明时，应当注明其所说明的内容，签字并加盖公证员的印章，同时将说明内容添加至副本中。

第四十九条　公证书

1. 公证员进行公证活动时，应制作相应的公证书，核对公证员姓名、公证书范围、公证行为的类型、年、月、制作的数量（文字数）、登记册中相应的编码，以及确认公证参与者的特征、是否具有法律行为能力。

2. 若公证中的文件是由外语书写的，公证员可以用相应的语言制作公证书。

3. 由司法部部长确认公证书的形式。

4. 亚美尼亚共和国 2016 年 11 月 12 日编号 ZR–18 立法，已经被废止。

5. 违反本条规定的公证书，不具有本法规定的公证效力。

第五十条　公证活动的登记

1. 公证员的一切公证活动均应在公证登记簿上登记。

2. 每一项公证活动都应有单独的编号，在公证文件和公证书中都应有对应的编号。

the notary, and also in the certified texts.

3. The form of the notarial register and procedure of registration in the register are established by the Minister of Justice.

3. 公证登记的形式和程序由司法部部长规定。

Article 51. Adjournment or suspension of making of notarial actions

1. Notarial actions are made in day of submission of documents necessary for this purpose.

2. According to the written reasoned statement of the interested person according to which it wishes to challenge the right of person to making of notarial action in court making of notarial action can be postponed for term no more than ten days. If during the specified term the notary does not receive from court of the decision on prohibition of making of this notarial action, then he makes notarial action. If during the specified term the notary receives the judgment about prohibition of making of this notarial action, making of notarial action stops before removal of prohibition by court.

Person who made the demand about suspension of notarial action for the basis provided by this Item shall indemnify the loss caused to the party owing to unreasonable suspension. The notary in writing warns about it the party which provided the requirement about suspension.

3. Making of notarial actions can be postponed:

1) in case of lack of stipulated by the legislation necessary data, documents, agreements or other documents or if requirements of the procedure for making of this notarial action established by the legislation are not observed;

2) in case of the direction the notary of documents for examination;

3) in case of need of detailed studying by the notary of the submitted documents;

4) in need of receipt by the notary of the corresponding data or documents from the organizations for making of notarial action;

5) in other cases provided by the law and for other terms.

The term of making of notarial actions on the bases provided by the subitem of 1 this Item is transferred about day of presentation to the notary of proofs about fulfillment of requirements of the procedure established for submission of necessary data, documents, agreements, stipulated by the legislation or making of notarial actions.

The term of making of notarial actions on the bases provided by the subitem 2 presents of Item is transferred

第五十一条　公证活动的暂停或中止

1. 公证程序的启动时间为公证申请人提交公证所需文件的当天。

2. 利害关系人在法庭上对请求权提出异议的，根据利害关系人的书面陈述，可以顺延不超过 10 日。在规定期限内，公证员未收到法院中止公证的裁定的，公证程序应当继续进行。在规定期限内，公证员收到中止公证程序的裁定的，在法院解除中止指令前应停止该公证程序。

若公证程序被不合理的中止，申请中止的一方应当赔偿因不合理中止给公证申请人造成的损失。公证员应以书面形式提示申请中止的一方。

3. 出现以下情形，公证程序可以被延期：

（1）法律没有规定，但应当提供必要的资料、文件、协议或者其他材料的；

（2）受委托作出的公证书，由公证机构审查；

（3）公证员需要对提交的文件进行详细审查的；

（4）公证程序需要依据有关机构的资料或文件方可进行的；

（5）法律规定的其他情形和条件。

根据本条第 3 款第 1 项提供公证材料的期限，持续到公证机构证明其所收到的材料已经完全满足了立法规定的完成公证程序所需的必要数据、文件、协议等的当日。

根据本条第 3 款第 2 项延期的期限，持续到公证员收到受托证明材料次日。

about one the day following receipt of experimental testimony by the notary.

The term of making of notarial actions on the bases provided by the subitem 3 presents of Item can be postponed for a period of up to ten days.

The term of making of notarial actions on the bases provided by the subitem 4 presents of Item is transferred about one the day following receipt by the notary of the corresponding data or documents, but no more than for 30 days.

4. In the presence of the bases for adjournment or suspension of making of notarial actions the notary upon the demand of the applicant issues the written decree on adjournment or suspension in which legal basis of adjournment or suspension, and in the case provided by the subitem 3 of Item 3 of this Article as well adjournment term is specified. One copy of the resolution on adjournment or suspension of making of notarial action is handed to persons who addressed for making of notarial actions. If during adjournment or suspension of making of notarial actions the notary receives documents from the applicant, then in the resolution on adjournment or suspension names of the received documents when also by whom they are constituted or issued also other necessary data shall be in detail specified.

根据本条第 3 款第 3 项延期的期限，最多可延期 10 日。

根据本条第 3 款第 4 项延期的期限，持续到公证员收到相应数据或文件后次日，但最多不得超过 30 日。

4. 根据公证申请人的要求，公证员自收到通知后中止公证程序，关于中止公证程序书面令状应载明中止的法律依据，以及注明中止事项，并对中止期限进行说明。关于暂停或中止公证程序的决议，其中一份副本交给负责公证的公证员。若在暂停或中止公证程序期间，公证员收到申请人提交的文件，还应详细说明其他必要的细节。

Article 52. Refusal in making of notarial actions

1. The notary refuses making of notarial action if:

1) making of notarial action contradicts the law, other legal acts or articles of organization;

2) the submitted document or required notarial action is not subject to the notarial certificate or witnessing;

3) according to the law notarial action is not subject to making by this notary;

4) the incapacitated person or person which does not have necessary powers either his incapacitated or not having necessary powers representative, the cases except for provided by the law requested making of notarial action;

5) person who addressed for making of notarial action though is capable, however is at present in condition when it does not realize value of the actions or cannot manage them;

6) the addressed person refuses to submit the documents, necessary for making of notarial action, provided by the law, other legal acts;

7) the addressed person does not pay the state fee provided for making of notarial action or the amount for

第五十二条　拒绝公证

1. 有下列情形之一的，公证员应拒绝公证：

（1）公证内容与本法、其他法律或者组织章程相抵触的；

（2）提交的文件或要求公证的内容不属于公证的范围；

（3）依照法律规定，公证事项不属于该公证机构管辖；

（4）公证申请人无民事行为能力或丧失民事行为能力，法律另有规定的除外；

（5）有职业资格的公证员受委托开展公证活动，但目前处于无法实现公证目的或者无法开展公证的状态；

（6）依据本法或其他法律的规定，公证申请人拒绝提交开展公证所必需的文件；

（7）公证申请人不缴纳公证费用或其他公证服务费用；

other services rendered by the notary.

8) notarial action shall not be made concerning person searched by a court decision, under the resolution of the prosecutor or investigator and avoiding criminal liability, or concerning its property. On the basis specified in this Item the notary refuses making of notarial action only if from the face or the body which issued the decree on search or from the Ministry of Justice official information on search of this person arrived.

2. In the presence of the bases for refusal in making of notarial actions the notary upon the demand of the applicant issues the written decree on refusal in which legal basis for refusal and procedure for protest is specified. One copy of the resolution on refusal in making of notarial action is handed to persons who addressed for making of notarial actions.

If the submitted documents do not require additional studying, then the notary makes the decision on refusal in accomplishment of notarial action in day of the address to him or next day submissions of the statement.

In case of need additional studying of the submitted documents the notary makes the decision on refusal in accomplishment of notarial action to the statement of day, the fifth after representation.

Article 53. Storage and provision of documents

1. Originals of notarial acts are stored at the notary who certified them. After making of notarial actions according to the statement of the parties the copies of documents or the statement from them having legal force, equal with the original, are provided to them.

2. The copy of the document or the statement from it shall correspond to the original also spelling, punctuation and reducings. The notary issues the statement from the document if other part of the document does not contradict contents of the statement.

3. The notary at written request of physical persons or organizations, from name or for benefit of which notarial actions are made shall issue statements from the notarial register.

4. Due to the criminal or civil cases which are in the pretrial or court investigation, connected with committed notarial action, the notary based on the written requirement of the prosecutor, court, the investigator or body of the inquiry issued according to the procedure established by the Code of penal procedure of the Republic of Armenia provides them the duplicate of the notarial act or the state-

（8）对于检察官或审查人员决议搜查，或是逃避刑事责任以及涉及财产犯罪的人提出的公证申请，公证员应当拒绝。但公证员只有从签发搜查令的机关或司法部获得正式文件时，才可拒绝公证。

2. 公证员拒绝公证时应出具书面拒绝令，明确拒绝的法律依据和申诉程序。

若提交的文件不需要另行审查，则公证员应在接收公证申请的当日，或者在接收公证申请的第 2 日作出拒绝公证的决定。

若需要对提交的文件进一步审查，公证员应在接收公证申请的第 5 日作出拒绝公证的决定。

第五十三条　公证书的保存和提供

1. 公证书的原件存放在作出公证的公证员处。依照申请人的申请开展公证活动后，公证员应向申请人提供具有同等法律效力的公证书副本或声明书。

2. 公证书副本或声明书应与原文件的书写内容相一致。公证员在公证书的其他部分与副本内容不抵触的情况下，应出具公证书副本。

3. 公证员应当根据申请公证的自然人、法人或者其他组织的书面请求，在公证登记簿上登记。

4. 根据亚美尼亚共和国刑事诉讼法规定的程序，若在刑事或民事案件审理过程中或在法庭调查中，公证员基于法官、检察官、法庭调查员或其他调查主体的书面要求，应提供公证书的复印件或公证登记簿上的登记内容。在法律规定的情况下，公证员将公证书原件移交指定的签字人员。在此情况下，公证员应当将移交公证书的副本保存在自己处，并在副本上注明

ment from the notarial register. The notary shall transfer the original document in the cases established by the law to specified persons who undersign for receipt of the document from the notary. In this case the notary shall store at himself the copy of the transferred document on which makes record that the original document is in relevant organ, having specified date of its provision. Also the resolution on reclamation of the original document is attached to the duplicate.

原文件持有人员，注明相应日期。此外，关于收回原件的决议也应附在该副本上。

After the end of production on the corresponding case or falling away of need of use of the original document the court or body which requested the original document shall return the original to three-day time to the notary.

相应案件已经完结或者不再需要使用原件的，使用原件的法院或者其他机关，应在 3 日内将原件返还至公证员处。

5. According to the written requirement of the bodies having the right within the competence to exercise control of making of notarial actions, the notary provides them the notarial act or its duplicate or the statement from the notarial register.

5. 在公证机构管理机关的书面要求下，公证员有权在其权限范围内，向其提供公证书的副本或者公证登记簿的登记内容。

6. The procedure for notarial clerical work is established by the Minister of Justice - according to the offer of notarial chamber.

6. 公证书的制作程序由司法部部长根据公证机构的提议制定。

7. The procedure for notarial clerical work is established by the Minister of Justice - according to the offer of notarial chamber.

7. 公证员文件的保管程序由司法部部长根据公证机构的建议制定。

8. The procedure for maintaining the electronic database of notarial acts, and also put by inheritance, is established by order of the Minister of Justice.

8. 公证电子数据库的维护、承接程序，根据司法部部长的命令确立。

Article 54. The notarial actions made by diplomatic representations and consular establishments of the Republic of Armenia

第五十四条　亚美尼亚共和国外交代表和领事机构的公证活动

1. Diplomatic representations and consular establishments of the Republic of Armenia make the following notarial actions:

1. 亚美尼亚共和国外交代表和领事机构有权对下列事项公证：

1) is certified by transactions (agreements, wills, powers of attorney and other), the agreements on the real estate which is in the territory of the Republic of Armenia except for signed;

（1）对协议、遗嘱、授权书等有权出具公证书，但在亚美尼亚共和国境内签署的不动产协议除外；

2) take measures to protection of heritable property;

（2）采取措施保护继承财产；

3) grant certificates on the right to inheritance;

（3）出具继承权公证书；

4) grant certificates on the property right to the relying share in the property belonging to persons on the right of common joint property;

（4）对共有财产权利人拥有的份额公证；

5) witness fidelity of copies of documents and statements from them;

（5）对文件与声明的副本的真实性公证；

6) witness authenticity of the signature on documents;

（6）对文件签名的真实性公证；

7) witness fidelity of the translation of documents;

8) certify the fact of finding of the citizen in live;

9) certify the fact of finding of the citizen in certain place;

10) certify identity of the citizen with person represented in the photo;

11) certify time of presentation of the document;

12) are accepted in the deposit, on storage, issued and return sums of money and securities, precious metals, stones and issues the certificate;

13) accept documents on storage;

14)Transfer to trusteeship;

15) grants certificates on approval of powers of the testamentary executor;

16) in the consent of all heirs nullifies earlier granted certificates on approval of powers of the testamentary executor;

17) issues copies of notarial acts.

2. On behalf of diplomatic representations and consular establishments of the Republic of Armenia notarial actions are made by their heads.

3. Diplomatic representations and consular establishments of the Republic of Armenia make notarial actions according to the procedure, established by this Law and other legal acts adopted according to it.

Chapter 6. Certificate of transactions

Article 55. The transactions certified in notarial procedure

1. The notary certifies transactions for which the law provides obligatory notarial form.

Upon the demand of one of the parties the notary can certify and other transactions even if by the law the notarial form for this type of the transaction is not required.

2. Transactions about modification or amendments in transactions or about their early termination make sure the notary who certified the main transaction, except as specified replacements or discharges from position of the notary.

In case of absence of the notary the notarial operation provided by part 2 of this Article is performed by the replacement notary.

3. For making of this transaction the notary shall request the parties to submit the necessary documents established by this Law, including proofs of accessory of property or the right to it to person disposing to them (al-

（7）对文件翻译的真实性公证；

（8）对公民行为事实的真实性公证；

（9）对公民在特定地点的事实公证；

（10）对公民与其身份证件中照片是否一致公证；

（11）对文件制作的时间公证；

（12）对存款以及转让、返还货币或者有价证券或保证金、贵金属、宝石公证；

（13）接受应储存的文件；

（14）转移托管；

（15）对遗嘱执行人权利公证；

（16）经全体继承人同意，承认之前授予的继承权属证书无效；

（17）出具公证书副本。

2. 由亚美尼亚共和国的外交或领事机构的负责人开展公证活动。

3. 亚美尼亚共和国的外交代表和领事机构依照本法制定的程序和其他法律规定开展公证活动。

第六章　公证证明

第五十五条　公证的证明程序

1. 法律规定必须以公证形式作出证明的，由公证机构出具证明。

根据公证申请人的要求，公证员可以对公证内容进行证明，即使法律上没有规定需要此种公证。

2. 修改、修正或提前终止公证前，应由公证员确认，但公证员被替换或被解雇的情形除外。

若无公证员，则依据本条第 2 款规定的公证程序更换公证员。

3. 公证员开展公证活动时，应当要求公证申请人提交本法规定的必要文件，包括财产附属物证明或者财产权利的物权证明（转让、质押、委托管理等）。

ienating, pledging use or trust management, etc.).

Article 56. Certificate of the will

1. The notary certifies wills of capable citizens.

2. The certificate of wills through representatives is not allowed.

3. In case of the certificate of the will from the testator the proofs confirming its property right or other rights to the bequeathed property are not required.

4. The will can be cancelled or changed by the testator by submission of the corresponding statement or creation of the new will. The statement for modification and amendments of the will, and also about cancellation of the will, is assured by the notary who certified the main will, except as specified replacements or discharges from position of the notary.

4.1. In case of replacement of the notary, the notarial operation provided by part 4 of this Article is performed by the replacement notary.

5. In case of receipt of the statement for cancellation of the will, and also receipt of the new will canceling or changing the will, the notary does about it mark in the will copy which is stored in notary office, and in the register of notarial actions. The statement for cancellation or change of the will is certified of the procedure established for assurance of the will.

6. The will makes sure the notary according to the procedure, provided by the Civil code and this Law.

7. From the moment of notification about opening of the will the notary reports to heirs about will availability.

8. The notary enters probate cases and wills into the electronic database of probate cases and wills.

Article 57. Certificate of the power of attorney

1. The notary certifies the power of attorney on behalf of one or several persons, addressed to one or several persons.

2. The power of attorney issued on the retrust right is subject to the notarial certificate in the procedure established by the law. The notary certifies the power of attorney issued on the retrust right in case of submission of the main power of attorney. The power of attorney issued on the retrust right does not may contain more rights, than it is provided under the main power of attorney. Effective period of the power of attorney issued on the retrust right cannot exceed effective period of the main power of attorney.

3. Powers in the power of attorney shall be stated accurately and clearly. Impersonal or ambiguous powers

第五十六条　遗嘱公证

1. 公证员对有行为能力公民的遗嘱进行公证。

2. 不允许通过代理人出具遗嘱证明。

3. 在遗嘱公证中，不需要证明遗嘱订立人对遗嘱财产的产权或其他权利。

4. 遗嘱订立人可以通过提交相应的声明，或新遗嘱的设立来撤销或变更遗嘱。遗嘱的修改和修改声明，以及关于撤销遗嘱的声明，由作出公证的公证员确认，但指定的公证员被替换或被解雇的情形除外。

4.1. 若更换公证员，依据本条第 4 款的规定进行。

5. 在收到撤销、变更遗嘱声明和新遗嘱时，公证员应对存放在公证机构的遗嘱副本进行登记。公证员应依据保护遗嘱的程序，对撤销或变更遗嘱的声明作出公证。

6. 公证员应依照民法和本法规定的程序对遗嘱进行确认。

7. 从遗嘱公告之日起，公证员应及时向继承人报告。

8. 公证员应将遗嘱录入遗嘱数据库。

第五十七条　委托书公证

1. 由一人或数人向公证员提出申请，公证员向其出具对委托书的公证书。

2. 依照法定程序出具的委托书的委托权利范围，以公证书为准。公证员对提交的委托书、委托权利进行公证。对转委托书公证时，所包含的权利不得超过主委托书所规定的范围。对转委托书有效期限的公证，不得超过主委托书的有效期限。

3. 委托书中的委托权利应当被明确、清晰地注明。与个人无关或不明确的权利不得被公证。

shall not be certified.

4.The procedure and conditions established for powers of attorney are applied to the announcements and (or) agreements certified or witnessed by the notary.

5. After assurance of the power of attorney the notary enters it into electronic base of powers of attorney.

6. In case of refusal from the power of attorney or receipt of the statement for the termination of the power of attorney, the notary enters the relevant data into electronic base of powers of attorney.

Chapter 7. Acceptance by the notary of measures to protection of heritable property

Article 58. Protection of heritable property

1. For protection of the rights of heirs, beneficiaries and other interested persons the notary in the place of servicing of the opened inheritance takes the measures established by the Civil code and this Law and inheritances, necessary for protection, and management of it.

2. The notary takes measures to protection of heritable property and on management of it based on the statement of the heir, the testamentary executor, the creditor, local government body or other persons acting for the benefit of protection of heritable property.

If necessary the notary has the right on the initiative to take measures to protection of heritable property and management of it.

Article 59. Inventory of mass of inheritance

1. The notary in the procedure established by the law makes the inventory of mass of inheritance for protection of heritable property and manages it.

The inventory of mass of inheritance is made with the assistance of the interested persons and at least two witnesses who wished to participate in case of this action.

2. In the protocol of the inventory shall be specified receipt date of the statement (message) on taking measures to protection of mass of inheritance; date of the inventory; names, surnames, the places of residence of persons participating in the inventory; name, surname, middle name of the testator, day of his death; the location of the described property; information on whether really belonging to the testator the apartment, the house or other structure were sealed before appearance of the notary and whom whether the seal or seal, and also the detailed characteristic of the described objects, assessment and degree of depreciation of each of them is broken.

4. 委托书制定的程序和条件，适用于公证员公证的程序和条件。

5. 公证员对委托书公证后，录入委托书电子数据库。

6. 拒绝委托书公证或收到终止委托书的声明，公证员应将相关情况录入委托书电子库。

第七章　公证员采取的遗产保护措施

第五十八条　遗产保护

1. 公证员有权采取民法和本法规定的措施，对继承人、受益人和其他利害关系人的权利进行必要的保护。

2. 公证员根据继承人、遗嘱执行人、债权人、地方政府机关，或者其他为保护遗产利益的人的声明，采取措施保护和管理遗产。

如有必要，公证员有权主动采取措施保护和管理遗产。

第五十九条　遗产的清点

1. 依照法定的程序，公证员为保护遗产而对遗产进行清点和管理。

遗产数量的清点需在公证申请人和至少两名愿意参加的见证人的协助下进行。

2. 在清单记录文件中应规定接收日期，注明采取措施保护的遗产的声明、存货清单日期、参与清点人员的姓名、住所、遗嘱订立人姓名、中间名、死亡日期、上述财产的地点，以及公证员介入之前，是否真正属于遗嘱订立人的信息、房屋或建筑物是否被封锁、是否是遗嘱订立人的印章，以及描述物品的详细特征，评估破坏折旧的程度。

For assessment of the described property the notary has the right on the initiative or upon the demand of participants of the inventory to invite the specialist in property assessment.

At the end of each page of the protocol the final quantity of the described objects, and upon termination of the inventory - total final quantity of objects is specified.

3. All property which is in the apartment, the house or other structure of the testator is entered in the protocol of the inventory. Statements of neighbors, relatives and other persons for accessory to the testator of separate objects are also entered in the protocol of the inventory, and the procedure for appeal to the court with the action for declaration about exception of this property of the inventory is explained to interested persons.

4. If the belongings list is interrupted for several days or several days, then the apartment, the house or other structure every time proceed are sealed by the notary. In the protocol of the inventory the reasons and time of the termination and renewal of the inventory, and also condition of seal and seal in case of the subsequent opening of the apartment, house or other structure are specified.

5. At the end of the protocol the name, surname, middle name, birth date and the place of residence of the citizen to which the property, the name, document number, proving his identity when also who issues this document is transferred to storage are entered.

6. The protocol is constituted at least in triplicate. All copies are signed by the notary, interested persons, witnesses, the appraiser of property (if he is invited) and person which accepted property on storage.

7. In case of impossibility of taking measures to protection of mass of inheritance (the heirs or other persons living together with the testator object to the inventory, do not show the mass of inheritance to the inventory or if it is withdrawn also other) the notary constitutes the relevant protocol and reports about it to interested persons and in notarial chamber.

8. If the heritable property is in different places, then the notary in the place of opening of inheritance sends to the notary in the location of the corresponding part of heritable property the order which is subject to obligatory execution about protection of inheritance or management of it, having informed on it notarial chamber.

为评估上述财产，公证员有权主动或根据参与人的要求，邀请财产评估专家作出评估报告。

在清单记录文件的每一页末尾，应明确所描述对象的最终数量，并在清点完成时注明总数。

3. 公寓、房屋或遗嘱订立人的其他建筑物财产均应在财产清单记录文件中登记。财产清单记录文件也应单独记录邻居、亲属和其他个人对遗嘱订立人财产的陈述，并向公证申请人说明向法院起诉的程序，以及关于财产清单记录文件例外情况的声明。

4. 若财产清点出现中断，则每次进行的公寓、房屋或其他建筑物财产清点都要由公证员封存。清单记录文件记录了储存终止和续期的原因和时间，以及在公寓、房屋或其他建筑物被再次使用的条件。

5. 在清单记录文件的末尾，记录该公民的姓名、中间名、出生日期和居住地、身份证件号码、财产类型，以及文件保存人的身份信息。

6. 清单记录文件至少一式三份。所有副本由公证员、公证申请人、证人、物业估价师（如获邀请）及接受存放的物业人员签署。

7. 若无法采取措施保护遗产（继承人或与立遗嘱人一起生活的其他人反对清点，不代表无须对遗产清点或者撤回清点表示），公证员应拟定相关文书作出说明，并向有关人员和公证机构报告。

8. 若遗产分属不同的地方，则遗产继承地的公证员应向部分遗产所在地的公证员发送代为保护或管理遗产的协助令，并通知公证机构。

Article 60. Acceptance by the notary of measures to protection of mass of inheritance

1. The cash or foreign currency entering the mass of inheritance are brought in the deposit of the notary, and currency, the property made of gemstones or metals checked in bank according to the procedure, established by the Civil code.

2. Protection of the inheritance of property entering weight which can be in circulation on permission or the license is performed by the notary according to the procedure, the established legislation on the corresponding property.

3. If the property which is not specified in Items 1 and 2 of this Article entering the mass of inheritance does not need management, then the notary under the agreement of storage reports its to one of heirs, and in case of impossibility of transfer to heirs - the specialized organization.

4. If in the mass of inheritance there is property needing not only in protection, but also in management (share in the authorized (share) capital of economic partnership or society, securities, exclusive rights and other), then the notary as the founder of trust management signs the agreement on trust management of this property.

5. The managing director, heirs or other persons to whom the property entering the mass of inheritance is transferred are warned about the responsibility for waste, spoil, concealment, alienation of heritable property and for causing provided by the law to heirs of damage.

Article 61. Application of measures to ensuring responsibility of heirs

1. Heirs after receipt of the certificate on the right to inheritance within the cost of the property which passed with it refund the expenses provided by the Civil code.

2. Both in case of direct opening of inheritance, and in case of transfer of the right to inheritance acceptance the heir who accepted inheritance bears responsibility within property value, received on these two bases.

Heirs bear joint liability within the cost of the heritable property which passed with it.

3. For the purpose of ensuring payment of expenses, stipulated in Item 1 this Article, the notary imposes prohibition on the corresponding property inherited by heirs, having notified on it heirs, their creditors and the state competent authorities.

The ban from the property specified in this Item can be withdrawn only in case of the consent of all creditors or

第六十条　公证员采取保护遗产的措施

1. 依照《民法典》规定的程序，公证员将现金、外币、宝石、金属等财产存入银行。

2. 公证员根据有关遗产的规定，对准予流转或者许可继承的遗产进行保护。

3. 若不属于本条第 1 款和第 2 款规定的遗产，则不需要管理，公证员则根据保管协议，向其中一名继承人报告。在无法转移给继承人的情况下，转移给专门组织保管。

4. 若继承的巨额财产不但需要保护，而且还需要管理（经济合作或社团组织中的资本份额、证券、排他性权利和其他），则公证员有权与信托管理公司签署关于该财产信托管理的协议。

5. 管理人、继承人或其他人存在挥霍、夺取、隐瞒、转移遗产以及对继承人造成损害的，应当依据法律规定承担责任。

第六十一条　继承人的义务

1. 继承人在收到继承权公证书后，应按照《民法典》规定的条文在继承财产的范围内缴纳相关费用。

2. 无论是直接继承权还是转受继承权的情形，接受遗产的继承人在遗产价值范围内承担责任。

继承人对其继承的财产承担连带责任。

3. 为确保缴纳本条第 1 款规定的费用，公证员通知继承人、债权人和国家主管机关后，保留与规定费用相应的财产。

仅能在征得所有债权人同意或由本条第 1 款规定的继承人缴纳费用的情形下，才能撤销对本条规定遗

execution by heirs of the obligations specified in Item 1 of this Article.

产的保留决定。

Chapter 8. Issue of the certificate on the right to inheritance

第八章 出具遗产继承权公证书

Article 62. Certificate on the right to inheritance

1. The certificate on the right to inheritance is granted to heirs based on the written application submitted to the notary in the place of opening of inheritance, according to the procedure and the terms established by the Civil code.

2. The heir who passed inheritance acceptance term can accept inheritance under the agreement of all other heirs who accepted inheritance which shall be provided in writing. This agreement of heirs is the basis for recognition of the certificate on inheritance which is earlier granted by the notary invalid and issues of the new certificate.

3. Upon transition of property on inheritance right to municipality the certificate on the right to inheritance is issued to municipality – on behalf of the head.

4. In the consent of all heirs the notary who granted the certificate on the right to inheritance nullifies earlier granted certificate on the right to inheritance, except as specified replacements and discharges from position of the notary.

第六十二条 遗产继承权公证书

1. 遗产继承权公证书是依照《民法典》规定的程序和条件，由继承人向公证员提出书面申请，由公证员在查明事实后出具的遗产权属证明。

2. 在继承期限届满后，指定继承人可以在其他继承人同意的情况下接受遗产。

3. 在将继承权的财产移交给政府时，继承权公证书移交给政府代表。

4. 在所有继承人的同意下，出具继承权公证书的公证员可以撤回先前授予的继承权公证书，但公证员的职位已被替代和被撤销的除外。

Article 63. Conditions of issue of certificates on the right to inheritance on the law and on the will

1. The notary in case of issue of certificates on the right to inheritance under the law or according to the will checks the fact of death of the testator, time and the place of opening of inheritance, the related relations or availability of the will, structure of mass of inheritance.

2. Before issue of the certificate on the right to inheritance according to the will the notary establishes also the group of people, having the right to obligatory share in inheritance, having warned beneficiaries under a will about responsibility for concealment of existence of legitimate heirs.

3. If one or several heirs are deprived of opportunity to produce the evidence of the related relations granting legitimate right for inheritance, then they can be included in the certificate on the right to inheritance from written consent of all other heirs, and in case of not reaching an agreement - judicially.

第六十三条 依法或者依照遗嘱出具继承权公证书的条件

1. 公证员依法或者依照遗嘱出具继承权公证书的，应当查验遗嘱人的死亡事实、继承的时间和地点、遗嘱法律关系是否成立、继承财产的数额等情况。

2. 公证员依照遗嘱出具遗产继承权公证书之前，也应确定具有法定继承权的人员，并根据遗嘱提示继承人，公证员对法定继承人的信息负有保密义务。

3. 一个或几个继承人未能提供相关关系证明，从而丧失合法继承权的，若没有达成司法上的协议，则可以通过其他所有继承人的书面同意，将其加入继承权公证书中。

Chapter 9. The certificate on the property right to the relying share of the property which is in general joint or common ownership

Article 64. The Section of the property which is in general joint either common ownership or allocation of share from it

1. The Section of common property between participants of common joint property or allocation of share from it one of them is made after preliminary determination of share of each of the participants having the right to common property.

The property which is in equity property can be divided between his participants from their consent.

2. The notary certifies the agreement signed between all participants of common joint or equity property on the Section of the property which is joint or equity property or allocation from it of share and on its basis grants certificates on the property right to respective share or part in the common or equity property belonging to them.

3. The certificate on the property right is granted only on the property which is joint or equity property of participants of joint or equity property and available in day of the certificate of the agreement and issue of the certificate.

4. In case of the death of one of participants of common joint property the notary office in the place of opening of inheritance issues to the survived participants or participants the certificate on the property right to the relying share in their common property based on the written application of all participants with the notice on it of the heirs who accepted inheritance.

5. With the consent of the survived participants of common joint property the notary can grant the certificate on the property right to share of the died participant in common property.

Chapter 10. Witnessing of authenticity of copies of documents or statements from documents

Article 65. Witnessing of authenticity of copies of documents or statements from documents

1. The notary witnesses compliance to originals of all copies of documents or statements from them issued by the organizations, assured by seal either signed in accordance with the established procedure or signed by physical persons if it is not forbidden by the law.

2. Fidelity of the statement can be attested only when

第九章 对一般共有财产或者共同共有财产份额的公证

第六十四条 一般共有财产份额，即指共有财产或从共有财产中分配的份额。

1. 对共有人之间的部分共有财产或共有财产中的一部分的分配，须在初步确定共同财产每个参与者的份额之后才能作出。

股权可以依照共有人之间的合意进行划分。

2. 财产共有人或股权财产的共有人之间签订财产分配协议时，公证员可以基于该财产分配协议对共有人各自的财产份额公证。

3. 该财产权公证书的出具仅针对共有人或股权共有人共同财产或股权财产，上述财产份额的权属变动发生于财产分配协议签订之日。

4. 若财产共有人之一死亡，继承权归属地的公证机构应向仍存活的共有人以书面形式出具基于共有财产中相应份额的财产权公证书。应当通知所有共有人和法定继承人。

5. 经财产共有人同意，公证员可以为已死亡的共有人应得的财产份额公证。

第十章 对文件副本真实性的公证

第六十五条 对文件副本真实性的公证

1. 公证员应对各单位组织出具的声明或文件原件的真实性予以确认，并按既定程序签字盖章。

2. 当声明文件中包含几个互不相关的独立问题的

the document of which the statement is made includes solutions of several separate questions which are not connected among themselves. The statement from the document shall reproduce the complete text of the document on certain question.

3. The copy shall correspond to the original the spelling, punctuation, reducings.

4. The copy of the document constituted in foreign language is witnessed only if the notary knows this foreign language. If the notary does not know the corresponding foreign language, then the copy of the document constituted in foreign language can be attested only after witnessing in the procedure for the translation of this document established by this Law.

5. Authenticity of the copy of the document issued by physical person is witnessed by the notary if authenticity of the signature of physical person on the document is certified by the notary.

6. The notary, witnessing authenticity of the copy of the document, does not certify or certifies the facts stated in the document, and only confirms that the copy of the document corresponds to the original.

Article 66. Witnessing of authenticity of the copy from the copy of the document

The notary witnesses authenticity of the copy from the copy of the document provided that authenticity of the copy is notarized or the copy of the document is issued by the organization from which the authentic document proceeds. In the latter case the copy of the document shall be stated on the form of this organization with the put-down seal and mark that the authentic document is at them.

Chapter 11. Witnessing of authenticity of signatures on documents

Article 67. Witnessing of authenticity of signatures on documents

1. The notary witnesses authenticity of signatures of physical persons on all documents which do not have nature of the transaction.

2. The notary, witnessing authenticity of the signature of physical person, does not certify or certifies the facts stated in the document, and only confirms that the signature is made by certain person.

解决方案时，公证员可以对该声明的真实性公证。该声明应对所涉问题作完整陈述。

3. 公证文件的副本应与原件的内容相对应。

4. 若公证员通晓外国语言，可以对该外文文件副本的真实性公证。公证员不通晓相应外国文字的，必须依据本法的规定指定翻译人员翻译，经公证员核对后，再对该外文文件副本的真实性公证。

5. 若公证员曾对自然人在文件中签名的真实性公证，则公证员可以对该文件副本的真实性公证。

6. 公证员对文件副本的真实性公证时，无须证明文件中所陈述的内容的真实性，只需证明文件副本与原件相符。

第六十六条　文件副本真实性的公证

文件副本的真实性必须经过公证，除非该文件的副本是由制作原文件的机构出具的。但在此种情形下，文件副本应在该机构的登记簿中注明，并加盖印章，注明原件在其机构内保存。

第十一章　对文件签名真实性的公证

第六十七条　对文件签名真实性的公证

1. 对不具有交易性质的文件，公证员可以对自然人签名的真实性作出公证。

2. 公证员对自然人签名的真实性公证时，不需要证明文件中内容的真实性，只需证明该签名是由本人作出的。

Chapter 12. Witnessing of authenticity of the translation of documents

Article 68. Witnessing of authenticity of the translation of documents

1. The notary witnesses authenticity of the translation of the document if he knows the corresponding languages. If he does not know the corresponding languages, the document is translated by the confidential translator of the notary whose authenticity of the signature is witnessed by the notary.

2. The notary, witnessing authenticity of the translation or authenticity of the signature of the translator, does not certify or certifies the facts stated in the document, and only confirms that content of the translation of the document corresponds to contents of its original.

Chapter 13. The certificate of the fact of finding of the citizen in certain place and in live, and also identity of the citizen with person represented in the photo

Article 69. Ascertaining of the fact of finding of the citizen in certain place

1. The notary, according to the petition from the citizen, confirms the fact of its stay in certain place and grants the certificate on it.

2. The stay fact in certain place of person recognized as incapacitated proves to be true based on the statement of his legal representatives (parents, adoptive parents, the guardian), and also those organizations on which care there is incapacitated person.

Article 70. The certificate of the fact of finding of the personality in live

The notary can certify that person is in live if it personally was to the notary or to whom the notary was personally. The notary identifies the personality of person and certifies the fact of its stay in live.

In the document certifying the fact of finding of the personality in live the surname, name, middle name of person (in the identity document, - is entered in case of its availability), year, month, number, the place of its birth, the place of residence, year, month, number, time of the certificate of the fact, the location of person, and also other data provided by this Law.

Article 71. The certificate of identity of the citizen with person represented in the photo

The notary certifies identity of the citizen with person

第十二章　对文件翻译的准确性的公证

第六十八条　对文件翻译的准确性的公证

1. 若公证员通晓外国文字，可直接对文件翻译的准确性公证。若公证员不通晓外国文字，由公证员指定的翻译人员翻译，在公证员核对后，再对文件翻译的准确性公证。

2. 公证员对译文的准确性或者译者签字的真实性公证时，不需要证明所公证文件中陈述的内容的真实性，只需证明翻译文件的内容与原文内容相符。

第十三章　对特定地点下公民行为事实的公证，以及对公民与身份证件中照片是否一致的公证

第六十九条　对特定地点公民行为事实的公证

1. 公证员根据公民的请求，对其在特定地点的在场事实予以公证。

2. 根据其法定代理人（父母、养父母、监护人）和无行为能力人监护组织的陈述，公证员对无行为能力人在特定地点下的行为事实的真实性公证。

第七十条　对现场发生的特定事实的公证

若某人亲自到公证员处，或公证员亲自到场，则公证员对某人在场的事实公证。

有关在场事实的公证书中，必须包含在场人的姓氏、名字、中间名、出生年月、出生地、居住地、时间、所在地及其他信息。

第七十一条　对公民与身份证件中照片是否一致的公证

公证员可以对公民与其身份证件中照片是否一致

represented in the photo.

进行公证。

Chapter 14. Transfer of statements, announcements and other documents of physical persons and legal entities to other physical persons and legal entities

第十四章　将自然人、法人的声明、公告或其他文件转交给其他自然人、法人

Article 72. Transfer of statements, announcements or other documents

1. The notary reports statements, announcements or other documents of the organizations or physical persons to other organizations or physical persons on receipt or sends by mail with the return notification.

2. Statements, announcements or other documents with the consent of persons who submitted them can be transferred with use of the fax, computer networks and other means of technical, electronic communication or personally. The expenses connected with transfer of statements, announcements or other documents are paid by person at the request of whom the statement, the announcement or other document is transferred.

3. Upon the demand of person who submitted the application, the announcement or other documents the relevant information on transfer of the statement, announcement or other documents is provided to it.

第七十二条　转交声明、公告或其他文件

1. 公证机构在收到邮件退回的通知时，应当向与邮件相关的组织或者自然人报告并说明情况。

2. 经申请人同意的声明、公告或其他文件，可通过传真、计算机网络和其他技术、电子通信手段及他人转交。与转交声明、公告或其他文件有关的费用，应由申请人支付。

3. 经申请人申请，公证员可以向其提供声明书、公告或者其他文件的有关资料。

Chapter 15. Acceptance in the deposit, storage, transfer and return of sums of money and securities

第十五章　接收存款，保管、转移、返还款项和有价证券

Article 73. Acceptance in the deposit, storage and return of sums of money and securities

1. In the cases provided by the law in execution by debtors of obligations, and also in other cases provided by the law the notary accepts in the deposit sums of money (dramas of the Republic of Armenia or foreign currency) or securities for transfer to their creditor. In case of acceptance in the deposit of sums of money or securities in obligation fulfillment the notary demands from debtors that person which brought them in the deposit, (debtor) in the statement except the name (name) and the place of residence (location), also accurately specified person having power on receipt of the deposit, and storage durations of money or securities as the deposit. Person who placed money or securities in the deposit according to the statement can make change or addition to deposit conditions. The deposit can be stopped according to the statement of person which brought in the deposit.

The notary in the cases provided by the regulatory legal

第七十三条　接收存款、保管、转移、返还款项和有价证券

1. 在法律规定的情形下，或在债务人履行义务时，公证员可以接收来自债务人的存款（亚美尼亚共和国币和外币）或证券，并向债权人代为转交。公证员接收债务人的存款金额或者有价证券时，应当要求债务人在有关清单中载明姓名（名称）、住所（地点）、所在地、存放的期限以及应收款的债权人名字。债务人可以改变或增加存款条件。

依据有关法律法规和证券交易的程序，以及亚美

acts establishing procedure for making of transactions with government securities and also with the securities issued by the Central bank of the Republic of Armenia accepts from the Central bank of the Republic of Armenia in the deposit the sums of money placed in pledge for the purpose of obligatory transfer to their creditor. In this case in the statement of the Central bank of the Republic of Armenia except the name and the location also data on subdepositaries of the mortgager and the pawnbroker and storage duration of money as the deposit are accurately specified. Central Bank of the Republic of Armenia according to the statement can make change or addition to deposit conditions. The deposit can be stopped according to the statement of the Central bank of the Republic of Armenia.

2. The notary informs the creditor on receipt of sums of money or securities and according to the statement of the creditor issues them to it.

3. Sums of money or securities can be returned to person which brought them in the deposit only with the consent of person for benefit of whom the contribution, or by a court decision is made.

Article 74. Storage of money or securities

1. The notary shall store the received money or securities. It registers in the special register the money or securities transferred it in which specifies the size of the transferred sum of money, quantity and cost of other securities, surname of person which transferred them, term and the purposes of transfer, the obligation in pursuance of which money or securities are transferred.

2. The notary without certificate transfers money or securities to body or person for which they are provided, having received the receipt on the translation.

Article 75. Impossibility of transfer of money and securities

If the notary for the objective reasons cannot make the transfer to the provided term charged to him, then within 15 days after receipt of money and securities it shall return them and if it is impossible, to bring them on storage to trial or to bring into the deposit account, the registered mail having notified about it person who transferred money and securities.

Article 76. Legal consequences of transfer of money and securities

1. Transfer of money and securities to the notary is obligation fulfillment.

2. The procedure provided by articles 73-75 of this

尼亚共和国中央银行发布的证券交易程序，公证员接收并存入亚美尼亚共和国中央银行的存款，是为了保证债权的顺利实现。在此情形下，在亚美尼亚共和国中央银行的报表中，应注明抵押人和典当商的名称、地点以及存款货币的存储期限。亚美尼亚共和国中央银行可以改变或增加存款条件。

2. 公证员收到存款或有价证券后，应通知债权人，公证员根据债权人的声明书向其偿还存款或有价证券。

3. 存款或有价证券仅能在获得利害关系人同意或经法院裁定后退还给存款者。

第七十四条　存储资金或有价证券

1. 公证员可以代为存储收到的资金或有价证券。在特定登记册中登记转移的资金或有价证券，其中载明转移资金的数额、证券的数额和本金、转移人的姓名、转移的期限和目的、资金或证券转移，以及依据的协议。

2. 不通晓外国文字的公证员在收到已被翻译的凭证后，将资金或有价证券转移给提供凭证的机构或个人。

第七十五条　无法转移的资金和有价证券

由于客观原因，公证员无法代为存储资金和有价证券时，公证员应当在 15 日内将收到的资金和有价证券归还。若归还有困难，需将该资金和有价证券存入指定账户，并通过邮件通知转移资金或有价证券的人。

第七十六条　资金和有价证券转移的法律效力

1. 向公证员转移资金和有价证券时应签订协议。

2. 本法第 73 条至第 75 条规定的程序，同样适用

Law is performed also in case the notary according to the law accepts documents, money, securities, heritable property or other objects on storage.

Chapter 16. Adoption of documents for storage

Article 77. Adoption of documents for storage

1. The notary has the right to accept any document which is not contradicting the law, including on the electronic medium. The notary accepts documents for storage according to the inventory. One copy of the inventory remains at the notary, and other copy is issued to person who checked documents.

The document is accepted on storage for the term of no more than one year. After the specified term according to the statement of its storage which handed over the document term every time can be prolonged no more than for one year.

2. Upon the demand of person the notary can accept on storage documents without inventory if these documents are packed properly. In this case packaging is fastened with notary's seal, signed by the notary and person checking documents. The notary bears responsibility for safety of packaging.

3. The receipt is issued to person which handed over documents.

Article 78. Return accepted on document storage and issue of statements from them

1. The documents accepted on storage return to checked them or legally authorized person upon presentation of the receipt and copy of the inventory or by a court decision.

The document returns handed over it in day of the expiration of storage, the stipulated in Article 77 these Laws, on specified handed over the document to the address. In this case the expenses of the notary connected with return of the document are compensated handed over it.

If the notary after storage duration of the document sent them it on specified handed over the document to the address, however not because of the notary he could not be transferred handed over the document, then the notary does not bear responsibility for further safety of this document.

2. The notary shall issue copies, statements, certificates of the documents stored in its archive to persons participating in their creation upon the demand of and at the expense of their heirs, and also by a court decision.

于公证员依法接收存单、货币、有价证券、遗产或者其他保管物的情形。

第十六章　文件的存储

第七十七条　文件的存储

1. 在不违反法律的前提下，公证员有权接收文件，包括电子媒介文件。公证员根据实际情况存储文件，并将其中一份留存于公证机构，另一份递交给文件审查人员。

文件存储的期限不超过一年。超过规定期限后，按照存储文件声明的期限，可以延长不超过一年。

2. 公证员可以接收并代为存储文件，但存储的文件需格式正确。在此情形下，加盖公证员的印章，由公证员和检查文件的人签字。由公证员对文件存储负责。

3. 按照既定程序，将文件归还给提交文件的人。

第七十八条　返还存储文件

1. 经接收存储的文件，在收到存储文件和副本，或经法院裁决后，返还给审查人或经法院授权的人。

依据本法第 77 条的规定，文件在存储期届满之日，应返还到指定地点。在此情形下，负责返还文件的公证员有权获得补偿费用。

若在文件存储期限届满后，非因公证员的个人原因，且无法将文件交到指定的地点，则公证员对文件不承担延迟返还的责任。

2. 根据继承人的申请，在考量继承人利益的基础上，公证员依据法院的裁决向参与文件制作的人员出具文件的副本、声明和有关证明。

Chapter 17. Providing proofs

Article 79. Providing the proofs necessary for initiation of proceedings in court or law enforcement agencies

1. According to the statement of interested persons the notary makes providing proofs which can be necessary for initiation of proceedings in court or law enforcement agencies if reasons to believe are had that production of evidence will become difficult or impossible subsequently.

2. The notary does not provide proofs on cases which are in production of court.

Article 80. Actions of the notary for providing proofs

1. For the purpose of providing proofs the notary interrogates witnesses, examines written or physical evidences, appoints examination, and also performs other operations on providing proofs provided by the Code of civil procedure of the Republic of Armenia.

2. In case of accomplishment of legal proceedings on providing proofs the notary is guided by the relevant standards of the Code of civil procedure of the Republic of Armenia and is given the appropriate authority provided by the Code.

3. The notary informs on time and the place of providing proofs of the party and interested persons, however their absence is not obstacle for accomplishment of actions for providing proofs.

4. In case of absence of the invited witness or the expert the notary reports about it in court at the place of residence of the witness or expert for acceptance of adequate measures.

5. The notary warns the witness and the expert about responsibility for making obviously false evidence or the conclusion and refusal of their giving.

Article 81. Certificate of time of presentation of the document

1. Time when the document is shown to the notary or with the assistance of the notary to other person, makes sure the notary.

2. Upon the demand of person the notary identifies the personality of person who showed the document, and the personality receiving the document.

第十七章　提供证据

第七十九条　向法庭或执法机构提起诉讼时，在以下情形中，公证员需提供必要的证据

1. 若有理由相信在未来证据提供具有困难或不可能，且根据利害关系人的陈述，该证据是在法庭或执法机构提起诉讼所必需的。

2. 公证员未向法庭提供审理案件的证据。

第八十条　公证员采集证据的行为

1. 为采集证据，公证员需询问证人、审查书面证据或实物证据、指定检查，并依据《亚美尼亚共和国民事诉讼法》的规定进行其他取证活动。

2. 在完成取证程序后，公证员应遵循《亚美尼亚共和国民事诉讼法》的规定进一步开展活动。

3. 公证员应及时通知公证申请人和利害关系人举证的时间和地点，但公证申请人和利害关系人的缺席并不妨碍举证行为的完成。

4. 若被邀请的证人或者专家缺席，公证员应当向证人或专家居住地的法庭报告，以便采取适当的措施。

5. 证人和鉴定人作出明显虚假的证言或者结论的，公证员有责任拒绝公证，并向上述主体提出警告。

第八十一条　提交文件的时间证明

1. 向公证员出示文件或在公证员协助下向他人出示文件时，应确保公证员知晓文件出示的过程。

2. 公证员根据公证申请人的要求，确定出具证明文件的人以及接收证明文件的人。

Chapter 17.1. Confirmation of the facts having legal value

Article 81.1. Confirmation of the facts having legal value

1. The notary confirms those facts on which depend origin, change or the termination of personal or property rights of citizens or legal entities.

2. The notary confirms the following facts:

1) family relations between persons;

2) finding of person dependent on other person;

3) registration of the birth, adoption (adoption), scrap, divorce and death;

4) inheritance acceptance and place of opening of inheritance;

5) accessory of the documents establishing the rights, except for the passport and military documents;

6) ownership of property by the property right;

7) oral announcements of persons.

3. The notary in the cases established by the Law confirms others of the facts, having legal value.

4. In the statement for confirmation of the fact of legal value it shall be specified for what purpose the applicant needs confirmation of this fact, and also the proofs confirming impossibility of receipt of proper documents or recovery of the lost documents shall be provided by the applicant.

5. The notary confirms the facts having legal value only if the applicant has no opportunity to receive the proper documents confirming these facts in other procedure or it is impossible to recover the lost documents.

6. The notarial act about confirmation of the facts having legal value is the basis for registration of this fact by relevant organs or for registration of the rights which arose in connection with the confirmed fact.

7. The notarial act about confirmation of the facts having legal value can be used only in the purposes specified in the notarial act.

8. The notarial act about confirmation of the facts having legal value shall contain:

1) the conditions established by part 2 of article 36.1 of this Law;

2) the fact having legal value which is confirmed by this notarial act;

3) the bases for confirmation or variation of the fact having legal value;

4) confirmations of the fact aiming legal value.

9. The notary adopts the notarial act about the fact

第十七章之一　具有法律意义的事实的公证

第八十一条之一　具有法律意义的事实的公证

1. 公证员确认公民或法人财产权利的来源、变更或终止事实。

2. 公证员可以对下列事实公证：

（1）家庭关系；

（2）依靠他人生存的人；

（3）出生登记、收养（收养）、离婚登记、死亡登记；

（4）接受继承和继承的地点；

（5）除护照、军事证件外，公证权利文件的附件；

（6）产权归属；

（7）口头通知。

3. 在法律规定的情形下，公证员可以对其他具有法律意义的事实进行公证。

4. 公证员在进行具有法律意义的事实公证时，应当说明申请人需要公证这一事实的目的。若公证申请人无法获得适当的文件或追回遗失的文件，应提供证明。

5. 必须在申请人无法通过其他程序，获得适当的文件或者无法追回遗失的文件的情况下，公证员对具有法律意义的事实作出公证。

6. 对具有法律意义事实进行公证时，由有关机关对该事实登记，或者对该事实所涉权利进行登记。

7. 具有法律意义的事实作出的公证仅能用于公证法律规定的目的。

8. 具有法律意义的事实包括：

（1）本法第 36 条之一第 2 款规定的情形；

（2）经公证确认具有法律意义的事实；

（3）对具有法律意义事实的确认或者变更依据；

（4）以法律意义为目的的事实。

9. 有下列情形之一的，公证员应对具有法律意义

having legal value if:

1) the submitted documents are sufficient for confirmation of the fact having legal value;

2) the subject to confirmation fact having legal value proceeds from the available data in the submitted documents;

3) there is no discrepancy with requirements of substantive law rules;

4) the applicant has no opportunity to receive or recover the documents confirming the fact having legal value in other procedure, or the possibility of it is exhausted;

5) requirements of part 4 of this Article are observed;

6) the fact having legal value is indisputable.

10. In case of non-compliance with requirements of part 9 of this Article, the notary rejects confirmation of the fact.

Article 81.2. Confirmation of oral announcements of persons by the notary

1. The notary confirms the oral announcement of person made in case of it to which confirmation of oath (oath) about truthfulness of the announcement made by this person is applied.

2. Confirmation of oath (oath) is performed in the presence of at least two witnesses, by means of the oral announcement and signing of confirmation of oath (oath) by person bringing oath (oath). Oath (oath) the physical person certifies truthfulness of the made announcement and signs the announcement and confirmation of oath of the oath). Witnesses confirm with the signatures that the announcement and confirmation of oath (oath) were made at their presence.

3. Person confirms with confirmation of oath (oath) that it is informed on criminal liability in case of gift of perjury (oath).

4. Confirmed with the notary in established by part of 1 this Article oral announcements have evidential force in court and in case of submission to other state bodies.

Chapter 18. Witnessing of the protocol of general meeting of the organization or meeting of other collegiate organ

Article 82. Witnessing of the protocol of general meeting of the organization or meeting of other collegiate organ

1. If the organization invites the notary for witnessing of protocols of the held meeting or meeting, then the notary witnesses only the minutes or meetings in which all that occurred is brought and time and the venue of meeting

的事实进行公证：

（1）提交的文件足以证明该事实具有法律意义；

（2）经确认的具有法律意义的事实；

（3）与实体法的规定不存在差异；

（4）其他程序中已被确认具有法律意义的文件；

（5）符合本条第 4 款的规定；

（6）被公认的具有法律意义的事实。

10. 若不符合本条第 9 款的规定，公证员应拒绝公证。

第八十一条之二　对口头声明的公证

1. 公证员可以对口头声明进行公证。

2. 确认口头声明（誓言）是在至少两名见证人在场的情况下，通过宣誓和誓言签署的方式进行的。对自然人口头声明（誓言）的真实性，通过签署公告和宣誓内容进行公证。见证人在签名时确认口头声明（誓言）是在其面前作出的。

3. 应当先告知见证人作伪证（誓言）的刑事责任，再宣誓确认。

4. 经公证员公证，口头声明在司法程序或行政程序中具有证据能力。

第十八章　证明组织成员会议或者其他会议的议定书

第八十二条　对组织成员会议或者其他会议的议定书公证

1. 若该组织邀请公证员见证所举行的会议或会议的议定书，则公证员可以对会议内容、时间、会议地点、会议作出的决定，以及会议的召开所获得的批准等事项进行公证。

or meeting, the decisions made at meeting or meeting was approved at its presence, and also.

2. The protocol is signed presiding over meeting or meeting and the secretary.

3. The notary makes record about the identity of the chairman at meeting or meeting and at his desire proves the identity of other participants.

2. 由会议主持人、与会人员以及秘书签署议定书。

3. 在会议中，公证员根据会议主席的介绍证明其他与会者的身份。

Chapter 18.1 Executive text

第十八章之一　执行文件

Article 82.1. General provisions about executive text

1. For accomplishment of the requirement of the creditor about collection of sums of money at the debtor or issue of property (things) or the document or transfer of the right to property, the notary about the transaction certified by it makes executive text.

2. The executive text is made if between the parties the agreement certified of notarial procedure by means of which the parties reached agreement on the work of executive text in case of failure to carry out proceeding from certified by the notary the this socklets of the requirement about payment of the amount or issue of property (document) or transfer of the right to property was signed.

3. The executive text is made if in the consent of obligation parties of the debtor on issue of sums of money or property (things) or the document or the right to property it is carried out by means of adoption of notarial acts or notarial actions.

4. The executive text is made based on the statement of the creditor, provision of leaf of executive text.

第八十二条之一　执行文件的一般规定

1. 为完成债权人向债务人催收款项、签署财产（物）或财产权利文件、转移财产等的要求，由作出公证的公证员出具执行文件。

2. 若公证申请人之间就公证内容签订了协议，且双方对公证执行文件的内容形成合意，则公证员应在执行文件中划去已经支付的数额，或已经签署转移的财产权。

3. 如果债务人对公证书中认定的债权债务关系、欠款金额等无异议，应按照公证书的内容出具执行文件。

4. 依据执行文件的出具程序，出具执行文件时应当听取债权人的陈述。

Article 82.2. Conditions of issue of leaf of executive text

1. The leaf of executive text is issued in case of simultaneous availability of the following conditions if:

1) the documents certified of notarial procedure which confirm the indisputable obligation of the debtor to the creditor are submitted, and is absent cross liabilities of the creditor;

2) there are bases provided by parts 2 and 3 of article 82.1 of this Law;

3) the creditor produces the evidence about the notification of the debtor as appropriate about the address to the notary for the work of executive text for debt collection or accomplishment of pending obligation.

2. The leaf of executive text is issued in duplicate, one of which together with the documents submitted by the creditor is attached to notarial case with the note "sec-

第八十二条之二　出具执行文件的条件

1. 出具执行文件的条件包括：

（1）经公证程序证明，确认债务人对债权人负有确定的义务，不存在债权人交叉责任的；

（2）存在本法第八十二条之一第 2 款、第 3 款规定的情形；

（3）债权人向公证员提供债务人地址有关的证据，以便进行债务催告或执行工作。

2. 执行文件一式两份，其中一份连同债权人提交的文件附于公证书后，附注“两份”，另一份交给债权人。

ond copy", another is issued to the creditor.

3. In each pending obligation the single sheet of executive text is issued.

4. Originals of the documents submitted to the notary return to the creditor, leaving the copy of the original document certified by notary's seal in notarial case.

5. The approximate form of leaf of executive text is approved by the Minister of Justice.

6. The leaf of executive text is issued within three days after submission of the statement.

Article 82.3. Procedure for collection on executive text

1. The leaf of executive text is carried out in the procedure established by the Law of the Republic of Armenia "About forced execution of court resolutions".

Chapter 19. Application by the notary of regulations of foreign law. International contracts and agreements

Article 83. Application of regulations of foreign law

The notary according to the legislation of the Republic of Armenia applies regulations of foreign law.

The notary accepts the documents constituted according to requirements of foreign law if it does not contradict the law or international treaties of the Republic of Armenia.

The notary makes certifying texts on the documents constituted in the form provided by the foreign legislation if it does not contradict the law or international treaties and if the notary knows the foreign legislation.

Article 84. Making of notarial action for foreign citizens or stateless persons

The foreign citizen or the stateless person can itself personally or through the representative to address for making of notarial action according to the procedure, established for citizens of the Republic of Armenia.

Article 85. Protection of heritable property and issue of the certificate on the right to inheritance

The actions connected with protection of the property which is in the territory of the Republic of Armenia which remained after the death of the foreign citizen or the stateless person, or the property relying the foreign citizen after the death of the citizen of the Republic of Armenia and also with issue of the certificate on the right to inheritance concerning such property are performed according to the legislation of the Republic of Armenia.

3. 针对每一项尚未履行的义务中，都需印发一份执行文件。

4. 向公证员提交的文件原件应当返还给债权人，公证员留存已经过盖章证明的原件复印件。

5. 执行文件的形式由司法部部长确定。

6. 执行文件在提交申请的 3 日内作出。

第八十二条之三　执行程序

1. 执行程序的依据是亚美尼亚共和国关于强制执行法院裁判的法律。

第十九章　对外国法律法规的适用，包括国际合约与协议

第八十三条　对外国法律的适用

公证员依据亚美尼亚共和国法律的规定适用外国法。

公证员在不违反亚美尼亚共和国的法律或国际条约的情形下，可以依据外国法的要求出具公证书。

依据外国法制作的文件，在不违反亚美尼亚共和国法律或者国际条约的情况下，若公证员通晓该外国法的，可以对上述文件进行公证。

第八十四条　为外国公民、无国籍人的公证

外国公民或者无国籍人可以亲自或者通过其代理人，依照为亚美尼亚共和国公民设立的程序办理公证。

第八十五条　对涉外遗产的保护和出具继承权公证书

外国公民或无国籍人死亡后留有遗产，且遗产位于亚美尼亚共和国境内，或者亚美尼亚公民死亡后在外国留有遗产，依据亚美尼亚共和国的法律，为保护亚美尼亚共和国财产，公证员有权对上述遗产的继承权进行公证。

Article 86. The power of attorney provided for making of actions abroad

The power of attorney certified by the notary provided for making of actions abroad and which is not containing specifying about effective period remains in force before its cancellation by person who issued the power of attorney.

第八十六条　委托书在国外的效力

经公证员公证的委托书在国外有效，不载明有效期限的委托书，在委托人撤销之前，始终有效。

Article 87. Acceptance by the notary of the documents constituted abroad

The documents constituted with participation of officials of competent authorities of other states or issued by them are accepted by the notary if they are in accordance with the established procedure certified by consular bodies of the Republic of Armenia, except as specified, provided by international treaties.

第八十七条　公证员接收在国外生成的文件

由其他国家主管官员签发的文件，若符合亚美尼亚共和国领事机构所确认的既有程序，则公证员应当接收，但国际条约另有规定的除外。

Article 88. Relations of the notary with judicial authorities of other states

The procedure for the relations of the notary with judicial authorities of other states is determined by the legislation and international treaties of the Republic of Armenia.

第八十八条　公证员与其他国家司法机关的关系

公证员与其他国家司法机关的关系，由亚美尼亚共和国的法律和国际条约规定。

Article 89. Providing the proofs which are required for business management in bodies of other states

The notary provides the proofs which are required for business management in bodies of other states.

第八十九条　为外国国家机构业务管理所需作出的公证

应外国国家机构的业务管理的需要，公证员可以为其提供公证服务。

Article 90. International agreements

If the international treaty refers to competence of the notary making of notarial actions, not stipulated by the legislation the Republic of Armenia, then the notary makes this notarial action according to the procedure, established by the Ministry of Justice.

第九十条　国际协议

若国际条约规定的公证员权限在亚美尼亚共和国法律中没有规定的，则公证员应按照司法部规定的程序开展公证活动。

Chapter 20. Transitional provisions

第二十章　过渡条款

Article 91. Transitional provisions

1. After the introduction of this Law in force the notaries public who are earlier appointed the Minister of Justice continue to perform the actions provided by this Law in the place of the activities before new appointments of notaries according to the procedure, stipulated in Item 3 these Articles.

The rights, obligations, guarantees and privileges provided by this Law for notaries extend to the notaries public who are earlier appointed the Minister of Justice and continuing the activities.

2. Advanced training of the notaries public who are

第九十一条　过渡条款

1. 本法生效后，已经接受司法部部长任命的公证员，按照本条第 3 款的规定，继续履行其公证员职务。

本法对公证员规定的权利、义务，也适用于本法生效前已接受司法部部长任命的公证员。

2. 司法部部长任命的公证员以及公证员候选人，

earlier appointed the Minister of Justice, and also new candidates for notaries is carried out in three months after the introduction of this Law to force.

在本法生效后的 3 个月内接受高级培训。

3. New appointments of notaries are performed by the Minister of Justice in four months from the date of adoption of this Law.

3. 新任命的公证员，由司法部部长在本法通过之日起 4 个月内批准任职。

The notaries who are earlier appointed the Minister of Justice and passed qualification examinations have the right to perform the notarial activities in premises of former notary offices which are provided to them in free use.

本法生效前已经接受司法部部长任命，并通过资格考试的公证员，有权在原公证机构继续开展公证活动。

4. The former notaries who did not pass qualification examinations continue to perform notarial activities three more months during which they have the right to pass qualification examinations in the procedure established by this Law. The notaries who did not pass qualification examinations in the specified time are relieved of the post.

4. 本法生效前未通过资格考试的公证员，可以在本法生效后的 3 个月内继续履行公证员职务，但在三个月内仍未通过资格考试的公证员，司法部部长应当免去其公证员职务。

5. In four months from the date of the introduction of this Law in force the Minister of Justice convokes the constituent assembly of notarial chamber in which have the right to participate only the notaries who passed qualification examinations.

5. 自本法施行之日起 4 个月内，司法部部长召开公证会议，所有通过资格考试的公证员均应参加。

6. Within one year from the date of the introduction of this Law in force the requirement about training at least one year, stipulated in Item 1 article 10 of this Law does not extend to persons who showed willingness to hold position of the notary.

6. 依据本法第 10 条第 1 项规定的"至少培训 1 年"，不包括有意愿担任公证员职务的人员。

7. When holding the qualification examinations provided by this Article requirements of Items 4 and 9 of article 11 of this Law are not applied.

7. 资格考试不适用本法第 11 条第 4 项、第 9 项的规定。

8. To the introduction of this Law in force the appointed training of trainees of the notary continues at the corresponding notaries before the termination of year of probation period.

8. 本法生效后，公证员指定培训期未终止前，应继续在原公证机构接受培训。

9. Within four months after the introduction of this Law in force the Government allocates to notarial chamber the corresponding territory.

9. 在本法生效后的 4 个月内，政府应为每一公证机构划定公证区域。

Chapter 21. Final provisions

第二十一章 最后条款

Article 92. The introduction of the Law in force

第九十二条 法律的效力

1. This Law becomes effective since March 1, 2002.
2. Declare invalid the Law Automated workplace. SSR "About the state notariate".

1. 本法自 2002 年 3 月 1 日起施行。
2. 相关法律自动无效。

President of the Republic of Armenia
R. Kocharyan

亚美尼亚共和国总统
R. 科恰良

阿塞拜疆

阿塞拜疆共和国公证法

LAW OF THE AZERBAIJAN REPUBLIC
of November 26, 1999 No. 762-IQ
About notariate
(The last edition from 30-12-2016)

阿塞拜疆共和国公证法
1999 年 11 月 26 日 第 762–IQ 号

（2016 年 12 月 30 日最新修订版）

Chapter I. General provisions

Article 1. Notariate in the Azerbaijan Republic

In the Azerbaijan Republic notariate it is necessary to understand as the word in total persons authorized on making of the legal actions provided by this Law (further - notarial actions).

In the Azerbaijan Republic the ji of the rights and facts of legal value and making of other notarial actions for execution of official and authentic documents belongs to notarial activities which can be performed only in the procedure established by this Law and persons provided in it.

Article 2. The legislation applied when making notarial actions

When making notarial actions it is necessary to be guided by the Constitution of the Azerbaijan Republic, this Law, other laws of the Azerbaijan Republic, and also regulations which are not contradicting this Law adopted by relevant organs executive within their competence.

Article 3. Notary

Person who is professionally engaged in notarial activities hereinafter is referred to as as the notary.

Any citizen of the Azerbaijan Republic, the person interested to work as the state or private notary (further - the citizen), shall have the higher legal education, have the

第一章　总则

第 1 条　阿塞拜疆共和国的公证员

阿塞拜疆共和国的公证员，是经授权开展本法所规定法律行为（即公证活动）的人员。

在阿塞拜疆共和国，公证是制作具有法律意义的权利和事实的公证书以及为执行官方的、可信的文件而开展的其他公证活动，只能按照本法规定的程序进行和由本法要求的人员开展。

第 2 条　开展公证活动时适用的法律

开展公证活动，必须遵循阿塞拜疆共和国宪法、本法、阿塞拜疆共和国其他法律以及有关行政机关在其职权范围内通过的与本法不相抵触的条例。

第 3 条　公证员

以下专业从事公证活动的人称为公证员。

有意从事国家或私营公证员工作的阿塞拜疆共和国公民，应接受过较高的法律教育，具有相应的道德素质和专业知识。

corresponding moral qualities and professional knowledge.

Persons having double citizenship, obligations to other states, the religious figures discharged earlier from office for violation of requirements of the legislation in connection with execution of the obligations, in the procedure established by the law recognized incapacitated or with special disability, committed earlier intended crime and condemned for it concerning which there is judgment which took legal effect about restriction for occupation with notarial activities or application of enforcement powers of medical nature, not capable to work as the notary based on the medical certificate owing to physical and intellectual defects, reached 65-year age and also concerning which is available the decision of investigating body or court on the termination of criminal case which took legal effect on crime execution in view of lack of the justificatory bases cannot be notaries.

The citizen meeting the specified requirements and the person interested to become the notary, shall receive the certificate on occupation notarial activities (further - the certificate).

The notary is forbidden to be engaged in business activity and to perform other paid works, except for scientific, pedagogical and creative activities.

The notary shall suspend the activities in any political party for the work.

Also the restrictions set by the Law of the Azerbaijan Republic "About service in judicial authorities" are applied to the notary public.

The notary shall observe requirements of the Code of ethical behavior of the notary approved by relevant organ of the executive authority of the Azerbaijan Republic.

Article 4. Procedure for issue of the certificate

Person wishing to receive the certificate on professional work by notarial activities shall file petition in relevant organ of the executive authority of the Azerbaijan Republic. Desire of person to perform activities as the state or private notary shall be specified in the statement.

The relevant organ of the executive authority of the Azerbaijan Republic within 1 month from the date of the address of the citizen shall check whether he answers the requirements established in article 3 of this Law and, depending on result, to submit collected documents to the qualification commission.

The citizen is in writing informed on result of consideration of its address.

不得担任公证员的人员：具有双重公民身份、对其他国家负有义务、之前由于违反关于履行义务的法律要求而被解职的宗教人士、依法定程序被确认无行为能力或有特殊残疾的、曾实施故意犯罪且法院的判决对从事公证活动进行了限制、适用强制医疗、基于体检证明因身体和智力缺陷无法从事公证员、达到65周岁、调查机关或法院作出终止刑事案件的决定但因缺乏正当性基础终止了犯罪执行的。

符合规定条件并有意向从事公证活动的公民，应当领取公证执业资格证书（即资格证）。

公证员不得从事商业活动和其他有偿工作，但是，从事科学、教学及创造性活动的除外。

公证员应当中止所有的政党工作。

此外，阿塞拜疆共和国《司法机关服务法》中规定的限制条件也适用于公证员。

公证员应遵守阿塞拜疆共和国行政机关有关部门批准的《公证员道德行为守则》的要求。

第 4 条　签发执业资格证书的程序

意欲获得公证执业资格证的人，应当向阿塞拜疆共和国行政机关有关部门提交申请。也应在申请中明确表明选择从事官方公证员或私营公证员的意向。

阿塞拜疆共和国行政机关的有关部门应在公民申请之日起 1 个月内，核查其是否符合本法第 3 条的规定，并根据结果提交所有相关文件至资格审查委员会。

申请结果将以书面形式通知申请人。

Level of knowledge of persons wishing to receive the certificate shall be checked by means of examination and interview then they are involved in compulsory education in educational scientific institution of relevant organ of the executive authority (further - compulsory education).

公证员申请人应接受考试和面试以考核其知识水平，然后在行政机关有关部门的科学教育机构参与法定培训。

Persons, at least 2 years which worked consultants or in higher positions in structure of relevant organ of the executive authority Azerbaijani the Republics exercising direct supervision over notarial activities and notary offices, are exempted from compulsory education.

在阿塞拜疆共和国行政机关有关部门担任顾问或更高职位不少于 2 年，且从事对公证活动和公证机构直接监管工作的人可以免除法定培训。

For receipt of the certificate of person, after compulsory education, shall have interview concerning their professional readiness for notarial activities.

为获得公证执业资格书，申请人在法定培训后，应参加有关公证执业资格面试。

The procedure for passing of examination and interviews is established by relevant organ of the executive authority of the Azerbaijan Republic.

由阿塞拜疆共和国行政机关有关部门负责制定审查和面试的程序。

Article 5. Qualification commission

第 5 条　资格审查委员会

The qualification commission is formed by relevant organ of the executive authority of the Azerbaijan Republic for a period of 5 years as a part of 7 members for the solution of the questions connected with check by means of examination and interview of level of knowledge of person wishing to receive the certificate on professional work by notarial activities, holding interview of rather professional readiness for notarial activities, issue of the certificate and offers to destination or refusal in issue of the certificate.

资格审查委员会由阿塞拜疆共和国行政机关有关部门组建，由 7 名成员组成，任期 5 年，通过考试和面试方式考核意欲获得公证执业资格证的人的知识水平。资格审查委员会负责组织面试，考核申请人对公证执业的准备情况，签发公证执业资格证或拒绝签发公证执业资格证。

The commission chairman is elected among her members.

委员会主席由委员会成员选举产生。

The relevant organ of the executive authority of the Azerbaijan Republic shall perform organizational support of activities of the qualification commission.

阿塞拜疆共和国行政机关有关部门应对资格审查委员会的工作提供组织上的支持。

The qualification commission considers the arrived documents, for the solution of question of the admission of person to compulsory education holds at it exam, conducts interview, conducts interview for check of professional readiness of persons exempted from compulsory education and depending on result makes the decision on issue of the certificate and offers to destination or on refusal in issue of the certificate.

资格审查委员会审查提交的文件，组织考核合格者参加法定培训的考试，组织面试，组织被豁免法定培训人员的面试，检查其专业准备情况，并根据结果决定签发公证执业资格证或拒绝签发公证执业资格证。

Questions according to the documents which arrived in the qualification commission shall be permitted on commission sessions no later than two months. The course of each meeting and the made decisions are subject to reflection in the constituted protocol.

提交到资格审查委员会的文件如有问题，应在 2 个月内于委员会会议上讨论。每次应在会议纪要中记录会议过程和作出的决定。

The meeting of the qualification commission is au-

至少指定 5 位成员参加资格审查委员会的会议。

thorized with the assistance of at least 5 of her members.

The qualification commission makes the decisions by a majority vote and within three days after that issues to person the copy of the decision.

In case of equality of votes the voice of the commission chairman is decisive.

Within 1 month after receipt of the copy of the decision of the commission on refusal in issue of the certificate person can file a lawsuit the claim concerning correctness of application of the legislation.

Persons who did not have interview of rather professional readiness can within 3 years with vacancy of the notary be allowed without passing of training to repeated interview for receipt of the certificate.

Article 6. Issue of the certificate. Prolongation of effective period of the certificate

After removal to the persons which successfully finished compulsory education or who had interview on professional training by the qualification commission of the decision on issue of the certificate the citizen brings for issue of the certificate to it the state fee.

The relevant organ of the executive authority of the Azerbaijan Republic in 10-day time after submission of the document on payment of the state fee grants to it the certificate on occupation notarial activities for a period of five years.

The notary wishing to continue notarial activities in three months prior to the expiration of the certificate files petition in relevant organ of the executive authority of the Azerbaijan Republic which estimates its activities with respect thereto.

Effective period of the certificate of the notary which activities are assessed positively is prolonged for five years. For prolongation of term of the certificate the notary brings the state fee.

Article 7. Cancellation of the certificate

The certificate can be cancelled by the judgment only in the following cases:

1) in case of violation by the notary of the requirements provided by Article part three 3, Item 3 of Article 9, Article part one 28, Article 30, Article 31, Article part four 32, Articles 33, 34 and 40 these Laws;

2) in case of numerous violation of the current legislation with causing essential damage to the state, physical person or legal entity when making by the notary of notarial actions;

资格审查委员会采用多数决投票的方式作出决定，并在作出决定后 3 日内向申请者发送决定的副本。

在票数相等的情况下，由委员会主席决定。

在收到委员会拒绝签发公证执业资格证的决定副本后 1 个月内，申请人可以提起诉讼，要求说明有关法律适用的正确性。

申请人未参加考核专业准备的面试的，可以在 3 年内公证职位有空缺时，不经培训重新面试以获得公证执业资格证书。

第 6 条　公证执业资格证的签发、延长公证执业资格证的有效期限

在申请人完成法定培训或者面试过专业技能后，由资格审查委员会决定向申请人签发公证执业资格证，申请人需要向国家缴纳规定的费用。

阿塞拜疆共和国行政机关的有关部门在申请人提交已缴纳法定费用的单据后 10 日内授予从事公证工作的公证执业资格证，为期 5 年。

意欲继续从事公证活动的公证员应在公证执业资格证有效期期满前 3 个月向阿塞拜疆共和国行政机关有关部门提出申请，由该部门进行评估。

经正式评估后公证执业资格证的有效期可延长 5 年。公证员应缴纳延长公证执业资格证期限的规定费用。

第 7 条　取消公证执业资格证

只有在下列情况时才能通过判决取消公证执业资格证：

（1）公证员违反本法第 3 条第 3 部分，第 9 条第 3 款，第 28 条第 1 部分，第 30 条，第 31 条，第 32 条第 4 部分，第 33 条，第 34 条和第 40 条的规定；

（2）公证员在开展公证行为时多次违反现行法律，对国家、自然人或法人造成重大损害；

3) in case of departure of the notary from the Azerbaijan Republic to other country on the permanent residence;

4) in case of condemnation of the notary for crime execution or availability of the judgment which took legal effect about application in its relation of enforcement powers of medical nature;

5) in case of decision about the termination concerning the notary of criminal case without justificatory motives;

6) in the presence of the judgment which took legal effect about legal incapacity of the notary or recognition by its incapacitated.

In the presence of one of the cases listed in Items 1-6 of part one of this Article, the relevant organ of the executive authority of the Azerbaijan Republic in the procedure established by the legislation of the Azerbaijan Republic with representation shall take a legal action about cancellation of the certificate. Right after the introduction in legal force of the judgment about cancellation of the certificate of the notary the relevant organ of the executive authority of the Azerbaijan Republic shall take necessary measures for the termination of activities of the notary.

The certificate of the notary can be cancelled by relevant organ of the executive authority of the Azerbaijan Republic in the following cases:

1) in case of submission of the written application by the notary about cancellation of the certificate at own will;

2) in case of not bringing of the oath of the notary by person who received the certificate;

3) in case of the death of the notary;

3-1) in case of the termination of citizenship of the Azerbaijan Republic of the notary;

4) in case of the announcement of the notary the dead or recognition it is unknown the absent court;

5) in case of not prolongation of term of the certificate;

6) in case of complete loss by the notary of working capacity it is continuous for the term of more than 6 months (in the presence of the conclusion of relevant organ of the executive authority);

7) in case of detection of obviously distorted data noted in the documents submitted by the notary for receipt of the certificate;

8) in case of achievement of 65-year age by the notary.

（3）公证员离开阿塞拜疆共和国并永久居住于其他国家；

（4）公证员因刑事犯罪而被定罪判刑或者被判决适用强制医疗；

（5）无正当理由终止对公证员刑事案件审理；

（6）存在对公证员的无行为能力的判决或承认其无行为能力的判决已发生法律效力。

在出现本条第 1 部分第 1 项至第 6 项所列情况之一时，阿塞拜疆共和国行政机关有关部门应按照阿塞拜疆共和国法律规定的程序，采取法律措施取消其公证执业资格证。具有法律效力的判决取消了公证员的公证执业资格证后，阿塞拜疆共和国行政机关有关部门应采取必要措施终止其公证活动。

在下列情况下，阿塞拜疆共和国行政机关有关部门可以取消公证员的公证执业资格证：

（1）公证员自愿提交了关于取消公证执业资格证的书面申请；

（2）收到公证执业资格证的人并未进行公证员宣誓；

（3）公证员去世；

（3-1）公证员丧失了阿塞拜疆共和国公民身份；

（4）公证员被缺席判决宣布死亡或失踪；

（5）未延长公证执业资格证的有效期；

（6）公证员完全丧失工作能力的时间超过连续的 6 个月（附有行政机关有关部门出具的证明）；

（7）公证员为获得公证执业资格证所提交的文件资料是经过篡改的；

（8）公证员已满 65 周岁。

Article 8. Rights of the notary

The notary can make the actions provided by this Law, constitute drafts of transactions, statements and other documents, to produce copies of documents and the statement from them, to make explanations in connection with making of notarial actions, to request from the documents and data necessary for making of the specified actions physical persons and legal entities.

By the legislation of the Azerbaijan Republic also other rights can be granted to the notary.

Article 9. Obligations of the notary

When implementing the obligations the notary shall:

1) to physical persons and legal entities of their right and obligation in connection with the made notarial actions, to render assistance in implementation of their rights and protection of legitimate interests;

2) to warn them about consequences of the made notarial actions legal lack of information could not be used by it to the detriment;

3) to observe this Law and other legal acts of the Azerbaijan Republic, to keep in secret data which became known to it in connection with implementation of its professional activity;

4) it is excluded.

Article 10. Personal seal, stamps and forms of the notary

Each notary of the Azerbaijan Republic has the official stamps belonging to him, stamps of certifying texts, angular stamps and forms of notary office in which he works.

On notary's seal surname, the name, middle name of the notary and the name of notary office in which it works shall be entered.

Article 10-1. Oath of the private notary

After receipt of the certificate prior to activities the private notary takes the oath of the following content in the procedure established by relevant organ of the executive authority of the Azerbaijan Republic:

"I swear to observe the Constitution and the laws of the Azerbaijan Republic, honesty, according to the law and for interests of people, without prejudice to perform the rights and obligations assigned to me granted to me by the state, to keep notarial secret".

Administration of oath is performed once. The text of the oath signed by the private notary is stored in its per-

第 8 条　公证员的权利

公证员可以依据本法的规定开展活动，制定交易草案、声明和其他文件，制作文件及声明的副本，对相关公证活动作出解释，要求自然人和法人在开展特定行为时提交必要的文件和资料。

公证员拥有根据阿塞拜疆共和国的法律授予的其他权利。

第 9 条　公证员的义务

公证员在履行义务时应：

（1）对于自然人和法人在公证中的权利和义务，应协助落实其权利和保护其合法利益；

（2）提醒他们关于公证活动的效果，以及缺乏对法律的了解不能作为造成损害的借口；

（3）遵守本法和阿塞拜疆共和国的其他法律，对在开展执业活动中知悉的有关资料保密；

（4）已删除。

第 10 条　公证员的印鉴、图章和表格

阿塞拜疆共和国的每一位公证员都有自己的官方图章、用以证明文本的图章、角形图章和所在公证机构的表格。

在公证员的印鉴上，应有公证员的姓氏、名字、中间名和所在公证机构的名称。

第 10–1 条　私营公证员的宣誓

私营公证员在收到公证执业资格证之后开展公证活动之前，应按照阿塞拜疆共和国行政机关有关部门制定的程序并按以下内容宣誓：

"我宣誓，将忠实遵守阿塞拜疆共和国的《宪法》和法律。根据法律和人民的利益，不偏不倚地行使国家授予我的权利和履行指派给我的义务，保障公证的保密性。"

宣誓程序只需开展一次。宣誓的内容由私营公证员签署后保存在其个人记录中。

sonal record.

Article 11. Financial responsibility of the notary

If as a result of illegal actions of the notary to individuals, material damage is caused to the organization or the state, he bears financial responsibility according to the procedure, stipulated by the legislation the Azerbaijan Republic.

The extent of the caused damage is established as agreed by the parties or judicially.

Chapter II. Basic provisions of implementation of notarial activities

Article 12. Clerical work and reporting under notarial activities

The instruction about record keeping on notarial activities affirms as the Azerbaijan Republic relevant organ of the executive authority of the Azerbaijan Republic.

The notaries and other officials making notarial actions keep statistic and accounting reports, provide in relevant organs of the executive authority of the Azerbaijan Republic reports and data on notarial actions and the collected state fees transferred into the budget taxes and other payments.

Article 13. Clerical work language on notarial activities

The clerical work on notarial activities in the Azerbaijan Republic is conducted in state language of the Azerbaijan Republic.

If person who addressed for making of notarial actions does not know language in which the clerical work is conducted, or asks to make notarial actions in any language, the notary whenever possible constitutes texts of the documents processed by it in desirable language or the text is translated to it by the translator.

Article 14. Control of notarial activities

The number of notary offices, notaries in the Azerbaijan Republic and involved in compulsory education for receipt of the certificate, and also the administrative territories of implementation by notaries of the activities, the locations of notary offices are determined by relevant organ of the executive authority of the Azerbaijan Republic taking into account population and notarial actions.

Control of notarial activities is exercised by relevant organ of the executive authority of the Azerbaijan Republic.

Notarial activities of each notary are performed at

第 11 条　公证员的赔偿责任

若公证员对个人实施了非法行为、对组织或国家造成了重大损害，则将按照阿塞拜疆共和国法律规定的程序承担赔偿责任。

造成损害的程度由当事方商定或由司法方式决定。

第二章　实施公证活动的基本规定

第 12 条　公证活动中的文书和报告

由阿塞拜疆共和国行政机关有关部门指导公证活动的记录。

公证员和其他公职人员开展公证活动时，应保留有关资料和会计报告，向阿塞拜疆共和国行政机关有关部门提交公证活动的报告和资料，并将收取的法定费用转入预算税收和其他款项。

第 13 条　公证活动的文书语言

阿塞拜疆共和国公证活动的文书中应使用阿塞拜疆共和国的官方语言。

若申请人提出以不知名的语言书写公证活动的文书，或者以其他任何语言开展公证活动，则公证员应尽可能使用所要求的语言书写公证文件或者由译者对文本进行翻译。

第 14 条　公证活动的管理

由阿塞拜疆共和国行政机关有关部门根据人口分布和公证业务数量决定阿塞拜疆共和国的公证机构、公证员、为获得公证执业资格证参加法定培训人员的数量，以及公证员负责的行政区域、公证机构的地点。

由阿塞拜疆共和国行政机关有关部门负责对公证活动进行管理。

每名公证员至少在两年内开展一次公证活动。

least once in two years.

The notary shall represent to person authorized on the conducting check, all data and documents concerning notarial activities.

Rules of conducting check are established by relevant organ of the executive authority of the Azerbaijan Republic.

公证员应向被授权进行检查的人员出示有关公证活动的所有资料和文件。

由阿塞拜疆共和国行政机关有关部门规定相关的检查规则。

Article 14-1. Professional training and advanced training of notaries

Notaries constantly are involved in professional training and advanced training in educational scientific institution of relevant organ of the executive authority.

第 14–1 条　公证员的专业培训和高级培训

公证员应经常参与科学教育机构组织的专业培训和高级培训。

Chapter III. Implementation of notarial activities in public institutions

第三章　在官方机构中从事公证活动

Article 15. The subjects performing notarial activities in public institutions

Notarial activities by means of the state are performed by the notaries public working in offices of notary public, relevant organs of the executive authority in settlements in which there are no notary offices, persons equated to the notary according to the Civil code of the Azerbaijan Republic, authorized officers of consulates of the Azerbaijan Republic according to the procedure, established by this Law.

第 15 条　在官方机构中从事公证活动的主体

国家公证活动由在官方机构的公证员执行。在没有公证机构的乡镇，根据《阿塞拜疆共和国民法典》的规定，行政机关有关部门人员等同于公证员。根据本法规定的程序授予阿塞拜疆共和国领事馆官员等同于公证员的权力。

Article 16. Notary public

Position assignment of the notary public performs relevant organ of the executive authority of the Azerbaijan Republic from among the citizens who received the certificate.

Questions of encouragement, attraction to disciplinary responsibility and dismissal of the notary public are solved by relevant organ of the executive authority of the Azerbaijan Republic according to the procedure, corresponding to the Law of the Azerbaijan Republic “About service in judicial authorities”.

第 16 条　官方公证员

由阿塞拜疆共和国行政机关有关部门对收到公证执业资格证的官方公证员进行职位分配。

由阿塞拜疆共和国行政机关有关部门根据与《阿塞拜疆共和国司法服务法》中的相应程序负责关于落实纪律责任和解雇公证员的问题。

Article 17. The notarial actions made by the notary public

The notary public makes the following notarial actions:

1) certifies transactions and powers of attorney;

2) takes measures to protection of heritable property;

3) grants certificates on the right to inheritance;

4) grants certificates on the property right to share in common property of spouses;

第 17 条　官方公证员的公证活动

官方公证员可开展以下公证活动：

（1）证明交易和授权书的真实性；

（2）采取措施以保管遗产；

（3）出具继承权公证书；

（4）出具夫妻共同财产的产权公证书；

5) grants certificates on acquisition of apartment houses and apartments on open auction;

6) is witnessed by fidelity of copies of documents and statements from documents;

7) is witnessed by authenticity of signatures on documents;

8) witnesses fidelity of the translation of documents from one language on another;

9) is certified by the fact of finding of person in live;

10) is certified by the fact of finding of person in certain place;

11) is certified by identity of person with person represented in the photo;

12) is certified by time of production of documents;

13) transfers statements of physical persons and legal entities to other physical persons and legal entities;

14) is accepted on storage by obligation fulfillment subject, and also on the deposit - sums of money, securities and wills;

15) makes executive texts;

16) makes protests of bills of exchange;

17) shows checks to payment and certifies non-payment of checks;

18) accepts documents on storage;

19) makes ship's protests;

20) provides proofs.

Certificates of the documents used abroad creation of ship's protests is assigned by relevant organ of the executive authority of the Azerbaijan Republic to certain notaries.

By the legislation of the Azerbaijan Republic making and other notarial actions can be assigned to the notary public.

Article 18. The notarial actions made by officials of relevant organs of the executive authority

In settlements where there are no notary offices, relevant organs of the executive authority make the following notarial actions:

1) take measures to protection of heritable property;

2) is certified by wills;

3) is certified by powers of attorney on use and the order of property, except powers of attorney on transfer of cars to temporary use;

4) witness fidelity of copies of documents and statements from documents;

5) is witnessed by authenticity of signatures on documents;

（5）出具在公开拍卖中购买的公寓和套房的公证书；

（6）证明文件副本和文件中声明的真实性；

（7）证明文件签名的真实性；

（8）证明文件从一种语言翻译成另一种语言的可信度；

（9）证明某人存活的事实；

（10）证明某人在某地的事实；

（11）证明照片中所载人员身份；

（12）证明文件的制作时间；

（13）将自然人和法人的声明转交给其他自然人和法人；

（14）接受履行义务主体的提存以及保管资金，证券和遗嘱；

（15）制作执行书；

（16）对汇票提出异议；

（17）提交付款支票，以及证明是拒付款支票；

（18）保管文件；

（19）对船舶提出抗议；

（20）提供证明。

用于在国外对船舶提出抗议的文件公证书由阿塞拜疆共和国行政机关有关部门委派特定的公证员办理。

官方公证员可以根据阿塞拜疆共和国的法律开展和被委派开展其他公证活动。

第 18 条　由行政机关有关部门官员开展的公证活动

在没有公证机构的乡镇，行政机关有关部门可开展如下公证活动：

（1）采取措施以保管遗产；

（2）证明遗嘱；

（3）证明使用和处置财产的授权书，但转让汽车临时使用的授权书除外；

（4）证明文件副本和文件中声明的可信度；

（5）证明文件签名的真实性；

6) is certified by agreements on transfer to lease and use of the parcels of land of agricultural purpose no more than five hectares for the term of no more than one year, and also the power of attorney concerning transfer to lease and use of these parcels of land which are in private property for the term of no more than two years.

（6）证明面积不超过 5 公顷，期限不超过 1 年的农业用地转让协议；证明期限不超过 2 年，转让私人财产用以租赁和使用的授权书。

Article 18-1. The notarial actions made by persons equated to the notary according to the Civil code of the Azerbaijan Republic

Persons, stipulated in Article 362 Civil codes of the Azerbaijan Republic, certify powers of attorney, and faces, stipulated in Article 1181, - wills.

第 18–1 条　由等同于公证员的人员根据《阿塞拜疆共和国民法典》所开展的公证活动

《阿塞拜疆共和国民法典》第 362 条中规定的人员，拥有《民法典》第 1181 条规定的授权书、权利表现、意志。

Article 19. The notarial actions made in consulates of the Azerbaijan Republic

Authorized officers of consulates of the Azerbaijan Republic make the following notarial actions:

1) is certified by transactions and powers of attorney, except agreements on alienation and pledge of the real estate which is in the territory of the Azerbaijan Republic;

2) take measures to protection of heritable property;

3) grant certificates on the right to inheritance;

4) grant certificates on the property right to share in common property of spouses;

5) is witnessed by fidelity of copies of documents and statements from documents;

6) is witnessed by authenticity of signatures on documents;

7) is witnessed by fidelity of the translation of documents from one language on another;

8) certifies the fact of finding of person in live;

9) is certified by the fact of finding of person in certain place;

10) is certified by identity of person with person represented in the photo;

11) is certified by time of production of documents;

12) is accepted on storage by obligation fulfillment subject, and also on the deposit - sums of money, securities and wills;

13) makes executive texts;

14) accepts documents on storage;

15) makes ship's protests;

16) provides proofs.

By the legislation of the Azerbaijan Republic on authorized officers of consulates of the Azerbaijan Republic making and other notarial actions can be assigned.

第 19 条　由阿塞拜疆共和国领事馆开展的公证活动

阿塞拜疆共和国领事馆经授权的官员可开展以下公证活动：

（1）证明交易和授权书，但在阿塞拜疆共和国境内转让和抵押房地产的协议除外；

（2）采取措施以保管遗产；

（3）授予继承权公证书；

（4）授予夫妻共同财产的产权公证书；

（5）证明文件副本和文件中声明的可信度；

（6）证明文件签名的真实性；

（7）证明文件从一种语言翻译成另一种语言的可信度；

（8）证明某人存活的事实；

（9）证明某人在某地的事实；

（10）证明照片中所载人员身份；

（11）证明文件的制作时间；

（12）接受履行义务主体的提存以及保管资金，证券和遗嘱；

（13）制作执行书；

（14）保管文件；

（15）对船舶提出抗议；

（16）提供证明。

阿塞拜疆共和国领事馆经授权的官员可以根据阿塞拜疆共和国法律开展和被委派开展其他公证活动。

Article 20. Offices of notary public

Offices of notary public are created and liquidated by relevant organ of the executive authority of the Azerbaijan Republic.

The staff list of offices of notary public with use of states of the senior notary public, notary public, consultant and necessary technical workers and procedure for their work establishes relevant organ of the executive authority of the Azerbaijan Republic.

Management of activities of office of notary public is performed by the senior notary public (notary public), and control - relevant organ of the executive authority of the Azerbaijan Republic.

Article 21. Public notarial Records Office

Under relevant organ of the executive authority of the Azerbaijan Republic the Public notarial Records Office for storage of notarial documents within 75 years functions.

The relevant organ of the executive authority of the Azerbaijan Republic determines the number of staff of the Public notarial Records Office and approves the Provision on the organization of work and powers of the Public notarial Records Office.

The Public notarial Records Office is legal entity. Management of its activities is performed by the manager appointed (exempted) by relevant organ of the executive authority of the Azerbaijan Republic.

The manager of the Public notarial Records Office (the official replacing it) issues duplicates of the documents which are stored in this archive, certifies fidelity of their copies and statements.

The Public notarial Records Office has seal with the image of the State Emblem of the Azerbaijan Republic and the name.

The Public notarial Records Office is financed by the payment received the services rendered by notaries public in connection with notarial actions and the executive authority of the Azerbaijan Republic arriving into the special account of relevant organ for content of offices of notary public and the Public notarial Records Office and also by the government budget of the Azerbaijan Republic.

Chapter IV. Implementation of notarial activities in private procedure

Article 22. Office insurance for implementation of notarial activities in private procedure

For the purpose of ensuring indemnification which

第 20 条　官方公证机构

官方公证机构由阿塞拜疆共和国行政机关有关部门设立和清算。

由阿塞拜疆共和国行政机关有关部门建立公证机构的工作人员名单，应包括国家高级官方公证员、官方公证员、顾问、必要的技术工人，工作程序。

官方公证机构的活动由国家高级官方公证员（官方公证员）负责开展，由阿塞拜疆共和国行政机关有关部门管理。

第 21 条　官方公证记录处

阿塞拜疆共和国行政机关有关部门下设的官方公证记录处，负责存储 75 年内的公证文件。

由阿塞拜疆共和国行政机关有关部门决定官方公证记录处的员工数量，并批准有关官方公证记录处的工作和权限的规定。

官方公证记录处是法人。由阿塞拜疆共和国行政机关有关部门任命（豁免）的主管负责管理其开展的活动。

由官方公证记录处的主管负责发布在此存档的文件副本（经官方复制），证明副本和声明的可信度。

官方公证记录处在密封时要附有阿塞拜疆共和国国徽的图案和名称。

官方公证记录处的资金来自公证员提供与公证活动有关的服务所得、阿塞拜疆共和国行政机关打入有关部门的特别账户供公证机构人员和公证记录处使用的资金，以及阿塞拜疆共和国的政府预算。

第四章　开展私营公证活动的程序

第 22 条　开展私营公证活动的官方保险

为了确保在开展私营公证活动时能够支付赔偿

can be put when implementing notarial activities in private procedure the citizen wishing to be engaged in such activities, shall insure the responsibility or transfer to the special bank account security deposit from three hundred thirty manats.

金，意欲从事此类活动的公民应当投保责任险或将330马纳特币转到特别银行账户保证金中。

Article 23. Warranty cash desks of private notaries

For the purpose of guaranteeing responsibility of private notaries to clients the warranty cash desk is created. The warranty cash desk consists of the special bank account. Means of this account constitute 5 percent of the monthly income of the private notary which it monthly translates in this respect.

In case of unintentional damnification by any private notary and insufficiency of means of security deposit for compensation of damage suffered based on the judgment means of warranty cash desk are used.

第 23 条　私营公证员的担保兑付服务机制

为了保证私营公证员对客户负责，建立了担保兑付机制。担保兑付机制有一个特别的银行账户。这个账户的资金来自私营公证员每月收入的 5%，并按月转入。

若私营公证员非故意造成损害，并且保证金不足以赔偿损失，则将根据情况判断是否启用担保兑付机制。

Article 24. Registration of private notaries

The citizen who received the appropriate certificate on implementation of notarial activities in private procedure and signed the agreement of office insurance (which transferred security deposit into the special account of bank institution) shall be registered by relevant organ of the executive authority of the Azerbaijan Republic and receive the registration certificate of the private notary.

The relevant organ of the executive authority of the Azerbaijan Republic shall issue the registration certificate of the private notary in 10-day time after acceptance from the citizen owning the certificate, the corresponding statement, the document on the place of implementation of activities of the private notary and the copy of the agreement of office insurance (the document on security deposit) approved with relevant organ of the executive authority of the Azerbaijan Republic.

In the registration certificate of the private notary the administrative territory of implementation of its activities, the address of place of employment and effective period shall be specified. The relevant organ of the executive authority of the Azerbaijan Republic can make changes to the territorial district of implementation of activities of the notary.

The relevant organ of the executive authority of the Azerbaijan Republic immediately after issue to the citizen of the registration certificate of the private notary shall transfer the corresponding data on it to relevant organ of the executive authority in the place of its work.

第 24 条　私营公证员的登记

已获得开展私营公证活动的执业资格证书并签署官方保险协议（将保证金转入特别银行账户）的公民，应当在阿塞拜疆共和国行政机关有关部门登记，并收到私营公证员的登记执照。

阿塞拜疆共和国行政机关有关部门应在收到公民所持的公证执业资格证书、相应的声明、关于私营公证员实施活动地点的文件、阿塞拜疆共和国行政机关有关部门批准的办公保险协议（保证金的文件）副本的 10 日内签发私营公证员的登记执照。

在私营公证员登记执照中，应当写明其实施活动的行政区域、工作地点和有效期。阿塞拜疆共和国行政机关有关部门可以更改公证员实施活动的区域。

阿塞拜疆共和国行政机关有关部门在向公民颁发私营公证员登记执照后，应立即将相应的资料转交给其工作地的行政机关有关部门。

If the private notary within six months after receipt of the registration certificate from relevant organ of the executive authority of the Azerbaijan Republic, having ignored the official written prevention of relevant organ of the executive authority of the Azerbaijan Republic, without reasonable excuse will not start implementation of notarial activities for the specified place of employment, its registration certificate is nullified.

如果私营公证员在收到阿塞拜疆共和国行政机关有关部门的登记执照后6个月内，无视阿塞拜疆共和国行政机关有关部门的官方书面禁止，在没有正当理由的情况下不在指定工作地点开展公证活动，其登记执照无效。

Unreasoned decision about recognition of the registration certificate can be appealed by invalid administratively and (or) in court after pronouncement of this decision.

认为有关登记执照的决定是不合理时，可以在该决定宣布后通过行政申诉以及（或者）法院上诉使其无效。

Article 25. Organization of work of the private notary

第25条 私营公证员的工作机构

The private notary performs the activities in the isolated place suitable for making of notarial actions belonging to it or leased and approved with relevant organ of the executive authority of the Azerbaijan Republic.

私营公证员应在经阿塞拜疆共和国行政机关有关部门批准的，自有或租赁的独立场所内开展公证活动。

The private notary can sign civil and employment contracts (contracts), open in banks settlement and other accounts, including currency. The private notary shall use the forms used by relevant organ of the executive authority of the Azerbaijan Republic for making of notarial actions.

私营公证员可以签署民事和雇佣合同，可以在银行开设结算账户和其他账户，包括流水账单。私营公证员应使用阿塞拜疆共和国行政机关有关部门规定用于公证活动的表格。

The operating mode of the private notary, the staff list of private notary office and the candidates employed as the private notary will be approved with relevant organ of the executive authority of the Azerbaijan Republic.

私营公证员的运作方式、私营公证机构的工作人员名单和将聘为私营公证员的候选人，应获得阿塞拜疆共和国行政机关有关部门的批准。

The main objective of activities of the notary is not directed to profit earning.

公证活动的主要目的不是获利。

The money remaining after tax payment and other obligatory payments from the payment levied for making of notarial actions and the payment levied for the services provided in article 20 of this Law remains at the disposal of the private notary.

税后剩余款项和为开展公证活动收取的必要费用外的剩余款项，以及因提供本法第20条官方公证机构的服务收取必要费用外的剩余款项由私营公证员支配。

Article 26. The notarial actions made by the private notary. Termination of activities of the private notary

第26条 私营公证员的公证活动以及私营公证员活动的终止

The private notary makes the notarial actions provided in article 17 of this Law.

私营公证员按本法第17条的规定开展公证活动。

By the legislation of the Azerbaijan Republic making and other notarial actions can be assigned to the private notary.

私营公证员可以根据阿塞拜疆共和国法律开展和被委派开展其他公证活动。

For violation of requirements of the legislation when making notarial actions the relevant organ of the executive authority of the Azerbaijan Republic can make to the private notary the written or oral prevention.

如果私营公证员在开展公证活动时违反法律的要求，阿塞拜疆共和国行政机关有关部门可以作出书面或口头制止令。

Activities of the private notary stop relevant organ of the executive authority of the Azerbaijan Republic with cancellation of its registration certificate in the following cases:

1) in case of submission of the written application by the private notary about the termination of the activities;

2) in case of cancellation of the certificate of the private notary;

3) in case of expiration of the certificate of the private notary;

4) in case of recognition of the registration certificate of the private notary invalid.

In case of cancellation of the executive authority of the Azerbaijan Republic by relevant organ of the certificate and the registration certificate of the private notary, its activities stop.

The notary office in which the private notary whose activities are stopped worked can be liquidated by relevant organ of the executive authority of the Azerbaijan Republic.

In case of liquidation of notary office person working as the private notary shall hand over no later than one month in the Public notarial Records Office documents on the notarial actions made by it.

Chapter V. Basic rules of making of notarial actions

Article 27. Rules of making of notarial actions

Rules of making of notarial actions are established by this Law, other legal acts of the Azerbaijan Republic and the corresponding instruction approved by relevant organ of the executive authority on their basis, rules of making of notarial actions in consulates of the Azerbaijan Republic and also the Consular charter of the Azerbaijan Republic, the instruction jointly approved by relevant organs of the executive authority of the Azerbaijan Republic.

Article 28. Restriction of the rights to making of notarial actions

The notary or other official making notarial actions is forbidden to make notarial actions on the name and on its own behalf, addressed to and on behalf of the spouse (spouse), his (her) and relatives (parents, children, c, grandfathers, grandmothers, and also brothers, sisters, uncles, aunts), their children, addressed to and on behalf of person working together with the notary or other official making notarial actions.

Relevant organs of the executive authority have also

在下列情况下，阿塞拜疆共和国行政机关有关部门将取消私营公证员的登记执照，停止其活动：

（1）私营公证员提交关于终止其活动的书面申请；

（2）私营公证员的公证执业资格证被取消；

（3）私营公证员的公证执业资格证到期；

（4）私营公证员的登记执照被认定无效。

如果阿塞拜疆共和国行政机关有关部门取消了私营公证员的公证执业资格证和登记执照，应该终止其活动。

阿塞拜疆共和国行政机关有关部门可以对被终止活动的私营公证员所在公证机构进行清算。

如果公证机构被清算，私营公证员应在 1 个月内向公证记录处转交其开展的公证活动的文件。

第五章　开展公证活动的基本准则

第 27 条　开展公证活动的准则

公证活动的准则由本法、阿塞拜疆共和国的其他法律、行政机关有关部门在此基础上作出的相应指示、阿塞拜疆共和国领事馆关于开展公证活动准则、阿塞拜疆共和国领事宪章、阿塞拜疆共和国行政机关有关部门联合批准的指示等进行规定。

第 28 条　对开展公证活动的限制

公证员或其他官员禁止以自己的名义以及代表自己开展公证活动，禁止代表和向他（她）的夫妻、亲属（父母、孩子、孙辈、祖父、祖母、兄弟、姐妹、叔叔、阿姨）、子女开展公证活动，禁止代表和向一起工作的其他公证员或官员开展公证活动。

行政机关有关部门也无权代表和向本机构开展公

no right to make notarial actions addressed to and on behalf of this body.

The notarial actions and actions equated to them made with violation of requirements of this Article are considered as invalid and are the basis for cancellation by the judgment.

Article 29. Service fee, rendered in connection with notarial actions

For services (consultation, designing of transactions, statements and other documents, accomplishment of technical works) rendered in connection with the notarial actions provided by Items 6 and 8 of the first part of article 17 of this Law, notaries public levy payment in the amount of the state fee established for making of these actions, and for the services specified in connection with notarial actions, stipulated in Item 1 article 17 of this Law - in the amount of 15 percent from the sum of the state fee determined for making of these actions.

If under the Law of the Azerbaijan Republic "About the state fee" exemption of the state fee for making of notarial actions is applied, the service fee, rendered in connection with notarial actions, is not levied.

Use of the means received for the services rendered in connection with notarial actions and the offices of notary public which arrived into the special account of relevant organ of the executive authority of the Azerbaijan Republic for content and the Public notarial Records Office is performed according to the rules established by relevant organ of the executive authority.

For making of notarial actions private notaries levy payment in the amount of the state fee established for making of notarial actions from notaries public.

The data on the amounts of service fee rendered in connection with notarial actions shall be placed in the form of sign in a visible place of the building (room) in which each office of notary public is placed, the Public notarial Records Office or the private notary works.

If the notary leaves workplace for making of notarial actions, the actual transportation expenses shall be refunded by interested persons.

Article 30. State fee

The notaries public and other officials making notarial actions collect the state fee for making of notarial actions.

Rates of the state fee are established by the Law.

Data on the amount of the state tax, shall be hung out

证活动。

违反本条要求作出的公证和等同于公证的行为将被视为无效，这也将成为通过判决撤销该公证行为的合法依据。

第 29 条　与公证活动有关的服务费

本法第 17 条第 1 款第 6 项至第 8 项规定了与公证活动有关的服务（咨询，交易设计，声明和其他文件，完成技术工作），官方公证员实施这些行为应缴纳的税金、本法第 17 条第 1 款规定的与公证活动有关服务的税金，都为法定费用的 15%。

若根据《阿塞拜疆共和国法定费用法》豁免了法定公证费用，则不向公证服务费征税。

应根据行政机关有关部门设立的准则使用公证活动的收入、阿塞拜疆共和国行政机关有关机构特别账户内供官方公证机构和官方公证记录处使用的资金。

私营公证员开展公证活动的税款按照官方公证员开展公证活动的法定费用进行征收。

与公证活动有关的服务费收取标准应以公开形式放置在官方公证机构、官方公证记录处、私营公证员所在的建筑物（房间）的明显位置。

如果公证员离开工作场所以开展公证活动，则实际的交通费用应由利害关系人承担。

第 30 条　法定费用

官方公证员和其他官员开展公证活动，收取开展公证活动的法定费用。

法定费用的收取比率由法律规定。

关于国家税额的资料，应用牌子挂在每个公证机

in the form of the plate in a visible place in each office of notary public, indoors, in which there is the Public notarial Records Office or the private notary works.

The state fee withheld by the notary for making of notarial actions is transferred during two banking days to the government budget.

Article 31.

It is excluded.

Article 32. Storage of mystery of notarial actions

References and documents on notarial actions shall be issued only to physical persons and legal entities to which making of notarial actions is entrusted or concerning which notarial actions are made.

In established by the Law of the Azerbaijan Republic "About fight against legalization of money or other property received in the criminal way, and terrorism financing" procedure and cases represents to body of financial monitoring of the data, connected with notarial actions.

Due to the specific criminal or civil cases which are in production of court, investigating bodies and bodies of inquiry based on the resolution of data of bodies documents on notarial actions are issued to them.

Before receipt of notarial documents in connection with specific criminal cases these bodies shall inform the notary of the resolution on obtaining. Receipt of notarial documents is drawn up by the relevant protocol, and its copy is issued to the notary.

Copies of documents on notarial actions are issued to the lawyer based on its written request and the order.

Due to the specific criminal or civil cases which are in production of court, investigating bodies and bodies of inquiry based on written requests of data of bodies, and to the lawyer - based on the written request and the order it issues data on notarial actions.

In case of the certificate of the agreements connected with real estate or issue of certificates on inheritance the notary, other officials who are carrying out notarial actions shall direct the relevant documents in the cases and procedure established by the Civil code of the Azerbaijan Republic to relevant organ of the executive authority of the Azerbaijan Republic.

The notaries, other officials making notarial actions, and persons informed on notarial actions in connection with accomplishment of service duties shall keep secret of these actions.

In case of the certificate of the agreement on the right

构、公证记录处或私营公证员办公处之内。

公证员因开展公证活动而收取的法定费用在两个银行工作日内转入政府预算。

第 31 条

已删除。

第 32 条　公证活动的保密性

公证活动的参考资料和文件，只应发给委托开展公证活动或与开展公证活动有关的自然人和法人。

按《阿塞拜疆共和国反洗钱与资助恐怖主义法》中规定的程序和情况，对与公证活动有关的资料进行金融监管。

在法院审理特定的刑事或民事案件中，应将其需要的公证活动文件资料发送给搜查机构和调查机构。

这些机构应先将允许其取得文件的决议通知公证员，才能收到与特定刑事案件有关的公证文件。还应根据相关条款起草收到公证文件的收据，并将该副本发给公证员。

公证文件的副本将根据书面请求和顺序发送给律师。

在法院审理的特定刑事或民事案件中，将根据搜查机构和调查机构书面请求发送公证资料，根据律师书面请求和顺序发送公证资料。

若是有关出具房地产协议的公证书或继承权公证书，则执行该公证活动的公证员或其他官员应按照《阿塞拜疆共和国民法典》规定的案件和程序向阿塞拜疆共和国行政机关有关部门提交相关文件。

公证员、其他官员开展公证活动，以及在履行职责时涉及的人员应对这些行为保密。

如果是有关租赁权协议或与车辆使用或处置有关

of lease or other corporeal rights in connection with the vehicle or powers of attorney in connection with the rights to use or the order of the vehicle the notary without delay directs data, and also according to part VI-I of article 27 of the Law of the Azerbaijan Republic "About traffic" the address of place of registration and residence, number of the mobile phone and, in the presence, the e-mail address and number of the car driver license of physical persons, and concerning legal entities - the corresponding information about person to whom vehicle control about the certificate of the agreement or the power of attorney is entrusted to relevant organ of the executive authority. The relevant organ of the executive authority by means of technical means within one day sends these data to relevant organ of the executive authority.

的授权书公证书，公证员应根据阿塞拜疆共和国《交通法》第 27 条第 VI-I 款，立即通过技术手段将注册地和居住地址、手机号码、现用电子邮箱、驾驶员驾驶证号码、相关的自然人和法人资料，即将委托行政机关有关部门车辆控制权协议或授权书公证书相关信息，在 1 日内发送给行政机关有关部门。

Certificates of wills can be issued only after the death of the testator.

遗嘱公证书只能在遗嘱人去世后出具。

Persons guilty of disclosure of mystery of notarial actions shall bear responsibility according to the procedure, established by the legislation of the Azerbaijan Republic.

泄露公证活动中的机密的人员应当按照阿塞拜疆共和国法律规定的程序承担责任。

In case of excitement concerning the notary of the criminal case connected with making of notarial actions, the court can exempt it from obligation to keep secret.

如果公证员的刑事案件与其开展的公证活动有关，法院可以免除其保密义务。

Article 33. Place of making of notarial actions

Notarial actions are made in all territory of the Azerbaijan Republic, except as specified, when they be made by the notary public, the private notary, officials of relevant organ of the executive authority or consulates of the Azerbaijan Republic based on the legislation of the Azerbaijan Republic in the appropriate place.

第 33 条　公证活动的开展场所

在阿塞拜疆共和国的所有领土内，除非另有规定，官方公证员、私营公证员、行政机关有关部门的官员或阿塞拜疆共和国领事馆应根据阿塞拜疆法律在适当的场所开展公证活动。

Notarial actions shall be made in office of notary public, relevant organ of the executive authority indoors in which there are consulates of the Azerbaijan Republic or the private notary works.

公证活动应当在公证机构、行政机关有关部门、阿塞拜疆共和国领事馆或私营公证机构内开展。

If person as a result of disease, in connection with disability, limited opportunities of health or in other cases, stipulated by the legislation the Azerbaijan Republic, cannot be in office of notary public, relevant organ of the executive authority, the room in which there are consulates of the Azerbaijan Republic or the private notary works, notarial actions can be made also out of these rooms after introduction of the state fee and payment according to in advance issued notice and providing with the vehicle.

如果由于疾病、残疾、健康问题或其他情况，不能根据阿塞拜疆共和国法律的规定，在行政机关有关部门、阿塞拜疆共和国领事馆或私营公证机构办公，可以在根据前述要求缴纳法定费用和付款，并提供车辆后，在上述场所之外开展公证活动。

Article 34. Terms of making of notarial actions

Notarial actions if the laws of the Azerbaijan Republic do not provide other, are made in day of representation

第 34 条　公证活动的开展期限

如果阿塞拜疆共和国其他法律没有规定，那么在缴纳法定费用和付款后，具备公证所需的所有文件的

of all of documents necessary for this purpose after introduction of the state fee and payment.

当天开展公证活动。

Making of notarial actions in case of need of reclamation of additional data or documents from officials, organizations, the companies and the organizations, or the direction of documents for examination can be postponed for term no more than one month.

若需要从官员、机构、公司和组织收集额外的资料或文件，或者需要检查文件，则可以延期开展公证活动，期限不超过 1 个月。

In case of obtaining from court of the message on receipt of the statement from other interested person challenging the right or the fact which shall be certified making of notarial actions stops to permission of case by court.

如果收到其他利害关系人通过法院发来的声明，质疑公证活动将要证明的权利或事实，应先暂停公证活动等待法院的许可。

At the request of other interested person wishing to challenge in court of the right or fact which shall be certified making of notarial actions shall be postponed for ten-day term. If during this term the message on receipt of the statement from the face concerning the right or the fact which shall be certified is not received from court, then suspension of the made notarial action is not allowed.

其他利害关系人在法庭上质疑公证活动将要证明的权利或事实时，应延期 10 日再开展公证活动。若在此期限内未收到法院关于权利或事实的声明，则不允许中止公证活动。

Other bases for adjournment or suspension of notarial action can be established only by the legislation of the Azerbaijan Republic.

仅限阿塞拜疆共和国的法律对延期或中止公证活动的其他情况作出规定。

Article 35. Identification addressed for making of notarial action, check of their capacity to act and authenticity of their signatures

第 35 条　公证活动中的审查身份、检查行为能力和签字真实性

When making the corresponding notarial actions the notaries and other officials making notarial actions in each separate case identify the personality of persons who addressed for this purpose, their representatives or representatives of organizations, the companies and the organizations.

在开展相应的公证行动时，公证员和其他官员在每个独立的案件中都要审查公证申请人、其代理人或机构代理人、公司和机构的身份。

In case of the certificate of transactions and making of some other notarial actions in cases, stipulated by the legislation the Azerbaijan Republic, authenticity of signatures of participants of the transactions and other persons who addressed for making of notarial actions is verified.

在制作交易公证书和开展其他公证活动时，按照阿塞拜疆共和国法律的规定，需要核实交易参与者以及其他公证申请人签名的真实性。

In case of the certificate of transactions capacity to act of persons who are taking part in transactions shall be found out and legal capacity of legal entities is checked.

交易公证书中应查明参与交易的人的行为能力，并检查法人的法律行为能力。

In case of transaction by the representative its powers shall be checked.

若交易由代理人进行，则应检查其权限。

Transactions, and also statements and other documents certified in notarial procedure shall be signed with participation of the notary or other official making notarial action. If the transaction, the statement or other document were signed without participation of the specified officials, person which signed them shall confirm personally that the

交易，以及在公证程序中证明的声明和其他文件，应由开展公证活动的公证员或其他官员签字。如果交易、声明或其他文件是在没有特定官员参与的情况下签署的，签字的人应亲自确认该文件是由其签署的。如果由于身体缺陷、疾病或其他原因无法在交易中签署申请、交易、声明或其他文件，可以根据其指

document is signed by it. If person owing to physical defects, due to illness or for other reasons has no opportunity to sign the transaction, the application or other document, the transaction, the statement or other document can according to its order, with its participation and participation of the notary or other official making notarial action to sign other person. In this case the reason for which person who addressed for making of notarial action, cannot sign the document shall be specified.

令，由参与的公证员或其他开展公证活动的官员代为签署。在这种情况下，应说明公证申请人不能签署文件的原因。

In case of availability of the specimen signatures received during personal addresses known to notaries and relevant organ of the executive authority of officials of organizations, the companies, the organizations which authenticity does not raise doubts direct participation every time of officials is not required.

如果在公证员和行政机关有关部门官员、公司、组织已知的个人地址内留有有效的签名样本且真实性无疑义，那么官员不需要每次都直接参与检查签名。

Article 36. Reclamation of the data and documents necessary for making of notarial actions

第 36 条　开展公证活动所需的资料和文件

The notaries and other officials making the notarial actions having the right to request organizations, the companies and the organizations of the data and the documents necessary for making of notarial actions, to send reasonable written requests in connection with receipt of data from the state real estate register according to the Law of the Azerbaijan Republic “About the state real estate register”.

公证员和其他官员开展公证活动时，有权要求机构、公司和组织提供开展公证活动所需的资料和文件。开展公证活动时如需国家房地产登记处的文件，应按照《阿塞拜疆共和国房地产登记法》的规定发送合理的书面请求。

The corresponding data and documents shall be submitted in time, specified by the notary or other official making notarial action. This term cannot exceed one month.

相应的资料和文件应在公证员或其他开展公证活动的官员指定期限内及时提交。该期限不能超过1个月。

When carrying out the notarial actions connected with the authorized capital of commercial legal entities, implementation by founders (participants) of powers of founders (participants) and their shares in the authorized capital, the notary receives the information about founders (participants) of commercial legal entities and their shares in the authorized capital on the basis of electronic request by means of information system to currents of day.

开展与商业法人额定股本相关的公证活动时，调查创始人（参与者）的权限及其在额定股本中的份额时，公证员应通过当前的信息系统发送电子请求，以收到有关商业法律的创始人（参与者）的信息和他们在额定股本中的份额信息。

Article 37. Requirements to texts of the certified transactions and documents

第 37 条　证明交易和文件的文本要求

Documents in which there are erasures and deletions not certified appendices, and also documents which reading the text is not possible in view of their damage, or performed by pencil are forbidden to be accepted for making of notarial actions.

开展公证活动时禁止接收有过删除和遗失且未经证明的附录，以及因损坏而无法阅读的文本或用铅笔书写的文件。

Texts of notarially certified transactions and documents shall be written clearly and accurately, the numbers relating to the text of the document and time frames are

证明交易和文件的文本应清晰准确地书写，文件文本中的数字和时限数字至少用文字说明一次，法人的名称不能简写，并注明其地址。

specified at least once by words, and names of legal entities without reducings, with indication of addresses of their bodies.

The name, surname and middle name of physical persons shall be written completely, specified their residences.

The documents consisting of two and more single sheets shall be stitched, numbered and under seal.

Article 38. Making of certifying texts and issue of certificates

The notary or other official making notarial action in case of the certificate of transactions, witnessing of fidelity of copies and statements of documents, authenticity of the signature on documents, fidelity of the translation of documents from one language on another, in case of the certificate of time of presentation of the document make certifying texts on these documents and seal them.

As a witness inheritance rights, the property rights, certificates of the fact of finding of person in live, identity of person with person represented in the photo, acceptances on document storage appropriate certificates are granted.

Article 39. The documents equated to notarially certified documents

Stipulated in Article 362 Civil codes of the Azerbaijan Republic powers of attorney and stipulated in Article 1181 wills belong to the documents equated to the documents certified in notarial procedure.

The officials certifying the documents specified in this Article certify wills and powers of attorney according to the procedure, established by relevant organ of the executive authority of the Azerbaijan Republic, with observance of the current legislation.

The officials certifying the documents listed in this Article shall transfer immediately in one copy the will certified by them to storage to the Public notarial Records Office or to the notary on the permanent residence of the testator.

According to this Law captains of ocean ships shall transfer in one copy the wills certified by them to management of seaport of the Azerbaijan Republic or to consulate of the Azerbaijan Republic in foreign port for sending to the Public notarial Records Office or to the notary on the permanent residence of the testator.

If the testator had no permanent residence in the Azerbaijan Republic or the residence of the testator is un-

自然人的姓氏、名字、中间名应当书写完整，并注明其住所。

由两张及以上的单张纸组成的文件应装订、编号和加盖印章。

第 38 条　制作公证书和出具公证书

公证员或其他官员针对交易公证书、证明复印件和文件声明的可信度、证明文件签名的真实性、证明文件从一种语言翻译成另一种语言的可信度、证明文件提交的时间而开展的公证活动，则应为这些文件制作公证书并加盖印章。

对于证明继承权、产权、某人存活的事实，以及证明照片中某人的身份、接受文件保管情况，应出具公证书。

第 39 条　等同于公证书的文件

《阿塞拜疆共和国民法典》第 362 条规定的授权书、第 1181 条规定的遗嘱，效力都等同于在公证程序中经证明的文件。

官员应根据阿塞拜疆共和国行政机关有关部门制定的程序，并遵守现行法律，确认本条规定的遗嘱和授权书文件的效力。

确认了本条所列文件效力的官员，应立即将其确认的遗嘱的复印件转交至官方公证记录处或者有永久居留权的遗嘱人。

根据本法，海洋船舶的船长应将其确认的遗嘱复印件转交一份至阿塞拜疆共和国海港管理部门或外国港口的阿塞拜疆共和国领事馆，以便交至官方公证记录处或有永久居留权的遗嘱人。

若遗嘱人在阿塞拜疆共和国没有永久居留权或遗嘱人的住所不明，则遗嘱将交至阿塞拜疆共和国官方

known, the will goes to the Public notarial Records Office of the Azerbaijan Republic.

The manager of the Public notarial Records Office or the notary shall check legality of the will which arrived on storage and in case of establishment of its discrepancy to the law to report about it to the testator and the official who certified the will.

The Public notarial Records Office or the notary issue the duplicate of the wills which arrived on storage from persons specified in this Article.

Article 40. Refusal in making of notarial actions

The notary and other official making notarial actions refuse from making of notarial actions cases if:

1) making of action contradicts the law;

2) action is subject to making by other notary or other official;

3)incapacitated person or the representative who does not have necessary powers requested making of action;

4) the transaction made on behalf of the legal entity contradicts the purposes specified in its charter or provision;

5) the concluded bargain does not conform to requirements of the law;

6) the documents submitted for making of notarial action contradict requirements of the legislation or contain data, touching honor and advantage of individuals;

7)contents of the transaction do not correspond to actual intent of the parties.

The notaries and other officials making notarial action at the request of person to whom it is refused action making shall issue the reasonable decree on refusal within three days and explain procedure for its appeal.

The body of financial monitoring can suspend in the procedure established by the law and cases execution of the notarial actions made concerning the transactions causing suspicions based on the Law of the Azerbaijan Republic "About fight against legalization of money or other property received in the criminal way, and terrorism financing".

Article 41. Appeal in court of notarial actions or refusal of making of notarial actions

The interested person can appeal committed notarial actions or refusal of making of notarial actions in court in the location of office of notary public, the private notary, relevant organ of the executive authority, place of employment or services of the officials listed in part one of article

公证记录处。

官方公证记录处的管理人员或公证员应当检查所保存遗嘱的合法性。存在与法律规定不一致的情况应向遗嘱人和确认遗嘱的官员报告。

本条规定人员所存放的遗嘱的副本应由官方公证记录处或公证员出具。

第 40 条　不予开展公证活动的情况

在下列情况下，公证员和其他官员将不予开展公证活动：

（1）开展的行为与法律相抵触；

（2）该行为应由其他公证员或其他官员开展；

（3）请求开展公证活动的是无行为能力人或是没有权限的代理人；

（4）代表法人进行的交易与其章程或条款中规定的目的相抵触；

（5）交易内容不符合法律要求；

（6）为开展公证活动提交的文件与法律要求相抵触或包含的资料涉及他人的荣誉和利益；

（7）交易内容与申请人的真实意图不符。

公证员和其他官员被请求开展公证活动，但属于不予开展的情况时，应当在 3 日内发出合理的拒绝令，并告知其上诉程序。

当公证活动中的交易涉嫌《阿塞拜疆共和国反洗钱与资助恐怖主义法》时，财务监督机构可以按法律规定的程序和情况暂停开展公证活动。

第 41 条　对公证活动和不予开展公证的行为上诉

利害关系人可以对公证活动或不予开展公证的行为向公证机构、私营公证员、行政机关有关部门、本法第 24 条第 1 款的官员工作或服务所在地、船舶登记港的所在地的法院提起上诉。

24 of this Law or to the location of port of registration of the vessel.

Claims to the notarial actions made by consulates of the Azerbaijan Republic or refusal of making of notarial actions by them are considered according to the procedure, established by the Consular charter of the Azerbaijan Republic.

对阿塞拜疆共和国领事馆作出的公证活动或不予开展公证活动的申诉应根据阿塞拜疆共和国领事宪章规定的程序进行审议。

Article 42. The measures taken by the notary or other official making notarial action in case of identification of violations of the law

第 42 条 公证员或其他官员开展公证活动中发现违法行为应采取的措施

The notary or other official making notarial action in case of identification of violations of the law when making such action, shall report about it in the relevant organization, the company, the organization or to the prosecutor for taking measures.

公证员或其他官员在开展公证活动中发现违法行为，应当向有关机构、公司、组织或检察机关报告以采取措施。

If authenticity of the submitted document raises doubts, the notary or other official making notarial action shall direct this document for examination.

如果对提交的文件真实性存疑，公证员或其他官员应对该文件进行审查。

Article 42-1. Prevention of legalization of money or other property received in the criminal way and terrorism financings

第 42–1 条 反洗钱与资助恐怖主义

Notaries shall in established by the Law of the Azerbaijan Republic “About fight against legalization of money or other property received in the criminal way, and terrorism financing” procedure and cases to observe, prepare and apply own internal control system, to perform in this sphere others stipulated by the legislation actions of the Azerbaijan Republic.

公证员应遵循《阿塞拜疆共和国反洗钱与资助恐怖主义法》规定的程序和情况，准备和应用自有的内部控制制度，并采取阿塞拜疆共和国法律针对此类情况规定的其他措施。

Article 43. Registration of notarial actions

第 43 条 公证活动的登记

All notarial actions made by the notary and other official making notarial action are registered in the notarial register and independent number is assigned to each action.

公证员和其他官员开展的所有公证活动都应在公证登记簿中登记，每个行为都应分配独立的编号。

Forms of registers of registration of notarial actions, notarial certificates, certifying texts on transactions and the witnessed documents are established by relevant organ of the executive authority of the Azerbaijan Republic.

由阿塞拜疆共和国行政机关有关部门规定公证活动登记表、公证书以及证明交易的文本和证明文件的格式。

Article 44. Issue of the duplicate of notarially certified document

第 44 条 出具公证员证明的文件的副本

In case of loss of the document issued or certified by the notary and relevant organ of the executive authority according to the written application of persons listed in part one of article 35 of this Law the duplicate of the lost document is issued.

若由公证员和行政机关有关部门出具或证明的文件丢失，则根据本法第 35 条第 1 款所列人员的书面申请，出具丢失文件的副本。

The duplicate of the lost document is issued by the

丢失文件的副本由官方公证记录处出具。由公证

Public notarial Records Office. Before delivery in the Public notarial Records Office of the copies of the documents issued or certified by the notary or relevant organ of the executive authority, the duplicate of the lost document it is issued respectively by the notary or relevant organ of the executive authority on the storage location of these documents.

员或行政机关有关部门出具或证明的文件在寄送给官方公证记录处之前丢失，则文件的副本应由文件存储地相应的公证员或者行政机关有关部门出具。

Chapter VI. Certificate of transactions

第六章 交易公证书

Article 45. The transactions certified in notarial procedure

第 45 条 按公证程序证明的交易

Notaries and relevant organs of the executive authority within the powers certify the transactions which are subject to the certificate in notarial procedure in cases, stipulated by the legislation the Azerbaijan Republic and other transactions on desire of the parties.

公证员和行政机关有关部门根据阿塞拜疆共和国法律的规定，在交易方自愿的情况下，在权限内按公证程序证明交易，制作公证书。

Notaries and relevant organs of the executive authority shall check compliance of contents of the transaction certified by them to the law and actual intents of the parties.

公证机关和行政机关有关部门应当审查其证明的交易内容是否符合法律以及申请人的真实意图。

Article 46. Certificate of transactions of alienation and of pledge of property

第 46 条 财产转让和质押的交易公证书

Transactions about alienation and about pledge of the property which is subject to registration can be certified after submission of the documents confirming the property right on the alienated or pledged property, and on vehicles, also certificates of passing of survey by them in relevant organ of the executive authority of the Azerbaijan Republic.

财产转让和质押的交易需要登记的，应先提交确认财产、车辆转让或抵押的财产权文件，并经阿塞拜疆共和国的行政机关有关部门调查之后再办理公证。

For the conclusion one of spouses of the transactions assured of notarial procedure and (or) registered about the order by real estate need the consent of other party certified of notarial procedure.

在公证程序中发现夫妻一方参与交易担保的和（或）房地产买卖登记，则需要在公证程序中确认另一方的同意。

In case of the certificate of transactions of alienation or of pledge of the apartment house, the apartment, giving, the garden house, garage, the parcel of land, other real estate availability or lack of prohibition on property acquisition or seizure of property is checked.

若是证明公寓、套房、赠与、花园洋房、车库、土地和其他不动产的转让和质押交易，则应检查这些财产是否可交易，或者没有该财产交易的禁令。

In case of prohibition the transaction about property acquisition makes sure only in case of the consent of the creditor and acquirer to transfer of debt on the acquirer.

在有禁令的情况下，只有在债权人和收购方同意将债务转移给收购方时，才能确认有关财产收购的交易。

Transactions about alienation or about pledge of the apartment house, apartment, giving, garden house, garage, parcel of land, other real estate make sure in the location of this property.

公寓、套房、赠与、花园洋房、车库，土地和其他不动产的转让和质押交易应确认该财产的位置。

Article 47. Certificate of wills

The notaries and other officials making notarial actions certify the wills of certain capable persons constituted according to requirements of the legislation, and personally provided to the notary or other officials making notarial actions.

The certificate of wills through representatives, and also the certificate of one will on behalf of several persons is forbidden. The certificate only of joint wills of spouses of mutual inheritance is allowed.

In case of the certificate of the will from the testator production of evidence, confirming their property rights to the bequeathed property is not required.

第 47 条 遗嘱公证书

公证员和其他官员开展公证活动，证明遗嘱符合法律要求，书写人是有行为能力人并且是亲自将遗嘱提供给公证员或其他官员，以开展公证活动的。

禁止通过代表出具遗嘱公证书，禁止一份遗嘱公证书代表若干人的遗志。只允许相互继承的夫妻共用一份遗嘱公证书。

遗嘱人可出具遗嘱公证书作为证据，不需要再证明其对遗产的权利。

Article 48. Procedure for cancellation and change of the will

The notary managing the Public notarial Records Office, relevant organ of the executive authority in case of receipt of the statement for cancellation or change of the will, and equally in the receipt of the new will canceling or changing the will constituted earlier and also in case of receipt of the order of the testator about destruction of all copies of the will do about it mark in the will copy which is stored in notary office, the Public notarial Records Office or indoors in which there is relevant organ of the executive authority, and in the register of registration of notarial actions.

The signature in the statement for change or cancellation of the will shall be without fail notarially certified.

If in case of the certificate of the will the notary or relevant organ of the executive authority knows of earlier certified will, they send to the Public notarial Records Office, to the notary or to relevant organ of the executive authority where the copy of earlier constituted will, the notice on committed notarial action is stored.

第 48 条 取消和更改遗嘱的程序

官方公证记录处、行政机关有关部门的公证员，如果收到取消或变更遗嘱的声明、收到新的遗嘱，以及收到遗嘱人销毁遗嘱的所有副本，包括存放在公证机构、官方公证记录处或行政机关有关部门内和在公证活动登记册中副本的指令时，将取消或变更先前的遗嘱。

变更或取消遗嘱声明中的签名必须经公证员公证。

若公证员或行政机关有关部门已知之前有公证的遗嘱，则应将更新的遗嘱公证书送至前份遗嘱副本所在的官方公证记录处、公证员或行政机关有关部门，并保存允许开展公证活动的通知。

Article 49. Certificate of powers of attorney and termination of their action

The notary or other official making notarial actions certify powers of attorney on behalf of one or several persons, addressed to one or several persons.

The power of attorney can be issued on any (except for to the power of attorney providing the right to the order the vehicle) term.

The power of attorney providing the right to the order the vehicle is issued for the term of no more than one year.

The power of attorney issued according to the procedure of the retrust entrusted other person is subject to the

第 49 条 授权书的公证和终止公证

公证员或开展公证活动的其他官员对授权代理一个人或若干人进行公证，则应将公证书出具给一个人或多个人。

授权书可以为任意期限（提供订购车辆权利的授权书除外）。

提供订购车辆权利的授权书期限不能超过 1 年。

根据委托程序出具的授权书，只有在提交了包含委托权的主要授权书或者在提交主要授权书下的代理

notarial certificate only after submission of the main power of attorney in which the retrust right, or after production of evidence of the fact that the representative under the main power of attorney is forced to it for protection of interests issued the power of attorney is stipulated.

人行为事实的证据之后，才能出具公证书。这是为了保护所出具的授权书中涉及的利益。

The power of attorney issued according to the procedure of retrust shall not comprise more rights, than it is provided under the main power of attorney. Effective period of the power of attorney issued according to the procedure of retrust cannot exceed effective period of the power of attorney based on which it is issued.

根据委托程序出具的授权书不得比主要授权书中包含更多的权利。根据委托程序出具的授权书有效期不得超过主要授权书的有效期。

Cancellation of the power of attorney is performed according to the procedure, provided by the civil legislation of the Azerbaijan Republic.

应根据阿塞拜疆共和国民事法律规定的程序取消授权书。

Article 50. Number of copies of documents in which contents of transactions are stated

Documents in which contents of the transactions certified in notarial procedure are stated are provided to the notary or in relevant organ of the executive authority at least in duplicate, one of which remains in cases of the notary or relevant organ of the executive authority.

第 50 条　与交易相关的文件副本数量

公证与交易相关的文件，至少在公证程序中一式两份提供给公证员或行政机关有关部门，其中一份由公证员或行政机关有关部门保留。

Chapter VII. Taking measures to protection of heritable property

第七章　采取措施以保管遗产

Article 51. Protection of heritable property

Before inheritance acceptance, in case of need the notarial body for the place of opening of inheritance takes measures for the purpose of its protection. This rule extends also to cases when the heir is unknown or data on acceptance of inheritance by it are absent.

第 51 条　遗产的保管

在遗产被接收之前，如果需要，公证机构将采取措施先行保管待处理的遗产。本条也适用于继承人未知或者缺乏遗产接收相关资料的情况。

Article 52. The inventory of heritable property and its transfer on storage

For protection of inheritance the notarial body can carry out its inventory.

For implementation of the measures provided by this Section, the notarial body can appoint the managing director of property.

The managing director of property is warned about responsibility for waste or concealment of heritable property, and also about liability for the caused losses.

第 52 条　遗产清单及其储存

公证机构可以制作遗产清单以保管遗产。

为实施本节规定的措施，公证机构可任命遗产管理负责人。

应警示遗产管理负责人滥用或隐藏遗产以及造成损失的法律责任。

Article 53. The expenses connected with the measures provided by this Section

The expenses connected with the measures provided by this Section are ranked as inheritance liability.

第 53 条　与本节规定的措施有关的费用

与本节规定的措施有关的费用将被列为遗产中的债务。

Article 54. Payment of necessary expenses at the expense of heritable property

The notary before inheritance acceptance by heirs and if the inheritance is not accepted, then before issue to the state of the certificate on the right to inheritance, gives the order about payment for the account of sum of money as a part of heritable property of the following expenses:

1) on care of the testator during his disease, and also on funeral of the testator;

2) on content of persons which were dependent on the testator;

3) on satisfaction of the requirements following from the labor law and other requirements equated to them;

4) on protection of heritable property and on management of it, and also on the message to heirs about opening of inheritance.

If as a part of heritable property there is no sum of money, the notary gives the order about issue of objects from the inherited property with condition of not excess of the amount of the actual expenses on requirements satisfaction specified in part one of this Article.

第 54 条　继承遗产要支付的必要费用

在继承人接受遗产之前以及如果遗产未被接收，则公证员在出具继承权公证书之前，应作出指令，将因下列情况产生费用总额归入遗产，包括：

（1）遗嘱人生病期间照顾及其葬礼的费用；

（2）提供给依赖遗嘱人而生活的人的费用；

（3）根据劳动法规定的要求和与其相等的其他要求产生的费用；

（4）保护和管理遗产以及给向继承人提供处理遗产的信息的费用。

如果遗产不是金钱，那么公证员对遗产中的物件进行处理，但不得超过因本条第 1 部分中实际费用的需要。

Article 55. The notice and search of heirs on the opened inheritance

The notary who received the message of heirs on the opened inheritance shall inform on it those heirs, the residence or works of which is known to it.

The notary can also make challenge of heirs by the room of the public notice or the message in seal.

The notarial body takes measures for search of the heirs who are absent on the place of opening of inheritance.

第 55 条　通知和寻找被处理遗产的继承人

公证员收到被处理遗产继承人的信息，则应按照已知的居住地或工作地通知继承人。

公证员也可以通过公告或密封的信件对继承人提出质疑。

公证机构可采取措施寻找被处理遗产缺席的继承人。

Article 56. Termination of protection of heritable property

Protection of heritable property continues before inheritance acceptance and if the inheritance is not accepted, - before the expiration of the terms for inheritance acceptance established by the legislation.

第 56 条　终止遗产保管

在遗产被接收之前应继续保管待继承财产，如果遗产被拒绝接收，那么可以在法律规定中接收遗产条款到期之前终止保管。

Chapter VIII. Issue of certificates on the right to inheritance

第八章　出具继承权公证书

Article 57. Certificate on the right to inheritance and terms of its issue

The notary in the place of opening of inheritance issues to heirs and the state the certificate on the right to inheritance of the property passing according to the procedure of inheritance. Issue of the certificate is made in the

第 57 条　继承权公证书和规定出具的条款

遗产所在地的公证员根据继承程序向继承人或国家出具遗产继承权公证书。公证书根据民事法律规定的条款出具。

terms established by the civil legislation.

Article 58. Procedure for issue of the certificate on the right to inheritance

The certificate on the right to inheritance is granted according to the procedure, stopped by the civil legislation, according to the written application of the heirs who accepted inheritance, or to everyone depending on their desire.

The heirs who passed term for inheritance acceptance can be included in the certificate on the right to inheritance from written consent of all other heirs who accepted inheritance. Consent shall be declared before issue by the notary of the certificate on the right to inheritance.

The notary reports about issue of the certificate on the right to inheritance addressed to minor and incapacitated heirs in relevant organ of the executive authority at the place of residence of the heir for the purpose of protection of their valuable interests.

Upon transition of heritable property to the state the certificate is granted to relevant organ of the executive authority of the Azerbaijan Republic.

Article 59. Issue of the certificate on the right to inheritance under the law

The notary in case of issue of the certificate on the right to inheritance under the law by reclamation of proofs checks the fact of death of the testator, the place and time of opening of inheritance, availability of the bases for calling to inheritance under the law of persons who submitted the application for issue of the certificate, structure and the location of heritable property.

If heirs are deprived of opportunity to submit the documents confirming availability at them of the bases for calling to inheritance under the law, they can be included in the certificate on inheritance right from written consent of all other heirs who accepted inheritance and produced the evidence of availability at them with the testator of the relations of relationship, marriage or other relations.

Article 60. Issue of the certificate on the right to inheritance according to the will

The notary in case of issue of the certificate on the right to inheritance according to the will checks the fact of death of the testator, will availability, the place and time of opening of inheritance, structure of heritable property.

The notary finds out also the group of people, having the right to obligatory share in inheritance.

第 58 条　出具继承权公证书的程序

继承权公证书是根据民事法律规定的程序，根据接受遗产的继承人的书面申请，或根据任何人的意愿申请出具。

超过接受遗产期限的继承人可以通过其他接受遗产的继承人书面同意书，纳入继承权公证书中。该同意书应在公证员出具继承权公证书之前予以公开。

公证员向未成年和无行为能力人的继承人出具了继承权公证书，应向其居住地的行政机关有关部门报告，以保护其利益。

遗产转移给国家的，应将该公证书授予阿塞拜疆共和国行政机关有关部门。

第 59 条　依法出具继承权公证书

公证员通过依法收集证据、检查遗嘱人死亡的事实、被处理遗产的地点和时间、申请继承权公证书的人请求遗产的可行性依据、遗产的结构和地点，出具继承权公证书。

若继承人被依法剥夺了提交确认其继承可行性依据的文件的机会，则可以通过其他接受遗产继承人的书面同意并提供他们和遗嘱人的亲属、婚姻或其他关系，将其纳入继承权公证书中。

第 60 条　根据遗嘱出具继承权公证书

公证员根据遗嘱出具继承权公证书时，将检查遗嘱人的死亡事实、遗嘱的可行性、被处理遗产的地点和时间、遗产的财产结构。

公证员应查明所有有权继承遗产份额的人。

Chapter IX. Issue of the certificate on the property right to share in common property of spouses

Article 61. Issue of the certificate according to the joint statement

The notary according to the joint written statement of spouses issues to one of them or both spouses the certificate on the property right to share in the common property acquired during scrap.

The certificate can be granted to each of spouses both during scrap, and after its termination.

The certificate on the property right to the apartment house, the apartment, giving, the garden house, garage, the parcel of land and other real estate is issued only by the notary in the location of this property.

Article 62. Issue of the certificate in case of the death of one of spouses

In case of the death of one of spouses the certificate on the property right to share in common property of spouses is granted only by the notary in the place of opening inheritance according to the statement of the surviving spouse with the notice of the heirs of the testator who accepted inheritance.

The certificate can be granted on half of common property.

The share of the died spouse in common property also can be determined by the written application of the heirs who accepted inheritance and with the consent of the surviving spouse in the certificate on the property right.

Chapter X. Issue of certificates on acquisition of apartment houses on open auctions

Article 63. Issue of the certificate on acquisition of the apartment house on open auctions

Acquisition of apartment houses of the house on open auctions is drawn up by the notary in the location of the house with issue to the acquirer of the certificate on it.

If the auction did not take place, the certificate on acquisition of the house is granted to the claimant.

The certificate is granted based on the copy of the act of sale of the house by open auction or transfer of the house to the claimant because the auction did not take place.

第九章　出具夫妻共同财产的产权公证书

第 61 条　根据共同声明出具公证书

公证员根据夫妻的共同书面声明向其中一方或双方出具夫妻在争议期间获得的共同财产的产权公证书。

公证书可以在争议期间和终止后授予夫妻任何一方。

公寓、套房、赠与物、花园洋房、车库、土地和其他房地产的产权公证书只能由该财产所在地的公证员出具。

第 62 条　夫妻一方死亡时出具公证书

如果夫妻一方死亡，只能由待处理遗产所在地的公证员根据未亡夫妻一方的声明出具夫妻共同财产的产权公证书，并通知接受遗嘱人遗产的继承人。

可以只对共同财产的一半出具公证书。

死亡的夫妻一方在共同财产中的份额也可以通过接受遗产的继承人书面申请来确定，并经产权公证书中未亡一方同意。

第十章　对公开拍卖中获得的公寓出具公证书

第 63 条　对公开拍卖中获得的公寓出具公证书

公开拍卖中获得的公寓由公寓所在地公证员向其收购人出具公证书。

若拍卖没有进行，则向索赔人出具房屋公证书。

如果拍卖没有进行，也可以根据公开拍卖或转让房屋的法律规定向索赔人出具公证书。

Chapter XI. Witnessing of fidelity of copies of documents and statements from documents, authenticity of the signature and fidelity of the translation

Article 64. Witnessing of fidelity of copies of documents

Notaries, relevant organs of the executive authority witness fidelity of copies of the documents issued by organizations, the companies and the organizations provided that these documents do not contradict the law, have legal value, witnessing of fidelity of copies of documents and statements from documents is not forbidden by the law.

Fidelity of the copy of the document issued by person is witnessed by the notary when authenticity of the signature of this person on the authentic document is certified by the notary, relevant organ of the executive authority or organization, the company, the organization for place of employment, studies or treatments of person.

Article 65. Witnessing of fidelity of the copy from the copy of the document

Fidelity of the copy from the copy of the document is witnessed by the notary or relevant organ of the executive authority provided that fidelity of the copy of the document is notarized or the copy of the document is issued by organization, the company, the organization from which the authentic document proceeds. In the latter case the copy of the document shall be made on the form of organization, company, organization, is under seal and to have mark that the authentic document is stored in this organization, the company, the organization.

Article 66. Witnessing of fidelity of statements from documents

Fidelity of statements from documents can be attested only in that case when contents of these documents concern several, the questions which are not connected among themselves. The statement shall reproduce the complete text of part of the document on certain question.

Fidelity of statements from documents is witnessed according to the procedure, provided by articles 64 and 65 of this Law.

Article 67. Witnessing of authenticity of the signature on documents

The notary or relevant organ of the executive authority witness authenticity of the signature on documents

第十一章　证明文件副本和文件中声明的可信度，签名的真实性和翻译的可信度

第 64 条　证明文件副本的可信度

公证员、行政机关有关部门对机构、公司和组织出具的文件副本证明可信度的前提是这些文件不违法、具有法律价值、法律未禁止证明文件副本和文件中声明的可信度。

个人在原件副本上签字的，如果能够由公证员、行政机关有关部门或者机构、公司、工作地或学习地或治疗地证明签字的可信度，公证员可以出具证明该文件副本的可信度的公证书。

第 65 条　证明文件副本的副本可信度

文件副本的副本可信度可由公证员或者行政机关有关部门公证，前提是文件副本的可信度已被证明，或者文件副本是在原件的基础上由机构、公司、组织出具。在后一种情况下，文件的副本应以机构、公司、组织的格式制作，并密封加盖印章，将原件存储在该机构、公司、组织中。

第 66 条　证明文件中声明的可信度

只有在这些文件的内容涉及多个问题，这些问题彼此之间没有联系时，才能证明文件中声明的可信度。该声明应完整再现文件特定问题的部分。

证明文件中声明的可信度应根据本法第 64 条和第 65 条规定的程序。

第 67 条　证明文件中签名的真实性

公证员或者行政机关有关部门证明文件中签名的真实性的，文件内容应不违法，也不替代交易声明，

which contents do not contradict the law and does not represent transaction statement, and also does not reflect the data discrediting honor and advantage of the person.

Authenticity of the signature of the face which was signed for other person who cannot personally be signed in the transaction in view of physical defects, disease or on other reasonable excuses can be attested.

The notary or relevant organ of the executive authority, witnessing authenticity of the signature, does not certify the facts stated in the document, and only certifies that the signature is made by certain person.

Article 68. Witnessing of fidelity of the translation

The notary witnesses fidelity of the translation from one language on another if knows the corresponding language.

If the notary does not know the corresponding languages, the translation of documents can be made by the translator, and authenticity of its signature is witnessed by the notary.

If the notary is familiar with the signature of the confidential translator, the document signed by him can be accepted by means of electronic communication. If the translation is accepted by means of electronic communication, its certificate as copies is not required.

If the translation of the document is organized by means of the stipulated in Article 20 these Laws of relevant organ of the executive authority of the Azerbaijan Republic, and the notary, the translation payment accepted by the notary during two banking days is transferred into the bank account of the legal entity who rendered translation service.

Chapter XII. Certificate of the facts

Article 69. The certificate of the fact of finding of person in live

The notary based on request of person certifies the fact of stay it in live and grants to interested persons the certificate confirming this fact.

The certificate of the fact of finding of the minor in live is made at the request of his legal representatives (parents, adoptive parents, guardians or custodians).

Article 70. The certificate of the fact of finding of person in certain place

The notary at the request of person certifies the fact of stay it in certain place and grants to interested persons

不含有损害他人名誉和利益的内容。

因身体缺陷、疾病或其他经证明的合理原因无法在交易中亲自签署，而由他人代为签署的签名是为真。

公证员或者行政机关有关部门，证明签名的真实性时，并不证明文件中声明的事实，只是证明签名是由个人签署的。

第 68 条　证明翻译的可信度

如果公证员知道相应的语言时，那么可以证明从一种语言翻译成另一种语言的可信度。

如果公证员不知道相应的语言，那么可以由翻译人员翻译文件，公证员证明签名的真实性。

如果公证员对信任的翻译人员的签名很了解，那么公证员可以通过电子通信的方式接收其签署的文件。如果通过电子通信方式接收了翻译文件，那么不需要该公证书的副本。

如果文件是按照《阿塞拜疆共和国行政机关法》第 20 条的规定翻译的，公证员应在两个银行工作日内将翻译费用转入提供翻译服务的法人实体的银行账户。

第十二章　事实类公证书

第 69 条　关于某人存活事实的公证书

公证员根据某人的要求证明其存活的事实，并向利害关系人出具确认此事实的公证书。

证明未成年人存活的事实由其法定代理人（父母、养父母、监护人或看管人）提出申请。

第 70 条　关于某人在某地的事实公证书

公证员根据某人的要求证明其在某地的事实，并向利害关系人出具确认此事实的公证书。

the certificate confirming this fact.

The certificate of the fact of stay in certain place of the minor is made at the request of his legal representatives (parents, adoptive parents, guardians or custodians).

证明未成年人在某地的事实由其法定代理人（父母、养父母、监护人或看管人）提出申请。

Article 71. The certificate of identity of person with person, represented in the photo

第 71 条　关于照片中的人的身份的公证书

If the notary does not doubt identity of person with person, represented in the provided photo, then based on request of person he shall certify this fact and grant to this person the certificate on it.

如果公证员对提供的照片中的人的身份无疑义，那么可以根据请求人的要求证明这一事实并向该人出具公证书。

If the notary doubts identity of person with person represented in the photo, he does not certify this fact and explains to person the right to take a legal action on the matter.

如果公证员对照片中的人的身份存疑，那么将不对此进行公证，并解释可对此采取法律行动的权利。

Article 72. Certificate of time of presentation of the document

第 72 条　关于文件制作时间的公证书

The notary on the basis statements of persons, organizations, the companies and the organizations certifies time of presentation of the document and makes in the document certifying text about it with indication of the shown his face.

公证员依据个人、机构、公司和组织的陈述证明文件的制作时间，并在提交的文件中对与制作时间相关的文本进行标记，以示证明。

Article 73. Transfer of statements of persons, organizations, companies and organizations

第 73 条　转交自然人、机构、公司和组织的声明

The notary reports to other persons, organizations, the companies and the organizations statements of persons, organizations, the companies and the organizations which content does not contradict the law and does not contain the data discrediting honor and advantage of the person.

公证员可以将自然人、机构、公司和组织的声明转交给其他自然人、机构、公司和组织。声明的内容必须合法，也不含有损害他人名誉和利益的内容。

Statements are sent by mail with the return notification, or transferred personally on receipt. Statements can be transferred also with use of technical means.

通过邮寄方式发送的声明应有回执通知，或在转交时亲自收到收据。声明也可以通过技术手段转交。

At the request of person who submitted the application to it the certificate on transfer of the statement is granted.

应提交申请人员的要求，可出具转交声明的公证书。

Chapter XIII. Acceptance on storage of subject of obligation fulfillment, and also on the official deposit of sums of money, securities and wills

第十三章　受理履行义务的债务人提存、存款、证券和遗嘱

Article 74. Acceptance in the deposit of sums of money and securities

第 74 条　存款和证券的受理

The notary in cases, stipulated by the legislation, accepts from the debtor on storage obligation fulfillment subject, on the deposit sums of money and securities for transfer to their creditor. The notary provides storage of wills, stipulated in Article 1187 Civil codes of the Azerbai-

公证员按法律的规定，从履行义务的债务人处接受提存、存款和证券以转移给债权人。公证员按《阿塞拜疆共和国民法典》第 1187 条的规定接受保管遗嘱。

jan Republic, by their acceptance on the deposit.

The notary informs the creditor on receipt of subject of obligation fulfillment, sums of money and securities and according to its requirement issues it these sums of money or securities.

Acceptance of subject of obligation fulfillment on storage, and also on the deposit of sums of money and securities is made by the notary in the place of obligation fulfillment.

Under the agreements certified in notarial procedure connected with the order real estate payment by one of the parties another of the means exceeding the sum of money determined by relevant organ of the executive authority of the Azerbaijan Republic is performed by means of the deposit account opened in bank by the notary.

The notary certifies such agreements after submission of the receipt on introduction of money into the deposit account opened in bank.

Opening of the deposit account shall be approved with relevant organ of the executive authority of the Azerbaijan Republic.

Article 75. Return of subject of the obligation fulfillment accepted on storage and also the sums of money and securities accepted on the deposit

The subject of obligation fulfillment accepted on storage returns according to the procedure, stipulated in Article 538 Civil codes of the Azerbaijan Republic.

Return of sums of money and securities to person who introduced them on the deposit (debtor) is allowed only from written consent of person for benefit of which it is made contribution (creditor), or by a court decision.

Chapter XIV. Executive texts

Article 76. Collection of sums of money and reclamation of property on executive texts

For collection of sums of money or reclamation of property from the debtor the notary in the location of the debtor makes executive texts on the documents establishing debt.

Executive texts are made only if the submitted documents confirm indisputability of debt or other responsibility of the debtor to the claimant and from the date of emergence of the right of reclamation there passed no more than three years, and in the relations between organizations, the companies and the organizations - no more than one year.

公证员收到履行义务的债务人的提存、存款和证券时应通知债权人，并按照要求分配资金和证券。

公证员在职责履行地接受提存、存款和证券。

经公证程序证明的不动产交易付款的协议中，若其中一方付款超过阿塞拜疆共和国行政机关有关部门规定的金额时，则通过公证员开立的银行存款账户支付。

公证员将在提交了向其开立的银行存款账户汇款收据后公证此类协议。

公证员开立的银行存款账户应经阿塞拜疆共和国行政机关有关部门批准。

第 75 条　归还保管的提存物、资金和证券

《阿塞拜疆共和国民法典》第 538 条规定了归还保管的提存物的程序。

只能通过收益人（债权人）的书面同意或法院判决，将退还资金和证券给存款人（债务人）。

第十四章　执行书

第 76 条　为收回资金和财产的执行书

为了从债务人处收回资金或财产，债务人所在地的公证员可对规定了债务的文件作出执行书。

只有在提交的文件能够证实确有债务或债务人对申请的人负有义务，并且求偿权自产生之日起不超过 3 年，如是组织、公司和机构则不超过 1 年时，才能制作执行书。

The executive text is made within this term if for reclamation on which the executive text is made other term is not established.

The list of documents according to which debt collection is made in indisputable procedure based on executive texts is established by relevant organ of the executive authority of the Azerbaijan Republic.

执行书本应按本条规定制作，但求偿权的执行书则遵循其他规定制作，无须按本条制作。

在执行书的基础上，经无争议性程序，由阿塞拜疆行政机关有关部门制作债务回收的文件清单。

Article 77. Content of executive texts

Executive texts shall bear the following data:

1) position, surname, name and middle name of the notary making executive texts;

2) name and address of the claimant;

3) name and debtor's address;

4) the amount which is subject to collection and the objects which are subject to reclamation including percent and penalty fee if those are due;

5) the amount of payment, the amount of the state fee paid by the claimant or the state fee which is subject to collection from the debtor;

6) date (year, month, number) making of executive text;

7) number at which the executive text is registered in the register;

8) the signature, notary's seal, making executive text.

第 77 条　执行书的内容

执行书应包含以下内容：

（1）制作执行书的公证员职位、姓氏、名字和中间名；

（2）申请人的姓名和地址；

（3）债务人的姓名和地址；

（4）应收回的金额和应收回的物品，如果逾期，应包括收取的罚金和百分比的罚息；

（5）申请人应支付的金额、应支付的法定费用或者应从债务人处收取的法定费用；

（6）制作执行书的日期（年、月、日）；

（7）执行书在登记册中登记的号码；

（8）制作执行书的公证员签名、印鉴。

Article 78. Procedure for collection on executive texts

Collection on executive texts is made according to the procedure, established by the legislation of the Azerbaijan Republic for execution of judgments.

第 78 条　收回执行书的程序

收回执行书的程序适用阿塞拜疆共和国关于执行判决书的法律中规定的程序。

Article 79. Term of presentation of executive texts

The executive text if claimant or the debtor are physical persons, can be shown to forced execution within three years from the date of its making, and according to other requirements - within one year if the legislation of the Azerbaijan Republic does not establish other terms.

Recovery of the passed term for presentation of executive text, is made according to the legislation of the Azerbaijan Republic.

第 79 条　执行书的提交期限

如果申请人或债务人是自然人，那么可以在自出具执行书的 3 年内提出强制执行。阿塞拜疆共和国法律如另无规定的，可在 1 年内提出其他要求。

应根据阿塞拜疆共和国的法律恢复超过提交期限的执行书的效力。

Chapter XV. Creation of protests on bills of exchange, submission of checks for payment and confirmation of non-payment of checks

第十五章　对汇票提出异议，提交付款支票和确认拒付款支票

Article 80. Protest of the bill of exchange

The protest of the bill of exchange in non-payment, the non-acceptance and not dating of the acceptance is

第 80 条　对汇票提出的异议

公证员根据阿塞拜疆共和国关于转换票据和本票的立法，对无力支付、拒绝承兑、无承兑日期的汇票

made by notaries according to the legislation of the Azerbaijan Republic on the translated and promissory note.

Article 81. Presentation of checks to payment and the certificate of non-payment of checks

Notaries in the location of the payer accept for presentation to payment the checks provided after ten days from the date of issue of the check, and foreign cheques - after six months from the date of issue of the check, but no later than 12 hours following after that the term of day.

In case of check non-payment the notary certifies check non-payment by text on the check in the established form and notes about it in the register. Along with text on the check the notification is sent to the issuer about non-payment of its check by bank and making of text on the check.

At the request of the payee the notary in case of non-payment of the check makes executive text.

Chapter XVI. Making of ship's protests

Article 82. Statement for the ship's protest

The notary adopts the statement of the ship master for the incident taking place during swimming or the parking of the vessel which can be the basis for presentation to the shipowner of property requirements.

The application for the ship's protest is submitted to the notary in seaport of the Azerbaijan Republic in time, established by the legislation of the Azerbaijan Republic.

In confirmation of the circumstances stated in the application for the ship's protest the logbook and the statement certified by the captain from the logbook shall be submitted within the term established by the legislation to the notary on review.

Article 83. Creation of the act of the ship's protest

The notary based on the statement of the ship master, data of the logbook, and also poll of the captain and whenever possible at least four witnesses from crew, including two witnesses from command structure of the vessel, draws up the statement of the ship's protest and assures him the sign and seal. One copy of the act is issued to the captain or person authorized by it.

Chapter XVII. Acceptance on document storage

Article 84. Acceptance on document storage

Notaries accept documents for storage according to the inventory. One copy of the inventory remains at the

提出异议。

第 81 条　提交付款支票和拒付款支票的证明

付款人所在地的公证员接受付款支票的提交，以便在支票签发之日起 10 日后提供支票，外国支票自支票签发之日起 6 个月后，但不迟于期限后 1 日的 12 小时提供。

如果是拒付款支票，公证员会用固定文本格式在支票上和登记册上注明，以证明是拒付款支票。公证员将会通过银行连同支票上的标注一起通知拒付款支票的签发人和填写支票文本的人。

根据收款人的要求，公证员对拒付款支票制作执行书。

第十六章　对船舶提出抗议

第 82 条　船舶抗议声明

公证员接受船长对船舶在航行或停泊发生事故时的声明，这可以作为向船主提出财产要求的依据。

根据阿塞拜疆共和国的法律，船舶抗议的申请应及时向阿塞拜疆共和国海港的公证员提出。

在确认船舶抗议申请中所述情况时，应在法律规定的期限内将航海日志和经船长证实的航海日志中的声明提交给公证员进行审查。

第 83 条　船舶抗议声明的制作

公证员根据船长的声明、航海日志的资料以及对船长的民意调查，并尽可能从全体船员中找出至少 4 名见证人，包括 2 名来自船舶指挥部门的见证人，起草船舶抗议声明，并确保有签名和印章。公证员将该声明的副本发 1 份给船长或其授权的人。

第十七章　接受文件的保管

第 84 条　接受文件的保管

公证员可以保管根据清单所列的文件。公证员留有一份清单的副本，第二份则发给检查文件的人。

notary, and the second is issued to person who checked documents.

At the request of person the notary can accept documents without inventory if they are packed properly with the assistance of the notary.

Packaging is fastened with notary's seal, signed by it and person who checked documents.

To person who checked documents the certificate of the established form is granted.

如果文件是在公证员的协助下被妥善包装的，那么公证员可以应申请人的要求接受保管未附有清单的文件。

包装由公证员的印鉴密封固定，由其和检查文件的人签字。

应向检查文件的人出具有固定格式的公证书。

Article 85. Return accepted on document storage

The documents accepted on storage, return upon the demand of person who checked them or the authorized person upon presentation of the certificate and copy of the inventory, or by a court decision.

第 85 条　归还保管的文件

根据检查人或经授权人的要求，在提交公证书和清单副本或经法院判决后归还保管的文件。

Chapter XIII. Providing proofs

第十八章　提供证据

Article 86. Providing the proofs necessary in case of cases in courts, investigating bodies and bodies of inquiry

At the request of interested persons the notary provides the proofs necessary in case of cases in court, investigating bodies and bodies of inquiry if reasons to believe are had that production of evidence will become impossible or complicated subsequently.

The notary does not provide proofs on cases which at the time of the address to him of interested persons are in production of court, investigating bodies or bodies of inquiry.

第 86 条　在法院、搜查机构和调查机构的案件中提供必要的证据

如果有理由相信提交的证据可能会灭失或之后难以得到，那么在利害关系人的要求下，公证员可以在法院，搜查机构和调查机构的案件中提供必要的证据。

若利害关系人是来自法院、搜查机构和调查机构的，公证员则不提供案件的相关证据。

Article 87. Actions of the notary in the field of providing proofs

According to the procedure of providing proofs the notary interrogates witnesses, examines written and physical evidences, appoints examination.

In case of accomplishment of legal proceedings in the field of providing proofs the notary is guided by the relevant standards of the civil procedural legislation of the Azerbaijan Republic.

The notary informs on time and the place of providing proofs of the party and interested persons, however their absence is not obstacle for accomplishment of actions in the field of providing proofs.

Providing proofs without notice of the parties and interested persons is made only in cases, being urgent or when it is impossible to determine who will participate in case subsequently.

第 87 条　公证员收集证据的行为

根据收集证据的程序，公证员可以询问见证人、检查书证和物证或派人检查。

公证员应遵守阿塞拜疆共和国民事诉讼法律的相关规定，完成收集证据的法律程序。

公证员将通知申请人和利害关系人提供证据的时间和地点，但是他们的缺席并不能阻碍提交证据行为的完成。

只有在紧急情况时或无法确定案件的参与者时才能在未通知申请人和利害关系人时提供证据。

In case of absence of the witness or the expert in challenge the notary reports about it in court at the place of residence of the witness or expert for taking measures, provided by the civil procedural legislation of the Azerbaijan Republic.

在见证人缺席时或专家受到质疑时，公证员应按照阿塞拜疆共和国民事诉讼法的规定，向见证人或专家居住地法院报告以采取措施。

The notary warns the witness and the expert about responsibility for making obviously false evidence or the conclusion and for refusal and evasion from making the indication or the conclusion.

公证员应警示见证人和专家提供虚假证据或结论的后果，以及拒绝指证或作出结论的责任。

Chapter XIX. Application of the legislation of foreign states. International agreements

第十九章　外国法律的适用以及国际条约

Article 88. Application of the legislation of foreign states

第 88 条　外国法律的适用

Notaries according to the legislation of the Azerbaijan Republic, international treaties supported by the Azerbaijan Republic apply regulations of the legislation of foreign states.

公证员根据阿塞拜疆共和国法律、阿塞拜疆共和国加入的国际条约适用外国法律的规定。

Notaries accept the documents constituted according to requirements of the legislation of foreign states and also make certifying texts in shape, stipulated by the legislation foreign states if it does not contradict the legislation of the Azerbaijan Republic.

公证员可以接受根据外国法律要求制作的文件，并且如果不违反阿塞拜疆共和国法律，也可以制作外国法律规定的证明文本。

Article 89. Application of the right during protection of heritable property and in case of issue of the certificate on the right to inheritance

第 89 条　在遗产保管和出具继承权公证书时的权利适用

The actions connected with protection of the property which is in the territory of the Azerbaijan Republic which remained after the death of the foreigner, or the property which is due to the foreigner after the death of the citizen of the Azerbaijan Republic and also with issue of the certificate on the right to inheritance of such property are carried out according to the legislation of the Azerbaijan Republic.

应根据阿塞拜疆共和国的法律保管外国人死后在阿塞拜疆共和国境内遗留的财产，或保管阿塞拜疆共和国公民死亡后由外国人继承的财产，并对此类财产出具继承权公证书。

Article 90. Acceptance by notaries of the documents constituted abroad

第 90 条　公证员接受在国外制作的文件

The documents constituted abroad with participation of foreign authorities or from them outgoing are accepted by notaries on condition of their legalization of the executive authority of the Azerbaijan Republic by relevant organ.

公证员可接受在国外制作的、来自外国机关或有外国机构参与的文件，前提是阿塞拜疆共和国行政机关有关部门已将其合法化。

In cases, stipulated by the legislation the Azerbaijan Republic or the international treaties and agreements supported by the Azerbaijan Republic, notaries accept such documents without legalization.

如阿塞拜疆共和国法律规定或阿塞拜疆共和国参与的国际条约和协定另有规定，公证员可以在没有合法化的情况下接受这些文件。

Article 91. Relations of notaries with judicial authorities of foreign states

The procedure for relations of notaries with judicial authorities of foreign states is determined by the legislation of the Azerbaijan Republic and international treaties supported by it.

Article 92. Providing the proofs which are required for business management in bodies of foreign states

Notaries provide the proofs which are required for business management in bodies of foreign states.

Actions in the field of providing proofs are performed according to the civil procedural legislation of the Azerbaijan Republic.

Article 93. International agreements

If the international treaty determines other rules, than those which are stipulated by the legislation the Azerbaijan Republic, when making notarial actions rules of the international treaty are applied.

If the international treaty refers to competence of notaries making of notarial actions, stipulated by the legislation the Azerbaijan Republic, they make these notarial actions according to the procedure, established by relevant organ of the executive authority of the Azerbaijan Republic.

Article 94. The introduction of the law in force

This Law becomes effective from the date of publication.

President of the Azerbaijan Republic
Heydar Aliyev

第 91 条　公证员与外国司法机关的联系

公证员与外国司法机关联系的程序由阿塞拜疆共和国法律和参与的国际条约规定。

第 92 条　提供外国机构业务管理所需的证据

公证员可以向外国机构提供业务管理所需的证据。

提供证据应根据阿塞拜疆共和国民事诉讼法的规定。

第 93 条　国际条约

如果国际条约确定了与阿塞拜疆共和国法律规定不一样的规则，那么在开展公证活动时适用国际条约的规则。

如果国际条约涉及阿塞拜疆共和国法律中公证员开展公证活动的权限，那么公证员应根据阿塞拜疆共和国行政机关有关部门制定的程序开展公证活动。

第 94 条　法律生效时间

本法自公布之日起生效。

阿塞拜疆共和国总统
盖达尔阿利耶夫

巴林

1971 年关于公证的第 14 号法令

مرسوم بقانون رقم (14) لسنة 1971 بشأن التوثيق

1971 年关于公证的第 14 号法令

نحن عيسى بن سلمان آل خليفة حاكم البحرين وتوابعها،

巴林岛及其附属岛屿统治者
尔萨・本・萨勒曼・阿勒哈利法

بعد الاطلاع على المرسوم رقم 1 لسنة 1970 بإنشاء مجلس الدولة، وبناء على عرض رئيس دائرة العدل، وبعد موافقة مجلس الدولة، رسمنا بالقانون الآتي:

根据国务院于 1970 年发布的第 1 号法令，并在司法部部长的提议下制定。

مادة – 1 -

ينشأ بدائرة العدل مكتب يتولى توثيق المحررات التي يقضي القانون أو يطلب المتعاقدون توثيقها، والتصديق على التوقيعات و إثبات التاريخ في المحررات العرفية، ووضع الصيغة التنفيذية على صور المحررات الواجبة التنفيذ، وحفظ أصول المحررات التي تم توثيقها وإعداد فهارس للمحررات التي توثق وإعطاء الصور التي تطلب من المحررات الموثقة وإعطاء الشهادات بحصول التصديق على التوقيعات أو إثبات التاريخ في المحررات العرفية. ويرأس هذا المكتب كاتب العدل ويساعده عدد من الموثقين يعينون بقرار من رئيس دائرة العدل.

第 1 条

建立司法部下辖的公证机构：公证法律要求的文件或缔约方申请公证的文件；公证非官方文件的签署和日期；制定文件执行副本；保存已公证文件原件；准备公证文件索引；提供公证文件要求的副本；出具对非官方文件中签署和日期的公证文书。公证机构办公室由公证机构主任管理，并由司法部部长决定任命的若干助理公证员协助。

مادة – 2 -

يؤدي كاتب العدل والموثقون المساعدون قبل مباشرة أعمالهم يمينا أمام رئيس دائرة العدل بأن يقوموا بأعمال وظائفهم بالذمة و الصدق.

第 2 条

在上任之前，公证机构主任和助理公证员应当向司法部部长作忠诚、尽职尽责的就职宣誓。

مادة – 3 -

لا يجوز لكاتب العدل أو أي موثق آخر أن يباشر توثيق محرر يخصه شخصيا أو تربطه بأصحاب الشأن فيه صلة قرابة أو مصاهرة إلى الدرجة الرابعة.

第 3 条

公证员不得对专属其本人或与其有四代内近亲或姻亲关系的申请人有关联的文件进行公证。

مادة – 4 -

لا يوقع الموثق بتوثيق أي محرر إلا إذا دفع الرسم

第 4 条

公证员不得对未支付费用的文件进行公证。

المستحق عنه.

مادة - 5 -

توثق المحررات باللغة العربية، وإذا كان أحد المتعاقدين يجهل هذه اللغة أو لا يجيدها استعان الموثق بمترجم يقدمه المتعاقدون ويكون محل ثقتهم، ويجب أن يوقع المترجم المحرر مع المتعاقدين والشهود والموثق.

مادة – 6 -

يختص كاتب العدل بتوثيق جميع المحررات الرسمية عدا ما كان منها متعلقا بالوقف أو بالأحوال الشخصية. ومع عدم الإخلال بأحكام قانون التسجيلات العقارية رقم 1 لسنة 1367هـ أو أي إعلان آخر نافذ المفعول بشأن رهن و قيد الحقوق العينية على الأموال غير المنقولة، يكون توثيق حجج الوقف وما يدخل عليها من تغييرات أمام أحد قضاة المحكمة الشرعية الكبرى. ويوثق المحررات المتعلقة بالأحوال الشخصية بالنسبة إلى المسلمين أحد قضاة المحكمة الشرعية الكبرى. على أنه يجوز لرئيس دائرة العدل أن يفوض مأذونين في توثيق عقود الزواج والمصادقة عليها وإشهادات الطلاق. أما غير المسلمين فيوثقون محرراتهم المتعلقة بالأحوال الشخصية أمام كاتب العدل أو أمام جهات التوثيق الخاصة بهم في قنصلياتهم.

مادة - 7 -

لرئيس دائرة العدل إصدار قرارات بتفويض ممثلي الحكومة بالخارج في القيام بما يفوضون به من أعمال التوثيق في الجهات الكائنين بها. ويقوم كاتب العدل بالتصديق على توقيع هؤلاء المفوضين.

مادة – 8 -

يجب على الموثق أن يتحقق من شخصية ذوي الشأن بشهادة شاهدين بالغين عاقلين معروفين له، أو بالاطلاع على جواز سفرهم أو ورقة رسمية أخرى تقوم مقامه وعليه أن يثبت هذا الاطلاع في المحرر ذاته.

مادة – 9 -

يجب على الموثق قبل إجراء التوثيق أن يتثبت – على قدر الإمكان – من أهلية المتعاقدين ورضائهم. فإذا اتضح له عدم توافر الأهلية أو الرضاء أو إذا كان المحرر ظاهر البطلان رفض التوثيق وأعاد المحرر إلى ذوي الشأن مع إبداء أسباب الرفض بكتاب مسجل.

مادة – 10 –

لمن رفض توثيق محرره أن يتظلم من قرار الموثق أمام رئيس دائرة العدل ، وذلك في خلال عشرة أيام من إبلاغ الرفض إليه. ولرئيس دائرة العدل أن يندب قاضيا لنظر التظلم. ويكون قرار القاضي نهائيا، ولكن لا يحوز هذا القرار قوة الشيء المقضى به في موضوع المحرر ذاته.

مادة - 11 –

لا تسلم صور المحررات التي تم توثيقها إلا

第 5 条

公证文件应以阿拉伯文编写，如果申请人不懂这种语言或不精通，公证员应允许由申请人提供的其认为可靠的翻译人员提供翻译服务，翻译人员应与申请人、证人和公证员一起在文件上签字。

第 6 条

公证员有权公证所有官方文件，但有关公益慈善捐赠的文件除外。在不违背伊历 1367 年（公历 1947 年）1 号不动产登记法和任何其他有效的不动产实物权限制的法令的前提下，可以在宗教大法院的一名法官面前，对公益慈善捐赠的证据和变更进行公证。穆斯林的个人状况由宗教大法院的法官记录。但司法部部长可以授权订立和公证结婚证书和离婚证书。非穆斯林在公证机构或领事馆公证他们的与个人状况有关的文件。

第 7 条

司法部长应颁布决定，授权政府的海外代表在其所在机构执行被委托的公证工作。公证员应当公证这些受委托人的签署。

第 8 条

公证员必须通过两位与申请人熟悉且理智健全的成年证人证词或护照或其他正式文件，核实申请人的身份，并且必须在该文件中表明证件验证。

第 9 条

在公证文件之前，公证员必须尽可能核实申请人的资格和意愿。如果发现申请人不具备资格或意愿，或者文件明显无效，公证员应拒绝公证，将文件用挂号信退回给申请人，并告之拒绝理由。

第 10 条

被公证员拒绝公证其文件的申请人可在收到拒绝通知 10 日内，向司法部部长提出申诉。司法部部长可以委派 1 名法官来听取申诉。法官的判决应当是最终判决，但这一判决对文件内容本身不具有法律效力。

第 11 条

已完成公证的文件副本只能交给申请人。文件的

لأصحاب الشأن. ويجوز تسليم صورة المحرر للغير بأمر من القاضي. ولايجوز تسليم صورة تنفيذية ثانية من المحرر الموثق إلا بقرار من المحكمة.

مادة – 12 –

ال يجوز أن تنقل من مكتب التوثيق أصول المحررات التي تم توثيقها الو الدفاتر أو الوثائق المتعلقة بها. ويجوز للسلطات القضائية الاطلاع عليها في مكان حفظها. الو يجوز ضم دفتر من دفاتر التوثيق إلى ملف دعوى منظورة.

مادة – 13 –

إذا أصدرت محكمة قرارا بضم أصل محرر موثق إلى دعوى منظورة أمامها، تندب أحد قضاتها لينتقل إلى مكتب التوثيق لتحرر بحضوره صورة مطابقة للأصل الرسمي ويعمل بذيلها محضر يوقعه القاضي وكاتب العدل، ثم يضم أصل المحرر إلى ملف الدعوى وتقوم الصورة مكانه لحين رده.

مادة - 14 –

يصدر قرار من رئيس دائرة العدل بالئحة تنفيذية تشمل بيان إجراءات التوثيق والتصديق على التوقيعات وإثبات التاريخ وتنظيم الدفاتر والفهارس والصور والشهادات. وتحدد الرسوم الواجب أداؤها.

مادة – 15 –

اعتبارا من تاريخ العمل بأحكام هذا القانون، ال يجوز لأية هيئة أو سلطة مزاولة أعمال التوثيق وذلك فيما عدا الأحوال التي ينص فيها القانون على خالف ذلك.

مادة – 16 –

على رئيس دائرة العدل تنفيذ هذا القانون. ويعمل به اعتبارا من تاريخ نشره في الجريدة الرسمية.

حاكم البحرين وتوابعها
عيسى بن سلمان آل خليفة
صدر في قصر الرفاع

بتاريخ 14 جمادى الثانية 1391 هـ
الموافق 7 أغسطس 1971 م

副本可以通过法官的命令交给第三方。除法院命令外，不得出具已公证文件的执行副本。

第 12 条

不得从公证机构转移已公证的文件、文本或与之相关的文件正本。司法机关可以在文件保管地对文件进行检查。所有公证文本不能纳入待审案件的卷宗中。

第 13 条

如果法院决定将公证文本原件纳入待审案件，那么由法院委托 1 名法官到公证机构，编写一份与正本相一致的副本，并在其结尾处做记录，由法官和司法部部长共同签署，然后将原件纳入待审案件的卷宗中。副本替代正本，直至正本被送回。

第 14 条

司法部长的决定应按执行条例形式发布，其中包括对公证程序、公证签署、公证日期以及文本、索引、照片和证书等的规范说明，并确定要支付的费用。

第 15 条

自本法规定实施之日起，除非法律另有规定，否则任何机构或当局均不得从事公证活动。

第 16 条

司法部部长应执行本法。本法自《官方公报》发布之日起实施。

巴林岛及其附属岛屿统治者
尔萨 · 本 · 萨勒曼 · 阿勒哈利法
发布于里法宫

伊历 1391 年 6 月 14 日
（公历 1971 年 8 月 7 日）

孟加拉国

1961 年公证员条例

THE NOTARIES ORDINANCE, 1961 (ORDINANCE NO. XIX OF 1961). ANCE, 1961

1[*]

An Ordinance to provide for and to regulate the profession of notaries Bangladesh. 1WHEREAS it is expedient to provide for and to regulate the profession of notaries in Bangladesh; NOW, THEREFORE, in pursuance of the Proclamation of the seventh day of October, 1958, and in exercise of all powers enabling him in that behalf the President is pleased to make and promulgate the following Ordinance:-

Short title, extent and commencement

1. (1) This Ordinance may be called the Notaries Ordinance, 1961

(2) It extends to the whole of Bangladesh.

(3) It shall come into force on such date as the Government may, by notification in the official Gazette, appoint.

Definitions

2. In this Ordinance, unless the context otherwise requires,-

(a) "instrument" includes every document by which any right or liability is, or purports to be, created, transferred, modified, limited, extended, suspended, extinguished or recorded;

(b) "legal practitioner" means any advocate or attorney of the Supreme Court 2[*] or any pleader authorised under any law for the time being in force to practise in any Court of law

1961 年公证员条例 条例编号（1961 年第十九号）

孟加拉国公证员职业规范条例

为有效规范孟加拉国公证员的职业行为，依据 1958 年 10 月 7 日公告的授权，总统依法行使权力，制定和颁布以下条例：

简称、适用范围和生效时间

1.（1）本条例可简称为《1961 年公证条例》。

（2）本条例适用于整个孟加拉国。

（3）本条例自政府在政府公报刊登之日起生效。

定义

2. 在本条例中，除文本中另有所指外：

（a）"文书" 包括任何创设、转让、修改、限制、延长、暂停、终止或记载权利或责任的文件；

（b）"法律从业者" 指最高法院第 2[*] 号文件中的辩护人或代理人，或依据当时有效的法律授权在法院执业的辩护人；

(c) "notary" means a person appointed as such under this Ordinance:

Provided that for a period of six months from the commencement of this Ordinance it shall include also a person who, before such commencement, was appointed a notary public by the Master of Faculties in England, and is, immediately before such commencement, in practice as a notary in any part of 3[*in the territory now comprised in Bangladesh];

(d) "prescribed" means prescribed by rules made under this Ordinance;

(e) "Register" means a Register of Notaries to be maintained under section 4.

Power to appoint notaries

3. The Government, for the whole or any part of 4[*Bangladesh], may appoint as notaries any legal practitioners or other persons who possess such qualifications as may be prescribed.

Registers

4. (1) The Government shall maintain, in such form as may be prescribed, a Register of the notaries appointed by 5[*the] Government and entitled to practise as such under this Ordinance.

(2) Every such Register shall include the following particulars about the notary whose name is entered therein, namely:-

(a) his full name, date of birth, residential and professional address;

(b) the date on which his name is entered in the Register;

(c) his qualification; and

(d)any other particulars which may be prescribed.

Entry of names in the Register and issue or renewal of certificates of practice

5. (1) Every notary who intends to practise as such shall, on payment to the Government of the prescribed fee, if any, be entitled-

(a) to have his name entered in the Register maintained by 6[the] Government under section 4, and（实在看懂不这里的 6）

(b) to a certificate authorising him to practise for a period of three years from the date on which the certificate is issued to him.

（c）“公证员”指依据本条例被委任具备公证资格的人：

但自本条例生效日期起 6 个月的过渡期内，在本条例生效日期前由英格兰大主教特许法院主事官委任为公证员，并在本条例生效日期前已经在孟加拉国境内执行公证员职务的，也应当属于公证员；

（d）“规定”指依据本条例所制定的规则；

（e）“登记簿”指根据本条例第 4 条进行保存的公证员登记簿。

任命公证员的权力

3. 孟加拉国政府有权任命具有规定资格的法律从业人员或其他人员为公证员。

登记簿

4.（1）依据本条例第 5 条的规定，政府应当按法定格式存档一份政府委任并依照本条例以公证员身份执业的公证员名册。

（2）每份登记簿应当记载登记在册的公证员的以下信息：

（a）全名、出生日期、家庭住址和执业地址；

（b）其名字被录入登记簿的日期；

（c）其从业资格；以及

（d）其他要求登记的信息。

注册、执业证书的颁发和续期

5.（1）任何想从事公证员职业的人，应当向政府缴纳注册费；

（a）政府依据本条例第 4 条的规定将公证员名字登记在册；

（b）颁发的执业证书有效期为 3 年，自颁发之日起计算。

(2) Every such notary who wishes to continue to practise after the expiry of the period for which his certificate of practice has been issued under this section shall, on application made to the Government and payment of the prescribed fee, if any, be entitled to have his certificate of practice renewed for three years at a time.

（2）公证员执业期满后，在向政府提出申请并缴纳了注册费后，有权获得 3 年续期的许可。

Annual publication of lists of notaries

每年公布一次的公证员名单

6. The Government shall, not later than the end of January each year, publish in the official Gazette, a list of notaries appointed by 7[the] Government and in practice at the beginning of that year together with such details pertaining to them as may be prescribed.

6. 政府应于每年 1 月底之前，在官方公报上公布政府于本年年初委任并执业的公证员名单，以及规定的与公证员有关的详细资料。

Seal of notaries

公证员印章

7. Every notary shall have and use, as occasion may arise, a seal of such form and design as may be prescribed

7. 每一位公证员均有权拥有并使用（视情况而定）规定形式及设计的印章。

Functions of notaries

公证员职能

8. (1) A notary may do all or any of the following acts by virtue of his office, namely:-

(a) verify, authenticate, certify or attest the execution of any instrument;

(b) present any promissory note, hundi or bill of exchange for acceptance or payment or demand better security;

(c) note or protest the dishonour by non-acceptance or non- payment of any promissory note, hundi or bill of exchange or protest for better security or prepare acts of honour under the Negotiable Instruments Act, 1881, or serve notice of such note or protest;

(d) note and draw up ship's protest, boat's protest or protest relating to demurrage and other commercial matters;

(e) administer oath to, or take affidavit from, any person;

(f) prepare bottomry and respondantia bonds, charter parties and other mercantile documents;

(g) prepare, attest or authenticate any instrument intended to take effect in any country or place outside Bangladesh in such form and language as may conform to the law of the place where such deed is intended to operate;

(h) translate, and verify the translation of, any document from one language into another;

(i) any other act which may be prescribed.

(2) No act specified in sub-section (1) shall be

8.（1）公证员凭借其职位，可实施下列全部或部分行为：

（a）就法律文件的签署进行核实、证实、证明、见证；

（b）就本票、信贷证券或汇票提示承兑、付款或要求更多保障；

（c）根据《1881 年可转让票据法》的规定，就本票、信贷证券、汇票的拒绝承兑或拒付等拒绝兑现行为进行签注或制作拒绝证书，或出具拒绝证书以要求更多保障，或送达上述签注或拒绝证书的通知；

（d）提示并起草海事声明、船舶声明或与滞期费及其他商业安排有关的声明；

（e）主持宣誓或接受宣誓书；

（f）起草押船借贷合同、货船抵押债券、租船合同以及其他商业文件；

（g）准备、证明或认证符合合同所在地法律规定的形式和语言的文书，使其在孟加拉国境外的任何国家或地方生效；

（h）跨语种翻译文件，或核实跨语种翻译的文件的译本；

（i）法律规定的其他任何行为。

（2）第（1）款指明的行为非经公证员实施并加

deemed to be a notarial act except when it is done by a notary under his signature and official seal.

盖其公章和签字，不得视为公证行为。

Bar of practice without certificate

9. (1) Subject to the provisions of this section, no person shall practise as a notary or do any notarial act under the official seal of a notary unless he holds a certificate of practice in force issued to him under section 5: Provided that nothing in this sub-section shall apply to the presentation of any promissory note, hundi or bill of exchange for acceptance or payment by the clerk of a notary acting on behalf of such notary.

(2) [Omitted by section 3 and the Second Schedule of the Bangladesh Laws (Revision And Declaration) Act, 1973 (Act No. VIII of 1973).]

禁止无证执业

9.（1）根据本条规定，除非持有根据第 5 条向其颁发的有效执业证书，任何人不得作为公证员执业或使用公证员公章实施公证行为；但本款不适用于公证员助理代表公证员提示承兑或提示支付本票、信贷证券、汇票的情形。

（2）被“1973 年孟加拉国法（第 8 号法）第 3 节和附表 2（修订和声明）”所遗漏的。

Removal of names from Register

10. The Government may, by order, remove from the Register maintained by it under section 4 the name of the notary if he-

(a) makes a request to that effect; or

(b) has not paid any prescribed fee required to be paid by him; or

(c) is an undischarged insolvent; or

(d) has been found, upon inquiry in the prescribed manner, to be guilty of such professional or other misconduct as, in the opinion of the Government, renders him unfit to practise as a notary.

从登记簿上除名

10. 公证员如有下列行为，任命公证员的政府可以以命令的形式，将公证员从由其根据第 4 条保存的登记簿上除名：

（a）公证员自行提出有效的除名申请；

（b）不支付要求其缴纳的规定费用；

（c）因为未清偿债务而发生破产；

（d）通过规定的方式进行调查后，政府认为其犯有不再适合担任公证员的罪行或其他不当行为。

Construction of references to notaries public in other laws

11. Subject to the provisions of section 16, any reference to a notary public in any other law shall be construed as a reference to a notary entitled to practise under this Ordinance. Penalty for falsely representing to be a notary, etc

12. Any person who-

(a) falsely represents that he is a notary without being appointed as such, or

(b) practises as a notary or does any notarial act in contravention of section 9, shall be punishable with imprisonment for a term which may extend to three months, or with fine, or with both.

其他法律中引用的公证员的解释

11. 在符合本条例第 16 条规定的前提下，任何其他法律对“公证员”概念的引用都应当解释为有资格根据本条例执业的公证员。

12. 任何人不得有下列行为之一：

（a）在其没有被授予公证资格的情况下不当地对外表示其为公证员，或者

（b）违反本条例第 9 条以公证员的身份行事或从事任何公证活动，处以 3 个月以下的监禁或罚款，或二者并行。

Cognizance of offences

13. (1) No Court shall take cognizance of any offence committed by a notary in the exercise or purported

犯罪的认定

13.（1）除非政府授权的官员以书面形式通过一般或特别指令，否则任何法院不得将公证员行使或准

exercise of his functions under this Ordinance save upon complaint in writing made by an officer authorised by the Government by general or special order in this behalf.

备行使本条例规定的职能认定为犯罪。

(2) No magistrate other than a magistrate of the first class shall try an offence punishable under this Ordinance.

（2）除一等地方法官外，任何地方法官不得审判根据本条例规定应予惩罚的罪行。

Reciprocal arrangements for recognition of notarial acts done by foreign notaries

关于承认外国公证员公证行为的互惠安排

14. If the Government is satisfied that by the law or practice of any country or place outside Bangladesh, the notarial acts done by notaries within Bangladesh are recognised for all or any limited purposes in that country or place, the Government may, by notification in the official Gazette, declare that the notarial acts lawfully done by notaries within such country or place shall be recognised within Bangladesh for all purposes or, as the case may be, for such limited purposes as may be specified in the notification.

14. 如果联邦政府认为根据孟加拉国境外任何国家或地区的法律或惯例，孟加拉国公证员作出的公证行为在该国家或地区能够被全部或部分承认，政府可以通过官方公报通知声明，就公证员在该国家或地区合法作出的公证行为，应当在孟加拉国境内承认其所有目的或在公报中可以载明承认的有限目的范围。

Power to make rules

制定规则的权力

15. (1) The Government may, by notification in the official Gazette, make rules to carry out the purposes of this Ordinance.

15.（1）为贯彻本条例之目的，政府可通过在官方公报上公告的方式制定规则。

(2) In particular, and without prejudice to the generality of the foregoing power, such rules may provide for all or any of the following matters, namely:-

（2）适用于个例，且不损害前述权力的广泛性的前提下，此类规则可就下列全部或部分事项进行规定：

(a) the qualifications of a notary, the form and manner in which applications for appointment as a notary may be made and the disposal of such applicants;

（a）公证员的资格、委任申请的形式和方式，以及对申请的处理；

(b) the certificates, testimonials or proofs as to character, integrity, ability and competence which any person applying for appointment as a notary may be required to furnish;

（b）任何申请成为公证员的人都需要提供可能关系其品格、诚信、能力和胜任资格的证书、鉴定书或证明；

(c) the fees payable for appointment as a notary and for the issue and renewal of a certificate of practice, and exemption, whether wholly or in part, from such fees in specified classes of cases;

（c）任命为公证员、颁发执业证明和执业证明续期需缴纳的费用，以及在特定类别的案件中对于前述费用的全部或部分免除；

(d) the fees payable to a notary for doing any notarial act;

（d）公证员从事任何公证行为的费用；

(e) the form of Registers and the particulars to be entered therein;

（e）登记簿的形式及其中记载的详情；

(f) the form and design of the seal of a notary;

（f）公证员印章的形式及设计；

(g) the manner in which inquiries into allegations or professional or other misconduct of notaries may be made;

（g）针对公证员犯有职业或其他不当行为的指控进行调查可采取的方式；

(h) the acts which a notary may do in addition to those specified in section 8 and the manner in which a

（h）除本条例第 8 条载明的行为外，公证员可以采取的行动和履行职责的方式。

notary may perform his functions.

Saving of Act XXVI of 1881

16. Nothing in this Ordinance affects the provisions of the Negotiable Instruments Act, 1881, or any appointment made in pursuance of section 138 of that Act or the powers of any person so appointed.

Note

1.Throughout this Ordinance, the words "Bangladesh" and "Government" were substituted for the words "Pakistan" and "Provincial Government" or "Central Government" respectively by section 3 and the Second Schedule of the Bangladesh Laws (Revision And Declaration) Act, 1973 (Act No. VIII of 1973)

2. The words "or any advocate of the High Court" were omitted by section 3 and the Second Schedule of the Bangladesh Laws (Revision And Declaration) Act, 1973 (Act No. VIII of 1973)

3 .The words "in the territory now comprised in Bangladesh" were substituted for the word "Pakistan" by section 3 and the Second Schedule of the Bangladesh Laws (Revision And Declaration) Act, 1973 (Act No. VIII of 1973)

4 .The word "Bangladesh" was substituted for the words "the Province" by section 3 and the Second Schedule of the Bangladesh Laws (Revision And Declaration) Act, 1973 (Act No. VIII of 1973)

5. The word "the" was susbtituted for the word "that" by section 3 and the Second Schedule of the Bangladesh Laws (Revision And Declaration) Act, 1973 (Act No. VIII of 1973)

对 1881 年第二十六号法令的保留

16. 本条例中的任何内容均不会影响《1881 年可流通票据法案》(1881 年第 26 号)的规定或根据该法令第 138 条作出的任何委任或委任任何人的权力。

备注

1. 本条例中，依据"1973 年孟加拉国法(第 8 号法)第 3 节和附表 2(修订和声明)"，分别将"巴基斯坦"和"省政府"或"中央政府"改为"孟加拉国"和"政府"(1973 年第 VIII 号法令公告)。

2. "1973 年孟加拉国法(第 8 号法)第 3 节和附表 2(修订和声明)"省略了"或高等法院的任何辩护人"一词。

3. "1973 年孟加拉国法(第 8 号法)第 3 节和附表 2(修订和声明)"用"现在包括孟加拉国领土内"取代了"巴基斯坦"一词(1973 年第 VIII 号法令公告)。

4. "1973 年孟加拉国法(第 8 号法)第 3 节和附表 2(修订和声明)"用"孟加拉国"一词取代了"省"一词。

5. "1973 年孟加拉国法(第 8 号法)第 3 节和附表 2(修订和声明)"第 3 条和附表 2，用"the"一词取代了"that"。

柬埔寨

公证法

KRAM LAW

We, Preah Bath Samdech Preah NORODOM SIHANOUK VARAMAN, THE KING OF CAMBODIA

Having Seen the Constitution of the Kingdom of Cambodia;

Having Seen the Protocol of Transferring the Judiciary Power dated August 29,1953;

Having Seen the Judicial Convention dated September 9, 1953;

Having Seen Royal Decree No. 521. ns, dated August 26, 1954, on the appointment of the Council of Ministers;

Having Seen the Comments of the National Council;

With the Approval from the Council of Ministers;

IT IS HEREBY DECIDED:

1. GENERAL PROVISION

Article 1.The Notary is a public officer appointed by the Royal Decree or Sub. Decree of the Government and instituted for the purpose of:

1. Drafting, Legalizing, Notarizing all documents or contracts that the parties would like, especially official and public documents.

2. Notarizing the date of the document, securing the documents and issuing the original or duplicated document.

The duty of the Notary is to clarify, notify and advise the parties about the document that is made or shall be

柬埔寨公证法

我们的，

柬埔寨国王诺罗敦•西哈努克

依据柬埔寨王国宪法

依据1953年8月29日的《司法权力移交议定书》；

依据1953年9月9日的《司法公约》；

依据1954年8月26日关于任命部长会议的第521.ns号皇家法令；

依据国民议会的审议；

经部长会议批准；

兹决定：

一、一般规定

第一条 公证员是由皇家法令或政府机关的附属法令任命的公职人员，任命的目的是：

1. 起草、合法化、公证当事人需要的文件或合同，特别是官方和公共文件。

2. 对文件日期进行公证，确保文件的效力，并出具原件或复印件。

公证员的职责是阐明、告知、建议当事人已经或者应当提交的文件。作为公职人员，公证员应确保文

made by them. As a public officer, the Notary shall ensure that the content of the document is true and accurate (authentic). In no case shall the public officer disclaim responsibility by alleging that he/she is only objectively writing or recording information according to the documents provided by the parties in order to make the document lawful.

Article 2.This Royal Kram shall not prejudice the rights of the parties who allow the civil servant to certify the document according to the procedures stated in Article 944 and further articles of the Civil Code and shall not prejudice the effectiveness of the certification of such document.

Article 3. However, in the future, the Notary is the only person who has the right to certify any documents concerning the value on the amount of equal to or more than 200,000.00 Riels according to his/her Ministerial Commission. For any document with the value on the amount of 50,000.00 to 200,000.00 Riels, the competent chief of the District where the Real Estate is located or the parties live shall have the right to certify the document.

For any document with the value on the amount of less than 50,000.00 Riels, the certification shall be made by the Chief of Sub. District or District with the approval of the Parties, according to paragraphs 1 and 2 of Articles 945 of the Civil Code, or by the Notary.

The precedent provision of Article 3 shall constitute paragraphs 3, 4 and 5 of Article 945 of the Civil Code. In addition, the following clause shall be added to the end of paragraph 1 of Article 945:

"However, the rights and exclusiveness stated in this article shall be withheld for the sake of other public officers."

The following clause shall be added at the beginning of paragraph 2 of Article 945:

"However, it shall not affect the rights and exclusiveness of the competent Notary. (The remaining part shall not be changed)".

Article 4. In the future, the law may require the certification of any contracts classified by the law in the presence of the Notary. Regarding a contract on mortgaging real estate as collateral, stated in Article 1365 of the Civil Code, the certification shall be made in the presence of the Notary according to the French law; otherwise this contract shall be of no legal value.

Moreover, it shall not affect the existing rights and other rights conferred on the consular or diplomatic official in the Royal Government to act as the Notary, that are

件内容真实、准确。在任何情况下，公职人员不得声称他/她仅根据当事人双方提供的文件客观地编写或记录资料，以使文件合法，从而免除责任。

第二条 皇家公证法不应损害当事人按照《民法典》第944条和其他条款规定的程序请求公证员核证文件的权利，也不应损害核证文件的效力。

第三条 根据其部长级委员会授权，今后只有公证员有权公证价值等于或超过200000.00里亚尔的文件。对于价值50000.00至200000.00里亚尔的文件，房地产所在地或当事人居住地的区行政首脑有权公证该文件。

任何价值低于50000.00里亚尔的文件，应由分区或地区的行政首脑在经双方同意后根据《民法典》第945条第1款和第2款作出公证，或由公证员公证。

第3条的先例条款应构成《民法典》第945条第3款、第4款和第5款。此外，应在第945条第1款末尾增加以下条款：

"但是，为了其他公职人员的利益，本条规定的权利和排他性应予保留。"

第945条第2款开头应增加以下条款：

"但是，它不影响主管公证员的权利和排他性（其余部分不得更改）"。

第四条 今后，法律可要求公证员在场的情况下对各类合同进行公证。关于《民法典》第1365条规定的不动产抵押合同，根据法国法律，应在公证员在场的情况下进行公证；否则，该合同无效。

此外，它不应影响赋予王国政府领事官员或外交官员作为公证员的既有权利和其他权利，该权利在该官员所属政府和王国政府同意的国际法或外交公约中

stated in the international law or diplomatic convention agreed by the Government of that official and the Royal Government.

The Royal Government may authorize a Cambodian Embassy or Consulate in a foreign country to act as the Notary according to the procedures stated in the Cambodian law, to certify any contracts whose parties are Cambodian Citizens. However, it is not compulsory for Cambodian citizens to choose this certification. Cambodian citizens have the right to choose the Competent Authority of the country where they live to certify their documents.

Article 5. Applying for the precedent provisions, Article 961 of the Civil Code shall be abrogated and replaced with the following:

"Article 961: Besides the documents stated in Article 944 and the following articles shall not be regarded as the documents to be certified":

1. Any documents made by a Cambodian Embassy or Consulate in a foreign country in accordance with the Cambodian law on the Notary to the extent that the Cambodian decision authorizes this agency.

2. Any documents made by the public officers in accordance with the law . the Notary and clerks of the Notary appointed or authorized by the Royal Government shall be responsible for issuing legal documents in provinces of the Kingdom for a temporary period till the next authorization.

3. Any documents certified by a competent authority in a foreign country according to the foreign law.

4. Any documents certified by a legally appointed foreign Embassy or Consulate to the Royal Government if the Embassy or Consulate is in charge of the function of the Notary in accordance with the international public law or has a diplomatic or consular convention agreed by the government of that agency and the Royal Government.

Documents stated in paragraphs 3 and 4 of this article shall be certified by a Cambodian Court in order to receive Cambodian Executory Formula.

2. CONDITIONS FOR APPOINTMENT OF NOTARIES

Article 6. A Notary Counsel shall be created in Phnom Penh and the President of the Notary Counsel shall have the competence to perform its functions throughout the Royal Territory of the Kingdom. If requested by the Minister of Justice, the Council of Ministers may provide an additional Royal Decree as deemed necessary to create five Notary Counsels throughout the Kingdom of Cam-

有所规定。王国政府可授权柬埔寨驻外国大使馆或领事馆按照柬埔寨法律规定的程序委任公证员，以公证当事人一方为柬埔寨公民的合同。然而，柬埔寨公民并非必须选择这一种公证方式。柬埔寨公民有权选择其居住国的主管当局来公证其文件。

第五条　为适用先例条款，应废除《民法典》第961条，代之以以下条款：

“第961条：除第944条所述文件和下列条款外，不得视为有待公证的文件”：

1. 柬埔寨驻外国大使馆或领事馆在授权范围内根据柬埔寨公证法提供的任何文件。

2. 公职人员依法出具的任何文件。王国政府任命或授权的公证员和书记员负责在王国各省临时签发法律文件，授权期限直至下一次重新授权。

3. 外国主管当局根据外国法律公证的文件。

4. 经合法任命的外国大使馆或领事馆向王国政府公证的文件，该大使馆或领事馆须根据国际公法拥有公证员的职能，或设立该机构的政府与王国政府签订了外交或领事公约。

本条第3款和第4款所述文件应由柬埔寨法院公证，以便在柬埔寨得以执行。

二、公证员的任命条件

第六条　应在金边设立公证机构，公证机构的负责人有权在王国的领土内履行其职能。如果司法部长提出要求，部长会议可在必要时再颁布一项皇家法令，以便在柬埔寨王国各地增设5个公证机构。关于设立公证机构的新的皇家法令也应确定每一个公证机构的管辖权。

bodia. The new Royal Decree on appointing the Notary Counsels shall also determine the jurisdiction of each Notary Counsel.

Article 7. Candidate of the position of Notary shall be 1. the Cambodian National, enjoying the civil and political rights, at least 30 years of age and with diplomas specified in paragraphs 2 and 3 of this article.

2.A candidate with a bachelor degree or doctor degree in law shall be trained for two years in a Notary Counsel located in Cambodia or any other country in the Union of France.

3.The training period shall be increased to five years for any candidate with a degree in law or a degree of the same value or a candidate with a national degree in jurisprudence and political economy.

Article 8. But as the interim provision:

Paragraph 1. During the maximum period of three years as of the date of enforcing this Royal Kram, regardless of the nature of training, the Government may only appoint any candidate who fully meets the requirement of age, nationality and moral conduct in accordance with Article 7 as a Notary and this candidate shall also hold a bachelor degree in law.

Paragraph 2. Any candidate who has a degree in law or a degree of the same value may be appointed as a Notary for a period of five years if this candidate fully meets the requirement of age, nationality and moral conduct. After completing this five year period, this candidate shall be regarded as fulfilling the training obligation and he/she shall be appointed as a Notary for life.

Paragraph 3. Any candidate who has no degree but who is certified that he/she has been in public service as a senior official for the Royal Government of the Kingdom of Cambodia may be appointed as a Notary for a period of five years and this candidate may be reappointed if he/she has fully fulfilled the requirement of age, nationality and moral conduct.

The candidate may be appointed for life if he/she has obtained a degree in law or a degree of the same value during his/her interim appointment. The appointment for life shall not be made unless the candidate has worked as the head of a Notary Counsel for five years.

Article 9. The Royal Decree on the appointment of a Notary, upon request of the Minister of Justice, shall determine the necessary bonds by the candidate before swearing an oath.

This bond shall be determined as follows for the first

第七条 公证员职位候选人应为：

1. 柬埔寨国民，享有民事权利和政治权利，30岁以上，并持有本条第2款和第3款规定的文凭。

2. 拥有法学学士或博士学位的候选人应在柬埔寨或法兰西联合会的其他国家的公证机构接受2年的培训。

3. 法科大学学历或同等学历的候选人或具有判例法和政治经济学的国家学历的候选人的培训期应延长至5年。

第八条 临时规定：

1. 在执行本皇家法令之日起的最长3年期间，不论培训的性质如何，政府只能任命完全符合第7条规定的年龄、国籍和道德行为准则要求的候选人为公证员，该候选人还应持有法学学士学位。

2. 任何具有法学学位或同等学位的候选人，如果完全符合年龄、国籍和道德行为准则的要求，可被任命为公证员，任期5年。在完成5年任期后，该候选人应被视为履行了培训义务，并应被任命为终身公证员。

3. 任何没有学位但经证明已担任柬埔寨王国政府高级官员的候选人可被任命为公证员，任期5年，如果他/她完全符合年龄、国籍和道德行为准则的要求，可继续任命该候选人。

如候选人在其临时任命期间获得了法学学位或同等学位，可终身任用。否则除非候选人已担任公证机构负责人5年，不得终身任用。

第九条 基于司法部长的要求，任命公证员的皇家法令应确定候选人宣誓前的必要保证。

根据本皇家法令第6条第1款设立的第一个公证

office holder of the Notary Counsel established according to paragraph 1 of Article 6 of this Royal Kram.

1. Depositing the secured amount of 500,000.00 Riels in an account of a bank or credit establishment authorized by the Minister of Finance.

2.Assuring that he/she has real estate in Cambodia that is free from any kind of mortgage and this real estate shall be calculated according to the procedural price and shall be deposited as security and registered up to at least 1,000,000.00 Riels. Before swearing an oath, the candidate shall deposit this real estate as security worth of 1,000,000.00 Riels for the benefit of the treasury. The contract on the deposit of real estate as security shall be made according to Article 10 of this Royal Kram.

机构负责人，应按下列方式确定保证书：

1. 将 500000.00 里亚尔的保证金存入财政部授权的银行或信贷机构账户。

2. 确保他 / 她在柬埔寨拥有不受任何抵押的不动产，该不动产应按规定价格计算，并应作为保证金存放，登记金额至少为 1000000.00 里亚尔。在宣誓之前，候选人应将该房产作为价值为 1000000.00 里尔的保证金，存入财政账户。房地产作为抵押物的保证合同应按照本法第 10 条的规定进行。

3. RIGHTS AND OBLIGATIONS OF THE NOTARY

Article 10. The Notary has no authority to receive any document whose parties are him/herself or his/her siblings, direct line relatives by marriage or close relatives, including nieces/nephews or relatives of this generation or any document considered to be of interest to him/herself or his/her relatives.

The chief of a tribunal shall allow the persons mentioned in the above paragraph to find another Notary who does not have a conflict of interest.

If there is only one Notary in Cambodia, or in case that all the Notaries mentioned in the above paragraph of this article have conflicts of interest, the chief of the Civil Section of the adjudicative Court in Phnom Penh shall appoint a Chief of District deemed appropriate in accordance with a request submitted by the Office of the Minister of Justice. This Chief of District shall act as a Notary with the same procedure and shall receive the same payment as a Notary.

Article 11. For any document that one or all parties is/are unable to sign, two authorized witnesses of legal age shall sign this document instead of them.

Article 12. For any document from which one party or more is/are of foreign nationality, the Notary shall have translators as his/her assistants. The number of translators shall be the same of that of foreign languages.

Article 13. Before taking the office, the Notary shall swear an oath in the presence of the Supreme Court of SALA VINICHHAY. The formula of the oath is as follows: "I would like to swear an oath of allegiance that I shall always perform my duties as a good public officer,

三、公证员的权利和义务

第十条 公证员无权接受当事人为其本人或兄弟姐妹、直系婚姻关系人或近亲属，包括侄子、侄女或这一代亲属在内的任何文件，或被认为与其本人或其亲属有利害关系的任何文件。

审判长应允许上诉人再委托与本人没有利害关系的其他公证员。

如果柬埔寨只有一名公证员，或者与本条上一款提到的所有公证员都有利害关系，金边民事法庭审判长应根据司法部长提出的请求，任命一名地区主管官员为公证员。该官员应按同样程序担任公证员，并应获得与公证员相同的报酬。

第十一条 对于任何一方或所有当事方均无法签署的文件，满足法定年龄且经授权的见证人应代替他们在文件上签字。

第十二条 对于一方当事人或多方当事人为外国国籍的文件，公证员应配备翻译人员担任其助理。翻译人员的数量应与外语语种数量相同。

第十三条 在就职前，公证员应在SALA VINICHHAY最高法院前宣誓。誓词如下："我宣誓效忠，我将永远履行作为一名优秀公证人员的职责，遵守法律，即使在我停止工作之后，也对我获得的所有信息严加保密。"

shall abide by the law and keep all information I've acquired as strictly confidential even after I stop my work".

Article 14. The Notary shall be subject to the disciplinary procedures of the Bar Association. In the event that the Notary is unavailable or is sick, he/she shall assign his/her duties to a person and the Notary shall be responsible for that person's duties. In the event that the Notary dies, resigns, is terminated or dismissed from office, the Minister of Justice shall appoint a person to temporarily hold the office in the Notary Counsel; this person shall swear an oath of allegiance as stated in Article 13 before taking the office. This person shall fulfill all requirements of the provisions for being appointed as a Notary, besides providing the secured amount of money.

第十四条 公证员应当接受律师协会的纪律处分。如果公证员缺席或生病，他 / 她应将其职责转给他人，公证员应就该人的工作负责。如果公证员死亡、辞职、终止职务或被免职，司法部长应任命一人担任临时公证机构负责人；此人在就职前应按照第 13 条的规定宣誓效忠。除提供保证金外，该人还应满足任命公证员的各项规定的要求。

Article 15. The Notary shall receive any work submitted to him/her except in the cases described in Article 10 and the follow; if one or all parties is/are of unsound mind or becomes/become physically or mentally disabled; the document is not appropriate in accordance with the procedure; the parties do not pay the stamp fee or other fees; the Notary does not know the parties or the parties can not prove their identity by showing legal papers or by having two witnesses; or eventually the Notary shall be unable to undertake the work due to insurmountable force majeure.

第十五条 公证员应当接受交予的任何工作，但第 10 条规定的情形外和以下情形除外：当事人一方或者各方系精神不健全或者身体、精神有残疾的；文件不符合程序规定的；当事人未支付印花税或者其他费用的；公证员不能确认当事人身份或者当事人不能通过出示法律文件或者两名证人证明其身份的；或者公证员因不可抗力不能承担该工作的。

Article 16. The Notary's remuneration from fees shall be subject to the procedure that has been used as of August 29, 1953 unless there is a revised Royal Decree made during a meeting of the Council of Ministers.

第十六条 公证员的收费标准应遵守 1953 年 8 月 29 日起适用的规定，除非在部长会议期间有经修订的皇家法令。

Article 17. If there is a Royal Decree in the future to provide the procedural administration of the Notary.

第十七条 如果将来有皇家法令规定公证员的管理程序，从其规定。

Article 18. The Notary Counsel shall be subject to the provisions of the Decree dated August 24, 1921 and all other French texts, which are not contrary to this Royal Kram, which had been properly promulgated in Indochina as of August 29, 1953 until there is a promulgation of the National Texts.

第十八条 公证机构应遵守 1921 年 8 月 24 日以来颁布的法令和不违背本法，且在 1953 年 8 月 29 日前已在中南半岛颁布生效的所有其他法国法律，直至颁布新的国家法令。

The Notary shall be prudent and intelligent, and shall notarize the original documents of the clients and keep the record.

公证员应当谨慎、理性，对申请人的原始文件进行公证，并保存记录。

However, the Notary has no authority to request the Government to appoint someone to replace him/her. According to the scope of this Law, the Government has the discretion to appoint a person as deemed appropriate.

但是，公证机构无权要求政府任命其他人接替他 / 她。根据本法的范围，政府有权酌情任命一名适格的人候补。

Made in the Royal Palace in Phnom Penh
on the 5th day of Waxing Moon of December,

本规定制定于金边皇宫
盈月 12 月 5 日

Year of Horse, Chhasaka, Buddhist era 2497,
falling on November 4, 1954.
The King of the Kingdom of Cambodia
Signed: NORODOM SIHANOUK

马年，查萨卡，佛历纪元 2497 年
1954 年 11 月 4 日
柬埔寨王国国王
诺罗敦·西哈努克签署

塞浦路斯

有关公证服务的规定

Notary Services in Cyprus

Public notaries in Cyprus

According to Chapter 2 in the Advocates Law, lawyers in Cyprus have the right to carry out notarial duties, as the public notary notion does not exist. All lawyers conducting notarial activities must be part of the Cyprus Bar Association. The only notarial activity admitted by Cypriot laws is that of certifying officers that have the right to authenticate documents. Cypriot certifying officers are nominated by the Ministry of the Interior and are not required to be lawyers in order to conduct their activity.

Legalization of documents in Cyprus

All documents drafted in Cyprus with the intention of being recognized by foreign authorities must be legalized. The legalization of documents in Cyprus is conducted by lawyers acting as public notaries. One way of legalizing a document is to place an apostille on the document or to legalize it with the local embassy or consulate of the country in Cyprus.

Cyprus is a signatory member of the Hague Convention on Private International Law, Convention that was also enacted as the national Law 178/86. The Convention allows a simplification in the formalities required to legalize documents. The Convention created a simplified procedure of authentication of documents finalized with a certificate, called an apostille, on the document. The apostille means a document carrying it is considered authentic under the provisions of the Hague Convention.

In case of Cypriot powers of attorney that are some of the most employed legalized documents, the authentica-

塞浦路斯的公证服务

塞浦路斯公证员

因为塞浦路斯并不存在“公证员”的概念，根据《辩护人法》第二章的规定，塞浦路斯的律师有权履行公证职责。从事公证活动的律师必须是塞浦路斯律师协会的会员。由被授权的人员认证文件是唯一获得塞浦路斯法律承认的公证活动。从事公证活动不要求具备律师身份。上述得到授权的人员由内政部提名任命。

塞浦路斯文件的合法化

所有在塞浦路斯起草的文件必须经合法化后才能得到外国有权机关的承认。在塞浦路斯，文件合法化的工作由履行公证员职责的律师负责。文件合法化的方式包括在文件上加注认证标识，或通过外国驻塞浦路斯的大使馆或领事馆将其合法化。

塞浦路斯是《海牙国际私法公约》的签署成员国，该公约同时是塞浦路斯第178/86号法令。《海牙国际私法公约》允许简化文件合法化所需的手续。《海牙国际私法公约》创设了认证文件的简化程序，即通过在文件上加注“认证”的标识认证文件。根据《海牙国际私法公约》的规定，“认证”标识表明附有该标识的文件是真实的。

在塞浦路斯，授权委托书是最常用的合法文件，授权委托书的认证包括以下步骤：

tion is comprised of few steps:

• first, the Cypriot notary will attest the power of attorney was signed before him,

• the power of attorney will then be presented to the commissioner's office where a specimen of the notary is kept,

• the commissioner will attest the signature and place a seal on the power of attorney.

Once these formalities are accomplished, the power of attorney will be delivered to the Ministry of Justice in Nicosia who will apostille the document.

• 首先，塞浦路斯公证员确认该授权委托书系在其见证下签署；

• 授权委托书随后将提交给保存公证文书样本的专员办公室；

• 专员将确认签名并在授权委托书上加盖印章。

以上手续完成后，将该授权委托书提交至位于尼科西亚的司法部认证。

Notary services available in Cyprus

Among the notary services provided by our law firm in Cyprus are:

• powers of attorney,
• contract authentication,
• house rental contract authentication,
• transfer of property at the Cypriot Land Register,
• certified copies of documents.

You can contact our attorneys in Cyprus for details about all available legal services.

塞浦路斯提供的公证服务

塞浦路斯的律师事务所提供的公证服务包括：

• 制作授权委托书；
• 合同认证；
• 房屋租赁合同认证；
• 在塞浦路斯土地登记部门办理财产转让；
• 制作经认证的文件副本。

您可以联系塞浦路斯的律师了解更多关于法律服务的详情。

东帝汶

东帝汶民主共和国公证法

DEMOCRATIC REPUBLIC OF TIMOR-LESTE GOVERNMENT

DECREE-LAW No. 3/2004 Of 4 February 2004

NOTARIES

The approval of a Notarial Code is an important tool for grounding the legislative framework of Timor-Leste, especially in regard to economic activity.

The notarial function is one of the parameters indispensable for the development of national wealth, given the fact that a Notary, more than a mere certifier of signatures, should strive to make the function he or she performs become a guarantor of security for legal acts and businesses performed between individuals and between the latter and the State, thus alleviating the arduous task to be carried out by judicial magistrates.

The norms that relate to the Notarial Services are formulated in such a way as to guarantee the principles of contractual freedom and of the legality of individual rights, of acts, of contracts and of legal businesses. The laws on the Notarial Services should be oriented towards the creation of notarial procedures ensuring simplicity, saving of time and resources, and efficiency, to the interested parties.

Defined in general terms, this decree-law is translated into the simplification of the procedures inherent in the performance of notarial acts and in the level of formalism, into the introduction of more rigorous and transparent rules into the notarial practice, and also into the streamlining of the exercise of the notarial function.

It enshrines the fundamental principles that comprise the civil-law notarial system, which Timor-Leste wants to

东帝汶民主共和国

2004 年第 3 号法令 /2004 年 2 月 4 日

公证法

颁布公证规则是完善东帝汶立法，特别有关经济立法的重要方面。

公证员不仅要公证签名，还应该尽职尽责，保证个人之间和个人与国家之间法律行为和商业行为的安全，从而减轻司法官员的工作压力。因此，发挥公证职能是推动国家经济发展不可或缺的环节。

与公证服务有关的规范以保证契约自由和个人权利、行为、合同以及合法商业行为的合法性为原则。与公证服务相关的法律应该以创设简单、省时、节约、高效的公证程序为目的。

一般而言，本法令具体表现为：形式上公证活动的简捷；公证实践中引入更严格透明的规则；公证职能的简单快捷的实现。

本法根据东帝汶公民的要求，确立了民法公证制度的基本原则。这些原则是保持不变的，主要目的是

become a part of. These principles obviously remain unchanged, principally the recognition of full credit and faith in the acts performed by the Notary, with the attendant consequences at the level of the probative value of documents.

保证公证员所采取的行为，以及文件验证后在价值层面产生具有足够的信用和信誉的效果。

Pursuant to the civil-law notarial principles, a general rule is established with the aim of defining the acts subject to solemnity, based on the creation, modification or abolition of subjective rights over immovable property, followed by the initiation of the typology, though not restrictive, of other acts that should be subject thereto.

本法令是根据民法中的公证原则制定的一般规则，旨在基于不动产主体权利的产生、变更或废除界定法律行为的类型，进而根据该界定划分其他行为的类型。上述类型划分不是限制性的。

At the level of the functioning of the services, notaries are now expected to be recruited from among lawyers with special qualification, and generic authority is exceptionally conferred upon certain entities for the performance of notarial acts.

在公证服务的具体运作层面，目前要求从具有特殊资质的律师中选任公证员，同时特别授予某些机构从事一般公证活动的权力。

Also bearing in mind the need to make every kind of notarial act, taken individually, more expeditious and simpler by removing from them those requirements considered superfluous, while always pursuing technical and legal certainty and rigour. This decree-law is meant to endow the notarial acts as a whole with a simpler technique, thereby transforming such acts into realities more accessible and intelligible to citizens. Results are thus envisaged at the level of efficiency and effectiveness of the daily notarial practice, for the benefit of both users and the notarial services themselves.

通过取消多余的规定，确保技术和法律的确定性和严谨性，使得各种类型的公证活动更简捷。本法令旨在将公证活动视为一个整体，赋予其更为简洁的形式，使其更易为公民理解和使用。因此，为了方便法律使用者和公证服务，力求提高日常公证活动的效率和有效性。

Pursuant to subsections 115.1(b) and 115.3 of the Constitution of the Democratic Republic of Timor-Leste, the Government enacts the following that shall have force of law:

根据《东帝汶民主共和国宪法》第 115 条之一（b）项和第 115 条之三，东帝汶政府颁布如下具有法律效力的法律：

HEADING INOTARIES

第一部分　公证

CHAPTER I Notaries, notarial practice and appointment for the exercise of notarial functions

第一章　公证员、公证活动及公证职能的委任

Section 1 Notary Public

A Notary Public is a notarial practitioner empowered by the State to draft and authorize under his or her signature all acts and contracts that should, with his or her intervention, be entered into between individuals or between the latter and a legal person of any kind.

第一节　公证员

公证员是国家授权、在其签名下起草及公证个人之间或个人与各种类型的法人之间基于其介入的各种行为及合同的公证从业人员。

Section 2 Notarial Practice

1. Notarial practice is meant for legal drafting of, and to give full credit and faith to, extra- judicial legal acts.

2. For the purposes of subsection 1 above, a Notary

第二节　公证活动

1. 公证活动旨在依法起草非司法性质的法律文件并保证其真实有效。

2. 就上述第 1 款而言，公证员可以向表示愿意协

may provide advice to the parties in expressing their willingness to negotiate.

Section 3 Notarial Competence

1. The notarial competence shall be exercised by the Notary.

2. All other notarial officers may only perform such acts as may be assigned to them by an express legal provision.

3. Exceptionally, notarial functions are performed by:

(a) Timorese consular agents;

(b) entities vested with notarial authority by law in relation to certain acts;

4. Acts performed while using the authority given to special notarial organs shall be in compliance with the provisions of this decree-law, to the extent applicable.

Section 4 Organs with authority to appoint notaries

It is incumbent upon the Minister of Justice, represented by the National Director for Registries and Notarial Services, to appoint notaries for the exercise of notarial functions.

Section 5 Appointment Requirements

The pre-requisites for appointment as a Notary are:

(a) university degree in law;

(b) completion of the specific course imparted by the Judicial Training Centre;

(c) be not less than 23 years of age;

(d) having been convicted of no criminal offence;

(e) be affected by no disability or incompatibility referred to in this decree-law;

(f) be a Timorese national.

Section 6 Notary's oath of office

The National Directorate of Registries and Notarial Services shall set the date and time at which the appointee shall take oath of office.

Section 7 Solemn act of oath of office

The oath shall be taken before the Minister of Justice and the text thereof shall read as follows: <<I swear to God and on my honour that I will fulfil satisfactorily and with loyalty the functions that have been invested in me, will abide by and enforce the Constitution and the laws of the Democratic Republic of Timor-Leste, and will never be undeserving of the trust owed to the nature of my occupation>>.

商的双方提供建议。

第三节 公证能力

1. 公证职能由公证员行使。

2. 其他从事公证活动的人员只能从事法律明文规定的可以从事的行为。

3. 在例外情况下，公证职能由以下人员履行：

（a）东帝汶领事代表；

（b）被法律授予公证权力的机构。

4. 经授权的特殊公证机构从事公证活动时，应符合本法的规定。

第四节 有权委任公证员的机关

司法部长负责任命公证员履行公证职责，由国家登记和公证服务部负责人代理。

第五节 委任要求

被委任为公证员的前提条件是：

（a）具有大学法律学位；

（b）完成司法培训中心的相应课程；

（c）23 周岁以上；

（d）无犯罪记录；

（e）不属于本法规定的无能力或无资格的人士；

（f）为东帝汶公民。

第六节 公证员的就职宣誓

国家登记和公证服务部应规定被委任者进行就职宣誓的日期和时间。

第七节 宣誓就职

公证员应在司法部长面前宣誓，宣誓内容如下："我以我的荣誉向上帝发誓，我将尽职尽责履行我的职能，遵守和执行东帝汶民主共和国的宪法和法律，永不辜负人民对我的信任。"

Section 8 Registration of the Notary's signature

Once the oath has been taken, the newly-sworn-in Notary shall record in the notaries' signature register, held by the National Directorate of Registries and Notarial Services, the handwritten signature and initials that he or she will use in the performance of his or her acts as a Notary, thus being authorized to engage in notarial practice.

第八节　公证员签名的登记

宣誓就职后，公证员应在国家登记和公证服务部的公证员签名登记簿上登记他／她在担任公证员期间将使用的手写签名和姓名缩写，方可从事公证活动。

Section 9 Secret Signature

1. A Notary may use a specific password to avoid the risk of his or her signature being vitiated or falsified.

2. To that effect, a specimen of such a secret signature shall be sent to the National Directorate of Registries and Notarial Services. The specimen signature shall be entered in a special register held and kept under strict vigilance by the latter, together with the respective notice.

第九节　秘密签名

1. 公证员可以使用特定密码以避免他／她的签名被篡改或伪造的风险。

2. 为此，应将此类秘密签名的样本送交国家登记和公证服务部。签名样本及其各自的提示应记载于由国家登记和公证服务部严格保管的特别登记簿。

Section 10 Functional competency

1. The Notary is vested with technical autonomy and independence in the exercise of his or her function and, upon appointment, is considered, from an administrative viewpoint, as an official of the Ministry of Justice, under the National Directorate of Registries and Notarial Services.

2. The remuneration of notaries shall be determined by a joint order from the Ministry of Planning and Finance, the Ministry of Justice, and the Ministry of State Administration.

第十节　专业职能

1. 公证员应独立自主地行使其职能，并且出于行政角度的考虑，公证员在就职后虽然是司法部的官员，但是接受国家登记和公证服务部的管理。

2. 公证员的报酬应由规划与财政部、司法部和国家行政部共同确定。

Section 11 Technical competency

1. It is generally incumbent upon the Notary to draft a public act in accordance with the express will of the parties and to verify, interpret and conform it to the legal system, clarifying matters related to its value and scope.

2. It is especially incumbent upon the Notary:

(a) to draft public wills;

(b) to draft other public acts;

(c) to write minutes;

(d) to authenticate private documents; or simply certify the authorship of the handwriting with which such documents are written or the signatures affixed thereto;

(e) to issue life and identity certificates, as well as certificates of public office; certificates of management or administration of a legal person or company;

(f) to issue certificates of other facts that he or she checked;

(g) to certify translations of documents written in a foreign language or have them certified;

(h) to issue copies of public acts and of other docu-

第十一节　公证员的权力

1. 通常情况下，公证员有责任根据当事人的明确意思表示起草公开的文书，核实、解释该文书并使其符合法律规定，澄清有关的事项。

2. 公证员有权：

（a）起草公开遗嘱；

（b）起草其他公开文书；

（c）撰写备忘录；

（d）公证私人文件与该文件起草者或签署者的身份；

（e）出具存活证明和身份证明、公职证明、法人或公司的经营理证明；

（f）出具经过公证员检查的其他事项的证明；

（g）证明用外文书写或经公证的文件的译文；

（h）出具公开的文书或其他文件的副本；

ments on file;

(i) to issue photocopies of acts and other documents, or to cross-check photocopies made by the persons concerned with their respective originals;

(j) toauthenticatephotocopies;

(k) to telecopy, in a certified form, to other public services, for purposes of attestation, the contents of public acts, records or other documents held in the files of the registry, and receive those sent to him or her by the public services, under the same conditions;

(l) to intervene in extra-judicial legal acts, to which the persons concerned intend to give special guarantees of certainty or of authenticity;

(m) to conserve the documents required by law to be kept in the notarial files and those entrusted to him or her for that purpose.

（i）制作文书和其他文件的复印件，或复核有关人员制作的复印件及其各自的原件；

（j）公证复印件；

（k）出于证明的目的，以公证的形式将保存于注册处档案中的公开的文书、记录或其他文件的内容通过传真发送给其他公共服务机构，并接收该等公共服务机构以相同条件向其发送的上述文件；

（l）干预非司法性质的法律行为，有关人员对此类行为提供确定性或真实性的特别保证；

（m）根据法律要求或应他人委托，将文件归入公证机构档案并妥善保管。

Section 12 Place of Notarial Practice

1. The Ministry of Justice shall, following a proposal by the National Directorate of Registries and Notarial Services, indicate to the Notary the place where he or she will habitually and principally conduct notarial business.

2. Except as where otherwise provided in this decree-law, the Notary may perform, within and outside the jurisdiction where the notarial service is located, all acts that fall within his or her remit, which he or she may be requested to perform, and also those acts relating to persons domiciled or property situated outside his or her jurisdiction.

3. A Notary is empowered within his or her jurisdiction to publicly attest to any acts, facts or statements authorized by him or her in that capacity or that must, in accordance with the law, be authorized by a Notary.

第十二节 公证活动的场所

1. 司法部应根据国家登记和公证服务部的提议，向公证员说明其开展公证业务的主要场所。

2. 除本法令另有规定外，公证员可以在公证机构所在的司法管辖区以内或以外从事所有属于其职权范围，且要求其履行的行为，以及与在公证机构所属的司法管辖区以外居住的人或财产有关的行为。

3. 在其所处的司法管辖区内，公证员有权公开证明其以公证员身份授权，或者根据法律规定必须由公证员授权的行为、事实或声明。

Section 13 Registration of notaries

Once the provisions of the preceding sections have been complied with, the National Directorate of Registries and Notarial Services must:

(a) enter the Notary in the register, assigning him or her a personal identification number;

(b) report to all the courts, and especially to those that comprise the judicial district where the Notary is based, his or her appointment, including the password, signature and initials of the newly-appointed Notary;

(c) publicise the notice of appointment in one local daily newspaper only once and attach to the appointee's file a copy of such notice confirming its publication.

第十三节 公证员的登记

如遵守上述各节的规定，国家登记和公证服务部必须：

（a）在登记簿中登记公证员并向其分配个人识别号码；

（b）向所有法院，特别是公证员所处司法管辖区的法院报告公证员的委任情况，包括新委任的公证员的密码、签名和姓名缩写；

（c）仅在一家当地日报上公布委任通知，并在被委任人的档案中附上此公告的副本。

CHAPTER II Disabilities, suspensions, incompatibilities and restrictions

Section 14 Disabilities

The persons below may not be appointed as a Notary:

(a) visually-impaired persons;

(b) speaking or hearing-impaired persons, even if they know how to read and write through a special system;

(c) those convicted of a criminal offence;

(d) those convicted of false testimony, given either in writing or orally.

Section 15 Administrative Oversight of Notaries

The National Directorate of Registries and Notarial Services may, while exercising its supervisory authority and defending the trust owed to the Notarial Services, administratively suspend or dismiss a Notary prosecuted or convicted of a felony or criminal offence committed in a premeditated way, where the illicit deed might, in its opinion, hinder the performance of his or her functions.

Section 16 Disqualifications

The persons below may not serve as a Notary:

(a) military personnel on active duty, church ministers and political party leaders;

(b) the President of the Republic;

(c) cabinet members;

(d) members of Parliament;

(e) all those who are prevented by law from engaging in notarial practice.

Section 17 Restrictions and prohibitions on notarial practice

Taking into account the contents of the acts, a Notary may not authorise:

(a) any act that constitutes, acknowledges or changes, transfers or abolishes rights in his or her favour or against him or her, his or her spouse or relative up to the fourth degree of consanguinity or second degree of affinity;

(b) open solemn wills containing provisions in his or her favour, in favour of his or her spouse or any relative up to the fourth degree;

(c) acts or businesses pertaining to legal persons or entities in which any of the relatives by consanguinity or affinity mentioned in paragraph (a) have held or are holding a post as a director, manager, administrator or legal representative;

(d) anyothercasesestablishedbylaw.

第二章　无能力、暂停、存在冲突及限制情形

第十四节　无能力的情形

以下人员不得担任公证员：

（a）视障人士；

（b）表达障碍或听障人士，即使此人知晓如何通过特殊方式阅读和书写；

（c）有犯罪记录的人士；

（d）因以书面或口头方式作虚假证言而被定罪的人士。

第十五节　对公证员的行政监督

国家登记和公证服务部在行使监督权及捍卫公证服务部门公信力时，公证员被起诉或判定故意犯下重罪或刑事罪行且国家登记和公证服务部认为此违法行为妨碍公证员履行职能，可以采取行政措施暂停或取消公证员的职业资格。

第十六节　不适格的情形

以下人员不得担任公证员：

（a）现役军人、教会牧师和政党领袖；

（b）共和国总统；

（c）内阁成员；

（d）议员；

（e）法律禁止从事公证活动的其他人士。

第十七节　公证活动的限制及禁止

鉴于公证活动的内容，公证员不能授权：

（a）任何创设、承认或变更、转移或废除对公证员自己、公证员的配偶、四代以内血亲或两代以内姻亲享有的权利有利或不利的行为；

（b）订立包含对公证员自己、公证员的配偶或四代以内血亲有利条款的遗嘱；

（c）与（a）项所述的血亲或姻亲关系的人士曾经或正在担任董事、经理、行政人员或法定代表人的法人或实体有关的行为或商业活动；

（d）法律规定的其他情形。

HEADING II NOTARIAL RECORDS

CHAPTER I Notarial registers

Section 18 Register

1. Every notarial act shall, in accordance with its nature, be entered in the following registers: A Docket and Document Register.

2. A Notary may not authorise the recording of documents in registers other than the ones mentioned in subsection 1 above.

3. Registers are opened on the first day of January of each year and are closed on the 31st day of December of the same year.

CHAPTER II Composition, opening and closure of a docket

Section 19 Docket

A docket means a register in which notaries and consuls and other officials enter, under the terms of section 3, the deeds to be issued, following the order of their respective dates.

Section 20 Docket System

1. The docket uses a loose-sheet notebook system, typewritten or printed.

2. Every docket shall have ten sheets, which shall all be initialled by the Office of the Inspector of Registries and Notarial Services.

3. Upon taking office and at the beginning of each calendar year, which shall extend from the 1st day of January until the 31st day of December, a Notary shall be given ten initialled dockets and the quantity of notarial paper sufficient for the exercise of his or her functions.

4. The Notary shall, in due course, request from the Office of the Inspector of Registries and Notarial Services initialled dockets in the event that the ten copies he or she has been given are not sufficient.

Section 21 Notarial paper

Every notarial activity shall be carried out using simple paper numbered and identified as notarial paper and bearing the security seal determined by the Office of the Inspector of Registries and Notarial Services.

Section 22 Regulating the docket entry system

The docket entry system, the year-closing system, the archiving system, and the system for returning any dockets

第二部分 公证记录

第一章 公证登记簿

第十八节 登记簿

1. 公证员应在备忘录和文件登记簿中记录所有的公证活动。

2. 公证员不得授权在第 1 小节所提及的登记簿以外的登记簿上记录文件。

3. 登记于每年 1 月 1 日开放，并于同年 12 月 31 日关闭。

第二章 备忘录的组成、开放及关闭

第十九节 备忘录

备忘录是指公证员和领事以及其他官员根据第三节的规定，按照时间顺序记录其出具的证书的登记簿。

第二十节 备忘录制度

1. 备忘录使用可用于打印或复印的活页笔记本。

2. 每一份备忘录应有十页，由登记和公证服务部门检查员办公室制作。

3. 就职后，公证员应在每个日历年度年初获得十份备忘录和足以行使其职能数量的公证书，使用时间自当年 1 月 1 日起至 12 月 31 日止。

4. 如果十份备忘录不够用，公证员应在适当的时候向登记和公证服务部门检查员办公室申请新备忘录。

第二十一节 公证书

公证活动应使用有编号和标识的简易文书，并应使用由公证和登记服务部门检查员办公室确定的安全封条。

第二十二节 规范备忘录记录制度

经司法部批准，国家登记和公证服务部应建立备忘录登记制度、年度汇总制度、归档制度及空白备忘

that have not been used shall be the object of regulatory arrangements proposed by the National Directorate of Registries and Notarial Services, and approved by an order of the Minister of Justice.

录的返还制度监督。

CHAPTER III On the document register, on entries and on the composition and closure of the register

第三章 文件登记簿，登记簿的录入、组成和终止

Section 23 Legal act of entering documents

Entering a document is the legal act of attaching documents to the Document Register, following the procedures determined by this decree-law and the respective regulations.

第二十三节 记录文件的法律行为

记录文件是根据本法令及相关法规确定的程序在文件登记簿中登记文件的法律行为。

Section 24 Document Register

1. A Document Register means a register comprised of documents, notarial minutes and special minutes of extra-registry interventions, attached thereto by the Notary holding them in the course of the calendar year, by virtue of the law, regulation or resolution from a court or administrative authority; or, at the request of the person concerned, for the general purpose of conservation or reproduction:

(a) voluntary attachment of documents, which have not been requested within the scope of preparing a public deed or notarial minutes;

(b) certified photocopies and certificates not authorized by the Notary shall be chronologically annotated each month, in special minutes, by clearly indicating the number of the intervention, the name of the applicant, the date and the number of sheets of paper used, and making a summary of the matter or content thereof;

(c) the omission of any document entered in the special minutes mentioned above, failure to attach such minutes, or any change to the data contained therein, shall be punished according to the circumstances, under the terms of the law;

(d) notarial minutes are drafted and authorized following the procedure established for public deeds, insofar as they are consistent with such acts and are attached once the act has been finalized;

(e) the Document Register follows the terms applicable to the Docket, with the exception of the procedures inconsistent with its nature and composition.

2. The following minutes must be attached:

(a) minutes and protest proceedings;

(b) notarial minutes, whatever their nature;

(c) general or specific powers of attorney awarded

第二十四节 文件登记簿

1. 文件登记簿是指根据法律、法规或法院或行政机关决议，由文件、公证备忘录及额外登记干预的特别备忘录组成，由公证员在每个日历年度持有的登记簿；或出于保存或复制的目的，应当事人要求：

（a）准备公共契约或公证备忘录时不需要附录而自愿附录的文件；

（b）经公证的复印件和未经公证的证书，应按时间顺序在特别备忘录中备注，并清楚地注明介入的次数、申请人的姓名、所用文书的日期及页数以及相应的事项或内容的总结；

（c）遗漏上述特别备忘录记录的、未附录该备忘录或忽视其中数据变化的，应当根据具体情况，依照法律规定予以处罚；

（d）公证备忘录根据公共契约制定的程序起草和授权，只要其与该等行为具有一致性并且在行为最终确定后进行附录；

（e）除非其性质及组成不一致，备忘录适用文件登记簿的有关规定。

2. 必须附录下列备忘录：

（a）备忘录及反对程序；

（b）任何性质的公证备忘录；

（c）在本国使用之前或使用时于海外取得的一般

overseas, prior to or concurrently with their use in the country;

(d) all other documents the attachment of which to the Document Register is determined by law or regulation.

Section 25 Power of national authorities to order attachment of documents

Judges and administrative authorities may, within their remit, order the attachment of documents, when deemed convenient.

Section 26 Voluntary attachments

Voluntary attachment of documents may be requested by the person interested in having the document in question attached.

Section 27 Content of the Document Register

The Document Register is comprised of:

(a) public or private documents attached under the terms of the preceding sections;

(b) notarial minutes stating facts or things;

(c) minutes indicating a request made by the person concerned and its attachment to the Register.

Section 28 Attachment of documents written in a language other than either of the official ones

1. For the purpose of attaching a document written in a language other than either of the official ones of the Democratic Republic of Timor-Leste, such a document is required to be translated either by the Notary or a sworn translator licensed by the Ministry of Justice.

2. In the absence of a professional translator, the translation shall be made by two translators, who will appear before the Notary upon request for the attachment of the document and will sign the respective minutes, assuming responsibility for such a translation.

Section 29 Document Registration System

The entry system of the Document Register shall be regulated by an order of the Minister of Justice.

Section 30 Removal of attached documents

1. An attached document may not be removed without prior court order and prior endorsement by the Public Prosecution Service, and the removal thereof may only occur on grounds of a compelling need, in case of error or improper attachment of documents.

2. The procedure for removing documents shall be the object of regulatory arrangements approved by ministerial order.

或特殊授权委托书；

（d）法律或法规确定的应登记于文件登记簿的所有其他附录文件。

第二十五节　国家机关要求附录文件的权力

法官和行政机关可以在其职权范围内，在其认为适当的时间要求附录文件。

第二十六节　自愿附录

当事人可以申请登记尚在协商中的文件。

第二十七节　文件登记簿的内容

文件登记簿的内容包括：

（a）根据上述条款附录的公共或私人文件；

（b）陈述事实或其他事宜的公证备忘录；

（c）表明当事人请求的备忘录。

第二十八节　用非官方语言编写的附录文件

1. 登记使用东帝汶民主共和国任何一种官方语言以外的语言起草的附录文件，必须由公证员或司法部许可的，并宣誓过的翻译人员翻译成东帝汶民主共和国官方语言。

2. 若没有专业的翻译人员，公证员应要求附录文件前，由两名翻译人员翻译成东帝汶民主共和国官方语言，并签署相应的备忘录。上述翻译人员承担此次翻译的责任。

第二十九节　文件登记簿制度

文件登记簿记录制度应受司法部的监督。

第三十节　附录文件的删除

1. 未经法院的事先指令和公诉机关的事先批准，不得删除附录的文件；只有存在错误或附录文件不当，且有迫切需要的情况下才能删除附录文件。

2. 删除文件的程序由部长令确定。

CHAPTER IV Secrecy, conservation and storage of Notarial Records

第四章 公证记录的保密、保护和保存

Section 31 Confidentiality of Records

Notarial records are generally confidential and may only be examined by:

(a) judges and public prosecutors, in compliance with court decisions;

(b) notarialinspectorsinthecourseofextraordinaryvisitsandmandatoryinspections;

(c) the parties, their heirs or attorneys empowered to do so;

(d) officials authorised by the National Directorate of Registries and Notarial Services, and for the purpose of monitoring the payment of emoluments due.

第三十一节 记录的保密性

公证记录通常是保密的，只能通过以下方式查阅：

（a）法官和检察官依照法院判决查阅；

（b）公证检查员在特殊视察和强制检查过程中查阅；

（c）当事人、当事人的继承人或律师有权查阅；

（d）由国家登记和公证服务部授权的官员，出于监督到期薪酬支付之目的，可以检查。

Section 32 Exhibition of Records

Records are exhibited by the Notary himself or herself and such an exhibition shall only cover the relevant acts or parts thereof.

第三十二节 记录的公示

记录由公证员自行公示，且该等公示应仅涵盖记录中的相关行为或部分内容。

Section 33 Refusal to Exhibit

Where a Notary refuses to exhibit a record, the interested person may appeal to the National Director of Registries and Notarial Services, under the terms provided for by Regulation.

第三十三节 拒绝公示

如果公证员拒绝公示记录，利害关系人可以根据法规规定的条款向国家登记和公证服务部提出申诉。

Section 34 Conservation and Integrity of Records

A Notary is required to take all action necessary for the conservation and integrity of the records in his or her custody and is administratively and civilly liable, in the event of damage to individuals or to the State, without prejudice to any criminal action that might be filed.

第三十四节 记录的保全和完整性

公证员应采取一切必要措施，妥善保管记录并确保其完整。在不影响可能提起的任何刑事诉讼的情况下，公证员对个人或国家受到的损害承担行政责任和民事责任。

Section 35 Supervision of Notarial Archives

The Notarial Archives are under the supervision of the National Directorate of Registries and Notarial Services, through a specialised department called Office of the Inspector of Registries and Notarial Services, the organic structure and competencies of which shall be the object of a specific regulation.

第三十五节 公证档案的监督

公证档案由国家登记和公证服务部通过其下设的检查员办公室监督，国家登记和公证服务部门具体规定该部门的组成和职权。

Section 36 Listing Authorised Wills

1. A Notary shall refer to the Wills Registry the minutes of authorised wills, within three days of the date on which such wills have been authorised.

2. Such a listing shall only be submitted to the Wills Registry in relation to authorised wills and shall contain the following elements:

第三十六节 经公证遗嘱的列示

1. 公证员应在遗嘱公证之日起 3 日内向遗嘱登记处提交经公证遗嘱的备忘录。

2. 公证遗嘱备忘录仅需提交至遗嘱登记处，且应包括以下内容：

(a) nature of the act;

(b) full names, nationality, marital status, domicile and occupation of the grantor and, where feasible, the date and place of his or her birth;

(c) place and date of the grant;

(d) fullnameanddomicileoftheNotaryandofthewitnesses.

（a）行为的性质；

（b）被继承人的全名、国籍、婚姻状况、住所和职业，可以确定的话，还包括出生日期和地点；

（c）继承的地点和日期；

（d）公证员和见证人的全名和住所。

HEADING III NOTARIAL DOCUMENTS

第三部分 公证文件

CHAPTER I Public Deeds

第一章 公共契约

Section 37 Public Deed

1. A Public Deed is a notarial instrument whereby a legal business is entered in the Docket, under the terms established by law and after having been authorised by the Notary.

2. In addition to other acts specifically provided for by law, the following are performed by public deed:

(a) acts that require certification, establishment, acquisition, modification, sharing or abolition of rights of ownership, usufruct, use and housing, emphyteusis and superficies, or of servitude over immovable property;

(b) acts that require the revocation, rectification or change of businesses that, by virtue of the law or at the discretion of the parties, have been performed by public deed;

(c) acts to constitute, modify or dissolve a voluntary mortgage or antichresis, and to determine or change the amount of monthly food supplies, when such acts encumber immovable property;

(d) acts to dispose of or repudiate inheritances or legacies, provided that these form part of immovable property;

(e) cession of a mortgage or of the degree of priority of its registration, cancellation of a mortgage bond and cession or pledge of mortgage credits;

(f) dealings for the transfer of ownership of commercial or industrial establishments;

(g) perpetual leases, or life leases where the item or right disposed of is over real property;

(h) notarial qualification;

(i) sharing of real property or sharing of stock of companies forming part of real property.

第三十七节 公共契约

1. 公共契约是根据法律规定，经公证员公证后，将法律事务记录在备忘录中的一种公证文书。

2. 除了法律明确规定的其他行为外，以下行为均应签订公共契约：

（a）需要公证、设立、取得、变更、共有或废除所有权、用益权、使用权和住房权、永佃权和地上权，或不动产地役权的行为；

（b）由法律规定或当事人自行决定，通过签订公共契约执行需要撤销、更正或变更事务的行为；

（c）设立、变更或解除自愿抵押或不动产抵押的行为，以及在该行为妨碍不动产时确定或改变每月物品供应量的行为；

（d）遗产包括不动产的一部分时，处置或放弃继承权或遗产的行为；

（e）转让抵押或经登记的优先权，放弃抵押债券以及转让或质押抵押贷款；

（f）商业或工业设施所有权转让；

（g）永久租赁或终生租赁的标的物或权利超出不动产自身的范畴；

（h）公证资格；

（i）不动产的共有或构成不动产一部分的公司股票的分享。

Section 38 Drafting Public Deeds

1. Public deeds are drafted in Portuguese and in a clear and precise manner.

第三十八节 起草公共契约

1. 公共契约应使用葡萄牙语，以明确具体的方式起草。

2. A Notary may translate a deed into Tetum, if requested by the interested parties to do so, and enter it in the Docket, by following the same procedure, and mention shall be made of the faithfulness of such a translation.

Section 39 Translation services

Where a public deed is issued by a person who does not know the Portuguese language, a sworn translator shall assist him or her, under the terms of section 28, no translator being used where the Notary knows the language of both parties.

Section 40 Numbering deeds

Deeds shall be numbered in sequential order and shall be titled.

Section 41 Faulty and void deeds

1. A faulty deed may have no title and, where it does, the number thereof is repeated in the immediately subsequent deed.

2. A void deed is titled and the number thereof is not repeated in the immediately subsequent deed.

3. A faulty deed is that which is not fully drafted and is rendered null by writing the term "FAULTY" therein; the Notary shall not sign such a deed, and no emoluments shall be levied on it.

4. A void deed is that which has been fully drafted by the Notary and which neither the parties nor the Notary has signed it, with a mention being made, nevertheless, that such a deed has been rendered void and that the applicants shall pay emoluments at the discretion of the Notary.

Section 42 Basic Information of a Public Deed

Any public deed shall contain:

(a) the place and date of drafting;

(b) full name of the grantor and of witnesses, where applicable, as well as other names by which the person is known in his or her private life and his or her ID number;

(c) nationality, marital status, age, full domicile, with a detailed mention thereof, of any person who appears in the deed, either as a grantor or witness or legal or voluntary representative;

(d) where the grantor is married, widowed or divorced the matrimonial property regime and full name of the spouse are mentioned;

(e) the identifying elements of the grantors, witnesses and grantees relate to the statements made by them before the Notary and the formers are liable for the veracity of such statements.

2. 如利害关系人提出要求，公证员可以将契约翻译为德顿语，并按照同样的程序将其记录在备忘录中，并注明翻译的准确性。

第三十九节　翻译服务

如果公共契约由不懂葡萄牙语的人士出具，经宣誓的翻译人员应根据第二十八节的规定对其提供帮助，如果公证员通晓当事人使用的语言，则不使用翻译人员。

第四十节　契约编号

公共契约应按顺序编号，并且应有标题。

第四十一节　有瑕疵的和无效的契约

1. 有瑕疵的契约可能没有标题，如果确实如此，有瑕疵契约的编号会在随后的契约上重复使用。

2. 无效的契约有标题并且标题的编号不会在随后的契约中重复使用。

3. 有瑕疵的契约是指没有完成并且通过在契约中写明“有瑕疵”而使其无效；公证员不得签署此类契约且不得对其收取任何酬金。

4. 无效契约是指由公证员起草完成，曾被视作有效契约，但当事人和公证员都没有签署，在契约中有关于该契约无效的说明，申请人应根据公证员的自由裁量支付酬金。

第四十二节　公共契约的基本信息

在公共契约中应包含以下信息：

（a）起草的地点和日期；

（b）出让人和见证人的全名，如有可能，还包括授予人和见证人在私生活中使用的其他姓名及其身份证号码；

（c）契约相关人（无论是出让人、见证人，还是法定代表人、委托代表人）的国籍、婚姻状况、年龄、具体住所以及契约中具体提及的内容；

（d）如果出让人已婚、丧偶或离婚，应说明婚姻财产制度和配偶的全名；

（e）出让人、见证人和受让人在见证人的见证下陈述情况时，应当提供与此次陈述相关的身份证明，并对陈述的真实性负责。

Section 43 Reading, Granting, Signing and Authorisation of Public Deeds

The Notarial Regulation shall regulate:

(a) the form that the reading, granting, signing or authorisation of public deeds should take on;

(b) how to move to the following page;

(c) where witnesses knowing the identity of the parties or acting as subscribing witnesses shall intervene in cases where the grantors are speaking or hearing-impaired persons, do not know how to sign their name, or are blind, and the characteristics that witnesses shall have;

(d) the clauses that the Notary may add to a deed after drafting or before signing;

(e) the reading, granting and signing of a deed shall, in principle, be done in a single act,except where otherwise provided for by the regulation.

第四十三节 查阅、授予、签署及公证公共契约

公证法规应规定下列事项：

（a）查阅、授予、签署和公证公共契约应采取的形式；

（b）如何转至下一页；

（c）如果见证人知道当事人的身份，或作为签署证人时，应在出让人具有表达障碍或听力障碍，不知如何签名，或出让人失明的情况下干预公共契约的签署，并且见证人应该不具有上述情况，见证人不得有上述身体缺陷或疾病；

（d）公证员可能在起草后或签署前在契约中增加的条款；

（e）原则上，查阅、授予和签署公共契约应单独进行，但法规另有规定的情况除外。

Section 44 Attesting witness

Where the Notary knows the grantors, he or she attests to that fact in the deed and where he or she does not know the grantors, he or she crosschecks the identity of the grantors against a statement made by the attesting witnesses who shall sign the deed.

第四十四节 证明见证人

如公证员了解出让人，应在契约中证明此事实；如果公证员不了解出让人，公证员应反复核实出让人的身份，确保签署契约的公证见证人的陈述的真实性。

Section 45 Witnesses

1. The Regulation shall establish the characteristics that both subscribing and attesting witnesses shall be required to have. Subscribing witnesses may only intervene in the following cases:

(a) open solemn wills;

(b) where any of the grantors does not know or is not able to sign, is blind, or uses a script other than Roman characters;

(c) where one of the grantors so requires;

(d) whenever the Notary deems it convenient.

2. The notarial regulation shall establish the conditions to be met by attesting or subscribing witnesses.

第四十五节 见证人

1. 法规应规定担任签署见证人和证明见证人的资格。签署见证人只能介入以下案件：

（a）设立遗嘱；

（b）出让人不知道或不能签名，或因失明或使用罗马字母以外的文本不能签名；

（c）任一出让人要求见证人介入；

（d）公证员认为合适的情况。

2. 公证法规应规定证明见证人和签署见证人应符合的条件。

CHPATER II Notarial Minutes

第二章 公证备忘录

Section 46 Notarial Minutes

A Notary shall authorise minutes in which facts or items witnessed by him or her or statements made in his or her presence are recorded, following the procedure established for public deeds, to the extent consistent with the nature of such acts and without prejudice to the modifications provided for in the section below.

第四十六节 公证备忘录

公证员应当在公证备忘录中记录其见证的事实或事项以及公证活动中的其他主体在其见证下作出的陈述。制作公证备忘录应符合公共契约的有关程序，且不妨碍下述章节中有关修改公证备忘录的规定。

Section 47 Drafting Notarial Minutes

The following principles shall be taken into account in drafting notarial minutes:

(a) to authenticate the identity of the persons signing the minutes, the ID card number is exhibited, and attesting witnesses may be waived, whenever such witnesses are not expressly required by law;

(b) the intervention of subscribing witnesses is not required, except where the declarant does not know how to sign or is not able to do it, or is blind, in which case the signature shall be affixed by one of the witnesses at the request of the declarant. Subscribing witnesses may intervene where the Notary, the declarant or the law so determines;

(c) a single act or the same context is not required;

(d) In the absence of legal impediment, the entry of the minutes in the docket is recommended.

第四十七节　起草公证备忘录

制作公证备忘录的原则：

（a）核实公证备忘录签署人的身份，并要求其出示身份证号，除非法律没有明确要求，证明见证人方可免除此项义务。

（b）除非声明人不知道如何签署或者无法签署，或者失明，否则不需要签署见证人的介入，在此情况下，应根据声明人的要求附录一名见证人的签名。签署见证人可在公证员、声明人或法律要求或确定的情况下介入。

（c）不需要以单独的行为进行或具有相同的内容。

（d）在没有法律障碍的情况下，建议在第二部分第二章第十九节定义的备忘录中记录本章规定的公证备忘录。

Section 48 Purpose of Notarial Minutes

1. The purpose of the minutes shall be:

(a) to notify or apply for, at the request of one of the parties or by legal or judicial determination;

(b) to list extra-registry interventions, with the aim of recompiling the key data of notarial acts, in case of issuance of notarial attestations by exhibition, minutes of sealed wills, or notarial certificates;

(c) minutes of attachment of voluntary documents, of public or private documents;

(d) to verify, with the aim of crosschecking facts occurred or situations recorded or witnessed by himself or herself;

(e) to obligatorily attach documents, by legal determination.

2. The Regulation shall establish the format such minutes shall have.

第四十八节　公证备忘录的目的

1. 备忘录的目的应为：

（a）根据当事人一方的请求或依据法律或司法判决通知或申请；

（b）为重新编制公证行为的关键数据，列明登记处管理之外的干预措施，以便通过公示、密封遗嘱备忘录或公证书的方式发布公证证明；

（c）附录自愿文件、公共或私人文件的备忘录；

（d）基于反复检查其记录或见证已发生事实或情况的目的进行核验；

（e）通过法律决定强制性附录文件。

2. 法规应规定公证备忘录的格式。

Section 49 Minutes for attaching documents

1. Minutes in which the attachment of a document is recorded shall contain:

(a) the title, specifying the corresponding attachment number in the document register;

(b) the place and date on which a document is attached;

(c) the nature of the minutes, where obligatory, indicating the legal provision; where judicial or administrative, stating the determination that imposes it and the document from which they were transcribed; where voluntary, mak-

第四十九节　附录文件备忘录

1. 记录文件附件的备忘录应包括：

（a）文件的标题，并注明在文件登记簿上相应的编号；

（b）附录文件的地点和日期；

（c）备忘录的性质，如果是强制性的，注明相应的法律规定；如果是司法性或行政性的，说明其中附录的决定及其文件来源；如果是自愿性的，提及利害关系人的要求；

ing mention of the interested party's request;

(d) the enumeration of documents being attached to register;

(e) the sheets occupied by the attachment;

(f) a reference to the previous one;

(g) the signature, initials and stamp of the Notary.

2. The application and the attachment proper, with the contents and procedures as established by the regulation and this decree-law, may be recorded in the same minutes.

（d）附录在登记簿上的文件的详情；

（e）附件使用的表格；

（f）对前一个备忘录的引用；

（g）公证员的签名、姓名缩写和印章。

2. 可以在同一份备忘录中记录适当的申请和附件以及法规和本法令规定的内容和程序。

CHAPTER III Copies, attestations and certificates

第三章 副本、证明和证书

Section 50 First copy of public deeds and attestations

1. A Notary shall deliver to the parties, whatever the nature of the act, a copy of the public deed or attestation of the attachment effected.

2. The delivery shall be effected within three days after the date of signature of the deed or of the entry thereof in the docket.

3. The fulfilment of the obligation to issue a first copy or attestation is not subject to a request from the parties.

4. The copy or attestation to be issued, under the terms of this section, is the one required to be entered at the Public Registries and shall be issued to the party benefiting from the entry thereof.

5. The other party(ies) may, at all times, request a copy of the deed or attestation of attachment to the document register.

第五十节 公共契约和证明的第一份副本

1. 无论行为的性质如何，公证员均应向当事人提供公共契约的副本或生效附件的证明。

2. 应在契约签署之日或记录于备忘录之日起 3 日内向当事人交付。

3. 履行出具第一份副本或证明的义务不受当事人要求的约束。

4. 根据本条款出具的副本或证明应在公共登记处登记，并应交付给此次登记中受益的当事人。

5. 其他当事人可能随时要求提供文件登记簿上的契约或附件证明的副本。

Section 51 Procedures for issuing copies

The notarial regulation shall establish the procedure and relevance for the issuance of copies, as well as the regulatory arrangements in case of loss of the first copy of the deed or attestation of attachment to the document register.

第五十一节 出具副本的程序

公证法规应规定出具副本的程序和相关要求，以及在第一份文件登记簿上的契约的副本或附件的证明丢失情况下的监督安排。

Section 52 Marginal Notes

1. A Notary shall take note of the copies and attestations he or she issues, upon the issuance thereof.

2. The note shall be written into the margin of the original deed or attachment that corresponds to the copy or attestation.

3. The notarial regulation arising out of this law shall establish the format and the contents of the marginal note.

第五十二节 旁注

1. 公证员在出具副本或证明时应在其出具的副本或证明上进行注释。

2. 公证员应在副本原件的页边空白处书写注释。

3. 基于本法制定的公证法规应规定旁注的形式和内容。

Section 53 Attestations by exhibition

1. In addition to the attestations referred to in the preceding sections, a Notary may issue an attestation by

第五十三节 公示证明

1. 除了上文各节所述的证明外，公证员还可以应利害关系人的要求，通过公示公共或私人文件的方

exhibition of a public or private document, at the request of the interested party and with the aim of certifying the existence, nature or contents of the document reproduced, and such does not imply superseding it in regard to its validity and effects.

2. In the authenticated photocopy, which is a document reproduced by using a photographic, electrostatic or similar procedure, is stated its compliance with the attestation by exhibition and not by certification.

式出具证明，证明所复制文件确实存在及其性质或内容，但这并不意味着副本在有效性和效力方面可以取代原文件。

2. 在经过公证的复印件（使用摄影、静电或类似程序复制的文件）中表明其符合通过公示进行证明而非通过公证的方式。

Section 54 Format and contents of attestation by exhibition

The notarial regulation shall establish the format and contents of the attestation by exhibition.

第五十四节 公示证明的形式和内容

公证法规应规定公示证明的形式和内容。

Section 55 The Object of Certificates

A Notary may issue a certificate the object of which is:

(a) to declare the existence of a legal situation, act or fact, known to the Notary or proved by the latter through the exhibition of a public or private document;

(b) to certify a signature affixed to a private document issued and signed in his or her presence.

第五十五节 公证书的对象

公证员可以出具公证书，公证书的对象为：

（a）公布公证员知悉的法律情况、法律行为或法律事实的存在，或由公证员通过公示公共或私人文件证明的法律情况、法律行为或法律事实。

（b）证明在公证员见证下出具和签署的私人文件上的签名。

Section 56 Elements of a Certificate

In the cases referred to in paragraph (a) of the preceding section, the Notary shall make a clear and precise list of the following elements:

(a) act or fact that is the object of the certificate;

(b) public or private document from which such an act or fact results, the date, the nature and its characteristics;

(c) the exhibition of the said documents or the personal perusal thereof, indicating, in thiscase, the registry or place where he or she perused them;

(d) where the Notary personally knows the certified act or fact, he or she shall mention this fact, assuming responsibility for its existence and compliance.

第五十六节 公证书的要件

在第五十五节（a）段所述的情况下，公证员应清楚准确地列示以下要素：

（a）公证书公证的行为或事实；

（b）与上述行为或事实相关的公共或私人文件的日期、性质及其特征；

（c）在上述文件的公示或个人查阅时，注明公示或查阅的登记处或地点；

（d）公证员了解经公证的行为或事实，其应提及这一事实，并对该等行为或事实的存在及合规性承担责任。

Section 57 Requirements for a Certificate

1. In the cases provided for in subsection 55(b) , the Notary shall meet the following requirements:

(a) a grantor applying for the authentication of his or her signature shall identify himself or herself through all his or her particulars;

(b) a grantor is identified either by personal knowledge or by attesting witnesses;

(c) the Notary shall read out the document to the grantor, and shall receive a confirmationthat it has been

第五十七节 证书的要求

1. 在第五十五节（b）段规定的情况下，公证员应符合下列要求：

（a）出让人申请公证自己的签名时，应通过其所有资料表明身份。

（b）公证员是通过个人了解或证明见证人确定出让人身份的。

（c）公证员应向出让人宣读文件，并应接受已经出具文件的确认书。

issued;

(d) a grantor shall sign the document in the presence of the Notary, at the same moment as the act is performed; where he or she has already signed it, he or she will acknowledge the signature affixed to the document as his or her own and shall subscribe a certificate drafted by the Notary indicating the reason for doing so;

(e) where a grantor does not know how to sign or is not able to sign, he or she shall declare it in the presence of the witnesses and shall request one of the witnesses to sign.

2. The witness shall sign the document stating that he or she is doing it at the request of the impaired grantor; and such a statement is written before the signature that acts in this two-fold capacity.

3. The Notary may require the grantor to affix to the document, in the space reserved for signatures, his or her right-hand thumbprint or, in the absence of his or her right-hand thumb, his or her left-hand thumbprint.

4. The certification of the signature of a person who has not expressly applied for such a notarial intervention shall be forbidden.

Section 58 Contents of a Certificate

Any notarial certificate shall include:

(a) the full name of the person who has requested its issuance, where these particulars do not result from the very certification modality, in conformity with the preceding sections;

(b) the Notary may require that an official identity document, national or foreign, proving the identity of the applicant, be exhibited;

(c) the requirements, particulars and proofs as established in the preceding sections in order to clearly demonstrate compliance with said sections;

(d) the mentions required by law or regulation, depending on the intervention applied for;

(e) the place and date of issuance of the certificate, the stamp and signature of the Notary.

HEADING IV MANAGAMENT AND DISPCIPLINE OF NOTARIAL SERVICES

CHPATER I Management

Section 59 Supervision of the Notarial Services

It is exclusively incumbent upon the National Directorate of Registries and Notarial Services to supervise

（d）被继承人应在公证员的见证下，在履行行为的同时签署文件；在出让人已经签署的文件上，出让人承认签名是自己的，应签署公证员起草的公证书以说明其这样做的原因。

（e）被继承人不知道如何签字或无法签字的，应在见证人见证下作出声明，并且应要求其中一位见证人签字。

2. 见证人应在受损害的出让人要求的情况下签署说明其证明的文件，此说明是在以该等双重身份行事的签名之前书写的。

3. 公证员可要求出让人在文件为签名预留的空白处按右手拇指手印，没有右手拇指的，按左手拇指手印。

4. 对于未明确申请公证介入人士的签名的证书应予以禁止。

第五十八节　公证书的内容

公证书中应包含以下内容：

（a）申请人的全名，若这些要求不是由证书方式产生的，则应符合上文章节的规定；

（b）公证员可以要求申请人出示证明其身份的国家或外国官方证明文件；

（c）上述各章节规定的要求、具体内容和证明，以便清楚证明公证书符合上述章节；

（d）根据申请人申请的公证干预类型，具备法律或法规要求提及的内容；

（e）出具公证书的地点和日期，以及公证员的印章和签名。

第四部分　公证服务部门的管理和纪律

第一章　管理

第五十九节　对公证机构的监督

国家登记和公证服务部通过对公证活动的监控、处罚和调控，全权负责对公证服务的监督。

the notarial services, through the exercise of monitoring, disciplinary and regulatory powers over notarial practice.

CHAPTER II Visit to Notarial Services

Section 60 Exposure of Notarial Registers

A Notary has the obligation to make the Dockets or Document Registers available to the Office of the Inspector of Registries and Notarial Services, wherever the registry is located.

Section 61 Annual Visit

1. The annual visit shall take place within the first two months of the year.

2. The Office of the Inspector of Registries and Notarial Services may attend without the need for a written notification, after prior consultation with the Department of Administration, Finance and Logistics, National Directorate of Registries and Notarial Services, to make sure that emoluments are levied and paid in the prescribed manner.

Section 62 Extraordinary visit

1. The Office of the Inspector of Registries and Notarial Services may, at all times, and without a need for justification, require the production of all or part of the notarial records.

2. The attendance shall be by an official designated by the National Directorate of Registries and Notarial Services, to act as the Inspector of Registries and Notarial Services.

Section 63 Officials empowered to pay the visit

The officials of the Office of the Inspector of Registries and Notarial Services empowered to pay such visits shall enter into the last sheet of each notebook of the Docket and of the Document Register a note of revision containing:

(a) the term 'VISITED';

(b) the day, the month and the year when the visit was paid;

(c) the signature or endorsement by the visiting official.

CHPATER III On the discipline of notaries

Section 64 Competency

1. It is incumbent upon the National Directorate of Registries and Notarial Services to enforce the code of

第二章 对公证机构的检查

第六十节 公证登记簿的公开

无论登记处位于何地，公证员有义务向登记和公证服务部门检查员办公室提供备忘录或文件登记簿。

第六十一节 年度检查

1. 年度检查应在每年的前两个月进行。

2. 在事先与行政、财政和后勤部门以及国家登记和公证服务部协商后，登记和公证服务部门检查员办公室可以在没有书面通知的情况下检查公证员的工作，以确保按规定的方式收取和支付酬金。

第六十二节 特别检查

1. 登记和公证服务部门检查员办公室无须特别理由，可随时要求公证员提供全部或部分公证记录。

2. 应由国家登记和公证服务部官方指定的登记和公证服务检查员检查。

第六十三节 授权参加检查的官员

授权检查的国家登记和公证服务部检查办公室的官员应在备忘录和文件登记簿的最后一页制作一份修订说明，其中包括：

（a）“检查”字样；

（b）检查的年、月、日；

（c）检查官员的签名或认可。

第三章 关于公证员的纪律

第六十四节 能力

1. 国家登记和公证服务部有权按照本章和适用于公务人员的其他法律，执行公证员纪律守则。

discipline of notaries, in conformity with this Chapter and with all other legislation applicable to civil servants.

2. The National Directorate of Registries and Notarial Services may, to that effect, appoint a disciplinary committee.

Section 65 Disciplinary Proceeding

The code of discipline applicable to officials of the National Directorate of Registries and Notarial Services shall be the same as the one applicable to all other civil servants, without prejudice to civil or criminal liability.

HEADING V SPECIAL DEEDS

Section 66 Qualification of heirs

1. Qualification of heirs may be sought through a Notary.

2. Qualification of heirs may not be sought through a Notary where one of the heirs is underage.

Section 67 Qualifying Deed

1. Notarial qualification consists of a statement made in a public deed by three persons the Notary deems trustworthy, attesting that the applicants are heirs of the deceased and that no one else takes precedence over, or competes with, them in the succession.

2. The statement shall indicate the full name, marital status, place of birth and the previous habitual residency of the person bequeathing the inheritance and of the applicants.

Section 68 Admissible Declarants

For the purposes of the preceding section, persons disqualified as witnesses, relatives that may succeed the applicants, or a spouse of either of the former, do not qualify as declarants.

Section 69 Attachments

The following documents shall be attached to a qualifying deed:

(a) death certificate of the person bequeathing the inheritance;

(b) documents proving the legitimate succession, where such succession is based on the capacity of any of the applicants as an inheritor;

(c) certificate of the full record of the will or bequest deed, even if the succession is not based on any of such acts.

2. 基于上述目的，国家登记和公证服务部可以组建一个纪律委员会。

第六十五节　纪律处分

国家登记和公证服务部官员与其他公务人员适用相同的纪律守则，对公证员给予纪律处分不影响其承担民事或刑事责任。

第五部分　特殊契约

第六十六节　继承人资格

1. 继承人可以通过公证员公证取得继承人资格。

2. 未成年的继承人不能通过公证员公证取得继承人资格。

第六十七节　合格契约

1. 具有公证资格的公共契约应当包括一份声明，此声明由三位公证员认为值得信赖的人作出，用以证明申请人是死者的继承人，并且没有其他继承顺位在先或相同的人。

2. 上述声明应说明遗产继承人和申请人的姓名、婚姻状况、出生地和曾经的经常居住地。

第六十八节　合格的声明人

为实现前述章节的目的，被取消见证人资格的人，可能继承该申请人资格的亲属及上述两类人的配偶，不得担任声明人。

第六十九节　附件

合格契约包括下列文件：

（a）被继承人的死亡证明；

（b）证明继承合法性的文件，证明继承是基于申请人具有继承人的能力；

（c）包括遗嘱或遗赠契约完整记录的证书，即使继承不是基于此类行为发生的。

Section 70 Effects

1. Notarial qualification has the same effects as judicial qualification and is a title in and of itself allowing that the following acts be collectively performed, on behalf of all heirs and of the surviving spouse:

(a) entering records at the real estate registration office;

(b) entering records at the company registration office and at the vehicle registration office;

(c) recording securities;

(d) recording the transfer of copyright in literary, scientific, artistic or industrial work;

(e) withdrawing money or other values.

2. The acts referred to in paragraphs (a) to (d) of subsection 1 above may be applied for by any of the qualified heirs or by the surviving spouse.

第七十节 效力

1. 公证资格与司法资格一样具有相同的效力，具有公证资格的继承人意味着允许代表所有继承人及其在世配偶共同履行下列行为：

（a）在房地产登记处登记；

（b）在公司登记处和车辆登记处登记；

（c）登记有价证券；

（d）登记文学、科学、艺术或工业作品的版权转让；

（e）收回现金或其他有价物。

2. 第 1 小节（a）段至（d）段所述的行为可由合资格的继承人或在世的配偶申请。

Section 71 Challenge

In addition to initiating legal action under the terms of the civil procedure law, an unqualified heir who wishes to challenge a notarial qualification shall request the court to immediately notify the relevant registry of the pendency of the case.

第七十一节 申诉

除根据民事诉讼法的有关条款提起诉讼外，对公证资格提起申诉的非合格继承人应请求法院立即通知相关登记处相关案件尚未判决。

Section 72 Qualification of Legatees

The provisions of the preceding sections shall apply, mutatis mutandis, to the qualification of legatees, where such legatees are unspecified or generically designated, or where the inheritance is all left as legacies.

第七十二节 受遗赠人资格

如果未确定或一般指定该等受遗赠人，或遗产全部留作遗赠财产的，上述章节的规定在经过必要的修正后适用于受遗赠人资格。

HEADING VI REBUTTALS AND APPEALS

第六部分 反驳与上诉

CHAPTER ION REBUTTALS AND APPEALS

第一章 关于反驳与上诉

Section 73 Refusal to Perform an Act

1. The Notary shall refuse to perform an act that he or she is required to perform by law, in the following cases:

(a) where the act is null;

(b) where the act does not fall within his or her competencies or where he or she is personally unable to perform it;

(c) where he or she has doubts that any of the intervening parties is in full possession of his or her mental faculties;

(d) where the parties have not made the required preparations.

2. Doubts about any of the intervening parties' being in full possession of all his or her mental faculties cease to

第七十三节 拒绝执行某一行为

1. 在下列情况下，公证员应拒绝履行法律要求其履行的行为：

（a）此行为无效；

（b）此行为不属于其能力范围或公证员无法履行；

（c）公证员怀疑当事人丧失心智；

（d）当事人尚未做好必要的准备。

2. 当事人能提出证明其心智正常的医疗文件，公证员不得以怀疑当事人丧失心智为由拒绝公证。

be a ground for refusal where a medical document attesting to the mental health of the parties is attach to the act.

3. In the case of a will, the absence of preparation does not constitute a ground for refusal.

4. The intervention of the Notary may not be refused on grounds of the act being voidable or ineffective.

5. In the cases contemplated in subsection (4) above, the Notary shall warn the parties of the existence of a defect and shall record in the act any warning he or she may have given.

3. 对于遗嘱而言，缺少准备并不构成公证员拒绝的理由。

4. 公证员的干预不得因该行为的无效而被拒绝。

5. 在第 4 款所述的情况下，公证员应提醒当事人存在瑕疵，并记录自己提醒的内容。

CHAPTER II Appeals

第二章 上诉

Section 74 Appeals

1. Where the Notary refuses to perform an act, the person concerned may appeal to the National Director of Registries and Notarial Services.

2. The person concerned may, acting in his or her discretion, lodge an appeal with the competent court.

第七十四节 上诉

1. 如果公证员拒绝公证的，利害关系人可以向国家登记和公证服务部负责人提出上诉。

2. 利害关系人可以自行决定向有管辖权的法院提出上诉。

Section 75 Refused Act the Performance of Which is Determined on Appeal

A refused act the performance of which is determined on appeal shall be effected by the respondent Notary pursuant to the decision rendered, as soon as the parties so request.

第七十五节 执行上诉决定

被上诉的公证员应执行国家登记和公证服务部负责人的决定。

HEADING VII FINAL AND TRANSITIONAL PROVISIONS

第七部分 最后条款和生效条款

CHAPTER ITransitional Provisions

第一章 生效条款

Section 76

The implementation of this decree-law shall begin on a date to be set by an order issued by the Minister of Justice, in accordance with a specific timeframe.

第七十六节

本法令自司法部长根据具体时间表确定的日期起实施。

CHAPTER II Final Provisions

第二章 最后条款

Section 77 Emoluments

Emoluments and charges to be levied by notaries shall be established by a joint order of the Ministry of Planning and Finance and of the Ministry of Justice, to be approved within 30 days.

第七十七节 酬金

公证员收取的酬金和费用应由规划财政部和司法部联合下发的指令规定，并在下达指令的 30 日内批准通过。

Section 78 Notarial Regulation

The Notarial Regulation shall be approved by order of the Minister of Justice within 30 days.

第七十八节 公证法规

公证法规应在 30 日内经司法部长批准。

Section 79 Entry into Force

This decree-law comes into force 30 days following the date of its publication.

Seen and approved by the Council of Ministers on 9 December 2003.

The Prime Minister
[Signed]
(Mari Bim Amude Alkatiri)

The Minister of Justice
[Signed]
(Domingos Maria Sarmento)

Promulgated on 22 January 2004.
To be published.

The President of the Republic
[Signed]
(Kay Rala Xanana Gusmão)

第七十九节　生效

本法令自公布之日起 30 日后生效。

2003 年 12 月 9 日由部长理事会审阅并批准。

总理
[签字]
（Mari Bim Amude Alkatiri）

司法部长
[签字]
（Domingos Maria Sarmento）

2004 年 1 月 22 日颁布。
待公布。

共和国总统
[签字]
（Kay Rala Xanana Gusmão）

格鲁吉亚

公证法

This law determines the legal basis of arrangement of the notariate and notarial activities as well as the basic requirements for execution of the notarial and other related activities.

本法确定了公证机构和公证活动的法律依据，以及执行公证和其他相关活动的基本要求。

Chapter I General Provisions

第一章　一般条款

Article 1. Notariate

1. Notariate is a public legal institution, the aim of which is to confirm legal relations between persons and juridical facts within the limits determined by the State.

2. State management of the notariate on the basis of Georgian legislation is performed by the Ministry of Justice of Georgia (hereinafter the Ministry of Justice).

第一条　公证机构

1. 公证机构是一个公共法律机构，其目的是在国家确定的范围内确认公民与司法事实之间的法律关系。

2. 格鲁吉亚司法部（下称“司法部”）依据格鲁吉亚法律对公证机构进行管理。

Article 2. Legal Basis of Notarial Activities

The Constitution of Georgia, this Law, international agreements and treaties of Georgia and other legislative and normative acts of Georgia shall constitute the legal basis for notarial activities.

第二条　公证活动的依据

格鲁吉亚宪法、本法、格鲁吉亚参与的国际协定和条约以及格鲁吉亚的其他法律和规范性文件构成公证活动的法律依据。

Article 3. Notary

1. A notary is free in its professional activities and exercises public authorities through notarial and other associated activities on the basis of this Law and other legal acts.

2. While performing its notary duties, a notary is independent and impartial.

3. Notary acts are performed in accordance with and within the scope of Georgian legislation. Notarial profession is not entrepreneurship and the source of profit.

4. Remuneration paid to a notary for his/her official activities belong only to him/her.

第三条　公证员

1. 公证员在其专业活动中是免费的，并依据本法和其他法律规定通过公证机构及其他相关机构行使公共权力。

2. 公证员独立且公正地履行公证员职责。

3. 公证依据格鲁吉亚法律并在其范围内进行。公证职业不是商业行为，不可以此盈利。

4. 为公务活动中向公证员支付的报酬仅属于他/她。

5. A notary is an employer for the employees of his/her notary office.

6. A notary is responsibility for any damage caused thereby during performing his/her official duties. The State shall not be responsible for the damage caused through any notary's fault.

7. Disciplinary liability against notaries shall be determined in special regulations to be approved by the Minister of Justice of Georgia (hereinafter the Minister of Justice) upon the recommendation of the Notary Chamber of Georgia.

8. A notary shall perform the duties specified by the Law of Georgia on Facilitating the Prevention of Illicit Income Legalization and relevant normative acts.

9. A notary is not a public servant.

Law of Georgia №3363, dated 6 July 2010 - Georgian Legislative Bulletin I, №40, 20.07.2010, art. 244

Article 4. Notary Chamber of Georgia and Other Notary Associations

1. The Notary Chamber of Georgia is an association of notaries formed on the principle of self-government and based on mandatory membership. Notaries may be the members of notary public associations on a voluntary basis.

2. The Notary Chamber of Georgia represents and protects the interests of notaries, assists them in their notarial activities, organizes the internships for candidate notaries, takes care of the capacity development of notaries.

3. The Notary Chamber of Georgia ensures the notaries' involvement in solving the problems related to the functioning of notariate and the implementation of common professional interests of notaries.

4. The supreme body of the Notary Chamber of Georgia is the General Meeting of the Members of the Notary Chamber of Georgia, while the executive and management body – the Board of the Notary Chamber of Georgia.

5. The Notary Chamber of Georgia is a legal entity of public law.

Article 5. Notarial Act

1. A notarial act is performed by a notary in the cases prescribed by this Law upon the request of an individual or legal entity and it has legal effect. Any notarized document has a true evidential force.

2. The procedure for performance of a notarial act shall be determined by the regulations to be approved by

5. 公证员是其公证机构雇员的雇主。

6. 公证员对履行公务期间造成的任何损害负责。国家不对任何公证员过错造成的损害负责。

7. 对公证员的约束责任应由格鲁吉亚司法部长根据格鲁吉亚公证协会的提议所批准的特别规定进行确定。

8. 公证员应履行格鲁吉亚禁止非法收入合法化法律和相关规范性文件规定的职责。

9. 公证员不是公务员。

2010 年 7 月 6 日，格鲁吉亚第 3363 号法令——格鲁吉亚立法公报 I，2010.7.20，第 40 版，第 244 条。

第四条　格鲁吉亚公证协会和其他组织

1. 格鲁吉亚公证协会是根据自治原则和强制会员资格组建的公证员协会。公证员可自愿成为公证协会会员。

2. 格鲁吉亚公证协会代表并保护公证员的利益，协助他们的公证活动，组织候选公证员的实习，关心公证员的职业发展。

3. 格鲁吉亚公证协会确保公证员参与解决与公证机构运作有关的问题和维护公证员共同的职业利益。

4. 格鲁吉亚公证协会的最高机构是格鲁吉亚公证协会会员大会，行政管理机构是格鲁吉亚公证协会董事会。

5. 格鲁吉亚公证协会是公法法人。

第五条　公证

1. 公证由公证员在个案中依据本法规定应自然人或法人的要求进行，具有法律效力。任何经过公证的文件都具有真实的证据效力。

2. 进行公证的程序应依据格鲁吉亚法律由司法部长根据格鲁吉亚公证协会的提议所批准的规定进行

the Minister of Justice upon the recommendation of the Notary Chamber of Georgia in the manner prescribed by the Georgian legislation.

确定。

Article 6. Language of Notarial Acts

1. Notarial acts shall be performed in the official language of the country.

2. If the person requesting a notarial act does not speak the national language, the notary shall perform the notarial act with the help of an interpreter.

第六条 公证语言

1. 公证应以国家通用的语言进行。

2. 如果公证申请人不使用国家通用的语言的，公证员应在翻译员的协助下进行公证。

Article 7. Legal Dispute Arising in the Performance of the Notarial Act

Any legal dispute that arises between the parties during the performance of any notarial act shall be resolved through the court.

第七条 公证活动产生的法律纠纷

申请人在进行公证的过程中产生的任何法律纠纷，应通过法院解决。

Article 8. Confidentiality of Notarial Acts

1. Unless otherwise stated in this article, a notary shall keep confidential the information that became known thereto in connection with his/her official activities. This obligation shall remain in force after the dismissal of any notary.

2. A notary may give information about a notarial act only to the individual or legal entity at whose request or in relation to whom the notarial act has been performed or any representative thereof. At the request of investigation bodies or courts, a notary shall provide information of criminal and civil cases which are in the process of consideration by investigation bodies or courts. In case of appropriate request, a notary shall provide information to tax authorities about the value of the property transferred to a person. Tax authorities are prohibited to disclose such information to third persons, including mass media, or to disclose such information at public speaking until the final judgement of court is delivered.

3. A notary may disclose the existence or content of any will only after the death of a testator.

4. Any person, at whose request the notarial act has been executed, or his/her successor or representative may release notary from the obligation of preserving the secrecy of notarial act based on written approval. If a person has deceased and he/she has no successor or it is impossible to contact the successor, the court may release notary from the obligation of preserving the secrecy of notarial act. The court may also release a notary from the obligation of preserving the secrecy of notarial acts for other reasonable excuses.

第八条 公证的保密性

1. 除本条另有规定外，公证员应对相关公务活动中获知的信息保密。该规定在公证员离职后仍有效力。

2. 公证员只能向要求公证或与进行公证、代理公证有关的自然人或法人提供公证信息。依调查机构或法院的要求，公证员应提供调查机构或法院正在审议的刑事和民事案件的信息。如要求合理，公证员应向税务机关提供向他人转让财产价值的信息。在法院作出最终判决前，税务机关不得向包括大众媒体在内的第三方披露此类信息，不得在公开演讲中披露此类信息。

3. 公证员只有在遗嘱人死亡后才可以披露遗嘱的存在或其内容。

4. 在公证申请人或其继承人或代理人书面批准的情况下，可免除公证员的公证保密义务。如申请人死亡且无继承人或无法联系继承人，法院可以免除公证员的公证保密义务。法院也可因其他合理事由免除公证员的公证保密义务。

5. A notary shall submit information on the deals foreseen by the Law of Georgia on Facilitating the Prevention of Illicit Income Legalization to the Financial Monitoring Service of Georgia in line with the procedure established by the same Law and relevant normative acts.

Law of Georgia №1732, dated December 11,2013 – website, 25.12.2013

Article 9. Notary's Right to Use the State Emblem

1. A notary has an official seal with an inscription of small state national emblem of Georgia. First and last names of a notary are set on the seal.

2. A notary is entitled to use the small state national emblem of Georgia on the signboards and printed forms.

Article 10. Supervision over Notary's Official Activities

1. A notary's official activities shall be supervised by the Ministry of Justice, which shall within the scope of its competence:

a. Control the compliance of a notary's activities with the Georgian legislation and the accuracy of having notarial fees paid for a notarial act;

b. Require from a notary all information and material being necessary for supervision;

c. Delegate the supervision authority to the Notary Chamber of Georgia on certain issues of a notary's official activities.

2. A notary may appeal the decisions of the Minister of Justice or the Notary Chamber of Georgia that are based on the supervision material to the court.

3. The Ministry of Justice shall make supervision over notaries in the manner prescribed by the Georgian Law on Facilitating the Prevention of Illicit Income Legalization and relevant normative acts.

Chapter II Notarial Service

Article 11. Terms and Conditions for Occupying the Post of Notary

1. Under this Law, the notary's position may be occupied by any capable Georgian citizen, who has a higher legal education, has undergone training or has at least one year length of service as a notary or at least 5 years length of service by his/her specialty in the public service and has passed a qualifying examination for notaries.

2. A person shall be released from the obligation of passing a qualifying examination for notaries, if he/she has

5. 公证员应以符合《格鲁吉亚防止禁止收入合法化法》和相关规范性文件规定的程序，向格鲁吉亚金融监管机构提交《格鲁吉亚防止禁止收入合法化法》中所规定的信息。

2013 年 12 月 11 日，格鲁吉亚第 1732 号法令——网页，2013.12.25。

第九条　公证员使用国徽的权利

1. 公证员拥有刻有格鲁吉亚小型国徽的官方印章。公证员的姓名也刻在印章上。

2. 公证员有权在公告牌和印制表格上使用格鲁吉亚小型国徽。

第十条　对公证员公务活动的监管

1. 司法部在其职权范围内对公证员的公务活动进行监管：

a. 针对公证活动对格鲁吉亚法律的遵守和公证费用支付的准确性进行管理；

b. 要求公证员提供监管所需的所有信息和材料；

c. 将与公证员公务活动有关的部分监管权授予格鲁吉亚公证协会。

2. 公证员可以就司法部长或格鲁吉亚公证协会根据监管材料作出的决定向法院提出上诉。

3. 司法部应依据《格鲁吉亚防止禁止收入合法化法》和相关规范性文件规定的方式对公证员进行监管。

第二章　公证业务

第十一条　担任公证员的条款和条件

1. 依据本法，公证员可由任何有能力的格鲁吉亚公民担任，他们有较高的法律教育背景，受过培训，或至少有 1 年的公证经验，或在公共领域有至少 5 年的公共服务经验并通过公证员资格考试。

2. 在民法、国际私法或民事诉讼法领域取得博士学位或同等学位的，可免于参加公证员资格考试。

a doctor's degree or equivalent degree specialized in Civil, International Private Law or Civil Procedural Law.

2.1. Newly appointed notary within first 3 years shall perform notarial activity in high altitude or such settlement, where notary services are not duly available. For the purpose of this Law, status of "high altitude settlement" shall be determined under the rules established by the Law of Georgia "on development of high mountainous regions".

2.1. 新就职的公证员在前 3 年内，应在高海拔或公证服务不便利的地区进行公证活动。依本法，"高海拔地区"应依据格鲁吉亚法律规定的《高山地区发展规则》确定。

2.2. List of settlements (including high mountainous settlements) where notary service is not duly available shall be determined by the Minister of Justice under the rule of par. 5 of Article 16 of the said Law.

2.2. 公证服务不便利的地区名录（包括高山区），由司法部长依据本法第 16 条第 5 款的规定确定。

2.3. A notary defined under par. 21 of this Article throughout the entire period of performing notarial activity in relevant settlement shall be provided by the financial aid by the Notary Chamber of Georgia. Rule of providing financial aid to the notary shall be defined by the Notary Chamber of Georgia upon agreement with the Minister of Justice.

2.3. 本条第 2.1 项规定的公证员在有关地区进行公证活动期间的费用应由格鲁吉亚公证协会提供支持。由格鲁吉亚公证协会与司法部长协商确定向公证员提供财政支持的规则。

2.4. After expiration of three-year term stated in par. 21 of this Article a notary may continue performing notarial activity at the same or any other settlement. If for the moment of continuing notarial activities by the notary such settlement is on the list stated in par. 22 of this Article, the notary shall be provided by due financial aid during the corresponding period by the Notary Chamber of Georgia, under the rule established by par. 23 of this Article.

2.4. 本条第 2.1 项规定的 3 年期限届满后，公证员可以继续在同一或任何其他地区进行公证活动。如果公证员继续进行公证活动的地区系本条第 2.2 项规定的地区，格鲁吉亚公证协会应依据本条第 2.3 项规定在相应期间向公证员提供相应的财政支持。

2.5 A notary who places his(her) office in the settlement foreseen by par. 21 of this Article, during the corresponding period of performing notarial activities shall be provided by due financial aid from the Notary Chamber of Georgia, under the rule established by par. 23 of this Article.

2.5. 办公场所位于本条第 2.2 项规定地区的公证员，在进行公证活动的相应期间，应由格鲁吉亚公证协会依据本条第 2.3 项规定提供相应的财政支持。

3. Age limit for occupying the notary's position shall align with the age limit in public service. Based on the proposal of the Notary Chamber, the Minister of Justice may extend a notary's term of office for no more than 5 years.

3. 公证员任期应与公职人员的任期相一致。司法部长可根据公证协会的提议将公证员任期延长，但不超过 5 年。

Georgian Law №4610, dated December 10, 2015 – website, 22.12.2015

2015 年 12 月 10 日，格鲁吉亚第 4610 号法令——网页，2015.12.22。

Article 12. Qualifying Examinations for Notaries

第十二条　公证员资格考试

1. A qualifying examination for notaries (testing) includes two stages – professional part and general skills (verbal and mathematical parts).

1. 公证员资格考试（测试）包括两个阶段——专业部分和一般技能（口头和数学部分）。

2. A person may be released from the obligation of

2. 如通过法律基础或民法和行政法的法官资格考

passing the professional part of qualifying examination if he/she has passed a qualifying examination for judges specialized in General or Civil and Administrative Laws, or has occupied a judge's position and no more than 2 years have passed since taking that examination/releasing from a judge's position to passing a qualifying examination for notaries, or if he/she is holding a judge's position.

试，或已担任法官职务且从法官到通过公证员资格考试不超过 2 年，或者担任法官职务，则可免于参加公证员资格考试。

3. Testing program for a qualifying examination for notaries shall be approved by the Minister of Justice.

3. 公证员资格考试的考核项目应由司法部长批准。

4. The procedure for conducting a qualifying examination, forming a qualifying examination committee and rules of its operation shall be determined by the regulations of the qualifying examination committee to be approved by the Minister of Justice of Georgia.

4. 组织资格考试的程序、资格考试委员会的组成及运作规则，应由格鲁吉亚司法部长批准的资格考试委员会条例确定。

5. Conduction of qualifying examination for notaries shall be provided by LEPL Training Centre of Justice of Georgia at the Ministry of Justice. A person shall pay 150 GEL in order to participate in the qualifying examination for notaries.

5. 公证员资格考试应由格鲁吉亚司法部 LEPL 训练中心组织。参加公证员资格考试须支付 150 拉里。

5.1. If a notary starts performing notarial activities in the settlement foreseen by par. 21 of Article 11 of this Law, the Notary Chamber of Georgia shall forthwith remunerate a fee being paid for participation in the qualifying examination for notaries.

5.1. 如果公证员在本法第 11 条第 2.1 项规定的地区进行公证活动，格鲁吉亚公证协会应立即支付其公证员资格考试费用。

6. Results of qualifying examination for notaries shall be void if a person having passed such examination fails to fulfil notarial activities during a two-year period. After expiration of this period, a person shall take the qualifying examination for notaries over again in order to hold a notary's position.

6. 通过公证员资格考试后 2 年内如未进行公证活动，则其公证员资格无效。2 年期满后应再次参加公证员资格考试，以取得公证员职位。

Article 13. Appointment to the Position of Notary

1. A notary is appointed to the position by the Minister of Justice. At appointing to the position the Minister of Justice shall indicate as a location of notary office the settlement foreseen by par. 21 of Article 11 of this Law.

2. Notary position may be occupied by any individual satisfying the requirements set forth in Paragraph 1 or 2 of Article 11 of this Law and having won a contest, the procedure and conditions of holding whereof shall be approved by the Minister of Justice.

3. The decision on rejection of appointing to the notary position may be appealed to the court in the manner prescribed by laws of Georgia.

第十三条　公证员职务的任命

1. 公证员职务由司法部长任命。司法部长在任命该职位时，应指定本法第 11 条第 2.1 项规定的地区作为其公证机构所在地。

2. 公证员职位可由符合本法第 11 条第 1 款或第 2 款规定条件且通过竞选的公民担任，任职程序和条件由司法部长批准。

3. 公证员可依据格鲁吉亚法律规定的方式就不予任命公证员职务的决定向法院提出上诉。

Article 14. Basis for Rejection of Appointment to the Position of Notary

A person shall not be appointed to the position of no-

第十四条　不予任命公证员职务的依据

以下人员不得被任命为公证员职务：

tary if he/she:

a) Fails to meet the requirements of Paragraph 1 or Paragraph 2 of Article 11 of this Law;

a.1) Fails to win the contest;

b) Has been convicted for committing a deliberate crime or criminal prosecution is pending against him/her for committing a deliberate crime;

b.1) Has been convicted for committing a crime immediately associated with notarial activities, notwithstanding the removal or cancellation of conviction;

c) Has been convicted for committing a deliberate crime but the criminal case against him/her terminated due to time limitation or amnesty;

d) Has been released from the public service and/or terminated the membership of the Georgian Bar Association due to disciplinary misdemeanour, grave and/or repeated breach of law, misuse of authority to the prejudice of justice and service interests or committing corruption offence (void the normative contents of par "d", banning the appointment of persons having been dismissed from public service for disciplinary misdemeanour on notary position with reference to Article 14 of the Constitution of Georgia);

e) Has been released from the notary position due to disciplinary misdemeanour;

f) Fails to meet the requirements set forth in Paragraph 1 of Article 20 of this Law;

g) Has been deprived of the right to conduct notarial activities under a conviction being enforced by the court;

h) If the notary positions are occupied for the year in question in accordance with the maximum number of notary positions determined by the Minister of Justice;

i) Denies to perform notary activities in the settlement foreseen by par. 2.1. of Article 11 of this Law.

Article 15. Application for Appointment to the Position of Notary

1. In order to occupy notary position, one shall submit an application to the Ministry of Justice together with the following documents:

a) Documents proving the circumstance foreseen by Paragraph 1 or Paragraph 2 of Article 11 of this Law;

b) Documents signed by an applicant, proving the existence of the circumstances foreseen by Article 14 of this Law;

c) (Deleted – 20.12.2011, №5573).

（a）不满足本法第 11 条第 1 款或第 2 款规定的条件；

（a.1）未通过选拔；

（b）因故意犯罪被判有罪或被提起刑事诉讼；

（b.1）因犯有与公证活动有关的罪行而被定罪，无论罪名被改变还是撤销；

（c）因故意犯罪被判有罪，但因时间限制或特赦而终止刑事诉讼；

（d）因违反纪律、严重和 / 或屡次违反法律、滥用权力损害司法和公共利益或犯贪污罪而被开除公职和 / 或被终止格鲁吉亚律师协会会员资格（d 项规范性内容的无效，禁止依据《格鲁吉亚宪法》第 14 条规定任命因违反公证员职务纪律被开除公职的人）；

（e）因违反纪律被开除公证员职务；

（f）不符合本法第 20 条第 1 款规定的条件；

（g）在法院执行有罪判决时被剥夺了进行公证活动的权利；

（h）依据司法部长确定的公证员职务的最大数量，该年度已无公证员职务；

（i）拒绝在本法第 11 条第 2.1. 项规定的地区进行公证活动。

第十五条　申请任命为公证员职务

1. 取得公证员职务应向司法部提交申请书及下列文件：

（a）符合本法第 11 条第 1 款或第 2 款规定条件的证明文件；

（b）申请人签署的符合本法第 14 条规定条件的证明文件；

（c）（2011 年 12 月 29 日根据第 5573 号法令删除）。

2. If the legal address of any notary office is changed, a notary shall immediately notify the Notary Chamber of Georgia thereof.

2. 公证机构住所地变更的，公证员应立即通知格鲁吉亚公证协会。

Article 16. Registration of Notary with the Notary Registry of Georgia and Commencement of Notarial Activities

第十六条 格鲁吉亚公证登记处公证员登记与公证活动开展

1. A notary shall within 2 months from appointment to the position submit to the Notary Chamber of Georgia:

a) Official seal and specimen signature certified in the manner prescribed by legislation;

b) Documents of compulsory professional liability insurance;

c) Document of possession/ownership of notary office equipped in accordance with the procedure prescribed by the Instructions for Notarial Acts Performance Procedure approved by the Order of the Minister of Justice.

1. 公证员应在被任命后 2 个月内向格鲁吉亚公证协会提交以下材料：

（a）以法律规定方式认证的正式印章和样本签名；

（b）强制性职业责任保险文件；

（c）依据司法部长命令批准的公证程序中应由公证机构占有 / 有所有权的文件。

2. After submitting all documents foreseen by Paragraph 1 of this Article, the Notary Chamber of Georgia shall immediately but no later than 5 business days register the notary with the Notary Registry of Georgia and grant the notary authority to access the electronic notary registry, and thereafter the notary is authorized to perform notarial activities.

2. 在提交本条第 1 款规定的所有文件后，格鲁吉亚公证协会应立即且不迟于 5 个工作日向格鲁吉亚公证登记处进行公证员登记，并授予公证员进行电子公证登记的权利，此后公证员即有权进行公证活动。

3. (Deleted – 22.05.2012, №6255).

4. The form and procedure for maintaining the Notary Registry of Georgia shall be determined by the Minister of Justice.

3.（2012 年 5 月 22 日依据第 6255 号法令删除）。

4. 格鲁吉亚公证登记处的形式和程序应由司法部长决定。

5. At the beginning of each year, no later than February 1, under appropriate order, the Minister of Justice shall fix the maximum number of notary positions (including those in high-altitude settlements, where the notary service is not duly available). Maximum number of notary positions shall not be less than the total number of the notaries being in office for the time of fixing.

5. 在每年年初，不迟于 2 月 1 日，在合理指令下，司法部长应确定公证员职务的最大数量（包括公证服务不便利的高海拔地区）。公证员职务的最大数量不得少于公证员在确定的时间内的总人数。

Article 17. Suspension of the Right of Notarial Activity

第十七条 公证员职务的中止

1. A notary's right of notarial activity shall be suspended if he/she:

(a) Has breached the requirement under Subparagraph "c" of Paragraph 1 of Article 16 of this Law. A notary shall, within reasonable term but no later than 10 days, ensure the compliance with the requirement under Subparagraph "c" of Paragraph 1 of Article 16 of this Law.

(b) Has committed misdemeanour foreseen by the Regulations on Disciplinary Liabilities of Notaries, entailing the suspension of right of notarial activity.

1. 如有以下情形，公证员公证员职务中止：

（a）违反本法第 16 条第 1 款第 c 项的规定。公证员应在合理期限但不晚于 10 日内确保遵守本法第 16 条第 1 款第 c 项的规定。

（b）违反公证员纪律条例的规定，致使公证员职务中止。

(c) Has been found guilty and criminal proceedings have been instituted against him/her - until passing final judgment on the criminal case.

2. If criminal proceedings have been instituted against a notary having been found guilty, the body conducting the criminal proceeding shall immediately but no later than the next business day notify the Notary Chamber of Georgia thereof.

3. The Notary Chamber of Georgia shall make relevant record on the suspension of the right of notarial activity in the Notary Registry. If the basis for suspension of the right of notarial activity has been removed, the Notary Chamber of Georgia shall revoke the relevant record, and thereafter the notary shall be authorized to proceed to the notarial activity.

Article 18. Dismissal of Notary

1. A notary's term of office shall cease if he/she has been dismissed.

2. Basis for the dismissal of a notary shall be as follows:

a) A notary's written application for resignation from the position to be submitted to the Minister of Justice;

b) Reaching the retirement age, save as the case foreseen by Paragraph 3 of Article 11 of this Law;

c) A notary's death, recognition by the court as lost without a trace, declared as deceased or recognition as handicapped/legally incapable;

d) Committing the misdemeanour foreseen by the Regulations on Disciplinary Liabilities of Notaries, entailing the suspension of right of notarial activity;

e) Notary's health status that excludes the due performance of official duties by him/her;

f) Enforcement of the verdict of "guilty" against a notary for committing a deliberate crime or ceasing of criminal case on committing a deliberate crime due to time limitation or amnesty;

g) Termination of citizenship of Georgia to a notary;

h) Depriving the right of notarial activity under the verdict of "guilty" having been enforced;

i) Performing the activities inconsistent with the notary position;

j) Failure to fulfil the requirements foreseen by Subparagraph "a" of Paragraph 1 of Article 17 of this Law within the established period;

k) Termination of notarial activities in certain settlement by the notary being appointed under the rule estab-

（c）被认定有罪并被提起刑事诉讼，直到刑事案件作出最终判决为止。

2. 如对被认定有罪的公证员提起刑事诉讼，提起刑事诉讼的机构应立即（不迟于下一个工作日内）通知格鲁吉亚公证协会。

3. 格鲁吉亚公证协会应在公证登记处就公证员职务中止进行登记。如公证员职务中止的事由不存在，格鲁吉亚公证协会应撤销登记，此后公证员有权继续进行公证活动。

第十八条　公证员的解雇

1. 如果公证员被解雇，其任期终止。

2. 解雇公证员的事由如下：

（a）公证员向司法部长提交书面辞职申请；

（b）依据本法第 11 条第 3 款的规定达到退休年龄；

（c）公证员死亡、被法院宣告失踪、宣告死亡或认定为无民事行为能力人；

（d）违反公证员纪律条例的规定，致使公证员职务中止；

（e）公证员的健康状况有碍其公务职责的履行；

（f）执行公证员故意犯罪的有罪判决，或因时限或特赦而终止执行故意犯罪的有罪判决；

（g）公证员丧失格鲁吉亚国籍；

（h）因执行有罪判决而被剥夺公证员职务；

（i）进行与公证员职务不相符的活动；

（j）规定期限内未满足本法第 17 条第 1 款第 a 项的规定；

（k）终止本法第 11 条第 2.1 项规定的公证机构指定公证员的公证活动。

lished by par 2.1 of Article 11 of this Law.

3. A notary having been released from the position shall be removed from the Notary Registry of Georgia.

4. Decisions on suspending the right of notarial activity or dismissing a notary shall be taken by the Minister of Justice.

5. Under appropriate order of the Minister of Justice, documents of the notary having been suspended the right of notarial activity or been dismissed shall be forwarded to the Notary Chamber of Georgia.

6. A notary having been suspended the right of notarial activity or been dismissed shall be entitled to appeal the decision of the Minister of Justice within 1 month from being officially informed thereof. An order shall be deemed as served if handed over to the notary or sent by registered mail to the notary's registered address. Appealing the order shall not cause the termination of its validity.

Article 19. Notary Office

1. A notary shall have a notary office as his/her work place. Location of a notary office shall be chosen by a notary by observing the terms and conditions foreseen by par. 2.1 of Article 11 of this Law. A notary is authorized to employ and dismiss officers in accordance with the labour legislation of Georgia and manage the income gained from the performance of notarial acts.

2. Two or more notaries may have a joint notary office. Duties and responsibilities of notaries in the joint notary office shall be defined by the agreement concluded among them. Each notary in the joint notary office shall execute notarial acts in his/her name and be personally responsible for his/her official activities. A joint notary office may be established as a business legal entity under the Law of Georgia on Entrepreneurs, except as a joint stock company. A notary acting as the partner of a business legal entity shall execute notarial acts in his/her name and together with the business legal entity, he/she shall be jointly and severally responsible for any damage inflicted as a result of any notarial act. A person employed under a labour contract at the business legal entity provided for by this Article shall not be a notary.

3. In order to organize notarial activities, under approval of the Ministry of Justice, a notary may establish a joint office together with a lawyer, private executor, translator and/or auditor. Rights and obligations of a notary and other joint office participants to such joint office, also the procedure for distribution of income and expenditure shall

3. 被解雇的公证员应在格鲁吉亚公证登记处进行核销登记。

4. 中止公证员职务或解雇公证员的决定应由司法部长作出。

5. 在司法部长适当指令下，中止公证员职务或解雇公证员的文件应提交给格鲁吉亚公证协会。

6. 被中止公证员职务或被解雇的公证员有权自接到通知之日起 1 个月内就司法部长的决定起诉。如该决定已送交公证员或邮寄至公证员登记地址，则视为送达。诉讼不中止决定的效力。

第十九条　公证机构

1. 公证员应在公证机构工作。公证机构所在地应由公证员依据本法第 11 条第 2.1 项选定。公证员有权依据格鲁吉亚劳动法雇佣及解雇工作人员，并管理进行公证的收入。

2. 两个或两个以上公证员可设立联合公证机构。联合公证机构公证员的职权和责任应由公证员签订的协议确定。联合公证机构的每位公证员应以自己的名义进行公证并对其公务活动负责。依据《格鲁吉亚公司法》的规定，联合公证机构除作为股份公司外，还可以作为商业法人。作为商业法人合伙人的公证员应以自己的名义进行公证，并与商业法人一起对因任何公证造成的任何损害承担连带责任。本法规定的商业法人依据劳动合同雇佣的人不得作为公证员。

3. 为开展公证活动，经司法部批准，公证员可与律师、私人遗嘱执行人、翻译人员和 / 或审计人员共同设立联合办公室。公证员和其他联合办公人员的权利和义务，以及收入和支出的分配方式，由其签订的协议确定。

be determined by the agreement concluded by and among them.

4. In order to obtain the approval set forth in Paragraph 3 of this Article, a notary and other joint office participants shall submit a service improvement plan to the Ministry of Justice of Georgia, the main evaluation criteria of which shall be determined by the Minister of Justice.

4. 为获得本条第 3 款中规定的批准，公证员和其他联合办公人员应向格鲁吉亚司法部提交服务改进计划，主要评估标准应由司法部长确定。

Article 191. Organization of Notarial Activities

1. A joint notary office provided for by Paragraph 3 of Article 19 of this Law may be established as a business legal entity under the Law of Georgia on Entrepreneurs, except as a joint stock company. Rights and obligations of the partners of a business legal entity shall be determined by the agreement concluded by and among them (partners' agreement/charter). Such agreement (partners' agreement/charter) shall provide for the casting vote of a notary when making a decision on the issues related to notarial activities at the meeting of partners or other governing body of a company. A notary acting as the partner of a business legal entity shall execute notarial acts in his/her name and together with the business legal entity, he/she shall be jointly and severally responsible for any damage inflicted as a result of any notarial act.

2. If a business legal entity under Paragraph 1 of this Article is established, its firm name shall include the name of at least one partner notary.

3. In order to obtain the approval set forth in Paragraph 3 of Article 19 hereof, the founders of a business legal entity shall submit a service improvement plan and draft agreement between partners (partners' agreement/charter). In order to register the business legal entity under this Article, the approval of the Ministry of Justice shall be submitted to LEPL National Agency of Public Registry at the Ministry of Justice.

4. A person employed under a labour contract at the business legal entity provided for by this Article shall not be a notary.

5. Other issues associated with the organization of notarial activities under this Article, also the guarantees for independence of a notary shall be determined by appropriate order of the Minister of Justice.

第十九条之一　公证活动的组织形式

1. 本法第 19 条第 3 款规定的联合公证机构可依据《格鲁吉亚公司法》设立为商业法人，但作为股份有限公司的除外。商业法人合伙人的权利和义务，应由其签订的协议（合伙人协议 / 章程）确定。此类协议（合伙人协议 / 章程）应在公司合伙人或其他管理机构会议上就公证活动相关问题作出决定时对公证员进行决定性投票。作为商业法人合伙人的公证员应以自己的名义进行公证，并与商业法人一起对因公证造成的任何损害承担连带责任。

2. 如设立本条第 1 款规定的商业法人，其公司名称应包括至少 1 名合伙公证员的姓名。

3. 为获得第 19 条第 3 款规定的批准，商业法人创始人应提交服务改进计划并起草协议（合伙人协议 / 章程）。为依据本条登记成为商业法人，应向司法部公证登记处的 LEPL 国家办公室提交司法部的批准书。

4. 本条规定下商业法人依据劳动合同雇用的人，不得作为公证员。

5. 与本条所规定的公证活动开展有关的其他事项，以及公证员独立性的保障，应由司法部长的指令确定。

Article 20. Notary's Incompatibility of Office

1. A notary shall not hold other position along with the performance of notarial activities or perform other paid work, except the pedagogic, scientific and creative activities.

第二十条　公证员的不当行为

1. 除进行教育、科学和创造性活动外，公证员进行公证活动时不得同时担任其他职务或从事其他有偿工作。

2. A notary is authorized to invest his/ her own capital.

3. A notary and other officers of his/her notary office are prohibited from being mediators of parties when concluding agreements.

4. Placing or extending undue advertisement, or advertising of notary's professional skills by notary is inadmissible. Notary shall be entitled to spread an information on its own notarial activity within the scopes of "Instruction About the Rule on Performing Notary Acts".

2. 公证员有权对自己的财产进行投资。

3. 在签订协议时，公证员和其公证机构的其他人员不得成为申请人的调解人。

4. 禁止发布或提供不正当广告或宣传公证员专业技能。公证员有权在《公证员行为准则》指引的规定下在其公证活动范围内传播信息。

Article 21. Remuneration of Notaries and Notary Office Finances

1. Performance of a notarial act by a notary, as well as rendering of legal advice and provision of technical service associated with such notarial act shall be paid, except the cases foreseen by the Law. The amount of notarial fee, the terms of service and the procedure for having the notarial fee paid, as well as the amount of fee due to the Notary Chamber of Georgia, the terms of service and the procedure for having the fee paid shall be determined by the Decree of the Government of Georgia.

2. A notary's income from official activities is the balance of notary's remuneration remained after the payment of expenses for maintaining notary office, all taxes established by law and other compulsory taxes associated with the notary's official activities. A notary's income may also be the other financial contributions not contradicting to the Georgian legislation, including the income gained as a financial aid from the Notary Chamber of Georgia during the period of notarial activity in the settlement foreseen by par. 21 of Article 11 of this Law.

第二十一条　公证员薪资和公证机构财务

1. 公证员进行公证，以及提供与该公证相关的法律咨询和技术服务，应当收费，但法律另有规定的除外。收取的公证费、服务条款和办理公证费的手续，以及格鲁吉亚公证机构的费用数额、服务条件和收取费用的手续由格鲁吉亚政府法令决定。

2. 公证员从公务活动中所得的收入，是支付公证机构运转费用、法律规定的所有税款以及与公证员公务活动有关的其他强制性税款后的公证员薪酬。公证员的收入也可能包括与格鲁吉亚法律不相抵触的其他财政援助，包括在本法第 11 条第 2.1 项的规定地区提供公证服务期间从格鲁吉亚公证协会获得的财政支持。

Article 22. Property Liability of Notaries

A notary shall be imposed a property liability for the damage caused by his/her deliberate or negligent acts.

第二十二条　公证员的赔偿责任

公证员对因其故意或过失所造成的损害应承担赔偿责任。

Article 23. Compulsory Professional Liability Insurance of Notaries

1. In order to secure the damage compensation set forth in Article 22 of this Law, a notary shall conclude agreement on compulsory professional liability insurance for the entire period of office.

2. The essential terms and conditions of a notary's professional liability insurance and the minimum limit of insurance amount shall be determined by the Minister of Justice upon the recommendation of the Notary Chamber of Georgia.

第二十三条　公证员强制职业责任险

1. 为保证本法第 22 条规定的损害赔偿，公证员应在整个任期内签订强制职业责任保险协议。

2. 公证员职业责任险的基本条款和条件以及保险金额的最低限额，应由司法部长根据格鲁吉亚公证协会的提议确定。

2.1. If a business legal entity under Article 191 of this Law is established, the essential terns and conditions of professional liability insurance and the minimum limit of insurance amount shall be determined by the Minister of Justice.

3. The Notary Chamber of Georgia may conclude insurance agreement for indemnification of damages inflicted by its member as set forth in Article 22 of this Law.

Article 24. Substitution of Notary

1. A notary is entitled to appoint his/her substitute for the period of his/her absence in agreement with the Notary Chamber of Georgia. Total period of substitution of notary during a calendar year shall not exceed 30 business days, save as the cases prescribed by Paragraphs 2 and 3 of this Article. A notary elected in or officially assigned to the management bodies of the Notary Chamber of Georgia or international notary associations, during his/her official assignment, may appoint his/her substitute additionally for no more than 30 business days during a calendar year.

2. A notary is authorized to determine his (her) substitute's term of authority for more than 30 but no more than 90 business days during a calendar year due to pregnancy, childbirth, infant adoption or a child care, whereon relevant documentation shall be submitted to the Notary Chamber of Georgia.

3. By the consent of the Ministry of Justice, in special cases (serious illness, study leave for the aim of raising qualification, etc) a substitute notary may be appointed for no more than 4 months period.

4. A notary is prohibited from notarial acting in the period when his/her substitute performs his/her official activities.

5. A notary shall conclude agreement with his/her substitute. A copy of the agreement shall be submitted to the Notary Chamber of Georgia. A notary shall enter the resolution on a substitute appointment in the electronic notary registry.

6. A person having passed qualifying examination for notaries may be appointed as a substitute notary.

7. When performing his/her official duties, a substitute notary shall guide from this Law.

8. A substitute notary shall acquire his/her official rights and duties from the date of appointment to the position, and such rights and duties shall terminate at dismissal from the position.

9. When performing notarial acts, a substitute notary

2.1. 如果建立本法第 19 条之一规定的商业法人，职业责任险的基本条件和保险金额的最低限额应由司法部长确定。

3. 格鲁吉亚公证协会可依据本法第 22 条的规定，签订赔偿其会员所造成损害的保险合同。

第二十四条　替补公证员

1. 公证员有权在与格鲁吉亚公证协会达成协议的前提下在其缺席期间指定一名替补公证员。如本条第 2 款和第 3 款规定的情形，一个日历年度内公证员的代任期限不得超过 30 个工作日。在正式任职期间被选为或正式指定为格鲁吉亚公证协会或国际公证协会管理机构的公证员，可另外指定一名替补公证员，在一个日历年度内代替其不超过 30 个工作日的工作。

2. 怀孕、分娩、收养婴儿或照看孩子的公证员有权将相关文件提交给格鲁吉亚公证协会授权他（她）的替补公证员在一个日历年度内超过 30 个但不超过 90 个工作日的任期。

3. 经司法部同意，公证员在特殊情况下（重病、为提高资历而进修等）可以指定一名替补公证员，时间不超过 4 个月。

4. 在替补公证员进行公务活动期间，公证员禁止公证。

5. 公证员应与其替补公证员签订协议。协议复印件应提交至格鲁吉亚公证协会。公证员应进入电子公证登记处提交替补任职决议。

6. 通过公证员资格考试的人可以被委任为替补公证员。

7. 替补公证员进行公务活动时应遵循本法。

8. 替补公证员自任命之日起获得正式的权利和义务，该权利和义务在其解雇时终止。

9. 进行公证时，替补公证员应使用其所代替的公

shall use the official seal and electronic notary registry of the notary he/she substitutes.

Law of Georgia №5573, dated 20 December 2011 – website, 28.12.2011

Article 24.1. Concluding Labor Contracts by Notary

1. A notary may conclude labor contract with the other notary.

2. Labor contract shall be submitted to the Notary Chamber of Georgia. A notary working under labor contract may perform all notarial acts as defined by law, unless otherwise prescribed by the labor contract.

3. A notary working under labor contract may carry out notarial activities in the name of the notary, with whom he/she has concluded labor contract. The latter shall be imposed a property liability for the damage inflicted by the notary working under labor contract. A notary working under labor contract shall be responsible for the performed notarial act in the manner prescribed by the Regulations on Disciplinary Liabilities of Notaries.

4. The notary office address of a notary working under labor contract shall be the notary office address of the notary, with whom he/she has concluded labor contract. By consent of the Notary Chamber of Georgia, the notary office address of a notary working under labor contract may be any other address as well. The terms and conditions for giving such consent shall be determined by appropriate order of the Minister of Justice.

5. The number of notaries working under labor contract with one notary may be limited by appropriate order of the Minister of Justice.

Article 25. Remuneration of Substitute Notary

A substitute notary shall get remuneration from the notary whom he/she substitutes. The amount of remuneration shall be determined by the notary.

Article 26. Property Liability of Substitute Notary

1. Property liability for the damage caused by the substitute notary's illegal official act shall be borne by the notary.

2. A notary is authorized to claim back from the substitute notary the amount of paid compensation.

Article 27. Candidate Notary

1. A candidate notary may be a citizen of Georgia having a higher legal education when the fact proving the inadequacy for working as a notary is not known.

2. A person wishing to become a candidate notary

证员的官方印章和电子公证登记。

2011 年 12 月 20 日，格鲁吉亚第 5573 号法令——网页，2011.12.28。

第二十四条之一　公证员签订劳动合同

1. 公证员可与其他公证员签订劳动合同。

2. 劳动合同应提交至格鲁吉亚公证协会。签订劳动合同的公证员可以进行法律规定的所有公证，劳动合同另有规定的除外。

3. 签订劳动合同的公证员可与其签订劳动合同的公证员一起以公证员的名义进行公证活动。后者应对签订劳动合同的公证员所造成的损害承担赔偿责任。签订劳动合同的公证员对其依据公证任职纪律责任条例规定进行的公证负责。

4. 公证员所在的公证机构应是与其签订劳动合同的公证机构。经格鲁吉亚公证协会批准，签订劳动合同的公证员所在的公证机构也可位于其他位置。批准的条款和条件应由司法部长适当指令确定。

5. 与一个公证员共同工作的劳动合同下公证员的数量可由司法部长合理指令限制。

第二十五条　替补公证员的薪酬

替补公证员应从所替补的公证员处获得薪酬。薪酬应由公证员决定。

第二十六条　替补公证员的赔偿责任

1. 因替补公证员违法的公务行为造成的财产损害赔偿责任应由公证员承担。

2. 公证员有权向替补公证员追偿。

第二十七条　公证员的候选人

1. 在尚未证明是否胜任公证员的工作时，候选公证员可以是具有较高法律教育背景的格鲁吉亚公民。

2. 意欲成为候选公证员的人（如果他 / 她没有至

(if he/she does not have at least 1 year length of service as a notary or at least 5 years length of service in the public service) shall pass an internship contest. After winning the contest, the person will be sent for internship training by the Notary Chamber of Georgia, whereof the Ministry of Justice shall be notified.

少1年的公证服务年限，或至少5年的公共服务年限）应通过实习竞争。在通过竞争后，其将被送至格鲁吉亚公证协会进行实习培训，该培训应通知司法部。

3. Internship contest shall be held by testing and/or interviewing. The procedure and terms and conditions of holding the contest shall be determined by the regulations developed by the Notary Chamber of Georgia and approved by the Minister of Justice.

3. 实习竞争应通过考试和/或面试进行。进行竞争的程序和条件应由格鲁吉亚公证协会制定的规则确定并经司法部长批准。

4. A person may be released from internship training if he/she has passed internship training before enactment of this Law and no more than 2 years elapsed from taking such training until the appointment of qualifying examinations for notaries under Paragraph 1 of Article 57 of this Law.

4. 如果在本法颁布前已通过实习培训且在自参加培训至通过本法第57条第1款规定的资格考试不超过2年，则不需要参加实习培训。

Article 28. Internship Training

1. Internship training means the training by the program approved by the Notary Chamber of Georgia in the Training Centre at the Notary Chamber of Georgia. Internship training consists of two stages and includes theoretical and practical parts.

2. Payment for taking the both stages of internship training due to the Notary Chamber of Georgia shall be determined by the Decree of the Government of Georgia.

3. The procedure for taking internship training shall be approved by the Minister of Justice upon the recommendation of the Notary Chamber of Georgia.

第二十八条　实习培训

1. 实习培训指由格鲁吉亚公证协会批准，在格鲁吉亚公证协会培训中心进行的培训项目。实习培训由两个阶段组成，包括理论和实践部分。

2. 格鲁吉亚公证协会承担的参加两个阶段实习培训的费用应由格鲁吉亚政府法令决定。

3. 实习培训的程序，应由格鲁吉亚公证协会提出，由司法部长批准。

Article 29. Termination of Internship Training

The basis for termination of internship training shall be:

a) the trainee's personal application;

b) the trainee's systematic failure to fulfil or improper fulfilment of the obligations imposed.

第二十九条　实习培训的终止

终止实习培训的事由应是：

（a）实习生的个人申请；

（b）实习生不履行或不适当地履行所承担的义务。

Chapter III Notary Chamber of Georgia

第三章　格鲁吉亚公证协会

Article 30. Notary Chamber of Georgia

1. The Notary Chamber of Georgia is a legal entity under public law established on the membership of notaries and carries out its activities by the principle of self-government.

2. The Notary Chamber of Georgia has a representative body in the Autonomous Republic of Adjara, the budget and authority of which is defined by the Charter of

第三十条　格鲁吉亚公证协会

1. 格鲁吉亚公证协会是公证员依据公法设立的法人，并以自治原则开展活动。

2. 格鲁吉亚公证协会在阿贾拉自治共和国设有一个代表机构，其预算和权力由格鲁吉亚公证协会章程规定。

the Notary Chamber of Georgia.

3. The Charter of the Notary Chamber of Georgia shall be approved by the General Meeting of the Notary Chamber of Georgia.

3. 格鲁吉亚公证协会章程应由格鲁吉亚公证协会全体会议批准。

Article 31. Composition of the Notary Chamber of Georgia

第三十一条　格鲁吉亚公证协会的组成

1. The Notary Chamber of Georgia is composed of all notaries.

1. 格鲁吉亚公证协会由所有公证员组成。

2. A notary shall become the member of the Notary Chamber of Georgia as soon as he/she is appointed to the position. The member of the Notary Chamber of Georgia shall be terminated the authority as soon as he/she is released from the position.

2. 公证员一被任命即成为格鲁吉亚公证协会的会员。格鲁吉亚公证协会会员一旦被解雇即终止会员权力。

Article 32. Membership Fee

第三十二条　会费

1. A notary shall pay the membership fee to the Notary Chamber of Georgia.

1. 公证员应向格鲁吉亚公证协会缴纳会费。

2. The amount of membership fee as well as the term for its payment shall be determined by the Charter of the Notary Chamber of Georgia.

2. 会费数额及支付条款应由格鲁吉亚公证协会章程确定。

Article 33. Authorities of the Notary Chamber of Georgia

第三十三条　格鲁吉亚公证协会职权

In order to fulfil the assigned tasks, the Notary Chamber of Georgia is authorized to:

为了完成所委任的工作，格鲁吉亚公证协会有权：

a) Represent a notary at any state agency, civil association; establish relations with other states and international organizations;

（a）在任何国家机构、民间协会中代表公证员与其他国家和国际组织建立关系；

b) Submit proposals to the Ministry of Justice for improvement of legal acts associated with the activities of the Notary Chamber of Georgia;

（b）向司法部提议改进与格鲁吉亚公证协会活动有关的法律行为；

c) Demand necessary information from notaries and hear their explanations;

（c）要求公证员提供必要信息并听取他们的意见；

d) Determine compulsory payments for notaries due to the Notary Chamber of Georgia;

（d）确定格鲁吉亚公证协会对公证员的薪酬；

e) Form the staff of the Notary Chamber of Georgia;

（e）组建格鲁吉亚公证协会工作人员；

f) For the purpose of unification of the notarial acts practice, generalize the notarial acts;

（f）统一公证执业标准，推广公证；

g) Carry out commercial activities for achieving the goals under its Charter;

（g）开展商业活动，实现章程规定的各项目标；

h) Exercise other authorities prescribed by the Georgian legislation.

（h）行使格鲁吉亚法律规定的其他权利。

Article 34. Convening of General Meeting of Members of the Notary Chamber of Georgia and Decision Making

第三十四条　格鲁吉亚公证协会会员大会的召开和决议

1. The General Meeting of members of the Notary Chamber of Georgia shall be convened once a year.

1. 格鲁吉亚公证协会会员大会应每年召开一次。

2. The Extraordinary General Meeting of Members of the Notary Chamber of Georgia shall be convened:

a) at the proposal of the Minister of Justice;

b) at the initiative of the Board of the Notary Chamber of Georgia;

c) at the request of one fifth of the total number of the members of the Notary Chamber of Georgia.

3. The General Meeting of Members of the Notary Chamber of Georgia shall be convened by the Board of the Notary Chamber of Georgia, by serving notice to the members of the Chamber 2 weeks in advance, specifying the place, time and agenda of the meeting.

4. A notary shall participate in the proceedings of the General Meeting of Members of the Notary Chamber of Georgia personally or through a proxy being at the same time the member of the Chamber and having a due written consent for it.

5. The General Meeting of Members of the Notary Chamber of Georgia shall be capable if more than half of total number of the members is present. Any decision of the General Meeting of Members of the Notary Chamber of Georgia shall be taken by the simple majority of votes present.

6. The Minister of Justice is authorized to make amendments to the decisions of the Notary Chamber of Georgia if they contradict the Georgian legislation.

Article 35. Competence of the General Meeting of Members of the Notary Chamber of Georgia

1. The General Meeting of Members of the Notary Chamber of Georgia may make amendments to the agenda and resolve any issue falling within the competence of the Notary Chamber of Georgia.

2. Only the General Meeting of Members of the Notary Chamber of Georgia is authorized to make decisions on the following issues:

a) Approving the Charter of the Notary Chamber of Georgia, making amendments and supplements thereto;

b) Approving annual report of the Notary Chamber of Georgia;

c) Determining compulsory payments by notaries due to the Notary Chamber of Georgia.

3. If valid reason exists, the General Meeting of Members of the Notary Chamber of Georgia is authorized to allow the Board of the Notary Chamber of Georgia to make amendments to the cost estimate of the Chamber that shall be submitted to the following General Meeting

2. 格鲁吉亚公证协会特别会议召开应由：

（a）司法部长提议；

（b）格鲁吉亚公证协会董事提议；

（c）格鲁吉亚公证协会 1/5 以上会员要求。

3. 格鲁吉亚公证协会会员大会应由格鲁吉亚公证协会董事会召集，提前 2 周向协会会员发出通知，具体说明会议的地点、时间和议程。

4. 公证员应亲自或书面委托同为协会会员的代理人参加格鲁吉亚公证协会会员大会。

5. 如超过半数的会员出席，则格鲁吉亚公证协会会员大会有效。格鲁吉亚公证协会会员大会的任何决议都应以出席会员的简单多数表决确定。

6. 如格鲁吉亚公证协会的决议与格鲁吉亚法律相抵触，司法部长有权对其进行修正。

第三十五条　格鲁吉亚公证协会会员大会权限

1. 格鲁吉亚公证协会会员大会可以对议程进行修改，并解决协会职权内的任何问题。

2. 只有格鲁吉亚公证协会会员大会有权对下列事项作出决议：

（a）通过格鲁吉亚公证协会章程，对其作出修正和补充；

（b）通过格鲁吉亚公证协会年度报告；

（c）确定格鲁吉亚公证协会对公证员的强制薪酬。

3. 如有合理事由，格鲁吉亚公证协会会员大会有权批准董事会对应提交至会员大会批准的成本估算作出修改。

of Members of the Chamber for approval.

Article 36. Composition and Meeting of the Board of the Notary Chamber of Georgia

1. The chairman of the Board of the Notary Chamber of Georgia shall be elected by the General Meeting of Members, upon the recommendation of the Minister of Justice, for the term of 3 years by secret vote of the majority of members present.

2. If the General Meeting of Members of the Notary Chamber of Georgia twice successively fails to appoint the candidate chairman nominated by the Minister of Justice to the position of the Chairman of the Board, the General Meeting of Members shall appoint the chairman within 2 weeks period

3. The deputy chairman and members of the Board of the Notary Chamber of Georgia shall be elected by the General Meeting of Members of the Notary Chamber of Georgia for the term of 3 years by secret vote of the majority of members present. The number of members of the Board shall be odd and not less than three. Number of Board members shall be determined by the Minister of Justice of Georgia.

4. The Meeting of the Board of the Notary Chamber of Georgia, as a rule, shall be held once a month. The meeting shall be convened by the Chairman of the Board of the Notary Chamber of Georgia.

Article 37. Competence of the Board of the Notary Chamber of Georgia

1. The Board of the Notary Chamber of Georgia shall ensure the execution of the Charter of the Notary Chamber of Georgia and the decisions made by the General Meeting of the Chamber.

2. The Board of the Notary Chamber of Georgia in the period between the General Meetings of Members of the Notary Chamber of Georgia shall carry out all tasks of the Notary Chamber of Georgia, save as the authorities prescribed by Paragraph 2 of Article 35 of this Law. The Board shall establish links with the state agencies and other organizations on behalf of the Notary Chamber of Georgia and submit proposals and findings.

3. The Board of the Notary Chamber of Georgia is authorized to involve the members of the Board in implementation of tasks and form the staff of the Notary Chamber of Georgia.

4. The Chairman, Deputy Chairman, other members and employees of the Notary Chamber of Georgia shall

第三十六条 格鲁吉亚公证协会董事会的组成和决议

1. 格鲁吉亚公证协会董事会主席应经司法部长推荐，由出席会议会员的无记名多数决选举，任期 3 年。

2. 若由司法部长提名的候选主席两次都未能通过格鲁吉亚公证协会会员大会被指派为董事会主席，则会员大会应在两周内重新任命董事会主席。

3. 格鲁吉亚公证协会董事会副主席和董事会成员由格鲁吉亚公证协会会员大会出席会议的成员无记名多数决选举产生，任期 3 年。董事会成员的数量应该是奇数，且少于 3 个。董事会成员人数应由格鲁吉亚司法部长决定。

4. 格鲁吉亚公证协会董事会会议依规定每月举行一次。会议应由格鲁吉亚公证协会董事会主席召集。

第三十七条 格鲁吉亚公证协会董事会职权

1. 格鲁吉亚公证协会董事会应严格执行格鲁吉亚公证协会章程及会员大会作出的决议。

2. 格鲁吉亚公证协会董事会在格鲁吉亚公证协会会员大会召开期间应承担格鲁吉亚公证协会的所有职责，如本法第 35 条第 2 款规定的职权。董事会应代表格鲁吉亚公证协会与国家机构和其他组织建立联系，并提交提案和调查结果。

3. 格鲁吉亚公证协会董事会有权让董事会成员履行职责，有权组建格鲁吉亚公证协会工作人员体系。

4. 格鲁吉亚公证协会主席、副主席、其他会员及雇员不得泄露在董事会活动中获知的公证信息（如

not disclose the information on notarial acts having learnt in connection with the activity of the Board (save as cases foreseen by part 4 of Article 50 of the Criminal Procedure Code of Georgia). They may make such information public only at the permission of the Board of the Notary Chamber of Georgia. Secrecy of the notarial act shall be protected even if the members leave the Board of the Notary Chamber of Georgia or have been dismissed from the office.

《格鲁吉亚刑事诉讼法》第 50 条第 4 款的规定）。只有在获得格鲁吉亚公证协会许可后才可公开这些信息。即使离开了格鲁吉亚公证协会董事会，或者被开除解雇，也要保守公证秘密。

Chapter IV Notarial Act and General Requirements for Execution Thereof

第四章 公证及履行的一般要求

Article 38. Notarial Act

1. A notary shall perform the following notarial acts:

a) Certifies contracts in the cases established by law or in agreement with the parties;

b) Issues certificates of title;

c) Issues certificates of inheritance;

d) Issues certificates of title over the share in community property;

e) Takes measures to protect inherited property;

f) Certifies the authenticity of any copy of or extract from the original document;

g) Certifies the authenticity of signature on the document;

h) Certifies the accuracy of the translation from one language to another;

i) Certifies the fact of a citizen being alive;

j) Certifies the fact of a citizen being at a certain place;

k) Certifies the identity of the person depicted in the photo;

l) Certifies the time of document submission;

m) Transfers an application and a certificate of one person to the other;

n) Takes money, securities and valuables on deposit;

o) Issues writs of execution;

p) Executes protest of promissory notes;

q) Submits checks for cashing and certifies non-cashability of checks;

r) Receives documents for deposition;

s) Executes maritime protest.

2. In addition to the notarial acts stipulated by this Law, a notary also fulfils other notarial acts prescribed by the Georgian legislation.

3. A notary gives legal advice to people in connection

第三十八条 公证

1. 公证员应进行下列公证：

（a）证明由法律或申请人协议达成的合同；

（b）出具所有权证明；

（c）出具继承证明；

（d）出具社区财产股份所有权证书；

（e）采取措施保护继承财产；

（f）证明原始文件的任何副本或摘要的真实性；

（g）证明文件上签名的真实性；

（h）证明从一种语言至另一种语言翻译的准确性；

（i）证明公民生存事实；

（j）证明公民在某一位置的事实；

（k）证明照片所载人员的身份；

（l）证明提交文件的时间；

（m）将一方的申请书和证明移交至另一方；

（n）寄存金钱、证券和贵重物品；

（o）出具执行文书；

（p）执行拒付本票；

（q）提交支票兑现和证明支票的不可兑现性；

（r）保全书面证据；

（s）执行海事声明。

2. 除本法规定的公证外，公证员还进行格鲁吉亚法律规定的其他公证。

3. 公证员向与公证相关的人提供法律咨询，并根

with the notarial acts and draws up draft documents at their request.

4. A notary is authorized to give legal advice to any interested person not associated with the performance of any notarial act.

4.1. A notary has the right of public offering of a thing. Public offering of a thing shall be provided by electronic auction and/or other electronic means. Forms of public offering, as well as the electronic means used for public offering shall be determined by the Minister of Justice. With regard to the right of public offering of a thing, a notary also may give advice to any interested party.

5. A notary issues a writ of execution based on a due claim for money debt enforcement, property rights transfer, also enforcement of the pledged/mortgaged property only if the parties have agreed thereon and the legal consequences of issuing a writ of execution are explained in writing by the notary in the notarial act.

Article 381. Notary Mediation

1. A notary may be a mediator between the contending parties in:

a) Family law disputes (except for adoption, adoption declared invalid, restriction of parental rights and seizure of parental rights);

b) Succession and inheritance related legal disputes;

c) Neighbour legal disputes;

d) Any other disputes unless the laws of Georgia define a special procedure for mediation in such disputes.

2. Mediation with the participation of a notary may be carried out with the consent of contending parties.

3. The procedure for notary mediation shall be determined by appropriate order of the Minister of Justice.

4. If in the process of mediation the dispute ends with agreement between parties, a notary draws up a deed of agreement to be certified notarially.

5. If any party fails to fulfil the obligations under a deed of agreement drawn up within the scope of notary mediation, enforcement shall be carried out on the basis of a writ of execution issued by a notary in the manner prescribed by the Law of Georgia on Enforcement Proceedings.

Article 39. Authority to Render Registration Service

A notary is authorized to provide the submission of application, registration document electronically and/or materially to the agency keeping the state registry in the manner prescribed by laws of Georgia if the notarially certified document is subject to registration, also within the

据他们的要求起草草案。

4. 公证员有权向与公证无关的任何利害关系人提供法律咨询。

4.1. 公证员有权向公众公开发行出版物。公开发行应以电子拍卖和/或其他电子方式进行。公开发行形式及电子方式由司法部长决定。公证员也可就公开发行权向利害关系人提出建议。

5. 公证员只有在申请人同意的情形下，且在公证中以书面形式说明出具执行文书的法律后果时，才能就金钱债务强制执行、产权转让及质押/抵押财产强制执行出具执行文书。

第三十八条之一　公证调解

1. 公证员可对以下情形进行调解：

（a）家庭法律纠纷（收养、收养被宣布无效、限制亲权、剥夺亲权的除外）；

（b）继承和继承相关的法律纠纷；

（c）相邻法律纠纷；

（d）任何其他争议，格鲁吉亚法律已对此类争议的调解规定特别程序的除外。

2. 公证员可在争议申请人同意时进行调解。

3. 公证调解程序应由司法部长适当的指令确定。

4. 如争议申请人在调解中达成和解，公证员将起草一份协议并公证证明。

5. 如任何一方不履行公证调解协议的义务，公证员应依据格鲁吉亚法律规定的执行程序强制执行。

第三十九条　公证登记服务职权

如经公证的文件需要登记，属于国家登记机构的职权范围，需要确保权利登记、权利变更和/权利的暂停[与格鲁吉亚法律规定的物权登记、公司和非公司（非商业）实体登记和其他登记一致]，公证员有权以格鲁吉亚法律规定的方式向国家登记机构提交电

scope of powers delegated by the agency keeping the state registry, ensure the registration of records on the right, changes in the right and/or suspension of the right (with the Register of Rights on Real Things, Register of Entrepreneurial and Non-entrepreneurial (Non-commercial) Legal Entities and other registers provided for by laws of Georgia).

子版和 / 或纸质版申请材料、注册文件。

Article 40. Enforcement on the Basis of Notarial Documents

第四十条　公证文书的执行

1. A notary issues a writ of execution on the basis of written application of a creditor (its successor). The application shall be attached with the document on the basis of which an applicant requires the issue of a writ of execution. Creditor's (its successor's) application for the issue of a writ of execution shall include:

1. 公证员根据债权人（其继承人）的书面申请签发执行令。申请书应附有申请人申请执行令的文件。债权人（其继承人）申请执行令的材料应包括：

a) Identity of the notary to whom the application is filed;

（a）接受提交申请的公证员的身份材料；

b) Identities/names of the parties and their representatives;

（b）申请人及其代理人的身份 / 姓名材料；

c) Information on the volume of unfulfilled principal and additional liabilities;

（c）未偿还本金的数额和其他债务的信息；

d) Indication that any unfulfilled liability, for the enforcement of which a writ of execution is to be issued, does not depend on the compliance with any reciprocal (cross) liability by the applicant, or that the latter has already fulfilled such liability;

（d）签发未偿还债务的执行令的执行将不会取决于申请人是否有遵守互负（交叉）债务或者后者已经履行了此类责任的说明；

e) Applicant's signature.

（e）申请人的签名。

2. If the grounds established by this Article exist, a notary issues a writ of execution without requesting the documents proving the failure to meet liabilities.

2. 如果存在本条规定的事由，那么公证员签发执行令不要求提供未偿还债务的证明文件。

3. The following persons are authorized to issue a writ of execution in the order as listed in this Paragraph:

3. 以下人员有权依据本款所列顺序签发执行令：

a) A notary or his/her substitute who has notarized agreement;

（a）公证员或有公证档案的替补公证员；

b) If the authority of the notary set forth in Subparagraph "a" of this Paragraph is suspended or terminated – other acting notary.

（b）如果在本款第 a 项中规定的公证员职权被暂停或终止——其他有权的公证员。

4. Enforcement shall be admitted only on the basis of the original writ of execution issued by a notary. If the writ of execution is lost, a copy (duplicate) of the writ of execution shall be issued by a notary in the order listed in Paragraph 3 of this Article, and if it is impossible to issue a duplicate in this manner - by the Notary Chamber of Georgia.

4. 执行应仅以公证员签发的原始执行令为依据。如执行令丢失，执行令状复印件（副本）应由公证员依据本条第 3 款所列顺序签发，如无法以此方式签发副本——由格鲁吉亚公证协会出具。

5. Based on a writ of execution issued by a notary, enforcement shall be carried out in the manner prescribed by the Law of Georgia on Enforcement Proceedings. Fur-

5. 基于公证员签发的执行令，执行应依据格鲁吉亚执法程序法规定的方式执行。此外，因签发的执行令已经执行，对执行令和 / 或公证文件提出上诉并不

thermore, appealing the writ of execution and/or notarial document, for the enforcement of which the writ of execution has been issued, does not suspend the enforcement.

会中止执行。

6. The procedure for issuing a writ of execution shall be established by the Instructions for Notarial Acts Performance Procedure.

6. 签发执行令的程序应按照公证程序的规定。

Article 401. Registration of Civil Acts by Notary

1. A notary shall within the scope of powers delegated by the agency keeping the state register make registration of marriages and divorces in the manner prescribed by the Law of Georgia on Civil Acts.

2. A notary may make registration of marriage solemnly in agreement with the persons wishing to get married.

第四十条之一　公证员民事行为登记

1. 公证员应在国家登记机构授权的范围内，依据格鲁吉亚民事法律规定的方式登记结婚和离婚。

2. 公证员可与结婚对象一起庄严地登记结婚。

Article 41. (Deleted)

第四十一条（已删除）

Article 42. Notarial Acts Performed by Officials of Diplomatic Missions and Consular Institutions

Notarial acts, besides notaries, may be performed by duly authorized officials of the Georgian diplomatic missions and consular institutions abroad acting under the legal acts regulating the activities of consular institutions and diplomatic missions and the requirements of this Law. Duly authorized officials of consular institutions and diplomatic missions shall be entitled to perform notarial acts only if the electronic notary registry is available.

第四十二条　外交使团和领事机构官员公证

除公证员外，格鲁吉亚外交使团和领事机构的正式授权官员可依据规范领事机构和外交使团活动的法律及本法的要求进行公证。领事机构和外交使团的正式授权官员只有在电子公证登记可用时才有权进行公证。

Article 43. Certifying Wills and Powers of Attorney by Officials, Being Equal to the Notary-certified Documents

1. The following documents are equal to the documents certified by a notary:

a) Wills of the citizens placed for treatment in hospital, other inpatient medical-prophylactic institution, sanatorium or those living in elderly and disabled persons home, certified by the head physician, deputy head in medical affairs or physician on call of such hospital, medical institution or sanatorium, and the director or head physician of the elderly and disabled persons home. Also wills and Powers of Attorney granted by military servants or other persons placed for treatment in hospital, sanatorium and other military-medical institution, certified by the head, deputy head in medical affairs or physician on call of such hospital, sanatorium or military-medical institution;

b) Wills of the persons being on the ships sailing or aircrafts flying under the Georgian flag, certified by the captain of the ship or commander of the aircraft;

第四十三条　官员代理人认证遗嘱和授权书的效力与公证员认证的文件效力相同

1. 以下文件与公证员认证的文件效力相同：

（a）在医院、其他医疗预防机构、疗养院或居住在老年人和残疾人家中接受治疗的公民的遗嘱，由这些医院、医疗机构或疗养院的主任医师、医疗副主任或值班医生，以及老人和残疾人家庭的主任或主任医师认证。由军人、疗养院和其他军事医疗机构接受治疗的军人或其他公民的遗嘱和授权书，由医院事务负责人或医生、医务人员或医疗机构的医生认证。

（b）格鲁吉亚国旗下的航行船舶或飞机上公民的遗嘱，由船长或飞机指挥官认证。

c) Wills of the citizens being on research reconnaissance or other similar expeditions, certified by the head of such expedition;

（c）在侦察或其他类似远征队中公民的遗嘱，由远征队的首领认证。

d) Wills and Powers of Attorney of the military servants, also wills and powers of attorney of the servants, their family members and military servants' family members in the places of deployment of military units, formations, institutions and military schools where there are no notary offices or other agencies performing notarial acts, certified by the commander (head) of such unit, formation, institution or school;

（d）军人的遗嘱和授权书，以及在没有公证机构或其他进行公证机构的军事单位、编队、机构和军事学校部署地点的军人、其家庭成员和军人家属的遗嘱和授权书，由该单位、编队、机构或学校的指挥官（负责人）认证。

e) Wills and Powers of Attorney of the persons placed in prison or correction facilities, certified by the director of such prison or correction institution.

（e）监狱或矫正机构公民的遗嘱和授权书，由该监狱或矫正机构的主任认证。

2. Persons set forth in Subparagraphs "a" "d" and "e" of Paragraph 1 of this Law shall be entitled to perform notarial acts prescribed by the relevant Subparagraph of Paragraph 1 of the same Article only if the electronic notary registry is available.

2. 本条第 1 款第 a 项、第 d 项和第 e 项规定的人员，只有在电子公证登记可用时才有权进行同一条第 1 款有关第 1 项规定的公证。

3. In the cases set forth in Subparagraphs "b" and "c" of Paragraph 1 of this Article, the testator shall present the will to a notary as soon as he/she returns to normal living conditions and the notary shall register appropriate notarial act in the electronic notary registry. If the testator dies before he/she returns to normal living conditions, the persons set forth in Subparagraph "b" and "c" of Paragraph 1 of this Article shall submit the wills preserved thereby to the notary for official deposition, who must register appropriate notarial act in the electronic notary registry.

3. 在本条第 1 款第 b 项和第 c 项规定的情况下，遗嘱人一旦恢复健康，应立即向公证员出示遗嘱，公证员应在电子公证登记处登记准确的公证。如果立遗嘱人在他 / 她恢复健康前死亡，则本条第 1 款第 b 项和第 c 项所述的人应将留存的遗嘱提交公证员进行正式认定，并且必须在电子公证登记处登记准确的公证。

Article 431. Fees Paid for Performing Notarial Acts by Authorized Officials

The officials set forth in Article 43 of this Law shall have notarial fees paid for performing notarial acts in the amount determined by the Decree of the Government of Georgia on the Procedure for Collection of Notarial Service Fees and Fees due to the Notary Chamber of Georgia and it will be fully transferred to the budget of local self-governing unit.

第四十三条之一 授权官员进行公证的费用

本法第 43 条规定的官员，应依据格鲁吉亚政府法令关于格鲁吉亚公证协会收取公证服务费和收费程序的规定收取公证费用，且将费用全部转交至地方自治单位预算中。

Article 44. Performance of Notarial Act

A notarial act may be performed by any notary at the request of a person.

第四十四条　进行公证

公证可由任何公证员依据公民的要求进行。

Article 45. Term of Performing Notarial Act

A notary act shall be performed after submission of all necessary documents.

第四十五条　进行公证的期限

公证应在提交所有必要文件后进行。

Article 46. Deferment and Suspension of Performing Notary Act

1. Performance of a notarial act may be deferred:

a) If additional information and documents are requested – until the receipt thereof;

b) If the examination is conducted – before the receipt of expert report;

c) At the request of any interested person wishing to apply to court for bringing a counterclaim for the right or the fact, the confirmation of which is claimed by the other person. In such case, a notary is authorized to defer the performance of a notarial act for no more than 10 days. Unless within the period established the notary receives from the court a notice of application filed by an interested person, the notary shall perform a notarial act.

2. Performance of a notarial act shall be suspended based on a relevant notice from the court until settlement of legal dispute.

3. When the performance of a notarial act is deferred or suspended, a notary shall not issue a certified document or a certificate and shall issue a resolution on deferment or suspension of the performance of a notarial act within 2 days from deferment or suspension. If necessary, a notary shall specify in the resolution that the authority and capacity of the parties has been checked and proved.

Article 47. Limitation of the Right to Perform Notarial Act

1. The notaries and persons performing notarial acts under Articles 42 and 43 of this Law shall not be entitled to perform such notarial acts, to which they, their parents, spouse, children, grandchildren, grandparents, brothers, sisters, parents-in-law (personally or by proxies) are the parties.

2. A notary shall not be authorized to certify an agreement, to which the company established with the capital of the notary, his/her spouse, parent, child, sister or brother is the party and such fact is known to the notary.

3. A notarial act performed in breach of this Article shall be void.

Article 48. Establishment of Person's Identity, Authority and Capacity, Verification of Representative Authority and Request of Documents

1. When performing a notarial act, a notary and other official performing the notary act shall establish the identity of the persons and their representatives requesting to perform notarial act against the identification documents

第四十六条　公证的延期和暂停

1. 公证可能因下列原因延期：

（a）如果要求提供补充信息和文件，公证程序延期至收到时；

（b）如果进行检查，那么公证程序延期至收到专家报告之前；

（c）应任何利害关系人的要求而向法院提出权利或事实的反诉申请。在这种情况下，公证员有权延期公证，但不超过 10 日。除非在此期间内公证员从法院收到接受利害关系人申请通知书，否则公证员应进行公证。

2. 进行公证应依据法院的相关通知暂停，直至法律纠纷解决为止。

3. 进行公证被延期或暂停时，公证员不得出具认证文件或证明，并应在延期或暂停后 2 天内签发延期或暂停进行公证的决议。必要时，公证员应在决议中具体说明已经对申请人的权限和行为能力进行了检查和证明。

第四十七条　公证权力限制

1. 公证员以及依据本法第 42 条和第 43 条进行公证的人员，不可为其父母、配偶、子女、孙子、祖父母、兄弟、姐妹、岳父母（本人或代理人）公证。

2. 公证员及其配偶、父母、子女、姐妹或兄弟作为申请人向公司出资，且公证员知道该事实时，公证员不得认证该出资协议。

3. 违反本条规定进行的公证无效。

第四十八条　确定申请人身份、权限和行为能力，核查代理人权限和所要求的文件

1. 在进行公证时，公证员和进行公证的其他官员应通过提交的身份文件确认申请人及其代理人的身份。

presented.

2. In the cases prescribed by law or under agreement between parties, when certifying a contract, a notary shall verify the authority and capacity of the parties to the contract.

3. If the contract is executed through a representative, a notary shall also verify the authority of the representative.

4. A notary is authorized to request all documents necessary for the performance of notarial acts from institutions, enterprises or companies.

Article 49. Explaining the Contents and Legal Consequences of Notarial Act

When performing a notarial act, a notary shall explain the contents and legal consequences of the notarial act to the persons requesting to perform a notarial act. Furthermore, a notary shall take care that the interests of the persons not knowing the Georgian legislation and being in need of legal advice are not infringed.

Article 50. Procedure for Signing Notarial Document

1. In the cases prescribed by law, any contract or other document shall be signed in the presence of a notary. If signing of a contract or other document has not been performed in the presence of a notary, signatories shall personally prove that signatures are theirs.

2. If a notarial document includes the will expressed by the party to a notarial deed, a notary shall, before signing the document, read the text of the document to the party.

3. If a person requesting to perform a notarial act is dumb, deaf, or deaf-and-dumb, if necessary, a notary shall explain the contents and legal consequences of the notarial act to such person with the help of appropriate specialist. By signing, the specialist must certify that the contents of the notarial act have been explained to the party and the text complies with his/her will.

4. If because of illness or physical disability or any other reason a person lacks an opportunity to sign the document, it shall be signed by another person on his/her behalf in the presence of an officer performing the notarial act, with an indication of the reason for which the person is unable to sign the document.

5. If a person requesting the performance of a notarial act is illiterate or blind, a notary shall read the text of the document out loud and make the appropriate reference in

2. 在法律规定或者申请人约定的情形下认证合同时，公证员应核查合同申请人的权限和行为能力。

3. 如果合同是通过代理人履行的，公证员还应核查代理人权限。

4. 公证员有权要求机构、企业或公司提供进行公证所需的全部文件。

第四十九条　释明公证内容及法律后果

在进行公证时，公证员应向申请人释明公证的内容及法律后果。此外，公证员应保障不了解格鲁吉亚法律且需要法律咨询的利害关系人的权利不受侵犯。

第五十条　公证程序

1. 在法定情况下，任何合同或其他文件应在公证员见证下签署。如合同或其他文件的签署没有在公证员的见证下进行，签署人应证明是他们的亲自签名。

2. 如公证文件包括申请人口述公证遗嘱，在签署文件前公证员应向申请人宣读该文件文本。

3. 如申请人是哑巴、聋人或聋哑人，必要时公证员应在相应专家的帮助下向申请人阐释公证的内容和法律后果。在签署的过程中，专家必须证实已向申请人阐释公证内容，且文本符合他 / 她的意愿。

4. 如果因疾病或身体残疾或任何其他原因一方无法签署该文件，那么应由代表他 / 她的人在公证员的见证下签字，并说明该方无法签署该文件的理由。

5. 如果申请人是文盲或盲人，公证员应大声宣读文件文本，并在文件中进行相应的标注。

the document.

Article 51. Registration of Notarial Act

1. A notarial act performed by the notaries and persons set forth in Articles 42 and 43 of this Law shall be registered in the electronic notary registry.

2. Any performed notarial act shall be assigned an individual number, which shall be specified in the issued documents and evidencing inscriptions.

3. A notary issues an extract from the electronic notary registry at the written application of the person having requested the performance of a notarial act or to whom the notarial act has been performed, unless otherwise prescribed by this Law.

Article 52. Refusal to Perform Notarial Act

1. The notaries and persons set forth in Articles 42 and 43 of this Law shall refuse to perform notarial acts if:

a) Performance of a notary act contradicts the laws of Georgia;

b) Documents submitted for the performance of a notary act do not meet the established requirements or contain the information humiliating the dignity and honour of persons, or contradict the generally recognized moral standards;

c) Party to a notarial act is unauthorized, incapable or the request for a notarial act is made in the language which the notary does not speak and an interpreter is not available.

2. Notary's decision on the refusal to perform a notarial act shall be substantiated in writing and delivered to the person having requested the notarial act within no later than 3 days from such decision.

3. A notary shall explain to the person being refused to perform a notarial act the procedure and time limits of appealing such decision.

Article 53. Appealing Notary's Act or Decision

1. A person, whose interests are concerned in the notarial act, or a person being refused to perform a notarial act, may appeal the notarial act or decision on the refusal to court according to the notary office location.

2. Complaint against the activities of notaries not covered by Paragraph 1 of this Article shall be considered by the Ministry of Justice or the Notary Chamber of Georgia at its assignment.

Article 54. Performance of Notarial Acts for Foreign Citizens or Stateless Individuals

Foreign citizens and stateless individuals may per-

第五十一条　公证登记

1. 公证员及本法第 42 条、第 43 条规定的人员所进行的公证，应在电子公证机构登记。

2. 进行的任何公证，都应配有一个单独编号，并在已签发文件和证据上注明。

3. 公证员在申请人书面申请后，自电子公证登记处发布摘要，本法另有规定的除外。

第五十二条　不予进行公证

1. 在下列情形下，公证员及本法第 42 条、第 43 条规定的人员不予进行公证：

（a）公证行为违背格鲁吉亚法律；

（b）为进行公证而提交的文件不符合既定要求或包含侮辱人格尊严和个人荣誉的内容，或违背公认的道德标准；

（c）公证的申请人未经授权、无行为能力或者是对公证的要求是以公证员不知晓的语言提出且没有翻译。

2. 公证员不予进行公证的决定应以书面形式作出，并在不迟于该决定作出后的 3 日内送交要求公证的人。

3. 公证员应向被不予进行公证的人释明该决定的上诉程序和时限。

第五十三条　对公证员的行为或决定提出申诉

1. 公证利害关系人，或者被不予进行公证的人，可根据公证机构的办公地点就公证或不予公证的决定向法院提出申诉。

2. 对本条第 1 款未涉及的公证员申诉，应由司法部或格鲁吉亚公证协会处理。

第五十四条　对外国公民或无国籍人进行公证

外国公民和无国籍人可自己或通过代理人以与格

sonally or through representatives request the performance of notarial acts in the same manner as the Georgian citizens do.

Article 55. Accepting Documents by Notary Issued in Other State

A notary shall accept the documents issued in other state if they are legalized or apostilled in the manner prescribed by the laws of Georgia.

Article 56. Validity of International Treaties and Agreements

If the international treaties and agreements concluded or joined by Georgia determine the procedure for performing a notarial act different from the one prescribed by the Georgian legislation, a notary shall accordingly act under the international treaties or agreements.

Chapter V Transitional and Final Provisions

Article 57. Transitional Provisions

1. For the purposes of Article 11 of this Law, qualifying examination for notaries means an examination to be held after enforcement of this Law in the manner prescribed by Article 12 of the same Law.

2. Before enactment of this Law, substitute notaries appointed by the Minister of Justice upon the recommendation of the Notary Chamber of Georgia to fill the notary vacancies shall be deemed appointed to the notary positions in accordance with this Law.

3. Notaries and substitute notaries appointed to the vacant notary positions by the Minister of Justice upon the recommendation of Notary Chamber of Georgia, having resigned from the position/expired the term of office as substitute notaries for the last two years before enactment of this Law and there is no basis to reject them to occupy the notary positions, are authorized to file an application to the Minister of Justice for appointment to the notary position after enactment of this Law. If the requirements set forth in this Law are met, they will be appointed to the notary positions and may perform notarial activities.

4. The Ministry of Justice, together with the Legal Entity of Public Law – Notary Chamber of Georgia, shall ensure the development of a new procedure for calculation of notarial fees and submit the bill on relevant amendments to the Law of Georgia on Fees for Performing Notarial Acts to the Parliament of Georgia by the Spring Session 2010 of the Parliament of Georgia.

鲁吉亚公民相同的方式申请公证。

第五十五条　承认其他国家出具的公证文件

如其他国家出具的公证文件是按照格鲁吉亚法律规定的方式进行的公证，公证员应承认该公证文件的效力。

第五十六条　国际条约和协定的有效性

如果格鲁吉亚签订或加入的国际条约和协定规定了与格鲁吉亚公证法律不同的程序，公证员应依据国际条约或协定进行公证。

第五章　过渡条款和最终条款

第五十七条　过渡条款

1. 本法第 11 条对公证员资格考试的规定，是指本法实施后依照本法第 12 条举行的考试。

2. 在本法颁布前，司法部长根据格鲁吉亚公证协会提议任命的替补公证员应被视为公证员。

3. 司法部长根据格鲁吉亚公证协会提议任命的公证员和替补公证员，在本法颁布前两年辞去职位，或替补公证员任期终止且没有合理原因拒绝他们担任公证员职务，则有权在本法颁布后向司法部长申请担任公证职位。如符合本法规定的要求，他们将被任命为公证员，并可以进行公证活动。

4. 司法部和作为公法法人的格鲁吉亚公证协会，应确保制定新的公证费用计算程序并在格鲁吉亚议会 2010 年春季会议上提交《格鲁吉亚公证费修正法案》的草案。

5. Upon enactment of this Law, the Ministry of Justice shall ensure the compliance of appropriate statutory acts with this Law.

5. 本法颁布后，司法部应确保公证行为符合本法。

6. Upon enactment of this Law, the Notary Chamber of Georgia and notaries appointed to the positions before enactment of this Law shall ensure to register the inheritance cases and wills maintained with the archives of the Notary Chamber of Georgia and the notary offices, and make appropriate entries in the electronic notary registry.

6. 本法颁布后，格鲁吉亚公证协会和本法颁布前被任命的公证员，应确保将遗产案件和遗嘱公证登记于格鲁吉亚公证协会和公证机构的档案中，并在电子公证登记处添加到相应的条目。

7. The Minister of Justice shall issue the Decree for the year of 2010 set forth in Paragraph 5 of Article 16 of this Law, no later than 1 month from the enactment of this Law.

7. 司法部长应在本法颁布后 1 个月内发布本法第 16 条第 5 款规定的 2010 年法令。

Article 58. Enactment of Law

1. This Law, except Articles 1-56, Paragraphs 1-3 of Article 57 and Paragraph 3 of Article 58, shall be enacted from the moment of publishing.

2. Articles 1-56, Paragraphs 1-3 of Article 57 and Paragraph 3 of Article 58 of this Law shall be enacted from 1 April 2010.

3. Notary Law of Georgia of 3 May 1996 (Parliamentary Bulletin №012, 31.05.96, p. 16) be deemed null and void.

第五十八条　本法的施行

1. 本法除第 1 条至第 56 条、第 57 条第 1 款至第 3 款和第 58 条第 3 款外，自颁布之日起施行。

2. 本法第 1 条至第 56 条、第 57 条第 1 款至第 3 款和第 58 条第 3 款自 2010 年 4 月 1 日起施行。

3.1996 年 5 月 3 日的格鲁吉亚公证法（一会公报第 012 版，96.05.31，第 16 页）视为无效。

President of Georgia Mikheil Saakashvili Tbilisi
December 4, 2009
№2283-IIs

格鲁吉亚总统米哈伊尔萨卡什维利第比利斯
2009 年 12 月 4 日
No.2283-IIs

中国

中华人民共和国公证法

（2005年8月28日第十届全国人民代表大会常务委员会第十七次会议通过　根据2015年4月24日第十二届全国人民代表大会常务委员会第十四次会议《关于修改〈中华人民共和国义务教育法〉等五部法律的决定》第一次修正　根据2017年9月1日第十二届全国人民代表大会常务委员会第二十九次会议《关于修改〈中华人民共和国法官法〉等八部法律的决定》第二次修正）

目　录

第一章　总　则

第一条　为规范公证活动，保障公证机构和公证员依法履行职责，预防纠纷，保障自然人、法人或者其他组织的合法权益，制定本法。

第二条　公证是公证机构根据自然人、法人或者其他组织的申请，依照法定程序对民事法律行为、有法律意义的事实和文书的真实性、合法性予以证明的活动。

第三条　公证机构办理公证，应当遵守法律，坚持客观、公正的原则。

第四条　全国设立中国公证协会，省、自治区、直辖市设立地方公证协会。中国公证协会和地方公证协会是社会团体法人。中国公证协会章程由会员代表大会制定，报国务院司法行政部门备案。

公证协会是公证业的自律性组织，依据章程开展活动，对公证机构、公证员的执业活动进行监督。

第五条　司法行政部门依照本法规定对公证机构、公证员和公证协会进行监督、指导。

第二章　公证机构

第六条　公证机构是依法设立，不以营利为目的，依法独立行使公证职能、承担民事责任的证明机构。

第七条　公证机构按照统筹规划、合理布局的原则，可以在县、不设区的市、设区的市、直辖市或者市辖区设立；在设区的市、直辖市可以设立一个或者若干个公证机构。公证机构不按行政区划层层设立。

第八条　设立公证机构，应当具备下列条件：

（一）有自己的名称；

（二）有固定的场所；

（三）有二名以上公证员；

（四）有开展公证业务所必需的资金。

第九条　设立公证机构，由所在地的司法行政部门报省、自治区、直辖市人民政府司法行政部门按照规定程序批准后，颁发公证机构执业证书。

第十条　公证机构的负责人应当在有三年以上执业经历的公证员中推选产生，由所在地的司法行政部门核准，报省、自治区、直辖市人民政府司法行政部门备案。

第十一条　根据自然人、法人或者其他组织的申请，公证机构办理下列公证事项：

（一）合同；

（二）继承；
（三）委托、声明、赠与、遗嘱；
（四）财产分割；
（五）招标投标、拍卖；
（六）婚姻状况、亲属关系、收养关系；
（七）出生、生存、死亡、身份、经历、学历、学位、职务、职称、有无违法犯罪记录；
（八）公司章程；
（九）保全证据；
（十）文书上的签名、印鉴、日期，文书的副本、影印本与原本相符；
（十一）自然人、法人或者其他组织自愿申请办理的其他公证事项。

法律、行政法规规定应当公证的事项，有关自然人、法人或者其他组织应当向公证机构申请办理公证。

第十二条 根据自然人、法人或者其他组织的申请，公证机构可以办理下列事务：
（一）法律、行政法规规定由公证机构登记的事务；
（二）提存；
（三）保管遗嘱、遗产或者其他与公证事项有关的财产、物品、文书；
（四）代写与公证事项有关的法律事务文书；
（五）提供公证法律咨询。

第十三条 公证机构不得有下列行为：
（一）为不真实、不合法的事项出具公证书；
（二）毁损、篡改公证文书或者公证档案；
（三）以诋毁其他公证机构、公证员或者支付回扣、佣金等不正当手段争揽公证业务；
（四）泄露在执业活动中知悉的国家秘密、商业秘密或者个人隐私；
（五）违反规定的收费标准收取公证费；
（六）法律、法规、国务院司法行政部门规定禁止的其他行为。

第十四条 公证机构应当建立业务、财务、资产等管理制度，对公证员的执业行为进行监督，建立执业过错责任追究制度。

第十五条 公证机构应当参加公证执业责任保险。

第三章 公证员

第十六条 公证员是符合本法规定的条件，在公证机构从事公证业务的执业人员。

第十七条 公证员的数量根据公证业务需要确定。省、自治区、直辖市人民政府司法行政部门应当根据公证机构的设置情况和公证业务的需要核定公证员配备方案，报国务院司法行政部门备案。

第十八条 担任公证员，应当具备下列条件：
（一）具有中华人民共和国国籍；
（二）年龄二十五周岁以上六十五周岁以下；
（三）公道正派，遵纪守法，品行良好；
（四）通过国家统一法律职业资格考试取得法律职业资格；
（五）在公证机构实习二年以上或者具有三年以上其他法律职业经历并在公证机构实习一年以上，经考核合格。

第十九条 从事法学教学、研究工作，具有高级职称的人员，或者具有本科以上学历，从事审判、检察、法制工作、法律服务满十年的公务员、律师，已经离开原工作岗位，经考核合格的，可以担任公证员。

第二十条 有下列情形之一的，不得担任公证员：
（一）无民事行为能力或者限制民事行为能力的；
（二）因故意犯罪或者职务过失犯罪受过刑事处罚的；
（三）被开除公职的；
（四）被吊销公证员、律师执业证书的。

第二十一条 担任公证员，应当由符合公证员条件的人员提出申请，经公证机构推荐，由所在地的司法行政部门报省、自治区、直辖市人民政府司法行政部门审核同意后，报请国务院司法行政部门任命，并由省、自治区、直辖市人民政府司法行政部门颁发公证员执业证书。

第二十二条 公证员应当遵纪守法，恪守职业道德，依法履行公证职责，保守执业秘密。

公证员有权获得劳动报酬，享受保险和福利待遇；有权提出辞职、申诉或者控告；非因法定事由和非经法定程序，不被免职或者处罚。

第二十三条 公证员不得有下列行为：
（一）同时在二个以上公证机构执业；
（二）从事有报酬的其他职业；
（三）为本人及近亲属办理公证或者办理与本人及近亲属有利害关系的公证；
（四）私自出具公证书；
（五）为不真实、不合法的事项出具公证书；
（六）侵占、挪用公证费或者侵占、盗窃公证专用物品；

（七）毁损、篡改公证文书或者公证档案；

（八）泄露在执业活动中知悉的国家秘密、商业秘密或者个人隐私；

（九）法律、法规、国务院司法行政部门规定禁止的其他行为。

第二十四条 公证员有下列情形之一的，由所在地的司法行政部门报省、自治区、直辖市人民政府司法行政部门提请国务院司法行政部门予以免职：

（一）丧失中华人民共和国国籍的；

（二）年满六十五周岁或者因健康原因不能继续履行职务的；

（三）自愿辞去公证员职务的；

（四）被吊销公证员执业证书的。

第四章 公证程序

第二十五条 自然人、法人或者其他组织申请办理公证，可以向住所地、经常居住地、行为地或者事实发生地的公证机构提出。

申请办理涉及不动产的公证，应当向不动产所在地的公证机构提出；申请办理涉及不动产的委托、声明、赠与、遗嘱的公证，可以适用前款规定。

第二十六条 自然人、法人或者其他组织可以委托他人办理公证，但遗嘱、生存、收养关系等应当由本人办理公证的除外。

第二十七条 申请办理公证的当事人应当向公证机构如实说明申请公证的事项的有关情况，提供真实、合法、充分的证明材料；提供的证明材料不充分的，公证机构可以要求补充。

公证机构受理公证申请后，应当告知当事人申请公证事项的法律意义和可能产生的法律后果，并将告知内容记录存档。

第二十八条 公证机构办理公证，应当根据不同公证事项的办证规则，分别审查下列事项：

（一）当事人的身份、申请办理该项公证的资格以及相应的权利；

（二）提供的文书内容是否完备，含义是否清晰，签名、印鉴是否齐全；

（三）提供的证明材料是否真实、合法、充分；

（四）申请公证的事项是否真实、合法。

第二十九条 公证机构对申请公证的事项以及当事人提供的证明材料，按照有关办证规则需要核实或者对其有疑义的，应当进行核实，或者委托异地公证机构代为核实，有关单位或者个人应当依法予以协助。

第三十条 公证机构经审查，认为申请提供的证明材料真实、合法、充分，申请公证的事项真实、合法的，应当自受理公证申请之日起十五个工作日内向当事人出具公证书。但是，因不可抗力、补充证明材料或者需要核实有关情况的，所需时间不计算在期限内。

第三十一条 有下列情形之一的，公证机构不予办理公证：

（一）无民事行为能力人或者限制民事行为能力人没有监护人代理申请办理公证的；

（二）当事人与申请公证的事项没有利害关系的；

（三）申请公证的事项属专业技术鉴定、评估事项的；

（四）当事人之间对申请公证的事项有争议的；

（五）当事人虚构、隐瞒事实，或者提供虚假证明材料的；

（六）当事人提供的证明材料不充分或者拒绝补充证明材料的；

（七）申请公证的事项不真实、不合法的；

（八）申请公证的事项违背社会公德的；

（九）当事人拒绝按照规定支付公证费的。

第三十二条 公证书应当按照国务院司法行政部门规定的格式制作，由公证员签名或者加盖签名章并加盖公证机构印章。公证书自出具之日起生效。

公证书应当使用全国通用的文字；在民族自治地方，根据当事人的要求，可以制作当地通用的民族文字文本。

第三十三条 公证书需要在国外使用，使用国要求先认证的，应当经中华人民共和国外交部或者外交部授权的机构和有关国家驻中华人民共和国使（领）馆认证。

第三十四条 当事人应当按照规定支付公证费。

对符合法律援助条件的当事人，公证机构应当按照规定减免公证费。

第三十五条 公证机构应当将公证文书分类立卷，归档保存。法律、行政法规规定应当公证的事项等重要的公证档案在公证机构保存期满，应当按照规定移交地方档案馆保管。

第五章 公证效力

第三十六条 经公证的民事法律行为、有法律意义的事实和文书，应当作为认定事实的根据，但有相反证据足以推翻该项公证的除外。

第三十七条 对经公证的以给付为内容并载明债务人愿意接受强制执行承诺的债权文书，债务人不履行或者履行不适当的，债权人可以依法向有管辖权的人民法院申请执行。

前款规定的债权文书确有错误的，人民法院裁定不予执行，并将裁定书送达双方当事人和公证机构。

第三十八条 法律、行政法规规定未经公证的事项不具有法律效力的，依照其规定。

第三十九条 当事人、公证事项的利害关系人认为公证书有错误的，可以向出具该公证书的公证机构提出复查。公证书的内容违法或者与事实不符的，公证机构应当撤销该公证书并予以公告，该公证书自始无效；公证书有其他错误的，公证机构应当予以更正。

第四十条 当事人、公证事项的利害关系人对公证书的内容有争议的，可以就该争议向人民法院提起民事诉讼。

第六章 法律责任

第四十一条 公证机构及其公证员有下列行为之一的，由省、自治区、直辖市或者设区的市人民政府司法行政部门给予警告；情节严重的，对公证机构处一万元以上五万元以下罚款，对公证员处一千元以上五千元以下罚款，并可以给予三个月以上六个月以下停止执业的处罚；有违法所得的，没收违法所得：

（一）以诋毁其他公证机构、公证员或者支付回扣、佣金等不正当手段争揽公证业务的；

（二）违反规定的收费标准收取公证费的；

（三）同时在二个以上公证机构执业的；

（四）从事有报酬的其他职业的；

（五）为本人及近亲属办理公证或者办理与本人及近亲属有利害关系的公证的；

（六）依照法律、行政法规的规定，应当给予处罚的其他行为。

第四十二条 公证机构及其公证员有下列行为之一的，由省、自治区、直辖市或者设区的市人民政府司法行政部门对公证机构给予警告，并处二万元以上十万元以下罚款，并可以给予一个月以上三个月以下停业整顿的处罚；对公证员给予警告，并处二千元以上一万元以下罚款，并可以给予三个月以上十二个月以下停止执业的处罚；有违法所得的，没收违法所得；情节严重的，由省、自治区、直辖市人民政府司法行政部门吊销公证员执业证书；构成犯罪的，依法追究刑事责任：

（一）私自出具公证书的；

（二）为不真实、不合法的事项出具公证书的；

（三）侵占、挪用公证费或者侵占、盗窃公证专用物品的；

（四）毁损、篡改公证文书或者公证档案的；

（五）泄露在执业活动中知悉的国家秘密、商业秘密或者个人隐私的；

（六）依照法律、行政法规的规定，应当给予处罚的其他行为。

因故意犯罪或者职务过失犯罪受刑事处罚的，应当吊销公证员执业证书。

被吊销公证员执业证书的，不得担任辩护人、诉讼代理人，但系刑事诉讼、民事诉讼、行政诉讼当事人的监护人、近亲属的除外。

第四十三条 公证机构及其公证员因过错给当事人、公证事项的利害关系人造成损失的，由公证机构承担相应的赔偿责任；公证机构赔偿后，可以向有故意或者重大过失的公证员追偿。

当事人、公证事项的利害关系人与公证机构因赔偿发生争议的，可以向人民法院提起民事诉讼。

第四十四条 当事人以及其他个人或者组织有下列行为之一，给他人造成损失的，依法承担民事责任；违反治安管理的，依法给予治安管理处罚；构成犯罪的，依法追究刑事责任：

（一）提供虚假证明材料，骗取公证书的；

（二）利用虚假公证书从事欺诈活动的；

（三）伪造、变造或者买卖伪造、变造的公证书、公证机构印章的。

第七章 附 则

第四十五条 中华人民共和国驻外使（领）馆可以依照本法的规定或者中华人民共和国缔结或者参加的国际条约的规定，办理公证。

第四十六条 公证费的收费标准由省、自治区、直辖市人民政府价格主管部门会同同级司法行政部门制定。

第四十七条 本法自 2006 年 3 月 1 日起施行。

附 1 中国委托公证人（香港）管理办法

第一章 总则

第一条 为进一步健全委托公证人制度，加强对委托公证人的管理，提高委托公证的质量，维护当事人的合法权益，促进内地与香港社会经济的稳定发展，根据国务院有关规定，制定本办法。

第二条 委托公证人由司法部考试、考核合格后委托。委托期为三年，特殊情况可适当变更委托期限。委托期满，本人提出申请，经司法部考核合格并接受业务培训后，可连续委托。

第三条 委托公证人的业务范围是证明发生在香港地区的法律行为、有法律意义的事实和文书。证明的使用范围在内地。

第四条 委托公证人必须按照司法部规定或批准的委托业务范围、出证程序和文书格式出具公证文书。

第五条 委托公证人出具的委托公证文书，须经中国法律服务（香港）有限公司（以下简称公司）审核，对符合出证程序以及文书格式要求的加章转递，对不符合上述要求的不予转递。公司应定期（7 月 15 日前报上半年，1 月 15 日前报上年度）将加章转递情况报司法部。

第六条 委托公证人接受当事人委托后，应亲自办理委托公证事项。特殊情况下，需要内地公证机构或其他机构协助办理的，应征得当事人的同意，委托费用由委托公证人支付，或由委托公证人与当事人协商支付。

第七条 委托公证人应定期接受业务培训。

第二章 委托条件及程序

第八条 具备下列条件的香港律师，可向司法部提出成为委托公证人的申请：

（一）拥护《中华人民共和国宪法》，拥护《中华人民共和国香港特别行政区基本法》；

（二）在香港具有永久居留权的中国公民；

（三）担任香港律师十年以上；

（四）职业道德良好，未有因不名誉或违反职业道德受惩处的记录；

（五）掌握内地有关法律、法规和办证规则；

（六）能用中文书写公证文书，能用普通话进行业务活动。

第九条 具备本办法第八条规定条件的香港律师申请担任委托公证人，由本人向司法部提出书面申请；向公司申领并据实填写申请委托公证人登记表。申请书、登记表原件，学历、经历等证件的影印件经委托公证人公证后交由公司一并报司法部。

第十条 司法部接到有关申请后，对申请人资格进行审查并征求有关部门的意见，对符合申请条件的，集中组织进行法律知识和公证业务的培训，经培训后方可参加司法部组织的考试。

第十一条 司法部每三年举行一次委托公证人考试。

考试分为笔试、面试。重点测试申请人对内地有关法律和规定及委托公证业务、普通话的掌握程度。

通过考试的人员由司法部进行考核。

考核合格者，由司法部颁发委托书并予以首次注册。

第三章 注册条件及程序

第十二条 委托公证人应于每年 12 月 15 日前向司法部申请年度注册。未经注册的，不得办理委托公证业务。

司法部于每年一月份对注册的委托公证人进行年度公告。

第十三条 委托公证人符合下列条件的准予注册：

（一）在上一年度无违纪和判工行为；

（二）职业道德良好，无违反本办法及协会章程的行为；

（三）能按要求办理委托事宜。

第十四条 委托公证人注册程序：

（一）委托公证人向协会提出注册申请；

（二）填写协会发给的注册申请表，连同本人上年度办证情况及司法部规定需报的材料递交协会；

（三）协会理事会对委托公证人的注册申请签注意见后，将上述材料转交公司，公司将委托公证人所办公证加章转递情况签注意见后报司法部；

（四）司法部根据委托公证人的注册申请及有关

材料并参考有关部门的意见，作出准予或不准予注册的书面决定。准予注册的，通知公司和协会，由协会代办注册手续。

第十五条 委托公证人受到本办法第十六条第二项处分期间应暂缓注册。

第四章 法律责任

第十六条 委托公证人有违反法律、法规、规章和执业纪律的行为分别给予以下处分：

（一）警告；

（二）中止委托；

（三）取消委托。

第十七条 委托公证人有下列行为之一的予以警告处分：

（一）发往内地使用的公证文书未按规定的时间送公司审核转递的；

（二）不按规定的程序、格式及要求出具公证书，经提示未及时改正的。

第十八条 委托公证人有下列行为之一的，根据不同情节，予以中止委托6个月至12个月的处分：

（一）发往内地使用的公证文书，不经加章转递的；

（二）因被投诉受到调查而不积极配合调查或经查实造成不良后果的；

（三）有判工行为但经提示及时改正的；

（四）不按规定的收费标准收费的；

（五）无正当理由不参加业务培训的；

（六）对协会理事会决议无正当理由不予执行的。

第十九条 委托公证人有下列行为之一的，取消委托：

（一）发往内地使用的公证文书不经加章转递，受警告或中止委托处分后仍不改正的；

（二）不按规定的程序要求出具公证书，经书面提示仍不改正的；

（三）被投诉业经查实，确已造成严重后果的；

（四）有判工行为经提示不及时改正的；

（五）受到两次中止委托处分的；

（六）在申请登记表及其他申请文书中做虚假陈述的；

（七）其他丧失第八条规定条件的。

第二十条 委托公证人接受委托一年内无正当理由不办理委托业务或不申请年度注册的，经协会书面提示仍不改变，视为自动中止委托。自动中止委托期限为6个月，到期经协会再次书面提示不申请恢复委托，视为自动放弃委托。申请恢复委托者，应说明理由。

因特殊原因，不能办理委托业务的应向司法部报告，经审查批准后，可予以注册。

第二十一条 司法部设立委托公证人纪律监督委员会（以下简称委员会），受理当事人对委托公证人的投诉，直接或委托有关单位进行调查。委员会应将调查结果及时向司法部报告并提出处理意见。

第五章 委托公证人协会

第二十二条 委托公证人协会由委托公证人依法组成，是委托公证人的自律性组织。委托公证人协会接受司法部的委托，承办与委托公证人有关的具体事项。

委托公证人在任期内必须参加协会成为协会会员。

第二十三条 委托公证人协会的职责由其章程作出规定。

第六章 附则

第二十四条 本办法由司法部解释。

第二十五条 本办法自2002年4月1日起施行。原司法部第34号令《中国委托公证人（香港）管理办法》同时废止。

附2 澳门公证法典

《公证法典》第1条至第50条

第一编
公证职能之行使

第一章 一般规定

第一条（公证职能）

一、公证职能之主要作用在于使非以司法途径作出之法律行为具备法定形式，并赋予该等行为公信力。

二、为着产生上款规定之效力，公证员得在当事人表达其法律行为意思之事宜上给予指导。

第二条（专职机关）

具公证职能之专职机关为公共公证员及私人公证员。

第三条（特别机关）

一、在例外情况下，下列者得行使公证职能：

a）专责公证员；

b）就特定行为获法律赋予公证员权限之其他实体。

二、专责公证员系指就特定行为获法律赋予公证员权限且具法律学士学位之公共机关之公务员、服务人员或工作人员。

三、具有公证职能之特别机关运用其权限而作出之行为，应受本法典内适用于该等行为之规定部分所约束。

第四条（实习员及助理员）

公证机构之实习员及助理员，仅得作出法律明确允许其作出之行为；该等行为受本法典内规范公证员行为之规定所约束。

第二章 公证员

第一节 权限及回避

第一分节 职权

第五条（一般权限）

一、公证员之一般权限为接收及理解当事人之意思，使有关意思符合法律规定及具备法定形式，作成与上述目的相符之文书及赋予该等文书真确性，并确保文书之保存、证明力及执行力。

二、公证员在行使其权限时，应就其所作行为之意义及涵盖范围向当事人作出说明。

第六条（特别权限）

一、公证员具下列特别权限：

（a）缮立公证遗嘱、废止遗嘱之公证书以及密封遗嘱之核准书、存放书及启封书，并就按照民法所定之某一特别方式而订立之遗嘱缮立存放书；

（b）缮立载于记录簿册内及非载于记录簿册内之其他公证文书；

（c）在私文书上缮立认证语，或就私文书上之笔迹或签名缮立作成人之认定语；

（d）发出生存证明书、身份证明书以及担任公共职务或法人管理职务之证明书；

（e）就已发生之其他事实发出证明书；

（f）证明文件之译本，或提供并证明文件之译本；

（g）发出公证文书及登记之证明，以及公证机构内其他存盘文件之证明，并就为作成认证缮本之目的而向其出示之文件发出认证缮本；

（h）为接收郑重声明或经宣誓作出之声明而缮立文书；

（i）按可予证实之方式透过图文传真，将公证文书及登记之内容，以及公证机构内其他存盘文件之内容传送至须向其作出证明之任何公共部门或公证机关；

（j）接收自公共部门或公证机构按可予证实之方式透过图文传真而传送之文件，并就该等文件发出证明书；

（l）按有关法津之规定认证商业企业主之簿册；

（m）参与非以司法途径作出之法律行为，以使其在确定性或真确性方面具备利害关系人所期望之特别保障；

（n）对依法应在有关公证机构内存盘之文件以及为存盘目的而交予公证员之文件加以保存。

二、应利害关系人之请求，公证员得为作成属其权限范围之行为而透过任一途径要求任何公共部门提供所需之文件。

第七条（对私人公证员权限之限制）

一、私人公证员有权限作出本法典规定之一切公证行为，但下列公证行为除外：

（a）公证遗嘱及废止遗嘱之公证书；

（b）密封遗嘱之核准书、存放书与启封书，以及按照民法所定之某一特别方式而订立之遗嘱之存放书；

（c）按法律规定应以公证书作出之抛弃遗产行为；

（d）公证确认继承资格及公证证明；

（e）婚姻协定；

（f）债权证券之拒绝证书；

（g）无行为能力人系当事人之行为，但在该行为中无行为能力人经适当代理或辅助者除外。

二、上款之规定不妨碍可按《民法典》第二千零五十一条之规定于私人公证员面前订立遗嘱。

第八条（权限范围）

除法律另有规定外，公证员得应请求而在本地区作出属其权限范围之一切行为，即使涉及非居住于澳门之人或非位于澳门之财产亦然。

第二分节　回避

第九条（公证员之回避）

一、若公证员本人、其配偶、任一直系血亲或姻亲、二亲等内之旁系血亲或姻亲，或与公证员在事实婚状况下生活之人，系行为之直接或间接当事人，又或系行为之直接或间接受益人，则公证员不得作出有关行为。

二、若上款所指之任一人系行为当事人或受益人之受权人或法定代理人，则上述之回避亦适用于有关行为。

三、行为之当事人或利害关系人为一股份有限公司，而公证员本人或第一款所指之人系该公司之股东者，公证员得参与有关行为；行为之当事人或利害关系人为一公益法人，而此法人系由公证员管理者，公证员亦得参与有关公证行为。

第十条（公证机构之实习员及助理员之回避）

一、公证机构之实习员及助理员处于上条所指之应回避状况时，不得作出公证行为。

二、公证员应回避时，其所属公证机构之实习员及助理员亦须回避。

第十一条（例外）

一、第九条及第十条之规定，不适用于以法庭上之单纯代理权为内容之授权及复授权，亦不适用于在不构成合同行为凭证之文书上所作之公证认定；但该等授权、复授权及认定涉及应回避之公证员、公证机构之实习员或助理员时，则第九条及第十条之规定仍予适用。

二、公证机构之实习员及助理员得作出上款所指之行为，即使其所属公证机构之公证员为被代理人、代理人或签署人亦然。

第二节　保守职业秘密及拒绝作出公证行为

第一分节　保守职业秘密及提供信息

第十二条（保守职业秘密）

一、对于为作出簿册认证或为作出认证而交予公证员之私文书之存在及内容，以及对于交予公证员供其准备及作出属其权限行为所用之数据，均须作为职业秘密加以保守。

二、在未经向公证员出示遗嘱人之死亡证明时，遗嘱及任何与其有关之资料均属秘密；但对遗嘱人本人或其具特别权力之受权人则除外。

三、仅在法律规定之情况下，公证员方有出示公证机构之簿册、文件及数据库内数据之义务；公证员亦有义务保管按照法律仍未移至其他档案库或未销毁之簿册、文件及数据库内数据。

第十三条（信息）

一、对于可发出证明之行为、登记或存盘文件，若利害关系人提出要求，则公证员应就该等行为、记录或文件之存在提供口头信息。

二、在上款所指情况下，应当事人或订立行为人之明确要求，公证员应就有关行为、登记或存盘文件提供不具证明效力而仅具信息用途之复印件。

三、应信用机构之要求，得以书面及简介方式就债权证券之拒绝证书簿册内所作之登记提供相关信息。

第二分节　拒绝作出公证行为

第十四条（拒绝之义务）

一、在下列情况下，公证员应拒绝作出被申请之公证行为：

（a）行为属无效；

（b）行为不属其权限范围或属其本人应回避作出者；

（c）就参与人之精神是否健全存有疑问。

二、若有经卫生司认可之两位医学鉴定人参与公证行为，并证实参与人精神健全，则就参与人之精神健全存有疑问即不构成拒绝作出公证行为之依据。

第十五条（说明拒绝之理由）

一、若公共公证员拒绝作出属其权限范围之行为，而利害关系人以口头或书面方式向其声明拟对该拒绝作出行为之决定提出争议，则公证员应在四十八小时内向利害关系人交出一份注明日期之书面报告，其中应详细说明拒绝之理由。

二、上款之规定，经作出必要配合后，适用于拒绝发出证明之情况。

三、为针对公证员拒绝作出公证行为之决定而提出争议，向利害关系人交出第一款所指说明拒绝理由之报告之日，视为就该决定作出通知之日。

第十六条（可撤销行为及不产生效力行为）

一、公证员不得以有关行为属可撤销或不产生效力为理由而拒绝参与。

二、在上款所指之情况下，公证员应将有关行为具有瑕疵或不产生效力一事提醒其订立人，并在文书内注明已作上述提醒。

第十七条（私人公证员拒绝作出公证行为之权能）

一、私人公证员有权拒绝作出任何属其权限范围之行为，而无须指出拒绝之理由。

二、若因行为之性质或依法律规定而仅得由某特定公证员或其代任人作出该行为，则此公证员或其代任人在被要求作出该行为时，即不得行使上款所指之权能。

三、在上款所指之情况下，对公证员之拒绝适用第十五条之规定。

第三节　对公证行为之责任

第十八条（一般原则）

一、就公证行为及由公证机构发出之文件，均由其签署人承担责任，但其缮立人仍须承担因欺诈或恶意而应负之责任。

二、按上款规定须对公证行为承担责任之人，基于所造成之损失而负有之责任，并不因该等行为已透过司法途径转为有效而获免除。

第十九条（连带责任）

一、公证员因缺乏监管或领导而导致其公证机构之工作人员在执行有关职务时不法实践某些作为或不作为者，须承担连带责任，但该等工作人员本身仍须承担其个人责任。

二、除上款规定外，私人公证员尚须就基于工作上之错误而对第三人造成之损失，以及就税务法律之不履行而向有关行为之订立人承担连带责任。

第二十条（刑事责任）

有关公务员须承担刑事责任之规定，适用于公证员就执行职务时所作出之行为而须承担之刑事责任。

第四节　法定制度

第二十一条（适用规定）

一、公共公证员职程之纳入，公共公证机构之组织及运作，以及在机构内工作之人员之职责，均受登记及公证机关组织架构所规范。

二、私人公证员之入职条件以及从事私人公证活动之条件，均受专门法规所规范。

第三章　公证活动之组织

第一节　簿册

第二十二条（公证行为之簿册）

一、公证行为须按性质而分别缮立于下列簿册内：

（a）公证遗嘱及废止遗嘱之公证书之记录簿册；

（b）杂项公证书之记录簿册；

（c）债权证券之拒绝证书之簿册；

（d）有关缮立于a项所指簿册内之行为、密封遗嘱之核准书及存放书，以及其他遗嘱之存放书之登记簿册；

（e）杂项公证书之登记簿册；

（f）独立文书及其他文件之登记簿册；

（g）手续费及印花税之登记簿册；

（h）簿册认证之登记簿册。

二、公证机构及其他具公证职能之特别机关，应备有为作出属其权限范围之公证行为所需、且属上款所指之簿册。

第二十三条（其他簿册）

除公证行为之簿册外，公证机构尚应备有下列簿册：

（a）目录簿册；

（b）公证员认为对公证机构之运作属必要之其他簿册。

第二十四条（式样）

一、公证员应采用经核准之簿册式样；无该式样时，应采用最适合于簿册用途之式样。

二、对供公证机构使用簿册之式样之核准，以及对使用中之式样之更改，均由司法事务司司长在听取登记暨公证委员会之意见后以批示作出。

第二十五条（簿册之计算机化）

一、司法事务司司长在听取登记暨公证委员会之意见后，得决定以适当之计算机储存数据取代簿册，即使仅为存档之目的亦然。

二、司法事务司司长有权订定取代簿册之程序，尤其得决定将两册或两册以上之登记簿册并入独一数据库。

三、本节内之规定，经作出必要配合后，适用于加载计算机储存数据内之簿册式样。

第二十六条（簿册分为数册）

一、若公证员行使第五十三条第一款最后部分所指之权能，则公证遗嘱及废止遗嘱之公证书之记录簿册应分为两册。

二、杂项公证书之记录簿册得按工作需要而分为数册。

三、手续费及印花税之登记簿册得分为两册，一册用作登记有关公证认定行为之收费账目，另一册用作登记有关其他行为之收费账目。

四、上款所指用作登记公证认定行为之收费账目之簿册，得视乎工作情况而分为数册。

第二十七条（公证遗嘱及废止遗嘱之公证书之记录簿册）

一、公证遗嘱、废止遗嘱之公证书以及相关附注，均缮立在第二十二条第一款 a 项所指之簿册内。

二、上述簿册按上条第一款之规定而分为两册者，一册用于手写之行为，另一册用于经打字或计算机处理之行为。

第二十八条（杂项公证书之记录簿册）

凡公证书及相关附注，均缮立在杂项公证书之记录簿册内，但上条所指之公证书除外。

第二十九条（债权证券之拒绝证书簿册）

对于因要求作出拒绝证书而提交债权证券所作之提交登记，及就作成之拒绝证书所作之登记，以及按第一百三十五条之规定就有关债权证券之提取所作之注记，均缮立在拒绝证书之簿册内。

第三十条（遗嘱及公证书之登记簿册）

在第二十二条第一款 d 项及 e 项所指之每一簿册内，均应对该簿册所登记之行为作出注录。

第三十一条（独立文书及其他文件之登记簿册）

在独立文书及其他文件之登记簿册内，须记入：

（a）密封遗嘱之启封书；

（b）不属于第二十二条第一款 c 项及 d 项所指簿册之登记范围但应存档之其他独立文书；

（c）设立社团之经认证文书及创立财团之经认证文书，以及有关更改之经认证文书；

（d）交予公证机构存盘之文件。

第三十二条（手续费及印花税之登记簿册）

手续费及印花税之登记簿册系用于：

（a）对因作出公证行为而应收取之手续费及印花税进行记账；

（b）对因完全免除费用而无须编制收费账目之行为进行登记，并在登记旁侧之一栏内注明该免除费用之情况。

第三十三条（簿册认证之登记簿册）

第二十二条第一款 h 项所指之簿册，系用于登记按有关法律规定为商业企业主之簿册进行认证之行为。

第三十四条（目录簿册）

一、在目录簿册内须将公证机构之各簿册列出，并标明其字母代号、编号及名称，并将每一簿册内首次及末次缮立之行为之日期及每一簿册之页数列出；目录簿册内亦须列出各档案组及注明所属年份或顺序编号，以及每一档案组所包括之文件数量及每一档案组之页数。

二、各簿册一经开始使用，即须列入目录簿册，档案组则在齐备文件后即须列入该簿册。

三、与记录簿册内缮立之行为有关之档案组，须在目录中涉及有关簿册之记录旁列出。

第三十五条（簿册之编号及认别）

一、任何簿册均有一顺序编号，而每类簿册均有其本身之编号顺序。

二、涉及被分为多册之簿册时，每一簿册均依字母顺序而以一字母代号表示，该代号置于编号之后面，此编号因此按各具同一字母代号之簿册而有其本身之编号顺序。

第三十六条（簿册之装订以及散册或散页之使用）

一、簿册得由散册或散页组成；使用完毕后，应将其装订成卷，每卷最多由一百五十页组成。

二、由散册或散页组成之公证遗嘱及废止遗嘱公证书之记录簿册，应在公证机构内装订，以便对载于其内之行为保守秘密。

三、在散册或散页上作出之公证书，得缮立于无衬格纸、留有页边空白及有二十五行可供书写之纸张上；该等公证书得仅缮立于纸张正面而弃用背面，但对同一簿册内之其他纸张须作相同处理。

四、按第二十五条之规定以计算机储存数据取代簿册时，司法事务司司长应定出磁盘之最大储存量及定出缮立公证行为之各页页面之编排。

第三十七条（簿册之认证）

一、不得使用未经预先认证之簿册。

二、认证簿册系指分别在首页及末页填写启用语及终结语，并在启用语及终结语内注明日期及签名，且在其余各页上作简签及将每一页编号。

三、每一页之编号均应连同相关簿册之顺序编号及字母代号。

四、由散册或散页组成之簿册之终结语，须在簿册内最后之行为被缮立后填写，而编号及简签则视乎需用之纸张而作出。

五、为认证簿册而作之记载得采用机械程序作出，但对由散册或散页组成之簿册则不得以印章替代簿册内之简签。

六、按第二十五条之规定以计算机储存数据取代簿册时，由司法事务司司长订定有关其认证之方式。

第三十八条（启用语及终结语）

一、启用语内须注明簿册之顺序编号、字母代号、用途及簿册所属之公证机构；终结语内须载明簿册之页数及所使用之简签。

二、若仅在纸张正面作成公证书而弃用背面，则须在终结语内注明此情况。

三、在公共公证机构内，终结语中所载之简签须由在有关簿册内缮立最后行为且在终结语内签名之公证员作出。

四、在私人公证机构内，若公证员不能在有关簿册上填写终结语，则须由其代任人在其之前所缮立行为之纸页后之一页上填写终结语，并在终结语内签名及注明此事。

第三十九条（认证簿册之权限）

一、认证簿册之权限属公证员或其代任人所有。

二、第三条所指特别机关之簿册，由有关部门之领导人或依法在有关实体担任领导职务之人认证；但法律另有规定者除外。

第二节 数据库

第一分节 公证机构之数据库

第四十条（数据库及其编排）

一、在任何公证机构内，均应就订立行为人设置一总数据库，有关数据须每日更新。

二、在上款所指之数据库内，应记入与下列者有关之资料：

（a）在该公证机构缮立之公证书；

（b）第四十五条第二款d项所指之授权书及复授权书；

（c）为归入某行为或作成某行为而提交之非仅以作出该行为作为授权内容之其他授权书；

（d）设立社团之经认证文书及创立财团之经认证文书，以及有关更改之经认证文书；

（e）应当事人要求而存盘之文件。

三、涉及公证证明、公证确认继承资格或财产分割之公证书之数据，以及与由代理人参与作成之文书有关之资料，应仅分别加载提出证明之人、被继承人及被代理人之数据卡内。

四、涉及商业企业主及法人以当事人身份参与之行为之数据，须加载标有其商业名称或法人名称之数据卡内，而非加载代表其订立有关行为之人之资料卡内；至于涉及商业企业主及法人之其他行为，有关资料仍须加载订立行为人之资料卡内。

五、在公共公证机构内，除第一款所指之数据库外，尚应就遗嘱及与其有关之一切文书，尤其系废止遗嘱之公证书以及密封遗嘱之核准书、存放书及启封书，设置一专门数据库。

第四十一条（资料卡之排列及内容）

一、数据卡内应加载卡主之全名，并按字母顺序排列。

二、数据卡内应载明被订立行为之类型或以文书作为凭证之行为之类型、缮立有关行为之簿册或存盘档案组之编号及页码；以上规定不影响下条第二款规定之适用。

三、若涉及应当事人要求而存盘之文件，则应简述文件之性质以作认别。

第四十二条（数据库之计算机化）

一、第四十条所指之数据库，得由计算机储存数据内之登记所组成之数据库取代。

二、司法事务司司长在听取登记暨公证委员会之意见后，得决定将公证机构之数据库计算机化，在此情况下，亦得以同样方式决定在有关登记内除应加载上条第二款所指者外，尚应加载其他数据。

三、本分节之规定，经作出必要配合后，适用于按以上两款规定进行计算机化之数据库。

第二分节 中心数据库

第四十三条（数据库及其编排）

一、司法事务司须就订立行为人设置一中心数据库，该数据库由载于计算机储存数据内之登记所组成，有关数据须按公证机构之数据库内容每月进行更新。

二、对中心数据库之编排，适用经作出必要配合之以上数条规定。

三、中心数据库之登记内，除应加载以上数条所指内容外，尚应就所登记之行为加载有关公证机构之认别数据。

第三分节 档案

第四十四条（簿册及文件）

除各簿册、不应交予当事人之独立文书及经认证文书须在公证机构存档外，为归入已在簿册内或非在簿册内作成之行为而提交之文件，又或为作成该等行为而提交之文件，均须在公证机构存盘；但法律另有规定或仅要求出示文件者除外。

第四十五条（档案组）

一、文件须按其所涉及行为之作出时间或文件之提交时间之顺序而分组存盘。

二、尤其应就下列文件编排各自之组别：

（a）与每一记录簿册内缮立之行为有关之文件；

（b）密封遗嘱之存放书及用作取回密封遗嘱之授权书；

（c）密封遗嘱之启封书及其相关遗嘱、遗嘱人之死亡证明以及第二百零七条第五款所指之证明之收据；

（d）第一百二十八条第二款所指之授权书，以及以该等授权书为基础按同样方式所作之复授权书；

（e）被登记之其他独立文书、与该等文书有关之文件以及应当事人要求而存盘之文件；

（f）设立社团之经认证文书及创立财团之经认证文书；

（g）供作附注依据用之公函、申请及文件；

（h）作出第一百三十四条所指通知之挂号存根，以及与制作拒绝证书工作有关之应存盘文件；

（i）就公证行为所作通知之复本；

（j）存放手续费及印花税之凭单之复本；

（l）不应归入其他档案组之透过图文传真而接收之文件及有关申请，以及用于发送图文传真之原件及发送注记；

（m）不应归入其他档案组之发出信函之复本及接收之信函。

三、用于归入公证行为或作成公证行为之文件，须按其相关文书内所载之顺序存盘。

四、档案组须按年编排；但第二款 a 项所指文件之档案组除外。

五、基于存盘文件之数量而导致有理由将档案组分为适当之分组者，得作出之。

第四十六条（编号）

一、涉及记录簿册内缮立之行为之每一档案组，均以其有关簿册之字母代号及顺序编号作认别。

二、按年编排之档案组尚须以其所属之年份作认别。

三、档案组有分组时，每一分组须有一数字编号。

四、档案组中之各页均有编号；文件归入档案组后，即须在其上标出一顺序编号及标出缮立有关行为之簿册之编号及此行为所在纸页之首页码。

五、在各档案组中应注明其所包括之文件数量及其页数。

第四十七条（信函）

一、发出信函之复本以及接收之信函，均须依时间顺序而按年以独立档案组存盘。

二、对于具有持久效力之工作批示或指示之公函及传阅文件，须将之集中及有序编成独立卷册。

第四十八条（簿册及文件之取离）

一、仅在公证员以书面及附有依据之方式给予许可后，方得将簿册及文件取离公证机构；但涉及在公证机构以外缮立之公证行为，或因不可抗力之情况而有必要影印或紧急迁移簿册及文件者除外。

二、就公证员不许可将簿册或文件取离公证机构一事，系由司法事务司司长进行审查，该司长得决定允许将有关簿册或文件取离公证机构。

三、司法事务司司长在行使监察权时，得索取任何公证机构之簿册及文件，以便进行查核，但不得影响该等机构之正常工作。

第四十九条（将簿册及文件转移至其他档案库）

一、公证机构之簿册及文件，自其完成或作成目录后之三十年内，不得转移至其他档案库，但不影响十一月二十八日第 54/97/M 号法令第十二条及第十六条规定之适用。

二、上述三十年之期间届满后，即可将有关簿册及文件转移至澳门历史档案室。

三、私人公证机构之簿册及文件，并不受第一款规定之约束，而可按照有关法律规定转移至原公证员之代任人所属之公证机构。

第二编
公证行为

第一章　一般规定

第一节　文书以及公证行为之作出

第五十条（文书类型）

一、公证员缮立或参与制作之文书得为公文书、经认证之文书或仅经公证认定之文书。

二、公文书系指公证员在有关簿册或独立文书内缮立之文书，以及由公证员发出之证明书、证明及其他类似之文书。

三、经认证之文书系指经当事人在公证员面前确认之私文书。

四、私文书经公证员按本法典规定认定其内之笔迹及签名或仅认定其内之签名者，即为经公证认定之文书。

第五十一条（缮立行为之所在）

一、凡公证遗嘱以及按法律或利害关系人之要求而须采用公证书形式作出之行为，均须缮立于记录簿册内。

二、若文书之缮立不能在其起首之簿册内完成，则须于下一顺序编号之簿册内继续缮立，并须在正文末处签名之上方注明此事。

三、凡应加载公文书之行为而法律或利害关系人未要求以公证书作出者，须缮立在非属于记录簿册之文书内。

四、法律要求公证员作出之登记，须缮立于登记专用之簿册内，但不影响第二十五条第二款最后部分规定之适用。

五、认证语及公证认定行为须缮立于相应之文书或其附页内。

第五十二条（编号）

一、就公证行为之登记之顺序编号须为按月编定，而对公证认定行为之顺序编号则得为按日编定。

二、独立文书内之附注、第二十二条第一款 a 项及 b 项所指簿册内之附注以及第二十二条第一款 c 项至 h 项所指簿册内缮立之行为或书录，须按缮立之顺序而编号。

三、附注之编号须具连续性，有关编号顺序属其相应行为所专有。

第五十三条（作成）

一、遗嘱、废止遗嘱公证书以及密封遗嘱核准书，均应以易于辨认之字迹手写作成；但若属由公证员执行职务之情况，则得以打字或通过计算机处理而作成上述文书，而随后须将有关计算机储存数据清除。

二、载于杂项公证书之记录簿册内之行为应以打字或通过计算机处理而作成；但该簿册分为多册时，其中一册内之行为得以手写作成。

三、对于其他公证行为，得使用任何书写方法或计算机程序，但字体应相当清晰。

第五十四条（使用之材料）

一、公证行为之作成及打印所使用之材料应为黑色，并应使所书写之文字具有不变性及持久性。

二、在任何情况下均禁止使用能使书写痕迹消失之材料。

三、司法事务司司长得在听取登记暨公证委员会之意见后，命令使用由其核准式样之印件缮立独立文书，以及命令或禁止在缮立行为时采用某些材料、书写方法或计算机程序。

第五十五条（钢印之使用）

一、任何公证行为之文书内均应盖上公证机构之钢印，但缮立于簿册内之行为除外。

二、钢印须盖于公证员之签名及简签上。

第五十六条（书写行为时应遵守之规则）

一、书写公证行为时所使用之名称须为全写；但属数词者除外，对此得使用数字符号。

二、在受法律保护之交易中惯用之简称，以及按行为之上下文显示意义明确之缩写，亦允许使用之；但涉及行为当事人或订立人之身份者除外。

三、在译本、内容证明以及非以复印件形式发出之认证缮本中，对原文之转录须保留原文内之简称、缩写及数字符号。

四、缮立公证文书、证明书、证明、其他类似之文书以及认证语时，均不得留有空白，对空白之处须加一横线以使其不得使用。

第五十七条（更改声明）

一、对经订正之字、经涂改之字、插行书写之字及删除之字，均应作出明确之更改声明。

二、删除已书写之字时，应在其上划线，划线方式须使被删之字仍可被辨认。

三、更改声明须在有关文本所载行为之签名上方作出；涉及在记录簿册内缮立之行为、其补充文件或授权书时，更改声明应由在上述文件上签名之公证员以手写作成。

四、若对经订正之字、经涂改之字及插行书写之字未作出更改声明，则该等文字视为不存在，但不影响民事法律中有关文书证明力之规定之适用。

五、若对已被划线但尚可辨认之字未作更改声明，则视其为未被删除。

第五十八条（行文）

一、公证行为须以任一正式语文作成，其行文应尽量完善、明确及准确。

二、在公证行为之行文中所使用之词汇须为在法律词汇中最能表达当事人以其作出之指示所显露之意思者，亦应避免在文书内作出多余或重复之记载。

三、司法事务司司长得在听取登记暨公证委员会之意见后，认可供选择性使用之公证行为文书之官方拟本，该等拟本应分别以两种正式语文作成。

第五十九条（拟本）

一、订立行为人得向公证员提交行为之拟本。

二、如拟本之行文符合上条第一款及第二款之规定，公证员应照该拟本复制；但对拟本中违反强制性法律规定之部分，则不应复制。

三、如拟本有不完善之处，公证员应将此事提醒利害关系人，并采纳其认为最能表达订立行为人意思之行文。

四、经公证员在提交之拟本上作简签后，拟本须交还提交人；但提交人要求将拟本存档者除外，在此情况下，提交人亦应在拟本之每一页上签名。

五、若就订立行为人拟作出之行为已具备适当之官方拟本，则第二款所指之义务即告终止。

第六十条（透过图文传真接收之文件）

一、由第六条第一款 j 项所指实体透过图文传真向公证员传送之文件或文书，得用以作成公证行为或用以归入公证行为内。

二、上款所指之文件或文书，只要具备下列要素，即具有与原件相同之证明力：

（a）发出部门或公证机构之名称、传走纸页之编号、发出日期及地点、有权限之工作人员或公证员之签名以及其在无其签名之纸页上之简签；

（b）一项终结注记，其内载有由发出部门或公证机构按相关法律发出之内容证明中应含有之各项数据。

三、透过图文传真接收之文件，若以感热纸印出，则应将之影印；在任何情况下，均应将所接收之文件编号及在其所有纸页上作简签并缮立接收注记，随后应立即将之归入本身之档案组；接收注记内须指出实际接收之纸页数目、接收地点及日期、接收之公证机构之有关工作人员或公证员之职级及签名。

第六十一条（透过计算机接收之文件）

一、司法事务司司长经听取登记暨公证委员会之意见后，得就透过计算机传送予公证员之文件决定是否可用以作成公证行为或用以归入公证行为内。

二、为在作出公证行为中使用透过电子方式接收之文件，司法事务司司长有权定出该等文件应符合之要件。

第六十二条（本地区以外地方发出之文件）

一、由本地区以外地方按当地法律发出之文件，得用以作成公证行为。

二、公证员得根据由本地区以外地方透过图文传真向公证员传送之文件而作成公证行为，但以嗣后有可能将之与原件核对者为限。

三、对按上款规定而接收之文件，适用第六十条第三款之规定。

四、透过图文传真所传送之文件，在尚未能核实系与原件相符时，公证员不得就按照第二款之规定而作成之公证行为发出证明；对于属不应存档之文书，公证员在尚未能核实其系与原件相符时，不得将该等文书交予利害关系人。

五、如公证员有充分理由怀疑所提交或透过图文传真所传送之文件之真确性，得要求提供补充书证以消除怀疑；以上规定不影响《民法典》第三百五十八条第二款最后部分规定之适用。

第六十三条（以非正式语文或公证员不谙之语文书写之文件）

一、以非正式语文书写之文件应附有相应之译本；该译本得由澳门之公证员、本地区之执业律师或适当之翻译提供，有关翻译须透过名誉宣誓或名誉承诺，在公证员面前确认译本忠于原文。

二、与某公司活动有关之文件，得附具经该公司之秘书按商法之规定而证明之译本。

三、如公证员不谙被提交文件所使用之正式语文，该等文件须依职权由公证员信任之传译作出翻译，无须进行任何手续。

第六十四条（存盘文件之使用）

一、对于在公证机构内存有之文件或公证文书，在未逾有效期且其缮立状况亦未改变之时，得用以归入在该机构缮立之公证行为内或用以作成公证行为。

二、除法律另有规定外，允许以官方实体发出、且已逾有效期之存盘于有关公证机构之文件为依据而作成公证行为，但仅以公证员能透过计算机通讯方法查核该等文件所载之数据是否符合现状及是否准确者为限。

三、在上款所指之情况下，公证员应在有关文书内注明上述情况；若属应予存盘之文件，则应就所作之查询取得一打印本并予存档。

第六十五条（其他档案之查阅）

一、为获取房地产之必要认别资料及关乎其法律状况之数据，得透过计算机直接查阅在澳门不动产所有权之规范程序中有所参予之公共部门之档案内信息；由此获取之资料即取代为作成有关公证行为所需之登记证明及地籍图。

二、按上款规定而获取之数据，其有效期为十日；公证员应就有关资料取得一打印本以供存盘。

三、司法事务司司长经咨询登记暨公证指引及查核部门之意见后，得就第一款规定之目的指定其他公共实体之档案可供查阅。

第二节　公证文书之要件

第一分节　一般要件

第六十六条（共同之形式要件）

一、公证文书应具备以下内容：

（a）签署文书之日期、月份、年份及地点，订立行为人有所要求时，亦应指出作成文书之时刻；

（b）参与作成文书之公证员或工作人员之全名、身份及其所属公证机构之名称；

（c）与行为有关之自然人之全名、婚姻状况、国籍及常居所，对于属自然人之商业企业主，应同时指出其商业名称；

（d）对于以当事人身份参与行为之属法人之商业企业主，按商法规定指出其认别资料及其住所，以及由订立行为人代表之其他法人之名称及其住所；

（e）以代理人身份订立行为之人、公证确认继承资格或公证证明之公证书内之声明人，以及应以证明人、传译、医学鉴定人、证人或文书宣读人身份参与行为之人之全名、婚姻状况及常居所；

（f）就订立行为人及上项所指之人指出证实身份之方式，或指出该等人为公证员本人所认识；

（g）指出证明受权人及代理人身份之授权书及各涉及有关公证文书之文件，并明确注明已证实该受权人或代理人具有作出有关行为所需之权力；

（h）借指出文件存盘一事而提及存盘之一切文件及说明其性质；

（i）注明单纯被出示之文件，并指出其性质及发出日期，若文书本身未指明发出文件之实体或未能因文件性质而确定其发出实体，则亦须注明该发出实体；

（j）若传译、医学鉴定人或文书宣读人参与行为，则指出其参与原因，并提及该等人士所作之名誉宣誓或名誉承诺，或注明属官方传译参与之情况；

（l）有关已遵守因出现第八十二条及第八十三条所指情况而要求遵守之程序之声明；

（m）载明已在所有参与人同时在场之情况下，向订立行为人高声宣读文书并解释文书内容；

（n）指出未签名或仅按上指模之订立行为人，以及就每一仅按上指模之订立行为人指出其所作因不会或不能签名而未签名之声明；

（o）订立行为人及其他参与人置于正文后之签名或指模，以及公证员或工作人员之签名，该签名为文书内最后之一个签名。

二、因公证员回避或缺勤而由其代任人参与公证行为时，应指出代任原因。

三、允许私人公证员不使用第一款 b 项所指之全名，而使用其在有关专业社团之登录中所采用之简名，但该简名必须与允许其从事公证职务之凭证内所载者相同。

四、若在认别当事人时使用中文姓名之罗马拼音，则应在姓名后置一括号以在其内指出有关身份证明文件所载与罗马拼音编码表对应之数字编号；若该文件内无此编号，或涉及商业企业主之商业名称或法人之名称，则应写出相应之中文字以替代该编号，书写上述中文字得以手写作出。

五、第一款 g 项之规定，不适用于以未成年子女代理人之身份订立行为之父母。

六、在抛弃遗产或遗赠之公证书内，应特别指出抛弃遗产或遗赠之人是否有直系血亲卑亲属。

七、可参与作成更正书之人，仅系与待更正之行为有正当利害关系之订立行为人，或属有关错误所涉及之人；若属后一情况，则该更正不可影响行为之内容。

第六十七条（在须作登记之行为之文书内应作出之特别载明）

一、供须作登记之行为作凭证用之文书，尤其应载明以下内容：

（a）若行为所涉及之人为已婚，则载明其配偶之全名及有关之夫妻财产制，若该人为未婚，则指出其系成年人或未成年人；

（b）公证员应向订立行为人所作之提醒，该提醒系指出若有关行为未经登记，则视乎情况而不在当事人之间产生效力或不对第三人产生效力。

二、对于订立行为人须促使有关行为被登记之情况，公证员应提醒订立行为人有义务按适用之法律所规定之方式及期间促使有关登记之作出，并在文书之正文内载明此提醒。

三、第一款 a 项之规定，适用于确认继承资格公证书内有关被继承人及待确认资格人之部分，亦适用于赋予作出须作登记行为之权力之授权书。

四、公证遗嘱、废止遗嘱公证书以及密封遗嘱核准书，均应特别载明遗嘱人之出生日期及其父母之全名。

第六十八条（身份之证实）

一、公证员应证实订立行为人及参与行为之其他人之身份；但该等人为公证员本人所认识者除外。

二、在有关行为中对订立行为人之身份作出证实，得以下列任一方式为之：

（a）出示澳门居民身份证或等同文件；

（b）出示护照；

（c）两名证明人作出声明，而证明人之身份须经公证员透过上两项所指之任一方式作证实，或为公证员本人所认识者。

三、对参与公证行为之其他人之身份，仅得以上款 a 项及 b 项所指之任一方式作出证实。

四、在证实身份时，不得接纳与利害关系人提供之身份数据不符之文件，亦不得接纳已逾有效期之文件。

五、文书证人得作为证明人。

第六十九条（法人之代理）

一、有效期为三个月之法人登记证明，为应作登记之法人之代理人身份之书证，以及该代理人具足够权力之书证，但不妨碍公证员尚可要求提供其他文件，以使其对代理人所主张之权力得以全面证实。

二、属已指定秘书之公司者，若向公证员提交经该秘书证明、其内指出声称为代理人之人具备代理人身份并列出其各项代理权之文件，则免除提供商业登记证明；以上规定不妨碍公证员尚可要求提供其他文件，以使其对代理人所主张之权力得以全面证实。

三、若法人代理人所主张之身份及法人代理人具备正当参与行为之权力系为公证员本人所认识，则可免除法人代理之书证，但须在有关文件之正文内明确注明此事。

第七十条（意定代理）

一、意定代理系以授权书证明，此授权书之原件或证明须交予公证员，其上须贴有适当之印花及符合

第一百二十八条所指之任一形式。

二、对符合上款规定并透过图文传真传送予公证员之授权书，须视乎情况而适用第六十条或第六十二条之规定。

三、对透过计算机传送予公证员之授权书，适用第六十一条之规定。

第七十一条（补充文件）

一、对于以公证文书为凭证之行为，作为其目标之财产得在附件中标示。

二、下列者亦得列入附件：

（a）按法律规定或当事人意思应以公证文书设立之社团、财团及法人商业企业主之章程；

（b）以信用机构作为利害关系人之行为之合同条款，或因条款内容之涵盖范围广而有理由加载独立文书者；

（c）与公证文书有关之投承规则或工程说明。

三、第五十四条至第五十六条，以及第五十八条第一款之规定，经作出必要配合后，适用于除第二款c项以外之上两款所指之文件。

第七十二条（文书之宣读及解释）

一、在签名前，应在所有参与人在场之情况下，宣读公证文书及附于该文书之补充文件，并随即解释有关文件之内容及其法律后果。

二、上款所指之宣读得由文员或传译在公证员在场之情况下作出；若订立行为人声明已阅读补充文件或完全了解其内容，则免除宣读补充文件，但须在有关文书内明确载明此事。

三、有关文书之内容及其法律后果之解释应由公证员为之，公证员应以扼要但能使订立行为人准确认识其所作行为之意义及后果之方式作出该解释。

第七十三条（签名及指模）

一、公证行为之文书应由订立行为人及参与行为之其他人在公证员在场之情况下签名，最后由公证员签名。

二、第七十一条所指之补充文件，仅须由与其直接有关之订立行为人以及公证员签名，有传译参与时亦须由其签名。

三、不会或不能签名之订立行为人，应按文书正文内所提及之顺序，以右手食指按上指模代替签名。

四、不能以右手食指按上指模之订立行为人，应以公证员指定之手指按上指模，而在指模旁须注明指模所属之手指。

五、若有订立行为人不能按上任何指模，则应在文书内指出此事以及不能按上指模之原因。

第七十四条（在无签名之纸页上之简签）

一、在由散页组成之记录簿册之纸页上，除已具有签名者外，均应由参与行为之人作简签；独立公证文书之纸页上尚应由公证员作简签。

二、在第七十一条所指之补充文件之纸页上，仅须由订立行为人及公证员作简签。

三、不会或不能签名之订立行为人，应在各纸页上按上指模。

第七十五条（行为之连续性）

文书之宣读、解释及签名应连续进行。

第二分节 特别要件

第七十六条（涉及物业登记之载明）

一、凡涉及须作物业登记之行为之文书，均须载明有关房地产在登记局之标示之编号，或声明有关房地产在登记局无标示，在后一情况下，须载明地籍编号以及一切为作出有关标示所需之内容。

二、在缮立分割或移转对房地产之权利之文书以前，或在缮立设定对房地产之负担之文书以前，均须先就该等属被继承人、移转权利之人或设定负担之人名下之权利指出有关确定登录。

三、上款之规定不适用于下列情况：

（a）在取得被分割、被移转或被设定负担之权利之同一日内，由取得权利之人在公证员知悉之情况下因移转其所得之权利或对其所得之权利设定负担而作出之文书；

（b）作为《物业登记法典》生效后所作之首个移转行为之凭证之文书，但仅以可出示证实移转权利之人所具权利之文件，或可在作出移转行为之同时就该移转权利之人所具权利作出证明者为限；

（c）因订立行为人有生命危险而造成之紧急情况，且经适当证实者，又或基于火灾、水灾或总督以批示方式认为属灾难之其他原因而造成失去登记或登记失去效用之情况，以致未能及时取得登记证明者。

四、在上款所指之情况下，应在文书内指出免除注明先前登记所依据之情况；涉及紧急情况时，尚应指出证实此情况之方式，若以总督之批示为依据，则应注明总督之批示。

五、有关登记局内房地产标示及登录之编号，系透过出示发出未逾三个月之内容证明以资证实。

六、房地产无标示之事实系透过出示有效期为三个月之证明以资证实，此证明并不得由透过计算机获取之数据所替代。

第七十七条（受分层所有权制度约束之房地产）

一、对于受分层所有权制度约束之房地产，在缮立移转其独立单位之物权或对其独立单位设定负担之文书以前，须先出示证实有关分层所有权之设定凭证在物业登记中之确定登录之文件。

二、上款之规定，不适用于在以公证方式设定分层所有权之同一日内因移转权利或对权利设定负担而缮立之文书，但仅以此情况为公证员本人所知悉者为限；有关文书内亦应明确注明此事。

三、对于受分层所有权约束之房地产，若其分层所有权之登记尚属临时性质，则有关移转分层建筑物之独立单位或对其独立单位设定负担之行为，仅在其文书内已指明有关分层所有权之登记移转为确定系此移转行为或设定负担行为具备完全效力之条件时，方可作出。

四、对于属批给性质之房地产，在批给尚属临时性质、且分层所有权之登记为临时登记之期间内，适用上款之规定；在此情况下，无须取得七月五日第6/80/M号法律第一百四十三条第一款所指之许可。

第七十八条（与财政司之房屋记录有关之载明事项）

一、对房地产作标示之文书内，应指出在财政司之有关房屋记录内之登录编号；若在该财政部门之房屋记录内无相应登录，则文书内须就应作之登录指出已报请该财政部门作登录之声明。

二、若在财政司之房屋记录内之登录编号，与按物业登记中房地产标示所载在财政司之房屋记录内之登录编号不符，则不得在涉及须作物业登记之事实之文书内对有关房地产作认别。

三、若向公证员提交证实财政司之房屋记录内之旧有编号与现有编号相符之证明，或在不能透过证明证实编号相符时利害关系人能说明两者不符之原因，则不适用上款之禁止，但须在有关文书内载明此事。

四、财政司之房屋记录内之编号，系透过出示发出未逾三个月之有关记录内登录之内容证明，或透过出示该财政部门发出之其他文件以资证实。

五、若涉及应在财政司之房屋记录内作登录但未予登录之房地产，则须透过出示已加上该财政部门收件注录之复本或出示有关声明之证明以证实已报请该财政部门作出登录，以上复本或证明之有效期为一年。

第七十九条（与地籍相符）

一、在涉及须作物业登记之事实之文书内对房地产所作之认别，不得在面积、地点及四至方面与房地产之标示不符。

二、若利害关系人可说明有关认别与房地产之标示不符系因嗣后之修改而造成，且公证员对所涉及者属同一房地产并无疑问，则不适用上款之禁止。

三、若认为有关房地产之标示就第一款所指之某些要素并不符合现状，则须作登记之事实，在未提交有关地籍图前不得成为有依据之事实。

四、若须作登记之事实会导致土地定界之修改，则涉及有关事实之文书，在未提交证实该修改之临时地籍图前不得缮立。

五、第三款及第四款之规定，不适用于经适当方式证实之紧急情况。

第八十条（适用于遗嘱之特别制度）

第七十六条至第七十九条之规定，不适用于遗嘱。

第八十一条（财产价值）

一、在须作物业登记之行为中，应就行为所涉及之每一房地产、涉及之未分割部分或涉及之权利指出其价值，若行为之价值系取决于所标示或列出之财产之总价值而确定，则亦应指出该总价值。

二、对非以当事人简单声明或官方公布为依据而定出之财产价值，应以提交必需文件或以财政部门发出之未逾三个月之证明或声明予以证实；在后一情况下，文书内须指出有关文件所载之财产税务价值。

第三分节　偶然参与者

第八十二条（由不谙作成公证文书所用语言之人参与之行为）

一、若在行为中有所参与之订立行为人不谙作成公证文书所用之语言，则须有一位由其选择之传译与其共同参与该行为，此传译应就文书之内容向该订立行为人作出口头翻译，并将该人之意思表示以口头形式传达予公证员。

二、对于懂得有别于作成公证文书所用语文之另一正式语文之订立行为人，若其明确表示得由公证员信任之传译参与有关行为，则须有此参与。

三、若订立行为人有多人，且无可能找出各人均懂得之一种语言，则由有必要参与之多位传译参与有关行为；若某一或某些订立行为人所懂之语文非为正式语文，且不谙任一正式语文，则得以间接方式进行翻译。

四、若公证员懂得订立行为人足以理解之语言，以致可向其口头翻译文书之内容及接收其意思之表示，则免除传译之参与。

第八十三条（由聋人、哑人及盲人参与之行为）

一、因耳聋而不能听取公证文书之宣读之订立行为人，应大声宣读该文书；不会或不能宣读时，有权指定一人在所有参与人在场之情况下第二次宣读有关文书，并向该订立行为人解释文书的内容。

二、既懂得亦能书写之哑人，应在有关文书内之签名上方作出承认该文书与其意思相符之书面声明；

不会或不能书写之哑人，应以公证员及其他参与者懂得之示意操作表达其意思，不能采用该方法时，应指定传译，此传译须能就订立行为人已理解行为之内容以及有关行为与其意思相符传达有关声明。

三、上条第三款之规定，经作出必要配合后，适用于上款所指传译之参与。

四、失明之订立行为人得指定一人进行第二次宣读文书。

第八十四条（证人及医学鉴定人之参与）

一、仅就下列文书之作成方可有文书证人之参与：

（a）公证遗嘱、密封遗嘱之核准书或启封书，以及废止遗嘱公证书；

（b）除债权证券之拒绝证书以外之其他文书，但仅以该参予系由公证员或某一当事人所要求者为限。

二、在紧急及难以寻求证人之情况下，公证员得就上款a项所指之文书免除证人之参与，但须在有关文书内明确载明此事。

三、若有文书证人之参与，则须为两名。

四、应订立行为人或公证员之要求，医学鉴定人亦得在有关行为中有所参与，以证明订立行为人精神健全。

第八十五条（无能力及无资格之情况）

一、下列者不得成为证明人、传译、医学鉴定人、文书宣读人或证人：

（a）缺乏完全判断力之人；

（b）亲权未解除之未成年人、聋人、哑人及盲人；

（c）任一订立行为人、代理人或被代理人之配偶、直系血亲及姻亲或二亲等内之旁系血亲及姻亲；

（d）与任一订立行为人、代理人或被代理人有事实婚关系之人；

（e）因有关行为而取得任何财产利益之人；

（f）不会或不能签名之人。

二、有关公证机构之工作人员及在该机构内提供服务之其他人员，均不得成为证明人、医学鉴定人或证人；丈夫及妻子亦不得同时成为证明人、医学鉴定人或证人。

三、任何偶然参与行为之人只能以一种身份参与行为；但属第六十八条第五款所规定者除外。

四、公证员有合理理由怀疑任何偶然参与行为之人之适当性时，应拒绝其参与行为，即使该等人非属第一款所禁止之人亦然。

五、证明人、医学鉴定人或证人不谙公证员所懂得之正式语文或不谙任一正式语文时，应适用经作出必要配合之第八十二条之规定。

第八十六条（法定宣誓）

一、传译、医学鉴定人及文书宣读人，均应在公证员面前作出良好执行职务之名誉宣誓或名誉承诺。

二、对于在公共公证机构工作之官方传译，不适用上款之规定。

三、对名誉宣誓或名誉承诺，适用程序法中经作出必要配合之相关规定。

第三节 公证文书之无效、补正及使公证文书转为有效

第一分节 无效

第八十七条（无效之情况）

一、公证文书仅在欠缺下列任一要件时，方因形式上之瑕疵而无效：

（a）缮立公证文书之日期、月份、年份或地点；

（b）已遵守第八十二条及第八十三条所定程序之声明；

（c）对第五十七条第二款规定之遵守；

（d）任一证明人、传译、文书宣读人、医学鉴定人或证人之签名；

（e）懂得及能够签名之任一订立行为人之签名，以及不会或不能签名之订立行为人之指模；

（f）公证员之签名。

二、由无权处理有关事宜或依法应回避之人所缮立之公证文书亦属无效，但不影响民法中有关文书证明力之规定之适用。

三、就任何偶然参与行为之人发生第八十五条所指之某一无能力或无资格之情况时，亦导致公证文书无效。

第八十八条（对某些无效之效果上之限制）

如行为所包括之某些处分系有利于第九条第一款所指之任何人，又或有利于有关行为之任一偶然参与人，其中包括偶然参与作成密封遗嘱核准书之人，则有关无效仅以该处分为限。

第八十九条（将宣告行为无效之裁决通知公证员）

一、法院须将宣告公证行为无效之经确定之司法裁决通知司法事务司司长，该司长应在二十四小时内将之传达缮立有关行为之公证机构。

二、在按上款规定所作之通知中，应载明有关司法卷宗之认别资料、裁决中作出规定部分之内容、作出裁决之日期及裁决已属确定。

三、上述通知应自导致其须被作出之裁决成为确定之日起四十八小时内作出。

第二分节　公证文书之补正及透过司法途径使公证文书转为有效

第九十条（补正）

一、公证文书不符合第八十七条第一款a项、b项、d项及e项所指要件时，其因形式上之瑕疵而造成之无效，得分别在下列情况下由公证员本人补正：

（a）欠缺指出订立行为之日期、月份、年份或地点，但可按第一百四十二条第二款之规定作出附注；

（b）订立行为人以公文书方式声明已遵守第八十二条及第八十三条所定之程序；

（c）偶然参与行为之人未签名，但其身份在有关行为中已作适当认别，且以公文书方式声明在宣读、解释及订立有关行为时在场并声明未拒绝在文书上签名；

（d）未签名或未按上指模之订立行为人以公文书方式声明在宣读及解释有关行为时在场，并声明有关行为符合其本人之意思，且未拒绝在文书上签名或按上指模。

二、司法事务司司长经听取登记暨公证委员会之意见后，得透过批示补正下列无效：

（a）因未遵守第五十七条第二款之规定以致出现形式上之瑕疵而造成之无效，只要当事人以公文书方式声明任何失去效用之字均不会改变行为之主要组成部分或实质内容；

（b）因证明人、医学鉴定人或证人之无能力或无资格而造成之无效，只要该瑕疵仅涉及其中一名参与人且可因另一参与人之适当性而视为被补正。

第九十一条（欠缺公证员签名以及传译或文书宣读人无能力或无资格）

一、因欠缺公证员签名或因传译或文书宣读人无能力或无资格而造成文书无效时，仅得透过司法途径使文书转为有效。

二、欠缺公证员签名之公证文书，仅在证明该文书符合法律，忠实反映当事人之意思，并由公证员主持缮立该文书且未拒绝在文书上签名时，方得转为有效。

三、若传译或文书宣读人无能力或无资格，则仅在证明已将文书内容忠实传达予利害关系人时，方得透过司法途径使该文书转为有效。

第九十二条（透过司法途径使公证文书转为有效之其他情况）

一、在第八十七条第一款b项至e项所指之情况下，只要能证明下列事项，尚得透过司法途径使有关公证文书转为有效：

（a）已遵守规定之程序；

（b）任何删除之字均不会改变行为之主要组成部分或实质内容；

（c）未签名之偶然参与人在宣读、解释及订立有关行为时在场，且未拒绝在文书上签名；

（d）未签名或未按上指模之订立行为人在宣读及解释有关行为时在场，同意缮立该文书，且未拒绝在文书上签名或按上指模。

二、公证文书因证明人、医学鉴定人或证人无能力或无资格而无效时，只要该瑕疵仅涉及其中一名参与人且可由另一名参与人之适当性所补正，即可透过司法途径使该文书转为有效。

三、在上两款所指之情况下，若利害关系人不能或不欲透过行政途径使公证文书转为有效，则得透过司法途径为之；属利害关系人不欲透过行政途径使公证文书转为有效之情况时，一经采取司法途径，即告丧失透过行政途径补正有关瑕疵之权利。

第九十三条（使公证文书转为有效之程序）

一、使公证文书转为有效之诉讼应向具有民事管辖权之初级法院提起。

二、诉讼得由任一利害关系人针对其余利害关系人及公证员提起，亦得由缮立公证文书之私人公证员提起，或应有关之公共公证员要求而由检察院提起。

三、起诉状须致予法院，并应详细指明请求、请求之理由及与请求有利害关系之人之身份。

四、法官须传唤各利害关系人，以便其在十日内提出反对。

五、如有反对提出，即须适用简易诉讼程序之规定；若无反对提出，则法官应命令采取其认为适宜之措施，然后就有关请求之实质问题作出决定。

六、就案件之判决得向中级法院提出上诉；上诉具中止效力，并须按诉讼法之规定而进行及审理。

七、当事人、公证员及检察院，均有提起上诉之正当性。

八、不得就中级法院的合议庭裁判向终审法院提起平常上诉。

九、裁决经确定后，法院须向司法局局长发出裁决内容证明，该证明应在二十四小时内传送至有关之公证机构，以便作出相应之附注。

十、透过司法途径使公证文书转为有效之诉讼程序，在有关请求被裁定理由成立之情况下，须免除诉讼费用及印花税。

第二章　公证书

第一节　一般规定

第九十四条（要求采用公证书）

一、凡构成对不动产之所有权、用益权、使用及居住权、地上权或地役权之确认、设定、取得、分割或消灭之行为，一般均须采用公证书之方式作出。

二、除法律规定之其他行为外，下列行为尤其须采用公证书之方式作出：

（a）公证确认继承资格；

（b）非在遗嘱内作出之使失格之人恢复权利之行为；

（c）不能或当事人不欲按民事登记法律之规定而订立之婚姻协议；

（d）公证证明；

（e）以法律行为设定分层所有权；

（f）永久定期金合同，以及让与物或让与权利之价值高于澳门币500000元或涉及应采用公证书作出让与之物或权利之终身定期金合同；

（g）商业企业拥有不动产时，移转商业企业之所有权或享益权之行为，以及对商业企业设定用益物权或担保物权之行为；

（h）遗产或遗赠中含有依法应采用公证书作出让与之财产时，让与、抛弃及放弃有关遗产或遗赠之行为；

（i）共有物、被继承财产、合营组织财产或其他共同财产中含有依法应采用公证书作出让与之财产时，对共有物、被继承财产、合营组织之财产或其他共同财产进行分割之行为；

（j）涉及依法应采用公证书作出让与之财产时，设立、分立或合并合营组织之行为，以及订立合营组织章程及对其作修改之行为；

（l）设立经济利益集团之行为、合作经营合同以及隐名合伙合同，只要其成员对集团或合作经营之出资或隐名合伙人之出资含有依法应采用公证书作出让与之财产；

（m）向债权人作出之财产交管，只要所交管之财产含有依法应采用公证书作出让与之财产；

（n）非透过司法途径而订立之和解合同，只要法律就其效果之产生定出公证书之要求；

（o）涉及不动产之移转时，设立社团及以生前行为创立财团之行为，包括订立有关章程及对其作修改之行为；

（p）设定及更改不动产上之抵押权之行为，对不动产上之抵押权或其登记之优先次序作出之让与，以及对载于物业登记之抵押债权作出之让与或出质；

（q）涉及对不动产设定负担时，设立、更改及解除对收益用途作指定之行为，以及订定及修改按月提供之扶养给付之行为；

（r）不动产融资租赁合同。

三、除法律另有规定者外，凡导致依法或按当事人意思而采用公证书作出之法律行为被废止或变更之行为，以及不能以附注方式作出之更正该等法律行为之行为，亦应以公证书作出；以上规定不影响《民法典》第二百一十三条及第二百一十四条规定之适用。

第九十五条（特别法例）

受特别法律规范约束之行为及合同，尤其以本地区、公共部门及其他公法人作为订立人而参与之行为，均须按相关法例之规定作出。

第二节　公证确认继承资格

第九十六条（继承人及受遗赠人资格之确认）

一、若无须进行强制性财产清册程序，或虽有未成年继承人或等同未成年人之继承人，但遗产中并无位于澳门之财产时，则得透过公证方式确认继承人之资格。

二、公证员应按下条第一款所指之人作出之声明及其提交之文件，审查是否发生上款所指之情况。

三、受遗赠人系以不确定或概括之方式被设定，或全部遗产均以遗赠方式分配时，本分节之规定，经作出必要配合后，适用于对受遗赠人资格之确认。

第九十七条（概念及须载明之事项）

一、公证确认继承资格，系指由三名人士或由待分割财产管理人作出声明，内容为指出待确认资格人为死者之继承人，且不存在任何较其优先继承或与其共同继承之人。

二、声明人须接受提醒，其内容为如声明人故意及为损害他人之目的作虚假声明，则会被处以适用于在官员面前作虚假声明罪之刑罚；以上提醒应于公证书内明确载明。

三、对于被继承人及待确认资格人，应以载明其全名、婚姻状况、国籍及常居所认别其身份，但不影响第六十七条第三款第一部分规定之适用。

四、对于旁系继承人，应就可继承被继承人遗产之兄弟姊妹载明其与被继承人属同父同母、同父异母或异父同母之兄弟姊妹关系。

第九十八条（声明人）

一、不能成为文书证人之人、待确认资格人之配偶及可继承待确认资格人之遗产之血亲，以及与待确认资格人在事实婚状况下生活之人，均不得作为旨在产生上条第一款所指效力之声明人，但属待分割财产管理人者除外。

二、公证员有充分理由怀疑某些人作为声明人之适当性时，亦不应接纳该等人为声明人。

第九十九条（必要文件）

一、确认继承资格公证书之作成，应附同下列文件：

（a）被继承人之死亡证明；

（b）证明特留份继承之文件，只要特留份继承系其中一名待确认资格人具有继承人资格之依据者；

（c）遗嘱内容证明或赠与书内容证明，只要全部或部分继承系以遗嘱或赠与为依据者。

二、若规范继承之法律非为澳门法律，则公证书之作成尚应附同有关国家之使馆人员或等同人员发出之文件，又或附同公证文件或其他适当文件，以视乎情况而证明按被继承人之属人法所定之有关继承之法定顺位，或证明被继承人之遗嘱能力。

第一百条（确认继承资格之效力）

一、公证确认继承资格与透过司法途径确认继承资格具有相同之效力，并构成享有共同财产半数之配偶或其余任一继承人为惠及各继承人而要求作出下列行为之足够凭证：

（a）物业登记；

（b）商业、汽车及航空器之登记；

（c）债权证券之附注；

（d）文学产权、科学产权、艺术产权及知识产权之移转之附注。

二、全部继承人及享有共同财产半数之配偶为惠及各继承人而要求或许可提取金钱或其他有价物时，公证确认继承资格公证书亦构成有关提取之足够凭证。

第一百零一条（对确认继承资格提起争议）

一、拟对公证确认继承资格提起争议之人，除应按民事诉讼法之规定提起诉讼外，亦应要求法院立即将有诉讼待决一事通知司法事务司司长，该司长应在二十四小时内将此事传达缮立有关公证书之公证机构。

二、就上述争议之诉所作之裁决一经确定，即须通知缮立有关公证书之公证机构。

三、第八十九条之规定适用于上述裁决之通知。

第三节 公证证明

第一百零二条（为在物业登记中继续建立连续性而作之证明）

一、为在物业登记中继续建立连续性而作之证明，旨在自物业登记之末次登录中之权利人起继续建立登记之连续性，目的为弥补利害关系人不能取得作为其所拥有权利之依据之某一或某些移转之证明凭证。

二、公证书内应加载自末次登录中之权利人起一切证明利害关系人所拥有权利之移转行为，并应详细指出移转之原因及有关主体之身份资料。

三、公证证明系透过利害关系人之声明作出，声明内应指出不能取得第一款所指凭证之原因。

第一百零三条（为在物业登记中重新建立连续性而作之证明）

一、为在物业登记中重新建立连续性而作之证明，系指利害关系人为着产生在物业登记中作登录之效力而就权利之原始取得所作出之确认。

二、在有关公证书内应就所证明之权利指出其取得所依据之具体情况，并指出在取得权利前后作出、且对权利之主张属必要之移转行为。

三、若系因以无依据之占有为基础之取得时效而取得权利，则须在文书内指出允许作出有关主张之事实状况。

四、对本条所指之证明，适用经作出必要配合之上条第二款及第三款之规定。

第一百零四条（同时作出之证明）

上两条所指之公证证明，得在作为取得权利之凭证之文书内作出；但在涉及让与行为之情况下，让与人须预先作出上两条所指之声明。

第一百零五条（允许作出证明之限制）

一、对于按税法规定应加载财政司之房屋记录内之权利，仅允许就该记录所登录之权利作出证明。

二、除在该记录内被登录之权利人外，因继承或生前行为而从该人取得权利之人，亦具有以提出证明人之身份作出有关行为之正当性。

第一百零六条（对所指出原因之审查）

对利害关系人所指出之原因是否会导致其不能透过一般非司法途径证实拟证明之事实，公证员有权作出决定。

第一百零七条（声明之确认；对订立行为人之提醒）

一、由提出证明人作出之声明，须经三人作出声明予以确认；对该三名声明人适用经作出必要配合之第九十八条之规定。

二、公证员应向各订立行为人作出第九十七条第二款所指之提醒，并在公证书之正文内明确载明此事。

第一百零八条（文件）

一、对于为物业登记之目的而缮立之有关公证证明之公证书，须附同下列文件以作成之：

（a）房地产标示之内容证明，以及现有全部登录之证明；

（b）财政司之房屋记录中相应登录之证明。

二、对于为继续建立连续性而缮立之有关公证证明之公证书，尚须附同证实所证明之移转行为已履行税法规定之文件，或附同证实不能取得有关证明之证明，以作成之。

三、上两款所指之证明，须属发出未逾三个月之证明。

四、在第一百零三条第二款所指之情况下，若提出证明人未能确认不可能取得证实在所证明之事实前后所作移转行为之文件，则尚须出示该等文件。

第一百零九条（对被登录之权利人作出之预先通知）

一、若欠缺由被登录之权利人参与行为之凭证，则在法院基于利害关系人之要求而向该权利人作出诉讼以外之通知前，不得缮立有关公证书。

二、法官须在有关批示内命令立即以公示方式通知被登录之权利人，或在证实该人已失踪或死亡时通知其继承人，而无论其继承人是否已被确认继承资格。

三、对上款所指之通知，适用经作出必要配合之民事诉讼法律中因地点不确定而作之公示传唤之规定。

四、公证书内应载明已作上述通知。

第一百一十条（公布）

一、有关公证证明之公证书须以内容摘要方式公布；摘要自公证书作成之日起五日内发出。

二、公布须在澳门报章中最多人阅读之其中一份中文报章及一份葡文报章上作出；公布费用由利害关系人承担。

第一百一十一条（对公证证明之争议）

一、如某一利害关系人就被证明之事实向法院提出争议，应同时要求法院立即将有诉讼待决一事通知司法事务司司长，该司长应在二十四小时内将此事传达缮立有关公证书之公证机构。

二、就争议之诉所作之裁决一经确定后，即须通知缮立有关公证书之公证机构，为此适用第八十九条之规定。

第一百一十二条（证明之发出）

一、若自有关公证证明之公证书之内容摘要公布之日起计三十日内，未收到有争议之诉待决之通知，则方可就该公证书发出证明。

二、上款之规定，不影响为用作对被证明之事实提出争议而发出证明，而证明内须明确载明此用途。

三、若已有争议提出，则仅在就有关诉讼之确定裁判作出附注后，方得发出证明。

第一百一十三条（其他证明）

一、本节之规定，经作出必要配合后，适用于对权利所作之为法律所允许及用作载入物业登记以外之其他登记内之公证证明。

二、若未向公证员提交可证实有关权利实际上有可能获得公证证明之证明，则公证证明即不应作出；以上规定不影响要求提交第一百零八条第二款及第四款所指之文件。

第三章 独立公证文书

第一节 一般规定

第一百一十四条（份数）

缮立独立文书时，仅须作成一份文书，但以一式两份之方式作出之遗嘱存放书除外。

第一百一十五条（每份文书之处置）

一、独立文书须交予订立行为人或利害关系人。

二、上款之规定不适用于密封遗嘱启封书、追认公证行为之文书，以及第一百二十八条第二款所指之授权书及相应之复授权书，上述文书均须予存档。

三、涉及遗嘱存放书时，一式两份中视作正本之一份须予存档，另一份则交予存放人。

第一百一十六条（依据之文件）

对作成公证行为所需之文件，须与文书正本作相同处置。

第二节 密封遗嘱之核准

第一百一十七条（密封遗嘱之作成）

一、密封遗嘱须由遗嘱人本人手写或由他人代其书写，且仅在遗嘱人不会或不能签名时方不应由其在遗嘱上签名，在此情况下得由他人代其签名。

二、在遗嘱上签名之人，应在遗嘱中无其签名之纸页上作简签。

三、对订正、涂改、划线、插行书写、墨迹、边页注记或删除之字所作之更改声明，仅得由书写遗嘱之人或由遗嘱人本人作出。

四、更改声明须于签名前作出，又或作为附加部分紧接于签名后作出，并须再次签名。

第一百一十八条（遗嘱之宣读）

一、仅在遗嘱人要求宣读时，方得由缮立密封遗嘱核准书之公证员宣读有关遗嘱。

二、若遗嘱人允许，则得在参与行为之其他人在场之情况下高声宣读有关遗嘱。

第一百一十九条（文书之形式要件）

一、密封遗嘱核准书，须缮立于遗嘱人提交公证员之遗嘱内紧接签名之部分。

二、核准书应特别提及由遗嘱人所作之下列声明：

（a）在所提交之遗嘱内载有作为其遗愿之处分；

（b）遗嘱由其本人书写及签名，或由他人代书而仅由其本人签名，或因其本人不会或不能签名而由他人代书及签名；

（c）遗嘱中并无经订正之字、删除之字、经涂改或插行书写之字、墨迹或边页注记；若有上述情况，则指出对此已作出适当之更改声明；

（d）在遗嘱内，除有签名之纸页外，其余各页均由在遗嘱上签名之人作简签。

三、若遗嘱非由遗嘱人本人书写，则核准书内尚应载有遗嘱人所作之因已阅读遗嘱而了解遗嘱内容之声明，遗嘱人因此须在公证员面前证明其懂得及能够阅读。

四、核准书内尚应载明遗嘱中整页占用之页数及非整页占用之纸页上之行数。

五、遗嘱之各页均须由公证员作简签，且应以确保遗嘱与其核准书合成一整体之适当机械方式，将有关纸页与核准书连接。

六、应利害关系人之要求，遗嘱得装入注明遗嘱人姓名之信封内，而公证员应将信封以火漆封口，并在火漆上盖上有关公证机构之印章。

第三节　遗嘱之存放及交还

第一百二十条（密封遗嘱之存放）

一、若遗嘱人拟将其密封遗嘱存放于公证机构，则应将之递交予公证员，以便公证员缮立载明上述情况之文书。

二、密封遗嘱之存放书内应载明该存放书系以一式两份之方式缮立。

三、对为存放于公证机构而递交之遗嘱，适用上条第六款之规定。

第一百二十一条（其他遗嘱之存放）

一、对于以民法规定之任一特别形式而订立之遗嘱之存放，适用经作出必要配合之上条规定。

二、存放人在作出存放时，应向公证员声明是否知悉遗嘱人之死亡，该声明须在存放书内明确载明。

三、公证员尚应在存放书内指明存放人之身份、存放遗嘱之份数，且在属航海日志或飞行日志内载有记录或属《民法典》第二千零五十一条所指之情况时，尚应载明有关记录内之数据。

第一百二十二条（遗嘱之交还）

一、遗嘱人得随时取回其已存放之遗嘱。

二、已存放之遗嘱，仅得交还予遗嘱人或具特别权力之受权人。

第四节　密封遗嘱之启封

第一百二十三条（有权限之公证机构）

任何公共公证机构均有权限将密封遗嘱启封，但不包括存放于公证机构之密封遗嘱，在此情况下，仅密封遗嘱所存放之公证机构方有权将之启封。

第一百二十四条（必要文件）

一、在遗嘱人已死亡之情况下，密封遗嘱之启封书应在遗嘱人死亡登记之证明被出示后缮立；属司法机关宣告遗嘱人被推定死亡并因此命令启封密封遗嘱之情况时，有关启封书应在司法机构命令启封之裁判之证明被出示后缮立。

二、若公证员本人获悉遗嘱人死亡之事实，则为着启封遗嘱之目的，对出示遗嘱人死亡登记之证明之要求予以免除。

三、然而，在上款所指之情况下，仅在向公证员出示证实遗嘱人死亡之文件后，方得获发遗嘱之证明。

第一百二十五条（启封程序）

一、密封遗嘱之启封按下列步骤为之：

（a）检查遗嘱之状况，尤其是否存在未作更改声明之瑕疵、涂改字、订正字、插行书写之字、删除之字、墨迹或页边注记；

（b）公证员在提交遗嘱之人或利害关系人，以及证人同时在场之情况下高声宣读遗嘱。

二、如遗嘱按第一百一十九条第六款之规定装入以火漆封口之信封内，公证员尚应检查火漆是否完整。

三、遗嘱启封后，须由提交遗嘱之人或利害关系人，以及由证人及公证员在遗嘱之各页上作简签，随后须将遗嘱存档。

第一百二十六条（启封书）

就遗嘱之启封须缮立启封书，其内特别载明已执行上条所指之程序，并视乎情况而载明遗嘱人死亡日期或司法机关作出命令启封遗嘱之裁判之日期。

第一百二十七条（依职权启封遗嘱）

一、若公证员获悉遗嘱存放于其公证机构内之某人在澳门死亡，则应向有权限之登记局索取遗嘱人之死亡证明；该证明须加快发出，且免除缴纳有关手续费。

二、公证员收到死亡证明后，须启封遗嘱并缮立启封书。

三、公证员按上款规定启封遗嘱后，应随即将存在遗嘱一事以挂号信通知遗嘱内提及之继承人及遗嘱执行人，已知遗嘱人有可继承遗产之亲等较近之血亲时，亦应通知该等血亲。

四、未付清包括遗嘱印花税之文书收费前，公证员不得就密封遗嘱提供任何信息或发出密封遗嘱之内容证明。

第五节　授权、复授权及配偶之同意

第一百二十八条（授权书之形式）

一、依法应由公证员参与之授权，得采用下列形

式作出：

（a）公证文书；

（b）经认证之文书；

（c）由被代理人签名且签名经当场认定之文书。

二、同时为受权人或第三人之利益而作出之授权，以及授予双方代理权之授权，均应以公证文书作出。

三、下列授权应采用上款a项及b项所指之其中一种形式作出：

（a）具民事或商事上之一般管理权力之授权；

（b）具承担汇票债务权力之授权；

（c）作出授权之目的与在司法争议中作出自认、撤回或和解有关；

（d）有关授权涉及应以公证书或其他公文书作出之行为之代理权，或涉及须以公文书证明之行为之代理权。

四、在第一款c项所指情况下，若授权书系以被代理人不谙之语言作成，则由其选定之一名传译与其共同参与有关行为，而认定语内须载明委托人应作之指出委托人了解及接纳授权书内容之声明。

第一百二十九条（复授权及配偶之同意）

对复授权及配偶之同意，适用经作出必要配合之有关授权之规则。

第六节　债权证券之拒绝证书

第一百三十条（汇票及其他债权证券之拒绝证书）

本节之规定，适用于汇票之拒绝证书；对本票、支票、赊账买卖票据或其他依法须就有关情况作出拒绝证书之债权证券，适用本节内与该等债权证券之性质及规范该等债权证券之特别制度不抵触之部分。

第一百三十一条（提交汇票以缮立拒绝证书）

一、提交人应将汇票交予公证机构，并附同为作出通知所需之符合已核准式样之通知信；通知信须适当填写，且贴上所需邮票。

二、即使提交人未附同上款所指之通知信，公证员亦不得拒绝其提交汇票。

三、收到为缮立拒绝证书而提交之汇票后，应将一份以式样经核准之印件作成及由提交人填写之收据交予提交人。

四、汇票之提交，须按其交予公证机构之顺序而在专用簿册内作登记。

五、汇票提交后，须在汇票上注录有关提交之编号及日期，并由公证员在汇票上作简签。

第一百三十二条（提交之期间及其推延）

一、为缮立拒绝证书，应在下列期间内提交汇票：

（a）若属拒绝承兑定日付款之汇票、出票日后定期付款之汇票或见票后定期付款之汇票，则提交期为直至得作提示承兑之日；

（b）若属承兑见票后定期付款之汇票或属按特别约定应在某一期间内作提示承兑之汇票，而在承兑时未注明日期，则提交期为直至为缮立拒绝承兑证书而提交汇票之期间届满之日；

（c）若属拒绝支付a项所指之汇票，则在紧接可作支付日后之两个工作日内之其中一日提交，或在可作支付之多日内之最后一日提交；

（d）若属拒绝支付见票即付之汇票，则在得作提示付款之期间内提交；

（e）若属《商法典》第一千一百九十九条及第一千二百零一条所指之情况时，持票人可随时提交。

二、在《商法典》第一千一百五十七条第一款及第一千一百七十七条第三款所指之情况下，若汇票之提示承兑或提示付款系在有关期间之最后一日作出，则为缮立拒绝证书而提交汇票尚得在翌日作出。

三、若提交汇票之期间届满之日为公共公证机构或信贷机构停止服务之日，则该期间届满之日延至紧接之第一个工作日。

四、对于银行及同类机构，本条所指期间届满之日延至紧接之第一个工作日。

五、为缮立拒绝证书而提交汇票，最迟应在正常工作时间结束前一小时作出。

六、在法定期间届满后提交汇票，并不构成拒绝缮立有关拒绝证书之理由。

第一百三十三条（不得被接纳以缮立拒绝证书之汇票）

一、不得就下列汇票缮立拒绝证书：

（a）欠缺《商法典》第一千一百三十四条所指某一要件之汇票，只要该欠缺不能按《商法典》第一千一百三十五条之规定弥补；

（b）以公证员不谙之语文作成之汇票，只要提交人未附同译本；但以正式语文作成之汇票除外，在此情况下，汇票之翻译须依职权作出；

（c）所指出之承兑地点或支付地点非为澳门特区之汇票。

二、上款b项第一部分所指之汇票译本，须发还予提交人，有关翻译得由任何人作出，而无须经特别程序；翻译为依职权作出时，须由公证员定出翻译之方式，如定出之方式为书面，尚须定出对译本之处置。

第一百三十四条（通知）

一、公证员应在提交汇票当日或紧接之第一个工作日，将提交汇票一事通知应承兑或支付汇票之人，包括所有对持票人承担责任之人。

二、通知系透过将附同汇票被提交之通知信以挂号邮递方式寄发而作出，挂号存根须存盘在专用之档案组内。

第一百三十五条（取回之汇票）

若提交人在拒绝证书作成前取回汇票，则应在提交汇票之登记旁注明提交人已收回汇票及收回之日期。

第一百三十六条（缮立拒绝证书之期间、顺序及效力）

一、若提交人未取回汇票，则汇票之拒绝证书须在寄出通知信之五日后、提交汇票后之十日内缮立。

二、拒绝证书须按汇票提交之顺序缮立。

三、拒绝证书自汇票提交之日起产生效力。

第一百三十七条（拒绝证书之形式要件）

一、拒绝证书应透过填写式样经核准之印件及以针对所有汇票债务人之方式缮立。

二、拒绝证书应载明以下内容：

（a）汇票之认别数据，包括发票日期、出票人姓名及相应的金额；

（b）有关第一百三十四条所指通知之注录，或注明因未附同通知信提交汇票而未作通知；

（c）注明被通知之人是否在场，以及被通知之人所提供未承兑或未付款之理由；

（d）公证员就有关拒绝证书之依据所作之声明，并指出申请缮立有关证书之人及证书所针对之人；

（e）提交汇票之日期；

（f）被通知并到场之人之签名，或由该等人所作之因不会签名、不能签名或不欲签名而未签名之声明。

三、有关拒绝承兑或拒绝付款之理由之声明得为口头声明，或为由被通知之人交予公证员之书面声明，而书面声明须予存档。

四、声明人得要求发出拒绝证书之认证缮本。

第一百三十八条（汇票之发还）

一、发还汇票前须收回第一百三十一条第三款所指之收据，并将之作废。

二、若上款所指之收据遗失，则在归还汇票前应向提交汇票之人索取收据，并将之存档。

第四章 附注

第一百三十九条（附注之定义及方式）

一、附注系指将后一行为扼要注录于前一行为，而在注录内载明所附注之事实及其凭证之认别资料。

二、附注须置于记载有关行为之纸页上方空白处或页边空白处，并经适当注明日期及由公证员签名。

三、对在记录簿册内缮立之行为所作之附注，须首先置于纸页上方空白处，其次置于留作缮立公证文书之部分内可能空白之处，最后置于外侧页边空白处。

四、如用完按以上两款规定可作附注之空位，须在同类之记录簿册内首张可使用之纸页上留作缮立公证文书之部分内作出附注，并须作出必要之承接说明。

第一百四十条（发起）

一、依职权作出附注之情况限于拟附注之行为适当指出识别前一行为之资料者，或法律明文规定须依职权作出该附注者。

二、不属应依职权作出附注之情况时，如认定两个行为处于第一百四十一条及第一百四十二条所指状况，得应任何利害关系人之请求作出附注。

三、为着上款规定之目的，利害关系人在有需要时应出示载有拟附注之事实之文书之复本或证明。

第一百四十一条（附注之事实）

下列事实须附注于与该等事实有关之文书内：

（a）遗嘱人死亡；

（b）赠与人死亡，只要有关赠与附有应于赠与人死后履行之为公益或为死后受悼念或近似目的而设定之负担；

（c）对授权之废止或对获授予权力之放弃，以及以第一百二十八条第二款所指之授权为基础所作之复授权；

（d）就针对公证确认继承资格或公证证明提出争议之诉讼待决一事所作之通知，以及按第一百一十条之规定就公证证明所作之公布；

（e）就上项所指诉讼作出之法院裁判，以及宣告公证行为无效及使公证行为转为有效之法院裁判；

（f）有关行为所具瑕疵之补正；

（g）所存放之遗嘱之交还；

（h）涉及接纳、追认、更正或废止前一行为或对前一行为作附加之公证行为；

（i）按下条规定所作之对缺漏之弥补及对不准确之处之更正。

第一百四十二条（缺漏之弥补及不准确之处之更正）

一、对在记录簿册内缮立之行为中出现、与下款所指事项有关且由经文件证实之错误所引致之缺漏及不准确之处，得随时透过附注予以弥补及更正，只要不会因此而对该行为之对象或参与者之身份产生疑问。

二、得透过附注弥补或更正与下列事项有关之缺漏或不准确之处：

（a）缮立公证行为之日期、月份、年份或地点；

（b）房地产标示及登录之编号、须作商业登记之实体之登记编号以及所涉之登记局；

（c）财政司房屋记录之登录以及财产之税务价值；

（d）房地产所处之堂区、公共街道及所在地之门牌号码；

（e）当事人、参与行为之人以及确认继承资格公证书内之继承人或受遗赠人之姓名之书写、罗马拼音及拼音编号、婚姻财产制及其他身份数据；

（f）按公证行为之文本显示属单纯之误算、误写或缺漏；

（g）特别法要求载明之事项及作出之提醒；

（h）存盘文件之记载。

三、若须缴纳物业转移税之差额，则利害关系人应证实已缴纳该差额；所作之更正引致有关行为之价值增加时，须制作新收费账目，以缴纳对应于增加之价值之手续费及印花税。

四、在第二款g项所指情况下，若未载明之事项为土地批出合同、受移转人接纳该合同之条款、就七月五日第6/80/M号法令第一百五十五条第三款之规定对受移转人所作之提醒、存在地租、法律要求载明之其他事项或作出之其他提醒，则附注须根据经认证之文书作出，而只有对拟更正之行为有直接利害关系之订立行为人方得参与作成该文书。

五、在记录簿册内缮立之行为中出现之缺漏或不准确之处，若与公证员应审查之税务规定之遵守情况有关或与存盘文件之记载有关，且该缺漏或不准确之处已根据该行为之内容予以证实，则得依职权透过附注予以改正。

六、若按公证文书之内容或公证机构存有之数据可确定作出公证行为之时间或地点，则对作出有关公证行为之日期、月份、年份或地点之缺漏或不准确之处，亦得依职权透过附注予以弥补或更正。

七、本条所指之附注应由公证员本人签名。

第一百四十三条（就遗嘱人及赠与人死亡所作之附注）

一、经任何出示遗嘱人死亡登记之证明人之请求，得于遗嘱内或废止遗嘱之公证书内附注遗嘱人之死亡。

二、公证员收到澳门某一公共部门就遗嘱人之死亡所作之正式通知时，若尚未就该遗嘱人之死亡作附注，则应要求有权限之登记局免费发出遗嘱人之死亡证明，并在收到该证明后依职权作有关附注。

三、附注应载明遗嘱人死亡之日期、死亡登记编号以及缮立该登记之登记局。

四、本条之规定，经作出必要配合后，适用于就赠与人之死亡所作之附注。

第一百四十四条（就交还存放之遗嘱所作之附注）

获交还存放之密封遗嘱之人，应在就交还该遗嘱所作之附注内签名，若不会或不能签名，则应在附注内按上指模。

第一百四十五条（就附注之事实所作之告知）

一、若某一公证机构应依职权就某项事实作附注，而载有所附注之事实之文书系由另一公证机构所缮立，则缮立该文书之公证员应向前者提供作附注所需之数据。

二、作附注所需之数据得透过以签收、挂号邮寄或图文传真之方式传送之公函提供；以图文传真提供数据时，须对已收到之数据作确认。

第一百四十六条（期间）

公证员应在三日内履行上数条所定之义务。

第一百四十七条（文件之处置）

一、附注所依据之文件必须存盘。

二、透过图文传真收到以感热纸印出之文件时，公证员亦应将影印该文件而得之复印件存盘。

三、非因依职权提出要求而获给予之遗嘱人或赠与人之死亡证明，不受第一款规定之约束。

第五章　登记

第一百四十八条（对象）

下列者须登记于用作登记之簿册内：

（a）缮立于第二十二条第一款a项及b项所指簿册内之文书；

（b）密封遗嘱之核准书、存放书及启封书，以及其他遗嘱之存放书；

（c）为缮立拒绝证书而作之债权证券之提交、债权证券之收回以及拒绝证书；

（d）第一百二十八条第二款所指之授权书以及相应之复授权书；

（e）公证行为之追认书；

（f）设立社团及创立财团之经认证之文书；

（g）对商业企业主簿册之认证行为；

（h）当事人拟在公证机构存盘之文件。

第一百四十九条（登记次序）

登记须按缮立文书或提交文件之次序每日作出。

第一百五十条（公证遗嘱及公证书之登记）

一、公证遗嘱及废止遗嘱之公证书之登记内应载有下列资料：

（a）缮立文书之簿册之编号及文书在簿册内所处之第一页之页码；

（b）文书之名称及缮立文书之日期；

（c）遗嘱人或订立行为人之全名。

二、杂项公证书之登记内除上款a项及b项所指之资料外，尚应载有下列资料：

（a）行为之目标及价值；

（b）与行为有关之商业企业主之商业名称及住所，或与行为有关之法人之名称及住所；

（c）各当事人之全名，当事人已婚时，配偶之姓名得按具体情况以"及妻子"或"及丈夫"一词代替；

（d）对因有关行为而须缴交之税捐及税项之缴纳情况之监察属必需之说明。

三、上款c项所指之有关当事人全名之记载，得透过指出首位权利主体及首位义务主体之姓名，并在其后按具体情况加上"及其他一人"或"及其他各人"一词为之。

第一百五十一条（与密封遗嘱有关之文书之登记）

一、密封遗嘱之核准书之登记须在交还遗嘱前作出；登记内应载有下列资料：

（a）文书之名称及缮立文书之日期；

（b）遗嘱人之全名、父母姓名、出生日期、婚姻状况及居所；

（c）指出对遗嘱有否按第一百一十九条第六款所指之程序处理。

二、密封遗嘱之存放书及启封书之登记内，以及第一百二十一条所指之存放书之登记内，应载有上款a项所指之数据、遗嘱人之全名以及存放书及启封书在档案组内之编号。

第一百五十二条（与债务证券之拒绝证书有关之登记）

一、为缮立拒绝证书而提交债权证券时，就提交所作之登记内，应载有提交日期及提交人、承兑人或受票人与出票人之姓名、居所或住所，以及债权证券之类型与所含债务之金额。

二、拒绝证书之登记，系指在就提交所作之登记旁作出之记明拒绝证书之依据及日期之注录。

三、就收回为缮立拒绝证书而提交之债务证券所作之登记，系透过在就提交所作之登记旁注明已收回债权证券及收回之日期而作出。

第一百五十三条（认证簿册之登记）

认证商业企业主簿册之登记内，尤应载有日期及商业企业主之认别资料，包括指出其住所，并应注明经认证之簿册之性质及页数。

第一百五十四条（其他行为之登记）

一、以上各条所指文件或文书以外之其他文件或独立文书之登记，系指提交文件日期或缮立文书日期之注明，以及该文件或文书之认别数据之指出，而后者系透过注明该文件或文书之类型或性质、利害关系人之全名或法人名称及文件或文书在档案组内之编号为之。

二、当事人请求存盘之文件经登记后，不得将之交还。

第六章　私文书之认证

第一百五十五条（经认证之文书）

私文书经当事人在公证员面前确认其了解文书内容且文书表达其意思后，即成为经认证之文书。

第一百五十六条（认证语）

一、公证员收到为获认证而提交之文书后，应缮立认证语。

二、本法典有关公证文书之规定中与认证语之性质不抵触之部分，均适用于认证语。

第一百五十七条（形式要件）

一、除应符合经作出必要配合之第六十六条第一款之规定之适用部分外，认证语尚应载有：

（a）当事人所作之已阅读文书或完全了解文书内容且该文书表达其意思之声明；

（b）就文书内未经适当作出更改声明之订正字、插行书写之字、涂改字、删除之字或划线所作之更改声明。

二、若拟认证之文书系由别人代为签名，则认证语除载有上款所指内容外，尚应载明代签人之身份数据，以及注明被代签人在认证行为中确认该代签行为，而被代签人应在认证语内按上指模。

第一百五十八条（社团及财团）

一、除法律要求其他更庄严之方式外，设立社团之凭证、以生前行为创立财团之凭证以及有关章程及章程之修改，均应加载经认证之文书，而有关文书须存档。

二、认证语内除应载有上条所指内容外，尚应注明：

（a）公证员应作之对设立凭证、章程及其修改之合法性之认定；

（b）就设立或创立文件、章程及章程之修改仅在《澳门政府公报》上公布后方对第三人产生效力一事，向利害关系人作出之提醒。

三、涉及财团之创立文件时，认证语尚应载有：

（a）就开始认可程序后创立文件即不可废止一事向创立人作出之提醒；

（b）财团仅在获有权限实体认可后方取得法律人格之注明。

四、公证员须依职权促使以摘录方式公布社团之设立文件、有关章程及其修改，公布费用由利害关系人承担；公证员应将公布一事通知有权限作出登记之实体。

五、涉及财团时，公证员应将创立文件之证明送交有权限作认可之实体。

第七章 认定

第一百五十九条（认定之类型）

一、公证认定得为对照认定、当场认定或作出特别注明之认定。

二、签名之对照认定系指将签名与下列任一文件上之签名作出比对：

（a）第六十八条第二款 a 项及 b 项所指之身份证明文件；

（b）上项所指文件之认证缮本；

（c）载有拟认定签名之样本之公司秘书之证明书；

（d）载有拟认定签名之样本之应利害关系人请求为认定签名而在公证机构存盘之文件。

三、当场认定系指认定在公证员面前书写及签名之文书内之笔迹及签名，或认定只在公证员面前签名之文书内之签名；在签署人于认定时在场之情况下作出之认定，亦为当场认定。

四、作出特别注明之认定系指认定时根据法律之规定或应利害关系人之请求，注明与利害关系人、签署人或被代签人有关且为公证员知悉或经公证员按向其出示之文件证实之任何特别情况。

五、公证认定须为对照认定，但法律明文规定须当场认定者除外。

第一百六十条（作出特别注明之认定）

特别注明签署人具有代表人身份之认定，得透过将文件上之签名与第一百五十九条第二款所指任一文件上之签名作出比对之方式为之。

第一百六十一条（代签）

一、只有在经公证员证实身份之被代签人在场且其不会或不能签名之情况下，方得对代签作认定。

二、应在认定签名之行为中，于向被代签人宣读有关文书后在公证员面前作出代签或确认代签。

第一百六十二条（形式要件）

一、在公证认定行为中，应载有以下内容：

（a）作出认定之日期、月份、年份及地点；

（b）作认定之人之身份及作认定之公证机构；

（c）签署人、被代签人及在认定行为中参与之其他人之全名，以及注明证实该等人士身份之方式或公证员认识该等人士；

（d）认定之类型，以及按具体情况注明第一百五十九条第五款或第一百六十条所指之情况；

（e）证明人及其他偶然参与者之签名，以及在其后加上公证员之签名。

二、作出特别注明之认定行为中，除应载有上款所指内容外，尚应指出第一百五十九条第三款所指之文件，或注明该认定系因公证员本人知悉在认定行为中特别指出之情况而作出。

三、代签之认定行为中尚应明确载明可作代签所依据之情况，并应按有被代签人之指模。

四、对签署人或被代签人身份之证实，以及任何偶然参与者身份之证实及其参与，适用本法典有关公证文书之规定。

第一百六十三条（不得作出之认定）

一、作成笔迹或签名时使用之书写材料无稳固性方面之保障时，以及笔迹或签名系置于含有空白行或空白处且未使空白行或空白处失去效用之文书内时，公证员应拒绝对该等笔迹或签名作认定。

二、签名置于全部空白之纸张内、未提供予公证员阅读之文书内或使用之书写材料无稳固性方面之保障之文书内时，公证员亦应拒绝对该等签名作认定。

三、涉及以公证员不谙之语言作成之文书时，仅在由公证员选定之传译将文件向其作翻译后，方得作出有关认定，文件之翻译得为口译。

四、涉及用作证明列入印花税总表但获豁免或减少印花税之行为或合同而未贴上印花之文书时，仅在该文书系载有给予上述税项优惠之法律规定之情况下，方得在该文书内作出认定。

第八章 证明书、证明及同类文件

第一节 一般规定

第一百六十四条（发起）

一、证明书、证明及其他同类文件须应利害关系人之请求，又或应公共当局或公共部门之要求发出，但法律另有规定者除外。

二、应公共当局或公共部门要求发出证明书、证明及其他同类文件时，免缴有关收费；该要求应向有权限之公证员提出，并指明要求发出之文件之用途。

三、属上款规定以外之情况时，若不能立即满足有关请求而发出证明书、证明或其他同类文件，则就该请求应填写一张式样经核准之领取凭单，领取凭单上应注明有关编号；须将该凭单之正本存档，而将复本交予申请人。

第一百六十五条（期间）

一、证明书、证明及同类文件须在自请求或要求之日起计之五个工作日内发出。

二、被请求或要求加快发出之文件应在二十四小时内发出。

三、被请求加快发出文件时，应提醒利害关系人手续费加倍。

第一百六十六条（共同之必备资料）

一、证明书、证明及同类文件内，应载有发出该等文件之公证机构之名称、页数之编号、发出日期及地点、有权限之公证员之签名以及在无签名之纸页上公证员之简签。

二、应公共当局或公共部门要求发出之证明书、证明及同类文件内，尚应载明其用途。

三、按第六条第一款 i 项之规定以图文传真方式传送之证明书、证明及同类文件内，除应载有以上两款所指之必备数据外，尚应含有一终结注记，其内载明就发出内容证明而规定应包括之事项。

第二节 证明书

第一百六十七条（生存证明书及身份证明书）

一、在生存证明书及身份证明书内，特别应指出利害关系人之身份资料，指出证实其身份之方式或注明公证员本人认识该人，以及载有其签名或其不会或不能签名之声明，而无论属何种情况，在该声明后均须按有利害关系人之指模。

二、在证明书内得贴上利害关系人之相片，公证员应在相片上盖上公证机构之钢印。

第一百六十八条（担任职务之证明书）

在担任公共职务或法人行政管理职务之证明书内，应声明公证员本人知悉所证明之事实或仅透过文件证实该事实，在后一情况下应指出获出示之文件之认别资料。

第一百六十九条（透过图文传真接收之文件之证明书）

一、若澳门公共部门或公证机构透过图文传真传送予公证员之文件符合第六十条第二款之规定，则得发出该等文件之证明书。

二、证明书内特别应指出收到文件之日期以及实收页数。

第一百七十条（其他事实之证明书）

其他证明书内应准确载明所证明之事实，特别应载明公证员知悉该事实之途径。

第三节 证明

第一百七十一条（证据价值）

一、公证机构之存盘公证文书、登记及文件之内容，系以所发出之证明予以证实。

二、以图文传真方式传送并符合第一百六十六条第三款规定之文件，具有与发出之证明相同之证据价值。

第一百七十二条（证明之申请及递交）

一、任何人均得申请发出证明，但属下款规定之情况除外。

二、就遗嘱人之死亡未作附注前，与公证遗嘱、废止遗嘱公证书、密封遗嘱存放书及相应登记有关之证明，仅得应遗嘱人或其具特别权力之受权人之申请而发出。

三、上款所指之证明仅得交予申请人本人或经其许可受领该证明之人。

四、无论有否申请，均须发出第二百零九条 d 项所指之获豁免手续费之证明；若该证明系由遗嘱人请求发出，应将之交予遗嘱人，在其他情况下，则应将之交予被公证员收取费用之人。

第一百七十三条（证明之类型）

一、证明得分为内容证明或叙述证明，以及整体证明或部分证明。

二、内容证明系指逐字逐句复制正本内容之证明；叙述证明系指以单纯之摘录方式复制正本内容之证明。

三、涉及正本之全部内容之内容证明或叙述证明为整体内容证明或整体叙述证明；涉及正本之部分内容之内容证明或叙述证明为部分内容证明或部分叙述证明。

四、从公证文书及公证机构之存盘文件发出之证明须为内容证明；与登记有关之证明、用以公布公证行为之证明，以及用以告知有关公证行为之证明，须为叙述证明。

第一百七十四条（证明之方式）

一、内容证明系以影印或获许可使用之其他照相复制方法作成；不能采用上述方法时，得以计算机处理、打字或手写之方法作成。

二、任何叙述证明，以及用以在本地区以外产生公信力或从文本显示不易阅读之手写公证文书及手写存盘文件之内容证明，均须以计算机处理或打字方法作成。

第一百七十五条（形式要件）

证明特别应载有以下内容：

（a）该证明所取自之簿册或档案组之编号及名称；

（b）正本在簿册或档案组内之首页及末页之页码；

（c）所作之与正本相符之声明；

（d）按第一百七十二条第四款之规定发出时，注明系免费发出之证明。

第一百七十六条（内容证明所包含之资料）

一、内容证明应显现或注明正本所载之印记、对正本作认证之其他注记、印花以及缴纳之印花税之款项，并应以显而易见之方式标出有关行为或文件之文本之一切不规范之处及瑕疵。

二、就正本发出证明时，须作成符合正本内之更改声明之证明。

第一百七十七条（整体内容证明）

一、整体内容证明应复制文书之内容、遗嘱全文及密封遗嘱之核准书与启封书、死因赠与公证书之全文以及第七十一条第一款及第二款 a 项及 b 项所指之补充文件之全文。

二、整体内容证明尚应载有附注、参考编号以及该证明所涉之文书及文件之收费账目；应利害关系人之请求，尚得复制作为被证明之行为之依据之其他文件。

第一百七十八条（部分内容证明）

一、公证文书载有多个法律上之行为，或仅载有一个法律上之行为但此行为所产生之权利及义务系涉及不同人或不同实体时，得请求发出仅涉及某个行为或某一当事人之证明，在此情况下须遵守以下数款之规定。

二、部分内容证明除应含有文书内涉及被指出之有关行为或当事人之内容外，尚应载有与制作该文书时之情况及该文书之一般必备数据有关以及与为作成该文书而附同之文件有关之一切资料。

三、对作为被证明之行为之依据之文件，适用上条之规定。

四、证明尚应以叙述方式记明对充分了解证明内容属必需之其他事项，以及载有扩大、限制、变更被证明之行为之订定内容或对该行为设置条件之订定内容。

第四节　认证缮本

第一百七十九条（概念及方式）

一、认证缮本系指公证员从为此目的而获递交之非存盘文件所发出之整体或部分内容副本。

二、认证缮本按第一百七十四条第一款之规定制作；但涉及身份证明文件、护照或驾驶执照者除外，在此情况下，认证缮本仅得以复印件方法制作。

第一百八十条（载明事项）

一、认证缮本应载有该缮本与正本相符之声明；对认证缮本，亦适用第一百七十六条第一款之规定。

二、在上条第二款最后部分所指之情况下，认证缮本亦应载明文件正本之编号、发出正本之日期及实体。

三、若上条第二款最后部分所指文件之有效期已过或保存状况不佳，则仅在认证缮本上载明此事时方得发出认证缮本，但属法院要求发出之情况除外。

第一百八十一条（以公证员不谙之语言作成之文书之认证缮本）

对以公证员不谙之语言作成之文书，得以认证缮本方式加以复制，但公证员得要求由其选定之传译对文书作翻译，文书之翻译得为口译。

第五节　译本

第一百八十二条（概念）

文件之翻译系指将以正式语文作成之文书之全部内容译成另一种正式语文，或将以非正式语文作成之文书之全部内容译成正式语文，又或将以正式语文作成之文书之全部内容译成非正式语文。

第一百八十三条（形式要件）

一、译本内应指出作成原文书所使用之语文，并须载有译文系忠于原文之声明。

二、如译本系由已作宣誓之翻译作成，应在置于译本或附页上之证明书内注明已进行第六十三条第一款最后部分所定程序。

第一百八十四条（制度）

第一百七十五条 c 项、第一百七十六条及第一百七十七条第二款首部分之规定适用于译本。

第三编
对公证员之决定提出之申诉

第一章　一般规定

第一百八十五条（可申诉之决定）

一、对公证员拒绝作出属其权限之行为之决定、拒绝发出证明之决定及公证行为之收费，均得以本法典规定之任一方式提出申诉。

二、对私人公证员之拒绝决定，仅得在第十七条第二款所指情况下提出申诉。

第一百八十六条（申诉之方式）

一、对上条所指之公证员之决定，得以下列任一方式提出申诉：

（a）向公证员提出声明异议；

（b）行政上诉；

（c）向法院之上诉。

二、行政上诉，须向司法事务司司长提起；向法院之上诉，须向具有民事管辖权之初级法院提起。

三、行政上诉系具任意性，且不取决于先前已否向公证员提出声明异议；但提起行政上诉后，即丧失声明异议权，并等同于撤回声明异议。

四、向法院提起上诉后，即丧失声明异议权或行政上诉权，并等同于撤回待决之程序。

五、对在声明异议待决期间提起之行政上诉或向法院之上诉，分别适用第一百九十一条及第二百条第二款及第三款之规定。

第一百八十七条（正当性）

直接受公证员之决定损害之利害关系人，具有对该决定提出申诉之正当性，但法律另有规定者除外。

第二章 行政申诉

第一节 声明异议

第一百八十八条（声明异议之程序及期间）

一、声明异议应采用书面形式，并应说明理由；声明异议须在就其所针对之决定通知利害关系人之日起三十日内，向负责公证机构之公证员提出。

二、对拒绝发出证明之决定或公证行为之收费提出申诉时，声明异议之期间为八日。

三、利害关系人应在声明异议之申请内力求论证声明异议所针对之决定理由不成立，最后并提出改正该决定之请求。

第一百八十九条（决定）

一、有关公证机构之有权限公证员或其代任人应在五日内审查声明异议并作出决定，即使声明异议所针对之决定非由该公证员或代任人本人作出亦然。

二、公证员作出决定时，应说明理由，并在决定中指明将声明异议所针对之决定予以改正或维持。

三、作出决定后，公证员应在二十四小时内将该决定以挂号信的形式通知声明异议人。

四、公证员在第一款所指期间未作出明示决定者，声明异议人之要求即视为被驳回。

第二节 上诉

第一百九十条（上诉之提起及期间）

一、提起上诉，须透过在有关公证机构呈交致予司法事务司司长之上诉申请为之，该上诉视为在公证机构接收申请之日提起。

二、呈交上诉申请时，须附同上诉人认为必要之文件，且在申请内应：

（a）指出上诉所针对之行为；

（b）完整列明上诉之依据；

（c）要求下令作出公证行为或更正收费。

三、对公证员之拒绝决定而提起之直接上诉，须在上诉人获通知该决定之日起三十日内为之。

四、对驳回先前提出之声明异议之决定而提起之上诉，应在就该决定通知利害关系人之日起二十日内为之；若属上条第四款所指之情况，则须在可作该通知之最后一日起二十日内提起该上诉。

五、对拒绝发出证明之决定或公证行为之收费提出申诉时，上诉之期间在任何情况下均为八日。

六、未提出声明异议之利害关系人，不得利用对在声明异议程序内所作决定提起上诉之期间。

第一百九十一条（先前未提出声明异议之上诉）

一、在上条第三款所指情况下，公证机构之有权限公证员或其代任人须于收到申请及附于申请之文件后五日内作出附理由说明之决定，维持或改正上诉所针对之原决定。

二、如公证员改正上诉所针对之原决定，应在二十四小时内将此事以挂号信通知上诉人，在此情况下，上诉即告终结。

三、公证员维持上诉所针对之原决定或可作出此行为之期间届满时，应在二十四小时内将有关卷宗送交司法事务司司长。

第一百九十二条（先前已提出声明异议之上诉）

一、在第一百九十条第四款所指之对有关决定提起上诉之情况下，公证员应在二十四小时内，将上诉申请及附于申请之文件，连同与上诉人有关之声明异议之卷宗，一并送交司法事务司司长。

二、上款之规定，适用于已提出声明异议但未在法定期间对此作决定之情况。

第一百九十三条（嗣后之步骤）

一、司法事务司司长收到有关卷宗后，须将之送交登记暨公证指引及查核部门，以便由该部门发出意见书。

二、上款所指之意见书须在十日内发出；因有关事宜之复杂性而有必要时，得将该期间延长五日。

三、对拒绝发出证明之决定提起上诉或对公证行为之收费提出申诉者，有关意见书须在五日内发出。

第一百九十四条（明示决定之嗣后作出）

一、如属对默示驳回声明异议之决定提起之上诉，公证员得在将有关卷宗送交司法事务司司长后四十八小时内，就声明异议作出明示批准之决定。

二、公证员之决定应告知司法事务司司长，该司长须在二十四小时内将该决定以挂号信的形式通知上诉人，在此情况下，上诉即告终结。

第一百九十五条（对上诉之决定）

一、如有关程序不应按上条第二款之规定终结，司法事务司司长须在第一百九十三条所指意见书发出之日起最长五日期间内，作出批准或驳回上诉之决定。

二、对上诉之决定应在司法事务司收到有关卷宗之日起二十日内作出，但若属对拒绝发出证明之决定或公证行为之收费提出申诉之情况，则应在十日内作出。

三、须在二十四小时内将司法事务司司长之决定以挂号信的形式通知上诉人，并将之告知上诉所针对之公证员。

四、在告知公证员之同时，或在任何情况下于第二款所指期间届满时，司法事务司司长应将与上诉人有关之卷宗之副本送交有关公证机构。

第一百九十六条（决定之效力）

一、就上诉作出批准之决定时，如利害关系人提出请求，即须作出被拒绝之行为，但公证员得在嗣后缮立之文书及发出之证明内载明该决定。

二、属涉及公证行为之收费之决定者，应按决定之内容重新编制收费账目，并在收费账目内载明此事。

第三章 向法院之上诉

第一百九十七条（可提起上诉之决定）

对第一百八十五条所指之公证员之决定，以及驳回先前提出之声明异议之决定，包括默示驳回之决定，得向法院提起上诉。

第一百九十八条（期间）

一、对第一百八十五条所指之公证员之决定而提起之上诉，应在作出有关通知之日起三十日内为之。

二、对驳回声明异议之决定提起上诉者，上诉期间为二十日，自就该决定通知利害关系人之日起或可作该通知之最后一日起计。

三、若先前提起之行政上诉被裁定理由不成立，或未在法定期间就该上诉作决定，则对公证员之决定而提出之申诉，在任何情况下其期间均为二十日，自就司法事务司司长之决定通知上诉人之日起或可作该通知之最后一日起计。

四、对拒绝发出证明之决定提起上诉或对公证行为之收费提出申诉者，在任何情况下其期间均为八日；对该期间之计算，适用以上数款之规定。

五、曾提出声明异议或先前曾提起行政上诉之人，方得利用按第二款及第三款之规定计算之期间。

第一百九十九条（上诉之提起）

一、提起上诉，须透过在有关公证机构呈交致予管辖法院之诉状为之，该上诉视为在公证机构接收诉状之日提起。

二、对上诉之诉状，适用经作出必要配合之本法典有关行政上诉申请之规定。

第二百条（将卷宗送交法院）

一、公证员应在收到上诉后二十四小时内将上诉文件送交管辖法院，并将倘有之与上诉人有关之声明异议及行政上诉之卷宗附同该文件一并送交；以上规定不影响以下数款规定之适用。

二、若公证机构之有权限公证员或其代任人未有机会在先前之行政申诉程序中就上诉事宜表明意见，则得在五日内作出明示决定，维持或改正上诉所针对之原决定。

三、对公证员按上款规定作出之决定，适用经作出必要配合之第一百九十一条第二款及第三款之规定。

四、公证员将卷宗送交法院时，应向司法事务司司长作出通知，以便适用第一百八十六条第四款之规定。

第二百零一条（明示决定之嗣后作出）

一、如属对默示驳回声明异议之决定提起之上诉，公证员得在第一百九十四条第一款所指期间届满前，就声明异议作出明示批准之决定。

二、有关决定告知法院后，法官须终结诉讼程序，并命令对利害关系人作出通知。

第二百零二条（对上诉之审判）

一、法院收到卷宗后，须将之交予法官作批示，而由该法官将之送交检察院作意见书，意见书应在十五日内发出。

二、若法院所收到之卷宗内无登记暨公证指引及查核部门之意见书，则法官须在上款所指批示内命令通知司法事务司司长，以便该部门在上款所指期间届满前发出意见书。

三、若诉讼程序不应按上条第二款之规定终结，则法官须在发出意见书之期间届满后十日内作出判决。

第二百零三条（对裁判之上诉）

一、利害关系人及检察院均得对有关判决向中级法院提起上诉，上诉具中止效力。

二、上诉须按民事诉讼法之规定进行及审判。

三、不得就中级法院的合议庭裁判向终审法院提起平常上诉。

第二百零四条（对确定裁判之执行）

一、对上诉作确定裁判后，法院书记长须对上诉人作出通知，并将所作裁判之证明送交有关公证员及司法事务司司长。

二、如上诉理由成立，司法事务司司长所作之驳回先前提起之行政上诉之决定即不生效力。

三、若法院之裁判要求被上诉所针对之公证员作出有关行为，且利害关系人提出请求，则该公证员应立即作出该行为，并在行为内载明已确定之裁判。

四、属涉及公证行为之收费之裁判者，应按裁判之内容重新编制收费账目，并在收费账目内载明此事。

第二百零五条（上诉利益值及诉讼费用之豁免）

一、上诉利益值为被拒绝作出之行为之价值；但如属对拒绝发出证明之决定提出申诉之情况，上诉利益值为上诉人给予而最终由法院定出之价值。

二、旨在对公证行为之收费提出申诉之上诉，其利益值为上诉所针对之收费之金额。

三、无论对上诉之裁判为何，上诉所针对之公证员均无须支付诉讼费用及预付金；但证明其行事出于故意或恶意者除外。

第四编 最后规定

第一章　就公证行为所作之告知

第二百零六条（就公证行为所作之告知）

一、公证员应最迟于每月之十五日，透过送交计算机储存媒体或副本作出下列行为：

（a）向司法事务司送交一份已于上月登录于有关公证机构之数据库内之公证行为之清单；

（b）向统计暨普查司送交一份上月所作之杂项公证书之登记列表；

（c）向财政司送交一份上月所作之杂项公证书之登记列表，以及上月所作之第一百二十八条第二款所指之授权书及其相应之复授权书之登记清单；

（d）向七月五日第 6/80/M 号法律第一百一十二条所指之部门送交一份该法规第一百五十八条第三款所指公证书之登记清单；

（e）向有权限之登记局送交一份上月缮立而用作证明须作强制性商业登记之事实之公证文书之登记清单。

二、除应作法律规定之告知外，公证员尚应作出司法事务司司长以传阅文件方式要求进行之通知。

第二百零七条（就为公益而设定之负担及为死后受悼念或近似目的而作之处分所作之告知）

一、公证员须向负责监察为公益而设定之负担之履行情况之实体及向负责监察为死后受悼念或近似目的而作之处分之执行情况之实体，送交载有具上述性质处分之遗嘱及赠与公证书之证明。

二、涉及为公益而设定之负担时，须将证明送交总督；涉及为死后受悼念或近似目的而作之处分时，须将证明送交有关宗教实体或负责监察该处分之执行情况之人。

三、无须为获发证明而缴纳手续费，但在证明内须载有使人能识别该证明之用途之一切必需资料；证明得为部分内容证明或叙述证明。

四、证明最迟须于附注遗嘱人或赠与人死亡后翌月之十五日送出。

五、收到证明之实体应以具收件回执之挂号信向公证员邮寄收据，但该证明系以签收形式送达者除外。

第二章　公证行为之费用

第二百零八条（手续费及开支）

一、对在澳门地区作出之任何公证行为，均征收手续费表内所定之相应费用，但属法律规定免费、减少或豁免手续费之情况除外。

二、上款所指手续费之外，另须计算邮费；若属在公证机构以外作出之公证行为，则除该费用及邮费外，尚须计算必需之交通费。

三、私人公证员所作公证行为之手续费，相当于有关手续费表内所定之一般数额之三分之二。

第二百零九条（手续费之豁免）

除法律特别规定豁免手续费之情况外，就作出下列行为或发出下列文件亦豁免手续费：

（a）公证员为更正不可归责于当事人之错误或缺漏而须作之行为；

（b）为作成上项所指行为所需之文件及证明；

（c）第一百一十二条第二款所指之证明；

（d）公证员就公证遗嘱、公证书、第一百二十八条第二款所指授权书及设立社团与创立财团之经认证文书而发出之第一份证明。

第二百一十条（印花税及物业转移税）

一、除第二百零八条所指费用外，公证员尚应向利害关系人征收印花税表内所定之对应于各种公证行为之印花税，但属豁免印花税之情况除外。

二、基于非透过司法途径作出之分割而进行之不动产移转所应缴纳之物业转移税，由有权结算继承及赠与税或物业转移税之实体根据公证员发出之凭单予以结算及征收。

第二百一十一条（要求发出之文件之费用）

一、公共当局或部门依职权要求发出之文件免缴任何费用。

二、公共部门或公证机构应利害关系人请求而要求发出之文件之费用，须由该部门或机构征收，而该部门或机构应在四十八小时内以支票或存入账户之方式，将文件本身之费用及发送之开支之有关款项送交发出文件之公证机构。

第二百一十二条（独立公证文书之费用）

就一式两份之独立公证文书，仅须缴纳正本之手续费。

第二百一十三条（收费账目之编制及记录）

一、公证行为之费用应加载于相应账目内，并须按法律规定之方式适当列出各项费用。

二、作出公证行为后须立即编制收费账目；但属依职权将存放于公证机构内之密封遗嘱启封之情况除外，在此情况下，仅于按第一百二十七条第四款之规定应缴付费用时方须制作收费账目。

三、与缮立于簿册内之行为或应归档之独立公证文书内之行为有关之收费账目，以及与不应交予利害关系人之其他文件有关之收费账目，须在符合正使用之式样之一式两份印件上编制，并须注明用作缮立行为之簿册及纸页编号。

四、涉及缮立于交予当事人之独立公证文书及其他文件内之行为之收费账目，须记入该文书或文件内，如有复本，亦须记入复本内。

五、与为缮立拒绝证书而提交债权证券有关之收费账目，在缮立该证书前收回债权证券之情况下，须在债权证券内编制及记录，而在已缮立该证书之情况下，须纳入与该证书有关之收费账目内。

六、涉及应利害关系人要求透过图文传真传送之文件之收费账目，由收到文件之公证机构编制，并按第三款之规定将该账目予以记录。

第二百一十四条（收费账目之核对及解释）

一、公证员或主持公证行为之人须核对收费账目，并在其内作简签；收费账目之复本应交予利害关系人，而在正本上应作成表示已交付复本之凭据。

二、若利害关系人以口头或书面形式声明拟对收费提出申诉，则公证员应在二十四小时内交予利害关系人清楚详细列明计算收费标准之书面说明。

三、为着对收费提出申诉之效力，该收费之通知视为在将上款所指说明交予利害关系人之日作出。

第二百一十五条（收费账目之登记）

一、编制收费账目后，须立即将之登录于手续费及印花税之登记簿册内。

二、如因疏忽而导致收费账目错误或未登记账目，得嗣后改正错误或作出登记。

三、在手续费及印花税之登记簿册终结之日，若对强制性存放之费用作决算时发现有收费账目内之款项尚未缴纳，则须将之从簿册终结时之总额内扣除，并在收费登记及备注栏内以红色注明该账目已注销。

四、在上款所指情况下，有关收费账目应在缴纳款项后重新登记于手续费及印花税之登记簿册内，并应在销账之注录旁侧注明获给予之新登记编号。

第二百一十六条（与收费账目登记有关之说明）

一、在每一收费账目末处，均须标明相应之登记编号。

二、如与公证文书有关之收费账目不应记入该文书内，须在该文书内之签名后注明收费账目之登记编号；如某一公证行为获豁免或减少手续费及印花税，应扼要注明有关法律依据。

三、在提及与公证认定行为有关之收费账目时，应指出收费账目之总额。

四、公证员或主持公证之人应在收费账目登记之记载及有关豁免或减少手续费及印花税之记载后作简签。

第三章　期间

第二百一十七条（期间之计算）

一、计算本法典所指期间时，须以连续计日数之方式为之，但第一百六十五条第一款之规定除外。

二、若作出某一行为之期间届满之日公共公证机构不办公，则该行为得于紧接之首个工作日作出，并视为有效及产生效力，即使该行为应由私人公证员作出者亦然。

三、对本法典所指期间之计算，适用民法有关期限之计算之规定。

第二百一十八条（期间之不遵守）

公证员不遵守就履行本法典所指义务而规定之法定期间者，须负纪律责任，且须承受法律就不遵守法定期间而规定之其他后果。

附 3 台湾地区“公证法”

法规名称：“公证法”
修正时间：2009 年 12 月 30 日

第一章 总则

第一条

公证事务，由法院或民间之公证员办理之。地方法院及其分院应设公证处；必要时，并得于管辖区域内适当处所设公证分处。民间之公证员应于所属之地方法院或其分院管辖区域内，“司法院”指定之地设事务所。

第二条

公证人因当事人或其他关系人之请求，就法律行为及其他关于私权之事实，有作成公证书或对于私文书予以认证之权限。公证人对于下列文书，亦得因当事人或其他关系人之请求予以认证：一、涉及私权事实之公文书原本或正本，经表明系持往境外使用者。二、公、私文书之缮本或复印件。

第三条

前条之请求，得以言词或书面为之。公证或认证请求书，应由请求人或其代理人签名；其以言词请求者，由公证人、佐理员或助理人作成笔录并签名后，由请求人或其代理人签名。前项请求书或笔录，准用非讼事件法关于声请书状或笔录之规定。

第四条

公证或认证之请求，得由代理人为之。但依法律规定或事件性质不得由代理人为之者，不在此限。

第五条

公证文书应以中国文字作成之。但经当事人请求时，得以外国文字作成。前项文书以中国文字作成者，必要时得附记外国文字或附译本。以外国文字作成公证文书或就文书之翻译本为认证之公证人，以经“司法院”核定通晓各该外国语文者为限。

第六条

当事人或其他关系人，除法律另有规定外，得向任何地区之公证人请求作成公证书或认证文书。

第七条

公证人应以所属之地方法院或其分院之管辖区域为执行职务之区域。但有急迫情形或依事件之性质有至管辖区域外执行职务之必要者，不在此限。违反前项规定所作成之公、认证文书，效力不受影响。

第八条

办理公证事务，应于法院公证处或民间之公证人事务所为之。但法令另有规定或因事件之性质，在法院公证处或民间之公证人事务所执行职务不适当或有其他必要情形者，不在此限。办理公证事务之时间，依一般法令之规定。但必要时，得于法令所定时间外为之。

第九条

公证人为职务上签名时，应记载其职称及所属之法院。民间之公证人并应记载其事务所所在地。

第十条

公证人有下列各款情形之一者，不得执行其职务：一、为请求人或就请求事项有利害关系者。二、为请求人或其代理人或就请求事项有利害关系者之配偶、前配偶、未婚配偶、四亲等内之亲属或同居之家长、家属者。其亲属或家长、家属关系终止后，亦同。三、为请求人或其代理人之法定代理人者。四、就请求事项现为或曾为代理人或辅佐人者。

第十一条

公证人作成之文书，非具备本法及其他法律所定之要件，不生公证效力。公证人违反本法不得执行职务之规定所作成之文书，亦不生公证效力。

第十二条

公证人办理公证事务，于必要时，得向有关机关、团体或个人查询，并得请求其协助。前项情形，亦得商请外国机关、团体或个人为之。

第十三条

当事人请求公证人就下列各款法律行为作成之公证书，载明应径受强制执行者，得依该证书执行之：一、以给付金钱或其他代替物或有价证券之一定数量为目标者。二、以给付特定之动产为目标者。三、租用或借用建筑物或其他工作物，定有期限并应于期限届满时交还者。四、租用或借用土地，约定非供耕作或建筑为目的，而于期限届满时应交还土地者。前项公证书，除当事人外，对于公证书作成后，就该法律行为，为当事人之继受人，及为当事人或其继受人占有请求之目标物者，亦有效力。债务人、继受人或占有人，主张第一项之公证书有不得强制执行之事由提起诉讼时，受诉法院得因必要情形，命停止执行，但声请人陈明愿供担保者，法院应定相当之担保额，命停止执行。

第十四条

公证人、佐理员及助理人，除法律另有规定外，对于经办事件，应守秘密。

第十五条

公证人非有正当理由，不得拒绝请求人之请求。公证人拒绝请求时，得以言词或书面为之。但请求人要求说明其理由者，应付与理由书。

第十六条

请求人或利害关系人，认为公证人办理公证事务有违法或不当者，得提出异议。公证人如认为异议有理由时，应于三日内为适当之处置；如认为无理由时，应附具意见书，于三日内送交所属之地方法院或其分院，法院应于五日内裁定之。

第十七条

法院认异议为有理由时，应以裁定命公证人为适当之处置；认异议为无理由时，应驳回之。前项裁定，应附具理由，并送达于公证人、异议人及已知之其他利害关系人。对于第一项之裁定，得于十日内抗告。但不得再抗告。抗告，除本法另有规定外，准用非讼事件法关于抗告之规定。

第十八条

公证人作成之公证书原本，与其附属文件或已认证之文书缮本、复印件，及依法令应编制之簿册，保存于公证处或事务所，不得携出。但经法院或其他有关机关依法律调阅或因避免事变而携出者，不在此限。公证文书依前项规定调阅而携出者，公证人应制作复印件留存。第一项文书、簿册之保存及销毁规则，由“司法院”定之。

第十九条

本法规定之各项金额或价额，均以新台币为单位。

第二十条

依本法所为罚款处分之议决，得为强制执行名义。

第二十一条

公证事件，除本法另有规定外，准用非讼事件法之规定，非讼事件法未规定者，准用民事诉讼法之规定。

第二章　公证人

第一节　法院之公证人

第二十二条

法院之公证人，应就具有司法人员人事条例第二十三条第一项所定资格之一者遴任之。公证人有两人以上者，以一人为主任公证人，处理并监督公证处之行政事务。法院之公证人，得由地方法院或其分院法官或具有第一项资格之司法事务官兼充之。

第二十三条

公证处置佐理员，辅助法院之公证人办理公证事务，应就具有法院书记官任用资格者遴任之。前项佐理员，得由地方法院或其分院书记官兼充之。

第二节　民间之公证人

第二十四条

民间之公证人为“司法院”依本法遴任，从事第二条所定公证事务之人员。有关公务人员人事法律之规定，于前项公证人不适用之。

第二十五条

民间之公证人，应就已成年之台湾地区公民具有下列资格之一者遴任之：一、经民间之公证人考试及格者。二、曾任法官、检察官，经铨叙合格者。三、曾任公设辩护人，经铨叙合格者。四、曾任法院之公证人，经铨叙合格，或曾任民间之公证人者。五、经高等考试律师考试及格，并执行律师业务三年以上者。

第二十六条

有下列情事之一者，不得遴任为民间之公证人：一、年满七十岁。二、曾受一年有期徒刑以上刑之裁判确定。但因过失犯罪者，不在此限。三、褫夺公权，尚未复权。四、曾任公务员而受撤职处分，其停止任用期间尚未届满。五、曾依本法免职或受撤职处分。六、曾受律师法所定除名处分。七、受破产之宣告，尚未复权。八、受监护或辅助之宣告，尚未撤销。九、因身体或精神障碍致不能胜任其职务。

第二十七条

交通不便地区无民间之公证人时，得依有关民间之公证人遴任办法之规定，就曾在公立或经立案之私立大学、独立学院法律学系、法律研究所或经教育部承认之国外大学法律学系、法律研究所毕业，并任荐任司法行政人员、荐任书记官办理民刑事纪录或委任第五职等公证佐理员四年以上，成绩优良，经审查合格者，遴任为候补公证人。候补公证人候补期间三年，期满成绩优良者，得遴任为民间之公证人。候补公证人，除本法另有规定外，准用关于民间之公证人之规定。

第二十八条

民间之公证人经所属地方法院或其分院之许可，得雇用助理人，辅助办理公证事务。前项许可，必要时得撤销之。第一项之助理人其资格、人数、处理事务之范围及撤销许可之事由等事项，由“司法院”定之。

第二十九条

民间之公证人于执行职务前，应经相当期间之研习。但具有第二十五条第二款或第四款之资格者不在此限。民间之公证人于执行职务期间内，得视业务需要，令其参加研习。

第三十条

民间之公证人之遴选、研习及任免办法，由“司法院”定之。

第三十一条

民间之公证人由“司法院”遴任之，并指定其所属之地方法院或其分院。但不得限制其人数。

第三十二条

民间之公证人于任命后，非经践行下列各款事项，不得执行职务：一、向所属地方法院或其分院登录。二、加入公证人公会。三、参加责任保险并缴纳保险费。四、向所属地方法院或其分院提出职章、钢印之印鉴及签名式。

第三十三条

民间之公证人任命后有下列情事之一者，应予免职：一、受刑事裁判确定。但因过失犯罪者，不在此限。二、受褫夺公权之宣告。三、曾任公务员而受撤职处分。四、受律师法所定除名处分。五、受破产之宣告。六、受监护或辅助之宣告。七、因身体或精神障碍致不能胜任其职务。民间之公证人于任命后，发见其在任命前有第二十六条所定各款情事之一者，亦应予免职。

第三十四条

民间之公证人未依本法规定缴纳强制责任保险费者，得予免职。

第三十五条

民间之公证人年满七十岁者，应予退职。

第三十六条

民间之公证人依本法执行公证职务作成之文书，视为公文书。

第三十七条

民间之公证人具有律师资格者，不得执行律师业务。但经遴任仅办理文书认证事务者，或因地理环境或特殊需要，经“司法院”许可者，不在此限。律师兼任民间之公证人者，就其执行文书认证事务相关之事件，不得再受委任执行律师业务，其同一联合律师事务所之他律师，亦不得受委任办理相同事件。除本法另有规定外，民间之公证人不得兼任有薪给之公职或业务，亦不得兼营商业或为公司或以营利为目的之社团法人代表人或使用人。但与其职务无碍，经“司法院”许可者，不在此限。

第三十八条

民间之公证人及其助理人，不得为居间介绍贷款或不动产买卖之行为。

第三十九条

民间之公证人因疾病或其他事故，暂时不能执行职务时，得委请所属之地方法院或其分院管辖区域内之其他民间之公证人或候补公证人代理之。民间之公证人依前项规定委请代理时，应即向所属之地方法院或其分院陈报。解除代理时，亦同。依第一项规定委请代理之期间逾一个月者，应经所属之地方法院或其分院许可。

第四十条

民间之公证人未依前条第一项规定委请代理时，所属之地方法院或其分院得命管辖区域内之其他民间之公证人或候补公证人代理之。前条第一项之民间之公证人得执行职务时，所属之地方法院或其分院应解除其代理人之代理。地方法院或其分院不能依第一项规定指定代理人时，得命法院之公证人至该地执行职务。

第四十一条

民间之公证人之代理人，执行前两条所定代理职务时，应以被代理人之事务所为事务所。前项代理人为职务上签名时，应记载被代理公证人之职称、姓名、所属法院、事务所所在地及其为代理之旨。

第四十二条

民间之公证人之代理人应自行承受其执行代理职务行为之效果；其违反职务上义务致他人受损害时，应自负赔偿责任。前项代理人使用被代理公证人之事务所、人员或其他设备，应给与相当的报偿，其数额有争议者，得声请法院裁定。前项裁定得为执行名义。

第四十三条

民间之公证人死亡、免职、撤职或因其他事由离职者，所属之地方法院或其分院认为必要时，得指派人员将其事务所之有关文书、对象封存。

第四十四条

民间之公证人死亡时，其继承人、助理人或其他使用人，应于知悉后十日内陈报该公证人所属之地方法院或其分院。

第四十五条

民间之公证人死亡、免职、撤职或因其他事由离职者，在继任人未就职前，所属之地方法院或其分院得指定管辖区域内其他民间之公证人兼任其职务。前项兼任职务之民间之公证人得在兼任之区域内设事务所。第一项兼任之职务，在继任人就职时，所属之地方法院或其分院应解除其兼任。

第四十六条

民间之公证人免职、撤职或因其他事由离职时，应与其继任人或兼任人办理有关文书、对象之移交；其继任人或兼任人应予接收。民间之公证人因死亡或其他事由不能办理移交者，其继任人或兼任人应会同所属之地方法院或其分院指定之人员接收文书、对象。依第四十三条规定封存之文书、物件，继任人或兼任人应会同所属之地方法院或其分院指定之人员解除封印，接收文书、对象。民间之公证人之交接规则，由"司法院"定之。

第四十七条

前条之规定，于兼任人将有关文书、对象移交其他民间之公证人时，准用之。

第四十八条

兼任人于职务上签名时，应记载其为兼任之旨。继任人依前任人或兼任人作成之公证书，而作成正本、缮本、复印件或节本时，应记明其为继任人。

第四十九条

民间之公证人死亡、免职、撤职或因其他事由离职并因名额调整而无继任人者，"司法院"得命将有关文书、对象移交于同一地方法院或其分院管辖区域内其他民间之公证人。第四十六条及前条第二项之规定，于依前项受命移交之民间之公证人准用之。

第五十条

第四十三条、第四十五条、第四十六条第三项及第四十八条第一项之规定，于民间之公证人停职时准用之。兼任人依前项规定执行职务时，以停职人之事务所为事务所。

第五十一条

民间之公证人之监督由"司法院"行之。前项监督，得由所属之高等法院、地方法院或其分院为之。前两项之监督，其办法由"司法院"定之。

第五十二条

依前条规定行使监督权之机关，得定期检查民间之公证人保管之文书、对象。

第五十三条

监督机关得对民间之公证人为下列行为：一、关于职务上之事项，得发命令促其注意。二、对有与其职位不相称之行为者，加以警告。但警告前，应通知该公证人得为申辩。

第五十四条

民间之公证人有下列情事之一者，应付惩戒：一、有违反第一条第三项、第七条第一项、第十条、第十四条、第十五条第一项、第十八条第一项、第三十二条、第三十七条、第三十八条、第四十一条第一项、第四十六条、第六十七条第一项、第六十九条、第七十条、第九十条第一项、第九十八条第二项，第一百零一条第一项、第四项，第一百零八条之行为者。二、经监督机关为第五十三条之惩处后，仍未改善者。三、因犯罪行为，经判刑确定者。但因过失犯罪者，不在此限。前项第三款行为，经依第三十三条规定免职者，免付惩戒。民间之公证人有下列情事之一者，得付惩戒：一、有违反第七十一条至第七十五条、第八十条之行为者。二、有其他违反职务上之义务或损害名誉之行为者。

第五十五条

民间之公证人惩戒处分如下：一、申诫。二、罚款一万五千元以上十五万元以下。三、停职两个月以上两年以下。四、撤职。前项第一款、第二款之处分得同时为之。

第五十六条

民间之公证人之惩戒，由民间之公证人惩戒委员会为之。

第五十七条

民间之公证人惩戒委员会，由高等法院或其分院法官四人及民间之公证人三人组织之，主任委员由委员互选之。民间之公证人惩戒覆审委员会，由"最高法院"法官五人及民间之公证人四人组织之；主任委员由委员互选之。

第五十八条

民间之公证人应付惩戒者，由高等法院或其分院依职权移送民间之公证人惩戒委员会审议。地方法院或其分院认其辖区内民间之公证人有应付惩戒之事由者，得报请高等法院或其分院审查移送民间之公证人惩戒委员会审议。地区公证人公会认其会员有应付惩戒之事由者，得经会员大会或理事、监事联席会议之决议，送请民间之公证人惩戒委员会审议。

第五十九条

民间之公证人惩戒委员会受理惩戒案件后，于议决前，应为相当之调查，并予被付惩戒人充分申辩之机会，亦得通知前条之移送机关或公会为必要之说明。前项之议决，应作成议决书。

第六十条

受惩戒处分人、依第五十八条第三项移送惩戒之公证人公会，对于民间之公证人惩戒委员会之议决有不服者，得于议决书送达之翌日起二十日内向民间之公证人惩戒覆审委员会请求覆审。前条之规定，于前项覆审程序准用之。关于停职、撤职之处分，经惩戒覆审委员会议决确定后，受惩戒处分人得向原惩戒覆审委员会请求再审议。其请求再审议之事由及程序，准用公务员惩戒法之规定。

第六十一条

民间之公证人惩戒程序规则，由“司法院”定之。

第六十二条

惩戒处分确定后，民间之公证人惩戒委员会或惩戒覆审委员会应将全卷函送受惩戒处分人所属高等法院或其分院，报请“司法院”分别命令执行；其惩戒处分为停职或撤职者，并应将议决书刊登公报。

第六十三条

民间之公证人依刑事诉讼程序被羁押，或依刑事确定判决，受拘役以上刑之宣告，在执行中者，其职务当然停止。民间之公证人应受惩戒之事由情节重大者，“司法院”得在惩戒程序终结前，先行停止其职务。民间之公证人依前两项规定停止其职务时，准用第五十条之规定。

第六十四条

依前条第一项、第二项停止职务之民间之公证人，有下列各款情形之一者，于停止职务之原因消灭后，应许其复职：一、未受免职、撤职或停职处分者。二、受拘役以上刑之宣告，经执行完毕而未受免职、撤职或停职处分者。

第六十五条

民间之公证人得请求辞去职务，“司法院”于其依本法规定移交完毕后，解除其职务。

第六十六条

民间之公证人经依本法免职、停职、撤职、停止职务、退职或辞职而解除其职务者，自命令送达之翌日起，不得继续执行职务；其依第六十三条第一项规定职务当然停止者，自被羁押或受刑之执行时起，不得继续执行职务。

第六十七条

民间之公证人于执行职务期间，应继续参加责任保险。前项保险契约于每一保险事故之最低保险金额，由“司法院”视情势需要，以命令定之。但保险人对同一保险年度内之最高赔偿金额得限制在最低保险金额之两倍以下。保险人于第一项之保险契约停止、终止、解除或民间之公证人迟延缴纳保险费或有其他足以影响保险契约效力之情形时，应即通知所属地方法院或其分院及地区公证人公会。

第六十八条

民间之公证人因故意违反职务上之义务，致他人之权利受损害者，负赔偿责任。其因过失者，以被害人不能依他项方法受赔偿时为限，负其责任。被害人不能依前项、前条、第一百四十五条规定或他项方法受赔偿或补偿时，得依“国家赔偿法”所定程序，请求赔偿。其赔偿义务机关为该民间之公证人所属之地方法院或其分院。前两项之规定，于第四十二条第一项之民间之公证人代理人准用之“国家赔偿法”第四条第二项之规定，于前两项情形准用之。民间之公证人之助理人或其他使用人，于办理有关公证事务之行为有故意或过失时，民间之公证人应与自己之故意或过失，负同一责任。

第六十九条

民间之公证人应按月于次月十日前，将作成之公证书、认证书缮本或影本，依受理时间之先后顺序汇整成册，送所属之地方法院或其分院备查。

第三章　公证

第七十条

公证人不得就违反法令事项及无效之法律行为，作成公证书。

第七十一条

公证人于作成公证书时，应探求请求人之真意及事实真相，并向请求人说明其行为之法律上效果；对于请求公证之内容认有不明了、不完足或依当时情形显失公平者，应向请求人发问或晓谕，使其叙明、补充或修正之。

第七十二条

公证人对于请求公证之内容是否符合法令或对请求人之真意有疑义时，应就其疑虑向请求人说明；如请求人仍坚持该项内容时，公证人应依其请求作成公证书。但应于公证书上记载其说明及请求人就此所为之表示。

第七十三条

公证人作成公证书，应令请求人提出居民身分证或其他身分证明文件，证明其实本人；如请求人为外国人者，应令其提出护照、其本国使领馆出具之证明书或其他身分证明文件。

第七十四条

请求人不通中国语言，或为聋、哑人而不能用文字表达意思者，公证人作成公证书，应由通译传译之。但经请求人同意由公证人传译者，不在此限。

第七十五条

请求人为盲者或不识文字者，公证人作成公证书，应使见证人在场。但经请求人放弃并记明笔录者，不在此限。无前项情形而经请求人请求者，亦应使见证人在场。

第七十六条

由代理人请求者，除适用前三条之规定外，应提出授权书；事件依法非受特别委任不得为之者，并须有特别之授权。前项授权书，如为未经认证之私文书者，应依下列方式之一证明之：一、经有关公务机关证明。二、于境外作成者，经台湾地区驻外使领馆或经外交部授权之驻外机构或经其他有权机关授权之团体证明。三、外国人或居住境外之人作成者，经该国驻台湾地区使领馆或经该国授权之机构或经该地区有权机关授权之团体证明。授权书附有请求人之印鉴证明书者，与前项证明有同一效力。

第七十七条

就须得第三人允许或同意之法律行为，请求作成公证书，应提出已得允许或同意之证明书。前条第二项、第三项之规定，于前项情形准用之。

第七十八条

通译及见证人，应由请求人或其代理人选定之，见证人得兼充通译。请求人或其代理人未选定通译者，得由公证人选定之。

第七十九条

下列各款之人，不得充本法所定之见证人。但第七十五条第二项之情形，不在此限：一、未成年人。二、受监护或辅助宣告之人。三、于请求事件有利害关系者。四、于请求事件为代理人或曾为代理人者。五、为公证人之配偶、直系血亲或直系姻亲者。六、公证人之佐理员及助理人。前项第四款至第六款规定之人，如经请求人全体同意者，仍得为见证人。

第八十条

公证人作成公证书，应记载其所听取之陈述与所见之状况，及其他实际体验之方法与结果。

第八十一条

公证书应记载下列各款事项：一、公证书之字号。二、公证之本旨。三、请求人之姓名、性别、出生地、出生年、月、日、职业、居民身分证或其他身分证明及其字、号、住、居所；为法人或其他团体者，其名称及事务所。四、由代理人请求者，其事由与代理人之姓名、性别、出生地、出生年、月、日、职业、居民身分证或其他身分证明与其字、号、住、居所及其授权书之提出。五、有应径受强制执行之约定者，其意旨。六、曾提出已得第三人允许或同意之证明书者，其事由，及该第三人之姓名、性别、出生地、出生年、月、日、职业、住、居所，该第三人为法人或其他团体者，其名称及事务所。七、有通译或见证人在场者，其事由，及其姓名、性别、出生地、出生年、月、日、职业、住、居所。八、作成之年、月、日及处所。

第八十二条

公证书应文句简明、字画清晰，其字行应相接续，如有空白，应以墨线填充或以其他方法表示其为空白。公证之本旨记载年、月、日及其他数目表示同一内容者，其第一次出现时，应以文字大写；作成公证书年、月、日之记载，亦应以文字大写。

第八十三条

公证书文字，不得挖补；如有增加、删除或涂改，应依下列方法行之：一、删除或涂改字句，应留存字迹，俾得辨认。二、公证书末尾或栏外应记明增删字数，由公证人、请求人或其代理人、见证人签名或盖章。违反前项规定所为之更正，不生效力。

第八十四条

公证人应将作成之公证书，向在场人朗读，或使其阅览，经请求人或代理人承认无误后，记明其事由。有通译在场时，应使通译将公证书译述，并记明其事由。为前两项之记载时，公证人及在场人应各自签名；在场人不能签名者，公证人得代书姓名，使本人盖章或按指印，并记明其事由，由公证人签名。公证书有数页者，公证人、请求人或其代理人、见证人，应于每页骑缝处盖章或按指印，或以其他方法表示其为连续。但公证书各页能证明全部连续无误者，虽缺一部分人盖章，其公证书仍属有效。

第八十五条

公证书内引用他文书或与文书有相同效用之对象为附件者，公证人、请求人或其代理人、见证人应于公证书与该附件之骑缝处盖章或按指印，或以其他方法表示其为连续。前三条之规定，于前项附件准用之。

第八十六条

依前条规定所为之附件，视为公证书之一部分。

第八十七条

公证人应将公证书、证明身分、代理人权限、第三人允许或同意之证明书及其他附属文件，编为卷宗保存之。前项卷宗，应逐页连续编号，如请求人请求返还附属文件时，得将其缮本或复印件替代原本保存之。

第八十八条

公证书之原本全部或一部分灭失时，公证人应征求已交付之正本、经证明与正本相符之缮本或复印件，或向所属地方法院或其分院请求调阅公证书缮本或复印件，经该院院长认可后，依该正本、缮本或复印件作成经认证之缮本，替代原本保存之。前项情形及认可之年、月、日，应记明于替代原本之缮本并签名。

第八十九条

请求人或其继受人或就公证书有法律上利害关系之人，得请求阅览公证卷内文书。第七十三条、第七十六条、第七十七条之规定，于依前项为请求时准用之。请求人之继受人及就公证书有法律上利害关系之人请求阅览时，应提出证明文件。第七十六条第二项、第三项之规定，于前项证明文件准用之。

第九十条

公证人应编制公证书登记簿及其他相关之簿册。前项簿册及其应记载之内容，由“司法院”定之。

第九十一条

公证人得依职权或依请求人或其继受人之请求，交付公证书之正本。第七十三条、第七十六条、第七十七条、第八十九条第三项之规定，于依前项为请求时准用之。

第九十二条

公证书正本应记载下列各款事项，由公证人签名并盖职章或钢印：一、公证书之全文。二、记明为正本字样。三、受交付人之姓名。四、作成之年、月、日及处所。违反前项规定者，无正本之效力。

第九十三条

一公证书记载数事件，或数人共一公证书时，得请求公证人节录与自己有关系之部分，作成公证书正本。前项正本，应记明系节录正本字样。

第九十四条

公证人交付公证书正本时，应于该公证书原本末行之后，记明受交付人之姓名、事由及年、月、日，并签名。

第九十五条

请求人或其继受人或就公证书有法律上利害关系之人，得请求交付公证书及其附属文件之缮本、复印件或节本。第七十三条、第七十六条、第七十七条、第八十九条第三项之规定，于依前项为请求时准用之。

第九十六条

公证书及其附属文件之缮本、复印件或节本，应记载下列各款事项，由公证人签名并盖职章或钢印：一、公证书及其附属文件之全文或一部分。二、记载为缮本、复印件或节本字样。三、作成之年、月、日及处所。

第九十七条

公证书正本或公证书及其附属文件之缮本、复印件或节本有数页时，公证人应于骑缝处盖章，或以其他方法表示其为连续。第八十二条、第八十三条之规定，于前项文书准用之。

第九十八条

公证遗嘱，除请求人外，不得请求阅览或交付正本、缮本、复印件或节本。但请求人声明愿意公开或于公证遗嘱后死亡者，不在此限。公证人应于作成公证遗嘱之日起十日内制作缮本一份，将其密封，于封面上记明遗嘱人之人别资料及作成之年、月、日，加盖职章后，送交公证人公会联合会保存之。于有第一项但书之情形，请求人之继受人或就公证遗嘱有法律上利害关系之人，亦得向公证人公会联合会查询有无第一项之遗嘱并请求阅览。前两项之规定，于其他遗嘱之公、认证，准用之。

第九十九条

公证人依票据法作成拒绝证书者，不适用第十八条、第七十三条至第七十七条及第八十一条之规定。

第四章　认证

第一百条

公证人认证文书，应作成认证书。

第一百零一条

公证人认证私文书，应使当事人当面于私文书上签名，或承认为其签名，并于认证书内记明其事由。认证公文书之原本或正本，应就其程序及意旨审认该文书是否真实。认证公文书或私文书之缮本或复印件，应与经审认为真实之原本、正本对照相符，并于缮本或复印件内记明其事由。认证文书之翻译本者，除依前三项规定办理外，应审查该翻译语文是否正确，并将原文连缀其后。公文书或私文书有增删、涂改、损坏或形式上显有可疑之点者，应记明于认证书内，必要时，并得为查证。

第一百零二条

公证人认证请求人陈述私权事实之私文书，以该文书系持往境外使用者为限，得命请求人亲自到场并为具结。请求人陈述私权事实之私文书，依法律或基于法律授权订定之命令，得提出于法院或其他机关为一定之证明者，请求人请求认证时，适用前项认证方法之规定。

第一百零三条

请求人依前条规定具结，应于结文内记载当据实陈述决无虚伪等语。公证人于请求人具结前，应告以具结之意义及虚伪陈述之处罚。

第一百零四条

请求认证文书，应提出文书之缮本或复印件。

第一百零五条

认证书应记载下列各款事项，由公证人及在场人签名，并盖公证人职章或钢印：一、认证书之字号。二、依第一百零一条规定为认证之意旨。三、认证之年、月、日及处所。为第一百零一条第一项之认证者，其认证书并应记载第八十一条第三款、第四款、第六款及第七款所定之事项。认证书应连缀于认证之文书；由公证人及在场人加盖骑缝章，或以其他方法表示其为连续。

第一百零六条

公证人得在认证之文书上以直接注记之方式为认证，记载前条第一项规定之事项，由其签名并盖职章或钢印。依前项方式为第一百零一条第一项之认证者，并应依前条第二项之规定为记载。但请求书或认证之文书上已有记载者，不在此限。

第一百零七条

认证，除本章有规定外，准用前章公证之规定。

第五章　公证费用

第一百零八条

公证费用，应依本章之规定收取之，不得增减其数额。

第一百零九条

请求就法律行为或涉及私权之事实作成公证书者，其费用除本法另有规定外，按其目标之金额或价额，依下列标准收取之：一、二十万元以下者，一千元。二、逾二十万元至五十万元者，两千元。三、逾五十万元至一百万元者，三千元。四、逾一百万元至两百万元者，四千元。五、逾两百万元至五百万元者，五千元。六、逾五百万元至一千万元者，六千元。七、逾一千万元至五千万元者，其超过一千万元部分，每一千万元加收两千元；不满一千万元者，按一千万元计算。八、逾五千万元者，其超过部分，每一千万元加收一千元；不满一千万元者，按一千万元计算。

第一百一十条

关于计算公证事件目标之价额，本法未规定者，准用民事诉讼费用有关之规定。

第一百一十一条

典权之价额，以其典价为准。

第一百一十二条

公证之法律行为或涉及私权之事实，其目标之价额不能算定者，收取费用一千元。

第一百一十三条

请求就婚姻、认领、收养或其他非因财产关系之法律行为或涉及私权之事实，作成公证书者，收取费用一千元。于非财产关系之公证，并请求为财产关系之公证者，其公证费用分别收取之。

第一百十四条

请求就下列各款事项作成公证书者，收取费用一千元：一、承认、允许或同意。二、契约之解除或终止。三、遗嘱全部或一部分之撤回。四、曾于同一公证处或公证人事务所作成公证书之法律行为之补充或更正。但以不增加目标金额或价额为限。其增加目标金额或价额者，就增加之部分，依第一百零九条之规定收取费用。

第一百一十五条

请求作成公证书，须实际体验者，依其所需之时间，按一小时加收费用一千元；不满一小时者，按一小时计算。

第一百一十六条

请求就股东会或其他集会之决议作成公证书者，依前条之规定收取费用。

第一百一十七条

请求就密封遗嘱完成法定方式者，收取费用一千元。

第一百一十八条

请求作成授权书、催告书、受领证书或拒绝证书者，收取费用一千元。

第一百一十九条

请求就法律行为作成公证书，并载明应径受强制执行者，依第一百零九条或第一百一十二条所定之费用额，加收二分之一。

第一百二十条

请求就文书为认证者，依作成公证书所定之费用额，减半收取之。

第一百二十一条

本法未规定公证费用之事项，依其最相类似事项之规定收取费用。

第一百二十二条

公证人因请求人之请求，于夜间、例假日或其他法令所定执行职务时间外之时间执行公、认证职务者，各依本法所定之费用额，加收二分之一。但加收部分最高不得超过五千元。

第一百二十三条

公证人在请求人病榻前或其他相类似场所执行公、认证职务者，加收费用两千元。

第一百二十四条

公证人作成之公证书，其张数如超过六张时，超过部分每一张加收费用五十元。前项之张数，以一行二十五字、二十行为一张，未满一张者，以一张计算。

第一百二十五条

公证人因请求人之请求以外文作成公证书或认证文书之翻译本者，依本法所定之费用额，加收二分之一。但加收部分最高不得超过一万元。

第一百二十六条

公证人已着手执行职务后，因请求人之请求停止其职务之执行，或因可归责于请求人或到场人之事由致不能完成职务之执行者，依本法所定之费用额，收取二分之一。但最高不得超过五千元。

第一百二十七条

请求人或其他就法律上有利害关系之人请求阅览公、认证卷内文书者，每阅览一次收取费用两百元。

第一百二十八条

请求交付公、认证书及其附属文件之缮本、复印件或节本者，每份收取两百元。其张数超过六张时，每一张加收五元。翻译费每百字收取费用一百元至四百元，由公证人酌定之，其酌定标准由“司法院”另以命令定之。未满百字者，按百字计算。邮电费、运送费、登载公报新闻纸费、送达公证文件费、法院之公证人、佐理员出外执行职务之旅费、民间之公证人、助理人出外执行职务及鉴定人、通译之日费及旅费，准用民事诉讼费用有关之规定。

第一百二十九条

本章所定之收费标准，“司法院”得按情势需要，以命令减至二分之一，或增至十倍。

第六章　公会

第一百三十条

公证人公会，以谋求公证理论与实务之研究发展，砥砺会员品德，增进共同利益，执行民间之公证人之研习、指导、监督及处理其他共同有关事项为宗旨。

第一百三十一条

公证人公会为法人。

第一百三十二条

公证人公会由民间之公证人依法组织之。民间之公证人除执行律师业务者外，应加入公证人公会，公证人公会不得拒绝其加入。法院之公证人及执行律师业务之民间之公证人，得加入其所属法院所在地之地区公证人公会为赞助会员。

第一百三十三条

公证人公会分为地区公证人公会及公证人公会联合会。高等法院或其分院所属地方法院或其分院登录之民间之公证人总数满九人者，应于该高等法院或其分院所在地组织地区公证人公会，并以该高等法院或其分院之管辖区域为组织区域；其未满九人者，应加入邻近高等法院或其分院管辖区域内之地区公证人公会，或共同组织之。公证人公会联合会，应由各地区公证人公会三个以上之发起，及全体过半数之同意，于政府所在地组织之。地区公证人公会应加入公证人公会联合会为会员。在同一组织区域内之同级公会，以一个为限。

第一百三十四条

公证人公会置理事、监事，由会员大会选举之，其名额如下：一、地区公证人公会，理事三人至十一人，监事一人至三人。二、公证人公会联合会，理事五人至十七人，监事一人至五人。前项理事名额不得超过全体会员人数之二分之一，监事名额不得超过理事名额之三分之一。公证人公会得置候补理事、候补监事，其名额不得超过理事、监事名额之三分之一。理事、监事名额在三人以上者，得分别互选常务理事及常务监事，其名额不得超过理事或监事总额之三分之一；并由理事就常务理事中选举一人为理事长，其不设常务理事者，就理事中互选之。第一项理事、监事任期三年，连选得连任，理事长之连任以一次为限。

第一百三十五条

公证人公会联合会由各地区公证人公会选派之代表，举行代表大会，行使会员大会职权；其代表之人数，依各地区公证人公会会员人数之比例，于章程中定之。

第一百三十六条

地区公证人公会应订立章程，报经所在地高等法院或其分院转送“司法院”核准后，向所在地社会行政主管机关报备；章程有变更时，亦同。公证人公会联合会应订立章程，报经“司法院”核准后，向社会行政主管机关报备；章程有变更时，亦同。

第一百三十七条

地区公证人公会章程，应载明下列事项：一、名称及会址。二、所属区域。三、组织。四、会员资格之取得与丧失。五、会员之权利与义务。六、理事、监事之名额、职权、任期、选任及解任。七、会员大会及理事、监事会议之召集程序及决议方法。八、经费及会计。九、章程修改之程序。十、其他有关会务之必要事项。前项章程，并得载明关于公证人互助基金之设置及运用事项。

第一百三十八条

地区公证人公会会员大会由理事长召集之，每年至少召集一次。理事长不为召集时，监事得召集之。如有全体会员五分之一以上之请求，表明会议目的及召集理由，请求召集时，理事长应召集之。理事长受前项之请求后，一个月内不为召集者，得由请求之会员，经法院之许可召集之。会员大会之召集，除章程另有规定外，应于三十日前对各会员发出通知。通知内应载明会议目的事项。

第一百三十九条

地区公证人公会之主管机关为该公会所在地之社会行政主管机关。但其目的事业，应受所属之高等法院或其分院之指导、监督。公证人公会联合会之主管机关为社会行政主管机关。但其目的事业应受“司法院”之指导、监督。

第一百四十条

地区公证人公会举行会议时，应陈报所在地社会行政主管机关及所属之高等法院或其分院。公证人公会联合会举行会议时，应陈报社会行政主管机关及“司法院”。前两项会议，各该主管机关得派员列席。

第一百四十一条

地区公证人公会应将下列各款事项，陈报所在地之社会行政主管机关及所属之高等法院或其分院：一、会员名册及会员之入会、退会。二、理事、监事选举情形及当选人姓名。三、会员大会，理事、监事会议开会之时间、地点及会议情形。四、提议、决议事项。前项陈报，所属之高等法院或其分院应转送“司法院”备查。

第一百四十二条

公证人公会联合会应订立民间之公证人规范，提经会员代表大会通过后，报请“司法院”备查，其修正亦同。

第一百四十三条

地区公证人公会会员大会之决议，以会员过半数之出席，出席人数过半数或较多数之同意行之。但下列事项之决议应以出席人数三分之二以上同意行之：一、章程之订定与变更。二、理事、监事及会员代表之罢免。三、财产之处分。四、其他与会员权利义务有关之重大事项。

第一百四十四条

公证人公会之行为或决议违反法令或公证人公会章程者，“司法院”或社会行政主管机关得分别施以下列之处分：一、警告。二、撤销其决议。三、整理。前项第一款、第二款之处分，所在地高等法院或其分院亦得为之。

第一百四十五条

地区公证人公会，应为该地区民间之公证人办理责任保险，以确保民间之公证人因执行职务依第六十七条规定参加责任保险所不能理赔之损害赔偿。前项保险契约于每一保险事故之最低保险金额，由“司法院”视情势需要，以命令定之。但保险人对同一保险年度内之最高赔偿金额得限制在最低保险金额之四倍以下。

第一百四十六条

第一百三十七条、第一百三十八条、第一百四十一条第一项、第一百四十三条之规定，于公证人公会联合会准用之。

第七章　罚则

第一百四十七条

冒充公证人或候补公证人而执行其职务者，处三年以下有期徒刑、拘役，或科或并科新台币三十万元以下罚金。

第一百四十八条

民间之公证人或候补公证人非亲自执行职务，而将事务所、章证或标识提供与无民间之公证人资格之人使用者，处二年以下有期徒刑、拘役，或科或并科新台币十五万元以下罚金。

第一百四十九条

依第一百零二条规定具结之人，就与认证之私文书内容本旨有关之重要事项，为虚伪之陈述者，处一年以下有期徒刑、拘役或科新台币三万元以下之罚金。

第八章 附则

第一百五十条

驻外领务人员，得依法令授权，于驻在地办理公证事务。前项人员办理公证事务时，除不得作成第十三条之公证书外，准用本法之规定。第一项之授权办法，由“司法院”会同“行政院”定之。

第一百五十一条

本法施行细则，由“司法院”定之。

第一百五十二条

本法自公布生效后二年施行。本法修正条文，除2009年12月15日修正之第二十六条、第三十三条、第七十九条自2009年11月23日施行外，自公布尔日施行。

印度

1952 年公证法

The Notaries Act, 1952

1. Short title, extent and commencement.—

(1) This Act may be called the Notaries Act, 1952.

(2) It extends to the whole of India .

(3) It shall come into force on such date2 as the Central Government may, by notification in the Official Gazette, appoint.

2. Definitions.

—In this Act, unless the context otherwise requires,

(a) "instrument" includes every document by which any right or liability is, or purports to be, created, transferred, modified, limited, extended, suspended, extinguished or recorded;

(b) "legal practitioner" means an advocate entered in any rollunder the provisions of the Advocates Act, 1961;

(c) "notary" means a person appointed as such under this Act:

Provided that for a period of two years from the commencement of this Act it shall include also a person who, before such commencement was appointed a notary public under the Negotiable Instruments Act, 1881 [XXVI of 1881], and is, immediately before such commencement, in practice in any part of India: Provided further that in relation to the State of Jammu and Kashmir the said period of two years shall be computed from the date on which this Act comes into force in that State;

(d) "prescribed" means prescribed by rules made under this Act;

(e) "Register" means a Register of Notaries maintained by the Government under section 4;

(f) "State Government", in relation to a Union territo-

1952 年公证法

1. 名称、效力范围及生效

（1）本法案可称为《1952 年公证法》。

（2）其效力范围覆盖整个印度。

（3）本法案自中央政府以通告形式在官方公报上指定日期的次日生效。

2. 定义

在本法中，除上下文另有规定外，

（a）"法律文件"包括所有用于或据称用于创设、转移、修改、限制、扩展、终止、消灭或记录权利、责任的文件。

（b）"法律从业者"是指按照《1961 年辩护律师法》规定登记于名册的辩护律师。

（c）"公证员"是指根据本法受任为公证员者：

就本法生效之日起两年内，"公证员"也应包括在本法生效前依据《1881 年可转让票据法》[XXVI of 1881] 受任为公证员，并恰于本法生效前已在印度任一地区执业者；就查谟 - 克什米尔邦而言，上述两年期限应自本法在该邦实际生效之日起起算。

（d）"规定的"是指根据本法制定的规则中已有的规定。

（e）"登记簿"是指根据第 4 条由政府负责维护的公证员登记簿。

（f）"邦政府"就联邦属地而言，是指其行政长官。

ry means the administrator thereof.

3. Power to appoint notaries.

—The Central Government, for the whole or any part of India, and any State Government, for the whole or any part of the State, may appoint as notaries any legal practitioners or other persons who possess such qualifications as may be prescribed.

4. Registers.—

(1) The Central Government and every State Government shall maintain, in such form as may be prescribed, a Register of the notaries appointed by that Government and entitled to practise as such under this Act.

(2) Every such Register shall include the following particulars about the notary whose name is entered therein, namely:—

(a) his full name, date of birth, residential and professional address;

(b) the date on which his name is entered in the Register;

(c) his qualifications; and

(d) any other particulars which may be prescribed.

State Amendment Gujarat: After section 4 insert the following new section:

— "4A.—Special provision regarding registered Notaries of Gujarat.

—(1) Notwithstanding anything contained in this Act, the State Government of Gujarat shall prepare in the form prescribed for a Register required to be maintained under section 4, a Register of Notaries for the State of Gujarat as hereinafter provided.

(2) The State Government of Gujarat shall, by an order published in the Official Gazette, enter in the Register the names of notaries and all particulars relating thereto appearing in the Register maintained immediately before the 1st May, 1960 by the State Government of Bombay (hereinafter referred to as 'the Bombay Register') after excluding from such names, the name of any notary whose professional address as recorded in the Bombay Register falls outside the State of Gujarat.

(3) Before making any Order under sub-section (2), the State government of Gujarat shall make such inquiry as a deems necessary, and give an opportunity to the person whose name is proposed to be excluded from the Register, to make his representation, if any.

(4) On preparation of the Register as aforesaid,—

(a) the Register as so prepared shall, for all purposes

3. 任命公证员的权力

中央政府可就印度全境或部分地区，邦政府可就本邦全境或部分地区，将法律从业者或其他具备规定的资格的人任命为公证员。

4. 登记簿

（1）中央政府和各邦政府应以规定的格式，维护一份登记簿，记载由政府根据本法任命并授权执业的公证员姓名。

（2）就登记入簿的公证员，所有此类登记簿应包含其下列详细信息，即：

（a）其全名，出生日期，家庭住址和工作地址；

（b）其名登记入簿之日；

（c）其资格；

（d）其他可能有所规定的详细信息。

古吉拉特邦修正案：在第 4 条之后插入以下新法条：

4A. 关于古吉拉特邦注册公证员的特别规定。

（1）无论本法作何规定，古吉拉特邦政府应按照下文规定编制古吉拉特邦公证员登记簿，其格式采用第 4 条规定应维护的登记簿的格式。

（2）古吉拉特邦政府应以在官方公报上发布命令的形式，向其登记簿中录入截至 1960 年 5 月 1 日前，孟买邦政府维护之登记簿（以下简称“孟买登记簿”）中，排除工作地址不位于古吉拉特邦的人后，剩余公证员的姓名和其他相关信息。

（3）在作出第 2 款规定的命令前，古吉拉特邦政府应进行其认为必要之调查，对姓名被提议排除在登记簿之外的人，如该人有意见陈述的话，应给予其机会陈述。

（4）就前述登记簿之编制：

（a）编制成的登记簿应视为古吉拉特邦维护的登

of this Act, be deemed to be the Register maintained for the State of Gujarat;

(b) all persons whose names have been entered in the Register shall, for the residue of the period for which they were appointed by the State Government of Bombay, be deemed to have been appointed by the State Government of Gujarat, and accordingly, the certificate of practice issued to them under section 5 shall be deemed to have been amended so as to restrict their area os practice to the State of Gujarat."

—Notaries Act (Gujarat Adaptation) Order, 1961, published in Guj. Govt. Gaz., 27-4-1961, Pt. IVA, p. 43.

记簿，可用于本法规定的一切用途；

（b）凡姓名录入登记簿者，就其经孟买邦政府任命的剩余任期内，视为经古吉拉特邦政府任命，与之相应，根据第5条颁发给他们的执业证书应视为已修正为限制其执业区域为古吉拉特邦。

《公证法》（古吉拉特邦之变通）

1961年命令，发布于古吉拉特邦政府1961年4月27日公报IVA部分第43页。

5. Entry of names in the Register and issue or renewal of certificates of practice.—

(1) Every notary who intends to practise as such may, on payment to the Government appointing him of the prescribed fee, if any, be entitled—

(a) to have his name entered in the Register maintained by that Government under section 4; and

(b) to a certificate authorising him to practise for a period of five yearsfrom the date on which the certificate is issued to him.

(2) The Government appointing the notary, may, on receipt of an application and the prescribed fee, renew the certificate of practice of any notary for a period of five years at a time.

5. 向登记簿录入姓名以及颁发或更新执业证书

（1）凡公证员意图作为公证员执业的，经向任命政府支付规定费用（如有的话）后，有权要求：

（a）将其姓名录入第4款规定的政府维护的登记簿中；

（b）获得证书，授权其自证书颁发之日起5年内执业。

（2）任命公证员的政府，经收到申请和规定费用后，每次可以以5年为期对执业证书进行续期。

State Amendment Section 5A:

Maharashtra: After section 5, insert the following:—

"5A. Special provision regarding Register of Notaries for the State of Maharashtra.

—(1) Notwithstanding anything contained in this Act, the State Government of Maharashtra may, by order published in the Official Gazette, amend the Register, maintained before the 1st day of May 1960 by the State Government of Bombay, by deleting therefrom the name of any notary whose professional address as recorded in the Register, falls outside the State of Maharashtra: Provided that, before passing any order as aforesaid, the State Government of Maharashtra shall make such inquiry as it deems necessary, and give an opportunity to the person concerned to make his representation, if any.

(2) After the amendment of the Register as aforesaid,—

(a) the Register as so amended shall, for all purposes of this Act, be deemed to be the Register for the State of

邦修正案第5A条：

马哈拉施特拉邦：在第5条后插入下文：

5A. 关于马哈拉施特拉邦的公证员登记簿的特别条款。

（1）无论本法作何规定，马哈拉施特拉邦政府可以以在官方公报上发布命令的形式，通过从其中删除所载工作地址位于马哈拉施特拉邦外的人的姓名，修正截至1960年5月1日前由孟买邦政府维护的登记簿：但在通过前述命令前，马哈拉施特拉邦政府应进行其认为必要之调查，对相关人士，如其有意见陈述的话，应给予其机会陈述。

（2）如前述修正登记簿后：

（a）经修正的登记簿应视为马哈拉施特拉邦的登记簿，可用于本法规定的一切用途；

Maharashtra; and

(b) all persons whose names remain thereon shall (for the residue of the period for which they were appointed by the State Government of Bombay) be deemed to have been appointed by the State Government of Maharashtra and accordingly, the certificates of practice issued to them under section 5 shall be amended so as to restrict their area of practice to the State of Maharashtra."

—The Central Acts on State and Concurrent Subjects (Maharashtra Adaptation) Order, 1960 (w.r.e.f. 1-5-1960).

（b）凡姓名继续保留在册者（就其经孟买邦政府任命的剩余任期内）视为经马哈拉施特拉邦政府任命，与之相应，根据第 5 条颁发给他们的执业证书应视为已修正为限制其执业区域为马哈拉施特拉邦。

《有关邦和兼任主体的中央法案》（马哈拉施特拉邦之变通）1960 年命令（w.r.e.f. 1-5-1960）

6. Annual publication of lists ofnotaries.

—The Central Government and every State Government shall, during the month of January each year, publish in the Official Gazette a list of notaries appointed by that Government and in practice at the beginning of that year together with such details pertaining to them as may be prescribed.

6. 公证员名单的年度公布

中央政府和所有邦政府应于每年 1 月间，在官方公报上公布该政府于该年 1 月任命和截至该年 1 月已执业的公证员的名单，规定要求的上述公证员的相关详细信息亦应一并公布。

7. Seal of notaries.

—Every notary shall have and use, as occasion may arise, a seal of such form and design as may be prescribed.

7. 公证员印章

所有公证员均应备有并按场合需要使用按规定的格式和外观制作的印章。

8. Functions of notaries.—

(1) A notary may do all or any of the following acts by virtue of his office; namely:—

(a) verify, authenticate, certify or attest the execution of any instrument;

(b) present any promissory note, hundi or bill of exchange for acceptance or payment or demand better security;

(c) note or protest the dishonour by non-acceptance or non-payment of any promissory note, hundi or bill of exchange or protest for better security or prepare acts of honour under the Negotiable Instruments Act, 1881 (XXVI of 1881), or serve notice of such note or protest;

(d) note and draw up ship's protest, boat's protest or protest relating to demurrage and other commercial matters;

(e) administer oath to, or take affidavit from, any person;

(f) prepare bottomry and respondentia bonds, charter parties and other mercantile documents;

(g) prepare, attest or authenticate any instrument intended to take effect in any country or place outside India in such form and language as may conform to the law of the place where such deed is entitled to operate;

(h) translate, and verify the translation of, any document from, one language into another;

8. 公证员的职能

（1）公证员凭借其职位，可实施下列全部或部分行为；即：

（a）就法律文件之签署进行核实、证实、证明、见证；

（b）就本票、信贷证券或汇票提示承兑、付款或要求更多保障；

（c）根据《1881 年可转让票据法》（XXVI of 1881），就本票、信贷证券、汇票的拒绝承兑或拒付等拒绝兑现行为进行签注或制作拒绝证书，或出具拒绝证书以要求更多保障，或送达上述签注或拒绝证书的通知；

（d）签注及起草海事报告或与滞期及其他商业事宜相关的抗议书；

（e）为他人主持宣誓仪式或从他人处提取宣誓书；

（f）起草押船借贷合同、货船抵押债券、租船合同以及其他商业文件；

（g）起草、见证或证实法律文件，该文件采用有权实施该行为地区的法律规定的格式和语言，欲于印度之外的国家或地区生效；

（h）跨语种翻译文件，或核实跨语种翻译的文件的译本；

(ha) act as a Commissioner to record evidence in any civil or criminal trial if so directed by any court or authority;

(hb) act as an arbitrator, mediator or conciliator, if so required;

(i) any other act which may be prescribed.

(2) No act specified in sub-section (1) shall be deemed to be a notarial act except when it is done by a notary under his signature and official seal.

9. Bar of practice without certificate.

—(1) Subject to the provisions of this section, no person shall practise as a notary or do any notarial act under the official seal of a notary unless he holds a certificate of practice in force issued to him under section 5: Provided that nothing in this sub-section shall apply to the presentation of any promissory note, hundi or bill of exchangefor acceptance or payment by the clerk of a notary acting on behalf of such notary.

(2) Nothing contained in sub-section (1) shall, until the expiry of two years from the commencement of this Act, apply to any such person as is referred to in the proviso to clause (d) of section 2: Provided that in relation to the State of Jammu and Kashmir the said period of two years shall be computed from the date on which this Act comes into force in that State.

10. Removal of names from Register.

—The Government appointing any notary may, by order, remove from the Register maintained by it under section 4 the name of the notary if he—

(a) makes a request to that effect; or

(b) has not paid any prescribed fee required to be paid by him; or

(c) is an undischarged insolvent; or

(d) has been found, upon inquiry in the prescribed manner, to be guilty of such professional or other misconduct as, in the opinion of the Government, renders him unfit to practise as a notary;

(e) is convicted by any court for an offence involving moral turpitude; or

(f) does not get his certificate of practice renewed.]

11. Construction of references to notaries public in other laws.

—Any reference to a notary public in any other law shall be construed as a reference to a notary entitled to practise under this Act.

（ha）根据法院或者当局的指示，作为专员记录民事或刑事审判中的证据；

（hb）应要求充当仲裁人、调停人或者调解人。

（i）法律规定的其他任何行为。

（2）第（1）款指明的行为非经公证员实施并加盖其签字、公章，不得视为公证行为。

9. 禁止无证执业

（1）根据本条规定，除非持有根据第 5 条向其颁发的有效执业证书，任何人不得作为公证员执业或使用公证员公章实施公证行为；但本款不适用于公证员助理代表公证员提示承兑或提示支付本票、信贷证券、汇票的情形。

（2）自本法实施之日起两年期满前，第 1 款之内容不适用于第 2 条第 d 款附文中提及的此类人员：但就查谟 - 克什米尔邦而言，上述 2 年期限应自本法在该邦实际生效之日起起算。

10. 从登记簿上除名

公证员如有下列行为，任命公证员的政府可以以命令的形式，将公证员从由其根据第 4 条维护的登记簿上除名：

（a）公证员自行申请除名；

（b）不支付要求其缴纳的规定费用；

（c）成为未偿清债务的破产者；或者

（d）经规定方式的调查后，发现其犯有职业不当行为或其他不当行为，政府认为足以致使其不适于作为公证员执业的；

（e）因违反公德之行为被任一法院认定为构成犯罪；或者

（f）不为其执业证书续期的。

11. 对其他法律中引用的公证员的解释

其他任何法律中提及公证员的，应理解为根据本法执业的公证员。

12. Penalty for falsely representing to be a notary, etc.—Any person who—

(a) falsely represents that he is a notary without being appointed as such, or

(b) practises as a notary or does any notarial act in contravention of section 9, shall be punishable with imprisonment for a term which may extend to one year, or with fine, or with both.

13. Cognizance of offence.—

(1) No court shall take cognizance of any offence committed by a notary in the exercise or purported exercise of his functions under this Act save upon complaint in writing made by an officer authorised by the Central Government or a State Government by general or special order in this behalf.

(2) No magistrate other than a presidency magistrate or a magistrate of the first class shall try an offence punishable under this Act.

14. Power to make rules.—

(1) The Central Government may, by notification in the official Gazette, make rules to carry out the purposes of this Act.

(2) In particular, and without prejudice to the generality of the foregoing power, such rules may provide for all or any of the following matters, namely:—

(a) the qualifications of a notary, the form and manner in which applications for appointment as a notary may be made and the disposal of such applications;

(b) the certificates, testimonials or proofs as to character, integrity, ability and competence which any person applying for appointment as a notary may be required to furnish;

(c) the fees payable for appointment as a notary and for the issue and renewal of a certificate of practice, area of practice or enlargement of area of practice and exemption whether wholly or in part, from such fees in specified classes of cases;

(d) the fees payable to a notary for doing any notarial act;

(e) the form of Registers and the particulars to be entered therein;

(f) the form and design of the seal of a notary;

(g) the manner in which inquiries into allegations of professional or other misconduct of notaries may be made;

(h) the acts which a notary may do in addition to those specified in section 8 and the manner in which a no-

12. 对虚假陈述其为公证员等行为的惩罚

任何人——

（a）未经任命，而虚假陈述其为公证员的，或者

（b）违反第 9 节规定，作为公证员执业或者为任何公证行为的，应判处最高 1 年的监禁或罚款，或并罚。

13. 犯罪行为的审理权

（1）除非中央政府或邦政府为其利益，通过概括命令或特别命令授权的官员以书面形式提起告诉，否则就公证员在行使或意图行使其职能的过程中作出的本法规定的犯罪行为，法院不得取得其审理权。

（2）非首席法官或一级法官不得审判本法规定的可罚犯罪行为。

14. 制定规则的权力

（1）为贯彻本法之目的，中央政府可通过在官方公报上公告的方式制定规则。

（2）在适用于个例，且不损害前述权力的广泛性的前提下，此类规则可就下列全部或部分事项进行规定，即：

（a）公证员的任职资格，申请任命为公证员可采取的格式与方式，对此类申请的处理；

（b）凡申请任命为公证员都要求提供的，用于证明品格、正直、能力和才干的证书、推荐书或证据；

（c）就任命公证员和颁发、续期执业证书所收取的费用，执业范围或执业范围之拓展，以及全部或部分免除指明种类案例的上述费用；

（d）因公证员实施公证行为而向其支付的费用；

（e）登记簿的格式以及需录入登记簿中的详细信息；

（f）公证员印章的格式与外观；

（g）针对公证员犯有职业或其他不当行为的指控进行调查可采取的方式；

（h）除第 8 条指明的行为外，公证员可以从事的其他行为，以及公证员行使其职能可采用的方式；

tary may perform his functions;

(i) any other matter which has to be, or may be, prescribed.

(3) Every rule made by the Central Government under this Act shall be laid, as soon as may be after it is made, before each House of Parliament, while it is in session, for a total period of thirty days which may be comprised in one session or in two or more successive sessions,

and if, before the expiry of the session immediately following the session or the successive sessions aforesaid, both Houses agree in making any modification in the rule or both Houses agree that the rule should not be made, the rule shall thereafter have effect only in such modified form or be of no effect, as the case may be;

so, however, that any such modification or annulment shall be without prejudice to the validity of anything previously done under that rule.

15. Amendment of Act XXVI of 1881.

—[Rep. by the Repealing and Amending Act, 1957 (36 of 1957), sec. 2 and Sch.I.]

（i）其他必须规定或可以规定的事项。

（3）所有由中央政府根据本法制定的规则，应自其制定后于会议期间尽早提交议会两院，审议时间总计 30 日，既可一次性连续 30 日审议，亦可分为连续的两段或更多段审议。

若在会期结束前，经过前述的时间段或连续时间段，两院同意就规则进行修改或两院均认为不应制定规则的，则该规则应视情况，按修改后的形式生效，或失去其效力。

但此类修改或废止并不影响此前根据该规则完成的事宜的有效性。

15.1881 年第 26 号法令修正案

[由《1957 年废止和修正法》（1957 年第 36 号）第 2 条和计划表 1 修正，修正]

印度尼西亚

2004 年印度尼西亚共和国第 30 号公证机构法

LAW OF THE REPUBLIC OF INDONESIA NUMBER 30 OF 2004 ON OFFICE OF NOTARY PUBLIC

2004 年印度尼西亚共和国第 30 号公证机构法

DIRECTORATE GENERAL OF LAWS AND LEGISLATION THE MINISTRY OF LAWS AND HUMAN RIGHTS OF THE REPUBLIC OF INDONESIA

印度尼西亚共和国立法局

印度尼西亚共和国法律与人权事务部

PREFACE

序言

The 1945 Constitution of the State of the Republic of Indonesia explicitly stipulates that the state of the Republic of Indonesia is a constitutional state. The principle of constitutional state is to secure the legal certainty, order and protection based on the truth and justice.

印度尼西亚共和国 1945 年《国家宪法》明确规定，印度尼西亚共和国是一个宪政国家。宪政国家的基本原则是在事实和正义的基础上，保证法律的确定性、维护法律秩序以及保护性要求。

Legal certainty, order, and protection require, among others, that legal traffic in the community requires evidences clearly determining the rights and obligations of an individual in the community. In various business relations, banking, land, social activities and other activities require written evidences, among others in the form of authentic deed. An authentic deed can clearly define the rights and obligations of the relevant parties thereby securing legal certainty and avoiding any dispute.

法律的确定性、法律秩序和保护性要求，法律适用要建立在证据的基础上，明确个人在社会中的权利和义务。在各种商业关系中，银行、土地、社会活动和其他活动都需要书面证据，其中包括以公证文书形式提供的证据。公证文书可以清楚界定有关各方的权利和义务，从而确保法律的确定性和避免纠纷。

Notary public is the competent public official to draw up an authentic deed as long as the drawing up of a certain deed is not specifically made to the other public officials. In addition to being required by the laws and legislation, the drawing up of an authentic deed is also required by

公证员是出具公证文书的公职人员，但其不能向其他公职人员出具文书。公证文书除了需要符合法律法规的要求外，还需要与当事人有利害关系，在法律的确定性、秩序性和保护性的范围内，明确有关各方的权利和义务，在保护当事人的同时向社会公众提供

the relevant party to ensure the rights and obligations of the parties for legal certainty, order, and protection to the relevant parties simultaneously to the community on the whole.

保障。

This Law stipulates in details general office of Notary Public, therefore an authentic deed drawn up by or before a Notary Public can expectedly secure legal certainty, order, and protection. Considering Notarial Deeds as authentic deeds are the strongest and fullest written evidences, this Law also stipulates the form and nature of Notarial deed, Minutes of Deed, Tenor of Deed, and Copy of Deed, or Excerpt of Notarial Deed.

本法详细规定了公证机构，公证员起草或当场制作的公证文书可预期确保法律的确定性、秩序性和保护性。鉴于公证作为真实行为最有力、最充分的书面证据，本法还规定了公证文书的形式、性质、文书记录、公证程序、文书副本或公证文书摘录等事项。

In accordance with one of the tasks of the Directorate General of Laws and Legislation of the Ministry of Laws and Human Rights of the Republic of Indonesia, it is deemed necessary to disseminate Law Number 30 Of 2004 on Office of Notary Public for understanding by the community.

根据印度尼西亚共和国立法局和法律与人权事务部的规定，有必要公开 2004 年第 30 号公证机构法，以供社会理解与运用。

May this book fulfil the expectations of all parties and be beneficial.

希望本法内容能满足各方预期并获得良好的效益。

Jakarta, December 2008
Director General of
Laws and Legislation
signed
ABDUL WAHID, S.H, M.H.

2008 年 12 月，雅加达
立法局局长
签名
阿卜杜勒·瓦希德，S.H，M.H.

Considering:

a. that the State of the Republic of Indonesia as a constitutional state based on Pancasila and the 1945 Constitution of the State of the Republic of Indonesia shall secure legal certainty, order, and protection based on the truth and justice;

b. that authentic written evidence on legal condition, event, or act through a certain office shall be required to secure legal certainty, order, and protection;

c. that notary public being a certain office holding a profession in legal services to the community shall receive protection an security for legal certainty;

d. that notarial services as one of the legal requirements in the development process shall be increasing more and more;

e. that Reglement op Het Notaris Ambt in Indonesie (Stb. 1860:3) on Office of Notary Public shall fail to conform to the legal development and community's needs anymore;

考虑到：

a. 印度尼西亚共和国作为宪政国家，坚决拥护建国五原则和印度尼西亚共和国 1945 年宪法，应当确保在事实和正义的基础上实现法律的确定性、秩序性和保护性；

b. 为确保法律的确定性、秩序性和保护性，真实书面证据建立于有关部门查明的法律规定、事件或行为的基础上；

c. 公证员是为社会提供专业法律服务的特定公职群体，应当受到法律保护，以保证法律的确定性；

d. 公证服务作为法律事务需求之一，在发展的过程中需求会越来越多；

e. 对公证机构的公证活动实行监管能够避免公证和法律的发展与社会需求脱节；

that, therefore, it is necessary to form Law of Office of Notary Public;

In view of : Articles 20, 21, and 24 paragraph (3) of the 1945 Constitution of the State of the Republic of Indonesia;

With Joint Approval of

THE HOUSE OF PEOPLE'S REPRESENTATIVESOF TH REPUBLIC OF INDONESIA and THE PRESIDENT OF THE REPUBLIC OF INDONESIA HAS STIPULATED:

To stipulate : LAW OF OFFICE OF NOTARY PUBLIC.

因此，有必要制定《公证机构法》；

依据：印度尼西亚共和国 1945 年宪法第 20 条、第 21 条和第 24 条第 3 款；

印度尼西亚共和国人民代表会议和印度尼西亚共和国总统共同批准

规定:《公证机构法》

CHAPTER I
GENERAL

In this Law, by:

1. Notary Public we mean a public official having an authority to draw up authentic deeds and other authorities as referred to in this Law.

2. Notary Public Temporary Official we mean an individual who for the time being holds the position of Notary Public to perform the office of a Notary Public who passes away, is dismissed, or suspended.

3. Substitute Notary Public we mean an individual who for the time being is appointed as a Notary Public to replace another Notary Public who takes leave, is sick, or for the time being indisposed.

4. Special Substitute Notary Public we mean an individual who is appointed as a Special Notary Public to draw up certain deeds as mentioned in his/her assignment letter as a Notary Public because there is only one Notary Public in one district or city, while the relevant Notary Public is not allowed to draw up the deed pursuant to this Law.

5. Notary Public Organization we mean a notarial profession organization in the form of corporate body association.

6. Supervisory Council we mean a body having authority and obligation to develop and supervise Notary Publics.

7. Notarial Deed we mean an authentic deed drawn up by or before a Notary Public according to the given form and procedure herein.

8. Minutes of Deed we mean the authentic Notarial

第一章 一般条款

在本法中：

1. 公证员是指有权出具本法规定的公证文书以及拥有本法规定的其他权力的公职人员。

2. 临时公证员是指当某一公证员去世、被解雇或被停职时，暂时担任公证员职位，履行公证员职责的个人。

3. 替补公证员是指暂时被委任为公证员的个人，以代替请假、生病或暂时不适格的公证员。

4. 特别替代公证员是指在某个区 / 市只有一个公证员，但该公证员依据本法规定不得为特定公证活动时，委任其他人为特别替代公证员，特别替代公证员依据委任内容从事特定公证活动。

5. 公证机构是指以法人为组织形式的公证行业实体组织。

6. 监察委员会是指有权力和职责去引导、发展和监督公证员的机构。

7. 公证文书是指依据本法规定的格式和程序，由公证员出具的、具有证明力的文书。

8. 文本记录是指具有证明力的公证文书。

Deed.

9. Copy of Deed we mean copy of word by word of the entire deed and the lower section thereof contains a phrase "issued as a copy".

10. Excerpt of Deed we mean excerpt of word by word of one or several sections of the deed and the lower section of the excerpt of the deed contains a phrase "issued as an excerpt".

11. Formation of Office of Notary Public we mean determination of the number of Notary Publics required in a Office of Notary Public area.

12. Notarial Protocols we mean a collection of documents being a state archive to keep and maintain by Notary Publics.

13. Minister we mean a Minister of which the tasks and responsibilities cover notarial affairs.

CHAPTER II
ASSIGNMENT AND DISMISSAL OF NOTARY PUBLIC

Part One
Assignment

Article 1. Notary Public we mean a public official having an authority to draw up authentic deeds.

Article 2. Notary Publics shall be assigned and dismissed by the Minister.

Article 3. Requirements of assignment of Notary Public as referred to in the Article 2 shall be:

a. Indonesian national;

b. being devoted to the One Supreme God;

c. attaining the minimum age of 27 (twenty seven) years;

d. being sound of mind and sound of body;

e. having a master of law's degree and MA's degree in notarial affairs;

f. already being apprenticed or decidedly already being an Notary Public's employee for 12 (twelve) consecutive months in a Notary Public's office on his/her own initiative or at the recommendation of Notary Public Organization after having MA's degree in notarial affairs; and

g. not being a civil servant, state's official, advocate, or not holding another position that the law prohibits the same from doubling the position.

Article 4.(1) Before performing his/her office, a Notary Public shall pronounce an oath according to his/her religion before the Minister or the appointed official.

9. 文书副本是指公证书的复制件，其文本末尾应印有“作为副本发布”的字样。

10. 文书摘录是指对公证书中的部分字句或者部分内容摘录，摘录文本末尾应印有“作为摘录发布”的字样。

11. 公证机构的构成是指区 / 市内公证机构公证员的数量。

12. 公证档案是由公证员保管和维护的一系列档案文件。

13. 本法所称的部长是指负责公证业务的部长。

第二章　公证员的任免

第一节　任职

第一条　公证员是指有权起草文书证明真实行为的公职人员。

第二条　公证员应当由部长指派或者免职。

第三条　第 2 条所称公证员任职的条件是：

a. 印度尼西亚公民；

b. 忠诚于至高无上的神；

c. 年满 27 周岁；

d. 身心健全；

e. 获得法学硕士学位和公证专业硕士学位；

f. 已经在公证机构自主实习或连续任职满 12 个月，或者在获得公证专业硕士学位后得到公证组织的推荐；

g. 没有担任公务员、政府官员、律师或法律禁止的其他职位。

第四条（1）公证员在履行职务前，应当根据其宗教信仰在部长或指定官员面前宣誓。

(2) The oath as referred to in the paragraph (1) shall read as follows:

"I swear:

that I will adhere to and loyal to the State of the Republic of Indonesia, Pancasila and the 1945 Constitution of the State of the Republic of Indonesia, Law of Office of Notary Public and other laws and legislation.

that I will perform my office trustworthily, honestly, accurately, independently, and non-unilaterally.

that I will maintain my attitude, behaviour, and perform my obligations in accordance with code of ethics of my profession, honour, dignity, and responsibility as Notary Public.

that I will keep secret the content of the deed and statement obtained in the performance of my office.

that to be assigned in this office, I, directly or indirectly, with any name or on any ground, never and will not give or promise anything t anybody."

Article 5.The taking of an oath of Notary Public as referred to in the Article 4 shall be made at the latest 2 (two) months as of date decision of assignment of Notary Public.

Article 6.In case of failure to take the oath within the given time as referred to in the Article 5,decision of assignment of Notary Public can be cancelled by the Minister.

Article 7.Within 30 (thirty) days as of date of taking of an oath of Notary Public, the relevant person shall:

a. really implement his/her office;

b. submit minutes of oath of Notary Public to the Minister, Notary Public Organization, and District / Municipal Supervisory Council; and

c. submit office address, sample of signature, and initial, as well as red-coloured seal of Office of Notary Public to the Minister and another official responsible for agrarian affairs, Notary Public Organization, chief judge of district court, District / Municipal Supervisory Council, as well as district head or mayor where the Notary Public is appointed.

Part Two
Dismissal

Article 8.(1) A Notary Public shall resign or be honourably dismissed from his/her office due to:

a. demise;

b. attaining the age of 65 (sixty five) years;

c. own request;

d. failing to spiritually and/or bodily perform his/her

（2）第 1 款所述誓词为：

"我宣誓：

我将遵守并忠于印度尼西亚共和国、建国五原则和 1945 年《印度尼西亚共和国宪法》、《公证机构法》以及其他法律。

我将诚实、信用、准确、独立和全面地履行我的职责。

我将坚守我的立场和行为，遵守职业道德准则，做一个有荣誉感、有尊严、有担当的公证员。

我将对履行职务时所获文书和陈述的内容保密。

任职期间，我绝不会直接或间接地，以任何名义或理由向任何人提供或承诺任何事情。"

第五条 第 4 条规定的就职宣誓应当在公证员任命决定作出之日起 2 个月内完成。

第六条 如果在第 5 条规定的时间内没有完成就职宣誓，部长可以取消对公证员的任命决定。

第七条 自公证员宣誓之日起 30 日内，有关人员应当：

a. 履行公证员职务；

b. 向部长、公证机构和区 / 市监督委员会提交公证员宣誓记录；

c. 将公证机构的办公地址、签字样本以及公证机构的原始印章模版提交给部长以及其他机关，如土地事务的管理部门、公证机构、地区法院的首席法官、区 / 市监督委员会以及公证员任职所在地的区长或市长。

第二节 职务解除

第八条 （1）公证员因下列原因解除职务：

a. 死亡；

b. 年满 65 周岁；

c. 主动申请辞职；

d. 连续 3 年以上在精神和（或）身体上无法胜任

Notarial tasks for more than 3 (three) consecutive years; or

e. doubling the position as referred to in the Article 3 point g.

(2) Provision on age as referred to in the paragraph (1) point b can be extended until attaining the age of 67 (sixty seven) years by considering the health of the relevant person.

Article 9. (1) A Notary Public can be suspended from his/her office due to:

a. being in an insolvency process or deferment of obligation to pay debt;

b. being under custody;

c. committing a disgraceful deed; and

d. violating his/her office obligations and prohibitions.

(2) Before the suspension as referred to in the paragraph (1), the Notary Public shall be given an opportunity for advocacy before the Supervisory Council gradually.

(3) The suspension of the Notary Public as referred to in the paragraph (2) shall be made by the Minister at the recommendation of the Central Supervisory Council.

(4) The suspension on the ground as referred to in the paragraph (1) points c and d shall become effective for not later than 6 (six) months.

Article 10.(1) The suspended Notary Public as referred to in the Article 9 paragraph (1) point a or b can be reassigned to be a Notary Public by the Minister after recovery of his/her rights.

(2) The suspended Notary Public as referred to in the Article 9 paragraph (1) point c or d can be reassigned to be a Notary Public by the Minister after expiry of the term of suspension.

Article 11.(1) Any Notary Public who is assigned to be a state official shall take leave.

(2) The leave as referred to in the paragraph (1) shall become effective as long as the Notary Public holds the position of state official.

(3) The Notary Public as referred to in the paragraph (1) shall appoint a Substitute Notary Public.

(4) If the Notary Public fails to appoint the Substitute Notary Public as referred to in the paragraph (3), the District / Municipal Supervisory Council shall appoint another Notary Public to take the Notarial Protocols having jurisdiction over the domicile of the Notary Public appointed to be a state official.

(5) The appointed Notary Public as referred to in the paragraph (4) shall temporarily hold the Notarial

公证员职务；

e. 同时担任本法第 3 条第 g 项规定的其他职务的。

（2）关于第 1 款第 b 项所述年龄的规定，可以根据具体人员的健康情况，延长至 67 周岁。

第九条 （1）由于以下原因，公证员可以被暂停公证员职务：

a. 进入破产程序或难以偿还个人债务的；

b. 被羁押的；

c. 作出可耻行为的；

d. 违反其工作义务和禁令的。

（2）依据第 1 款规定被暂停职务前，公证员有权向监督委员会提出申辩。

（3）第 2 款所述的公证员暂停职务的决定应当由部长根据中央监督委员会的建议作出。

（4）第 1 款第 c 项和第 d 项所述的暂停职务决定有效期间不超过 6 个月。

第十条（1）公证员因为第 9 条第 1 款第 a 项、第 b 项被暂停职务的，可以在其恢复权利后，由部长重新恢复其公证员职务。

（2）公证员因第 9 条第 1 款第 c 项、第 d 项被暂停职务的，可以在暂停期限届满后，由部长重新恢复其公证员职务。

第十一条（1）被任命为政府官员的公证员应当辞去公证员职务。

（2）一旦公证员担任政府官员，第 1 款即刻生效。

（3）第 1 款中的公证员应当指定一名替补公证员。

（4）公证员未按照第 3 款的规定指定替补公证员的，由区、市监督委员会另行指定一名公证员，接管被任命为政府官员的公证员之前负责的公证事务。

（5）第 4 款中的被指定的替补公证员应当暂时保管公证档案。

Protocols.

(6) Any Notary Public no longer holding the position of state official as referred to in the paragraph (1) can perform the Office of Notary Public back and the Notarial Protocols as referred to in the paragraph (4) shall be submitted back to him/her.

Article 12.A Notary Public shall be dishonourably dismissed by the Minister at the recommendation of the Central Supervisory Council in case of:

a. declaration of insolvency based on court's order already having a permanent force of law;

b. being under custody for more than 3 (three) continuous years;

c. committing any action humiliating the honour and dignity of Office of Notary Public; or

d. committing a severe violation to Office of Notary Public obligations and prohibitions.

Article 13.A Notary Public shall be dishonourably dismissed by the Minister in case of committing a criminal act threatened with imprisonment of 5 (five) years or more based on court's order already having a permanent force of law.

Article 14.Any further provisions on the terms of and procedures for appointment and dismissal as referred to in the Article 3, Article 8, Article 9, Article 10, Article 11, Article 11, an Article 13 shall be contained in a Ministerial Regulation.

CHAPTER III AUTHORITIES,OBLIGATIONS,AND PROHIBITIONS

Part One Authorities

Article 15 .(1) A Notary Public shall be authorized to draw up an authentic deed on all actions, agreements, and decisions required by the laws and legislation and/or the relevant parties to contain in an authentic deed, guarantee the certain date of drawing up of deed, keep deed, as long as the drawing up of the deed is not assigned or excepted to another official or person stipulated by the law.

(2) A Notary Public shall also be authorized to:

a. ratify signature and determine certain dates of documents privately made by registering the same in a special register;

b. register any documents privately made in a special

（6）不再担任第 1 款所称政府公职的公证员，其公证员的身份可以重新恢复，替补公证员应当向其返还第 4 款规定中的公证档案。

第十二条 在下列情况下，部长应当根据中央监督委员会的建议，解除公证员的公证员职务：

a. 具有永久法律效力的法院文书已经宣布公证员破产；

b. 被连续羁押超过 3 年；

c. 犯有任何有损公证机构荣誉和尊严的罪行的；

d. 严重违反公证的义务和禁令。

第十三条 根据法院的生效判决，公证员被判处 5 年及以上刑期的刑罚的，部长应当解除公证员的职务。

第十四条 关于第 3 条、第 8 条、第 9 条、第 10 条、第 11 条、第 13 条中的任命和解除职务的具体程序及其进一步规定详见相关行政条例。

第三章 权力、义务和禁令

第一节 权力

第十五条 （1）公证员有权根据法律、法规和/或有关各方所要求的各种行动、协议和决定，出具一份公证文书，公证该行动、协议和决定的日期，并保存该文书。只要上述出具文书的权力没有被授予其他机构或者排除其他机构根据法律规定获得授权。

（2）公证员还应当有权：

a. 批准签署，并公证在特别登记册上登记的私人文件的确切日期；

b. 为在特别登记册上登记的任何私人文件注册；

register;

c. make copies of the authentic documents privately made in the form of copies as written and described in the relevant documents;

d. verify the copies to the authentic documents;

e. give a legal extension on drawing up of deeds;

f. draw up deeds relating to agrarian affairs; or

g. make deeds of minutes of bid.

(3) In addition to the authorities as referred to in the paragraphs (1) and (2), a Notary Public shall have other authorities stipulated by the laws and legislation.

c. 根据相关文件相互印证的情况，为真实的私人文本制作副本；

d. 对副本文件来源的真实性进行核实；

e. 为公证书的履行设定宽限期；

f. 出具与土地有关的公证书；或

g. 对投标记录出具公证书。

（3）除第 1 款、第 2 款规定的权力外，公证员的其他权力应当由法律、法规明确规定。

Part Two
Obligations

第二节　义务

Article 16.(1) In performing his/her office, a Notary Public shall be obligated to:

a. act honestly, accurately, independently, non-unilaterally, and maintain the interests of the relevant parties in any legal action;

b. draw up deeds in the form of Minutes of Deed and keep the same as a part of Notarial Protocols;

c. issue Tenor, Copy, or Excerpt of Deeds based on Minutes of Deed;

d. serve pursuant to this Law, unless there is any reason to refuse the same;

e. keep secret anything on deeds he/she draws up and any information he/she receives to draw up the deeds in accordance with oath of office, unless stipulated otherwise by the law;

f. bind any deeds he/she draw up in 1 (one) month into a book containing not more than 50 (fifty) deeds, and in case of failure to contain the number of the deeds in one book, the deeds can be bound into more than one book, and record the number of Minutes of Deeds, month, and year of drawing up of the same in the envelope of each book;

g. make a list of deeds of protest against non payment or non receipt of securities;

h. make a list of deeds relating to testament according to the sequence of time of drawing up of deeds each month;

i. submit the list of deeds as referred to in the point h or the list of nihilism relating to testament to the Central Testament Department of which the tasks and responsibilities are in notarial affairs within 5 (five) years in the first week in the following month;

第十六条　（1）公证员在履行职务时，有义务：

a. 诚实、准确、中立、全面地履行职责，并在任何行动中维护公证各方的利益；

b. 文书以记录的形式制作，并与公证档案的部分内容保持一致；

c. 依据文书记录确认相关文书的日期、副本或摘录；

d. 依照本法提供服务，有理由拒绝的除外；

e. 对他 / 她制作的文书和他 / 她收到的与文书有关的任何信息保密，但法律另有规定的除外；

f. 将他 / 她在 1 个月内制作的文书以 50 份为 1 本装订成册，如果 1 册无法装订所有的文书，那么可以装订多册，并在每册中标明文书的数量以及每份文书出具的年、月等信息；

g. 对未支付费用或者没有收据的文书列出清单；

h. 按照出具文书的先后顺序，每月列出与遗嘱有关的文书的清单；

i. 在每个月的第一个星期，将第 h 项所述的清单向中央遗嘱部门提交，在接下来的 5 年内，上述任务属于公证事务；

j. record the same in the repertory of date of submission of list of testament at each end of the month;

k. read out the deed before the appearer(s) in the presence of at least 2 (two) witnesses and signed at the same by the appearer(s), witnesses, and Notary Public;

l. accept the apprenticeship of the prospective Notary Publics.

(2) Keeping of Minutes of Deed as referred to in the paragraph (1) point b shall not apply, in case a Notary Public issues original deeds.

(3) The original deeds as referred to in the paragraph (2) shall be:

a. deeds of payment of rent, interest, and pension;

b. offering of cash payment;

c. deeds of protest against non payment or non receipt of securities;

d. deeds of power;

e. deeds of statement of ownership; or

f. other deeds by virtue of laws and legislation.

(4) The original deeds as referred to in the paragraph (2) can be drawn up more than 1 (one) duplicate, signed at the same time, with the same form, and content, provided that each deed is written “apply as one and one applies for all”.

(5) The original deed containing a power where the name of the proxy is not yet filled can only be made in 1 (one) duplicate.

(6) The reading of deed as referred to in the paragraph (1) point 1 shall not be required, if the appearers wish that the deed is not read because the appearers have read, known, and understood the content thereof on their own.

(7) In case of failure to fulfil one of the requirements as referred to in the paragraph (1) point a and paragraph (7), the relevant deed shall only have power of evidencing as a deed privately made.

(8) The provision as referred to in the paragraph (7) shall not apply for the drawing up of deed of testament.

Part Three
Prohibitions

Article 17.A Notary Public shall be prohibited from:

a. implementing an office outside his/her office area;

b. leaving his/her office are for 7 (seven) consecutive days without any acceptable reason.

c. doubling as a civil servant;

j. 在每个月末提交遗嘱清单的汇编中相同的内容；

k. 在至少 2 名见证人面前宣读公证文书，并由申请人、见证人和公证员签名确认。

l. 训练公证员学徒。

（2）第 1 款第 b 项规定不适用于文书记录保存，除非公证员出具原始文件。

（3）第 2 款所称原始文件为：

a. 租金、利息及退休金的缴付凭据；

b. 现金支付凭证；

c. 拒付或无担保的抗辩文书；

d. 与政治权力相关的文书；

e. 声明所有权的文书；

f. 法律法规规定的其他文书。

（4）第 2 款规定的原始文书可以制作形式和内容相同的多份副本，并需要签名，但每份文书均应当注明“一对一申请且适用于所有人”。

（5）没有注明代理人姓名的原始文书只能制作一份副本。

（6）如果当事人希望该文书不被查阅是因为当事人已经阅读、了解和知晓了其内容仅涉及其自身，第 1 款第 1 项所述文书应当禁止查阅。

（7）如果未能满足第 1 款第 a 项和第 7 款所述的要求之一，那么相关文书与当事人私下制作的文书效力等同。

（8）第 7 款不适用于遗嘱文书。

第三节 禁令

第十七条 禁止公证员从事下列行为：

a. 在其办公领域以外从事公务活动；

b. 无正当理由离职连续超过 7 日；

c. 同时兼任公务员；

d. doubling as a state official;

e. doubling as an advocate;

f. doubling as a manager or an employee to the state-owned company, regionowned company or private company;

g. doubling as a Land Deed Official outside his/her office area;

h. perform another job in contravention of religious, ethical, or appropriateness norms that can influence the honour and dignity of office of Notary Public.

d. 同时兼任政府官员；

e. 同时兼任律师；

f. 同时兼任国有企业、地方国企或私营企业的经理或雇员；

g. 同时兼任他/她的办公区域之外的土地事务官员；

h. 兼任其他职务，且该职务违反宗教、道德或其他规范，可能影响公证员职业的荣誉和尊严。

CHAPTER IV
DOMICILE, FORMATION, AND OFFICE AREA OF NOTARY PUBLIC

第四章　公证员的住所、设置和办公场所

Part One
Domicile

第一节　住所

Article 18.(1) A Notary Public shall have domicile in district or municipality.

(2) A Notary Public shall have office area throughout the province of his/her domicile.

第十八条　（1）公证员应当在本区或市内有固定住所。

（2）公证员应当在其居住的省内设有办公场所。

Article 19.(1) A Notary Public shall only have one office, namely in his/her domicile.

(2) A Notary Public shall not be authorized to regularly implement his/her office outside his/her domicile.

第十九条　（1）公证员在其居住地范围内只有一个办公场所。

（2）公证员无权在其住所地之外的区域履行职务。

Article 20.(1) A Notary Public can implement his/her office in the form of civil association by remaining taking into account independence in implementing his/her office.

第二十条　（1）公证员可以以民间社团的形式组织办公场所，但是应当考虑到其职务的独立性。

(2) The form of civil association as referred to in the paragraph (1) shall be arranged by Notary Publics by virtue of laws and legislation.

（2）第1款所述的民间社团组织形式应当依照法律的规定。

(3) Any further provisions on the requirements of implementing Office of Notary Public as referred to in the paragraph (1) shall be stipulated in Ministerial Regulation.

（3）关于第1款组建公证办公场所的任何进一步要求，应当在《部长条例》中作出规定。

Part Two
Formation of Office of Notary Public

第二节　公证办公场所的设立

Article 21. The Minister shall be authorized to determine the Formation of Office of Notary Public in a region as referred to in the Article 18 paragraph (1) by considering a recommendation from Notary Public Organization.

第二十一条　应授权部长通过审议公证办公场所的设立的建议，批准第18条第1款所述区域的公证办公场所的设立。

Article 22.(1) Formation of Office of Notary Public shall be determined based on:

a. business world activity;

b. total population; and/or

c. average number of deeds drawn up by and/or before Notary Public each month.

第二十二条　（1）公证办公场所的设立应根据下列因素确定：

a. 商业活动范围；

b. 区域总人口；

c. 此前公证机构每月出具文书的平均数量。

(2) Any further provisions on Formation of Office of Notary Public as referred to in the paragraph (1) shall be stipulated in Ministerial Regulation.

（2）第 1 款所述的公证员办事处设立的任何进一步规定，由《部长条例》规定。

Part Three
Removal of Notary Public Officer Area

第三节　公证办公场所的撤销

Article 23.(1) A Notary Public can submit a request for removal of his/her office area in writing to the Minister.

(2) The requirements of removal of office area as referred to in the paragraph (1) shall be he/she has performed his/her office tasks in a certain district or municipality being his/her domicile for 3 (three) consecutive years.

(3) The request as referred to in the paragraph (1) shall be submitted after receiving a recommendation from Notary Public Organization.

(4) The time as referred to in the paragraph (2) shall exclude leave already taken by the relevant Notary Public.

(5) Any further provisions on request for removal of Office area of Notary Public shall be stipulated in Ministerial Regulation.

第二十三条　（1）公证员可以书面向部长提出撤销其办公场所的请求。

（2）公证员根据第 1 款提出的请求，应当满足其已在某一特定的区域内连续任职满 3 年的要求。

（3）第 1 款所述的请求应当在收到公证机构的建议后提交。

（4）第 2 款所述的时间不包括相应公证员的已休假期。

（5）有关撤销公证员办公场所的任何进一步规定，应当在部长条例中予以规定。

Article 24. In a certain condition and at the request of the relevant Notary Public, the Minister can remove a Notary Public from one office area to another one.

第二十四条　在一定条件下，应有关公证员的要求，部长可以决定将公证员办公场所迁移到另一地区。

CHAPTER V
LEAVE FOR NOTARY PUBLIC AND SUBSTITUTE NOTARY PUBLIC

第五章　公证员休假及替补公证员

Part One
Leave for Notary Public

第一节　公证员休假

Article 25.(1) A Notary Public shall have a right to leave.

(2) The right to leave is referred to in the paragraph (1) can be taken after the Notary Public implements his/her office for 2 (two) years.

(3) During taking leave, the Notary Public shall appoint a Substitute Notary Public.

第二十五条　（1）公证员享有休假权。

（2）行使第 1 款所述权利的条件是公证员连续任职满两年。

（3）在公证员休假期间，应当任命一名替补公证员。

Article 26.(1) The right to leave as referred to in the Article 25 paragraph (1) can be taken each year or simultaneously for several years.

(2) A leave can be taken for maximum 5 (five) years including the extension.

(3) During the term of office of Notary Public, total leave shall be maximum 12 (twelve) years.

第二十六条　（1）第 25 条第 1 款规定的休假权可以每年申请或数年假期一次性申请。

（2）可一次性申请最多 5 年的休假，包括延长期。

（3）公证员任职期间，总休假时间最高不超过 12 年。

Article 27.(1) A Notary Public can submit a request for leave in writing accompanied with the recommenda-

第二十七条　（1）公证员休假应当提交书面申请，并附上任命替补公证员的建议。

tion of appointment of Substitute Notary Public.

(2) The request for leave as referred to in the paragraph (1) shall be submitted to the competent official, namely:

a. District / Municipal Supervisory Council, in case the leave is not more than 6 (six) months;

b. Provincial Supervisory Council, in case the leave is more than 6 (six) months to 1 (one) year;

c. Central Supervisory Council, in case the leave is more than 1 (one) year.

(3) The request for leave can be approved or refused by the competent official to give leave permit.

(4) Carbon copy of the request as referred to in the paragraph (2) point b shall be submitted to the Central Supervisory Council.

(5) Carbon copy of the request as referred to in the paragraph (2) point c shall be submitted to the District / Municipal Supervisory Council and Provincial Supervisory Council.

Article 28. In urgency, a Notary Public's spouse or relative in vertical line can submit a request for leave to the Supervisory Council as referred to in the Article 27 paragraph (2).

Article 29.(1) Leave permit certificate shall at least contain:

a. Notary Public's name;

b. date of commencement and expiry of leave; and

c. name of Substitute Notary Public accompanied with documents supporting the Substitute Notary Public as stipulated in the laws and legislation.

(2) Carbon copy of leave permit certificate from the District / Municipal Supervisory Council shall be submitted to the Minister, Central Supervisory Council, and Provincial Supervisory Council.

(3) Carbon copy of leave permit certificate from the Provincial Supervisory Council shall be submitted to the Minister and Central Supervisory Council.

(4) Carbon copy of leave permit certificate from the Minister shall be submitted to the Central Supervisory Council, Provincial Supervisory Council, District / Municipal Supervisory Council.

Article 30.(1) The Minister or the appointed official shall be authorized to issue leave certificate.

(2) The leave certificate as referred to in the paragraph (1) shall contain data on taking of leave.

(3) Data of taking of leave as referred to in the paragraph (2) shall be recorded by the Supervisory Council as

（2）第 1 款规定的休假申请应当提交给相应的主管官员，即：

a. 如果休假期不超过 6 个月，向区 / 市监督委员会提出休假申请；

b. 如果休假期为 6 个月以上 1 年以下，向省级监督委员会提出休假申请；

c. 如果休假期超过 1 年，向中央监督委员会提出休假申请。

（3）主管官员可以批准或拒绝许可公证员的休假申请。

（4）第 2 款第 b 项规定的申请函副本应当提交至中央监督委员会。

（5）第 2 款第 c 项规定的申请函副本应提交至区 / 市监督委员会和省级监督委员会。

第二十八条　在紧急情况下，公证员的配偶或直系亲属可以向监督委员会提出第 27 条第 2 款规定的休假申请。

第二十九条　（1）休假许可证书应当至少包括以下内容：

a. 公证员姓名；

b. 休假开始日期和结束日期；

c. 替补公证员的姓名，并附有法律法规规定的符合替补公证员要求的有关文书。

（2）由区 / 市监督委员会批准的休假许可证书副本应当提交至部长、中央监督委员会和省级监督委员会。

（3）由省级监督委员会批准的休假许可证书副本应当提交至部长和中央监督委员会。

（4）由部长批准的休假许可证书副本应当提交至中央监督委员会、省级监督委员会、区 / 市监督委员会。

第三十条　（1）部长或指定官员有权签发休假许可证书。

（2）第 1 款规定的休假许可证书应当包含准予休假的具体内容。

（3）第 2 款所述的休假数据，应由第 27 条第 2 款所述的监督委员会记录。

referred to in the Article 27 paragraph (2).

(4) Each request for leave shall enclose leave certificate as referred to in the paragraph (2).

(5) The Minister or the appointed official can issue duplicate of unusable or lost leave certificate at the request of the relevant Notary Public.

Article 31.(1) Request for leave can be refused by the competent official to the leave.

(2) Refusal of request for leave shall be furnished with reason(s) thereof.

(3) Refusal of request for leave by the District / Municipal Supervisory Council can be appealed to the Provincial Supervisory Council.

(4) Refusal of request for leave by the Provincial Supervisory Council can be appealed to the Central Supervisory Council.

Article 32.(1) In case of on leave, a Notary Public shall submit Notarial Protocols to the Substitute Notary Public.

(2) The Substitute Notary Public shall submit the Notarial Protocol back to the Notary Public after expiry of leave.

(3) The submission as referred to in the paragraphs (1) and (2) shall be drawn up in a minutes and submitted to the Provincial Supervisory Council.

Part Two
Substitute Notary Public, Special Substitute Notary Public, and Notary Public Temporary Official

Article 33.(1) Requirements of appointment of Substitute Notary Public, Special Substitute Notary Public, and Notary Public Temporary Official shall be Indonesian nationals with master of law degree and already working to Notary Public's office for at least 2 (two) consecutive years.

(2) Provisions applicable to Notary Publics as referred to in the Articles 15, 16, and 17 shall also apply to Substitute Notary Public, Special Substitute Notary Public, and Notary Public Temporary Official, unless stipulated otherwise inthis Law.

Article 34.(1) In case there is only 1 (one) Notary Public in one office area, the District / Municipal Supervisory Council can appoint A Special Substitute Notary Public competent to draw up deeds in the personal interest of the Notary Public or his/her family.

(2) The temporary appointment as referred to in the

（4）每项休假申请应当附上第 2 款规定的休假证书。

（5）部长或指定官员可以应有关公证员的申请，签发无效或遗失休假证书的复印件。

第三十一条 （1）主管官员有权拒绝休假申请。

（2）拒绝休假申请的，应当说明原因。

（3）区 / 市监督委员会拒绝休假申请的，申请人可以向省级监督委员会申诉。

（4）省级监督委员会拒绝休假申请的，申请人可以向中央监督委员会申诉。

第三十二条 （1）开始休假之前，公证员应当向替补公证员移交公证档案。

（2）休假结束后，替补公证员应当将公证档案交回至公证员。

（3）第 1 款和第 2 款所述的公证档案应在短时间内制定出来并提交至省级监督委员会。

第二节　替补公证员、特殊替代公证员和临时公证员

第三十三条 （1）担任替补公证员、特殊替代公证员或临时公证员应当是具有法学硕士学位的印度尼西亚公民，且连续从事公证实务至少满 2 年。

（2）除非本法另有规定，否则第 15 条、第 16 条和第 17 条适用于公证员的规定也适用于替补公证员、特殊替代公证员和临时公证员。

第三十四条 （1）若某区域内只有一名公证员，则区 / 市监督委员会可临时任命一名特殊替代公证员，其有权根据公证员职务内容制作相关文书。

（2）第 1 款中的临时任命无须同时提交公证档案。

paragraph (1) shall not be accompanied with submission of Notarial Protocols.

(3) The Special Substitute Notary Public as referred to in the paragraph (1) shall take an oath before the Minister or the appointed official.

Article 35.(1) In case of demise of Notary Public, his/her spouse or relative in vertical line shall notify the District / Municipal Supervisory Council of the same.

(2) The notification as referred to in the paragraph (1) shall be submitted at the latest 7 (seven) working days.

(3) In case of demise on leave, the office tasks of the Notary Public performed by Substitute Notary Public as a Notary Public Temporary Official shall be maximum 30 (thirty) days as of date of demise.

(4) The Notary Public Temporary Official shall submit Notarial Protocols of the late Notary Public to the District / Municipal Supervisory Council at the latest 60 (sixty) days as of date of demise.

(5) The Notary Public Temporary Official as referred to in the paragraphs (3) and (4) can draw up a deed in his/her own name and have Notarial Protocols.

CHAPTER VI
HONORARIUM

Article 36.(1) A Notary Public shall be entitled to receive honorarium for legal services he/she gives in accordance with his/her competence.

(2) The amount of honorarium received by the Notary Public shall be based on economic and sociologic values of each deed he/she draws up.

(3) The economic value as referred to in the paragraph (2) shall be determined from the object of each deed as follows:

a. up to Rp. 100,000,000.00 (one hundred million rupiah) or equivalent to gram of gold at that time, honorarium he/she receives shall be maximum 2,5% (two point five percent);

b. above Rp. 100,000,000.00 (one hundred million rupiah) up to Rp. 1,000,000,000.00 (one billion rupiah), honorarium he/she receives shall be maximum 1.5% (one point five percent); or

c. above Rp. 1,000,000,000.00 (one billion rupiah), honorarium he/she receives shall be as agreed between the Notary Public and the parties, but not more than 1% (one percent) of the object of deed he/she draws up.

(4) The sociologic value shall be determined based

（3）第 1 款所述的特殊替代公证员应当在部长或指定官员面前进行就职宣誓。

第三十五条 （1）如果公证员死亡，其配偶或直系亲属应当及时通知区 / 市监督委员会。

（2）第 1 款所述的通知应当在 7 个工作日内提交。

（3）如果公证员在休假期间死亡，由替补公证员作为临时公证员处理公证事务的最长期限为自公证员死亡之日起 30 日。

（4）临时公证员应当自公证员死亡之日起 60 日内向区 / 市监督委员会提交已故公证员的公证档案。

（5）第 3 款和第 4 款所述的临时公证员可以以自己的名义出具公证文书，并保管公证档案。

第六章　酬金

第三十六条 （1）公证员有权获得其提供法律服务的酬金。

（2）公证员所获酬金的数额，应当根据他 / 她所出具的每份文书的经济价值及社会价值确定。

（3）第 2 款所述的经济价值，应当以每项文书的标的额确定，具体如下：

a. 若标的额在 100000000.00 卢比以下或相当于当时的一克金，其酬金最高可达标的额的 2.5%；

b. 若标的额在 100000000.00 卢比至 1000000000.00 卢比，酬金最高可达标的额的 1.5%；或

c. 若标的额超过 1000000000.00 卢比，公证员收取的酬金应按照公证员和当事人之间双方商定的方式达成，但最终收取的酬金不超过标的额的 1%。

（4）社会价值应当根据每份文书的社会功能决

on social function of the object of each deed and the honorarium he/she receives shall be maximum Rp. 5,000,000.00 (five million rupiah).

定，其收取的酬金应最高为 5000000.00 卢比。

Article 37.Each Notary Public shall provide the poor with free notarial legal services.

第三十七条 公证员应向经济困难群体免费提供公证法律服务。

CHAPTER VII NOTARIAL DEED

第七章 公证书

Part One Form and Nature of Deed

第一节 公证书的形式和实质

Article 38.(1) Each deed shall consist of:

a. heading;

b. body; and

c. closing.

(2) Heading shall contain:

a. title;

b. number;

c. hour, day, date, month, and year; and

d. full name and domicile of Notary Public.

(3) Body shall contain:

a. full name, birth place and date, nationality, occupation, domicile, residence of the appearers and/or those they represent;

b. statement on position to act as appearers;

c. content of deed being the desire and intention of the relevant parties; and

d. full name, birth place and date, occupation, position, domicile, and residence of each knowing witness.

(4) Closing shall contain:

a. description of reading of deed as referred to in the Article 16 paragraph(1) point a or Article 16 paragraph (7);

b. description of signing and place of signing r translation of deed, if any;

c. full name, birth place and date, occupation, position, domicile, and residence of each witness of deed; and

d. description of absence of change in the drawing up of deed or description of change that can be in the form of addition, deletion, or substitution.

(5) In addition to containing provisions as referred to in the paragraphs (2), (3), and (4), Deed of Substitute Notary Public, Special Substitute Notary Public, and Notary Public Temporary Official shall also contain number and date of stipulation of appointment, and the appointing official.

第三十八条 （1）每份公证书应包含：

a. 标题；

b. 主体内容；

c. 结尾。

（2）标题应包含：

a. 题目；

b. 编号；

c. 小时、天数、日期、月份和年份；

d. 公证员的全名和住所。

（3）主体内容应包含：

a. 当事人的全名、出生地点及日期、国籍、职业、住所、居住地和 / 或他们所代表的人；

b. 各方当事人的陈述；

c. 文书的内容是有关各方当事人的目标和意图；

d. 见证人的全名、出生地点及日期、职业、岗位、住所、居住地。

（4）结尾应包含：

a. 第 16 条第 1 款第 a 项或第 16 条第 7 款所述的文书解释说明；

b. 如果公证书需要签字或者翻译，应标明地点和对签字情况的说明；

c. 所有公证见证人的全名，出生地和日期，职业，住所和居住地；

d. 对文书起草过程中采用添加，删除或替换等形式对文书进行的更改情况作出说明。

（5）除包含第 2 款、第 3 款和第 4 款所述的规定外，替补公证员，特殊替代公证员和临时公证员出具的文书还应包含其编号、任命日期和任命官员的姓名。

Article 39.(1) The appearers shall fulfil the following

第三十九条 （1）当事人应当符合下列要求：

requirements:

a. attaining the minimum age of 18 (eighteen) years or already married; and

b. being capable of taking legal actions.

(2) The appearers shall be known to Notary Public or introduced to him/her by 2 (two) knowing witnesses attaining the minimum age of 18 (eighteen) years or already married and being capable of taking legal actions or introduced by other 2 (two) appearers.

(3) The introduction as refered to in the paragraph (2) shall be explicitly declared in a deed.

Article 40.(1) The reading out of deed by Notary Public shall be in the presence of at least 2 (two) witnesses, unless the laws and legislation stipulate otherwise.

(2) The witnesses as referred to in the paragraph (1) shall fulfil the following requirements|

a. attaining the age of minimum 18 (eighteen) years or already married;

b. being capable of taking legal actions;

c. understanding the language used in the deed;

d. being able to affix signature and initial; and

e. not having any marriage relation or blood relation in upper or lower straight line without any degree limitation and until the third degree with the Notary Public or the parties.

(3) The witnesses as referred to in the paragraph (1) shall be known to the Notary Public or introduced to the Notary Public or the appearers shall explain their identities and competence to the Notary Public.

(4) The introduction or explanation of the identity and competence of the witnesses shall be explicitly contained in a deed.

Article 41.In case of failure to fulfil the Articles 39 and 40, the deed shall only have a power of evidencing as a deed privately made.

Article 42.(1) A Notarial Deed shall clearly contain mutual relationship uninterruptedly and not use any abbreviation.

(2) All numbers shall be intended to determine the number of anything mentioned in deed, the mentioning of date, month, and year shall be stated in letters and preceded with figure.

Article 43.(1) Deeds shall be drawn up in Indonesian.

(2) In case the appearer fails to understand the language used in a deed, Notary Public shall translate or explain the content thereof in a language understandable by

a. 已满 18 周岁或已婚；

b. 有民事行为能力。

（2）当事人应当是公证员知悉的人或者由 2 名见证人向公证员引荐，见证人应当年满 18 周岁或已经结婚，并有民事行为能力。

（3）第 2 款所述的引荐应当在文书中进行说明。

第四十条　（1）除非法律另有规定，公证员应当在至少 2 名见证人在场的情况下宣读文书。

（2）第 1 款所述的见证人应当符合下列要求：

a. 已满 18 周岁或已婚；

b. 有民事行为能力；

c. 能够理解文书中使用的语言；

d. 有能力签名；

e. 与参与公证的各方当事人不存在婚姻、直系血亲或三代以内旁系血亲关系。

（3）第 1 款所述的见证人，应当向公证员公开或向公证员介绍，或由当事人向公证员解释他们的身份及能力。

（4）对见证人的身份和能力的介绍或说明应当写入文书。

第四十一条　如果违反第 39 条和第 40 条，所制作的文书仅具有私人契约的证明效力。

第四十二条　（1）公证文书应当包含本法规定的内容，不得使用缩写或出现缺漏。

（2）文书中涉及的数量应以数字表示，所有日期、月份和年份应以字母注明。

第四十三条　（1）公证文书应当以印度尼西亚语书写。

（2）如果当事人不通晓公证文书使用的语言，公证员应当以当事人通晓的语言作出翻译或解释其内容。

the appearer.

(3) If the Notary Public fails to translate or explain the same, the deed shall be translated or explained by an authorized translator.

(4) Deeds can be drawn up in another language understandable by the Notary Public and witnesses if the relevant parties require the same, unless stipulated otherwise by the laws and legislation.

(5) In case the deeds are drawn up as referred to in the paragraph (4), Notary Public shall translate the same in Indonesian.

Article 44.(1) A deed having been duly read out shall be signed by the appearers, witnesses, and Notary Public, unless one of the appearers fails to affix his/her signature by mentioning the reason(s).

(2) The reason(s) as referred to in the paragraph (1) shall be explicitly contained in a deed.

(3) The deed as referred to in the Article 43 paragraph (3) shall be signed by the appearers, Notary Public, witnesses, and sworn translator.

(4) The reading out, translation or explanation, and signing as referred to in the paragraphs (1) and (3) and Article 43 paragraphs (2), (3), and (5) shall be explicitly contained at the end of the deed.

Article 45.(1) In case the appearers are only interested in a certain part of the deed, only the certain part shall be read out to them.

(2) If the certain part as referred to in the paragraph (1) translated or explained, the appearers shall affix their initial and signature on the part.

(3) The reading out, translation or explanation, and signing as referred to in the paragraphs (1) and (2) shall be explicitly mentioned at the end of the deed.

Article 46.(1) If in the making of recording of wealth or minutes on an action or event, the appearers:

a. refuse to affix their signature; or

b. are absent in the closing of the deed, while the appearers do not yet sign the deed;

The refusal or absence shall be contained in a deed and the deed shall remain being an authentic deed.

(2) The refusal as referred to in the paragraph (1) point a shall be contained in a deed by mentioning the reason(s) thereof.

Article 47.(1) Authentic power of attorney or another document being a basis to draw up a deed issued in the form of original deed or power of attorney privately made shall be attached to the Minutes of Deed.

（3）如果公证员不能翻译或解释，应当指派翻译人员翻译或解释。

（4）除非法律另有规定，若当事人提出要求，可以用公证员、见证人通晓的另一种语言制作公证文书。

（5）如果按照第 4 款出具公证文书，公证员应当将其翻译成印度尼西亚语。

第四十四条 （1）经正式宣读的文书应当由当事人、见证人和公证员签字确认，除非其中一名当事人因特殊原因而未签名。

（2）第 1 款所述的原因应当明确记载于公证文书内。

（3）第 43 条第 3 款所述的文书应当由当事人、公证员、见证人和翻译人员签字确认。

（4）本条第 1 款和第 3 款，第 43 条第 2 款、第 3 款和第 5 款所述的宣读、翻译、解释及签字，应当在文书结尾处注明。

第四十五条 （1）如果当事人只对文书的某一部分有利害关系，那么只应向他们宣读该部分。

（2）如果第 1 款所述的内容已被翻译或由公证员作出解释，当事人应当在该部分处签字。

（3）第 1 款和第 2 款所述的宣读、翻译、解释和签字应当在文书结尾处注明。

第四十六条 （1）如果在某事件或活动中记录财产或者时间时，当事人：

a. 拒绝签名；

b. 在签署文书时当事人因缺席而未签署；

拒绝或缺席的情况应当记载于文书中，但文书仍然真实可信。

（2）应当将第 1 款中的拒绝理由记载于文书内。

第四十七条 （1）授权委托书、起草文书依据的原始文本或代理人材料应当附于公证书结尾。

(2) The authentic power of attorney drawn up in the form of Minutes of deed shall be described in a deed.

(3) Provisions as referred to in the paragraph (1) shall not be required if the power of attorney is attached to the a deed drawn up before the same Notary Public and it is contained in a deed.

Article 48.(1) Content of the deed shall not be changed or added, both in the form of overlapped writing, insertion, deletion, or deletion and replace the same with another one.

(2) Change of deed in the form of addition, substitution, or deletion shall be lawful if the change is initialized or given another validation mark by the appearers, witnesses, and Notary Public.

Article 49.(1) Each change of deed shall be made on the left side of the deed.

(2) If the change can not be made on the left side of the deed, the change shall be made at the end of the deed, before closing of deed, by indicating the changed part or inserting additional sheet.

(3) Any change without indicating the changed part shall make the change null and void.

Article 50.(1) If words, letters, or numbers in a deed shall be deleted, the deletion shall be made in such a way so that it can be read as originally contained, and the number of the deleted words, letters, and numbers shall be contained on the side of the deed.

(2) The deletion as referred to in the paragraph (1) shall be considered valid if the deletion is initialized or given another validation mark by the appearers, witnesses, and Notary Public.

(3) In case of another change in the change as referred to in the paragraph (2), the change shall be made on the side of the deed in accordance with Article 49.

(4) The number of change, deletion, and addition shall be contained in the closing of each deed.

Article 51.(1) A Notary Public shall be authorized to revise any miswriting and/or mistyping in the Minutes of Deed already signed.

(2) The revision as referred to in the paragraph (1) shall be made by making a minutes and giving a notation on the same in the original Minutes of Deed by mentioning date and number of deed of minutes of revision.

(3) Copy of deed of minutes as referred to in the paragraph (2) shall be submitted to the parties.

Article 52.(1) A Notary Public shall not draw up a deed on his/her own, for his/her spouse, or for the others

（2）如果授权委托书以文书记录的形式出具，那么应当在公证书中作出说明。

（3）如果在公证员见证下起草的文书附有授权书，并且授权内容载于该文书内，那么不适用第 1 款的规定。

第四十八条（1）文书内容不得改变或增加，即包括重复、插入、删除以及替换原有内容。

（2）文书变更以补充、替换或删除形式进行，如果变更内容由当事人、证人和公证员签字认可，那么是合法有效的。

第四十九条（1）文书的每项变更应当在文书的左侧标明。

（2）如不能在文书的左侧作出更改，那么应当在文书的结尾处作出更改，并在结尾之前注明更改的部分或插入另外的表格注明。

（3）任何不作注明的变更皆为无效。

第五十条（1）如某文书中的文字、数字需予以删除，应当将删除内容载明于文书一侧，以使其可以被包含在最初出现处。

（2）第 1 款中的删除，如果符合形式要求或者由当事人、见证人和公证员对删除的内容签字认可，视为有效。

（3）如对第 2 款规定的变更内容再次更改，应当按照第 49 条的规定在文书的边侧作出记录。

（4）数字的变更、删除和增加应当载于每项文书的结尾。

第五十一条（1）公证员有权以文书记录的形式修改文书中的书写错误和 / 或排版错误。

（2）第 1 款规定的修改，应当由公证员制作一份修改记录，并且在原文书记录中注明修改记录的时间和数量。

（3）第 2 款所述的修改记录副本应当提交至参与公证程序的各方主体。

第五十二条（1）公证员不得为自己及其配偶，或与公证员因婚姻或血缘关系而形成的直接或间接不

having a family relationship with the Notary Public both due to marriage or blood relationship in lower and/or upper straight line without any degree limitation.

受亲等限制的直系亲属关系的当事人出具公证文书。

(2) Violation of the provision as referred to in the paragraph (1) shall make the deed only have a power of evidencing as a deed privately made if the deed is signed by the appearers, without prejudice to the obligations of the Notary Public drawing up the deed to pay any expense, compensation, and interest to the relevant person.

（2）违反第 1 款的规定，如果文书由当事人签署，那么该文书仅具有私人行为的证明效力，公证员应当向有关当事人公平补偿相关费用、损失和利息。

Article 53.A Notarial Deed shall not contain a provision giving a right and/or profit to:

a. Notary Public, his/her spouse;

b. witness, his/her spouse; or

c. persons with family relationship with the Notary Public or witness, both blood relationship in upper or lower straight line without any degree limitation or marriage relationship until the third degree.

第五十三条 公证文书中不得出现赋予以下人员权利和 / 或利益的条款：

a. 公证员及其配偶；

b. 证人及其配偶；

c. 与公证员或证人有家庭关系的人、与公证员或证人无亲等限制的直系血亲或三代以内的旁系姻亲关系的人。

Part Two
Tenor, Copy, and Excerpt of Deed

第二节 文书的日期、副本与摘录

Article 54.A Notary Public can only provide, introduce, or inform the Content, Tenor, Copy, or Excerpt of Deed to the persons directly related to the deed, beneficiaries, or persons receiving the rights, unless stipulated otherwise the laws and legislation.

第五十四条 除非法律法规另有规定，公证员只能向与文书具有直接利害关系的人、受益人或享有相关权利的人提供、解释或告知文书的内容、日期或文书副本与摘录的内容。

Article 55.(1) A Notary Public issuing Tenor of Deed shall make a notation on the minutes of deed of the receipt of Tenor of Deed and date of issue and the notation shall be signed by the Notary Public.

第五十五条 （1）公证书的有关时间应当被明确记录，在文书记录中标明收到文书的日期和出具日期，而且记录事项应当由公证员完成。

(2) Tenor of Deed of debt acknowledgment drawn up before Notary Public shall be a Copy of Deed with executorial power.

（2）由公证员制作的债权承认文书，应当视为具有强制执行效力的文书。

(3) The second Tenor of Deed and so forth can only be given to the persons as referred to in the Article 54 at the court's order.

（3）文书的时间等内容只能向本法第 54 条规定的人通告。

Article 56.(1) Original deed, Tenor of Deed, Copy of Deed, or Excerpt of Deed issued by a Notary Public shall be sealed / stamped.

第五十六条 （1）公证文书原本、副本或公证员出具的文书摘录应当加盖印章。

(2) The seal as referred to in the paragraph (1) shall also be affixed to the copy of document attached to the Minutes of Deed.

（2）第 1 款的规定同时适用于文书记录的副本文件。

(3) Privately made document so legalized and registered and verification of copy by Notary Public shall be sealed/stamped and initialized and signed by the Notary Public.

（3）私下制作的文件的合法性以及文件副本的注册、登记，都应当由公证员盖章和签字。

Article 57.Tenor of Deed, Copy of Deed, Excerpt of

第五十七条 文书时间、文书副本、公证文书

Notarial Deed, or validation of privately made document attached to the deed kept in the Notarial Protocols, can only be issued by the Notary Public drawing up the same, Substitute Notary Public, or the valid holder of Notarial protocols.

摘录或公证档案所附的私人文件的审定，只能由公证员、替补公证员等持有公证档案的主体出具。

Part Three
Making, Keeping, and Submission of Notarial Protocols.

第三节　公证文书的制作、保存和提交

Article 58.(1) A Notary Public shall make register of deeds, register of privately made documents so legalized, list of privately made documents so recorded, and other registers of documents required by this Law.

(2) In the register of deeds as referred to in the paragraph (1), the Notary Public shall each day register all deeds drawn up by or before him/her, both in the form of Minutes of Deed and original deeds, without any empty gaps, each in a space covered with ink lines, by mentioning serial number, monthly number, date, nature of deed, and names of all persons acting both on their own and as proxies of the others.

(3) Deeds issued in the form of original deeds shall be recorded in a register in one number.

(4) Each page in the register shall be given serial number and initialized by the District / Municipal Supervisory Council, but the first and last pages shall be signed by the District / Municipal Supervisory Council.

(5) Pages before the first page shall contain information on total pages on the register of deeds signed by the District / Municipal Supervisory Council.

Article 59.(1) A Notary Public shall make a clapper register for register of deeds and register of privately documents so legalized as referred to in the Article 58 paragraph (1) shall be prepared alphabetically and make the same each month.

(2) The clapper register as referred to in the paragraph (1) shall contain the names of the appearers by mentioning behind the names the nature, and numbers of deeds, or documents registered in the register of deeds and register of privately made documents.

Article 60. Deeds drawn up by or before Substitute Notary Public or Special Substitute Notary Public shall be registered in the register of deeds.

Article 61.(1) A Notary Public shall severally or through his/her proxy submit in writing a legalized copy of register of deeds and other registers made in the previous month within no later than 15 (fifteen) days in the follow-

第五十八条　（1）公证员负责文书登记，包括对私人制作的合法文件进行登记，并对登记在案的私人文件列出清单，以及对本法规定的其他文件进行登记。

（2）对于第 1 款所述的文书登记，公证员应当对其每天出具的文书进行登记，具体登记方式可以采用文书记录形式，也可以采用原始文书的形式。登记册应当采用墨线装订，并标明序列号、月份、日期、文书的性质、所有当事人及其代理人的姓名。

（3）原始文本应当以数字标序的形式登记入册。

（4）登记册内的每一页应当标明序号，并由区 / 市监督委员会进行审核，但第一页和最后一页应当由区 / 市监督委员会签署。

（5）在第一页之前应当标明被区 / 市监督委员会签署的已经被登记的文书的总页数。

第五十九条　（1）公证员应当每个月按照第 58 条第 1 款所述的规定，并按字母顺序编制文书登记册和私人文件登记册。

（2）第 1 款所述的登记册，应当记载有当事人的名称，并在名称后标注登记注册的性质、文书登记和私人文件登记的数量。

第六十条　由替补公证员或特殊替代公证员出具的文书应当在文书登记册内登记。

第六十一条　（1）公证员应当亲自或通过其代理人，将上一个月编制的文书登记册及其他登记册的副本，在下一个月开始后的 15 日内提交至区 / 市监督委员会。

ing month to the District / Municipal Supervisory Council.

(2) If the Notary Public fails to draw up a deed within 1 (one) month, the Notary Public shall severally or through his/her proxy submit the same in writing to the District / Municipal Supervisory Council within the time as referred to in the paragraph (1).

（2）如果公证员未能在1个月内出具公证文书，公证员应当在第1款规定的时间内，亲自或通过其代理人将文书以书面形式提交至区/市监督委员会。

Article 62.A Notary Public shall submit Notarial Protocols in case of:

a. demise;

b. expiry of term of office;

c. own request;

d. failing to spiritually and/or bodily implement office tasks as a Notary Public for 3 (three) consecutive years;

e. appointment of a state official;

f. removal of office area;

g. suspension; or

h. dishonourably dismissal.

第六十二条 公证员在下列情况下应提交公证档案：

a. 死亡；

b. 任期届满；

c. 自我请辞；

d. 连续3年未履行公证员的职责；

e. 被任命为政府官员；

f. 搬离办公场所；

g. 被停职；或

h. 被不光彩地解雇。

Article 63.(1) Submission of Notarial Protocols as referred to in the Article 62 shall be made within no later than 30 (thirty) days by making a minutes of submission of Notarial Protocols signed by the persons submitting and receiving the Notarial Protocols.

第六十三条 （1）第62条规定的公证档案的提交应当在30日内作出，并制作与提交公证档案有关的记录，提交和接受公证档案的人都要签字确认。

(2) In case of condition as referred to in the Article 62 point a, the submission of Notarial Protocols shall be made by the Notary Public's beneficiary(-ies) to another Notary Public appointed by the District / Municipal Supervisory Council.

（2）在满足第62条第a款的情形时，公证员应当向由区/市监督委员会委任的另一名公证员提交公证档案。

(3) In case of condition as referred to in the Article 62 point g, the submission of Notarial Protocols shall be made by the Notary Public to another Notary Public appointed by the District / Municipal Supervisory Council if the suspension is more than 3 (three) months.

（3）在满足第62条第g款的情形时，如果停职超过3个月，公证员应当向由区/市监督委员会委任的另一名公证员提交公证档案。

(4) In case of condition as referred to in the Article 62 point b, c, d, f, or h, the submission of Notarial Protocols shall be made by the Notary Public to another Notary Public appointed by the Minister at the recommendation of the District / Municipal Supervisory Council.

（4）在满足第62条第b款、第c款、第d款、第f款、第h款中的任一情形时，公证员应当向由区/市监督委员会委任的另一名公证员提交公证档案。

Article 64.(1) Notarial Protocols from Notary Public appointed to be a state official shall be submitted to a Notary Public appointed by the District / Municipal Supervisory Council.

第六十四条 （1）公证员因被任命为政府官员而需交回公证档案，该公证档案应当提交给区/市监督委员会任命的公证员。

(2) Notary Public holding the Notarial protocols as referred to in the paragraph (1) shall be authorized to issue Tenor of Deed, Copy of deed, or Excerpt of Deed.

（2）持有第1款规定的公证档案的公证员，应当有权出具文书、文书副本或文书摘录本。

Article 65. Notary Public, Substitute Notary Public, Special Substitute Notary Public, and Notary Public Tem-

第六十五条 公证员、替补公证员、特殊替代公证员和临时公证员应对其出具的每一份文书负责，即

porary Official shall be responsible for each deed they draw up even though the Notarial Protocols have been submitted or transferred to a party keeping the Notarial protocols.

使公证档案已经提交或转让给公证档案的保管方。

CHAPTER VIII
TAKING OF MINUTES OF DEED AND SUMMONS OF NOTARY PUBLIC

第八章　文书记录和公证员传唤

Article 66.(1) In the interest of judicial process, the investigators, general prosecutors, or judges with the approval from the District / Municipal Supervisory Council shall be authorized to:

a. take copy of Minutes of Deed and/or documents attached to the Minutes of Deed or Notarial Protocols kept by the Notary Public; and

b. summon the Notary Public to be present in the hearing relating to the deeds he/she draw up or Notarial Protocols kept by the Notary Public.

(2) Taking of copy of Minute of Deed or documents as referred to in the paragraph (1) point a, shall be made in a minutes of submission.

第六十六条　（1）为了司法程序利益，经区 / 市监督委员会批准的调查员、总检察官或法官有权：

a. 查阅公证记录副本、公证员保存的与公证记录或公证档案有关的文件；和

b. 召集公证员出席与他 / 她出具的文书或公证员保管的公证档案有关的听证会。

（2）查阅第 1 款第 a 项所述的文书纪录副本或文件，应当制作查阅记录。

CHAPTER IX
SUPERVISION

第九章　监督

Part One
General

第一节　一般规定

Article 67.(1) Notary Publics shall be supervised by the Minister.

(2) In the supervision as referred to in the paragraph (1), the Minister shall form a Supervisory Council.

(3) The Supervisory Council as referred to in the paragraph (2) shall consist of 9 (nine) as follows:

a. 3 (three) persons from the government;

b.3 (three) persons from Notary Public Organization; and

c. 3 (three) experts/academicians.

(4) In case of absence of the government's elements in one region as referred to in the paragraph (3) point a, membership in the Supervisory Council shall be filled from the other elements appointed by the Minister.

(5) The supervision as referred to in the paragraph (1) shall cover behaviour of Notary Publics and performance of the office of Notary Public.

(6) Provisions on the supervision as referred to in the paragraph (5) shall apply to Substitute Notary Public,

第六十七条　（1）公证员受部长监督。

（2）依据第 1 款的规定，部长应当组织成立监督委员会。

（3）第 2 款所述的监督委员会应当由下列 9 位成员组成：

a. 3 名政府人员；

b. 3 名公证机构的成员；

c. 3 名专家 / 学者。

（4）如第 3 款第 a 项所述的监督委员会内政府成员缺席，缺席的监督委员会成员应当由部长委任的其他人员补充。

（5）第 1 款所述的监督内容，应当涵盖公证员的行为和公证员的职业表现。

（6）第 5 款所述的监督条款，适用于替补公证员、特殊替代公证员、临时公证员。

Special Substitute Notary Public, and Notary Public Temporary Official.

Article 68.The Supervisory Council as referred to in the Article 67 paragraph (2) shall consist of:

a. District / Municipal Supervisory Council;

b. Provincial Supervisory Council; and

c. Central Supervisory Council.

Part Two
District / Municipal Supervisory Council

Article 69.(1) District / Municipal Supervisory Council shall be formed in district or municipality.

(2) Membership of District / Municipal Supervisory Council shall consist of the elements as referred to in the Article 67 paragraph (3).

(3) Chairman and Vice Chairman of District / Municipal Supervisory Council shall be elected from and by members as referred to in the paragraph (2).

(4) Term of office of chairman, vice chairman, and members of District / Municipal Supervisory Council shall be 3 (three) years and they can be reassigned.

(5) District / Municipal Supervisory Council shall be assisted by a secretary or more appointed in a Meeting of District / Municipal Supervisory Council.

Article 70.District / Municipal Supervisory Council shall be authorized to:

a. hold meetings to investigate alleged violation of Code of Ethics of Notary Public or violation of performance of office of Notary Public;

b. gradually investigate the Notarial Protocols;

c. give leave permit for up to 6 (six) months;

d. determine Substitute Notary Public by taking into account the recommendation of the relevant Notary Public;

e. appoint a Notary Public to serve as a temporary holder of Notarial Protocols assigned as a state official as referred to in the Article 11 paragraph (4);

f. receive reports from the public on alleged violation of Code of Ethics of Notary Public or violation of any provisions herein; and

g. make and submit reports as referred to in the points a, b, c, d, e, f, and g to Provincial Supervisory Council.

Article 71. District / Municipal Supervisory Council shall be obligated to:

a. record in a register contained in Notarial Protocols by mentioning date of investigation, number of deeds and

第六十八条 第67条第2款所述的监督委员会应包括：

a. 区 / 市监督委员会；

b. 省监督委员会；

c. 中央监督委员会。

第二节 区 / 市监督委员会

第六十九条 （1）区 / 市监督委员会应当在区 / 市设立。

（2）区 / 市监督委员会成员应由第67条第3款中的成员组成。

（3）区 / 市监督委员会的主席和副主席应当由第2款中的成员中选举产生。

（4）区 / 市监督委员会的主席、副主席及委员任期为3年，可以连选连任。

（5）区 / 市监督委员会应由区 / 市监督委员会会议选出的秘书或其他人组织运作。

第七十条 区 / 市监督委员会有权：

a. 举行会议调查涉嫌违反公证员道德守则或公证员职务的案件；

b. 调查公证档案；

c. 批准6个月的休假申请；

d. 考虑相关公证员的建议，确定替补公证员；

e. 任命1名公证员担任第11条第4款规定的公证档案的临时持有人；

f. 接收公众关于涉嫌违反公证员道德守则或其他规定的举报；

g. 制作并向省级监督委员会提交第a项、第b项、第c项、第d项、第e项、第f项和第g项中的报告。

第七十一条 区 / 市监督委员会有义务：

a. 在载有公证档案的登记册中，记录调查日期、合法制作的私人文书和文件数量，并于调查期间的结

documents privately made so legalized and made as of the last date of investigation;

b. make minutes of investigation and submit the same to the Provincial Supervisory Council, with carbon copy to the relevant Notary Public, Notary Public Organization, and Central Supervisory Council;

c. keep secret the content of the deed and the result(s) of investigation;

d. receive the legalized copies of register of deeds and other deeds from Notary Public and keep them secret;

e. investigate the reports from the public on Notary Public and submit the results of investigation to Provincial Supervisory Council within 30 (thirty) days, with carbon copy to the reporting party, the relevant Notary Public, Central Supervisory Council, and Notary Public Organization.

Part Three
Provincial Supervisory Council

Article 72.(1) Provincial Supervisory Council shall be formed and domiciled in Capital of Province.

(2) Membership of Provincial Supervisory Council shall consist of the elements as referred to in the Article 67 paragraph (3).

(3) Chairman and Vice Chairman of Provincial Supervisory Council shall be elected from and by the members as referred to in the paragraph (2).

(4) Term of office of chairman, vice chairman, and members of Provincial Supervisory Council shall be 3 (three) years and they can be reassigned.

(5) Provincial Supervisory Council shall be assisted by a secretary or more appointed in a Meeting of Provincial Supervisory Council.

Article 73.(1) Provincial Supervisory Council shall be authorized to:

a. hold meetings to investigate and make decision on a public report submitted through Provincial Supervisory Council;

b. summon the reported Notary Public for investigation as referred to in the point a;

c. give a leave permit for more than 6 (six) months to 1 (one) year;

d. investigate and judge the decision of District / Municipal Supervisory Council refusing a request for leave submitted by the reporting Notary Public;

e. impose sanctions in the form of oral or written warnings;

束日作出；

b. 制作调查记录，并向省级监督委员会提交，将副本送交有关公证员、公证机构和中央监督委员会；

c. 对文书的内容和调查结果保密；

d. 保存从公证员处收到的文书登记册以及其他文书的副本，并对此保密；

e. 根据公众对公证员的举报开展调查工作，并在30日内向省级监督委员会提交调查结果，并向举报方、有关当事人、中央监督委员会和公证机构送达调查结果的副本。

第三节　省级监督委员会

第七十二条　（1）省级监督委员会应当在省会城市设立。

（2）省级监督委员会成员应当由第67条第3款所述人员组成。

（3）省级监督委员会主席、副主席由第2款中的成员选举产生。

（4）省级监督委员会主席、副主席、委员任期为3年，可以连任。

（5）省级监督委员会由省级监督委员会会议任命的秘书或者其他人员组织运作。

第七十三条　（1）省级监督委员会有权：

a. 召开会议，对向省级监督委员会递交的举报报告进行调查和作出决定；

b. 为了展开调查，传唤第a项所述的被举报的公证员；

c. 对时间为6个月至1年的休假申请作出是否批准的决定；

d. 调查和复核区 / 市监督委员会作出的拒绝公证员休假请求的决定；

e. 以口头或书面警告的形式对违法的公证员实施惩罚；

f. recommend the imposition of sanctions against the Notary Public to the Central Supervisory Council in he form of:

1) suspension for 3 (three) months to 6 (six) months; or

2) dishonourably dismissal.

g. make a minutes for any decision of imposition of sanctions as referred to in the points e and f.

(2) Decision of Provincial Supervisory Council as referred to in the paragraph (1) point e shall be final in nature.

(3) Each decision of imposition of sanction as referred to in the paragraph (1) points e and f shall be drawn up in a minutes.

Article 74.(1) The investigation in the meeting of Provincial Supervisory Council as referred to in the Article 73 paragraph (1) point a shall be closed to the public.

(2) Notary Public shall be entitled to advocacy in the meeting of Provincial Supervisory Council.

Article 75. The Provincial Supervisory Council shall be obligated to:

a. submit the decisions as referred to in the Article 73 paragraph (1) points a, b, c, d, e, and f to the relevant Notary Public with carbon copy to the Central Supervisory Council, and Notary Public Organization; and

b. submit an appeal from the Notary Public to the Central Supervisory Council against the imposition of sanction and refusal of leave.

Part Four
Central Supervisory Council

Article 76.(1) Central Supervisory Council shall be formed and domiciled in the capital of the state.

(2) Membership of Central Supervisory Council shall consist of the elements as referred to in the Article 67 paragraph (3).

(3) Chairman and Vice Chairman of Central Supervisory Council shall be elected from and by the members as referred to in the paragraph (2).

(4) Term of office of chairman, vice chairman, and members of Central Supervisory Council shall be 3 (three) years and they can be reassigned.

(5) Central Supervisory Council shall be assisted by a secretary or more appointed in a meeting of Central Supervisory Council.

Article 77. Central Supervisory Council shall be authorized to:

a. hold meetings to investigate and make decision at appeal instance against the imposition of sanction and

f. 向中央监督委员会提出对公证员实施惩罚的建议，其形式包括：

1）停职 3 至 6 个月；或

2）被不光彩地解雇。

g. 就第 e 项和第 f 项规定的惩罚作出决定并记录。

（2）第 1 款第 e 项规定的省级监督委员会的决定具有终局性。

（3）第 1 款第 e 项、第 f 项规定的惩罚决定，应当立即作出。

第七十四条 （1）第 73 条第 1 款第 a 项规定的省级监督委员会会议的调查结果，应当向社会公开。

（2）公证员在省级监督委员会会议上有权进行申辩。

第七十五条 省级监督委员会有义务：

a. 将第 73 条第 1 款第 a 项、第 b 项、第 c 项、第 d 项、第 e 项、第 f 项中的决定送达至相关公证员，并向中央监督委员会和公证机构送达副本；及

b. 向中央监督委员会提交公证员对实施惩罚和拒绝休假许可决定的申诉文件。

第四节 中央监督委员会

第七十六条 （1）中央监督委员会应当在国家首都组建和设立。

（2）中央监督委员会的组成人员应由第 67 条第 3 款中的人员组成。

（3）中央监督委员会主席和副主席由第 2 款中的成员选举产生。

（4）主席、副主席和中央监督委员会成员的任期为 3 年，可以连选连任。

（5）中央监督委员会由中央监督委员会会议指定的秘书或其他人员组织运作。

第七十七条 中央监督委员会有权：

a. 举行会议，在反对实行惩罚和拒绝休假申请的上诉案件中展开调查并作出裁决；

refusal of leave;

b. summon the reported Notary Public for investigation as referred to in the point a;

c. impose a sanction in the form of suspension; and

d. recommend the imposition of a sanction in the form of dishonourably dismissal to the Minister.

Article 78.(1) The investigation in a meeting of Central Supervisory Council as referred to in the Article 77 point a shall be open to the public.

(2) The Notary Public shall be entitled to advocacy in the meeting of Central Supervisory Council.

Article 79.Central Supervisory Council shall submit the decision as referred to in the Article 77 point a to the Minister and the relevant Notary Public with carbon copy to the relevant Provincial Supervisory Council and District / Municipal Supervisory Council as well as Notary Public Organization.

Article 80.(1) During suspension, the Central Supervisory Council shall recommend a temporary official to the Minister.

(2) The Minister shall appoint a Notary Public to receive the Notarial Protocols from the suspended Notary Public.

Article 81.Any further provisions on procedures for appointment and dismissal of members, organizational structure and work system, as well as procedure for investigation by the Supervisory Councils shall be contained in a Ministerial Regulation.

CHAPTER X NOTARY PUBLIC ORGANIZATION

Article 82.(1) Notary Publics shall associate in one Organization.

(2) Provisions on purposes, tasks, authorities, work systems, and organizational structure shall be contained in Articles of Association and Bylaws.

Article 83.(1) Notary Public Organization shall determine and maintain Code of Ethics of Notary Public.

(2) A Notary Public Organization shall have a register of members and the copy thereof shall be submitted to the Minister and Supervisory Council.

CHAPTER XI SANCTION

Article 84.Violation by a Notary Public of the provisions as referred to in the Article 16 paragraph (1) point

b. 为了开展调查，传唤第 a 项所述的被举报的公证员；

c. 实施停职惩罚；及

d. 向部长建议以非公开方式行使惩罚。

第七十八条 （1）第 77 条所指的中央监督委员会会议的调查结果，应向社会公开。

（2）公证员有权在中央监督委员会会议上进行申辩。

第七十九条 中央监督委员会应当向部长和有关公证员提交第 77 条第 a 款所述的决定，并将其副本抄送至省级监督委员会、区 / 市监督委员会和公证机构。

第八十条 （1）在停职期间，中央监督委员会应当向部长推荐一名临时公证员。

（2）部长应当任命一名公证员接受由停职的公证员递交的公证档案。

第八十一条 关于成员任免程序、组织结构、工作制度以及监督委员会的调查程序等任何进一步规定均应载于部长级条例中。

第十章 公证机构

第八十二条 （1）公证员隶属于某一公证机构。

（2）有关目的、职责、权力分配、工作制度和组织结构的规定应当载于章程和细则。

第八十三条 （1）公证机构应当制定和维护公证员的道德守则。

（2）公证机构应当拥有成员登记册，并将其副本提交至部长和监督委员会。

第十一章 惩罚

第八十四条 公证员违反第 16 条第 1 款第 a 项，第 16 条第 1 款第 k 项，第 41 条，第 44 条，第 48 条，

I, Article 16 paragraph (1) point k, Article 41, Article 44, Article 48, Article 49, Article 50, Article 51, or Article 52 making a deed only have a power of evidencing as a deed privately made or making the same null.

第49条，第50条，第51条或第52条的规定的，所出具的文书只具有私人文书的证明效力或者无效。

Article 85.Violation of the provisions as referred to in the Article 7, Article 16 paragraph (1) point a, Article 16 paragraph (1) point b, Article 16 paragraph (1) point c, Article 16 paragraph (1) point d, Article 16 paragraph (1) point e, Article 16 paragraph (1) point

f, Article 16 paragraph (1) point g, Article 16 paragraph (1) point h, Article 16 paragraph (1) point i, Article 16 paragraph (1) point j, Article 16 paragraph (1) point k, Article 17, Article 20, Article 27, Article 32, Article 37, Article 54, Article 58, Article 59, and/or Article 63, can be sanctioned in the form of:

a. oral warning;
b. written warning;
c. suspension;
d. honourably dismissal; or
e. dishonourably dismissal.

第八十五条 违反第7条、第16条第1款第a项，第16条第1款第b项，第16条第1款第c项，第16条第1款第d项，第16条第1款第e项，第16条第1款第f项，第16条第1款第g项，第16条第1款第h项，第16条第1款第i项，第16条第1款第j项，第16条第1款第k项，第17条，第20条，第27条，第32条，第37条，第54条，第58条，第59条和/或第63条，可以作出下列形式的惩罚：

a. 口头警告；
b. 书面警告；
c. 暂停职务；
d. 辞退；或
e. 被不光彩地解雇。

CHAPTER XII TRANSITIONAL PROVISION

第十二章　过渡条款

Article 86.Upon effectiveness of this Law, the implemental regulation relating to the office of Notary Public shall remain effective as long as not contravening or replaced yet by virtue of this Law.

第八十六条 在本法仍有效的情况下，与公证员职务有关的规定，只要不违反本法或其他法律的替代规定，仍为有效。

Article 87.Notary Publics already appointed upon effectiveness of this Law shall be declared as Notary Publics as contained herein.

第八十七条 在本法生效之前任命的公证员仍然有效。

Article 88.Upon effectiveness of this Law, a request for appointment of Notary Public already fulfilling the requirements shall remain processed by virtue of the existing laws and legislation.

第八十八条 在本法生效前已经满足要求的公证员的任命请求仍应依据之前法律和法规进行处理。

Article 89.Upon effectiveness of this Law, the existing Code of Ethics of Notary Public shall remain effective until stipulation of the new Code of Ethics of Notary Public by virtue of this Law.

第八十九条 在本法生效时，现行的公证员道德规范在依据本法通过新的公证员道德规范之前仍然有效。

Article 90.Any graduate of Notarial Specialist education not yet appointed as a Notary Public upon effectiveness of this Law can remain appointed as a Notary Public pursuant to this Law.

第九十条 任何尚未被委任为公证员的公证专业毕业生，在本法生效后，仍可根据本法规定被委任为公证员。

CHAPTER XIII CLOSING

第十三章　结束

Article 91.Upon effectiveness of this Law:

第九十一条 本法以下述法律法规为基础：

1. Reglement op het Notaris Ambt in Indonesie (Stlb 19860:3) as already amended recently in State Gazette Of 1945 Number 101;

2. Ordonantie 16 September 1931 on Honorarium for Notary Public;

3. Law Number 33 Of 1954 on Notary Public Representative and Temporary Notary Public Representative (State Gazette Of 1954 Number 101, Supplement to State Gazette Number 700);

4. Government Regulation Number 11 of 1949 on Oath of Office of Notary Public, shall be revoked and declared null and void.

Article 92.This law shall become effective as of date of stipulation. For people cognizance, it is instructed to promulgate this Law by inserting the same in the State Gazette of the Republic of Indonesia.

1.1945 年第 101 号国家公报中印度尼西亚公证法的修订本；

2.1931 年 9 月 16 日的公证员收费条例；及

3.1954 年关于公证员代理和临时公证员代理的 33 号法律（1954 年第 101 号国家公报，第 700 号国家公报补充）；

4.1949 年政府关于公证机关宣誓的第 11 号规定。

第九十二条 本法自规定之日起生效，并在印度尼西亚共和国国家公报中公开发布。

Ratified in Jakarta on October 16, 2004
THE PRESIDENT OF THE REPUBLIC OF INDONESIA
Signed
MEGAWATI SOEKARNOPUTRI

2004 年 10 月 16 日批准于雅加达
印度尼西亚共和国总统

签字
梅加瓦蒂 • 苏加诺普特丽

Enacted in Jakarta on October 6, 2004
STATE SECRETARY OF THE REPUBLIC OF INDONESIA,
signed
BAMBANG KESOWO

2004 年 10 月 6 日颁布于雅加达
印度尼西亚共和国国务卿

签字
班邦 • 哥索沃

STATE GAZETTE OF THE REPUBLIC OF INDONESIA OF 2004 NUMBER 117 ELUCIDATION OF LAW OF THE REPUBLIC OF INDONESIA NUMBER 30 OF 2004 ON OFFICE OF NOTARY PUBLIC

2004 年印度尼西亚共和国公报 117 号文

2004 年第 30 号印度尼西亚共和国法律委员会关于公证法的解释

I. GENERAL

The 1945 Constitution of the State of the Republic of Indonesia explicitly stipulates that the state of the Republic of Indonesia is a constitutional state. The principles of constitutional state are to secure the legal certainty, order and protection based on the truth and justice.

Legal certainty, order, and protection require, among others, that legal traffic in the community requires evi-

I. 一般规定

印度尼西亚共和国 1945 年《国家宪法》明确规定，印度尼西亚共和国是一个宪政国家。宪政国家的基本原则是在事实和正义的基础上，保证法律的确定性、维护法律秩序以及保护性要求。

法律的确定性、法律秩序性和保护性要求，社会交往的法律纠纷要建立在证据的基础上，明确个人在

dences clearly determining the rights and obligations of an individual in the community.

Authentic deeds as the strongest and fullest written evidences have the significant role in any legal relationship in the community. In various business relationships, banking, agrarian, social activities and other activities, the need for written evidencing increase more and more in line with the growing demand for legal certainty in various economic and social relationships, in national, regional, or global level. Authentic deeds explicitly stipulate the rights and obligations, secure legal certainty, and simultaneously avoid any dispute. Despite the inevitability, in a dispute settlement process, an authentic deed being the strongest and fullest evidence rally contributes to the settlement of case less expensively and immediately.

As long as the drawing up of certain deeds, authentic deeds are not made special for the other public officials. In addition to being required by the laws and legislation, the drawing up of an authentic deed is also required by the relevant party to ensure the rights and obligations of the parties for legal certainty, order, and protection to the relevant parties simultaneously to the community on the whole.

Authentic deeds basically contain the formal truth as informed by the parties to Notary Public. But, Notary Public must indicate that what is contained in a Notarial Deed is really understood and as wished by the parties, namely by reading out the same thereby clarifying the content of Notarial Deed and giving an access to information, including access to the relevant laws and legislation to the parties signing the deed. Therefore, the parties can freely determine to agree or disagree the content of Notarial Deed to sign.

Part of the applicable legislation of Office of Notary Public is the inheritance of the Netherlands East Indies and another one is the national legislation, namely:

1. Reglement Op Het Notaris Ambt in Indonesie (Stlb 19860:3) as already amended recently in State Gazette Of 1945 Number 101;

2.Ordonantie 16 September 1931 on Honorarium for Notary Public;

3. Law Number 33 Of 1954 on Assistant to Notary Public and Assistant to Temporary Notary Public (State Gazette Of 1954 Number 101, Supplement to State Gazette Number 700);

4. Government Regulation Number 11 Of 1949 on Oath of Office of Notary Public.

The legislation fails to conform to the legal development and need of Indonesians. Therefore, it is necessary to

交往关系中的权利和义务。

公证书作为最有力和最全面的书面证据，在社会中的任何法律关系中都发挥着重要的作用。在各种商业关系中，在银行、农业、社会活动和其他活动中，对书面证据的需求越来越多，这与国家、区域或全球各种经济和社会关系中对法律确定性不断增长的需求一致。公证书明确了权利和义务，确保了法律的确定性，同时避免争议。虽然争议在所难免，但是在争端解决程序中，公证书通常作为最有力和最充分的证据集，对高效和快速解决纠纷做出重要的贡献。

公证书不得为特殊的政府官员谋求特殊的利益。除了法律和立法的要求外，在整个社会关系交往的同时，为了实现法律的确定性、秩序性和保护性，公证书的制作必须能够明确有关利益各方的权利和义务。

公证书基本上包含了公证员对利益相关方行为事实的确认。但是，公证员必须保证公证书中所包含的内容是当事人所希望的，且能够为各方真正理解，即通过解读文书的内容，从而澄清公证书的内容并提供相关信息，包括获取与当事方签署文书有关的法律依据。因此，当事人可以自由决定在同意或不同意公证书的内容基础上进行签字确认。

公证员职务适用的法律一部分是继承荷属东印度群岛的立法，另一部分是印度尼西亚国家立法，即：

1.1945 年第 101 号国家公报中印度尼西亚公证法的修订本；

2.1931 年 9 月 16 日关于公证员收费条例；及

3.1954 年关于公证员代理和临时公证员代理的第 33 号法律（1954 年第 101 号国家公报，第 700 号国家公报补充）；

4.1949 年政府关于公证机关宣誓的第 11 号规定。

立法有时不能符合印度尼西亚法律的发展和需要。因此，有必要对立法进行更新和进一步完善，从

renew and re-stipulate the same on the whole in one law on office of notary public thereby creating a legal unification applicable to all inhabitants throughout the state of the Republic of Indonesia. To realize the legal unification in notarial affairs, Law of Office of Notary Public shall be formed.

而促进印度尼西亚共和国境内的法律统一。为实现公证事务立法的统一，应当出台一部公证法。

This Law stipulates in details genera office of Notary Public thereby expectedly making the authentic deeds drawn up by or before a Notary Public able to secure legal certainty, order, and protection. Considering Notarial Deeds as authentic deeds are the strongest and fullest written evidences, this Law also stipulates the form and nature of Notarial deed, Minutes of Deed, Tenor of Deed, and Copy of Deed, or Excerpt of Notarial Deed.

本法详细规定了公证员的职责，从而使公证员出具的文书能够确保法律的确定性、秩序性和保护性。考虑到公证书是真实的文书，是最强有力和最全面的书面证据，本法还规定了公证文书的形式和性质、文书记录、文书时间、文书副本、公证文书的摘录。

As the strongest and fullest written evidences, what is contained in a Notarial Deed shall be accepted, unless the relevant parties can prove otherwise before the court. Functions of Notary Public outside the drawing up of authentic deeds are comprehensively stipulated for the first time herein. In addition to involving the Agency assigned to and responsible for notarial affairs and Notary Public Organization, the supervision of office of Notary Public shall also involve the experts/academicians. This Law shall be intended to improve legal services and protection to the community.

作为最有力和最全面的书面证据，除非有关各方能够在法庭上另行举证证明，否则公证文书所载的内容具有绝对的证明能力。本法第一次全面规定了公证员的职能。除了涉及公证事务的代理和责任内容、公证机构外，对公证员的监督还应包括专家 / 学者的参与。本法旨在改善公证服务的质量和保护社会公共利益。

II. BY ARTICLES

Article 1.Self-explanatory.

Article 2.Self-explanatory.

Article 3.

Point a

Self-explanatory.

Point b

Self-explanatory.

Point c

Self-explanatory.

Point d

By “sound of body and sound of mind” we mean being able to bodily and spiritually perform the authorities and obligations as a Notary Public.

Point e

Self-explanatory.

Point f

By “own initiative” we mean that the prospective notary public can choose his/her office on his/her own by

II. 具体条文

第一条　无须解释。

第二条　无须解释。

第三条

a 款

无须解释。

b 款

无须解释。

c 款

无须解释。

d 款

“身体和心灵的声音”，我们指的是能够在行动上和精神上履行公证员职责。

e 款

无须解释。

f 款

“自己的行动”指的是未来公证员在接受公证机构的建议后，仍可以自行选择办公场所。

remaining receiving a recommendation from Notary Public Organization.

Point g

By "civil servants" and "state officials" we mean those as referred to in Law Number 43 Of 1999 on Amendment to Law Number 8 Of 1974 on Principles of Personnel Affairs. By "advocate" we mean those as referred to in Law Number 18 Of 2003 on Advocates.

Article 4.Self-explanatory.

Article 5.Self-explanatory.

Article 6.Self-explanatory.

Article 7.

Point a

Self-explanatory.

Point b

Self-explanatory.

Point c

This provision shall be intended to know whether or not the relevant Notary Public has really implemented his/her tasks.

Article 8.Paragraph (1)

Point a

Self-explanatory.

Point b

Self-explanatory.

Point c

Self-explanatory.

Point d

Continuous incapability, both spiritually and bodily, in this provision shall be proven with expert medical certificate.

Point e

Self-explanatory.

Paragraph (2)

Self-explanatory.

Article 9.

Paragraph (1)

Point a

Self-explanatory.

Point b

Self-explanatory.

Point c

By "committing disgraceful deed" we mean committing an action in contravention of religious, ethical, and traditional norms.

Point d

Self-explanatory.

g 款

"公务员"和"政府官员"是指 1999 年第 43 号关于人事事务原则（对 1974 年第 8 号法案的修正）中的人员。"宣誓"是指 2003 年关于宣誓的第 18 号法律中的内容。

第四条 无须解释。

第五条 无须解释。

第六条 无须解释。

第七条

a 款

无须解释。

b 款

无须解释。

c 款

该条款旨在了解相关公证员是否真正履行了他 / 她的职责。

第八条 第（1）款

a 项

无须解释。

b 项

无须解释。

c 项

无须解释。

d 项

在这项规定中，精神上和身体上的持续无能，需经有关医疗专家证明。

e 项

无须解释。

第（2）款

无须解释。

第九条

第（1）款

a 项

无须解释。

b 项

无须解释。

c 项

"犯不光彩的罪行"是指违反宗教、伦理和传统规范的行为。

d 项

无须解释。

Paragraph (2)

By "gradually" in this provision we mean starting from District / Municipal Supervisory Council, Provincial Supervisory Council, to Central Supervisory Council.

Paragraph (3)

Self-explanatory.

Paragraph (4)

Self-explanatory.

Article 10.Self-explanatory.

Article 11.

Paragraph (1)

This provision shall be intended to avoid conflict of interest because as a Notary Public, he/she has to be independent and non-unilateral.

Paragraph (2)

Self-explanatory.

Paragraph (3)

Self-explanatory.

Paragraph (4)

Self-explanatory.

Paragraph (5)

Self-explanatory.

Paragraph (6)

Self-explanatory.

Article 12.

Point a

Self-explanatory.

Point b

Self-explanatory.

Point c

By "action humiliating the honour and dignity" we mean for example gambling, being intoxicated, misusing drugs, and committing adultery.

Point d

By "severe violation" we mean failing to fulfil the obligations and violating the prohibitions in the office of Notary Public.

Article 13. Abolished.

Article 14.Self-explanatory.

Article 15.

Paragraph (1)

Self-explanatory.

Paragraph (2)

Point a

This provision shall be a legalization of private deed drawn up by an individual on his/her own or by the parties on their own on a duly stamped paper by registering the

第（2）款

在本款中，"逐步"是指从区/市监督委员会，到省级监督委员会再到中央监督委员会。

第（3）款

无须解释。

第（4）款

无须解释。

第十条 无须解释。

第十一条

第（1）款

本款旨在避免利益冲突，因为公证员必须独立且全面地履行公证员职务。

第（2）款

无须解释。

第（3）款

无须解释。

第（4）款

无须解释。

第（5）款

无须解释。

第（6）款

无须解释。

第十二条

a 款

无须解释。

b 款

无须解释。

c 款

"有损名誉和尊严的行为"指的是赌博、酗酒、滥用毒品和通奸。

d 款

"严重违反"是指未能履行公证员的义务和违反禁令。

第十三条 已废止。

第十四条 无须解释。

第十五条

第（1）款

无须解释。

第（2）款

a 项

本规定涉及由个人制定的私人文件或由当事人自行制定的私人文书，并在公证员指定的登记册中进行登记。

same in a book specifically appropriated by Notary Public.

Point b

Self-explanatory.

Point c

Self-explanatory.

Point d

Self-explanatory.

Point e

Self-explanatory.

Point f

Self-explanatory.

Point g

Self-explanatory.

Paragraph (3)

Self-explanatory.

Article 16.

Paragraph (1)

Point a

Self-explanatory.

Point b

Self-explanatory.

Point c

Tenor of Deed issued based on this provision shall be the first Tenor, while the subsequent ones shall only be issued at the court's order.

Point d

By "any reason to refuse the same" we mean any reason making a Notary Public non-unilateral, such as blood or family relationship with the Notary Public or with his/her spouse, one of the parties has no capability to take any action or anything not allowed by the law.

Point e

Obligation to keep secret anything relating to deeds or other documents shall be to protect the interests of all parties related o the deeds.

Point f

Deeds and documents made by a notary public as authentic official documents shall be secured both the deeds themselves and the content thereof to prevent the misuse.

Point g

Self-explanatory.

Point h

Obligations contained in this provision shall be important to protect the interests of the beneficiaries where the correctness of a deed of testament already drawn up before a Notary Public that can be traced.

b 项

无须解释。

c 项

无须解释。

d 项

无须解释。

e 项

无须解释。

f 项

无须解释。

g 项

无须解释。

第（3）款

无须解释。

第十六条

第（1）款

a 项

无须解释。

b 项

无须解释。

c 项

根据本条出具的文书时间应是第一时间，而第二时间仅应在法院命令中发出。

d 项

“任何可拒绝的理由”是指与公证员存在特定关系，例如配偶及血缘或其他家庭关系，以上各方无权采取任何行动或为法律不允许的任何事情。

e 项

任何与文书或其他文件有关的保密义务，是指保护与文书有关的当事人的利益。

f 项

公证员出具的文书和文件，应当保证其内容的真实性，禁止公证员滥用权力。

g 项

无须解释。

h 项

本条款所载义务对于保护受益人的利益是重要的，因为公证员出具的公证书具有确定性。

Point i

Self-explanatory.

Point j

Recording in the repertory shall be made on day of submission, it is important to prove that the obligations of Notary Public as referred to in the points f and g have been fulfilled.

Point k

Self-explanatory.

Point l

That Notary Public shall be physically present and sign the deed before the appearers and witnesses.

Point m

Self-explanatory.

Paragraph (2)

Self-explanatory.

Paragraph (3)

Self-explanatory.

Paragraph (4)

Self-explanatory.

Paragraph (5)

Self-explanatory.

Paragraph (6)

Self-explanatory.

Paragraph (7)

Self-explanatory.

Paragraph (8)

Self-explanatory.

Paragraph (9)

Self-explanatory.

Article 17.This prohibition shall be intended to secure the public interests requiring Notarial services.

Point a

The prohibitions in this provision shall be intended to give legal certainty to the public and simultaneously prevent the unfair competition between the Notary Publics in implementing their tasks.

Point b

Self-explanatory.

Point c

Vide the Explanation of Article 3 point g.

Point d

Vide the Explanation of Article 3 point g.

Point e

Vide the Explanation of Article 3 point g.

Point f

Self-explanatory.

i 项

无须解释。

j 项

记录汇编应在提交当天制作，同时有必要证明第 f 项和第 g 项中提到的公证员的义务已经被履行。

k 项

无须解释。

l 项

公证员应亲自到场并在当事人和证人面前签署文书。

m 项

无须解释。

第（2）款

无须解释。

第（3）款

无须解释。

第（4）款

无须解释。

第（5）款

无须解释。

第（6）款

无须解释。

第（7）款

无须解释。

第（8）款

无须解释。

第（9）款

无须解释。

第十七条　该禁令旨在确保公证服务能够保护公共利益。

a 款

本条款中的禁令应旨在为公众提供法律上的确定性，同时防止公证员之间在履行职务时的不公平竞争。

b 款

无须解释。

c 款

参见第 3 条第 g 款的解释。

d 款

参见第 3 条第 g 款的解释。

e 款

参见第 3 条第 g 款的解释。

f 款

无须解释。

Point g

Self-explanatory.

Point h

Prohibition from becoming a "Substitute Notary Public" shall apply to Notary Publics not yet implementing their office, those taking leave, and those in office area removal process.

Point i

Self-explanatory.

Article 18.Self-explanatory.

Article 19.Paragraph (1)

By only having one office we mean a Notary Public shall be prohibited from having branch, representative office, and/or any other forms.

Paragraph (2)

A Notarial Deed shall as much as possible be drawn up in Notary Public's office except the drawing up of certain deeds.

Article 20.Paragraph (1)

By "civil association" in this provision we mean Notary Public joint office.

Paragraph (2) Self-explanatory.

Paragraph (3) Self-explanatory.

Article 21.Self-explanatory.

Article 22.Provision on Formation of Office of Notary Public shall apply to the first appointment or removal of office area of Notary Public.

Article 23.Paragraph (1)

Self-explanatory.

Paragraph (2)

By "certain district or municipality" in this provision we mean a district or municipality where a Notary Public implements his/her office tasks upon submission of request for removal of his/her office area.

Paragraph (3)

Self-explanatory.

Paragraph (4)

Self-explanatory.

Paragraph (5)

Self-explanatory.

Article 24.By "certain conditions" we mean among others due to natural disaster, security.

Article 25.Self-explanatory.

Article 26.

Paragraph (1)

"Taking of annual leave" in this paragraph shall mean without prejudice to the rights of Notary Public to

g 款

无须解释。

h 款

"替补公证员"的条款适用于尚未执行职务的公证员、休假的公证员以及离职的公证员。

i 款

无须解释。

第十八条 无须解释。

第十九条

第（1）款

只有一个办公场所是指公证员不得有分支机构，代表处和 / 或任何其他形式的机构驻处。

第（2）款

除了出具某些其他文书外，公证员应尽可能地在公证机构制作、出具公证书。

第二十条 第（1）款

"民间协会"是指公证公共组织。

第（2）款 无须解释。

第（3）款 无须解释。

第二十一条 无须解释。

第二十二条 关于公证办事处构成的规定适用于公证员的首次任免。

第二十三条

第（1）款

无须解释。

第（2）款

在本款中，"某些地区或市政"是指公证员在提交搬迁其办公区域请求时执行其职务的地区。

第（3）款

无须解释。

第（4）款

无须解释。

第（5）款

无须解释。

第二十四条 "特定条件"是指自然灾害或出于安全考虑等。

第二十五条 无须解释。

第二十六条

第（1）款

本段中的"休年假"与公证员在 1 年内休假超过 1 次的权利不冲突。

take leave for more than 1 (one) times in 1 (one) year.

Paragraph (2)

Self-explanatory.

Paragraph (3)

Self-explanatory.

Article 27.Self-explanatory.

Article 28.By "urgency" we mean if a Notary Public has no opportunity to submit a request for leave due to temporary indisposition.

Article 29.Paragraph (1)

Point a

Self-explanatory.

Point b

Self-explanatory.

Point c

Documents supporting Substitute Notary Public shall be:

1. copy of master of law certificate legalized by the relevant university;

2. copy of identity card ratified by Notary Public;

3. copy of birth certificate ratified by Notary Public;

4. copy of marriage certificate ratified by Notary Public, if already married;

5. certificate of good conduct from the local police;

6. certificate of sound body from the government doctor;

7. 4 recent colour photos, 3x4cm size; and

8. curriculum vitae.

Paragraph (2)

Self-explanatory.

Paragraph (3)

Self-explanatory.

Paragraph (4)

Self-explanatory.

Article 30.Self-explanatory.

Article 31.Self-explanatory.

Article 32.Self-explanatory.

Article 33.Self-explanatory.

Article 34.Self-explanatory.

Article 35.

Paragraph (1)

Self-explanatory.

Paragraph (2)

Self-explanatory.

Paragraph (3)

Self-explanatory.

第（2）款

无须解释。

第（3）款

无须解释。

第二十七条　无须解释。

第二十八条　“紧急”是指公证员由于紧急不适而无法提交休假申请。

第二十九条　第（1）款

a 项

无须解释。

b 项

无须解释。

c 项

替补公证员应提交的文件为：

1. 相关大学颁发的法学硕士证书复印件；

2. 公证员已确认过的身份证复印件；

3. 公证员已确认过的出生证明复印件；

4. 如已结婚，还需提交公证员已确认过的结婚证复印件；

5. 当地警局出具的无不良行为的证明书；

6. 政府指定医生出具的健康证明书；

7. 最近的 4 张 3x4cm 的彩色证件照；及

8. 简历。

第（2）款

无须解释。

第（3）款

无须解释。

第（4）款

无须解释。

第三十条　无须解释。

第三十一条　无须解释。

第三十二条　无须解释。

第三十三条　无须解释。

第三十四条　无须解释。

第三十五条

第（1）款

无须解释。

第（2）款

无须解释。

第（3）款

无须解释。

Paragraph (4)

Based on this provision, "Notary Public Temporary Officials" shall be responsible for what they do in implementing their tasks and office.

Paragraph (5)

Self-explanatory.

Article 36.

Paragraph (1)

Self-explanatory.

Paragraph (2)

Self-explanatory.

Paragraph (3)

Self-explanatory

Paragraph (4)

Deeds with social function shall be, for example deed of incorporation of foundation, deed of incorporation of school, deed of wakaf land, deed of incorporation of house of worship, or deed of incorporation of hospital.

Article 37.Self-explanatory.

Article 38.

Paragraph (1)

Self-explanatory.

Paragraph (2)

Self-explanatory.

Paragraph (3)

Point a

Self-explanatory.

Point b

Self-explanatory.

Point c

Self-explanatory.

Point d

Self-explanatory.

Paragraph (4)

Self-explanatory.

Paragraph (5)

Self-explanatory.

Article 39.Self-explanatory.

Article 40.Self-explanatory.

Article 41.Self-explanatory.

Article 42.

Paragraph (1)

Self-explanatory.

Paragraph (2)

Self-explanatory.

Paragraph (3)

Self-explanatory.

第（4）款

根据这一规定，“临时公证员”应对其在履行职责时作出的行为负责。

第（5）款

无须解释。

第三十六条

第（1）款

无须解释。

第（2）款

无须解释。

第（3）款

无须解释。

第（4）款

与社会功能有关的行为应当包括基金会成立有关的文书、学校注册有关的文书、土地有关的文书、教堂成立有关的文书或医院注册有关的文书等。

第三十七条　无须解释。

第三十八条

第（1）款

无须解释。

第（2）款

无须解释。

第（3）款

a 项

无须解释。

b 项

无须解释。

c 项

无须解释。

d 项

无须解释。

第（4）款

无须解释。

第（5）款

无须解释。

第三十九条　无须解释

第四十条　无须解释。

第四十一条　无须解释。

第四十二条

第（1）款

无须解释。

第（2）款

无须解释。

第（3）款

无须解释。

Paragraph (4)

Self-explanatory.

Article 43.

Paragraph (1)

Indonesia Language as referred to in this deed shall be Indonesia language adhering to the standard principle of Indonesia language.

Paragraph (2)

Self-explanatory.

Paragraph (3)

By "authorized translator" we mean a sworn translator.

Paragraph (4)

By the relevant parties" we mean the appearers or those represented by the appearers.

Paragraph (5)

Self-explanatory.

Article 44.Self-explanatory.

Article 45.Self-explanatory.

Article 46.Self-explanatory.

Article 47.Self-explanatory.

Article 48.Self-explanatory.

Article 49.Self-explanatory.

Article 50.Self-explanatory.

Article 51.Self-explanatory.

Article 52.Self-explanatory.

Article 53.Self-explanatory.

Article 54.Self-explanatory.

Article 55.Self-explanatory.

Article 56.Self-explanatory.

Article 57.Self-explanatory.

Article 58.Self-explanatory.

Article 59.Self-explanatory.

Article 60.Self-explanatory.

Article 61.

Paragraph (1)

By "15 (fifteen) working days" we mean from the 1st day to the 15th day.

Paragraph (2)

Self-explanatory.

Article 62.Notarial Protocols shall consist of:

a. minutes of Deed;

b. register of deeds or repertory;

c. register of privately made deeds of which the signing is made before a Notary Public or privately made deeds so registered;

d. register of names of the appearers;

第（4）款

无须解释。

第四十三条

第（1）款

文书中提到的语言应为印度尼西亚语，符合印度尼西亚语的语法规则。

第（2）款

无须解释。

第（3）款

这里的"有权翻译"人是已经宣誓且忠实的翻译人员。

第（4）款

有关各方指的是当事人或相关代理人。

第（5）款

无须解释。

第四十四条　无须解释。

第四十五条　无须解释。

第四十六条　无须解释。

第四十七条　无须解释。

第四十八条　无须解释。

第四十九条　无须解释。

第五十条　无须解释。

第五十一条　无须解释。

第五十二条　无须解释。

第五十三条　无须解释。

第五十四条　无须解释。

第五十五条　无须解释。

第五十六条　无须解释。

第五十七条　无须解释。

第五十八条　无须解释。

第五十九条　无须解释

第六十条　无须解释。

第六十一条

第（1）款

"15 个工作日"是指从第 1 天到第 15 天。

第（2）款

无须解释。

第六十二条　公证档案应包括：

a. 文书记录；

b. 文书或相关汇编的登记；

c. 对在公证员面前签署的或私下制作的文书的登记；或

d. 对当事人名字的登记；

e. register of protests;

f. register of testament; and

g. other registers to keep by the Notary Public by virtue of the laws and legislation.

Article 63.Self-explanatory.

Article 64.Self-explanatory.

Article 65.Self-explanatory.

Article 66.Self-explanatory.

Article 67.

Paragraph (1)

Self-explanatory.

Paragraph (2)

Self-explanatory.

Paragraph (3)

Point a

The government elements shall be stipulated by the Minister.

Point b

Self-explanatory.

Point c

By “experts/academicians” in this provision shall be legal experts/academicians.

Paragraph (4)

Self-explanatory.

Paragraph (5)

Self-explanatory.

Paragraph (6)

Self-explanatory.

Article 68.Self-explanatory.

Article 69.Self-explanatory.

Article 70.

Point a

Self-explanatory.

Point b

Self-explanatory

Point c

Self-explanatory.

Point d

Self-explanatory.

Point e

Self-explanatory.

Point f

Self-explanatory.

Point g

By “report from the public” shall include reports from the other Notary Publics.

e. 抗辩登记；

f. 遗嘱登记；及

g. 由公证员根据法律和立法保留的其他登记。

第六十三条　无须解释。

第六十四条　无须解释。

第六十五条　无须解释。

第六十六条　无须解释。

第六十七条

第（1）款

无须解释。

第（2）款

无须解释。

第（3）款

a 项

政府人员应由部长任命。

b 项

无须解释。

c 项

本项中的“专家 / 学者”应是法律专家 / 学者。

第（4）款

无须解释。

第（5）款

无须解释。

第（6）款

无须解释。

第六十八条　无须解释。

第六十九条　无须解释。

第七十条

a 项

无须解释。

b 项

无须解释。

c 项

无须解释。

d 项

无须解释。

e 项

无须解释。

f 项

无须解释。

g 项

“公开报告”应包括其他公证员的报告。

Point h

Self-explanatory.

Article 71.Self-explanatory.

Article 72.Self-explanatory.

Article 73.Paragraph (1)

Self-explanatory.

Paragraph (2)

By "final in nature" we mean binding and can not be appealed to the Central Supervisory Council.

Paragraph (3)

Self-explanatory.

Article 74.Self-explanatory.

Article 75.Self-explanatory.

Article 76.Self-explanatory.

Article 77.Self-explanatory.

Article 78.Self-explanatory.

Article 79.Self-explanatory.

Article 80.Self-explanatory.

Article 81.Self-explanatory.

Article 82.Self-explanatory.

Article 83.Self-explanatory.

Article 84.Sanctions imposed on Notary Publics shall also apply to Substitute Notary Publics, Special Substitute Notary Publics, and Notary Public Temporary Officials.

Article 85.Self-explanatory.

Article 86.Self-explanatory.

Article 87.Self-explanatory.

Article 88.Self-explanatory.

Article 89.Self-explanatory.

Article 90.Self-explanatory.

Article 91.Self-explanatory.

Article 92.Self-explanatory.

SUPPLEMENT TO STATE GAZETTE OF THE REPUBLIC OF INDONESIA NUMBER 4432

h 项

无须解释。

第七十一条　无须解释。

第七十二条　无须解释。

第七十三条　第（1）款

无须解释。

第（2）款

具有最终性质是指具有约束力，不能向中央监督委员会申诉。

第（3）款

无须解释。

第七十四条　无须解释。

第七十五条　无须解释。

第七十六条　无须解释。

第七十七条　无须解释。

第七十八条　无须解释

第七十九条　无须解释。

第八十条　无须解释。

第八十一条　无须解释。

第八十二条　无须解释。

第八十三条　无须解释。

第八十四条　对公证员实施的惩罚也适用于替补公证员、特殊替代公证员及临时公证员。

第八十五条　无须解释。

第八十六条　无须解释。

第八十七条　无须解释。

第八十八条　无须解释。

第八十九条　无须解释。

第九十条　无须解释。

第九十一条　无须解释。

第九十二条　无须解释。

《印度尼西亚共和国公报》补编 4432 号

2014 年公证机构法修正案

LAW OF THE REPUBLIC OF INDONESIA NUMBER 2 2014 ABOUT CHANGES TO THE LAW NUMBER 30 OF 2004

BY THE GRACE OF GOD ALMIGHTY

PRESIDENT OF THE REPUBLIC OF INDONESIA,

Considering: a. that the Republic of Indonesia as a state of law based on Pancasila and the Constitution of the Republic of Indonesia Year 1945 guarantees certainty, order, and legal protection for every citizen;

b. that in order to ensure certainty, order, and the legal protection required written evidence is authentic about deeds, agreements, determination, and legal events, made before or by the competent authority;

c. that the Notary as public officials who run the profession in providing legal services to the public, need to get protection and guarantees in order to achieve legal certainty;

d. that some provisions of Law No. 30 Year 2004 concerning Notary is no longer compatible with the development of the law and the needs of the community that needs to be changed;

e. that based on the considerations set forth in paragraphs a, b, c, and d, it is necessary to form the Law on Amendments to the Law No. 30 Year 2004 concerning Notary;

1. Article 20 and Article 21 of the Constitution of the Republic of Indonesia Year 1945;

2. Law No. 30 of 2004 concerning Notary (State Gazette of the Republic of Indonesia Year 2004 Number 117, Supplement to State Gazette of the Republic of Indonesia Number 4432);

With agreement between
HOUSE OF REPRESENTATIVES OF THE REPUBLIC OF INDONESIA
and
PRESIDENT OF THE REPUBLIC OF INDONESIA
DECIDE:

印度尼西亚共和国 2014 年第 2 号法律

关于
对 2004 年第 30 号法律的修订

真祖的恩典

印度尼西亚共和国总统，

鉴于：a. 印度尼西亚共和国作为一个法治国家，以建国五原则与《印度尼西亚 1945 年宪法》为基础，确保国家稳定、秩序和对每个公民提供法律保护；

b. 为了保证确定性、秩序性以及法律保护性，所有的关于行为、协议、决定、法律事件都需要书面证据，这些书面证据由有权者作出；

c. 公证员作为公职人员，从事向公众提供法律服务的职业，需要得到保护和保障，以实现法律的确定性；

d. 关于公证的第 30 号法律的某些规定已不再符合法律的发展以及社会的需要，尚需被改变；

e. 根据第 a 项、第 b 项、第 c 项和第 d 项所述，有必要制定第 30 号公证法的修正案；

1.1945 年《印度尼西亚共和国宪法》第 20 条和第 21 条；

2.2004 年第 30 号公证法（印度尼西亚共和国国家公报 2004 年第 117 号文件，印度尼西亚共和国国家公报补编第 4432 号文件）；

由印度尼西亚共和国总统和印度尼西亚共和国众议院共同达成最终协议

决定

Assign: LAW ON AMENDMENT TO THE LAW NUMBER 30 OF 2004 ON POSITION NOTARY.

Article 1

Several provisions in the Act No. 30 of 2004 concerning Notary (State Gazette of the Republic of Indonesia Year 2004 Number 117, Supplement to State Gazette of the Republic of Indonesia Number 4432) is amended as follows:

1. The provisions of Article 1 number 1, number 2, number 5, number 6, number 7, number 8, number 9, number 10, number 12, and number 13, was changed, the number 4 and number 14 were removed so that Article 1 reads as follows :

Article 1

In this Act, referred to as:

1. The Notary is a public official who is authorized to make an authentic deed and have more authority as referred to in this Act or under other laws.

2. Acting Notary is a temporarily served as Notary to run the office of Notary who died.

3. Substitute Notary is a temporarily appointed to replace Notary Notary on leave, sick or temporarily unable to run his position as a Notary.

4. Removed.

5. Organizations Notary Public office is a professional organization in the form of legal entity associations.

6. Notary Supervisory Council hereinafter referred to as the Supervisory Council is a body that has the authority and obligation to implement the guidance and supervision of a Notary.

7. Deed hereinafter referred authentic deed is a deed made by or in the presence of a Notary according to the forms and procedures stipulated in this Law.

8. Minuta Deed is the original deed specifying the penghadap signatures, witnesses, and Notary, which is stored as part of Notary Protocol.

9. A copy of the deed is word for word copy of the entire Act and the bottom copy of deed contained the phrase “given as the same sound COPY”.

10. Excerpts deed is quote verbatim from one or several parts of the Act and on the bottom of the citations listed Deed phrase “given as QUOTES”.

11. Formation Notary Notary is the amount needed in a district / city.

文件名：2004 年第 30 号公证法的修正案

第一条

对 2004 年第 30 号法律关于公证的若干规定（印度尼西亚共和国国家公报 2004 年第 117 号文件，印度尼西亚共和国国家公报补编第 4432 号文件）修订如下：

1. 第 1 条第 1 款、第 2 款、第 5 款、第 6 款、第 7 款、第 8 款、第 9 款、第 10 款、第 12 款、第 13 款已被重新修订，第 4 款和第 14 款已被删除，具体如下：

第一条

在该条中，修改的内容有：

1. 公证员作为公职人员，有权作出真实的文书，并有权依据本法或其他法律享有更多的职权。

2. 临时公证员是临时担任公证员的人员，负责接替已经去世的公证员的职务。

3. 替补公证员是在公证员请假、生病或暂时无法履行公证员职务时被临时任命的。

4. 已被删除。

5. 公证机构是以法人团体的形式设立的专业组织。

6. 公证监督委员会（以下简称“监督委员会”），是有权力和义务对公证员进行指导和监督的机构。

7. 下文所述的文书是指根据本法规定的形式和程序，由公证员或在公证员在场的情况下出具的真实文书。

8. 文书记录是指由当事人、证人和公证员签署的原始文书，作为公证档案的一部分被保存。

9. 文书副本是整个文书的复印本，而文书副本结尾处需标明“与正本无异”的字样。

10. 文书摘录是对该文书中的一个或几个部分逐字引述，并在引用结尾处标明“作为引用”的字样。

11. 公证员编制是区 / 市所需的公证员数量。

12. Protocol Notary is a collection of documents that constitute the state archives to be kept and maintained by the Notary in accordance with the provisions of the legislation.

13. Minister is the minister who held government affairs in the field of law.

2. The provisions of Article 3 letter d and f amended, and plus 1 (one) point, the letter h, so that Article 3 reads as follows:

Article 3

Requirements to be appointed as a Notary as referred to in Article 2 is:

a. Indonesian citizens;

b. fear of God Almighty;

c. be at least 27 (twenty-seven) years;

d. physical and spiritual health are expressed by a health certificate from a doctor and a psychiatrist;

e. law degree and a graduate degree in undergraduate level two notaries;

f. have undergone internships or obviously been working as an employee within the shortest Notary 24 (twenty four) months in a row at the Notary's office on their own initiative or upon the recommendation of a Notary Organization after graduating strata two notaries;

g. is not a civil servant, state officials, advocates, or not being held other positions that by law forbidden to concurrently with the Notary office; and

h. never been sentenced to imprisonment by a court decision that has gained legal force remained for a criminal offense punishable by imprisonment of 5 (five) years or more.

3. The provisions of Article 7 are amended to read as follows:

Article 7

(1) In the period of 60 (sixty) days from the date of taking the oath / pledge Notary office, concerned shall:

a. run with the real position;

b. convey the minutes oath / pledge Notary office to the Minister, Notary Organization and Assembly Regional Supervisor; and

c. deliver office address, specimen signatures and initials, and date-stamp or stamp red Notary office to the Minister and other officials in charge of land, Notary Organization, Chairman of the Court, the Regional Supervisory Council, as well as the Regent / Mayor at the Notary lifted.

12. 公证档案是由公证员根据法律规定保存的国家档案的集合。

13. 部长是在法律领域主持政府事务的首长。

2. 第 3 条第 d 款、第 f 款已经被修改，并增加第 h 款，第 3 条具体修改如下：

第三条

第 2 条规定的被任命为公证员的要求如下：

a. 印度尼西亚公民；

b. 敬畏全能的真主；

c. 年满 27 周岁；

d. 由医生和精神病医生对其身体和精神健康状况出具证明；

e. 获得法学学位和二级公证员证书；

f. 已在公证机构实习或连续受雇任职至少 24 个月，或者在获得公证专业硕士学位后得到公证组织的推荐；

g. 没有担任公务员、政府官员、律师或没有担任其他本法禁止与公证员岗位同时兼任的职务；及

h. 从未受过法院判决 5 年以上监禁刑的刑事处罚。

3. 对第 7 条的修改如下：

第七条

（1）自公证员宣誓之日起 60 日内，其应：

a. 从实质上开始履行职务；

b. 向部长、公证机构和监督委员会提交宣誓会议记录；及

c. 向部长和其他负责土地事务的官员、公证机构，法院院长、区域监督委员会以及公证业务所在地的区 / 市长提供办公地址、签名样本、姓名首字母以及盖章样本。

(2) Notary who violates the provisions referred to in paragraph (1) may be subject to sanctions in the form:

a. written warning;

b. layoffs;

c. honorable discharge; or

d. dishonorable discharge.

4. The provisions of Article 9 paragraph (1) letter d changed and plus 1 (one) point, the letter e, so that Article 9 reads as follows:

Article 9

(1) Notary suspended from his post as:

a. in the process of bankruptcy or suspension of payment of debts;

b. are under guardianship;

c. misconduct;

d. violation of obligations and prohibitions Notary office and code of ethics; or

e. is undergoing a period of detention.

(2) Before a suspension referred to in paragraph (1) shall, Notary given the opportunity to defend himself before the Council of Trustees in stages.

(3) Suspension Notary referred to in paragraph (2) made by the Minister at the proposal of the Supervisory Council of the Centre.

(4) Suspension on grounds referred to in paragraph (1) letter c and d, valid for a period of 6 (six) months.

5. The provisions of Article 11 is amended to read as follows:

Article 11

(1) Notaries are appointed state officials are required to take leave.

(2) Leave referred to in paragraph (1) applies for Notary took office as state officials.

(3) Further provisions on leave Notary referred to in paragraph (1) is regulated by the Minister.

6. The provisions of Article 16 be amended to read as follows:

Article 16

(1) In carrying out his post, Notary shall:

a. act trustworthy, honest, thorough, independent, impartial, and safeguard the interests of the parties involved in legal actions;

b. Deed in Minuta Deed form and save it as part of a Notary Protocol;

c. attach a letter and documents and fingerprints

（2）违反第 1 款所述的规定，公证员将受到以下形式的惩罚：

a. 书面警告；

b. 停职；

c. 辞退；或者

d. 被不光彩地解雇。

4. 第 9 条第（1）款第 d 项被修改，并增加第 e 项，具体修改如下：

第九条

（1）公证员因下列原因停职：

a. 进入破产程序或难以偿还个人债务的；

b. 被羁押的；

c. 作出不当行为的；及

d. 违反法定义务和公证员禁令，违反道德规范；

e. 正处于拘留期间。

（2）实行第（1）款规定的暂停职务前，公证员有权向监督委员会提出申辩。

（3）第（2）款所述的公证员暂停职务的决定应由部长根据中央监督委员会的动议作出。

（4）第（1）款第 c 项和第 d 项所述的暂停职务有效期为 6 个月。

5. 第 11 条被修改的内容如下：

第十一条

（1）公证员被任命为政府官员时需辞去公证员职务。

（2）第（1）款中的辞职适用于公证员就任政府官员的情况。

（3）第（1）款中的关于公证员辞职的进一步规定由部长作出。

6. 对第 16 条的修改内容如下：

第十六条

（1）公证员在执行职务时应当：

a. 诚信、尽职、严谨、独立、公正，在法律范围内维护当事各方的利益；

b. 文书以记录的形式制作，并将其作为公证档案的一部分保存；

c. 在文书记录中附上相关文件、信件，并由当事

penghadap on Minuta Deed;

d. Grosse issued Deed, Deed copy, or citation based Minuta Deed Deed;

e. provide services in accordance with the provisions of this Act, unless there is a reason to reject it;

f. keep everything on the deed he made and all information obtained in order to manufacture in accordance with the Deed of oath / pledge of office, unless the statute otherwise provides;

g. binding deed he made in 1 (one) month into a book that contains no more than 50 (fifty) Act, and if the number of deed can not be loaded in a single book, the deed can be bound to more than one book, and record the number of Minuta Deed , month, and year of manufacture on the cover of each book;

h. make a list of the Deed of protest against not being paid or non-receipt of securities;

i. make a list Deed relating to wills chronological Deed manufacture each month;

j. send list deed referred to in the letter i or register zero with respect to the center of the will to the will list the ministry held government affairs in the field of law within 5 (five) days in the first week of the next month;

k. repertorium delivery dates noted in the list of probate at the end of each month;

l. have a seal or stamp which contains the symbol of the Republic of Indonesia and the space encircling written the name, position, and the locus in question;

m. Deed read before penghadap in the presence of at least two (2) witnesses, or four (4) witnesses specifically for the manufacture of testamentary deed under the hand, and signed at that time by penghadap, witnesses, and Notary; and

n. Notary accepts internship candidates.

(2) The obligation to keep Minuta Deed referred to in paragraph (1) letter b does not apply, in the case of the Notary Deed issued in originali.

(3) Act in originali referred to in paragraph (2) shall include:

a. Deed payment of rent, interest, and retirement;

b. Deed offers cash payments;

c. Deed of protest against non-payment or nonreceipt of securities;

d. Deed of power;

e. Deed of ownership information; and

f. Other Acts in accordance with the provisions of the legislation.

人捺印；

d. 公证员依据公证书出具文书副本、文书摘录本；

e. 若无正当理由拒绝，应按照本法的规定提供公证服务；

f. 除非法规另有规定，为保证公证书的全面性，公证员需依据其所查明的事实以及相关信息，遵循其宣誓内容出具公证书；

g. 按月为单位制作的文书以 50 份为一本装订成册，如果一册无法装订所有的文书，则可以装订多册，并在每一册中标明文书的数量以及制作的年、月等信息；

h. 对未付费用或者没有收据的文书列出清单；

i. 每月列明一份与遗嘱有关的公证文书的清单，并按文书制作的时间先后编排；

j. 在每个月的第一个星期的 5 个工作日内，将第 i 项所述的清单向中央遗嘱部提交，在接下来的 5 年内，上述任务属于公证事务；

k. 在每个月末提交遗嘱清单的汇编中记录相同的内容；

l. 制作印章，印章上面印有印度尼西亚共和国的标志，并标明名称及所涉及的地点；

m. 遗嘱文书的制作必须在公证员在场的情况下作出，并且至少有 2 名证人在场；或者至少有 4 名证人在场，并由公证员和证人共同签字；

n. 训练实习公证员。

（2）第（1）款第 b 项规定不适用于文书记录保存，除非公证员出具原始文件。

（3）第（2）款所称原始文件包括：

a. 租金、利息及退休金的缴付凭据；

b. 提供现金支付凭证；

c. 拒付或无担保的文书凭证；

d. 权力行为；

e. 所有权声明文书；或

f. 法律规定的其他行为。

(4) Deed in originally referred to in paragraph (2) can be made more than 1 (one) copy, signed at the time, form, and content of the same, with the provisions of any Act the words "APPLY AS ONE AND ONE FOR ALL APPLICABLE".

(5) Deed in originali which contains the power that has not been filled in the name of the authorized person can only be made within 1 (one) copy.

(6) The shape and size of the seal or stamp referred to in paragraph (1) letter l determined by the Regulation.

(7) The reading of Act referred to in paragraph (1) letter m not mandatory, if penghadap wants Deed not be read because penghadap have read yourself, know, and understand its contents, provided that it is stated in the Deed cover and on each page minuta Deed initialed by penghadap, witnesses, and Notary.

(8) The provisions referred to in paragraph (7) excluded the reading head Deed, comparison, principal explanation Deed briefly and clearly, and cover Deed.

(9) If one of the conditions referred to in paragraph (1) letter m and (7) are not met, the Act is concerned only has the strength of evidence as the deed under the hand.

(10) The provisions referred to in paragraph (9) does not apply to the making of a will Deed.

(11) Notaries in violation of the provisions referred to in paragraph (1) letter a to letter l may be subject to sanctions in the form:

a. written warning;

b. layoffs;

c. honorable discharge; or

d. dishonorable discharge.

(12) In addition to the sanctions referred to in paragraph (11), violation of the provisions of Article 16 paragraph (1) letter j can be the reason for the injured party to demand reimbursement of losses, damages, and interest to the Notary.

(13) Notaries in violation of the provisions referred to in paragraph (1) letter n may be subject to sanctions in the form of a written warning.

7. In between Article 16 and Article 17, 1 (one) article, namely Article 16A to read as follows:

Article 16A

(1) Candidates who are doing internship Notary shall implement the provisions referred to in Article 16 paragraph (1) letter a.

(2) In addition to the obligations referred to in par-

（4）第（2）款规定的原始文书可以制作多份副本，并需签署，且形式和内容相同，但每份文书均应标明“一对一申请且适用于所有人”。

（5）没有标明代理人名称的原始文书只能制作一份副本。

（6）第 1 款规定的印章的大小和形状由相关条文规定。

（7）如果当事人希望该文书不被查阅是因为当事人已经阅读、了解和知晓了其内容，第（1）款第 m 项中的文书将被禁止查阅。

（8）依据第（7）款所禁止查阅的内容，包括文件标题、主体部分及内容解释等。

（9）如果未能满足第（1）款第 m 项和第（7）款所述的要求之一，那么相关文书仅具有私人行为的证明效力。

（10）第（9）款不适用于起草遗嘱文书。

（11）公证员违反第（1）款第 a 项至第 I 项的规定，应受到以下形式的惩罚：

a. 书面警告；

b. 停职；

c. 辞退；

d. 不光彩地被解雇。

（12）除第（11）款规定的惩罚外，违反第 16 条第（1）款第 j 项的规定，可成为受害方向公证员主张赔偿损失、损害及利益的事由。

（13）公证员违反第（1）款第 n 项的规定，可以书面警告形式予以惩罚。

7. 在第 16 条和第 17 条之间，新增条款第 16(A)条：

第十六（A）条

（1）从事公证实习的候选人须履行第 16 条第（1）款规定的义务。

（2）除第（1）款规定的义务外，还须要求候选

agraph (1), candidates are also required to keep Notary everything about the deed he made and all information obtained in order to manufacture Deed.

8. The provisions of Article 17 be amended to read as follows:

Article 17

(1)Notaries are prohibited:

a. running position outside the office;

b. leaving the office area of more than seven (7) consecutive working days without a valid reason;

c. doubles as a public servant;

d. doubled as state officials;

e. doubled as an advocate;

f. concurrent positions as leaders or employees of state-owned enterprises, locally-owned enterprises or private entities;

g. doubled as the Land Deed Officer and / or Officer Class II Auction outside the seat of the Notary;

h. become a Notary Substitute; or

i. perform other work that is contrary to the norms of religion, ethics, or propriety which may affect the honor and dignity of the office of Notary.

(2) Notary who violates the provisions referred to in paragraph (1) may be subject to sanctions in the form:

a. written warning;

b. layoffs;

c. honorable discharge; or

d. dishonorable discharge.

9. The provisions of Article 19 be amended to read as follows:

Article 19

(1) Notary shall have only one office, which is in the position.

(2) The position of Notary as the Land Deed Officer shall follow the seat of the Notary.

(3) Notaries are not authorized in a row to keep running position outside the domicile.

(4) Notaries in violation of the provisions referred to in paragraph (2) may be subject to sanctions in the form:

a. written warning;

b. layoffs;

c. honorable discharge; or

d. dishonorable discharge.

10. The provisions of paragraphs (1) and paragraph (2) of Article 20 are amended and paragraph (3) is removed so that Article 20 reads as follows:

人将其所作的文书及所获取的所有信息按顺序制作成册，以便制作文书。

8. 对第 17 条的修改内容如下：

第十七条

（1）禁止公证员从事下列行为：

a. 在其办公区域以外履行职务；

b. 无正当理由离职连续超过 7 日；

c. 同时兼任公务员；

d. 同时兼任政府官员；

e. 同时兼任律师；

f. 同时兼任国有企业、地方国企或私营企业的经理或雇员；

g. 同时兼任土地事务官员及 / 或在公证员职务以外的二级拍卖官；

h. 成为替补公证员；

i. 兼任其他职务，但该职务违反宗教、道德或其他规范，可能影响公证员及其职业的荣誉和尊严。

（2）违反第（1）款的规定，公证员应受以下形式的惩罚：

a. 书面警告；

b. 停职；

c. 辞退；或

d. 不光彩地解雇。

9. 对第 19 条的修改内容如下：

第十九条

（1）公证员在其居住地范围内只有一个办公场所。

（2）公证员处理土地公证事务应当善尽其责。

（3）公证员不得持续在住所外履行职务。

（4）违反第（2）款规定的公证员可能受以下形式惩罚：

a. 书面警告；

b. 停职；

c. 辞退；

d. 不光彩地解雇。

10. 第 20 条第（1）款和第（2）款已被修订，删除第（3）款，修改后的内容如下：

Article 20

(1) Notaries can run the office in the form of a civil union with regard to the independence and impartiality in carrying out his post.

(2) The form of civil partnership referred to in paragraph (1) shall be regulated by the Notary under the provisions of the legislation.

(3) Deleted.

11. The provisions of Article 22 be amended to read as follows:

Article 22

(1) Formation Notary determined by:

a. business activities;

b. population; and / or

c. the average number of Deed made by and / or in the presence of a Notary every month.

(2) Formation Notary referred to in paragraph (1) is a guideline to determine the category of the area.

(3) Further provisions concerning the formation and determination Notary area categories referred to in paragraph (1) and paragraph (2) is regulated by the Minister.

12. The provisions of Article 32 plus 1 (one) paragraph, namely paragraph (4), so that Article 32 reads as follows:

Article 32

(1) Notaries who run off shall submit to the Substitute Notary Notary Protocol.

(2) Substitute Notary handed back to the Notary Notary Protocol after the leave ends.

(3) The receipt is referred to in paragraph (1) and (2) made an official report and submitted to the Supervisory Council of the Territory.

(4) Notaries in violation of the provisions referred to in paragraph (1), paragraph (2), and paragraph (3) may be subject to sanctions in the form:

a. written warning;

b. layoffs;

c. honorable discharge; or

d. dishonorable discharge.

13. Title Part Two CHAPTER V amended to read as follows:

Part Two
Substitute and Acting Notary Notary

14. The provisions of Article 33 be amended to read as follows:

第二十条

（1）公证员可以以民间社团的形式组建办公场所，但是应考虑到其职务的独立性和公正性。

（2）第（1）款中的民间社团组织需依据法律的规定接受公证员的监督。

（3）已删除。

11. 对第 22 条的修改如下：

第二十二条

（1）公证员编制安排原则如下：

a. 商业活动；

b. 总人口；和 / 或

c. 公证员每月制作或者在公证员见证的情况下制作的文书的平均数量。

（2）有关第（1）款的公证员编制安排原则作为确定区域范围的指导。

（3）有关第（1）款及第（2）款中的公证员的编制安排和最终确定的进一步规定由部长决定。

12. 第 32 条增加第（4）款，规定如下：

第三十二条

（1）如果休假，公证员应向替补公证员移交公证档案。

（2）替补公证员应在公证员休假结束后将公证档案交回至公证员。

（3）对于第（1）款和第（2）款规定的公证档案，公证员应在短时间内制定报告并提交至省级监督委员会。

（4）公证员违反第（1）款、第（2）款及第（3）款的条文，将受到以下形式的惩罚：

a. 书面警告；

b. 停职；

c. 辞退；或

d. 不光彩地解雇。

13. 对第五章第二节的修改内容如下：

第二节　替补公证员

14. 对第 33 条的修改内容如下：

Article 33

(1)Requirements to be appointed as Substitute and Acting Notary Notary is an Indonesian citizen who graduate degree in law and has worked as an employee of the Notary office at least two (2) consecutive years.

(2) The provisions applicable to the Notary as referred to in Article 4, Article 15, Article 16, and Article 17 shall apply for and Acting Substitute Notary Notary, unless this Act otherwise provides.

15. Article 34 is deleted.

16. The provisions of paragraph (1) of Article 35 be amended to read as follows:

Article 35

(1) If the Notary died, the husband / wife or relatives by blood in a straight line of descent by marriage to the second degree shall notify the Regional Supervisory Council.

(2) The notification referred to in paragraph (1) shall be submitted within a period of seven (7) working days.

(3) If the Notary died during the run off, the task is executed by a Notary Notary office as Acting Notary Substitute later than 30 (thirty) days from the date of Notary died.

(4) Acting Notary Notary Notary handed Protocol deceased to the Regional Supervisory Council not later than 60 (sixty) days from the date of Notary died.

(5) Acting Notary referred to in paragraph (3) and (4) can make a deed in his own name and has a Notary Protocol.

17. The provisions of Article 37 be amended to read as follows:

Article 37

(1) Notary shall provide legal services in the field of notaries for free to people who can not afford.

(2) Notary who violates the provisions referred to in paragraph (1) may be subject to sanctions in the form:

a. verbal warning;

b. written warning;

c. layoffs;

d. honorable discharge; or

e. dishonorable discharge.

18. The provisions of paragraph (1), paragraph (4), and paragraph (5) Article 38 amended to read as follows:

Article 38

(1) Every Act shall consist of:

a. early Deed or Deed head;

b. Deed body; and

第三十三条

（1）替补公证员应当是获得法学学位的印度尼西亚公民，且至少连续 2 年从事公证工作。

（2）除非本法另有规定，第 4 条、第 15 条、第 16 条及第 17 条适用于公证员的规定也适用于替补公证员。

15. 删除第 34 条。

16. 第 35 条第（1）款已被修改，修改内容如下：

第三十五条

（1）如果公证员死亡，其配偶、直系血亲或两代以内旁系姻亲应当通知区 / 市监督委员会。

（2）第（1）款规定的通知应在 7 个工作日内提交。

（3）如果在休假期间死亡，应当由替补公证员作为临时公证员，自公证员死亡之日起，在 30 日以上的时间内代为处理未完成的公证事务。

（4）临时公证员应当公证员自死亡之日起最迟 60 日向区 / 市监督委员会提交已故公证员的公证档案。

（5）第（3）款及第（4）款中的临时公证员可以以自己的名义出具公证书，并持有公证档案。

17. 对第 37 条的修改内容如下：

第三十七条

（1）公证员应当为不能承受相关费用的困难群众免费提供一定范围内的公证服务。

（2）凡违反第（1）款规定的公证员可能受到以下形式的惩罚：

a. 口头警告；

b. 书面警告；

c. 停职；

d. 辞退；

e. 不光彩地解雇。

18. 第 38 条第（1）款、第（4）款及第（5）款已被修订，具体内容如下：

第三十八条

（1）每项文书应包含：

a. 前言及标题；

b. 主体内容；

c. end Deed.

(2) Initial Deed or Deed head includes:

a. title deed;

b. number Deed;

c. hour, day, date, month, and year; and

d. full name and domicile of the Notary.

(3) Agency Act includes:

a. full name, place and date of birth, nationality, occupation, position, position, place of residence of the penghadap and / or the people they represent;

b. information regarding the position to act penghadap;

c. Deed contents which is the will and desire of the parties concerned; and

d. full name, place and date of birth, and occupation, position, status, and residence of each witness identification.

(4) End or closing Deed contains:

a. description of readings Act referred to in Article16 paragraph (1) letter m or Article 16 paragraph (7);

b. description of the signing and signing a deed or translation if any;

c. full name, place and date of birth, occupation, position, status, and residence of each witness Deed; and

d. description of the absence of changes occurring in the manufacture of the Deed or a description of any changes that may be the addition, deletion, or replacement as well as the number of changes.

(5) Deed in Lieu and Acting Notary, besides including the provisions referred to in paragraph (2), paragraph (3), and paragraph (4), also contain the number and date of appointment-setting, as well as the officials who appointed him.

19. The provisions of paragraph (1) and (2) Article 39 amended to read as follows:

Article 39

(1) penghadap must meet the following requirements:

a. minimum age of 18 (eighteen) years or has been married; and

b. legally competent.

(2) penghadap should be known by the Notary or introduced to it by 2 (two) witnesses the lowest identifier aged 18 (eighteen) years or has been married and legally competent or were introduced by two (2) other penghadap.

(3) The introduction referred to in paragraph (2) expressly provided in the Act.

c. 结尾

（2）标题部分或文书开头应包含：

a. 题目；

b. 编号；

c. 时、日期、月份和年份；及

d. 公证员的全名和住所。

（3）主体内容应包含：

a. 当事人和 / 或他们所代表的人的全名、出生地点及日期、国籍、职业、住所、居住地；

b. 各方当事人陈述的信息；

c. 文书的内容应符合有关各方当事人的目标和意图；

d. 每位证人的全名、出生地点和日期、职业、住所、居住地。

（4）文书结尾应包含：

a. 第 16 条第（1）款第 m 项或第 16 条第（7）款所述的文书解释说明；

b. 对签字、签署文书及翻译的说明；

c. 文书中所有证人的全名、出生地、出生日期、职业、地位、住所和居住地；及

d. 对文书起草过程缺失内容的说明，采用添加、删除或替换等形式对文书进行的更改情况和次数的说明。

（5）除包含第（2）款、第（3）款和第（4）款规定的内容外，替补公证员出具的文书还应包含其编号、任命日期和作出任命决定的官员的姓名。

19. 对第 39 条第（1）款、第（2）款的修改内容如下：

第三十九条

（1）当事人应符合下列要求：

a. 已满 18 周岁或已婚；

b. 具有完全民事行为能力。

（2）当事人应当被公证员熟知或者由 2 名证人向公证员引荐，证人需年满 18 周岁或已经结婚，并具有完全民事行为能力。当事人也可以由另外的其他 2 名当事人引荐。

（3）第（2）款中的引荐情况须在文书中进行注明。

20. The provisions of paragraph (2) of Article 40 be amended to read as follows:

Article 40

(1) Every deed which was read by the Notary attended at least two (2) witnesses, unless the regulations specify otherwise.

(2) The witness referred to in paragraph (1) shall meet the following requirements:

a. minimum age of 18 (eighteen) years of age or have previously been married;

b. legally competent;

c. understand the language used in the Act;

d. can put your signature and initials; and

(3) The witness referred to in subsection (1) must be known by the Notary Notary or introduced or explained about the identity and authority to the Notary by penghadap.

(4) The introduction or statement of identity and authority of the witnesses stated explicitly in the Act.

21. The provisions of Article 41 be amended to read as follows:

Article 41

Violation of the provisions referred to in Article 38, Article 39, and Article 40 resulted Act only have the force of proof as a certificate under the hand.

22. The provisions of paragraph (1), paragraph (3), (4), and paragraph (5) Article 43 is amended and supplemented 1 (one) paragraph, namely paragraph (6) so that Article 43 reads as follows:

Article 43

(1) Act shall be made in Indonesian.

(2) In the case penghadap do not understand the language used in the Act, the Notary shall translate or explain the contents of the deed in a language understood by penghadap.

(3) If the parties want, Deed can be made in a foreign language.

(4) In terms of the Deed made as referred to in paragraph (3), Notary shall translate into Indonesian.

(5) If the Notary can not translate or explain, the Deed translated or explained by an official translator.

(6) In the event of any differences in the interpretation of the content of the Deed referred to in paragraph (2), then the use is made in the deed of Indonesian.

23. The provisions of paragraph (2) and paragraph

20. 第 40 条第（2）款已被修改，具体修改内容如下：

第四十条

（1）除非法律和立法另有规定，公证员宣读文书应至少有 2 名证人在场。

（2）第（1）款所述的证人应符合下列要求：

a. 已满 18 周岁或已婚；

b. 具有完全民事行为能力；

c. 能够理解文书中使用的语言；

d. 有能力签名。

（3）第（1）款所述的证人，应当是公证员知悉的或者由当事人向公证员介绍他们的身份及能力。

（4）对证人的身份和能力的介绍或解释应明确载入文书。

21. 对第 41 条的修改内容如下：

第四十一条

违反第 38 条、第 39 条及第 40 条的规定，仅具有手写文件的证明效力。

22. 第 43 条第（1）款、第（3）款、第（4）款及第（5）款已被修订，并新增第（6）款，修改后的第 43 条内容如下：

第四十三条

（1）公证书须以印度尼西亚语书写。

（2）如果当事人不能理解文书中使用的语言，公证员应以当事人可以理解的语言作出翻译或解释其内容。

（3）如果当事人提出要求，文书可以用其他语言制作。

（4）如果文书以第（3）款的语言制作，公证员需翻译成印度尼西亚语。

（5）如果公证员不能作出翻译或解释，那么应当指派官方翻译人员翻译或解释。

（6）如在解释第（2）款中的协议内容时有任何差异，以印度尼西亚语版本的文书为准。

23. 第 44 条第（2）款及第（4）款已被修改，并

(4) of Article 44 is amended and supplemented 1 (one) paragraph, namely paragraph (5), so that Article 44 reads as follows:

Article 44

(1) Immediately after the Act was read, the deed is signed by each penghadap, witnesses, and Notary, unless there penghadap can not put your signature stating the reasons.

(2) The reasons referred to in paragraph (1) explicitly stated at the end of Act.

(3) Act as referred to in Article 43 paragraph (3) shall be signed by penghadap, Notary, witnesses, and an official translator.

(4) The reading, translation or explanation, and the signing referred to in paragraph (1) and paragraph (3) and in Article 43 paragraph (3) expressly provided at the end of Act.

(5) Any violation of the provisions referred to in paragraph (1), paragraph (2), paragraph (3), and paragraph (4) resulted in a deed only has the strength of evidence as the deed under the hand and can be the reason for the party who suffered loss to demand reimbursement, compensation, and interest to the Notary.

24. The provisions of paragraph (1) and (2) Article 48 is amended and supplemented 1 (one) paragraph, namely paragraph (3), so that Article 48 reads as follows:

Article 48

(1) The Act prohibited to be changed to:

a. replaced;

b. plus;

c. crossed out;

d. inserted;

e. removed; and / or

f. written overlap.

(2) Changes in the contents of the Deed referred to in paragraph (1) letter a, b, c, and d can be legitimate if the change initialed or marked another endorsement by penghadap, witnesses, and Notary.

(3) Violation of the provisions referred to in paragraph (1) and paragraph (2) resulted in a deed only has the strength of evidence as the deed under the hand and can be the reason for the injured party to demand reimbursement of losses, damages, and interest to the Notary.

25. The provisions of paragraph (1) and (2) Article 49 is amended and supplemented 1 (one) paragraph, namely paragraph (4), so that Article 49 reads as follows:

新增第（5）款，修改后的内容如下：

第四十四条

（1）经正式宣读的文书应当由每位当事人、证人和公证员签署，若有当事人未能签名需注明理由。

（2）第（1）款所述的理由应当在文书结尾处载明。

（3）第43条第（3）款所述的文书应由当事人、公证员、证人和翻译人共同签署。

（4）本条第（1）款、第（3）款及第43条第（3）款中的宣读、翻译、解释及签署应当在文书结尾处载明。

（5）若违反第（1）款、第（2）款、第（3）款和第（4）款的规定，制作的文书只有作为手写文书的证明效力，并且可以成为当事方向公证员主张赔偿损失、补偿、利益的理由。

24. 第48条第（1）款和第（2）款已被修改，并且新增第（3）款，修改后的内容如下：

第四十八条

（1）文书内容不得以以下形式改变：

a. 替换；

b. 增加；

c. 删除；

d. 插入；

e. 移除；及 / 或

f. 重复叙述。

（2）对于第（1）款第a项、第b项、第c项、第d项规定的改变，如果变更内容由当事人、证人和公证员签字认可，那么是合法的。

（3）违反第（1）款和第（2）款的规定，将导致文书只具有手写文书的证明效力，并且可以成为受害方向公证员主张损害赔偿或利益损失的理由。

25. 第49条第（1）款、第（2）款已被修订，并新增第（4）款，已修改后的内容如下：

Article 49

(1) Any changes to the Act referred to in Article 48 paragraph (2) is made on the left side of the Deed.

(2) In the event of a change can not be made on the left side of the Deed, the change was made at the end of the Act, before closing Deed, to designate parts that are changed or by inserting an additional sheet.

(3) Changes made without pointing amended section resulted in changes in the void.

(4) Violation of the provisions referred to in paragraph (1) and paragraph (2) resulted in a deed only has the strength of evidence as the deed under the hand and can be the reason for the injured party to demand reimbursement of losses, damages, and interest to the Notary.

26. The provisions of paragraph (1), paragraph (3), and paragraph (4) of Article 50 is amended and supplemented 1 (one) paragraph, namely paragraph (5), so that Article 50 reads as follows:

Article 50

(1) If the deed is necessary to the exclusion of words, letters, or numbers, deletion is done in a way that can still be read in conjunction with the previously listed, and the number of words, letters, or numbers that crossed expressed on the left side of the Deed.

(2) The crossing referred to in paragraph (1) shall be declared valid after initialed or marked another endorsement by penghadap, witnesses, and Notary.

(3) In the case of any other changes to the exclusion referred to in paragraph (2), the change was made on the left side of the Act in accordance with the provisions referred to in Article 49 paragraph (2).

(4) On the cover of every deed expressed about the presence or absence of changes in the write-off.

(5) In the case of the provisions referred to in paragraph (1), paragraph (2), paragraph (3), and paragraph (4), and in Article 38 paragraph (4) letter d is not met, the Act only have the strength of evidence as certificate under the hand and can be the reason for the party that suffered the loss to claim reimbursement, compensation, and interest to the Notary.

27. The provisions of paragraph (2) Article 51 is amended and supplemented 1 (one) paragraph, namely paragraph (4) so that Article 51 reads as follows:

Article 51

(1) Notary authorized to correct typographical errors and / or typographical errors contained in the Act that was

第四十九条

（1）第48条第（2）款中的每项变更内容须在文书的左边侧作出。

（2）若不能在文书的左侧作出更改，则须在文书结尾处作出更改，并在结尾之前注明更改的部分或者插入添加的表格。

（3）任何不作注明的变更都是无效的。

（4）违反第（1）款和第（2）款的规定，将导致文书仅具有手写文书的证明效力，并且可以成为受害方向公证员主张损害赔偿或利益损失的理由。

26. 第50条第（1）款、第（3）款和第（4）款已被修订，并新增第（5）款，修改后的内容如下：

第五十条

（1）若某文书中的文字、数字须予删除，则应对修改的内容列表标明，同时将修改的文字、数字的具体数量载明于文书左侧。

（2）如果删除符合形式要求和经过当事人、证人、公证员对删除内容签字认可，第（1）款中的删除在以下情形被视为有效。

（3）若需对第（2）款规定的更改内容再次更改，则须在文书左侧进行注明，具体遵循第49条第（2）款的规定。

（4）在每项文书的封面作出修改或者没有修改的说明。

（5）如果违反第（1）款、第（2）款、第（3）款、第（4）款以及第38条第（4）款第d项的规定，将导致文书仅具有手写文书的证明效力，并且可以成为受害方向公证员主张损害赔偿或利益损失的理由。

27. 第51条第（2）款已被修订，并新增第（4）款，已修改后的内容如下：

第五十一条

（1）公证员有权以文书记录的形式纠正文书中的书写错误和/或排版错误，并经当事人签字确认。

signed Minuta.

(2) The correction referred to in paragraph (1) shall be conducted in the presence of penghadap, witnesses, and Notary as outlined in the minutes and provide a record of it in the original deed Minuta specifying the date and number of the minutes of the rectification deed.

(3) A copy of the deed of the minutes referred to in paragraph (2) shall be submitted to the parties.

(4) Violation of the provisions referred to in paragraph (2) resulted in a deed only has the strength of evidence as the deed under the hand and can be the reason for the injured party to demand reimbursement of losses, damages, and interest to the Notary.

28. The provisions of Article 54 be amended to read as follows:

Article 54

(1) Notaries can only give, show, or notify the contents of the Deed, Grosse Deed, copy of Deed or Deed citation, the person concerned directly on the deed, heirs, or persons who are entitled, unless otherwise provided by legislation.

(2) Notary who violates the provisions referred to in paragraph (1) may be subject to sanctions in the form:

a. written warning;

b. layoffs;

c. honorable discharge; or

d. dishonorable discharge.

29. The provisions of paragraph (1) of Article 60 be amended to read as follows:

Article 60

Deed made by or in the presence of Notary deed in lieu of note in the list.

30. The provisions of Article 63 plus 1 (one) paragraph, namely paragraph (6) so that Article 63 reads as follows:

Article 63

(1) Submission of the Protocol referred to in Article 62 be done not later than 30 (thirty) days to manufacture news Notary handover protocol signed by the submitting and receiving Notary Protocol.

(2) In the case referred to in Article 62 letter a Notary Protocol submission made by the heirs to the Notary Notary appointed by the Supervisory Council of Regions.

(3) In the case referred to in Article 62 paragraph g, the submission made by the Protocol Notary Notary Nota-

（2）对于第（1）款中的修改，需在当事人、证人及公证员在场的情况下进行，并制作一份修改记录，在原文书记录中注明制作修改记录的时间及具体的修改数量。

（3）第（2）款中的修改记录的副本须提交至各方。

（4）如果违反第（2）款的规定，将导致文书仅具有手写文书的证明效力，并且可以成为受害方向公证员主张损害赔偿或利益损失的理由。

28. 对第 54 条的修改内容如下：

第五十四条

（1）除非法律法规另有规定，公证员只能向与文书有直接利害关系的人提供、展示或通知文书的内容、日期、副本或摘录。

（2）公证员违反第（1）款的规定，可能受到以下形式的惩罚：

a. 书面警告；

b. 停职；

c. 辞退；

d. 不光彩地解雇。

29. 对第 60 条第（1）款修改后的内容如下：

第六十条

应当注明文书是否是在公证员在场的情况下作出。

30. 第 63 条新增第（6）款，修改后的内容如下：

第六十三条

（1）第 62 条规定的公证档案的提交应在不迟于 30 日内作出，并制作与提交公证档案相关的记录，由提交和接受公证档案的人签署。

（2）在满足第 62 条第 a 款规定的情况下，公证员须向区 / 市监督委员会委任的另一名公证员提交公证档案。

（3）在满足第 62 条第 g 款规定的情况下，如果停职超过 3 个月，公证员须向区 / 市监督委员会委任

ry to others appointed by the Council of Regional Supervisor if a suspension of more than 3 (three) months.

(4) In the case referred to in Article 62 letter b, c, d, f, or h, the submission made by the Protocol Notary Notary Notary to others appointed by the Council of Ministers upon the recommendation of the Regional Supervisor.

(5) In the case of Notary Protocol is not submitted within 30 (thirty) days referred to in paragraph (1), the Regional Supervisory Council is authorized to take Notary Protocol.

31. The provisions of Article 65 be amended to read as follows:

Article 65

Notary, Notary Substitute, and Acting Notary responsible for any deed that made despite Notary Protocol has been submitted or transferred to the storage Notary Protocol.

33. In between Article 65 and Article 66, 1 (one) article, namely Article 65A, which reads as follows:

Article 65A

Notary who violates the provisions of Article 58 and Article 59 may be subject to sanctions in the form:

a. written warning;

b. layoffs;

c. honorable discharge; or

d. dishonorable discharge.

33. Title Chapter VIII amended to read as follows:

CHAPTER VIII
DECISION PHOTOCOPYING minuta DEED and invitation NOTARY

34. The provisions of paragraph (1) of Article 66 is amended and supplemented 2 (two) paragraph, namely paragraph (3) and (4) so that Article 66 reads as follows:

Article 66

(1) For the purposes of judicial proceedings, investigators, prosecutors, or judges with the approval of the competent Notary honor assemblies:

a. take a photocopy of Minuta Deed and / or letters attached to Minuta Deed or in storage Notary Notary Protocol; and

b. Notary summoned to be present in the examination relating to the Deed or protocols that are in storage Notary Notary.

(2) Making photocopies Minuta Deed or securities referred to in paragraph (1) letter a, made news handover.

的另一名公证员提交公证档案。

（4）在满足第62条第b款、第c款、第d款、第f款、第h款规定的情况下，公证员应向由区/市监督委员会推荐并由部长任命的另一名公证员提交公证档案。

（5）如果公证档案未在第（1）款规定的30日内提交，那么区/市监督委员会有权收回公证档案。

31. 第65条修改后的内容如下：

第六十五条

公证员、替补公证员应对其出具的每一份文书负责，即使公证档案已经提交或移交给公证档案保管处。

32. 在第65条至第66条之间，新增第65（A）条，具体修改内容如下：

第六十五（A）条：

公证员违反第58条及第59条的规定，可能受到以下形式的惩罚：

a. 书面警告；

b. 停职；

c. 辞退；

d. 不光彩地解雇。

33. 第八章修改后的内容如下：

第八章　文书记录和公证员传唤

34. 第66条第（1）款已被修订，并新增第（3）款、第（4）款，修改后的内容如下：

第六十六条

（1）因为司法程序的需要，经公证员荣誉大会批准的调查员，总检察官或法官有权：

a. 查阅公证员保存的文书及相关文件或保存的公证档案副本；和

b. 传唤公证员出席与他/她出具的文书或公证员保管的公证档案有关的听证会。

（2）取得第（1）款第a项中的文书纪录或文件副本，但应当制作移交记录。

(3) Notary honor Assembly within a period of 30 (thirty) working days from the receipt of the request for approval referred to in paragraph (1) shall provide answers to accept or reject the request for approval.

(4) In the case of honor assemblies Notary does not give an answer within the period referred to in paragraph (3), the panel considered the honor Notary receives a request for approval.

35. In between Article 66 and Article 67, 1 (one) article, namely Article 66A to read as follows:

Article 66A

(1) In carrying out the development, the Minister establishing an honor Notary.

(2) Assembly Notary honor totaled seven (7) persons, consisting of elements:

a. Notary three (3) persons;

b. Government of 2 (two); and

c. experts or academics as much as two (2) persons.

(3) Further provisions on the duties and functions, requirements and procedures for the appointment and dismissal, organizational structure, work procedures, and budget assemblies honor Notary governed by Regulation.

36. The provisions of paragraph (3) and (6) Article 67 amended to read as follows:

Article 67

(1) Supervision over the Notary made by the Minister.

(2) In implementing the supervision referred to in paragraph (1) The Minister formed the Assembly of Trustees.

(3) The Supervisory Council referred to in paragraph (2) amounted to 9 (nine) members, consisting of elements:

a. Government of 3 (three);

b. Notary Organization for three (3) persons; and

c. experts or academics as much as three (3) persons.

(4) In the event that there is an area of government agencies referred to in paragraph (3) letter a, membership in the Council of Trustees filled from other elements designated by the Minister.

(5) Supervision referred to in paragraph (1) covers the behavior and implementation Notary Notary office.

(6) The provisions concerning the supervision referred to in paragraph (5) applies to Substitute and Acting Notary Notary.

37. The provisions of paragraph (1) and (2) Article 69 is amended and in between paragraphs (2) and paragraph (3), 1 (one) paragraph, namely paragraph (2a) so that Arti-

（3）在收到第（1）款规定的批准请求后，荣誉大会应在 30 个工作日内答复接受或拒绝批准请求。

（4）若在第（3）款规定的期间内未给予答复，则视为批准。

35. 在第 66 条至第 67 条之间，新增第 66(A)条，具体内容如下：

第六十六（A）条

（1）在未来发展过程中，由部长设立荣誉公证员大会。

（2）荣誉公证大会共由 7 人组成，其中包括：

a. 3 名公证员；

b. 2 名政府官员；

c. 2 名专家或学者。

（3）有关职责、功能、任免条件、任免程序、组织结构、工作程序和预算安排等的进一步规定详见相关条例。

36. 第 67 条第（3）款、第（6）款已被修改，修改后的内容如下：

第六十七条

（1）公证员应由部长监督。

（2）依据第（1）款的规定，部长应组织成立监督委员会。

（3）第（2）款规定的监督委员会须由下列 9 位成员组成：

a. 3 名政府人员；

b. 3 名来自公证机构的成员；

c. 3 名专家 / 学者。

（4）如第（3）款第 a 项中的某政府成员缺席，由部长委任的其他人员补充。

（5）第（1）款中的监督内容涵盖公证员的行为及公证员的职业表现。

（6）第（5）款所述的监督条款，适用于替补公证员。

37. 第 69 条第（1）款、第（2）款已被修订，在第（2）款与第（3）款之间，新增第（2a）款，修改后的内容如下：

cle 69 reads as follows:

Article 69

(1) Regional Supervisory Council was formed in the District / City.

(2) The membership of the Regional Supervisory Council consists of the elements referred to in Article 67 paragraph (3).

(2a) In the case of a district / city, the number of Notary is not proportional to the number of members of the Supervisory Council of Regions, Regional Supervisory Council can be formed joint for some regencies / cities.

(3) The Chairman and Vice-Chairman of the Regional Supervisory Council elected from and by the members referred to in paragraph (2).

(4) The term of office of the chairman, vice chairman, and members of the Supervisory Council of Regions is 3 (three) years and may be reappointed.

(5) Regional Supervisory Council is assisted by a secretary or more designated in the Regional Meeting of the Supervisory Council.

38. The provisions of Article 73 paragraph (1) letter a and e are amended and paragraph g removed so that Article 73 reads as follows:

Article 73

(1) Council of Regional Supervisory authorities:

a. held a hearing to examine and take decisions on the public reports that can be delivered through the Regional Supervisory Council;

b. call Notary reported for assessment in the report referred to in paragraph a;

c. give permission leave more than 6 (six) months to 1 (one) year;

d. examine and decide on the Regional Supervisory Council decision refusing leave filed by the reporting Notary;

e. sanction both verbal warning and a written warning;

f. proposing sanctions against the Central Supervisory Council of Notaries to the form:

1) a suspension of 3 (three) months up to 6 (six) months; or

2) dishonorable discharge.

g. removed.

39. The provisions of Article 81 be amended to read as follows:

第六十九条

（1）区监督委员会应当在区 / 市设立。

（2）区监督委员会成员应由第 67 条第（3）款中的成员组成。

（2a）在区 / 市，公证员人数与区 / 市监督委员会成员数不成比例时，区 / 市监督委员会可以设立联合会。

（3）区 / 市监督委员会的主席和副主席由第（2）款中的成员中选举产生。

（4）区 / 市监督委员会的主席、副主席及委员任期为 3 年，可以连任。

（5）区 / 市监督委员会应由区 / 市监督委员会会议选出的秘书或其他人组织运作。

38. 第 73 条第（1）款第 a 项、第 e 项已被修订，第 g 项已被删除，修改后的内容如下：

第七十三条

（1）省级监督委员会有权：

a. 召开会议，对通过区监督委员会递交的公开报告进行调查和作出决定；

b. 传唤第 a 项规定的被举报的公证员进行调查；

c. 对期限为 6 个月至 1 年的休假请求作出决定；

d. 复核区 / 市监督委员会拒绝公证员休假请求的上诉，并作出决定；

e. 以口头或者书面警告的形式实施惩罚；

f. 向中央监督委员会提出对公证员实施惩罚的建议，其形式为：

1）停职 3 至 6 个月；或

2）被不光彩地解雇。

g. 已被删除。

39. 对第 81 条修改后的内容如下：

Article 81

Further provisions on the procedure for the appointment and dismissal of members, organizational structure and working procedures, budget and examination procedure is regulated by the Supervisory Council of Ministers.

40. The provisions of paragraph (2) Article 82 is amended and supplemented three (3) paragraph, namely paragraph (3), (4), and paragraph (5), so that Article 82 reads as follows:

Article 82

(1) Notary come together in one container Notary Organization.

(2) Containers Notary Organization referred to in paragraph (1) is the Indonesian Notary Association.

(3) Organizations Notary referred to in paragraph (1) is the only profession is free and independent Notary formed with the intent and purpose to improve the quality of the Notary profession.

(4) The provisions concerning the objectives, tasks, authority, work procedures, and organizational structures set out in the Articles of Association and Bylaws Notary Organization.

(5) The provisions concerning the establishment, development, and supervision of Notary Organization governed by the Regulation.

41. Provisions Chapter XI deleted.

42. The provisions of Article 88 be amended to read as follows:

Article 88

At the time this Act comes into force:

a. Notary filing as being processed, will be processed pursuant to Act No. 30 of 2004 concerning Notary.

b. apprenticeship candidates who have lived Notary still be calculated based on the requirements laid down in this Act.

43. In between Article 91 and Article 92 inserted two (2) Article, namely Article 91A and Article 91B, which reads as follows:

Article 91A

Provisions concerning the procedures for the imposition of sanctions referred to in Article 7 (2), Article 16, paragraph (11) and (13), Article 17 paragraph (2), Article 19 paragraph (4), Article 32 paragraph (4), Article 37 paragraph (2), Article 54 paragraph (2), and Article 65A.

第八十一条

有关成员的任免程序、组织结构、工作程序、预算及检查程序等由部长组织下的监督委员会监督开展。

40. 第 82 条第（2）款已经被修订，并新增第（3）款、第（4）款及第（5）款，修改后的内容如下：

第八十二条

（1）公证员隶属于某一公证机构。

（2）第（1）款中的公证机构是印度尼西亚公证员协会。

（3）第（1）款中的公证机构是自由且独立的专业机构，提高公证员的职业水平是其责任之一。

（4）公证机构的章程包括目标、任务、职权、工作程序和组织结构。

（5）有关于公证机构的设立、发展和监督的条款见相关规定。

41. 第十一章已被删除。

42. 第 88 条修改后的内容如下：

第八十八条

关于本法的效力：

a. 公证备案程序按照 2004 年第 30 号公证法予以处理。

b. 已经成为公证候选人的，按照本法规定的要求继续有效。

43. 在第 91 条与第 92 条之间，新增第 91（A）条、第 91（B）条，修改后的内容如下：

第九十一（A）条

有关实施惩罚的程序的规定详见第 7 条第（2）款、第 16 条第（11）款及第（13）款、第 17 条第（2）款、第 19 条第（4）款、第 32 条第（4）款、第 37 条第（2）款、第 54 条第（2）款和第 65（A）条。

Article 91B

Regulations implementation of this Law shall be established no later than 1 (one) year from the date of this Act is enacted.

This Act shall take effect on the date of promulgation.

Ordering the promulgation of this Law shall be published in the State Gazette of the Republic of Indonesia.

Enacted in Jakarta
on January 15, 2014

PRESIDENT OF THE REPUBLIC OF INDONESIA,
DR. H. Susilo Bambang Yudhoyono

Promulgated in Jakarta
on January 15, 2014

MINISTER OF JUSTICE AND HUMAN RIGHTS REPUBLIC OF INDONESIA,
AMIR SYAMSUDIN

第九十一（B）条

本法中规定的补充措施应在本法颁布之日起 1 年内实施。

本法自公布之日起生效。

本法应当在印度尼西亚共和国国家公报上同时公布。

于雅加达通过
2014 年 1 月 15 日

印度尼西亚共和国总统，
苏西洛·班邦·尤多约诺

于雅加达颁布
2014 年 1 月 15 日

印度尼西亚共和国法律与人权事务部部长，

阿米尔·善苏汀

以色列

公证法

יושיר :'א קרפ

1. רש הנמיש העבש לש תונוישר תדעו תאמ ןתניי ןוירטונ ןוישר שאר בשויה ;ןידה יכרוע תכשל תעצה יפ לע םיינש םהמ ,םיטפשמה רבחו רוביצ יגיצנ ויהי תוחפל םירבח ינש ,הנידמה דבוע ןטפשמ היהי ןוירטונ היהי תוחפל דחא.

2. (א) ןוירטונ תויהל רישכ הלא לכ וב ומייקתנש ימ:

(1) אוה חרזא ילארשי וא בשות עבק בלארשי; לעניו ןזה ,"בשות עבק בלארשי" – ימ אוהש בעל רישיון לישיבת קבע בלארשי לפי חוק הכניסה לישראל, התשי"ב-1952;

(2) אוה רבח לשכת עורכי הדין ונתמלא בו אחת מאלה:

(א) עסק במקצוע של עורך דין 10 שנים לפחות, מתוכן חמש שנים וחצי לפחות בישראל;

(ב) (נמחקה);

(ג) עסק במקצוע של עורך דין 10 שנים לפחות, מהן שנתיים בישראל ,והגיש את בקשתו לרשיון תוך שבע שנים מהיום שבו היה לתושב ישראל.

(3) לא הורשע בישראל או מחוצה לה בעבירה פלילית שיש בה משום קלון;

(4) לא הוצא אלו העשוה תכשלמ עורכי הדין בישראל על פי פסק דין סופי בהליכים משמעתיים, למעט הליך על פי סעיף 78 לחוק לשכת עורכי הדין, תשכ"א-1961 (להלן – חוק הלשכה), ולא בוטל רשיונו אלו התולה וקפת בהליכים משמעתיים לפי חוק נוטריונים למסמכים יוצאי חוץ, תש"י-1950;

(5) ועדת הרשיונות מצאה אותו ראוי להיות נוטריון, לאחר שנתנה את דעתה, בין השאר, לעונשים משמעתיים שהוטלו עליו לפי חוק הלשכה או חוק נוטריונים למסמכים יוצאי-חוץ, תש"י-1950, תוך 10 שנים לפני מתן הרשיון, פרט לאלה האמורים בפסקה (4).

第一章　许可

第一条　公证员执照由司法部长任命的七人许可委员会颁发。

该委员会组成中，其中两人由律师协会推荐，主席需拥有法学专家和国家公职人员的双重身份，委员会至少有两名委员为公众代表，且至少有一名委员为公证员。

第二条

（一）成为公证员，应当具备下列条件：

（1）属于以色列公民或以色列永久居民；此处的“以色列永久居民”是指根据《进入以色列法》（犹太历5712年，即公元1952年）规定的在以色列持有永久居住许可证的人；

（2）属于以色列律师协会的一员，且符合以下任一条件：

①从事律师职业10年以上，其中至少5年半在以色列；

②（已删除）；

③从事律师职业10年以上，在以色列居住超过两年，并在他成为以色列居民当日起7年内提出申请执照。

（3）未曾有在以色列或境外触犯涉及道德败坏的犯罪；

（4）在惩罚措施中，没有被最终判决吊销或暂停使用以色列律师协会颁发的执照，除律师协会法律（犹太历5721年，即公元1961年）第78节规定的程序外，根据《以色列外国文件公证法》（犹太历5710年，即公元1950年）其执照未被吊销，或在纪律处分程序中未被停职；

（5）许可委员会认为他有资格成为公证员，在给出其意见后，除其他举措外，在许可授予的前10年内，许可委员会应根据《律师法》或《外国文件公证法》（犹太历5710年，即公元1950年）有权对其实

מא ןא ןוירטונ ןוישר םדאל תתל תיאשר תונוישרה תדעו (ב)
רמגש םוימ םינש רשע ורבע םא (3)(א) ןטק ןיעסב רומאכ עשרוה
ןטק ןיעסב םירומאה םישנעה דחא וילע לטוה םא ןאו ,ושנע תא תוצרל
(א)(4) םא ורבע רשע םינש םוימ ובש לטוה שנועה.

ןוירטונ ןוישיר ןתמ תונתהל תיאשר תונוישירה תדעו (ג)
אשיי ןתתשמה ;הדעוה עבקתש תונוכתמב הרצק תומלתשהב תופתתשהב
הדעוה עבקתש יפכ ,הקלח וא הלוכ ,תומלתשהב ותופתתשה תולעב.

3. טפושכ הנוהכ תפוקת ןיד ,(2)(א)2 ןיעסב רומאה ןינעל,
ותוא רשיא םיטפשמה רשש רחא יטפשמ דיקפתב וא יתד ןיד-תיב רבחכ
לארשיב ןיד ךרוע לש עוצקמב קוסיע תפוקת ןידכ ,הז ןיעס ךרוצל וצב,
קוסיע תפוקת ןידכ ץראל ץוחב ןוירטונכ וא טפושכ הנוהכ תפוקת ןידו
ץראל ץוחב ןיד ךרוע לש עוצקמב.

4. (א) תורישכה יאנת ןוישרה שקבמב ואלמתנש הדעוה האצמ
יפל תוכמסב שמתשהל םוקמ שיש הטילחה וא ,(א)2 ןיעסב םיטרופמה
תונקתב ועבקנש ךרדבו דעומב השקבה תא םסרפת ,(ב)2 ןיעס.

ךרדבו דעומב ,תונוישרה תדעול שיגהל יאשר םדא לכ (ב)
אל ךא ,שקבמל ןוישרה תקנעהל תקמונמ תודגנתה ,תונקתב ועבקנש
שקבמל הנתנש ינפל תודגנתהה ךמס לע השקבה תא הדעוה החדת
ויתונעט עימשהל תונמדזה.

5. והכל ןוירטונ ליחתי םרטב –

(1) ותחי םושמ תא םושיב ןוירטונה סקנפב להוניש וחוקיפב לש רש
םיטפשמה;

(2) ימסור למי רשש םיטפשמה וכימסה לכ ךדגומה לש ותמיתח
ושל ותמוח ,ךרדב העבקנש תונקתב;

(3) ישלם תא הרגאה העבקנש תונקתב.

6. (א) לעב ןוישר ןוירטונ םלשי ,אל יאוחר מ-31 ביונואר לש לכ
הנש ,אגרה תיתנש שישערוה ןקבע תונקתב ;אל שולמה הרגאה כאמור,
יוספו לה תופסות אלה:

(1) שולמה הרגאה בתקופה שביון 1 בפברואר ו־31 במרס –
10%;

(2) שולמה הרגאה בתקופה שביון 1 באפריל ו־30 בספטמבר –
50%;

(3) שולמה הרגאה אחרי 30 בספטמבר – 100%;

(4) שולמה הרגאה אחרי תום שנה פלונית שאית, בנוסף
לתשלום כפל הרגאה כאמור בסקפה (3), גם הפרשי הצמדה על סכום
הרגאה שנקבע לפי מדד המחירים לצרכן שמפרסמת הלשכה המרכזית
לסטטיסטיקה, מן המדד שפורסם בחודש שצדמבר שקדם למועד תשלום
הרגאה של אותה השנה עד המדד שפורסם לאחרונה לפני תשלום
בפועל.

施惩罚措施。

（二）即使一人已根据第（一）（3）款被定罪，且其已在判决执行完毕之日起已过去10年，或第（一）（4）款所指明的其中一项刑罚已被执行，许可委员会仍可给予其公证许可证；

（三）许可委员会可以规定，以委员会指定的途径参加短期研究者应当被授予公证许可；参加者须承担其参加课程的全部或部分费用，该费用由委员会决定。

第三条

为了达成第二条第（一）（2）款的要求，即在一段时间内从事法官职业这一条款，从事作为宗教法庭的成员或司法部长根据本部分的命令而批准的其他法律职业的工作时间，也应该被计入从事法官职业的总时间内，国外法官或公证员的任期应视为与国外律师的任期相同。

第四条

（一）如果委员会发现被发给执照者符合第二条第（一）（1）款所规定的条件，或认为可在第二条第（一）（2）款下行使权力，那么应按规定的时间和方式公布申请。

（二）任何人都可以按照实施细则规定的日期和方式向许可委员会提交合理的反对意见，但委员会在给予申请人陈述其论点的机会之前不应拒绝其基于异议的申请。

第五条

在公证员开始履职之前：

（一）在由司法部长监督管理的公证登记处登记；

（二）按照本条例所规定的方式，向司法部长授权签名的人提供签名和签名的范例；

（三）应当按照规定缴纳费用。

第六条

（一）公证员应不迟于每年1月31日支付年费，年费费率由规章规定；未缴纳上述费用的，应当增加下列费用：

（1）在2月1日至3月31日期间增加支付10%的费用；

（2）在4月1日至9月30日之间增加支付50%的费用；

（3）9月30日以后增加支付100%；

（4）未缴纳费用超过一年，除支付根据第（3）款规定的加倍费用外，还应支付根据其实际付款前中央统计局最后公布的消费者价格指数确定的费用金额。

(א1) אל םליש לעב ןוישר ןוירטונ תא הרגאה דעב הנש תינולפ דע םות שדוח סרמ לש הנשה הירחאלש, אל היהי יאשר שמשל ןוירטונ לכ דוע אל םליש תא הרגאה התואב הנשה, רומאכ ףיעסב ןטק (א)(4).

(ב) ןוירטונ אלש םליש הרגא תיתנש שמחל םינש, עקפי ופקת לש ונוישר.

(ג) רש םיטפשמה יאשר עובקל תונקתב רועיש הנוש לש הרגא תיתנש לעבל ןוישר ןוירטונ אוהש ליגב םיעבש הנש וא רתוי.

קרפ 'ב: תויוכמס ןוירטונה

7. ןוירטונ ךמסומ

(1) תמאל המיתח לע ךמסמ;

(2) רשאל םתוחהש לע ךמסמ, םשב ותלוז, היה ךמסומ ךכל;

(3) רשאל ותונוכנ לש קתעה ךמסמ;

(4) רשאל ותונוכנ לש םוגרת ךמסמ;

(5) לבקל רשאלו ריהצת הרהצהו תרחא;

(6) רשאל םדאש ינולפ יח;

(7) רשאל התונוכנ לש תמישר יאצמ;

(8) ךורעל הדעה לש ךמסמ ריחס;

(9) ךורעל ךמסמ וא תושעל וב הלועפ תרחא הכירעהשכ וא תיישע הלועפה ידיב ןוירטונ השורד וא תרתומ לע יפ ןיד, תוברל ןיד לש תנידמ ץוח, וא לע יפ ךמסמ רחא;

(10) שמתשהל תוכמסב לש ןוירטונ ירוביצ לע יפ ןיד רחא;

(11) תמאל םכסה ןוממ ןיב ינב גוז, שנכרת ינפל ןיאושינה.

8. הלועפ ןמ תולועפה תוטרופמה ףיעסב 7(1), (3), (7), (8) ו-(9), ךמסמהשכ ינוירטונה שורד יכרצל שומיש ץוחב ץראל, תוברל תוגיצנ לש תנידמ ץוח לארשיב, אל השעית אלא ידיב ןוירטונ.

9. ןיא תוארוהב קרפ הז ידכ עונמל תיישע הלועפ ידיב דבוע ירוביצ ךמסומה ךכל יולימב ודיקפת, וא ידיב םדא רחא ךמסומה ךכל לע יפ קוקיח.

קרפ 'ג: םיכרד םיאנתו עוציבל הלועפ תינוירטונ

10. (א) אל שמתשי ןוירטונ תוכמסב ויתויוכמסמ ןינעב לש ומצע, לש ובורק, לש ופתוש, לש ודבוע וא לש דיגאת אוהש ותטילשב.

(ב) ןינעל ףיעס הז, ״בורק״ לש ןוירטונה –

(1) ןב גוז;

(2) הרוה, הרוה הרוה, הרוה ןב-גוז, אצאצ, אצאצ ןב-גוז ינבו םגוז לש לכ דחא הלאמ;

(3) חא וא תוחא ינבו םגוז.

11. אל תמאי ןוירטונ ותמיתח לש םדא לע ךמסמ אלא םא םתוחה דמע וינפל, ההוז םתחו וינפב לע ךמסמה.

12. אל רשאי ןוירטונ ךמסמש ינולפ אוה קתעה ןוכנ רוקמהמ, אלא םא רוקמה גצוה וינפל אוהו הוושה הז לא הז ואצמו םיווש.

13. אל רשאי ןוירטונ תא התונוכנ לש תמישר יאצמ אלא םא ךרע

（-1）［是对（一）的补充］若公证员于次年 3 月底前未缴付去年的费用，则他在缴付该年由本条第（一）（4）款所规定的费用之前，无权担任公证员。

（二）公证员 5 年内未缴纳年费的，其执照有效期将过期；

（三）司法部长可按规定对 70 岁以上的公证执照持有人收取不同的年费。

第二章　公证员的权力

第七条　公证员的认证

（1）核实文件签名的真实性；

（2）证明代表他人签署的文件是被代表人授权的；

（3）确认文件副本的准确性；

（4）确认文件翻译的正确性；

（5）接收并确认一份宣誓书和其他声明；

（6）确认某个人还活着；

（7）确认库存清单的正确性；

（8）编辑可转让单证的公证文书；

（9）当编辑或公证员被法律要求或允许时，包括外国法律或其他文件的允许可以执行任何其他行为；

（10）根据任何其他法律行使公证员的权力；

（11）验证配偶之间基于婚姻协议签署的财务协议。

第八条　依照第七条第（1）项、第（3）项、第（7）项、第（8）项和第（9）项的规定采取行动，为了在国外使用的目的公证文件，包括在以色列的外国代表，只能由公证员完成。

第九条　本章的规定不应阻止获得授权的公务员或由法律授权的其他人在履行其职责时采取行动。

第三章　公证的方式和条件

第十条

（一）公证员不应当对其本人、亲属、伴侣、雇员或其控制下的公司履行公证员职务；

（二）就本节而言，公证员的“亲属”包括：

（1）配偶；

（2）父母，父母的父母，配偶的父母，后代，配偶的后代和以上任何一方的配偶；

（3）兄弟姐妹及其配偶。

第十一条　公证员应当认证在文件上的签名，除非签字人在场，且已经在他的文件上签署和被识别。

第十二条　除非公证员得到源文件，并将两份文件相互比较发现它们确实是一致的。公证员不得证明某一特定文件是原件的正确副本。

第十三条　除非在公证员面前进行清单的编辑和

יאצמה אשונב יקב אוהו וינפב הכרענ וא התוא.

14. מותחל יאכז ותלוז םשב ךמסמ לע םותחהש ןוירטונ רשאי אל שיש םיכמסמ ידי לע ןוירטונל החכוה םותחל ותוכז םא אלא ,ךכ וילע יפ לע להנתמה סקנפ ידי לע – דיגאת םשב םתח םאו ,רבדל היאר םהב רחא ךמסמ ידי לע וא ,תרחא ךרדב ןיבו ירוביצ דבוע ידיב ןיב ,קוקיח רבדל היאר וב שיש.

15. טלוש אוה םא אלא םוגרת לש ותונוכנ ןוירטונ רשאי אל תא ךרע ומצע אוהו ,םגרות היאלש הפשבו רוקמה ךרענ הבש הפשב ותונוכנ תא קדב וא םוגרתה.

16. אלא םייחב ינולפ םדא היה ינולפ םויב יכ ןוירטונ רשאי אל ההוזו םוי ותואב םדאה וינפל דמע םא.

17. ןידכ לייובמ וניאש ךמסמ יבגל ותוכמסב ןוירטונ שמתשי אל.

18. םיפסונ םיאנתו םיכרד תונקתב עובקל יאשר םיטפשמה רש עובקל אוה יאשר ראשה ןיבו תינוירטונ הלועפ ןוירטונ עצבי םהבש – רבדב תוארוה

(1) לש עוציב םשל וינפל בצייתמה לש תיטפשמה ותורשכ רוריב הלועפה תועמשמ תא ןוכנ לא ןיבמ ותויה תאו תינוירטונה הלועפה;

(2) תוינוירטונה תולועפה לע להנל ןוירטונה לעש תומושר יכרדו ,ודיב ריאשהל וילעש ,םהב לעפש םיכמסממ םיקתעה ,עציבש הנמז ךשמו הלא לכ לש הרימשה.

תינוירטונ הלועפ לש תואצותה :'ד קרפ

19. היאר היהי ,ויפ לע תונקתהו הז קוח יפל ןוירטונ לש ורושיא ןוירטונה ירבדל ,תפסונ היארב ךרוצ אלל ,יטפשמ ךילהב תקפסמ רומאכ לכה ,וינפב ושע וא ורמאש םהישעמלו םירחא ירבדלו וישעמלו רושיאב.

20. (א) יופי-חוכ יללכ ויופי-חכ עוציבל תואקסע ןיעקרקמב ךרע םא אלא ףקות-ינב ויהי אל ,ןיעקרקמה םשרמב םושיר תונועטה תונקתבו הז קוחב רומאכ ,םהילעש תומיתחה תא תמיא וא ןוירטונ םתוא הכשלה קוחל 91 ףיעסמ תערוג הניא וז הארוה ;ויפ לע.

(ב) ףיעס הז וניא לח לע יופי-חוכ ןתינש ץוחב ץראל יפל ינידה ןתינ ובש םוקמה.

תיעוצקמ הקיתא :'ה קרפ

21. ןוירטונ רומשי לע דובכ הקצועמ ויימנע לכמ רבד העולול עוגפל בכבוד הקצועמ.

22. במילוי תפקידיו יפעל ןוירטונ בנאמנות ובמסירות; נתבקש הנוטריון לבצע פעולה בשביל יותר מאדם אחד, חב הוא בנאמנות שווה לכל הצדדים ואין נפקא מינה מי מהם משלם את שכרו.

23. ןוירטונ אל יעשה ,במישרין או בעקיפין ,פרסומת לעיסוק אלא בהתאם לכללים שהותקנו לפי סעיף 55 לחוק הלשכה; כן יחולו על ןוירטונ הכללים שהותקנו לפי הסעיף האמור ,לעניין ציון שם המקצוע.

制作，且公证员熟悉清单的主题，否则公证员不得确认清单的正确性。

第十四条 公证员不得证明获得授权者以他人名义签署的文件，除非其签署的权利由公证员证明，该文件由证人作证；如果他以公司名义签署，基于法律依据，无论是由公职人员还是其他人签署，均需要另一份包含证据的文件进行佐证。

第十五条 公证员不得认证翻译的正确性，除非公证员能流利地使用原文和所译的语言，并且公证员自己可以编辑译文或检查其正确性。

第十六条 公证员不得公证某人在某一天活着，除非该人在当天站在他面前并被确认身份。

第十七条 公证员不得对未经盖章的文件进行公证。

第十八条 司法部长可以在条例中规定公证员执行公证行为的其他方式和条件，还可以规定其他有关条件：

（1）澄清证人出庭对履行公证行为的法律效力及其对诉讼的意义；

（2）公证员必须对他所作出的公证行为、他所出具的公证文书及其复印件、他所保管的文件以及保管期限进行记录。

第四章 公证行为的结果

第十九条 根据本法，公证员根据公证员的行为和他人的言行，以及当事人对公证员所说或做的行为，所作出的公证行为能够在法律程序中充当充分证据，而无须进一步证明。

第二十条

（一）除非公证员已根据本法及其他规定制作或核实其签名，否则一般授权书和在土地登记处登记的房地产交易行为的授权书均无效；且该规定并未违反《主席团法》第 91 条；

（二）根据所在地的法律，本章不适用于国外授权书。

第五章 职业道德

第二十一条 公证员应当保持职业尊严，不得做有可能损害职业尊严的任何事情。

第二十二条 在履行职责时，公证员将以忠诚和奉献的方式行事；如果公证员被要求对不止一个人实施公证，他应当同样忠于所有各方，并且与他们中的一方是否支付他的工资无关联。

第二十三条 公证员不得直接或间接地宣传他的职业，除非按照《律师法》第 55 条规定的规则；根据上述条款颁布的规则，在名称和专业方面也适用于

24. אל לדשי ןוירטונ, בעצמו או על ידי אחר, למסור לו הדובע
מקצועית.

25. אל ישתמש נוטריון בציון "נוטריון" או במקצוע אלא בתואר
תואר לועזי מקביל בשם נקבע בתקנות ובתואר זה בלבד; אין בו
כדי למנוע את השימוש בתואר אקדמי או בתואר שדין אחר מסדיר את
השימוש בו.

26. (א) נוטריון לא יעסוק במקצועו בשותפות עם מי שאינו
נוטריון, ולא ישתף בהכנסותיו במתמורה לשירותים, סיוע או תועלת
אחרת למקצועו; ואולם רשאי נוטריון לחלק בהכנסותיו את אלמנתו ואת
יתומים קטינים של כל אחד מאלה:

(1) שותפו או שותף שפרש, אם נפטר בעוד נוטריון;

(2) נוטריון שאת משרדו רכש.

(ב) נוטריון יפעל עצמו בשותפות נוטריונית בשם ובלבד, אף אם הוא עוסק
בשותפות עם נוטריון אחר.

(ג) אין בסעיף זה כדי למנוע שותפות בין עורך דין שהוא נוטריון
בין עורך דין שאינו נוטריון.

27. לא יעשה נוטריון פעולה נוטריונית במילוי תפקידו כשכיר.

28. (א) נוטריון ישמור בסוד כל דבר שהובא לידיעתו על ידי מי
שנזקק לשירותיו ושנעשה על פי דין, זולת אם נאמר אחרת בחיקוק או אם
ויתר הלקוח בכתב על שמירת הסודיות.

(ב) העובד בשירותו של נוטריון ישמור על סודיות העניינים
המגיעים לידיעתו ושירות במהלך עבודתו כמו שהיה חייב נוטריון
בעצמו לשמור על סודיות.

(ג) נוטריון חייב לנקוט אמצעים סבירים כדי להבטיח שעובדיו
ישמרו על הסודיות כאמור בסעיף זה.

(ד) סעיף זה לא יחול על גילוי שנצטווה עליו הנוטריון או עובדו
לפי צו בית משפט או בהליך משפטי.

29. לא ישתמש נוטריון בידיעה שהגיע אליו במילוי תפקידו
ממי שנזקק לשירותיו לכל מטרה זולת לעניין ואותו אדם שנזקק לשירותיו
כאמור או ברשותו.

פרק ו': ניהול ושימור מסמכים

30. השר רשאי להקים ארכיון מרכזי למסמכים
נוטריוניים ולחייב נוטריונים לשלוח לארכיון זה, במועד שנקבע בתקנות,
העתק ממסמכים או מסוגים מסמכים כפי שנקבע בתקנות באישור ועדת
החוקה חוק ומשפט של הכנסת.

31. נוטריון יפרסם בקשר למילוי תפקידו, ובהם רישום
פעולותיו בדרך שנקבעה בתקנות.

32. השר רשאי לקבוע בתקנות –

(1) את סוגי המסמכים שעליהם בארכיון יכולו לראות את הארכיון

公证员。

第二十四条 公证员不得由任何其他人代替他提供专业工作。

第二十五条 公证员不得将其职业用作其他法规和本法律规定之外的“公证”或与之平行的外国职称；该规定不得妨碍使用学位或其他法律规定允许其使用的范围。

第二十六条

（一）公证员不得与非公证员合伙履行其职务，不得分享其收入以换取其专业的服务、协助或其他利益。但下列情况下，公证员可以与合伙公证员的遗孀和他们每个人的未成年子女分享他的收入：

（1）他的合伙人或已经退休的合伙人，如果在公证时已经去世；

（2）共同出资设立办公室的公证员。

（二）公证员只能代表自己行使公证行为，即使他与另一名公证员合伙。

（三）本部分不是为了禁止公证员与非公证员之间的合作关系。

第二十七条 在履行职责时，公证员不能为员工实施公证行为。

第二十八条

（一）除非法律另有规定或客户以书面形式放弃保密，公证员应对其知道的来自其服务对象的任何事情予以保密；

（二）为公证员工作的人员应当在其服务过程中将自己接触到的事项与公证员的保密义务保持一致；

（三）公证员必须采取合理措施确保其员工遵守本节规定的保密要求；

（四）本条不适用于公证员依据命令披露的信息，也不适用于法院或法律程序要求。

第二十九条 在未经要求提供此类服务的人许可的情况下，公证员不得利用他在履行职责时所获得的商业秘密，这些商业秘密是出于其他目的的需要专属于其服务的人。

第六章　管理和维护文件

第三十条 司法部长建立公证文件的中央档案馆，并要求公证员在条例规定的日期向该档案馆递送“各类文件副本或者各类经以色列议会、宪法、法律和司法委员会批准的法规文件”。

第三十一条 公证员应当履行其职责，并按照《实施细则》规定的方式记录其活动。

第三十二条 司法部长根据条例：

（1）有权审阅中央档案馆中的公证文件，包括根

יגוס תא 54, ףיעס יפל ורסמנש םיכמסמ תוברל ,םיינוירטונ םיכמסמל
םיאכזה לבקל םיקתעה םהמ, תאו ירדס ןויעה תלבקו םיקתעהה;

(2) תא הרוצה םוקמהו תזינגל םיכמסמ, תוברל םירפס רומאכ
ףיעסב 31, רשא ויה ידיב ןוירטונ.

33. (א) ןוירטונ דימעי תא םיכמסמה וילעש רומשל תאו םירפסה
וילעש

להנל, הז קוח יפל ,תרוקיבל ימ רשש םיטפשמה והנימ ךכל.

(ב) יכרד תרוקבה ועבקיי תונקתב.

(ג) ימ שנתמנה ךורעל תרוקב יפל ףיעס הז, רומשי דוסב לכ רבד
שבא ותעידיל ודיקפת יולימב אלו שמתשי העידיב רומאכ אלא יולימל
ודיקפת; הארוה וז הניא הלח לע יוליג שנצטווה וילע בחקירה לע יפ ןיד
וא ךילהב יטפשמ.

יתעמשמ טופיש :'ז קרפ

34. ןוירטונ אשמ תריבעב תעמשמ םא –

(1) רבע לע יללכ האתיקה תיעוצקמה יפכ ועבקנש קרפב ה';

(2) אל םייק תא הטומל וילע יפל תוארוה הז קוח ותקנותה
ושהוקנו יפל וא התרשל םויקב הטומל וילע רומאכ;

(3) השע יולימב וידיקפת ןוירטונכ הלועפ אלש היה הל דמסומ
בקוקיח;

(4) ןתנ רושיא עדיש וא היה בייח תעדל אוהש בזוכ;

(5) הבג וא שרד דעב ויתוריש רכש אוהש הלעמל ןמ עובקה
וחוכמ לש הז קוח, וא הבג וא שרד, אלל טעם קיפסמ, רכש אוהש הטמל
ןמ עובקה וחוכמ לש הז קוח;

(6) עשרוה, בישראל וא הצוחמ לה, בעבירה שיש הב םושמ
קלון.

35. ןוידה תיב ינפל אהי הז קרפ יפל תעמשמ תוריבעב ןוידה
יתעמשמה יזוחמה שהוקם יפל קוח הלשכה (ולהל – תיב ןוידה) והרכבו
ןינעל הז יכלול ינש םינוירטונ לפחות.

36. ץעויה יטפשמה לממשלה וא ונציג רשאים, ביןּ ביוזמתם ויבן
לע יפ תלונת אדם רחא, להגיש קובלנה לבית ןוידה לשב עבירת משמעת
ולהתייצב ולטעון בכל הליך יפל קרפ הז.

37. (א) הסמכויות לש תיב ןוידה וסדרי ןוידה בדיון יפל קרפ הז
יהיו כסמכויות וסדרי ןוידה בדיון יפל הקרפ הששי לחוק הלשכה, זולת
אם נקבע אחרת בחוק הז וא על פיו; כן יחולו םיפיעס 64 ו-80 לחוק
הלשכה בשינויים המחויבים.

(ב) שר המשפטים רשאי לקבוע בתקנות סדרי דין מיוחדים
להליכים יפל קרפ הז.

38. ראה תיב ןוידה שיש לערוך חיפוש כדי להבטיח הצגה לש
תעודה וא מסמך הדרושים לחקירה בעבירת משמעת וא לדיון, רשאי
הוא ליתן צו חיפוש; הצו יבוצע כדרך צו חיפוש יפל פקודת סדר הדין
הפלילי (מעצר וחיפוש) [נוסח חדש], תשכ"ט-1969.

39. (א) אלה הם אמצעי המשמעת שבית ןוידה מוסמך להטיל על
הנוטריון:

据第 54 条规定提交文件，有权接收这些文件，并且审查接收程序；

（2）设置公证员持有的公证文件的格式和具体地点，包括第 31 条规定的相关文书。

第三十三条

（一）公证员应根据本法将其必须保留的文件和他必须管理的文书交由司法部长任命的人员进行审查。

（二）审查方法由法规规定。

（三）根据本条被指定进行审查的人员应对其履行职责时所知悉的一切内容保密，除履行其职责外不得使用该等资料；本条款不适用于根据法律或法律程序进行的调查。

第七章　纪律

第三十四条　如公证员有以下情况，即属违纪行为：

（1）违反了第五章规定的职业道德规则；

（2）未履行本法规定的条例和依照条例制定的规定，或者履行职责疏忽；

（3）在履行其公证员的职责时没有获得立法授权；

（4）提供了他知道或应当知道有错误的证明；

（5）其服务的收费要求高于依照本法规定的收费，或者没有充分理由收取或者要求的收费低于依照本法规定的收费；

（6）在以色列或国外被判犯有构成道德败坏的罪行。

第三十五条　本章规定的违反纪律罪的听讯应在根据《律师法》设立的地区纪律法庭（下称“法庭”）审理，其组成至少应包括两名公证员。

第三十六条　总检察长或其代表可以自行或通过另一人的申诉向法庭提出申诉，以处理违纪行为，以及根据本章提交的任何诉讼。

第三十七条

（一）法院的审理和根据本章进行的诉讼程序应按照《律师法》第六章的规定进行听证。本法另有规定除外，《律师法》第 64 条和第 80 条也将参照适用。

（二）司法部长可根据本章规定的程序制定特别程序。

第三十八条　如果法庭认为必须进行搜查以确保在违纪行为的听证会上出示调查所需的证据或文件，可以发出搜查令；该命令将根据《刑事诉讼程序（逮捕和搜查）条例》（新版本 1964—1969）作为搜查令执行。

第三十九条

（一）这些是法庭有权对公证员施加的纪律手段：

(1) הרהזא;

(2) הפיזנ;

(3) הריבע לכל תוריל 20,000 לע הלעי אלש םוכסב סנק;

(4) לע הלעת אלש הבוצק הפוקתל ןוישרה לש ופקת תיילתה םינש שמח;

(5) ןוישרה לוטיב.

(ב) טפשמ תיב ליטהש סנק ומכ הבגיי הז ףיעס יפל לטוהש סנק ילילפ ךילהב.

40. תויוכמסה םג 39 ףיעסב רומאל ףסונב ויהי ןידה תיבל קוחל 74-ו 73 םיפיעס ולוחי ןכ ,הכשלה קוחל 69 ףיעסב תורומאה הכשלה.

41. (א) ןוירטונה ץעויהו יטפשמה הלשממל וא הציגנו גירש םיאשר לע רערעל ,יצראה יתעמשמה ןידה תיב ינפל ןידה תיב לש ןידה קספ לע ,הכשלה קוח יפל םקוהש דעומב ךרדבו םירערעמש קספ לע ןיד לש תיב הכשלה קוח יפל םיכילהב ןתינש ןידה.

(ב) לולכי הז ףיעס יפל רוערעב יצראה יתעמשמה ןידה תיב בכרה .תוחפל םינוירטונ ינש

(ג) לע קספ ןידה לש תיב ןידה יתעמשמה יצראה יפל ףיעס הז ןוירטונה ץעויהו יטפשמה הלשממל וא הציגנו גירש םיאשר תיב ינפל רערעל ןידה קספ םהל עדוהש םוימ םוי םישולש ךות םילשוריב יזוחמה טפשמה .יצראה ןידה תיב לש

(ד) (לטוב).

42. (א) תיב ןידה רשאי תועשהל ןוירטונ –

(1) שגוהש דגנו בתכ אישום תיבב טפשמ לשב עבירה תילילפ רבעש םילוית תפקידו ושבנסיבות הנעין היה הב םשמוש ןולק;

(2) שהועמד ינפלו לדין יפל חוק הז בעניו ושב עולול תיב ןידה להחליט לע תיילתה תפקו לש ןוישרה וא לע ביטולו.

(ב) השעייתו לש ןוירטונ יפל סעיף קטן (א)(1) תחא דע ספקל ןידה תיב ינפל העשרהה רבד אבוהו הרושע םאו ,טפשמה תיבב ןידו ןידה תיבל רבדה אבוה אל ;הז קוח יפל ןידה תיב לש ןידה קספל דע – ךות םישולש םוי םוימ ובש הנעש הספקה המרשיע ,סופי וא ובטולה העשרהה – הלטב השעהיה.

(ג) השעייתו לש ןוירטונ יפל סעיף קטן (א)(2) תחא דע למתן ספק ןידה תיבב ןידה.

(ד) (לטוב).

(ה) רשאי ןוירטונ לערער לע החלטת תיב ןידה להשעות ואילו היה ספק ןיד ,ועסיף 41 יחולו בשינויים המחויבים; ואלם הגשת ערעור לא תעכב את ההשעיה.

התקספהו הנוהכה םויס :'ח קרפ

43. רשונו לש ןוירטונ בטל םא נתקיימה אחת מאלה:

(1) רש םיטפשמה ביטל תא ןוישרה לע יפ תשקב ןוירטונה;

(2) ןוירטונה לדח תויהל חרזא ישראלי;

（1）警告；

（2）责备；

（3）每项罪行罚款不超过 20000 英镑；

（4）暂停执照的期限不超过 5 年；

（5）吊销执照。

（二）根据本条规定的罚款应作为法院在刑事诉讼中罚款的一部分。

第四十条 除第 39 条规定外，法庭还应具有《律师协会法》第 69 条规定的权力，《律师法》第 73 条和第 74 条也同样适用。

第四十一条

（一）公证员和总检察长或其代理人可以根据《律师法》制定的“国家纪律条例”提出对法院判决的质疑，依据律师协会的法律程序，向法院提出上诉；

（二）国家纪律法院审理根据本条提出的上诉，组成人员中应至少包括两名公证员；

（三）根据本条规定，国家纪律法庭的判决，公证员和司法部长或其代表可在收到国家劳动法院判决之日起 30 日内向耶路撒冷地区法院提出上诉；

（四）（已删除）。

第四十二条

（一）法院可暂停公证员职务：

（1）在法庭上对他提起刑事诉讼，指控他在执行公务时犯了罪，在具有案件的情况下，这构成了一种耻辱；

（2）由法院决定暂停或吊销执照的，可依法起诉。

（二）根据该条第（一）（1）款的规定，公证员的职务中止应由法院作出裁决，如果裁决将被提交至法院进行诉讼，直至法院根据本法作出判决；如果在作出最终裁决之日起 30 日内未向法院提起诉讼，或者撤销裁决，则暂停中止。

（三）根据该条第（一）（2）款暂停公证，直至法院作出判决。

（四）（已删除）。

（五）公证员可以对法院的判决提出上诉，其作出的判决暂缓执行，第 41 条应比照适用；但是，提起上诉不会延迟暂停。

第八章　服务的暂停和终止

第四十三条 如果出现以下情况之一，公证执照应予撤销：

（1）司法部长应公证员的要求吊销执照；

（2）公证员不再是以色列公民；

(3) העקפ ןידה יכרוע תכשלב ןוירטונה לש ותורבח.

44. ןוירטונ שנתקיימה וב תחא מאלה:

(1) ףיעסב רומאה חוכמ הקספוה ןידה יכרוע תכשלב ותורבח א52 קוחל הכשלה;

(2) ב52 ףיעסב רומאכ ןידה יכרוע תכשלב ותורבח תא ליבגה הכשלה קוחל;

(3) קוחל 49 ףיעס יפל ,התעשוה ןידה יכרוע תכשלב ותורבח הכשלה;

(4) הכשלה קוחל 78 ףיעס יפל תינמז העשוה;

וא תורבחה תלבגה ,הקספהה דוע לכ הלתומ ונוישר ףקות אהי תודמוע ןניעב היעשהה.

ןוירטונ תמיתח תומיא :'ט קרפ

45. (א) תונקתהו הז קוח יפל ודיקפת ףקותב ,ןוירטונ לש ותמיתח יפ לע ,תמואת ,לארשיל ץוחמ שומישל דעונה ךמסמ יבג לע ,ויפ לע ךכל ונומש הנידמה דבוע וא םולש טפשמ-תיב םשר ידיב ,ןינועמ תשקב םיטפשמה רש ידיב.

(ב) (קחמנ).

תונוש :'י קרפ

46. םיטפשמה רש יאשר עובקל תונקתב –

(1) הז קוח יפל ויתוריש דעב ןוירטונ לבקיש רכשה רועיש תא רכשמ רוטפה ירקמ תאו;

(2) םיכמסמל יזכרמה ןויכראה יתוריש דעב ומלושיש תורגאה תא םיינוירטונ.

47. ןוירטונ השמתשמה ךמסמ יבגל ותוכמסב ויעדויב ךמסמה יכ דעונ ,תיליל פהריבע עוציבל וא תיליל פהריבע ותכירעבש היה ושמש ,הריבע התואב םשאה לש ונידכ וא םינש שולש רסאמ – ונידיפל לכה ,רתוי רומחה שנועה.

48. ימ ןיאשו ךמסומ והכל ןוירטונכ ןוירטונ תויהל הזחתמו ,ונידסאמ שולש םינש. –

49. (א) ימ עשוהש הלועפה ןמ תולועפה שנתייחדו יפל ףיעס 8 ןוירטונל ילב תויהל ךמסומ לע יפ ןיד –

(1) ןיד – סנק 10,000 תוריל;

(2) ןיא וכזא לשכר דעב הלועפה ,מאו םלוש רכש – יזחר ותוא ימל שילמו.

(ב) ןעוטה שהוא ךמסומ לעשיית הלועפה ,וילע הארה.

50. בתחום לש רשות מקומית שב בית משפט שלום ואין בו ןוירטונ ,רשאי שר המשפטים למנות עובד המדינה המלא תפקיד ובאות תיב טפשמ להשתמש בסמכויות ןוירטונ ,כולן או מקצתן ,ודין פעולה של עובד המדינה שהשתמש בסמכויות אלה כדין פעולה של ןוירטונ.

（3）以色列律师协会的会员资格过期。

第四十四条　有下列其中一项的公证员，只要律师协会成员资格中断、限制或暂停执行，其许可证的有效期将被中止：

（1）根据《律师协会法》第 52 条第（一）款的规定，以色列律师协会成员资格被终止；

（2）根据《律师协会法》第 52 条第（二）款的规定，在律师协会的成员资格受到限制；

（3）根据《律师法》第 49 条的规定，在以色列律师协会的成员资格被暂停；

（4）根据《律师协会法》第 78 条的规定暂时中止。

第九章　公证员签名的验证

第四十五条

（一）根据本法及其他法律规定，公证员在以色列境外使用的文件上签字，应经过利益关系方的请求，由裁判法院司法常务官或由司法部长任命的公务员核实验证。

（二）（已删除）。

第十章　附则

第四十六条　司法部长可以通过条例来规定：

（1）公证员根据本法其服务所得到的报酬率和豁免收费的情况；

（2）公证文件的中央档案服务费用。

第四十七条　对明知该文件拟用于实施刑事犯罪或其准备实施刑事犯罪，而对文件实施公证的公证员，应判处 3 年徒刑或与指控犯处同一罪，从重处罚。

第四十八条　没资格担任公证员而伪装成公证员的人应被判处 3 年徒刑。

第四十九条

（一）未经法律授权，做了《公证法》第八条规定行为的公证员，将被：

（1）处以 10000 英镑罚款；

（2）无权获得该案的报酬，并且如果支付了报酬，应当将其退还给当事人。

（二）声称被授权执行公证行为的人，需要证据。

第五十条　在地方领域，地方法院没有公证机构，司法部长可以任命一名在该法院工作的公务员行使公证员的全部或部分权力，并且凭借这种权力行事的公务员的行为应被视为公证行为。

50א. (א) םיגיצנ םייטמולפיד םיגיצנו םיירלוסנוק לש לארשי
תועמשמכ ףיעסב 29 תדוקפל תויארה [חסונ שדח], תשל"א-1971,
םיכמסומ להשתמש בחוק-לארץ תויוכמסב תונירטו, ידו ןפועל השנעשת
ידיב ציגנ כאמור םכמוח תויוכמס אלה כדין פועל של תונירטו. ציגנ
כאמור אל ישתמש תויוכמסב תונירטו, אלא לאחר שישתתף בהשתלמות
קצרה, במתכונת שיקבע המנהל הכללי של משרד החוץ, או מי שהוא
הסמיך לכך, בהתייעצות עם ועדת הרישיונות.

(ב) על אף האמור בסעיף קטן (א) רשאי שר המשפטים, בהסכמת
שר החוץ, לקבוע בתקנות את שיעור השכר לקבל ציגנ דיפלומטי או
קונסולרי בעד שירותיו לפי חוק זה, בשינוי מהשכר שנקבע לפי סעיף
46(1); שכר כאמור ישולם לאוצר המדינה ויכול שיהא שונה במדינות
שונות הבא והבא ןייגבה ושייקבע במטבע המדינה הבא ייגבה.

51. בטלים –

(1) חוק העותמאני בדבר הנוטריון מיום 27 בזילקעדה שנת
1331 (1913);

(2) סעיף 18 לפקודת הרשמים [נוסח חדש], תשל"א-1971;

(3) חוק נוטריונים למסמכים יוצאי חוץ, תש"י-1950;

(4) חוק האגרות (נוטריון ציבורי), תשט"ז-1956;

(5) תקנות הנוטריון הציבורי מיום 4.7.1918;

אך אין בביטולם כדי להשפיע על הליכים ועל תרופות שיינקטו או
ייתנו לגבי מסמכים שנערכו לפני תחילתו של חוק זה.

52. בסעיף 29 לפקודת הראיות [נוסח חדש], תשל"א-1971,
בהגדרת "תעודה ציבורית", אחרי המלים "גוף אחר בעל סמכות
שיפוטית או מעין שיפוטית" בסקפה (2) להגדרה, יבוא "נוטריון".

53. בסעיף 22 לחוק הירושה, תשכ"ה-1965, אחרי סעיף קטן (ו)
יבוא:

"(ז) לענין סעיף זה דין נוטריון כדין שופט."

54. (א) הקום ארכיון מרכזי למסמכים נוטריוניים, ימסרו לו
למשמרת בכפוף לאמור בחוק הארכיונים, תשט"ו-1955, המסמכים
הנוטריוניים ספרי הנוטריון הציבורי שעל יד בית המשפט.

(ב) מי שלפני תחילתו של חוק זה היה כדין כנוטריון למסמכים
יוצאי חוץ, רואים אותו כאילו נתמנה נוטריון ביום תחילתו של חוק זה,
אף אם אין לו הכשירויות לפי סעיף 2.

(ג) מי שהיה נוטריון למסמכים יוצאי חוץ בתוקף לפני תחילתו של
חוק זה, ינהג בהעתקים של אישורים נוטריוניים שעליו לשמור אותה
שעה, כאילו חוק זה לא נתקבל.

(ד) חתימות על מסמכים יוצאי חוץ שנערכו כדין בידי נוטריון
למסמכים יוצאי חוץ לפני תחילתו של חוק זה, יאומתו בדרך האמורה
בפרק ט'.

(ה) מי שהיה נוטריון למסמכים יוצאי חוץ ועבר לפני תחילתו של
חוק זה עבירת משמעת לפי חוק נוטריונים למסמכים יוצאי חוץ, תש"י-
1950, יראו אותה עבירה כעבירת משמעת לפי חוק זה.

(ו) מיום ב' בסיון תשל"ו (31 במאי 1976) עד יום תחילתו

第五十一条之一 （第五十条的补充）

（一）根据《证据法令》（新版本，1971 年颁布）第 29 条的规定，以色列外交代表和领事代表有权在国外使用公证员的权力，并且该代表根据这些权力采取的行动应被视为公证员的行为；除非他参加短期培训课程，否则代表不得行使公证员的权力，培训形式由外交部总干事或由他授权的人员与许可证委员会协商确定。

（二）尽管有本条第（一）款的规定，司法部长可在外交部长的同意下，按照本法第 46 条第（一）款的规定，外交代表或领事代表根据本法提供服务而收到报酬；这种报酬应交给国库，在收取报酬的各个国家可能会有所不同，根据各个国家的规定确定。

第五十一条 取消：

（1）1331 年 8 月 27 日（1913 年）奥斯曼公证法；

（2）《注册服务机构条例》［新版］第 18 条（1971 年发行）；

（3）《外国文件公证法》（1950 年声明）；

（4）公证费用法（1916—1956）；

（5）1918 年 7 月 4 日公布的《公证条例》。

但是，它们的取消不影响本法生效前已经完成的文件的程序和补救措施。

第五十二条 在 1971 年发行的《证据法令》（新版本）第 29 条“公共证明”的定义中，在定义第二章中“具有司法或准司法权力的另一个机构”之后应插入“公证”。

第五十三条 在 1965 年《继承法》第二十二章中，在第（六）条之后，应增加以下内容：

“（七）就本条而言，公证员须被视为法官。”

第五十四条

（一）根据《档案法》（1955 年）的规定，公证文件和法院的公证文书应上交至中央档案馆以便妥善保管。

（二）在本法生效之前已经担任外国文件的公证员的，自本法施行之日起即被认定为公证员，即使他没有根据本法第 2 条规定的资格。

（三）在本法生效之前，外国文书的公证员应当以公证书复印件为准，恰如该法未被批准生效之前。

（四）在本法生效前由公证员合法准备的外国文件的签字，应按照第九章的规定进行核实。

（五）在本法生效之前，根据《公证员外国文件公证法》（1950 年），作为外国文件公证员并已认定为违法行为的应被视为本法规定的违纪行为。

（六）自本法生效之日起（1976 年 5 月 31 日），

סינוירטונ קוח יפל ןוירטונכ ןהכל ןוישר סדאל ןתניי אל הז קוח לש
תשקבב תוצלמהה תדעו ןודת אלו ,1950-י"שת ,ץוח יאצוי סיכמסמל
התצלמה תא תוצלמהה תדעו הנתנ סא אלא ,רומאכ ןוישר תלבקל סדא
סוי דע השקבה השגוה וא (1972 יאמב 30) ב"לשת ןויסב ז"י סוי דע
וינעה יפל לכה ,הז.

55. ןיקתהל יאשר אוהו הז קוח עוציב לע הנוממ סיטפשמה רש
ועוציבל עגונה לכב תונקת.

56. תומושרב ומוסרפ סוימ תחא הנש סותב הז קוח לש ותליחת,
זלות קיעס 54(ו) ותליחתש ב' סויב ןויסב ו"לשת (31 יאמב 1976).

根据《外国豁免公证法》，外国人将不被授予公证员执照而且侵权委员会不考虑其申请，除非建议委员会在 1972 年 5 月 30 日前提出建议，或者直到当天提交请求，一切视情况而定。

第五十五条 司法部长负责执行本法，并可能就其执行情况制定条例。

第五十六条：本法自公布之日一年后生效，但第五十四条第（六）款除外，该条于 1976 年 5 月 31 日星期一生效。

日本

公证员法

公証人法
明治四十一年 (1908 年) 四月十四日法律第五十三号

最終改正：平成二三年 (2011 年) 六月二四日法律第七四号

第 1 章　総則

第 1 条　公証人は当事者其の他の関係人の嘱託に因り左の事務を行ふ権限を有す

一　法律行為其の他私権に関する事実に付公正証書を作成すること

二　私署証書に認証を与ふること

三　会社法（平成 17 年法律第 86 号）第 30 条第 1 項及其の準用規定並一般社団法人及び一般財団法人に関する法律（平成 18 年法律第 48 号）第 13 条及第 155 条の規定に依り定款に認証を与ふること

四　電磁的記録（電子的方式、磁気的方式其の他人の知覚を以て認識すること能はざる方式（以下電磁的方式と称す）に依り作らるる記録にして電子計算機に依る情報処理の用に供せらるるものを謂ふ以下之に同ジ）に認証を与ふること但し公務員が職務上作成したる電磁的記録以外のものに与ふる場合に限る

第 2 条　公証人の作成したる文書又は電磁的記録は本法及他の法律の定むる要件を具備するに非されは公正の効力を有せす

第 3 条　公証人は正当の理由あるに非されは嘱託を拒むことを得す

第 4 条　公証人は法律に別段の定ある場合を除くの外其の取扱ひたる事件を漏泄することを得す但し嘱託人の同意を得たるときは此の限に在らす

公证员法
明治四十一年（1908 年）四月十四日第五十三号法令

最终修订：平成二十三年（2011 年）六月二十四日第七十四号法令

第一章　总则

第一条　公证员拥有受托为当事人或其他相关人员办理下列事务的权限：

（一）就法律行为及其他有关私权的事实出具公证书；

（二）对私署文书予以认证；

（三）根据《公司法》[平成十七年（2005 年）第八十六号法令] 第三十条第一款及其准用规定，以及《一般社团法人和一般财团法人的相关法律》[平成十八年（2006 年）第四十八号法令] 第十三条及第一百五十五条的规定对公司章程予以认证；

（四）对电磁记录 [以电子方式、磁性方式以及凭借他人知觉无法认知的方式（以下统称为“电磁方式”）制作的记录，可用于电子计算机进行情报处理] 进行认证，但限于除公务员职务上制作的电磁记录以外的记录。

第二条　公证员制作的文件及电磁记录，如不具备本法及其他法律所规定的条件，没有公证效力。

第三条　公证员无正当理由不得拒绝委托。

第四条　除法律另有规定外，公证员不得泄露所办理的案件，但经委托人同意的除外。

第５条　公証人は他の公務を兼ね、商業を営み又は商事会社若は営利を目的とする社団法人の代表者若は使用人と為ることを得す　但し法務大臣の許可を得たるときは此の限に在らす

第６条　削除

第７条　公証人は嘱託人より手数料、送達に要する料金、第 57 条の３の登記の手数料相当額（第３項に於て登記手数料と称す）、日当及旅費を受く

２　公証人は前項に記載したるものを除くの外何等の名義を以てするも其の取扱ひたる事件に関して報酬を受くることを得す

３　手数料、送達に要する料金、登記手数料、日当及旅費に関する規程は政令を以て之を定む

第７条の２　本法及他の法令に依り公証人が行ふこととせられたる電磁的記録に関する事務は法務大臣の指定したる公証人（以下指定公証人と称す）之を取扱ふ

２　前項の指定は告示して之を為す

３　第６章の規定は本法及他の法令の定むるところに依り指定公証人が行ふ電磁的記録に関する事務に付ては之を適用せず

４　本法に規定するものの外指定公証人が行ふ重磁的記録に関する事務に付ては法務省令を以て之を定む

第８条　法務局若は地方法務局又は其の支局の管轄区域内に公証人なき場合又は公証人其の職務を行ふこと能はさる場合に於ては法務大臣は当該法務局若は地方法務局又は其の支局に勤務する法務事務官をして管轄区域内に於て公証人の職務を行はしむることを得

第９条　本法及他の法令中公証人の職務に関する規定は公証人の職務を行ふ法務事務官に之を準用す　但し第７条に依る手数料、日当及旅費は国庫の収入とす

第２章　任免及所属

第 10 条　公証人は法務局又は地方法務局の所属とす

２　各法務局又は地方法務局に所属する公証人の人数は法務局若は地方法務局又は其の支局の管轄区域毎に法務大臣之を定む

第 11 条　公証人は法務大臣之を任し及其の属すへき法務局又は地方法務局を指定す

第 12 条　左の条件を具備する者に非されは公証人に任せらるることを得す

一　日本国民にして成年者たること

第五条　公证员不得兼任其他公务，经营商业或作为商事公司、以营利为目的的社团法人的代表人或雇员，但得到法务大臣许可的除外。

第六条　删除。

第七条　公证员向委托人收取手续费、邮寄费、第五十七条之三所述登记手续费用相当的款项（第三款所称登记手续费）、日薪及旅费。

公证员除前款记载的费用外，不得以任何名义，就其办理的案件收受报酬。

手续费、邮寄费、登记手续费、日薪及旅费的有关规程由政令加以规定。

第七条之二　依照本法及其他法令公证员所从事的电磁记录相关认证事务，由法务大臣指定的公证员进行。

前款指定需予以公告。

第六章的规定不适用于依照本法及其他法令公证员所从事的电磁记录相关认证事务。

本法规定之外的指定公证员所从事的电磁记录相关事务由法务省令加以规定。

第八条　在法务局或地方法务局及其支局管辖区域内，如无公证员或公证员不能执行其职务时，法务大臣可指定在该法务局或地方法务局及其支局工作的法务事务官，在其管辖区域内执行公证员的职务。

第九条　本法及其他法令中有关公证员职务的规定适用于执行公证员职务的法务事务官，但根据第七条收取的手续费、日薪及旅费应作为国库收入。

第二章　任免及隶属

第十条　公证员隶属于法务局或地方法务局。

隶属于各法务局或地方法务局的公证员的人数，由法务大臣根据法务局或地方法务局及其支局管辖区域的情况而分别规定。

第十一条　公证员由法务大臣任命并指定其所隶属的法务局或地方法务局。

第十二条　不具备下列条件的，不得任命为公证员：

（一）成年的日本国民；

二　一定の試験に合格したる後６月以上公証人見習として実地修習を為したること

２　試験及実地修習に関する規程は法務大臣之を定む

第 13 条　裁判官（簡易裁判所判事を除く）、検察官（副検事を除く）又は弁護士たるの資格を有する者は試験及実地修習を経すして公証人に任せらるることを得

第 13 条の２　法務大臣は当分の間多年法務に携はり前条の者に準する学識経験を有する者にして政令を以て定むる審議会等（国家行政組織法（昭和 23 年法律第 120 号）第８条に定むる機関を謂ふ）の選考を経たる者を試験及実地修習を経すして公証人に任することを得　但し第８条に規定する場合に限る

第 14 条　左に掲くる者は公証人に任せらるることを得す

一　禁錮以上の刑に処せられたる者但し２年以下の禁錮に処せられたる者にして刑の執行を終り又は其の執行を受くることなきに至りたるときは此の限に在らす

二　破産手続開始の決定を受け復権せさる者

三　罷免の裁判を受けたる者、懲戒の処分に因り免官若は免職せられたる者又は弁護士法に依り除名せられたる者にして罷免、免官、免職又は除名後２年を経過せさる者

第 15 条　法務大臣は左の場合に於て公証人を免することを得

一　公証人免職を願出てたるとき

二　公証人期間内に身元保証金又は其の補充額を納めさるとき

三　公証人年齢 70 歳に達したるとき

四　公証人身体又は精神の衰弱に因り其の職務を執ること能はさるに至りたるとき

２　前項第４号の場合に於ては第 13 条の２の政令を以て定むる審議会の議決を経へし

第 16 条　公証人第 14 条第１号又は第２号に該当するに至りたるときは当然其の職を失ふ

第 3 章　職務執行に関する通則

第 17 条　公証人の職務執行の区域は其の所属する法務局又は地方法務局の管轄区域に依る

第 18 条　公証人は法務大臣の指定したる地に其の役場を設くへし

２　公証人は役場に於て其の職務を行ふことを要す但し事件の性質か之を許ささる場合又は法令に

（二）经一定的考试合格后，在实地进行六个月以上的公证员实习。

考试及实地实习的有关规程由法务大臣加以制定。

第十三条　法官（简易法院的判事除外）、检察官（副检事除外）或具有律师资格者可以不经考试及实地见习而被任命为公证员。

第十三条之二　最近多年从事法务，具有前条所述人员的学识经验，并经政令规定的审议会｛《国家行政组织法》［昭和二十三年（1948 年）第一百二十号法令］第八条规定的机关称谓｝选考者，可以不经考试及实地见习，由法务大臣任命为公证员，但仅限于第八条所规定的情形。

第十四条　下列人员不得被任命为公证员：

（一）被判处监禁以上刑罚的，但被判处二年以下监禁且刑期已满，或未被执行的除外；

（二）被宣告破产程序开始尚未复权的；

（三）受到罢免裁判，因惩戒处分被免官或免职，根据《律师法》被除名的，其被罢免、免官、免职或除名后不满两年的。

第十五条　下列情形下，法务大臣可以免去公证员职务：

（一）公证员提出辞呈时；

（二）担任公证员期间不交纳身份保证金或补充金额时；

（三）公证员年满七十岁时；

（四）公证员因身体或精神衰弱不能履行职务时。

前款第（四）项的情形需经第十三条之二中政令所规定的审议会议决。

第十六条　符合《公证法》第十四条第（一）款或第（二）款的情形时，公证员当然丧失其职务。

第三章　关于执行职务的通则

第十七条　公证员执行职务的区域为其隶属的法务局或地方法务局的管辖区域。

第十八条　公证员应在法务大臣指定的地点设立事务所。

公证员应在事务所内执行职务，但事件性质不允许或法令另有规定的情形除外。

別段の定ある場合は此の限に在らす

第 19 条 公証人は任命の辞令書を受けたる日より 15 日以内に其の所属する法務局又は地方法務局に身元保証金を納むへし

2 身元保証金の額は政令を以て之を定む

3 身元保証金の額に不足を生し補充の命令を受けたるときは其の命令を受けたる日より 30 日以内に其の不足額を補充すへし

4 公証人身元保証金を納めさる間は其の職務を行ふことを得す

第 20 条 身元保証金を還付すへき場合に於ては其の身元保証金の上に権利を有する者に対し 6 月を下らさる期間内に申出つへき旨を公告すへし

2 身元保証金は前項の期間を経過するに非されは之を還付せす

3 身元保証金は他の公課及債権に先チて之を第 1 項の公告費用に充つ

第 21 条 公証人は其の職印の印鑑に氏名を自署し之を其の所属する法務局又は地方法務局に差出すへし

2 公証人前項の印鑑を差出ささる間は其の職務を行ふことを得す

第 22 条 公証人は左の場合に於て其の職務を行ふことを得す

一 嘱託人、其の代理人又は嘱託せられたる事項に付利害の関係を有する者の配偶者、4 親等内の親族又は同居の親族たるとき親族関係か止みたる後亦同し

二 嘱託人又は其の代理人の法定代理人、保佐人又は補助人たるとき

三 嘱託せられたる事項に付利害の関係を有するとき

四 嘱託せられたる事項に付代理人若は輔佐人たるとき又は代理人若は輔佐人たりしとき

第 23 条 公証人職務上署名するときは其の職名、所属及役場所在地を記載すへし

第 24 条 公証人は其の所属する法務局又は地方法務局の長の認可を受けて書記を置き執務の補助を為さしむることを得

2 前項の認可は必要なる場合に於ては何時にても之を取消すことを得

第 25 条 公証人の作成したる証書の原本及其の附属書類、第 58 条の 2 第 4 項の規定に依り公証人の保存する証書及其の附属書類、第 62 条の 3 第 3 項の規定に依り公証人の保存する定款及其の附属書類並法令に依り公証人の調製したる帳簿は事変を避くる為にする場合を除くの外之を役場外に持出す

第十九条 公证员须在收到任命书十五日内，向其隶属的法务局或地方法务局交纳身份保证金。

身份保证金的数额由政令规定。

因身份保证金交纳不足，而接到补交命令时，应在接到命令之日起三十日内补足。

未交纳公证员身份保证金期间不得执行职务。

第二十条 在应当退还身份保证金时，应向对身份保证金拥有权利的人发出公告，命其在不少于六个月的期间内提出申请。

未满前款期间的，不得退还身份保证金。

身份保证金应优先于其他由政府征收的费用及债权，而用于第一款所述公告费。

第二十一条 公证员须向隶属的法务局或地方法务局提交其职务印鉴及亲笔签名。

公证员在未提交前款印鉴期间，不得执行职务。

第二十二条 下列情形下公证员不得执行其职务：

（一）公证员是委托人或其代理人或与受委托事项有利害关系人的配偶、四亲等内的亲属或同居的亲属（亲属关系终止后亦同）；

（二）公证员是委托人或其代理人的法定代理人、保佐人或辅助人时；

（三）公证员与受委托事项有利害关系时；

（四）公证员是或曾经是受委托事项的代理人或辅佐人时。

第二十三条 公证员因职务需要署名时，须记明其职称、隶属及事务所所在地。

第二十四条 公证员在隶属的法务局或地方法务局局长的认可下，可设置书记员以辅助其执行职务。

前款认可，在必要时可随时撤销。

第二十五条 公证员出具公证书的原本及附属文件、依据第五十八条之二第四款的规定由公证员保存的公证书及附属文件、依据第六十二条之三第三款的规定由公证员保存的公司章程及附属文件以及公证员依据法令制作的账簿，除为躲避意外事件外，不得带出事务所，但在法院有命令或委托时除外。

ことを得す　但し裁判所の命令又は嘱託ありたるときは此の限に在らす

２　前項の書類の保存及廃毀に関する規程は法務大臣之を定む

有关前款文件的保存和销毁规程，由法务大臣制定。

第4章　証書の作成

第四章　公证书的出具

第26条　公証人は法令に違反したる事項、無効の法律行為及行為能力の制限に因りて取得すことを得へき法律行為に付証書を作成することを得す

第二十六条　对违反法令的事项、无效法律行为及因行为能力欠缺需要撤销的法律行为，公证员不得出具公证书。

第27条　公証人は日本語を用ウる証書に非されは之を作成することを得す

第二十七条　公证员不得使用日语以外的语言出具公证书。

第28条　公証人証書を作成するには嘱託人の氏名を知り且之と面識あることを要す

第二十八条　公证员出具公证书时，须了解委托人的姓名并与其认识。

２　公証人嘱託人の氏名を知らす又は之と面識なきときは官公署の作成したる印鑑証明書の提出其の他之に準すへき確実なる方法に依り其の人違なきことを証明せしむることを要す

公证员不知道委托人的姓名或与其并不认识时，须令其提交官方机关出具的盖有印鉴的证明，或通过其他类似可靠方法，证明确为此人无误。

３　急迫なる場合に於て公証人証書を作成するときは前項の手続は証書を作成したる後３日内に証書の作成に関する規定に依り之を為すことを得

公证员在紧急状况下出具公证书时，可在公证书作成后三日内，依照出具公证书的有关规定，履行前款手续。

４　前項の手続を為したるときは証書は急迫なる場合に非さるか為其の効力を妨けらるることなし

在完成前款手续后，公证书的效力不因其情况并不紧急而受到影响。

第29条　嘱託人日本語を解せさる場合又は聾者若は唖者其の他言語を発すること能はさる者にして文字を解せさる場合に於て公証人証書を作成するには通事を立会はしむることを要す

第二十九条　如委托人不懂日语或是聋哑人，或是其他不能说话、不通文字的人，公证员出具公证书时须有翻译在场。

第30条　嘱託人盲者なる場合又は文字を解せさる場合に於て公証人証書を作成するには立会人を立会はしむることを要す

第三十条　如委托人是盲人或不通文字的人，公证员出具公证书时须有见证人在场。

２　前項の規定は嘱託人立会人を立会はしむることを請求したる場合に之を準用す

前款规定适用于委托人要求见证人在场的情形。

第31条　代理人に依り嘱託せられたる場合に於ては前３条の規定は其の代理人に之を適用す

第三十一条　受代理人委托时，前三条的规定适用于该代理人。

第32条　代理人に依り嘱託せられたる場合に於て公証人証書を作成するには其の代理人の権限を証すへき証書を提出せしめ其の権限を証明せしむることを要す

第三十二条　公证员受代理人委托出具公证书时，须要求其提供代理人代理权限证明。

２　前項の証書か認証を受けさる私署証書なるときは其の証書の外官公署の作成したる印鑑又は署名に関する証明書を提出せしめ証書の真正なることを証明せしむることを要す　但し当該公証人の保存する書類に依り証書の真正なること明なる場合は此の限に在らす

前款公证书如为未经认证的私署文书，为证明该私署文书确实无误，除文书外还须令其提供由官方机关制作的关于印鉴或署名的证明，但根据该公证员所保存的文件足以证明该文书确实无误的除外。

３　証書の作成に関する規定に依り代理又は其の方式の欠缺を追完したるときは証書は其の欠缺ありたるか為効力を妨けらるることなし

根据出具公证书的有关规定，代理或其代理方式的瑕疵已得到弥补时，公证书的效力并不因其曾有过瑕疵而受到影响。

第33条　第三者の許可又は同意を要すへき法律行為に付公証人証書を作成するには其の許可又は同意ありたることを証すへき証書を提出せしめ其の許可又は同意を証明せしむることを要す

2　前条第2項及第3項の規定は前項の場合に之を準用す

第34条　通事及立会人は嘱託人又は其の代理人之を選定することを要す

2　立会人は通事を兼ぬることを得

3　左に掲くる者は立会人たることを得す　但し第30条第2項の場合は此の限に在らす

一　未成年者

二　第14条に掲けたる者

三　自ら署名すること能はさる者

四　嘱託事項に付利害の関係を有する者

五　嘱託事項に付代理人若は輔佐人たる者又は代理人若は輔佐人たりし者

六　公証人又は嘱託人若は其の代理人の配偶者、四親等内の親族、法定代理人、保佐人、補助人、雇人又は同居人

七　公証人の書記

第35条　公証人証書を作成するには其の聴取したる陳述、其の目撃したる状況其の他自ら実験したる事実を録取し且其の実験の方法を記載して之を為すことを要す

第36条　公証人の作成する証書には其の本旨の外左の事項を記載することを要す

一　証書の番号

二　嘱託人の住所、職業、氏名及年齢若法人なるときは其の名称及事務所

三　代理人に依り嘱託せられたるときは其の旨並其の代理人の住所、職業、氏名及年齢

四　嘱託人又は其の代理人の氏名を知り且之と面識あるときは其の旨

五　第三者の許可又は同意ありたるときは其の旨及其の事由並其の第三者の住所、職業、氏名及年齢若法人なるときは其の名称及事務所

六　印鑑証明書の提出其の他之に準すへき確実なる方法に依り人違なきことを証明せしめ又は印鑑若は署名に関する証明書を提出せしめて証書の真正なることを証明せしめたるときは其の旨及其の事由

七　第32条第2項但書の場合は其の旨及其の事由

八　急迫なる場合に於て人違なきことを証明せしめさりしときは其の旨

九　通事又は立会人を立会はしめたるときは其の旨及其の事由並其の通事又は立会人の住所、職

第三十三条　公证员就需要得到第三人许可或同意的法律行为出具公证书时，为证明已得到其许可或同意，须令委托人提交已经得到其许可或同意的证明。

前条第二款及第三款的规定适用于前款的情形。

第三十四条　翻译及见证人须由委托人或其代理人选定。

见证人可兼任翻译。

下列人员不得担任见证人（但第三十条第二款的情形除外）

（一）未成年人；

（二）第十四条所述人员；

（三）不能自己签名的；

（四）同委托事项有利害关系的；

（五）是或曾经是委托事项的代理人或辅佐人的；

（六）公证员或委托人或其代理人的配偶、四亲等内的亲属、法定代理人、保佐人、辅助人、雇用人或同居人；

（七）公证员的书记员。

第三十五条　公证员出具公证书须记录其听取的陈述、其目击的状况以及其亲身体验到的事实，并载明其考察的方法。

第三十六条　公证员出具的公证书除主要内容外，还应记明下列事项：

（一）公证书的编号；

（二）委托人的住所、职业、姓名和年龄，（委托人是法人时）法人的名称及办事处；

（三）代理人委托时的情况以及该代理人的住所、职业、姓名和年龄；

（四）了解委托人或其代理人的姓名，并与其相识的情况；

（五）得到第三人的许可或同意的情况及其事由以及第三人的住所、职业、姓名及年龄，（第三人是法人时）法人的名称及办事处；

（六）使之提供印鉴证明或通过其他类似的可靠方法证明其人无误，或使之提供关于印鉴或署名的证明以证明文书确实无误的情况及其事由；

（七）符合第三十二条第二款但书规定的情况及其事由；

（八）紧急情况下未使之证明其人确实无误的情况及其事由；

（九）使翻译或见证人在场的情况及其事由，以及翻译、见证人的住所、职业、姓名及年龄；

業、氏名及年齢

十　作成の年月日及場所

第 37 条　公証人証書を作成するには普通平易の語を用ヰ字画を明瞭ならしむへし

2　接続すへき字行に空白あるときは墨線を以て之を接続せしむへし

3　数量、年月日及番号を記載するには壱弐参拾の字を用ウへし

第 38 条　証書の文字は之を改竄することを得す

2　証書に文字を挿入するときは其の字数及其の箇所を欄外又は末尾の余白に記載し公証人及嘱託人又は其の代理人之に捺印することを要す

3　証書の文字を削除するときは其の文字は尚明に読得へき為字体を存し削除したる字数及箇所を欄外又は末尾の余白に記載し公証人及嘱託人又は其の代理人之に捺印することを要す

4　前３項の規定に違反して為したる訂正は其の効力を有せす

第 39 条　公証人は其の作成したる証書を列席者に読聞かせ又は閲覧せしめ嘱託人又は其の代理人の承認を得且其の旨を証書に記載することを要す

2　通事を立会はしめたる場合に於ては前項の外通事をして証書の趣旨を通訳せしめ且其の旨を証書に記載することを要す

3　前２項の記載を為したるときは公証人及列席者各自証書に署名捺印することを要す

4　列席者にして署名すること能はさる者あるときは其の旨を証書に記載し公証人之に捺印することを要す

5　証書数葉に渉るときは公証人は毎葉の綴目に契印を為すことを要す

第 40 条　公証人の作成する証書に他の書面を引用し且之を其の証書に添附するときは公証人其の証書と添附書面との綴目に契印を為すことを要す

2　前３条の規定は前項の添附書面に之を準用す

3　前２項に依る添附書面は公証人の作成したる証書の一部と看做す

第 41 条　代理人の権限を証すへき証書、官公署の証明書、第三者の許可又は同意を証すへき証書其の他の附属書類は公証人の作成したる証書に之を連綴すへし　但し嘱託人より附属書類の原本の還付を請求したるときは其の謄本を原本に代へて連綴することを得

2　公証人は証書と其の附属書類との綴目及附属書類相互の綴目に契印を為すへし

第 42 条　証書の原本滅失したるときは公証人

（十）出具的年月日及地点。

第三十七条　公证员在出具公证书时须使用通俗易懂的语言，笔画清晰明了。

在需要连接的字行间留有空白时，须用墨线连接。

记载数量、年月日及编号时须用壹贰叁拾等字样。

第三十八条　公证书上的文字不得涂改。

增补公证书的文字，应将其字数及位置记载在栏外或末尾空白处，并加盖公证员及委托人或其代理人的印章。

删减公证书的文字，应原处保留该文字，使人可以明白读出。应将删减的字数及位置记载在栏外或末尾空白处，并加盖公证员及委托人或其代理人的印章。

违反前三款规定所作的修改无效。

第三十九条　公证员应将其出具的公证书向列席人宣读或交其阅读，经委托人或其代理人承认后，将该情况记入公证书。

翻译在场的情况下，除前款规定外，还须让翻译人员翻译公证书的内容，并将该情况写入公证书。

记载前两款情况时，应由公证员及列席人各自在公证书上签名盖章。

列席人如不能签名，须在公证书中写明，并由公证员盖章。

公证书有多页时，公证员须在每一页的装订处加盖骑缝章。

第四十条　公证员出具的公证书引用其他文件作为其公证书的附件时，公证员须在公证书和附件的装订处加盖骑缝章。

前三条的规定适用于前款的附件。

依据前两款制作的附件视为公证员所出具公证书的一部分。

第四十一条　代理人权限证明、官方机关的证明文书、证明已经第三人许可或同意的文书及其他附属文件应同公证员出具的公证书连缀，但委托人请求退回附属文件的原件时，可连缀抄本以代替原件。

公证员须在公证书和其附属文件的装订处及附属文件的相互装订处加盖骑缝章。

第四十二条　公证书的原件丢失时，公证员可收

は既に交付したる証書の正本又は謄本を徴し其の所属する法務局又は地方法務局の長の認可を受け滅失したる証書に代へて之を保存することを要す

2　前項の証書には其の所属する法務局又は地方法務局の長の認可を受け滅失したる証書に代へて之を保存する旨及其の認可の年月日を記載し公証人之に署名捺印することを要す

第 43 条　公証人は嘱託人をして印紙税法に依り証書の原本に印紙を貼用せしむへし

第 44 条　嘱託人、其の承継人又は証書の趣旨に付法律上利害の関係を有することを証明したる者は証書の原本の閲覧を請求することを得

2　第 28 条第 1 項及第 2 項、第 31 条並第 32 条第 1 項の規定は前項に依り公証人証書の原本を閲覧せしむへき場合に之を準用す

3　公証人嘱託人の承継人に証書の原本を閲覧せしむへき場合に於ては承継人たることを証すへき証書を提出せしめ其の承継人たることを証明せしむへし

4　検察官は何時にても証書の原本の閲覧を請求することを得

第 45 条　公証人は証書原簿を調製すへし

第 46 条　証書原簿には証書の作成毎に進行の順序を遂ひ左の事項を記入すへし

一　証書の番号及種類

二　嘱託人の氏名若法人なるときは其の名称

三　作成の年月日

2　前項の規定は証書の作成を記入すへき帳簿に関し法令に別段の定ある場合に之を適用せす

第 47 条　嘱託人又は其の承継人は証書の正本の交付を請求することを得

2　第 28 条第 1 項及第 2 項、第 31 条、第 32 条第 1 項及第 2 項並第 44 条第 3 項の規定は前項に依り公証人証書の正本を作成すへき場合に之を準用す

3　第 32 条第 2 項の規定は嘱託人の承継人か証書の正本の交付を請求する場合に提出すへき証書に之を準用す

第 48 条　証書の正本には左の事項を記載し公証人之に署名捺印することを要す

一　証書の全文

二　正本たること

三　交付を請求したる者の氏名

四　作成の年月日及場所

2　前項の規定に違反するものは証書の正本たるの効力を有せす

回已经提交的公证书正本或抄本，经其隶属的法务局或地方法务局局长许可后加以保存，以代替丢失的公证书。

前款公证书须写明已经所属法务局或地方法务局局长许可，可以保存以代替丢失的公证书，并写明征得许可的年月日，由公证员签名盖章。

第四十三条　公证员应让委托人依照印花税法在公证书原件上粘贴印花。

第四十四条　委托人及其继承人，或已证明同公证书内容在法律上有利害关系的人，可要求阅读公证书原件。

第二十八条第一款及第二款、第三十一条及第三十二条第一款的规定适用于根据前款阅读公证员公证书原件的情况。

公证员让委托人的继承人阅读公证书原件时，应让继承人提供其继承人身份证明。

检察官有权随时要求阅读公证书原件。

第四十五条　公证员应当编制公证书簿册。

第四十六条　公证书簿册须按照公证书制作的顺序逐一记明下列事项：

（一）公证书的编号及种类；

（二）委托人的姓名，（委托人是法人时）法人的名称；

（三）制作的年月日。

有关记载公证书制作情况的簿册，法令另有规定时前款规定不再使用。

第四十七条　委托人或其继承人可要求交付公证书的正本。

第二十八条第一款及第二款、第三十一条、第三十二条第一款及第二款、第四十四条第三款的规定适用于依前款出具公证书正本的情况。

第三十二条第二款的规定，适用于委托人的继承人要求交付公证书正本时必须提交的文书。

第四十八条　公证书的正本须记明下列事项，并由公证员签名盖章：

（一）公证书全文；

（二）本文件系正本；

（三）要求交付正本者的姓名；

（四）制作的年月日及地点。

违反前款规定时，公证书正本失去效力。

第 49 条　数事件を列記する証書又は数人各自に関係を異にする証書に付ては有用の部分及証書の方式に関する記載を抄録して其の正本を作成することを得

２　前項の正本には抄録正本たることを記載し前条第１項第２号の記載に代ふることを要す

第 50 条　公証人証書の正本を交付したるときは其の証書の末尾に嘱託人又は其の承継人何某の為正本を交付したる旨及其の交付の年月日を記載し之に署名捺印すへし

第 51 条　嘱託人、其の承継人又は証書の趣旨に付法律上利害の関係を有することを証明したる者は証書又は其の附属書類の謄本の交付を請求することを得

２　第 28 条第１項及第２項、第 31 条、第 32 条第１項並第 44 条第３項の規定は前項に依り公証人証書の謄本を作成すへき場合に之を準用す

第 52 条　証書の謄本には左の事項を記載し公証人之に署名捺印すへし

一　証書の全文

二　謄本たること

三　作成の年月日及場所

第 53 条　証書の謄本は其の一部に付之を作成することを得

２　前項の謄本には抄録謄本たることを記載すへし

第 54 条　前２条の規定は証書の附属書類の謄本の作成に之を準用す

第 55 条　証書の正本若は謄本又は其の附属書類の謄本を請求する者は之に記載すへき事項を自ら記載し公証人の署名捺印のみを請求することを得

２　公証人前項の正本又は謄本に署名捺印したるときは其の正本又は謄本は公証人自ら之を作成したると同一の効力を有す

第 56 条　証書の正本若は謄本又は其の附属書類の謄本数葉に渉るときは公証人は毎葉の綴目に契印を為すへし

２　第 37 条及第 38 条の規定は証書の正本及謄本並其の附属書類の謄本の作成に之を準用す

第 57 条　第 18 条第２項の規定は公証人遺言書を作成する場合に、第 28 条乃至第 32 条の規定は公証人拒絶証書を作成する場合に之を適用せす

第 57 条の２　民事執行法（昭和 54 年法律第４号）第 22 条第５号に掲ぐる債務名義に付ては其の正本若は謄本又は同法第 29 条後段の執行文及文書の謄本の送達は郵便又は最高裁判所規則の定むる方法に依る

第四十九条　关于记载数个事件的公证书或几个人各自拥有不同关系的公证书，可以抄录其有用部分及关于公证书方式的有关记载制作正本。

前款正本应写明本件系抄录正本，并取代前条第一款第（二）项的记载。

第五十条　交付公证员公证书正本时，应在该公证书结尾处写明已将正本交给委托人或其继承人某某，以及交付的年月日，并签名盖章。

第五十一条　委托人、其继承人或能够证明同公证书内容在法律上有利害关系的人，可以要求交付公证书或其附属文件的抄本。

第二十八条第一款及第二款、第三十一条、第三十二条第一款及第四十四条第三款的规定适用于依前款出具公证书抄本的情况。

第五十二条　公证书的抄本须记明下列事项，并由公证员签名盖章：

（一）公证书全文；

（二）本文件系抄本；

（三）制作的年月日及地点。

第五十三条　公证书的抄本可以只制作一部分。

前款抄本应注明系摘录抄本。

第五十四条　前两条的规定适用于出具公证书附属文件的抄本。

第五十五条　请求交付公证书正本、抄本或其附属文件的抄本者，可以自行记载必须记明的事项，只要求公证员签名盖章。

公证员在前款正本或抄本上签名盖章后，其正本或抄本同公证员亲自制作的文件具有同等效力。

第五十六条　如公证书的正本或抄本或其附属文件的抄本有数页时，公证员须在每页的装订处加盖骑缝章。

第三十七条及第三十八条的规定，适用于出具公证书正本、抄本及其附属文件抄本。

第五十七条　第十八条第二款的规定不适用于公证员制作的遗嘱，第二十八条至第三十二条的规定不适用于公证员制作的拒绝公证书。

第五十七条之二　《民事执行法》［昭和五十四年（1979 年）第四号法令］第二十二条第五款所述债务名义的正本或抄本，或该法第二十九条后半段执行文书及其抄本的送达，可通过邮寄或按最高法院规则规定的办法进行。

2　郵便に依る送達は申立に因り公証人之を為す

3　民事訴訟法（平成8年法律第109号）第99条第2項、第101条乃至第103条、第105条、第106条、第107条第1項及第3項並第109条の規定は前項の場合に之を準用す

第57条の3　公証人任意後見契約に関する法律（平成11年法律第150号）第3条に規定する証書を作成したるときは登記所に任意後見契約の登記を嘱託することを要す

2　前項の登記の嘱託書には証書の謄本を添付することを要す

第5章　認　証

第58条　公証人私署証書に認証を与ふるには当事者其の面前に於て証書に署名若は捺印したるとき又は証書の署名若は捺印を自認したるとき其の旨を記載して之を為すことを要す

2　私署証書の謄本に認証を与ふるには証書と対照し其の符合することを認めたるとき其の旨を記載して之を為すことを要す

3　私署証書に文字の挿入、削除、改竄、欄外の記載其の他の訂正あるとき又は破損若は外見上著く疑ふへき点あるときは其の状況を認証文に記載することを要す

第58条の2　公証人私署証書に認証を与ふる場合に於て当事者其の面前に於て証書の記載の真実なることを宣誓したる上証書に署名若は捺印し又は証書の署名若は捺印を自認したるときは其の旨を記載して之を為すことを要す

2　前項の認証の嘱託は証書2通を提出して之を為すことを要す

3　第1項の認証の嘱託は代理人に依りて之を為すことを得ず

4　公証人は第1項の規定に依る記載を為したる証書の中1通を自ら保存し他の1通を嘱託人に還付することを要す

第59条　認証を与ふへき証書には登簿番号、認証の年月日及其の場所を記載し公証人及立会人之に署名捺印し且公証人其の証書と認証簿とに契印を為すことを要す　此場合に於て嘱託人の申立あるときは第36条第4号及第6号乃至第8号に掲ぐる事項を記載することを要す

第60条　第26条乃至第34条、第37条、第38条及第39条第5項の規定は私署証書に認証を与ふる場合に之を準用す

邮寄送达，根据申请由公证员办理。

《民事诉讼法》[平成八年（1996年）第一百零八号法令]第九十九条第二款、第一百零一条至第一百零三条、第一百零五条、第一百零六条、第一百零七条第一款及第三款，以及第一百零九条的规定适用于前款所述情形。

第五十七条之三　公证员在依据委托代理合同的相关法律出具公证书时，须委托登记所进行委托代理合同的登记。

前款登记的委托书须添加公证书的抄本。

第五章　认证

第五十八条　公证员对私署文书予以认证时，如当事人当面于公证书上签名或盖章或自认对公证书签名或盖章，应记明这一情况。

对私署文书的抄本予以认证时，在对照私署文书确认无误后，应记明这一情况。

私署文书中如有文字的增补、删减、涂改、栏外记载或其他订正，或有破损或外观上的明显疑点时，须在认证文书上记明这一情况。

第五十八条之二　公证员对私署文书予以认证时，如当事人当面对证书记载的真实性宣誓后于证书上签名或盖章，或自认对证书签名或盖章，应记明这一情况。

前款认证的委托须提交两份证书。

第一款认证不得委托代理人代办。

对于第一款所规定的记明（签字或盖章情况的）证书，须一份由公证员自己保存，一份交还委托人。

第五十九条　应当予以认证的文书，应记明登记编号、认证年月日及地点，由公证员及见证人签名盖章，并由公证员在其公证书及认证簿上加盖骑缝章。此情形下委托人申请时须记明第三十六条第（四）项及第（六）项至第（八）项所载事项。

第六十条　第二十六条至第三十四条、第三十七条、第三十八条及第三十九条第五款的规定，适用于对私署文书予以认证的情形。

第60条の2　官公署の証明書、第三者の許可又は同意を証すべき証書其の他の附属書類は第58条の2第4項の規定に依り公証人の保有する証書に之を連綴すべし

2　第41条第1項但書及第2項の規定は前項の場合に之を準用す

第60条の3　第58条の2第4項の規定に依りて保存する証書滅失したるときは公証人は嘱託人に還付したる証書に依りて謄本を作成し又は既に交付したる証書の謄本を徴し其の所属する法務局又は地方法務局の長の認可を受け滅失したる証書に代へて之を保有することを要す

2　第42条第2項の規定は前項の場合に之を準用す

第60条の4　第44条及第51条乃至第56条の規定は第58条の2第4項の規定に依り公証人の保存する証書及其の附属書類に之を準用す

第60条の5　証書の記載が虚偽なることを知りて第58条の2第1項に規定する宣誓を為したる者は10万円以下の過料に処す

第61条　公証人は認証簿を調製すへし

第62条　認証簿には認証を与ふる毎に進行の順序を逐ひ左の事項を記入すへし

一　登録番号

二　嘱託人の住所及氏名若法人なるときは其の名称及事務所

三　証書の種類及署名捺印者

四　認証の方法

五　立会人の住所及氏名

六　認証の年月日

第62条の2　会社法第30条第1項及其の準用規定並一般社団法人及び一般財団法人に関する法律第13条及第155条の規定に依る定款の認証の事務は法人の本店又は主たる事務所の所在地を管轄する法務局又は地方法務局の所属公証人之を取扱ふ

第62条の3　前条の定款（其の定款が電磁的記録を以て作られたる場合に於ける其の電磁的記録を除く以下之に同ジ）の認証の嘱託は定款2通を提出して之を為すことを要す

2　公証人前条の定款の認証を与ふるには嘱託人をして其の面前に於て定款各通に付其の署名又は記名捺印を自認せしめ其の旨を之に記載することを要す

3　公証人は前項の記載を為したる定款の中1通を自ら保存し他の1通を嘱託人に還付することを要す

第六十条之二　官方机关的证明文书、证明已经第三人许可或同意的文书及其他附属文件应依据第五十八条之二第四款的规定同公证员保存的公证书连缀。

第四十一条第一款但书及第二款的规定适用于前款之情形。

第六十条之三　依据第五十八条之二第四款的规定保存的公证书灭失时，须由公证员根据交还委托人的公证书制作抄本，或征收其已交付公证书的抄本，经由其隶属的法务局或地方法务局局长的许可后代替已灭失公证书加以保存。

第四十二条第二款的规定适用于前款之情形。

第六十条之四　第四十四条及第五十一条至第五十六条的规定，适用于依据第五十八条之二第四款规定的公证员保存的公证书及附属文件。

第六十条之五　明知文书记载事项虚假仍进行第五十八条之二第一款规定的宣誓的，处十万日元以下罚款。

第六十一条　公证员须制作认证簿。

第六十二条　认证簿须按照认证的顺序逐一记明以下事项：

（一）登记编号；

（二）委托人的住所及姓名，（委托人是法人时）法人的名称及办事处；

（三）文书的种类及签名盖章人；

（四）认证方法；

（五）见证人的住所及姓名；

（六）认证的年月日。

第六十二条之二　根据《公司法》第三十条第一款及其准用规定，以及《一般社团法人和一般财团法人相关法律》第十三条及第一百五十五条规定的公司章程的认证事务，应由法人总部或主要办事机构所在地的主管法务局或地方法务局所属的公证员进行。

第六十二条之三　委托认证前条事务，须提交公司章程两份（公司章程是以电磁记录的方式制作的情形除外，下述规定亦同）。

公证员对前条的公司章程予以认证时，须使委托人当面确认其在每一份章程上签字或记名盖章，并记明这一情况。

对于前款所载的公司章程，一份由公证员自行保存，另一份交还委托人。

4 第58条第3項、第59条、第60条、第61条及第62条の規定は第2項の場合に之を準用す

第五十八条第三款、第五十九条至第六十二条的规定适用于第二款的情形。

第62条の4 代理人の権限を証すへき証書、官公署の証明書、第三者の許可又は同意を証すへき証書其の他の附属書類は前条第3項の規定に依り公証人の保存する定款に之を連綴すへし

第六十二条之四 代理人权限证明、官方机关的证明文书、证明已经第三人许可或同意的文书及其他附属文件应与依据前条第三款的规定与公证员保存的公司章程连缀。

2 第41条第1項但書及第2項の規定は前項の場合に之を準用す

第四十一条第一款但书及第二款的规定适用于前款之情形。

第62条の5 第60条の3及第60条の4の規定は第62条の3第3項の規定に依り公証人の保存する定款及其の附属書類に之を準用す

第六十二条之五 第六十条之三及第六十条之四的规定适用于依据第六十二条之三第三款的规定由公证员保存的公司章程及其附属文件。

第62条の6 指定公証人電磁的記録に認証を与ふるには法務省令の定むるところに依り当事者其の面前に於て嘱託に係る電磁的記録に記録せられたる情報に付左の行為（第62条の2の定款が電磁的記録を以て作られたる場合に於ける其の電磁的記録に記録せられたる情報に付ては第2号の行為に限る）を為したるとき其の旨を内容とする情報を電磁的記録に記録せられたる情報に電磁的方式に依り付して之を為すことを要す

第六十二条之六 指定公证员对电磁记录予以认证，根据法务省省令的规定，委托人当面对于电磁记录中的信息作出下述行为时［第六十二条第（二）项所述公司章程是以电磁记录的方式记录时，仅限于第（二）项情形］，公证员应将这一情况以电磁形式添加到电磁记录中：

一 嘱託に係る電磁的記録に記録せられたる情報が其の者の作成に係るものなることを示す措置にして当該情報が他の情報に改変せられたるや否やを確認し得る等作成者を確実に示すことを得るものとして法務省令に定むるものを為したるとき

（一）根据法务省省令的规定，委托人对于委托认证的电磁记录相关的信息，与制作该信息有关的措施，确认该信息未经更改等事项向公证员实际说明时；

二 前号に規定する措置を為したることを自認したるとき

（二）委托人自认已经作出前项规定的行为时。

2 指定公証人電磁的記録に認証を与ふる場合に於て当事者其の面前に於て嘱託に係る電磁的記録の内容の真実なることを宣誓したる上前項各号の行為を為したるときは其の旨を内容とする情報を電磁的記録に記録せられたる情報に電磁的方式に依り付して之を為すことを要す此場合に於ては第58条の2第3項の規定を準用す

2 指定公证员对电磁记录进行认证，当事人在其面前对于委托认证的电磁记录内容的真实性予以宣誓，需要将这一情况记录在电磁记录中时适用第五十八条之二第三款的规定。

3 前2項の認証の嘱託は法務省令の定むるところに依り之を為すことを要す

前两款认证的委托应当遵循法务省省令的相关规定。

4 第26条及第29条乃至第31条の規定は第1項及第2項の規定に依り電磁的記録に認証を与ふる場合に之を準用す

第二十六条及第二十九条至第三十一条的规定适用于第一款及第二款规定的有关对电磁记录予以认证的情形

5 嘱託に係る電磁的記録の内容が虚偽なることを知りて第2項の宣誓を為したる者は10万円以下の過料に処す

明知委托认证的电磁记录内容虚假仍进行第二款所述宣誓的，处十万日元以下罚款。

第62条の7 指定公証人は法務省令の定むるところに依り前条第1項又は第2項の規定に依り認証を受けたる電磁的記録に記録せられたる情報の同一性を確認するに足る情報を保存す

第六十二条之七 指定公证员依据法务省省令以及前条第一款及第二款的规定，对于获得认证的电磁记录应保存足以确认信息同一性的信息。

2 嘱託人は前条第1項又は第2項の規定に依

委托人对于依据前条第一款及第二款的规定获得

り認証を受けたる電磁的記録に記録せられたる情報と同一の情報を記録したる電磁的記録の保存を請求することを得

3　嘱託人、其の承継人又は電磁的記録の趣旨に付法律上利害の関係を有することを証明したる者は左の証明又は情報の提供を請求することを得

一　自己の保有する電磁的記録に記録せられたる情報と第1項に規定する電磁的記録に記録せられたる情報とが同一なることに関する証明

二　第2項の規定に依り保存せられたる電磁的記録に記録せられたる情報と同一の情報の提供

4　前項第2号の情報の提供は法務省令の定むるところに依り同号の電磁的記録の内容を証する書面の交付を以て之を為すことを得

5　前条第3項の規定は第2項及第3項の請求に之を準用す

第62条の8　指定公証人前2条の規定に依り認証を与へ又は電磁的方式に依る証明若は情報の提供を行ふ場合に於ては認証を与ふる電磁的記録に記録せられたる情報及第62条の6の規定に依り之に付せられたる情報又は当該証明を内容とする情報若は提供する情報に左の措置を為すことを要す

一　電磁的記録に記録せられたる情報が其の指定公証人の作成に係るものなることを示す措置にして当該情報が他の情報に改変せられたるや否やを確認し得る等作成者を確実に示すことを得るものとして法務省令に定むるものを為すこと

二　指定公証人が前号に規定する措置を為したるものなることを確認する為必要なる事項を証明する情報を電磁的方式に依り付すること

2　前項第2号の情報は法務大臣又は法務大臣の指定したる法務局若は地方法務局の長之を作る

3　前項の指定は告示して之を為す

第6章　代理兼務及受継

第63条　公証人疾病其の他已むことを得さる事由に因り職務を行ふこと能はさるときは同一の法務局又は地方法務局の管轄区域内の公証人に代理を嘱託することを得

2　公証人前項に依り代理を嘱託したるときは遅滞なく其の旨を其の所属する法務局又は地方法務局の長に届出つへし　其の代理を解きたるとき亦同し

第64条　公証人前条第1項に依り代理を嘱託せす又は之を嘱託すること能はさるときは其の所属する法務局又は地方法務局の長は同一の法務局又は地方法務局の管轄区域内の公証人に代理を命するこ

认证的电磁记录，可以请求保存足以确认信息同一性的信息。

委托人或其继承人，或能够证明对于电磁记录的内容有法律上利害关系的人，可以要求提供下列证明或信息：

（一）有关自己保存的电磁记录所记录的信息与第一款规定的电磁记录所记录的信息具有同一性的证明；

（二）依据第二款的规定保存的电磁记录所记录的信息具有同一性的信息。

提供前款第（二）项信息时，依据法务省省令的规定需交付同项电磁记录内容的书面证明。

前条第三款的规定适用于第二款及第三款所述要求。

第六十二条之八　指定公证员依据前两条的规定进行认证或提供电磁方式的证明或以该证明为内容的信息时，对于认证电磁记录的信息以及第六十二条之六所规定的证明或信息的提供，应该采用下列方式：

（一）电磁记录所记录的信息与指定公证员提供的认证相关，该认证信息或证明与委托人所提供的信息没有不同之处。

（二）指定公证员以电磁方式记录对于确认前项规定的措施所作的相关证明信息。

前款第（二）项信息由法务大臣或法务大臣指定的法务局或地方法务局局长提供。

前项指定须予以公示。

第六章　代理、兼任及继任

第六十三条　公证员因病及其他不得已的原因不能履行职务时，可委托其隶属的同一法务局或地方法务局管辖区域内的公证员代理。

公证员依据前款规定委托代理时，应及时向其隶属的法务局或地方法务局局长报告；解除代理时亦同。

第六十四条　当公证员不能根据前条第一款规定委托代理，或不具备委托代理的能力时，其隶属的法务局或地方法务局局长可命令同一法务局或地方法务局管辖区域内的公证员代理。

とを得

2　公証人其の職務を行ふことを得るに至りたるときは其の所属する法務局又は地方法務局の長は前項の代理を解くへし

第65条　公証人の代理者前2条に依り其の職務を行ふの役場は代理せらるる公証人の役場とす

2　公証人の代理者職務上署名するときは代理せらるる公証人の職氏名、所属、役場所在地及其の代理者たることを記載すへし

3　第22条の規定は代理せらるる公証人の外其の代理者にも之を適用す

第66条　公証人の死亡、免職、失職又は転属の場合に於て其の所属する法務局又は地方法務局の長必要と認むるときは其の指定したる官吏をして遅滞なく役場の書類に封印を為さしむへし

第67条　公証人の死亡、免職、失職又は転属の場合に於て直に後任者の任命せられさるときは其の所属する法務局又は地方法務局の長は同一の法務局又は地方法務局の管範区域内の公証人に兼務を命することを得

2　後任者其の職務を行ふことを得るに至りたるときは其の所属する法務局又は地方法務局の長は前項の兼務を解くへし

第68条　公証人の免職、失職又は転属の場合に於ては後任者又は兼務者は前任者と立会ひ遅滞なく書類の授受を為すへし

2　死亡其の他の事由に因り書類の授受を為すこと能はさる場合に於ては後任者又は兼務者は其の所属する法務局又は地方法務局の長の指定したる官吏の立会を以て書類を受取るへし

3　第66条に依る書類の封印後に命せられたる後任者又は兼務者は其の所属する法務局又は地方法務局の長の指定したる官吏の立会を以て封印を解き書類を受取るへし

第69条　前条の規定は兼務者か書類を更に他の公証人に引渡すへき場合に之を準用す

第70条　兼務者職務上署名するときは兼務者たることを記載すへし

2　前任者又は兼務者の作成したる証書に依り後任者か其の正本又は謄本を作成する場合に於て署名するときは後任者たることを記載すへし

第71条　公証人の死亡、免職、失職又は転属の場合に於て定員の改正に因り後任者を要せさるときは法務大臣は同一の法務局若は地方法務局又は其の支局の管轄区域内の公証人に書類の引継を命すへし

2　第68条及前条第2項の規定は前項に依り書類の引継を命せられたる公証人に之を準用す

公证员可以履行职务时，其隶属的法务局或地方法务局局长应解除前款代理。

第六十五条　公证员的代理人依前两条执行职务时的事务所，以被代理的公证员的事务所为准。

公证员的代理人在作职务上的签名时，应记明被代理公证员的职称、姓名、隶属、事务所所在地及其代理人等事项。

第二十二条的规定除适用于被代理的公证员外，也适用于代理人。

第六十六条　公证员在死亡、免职、职位丧失或调动的情况下，其隶属的法务局或地方法务局局长认为必要时，应命令其指定的官员及时封存事务所的文件。

第六十七条　在公证员死亡、免职、职位丧失或调动而尚未任命继任人时，其隶属的法务局或地方法务局局长可命令同一法务局或地方法务局管辖区域内的公证员兼任。

继任人可以执行职务时，其隶属的法务局或地方法务局局长应解除前款中的兼任职务。

第六十八条　在公证员免职、职位丧失或调动时，前任者应及时会同继任人或兼任人移交文件。

公证员因死亡或其他事由不能移交文件时，继任人或兼任人应在其隶属的法务局或地方法务局局长指定的官员在场的情况下接受文件。

依据第六十六条的规定在封存文件后被任命的继任人或兼任人，应在其隶属的法务局或地方法务局局长指定的官员在场的情况下启封接受文件。

第六十九条　前条规定适用于兼任人再向其他公证员移交文件时的情形。

第七十条　兼任人在作职务上的签名时应当记明兼任人的身份。

继任人根据前任者或兼任人出具的公证书，制作其正本或抄本，在签名时应当记明继任人的身份。

第七十一条　在公证员死亡、免职、职位丧失或调动，因修改定员不再需要继任人时，法务大臣应命令同一法务局或地方法务局或其支局管辖区域内的公证员接收其文件。

第六十八条及前条第二款的规定适用于前款中被命令接收文件的公证员。

第 72 条　第 66 条、第 67 条、第 68 条第 3 項及第 70 条第 1 項の規定は公証人の停職の場合に之を準用す

2　兼務者前項に依り其の職務を行ふの役場は停職者の役場とす

第 73 条　第 68 条及第 69 条の規定は法務事務官か第 8 条に依り公証人の職務を行ふ場合に之を準用す

第 7 章　監督及懲戒

第 74 条　公証人は法務大臣の監督を受く

2　法務大臣は其の定むるところに依り法務局又は地方法務局の長をして其の管轄区域内の公証人に対する監督事務を取扱はしむ

第 75 条　削除

第 76 条　第 74 条の監督権は左の事項を包含す

一　公証人の不適当に取扱ひたる職務に付其の注意を促し及適当に其の職務を取扱ふへきことを之に訓令すること

二　職務の内外を問はす公証人の地位に不相応なる行状に付之に諭告すること但し諭告を為す前其の公証人をして弁明を為すことを得せしむへし

第 77 条　監督官は公証人の保存する書類を検閲し又は其の指定したる官吏をして之を検閲せしむることを得

2　前項の規定は指定公証人の保存する電磁的記録に之を準用す

第 78 条　嘱託人又は利害関係人は公証人の事務取扱に対し其の所属する法務局又は地方法務局の長に異議を申出ることを得

2　前項の異議に付為したる処分に対し不服ある者は更に法務大臣に異議を申出ることを得

第 79 条　公証人職務上の義務に違反したるとき又は品位を失墜すへき行為ありたるときは懲戒に付す

第 80 条　懲戒は左の 5 種とす

一　譴責

二　10 万円以下の過料

三　1 年以下の停職

四　転属

五　免職

第 81 条　過料、停職、転属及免職は第 13 条の 2 の政令を以て定むる審査会の議決に依り法務大臣之を行ふ

2　譴責は法務大臣之を行ふ

第七十二条　第六十六条、第六十七条、第六十八条第三款及第七十条第一款的规定适用于公证员停职的情形。

兼任人依照前款规定执行职务时以停职人的事务所为其事务所。

第七十三条　第六十八条及第六十九条的规定适用于法务事务官依第八条执行公证员职务的情形。

第七章　监督及惩戒

第七十四条　公证员接受法务大臣的监督。

法务大臣根据其规定，指定法务局或地方法务局局长负责对其管辖区域内公证员的监督事务。

第七十五条　删除。

第七十六条　第七十四条的监督权包含下列事项：

（一）在公证员不适当地履行职务时提请其注意，并训令其适当地履行职务；

（二）在公证员无论职务内外出现与其地位不相符的行为时提出警告，但在提出警告前应允许公证员进行辩解。

第七十七条　监督官可对公证员保存的文件进行审阅，或命令其指定的官员进行审阅。

前款规定适用于指定公证员保存的电磁记录。

第七十八条　委托人或利害关系人对公证员负责的事务，可向其隶属的法务局或地方法务局局长提出异议。

对前款异议所作的处分存在异议，（委托人、利害关系人、公证员）可再向法务大臣提出异议。

第七十九条　公证员违反职务上的义务或有品行不端的行为时，应施以惩戒。

第八十条　惩戒有以下五种形式：

（一）谴责；

（二）罚款 10 万元以下；

（三）停职一年以下；

（四）职务调动；

（五）免职。

第八十一条　罚款、停职、调动及免职须依据第十三条之二的政令规定的公证员审查会进行决议，由法务大臣执行。

第 82 条　削除

第 83 条　公証人勾留せられ又は拘留の刑に処せられたるときは釈放に至るまで当然其の職務を停止せらる

2　法務大臣は懲戒事件停職、転属又は免職に該当するものと思料するときは懲戒手続結了に至るまで公証人の職務を停止することを得

3　公証人の停職に関する規定は其の事務停止の場合に之を準用す

第 84 条　過料を完納せさるときは検察官の命令を以て之を執行す

2　前項の執行に付ては非訟事件手続法（平成 23 年法律第 51 号）第 121 条の規定を準用す

3　公証人の納めたる身元保証金は第 20 条第３項の場合を除くの外他の公課及債権に先チて之を過料に充つ

第八十二条　删除。

第八十三条　公证员被羁押或被判拘留刑罚时，在其获释前当然予以停职。

法务大臣认为对公证员的惩戒事件足以适用停职、调动或免职惩罚时，在惩戒程序完结前，可以停止公证员的职务。

公证员停职的有关规定，适用于事务停止的情形。

第八十四条　公证员不交纳罚款时，可由检察官命令执行。

前款的执行适用《非讼案件程序法》[平成二十三年（2011 年）第五十一号法令] 第一百二十一条的规定。

公证员交纳的身份保证金，除第二十条第三款规定的情形外，应优先于其他由政府征收的费用及债权，而用于罚款。

公证员法施行规则

公証人法施行規則
昭和二十四年（1949 年）六月一日法務府令第九号
最終改正：平成一九年（2007 年）三月八日法務省令第七号

第一条　公証人は、法務大臣の指定した地にその役場を設けようとするときは、その位置、建物の構造及び周囲の状況を記載した書面を添附して、その所属する法務局又は地方法務局の長の認可を受けなければならない。

２　公証人は、役場を設けたときは、遅滞なくその旨を法務大臣に届け出なければならない。

３　前二項の規定は、役場を移転する場合に準用する。

第二条　公証人は、その役場に、公証人某役場と記載した表札を掲げなければならない。

第三条　公証人法（明治四十一年法律第五十三号）第二十条第一項の公告は、当該公証人の所属する法務局又は地方法務局の長が官報でする。

第四条　公証人の職印は、十八ミリメートル平方とし、公証人何某と彫刻しなければならない。

２　公証人法第三十九条第五項（第四十条第二項、第六十条及び第六十二条の三第四項において準用する場合を含む。）、第四十条第一項、第四十一条第二項（第六十条の二第二項及び第六十二条の四第二項において準用する場合を含む。）又は第五十六条第一項（第六十条の四及び第六十二条の五において準用する場合を含む。）の規定により契印をする場合には、附録第一号の様式による文様を打ち抜く方法によることができる。

第五条　書記の認可を申請するには、その申請書に本人自筆の履歴書及び戸籍抄本又は住民票の写しを添附しなければならない。

第六条　公証人は、あらかじめ書記に、その役場で取り扱う事務について、公証人が職務上漏らすことのできない事項を漏らさない旨を誓約させなければならない。

第七条　公証人は、書記を解雇し、又は書記が死亡したときは、遅滞なくその旨をその所属する法務局又は地方法務局の長に届け出なければならない。

第八条　公証人の作るべき証書その他の書面（第二項の書面を除く。）の用紙は、公証人役場と印

公证员法施行规则
昭和二十四年（1949 年）六月一日第九号法务府令
最终修订：平成十九年（2007 年）三月八日第七号法务省令

第一条　公证员在法务大臣指定的地点设立事务所，须提交记明其位置、建筑构造和周边状况的文件，获得其隶属的法务局或地方法务局局长的认可。

公证员在设立事务所后，应及时向法务大臣报告该事项。

前两款规定适用于事务所搬迁时的情形。

第二条　公证员须在其事务所设置公证员某某事务所的标记。

第三条　《公证法》[明治四十一年（1908 年）第五十三号法令] 第二十条第一款的公告，由该公证员隶属的法务局或地方法务局局长作官方宣布。

第四条　公证员的职称印鉴应为十八毫米见方，刻有公证员某某的字样。

按照《公证法》第三十九条第五款（包含适用于第四十条第二款、第六十条及第六十二条之三第四款的情形）、第四十条第一款、第四十一条第二款（包含适用于第六十条之二第二款及第六十二条之四第二款的情形）以及第五十六条第一款（包含适用于第六十条之四及第六十二条之五的情形）加盖骑缝章时，其模印可以附录第一号样式的文样为准。

第五条　申请书记员时，除申请书外，须附有本人亲笔书写的履历书及户籍或居民证的抄本。

第六条　公证员须事先令书记员就事务所办理的事务宣誓，保证其不泄露公证员在职务中不能泄露的事项。

第七条　公证员在解雇书记员或书记员死亡时，须及时向其隶属的法务局或地方法务局局长报告。

第八条　公证员出具公证书和其他文件（第二款文件除外）的用纸须使用印有公证员事务所的日本工

刷した日本工業規格A列四番の丈夫なけい紙とする。ただし、A列四番の用紙に代えて、B列四番の用紙とすることを妨げない。

2　公証人法第五十七条の三第二項の登記の嘱託書の用紙は、日本工業規格A列四番の丈夫な紙を用いなければならない。

第九条　公証人の執務時間は、法務省職員の勤務時間による。

2　前項の規定にかかわらず、急を要する場合には、公証人は、休日又は執務時間外でも嘱託に応じなければならない。

第十条　役場には、見やすい場所に、手数料、送達に要する料金、登記手数料、日当及び旅費の標準額並びに執務時間及び急を要する場合には休日又は執務時間外でも嘱託に応ずる旨（指定公証人の行う電磁的記録に関する事務に関する省令（平成十三年法務省令第二十四号）に基づく事務を除く。）を掲示しなければならない。

第十一条　公証人は、特別の事情がない限り、嘱託の順序に従つて事務を取り扱わなければならない。

第十二条　公証人は、嘱託を拒んだ場合に嘱託人の請求があるときは、その理由書を交付しなければならない。

第十三条　公証人は、法律行為につき証書を作成し、又は認証を与える場合に、その法律行為が有効であるかどうか、当事者が相当の考慮をしたかどうか又はその法律行為をする能力があるかどうかについて疑があるときは、関係人に注意をし、且つ、その者に必要な説明をさせなければならない。

2　公証人が法律行為でない事実について証書を作成する場合に、その事実により影響を受けるべき私権の関係について疑があるときも、前項と同様とする。

第十三条の二　公証人は、代理人の嘱託により証書を作成した場合には、証書を作成した日から三日以内に次の各号に掲げる事項を本人に通知しなければならない。ただし、代理人が本人の雇人又は同居者である場合には、この限りでない。

一　証書の件名、番号及び証書作成の年月日

二　公証人の氏名及び役場

三　代理人及び相手方の住所及び氏名

四　債務者が直ちに強制執行に服する旨の陳述の記載の有無

2　前項の通知は、同項第四号の記載のある証書については附録第一号の二の様式による書面により、同項第四号の記載のない証書については附録第

业规格A列第四号结实的格纸。然而，也可以用B列第四号用纸代替A列第四号用纸。

《公证法》第五十七条之三第二款的登记的委托书用纸，必须用日本工业规格A列四号结实的纸。

第九条　公证员的工作时间，参照法务省职员的工作时间。

紧急情况下，公证员必须在休息日或上班时间之外接受委托。

第十条　事务所内须在明显的地方标明手续费、邮寄费用、登记手续费、日薪及旅费的标准金额和工作时间，以及紧急情况下休息日和上班时间以外同样接受委托的事项｛基于《有关指定公证员办理电磁记录相关事务的省令》[平成十三年（2001年）法务省省令第二十四号]规定的事务除外｝。

第十一条　公证员除有特别事项外，须按照委托的顺序办理公证事务。

第十二条　公证员拒绝委托时，应委托人请求须出具理由书。

第十三条　公证员在对法律行为出具公证书或给予认证时，如对该法律行为的有效性、当事人是否充分考虑以及有无法律行为能力等事项存疑，须提请相关人注意并使其做必要的说明。

公证员对非法律行为的事实出具公证书时，如对受该事实影响的私权关系存疑，比照前款处理。

第十三条之二　公证员接受代理人的委托出具公证书时，须在公证书制作后三日内将下述列明事项通知本人，但代理人如为本人的雇用人或同居人时不受此规定限制：

（一）公证书的名称、编号及公证书制作的年月日；

（二）公证员的姓名和事务所；

（三）代理人及相对人的住所和姓名；

（四）有无债务人被强制执行事项的陈述的记载。

前款所述通知，如有该款第四项的记载，其文书须使用附录第一号之二的样式；如无该款第四项的记载，其文书须使用附录第一号之三的样式。

一号の三の様式による書面によりしなければならない。

3　公証人は、第一項の通知をしたときは、証書原簿の備考欄に同項の通知をした旨及び通知の方法、年月日を記載しておかなければならない。

第十三条の三　公証人法第五十八条の二の規定による宣誓は、良心に従って証書の記載が真実であることを誓うものとする。

2　宣誓は、起立して厳粛に行わなければならない。

3　公証人は、宣誓の前に、当事者に対し、宣誓の趣旨を説明し、かつ、証書の記載が虚偽であることを知って宣誓したときは過料の制裁があることを告げなければならない。

第十四条　同時に数箇の嘱託をする場合には、公証人法第二十八条第二項（第六十条及び第六十二条の三第四項において準用する場合を含む。）又は第三十二条第二項（第三十三条第二項、第六十条及び第六十二条の三第四項において準用する場合を含む。）の規定により提出する印鑑その他に関する証明書は、一通で足りる。

2　前項の場合には、一の嘱託にその証明書をつづり、その他の嘱託には、その旨を記載した書面を作つてつづらなければならない。

第十五条　公証人法第四十一条第一項に掲げる附属書類の原本の還付を請求する場合には、嘱託人は、その原本とともに原本と相違ない旨を記載した謄本を提出しなければならない。

2　公証人が附属書類の原本を還付するときは、その謄本に原本還付の旨を記載して印をおさなければならない。

第十六条　法律行為についての証書の再度の正本の交付を請求する者がある場合に、その正本を要する事由について疑があるときは、公証人は、その者にその事由を証明させなければならない。

第十七条　公証人は、嘱託人に手数料、送達に要する料金、登記手数料、日当又は旅費の概算額を予納させたときは、領収証を交付しなければならない。

第十八条　公証人役場には、証書原簿、認証簿、確定日附簿及び信託表示簿のほか、次の帳簿を備えて置かなければならない。

一　拒絶証書謄本綴込帳
二　抵当証券支払拒絶証明書謄本綴込帳
三　送達関係書類綴込帳
四　計算簿

第十九条　証書原簿、認証簿及び計算簿は、附

公证员在作第一款的通知时，须在公证书总簿册的备考栏中记明已作前项通知及通知的方法和年月日。

第十三条之三　根据《公证法》第五十八条之二所作的宣誓，须顺从良心对公证书记载事项的真实性起誓。

宣誓时须起立肃穆。

公证员在宣誓前须向当事人说明宣誓的主旨，以及明知公证书记载事项虚伪仍宣誓时会受到罚金处罚等事项。

第十四条　同时进行数件委托时，根据《公证法》第二十八条第二款（包含适用于第六十条及第六十二条之三第四款的情形）以及第三十二条第二款（包含适用第三十三条第二款、第六十条和第六十二条之三第四款的情形）的规定提交的印鉴和相关证明文件，只需一件即可。

前款情形下，将证明文件与其中一份委托连缀，其他的委托须同记载证明事项的文件连缀。

第十五条　《公证法》第四十一条第一款所述当委托人请求退还附属文件的原件时，须与原件一并提交记载相同内容的抄本。

公证员在退还附属文件的原件时，须在抄本上记明原件已退还并盖章。

第十六条　委托人再度请求交付有关法律行为的公证书的正本时，公证员如对请求交付正本的事由存疑，应要求委托人证明该事由。

第十七条　公证员预收委托人交纳的手续费、邮寄费用、登记手续费、日薪及旅费的概算金额时，应开具收据。

第十八条　公证员事务所除公证书总簿、认证簿、确定日期簿及信托表示簿外，还应设置下列账簿：

（一）拒绝证书抄本合订册；
（二）拒绝支付抵押证券证明书抄本合订册；
（三）送达相关文件合订册；
（四）计算簿。

第十九条　公证书总簿、认证簿及计算簿，须按

録第二号から第四号までの様式により調製しなければならない。

2 証書原簿及び認証簿には、公証人においてその枚数を表紙の裏面に記載し、職氏名を署し、職印を押し、且つ、毎葉のつづり目に職印で契印をしなければならない。

第二十条 公証人手数料令（平成五年政令第二百二十四号）第四条第二項（同令第六条第一項後段において準用する場合を含む。）の規定により交付すべき計算書は、附録第四号の様式に準じて作らなければならない。

第二十一条 公証人は、閲覧又は証書の正本若しくは謄本の交付の請求を受けた場合に、印鑑その他に関する証明書の提出によらないで人違でないことを証明させたときは、その旨及びその事由を計算簿の備考欄に記載しなければならない。

第二十二条 公証人は、認証の付与の嘱託を受けた場合に、前条に規定する証明をさせたときは、その旨及びその事由を認証簿の備考欄に記載しなければならない。

第二十三条 公証人は、嘱託人から手数料、送達に要する料金、登記手数料、日当又は旅費を受領したときは、公正証書の作成又はその嘱託と同時に嘱託された正本、謄本若しくは附属書類の謄本の交付に関するものは、附録第四号の甲の様式による計算簿に、その他に関するものは、同号の乙の様式による計算簿に、当該手数料、送達に要する料金、登記手数料、日当又は旅費の額その他の事項を記載しなければならない。ただし、相当と認めるときは、確定日附に関するものは、別に同号の丙の様式による計算簿に記載することを妨げない。

2 公証人は、公証人手数料令第五条の規定により手数料、送達に要する料金、登記手数料、日当又は旅費の全部又は一部の支払を猶予したときは、前項の場合に準ずる記載をするほか、その旨を計算簿の備考欄に記載しなければならない。

第二十四条 証書原簿又は計算簿に嘱託人の氏名を記載する場合に、嘱託人が多数であるときは、証書原簿については当事者双方各一人だけの氏名及び他の人員を、計算簿については当事者中その一人だけの氏名及び他の人員を記載すれば足りる。

2 前項の規定は、定款の認証について認証簿に嘱託人の氏名及び住所又は署名押印者の氏名を記載する場合に、それらの者が多数であるときに準用する。

3 定款の認証の嘱託があつた場合には、認証簿の備考欄に会社の商号を記載しなければならない。

照附录第二号至第四号标明的样式制作。

公证书总簿及认证簿须由公证员在簿册封内写明页数，签上职称姓名，加盖职称印鉴，并且在每一页的装订处用职称印鉴加盖骑缝章。

第二十条 按照《公证员手续费令》[平成五年（1993年）证明第二百二十四号]第四条第二款（同令第六条第一款包含适用于后半段的情形）的规定所应交付的计算书，须以附录第四号的样式为准制作。

第二十一条 公证员收到调阅或提交公证书正本或抄本的请求，如是通过提交印鉴及其他相关证明以外的方法证明其人无误时，须在计算簿的备考栏处记明该情况及事由。

第二十二条 公证员收到请求认证的委托，在依前条规定使委托人证明身份时，须将该情况及其事由在认证簿的备考栏中记明。

第二十三条 公证员向委托人收取的手续费、邮寄费用、登记手续费、日薪及旅费等费用如果与出具公证书或在接受委托的同时收到的交付正本、抄本或附属文件抄本的请求相关，须在按照附录第四号甲种格式制作的计算簿上记明该手续费、邮寄费用、登记手续费、日薪及旅费的金额和其他事项；其他相关事项应在按照同号乙种格式制作的计算簿上记明。但在认为必要时，不妨将有关确定日期的事项记入按照同号丙种格式制作的计算簿上。

公证员暂免《公证员手续费令》第五条规定的手续费、邮寄费用、登记手续费、日薪及旅费的全部或部分费用时，除按照前款的情形予以记明外，须将暂免情况记入计算簿的备考栏。

第二十四条 在公证书总簿或计算簿记明委托人姓名，而委托人有多人时，在公证书总簿中只需记明当事人双方各一人的姓名及其他人员，在计算簿中只需记明当事人中的一人及其他人员即可。

对于公证员认证公司章程，在认证簿中记明委托人的姓名、住所或签名盖章者的姓名，当委托人有多名时适用前款规定。

第二十五条　証書の原本又は公証人の保存する私署証書又は定款は、表紙を附け、証書の番号又は登簿番号の順序に従つてつづつて置かなければならない。

2　嘱託に関して提出した書類であつて、私署証書（公証人の保存する私署証書を除く。）の認証の付与の嘱託における人違いでないことを証明すべき印鑑その他に関する証明書、代理人の権限を証明すべき証書その他の原本に続けてつづるべきでないものは、表紙を付け、件名、受付の年月日及び証書の番号又は登簿番号を記載し、事件処理の順序に従つてつづつて置かなければならない。

第二十六条　公証人は、その役場に附属する倉庫又は堅ろうな建物内に書類を保管して置かなければならない。

2　書類が滅失し、又は滅失の虞があるときは、遅滞なくその旨をその所属する法務局又は地方法務局の長に報告しなければならない。事変を避けるため書類を役場外に持ち出したときも同様とする。

第二十七条　公証人は、書類及び帳簿を、次の各号に掲げる区分に応じ、それぞれ当該各号に掲げる期間保存しなければならない。ただし、履行につき確定期限のある債務又は存続期間の定めのある権利義務に関する法律行為につき作成した証書の原本については、その期限の到来又はその期間の満了の翌年から十年を経過したときは、この限りでない。

一　証書の原本、証書原簿、公証人の保存する私署証書及び定款、認証簿（第三号に掲げるものを除く。）、信託表示簿　二十年

二　拒絶証書謄本綴込帳、抵当証券支払拒絶証明書謄本綴込帳、送達関係書類綴込帳　十年

三　私署証書（公証人の保存する私署証書を除く。）の認証のみにつき調製した認証簿、確定日付簿、第二十五条第二項の書類、計算簿　七年

2　前項の書類の保存期間は、証書原簿、認証簿、信託表示簿、確定日附簿及び計算簿については、当該帳簿に最終の記載をした翌年から、拒絶証書謄本綴込帳、抵当証券支払拒絶証明書謄本綴込帳及び送達関係書類綴込帳については、当該帳簿に最終のつづり込みをした翌年から、その他の書類については、当該年度の翌年から、起算する。

3　第一項の書類は、保存期間の満了した後でも特別の事由により保存の必要があるときは、その事由のある間保存しなければならない。

第二十八条　公証人が保存期間の満了した書類を廃棄しようとするときは、目録を作り、その所属

第二十五条　公证书原件及公证员所保存的私署文书和公司章程，须附贴封面，按照证书编号或登记编号的顺序加以装订。

与委托有关而提交的文件、对于认证私署文书（公证员保存的私署文书除外）时证明身份所需的印鉴和其他相关证明以及代理人权限证明，若不必装订在原件后面，则须附贴封面，写明文件名称、接收委托的年月日及证书编号或登记编号，按照案件办理的顺序加以装订。

第二十六条　公证员须将文件放置在事务所的附属仓库或坚固的建筑物内保管。

文件灭失或存在灭失的隐患时，公证员须立即向其隶属的法务局或地方法务局局长报告。为躲避意外事件而将文件带出事务所之外时亦同。

第二十七条　公证员须按照下述列明的期间分别保存文件及簿册。然而，对于有确定履行期限的债务及与存续期间确定的权利义务相关的法律行为出具的公证书原件，已经过其期限到来或期间已满第二年起始的十年时，不受此限制：

（一）公证书原件、公证书总簿、公证员保存的私署文书及公司章程、认证簿（第三项所列事项除外）、信托表示簿二十年；

（二）拒绝证书抄本合订册、拒绝支付抵押证券证明书抄本合订册、送达相关文件合订册十年；

（三）认证（除公证员保存的私署文书外）私署文书而编制的认证簿、确定日期簿、第二十五条第二款的文件、计算簿七年。

前款文件的保存期间，公证书总簿、认证簿、信托表示簿、确定日期簿及计算簿，从该簿册最后几名的第二年起算；拒绝证书抄本合订册、拒绝支付抵押证券证明书抄本合订册及送达相关文件合订册从该簿册最后合订的第二年起算；其他文件从当年的第二年起算。

第一款第（一）项文件在保存期满后，因特别事由需要保存时，须在该事由存在期间加以保存。

第二十八条　公证员销毁保存期满的文件，须制定目录，并经其隶属的法务局或地方法务局局长认可。

する法務局又は地方法務局の長の認可を受けなければならない。

第二十九条　公証人法第六十八条（第六十九条及び第七十一条から第七十三条までにおいて準用する場合を含む。）の規定により書類の授受をする場合には、目録を作り、その末尾に授受の事由及び年月日を記載し、授受者及び立会官吏がこれに署名し、印をおさなければならない。

2　前項の目録は、作成の日から一箇月内に、その謄本をその所属する法務局又は地方法務局の長に差し出さなければならない。

第三十条　公証人法第六十七条第一項の兼務者は、自己の役場で前任者の事務を取り扱うことができる。

2　前項の場合には、遅滞なくその旨をその所属する法務局又は地方法務局の長に届け出なければならない。

第三十一条　代理者又は公証人法第七十二条の兼務者は、その職務を行う役場の見易い場所に、代理者某又は兼務者某である旨を掲示しなければならない。

2　後任者又は公証人法第六十七条第一項の兼務者は、その職務を行う役場の見易い場所に、公証人某の後任者又は公証人某の取り扱つた事務についての兼務者である旨を掲示しなければならない。但し、後任者のすべき掲示の期間は、一年とする。

第三十二条　後任者の作成する文書の番号は、前任者又は兼務者の作成した文書の番号の順序を追つて記載しなければならない。

第三十三条　公証人は、疾病その他やむを得ない事由により職務を行うことができない場合に、他の公証人に代理を嘱託せず又はこれを嘱託することができないときは、遅滞なくその所属する法務局又は地方法務局の長にその旨を届け出なければならない。その職務を行うことができるに至つたときも同様とする。

第三十四条　公証人はその氏名若しくは住所を変更し、又は失職したときは、遅滞なくその旨をその所属する法務局又は地方法務局の長に届け出なければならない。

2　前項の規定は、公証人が死亡した場合に、その四親等内の親族について準用する。

第三十五条　公証人は、公証事務の取扱に関して疑義を生じたときは、法務大臣にその指示を求めることができる。

第三十六条　公証人が法務大臣に書面の提出をするには、その所属する法務局又は地方法務局の長

第二十九条　按照《公证法》第六十八条（包括适用于第六十九条及第七十一条至第七十三条的情形）的规定移交和接受文件，须制作目录，在其结尾记明移交的事由和年月日，移交和接受双方及在场官员须签名盖章。

在从前项目录制作之日起的一个月内，须将其抄本提交至隶属法务局或地方法务局局长。

第三十条　《公证法》第六十七条第一款中的兼任人可在自己的事务所处理前任者的事务。

在前款情形下，应立即将该情况向其隶属的法务局或地方法务局局长报告。

第三十一条　代理人或《公证法》第七十二条中的兼任人，须在其执业的事务所中明显的位置标明其为代理人某某或兼任人某某。

后任者或《公证法》第六十七条第一款的兼任人，须在其执业的事务所明显的位置，标明是公证员某某的后任者或公证员某某处理的事务的兼任人。但后任者所应标记的期限为一年。

第三十二条　后任者制作的文件的编号，须按照前任者或兼任人制作的文件的编号顺序记载。

第三十三条　公证员因疾病或其他不可抗拒的事由不能履行职务，其他公证员无法代理或公证员无法委托代理时，须立即向其隶属的法务局或地方法务局局长报告。能够履行职务时亦同。

第三十四条　公证员变更姓名或住所，亦或失去职务时，应立即向其隶属的法务局或地方法务局局长报告。

公证员死亡时，前款规定适用于公证员四亲等内的亲属。

第三十五条　公证员对于公证事务的处理如有疑问，可以向法务大臣寻求指示。

第三十六条　公证员向法务大臣提交文件时，须经由其隶属的法务局或地方法务局局长转交。但紧急

を経由しなければならない。但し、急を要する場合は、この限りでない。

2　前項但書の場合には、同時にその旨を法務局又は地方法務局の長に届け出なければならない。

第三十七条　法務局又は地方法務局の長は、公証人名簿を備え、これにその所属する公証人の氏名、住所、生年月日及び役場所在地を記載して置かなければならない。

第三十八条　法務局又は地方法務局の長は、その所属する公証人に公証人法第十五条第一項第二号から第四号まで又は第七十九条に掲げる事由があると認めるときは、速かにその事情を具して、その旨を法務大臣に報告しなければならない。公証人がその氏名を変更し、又は死亡若しくは失職したときも同様とする。

第三十九条　法務局又は地方法務局の長は、少くとも毎年一回当該法務局又は地方法務局に所属する公証人の役場に臨み、その保存する書類の検閲及び執務の状況の調査をし、又は当該法務局又は地方法務局に勤務する法務事務官にこれをさせ、その結果を速かに法務大臣に報告しなければならない。

第四十条　法務局又は地方法務局の長は、その所属する公証人に対し注意を促し、且つ、訓令をしたとき、又は諭告をしたときは、速かにその事情を具して、その旨を法務大臣に報告しなければならない。公証人法第七十八条第一項の異議について処分をしたときも同様とする。

第四十条の二　法務局又は地方法務局の長は、所属の公証人の間における事務の負担が著しく均衡を失し、公証人の事務の適正迅速な処理又は品位の保持を害する虞があると認めるときは、法務大臣の認可を受け、事務の負担を調整することができる。

第四十一条　法務大臣は、特に必要があると認めるときは、法務局又は地方法務局の長の外、その都度法務省の職員に公証人に対する監督事務を取り扱わせるものとする。

第四十二条　公証人手数料令第七条の規定によつて手数料、日当又は旅費を印紙で納付させる場合には、納付書に収入印紙をはつて差し出させなければならない。

第四十三条　公証人は、法務局又は地方法務局の管轄区域ごとに公証人会を設立することができる。

2　公証人会は、公証事務の改善及び統一並びに公証人の品位の保持を図るため、公証人の指導及び連絡に関する事務を行うことを目的とする。

第四十四条　公証人は、その所属する法務局又は地方法務局の管轄区域内に設立された公証人会の

情况下不受此限制。

适用前款但书的情形时，须同时将该事项向法务局或地方法务局局长报告。

第三十七条　法务局或地方法务局局长须置备公证员名簿，记明其所属公证员的姓名、住所、出生年月及事务所所在地。

第三十八条　法务局或地方法务局局长如认为其所属公证员有《公证法》第十五条第一款第（二）项至第（四）项或第七十九条所述事由，须立即将该事项详情向法务大臣报告。公证员变更姓名、死亡或失去职务时亦同。

第三十九条　法务局或地方法务局局长，须每年至少到该法务局或地方法务局所属公证员的事务所视察一次，审阅该所保存的文件，调查执业的状况，或指使在该法务局或地方法务局工作的法务事务官为上述事项，并将结果迅速报告至法务大臣。

第四十条　法务局或地方法务局局长向其所属公证员提请注意、发出训令或提出警告时，应迅速报告法务大臣。在处置《公证法》第七十八条第一款所述异议时亦同。

第四十条之二　法务局或地方法务局局长认为其所属公证员之间的事务负担显然已失去均衡，并可能有害于公证员对事务的适当迅速处理或保持品德时，在获得法务大臣认可后可以调整事务负担。

第四十一条　法务大臣在认为有特殊必要时，除法务局或地方法务局局长外，还可命令法务省职员负责对公证员的监督事务。

第四十二条　根据《公证员手续费令》第七条的规定用印花税票缴纳手续费、日薪和旅费时，须使其在缴纳书上粘贴印花税票后提交。

第四十三条　公证员可以在法务局或地方法务局管辖区域内设立公证员会。

公证员会为谋求改善和统一公证事务，保持公证员的品德而从事公证员指导和联络的相关事务。

第四十四条　公证员是其隶属的法务局或地方法务局管辖区域内设立的公证员会的会员。

会員となる。

第四十五条　公証人会を設立しようとするときは、その会員となるべき公証人の過半数の同意を得て会則を定め、法務大臣の認可を受けなければならない。

２　会則には、左の事項を定めなければならない。

一　名称及び事務所

二　役員に関する事項

三　会員に関する事項

四　会議に関する事項

五　会計に関する事項

六　その他必要な事項

３　公証人会は、会則を変更しようとするときは、法務大臣の認可を受けなければならない。

第四十六条　公証人会は、役員を選任し、又は解任したときは、遅滞なくその旨を当該公証人会の事務所の所在地を管轄する法務局又は地方法務局の長に届け出なければならない。

第四十七条　公証人会は、公証事務に関し、当該公証人会の事務所の所在地を管轄する法務局又は地方法務局の長に建議し、又はその諮問に答申することができる。

２　法務局又は地方法務局の長は、前項の諮問をし、又は同項の建議若しくは答申があつたときは、速やかにその事情を具して、その旨を法務大臣に報告しなければならない。

第四十八条　公証人会は、公証人に非違又は品位を害する行状があると認めるときは、その旨をその所属する法務局又は地方法務局の長に報告しなければならない。

第四十九条　全国の公証人会は、日本公証人連合会を設立することができる。

２　日本公証人連合会は、公証事務の改善及び統一並びに公証人の品位の保持を図るため、公証人会及び公証人の指導及び連絡に関する事務を行うことを目的とする。

第五十条　公証人会及び公証人は、日本公証人連合会の会員となる。

第五十一条　日本公証人連合会を設立しようとするときは、その会員となるべき公証人会及び公証人の過半数の同意を得て会則を定め、法務大臣の認可を受けなければならない。

第五十二条　日本公証人連合会は、公証事務に関し、法務大臣に建議し、又はその諮問に答申することができる。

第五十三条　第四十五条第二項及び第三項並び

第四十五条　设立公证员会时，须征得作为其会员的公证员过半数同意后制订会则，并获得法务大臣的认可。

会则须规定下列事项：

（一）名称及事务所；

（二）雇员有关事项；

（三）会员有关事项；

（四）会议有关事项；

（五）会计有关事项；

（六）其他必要事项。

公证员会如更订会则，须征得法务大臣的许可。

第四十六条　公证员会在选任及解聘雇员时，须及时将该事项报告至该公证员会事务所所在地的主管法务局或地方法务局局长。

第四十七条　公证员会可以就公证事务向该公证员会事务所所在地的主管法务局或地方法务局局长提出建议，并答复其询问。

法务局或地方法务局局长，在提出询问，收到建议或答复时，须迅速将具体情况向法务大臣报告。

第四十八条　公证员会在认为公证员存在违法或有损品德的行为时，须报告其隶属的法务局或地方法务局局长。

第四十九条　全国的公证员会可以设立日本公证员联合会。

日本公证员联合会以谋求改善和统一公证事务，保持公证员的品德而从事公证员指导和联络的相关事务为设立目的。

第五十条　公证员会及公证员是日本公证员联合会的会员。

第五十一条　设立日本公证员联合会时，须征得作为其会员的公证员会及公证员过半数同意后制订会则，并获得法务大臣的认可。

第五十二条　日本公证员联合会可以就公证事务向法务大臣提出建议，并答复其询问。

第五十三条　第四十五条第二款和第三款以及第

に第四十六条の規定は、日本公証人連合会について準用する。この場合において、第四十六条中「当該公証人会の事務所の所在地を管轄する法務局又は地方法務局の長」とあるのは、「法務大臣」と読み替えるものとする。

第五十四条 二人以上の公証人は、事務の合理化及び品位の向上を図るため必要があるときは、役場又は収支の全部若しくは一部を共にする合同役場を設けることができる。

第五十五条 公証人は、合同役場を設けようとするときは、その規約を定め、あらかじめ法務大臣の認可を受けなければならない。

2 前項の規約には、左に掲げる事項を定めなければならない。

一 名称

二 役場の所在

三 構成員に関する事項

四 役員に関する事項

五 収入に関する事項

六 経費に関する事項

七 加入及び脱退に関する事項

3 規約を変更しようとするときは、法務大臣の認可を受けなければならない。

四十六条的规定适用于日本公证员联合会。在此情形下，将条款中的“该公证员会事务所所在地的主管法务局或地方法务局局长”换作“法务大臣”。

第五十四条 两人以上的公证员为谋求事务合理化及提高品德，必要时可以合并事务所或收支的全部或部分，设立联合事务所。

第五十五条 公证员设立联合事务所时须制订规则，并事先得到法务大臣的认可。

前款所述规则须记明下列事项：

（一）名称；

（二）事务所所在地；

（三）成员有关事项；

（四）雇员有关事项；

（五）收入有关事项；

（六）经费有关事项；

（七）加入及退出有关事项。

更订规则时，须得到法务大臣的认可。

哈萨克斯坦

哈萨克斯坦共和国公证法

Law of the Republic of Kazakhstan on Notaries

dated 14 July 1997, No. 155

Unofficial translation

Footnote. Throughout the text after the word "Section" the numbers "I – II" shall be respectively substituted by the numbers "1 – 2", by Law of the Republic of Kazakhstan dated 20 December 2004 No 13 (enforced from 1 January, 2005)

Footnote. Throughout the text, the word "termination" is, in all contexts, substituted by the word "forfeit", by Law of the Republic of Kazakhstan dated 12 January, 2007 No 222 (enforced upon expiry of 6 months after official publication);

the words "personal seal" are in all contexts, substituted by the word "seal", by Law of the Republic of Kazakhstan dated 28.06.2012 No 24-V (enforced upon expiry of ten calendar days after first official publication).

Footnote. Throughout the text, the words "aul(s) (village(s))" are respectively substituted by the word "village(s)", by Constitutional Law of the Republic of Kazakhstan dated 03.07.2013 No 121-V (enforced upon expiry of ten calendar days after first official publication).

Section 1
Organization and legal basis of activities of notaries

Chapter 1. General provisions

Article 1. Kazakhstan Notary Profession

1. The Kazakhstan Notary Profession is a legal insti-

哈萨克斯坦共和国
公证法
颁布于 1997 年 7 月 14 日，155 号文

非官方翻译

脚注 依据哈萨克斯坦共和国 2004 年 12 月 20 日第 13 号法令（2005 年 1 月 1 日起施行）的规定，本法案中，“I-II”分别由“1-2”取代。

脚注 依据哈萨克斯坦共和国 2007 年 1 月 12 日第 222 号法令（正式公布后 6 个月届满时施行）的规定，在本法案中，“终止”均由“丧失”取代；依据哈萨克斯坦共和国 2012 年 6 月 28 日第 24-V 号法令（自首次公布之日起 10 日后开始施行）的规定，“自然人印章”由“印章”一词取代。

脚注 依据《哈萨克斯坦共和国宪法》(颁布于 2013 年 7 月 3 日）第 121-V 号（自首次公布之日起 10 日后开始施行）的规定，在本法案中，“aul（s）（village（s））”由“village（s）”取代。

第一部分
公证活动的组织和法律依据

第一章　一般规定

第一条　哈萨克斯坦公证业

1. 哈萨克斯坦公证机构是开展公证活动，提供合

tution providing qualified legal assistance and protection of rights and legal interests of individuals and legal entities by carrying out notarial activities.

2. The right to carry out notarial activities in the cases and within the limits established by this Law, shall be held by:

1)notaries working state notary offices (state notary), and notaries engaging in private practice (private notary);

2) civil servants in authorities in cities of regional significance, municipalities, villages and rural districts, authorized to carry out notary activities;

3) persons fulfilling consular functions in the name of Republic of Kazakhstan;

3-1) (excluded);

4) other persons authorized by this Law to carry out notarial activities.

Footnote. Article 1 as amended by Laws of the Republic of Kazakhstan dated 24.12.2001 No 276; 05.05.2003 No 408; 20.12.2004 No 13 (enforced from 01.01.2005); and 26.12.2011 No 516-IV (enforced upon expiry of ten calendar days after first official publication).

Article 2. Legislation concerning notaries

The legislation concerning notaries consists of Civil Code standards, this Law and other Kazakh legislation regulating notarial activity.

Article3.Notarial activity and its guarantees

1. Notarial activity is carrying out of notarial activities provided for by this Law and other Kazakh legislative acts, by the notary. In the cases and within the limits established by this Law, specially authorized civil servants may carry out separate notarial activity. Notarial activity in the Republic of Kazakhstan shall be based on principles of legality, independence and secrecy of notarial activities.

Notarial activity is not a business activity.

2. In carrying out notarial activities, notaries and other persons licensed to carry out notarial activities are independent and subject only to the Law. They shall thus be guided by this Law and other regulatory legal acts, and by international treaties ratified by the Republic of Kazakhstan, regulating such activities.

3.Individuals and legal entities shall be guaranteed secrecy for the notarial activities carried out by them.

4.Ensuring secrecy of notarial activities is obligatory for persons no longer working as notaries.

4-1.Responsibility of confidentiality of notarial activities shall extend to trainees and clerks of notaries.

格的法律援助，保护自然人或法人的权利和合法利益的法律机构。

2. 下列人员有权在一般情形和本法规定的范围内开展公证活动：

（1）在国家公证机构工作的国家公证员和在私营公证机构工作的私营公证员；

（2）在特定的区域、城市、村庄和偏远地区，被授权开展公证活动的地方政府当局的公务员；

（3）以哈萨克斯坦共和国名义履行领事职能的人员；

（3-1）（删除）；

（4）本法授权的其他人。

脚注 第1条经哈萨克斯坦共和国2001年12月24日第276号、2003年5月5日第408号、2004年12月20日第13号（2005年1月1日起施行）和2011年12月26日第516-IV号（自首次公布之日起10日后开始施行）的法律修订。

第二条 关于公证的法律

有关公证的法律包括《民法典》、哈萨克斯坦《公证法》（本法）、哈萨克斯坦规范公证活动的其他法律。

第三条 公证活动及其规范

1. 公证员有权开展本法和哈萨克斯坦其他法律规定的公证活动。依据本法规定，经特别授权的公务员可以开展公证活动。哈萨克斯坦共和国的公证活动应以合法性、独立性和保密性为原则。

公证活动不是商业行为。

2. 公证员和其他经授权开展公证活动的人员应依法、独立行使职权，只受法律约束。他们应遵守本法、其他法律规范、哈萨克斯坦共和国批准的国际条约的规定。

3. 自然人或法人开展公证活动时，应当保守在公证活动中知悉的秘密。

4. 不再从事公证的人员有义务保守从事公证活动期间知悉的秘密。

4-1. 受培训的公证员和公证文员同样负有上述保密的义务。

5.Information on notarial activities, and copies or duplicates issued by a notary, shall be issued only to legal entities and individuals under whose instructions the notarial activities were carried out, or their authorized bodies.

6.Information on notarial activities and documents shall be issued at the written request of courts, investigation and inquiry authorities according to proceedings, executive bodies according to proceedings, prosecution authorities according to proceedings, and judicial bodies and notary associations, authorized by this Law to inspect notaries' activities.

Information on notarial activities, necessary for carrying out advocacy activities shall be issued at the written request of a defence lawyer representative of an applicant for legal assistance.

7.Persons intentionally disclosing information on performance of notarial action, shall be liable in accordance with the legislation.

8. Legal entities and civil servants must send the notary information and documents necessary for carrying out notarial activities, not later than ten calendar days from the date of the notary's demand.

9.Information on wills, and copies and duplicates, shall be issued to the interested persons only after death of the testator, unless otherwise established by the legislation.

Footnote. Article 3 as amended by Laws of the Republic of Kazakhstan dated 22.06.2006 No 147; 26.12.2011 No 516-IV (enforced upon expiry of ten calendar days after first official publication); 27.04.2012 No 15-V (enforced upon expiry of ten calendar days after first official publication); and by Constitutional Law of the Republic of Kazakhstan dated 03.07.2013 No 121-V (enforced upon expiry of ten calendar days after first official publication).

Article 4. Notarial clerical correspondence

1. Notarial clerical correspondence shall be carried out in accordance with the rules of notarial clerical correspondence (hereinafter – the Rules), confirmed by the Kazakh Ministry of Justice by agreement with the authorized Kazakh state body for management of archives and documentation involvement of the state notary association.

2. The territorial justice authorities and the notary association shall monitor compliance with the requirements of the Rules.

3. Documents of state notaries must be entered into the state archive according to the procedure established by

5. 公证活动的资料和公证员出具的关于公证资料的复印件、副本，应当只提供给开展公证活动的法人和自然人或者其授权机构。

6. 根据本法得到授权的法院、侦查询问机关、诉讼行政机关、诉讼检察机关、司法机关和公证协会的书面请求，公证员应向其出具公证活动的资料和公证文件。

根据法律援助申请人的辩护律师的书面请求，公证员应当出具开展辩护活动所必需的公证活动资料。

7. 公民故意泄露公证活动信息的，应当依法承担责任。

8. 法人和公务员必须自公证员申请之日起 10 日内，将公证所需的资料和文件送交公证员。

9. 关于遗嘱的资料、复印件、副本，应当自立遗嘱人死亡后送交利害关系人，法律另有规定的除外。

脚注 第 3 条经哈萨克斯坦共和国 2006 年 6 月 22 日第 147 号法令、2011 年 12 月 26 日第 516-IV 号法令（自首次公布之日起 10 日后开始施行）、2012 年 4 月 27 日第 15-V 号法令（自首次公布之日起 10 日后开始施行）和 2013 年 7 月 3 日第 121-V 号哈萨克斯坦共和国宪法（第 121-V 号“宪法法律”于自首次公布之日起 10 日后开始施行）修订。

第四条 公证文书

1. 公证文书应当依照经授权的国家公证协会档案和文件管理机构与哈萨克斯坦司法部协商确定的公证文书规则（以下简称“规则”）制作。

2. 有管辖权的司法机关和公证协会应当监督规则的遵守情况。

3. 国家公证员的文件应当依照哈萨克斯坦法律规定的程序输入国家档案馆。私营公证员的文件应当按

Kazakh legislation. Documents of private notaries must be entered into a private notarial archive according to the procedure established by Kazakh legislation.

照哈萨克斯坦法律规定的程序存入私营公证档案馆。

Footnote. Article 4 as amended by Laws of the Republic of Kazakhstan dated 05.05.2003 No 408; and 26.12.2011 No 516-IV (enforced upon expiry of ten calendar days after first official publication).

脚注 第4条经哈萨克斯坦共和国2003年5月5日第408号和2011年12月26日第516-IV号法令修订（自首次公布之日起10日后开始施行）。

Article 4-1. Unified notarial information system.

The unified notarial information system is a hardware and software complex, intended for automation of notarial activities and interaction of judicial bodies and notary associations.

4-1 统一公证信息系统

统一公证信息系统是一个软硬件相结合的系统，旨在实现公证活动的自动化和司法机关与公证协会的互动。

Footnote. Law supplemented by Article 4-1 in accordance with Law of the Republic of Kazakhstan 15.07.2010 No 337-IV (for method of enforcement see Article 2).

脚注 第4-1条依据哈萨克斯坦共和国法律2010年7月15日第337-IV号（施行方法见第2条）补充。

Article5.Language of clerical correspondence

1. Notarial clerical correspondence shall be conducted in accordance with Kazakh legislation concerning languages.

第五条 公证文书语言

1. 公证文书应依据哈萨克斯坦有关语言的法律制作。

2.If an applicant for notarial action, does not speak the language of the clerical correspondence, the texts of the documents formulated shall be translated for him/her, at his/her request, for a fee in accordance with Article 80 of this Law.

2. 申请公证的申请人不会使用文书要求的语言时，应当依据申请人的请求，为其翻译公证文件，并按照本法第80条的规定，收取相关费用。

Chapter 2. LEGAL STATUS OF NOTARY

第二章 公证员的法律地位

Article 6. Notary in the Republic of Kazakhstan

1. A notary may be a Kazakh citizen who has reached the age of twenty five years and has higher legal education, not less than two years' work experience in the legal profession, has undertaken a notary internship lasting not less than one year, is certified by the certification commission of justice, and has obtained a license for the right to carry out notarial activity, unless this Law provides otherwise.

第六条 哈萨克斯坦共和国公证员

1. 除本法另有规定外，年满二十五周岁、受过高等法律教育、从事法律工作不少于两年、公证实习时间不少于一年、经司法委员会认证、并取得公证职能执照的哈萨克斯坦公民，可以担任公证员。

A state notary shall be a state employee, holding a post according to the procedure established by Kazakh legislation concerning state service.

国家公证员为国家工作人员，依据哈萨克斯坦国家公务法律规定的程序履职。

A state notary shall be bound by the requirements mentioned in the first part of this Article, except for receipt of a licence for the right to carry out notarial activities.

国家公证员受本条第一部分规定的约束但不需要取得公证执照。

A notary may not be a person with unspent or undischarged convictions as established by the Law procedure, or recognized in established procedure as partly or fully incapacitated.

依据法律程序有犯罪嫌疑或未解除犯罪的人，或经法定程序被认定为限制民事行为能力人或无民事行为能力人，不得担任公证员。

A notary may not be a person for whom a criminal case has been terminated on grounds of non-rehabilitation, or whose notarial activity has been terminated through loss of licence or dismissal from office of state notary for breach of Kazakh legislation concerning fulfilment of notarial activities for five years after the occurrence of such events.

2. Private and state notaries shall have equal rights and responsibilities when carrying out notarial activity. Documents formulated by them shall have equal legal force.

3. Performance of notarial activities by persons unlicensed as per paragraph 1 of this Article (except for state notary and persons mentioned in subparagraph 2), 3) of paragraph 2 of Article 1 of this Law), or violation of other requirements of legislation concerning notaries and income from notarial activities shall lead to responsibility in accordance with Kazakh legislation.

4.Territorial body of justice shall have specific responsibility for notarial activities of state notaries.

Footnote. Article 6 as amended by Laws of the Republic of Kazakhstan dated 13.11.1998 No 302; 11.07.2001 No 235; 24.12.2001 No 276; 05.05.2003 No 408; and 26.12.2011 No 516-IV (enforced upon expiry of ten calendar days after first official publication).

Article 7. Clerks and trainees of notary

1. Notary may have clerks and trainees.

2. Clerks of notaries may Kazakh citizens only.

3. Clerks of notaries may work on the basis of an employment agreement with a notary engaged in private practice or be a staff member of a state notarial office.

4. Trainee notaries may be Kazakh citizens with higher legal education.

Trainees shall be trained by a notary engaged in private practice, or by state notaries on the basis of a training agreement.

Persons claiming the right to carry out notary activities shall conclude a training agreement with a territorial justice authority or notary association.

5. Clerks and trainees may, by order and under the supervision of the notary, carry out the notary's orders, which shall not take the place of notarial activities and instead be auxiliary to the maintenance of notarial clerical correspondence.

6. Training periods may be reduced by coordinated decision of the territorial body of justice and notarial

下列人员不得担任公证员：因身体未康复的原因导致犯罪案件被终结的，被吊销公证执照，或因违反哈萨克斯坦关于履行公证活动的法律被解除职务未满五年的。

2. 私营公证员和国家公证员开展公证活动时，享有平等的权利和义务。他们出具的文件具有同等的法律效力。

3. 本条第 1 款中无公证执照的人（国家公证员和本法第 1 条第 2 款第 3 项所述人员除外）从事公证活动，或违反有关公证员和公证活动收入的其他法律规定，应依据哈萨克斯坦法律追究上述人员的责任。

4. 有管辖权的司法机关对国家公证员的公证活动负责。

脚注 第 6 条经哈萨克斯坦共和国 1998 年 11 月 13 日第 302 号、2001 年 7 月 11 日第 235 号、2001 年 12 月 24 日 第 276 号、2003 年 5 月 5 日 第 408 号 和 2011 年 12 月 26 日第 516-IV 号法令（自首次公布之日起 10 日后开始施行）修订。

第七条　公证文员和见习公证员

1. 公证机构可以配备公证文员和见习公证员。

2. 公证文员应当是哈萨克斯坦共和国公民。

3. 公证文员可以是与私营公证机构签订雇佣协议的工作人员，也可以是国家公证机构的工作人员。

4. 见习公证员由受过较高法律教育的哈萨克斯坦共和国公民担任。见习公证员的培训应由私营公证员或国家公证员依据培训协议进行。

有权开展公证活动的人员应当与当地司法机关或公证协会签订培训协议。

5. 公证文员和见习公证员可以依据指示，并在公证员的监督下执行职务，但该行为不能取代公证活动，公证文员和见习公证员应协助维持公证文书的通信往来。

6. 有管辖权的司法机关和公证协会可以决定缩短培训时间，法律行业从业经验不少于五年的人员，其

chamber for persons, with not less than five years' experience in the legal profession. Duration of training periods may not be less than three months.

培训期不得少于三个月。

7. The aim of training shall be to provide the trainee with professional knowledge and practical skills in carrying out notarial activities and organizing the work of a notary.

7. 培训的目的是为学员提供开展公证活动、组织公证工作的专业知识和实践技能。

8. Not more than two trainees at the same time may undergo training with a notary.

8. 一名公证员不可以同时培训两名以上见习公证员。

9. Training hall be carried out according to unified program of professional preparation of trainees, confirmed by order of the Kazakh Ministry of Justice by agreement with the state notary association.

9. 培训厅按照国家公证协会经哈萨克斯坦司法部批准的《统一职业培训方案》开展工作。

The professional training programme shall be obligatory for all trainees and contain a list of measures aimed at giving trainees special theoretical skills, practical skills in notarial activities and organization of work of notary, and learning of professional and ethic regulations of behaviour of notary and attending seminars organized for notaries or specially for trainees.

职业培训具有强制性并伴随着一系列措施，旨在传授见习公证员专门的理论知识、公证活动的实践技能和组织技能，学习公证员职业道德规则，并参加为公证员或见习公证员举办的研讨会。

Reduction of duration of training shall not release trainees from responsibility to pass through the training program.

缩短培训时间不免除学员应当参加并通过培训方案的责任。

10. On completion of internship the notary shall prepare conclusion, reflecting completion of the professional training programme and be confirmed within ten business days by coordinated decision of the territorial body of justice and notarial chamber. If the trainee has not completed the study under the professional training programme, additional time shall be granted to him/her.

10. 实习结束后，公证员应编写报告，反映专业培训方案的完成情况，并由有管辖权的司法机关和公证协会协商，在 10 个工作日内予以确认。如果见习公证员没有完成专业培训方案下的学习要求，应延长其培训时间。

11. Completion of the professional training programme shall be a compulsory condition of training.

11. 完成专业培训方案的规定具有强制性。

12. The requirements of this Article shall not apply to persons with work experience as a state notary, except those dismissed from duty on negative grounds.

12. 本条的规定不适用于有公证经验的国家公证员，但被免除公职的人除外。

Footnote. Article 7 is in the wording of Law of the Republic of Kazakhstan dated 26.12.2011 No 516-IV (enforced upon expiry of ten calendar days after first official publication).

脚注 第 7 条采用哈萨克斯坦共和国 2011 年 12 月 26 日第 516-IV 号法令的措辞（自首次公布之日起 10 日后开始施行）。

Article 7-1. Certification commission of justice for the right to carry out notarial activities

7-1 司法认证委员会

1. Persons claiming the right to carry out notarial activity, shall be certified by the certification commissions of justice for the right to carry out notarial activity created in territorial bodies of justice in the regions and cities of national significance, and the capital.

1. 声称有权开展公证活动的人员，应由公证委员会确认其资格，以便其可在有司法管辖权的地区和国家重点城市以及首都开展公证活动。

The certification commission of justice for the right to carry out notarial activity shall consist of seven members: two notaries, including the dean of the notarial chamber, two representatives of territorial body of justice, a legal scholar and two maslikhat deputies.

司法认证委员会由七名成员组成：两名公证员（包括一名公证协会主任），两名地区司法代表，一名法律学者和两名代理人。

The composition of the certification commissions of justice for the right to carry out notarial activity and regulate its works shall be confirmed by orders of the Kazakh Minister of Justice.

司法认证委员会有权开展公证活动和管理工作，其组成成员应由哈萨克斯坦司法部长任命。

2. The basic tasks of certification commission of justice for the right to carry out notarial activity shall be:

2. 司法认证委员会的基本任务是：

1) ensuring quality selection of applicants toe licence to carry out notarial activity;

2) ensuring openness and publicity of sessions.

（1）为开展公证活动，对申请公证员执照的申请人进行高质量的考核、选拔；

（2）确保会议的公开性。

3. Representatives of mass media may attend the session of commission of justice certification for the right to carry out notarial activity.

3. 大众媒体的代表可参加司法认证委员会的会议。

4. In order to ensure openness and publicity of the certification commission of justice sessions for the right to carry out notarial activity, an audio and/or video or stenograph shall be produced. The stenograph or audio and/or video record made during the session shall be attached to the minutes of the session and remain together with the material of the certification commission of justice for the right to carry out notarial activity.

4. 为了确保司法认证委员会会议的公开性，应制作录音录像或记录。会议期间所作的记录或录音、录像应附在会议记录之后，并应与司法认证委员会的材料一起保存。

Footnote. Chapter 2 supplemented by Article 7-1 in accordance with Law of the Republic of Kazakhstan dated 26.12.2011 No 516-IV (enforced upon expiry of ten calendar days after first official publication).

脚注 第二章，依据哈萨克斯坦共和国 2011 年 12 月 26 日第 516-IV 号法令，由第 7-1 条加以补充（自首次公布之日起 10 日后开始施行）。

Article 7-2. Method and conditions of certification

7-2. 认证的方法和条件

1. The method and conditions for certifying persons undergoing training and claiming the right to carry out notarial activity shall be determined by rules confirmed by the Government of the Republic of Kazakhstan.

1. 对接受过培训并主张有权开展公证活动的人进行认证的方法和条件应由哈萨克斯坦共和国政府颁布的规则确定。

2. Persons claiming the right to carry out notarial activity shall, after undergoing training, submit an application according to place of residence to the corresponding certification commission of justice for the right to carry out notarial activity, for his/her certification by territorial bodies of justice in the regions, cities of national significance and the capital, with attachment of documents, provided for by Kazakh legislation.

2. 声称有权开展公证活动的人，应该在培训完成后，向其居住地的司法认证委员会提出申请，以便开展公证活动，由有司法管辖权的地区、国家重点城市以及首都的司法认证委员会认证，并附上哈萨克斯坦法律规定的文件。

3. In case of inappropriate formulation, or submission of an incomplete package of documents, the application and presented documents shall be returned to the applicant by the territorial bodies of justice in the region, cities of

3. 如以不恰当的方式提出或提交不完整的文件，申请书和提交的文件应由有司法管辖权的地区、国家重点城市以及首都的司法认证协会于收到之日起 5 个工作日内退还申请人，并附上书面理由。

national significance and the capital, without examination, no later than five business days from the date of receipt with written notification of reason for return.

4. Certification shall be refused if the applicant does not comply with the requirements of this Law. In certification is refused, the territorial bodies of justice in the regions, cities of national significance and the capital city shall send a well-grounded decision to the contender not less than fifteen business days from date of receipt of application.

Refusal of certification may be appealed against before a court according to the procedure established by the Law.

5. Applicants accepted for certification shall be notified in writing by the territorial bodies of justice in the regions, cities of national significance and the capital city of the place, date, time and procedure of certification at least ten calendar days before the ceremony.

6. Certification shall be conducted by the certification commission of justice for the right to carry out notarial activity as and when necessary, but at least once every quarter.

7. Certification consists of two stages:

1) passing a computer test on awareness of Kazakh legislation;

2) oral test on exam papers.

8. Applicants may, if they wish, undergo a test in the Kazakh and Russian languages. The test shall be conducted using computer technology.

9. According to the results of certification, the certification commission of justice for the right to carry out notarial activity shall issue a well-grounded decision on whether or not to certificate not later than the day following certification.

The decision of the certification commission shall be effective for three years from the date of issue. Decisions of the certification commission of justice may be appealed against before a court according to the procedure established by the Law.

10. During certification, the applicant may not any information, specialist and other literature, communication tools, or notes.

Breach of these requirements shall exclude an applicant from certification by the certification commission of justice for the right to carry out notarial activity.

Applicants excluded from certification may send a repeat application for certification according to the proce-

4. 申请人不符合本法规定的，司法认证委员会不得受理其申请。有司法管辖权的地区、国家重点城市以及首都的司法认证委员会拒绝认证的，应当自收到申请之日起至少 15 个工作日内，将理由充分的不予受理决定书送交申请人。

被拒绝认证的申请人可依据法律规定的程序向法院提出上诉。

5. 地区、国家重点城市以及首都的司法认证委员会应当在就职典礼举行前 10 日内书面通知得到认证的申请人就职典礼的地点、时间和程序。

6. 由司法认证委员会每个季度至少开展一次认证公证员有从事公证活动的权力的工作。

7. 认证分两个阶段：

（1）通过关于哈萨克斯坦法律的计算机测试；

（2）通过面试。

8. 申请人可以选用哈萨克语或俄语进行测试。测试以机考形式进行。

9. 依据认证结果，司法认证委员会应当在认证后第二天作出是否通过的决定，该决定应当有充分的理由。

司法认证委员会的决定自签发之日起三年内有效。可依据该法规定的程序，就司法认证委员会的决定向法院提出上诉。

10. 在认证期间，申请人不得携带任何信息、专业资料、文献、交流工具或笔记。违反上述规定的，司法认证委员会不得对其进行认证。

未被认证的申请人，可以依照本法规定的程序，自司法认证委员会作出决定之日起三个月后，再次提出认证申请。

dure provided by this Law, upon expiry of three months from the date of issue of decision by the certification commission of justice for the right to carry out notarial activity.

11. Applicants presented for certification for a valid reason shall be called for the next session of certification by the commission of justice for the right to carry out notarial activity, according to the procedure provided by paragraph 5 of this Article.

11. 依据本条第5款规定的程序，申请人以正当理由提交认证申请的，由司法认证委员的下一届会议进行认证。

In case of repeated non-attendance by the applicant, his/her application shall remain unexamined and be returned together with their submitted documents.

申请人多次缺席认证会议的，他/她的申请将保持未审查状态，连同提交的文件一并退回。

Footnote. Chapter 2 supplemented by Article 7-2 in accordance with Law of the Republic of Kazakhstan dated 26.12.2011 No 516-IV (enforced upon expiry of ten calendar days after first official publication).

脚注 第二章，依据哈萨克斯坦共和国2011年12月26日第516-IV号法令（自首次公布之日起10日后开始施行），由第7-2条加以补充。

Article 8. Licence to carry out notarial activity

第八条 公证执照

1. A licence to carry out notarial activity (notary licence), issued by the Ministry of Justice of the Republic of Kazakhstan according to the results of certification, shall authorize a private notary to carry out notarial activities.

1. 哈萨克斯坦共和国司法部依据认证结果颁发开展公证活动的许可证（公证执照），该执照授予私营公证员开展公证活动的权力。

2. The list of documents necessary for granting a notary licence, and the terms and procedure for issuing a licence, shall be established by the relevant regulatory legal acts.

2. 颁发公证执照所需的文件清单、颁发的条件和程序，由有关法律法规规定。

3. A notary licence shall be general, issued without limitation of, and valid throughout Kazakh territory.

3. 公证执照具有普遍性，签发不受限制，并在哈萨克斯坦境内有效。

4. A charge, the amount and payment method of which shall be determined by tax legislation, shall be applied for the issue of a notary licence.

4. 签发公证执照时，应当适用税法规定的收费标准和支付方式。

5. The Ministry of Justice of the Republic of Kazakhstan shall keep a State register of licenses to carry out notarial activity and publish information on persons to be issued with licences to carry out notarial activity in the departmental press, specifying:

5. 哈萨克斯坦共和国司法部应当保存记载公证执照颁发情况的国家登记册，并在省级报刊上公布获得公证执照人员的相关信息，具体内容包括：

1) the surname, forename patronymic of a notary;

2) the licence date and number.

（1）公证员的姓、名；

（2）执照的日期及号码。

6. Persons, passing the qualifying examinations in the qualifications body of justice of the Republic of Kazakhstan or in the qualifications commission of the Supreme Judicial Council of the Republic of Kazakhstan, regular judges and persons working as regular judges except for judges dismissed from judicial appointment for detractive offences and violation of law in fulfilment of their obligations, as well as state notaries, may obtain a licence to carry out notarial activity without undergoing certification.

6. 通过哈萨克斯坦共和国司法部资格考试或哈萨克斯坦共和国最高司法委员会资格考试的人、正式法官和准正式法官（因违法履行义务而被解除司法任命的除外），以及国家公证员，可不经认证，而获得开展公证活动的执照。

6-1. Excluded by Law of the Republic of Kazakhstan

6-1. 本条被哈萨克斯坦共和国2011年12月26

dated 26.12.2011 No 516-IV (enforced upon expiry of ten calendar days after first official publication).

Footnote. Article 8 as amended by Laws of the Republic of Kazakhstan dated 13.11.1998 No 302; 11.07.2001 No 235; 05.05.2003 No 408; 20.12.2004 No 13 (enforced from 01.01.2005); 29.04.2009 No 154-IV (for method of enforcement see Article 2); and 26.12.2011 No 516-IV (enforced upon expiry of ten calendar days after first official publication).

日第 516-IV 号法令（自首次公布之日起 10 日后开始施行）删除。

脚注 第 8 条依据哈萨克斯坦共和国 1998 年 11 月 13 日第 302 号法令、2001 年 7 月 11 日第 235 号法令、2003 年 5 月 5 日第 408 号法令、2004 年 12 月 20 日第 13 号法令（从 2005 年 1 月 1 日起施行）、2009 年 4 月 29 日第 154 号 -IV 法令（执法方法见第 2 条）和 2011 年 12 月 26 日第 516-IV 号法令（在自首次公布之日起 10 日后开始施行）修订。

Article 9. Refusal to issue notary licence

1. Grounds for refusal to issue a notary licence shall be established by legislation concerning licensure.

2. A well-grounded written decision specifying the reasons for refusal shall, within three days from the date of its adoption, be issued following refusal to issue a notary licence.

3. The decision of refuse may be appealed against before a court.

第九条 不予颁发公证执照

1. 不予颁发公证执照的情形由有关法律规定。

2 不予颁发公证执照的书面决定应当有充分的理由，并自作出决定之日起 3 日内发出。

3. 申请人可就拒绝颁发的决定向法院提出上诉。

Article 10. Suspension of notary licence

1. Notary licences shall be suspended by decision of the Ministry of Justice of the Republic of Kazakhstan on the basis of applications from citizens, territorial bodies of justice, notary associations and prosecution, investigation and inquiry authorities.

2. Validity of a notary licence shall be suspended for up to six months in the following cases:

1) commencement of action proceedings for termination of a licence to carry out notarial activity;

2) implication of a notary as a defendant in a criminal case;

3) failure by the notary to report information on change of surname, forename or patronymic to the territorial body of justice within one month;

3-1) systematic (three or more times during twelve continuous calendar days) violation of requirements provided by Kazakh legislation to combat legitimization (laundering) of illegally received income, and financing of terrorism;

4) violation by the notary of an area of activity delegated to him/her in accordance with this Law;

5) violation of Kazakh legislation in fulfilment of notarial activities, involving violation by a notary of laws and the legal interests of the state, individuals and legal entities;

6) physical absence of the notary from the address specified in the judicial bodies' registration record;

第十条 暂停公证执照

1. 哈萨克斯坦共和国司法部应依据公民、地区司法机关、公证协会以及起诉、调查和询问当局的申请，作出暂停公证执照的决定。

2. 出现下列情况，公证执照最长可暂停六个月：

（1）因终止公证执照而启动诉讼程序；

（2）公证员在刑事案件中作为被告；

（3）公证员未在一个月内向司法机关报告姓、名、姓名变更情况的；

（3-1）多次（连续 12 日内三次或三次以上）违反哈萨克斯坦法律规定的，该法旨在打击洗钱和资助恐怖主义行为；

（4）违反执业地区的法律；

（5）违反哈萨克斯坦法律开展公证活动，包括公证员违反法律，损害国家利益、自然人或法人的合法利益；

（6）公证员不在司法机关登记记录中指定地址的；

7) failure by the notary to comply with the requirements of paragraph 4 of Article 15 of this Law;

8) failure to observe the restrictions, provided by Article 19 of this Law;

9) failure by the notary to carry out practical notary activity after three months from the date of his/her placing on the register.

3. The reasons for and period of suspension of licence shall be specified in the licence suspension decision. Validity of licence shall be suspended from the date of advice of decision to a notary. Decision restore validity of licence shall be advised to the notary upon removal of grounds for suspension, within three calendar days from the date of sending of information on removal of grounds for suspension of notary.

4. Suspension of a notary licence shall lead to prohibition of notarial activities and delivery of a seal to the territorial body of justice for the notary's period of suspension.

5. The decision to suspend or restore a license shall be published in the departmental press of the Ministry of Justice of the Republic of Kazakhstan.

6. Decision to suspend a notary licence may be appealed against in a court.

7. The territorial body of justice and notary association shall be obliged to take measures to transfer documents from a notary whose licence is suspended to another notary, according to the procedure provided by the rules on notarial clerical correspondence.

Footnote. Article 10 as amended by Laws of the Republic of Kazakhstan dated 05.05.2003 No 408; 28.08.2009 No 192-IV (enforced from 08.03.2010); and 26.12.2011 No 516-IV (enforced upon expiry of 10 calendar days after first official publication); and by Constitutional Law of the Republic of Kazakhstan dated 03.07.2013 No 121-V (enforced upon expiry of ten calendar days after first official publication).

Article 11. Loss of notary licence

Notary licences shall be terminated by the court decision following action of prosecution authorities, the Ministry of Justice of the Republic of Kazakhstan, or the state notary association, in the following cases:

1) (excluded)

2) repeated infringement of the Notary's Code of Honour by a private notary;

3) repeated infringement of Kazakh legislation con-

（7）公证员不遵守本法第 15 条第 4 款规定的；

（8）不遵守本法第 19 条的限制规定的；

（9）自登记之日起 3 个月内，公证员未开展实际公证活动的。

3. 司法部应当在暂停公证执照的决定中释明暂停公证执照的理由及期限。

执照的有效性自公证员知悉暂停公证执照的决定之日起暂停。执照恢复有效的，司法部应当自发出撤销暂停公证执照理由起 3 日内通知公证员。

4. 暂停公证执照将会导致公证活动的停止，公证员应在停职期间向有管辖权的司法机关交付印章。

5. 司法部应在哈萨克斯坦共和国司法部的部门报刊上公布暂停或恢复公证执照的决定。

6. 公证员不满暂停公证执照的决定，可向法院提出上诉。

7. 地区司法机关和公证协会有义务采取措施，按照公证文书规则规定的程序，将被暂停公证执照的公证员的证件移送给另一名公证员。

脚注 第 10 条经哈萨克斯坦共和国 2003 年 5 月 5 日第 408 号、2009 年 8 月 28 日第 192-IV 号（2010 年 3 月 8 日起施行）和 2011 年 12 月 26 日第 516-IV 号法令（自首次公布之日起 10 日后开始施行）和哈萨克斯坦共和国 2013 年 7 月 3 日第 121-V 号"宪法"（自首次公布之日起 10 日后开始施行）修正。

第十一条 吊销公证执照

发生下列情况，法院应在检察机关、哈萨克斯坦共和国司法部或公证协会采取措施后作出决定，吊销公证执照：

（1）（删除）；

（2）私营公证员屡次违反公证员荣誉守则的；

（3）公证员屡次违反哈萨克斯坦法律开展公证活

cerning fulfilment of notarial activities, or law violation by the notary with damage to the interests of the state, individuals and legal entities;

4) failure to remove grounds for suspension of a licence;

5) confirmation of provision by the notary of unreliable or intentionally distorted information in the documents constituting grounds for the issue of a notary licence;

6) suspension of licence thrice;

7) excluded by Law of the Republic of Kazakhstan dated 26.12.2011 No 516-IV (enforced upon expiry of 10 calendar days after first official publication);

8) carrying out by the notary of professional activity without relevant registration in the territorial bodies of justice.

Footnote. Article 11 as amended by Laws of the Republic of Kazakhstan dated 11.07.2001 No 235; 05.05.2003 No 408; and 26.12.2011 No 516-IV (enforced upon expiry of 10 calendar days after first official publication).

动的，或者损害国家、自然人或法人利益的；

（4）暂停执照的情形未结束的；

（5）公证员在申请公证执照的文件中提供虚假信息或故意编造虚假信息的；

（6）公证员曾被暂停执照三次的；

（7）本条被哈萨克斯坦共和国 2011 年 12 月 26 日第 516-IV 号法令（自首次公布之日起 10 日后开始施行）删除；

（8）公证员开展专业公证活动，未在有管辖权的司法机关进行相应登记的。

脚注 第 11 条经哈萨克斯坦共和国 2001 年 7 月 11 日第 235 号、2003 年 5 月 5 日第 408 号和 2011 年 12 月 26 日第 516-IV 号法令（自首次公布之日起 10 日后开始施行）修订。

Article 12. Termination of notary licence

1. Validity of a notary licence shall be terminated when the licence is lost, or following decision of the Ministry of Justice of the Republic of Kazakhstan, in the following cases:

1) filing of application by the notary's own volition;

2) changing of citizenship of notary, or his/her departure to a permanent place of residence outside Kazakhstan;

3) death of notary;

4) conviction of notary for offence following passing of judgment;

4-1) decree to terminate criminal case with non-rehabilitating grounds in relation to the notary;

5) recognition of a notary as totally or partly incapacitated for work, according to the procedure established by legislation;

6) impossibility of fulfilment by the notary of professional duties for health reason (subject to medical report);

7) recognition of a notary as missing or declared dead.

2. Applications for termination of a notary licence shall be proposed by the relevant notary association and territorial body of justice.

3. the territorial body of justice and notary association shall be obliged to take measures to transfer documents from a notary whose licence is terminated to another nota-

第十二条 终止公证执照

1. 因公证执照的丢失，或哈萨克斯坦共和国司法部因下列情形作出裁定，执照的有效性终止：

（1）公证员自愿提出申请的；

（2）公证员变更国籍的，或离开哈萨克斯坦境内在他国永久性居住的；

（3）公证员死亡的；

（4）依生效判决，认定公证员有罪的；

（4-1）依据法令，无正当理由终止与公证员有关的刑事案件的；

（5）依据法律规定的程序，裁定公证员完全或部分丧失工作能力的；

（6）公证员因健康原因不能履行专业职责的（须提交医疗报告）；

（7）公证员被宣告失踪或宣告死亡的。

2. 终止公证执照的申请应由相应的公证协会和地区司法机关提出。

3. 地区司法机关和公证协会应当将执照被终止的公证员的文件转交给其他公证员或私营公证档案馆，同时收回执照，将其移交给颁发执照的机关，同时销

ry or to the private notarial archive, and, on revocation of a license, for transferring it to the licensor and destroying the notary's seal.

4.Disputes linked with termination of notary licences shall be settled in a judicial procedure.

Footnote. Article 12 as amended by Law of the Republic of Kazakhstan dated 5 May, 2003 No 408.

Article 13. State notary

Footnote. Article 13 is excluded by Law of the Republic of Kazakhstan dated 26.12.2011 No 516-IV (enforced upon expiry of 10 calendar days after first official publication).

Article 14. State notary office

1. The state notary office shall be a structural subdivision of the territorial body of justice without legal entity rights, and shall act on the basis of the Provisions confirmed by this body.

2. State notary offices shall be located in districts/cities of the Republic of Kazakhstan.

Article 15. Notary in private practice

1. Notaries in private practice, shall be recognized citizens in private practice without legal entity formation on the basis of a license, with his/her civil liability insured for obligations arising resulting from civil damages in the fulfilment of notarial activities, and shall be members of the notary association and registered with the territorial body of justice.

2. Notaries in private practice shall have the right to open a current account with banking institutions, hire and dismiss clerks and technical workers according to labour legislation, manage income earned from carrying out notarial activities, appear in court in his/her own name, and perform other actions in accordance with Kazakh legislation.

3. (Regulations of paragraph 3 lose effect and are not subject to application of Regulations of the Constitutional Council of the Republic of Kazakhstan dated 31 January 2005, No 1)

4. Notaries engaging in private practice shall be obliged to have one office suitable for unimpeded access by individuals and representatives of legal entities, confidentiality of performance of notarial activities, and conditions capable of ensuring security of notarial clerical correspondence.

The notary's office shall be the place of his/her re-

毁公证员的印章。

4. 与终止公证执照有关的争议按司法程序解决。

脚注 第 12 条经哈萨克斯坦共和国 2003 年 5 月 5 日第 408 号法令修订。

第十三条 国家公证员

脚注 本条被哈萨克斯坦共和国 2011 年 12 月 26 日第 516-IV 号法令（在自首次公布之日起 10 日后开始施行）删除。

第十四条 公证机构

1. 公证机构是地区司法部的分支机构，无法人资格，应当依据司法部的规定开展业务。

2. 公证机构设在哈萨克斯坦共和国各地区 / 城市。

第十五条 私营公证员

1. 私营公证员系从事私人执业的公民，而非有执照的法人，是公证协会的成员，在当地司法部注册登记，且应对其执行公证活动所造成损害的民事责任投保。

2. 私营公证员有权在银行开立活期存款账户，依据劳动法雇用和辞退办事员和技术工人，管理公证活动所得收入，以自己的名义出庭，并依据哈萨克斯坦法律从事其他活动。

3.（第 3 条失效，不适用于哈萨克斯坦共和国宪法委员会 2005 年 1 月 31 日第 1 号法令）

4. 私营公证员应配备可让自然人或法人代表自由进入，并能够确保公证活动的机密性和公证办事员的通信安全的办公室。

公证机构所在地为其注册所在地。公证机构搬迁

cord registration. Repeated record registration shall not be required if the notary office moves within the notary's designated territory. The territorial body of justice shall be obliged to make enquiries with a view to determining that the office complies with the requirements of Kazakh legislation within five business days of date of receipt of application for relocation of the notary's office within the designated territory.

至指定地区内的，不需要重复登记。当地司法机关有义务进行调查，以确定该公证机构在收到同意其迁往指定地区的申请之日起5个工作日内符合哈萨克斯坦法律的要求。

5. (Excluded).

6. (Excluded).

7. One or more notaries may work in one office when they comply with the requirements of paragraph 4 of this Article.

5.（删除）。

6.（删除）。

7. 一名或多名符合本条第4款要求的公证员可以在一个办公室工作。

Footnote. Article 15 as amended by Laws of the Republic of Kazakhstan dated 24.12.2001 No 276; 05.05.2003 No 408; 11.07.2009 No 185-IV (shall be enforced from 30.08.2009); and 26.12.2011 No 516-IV (enforced upon expiry of 10 calendar days after first official publication).

脚注 第15条经哈萨克斯坦共和国2001年12月24日第276号、2003年5月5日第408号、2009年7月11日第185-IV号法令（从2009年8月3日起施行）和2011年12月26日第516-IV号法令（在自首次公布之日起10日后开始施行）修订。

Article 16. Insurance of activity of private notary

1. Private notaries shall be obliged to take out civil liability insurance for obligations arising from civil damages arising from the execution of notarial activities, as provided in paragraph 1 of Article 34 of this Law, and shall not have a right to carry out notarial activities in the absence of such policy.

2. The procedure and conditions of civil liability insurance for notaries against obligations arising from civil damages arising from the execution of notarial activities shall be established by Kazakh legislative acts.

Footnote. Article 16 as amended by Law of the Republic of Kazakhstan dated 5 May 2003, No 408.

第十六条　私营公证员的保险

1. 私营公证员有义务按照本法第34条第1款的规定，为执行公证活动可能造成的民事损害所承担民事责任投保，没有保险的，无权开展公证活动。

2. 公证员购买本条第1款规定的保险的条件和程序由哈萨克斯坦法律规定。

脚注 第16条经哈萨克斯坦共和国2003年5月5日第408号法令修订。

Article 17. Rights of notary

Notaries shall have the right to:

1) Carry out notarial activities, provided for by this Law and other Kazakh legislative acts, in the interest of individuals and legal entities approaching them;

2) produce drafts of contracts, applications and other documents;

3) prepare copies of documents and abridged versions of them;

4) provide consultation on issues of fulfilment of notarial activities;

5) claim from individuals and legal entities the documents and information necessary for fulfilment of notarial activities, in accordance with established requirements for

第十七条　公证员的权利

公证员有权：

（1）开展本法和其他哈萨克斯坦法律规定的公证活动，为自然人或法人的利益而接触相关人员；

（2）起草合同草案、申请书和其他文件；

（3）准备文件副本和删节版本；

（4）就公证活动的履行问题提供咨询；

（5）向自然人、法人索要履行公证活动所需的文件和资料，包括受哈萨克斯坦法律所保护的商业秘密、银行秘密和其他秘密，该行为应当符合信息披露

disclosure of information, including commercial, banking and other secrets legally protected by Kazakh legislative acts;

6) practice a scientific, educational and creative activity;

7) (excluded).

Footnote. Article 17 as amended by Laws of the Republic of Kazakhstan dated 29.03.2000 No 42; 05.05.2003 No 408; and 26.12.2011 No 516-IV (enforced upon expiry of 10 calendar days after first official publication).

Article 18. Obligations of notary

1. Notaries shall be obliged to:

1) carry out notarial activities in accordance with requirements of this Law and other Kazakh regulatory legal acts governing activity of notaries;

2) explain rights and obligations to citizens and legal entities, and warn of consequences of performed notarial activities so that lack of legal information cannot be used to their detriment;

3) keep under seal of secrecy information made known to them in the context of professional activity;

4) refuse to carry out notarial activity that contravenes Kazakh legislation;

5) comply with professional ethics;

6) submit information on fulfilment of notarial action, other documents, and where necessary personal explanations, including issues of noncompliance with the requirements of professional ethics in the event of complaints about their action to judicial authorities and/or the notary association;

7) transfer documents being produced to another notary in the event of suspension of license, according to the procedure provided for by the rules concerning notarial clerical correspondence;

8) send all notarial documents held to the private notarial archive in the event of termination of licence on grounds, provided by subparagraphs 1), 2), 4), 4-1) and 6) of paragraph 1 of Article 12 of this Law;

9) provide information on change of surname, name, patronymic and location of office to the territorial body of justice within one month.

2. Provision of data and information on notarial activities to the authorized financial monitoring body according to the order and procedure provided for in the Law of the Republic of Kazakhstan "Concerning countering of legitimization (laundering) of illegally received income

的要求；

（6）开展科学、教育、创新活动；

（7）（删除）。

脚注 第 17 条经哈萨克斯坦共和国 2000 年 3 月 29 日第 42 号、2003 年 5 月 5 日第 408 号和 2011 年 12 月 26 日第 516-IV 号法令修订（在自首次公布之日起 10 日后开始施行）。

第十八条 公证员的义务

1. 公证员有义务：

（1）依照本法和其他哈萨克规范公证活动的法律开展公证活动；

（2）向公民和法人阐述权利和义务，并告知开展公证活动的效力，以避免当事人因欠缺法律知识而损害自身利益；

（3）保守在公证活动中知悉的秘密；

（4）拒绝从事违反哈萨克斯坦法律的公证活动；

（5）遵守职业道德；

（6）向司法当局和（或）公证协会提交关于公证活动的资料、其他文件，并在被投诉不遵守职业道德等必要的情形时提供解释；

（7）在暂停公证执照的情况下，依照公证文书通信规则的程序，向另一名公证员转交公证文件；

（8）以本法第 12 条第 1 款第 1 项、第 2 项、第 4 项、第 4-1 项和第 6 项规定的理由终止执照时，将持有的所有公证文件送交私营公证档案馆；

（9）姓氏、名字或办公地点发生变化的，应在一个月内向地方司法机关提供相关资料。

2. 依据《哈萨克斯坦共和国打击洗钱和资助恐怖主义行为法》的命令和程序，向获得授权的金融监督机构提供公证活动的数据和信息；依据《哈萨克斯坦共和国不动产登记法》规定的程序，通过统一公证信息系统向法律登记信息系统，移交经公证员电子签字

and financing of terrorism", and sending a soft copy of the title document certified by the notary's electronic digital signature, via the unified notarial information system to the legal register information system according to the procedure provided for in the Law of the Republic of Kazakhstan "Concerning state registration of rights on immovable property", shall not constitute disclosure of notarial activity secrets.

Footnote. Article 18 as amended by Laws of the Republic of Kazakhstan dated 28.08.2009 No 192-IV (enforced from 08.03.2010); 26.12.2011 No 516-IV (enforced upon expiry of 10 calendar days after first official publication); 21.06.2012 No 19-V (enforced upon expiry of ten calendar days after first official publication); and 08.01.2013 No 64-V (enforced from 01.01.2013).

Article 19. Restrictions of activities of notary

1. Notaries may not:

1) carry on business activities;

2) provide intermediary services during the completion, amendment and dissolution of a treaty;

3)perform notarial duties in cases of election of representative body by deputy;

4)perform their duties without a compulsory notary's civil liability insurance contract;

5)use a facsimile or transfer seal or electronic digital signature to another person, except when sending a seal to the territorial body of justice for the period of suspension of notary's licence;

6) carry out activity away from the place of registration, except in cases, provided for by this Law.

2. Notaries in private practice may not be in working relationships as employees, unless otherwise provided by this Law.

Footnote. Article 19 as amended by Laws of the Republic of Kazakhstan dated 24.12.2001 No 276; 05.05.2003 No 408; 26.12.2011 No 516-IV (enforced upon expiry of 10 calendar days after first official publication); and 28.06.2012 No 24-V (enforced upon expiry of ten calendar days after first official publication).

Article 20. Notarial district

A notarial district shall be recognized as a territory of one region, city of national significance or the capital city, in accordance with the administrative territorial division of the Republic of Kazakhstan.

Footnote. Article 20 as amended by Law of the Republic of Kazakhstan dated 5 May 2003, No 408.

认证的所有权文件的副本。上述两项制度不构成泄露公证活动的秘密。

脚注 第18条经哈萨克斯坦共和国2009年8月28日第192-IV号法令（2010年3月8日起施行）、2011年12月26日第516-IV号法令（第516-IV号法令在自首次公布之日起10日后开始施行）、2012年6月21日第19-V号法令（自首次公布之日起10日后开始施行）和2013年1月8日第64V号法令（2013年1月1日起施行）修订。

第十九条 公证活动的限制

1. 公证员不得：

（1）开展商业活动；

（2）在条约的完成、修改和解除过程中提供中介服务；

（3）在代理人选举代表的情况下，履行公证职责；

（4）在没有强制性民事责任保险合同的情况下履行职责；

（5）使用传真、向他人转让印章或者电子签名，但在公证执照被暂停期间向司法机关转送印章的除外；

（6）在登记地以外公证，但本法规定的情况除外。

2. 除本法另有规定外，私营公证员不得以雇员身份与他人建立劳动关系。

脚注 第19条经哈萨克斯坦共和国2001年12月24日第276号法令、2003年5月5日第408号法令、2011年12月26日第516-IV号法令（自首次公布之日起10日后开始施行）和第2012年6月28日第24-V号法令（自首次公布之日起10日后开始施行）修订。

第二十条 公证区

依据哈萨克斯坦共和国的行政领土划分，公证区是地区，一个具有国家意义的城市或首都的一部分地区。

脚注 第20条经哈萨克斯坦共和国2003年5月5日第408号法令修订。

Article 21. Activity area of notary

1. A notary's activity area of shall be determined by the territorial body of justice within the notarial district.

2. A private notary's activity area shall be determined by the territorial body of justice jointly with the notary association within the notarial district. Notaries may not place their office outside the territory designated territory to them. Requirements concerning the notary's office shall be established by the ministry of justice of the Republic of Kazakhstan at the suggestion of the state notary association. The territorial body of justice shall regularly inform the population of the activity area of state and private notaries.

3.The notary's activity area shall be observed upon fulfilment of actions provided for by subparagraphs 3), 4), 5) of paragraph 1 of Article 34 and Article 54 of this Law by the notary. In all other cases, individuals and legal entities requiring notarial activities may apply to any notary.

4.The office for carrying out notarial activities shall be within the territory, designated according to the procedure provided for by paragraphs 1 and 2 of this Article.

5. Notarial activity may be carried out away from the office of a state or private notary.

6. Notarial activity with outside visit shall be performed for specific persons on the basis of an application by those persons, and shall not be regular. If the notarial activity is carried out in a state notary's or private notary's office, the precise location, address and time of this notarial activity shall be noted in the document certificate in the notarial activities register.

Footnote. Article 21 as amended by Laws of the Republic of Kazakhstan dated 05.05.2003 No 408; and 26.12.2011 No 516-IV (enforced upon expiry of 10 calendar days after first official publication).

Article 21-1. Criteria for determining minimum number of notaries in notarial district

1. The minimum number of notaries in the notarial district shall be confirmed by the Ministry of justice of the Republic of Kazakhstan following application from the territorial body of justice jointly with the territorial notary association, on the basis of the following criteria:

1) number and density of population in the notarial district;

2) economic development, geographical location, existence of infrastructure and other peculiarities of district.

2. The territorial body of justice may introduce a state

第二十一条　公证活动辖区

1. 公证员的公证活动辖区由公证区内的司法机关确定。

2. 私营公证员的活动范围由地方司法机关与公证区内的公证协会共同确定。公证员不得将公证机构设在指定区外。有关公证机构的要求应由哈萨克斯坦共和国司法部依据国家公证协会的建议确定。当地司法机关应定期向民众告知国家和私营公证员的活动辖区。

3. 公证员的活动范围应符合公证员在施行第 34 条第 1 款第 3 项、第 4 项、第 5 项和本法第 54 条的规定，在其他情况下，自然人或法人可向公证员申请公证。

4. 开展公证活动的机构应按照本条第 1 款和第 2 款规定的程序在规定的范围内进行。

5. 公证活动可以在国家公证机构或者私营公证机构以外的地方进行。

6. 公证员应当根据特定人员的申请在公证区外开展公证活动，不得主动、定期开展。在国家公证机构或者私营公证机构开展公证活动的，应当在公证活动登记簿的证明文件上注明公证活动的准确地点、地址和时间。

脚注　第 21 条经哈萨克斯坦共和国 2003 年 5 月 5 日第 408 号法令和 2011 年 12 月 26 日第 516-IV 号法令（在自首次公布之日起 10 日后开始施行）修订。

21-1. 公证区内最低公证员人数

1. 哈萨克斯坦共和国司法部依据地方司法机关与当地公证协会共同提出的申请，并参照下列标准，确定公证区的最低公证员人数：

（1）公证区的人口数量和密度；

（2）区域经济发展、地理位置、现有基础设施等其他特点。

2. 私营公证员的职位空缺在三个月内没有得到填

notary into staff numbers when a vacancy is not filled for three months by the private notaries.

3. If a specified vacancy is subsequently filled by the private notary, the territorial body of justice shall be obliged to cancel one state notary within a month.

The territorial body of justice shall thus be obliged to take measures concerning:

1) monitoring of legality of notarial activities and correction of breaches by state notaries as revealed;

2) receipt and transfer of documents depending on state notary to private notary;

3) removal and elimination of a state notary's seal.

Footnote. Article 2 is supplemented by Article 21-1 in accordance with Law of the Republic of Kazakhstan dated 26.12.2011 No 516-IV (enforced upon expiry of 10 calendar days after first official publication).

Article 22. Notary's seal, stamp and forms

1. Notaries shall have a seal bearing the StateEmblem of the Republic of Kazakhstan and their surname, forename and patronymic (where applicable), the name of the state notary office (seal of state notary) or licence number and issue date(seal of private notary), and stamps for certificates of acknowledgments and private forms.

2. The stamps and sample signatures of the notaries shall be held by the Ministry of Justice of the Republic of Kazakhstan, territorial body of justice, and the notary association.

3. Orders for and issues of seals to notaries for carrying out notarial activities shall be fulfilled by the territorial body of justice.

Private notaries' seals shall be produced at the expense of their funds, and state notaries' seals – at the expense of budget funds.

Footnote. Article 22 is in the wording of Law of the Republic of Kazakhstan dated 28.06.2012 No 24-V (enforced upon expiry of ten calendar days after first official publication).

Article 23. Certificate of civil servants in cities of regional significance, rural settlements, villages and rural districts, authorized to carry out notarial activities

Persons, mentioned in subparagraph 2) of paragraph 2 of Article 1 of this Law, shall be certified in the territorial body of justice for carrying out notarial activities in accordance with the certification provision approved by the Ministry of Justice of the Republic of Kazakhstan.

Footnote. Article 23 as amended by Law of the Re-

补的，地方司法机关可以引入国家公证员。

3. 如某一特定空缺随后由私营公证员填补，地方司法机关应当在一个月内减少一名国家公证员。

因此，地方司法机关有义务在以下方面采取措施：

（1）监督公证活动的合法性，纠正国家公证员的违法行为；

（2）国家公证员向私营公证员转让证件或接受私营公证员转让的证件；

（3）取消国家公证员印章。

脚注　第 2 条由第 21-1 条补充，依据哈萨克斯坦共和国 2011 年 12 月 26 日第 516-IV 号法令（在自首次公布之日起 10 日后开始施行）。

第二十二条　公证员印章、图章及表格

1. 公证员印章应包括哈萨克斯坦共和国国徽及其姓、名和父姓（如适用）、国家公证机构名称（国家公证员印章）或执照号码和颁发日期（私营公证员印章），以及图章确认书和私人表格。

2. 公证员的图章和签名样本应由哈萨克斯坦共和国司法部、当地司法机关和公证协会持有。

3. 公证员为进行公证活动而需要出具印章的，应由地方司法机关负责。

制作私营公证员印章的费用，由自有资金支付，制作国家公证员印章的费用，由预算资金支付。

脚注　第 22 条载于哈萨克斯坦共和国 2012 年 6 月 28 日第 24-V 号法令（在首次正式公布后的 10 日届满时施行）。

第二十三条　重要城市、城乡居住区、村庄和偏远地区的地方政府公务员，有权开展公证活动

本法第 1 条第 2 款第 2 项所述人员，应依照哈萨克斯坦共和国司法部批准的公证条款，在当地司法机关进行公证活动。

脚注　第 23 条经哈萨克斯坦共和国 2004 年 12

public of Kazakhstan dated 20.12.2004 No 13 (enforced from 01.01.2005).

月 20 日第 13 号法令修订（2005 年 1 月 1 日起施行）。

Article24. Responsibility of notaries and civil servants, authorized to carry out notarial activities

1. Notaries and civil servants authorized by this Law to carry out notarial activities, shall bear criminal, administrative, financial, disciplinary and other liability provided for by Kazakh legislation in the event of illegal acts on their part.

2. Notaries in private practice shall be held liable by the notary association in accordance with the Notary's Code of Honour in the event of violation of their professional duties and ethical regulation.

3. The state shall decline liability for damage caused to individuals and legal entities through notarial activities carried out by private notaries.

Footnote. Article 24 as amended by Laws of the Republic of Kazakhstan dated 28.06.2012 No 24-V (enforced upon expiry of ten calendar days after its first official publication); and by Constitutional Law of the Republic of Kazakhstan dated 03.07.2013 No 121-V (enforced upon expiry of ten calendar days after first official publication).

第二十四条　开展公证活动的公证员和公务员的责任

1. 经本法授权，开展公证活动的公证员和公务员，如有违法行为，应当承担哈萨克斯坦法律规定的刑事、行政、经济、纪律和其他责任。

2. 私营公证员违反职责和道德规范的，应依据公证协会的荣誉守则承担责任。

3. 私营公证员的公证活动给自然人或法人造成损害的，国家应减轻其赔偿责任。

脚注　第 24 条经哈萨克斯坦共和国 2012 年 6 月 28 日第 24-V 号法令（自首次公布之日起 10 日后开始施行）和哈萨克斯坦共和国 2013 年 7 月 3 日第 121-V 号宪法修正案（自首次公布之日起 10 日后开始施行）。

Article25. Complaints concerning, or refusal to accept, notarial activities

Complaints concerning, or refusal to accept, notarial activities shall be considered by the courts in accordance with regulations of civil procedure legislation.

第二十五条　对公证活动的投诉或拒绝接受公证活动的案件

对公证活动的投诉或者拒绝接受公证活动的案件，由法院依照民事诉讼法的规定审理。

Chapter 3. NOTARY ASSOCIATION

第三章　公证协会

Article 26. Notary association

1. The notary association is an uncommercial professional self-financing organization, created for expressing and protecting the rights and legal interests of notaries in private practice and monitoring observance of legislation on notaries in provision of notarial activities.

2. The activity of the notary association shall be regulated by this Law and the charter. The notary association shall be a legal entity and subject to registration according to the procedure established by the Law.

3. A notary association shall be formed in the territory of each region, city of national significance and the capital of the Republic of Kazakhstan.

4. The state notary association shall be a non-commercial professional self-financing organization combining territorial notary associations.

第二十六条　公证协会

1. 公证协会是一个非商业性、专业性、自负盈亏的组织，旨在表达和保护私营公证员的权利和合法利益，并监督公证员开展公证活动的情况。

2. 公证协会的活动由本法和公证协会章程规定。公证协会系法人，依照本法规定的程序登记注册。

3. 每一地区、重要的城市和哈萨克斯坦共和国首都应成立一个公证协会。

4. 国家公证协会是联合地区公证协会的非商业性、专业性、自负盈亏的组织。

5. Person, licensed to carry out notarial activity cannot be refused membership of notary association, unless they fail to comply with the requirements of Article 6 of this Law.

Charging of membership fees by the notary associations is not allowed.

Footnote. Article 26 as amended by Law of the Republic of Kazakhstan dated 26.12.2011 No 516-IV (enforced upon expiry of ten calendar days after first official publication).

Article 26-1. Regulatory bodies of notary association

1. The general meeting of members shall be the supreme body of the notary association.

The following shall be within the exclusive competence of the general meeting:

1) adoption of charter of notary association, introduction of amendments and supplements;

2) election of dean of notary association, corporate executives and audit commission;

3) determination of guidelines for activity of the notary association;

4) adoption of budget of the notary association.

Other issues and decision-making processes within the exclusive competence of the general meeting may be listed in the charter of the notary association.

2. The government and dean of the notary association, elected by the general meeting of members of the notary association, shall manage the notary association. The competence of the general meeting of members, and the government and dean, of the notary association shall be regulated by the charter of the notary association.

3. Corporate executives shall be elected by secret voting for a four-year term.

4. The government shall be a regulatory body of the notary association, and shall include not less than five persons.

5. The procedure and terms of convening meetings of the notary association, and the powers of the dean and regulatory bodies of the notary association, shall be determined by the charter of the notary association.

Chapter 3 is supplemented by Article 26-1 in accordance with Law of the Republic of Kazakhstan dated 26.12.2011 No 516-IV (enforced upon expiry of ten calendar days after first official publication).

5. 被许可从事公证活动的人，除不符合本法第 6 条的规定外，不得拒绝加入公证协会。公证协会不得收取会员费。

脚注 第 26 条经哈萨克斯坦共和国 2011 年 12 月 26 日第 516-IV 号法令修订（在自首次公布之日起 10 日后开始施行）。

26-1. 公证协会的监督机构

1. 会员大会是公证协会的最高权力机构，有权对下列事项作出决定：

（1）通过公证协会章程，提出修正案和补充条款；

（2）选举公证协会主任、管理人员和审计委员会；

（3）制定公证协会活动准则；

（4）通过公证协会预算。

公证协会章程中可以列出由会员大会决策的其他事项和程序。

2. 公证协会会员大会选举产生的管理部门和主任负责管理公证协会。公证协会会员大会、管理部门和主任的职权，由公证协会章程规定。

3. 公证协会高级管理人员应以无记名投票方式选出，任期四年。

4. 管理部门是公证协会的管理机构，组成人数不少于五人。

5. 公证协会召开会议的程序和条件，以及公证协会主任和管理部门的权力，由公证协会章程规定。

第三章由第 26-1 条补充，依据哈萨克斯坦共和国 2011 年 12 月 26 日第 516-IV 号法令（在自首次公布之日起 10 日后开始施行）。

Article 26-2. Dean of notary association

1. A notary who is a direct member of the notary association for not less than five years shall be elected dean of the notary association.

The dean of the notary association shall be elected by secret voting for a four-year term.

2. The dean of the notary association shall:

1) organize the work of the notary association and ensure completion of tasks assigned to the notary association;

2) manage the work of the notary association and hire and dismiss employees of the notary association;

3) represent the interests of the notary association in state bodies, public associations, and other organizations;

4) exercise other powers, provided by the charter of the notary association and not inconsistent with Kazakh legislation.

Footnote. Chapter 3 supplemented by Article 26-2 in accordance with Law of the Republic of Kazakhstan dated 26.12.2011 No 516-IV (enforced upon expiry of ten calendar days after first official publication).

Article 27. Powers of notary association

1. The notary association shall:

1) generally manage and coordinate the activity of private notaries;

2) represent and protect the rights and legal interests of their members in state bodies and non-governmental organizations, assist them and work together in developing a notarial case;

3) carry out compliance control of the legislation on notaries upon performance of notarial activities by the private notaries;

4) introduce applications for suspension, loss or termination of a private notary's licence;

5) arrange civil liability insurance obligations arising from damages caused while carrying out injure notarial activities;

5-1) inform territorial bodies of justice on cases of failure by private notaries to take out compulsory civil liability insurance of and violations of other requirements of Kazakh legislation concerning compulsory civil liability insurance for private notaries;

6) organize training of persons licensed to carry out notary activity, and training of private notaries;

7) reimburse the costs of expert examinations called by a court in cases linked with its members' activity;

26-2. 公证协会主任

1. 公证协会主任应当为公证协会的成员，且加入协会的时间不少于五年，公证协会主任由无记名投票选举产生，任期四年。

2. 公证协会主任应行使下列职权：

（1）组织公证协会的工作，确保公证协会任务的完成；

（2）管理公证协会的工作，录用、辞退公证协会的职工；

（3）在国家机关、社会团体和其他组织中代表公证协会的利益；

（4）行使公证协会章程规定的且不违反哈萨克斯坦法律规定的职权。

脚注 第三章依据哈萨克斯坦共和国 2011 年 12 月 26 日第 516-IV 号法令，由第 26-2 条补充（在首次正式公布后的 10 日届满时施行）。

第二十七条 公证协会的权力

1. 公证协会拥有以下权力：

（1）管理和协调私营公证员的活动；

（2）在国家机关和非政府组织中代表和保护其成员的权利和合法利益，协助他们处理公证案件；

（3）对私营公证员的公证活动进行公证法律的合规控制；

（4）提出暂停、吊销或终止私营公证执照的申请；

（5）界定因公证活动造成损害所引起的民事责任所承担保险的义务；

（5-1）向当地司法机关通报私营公证员未购买强制性民事责任保险的案件和违反哈萨克斯坦法律中关于私营公证员强制性民事责任保险的其他要求的案件；

（6）组织持执照的公证员和私营公证员的培训活动；

（7）给付与协会会员有关的案件中法院要求进行专家审查的费用；

8) hold private notaries liable for violation of professional duty and ethics in accordance with the Notary's Code of Honour;

9) administer complaints and applications by citizens and legal entities concerning service acts of private notaries.

2. The notary association may demand explanations concerning notarial activities carried out, obtaining personal explanations where necessary, and concerning issues of non-observance of professional ethics by the notary, when examining questions of legality of actions carried out by a private notary.

3. The notary association shall send information on its activity in hard copy and electronic formats to the state notary association and the territorial body of justice, according to yearly and half-yearly results.

Footnote. Article 27 as amended by Laws of the Republic of Kazakhstan dated 05.05.2003 No 408; 11.06.2003 No 437; 15.07.2010 No 337-IV (for method of enforcement see Article 2); and 26.12.2011 No 516-IV (enforced upon expiry of 10 calendar days after first official publication).

Article 28. Charter of notary association

1. The charter of the notary association shall include:

1) its name, aims and main types of activity;

2) the rights and obligations of the Board;

3) conditions and procedures for acquisition, suspension and forfeit of membership;

3-1) rights, obligations and responsibility of members;

4) procedure of formation, function and duration of powers of governing bodies;

5) sources of formation of assets and method of use of assets;

6) procedure for introduction of amendments and supplements to the charter;

7) procedure for reorganizing and liquidating the Board, and fate of assets following liquidation.

2. The charter of the notary association may also embody other regulations, not inconsistent with legislation.

Footnote. Article 28 as amended by Law of the Republic of Kazakhstan dated 5 May 2003, No 408.

Article 29. Powers of state notary association

1. The activity of the state notary association shall be determined by this Law and its charter. The state notary association shall be registered in accordance with the pro-

（8）依照《公证员荣誉守则》追究私营公证员违反职业道德的责任；

（9）受理公民和法人关于私营公证员服务行为的投诉和申请。

2. 公证协会审查私营公证员的行为合法性问题时，可以要求该公证员对公证活动作出解释，必要时可要求公证员为自己辩护，以及对不遵守职业道德的问题作出解释。

3. 公证协会应当以拷贝和电子的形式向国家公证协会和地区司法机关报告年度和半年度公证活动的情况。

脚注 第 27 条经哈萨克斯坦共和国 2003 年 5 月 5 日第 408 号法令、2003 年 6 月 11 日第 437 号法令、2010 年 7 月 15 日第 337-IV 号法令（执法方法见第 2 条）和 2011 年 12 月 26 日第 516-IV 号法令（自首次公布之日起 10 日后开始施行）修订。

第二十八条　公证协会章程

1. 公证协会章程应当包括：

（1）公证协会的名称、目的和主要活动类型；

（2）委员会的权利和义务；

（3）取得、中止和终止成员资格的条件和程序；

（3-1）成员的权利、义务和责任；

（4）管理机构的组成程序、职能和权力期限；

（5）资产的来源和使用资产的方法；

（6）对章程作出修正和补充的程序；

（7）改组和清算委员会的程序，以及清理后资产的处理。

2. 公证协会章程可包括其他规定，但不得违反法律。

脚注 第 28 条经哈萨克斯坦共和国 2003 年 5 月 5 日第 408 号法令修订。

第二十九条　国家公证协会的权力

1. 国家公证协会的公证活动依本法及其章程确定，国家公证协会依照法律规定的程序注册。

cedure established by Law.

2. The state notary association shall:

1) coordinate the activity of the notary association;

2) represent the interests of the notary association and notaries in the state bodies and non-governmental organizations including foreign and international organisations;

3) participate in legislative drafting and expert activity of the Ministry of Justice of the Republic of Kazakhstan concerning notarial issues;

4) organize training of notaries;

5) participate in the development of regulatory legal acts and develop methodological materials concerning notarial issues;

6) develop and confirm the Notary's Code of Honour;

7) carry out other activity, not inconsistent with legislation and international treaties.

3.The state notary association shall annually present information on its activity, in hard copy and electronic formats, to the Ministry of Justice of the Republic of Kazakhstan.

4. A notary shall be elected dean of the state notary association, if he has been a member of the notary association not less than five continuous years until the date of election.

The dean of the state notary association shall be elected by secret voting for a four-year term. The procedure electing and empowering the dean of the state notary association shall be determined by this Law and the charter of the state notary association.

Footnote. Article 29 as amended by Laws of the Republic of Kazakhstan dated 15.07.2010 No 337-IV (for method of enforcement see Article 2); and 26.12.2011 No 516-IV (enforced upon expiry of 10 calendar days after first official publication).

Article 29-1. Private notarial archive

The private notarial archive shall be a branch of the territorial notary association.

The private notarial archive shall accumulate, store and use of notarial documents in accordance with Kazakh legislation concerning national funds and archives.

Footnote. Supplemented by Article 29-1, Law of the Republic of Kazakhstan dated 5 May 2003, No. 4IES

Article 30. Payment for notarial activities

1. Notaries working in the state notarial office and akim civil servants in cities of regional significance, rural settlements, villages and rural districts shall collect the

2. 国家公证协会应当：

（1）协调公证协会的活动；

（2）在国家机关和非政府组织，包括在外国和国际组织中代表公证协会和公证员的利益；

（3）参与哈萨克斯坦共和国司法部关于公证问题的法律起草和专家活动；

（4）组织公证员培训；

（5）参与制定关于公证问题的监督法律和方法论资料；

（6）制定《公证员荣誉守则》；

（7）开展不违反法律和国际条约的其他活动。

3. 国家公证协会应每年以拷贝和电子的形式向哈萨克斯坦共和国司法部提交关于其公证活动的资料。

4. 国家公证协会主任应当是国家公证协会成员，且至选举之日止，加入公证协会的时间不少于五年。国家公证协会主任由不记名投票选举产生，任期四年。国家公证协会主任的选举和授权程序由本法和国家公证协会章程规定。

脚注 第 29 条经哈萨克斯坦共和国 2010 年 7 月 15 日第 337-IV 号法令（执法方法见第 2 条）；2011 年 12 月 26 日第 516-IV 号法令（在自首次公布之日起 10 日后开始施行）修订。

29-1. 私营公证员档案馆

私营公证员档案馆是地方公证协会的分支机构。私营公证员档案馆应依据哈萨克斯坦关于国家资金和档案的法律，收集、储存和使用公证文件。

脚注 经 2003 年 5 月 5 日哈萨克斯坦共和国第 4IES 号法令第 29-1 条补充。

第三十条 公证活动的费用

1. 国家公证机构的公证员和重要城市、城乡居住区、村庄、偏远地区的地方政府公务员，应按照哈萨克斯坦税法中关于公证活动的税率收取费用。

state duties at the rate established by the Kazakhstan Tax Code for carrying out notarial activities.

2. Notarial activities carried out by a private notary shall be paid for at the appropriate level of state duty established by Kazakh tax legislation.

3. (Is excluded)

Note by RCLI!

Paragraph 4 shall be enforced from 01.01.2010.

4. Civil servants of a Kazakh consular institution shall, for carrying out notarial activities, collect a consular fee according to the procedure and amounts provided for by Kazakh tax legislation.

5. Reduced payment of notarial fees for individuals and legal entities, as provided by Kazakh tax legislation, shall be allocated to these persons and upon carrying out of notarial activities by the notaries in private practice.

6.Interested persons shall reimburse the notary for actual transport costs following travel from place of work for carrying out notarial activity.

7. (excluded)

Footnote. Article 30 as amended by Laws of the Republic of Kazakhstan dated 24.12.2001 No 276; 05.05.2003 No 408; 20.12.2004 No 13 (enforced from 01.01.2005); and 16.11.2009 No 200-IV (enforced from 01.01.2010).

Article 30-1. Payment for legal and technical services within activities carried out by private notary

1. Private notaries shall collect payment for provision of auxiliary technical and legal services as provided by this Article for carrying out notarial activities:

1) upon certification of sale agreements for fixed assets (plots of land, dwelling houses, apartments, country-houses, garages, constructions and other fixed assets) in urban areas:

if one party is a legal entity: 7 monthly calculation indexes; children, spouse, parents, full brothers and sisters, grandchildren: 2 monthly calculation indexes; other persons: 5 monthly calculation indexes; if the transaction is made for acquisition of immovable assets received under a residential mortgage loan: 2 monthly calculation indexes;

2) upon certification of sale agreements for fixed assets (plots of land, dwelling houses, apartments, country-houses, garages, constructions and other fixed assets) in rural areas:

if one party is a legal entity: 2 monthly calculation indexes; children, spouse, parents, full brothers and sisters,

2. 私营公证员开展的公证活动，应按照哈萨克斯坦税法规定的相应国家税率，收取费用。

3.（已删除）。

RCLI 提示！

第 4 款应自 2010 年 1 月 1 日起施行。

4. 哈萨克斯坦领事机构的公务员开展公证活动的，应当按照哈萨克斯坦税法规定的程序和数额收取领事费用。

5. 依据哈萨克斯坦税法的规定，自然人或法人减少的公证费用，在私营公证员完成公证业务后重新分配给他们。

6. 利害相关人应补偿公证员交通费用，即从工作地到公证活动开展地的旅途费用。

7.（已删除）。

脚注 第 30 条经哈萨克斯坦共和国 2001 年 12 月 24 日第 276 号法令、2003 年 5 月 5 日第 408 号法令、2004 年 12 月 20 日 第 13 号 法 令（2005 年 1 月 1 日起施行）和 2009 年 11 月 16 日第 200-IV 号法令（2010 年 1 月 1 日起施行）修订。

30-1. 私营公证员开展公证活动，收取法律和技术服务费用的规定

1. 私营公证员为开展下列公证活动，提供本条规定的辅助技术和法律服务，应当收取费用：

（1）对城市固定资产（土地、住宅、公寓、农舍、车库、建筑、其他固定资产）的销售协议进行公证的：

如果当事人一方是法人：7 个月计算指数；当事人一方系子女、配偶、父母、亲兄弟姐妹、孙辈关系的：2 个月计算指数；其他人员：5 个月计算指数；基于住房抵押贷款取得的不动产进行交易的：2 个月计算指数。

（2）对农村地区固定资产（土地、住宅、公寓、农舍、车库、建筑和其他固定资产）的销售协议进行公证的：

当事人一方为法人的：2 个月计算指数；当事人一方系子女、配偶、父母、亲兄弟姐妹、孙辈：1 个

grandchildren: 1 monthly calculation index;

other persons: 2 monthly calculation indexes;

3) upon certification of treaties for sale of motor vehicles:

if one party is a legal entity: 5 monthly calculation indexes;

children, spouse, parents, full brothers and sisters, grandchildren: 2 monthly calculation indexes;

other persons: 5 monthly calculation indexes;

4) upon certification of rent/loan agreements (except for residential mortgage loan), deposit, lease, work contract, marriage contract, division of commonly owned property, division of inherited property, alimony agreements, foundation agreements: 5 monthly calculation indexes;

5) upon certification of residential mortgage agreements: 2 monthly calculation indexes;

6)upon certification of wills: 2 monthly calculation indexes;

7)upon issue of inheritance right certificates: 2 monthly calculation indexes for each certificate issued;

8) upon issue of certificate of ownership right to share in common property and other persons having rights to jointly owned property: 4 monthly calculation indexes;

9) upon certification of powers of attorney for right of use and disposition of property: 2 monthly calculation indexes;

10) upon certification of powers of attorney for right of use and management of motor vehicles without right of sale: 1 monthly calculation index;

11) upon certification of powers of attorney for sale, granting, exchange of motor vehicles: 2 monthly calculation indexes;

12) upon certification of other powers:

for individuals - 1 monthly calculation index;

for legal entities - 2 monthly calculation indexes;

13) upon execution of marine protest - 5 monthly calculation indexes;

(per page):

14) upon certification of accuracy of copies of documents and extracts from documents for individuals – 0,05 monthly calculation index;

for legal entities – 0.07 monthly calculation index;

15) upon certification of authenticity of signature on documents and accuracy of translation of documents from one language to another (per document):

for individuals - 0.05 monthly calculation index; for

月计算指数；其他人员：2个月计算指数。

（3）对机动车买卖协议进行公证：当事人一方是法人：5个月计算指数；子女、配偶、父母、亲兄弟姐妹、孙辈：2个月计算指数；其他人员：5个月计算指数。

（4）对租金/贷款协议（住宅按揭贷款除外）、定金、租赁、劳动合同、婚约、共有财产分割、财产继承分割、赡养费协议、基础协议进行公证：5个月计算指数。

（5）对住房抵押贷款协议进行公证：2个月计算指数。

（6）对遗嘱进行公证：2个月计算指数。

（7）对遗产继承权证书的出具进行公证的：每张证书2个月计算指数。

（8）对共同财产所有权证书公证，其他共有财产权利人：4个月计算指数。

（9）对取得使用权、处分权的授权委托书进行公证：2个月计算指数。

（10）对无销售权的机动车进行使用权和管理权的公证：1个月计算指数。

（11）对机动车的买卖、赠予、交换协议进行公证：2个月计算指数。

（12）对其他权力进行公证：自然人按1个月计算指数；法人按2个每月计算指数；

（13）对海事声明的执行进行公证：5个月计算指数。

（14）对文件副本和文件摘录（每页）的准确性进行公证：自然人按0.05个月计算指数；法人按0.07个月计算指数。

（15）对在证明文件上签字的真实性和翻译文件的准确性进行公证的（每份文件）：自然人按0.05个月计算指数；法人按1个月计算指数。

legal entities - 1 monthly calculation index;

16) upon transfer of applications by individuals and legal entities to other individuals and legal entities - 0.05 monthly calculation index;

（16）自然人或法人向其他自然人或法人转达声明的：0.05 个月计算指数。

17) upon issues of notarized copies of documents – 0.05 monthly calculation index;

（17）公证文件副本：0.05 个月计算指数。

18) upon issue of duplicate - 2 monthly calculation indexes;

（18）出具复印件：2 个月计算指数。

19) upon certification of authenticity of signature in opening of bank account (per document):for individuals – 0.3 monthly calculation index;for legal entities – 0.5 monthly calculation index;

（19）对开立银行账户时签字的真实性进行公证的（每份）：自然人按 0.3 个月计算指数；法人按 0.5 个月计算指数。

20) upon certification of real estate mortgage agreements, rights of reclaim and mortgage certificate for residential mortgage loans - 2 monthly calculation indexes;upon consideration of other treaties of pledge - 3 monthly calculation indexes;

（20）对房地产抵押协议、住房抵押贷款收回权和抵押证书进行公证的按 2 个月计算指数；经审议的其他质押条约按 3 个月计算指数。

21) upon execution of appeal against bill and certification of non-payment of cheque: 1 monthly calculation index;

（21）公证上诉票据的执行书和未支付支票的证明件，按 1 个月计算指数。

22) upon custody of documents and security papers – 0.5 monthly calculation index per month;

（22）保管文件和证券，每月按 0.5 个月计算指数。

23) upon certification of surety and guarantee agreements – 1 monthly calculation index per month;

（23）对担保书和担保协议进行公证，按每月 1 个月计算指数。

24) upon execution of other notarial activities, provided for by this Law and other Kazakh legislative acts: 7 monthly calculation indexes.

（24）执行本法和其他哈萨克斯坦法律规定的其他公证活动的，按 7 个月计算指数。

2. The following shall be exempt from payment for legal and technical services by the private notary, on completion of those services:

2. 以下情形，免除支付私营公证员的法律和技术服务费用：

1) individuals and legal entities, independently preparing drafts of documents, subject to notarial certification;

（1）自然人或法人独立起草需要公证的文件；

2) persons, mentioned in subparagraphs 4), 8) and 9) of Article 542 of the Kazakh Tax Code;

（2）《哈萨克斯坦税法》第 542 条第 4 款、第 8 款和第 9 款所述人员；

3) elderly and disabled people residing in medico-social institutions for elderly and generally disabled people;

（3）居住在医疗社会机构的老年人和残疾人；

4) orphans and children without parental support;

（4）孤儿和无父母抚养的儿童；

5) disabled persons of groups I and II;

（5）第一类和第二类中的残疾人；

6) retirement pensioners.

（6）退休养恤金领取者。

Footnote. Chapter 4 is supplemented by Article 30-1 in accordance with Law of the Republic of Kazakhstan dated 26.12.2011 No 516-IV (enforced upon expiry of 10 calendar days after first official publication).

脚注 第四章经哈萨克斯坦共和国 2011 年 12 月 26 日第 516-IV 号法令（自首次公布之日起 10 日后开始施行）第 30-1 条补充。

Chapter 4. CONTROL OF NOTARY ACTIVITY: COMPETENCE OF JUDICIAL BODY REGARDING REGULATION OF NOTARIES

Article 31. Control of notary activity

1.Control of notarial activities and observance of rules of clericalcompliance by state notaries and akim civil servants in cities of regional significance, rural settlements, villages and rural districts shall be carried out by the territorial body of justice.

2. Control of notarial activities and observance of rules of clerical compliance by notaries engaging in private practice, shall be carried out by the territorial body of justice and the notary association.

3. Authorities of the Kazakh Revenue Service shall monitor the tax compliance of notaries and akim civil servant in cities of regional significance, rural settlements, villages and rural districts in Kazakhstan.

3-1. Control of compliance with Kazakh legislation concerning countering of legitimization (laundering) of illegally-earned incomes and financing of terrorism shall be carried out by the territorial body of justice.

4. Civil servants of the body of justice and the notary association must maintain secrecy of notarial activities carried out and made known during inspections of notarial activity. These persons shall be liable in accordance with Kazakh legislation for disclosure of secrets and damages caused to notaries.

5. Control of notary activity shall be carried out according to the procedure, established by the Law of the Republic of Kazakhstan "Concerning state control and supervision in the Republic of Kazakhstan".

Footnote. Article 31 as amended by Laws of the Republic of Kazakhstan dated 05.05.2003 No 408; 20.12.2004 No 13 (enforced from 01.01.2005); 28.08.2009 No 192-IV (enforced from 08.03.2010); and 26.12.2011 No 516-IV (enforced upon expiry of 10 calendar days after first official publication).

Article 31-1. Control of activity of territorial notary associations

1. Control of activity of territorial notary associations shall be carried out by the territorial bodies of justice according to the procedure established by the Law of the Republic of Kazakhstan "Concerning state control and supervision in the Republic of Kazakhstan".

2. Control shall be carried out with a view to estab-

第四章　公证活动的监督：司法机关有权对公证活动进行监督

第三十一条　对公证活动的监督

1. 地方司法机关有权对重要城市、城乡居住区、村庄、偏远地区的国家公证员和地方政府公务员就其开展公证活动和遵守神职人员守则的情况进行监督。

2. 地方司法机关和公证协会一同对私营公证员开展公证活动和遵守神职人员守则的情况进行监督。

3. 哈萨克斯坦税务局主管部门应对哈萨克斯坦的重要城市、城乡居住区、村庄、偏远地区的公证员和地方政府公务员的遵守税法的情况进行监督。

3-1. 当地司法机关有权监督哈萨克斯坦法律中关于打击洗钱和资助恐怖主义活动的情况。

4. 司法机关和公证协会的公务员在监督公证活动时，必须保守公证活动的秘密并保持监督活动的公开性。上述人员因违反哈萨克斯坦法律泄露秘密，给公证员造成损害的，应当承担责任。

5. 对公证活动的监督应依照《哈萨克斯坦共和国国家监督法》规定的程序进行。

脚注　第 31 条经哈萨克斯坦共和国 2003 年 5 月 5 日第 408 号法令、2004 年 12 月 20 日第 13 号法令（从 2005 年 1 月 1 日起施行）、2009 年 8 月 28 日第 192-IV 号法令（2010 年 3 月 8 日起施行）和 2011 年 12 月 26 日第 516-IV 号法令（自首次公布之日起 10 日后开始施行）修订。

31-1. 对区域性公证协会活动的监督

1. 当地司法机关依照《哈萨克斯坦共和国国家监督法》规定的程序对当地公证协会开展的活动进行监督。

2. 进行监督的目的是确保当地公证协会开展的下

lishing compliance with the activity requirements of the territorial notary associations of the Republic of Kazakhstan:

1) concerning creation of private notarial archives and organization of the accumulation, storage and use of notarial documents;

2) concerning arrangement of civil liability insurance by private notaries;

3) concerning organization of training of persons applying for the right to carry out notary activity, and training of private notaries.

3. The territorial body of justice shall send details of correction of breaches to the territorial notary association if a breach of Kazakh legislation is revealed. The territorial body of justice nay bring court action with a lawsuit to enforce rectification of the breaches of Kazakh legislation if the breach is not rectified at the stated time.

Footnote. Chapter 5 is supplemented by Article 31-1 in accordance with Law of the Republic of Kazakhstan dated 26.12.2011 No 516-IV (enforced upon expiry of 10 calendar days after first official publication).

Article 32. Competence of Ministry of Justice of the Republic of Kazakhstan to regulate notaries

The Ministry of Justice of the Republic of Kazakhstan shall:

1) Manage, coordinate and control the activity of territorial bodies of justice in organizing and ensuring the legality of public services provided by notaries;

2) confirm the rules for provision of notarial activities by notaries;

3) confirm the rules on notarial clerical correspondence by agreement with the authorized Kazakh state body for management of archives and documentation, with participation by the state notary association;

4) confirm the provision concerning certification of civil servants carrying out notarial activities in cities of regional significance, rural settlements, villages and rural districts;

5) excluded by Law of the Republic of Kazakhstan dated 26.12.2011 No 516-IV (enforced upon expiry of 10 calendar days after first official publication);

5-1) confirm a unified program of professional training of applicants in coordination with the state notary association;

5-2) establish the procedure and payment for training applicants for the profession of notary;

列活动符合哈萨克斯坦法律的要求：

（1）建立私营公证员档案，组织公证文件的汇总、保管和使用；

（2）安排私营公证员的民事责任保险；

（3）组织准公证员（申请开展公证活动的人员）的培训，组织私营公证员的培训。

3. 公证协会违反哈萨克斯坦法律的，当地司法机关应告知并要求公证协会纠正其违法行为。如果公证协会未在规定的时间内纠正该违法行为，当地司法机关有权向法院提起诉讼，要求强制纠正。

脚注 第五章经第 31-1 条补充，依据哈萨克斯坦共和国 2011 年 12 月 26 日第 516-IV 号法令（自首次公布之日起 10 日后开始施行）修订。

第三十二条 哈萨克斯坦共和国司法部拥有管理公证员的权力

哈萨克斯坦共和国司法部拥有下列权力：

（1）管理、协调和监督地区司法机关的活动（即组织和确保公证员开展的公证活动具有合法性）；

（2）确认规范公证员开展公证活动的规则；

（3）在国家公证协会的参与下，与经授权的哈萨克斯坦国家档案管理机构达成协议，确认公证文书通信规则；

（4）确认关于在重要城市、城乡居住区、村庄和偏远地区开展公证活动的地方政府公务员认证规定；

（5）第 5 条被哈萨克斯坦共和国 2011 年 12 月 26 日第 516-IV 号法令（在自首次公布之日起 10 日后开始施行）删除；

（5-1）与国家公证协会协调，确定对公证执业申请人进行职业培训的统一方案；

（5-2）确定对公证执业申请人进行培训的程序和费用；

6) confirm the provision concerning the State register of licenses to carry out notarial activity;

7) Confirm the rules for accounting registration of private notaries;

7-1) confirm the minimum number of notaries for each notarial district;

8) develop methodological, instructional and explanatory materials on issues concerning work as a notary;

9) license the activity of notaries;

10) maintain the State register of licenses for carrying out notary activity and publish information on persons issued with licenses in the departmental press;

11) make decisions to suspend or terminate a license for carrying out notary activity, and instigate suits following termination of a notary's licence;

12) establish the form of notarial activities registers (and electronic register of unified notarial information system), notarial certificates and regulations, certificates of acknowledgments of transactions, and documents certified by notaries;

13) excluded by Law of the Republic of Kazakhstan dated 26.12.2011 No 516-IV (enforced upon expiry of 10 calendar days after first official publication);

14) excluded by the Law of the Republic of Kazakhstan dated 26.12.2011 No 516-IV (enforced upon expiry of 10 calendar days after first official publication);

14-1) confirm criteria for assessing of degree of risk;

15) is excluded by the Law of the Republic of Kazakhstan dated 26.12.2011 No 516-IV (shall be enforced upon expiry of 10 calendar days after its first official publication);

16)regulation notarial activity in accordance with this Law and within its competence;

17) exercise other powers, provided by this Law, other Kazakh Laws, and acts of the President of the Republic of Kazakhstan and of the Government of the Republic of Kazakhstan.

Footnote. Article 32 as amended by Laws of the Republic of Kazakhstan dated 05.05.2003 No 408; 20.12.2004 No 13 (enforced from 01.01.2005); 15.07.2010 No 337-IV (for method of enforcement see Article 2); 05.07.2011 No 452-IV (enforced from 13.10.2011); 26.12.2011 No 516-IV (enforced upon expiry of 10 calendar days after first official publication); and by Constitutional Law of the Republic of Kazakhstan dated 03.07.2013 No 121-V (enforced upon expiry of ten calendar days after first official publication).

（6）确认国家公证执照登记制度的规则；

（7）确认私营公证员会计登记规则；

（7-1）确定每个公证区的最低公证员人数；

（8）编写关于公证工作中的方法性，指导性和解释性资料；

（9）许可公证员的活动；

（10）维护国家公证执照登记制度，并在省级报刊上公布获得公证执照人员的情况；

（11）有权决定暂停或者吊销公证执照，并有权在公证执照效力终止后提起诉讼；

（12）建立公证活动登记册（和统一公证信息系统电子登记册）、公证书和规范、交易确认书和经公证员公证的文件的样本；

（13）本条被哈萨克斯坦共和国 2011 年 12 月 26 日第 516-IV 号法令（在自首次公布之日起 10 日后开始施行）删除；

（14）本条被哈萨克斯坦共和国 2011 年 12 月 26 日第 516-IV 号法令（在自首次公布之日起 10 日后开始施行）删除；

（14-1）确定评估风险等级的标准；

（15）本条被哈萨克斯坦共和国 2011 年 12 月 26 日第 516-IV 号法令（自首次公布之日起 10 日后开始施行）删除；

（16）依照本法并在其职权范围内规范公证活动；

（17）行使本法和其他哈萨克斯坦法律规定的其他权力，以及开展哈萨克斯坦共和国总统和哈萨克斯坦共和国政府授权的行为。

脚注 第 32 条经哈萨克斯坦共和国 2003 年 5 月 5 日第 408 号法令、2004 年 12 月 20 日第 13 号法令（从 2005 年 1 月 1 日起施行）、2010 年 7 月 15 日第 337-IV 号法令（执法方法见第 2 条）、2011 年 7 月 5 日第 452-IV 号法令（2011 年 10 月 13 日起施行）、2011 年 12 月 26 日第 516-IV 号法令（首次正式公布后 10 日施行）和哈萨克斯坦共和国 2013 年 7 月 7 日第 121-V 号宪法修正案（首次正式公布后 10 日施行）修订。

Article 33. Competence of territorial body of justice to regulate notaries

1. The territorial body of justice shall:

1) open and close state notary offices;

2) consider applications by citizens and legal entities for actions by notaries;

2-1) organize control of compliance with the requirements of Article 16 of this Law by the private notary and take measures against private notaries failing to conclude a compulsory insurance policy for civil liability and violations of other Kazakh legislative requirements concerning compulsory insurance of civil liability of private notaries;

3) provide methodical and practical assistance to civil servants carrying out notarial activities in cities of regional significance, rural settlements, villages and rural districts;

4) monitor the legality of notarial activities carried out by notaries and civil servants in cities of regional significance, rural settlements, villages and rural districts;

4-1) control compliance with Kazakh legislation concerning countering of legitimization (laundering) of illegally-received income and financing of terrorism;

5) introduce reports on suspension, loss and termination of a notary's licence;

6) introduce reports on holding private notaries liable before the notary association;

7) check the existence of the notary's selected office and its compliance with requirements of legislation and then register the private notary. Registration shall be carried out at the notary's office;

8) carry out an order to produce seals of notaries and issue this report in accordance with Kazakh legislative requirements;

9) excluded by Law of the Republic of Kazakhstan dated 13.01.2014 No 159-V (enforced upon expiry of ten calendar days after first official publication);

10) certify civil servants authorised to carry out notarial activities in cities of regional significance, rural settlements, villages and rural districts;

11) excluded by Law of the Republic of Kazakhstan dated 26.12.2011 No 516-IV (enforced upon expiry of 10 calendar days after first official publication).

2. The territorial body of justice, together with the notary association, shall:

1) excluded by Law of the Republic of Kazakhstan dated 26.12.2011 No 516-IV (enforced upon expiry of 10 calendar days after first official publication);

2) introduce report on minimal number of notaries in

第三十三条 地区司法机关拥有监督公证员的权限

1. 地区司法机关拥有以下权限：

（1）设立、撤销国家公证机构；

（2）审议公民和法人主张公证员采取行动的申请；

（2-1）对私营公证员是否遵守本法第 16 条行为进行监督，并采取措施，防止私营公证员未能就民事责任缔结强制性保险单，以及违反哈萨克斯坦关于私营公证员民事责任强制保险的其他法律要求；

（3）向在重要城市、城乡居住区、村庄和偏远地区开展公证活动的地方政府公务员提供理论和实践帮助；

（4）监督公证员和地方政府公务员在具有重要意义的城市、城乡居住区、村庄和偏远地区开展公证活动的合法性；

（4-1）监督遵守哈萨克斯坦关于打击洗钱和资助恐怖主义法律的情况；

（5）公布公证执照被暂停、吊销和终止的情况；

（6）公布向公证协会追究私营公证员责任情况的报告；

（7）检查公证机构的选址和守法情况，并对私营公证员进行登记，登记应当在公证机构办理；

（8）依据哈萨克斯坦法律的要求，制作公证员印章，发布报告；

（9）本条被哈萨克斯坦共和国 2014 年 1 月 13 日第 159-V 号法令（自首次公布之日起 10 日后开始施行）删除；

（10）确认地方政府公务员有权在重要城市、城乡居住区、村庄和偏远地区开展公证活动；

（11）本条被哈萨克斯坦共和国 2011 年 12 月 26 日第 516-IV 号法令（在首次正式公布后 10 日施行）删除。

2. 地区司法机关与公证协会应：

（1）本条被哈萨克斯坦共和国 2011 年 12 月 26 日第 516-IV 号法令（在自首次公布之日起 10 日后开始施行）删除；

（2）公布公证员人数最少地区的报告，报司法部

notarial district for approval by the Ministry of Justice;

3) excluded by Law of the Republic of Kazakhstan dated 26.12.2011 No 516-IV (enforced upon expiry of 10 calendar days after first official publication);

4) organize provision of notarial activities in temporary absence of the notaries in the notarial district;

5) provide methodical and practical assistance to notaries;

6) generalize notarial practice;

7) excluded by Law of the Republic of Kazakhstan dated 26.12.2011 No 516-IV (enforced upon expiry of 10 calendar days after first official publication);

8) excluded by Law of the Republic of Kazakhstan dated 26.12.2011 No 516-IV (enforced upon expiry of 10 calendar days after first official publication);

9) excluded by Law of the Republic of Kazakhstan dated 26.12.2011 No 516-IV (enforced upon expiry of 10 calendar days after first official publication);

10) for notaries terminating their activity in the relevant notarial district, take measures to ensure destruction of seal and transfer of documents to another notary or private notarial archive, and transferring a terminated notary's licence to the licensor in cases of termination.

Footnote. Article 33 is in the wording of Law of the Republic of Kazakhstan dated 05.05.2003 No 408; as amended by Laws of the Republic of Kazakhstan dated 11.06.2003 No 437; 20.12.2004 No 13 (enforced from 01.01.2005); 28.08.2009 No 192-IV (enforced from 08.03.2010); 26.12.2011 No 516-IV (enforced upon expiry of 10 calendar days after first official publication); and 13.01.2014 No 159-V (enforced upon expiry of ten calendar days after first official publication).

Section 2. NOTARIAL ACTIVITIES AND RULES FOR ITS PROVISION

Chapter 5. NOTARIAL ACTIVITIES CARRIED OUT BY NOTARIES AND AUTHORIZED CIVIL SERVANTS

Article 34. Notarial activities carried out by notaries

1. Notaries shall carry out the following notarial activities:

1) certify transactions;

2) certify constitutional documents of economic partnerships;

批准；

（3）本条被哈萨克斯坦共和国 2011 年 12 月 26 日第 516-IV 号法令（在自首次公布之日起 10 日后开始施行）删除；

（4）在公证员临时缺席的情况下组织公证活动；

（5）为公证员提供理论上和实践上的帮助；

（6）推广公证实践；

（7）本条被哈萨克斯坦共和国 2011 年 12 月 26 日第 516-IV 号法令（自首次公布之日起 10 日后开始施行）删除；

（8）本条被哈萨克斯坦共和国 2011 年 12 月 26 日第 516-IV 号法令（自首次公布之日起 10 日后开始施行）删除；

（9）本条被哈萨克斯坦共和国 2011 年 12 月 26 日第 516-IV 号法令（自首次公布之日起 10 日后开始施行）删除；

（10）对于在公证地区终止其活动的公证员，应采取措施确保销毁印章并将文件移交给另一公证员或移交至私营公证档案馆，并在终止的情况下将终止的公证执照移交给许可人。

脚注 第 33 条是哈萨克斯坦共和国 2003 年 5 月 5 日第 408 号法令的措辞；经哈萨克斯坦共和国 2003 年 6 月 11 日第 437 号、2004 年 12 月 20 日第 13 号（2005 年 1 月 1 日起施行）法令、2009 年 8 月 28 日第 192-IV 号（2010 年 3 月 8 日起施行）法令、2011 年 12 月 26 日第 516-IV 号（自首次公布之日起 10 日后开始施行）法令和 2014 年 1 月 13 日第 159-V 号法令（自首次公布之日起 10 日后开始施行）修正。

第二部分 公证活动及其规定

第五章　公证活动由公证员和被授权的公务员进行

第三十四条　公证员开展公证活动

1. 公证员有权开展下列公证活动：

（1）公证交易；

（2）公证经济合伙关系的合法性文件；

3) assign an inheritance trust manager;

4) issue a certificate on right to inheritance;

5) issue a certificate on right of ownership of share in common property by spouses and other persons having joint ownership of assets;

6) impose and remove prohibition of assignment of assets;

7) certify accuracy of copies of documents and extracts from them;

8) certify genuineness of signatures in documents;

9) certify accuracy of translation of documents from one language to another;

10) certify the fact that a citizen is alive;

11) certify the fact that a citizen is in a particular place;

12) certify time of presentation of documents;

13) transfer declarations of individuals and legal entities to other individuals and legal entities;

14) receive money on deposit;

15) (excluded - No 42 dated 29 March, 2000)

16) execute bill protests;

17) accept documents and security papers for storage;

18) execute marine protests;

19) provide evidence.

2. Other notarial activities carried out by notaries shall be provided by Kazakh legislative acts.

Footnote. Article 34 as amended by Laws of the Republic of Kazakhstan dated 13 November 1998 No 302; 29 March 2000 No 42; and 5 May 2003, No 408.

Article35. Notarial activities carried out by civil servants in cities of regional significance, rural settlements, villages and rural districts

1. civil servants in cities of district significance, rural settlements, villages and rural districts, authorized to carry out notarial activities in cases of absence of the local notary, shall carry out the following notarial activities:

1) certify wills;

2) certify powers of attorney;

3) certify accuracy of copies of documents and accuracy of extracts from them;

4) certify genuineness of signatures on applications;

5) (excluded);

2. Other notarial activities carried out by civil servants of local executive bodies shall be provided by Kazakh legislative acts.

Footnote. Article 35 as amended by Law of the Re-

（3）指定遗产信托管理人；

（4）出具继承权证书；

（5）出具配偶和其他人对共同财产享有所有权的证书；

（6）强制执行和取消资产转让命令；

（7）公证文件副本及其摘录的准确性；

（8）公证文件中签名的真实性；

（9）公证翻译文件的准确性；

（10）公证公民生存的事实；

（11）公证公民在某一特定地点的事实；

（12）公证提交文件的时间；

（13）为自然人或法人向其他自然人或法人转达声明；

（14）接受提存；

（15）（已被2000年3月29日第42号法令删除）；

（16）开展案件异议；

（17）接受文件和证券储存；

（18）执行海事声明；

（19）提供证据。

2. 公证员开展的其他公证活动，由哈萨克斯坦法律规定。

脚注 第34条经哈萨克斯坦共和国1998年11月13日第302号、2000年3月29日第42号和2003年5月5日第408号法令修订。

第三十五条　在重要城市、城乡居住区、村庄和偏远地区的地方政府公务员有权开展公证活动

1. 重要城市、城乡居住区、村庄和偏远地区的地方政府公务员，在当地无公证员的情况下，经授权可以从事下列公证活动：

（1）公证遗嘱；

（2）公证授权委托书的效力；

（3）公证文件副本及其摘录的准确性；

（4）公证签名的真实性；

（5）（已被删除）；

2. 地方行政机关公务员进行的其他公证活动，由哈萨克斯坦法律规定。

脚注 第35条经哈萨克斯坦共和国2003年5月

public of Kazakhstan dated 5 May 2003, No 408; and 20 December 2004, No 13 (enforced from 1 January 2005).

5日第408号法令和2004年12月20日第13号法令（2005年1月1日起施行）修订。

Article 36. Notarial activities carried out by performing consular duties

第三十六条　领事人员开展公证活动

1. Civil servants performing consular duties in the name of the Republic of Kazakhstan shall carry out the following notarial activities:

1) certify transactions, except agreements for assignment of fixed assets located in Kazakh territory;

2) (excluded)

3) issue certificates of right to inheritance;

4) issue a certificate on right of ownership of share in common property by spouses and other persons having joint ownership of assets;

5) certify accuracy of copies of documents and extracts from them;

6) certify the genuineness of signatures in documents;

7) certify accuracy of translation of documents from one language to another;

8) certify the fact that a citizen is alive;

9) certify the fact that a citizen is in a particular place;

10) certify time of presentation of documents;

11) transfer declarations of individuals and legal entities to other individuals and legal entities;

12) receive money on deposit;

13) (excluded - No 42 dated 29 March 2000)

14) accept documents and security papers for storage;

15) execute marine protests;

16) provide evidence.

2. Other notarial activities carried out by notaries shall be provided by Kazakh legislative acts.

1. 以哈萨克斯坦共和国名义履行领事职责的公务员有权开展下列公证活动：

（1）公证交易，但哈萨克斯坦境内固定资产转让协议除外；

（2）（已被删除）；

（3）出具继承权证书；

（4）出具配偶和其他人对共同财产享有所有权的证书；

（5）公证文件副本及其摘录的准确性；

（6）公证文件中签名的真实性；

（7）公证翻译文件的准确性；

（8）公证公民生存的事实；

（9）公证公民在特定地点的事实；

（10）公证提交文件的时间；

（11）将自然人或法人的申报转让给其他自然人或法人；

（12）接受提存；

（13）（已被2000年3月29日第42号法令删除）；

（14）接受文件和证券以供储存；

（15）开展海事案件异议；

（16）提供证据。

2. 公证员开展的其他公证活动，由哈萨克斯坦法律规定。

Footnote. Article 36, as amended by Laws of the Republic of Kazakhstan dated 13 November 1998, No 302; 29 March 2000, No 42; and 5 May 2003, No 408.

脚注　第36条经哈萨克斯坦共和国1998年11月13日第302号法令、2000年3月29日第42号法令和2003年5月5日第408号法令修订。

Article 37. Attestation by civil servants of wills and powers of attorney equated to notarially certified documents. The following shall be equated to notarially certified documents:

第三十七条　经公务员证明的遗嘱及授权委托书，其效力等同于经公证的文件。下列文件的效力应等同于经公证的文件的效力：

1) wills of citizens undergoing treatment in hospitals, health resorts and other medical and preventive institutions, and resident in centres for elderly and disabled people, certified by the head and duty doctors of the said hospitals, health resorts and other medical and preventive institutions, and by directors and head doctors centres for

（1）在医院、疗养院和其他医疗和预防机构接受治疗的公民设立的遗嘱，以及经上述医院、医疗机构和其他医疗和预防机构的主任、值班医生以及老年人和残疾人中心主任、主任医生证明的老年和残疾人中心居民设立的遗嘱；

elderly and disabled people;

2) wills and powers of attorney of military and other persons undergoing treatment in hospitals, health resorts and other medical and preventive institutions, certified by the heads and assistant heads of medical unit, and by head and duty doctors of the said hospitals, health resorts and other medical and preventive institutions;

3) wills and powers of attorney of military personnel in home stations of military installations, units, departments and educational institutions, where no notaries and civil servants are authorized to carry out notarial activities, as well as wills and powers of attorney of workers and servants, members of their families and family members of military personnel, certified by the command officers (heads) of the installations, units, departments and facilities in question;

4) wills and powers of attorney of persons in the places of detention, certified by the heads of those places of detention;

5) wills of citizens on ocean-going or inland-waterway ships, sailing under the flag of the Republic of Kazakhstan, certified by the captains of these ships;

6) wills of citizens on exploratory and other expeditions, certified by the commanders of those expeditions;

7) powers of attorney of capable citizens, of age, in social welfare institutions, certified by the director of the institution or of the relevant body for social protection of population. Wills, provided for by this Article shall be signed by the testator in the presence of a witness, who shall also sign the will.

Footnote. Article 37 as amended by Law of the Republic of Kazakhstan dated 5 May 2003, No 408.

Article 38. Transfer of will certified by civil servants to notary

1. Civil servants listed in Article 37 of this Law must within ten calendar days of certification of will, and immediately if this is not possible for good reason, transfer one copy of the certified will to the notary for safe custody at the permanent location of the notary for the testator's district.

2. If the testator is not permanently resident in the Republic of Kazakhstan or his/her place of residence is unknown, the will shall be transferred to a notary appointed by the Ministry of Justice of the Republic of Kazakhstan.

3. The notary must check the wills delivered for safe storage, and if non-compliance with the law is established,

（2）经医疗单位的主任和副主任以及上述医院、疗养院和其他医疗和预防机构的主任、值班医生证明的，在医院、疗养院和其他医疗预防机构接受治疗的军人和其他人员的遗嘱和授权委托书；

（3）军事设施、单位、部门、教育机构所在地的军事人员的遗嘱和授权委托书，未经公证员和授权公务员公证的；以及经有关设施、单位、部门的指挥员（首长）证明的职工、公务员、家属和军人家属的遗嘱和授权委托书；

（4）经拘留场所负责人证明的被拘留的人的遗嘱和授权委托书授权；

（5）公民在有哈萨克斯坦共和国旗帜的远洋或内河船舶上设立的，并经船长证明的遗嘱；

（6）经探险队或考察团指挥员证明的，其他队员设立的遗嘱；

（7）经社会福利机构负责人或有关人口社会保护机构的主任证明的，有行为能力的老年人的授权委托书。

本条规定的遗嘱，应当由立遗嘱人在证人在场的情况下签名，见证人也应当在遗嘱上签名。

脚注 第 37 条经哈萨克斯坦共和国 2003 年 5 月 5 日第 408 号法令修订。

第三十八条 将经公务员公证的遗嘱移交公证员

1. 除有正当理由无法移交外，本法第 37 条所列公务员必须在遗嘱得到证明之日起 10 日内，将经证明的遗嘱副本移交给公证员立遗嘱人所在地区的公证员，在其常住地保管。

2. 立遗嘱人不是哈萨克斯坦共和国永久居民，或他 / 她的居住地不详，应将遗嘱移交给哈萨克斯坦共和国司法部指定的公证员。

3. 公证员必须检查立遗嘱人交付的遗嘱，以确保其得到安全保管。如果遗嘱不符合法律规定，应通知

inform the testator and civil servant who certified the will, for proper formulation.

4. The civil servant shall be liable in accordance with Kazakh legislation for losses and damaged caused to the heir(s) through late transfer of the certified will.

Footnote. Article 38 as amended by Constitutional Law of the Republic of Kazakhstan dated 03.07.2013, No 121-V (enforced upon expiry of ten calendar days after first official publication).

Chapter 6. BASIC RULES FOR CARRYING OUT NOTARIAL ACTIVITIES

Article 39. Procedure for carrying out notarial activities

The procedure for carrying out notarial activities shall be established by this Law, other legislative acts and rules for carrying out of notarial activities by notaries, certified by the Ministry of Justice of the Republic of Kazakhstan.

Footnote. Article 39 as amended by Law of the Republic of Kazakhstan dated 26.12.2011, No 516-IV (enforced upon expiry of 10 calendar days after first official publication).

Article 40. Timing of performance of notarial activities

Notarial activities shall be performed on the date of presentation of all necessary documents and payment of state duty upon carrying out of notarial activities by state notary or persons authorized by this Law to carry out notarial activities, or payment for notarial activities of private notary.

Article 41. Grounds and terms for postponement and suspension of notarial activities

1. Notarial action may be postponed on the following grounds:

1) Need to obtain additional information from individuals and legal entities;

2)sending documents for expert examination;

2. The length of postponement of notarial action may not exceed one month from date of pronouncement of regulation concerning postponement of notarial action.

3. Notarial action shall be postponed for no more than ten calendar days at the request of the interested party disputing a right or fact for certification of which another interested person shall be called on. If during this term the

立遗嘱人和证明遗嘱的公务员修改。

4. 公务员因迟交经证明的遗嘱给继承人造成损失和损害的，依据哈萨克斯坦法律承担责任。

脚注 第 38 条经 2013 年 7 月 3 日哈萨克斯坦共和国宪法法律第 121-V 号（在自首次公布之日起 10 日后开始施行）修订。

第六章 公证活动基本规则

第三十九条 开展公证活动的程序

开展公证活动的程序由本法、其他法律法规和经哈萨克斯坦共和国司法部确认的公证员开展公证活动的规则确定。

脚注 第 39 条经 2011 年 12 月 26 日哈萨克斯坦共和国法律第 516-IV 号（自首次公布之日起 10 日后开始施行）修订。

第四十条 开展公证活动的时间

公证活动应当自向国家公证员或者经本法授权的人员提交一切必要的文件和缴纳国家税款之日时进行；或自向私营公证员支付款项时进行。

第四十一条 公证活动延期、中止的原因和条件

1. 公证活动可因下列原因延期：

（1）需要更多有关自然人或法人的更多信息；

（2）发送文件以供专家审查。

2. 公证活动延期的期限：自公证活动延期的决定公布之日起，不得超过一个月。

3. 利害关系人与公证申请人申请公证的权利和事实产生争议的，利害关系人可以申请延期，但延期时间不得超过 10 日，如果在此期间利害关系人没有向法院起诉，那么应取消。

message of receipt of application is not received from the court, notarial action shall be postponed.

4. In case of receipt from the court of a message of receipt of application of interested person disputing a right or fact for certification of which another interested person is called on, performance of notarial action shall be suspended until the court resolves the matter.

Footnote. Article 41 as amended by Constitutional Law of the Republic of Kazakhstan dated 03.07.2013 No 121-V (enforced upon expiry of ten calendar days after first official publication).

4. 公证员得知利害关系人就第 3 款所述事项向法院起诉的，应暂停开展公证行为，直至法院解决此事。

脚注 第 41 条经哈萨克斯坦共和国 2013 年 7 月 3 日第 121-V 号宪法修正案（自首次公布之日起 10 日后开始施行）修正。

Article 42. Identification of applicant for notarial action

1. The notary or civil servant shall identify the citizen applying for notarial action, his/her representative or the representative of the legal entity when notarial action is carried out.

2. Identification shall be based on the identity document or passport of the citizen, applying for notarial action.

第四十二条 公证活动申请人的身份

1. 公证员或者得到授权开展公证活动的公务员进行公证时，应当查验申请公证的公民及其代理人、申请公证的法人的法人代表的身份。

2. 申请公证的身份证明应当以公民的身份证件或者护照为依据。

Article 43. Clarification of capacity of individuals and legal capacity of entity involved in transactions

Capacity of citizens shall be clarified legal capacity of entities shall be examined during certification of transactions.

第四十三条 核实参与交易的自然人或法人的民事行为能力

公证员在交易公证期间应审查公民和法人的行为能力。

Article 44. Procedure for signature of notarial documents

1. Content of notarially certified documents may be read aloud if the participants wish.

2. Transactions and applications certified by notary shall be signed by the participants before a notary.

3. If the citizen cannot personally sign due to physical disability, illness or any other reasons, then at his/her request and in his/her presence, and before the notary, another citizen may sign a transaction, application or other document with specification of reasons why the document cannot be signed personally by the citizen applying for notarial action.

第四十四条 公证文件的签署程序

1. 经当事人同意，公证员可当众宣读经公证证明的文件的内容。

2. 经公证员公证的交易和申请，应当由当事人在公证员面前签字确认。

3. 公民因身体残疾、疾病或其他原因不能亲自签字，依据该公民的请求并在该公民和公证员的见证下，可由另一公民代其签署交易申请书或其他文件，并说明该公民不能亲自签署文件的理由。

Article 45. Requirements applicable to texts of certified transactions and certified documents

1. Texts of notarially certified transactions must be written or printed clearly and well defined with regard to the content of the transaction; dates and terms shall be specified in words at least once, and names of legal entities shall be unabridged with specification of location.

第四十五条 关于经公证的交易文件及其他文件

1. 经过公证的交易文件应手写或打印而成，并应保证书面清晰，文件内容与交易相关；文件中应用文字特别标识说明日期和术语，法人的名称和所在地，公民的姓名及住所地。

Surnames, forenames and patronymics of citizens, and the addresses of their places of residences, shall be written in full.

2. Texts of transactions or certified documents with erasures, notices, deleted words or other unspecified corrections, and documents written in pencil, may not be certified.

3. Sheets in document containing more than one sheet shall be bound, tied and sealed.

Article 46. Limitation of rights to carry out notarial activities

1. Notaries and civil servants cities of regional significance, rural settlements, villages and rural districts shall may not carry out notarial activities in their own name or on their own behalf, or in the name and on behalf of their spouse or their relatives (parents, children, brothers, sisters, grandchildren, grandfather, grandmother).

2. In these cases, notarial activities shall be carried out by any other notary.

3. Notarial activities carried out in breach of the rules established by this Article shall be invalid.

Footnote. Article 46 as amended by Law of the Republic of Kazakhstan dated 20 December 2004, No 13 (enforced from 1 January, 2005)

Article47. Production of certificate of acknowledgments, issue of certificates and pronouncement of regulations

1. Certificates of acknowledgment shall be produced upon issue of duplicates of notarially certified documents and certification of accuracy of copies of documents and extracts from them, accuracy of translation of documents from one language to another, upon certification of time of presentation of documents on relevant documents.

2. Relevant certificates shall be issued for acceptance of inheritance, right of property, certification of facts of a citizen being alive and in a particular place, transfer of applications from individuals and legal entities to other individuals and legal entities, and acceptance of documents for safe storage.

3. Relevant regulations shall be pronounced when an inheritance trust manager is appointed.

Footnote. Article 47 as amended by Law of the Republic of Kazakhstan dated 5 May 2003, No 408.

Article48. Refusal to carry out notarial action

1. Notarial action shall be refused if:

2. 公证员不得公证有擦除、标注、删除痕迹或其他未明确更正的交易文件或公证文件，以及用铅笔书写的文件。

3. 两页以上的文本，须装订、密封。

第四十六条　开展公证活动的权利限制

1. 公证员和在重要城市、城乡居住区、村庄和偏远地区任职的地方政府公务员，不得以自己的名义或以配偶、亲属（父母、子女、兄弟、姐妹、孙辈、祖父、祖母）的名义，或代表自己或其配偶、亲属开展公证活动。

2. 出现上述情况的，公证活动应由其他公证员进行。

3. 违反本条规定的公证活动无效。

脚注　第46条经哈萨克斯坦共和国2004年12月20日第13号法令（2005年1月1日起施行）修订。

第四十七条　制作确认证书，颁发证书和颁布法规

1. 公证员出具证明文件时，应出具公证文件副本、文件副本及其摘录的准确性证明，翻译文件的准确性证明，相关文件提交时间的证明。

2. 公证员应就下列事项出具相关证书：遗产继承、财产权事实、公民生存事实的证明、代自然人或法人向其他自然人或法人转达声明；接收文件并妥善保管。

3. 公证员指定继承信托管理人的，应当遵守有关规定。

脚注　第47条经哈萨克斯坦共和国2003年5月5日第408号法令修订。

第四十八条　拒绝公证活动

1. 有下列情形之一的，当事人有权拒绝公证活动：

1) such action is contrary to laws;

2) the action should be carried out by another notary;

3) the citizen or representative is incapable and does not have the necessary powers to apply for notarial action;

4) the transaction performed on behalf of a legal entity is inconsistent with the goals specified in its charter or provision;

5) the transaction does not comply with requirements of legislation;

6) the documents presented for notarial action, do not comply with requirements of legislation.

2. A well-grounded written explanation specifying reasons for rejection shall be issued by the notary upon refusal of persons applying for notarial action within ten calendar days from the date of application for notarial action.

3. Refusal to carry out notarial action or incorrect performance of notarial action may be appealed against by judicial procedure.

Footnote. Article 48 as amended by Laws of the Republic of Kazakhstan dated 05.05.2003 No 408; and by Constitutional Law of the Republic of Kazakhstan dated 03.07.2013 No 121-V (enforced upon expiry of ten calendar days after first official publication).

Article 49. Registration of notarial activities

All notarial activities performed by the notary or civil servants mentioned in Articles 34-36 of this Law, shall be entered in registers (and in the electronic register of the unified notarial information system).

Footnote. Article 49 is in the wording of Law of the Republic of Kazakhstan dated 15.07.2010 No 337-IV (for method of enforcement, see Article 2).

Article50. Form of registers of notarial activities (and of electronic register of unified notarial information system), notarial certificates, certificates of acknowledgment

Footnote. Title amended by Law of the Republic of Kazakhstan dated 15.07.2010 No 337-IV (for method of enforcement see Article 2).

The form of registers of notarial activities (and of the electronic register of the unified notarial information system), notarial certificates and regulations, certificates of acknowledgments of transactions and certificated documents shall be established by the Ministry of Justice of the Republic of Kazakhstan.

Footnote. Article 50 as amended by Laws of the

（1）申请公证的事项违反法律规定；

（2）公证事项应当由另一名公证员办理；

（3）公民或者代理人无行为能力的或无权申请公证的；

（4）法人代表进行的交易不符合其法人章程的规定或目标的；

（5）交易不符合法律规定的；

（6）公证文件不符合法律规定的。

2. 公证员拒绝公证的，应当自公证申请之日起10日内，向申请人出具合理的书面说明，说明拒绝理由。

3. 公证员拒绝开展公证活动或者不正确开展公证活动的，申请人可以通过司法程序提出上诉。

脚注 第48条经哈萨克斯坦共和国2003年5月5日第408号法令和哈萨克斯坦共和国2013年7月3日第121-V号宪法修正案（在自首次公布之日起10日后开始施行）修订。

第四十九条 公证活动的登记

本法第34条至第36条规定的公证员进行的一切公证活动，均应当进行公证登记（以及统一公证信息电子登记）。

脚注 第49条载于哈萨克斯坦共和国2010年7月15日第337-IV号法令（执行方法见第2条）。

第五十条 公证登记簿（和统一公证信息电子登记簿）、公证书、确认书的格式。

脚注 标题经哈萨克斯坦共和国2010年7月15日第337-IV号法令（施行方法见第2条）修订。

哈萨克斯坦共和国司法部应统一公证登记簿和公证信息电子登记簿、公证书、交易确认证书和公证文件的格式。

脚注 第50条经哈萨克斯坦共和国2003年5月

Republic of Kazakhstan dated 05.05.2003 No 408; and 15.07.2010 No 337-IV (for method of enforcement, see Article 2).

Article 51. Issue of duplicate of notarially certified document

1. In the event of loss of a document a copy of which is stored in the notarial office or by the notary, citizens and representatives of legal entities for whom the notarial activities were carried out, shall be issued with a duplicate of the lost document.

2. Duplicate documents shall be issued in accordance with requirements of Article 3 of this Law.

Chapter 7. CERTIFICATE OF TRANSACTIONS

Article 52. Notarially certified transactions

The notary shall certify transactions for which notarial certification is required by legislation. The notary may certify other transactions if the parties so wish.

Article53. Explanation to parties of meaning and significance of draft transaction

Notaries and civil servants carrying out notarial activities must clarify the meaning and significance of the draft transaction presented and shall check that the content reflects the parties' actual intent and is not inconsistent with the requirements of legislation.

Article 54. Certification of property alienation and pledge documents subject to registration

1. Property alienation and pledge documents subject to registration may be certified upon presentation of documents confirming right of ownership to alienated or mortgaged property.

2. Property alienation and pledge certificates subject to registration shall be produced at the location of this property.

3. The notary shall establish a legal document for the land plot, whereon the alienable real estate properties are located, once the property alienation certificates are completed.

The notary shall claim the documents of title to the plot and determine the powers of the landowner (land user) on assignment of its rights when the property alienation certificates are completed.

Land plot title documents shall not be reclaimed when housing units and non-living premises located in condominium are alienated.

5 日第 408 号法令和 2010 年 7 月 15 日第 337-IV 号法令修订（施行方法见第 2 条）。

第五十一条　出具经公证的文件的副本

1. 如果遗失文件的副本由公证机构或公证员保管，经公民和法人代表申请，公证机构或公证员应出具遗失文件的副本。

2. 公证员应当依照本法第 3 条的规定出具副本。

第七章　公证交易

第五十二条　公证交易

公证员应当对依照法律规定必须公证的交易进行公证，依据双方当事人意愿，公证员可对其他交易进行公证。

第五十三条　向当事人解释交易草案的含义和意义

公证员和从事公证活动的公务员必须向当事人说明当事人提交的交易草案的含义和意义，并检查文件内容是否反映当事人的真实意愿，是否符合法律要求。

第五十四条　未办理登记的财产转让和抵押公证书

1. 未办理登记的财产转让和抵押文件，在提交证明转让财产或抵押财产所有权的文件后，可予以公证。

2. 公证员应在财产所在地的公证机构办理财产转让登记、制作抵押公证书。

3. 财产转让公证书一经出具，公证员就应转让不动产所在地的土地所有权凭证。

公证员应当取得该土地的所有权凭证，并在出具财产转让公证书后，确定土地所有人（土地使用者）转让的权利。

共同所有的区域和非住宅转让时，不得收回土地所有权文件。

Footnote. Article 54 as amended by Laws of the Republic of Kazakhstan dated 05.05.2003 No 408; and 26.12.2011 No 516-IV (enforced upon expiry of 10 calendar days after first official publication).

Article 55. (Article 55 excluded by Law of the Republic of Kazakhstan dated 5 May 2003, No 408)

Article 56. Certification of wills

1. The notary and other civil servants carrying out notarial activities shall certificate the wills of capable citizens composed in accordance with the requirements of Kazakh legislation and personally presented to the notary by them. Wills may not be certificated through representatives.

2. Presentation of evidences confirming right to property bequeathed shall not be required upon certification of wills from testators.

Article 57. Procedure for change and revocation of wills

When an application for revocation of will, or a new will revoking or changing a previously composed will is received, the notary and other civil servants carrying out the notarial activities shall make a note on a copy of the will kept by the notary and in the register of notarial activities (and in the electronic register of the unified notarial information system). Application for revocation or change of will shall be notarially certified.

Footnote. Article 57 as amended by Laws of the Republic of Kazakhstan dated 15.07.2010 No 337-IV (for method of enforcement see Article 2); and 26.12.2011 No 516-IV (enforced upon expiry of 10 calendar days after first official publication).

Article 58. Certification of powers of attorney

1. Notaries and civil servants carrying out notarial activities shall certificate powers of attorney on behalf of one or more persons in the name of one or more persons.

2. Powers of attorney issued according to the sub-delegation procedure, shall be subject to notarial certification on presentation of the basic power in which sub-delegation of right is specified. The power issued according to the sub-delegation procedure shall not contain more rights than the basic power presents. Duration of powers of attorney issued according to the sub-delegation procedure shall not exceed the duration of the power under authority of which it issued.

脚注 第 54 条经哈萨克斯坦共和国 2003 年 5 月 5 日第 408 号和 2011 年 12 月 26 日第 516-IV 号法令修订（在自首次公布之日起 10 日后开始施行）。

第五十五条 （第 55 条被哈萨克斯坦共和国 2003 年 5 月 5 日第 408 号法令删除。）

第五十六条 公证遗嘱

1. 公证员和其他从事公证活动的公务员应当依照哈萨克斯坦法律，对有民事行为能力的公民设立的遗嘱进行公证。立遗嘱人应当亲自向公证员提交遗嘱，他人代为递交的不予公证。

2. 对遗赠进行公证时，立遗嘱人无须出示关于遗赠财产权的归属的证据。

第五十七条 变更及撤销遗嘱的程序

公证员和其他从事公证活动的公务员收到撤销遗嘱的申请或者变更原有遗嘱的新遗嘱时，应当在公证机构保存的遗嘱副本和公证活动登记簿（以及统一公证信息电子登记簿）上注明。撤销或更改遗嘱的申请须予以公证。

脚注 第 57 条经哈萨克斯坦共和国 2010 年 7 月 15 日第 337-IV 号法令（执行方法见第 2 条）；2011 年 12 月 26 日第 516-IV 号法令（在自首次公布之日起 10 日后开始施行）修订。

第五十八条 公证授权委托书

1. 公证员和从事公证活动的公务员应当以一人或者多人的名义代表一人或者多人公证授权委托书。

2. 依据转委托程序出具的授权委托书，该授权委托书包含特定转授权的基本权力时，应接受公证；依据转授权程序产生的权力，不得超过基本权力；依据转授程序出具的授权委托书的期限，不得超过原授权委托书的期限。

Article 59. Number of copies of documents setting out context of transaction

The number of copies of documents setting out the context of the transaction certified in the notarial procedure shall be determined by the persons applying for notarial action but shall not be less than two, one of these copies being in the notary's notarial office.

第五十九条 交易文件副本数量

公证申请人可以自主决定公证活动中会用到的，列明交易内容的文件副本的数量，但不得少于两份，其中一份留存公证机构。

Chapter 8. Issue of certificate of right to inheritance

第八章 出具遗产继承权公证书

Footnote. The title of chapter 9 is in the wording of Law of the Republic of Kazakhstan dated 5 May, 2003 No 408.

脚注 第九章的标题是哈萨克斯坦共和国 2003 年 5 月 5 日第 408 号法令的措辞。

Article 60. Notification of heirs and legatees on opening of inheritance

1. Notaries receiving an advice of opening of inheritance shall be obliged to notify the heirs whose place of residence or work they know accordingly.

Notaries shall be obliged to notify the opening of inheritance by will to legatees whose place of residence or work they knows, when the will contains a legate.

2. If the place of residence or work of heirs or legatees is unknown, the notary shall advise the opening of inheritance through mass media.

Footnote. Article 60 is in the wording of Law of the Republic of Kazakhstan dated 27.04.2012 No 15-V (enforced upon expiry of ten calendar days after first official publication).

第六十条 继承开始时，通知继承人和受遗赠人

1. 公证员接到继承开始的通知后，有义务通知居住地或者工作地点已为公证员知悉的继承人。遗嘱包含受遗赠人时，公证员有义务通知居住地或工作地点已为公证员知悉的受遗赠人。

2. 继承人、受遗赠人的住所、工作地点不详的，公证员应当通过传播媒介告知继承开始。

脚注 第 60 条是哈萨克斯坦共和国 2012 年 4 月 27 日第 15-V 号法令的措辞（在首次正式公布后的 10 日届满时施行）。

Article 61. Acceptance of applications for renunciation of inheritance or issue of certificate of right to inheritance.

The notary shall accept applications for renunciation of inheritance or issue of certificate of right to it in writing, according to place of opening of inheritance, in accordance with Kazakh legislation.

Footnote. Article 61 is in the wording of Law of the Republic of Kazakhstan dated 5 May 2003, No 408.

第六十一条 接受放弃继承权的申请或者出具继承权证明。

依据哈萨克斯坦法律和继承开始的地点，公证员应以书面形式接受放弃继承权的申请或出具继承权证明的申请。

脚注 第 61 条采用哈萨克斯坦共和国 2003 年 5 月 5 日第 408 号法令的法律措辞。

Article 62. (Articles 62-68 are excluded by Law of the Republic of Kazakhstan dated 5 May 2003, No 408)

第六十二条 （第 62 条至第 68 条被哈萨克斯坦共和国 2003 年 5 月 5 日第 408 号法令删除）。

Article 69. Places and terms of issue of certificate of right of inheritance

1. The notary shall issue a certificate of right to inheritance at the place of opening of inheritance, following written application from the heirs.

2. Certificates of right to inheritance shall be issued within the periods provided by the Civil Code of the Re-

第六十九条 出具继承权公证书的地点和条款

1. 公证员收到继承人书面申请后，应当在财产继承地出具继承权公证书。

2. 公证员应当在《哈萨克斯坦共和国民法典》规定的期限内出具继承权公证书。

public of Kazakhstan.

Article 70. Procedure of issue of certificate of right of inheritance

1. Certificates of right of inheritance shall be issued to heirs accepting the inheritance, in accordance with Kazakh civil legislation regulations.

2. (Excluded)

3. Certificates of right of inheritance shall be issued together or to each heir individually, depending on their wish.

4. When a certificate of right to inheritance of is issued to guardianship and trusteeship authorities in the name of a ward of court or minor or disabled heir at the place of residence of heir for the protection of his/her property interest, the notary shall advise accordingly.

5. Certificates of right of inheritance shall be issued to the authorized state body when property is transferred by right of inheritance to the state.

6. Work concerning accounting, storage, valuation, further use and realization of property made state property by right of inheritance, shall be organised by the authorized state body.

The work procedure for accounting, storage, valuation, further use and realization of property made state property by right of inheritance shall be determined by the government of the Republic of Kazakhstan.

Footnote. Article 70 as amended by Law of the Republic of Kazakhstan dated 24 December 2001, No 276; 5 May 2003, No 408; and 22 June 2006, No 147.

Article 71. Conditions of issue of certificate of right to inheritance under law

1. The notary shall verify the death of testator, the time and place of opening of inheritance, the existence of relations constituting the basis for allocating the inheritance to persons applying for issue of certificate of right of inheritance under the Law, and the composition and location of inheritance property upon issue of certificate of right of inheritance under law, by demanding relevant items of evidence.

2. If one or more heirs are denied the opportunity to introduce evidence of relations as a basis for bringing inheritance, they may be included in the certificate of right of inheritance by agreement of all other heirs accepting the inheritance and introducing such evidence.

第七十条　出具继承权公证书的程序

1. 对接受继承的继承人，公证员应依照哈萨克斯坦民法的规定出具继承权公证书。

2.（已被删除）。

3. 公证员应依据各继承人的意愿，一同或分别向各继承人出具继承权公证书。

4. 为保护继承人的财产权益，以被监护人、未成年继承人、残疾继承人的名义向其居住地的监督、托管机关出具继承权证明的，应当由公证员告知。

5. 财产继承权转让给国家的，公证员应当向被授权的国家机关出具继承权公证书。

6. 经授权的国家机关组织实施继承国有财产的会计、保管、估价、进一步使用和变现工作。

对成为国有财产的遗产的清点、储存、估价、进一步使用和变现的工作程序应由哈萨克斯坦共和国政府决定。

脚注　第 70 条经哈萨克斯坦共和国 2001 年 12 月 24 日第 276 号法令、2003 年 5 月 5 日第 408 号法令和 2006 年 6 月 22 日第 147 号法令修订。

第七十一条　依据法律规定，出具继承权公证书的条件

1. 公证员应当依据相关证据，依法核实遗嘱人的死亡、遗嘱继承的时间、地点，或依据法律规定，核实申请出具继承权公证书的人与遗嘱人所存在的法律关系，以及在依法出具继承权公证书时财产的构成和地点。

2. 如果一名或多名继承人因无法提供亲属关系的证据而丧失继承权，他们可在其他继承人都同意并提出此类证据的情况下，取得继承权公证书。

Article 72. Conditions of issue of certificate of right to inheritance under will

1. The notary shall verify the death of testator, the testacy, the time and place of opening of inheritance, and the composition and location of inheritance property, upon issue of certificate of right of inheritance under the will by demanding relevant evidence.

2. The notary shall also clarify the scope of persons, having a hereditary right to portion of inheritance.

3. The notary shall invite legatees and explain the content of the will and their right to obtain a proper share from the heirs) when a legate is present.

Footnote. Article 72 as amended by Law of the Republic of Kazakhstan dated 27.04.2012 No 15-V (enforced upon expiry of ten calendar days after first official publication).

第七十二条　依据遗嘱，出具继承权公证书的条件

1. 公证员依据遗嘱内容出具继承权公证书时，应依据相关证据，核实遗嘱人的死亡、遗嘱继承、开始继承的时间、地点、继承财产的构成、地点。

2. 公证员还应当宣告继承人的身份。

3. 当遗嘱内容涉及遗赠时，公证员应当通知受遗赠人，并说明遗嘱的内容及受遗赠人获得适当份额的遗产的权利。

脚注　第 72 条经哈萨克斯坦共和国 2012 年 4 月 27 日第 15-V 号法令修订（在自首次公布之日起 10 日后开始施行）。

Chapter 9. ISSUE OF CERTIFICATES OF RIGHT TO SHARE IN JOINT PROPERTY, ATTACHMENT AND REMOVAL OF PROHIBITION OF ALIENATION OF PROPERTY

第九章　出具共同财产份额继承权公证书，扣押和解除财产转让禁令

Article 73. Issue of certificate of right of inheritance of share in joint property

1. The notary shall issue a certificate of right to inheritance to the person(s) with jointly owned property and wishing the certificate of right to inheritance on such share following the joint written application of persons, having a property or right of joint property.

2. The certificate of right of inheritance to share in joint property shall be issued according to location of this property.

第七十三条　出具共同财产份额继承权公证书

1. 公证员应当根据财产权人或共同财产权人的书面申请，向共同财产份额继承人（该继承人也希望获得该公证书）出具继承权公证书。

2. 公证员应当在该财产所在地出具共同财产份额继承权公证书。

Article 74. Issue of certificate of right to inheritance of a share in common property on application of surviving spouse

1. Certificates of right to inheritance of a share in common property shall be issued by the notary at the location of opening of inheritance following the written application of surviving spouse, with notification of heirs accepting the inheritance.

2. Certificates of right to inheritance of a share in common property may be issued for half of common property acquired during marriage by the surviving spouse, unless the marriage contract established otherwise.

3. Certificates of right to inheritance to the deceased spouse's share in their common property may be issued to the heirs of the deceased spouse following their application.

第七十四条　依据尚在人世的配偶的申请，出具共同财产份额继承权公证书

1. 尚在人世的配偶提出书面申请后，公证员在继承开始的地点出具共有财产份额继承权公证书，并通知继承人。

2. 对尚在人世的配偶在婚姻存续期间取得的一半共同财产，可以出具共有财产份额继承权公证书，但另有规定的除外。

3. 已故配偶的继承人提出申请的，公证员可向其出具已故配偶在共同财产中所占份额的继承权证书。

Article 75. Attachment and removal of prohibition of alienation of property

1. The notary shall attach prohibition of property to notifications from banking institutions or legal entity regarding issue of loan for the construction, capital repair or purchase of a house or apartment or for purchase of other movable and immovable property, and when a pledge contract is produced.

2. A notary shall send prohibition of alienation of property in writing to the movable and immovable property registration authorities.

3. On receipt of notification from banking institutions or legal entities for repayment of loan or termination of pledge contract, the notary shall remove the prohibition of alienation and inform the movable and immovable property authorities in writing.

第七十五条　附加和解除财产转让禁令

1. 公证员应附加财产转让禁令以便通知银行或法人机构，在发放建设、修缮、购买房屋或者购买其他动产或不动产的贷款，或者设立质押合同时，考虑上述情况。

2. 公证员应当将禁止转让财产的书面通知送交动产和不动产登记机关。

3. 公证员收到银行机构或者法人要求偿还贷款或者终止抵押合同的通知后，应当解除转让禁令，并书面通知动产和不动产主管机关。

Chapter 10. CERTIFICATION OF ACCURACY OF COPIES OF DOCUMENTS AND EXTRACTS FROM THEM, AUTHENTICITY OF SIGNATURE AND ACCURACY OF TRANSLATION

第十章　公证文件副本和摘录的准确性证明、签字的真实性和翻译的准确性证明

Article 76. Certification of accuracy of copies of documents and extracts from them

1. Notaries or civil servants authorized to carry out notarial activities shall certificate the accuracy of copies of documents and extracts from them issued by legal entities and citizens provided that these documents and their content shall not contradict legislation and have legal significance.

2. Accuracy of extracts may be certified only if the document from which the extract is made contains the resolution of several separate, unlinked issues. An extract shall reproduce the comprehensive text of the part of document concerned.

第七十六条　公证文件副本及其摘录的准确性

1. 公证员或被授权开展公证活动的公务员应当证明法人和公民出具的公证文件副本和摘录的准确性，且这些文件及其内容不得违反法律，并具有法律意义。

2. 公证员应通过制作摘录时所依据的文件证实摘录的准确性，且该文件应包含若干独立且无关联的问题的解决方案。摘录应反映文件部分内容的整体背景。

Article 77. Certification of accuracy of copy of document issued by citizen

Accuracy of copies of documents issued by citizens shall be certified by the notary in cases where the accuracy of a citizen's signature is certified on a document by the notary or civil servant authorized by this Law to carry out notarial activities.

第七十七条　公民签字的文件副本的准确性证明

公民签字的文件副本的准确性由证明该公民签字的准确性的公证员或被授权开展公证活动的公务员证明。

Article 78. Certification of accuracy of copy from copy of document

Accuracy of copies from copy of document shall be certified by the notary provided the accuracy of the copy is notarially certified or the copy document is issued by the

第七十八条　文件副本的复印件的准确性证明

文件副本复印件的准确性应由公证员证明，前提是副本的准确性经过公证，或副本由签发原始文件的法人签发。在后一种情况下，副本应写在信头纸上且

legal entity that issued the original document. In the latter case the copy document shall be made on this legal entity's headed paper and sealed and mention that the legal entity holds the original document.

密封，并注明该法人留存原始文件。

Article 79. Certification of authenticity of signature on document

1. Notaries shall certify authenticity of signature on documents provided that their content does not contradict legislative acts and the exposition of transaction is not certified.

2. Notaries certifying authenticity of signature shall not certificate the facts shown in the documents, and instead only confirm that the signature is made by the particular person.

Footnote. Article 79 as amended by Law of the Republic of Kazakhstan dated 5 May 2003, No 408.

第七十九条　文件上签字的真实性证明

1. 公证员公证文件签名的真实性的前提条件是文件内容不违反法律，且交易的内容未经公证。

2. 公证签字真实性的公证员不得证明文件中所示的事实，其职权仅限于确认签字是由特定的人作出的。

脚注　第 79 条经哈萨克斯坦共和国 2003 年 5 月 5 日第 408 号法令修订。

Article 80. Certification of accuracy of translation

1. A notary shall certify accuracy of translation from one language to another if the notary speaks the relevant language.

2. If a notary does not speak the relevant language, a translation may be made by a translator, and then certified as authentic by the notary.

第八十条　翻译准确性的证明

1. 公证员通晓有关语言的，应当证明翻译的准确性。

2. 公证员尚不通晓有关语言的，可以由翻译人翻译，再由公证员公证其翻译文本的准确性。

Chapter 11. CERTIFICATION OF FACTS

第十一章　事实证明

Article 81. Certification of fact that a citizen is alive

1. A notary shall certify the fact that a citizen is alive.

2. The fact that a minor is alive shall be certified at the request of his/her legal representatives (parents, adoptive parents, guardians, trustees) and by institutions and organizations in whose protection the minor is held. A certificate shall be issued to the interested persons in confirmation of that fact.

第八十一条　公民存活的事实证明

1. 公证员应就公民存活的事实进行公证。

2. 公证员应依据未成年人的法定代理人（父母、养父母、监护人、受托人）以及未成年保护机构和组织的申请，证明未成年人存活的事实。公证员应当向利害关系人出具公证书。

Article 82. Certification of facts that citizen is in a particular place

1. A notary shall certify the fact that a citizen is in a particular place at that citizen's request.

2. The fact that a minor is in a particular place shall be certified at the request of his/her legal representatives (parents, adoptive parents, guardians, trustees) and by institutions and organizations in whose protection the minor is held. A certificate shall be issued to the interested persons in confirmation of that fact.

第八十二条　公民在特定地点的事实证明

1. 公证员应当依据公民的申请，对该公民在特定地点的事实进行公证。

2. 公证员应依据未成年人的法定代理人（父母、养父母、监护人、受托人）以及未成年保护机构和组织的申请，证明未成年人在特定地点的事实。公证员应当向利害关系人出具公证书。

Article 83. Certification of time of presentation of documents

A notary shall certify the time of presentation of document to him/her. Acknowledgment on this shall be shown on the documents with specification of surname, forename and patronymic the person presenting it.

第八十三条　文件提交时间的证明

公证员应就文件提交的时间进行证明，应通过文件显示，文件中应注明提交人的姓名。

Chapter 12. TRANSFER OF DECLARATIONS BY INDIVIDUALS AND LEGAL ENTITIES. ACCEPTANCE OF MONEY ON DEPOSIT

第十二章　为自然人或法人转达声明、接受提存

Footnote. Wording of title changed Law of the Republic of Kazakhstan dated 13 November 1998, No 302.

脚注　标题的措辞由哈萨克斯坦共和国 1998 年 11 月 13 日的第 302 号法令改变。

Article 84. Transfer of declarations

1. Transfer of declarations of individuals and legal entities to other individuals and legal entities shall be personally carried out by the notary on receipt or by post with return notification. Declarations may also be transferred by fax machine, computer network or other technical facilities.

2. The expenses linked with use of technical facilities for transfer of declarations shall be paid by the person at whose request the notarial action is carried out.

3. At the request of person filing the declaration, a certificate of transfer of declaration shall be issued to him/her.

第八十四条　转达声明

1. 自然人或法人向其他自然人或法人转达声明，应由公证员在收到通知后亲自办理，或以附回执的邮件的方式通知。

公证员也可通过传真机、计算机网络或其他技术设施转达声明。

2. 因转达声明使用相关设备所产生的费用，应由申请公证的人支付。

3. 应申请转达者的请求，公证员应向其出具转达声明证书。

Article 85. Acceptance of money on deposit

1. A notary shall receive money on deposit from a debtor for transfer to a creditor in cases provided for by legislation.

2. A notary shall notify a creditor of receipt of money and at his/(her/its request issue the money to him/her/it.

3. Money shall be accepted on deposit by the notary at the place of fulfilment of obligations.

Footnote. Article 85 as amended by Law of the Republic of Kazakhstan dated 13 November 1998, No 302.

第八十五条　接受提存

1. 按照法律的规定，公证员应从债务人处接受提存，以便实现债权人的债权。

2. 公证员接受提存后，应当通知债权人，并依照债权人的要求，向其提存钱款。

3. 公证员应当在义务履行地接受提存。

脚注　第 85 条经 1998 年 11 月 13 日哈萨克斯坦共和国第 302 号法令修订。

Article 86. Repayment of money to person placing it on deposit

Repayments to persons placing money on deposit shall be allowed only with the written consent of the person or by court decision.

Footnote. Article 86 as amended by Law of the Republic of Kazakhstan dated 13 November 1998, No 302.

第八十六条　向存款人返还提存物

只有在债务人书面同意或法院裁决返还的情况下，公证员方可向债务人返还提存物。

脚注　第 86 条经 1998 年 11 月 13 日哈萨克斯坦共和国第 302 号法令修订。

Chapter 13. EXECUTION OF PROTEST OF BILL

第十三章　票据的抗辩

Footnote. Title as amended, Articles 87-91 excluded

脚注　该标题经过修正，第 87 条至第 91 条被哈

by Law of the Republic of Kazakhstan dated 29 March 2000, No 42.

Article 92. Protest of a bill

Protest of a bill in non-payment, non-acceptance and failure to date shall be performed by the notary in accordance with Kazakh legislative acts concerning exchange and promissory bills.

Chapter 14. ACCEPTANCE OF DOCUMENTS AND SECURITY PAPERS FOR STORAGE

Footnote. Title of chapter substituted by Law of the Republic of Kazakhstan dated 13 November 1998, No 302.

Article 93. Acceptance of documents and security papers for storage

1. A notary shall accept documents and security papers listed in an inventory for storage. One copy of the inventory shall be remained by the notary, another copy shall be issued to the person surrendering the documents and security papers for storage.

2. A notary may accept documents and security papers without inventory if they are properly packed (packing shall be under the seal of the notary, signed by him/her and the person surrendering the documents and security papers). In these cases a notary shall be responsible for safety of packing.

3. A certificate shall be issued to the person surrendering the documents and security papers.

Footnote. Article 93 as amended by Law of the Republic of Kazakhstan dated 13 November 1998, No 302.

Article 94. Return of documents and security papers accepted for storage

Documents and security papers accepted for storage shall be returned to the person surrendering them for storage or legally to an authorized body on presentation of certificate and its inventory or by a court decision.

Footnote. Article 94 as amended by Law of the Republic of Kazakhstan dated 13 November 1998, No 302.

Chapter 15. EXECUTION OF MARINE PROTESTS

Article 95. Declaration of marine protest

1. A notary shall accept a declaration by a ship's captain of an event occurring while the ship is sailing or in dock, if this is a basis for specifying the ship owner's

萨克斯坦共和国 2000 年 3 月 29 日第 42 号法令删除。

第九十二条　票据的抗辩

公证员对拒付、未承兑和未按期承兑的票据提出抗辩，应当符合哈萨克关于汇票和本票的法律规定。

第十四章　保管文件

脚注　本章标题被 1998 年 11 月 13 日哈萨克斯坦共和国第 302 号法令取代。

第九十三条　接受并保管文件和证券

1. 公证员应当接受并保管清单上所列的文件和证券。

公证员应为上述清单制作两份副本，一份由公证员保留，另一份由提交文件的人保留。

2. 公证员有权接受未在清单内的文件和证券，前提是这些文件已妥善包装（公证员和提交文件的人应在包装上签名，公证员应加盖印章）。公证员应妥善保管已包装的文件。

3. 公证员应向提交文件和证券的人出具公证书。

脚注　第 93 条经 1998 年 11 月 13 日哈萨克斯坦共和国第 302 号法令修订的。

第九十四条　退还保管的文件和证券

保管的文件和证券应退还给交存的人，或者退还给出示证书及文件清单或法院裁决退还的被授权机构。

脚注　第 94 条经 1998 年 11 月 13 日哈萨克斯坦共和国第 302 号法令修订。

第十五章　海事声明的执行

第九十五条　海事声明

1. 公证员应当接受船长主张船舶在航行中或者在码头上发生事件的声明，该声明可能是船主主张财产权的基础，是保护船主权利和合法权益的证据。船长

property requirements in order to provide evidence for protection of the ship holder's rights and legal interests.

关于船舶在航行期间或在港期间发生的事件的声明是船主主张财产权的基础，是保护船主权利和合法权益的证据。公证员应当接受上述声明。

2. A notice of marine protest shall contain a description of circumstances of occurrence and the measures adopted by the captain for protecting the property entrusted to him/her.

2. 海事声明通知书应说明发生的情况和船长为保护托付给他 / 她的财产而采取的措施。

3. A ship's captain shall be obliged to present a ship's journal and certified extract from the ship's journal confirming the circumstances listed in the notice of marine protest, in accordance with merchant shipping legislation, together with a notice or not later than seven calendar days from the date of port call or from the date of the event if it occurred in a port.

3. 船长应按照商船法的规定，提交航海日志及经公证的航海日志摘录，以确认海事声明通知书所列明的情况，并连同海事通知书一并提交。该事件发生在港口的，应自港口停靠日或事件发生之日起计的 7 日内提交文件。

Footnote. Article 95 as amended by Constitutional Law of the Republic of Kazakhstan dated 03.07.2013 No 121-V (enforced upon expiry of ten calendar days after first official publication).

脚注 第 95 条经哈萨克斯坦共和国 2013 年 7 月 3 日第 121-V 号宪法修正案（在自首次公布之日起 10 日后开始施行）修订。

Article 96. Deadline for declaring marine protest

1. A notice of marine protest shall, in accordance with merchant shipping legislation, be filed within twenty-four hours of the ship's arrival in port.

If the event triggering the need for the notice of marine protest occurred in the port, the protest shall be made within twenty-four hours of occurrence.

2. If notice of protest cannot be issued within the established period, the reason for this shall be specified in the notice of marine protest.

第九十六条 主张海事声明的最后期限

1. 依据商船法的规定，公证员应在船舶抵达港口后二十四小时内出具海事声明书。

港口发生纠纷，需要出具海事声明书的，公证员应当在事发后二十四小时内出具。

2. 公证员在规定期限内不能提交海事声明书的，应当在海事声明书中说明理由。

Article 97. Compilation of marine protest act

A notary shall compile a marine protest act and certify it with his/her own signature and seal on the basis of the captain's declaration and materials from the ship's journal, at the request of the captain and where possible, not less than two witnesses from the list of crew.

第九十七条 制作海事声明书

基于船长的请求，并在不少于两名船员的见证下，公证员可依据船长的声明和航海日志上的材料，撰写一份海事声明书，并签字盖章。

Chapter 16. PROVISION OF EVIDENCE

第十六章 证据的提供

Article 98. Provision of evidence necessary in a case arising in a court or other component body

1. A notary shall provide the evidence necessary in a case arising in a court or other component body at the request of the interested persons, if there are grounds for considering that presentation of the evidence will be impossible or difficult in the future.

2. A notary shall not provide evidence in a case that at the time when the interested persons apply to the notary

第九十八条 对法院或其他机构审理的案件提供必要的证据

1. 公证员有充分理由认为利害关系人今后不可能或提出相应的证据有困难的，应公证员基于利害关系人的请求，对法院或其他机构审理的案件提供必要的证据。

2. 利害关系人向公证员提出申请时，法院或其他主管机构已经开始审理此案件的，公证员不得提供证据。

is already in the court or other competent body.

Article 99. Activity of notary in provision of evidence

1.A notary shall question citizens, inspect documents and other items, and if necessary commission an expert examination, in order to provide evidence.

2.A notary shall governed by the relevant regulations of Kazakh civil procedure legislation when carrying out procedural actions to provide evidence.

3. A notary shall notify the time and place for provision of evidences from the party and interested persons, but their failure to appear shall not constitute a stay of execution of action to provide evidence.

4.Evidence shall only be provided without notification of one of the parties and interested persons only in emergency cases, or when it cannot be determined who shall participate in the case in future.

5.In case of failure by a witness or commissioned expert to appear, a notary shall inform the court for the place of residence of the witness or expert for adoption of measures provided for by Kazakh legislative acts.

6.A notary shall warn citizens and specialists on penalties for false evidence or conclusion and for failing or deliberately omitting to give evidence or conclusion.

第九十九条　公证员提供证据

1. 公证员可采取向公民咨询，检查文件和其他物品，以及必要时委托专家审查的方式来提供证据。

2. 公证员提供证据应遵守哈萨克斯坦民事诉讼法的有关规定。

3. 公证员应当通知当事人和利害关系人提供证据的时间和地点，当事人和利害关系人不出庭不中止提供证据。

4. 只有在紧急情况下，或无法确定案件当事人的情况下，公证员才可以在不通知当事人和利害关系人的情况下提供证据。

5. 目击证人或受委托的专家不出庭的，公证员应当告知法院证人或专家的居住地，以便采取哈萨克斯坦法律规定的措施。

6. 公证员应当警示公民和专家提供虚假证据、虚假结论或过失、故意遗漏证据或结论的责任。

Chapter 17. APPLICATION OF NORMS OF LAW OF OTHER STATES BY NOTARY. INTERNATIONAL TREATIES.

第十七章　公证员适用外国法律、国际条约

Article 100. Application of norms of law of other states by notary

1. A notary shall apply the norms of law of other states in accordance with Kazakh legislation.

2. A notary shall accept documents drawn up in accordance with the requirements of the international treaties of the Republic of Kazakhstan, and produce certificates of acknowledgments in the form established by the legislation of other states, unless otherwise provided by international treaties ratified by the Republic of Kazakhstan.

第一百条　公证活动中外国法律的适用

1. 公证员应当依照哈萨克斯坦法律适用外国法律。

2. 除哈萨克斯坦共和国批准的国际条约另有规定外，公证员应当接受哈萨克斯坦共和国参与的国际条约规定的文件，并根据外国法律规定的形式出具公证书。

Article101.Protection of inherited property and issue of certificate of right to inheritance

Actions linked with protection of property in Kazakh territory and left after the death of a foreign citizen or property coming to a foreign citizen after the death of a Kazakh citizen, and assignment of trustee of inheritance and issue of right of inheritance in relation to such property, shall be carried out in accordance with Kazakh legislation.

第一百零一条　保护遗产和出具继承权公证书

外国公民死亡后遗留在哈萨克斯坦境内的财产、哈萨克斯坦共和国公民死亡后遗留给他国公民的财产的保护，以及继承权的转让和与该财产有关的继承权的转让，应符合哈萨克斯坦法律。

Footnote. Article 101 as amended by Law of the Republic of Kazakhstan dated 5 May 2003, No 408.

Article102. Acceptance of notarial documents drawn up abroad

1. Documents drawn up abroad with participation by civil servants of competent bodies in other states or issued by those bodies, shall be accepted by the notary subject to their legalization by the Ministry of Foreign Affairs of the Republic of Kazakhstan.

2. Documents not legalized shall be accepted only in cases provided for by the legislation and international treaties of the Republic of Kazakhstan.

Article103. Provision of evidence necessary for conducting cases in the authorities of other states

A notary shall provide the evidence necessary for conducting cases in the authorities of other states.

Article 104. International treaty

1. If an international treaty ratified by the Republic of Kazakhstan established rules on notarial activities different from those provided by Kazakh legislative acts for carrying out notarial activities, the rules of the international treaty shall be applied when carrying out notarial activities.

2. If an international treaty ratified by the Republic of Kazakhstan includes within the competence of a notary the carrying out of notarial activities not provided by Kazakh legislation, a notary shall carry out the notarial activities according to the procedure established by the Ministry of Justice of the Republic of Kazakhstan.

Article 105. Ensuring fulfilment of this Law

1. (Excluded).

2. (Excluded).

3. Current regulatory legal acts regulating organization and activities of notaries prior to 1 January 1998 shall be brought into conformity with this Law and during this term shall be applied in the parts that do not contradict it.

4. Excluded by Law of the Republic of Kazakhstan dated 26.12.2011 No 516-IV (enforced upon expiry of 10 calendar days after first official publication).

Footnote. Article 105 as amended by Laws of the Republic of Kazakhstan dated 05.05.2003 No 408; and 26.12.2011 No 516-IV (enforced upon expiry of 10 calendar days after first official publication).

The President of the Republic of Kazakhstan

脚注 第 101 条经哈萨克斯坦共和国 2003 年 5 月 5 日第 408 号法令修订。

第一百零二条 境外公证文书的认可

1. 外国主管机构的公务员参与起草或外国主管机关签发的文件，应由哈萨克斯坦共和国外交部指定的公证员认可。

2. 公证员接受未合法化的文件应当符合哈萨克斯坦共和国法律和国际条约的规范。

第一百零三条 向外国主管机关提供证据

公证员应当向外国主管机关提供其办理案件所需的证据。

第一百零四条 国际条约

1. 哈萨克斯坦共和国批准的国际条约规定的公证活动规则与哈萨克斯坦公证法冲突时，公证员开展公证活动时应当适用国际条约的规则。

2. 如果哈萨克斯坦共和国批准的国际条约将开展哈萨克斯坦法律未规定的公证活动纳入公证员的职权范围，那么公证员应按照哈萨克斯坦共和国司法部规定的程序开展公证活动。

第一百零五条 确保本法的施行

1.（已被删除）。

2.（已被删除）。

3.1998 年 1 月 1 日之前规范公证员组织和活动的监督法律应符合本法的规定，并且在此期限内与本法不相抵触的部分可以适用。

4. 本条经哈萨克斯坦共和国 2011 年 12 月 26 日第 516-IV 号法令删除（自首次公布之日起 10 日后开始施行）。

脚注 第 105 条经哈萨克斯坦共和国 2003 年 5 月 5 日第 408 号法令和 2011 年 12 月 26 日第 516-IV 号法令修订（自首次公布之日起 10 日后开始施行）。

哈萨克斯坦共和国总统签署

朝鲜

朝鲜民主主义人民共和国公证法

NOTARY PUBLIC LAW OF THE DEMOCRATIC PEOPLE'S REPUBLIC OF KOREA

Adopted by Decision No. 51 of Lhe Standing Committee of tlie Supreme People's Assembly on February 2, 1995 and amended by Decree No. 808 of the Presidium of the Supreme People's Assembly on December 7, 2004

Chapter 1 Fundamentals

Article1 (Objective): This Iaw is enacted for the purpose of protecting the civil rights and interests of the institutions, enterprises, organizations and citizens and ensuring security in civil affairs by providing truthful authentication of facts or documents of legal significance.

Article2 (Affording convenience to applicants): A notarial act shall be performed upon application by an institution, enterprise, organization or citizen.

The Slate shall ensure that, all possible facilities are afforded to the institutions, enterprises, organizations and citizens presenting applications for a notarial act.

Article3 (Accuracy and lawfulness): The State shall ensure that notarial act is based on scientific and objective evidence so that accuracy and lawfulness may be guaranteed.

Article4 (Exercise of civil rights, performance of obligations): The State shall ensure that the applicants for a notarial act properly exercise the civil rights vested with them on an equal footing and perform their respective obligations in good faith.

Article5 (Notary institutions): Notarial acts shall be performed by the State notary offices.

朝鲜民主主义人民共和国公证法

1995年2月2日经最高人民大会常设委员会第51号决议通过

2004年12月7日经最高人民大会常设委员会第808号政令修正

第一章　公证法的基本内容

第一条（公证法的使命）：立法目的在于通过对具有法律意义的事实及文书真实性进行证明，以保护机关单位、企业、团体以及公民的民事权利和利益，致力于保障民事交易的安全。

第二条（为申请人提供便利的原则）：公证必须由机关单位、企业、团体或公民提交申请。

国家须积极为公证申请机关单位、企业、团体和公民提供必要的便利。

第三条（保障公证的准确性、合法性原则）：国家在公证的过程中，须根据科学客观的证据，保障公证的准确性以及合法性。

第四条（申请人履行权利义务的原则）：申请公证的当事人在平等的原则上，可正当行使自身的民事权利，并诚实履行自身的义务。

第五条（公证机构）：公证活动由国家公证机构执行。

Any notarial act, for which a citizen of the DPRK residing in a foreign country has filed an application, shall be performed by the DPRK consular mission accredited to the country concerned.

Article6 (Location): The State notary offices shall be established in the seats of provinces (or municipality directly under the central authority). They may also be established in the seats of municipalities (or districts) or counties, as may be required.

Article7 (Guidance): Unified guidance of notarial work shall be undertaken by the Supreme Court. Provincial (or municipality directly under the central authority) courts shall provide guidance in respect of notarial acts in the areas within their respective jurisdiction.

Article8 (Applicability) : This Law shall be applicable to the institutions, enterprises, organizations and citizens of the DPRK, as well as to foreign-invested businesses and foreigners within the territory of the DPRK.

Chapter 2 Objects of Notarial Act

Article9 (Objects of authentication): The Stale notary offices shall provide authentication to such facts and documents as stipulated hereunder:

1.A person' s identity and family relations;

2.Technical and professional qualifications, academic degrees, honorary titles and intellectual properties;

3.Missing and deceased persons;

4.Property ownership;

5.Inheritance;

6.Contracts;

7.Corporate body, entrust or agent;

8.Obligations and compensation for damage;

9.Trademarks;

10.Accidents and investigation;

11.Names of institutions, bank accounts, signatures and seals;

12.Articles of association of enterprises;

13.Originals, copies or translation of documents;

14.Preservation of evidence and deposit of property; and

15.Any other facts or documents of legal significance.

Article10 (Registration): The State notary offices shall register important properties of individuals and foreign- invested businessevs as well as corporate bodies.

Any change to the registered property or corporate

在国外居住的公民申请公证时，由驻该国的朝鲜民主主义人民共和国领事代表机构进行。

第六条（公证机构设置的地区）：国家公证机构设于道（直辖市）所在地。也可根据需要设于市（区域）、郡所在地。

第七条（对公证事业的指导）：最高法院统一指导公证活动。道（直辖市）法院指导管辖地区内的公证活动。

第八条（公证法的适用对象）：本法适用于我国机关单位、企业、团体以及公民。同样适用于在朝鲜民主主义共和国领域内的外国投资企业及外国人。

第二章　公证的对象

第九条（公证的对象）：国家公证机构将对下列事实及文书进行公证：

1. 身份及亲属关系；

2. 技术及专家资格、学位、荣誉称号、知识产权；

3. 失踪及死亡的人；

4. 财产所有权；

5. 继承；

6. 合同；

7. 法人、委托或代理；

8. 损害的赔偿和义务；

9. 商标；

10. 事故、调查；

11. 机构名称、银行账户、签名和印鉴；

12. 企业章程；

13. 文书的原本、副本、译文；

14. 保存证据或托管财产；

15. 其他具有法律意义的事实及文书的公证。

第十条（注册）：国家公证机构可对重要的个人财产、外国投资企业的财产及法人进行登记注册。

已注册的财产或法人发生变化时，须在 20 日内

bodies shall be re-registered within 20 days.

Article11 (Entrust): The State notary offices shall be entrusted with property deposited for the purpose of debt payment, objects of civil disputes, security for compensation of damage and ownerless articles.

Article12 (Preservation of evidence): The State notary offices shall preserve such evidence in civil cases as is liable to become extinct before the institution of a lawsuit or impossible to be recollected.

Chapter 3 Jurisdiction of Notarial Act

Article13 (Regional notary offices): The State notary offices located in the seats of municipalities (or districts) and counties shall conduct the notarial acts, the application for which is intended to be used'- in the territory of the DPRK and/or any other foreign country.

Article14 (Notarial act in applicant's place of residence): A notarial act shall be performed by the State notary office that has jurisdiction over the place of residence or location of the applicant concerned.

In case applications are submitted by several applicants for notarization of the same object, any State notary office that has jurisdiction over the place of residence or location of any one. of the parties concerned may undertake to perform the notarial act.

Article15 (Building, •property, evidence): Any notarial act shall be carried out by the competent State notary office, i. e., a notarial act for any building by the State notary office having jurisdiction over the location of such building, any property which is registered with an institution, enterprise or organization by the office having jurisdiction over the seat of any of the foregoing and any preserved evidence or deposited property by the office having jurisdiction over the place where the said evidence or property lies.

Article16 (The missing, the deceased, testament): The authentication of the missing or the deceased shall be undertaken by the State notary office that exercises jurisdiction over the last place of residence of the person in question, while that of testament shall be conducted by the State notary office that exercises. jurisdiction over the place where the act of testament has taken place.

Article17 (Natural disaster, accident, conclusion of contract): Any authentication concerning a natural disaster, an accident or conclusion of a contract shall be performed by the State notary office that has jurisdiction over the

重新注册。

第十一条（保管）：国家公证机构对用于偿还债务为目的的财产、涉及民事纠纷的物品、用于赔偿损害的保证金以及无人认领的物品进行保管。

第十二条（证据保存）：国家公证机构应当保存在提出诉讼前有可能灭失或无法二次搜集的民事案件证据。

第三章　公证活动的管辖

第十三条（各地区公证机构的管辖范围）：市（区域）、郡所在地的国家公证机构主要办理为在共和国境内使用的公证。

设于道（直辖市）所在地的国家公证机构主要办理为在共和国境内和国外使用的公证。

第十四条（申请人居住地、所在地的公证活动）：申请人申请的公证由管理申请人居住地或所在地有管辖权的国家公证机构进行公证。

当多个当事人同时对同一个公证对象申请公证时，可由其中任何一个当事人居住地或所在地有管辖权的国家公证机构进行公证。

第十五条（公证不动产、财产、证据）：不动产由不动产所在地的国家公证机构进行公证；机关单位、企业、团体注册的财产由该机关单位、企业、团体注册地的国家公证机构进行公证；保存证据和保管财产由保存证据及财产的国家公证机构进行公证。

第十六条（公证失踪者、死亡者、遗嘱）：失踪者或死亡者公证由该失踪者或死亡者的最后居住地的国家公证机构进行公证；遗嘱公证由遗嘱订立地的国家公证机构进行公证。

第十七条（公证自然灾害、事故、合同签署）：自然灾害、事故、合同签署的公证由自然灾害事故发生地的国家公证机构进行公证，签署合同由签署地的国家公证机构进行公证。

location of such natural disaster or accident or the place where the contract was concluded.

Chapter 4 Procedures and Methods of Notarial Act

Article18 (Application): An application for a notarial act shall be submitted to the relevant State notary office by the party concerned.

In an unavoidable circumstance, however, an application may be made either by an agent or by inviting a notary public to the place in question.

Article19 (Documents to be submitted): The applicant for a notarial act shall submit to the competent State notary office a written application, a documentary evidence and a bill of payment of State notarial fee.

The application for a notarial act shall specify such details as the appUcant's name, date of birth, occupation, place of residence and the subject in question.

Article20 (Rectification of errors): The State notary office shall, in case any written application proves imperfect, have it amended or supplemented within 5 days-.

The date on which the application is submitted for the first time shall be regarded as the date of application, provided that such an application has been amended or supplemented within the' prescribed period of time.

Article21 (Term of disposal): The State notary office shall deal with the application within 1 month of receipt.

Article22 (Evaluation of application): The State notary office shall check the capacity of the applicant, the authenticity and lawfulness of details of application and evidentiary document, summon a necessary witness or demand any exhibit from an institution, enterprise, organization or citizen. It may refer the exhibit to a relevant specialized organ for expert appraisal.

The relevant institutions, enterprises, organizations and citizens shall comply with any demand of the State notary office with regard to the performance of a notarial act.

Article23 (Preparation of notarial deed): The State notary office shall draft a notarial deed, provided that the details of application prove accurate and conform to legal requirements.

The original of a notarial deed shall be retained and the copy shall be handed over to the party concerned.

Article24 (Rejection): A notarial act shall not be provided in cases where:

1.There arises a dispute between the parties con-

第四章　公证程序及方式

第十八条（申请公证）：公证由当事人直接向国家公证机构提交申请。

在特殊的情况下，可通过代理人申请公证，或邀请公证员到当地进行公证。

第十九条（公证申请文件）：申请公证的当事人须向国家公证机构提交书面公证申请书、证据文件、费用支付凭证。

公证申请书必须载明申请人姓名、出生日期、单位职务、住址、申请项目等内容。

第二十条（勘误）：若公证申请书有误，国家公证机构应当要求 5 日内进行补充或修正。

若当事人在规定时间内进行补充和修改，可将首次接收公证申请书的日期视为申请日。

第二十一条（公证申请的处理期限）：国家公证机构须在接收公证申请书起 1 个月之内给予处理。

第二十二条（申请审核）：国家公证机构须确认并审核公证申请人的资格、申请内容，以及证据文书的真实性和合法性，有必要时可传召证人，向机关单位、企业、团体或公民要求提交物证，并交至专业部门进行鉴定。

有关机关单位、企业、团体和公民应遵守国家公证机构的要求。

第二十三条（制作公证文书）：若当事人申请公证的内容准确并符合国家法律法规，国家公证机构应制作公证文书。

公证文书正本必须由公证机构进行保管，申请人可获得公证文书副本。

第二十四条（拒绝公证）：下列情况下，国家公证机构有权拒绝公证：

1. 当事人之间对申请公证的事项有争议的；

cerned as regards the subject of application;

2.Thd subject of application proves inconsistent with facts;

3.There exists no evidence, or the evidence, if any, has been faked;

4.The subject of application is of confidential nature;

5.The application has been withdrawn by the applicant; or

6.The Stale charges have not been paid.

Article25 (Notification of rejection): Where any notarial act is to be refused, the reason and justifications thereof shall be notified to the applicant.

Article26 (Deposit of property, preservation of evidence): Any dejposit of property or preservation of evidence shall be undertaken either by the State notary j office or by referring to any other relevant organ.

Cash, securities and precious metals shall be in the custody of a relevant bank; any poisonous substance in the custody of a relevant supervision body; and any perishable goods sh^ll be1 sold and exchanged into cash to be deposited in a bank account; while any evidence shall be preserved in the form of filed records of interrogation of a witness, or a record of on-site 'inspection, an expert opinion in writing, or a picture taken thereof.

Article27 (Disposal of deposited property and preserved evidence): Ariy deposited property and preserved evidence shall be disposed of, pursuant to a judgment or award rendered by the court, or be returned to the rightful person at the expiry of a specified time limit.

Article28 (Issuance of writ of execution): In case the owner of a deposited property fails to collect the property in question within the specified time limit, the State notary office may issue a writ of execution.

The executioner of the People' s Court of a municipality (or district), or county shall serve the writ.

Article29 (Language): A notarial document shall be written in Korean.

A foreigner may write a notarial document in his national language;

Article30 (Replacement of notary public): A notary public, who has an interest in a notarial act for which application has been made, shall not conduct the notarial act in question.

An applicant for a notarial act may request the replacement of a notary public if the person in question has been known as not being fair in carrying out the notarial act concerned.

2. 申请公证的内容不符合事实的；

3. 申请公证的内容没有任何证据或证据属于伪造的；

4. 申请公证的内容为机密的；

5. 申请公证的申请人撤回申请的；

6. 没有按照规定支付公证费用的。

第二十五条（拒绝公证的通知）：拒绝申请人的公证申请时，须告知申请人拒绝公证的原因和根据。

第二十六条（财产保管和证据保存）：财产保管或证据保存由国家公证机构或其他有关机关进行。

现金、有价证券、贵金属等物品应交至银行保管；有毒物质应交至相关监督机构进行保管；易变质腐蚀的物品则销售后转换为现金储存至银行账户；证据应以证人笔录、现场检验调查书、专家鉴定书等形式进行保管，或通过拍照的方法进行保管。

第二十七条（保管财产和保存证据的处理）：应根据法院的判决处理当事人委托保管的财产和保存的证据。当超过规定期限时，可交还给适格人员。

第二十八条（执行文书的送达）：在规定期限内没有取回托管财产时，国家公证机构须发送执行文书。

由市（区域）、郡人民法院的执行官执行该文书的内容。

第二十九条（语言）：公证文书须用朝鲜语制作。

外国人可以使用本国语言制作公证文书。

第三十条（公证员回避）：若公证员与申请人申请的公证内容具有利害关系，公证员则不能进行该公证项目。

申请公证的申请人认为公证员无法公平公正地进行公证时，有权要求更换公证员进行公证。

The relevant State notary office shall either replace the said notary public with another person in case the above-mentioned request proves to be reasonable, or otherwise, reject it.

In case a notary public is to be replaced, a person authorized by the relevant court shall conduct the notarial act.

Article31 (Fees): An applicant for a notarial act shall pay the State charges and other prescribed fees.

Chapter 5 Complaints against Notarial Act

Article32 (Complaints, settlement): A party who has a complaint about a notarial act may, within 5 days of receipt of the notarial deed or the notice of rejection, lodge a complaint with a court that is located in the seat of the relevant State notary office.

The court with which the complaint has been lodged shall, within 10 days, review and settle it by an award.

Article33 (Appeal): A party who is still aggrieved at the award passed by the court may appeal to a higher court within 10 days of receipt of the copy of award.

Article34 (Examination, settlement)

The higher court with which the appeal has been filed shall, within 1 month, examine it and pass an award in support or rejection of the appeal.

Article35 (Reinvestigation): The State notary office may reinvestigate the subject of application pursuant to the award of the court or settle it on the basis of information and evidence certified by the court.

相关国家公证机构认定申请人的要求正当时，应予以更换公证员；若认定申请人的要求为非正当时，则有权拒绝更换公证员的要求。

当更换公证员时，可由该机构任命的其他公证员进行公证。

第三十一条（费用）：申请公证的申请人须根据相关规定支付相关费用。

第五章　对公证的异议

第三十二条（异议及解决）：若当事人对公证有异议，可在收到公证文书或拒绝通知书起 5 日内，向相关国家公证机构所在地区的法院提起诉讼。

法院须在接收异议日起 10 日内进行审理和判决。

第三十三条（上诉）：若当事人不服法院的审理结果，可在接收法院判决书日起 10 日内向上级法院提起上诉。

第三十四条（检查与处理）：接收上诉的法院须在 1 个月内进行审理，作出支持或拒绝的审判结果。

第三十五条（再次审核）：国家公证机构可根据法院的审理结果，对申请的公证内容进行再次审核，或根据法院的信息和认定的证据予以处理。

韩国

公证法

증인법

[시행 2013.11.29.] [법률제 11823 호 , 2013.5.28., 일부개정]

법무부 (법무과) 02-2110-3178~9

제 1 장총칙

(개정 2009. 2. 6.)

제 1 조 (목적)

이법은공증인 (公證人) 의지위와그직무에관한사항을규율하여공증사무의적절성과공정성을확보함을목적으로한다 .

[전문개정 2009.2.6.]

제 1 조의 2(용어의뜻)

이법에서사용하는용어의뜻은다음과같다 . < 개정 2012.6.1.>

1. "공증인" 이란제 2 조에서정하는공증 (公證) 에관한직무를수행할수있도록 법무부장관으로부터 제 11 조에따라임명을받은사람 (이하 "임명공증인" 이라한다) 과제 15 조의 2 에따라공증인가를받은자 (이하 "인가공증인" 이라한다) 를말한다 .

2. "전자문서" 란「전자문서및전자거래기본법」제 2 조제 1 호의전자문서를말한다 .

3. "전자화문서" 란종이문서나그밖에전자적형태로작성되지아니한문서 (이하" 전자화대상문서" 라한다) 를정보처리시스템이처리할수있는형태로변환한문서를말한다 .

4. "전자서명" 이란「전자서명법」제 2 조제 2 호의전자서명을말한다 .

5." 지정공증인" 이란공증인중에서전자문서및

公证法

（2013 年 11 月 29 日施行，第 11823 号法令，2013 年 5 月 28 日，部分公开）

法务部（法务科）(02–2110–3178–9)

第一章　总则

（2009 年 2 月 6 日修订）

第一条（目标）

为了规范公证员的地位和与职务相关的事项，保证公证事务的适当性和公正性制定本法。

（2009 年 2 月 6 日修订）

第一条第二款（用语的含义）

本法中所用的用语的含义如下（2012 年 6 月 1 日修订）：

1. 公证员是指为了执行第二条中规定的与公证有关的职务，根据第十一条规定从司法部长官中接受任命的人（以下称任命公证员）和根据第十五条第二款接受认可的公证员（以下称认可的公证员）。

2. 电子文书是指《电子文书和电子交易基本法》第二条第二款规定的电子文书。

3. 电子化文书是指以纸质文书之外的电子形态制成的文书（以下称电子化对象文书），并且是可以被信息处理系统处理的变换了形态的文书。

4. 电子签名是《电子签名法》中第二条第二款中规定的电子签名。

5. 指定公证员是指为了处理和电子文件和电子化

전자화문서 (이하 “전자문서등” 이라한다) 에관한 공증사무를취급할수있도록법무부장관이제 66 조의 3 에따라지정한자를말한다 .

[본조신설 2009.2.6.]

文书（以下称电子文书等）相关的公证事务，并且由司法部长根据第二条第三款指定的人。

（本条于 2009 年 2 月 6 日新增）

제 2 조 (공증인의직무)

공증인은당사자나그밖의관계인의촉탁 (囑託) 에따라다음각호의사무를처리하는것을직무로한다 . 공증인은위직무에관하여공무원의지위를가지는것으로본다 .

1. 법률행위나그밖에사권 (私權) 에 관한사실에대한 공정증서 (公正證書) 의작성

2. 사서증서 (私署證書) 또는 전자문서등 (공무원이직무상작성한것은 제외한다) 에대한인증

3. 이법과그밖의법령에서공증인이취급하도록정한사무

[전문개정 2009.2.6.]

第二条（公证员的职权）

公证员根据当事人或者其他的关系人的委托处理下列各项事务。公证员在职务方面拥有公务员的地位。

1. 对法律行为或者其他与私权相关的事实出具公证书。

2. 对私署证书和电子文书（公务员依职务制作的除外）等相关的认证。

3. 本法和其他法令中规定的公证员应该履行的职责。

（全文于 2009 年 2 月 6 日修订）

제 3 조 (문서의공증력의요건)

공증인이작성하는문서 (전자문서등을포함한다) 는이법이나그밖의법률에서정하는요건을갖추지아니하면공증의효력을가지지아니한다 .

[전문개정 2009.2.6.]

第三条（文书的公证力的要件）

公证员出具的文书（包括电子文书等）若不符合本法或者其他法律规定的要件，则不具备公证的效力。

（全文于 2009 年 2 月 6 日修订）

제 4 조 (촉탁인수의무)

① 공증인은정당한이유없이제 2 조에따른촉탁 (이하 “촉탁” 이라한다) 을거절하지못한다 .

② 공증인이촉탁을거절하는 경우에는촉탁을한자 (이하 “촉탁인” 이라한다) 나그대리인에게거절의이유를알려야한다 .

[전문개정 2009.2.6.]

第四条（接受委托的义务）

（一）公证员如果没有正当的理由，不能拒绝依据本法第二条所提出的委托（以下称委托）。

（二）公证员在拒绝委托的情况下应该向委托人（以下称委托人）或者他的代理人说明拒绝委托的理由。

（2009 年 2 月 6 日修订）

제 5 조 (비밀누설금지)

공증인은법률에특별한규정이있는경우가아니면직무상알게된비밀을누설하지못한다 . 다만 , 촉탁인의동의를받은경우는그러하지아니하다 .

[전문개정 2009.2.6.]

第五条（禁止泄露秘密）

公证员在法律没有特殊规定的情况下，不能泄露因其职务获知的秘密。但得到委托人同意的除外。

（全文于 2009 年 2 月 6 日修订）

제 6 조 (겸직금지)

임명공증인은다른공무 (公務) 를겸하거나상업을경영할수없고 , 상사회사나영리를목적으로하는사단법인의대표자또는사용인이될수없다 . 다만 , 상시근무가필요하지아니하고공증인의직무수행을방해하지아니하는업무로서법무부장관의허가를받은경우는그러하지아니하다 .

[전문개정 2009.2.6.]

第六条（禁止兼职）

任命的公证员不能兼顾其他公务或者从事商业活动，不能成为商事商社或者营利性的社团法人的代表和雇员。但是，对平时不需要执行职务和不会妨碍职务行为的业务，经司法部长允许，可以兼任。

（2009 年 2 月 6 日修订）

제 7 조 (수수료 , 일당 , 여비등)

① 공증인은촉탁인으로부터수수료 , 일당및여

第七条（手续费、日薪、差旅费等）

（一）公证员从委托人处收取手续费、日薪和差

비를받는다.

② 공증인은공증에관하여통지또는송달을하여야할경우에는촉탁인이나그의승계인, 그밖의통지또는송달의신청인으로부터그에필요한실비(實費)를받는다.

③ 지정공증인은제 66 조의 8 제 2 항의청구에따라전자문서등을보관하는경우촉탁인으로부터보관료를받는다.

④ 공증인은제 1 항부터제 3 항까지에서규정한것외에는그밖에어떠한명목으로도취급한사건에관하여보수를받지못한다.

⑤ 제 1 항부터제 3 항까지의규정에따른수수료, 일당, 여비, 실비및보관료에관한사항은법무부령으로정한다.

[전문개정 2009.2.6.]

제 8 조(공증사무의대행)

법무부장관은지방검찰청의관할구역에공증인이없거나공증인이그직무를수행할수없는경우또는주민의편의를위하여필요하다고인정하는경우에는그관할구역의검사나등기소장에게공증인의직무를수행하게할수있다.

[전문개정 2009.2.6.]

제 9 조(공증인의직무에관한규정의준용)

제 8 조에따라공증인의사무를취급하는검사나등기소장에대하여는이법이나그밖의법령중공증인의직무에관한규정을준용한다. 다만, 제 7 조제 1 항부터제 3 항까지의규정에따른수수료, 일당, 여비, 실비및보관료는국고의수입(收入)으로한다.

[전문개정 2009.2.6.]

제 2 장공증인의임명 · 인가등

(개정 2009. 2. 6.)

제 10 조(공증인의소속과정원)

① 공증인은지방검찰청소속으로한다.

② 각지방검찰청소속공증인의정원(定員)은지방검찰청의관할구역마다법무부장관이정한다. 이경우지방검찰청관할구역의면적, 인구등을고려하여필요하다고인정하면관할구역을세분하여정원을정할수있다.

[전문개정 2009.2.6.]

제 11 조(임명공증인의임명)

① 법무부장관은임명공증인을임명하고그소속지방검찰청을지정할수있다.

② 제 1 항에따라임명을받으려는사람은법무부령으로정하는바에따라법무부장관에게임명신청을하

旅费。

（二）公证员在需要下发与公证相关事项的通知和送达文书的情况下，会从委托人或者承继人，或者以外的通知和送达的申请人处收取必要的实际费用。

（三）指定公证员，根据本法第六十六条第八款第二项的规定，保存电子文书时，从委托人处收取保管费。

（四）公证员不能在第一项至第三项规定的范围之外，以某种名目收取相关的费用。

（五）从第一项至第三项所规定的手续费、日薪、差旅费、实际费用和保管费皆由司法部令规定。

（全文于 2009 年 2 月 6 日修订）

第八条（公证事务的代理）

在地方检察厅的辖区内如公证员空缺或者公证员不能执行职务时，以及为便利群众必要时，司法部长可以指定地方检察官或者法院登记所的书记官，在其辖区内代行公证员的职务。

（全文于 2009 年 2 月 6 日修订）

第九条（与公证员职务相关的规定的适用）

对根据第八条办理公证员事务的检察官或者法院登记所书记官，适用本法或者其他的法令中关于公证员职务的相关规定。但是，本法第七条第一项至第三项规定的手续费、日薪、差旅费、实际费用和保管费应作为国库收入。

（全文于 2009 年 2 月 6 日修订）

第二章　公证员的任命、认可

（2009 年 2 月 6 日修订）

第十条（公证员的隶属和定员）

（一）公证员隶属于地方检察厅。

（二）各个地方检察厅所属的公证员的人数，在地方检察厅的辖区内是由每个地方的司法部长决定的。在这种情况下，需要考虑到地方检察厅辖区的面积、人口等因素，具体分析所管辖的区域来决定公证员的人数。

（全文于 2009 年 2 月 6 日修订）

第十一条（公证员的任命）

（一）司法部长任命公证员，并且指定其所属的地方检察厅。

（二）如欲根据第一项接受任命，必须根据司法部法令的规定向司法部长提出任命申请。

여야한다.

[전문개정 2009.2.6.]

제 12 조 (임명공증인의자격)

임명공증인에임명될수있는사람은통산하여 10 년이상「법원조직법」제 42 조제 1 항각호의직에재직했던사람으로한다.

[전문개정 2009.2.6.]

제 13 조 (임명공증인의결격사유)

다음각호의어느하나에해당하는사람은임명공증인이될수없다.

1. 금치산자또는한정치산자
2. 파산선고를받고복권(復權)되지아니한사람
3. 금고이상의형을선고받고그집행이끝나거나집행을받지아니하기로확정된후 5 년이지나지아니한사람
4. 금고이상의형의집행유예를선고받고그유예기간이끝난날부터 2 년이지나지아니한사람
5. 금고이상의형의선고유예를받고그유예기간중에있는사람
6. 법원의판결에따라자격이상실되거나정지된사람
7. 탄핵이나징계에의하여파면또는면직처분을받거나「변호사법」에따라제명된날부터 5 년이지나지아니한사람
8. 징계에의하여해임처분을받은날부터 3 년이지나지아니한사람

[전문개정 2009.2.6.]

제 13 조의 2 (임명공증인의사무소)

임명공증인은임명을받으면법무부령으로정하는공증사무소의시설을갖추어야한다.

[본조신설 2009.2.6.]

제 14 조 (임명공증인의면직)

①법무부장관은임명공증인이다음각호의어느하나에해당하면면직시킬수있다.

1. 스스로사임을원하는경우
2. 제 13 조의 2 에따른공증사무소의시설을갖추지못하는경우
3. 제 18 조에따른기간내에신원보증금이나그보충액을내지아니한경우
4. 신체또는정신상의장애로인하여직무를수행할수없게된경우

②제 1 항제 4 호의경우에는제 85 조에따른공증인징계위원회의의결을거쳐야한다.

③ 지방검찰청검사장은소속임명공증인에게제 1 항각호의어느하나에해당하는사유가있으면지체없

(全文于 2009 年 2 月 6 日修订)

第十二条（任命公证员的资格）

欲受任为任命公证员的人，必须在《法院组织法》第四十二条第一项规定的职位上工作十年以上。

（全文于 2009 年 2 月 6 日修订）

第十三条（排除任命公证员的事由）

凡符合下列规定之一者，不得任命为公证员。

1. 禁治产人或者准禁治产人；
2. 进行破产宣告尚未复权者；
3. 被判处监禁以上刑罚，且刑罚执行完毕后或者是确定不受执行刑罚后，不满五年的人；
4. 被判处监禁以上刑罚，判决缓期执行，在缓刑执行期间结束后，不满两年的人；
5. 被判处监禁以上刑罚，判决缓期执行，在缓刑执行期间的人；
6. 根据法院的判决，被剥夺或者暂时停止其公民权者；
7. 根据弹劾或者惩戒而被罢免或者免职的或者是根据《律师法》被开除不满五年的人；
8. 因惩戒被免职不满三年的人。

（全文于 2009 年 2 月 6 日修订）

第十三条第二款（任命公证员的事务所）

如欲受任公证员，申请人必须具备可用作司法部法律规定的公证事务所的设施。

（本条于 2009 年 2 月 6 日修订）

第十四条（任命公证员的免职）

（一）在任公证员有下列情形之一，司法部长可以直接免除其职务。

1. 公证员自己主动辞职；
2. 根据本法第十三条第二款不具备公证事务所要求的设施；
3. 根据第十八条，在限期内没有上交身份保证金或者补充数额；
4. 由于身体或者精神上的障碍，不能履行职务。

（二）第一项第四点之情形，应由本法第八十五条规定的公证员惩戒委员会判定。

（三）对符合第一项任何一点的所管辖的任命公证员，地方检察厅的厅长不应有任何迟疑，要直接向

이법무부장관에게보고하여야한다.

④법무부장관은제 1 항제 2 호부터제 4 호까지의사유로공증인을면직하려면청문을거쳐야한다.

[전문개정 2009.2.6.]

제 15 조 (임기와당연퇴직)

① 임명공증인의임기는 5 년으로하되, 재임명할수있다.

② 법무부장관은다음각호의어느하나에해당한다고인정되는임명공증인은재임명을하지아니한다.

1. 신체또는정신상의장애로인하여직무를수행할수없는경우

2. 직무수행의태도ㆍ방식ㆍ결과등이현저히불량하여공증인으로서의적절한직무수행이곤란한경우

③임명공증인의정년은 75 세로한다.

④임명공증인은그정년이되는날이 1 월에서 6 월사이에있는경우에는 6 월 30 일에, 7 월에서 12 월사이에있는경우에는 12 월 31 일에당연퇴직한다.

⑤임명공증인이제 13 조각호의결격사유중어느하나에해당하게된경우에는당연퇴직한다.

[전문개정 2009.2.6.]

[시행일 :2012.2.7.] 제 15 조제 3 항ㆍ제 4 항개정규정중정년에관한부분

제 15 조의 2 (공증인가)

①법무부장관은다음각호의요건을모두갖춘자에대하여공증인가를하고그소속지방검찰청을지정할수있다.

1.「변호사법」에따라설립된법무법인, 법무법인 (유한) 또는법무조합 (이하 "법무법인등" 이라한다) 일것

2. 해당법무법인등의구성원변호사중 2 명이상이제 15 조의 4 에따른공증담당변호사자격이있을것

②제 1 항의인가를받으려는자는법무부령으로정하는바에따라법무부장관에게인가신청을하여야한다.

[본조신설 2009.2.6.]

제 15 조의 3 (공증담당변호사의지정등)

① 인가공증인은구성원변호사중에서 2 명이상의공증담당변호사를지정하여소속지방검찰청을거쳐법무부장관에게신고하여야한다. 공증담당변호사의지정에변경이있을때에도또한같다.

② 인가공증인은공증담당변호사가 1 명만남게된경우에는 3 개월이내에보충하여야한다.

[본조신설 2009.2.6.]

제 15 조의 4 (공증담당변호사의자격)

① 공증담당변호사는제 12 조의자격을갖추어야

司法部长报告。

（四）法务部长官，如果根据第一项第二点至第四点而决定免除公证员的职务的话必须公开进行。

（全文于 2009 年 2 月 6 日修订）

第十五条（任期和当然失去职务）

（一）任命公证员的任期是五年，可以连选连任。

（二）如果认为任命的公证员有下列情形之一，司法部长就可以取消其连选连任的资格。

1. 因身体上或者精神上的障碍导致不能正常行使职务；

2. 职务行为的态度、方式、结果等完全是不良的，完全不符合公证员职务行为规范的要求。

（三）达到任命公证员的退休年龄 75 岁。

（四）任命公证员于 1 月至 6 月间达到退休年龄的,6 月 30 日退职;于 7 月至 12 月间达到退休年龄的，12 月 31 日退职。

（五）任命公证员如果具备本法第十三条各点规定的排除事由之一，当然失去其职务。

（全文于 2009 年 2 月 6 日修订）

（第十五条第三项、第四项，修订规定中关于退休年龄的规定于 2012 年 2 月 7 日实行）

第十五条第二款（公证认可）

（一）司法部长对满足下列各条件者，予以公证认可并且指定其所属的地方检察厅。

1. 根据《律师法》建立的法务法人，法务法人（有限）和法务合作社（以下称法人等）；

2. 在现有的法务法人中，组成人员律师有两名以上，并且根据第十五条第四款的规定，具备公证律师的资格的。

（二）在第一项中，如果想要获得认可的人必须根据司法部法令向司法部长提出申请。

（本条于 2009 年 2 月 6 日修订）

第十五条第三款（公证律师的指定等）

（一）认可公证员是指从所组成的律师中指定两名以上的公证律师，并应该由所属的地方检察厅同意，并向司法部长申告。变更指定的公证律师时应适用相同的程序。

（二）在认可公证员中，如果只剩下一名公证律师的情况下，在三个月以内要补选。

（本条于 2009 年 2 月 6 日修订）

第十五条第四款（公证律师的资格）

（一）公证律师应该具备本法第十二条的资格。

한다 .

② 다음각호의어느하나에해당하는사람은공증담당변호사가될수없다 .

1. 제 13 조각호의결격사유중어느하나에해당하는사람

2.「변호사법」제 90 조제 3 호또는제 102 조제 2 항에따라정직또는업무정지중인사람

③공증담당변호사에관하여는제 15 조제 3 항부터제 5 항까지의규정을준용한다 .

④인가공증인은공증담당변호사에게제 2 항각호및제 15 조제 2 항각호의어느하나에해당하는사유가있을때에는지체없이 , 제 15 조제 3 항의사유가있을때에는같은조제 4 항에서정한날까지공증담당변호사의지정을철회하여야한다 .

[본조신설 2009.2.6.]

[시행일 :2012.2.7.] 제 15 조의 4 제 3 항 · 제 4 항의개정규정중정년에관한부분

제 15 조의 5(공증담당변호사의지위)

공증에관한법령을적용할때에는그성격에반하지아니하는한공증담당변호사를공증인으로본다 .

[본조신설 2009.2.6.]

제 15 조의 6(인가공증인의사무소)

인가공증인은인가를받으면법무부령으로정하는공증사무소의시설을갖추어야한다 .

[본조신설 2009.2.6.]

제 15 조의 7(공증인가의취소)

①법무부장관은인가공증인이다음각호의어느하나에해당하면공증인가를취소할수있다 .

1. 스스로인가취소를원하는경우

2. 공증담당변호사가전혀없거나제 15 조의 3 제 2 항의기간내에보충하지아니한경우

3. 제 15 조의 4 를위반하여공증담당변호사를지정하여공증사무를수행하게한경우

4. 제 15 조의 6 에따른공증사무소의시설을갖추지못하는경우

5. 제 18 조에따른기간이내에신원보증금이나그보충액을내지아니한경우

②법무부장관은인가공증인이해산하면즉시공증인가를취소하여야한다 .

③지방검찰청검사장은소속인가공증인에게제 1 항각호의어느하나에해당하는사유가있으면지체없이법무부장관에게보고하여야한다 .

④법무부장관은제 1 항제 2 호부터제 5 호까지의사유로공증인가를취소하려면청문을거쳐야한다 .

（二）有下列情形之一者，不能成为公证律师。

1. 具备本法第十三条排除事由之一者；

2. 根据《律师法》第九十条第三项和第一百零二条第二项正在停职，暂停执业者。

（三）与公证律师相关的适用第十五条从第三项至第五项的规定。

（四）认可公证员，作为公证律师的话，有第二项各点和第十五条第二项各点的任何一种事由的时候，应该立即撤回或者到第十五条第三项的事由的时候到第四项规定的时间为止应该撤回对公证律师的指定。

（本条于 2009 年 2 月 6 日修订）

（实施日：2012 年 2 月 7 日）

本法第十五条第四款第三项和第四项关于退休年龄的改革规定从 2012 年 2 月 7 日开始实行。

第十五条第五款（公证律师的地位）

适用关于公证的法令的时候，要挑选性格不与法令相违背的公证律师做公证员。

（本条于 2009 年 2 月 6 日修订）

第十五条第六款（认可公证员的事务所）

认可公证员如果想要得到认可的话，应该具备司法部法令规定的可用作公证事务所的设施。

（本条于 2009 年 2 月 6 日修订）

第十五条第七款（认可公证员的取消）

（一）对于有下列情形之一的认可公证员，司法部长可取消其公证员认可：

1. 公证员自己主动申请取消认可；

2. 完全没有公证律师或者在第十五条第三款第二项规定的时间内，没有补选；

3. 违反第十五条第四款的规定，没有指定的公证律师执行公证事务；

4. 根据第十五条第六款不具备可用作公证事务所的设施；

5. 根据本法第十八条的规定，在限期内没有上交身份保证金或者补充金额。

（二）司法部长如果解散认可公证员的话，即应取消公证认可。

（三）地方检察厅事务长，对所属的认可公证员如出现第一项中任何一点情形的，应该立即向司法部长报告。

（四）司法部长如果根据第一项第二点至第五点的事项取消公证认可的话应公开进行。

[본조신설 2009.2.6.]

제 15 조의 8(인가의유효기간)

① 공증인가의유효기간은 5 년으로하되 , 재인가할수있다 .

② 제 1 항의재인가에관하여는제 15 조제 2 항제 2 호를준용한다 .

[본조신설 2009.2.6.]

제 15 조의 9(변호사업무와의관계)

인가공증인은해당법무법인등또는공증인가합동법률사무소가대리한소송사건과관련하여다음각호와같은공증업무를수행할수없다 .

1. 법률행위나그밖에사권에관한사실에대한공정증서의작성

2. 어음・수표또는이에부착된보충지에강제집행할것을기재한증서의작성

3. 법인의등기절차에첨부되는의사록의인증

4.「상법」제 292 조및그준용규정에따른정관의인증

[본조신설 2009.2.6.]

제 15 조의 10(공증인의직무교육)

① 임명공증인은임명일부터 3 개월이내에법무부장관이정하는바에따라공증인직무교육을받아야한다 .

② 제 15 조의 3 제 1 항에따라법무부장관에게신고된공증담당변호사도제 1 항과같다 .

[본조신설 2009.2.6.]

제 15 조의 11(위임규정)

공증인의임명이나인가의절차및그밖에필요한사항은대통령령으로정한다 .

[본조신설 2009.2.6.]

제 3 장직무집행에관한통칙

(개정 2009. 2. 6.)

제 16 조 (직무집행구역)

공증인의직무집행구역은그소속지방검찰청의관할구역에따른다 . 다만 , 서울특별시는하나의직무집행구역으로한다 .

[전문개정 2009.2.6.]

제 17 조 (사무소)

① 공증인은사무소를설치하거나이전하려면법무부장관의인가를받아야한다 .

② 임명공증인의합동사무소의설치 , 운영및그밖에필요한사항은대통령령으로정한다 .

③ 공증인은그사무소에서직무를수행하여야한

（本条于 2009 年 2 月 6 日修订）

第十五条第八款（认可的有效期间）

（一）公证认可的有效期间是五年，可以再认可。

（二）第一项规定的与再认可相关的适用于第十五条第二项第二点的规定。

（本条于 2009 年 2 月 6 日修订）

第十五条第九款（公证律师的业务和关联）

认可公证员不能从事，正当的法务法人和公证认可联合法律事务所所代理的诉讼案件和相关联的以下公证业务。

1. 法律行为或者其他与私权相关的事实的公证书的出具；

2. 票据、支票和与之相关的补充材料的强制执行的记载证书的制作；

3. 法人的登记程序的补充记事录的公证事项；

4.《商法》第二百九十二条和根据其准用规则规定的章程的认证。

（本条于 2009 年 2 月 6 日修订）

第十五条第十款（公证员的职务培训）

（一）任命公证员，自任命之日起三个月内应根据司法部长的规定接受职务培训。

（二）根据本法第十五条第三款第一项向司法部长申告的公证律师应该和第一项相同。

（本条于 2009 年 2 月 6 日修订）

第十五条第十一款（委任规定）

公证员的任命或者认可程序和其他必要事项应该由大总统令决定。

（本条于 2009 年 2 月 6 日修订）

第三章　关于职务执行的规则

（2009 年 2 月 6 日修订）

第十六条（职务执行区域）

公证员的职务执行区域是根据他所属的地方检察厅而决定的。但是，首尔特别市就只有一个职务执行区域。

（全文于 2009 年 2 月 6 日修订）

第十七条（事务所）

（一）公证员如果想要设立或者移交事务所，应该得到司法部长的许可。

（二）认可公证员设立、运营联合事务所及其他事项需由大总统令规定。

（三）公证员应该执行事务所的职务。但是，案

다. 다만, 사건의성질상사무소에서직무를수행할수없을때와법령에다른규정이있을때에는예외로한다.

[전문개정 2009.2.6.]

제 17 조의 2(인가공증인의직무수행)

① 인가공증인의직무는그주사무소에서공증담당변호사가수행한다.

② 인가공증인의직무에관하여는공증담당변호사가각자인가공증인을대표한다.

[본조신설 2009.2.6.]

제 18 조(신원보증금의납부)

① 공증인은임명장또는인가증을받은날부터 15 일이내에소속지방검찰청에신원보증금을내야한다.

② 신원보증금의금액은법무부령으로정한다.

③ 제 1 항에따라낸금액이제 2 항에따라결정된금액에미달하여보충할것을명령받은경우에는그명령을받은날부터 30 일이내에그부족액을보충하여야한다.

④ 공증인은신원보증금을낼때까지는그직무를수행할수없다.

[전문개정 2009.2.6.]

제 19 조(신원보증금의환급)

① 신원보증금을환급(還給)하는경우에는그신원보증금에대한권리를가진자에게 6 개월이내에환급신청을할것을공고하여야한다.

② 신원보증금은제 1 항에서정한기간이지나지아니하면환급하지아니한다.

③ 신원보증금은다른공과금(公課金)이나채권(債權)보다우선하여제 1 항의공고비용에충당한다.

[전문개정 2009.2.6.]

제 20 조(서명·직인의신고)

① 공증인은그직무를수행하기전에그가사용할서명과직인(職印)의인영(印影)을소속지방검찰청검사장에게신고하여야한다.

② 공증인이신고한서명이나직인을변경하려면미리소속지방검찰청검사장에게신고하여야한다.

③ 지방검찰청검사장은제 1 항및제 2 항에따라서명과직인의인영을신고받으면지체없이법무부장관에게보고하여야한다.

④ 공증인은하나의직인을사용하여야한다.

[전문개정 2009.2.6.]

제 21 조(공증인의제척)

공증인은다음각호의어느하나에해당하면그직무를수행할수없다.

1. 촉탁인, 그대리인, 촉탁받은사항에관하여이해관계가있는사람의친족인경우. 친족관계가끝난경

件在性质上与事务所的职务相背离或者与法律相抵触时除外。

（全文与 2009 年 2 月 6 日修订）

第十七条第二款（认可公证员的职务执行）

（一）认可公证员的职务由其主事务所中的公证律师行使。

（二）与认可公证员的职务相关的公证律师代表各自认可的公证员。

（本条于 2009 年 2 月 6 日修订）

第十八条（身份保证金的缴纳）

（一）公证员从任命和得到认可之日起十五日内应向所属的地方检察厅上交身份保证金。

（二）身份保证金的金额由司法部令决定。

（三）根据第一项规定缴纳身份保证金，未达到根据第二项确定的金额的，应于接到补缴命令之日起三十日内，补足不足的金额。

（四）公证员在缴纳完身份保证金之前不能行使职务。

（全文于 2009 年 2 月 6 日修订）

第十九条（身份保证金的返还）

（一）返还身份保证金时，应对拥有身份保证金返还请求权的权利人发出公告，命其在六个月内提出申请。

（二）身份保证金自前款规定期限届满后，开始返还。

（三）身份保证金应该优先于国家税费及债券，用于充抵第一项规定的公告费。

（全文于 2009 年 2 月 6 日修订）

第二十条（签名和职务印章的提交）

（一）公证员在执行职务之前应该把他使用的签名和职务印章的影印件提交其所属的地方检察厅。

（二）公证员提交过的签名或者职务印章如欲变更，必须提前向所属的地方检察厅检察长申告。

（三）地方检察厅检察长根据第一项和第二项接受其申告的签名和职印的影印件后，应该立即向司法部长报告。

（四）公证员应该只用一个职务印章。

（全文于 2009 年 2 月 6 日修订）

第二十一条（公证员不得执行职务的情况）

公证员有下列情形之一的，不能执行职务。

1. 委托人，他的代理人，和与委托事项有利害关系人的近亲属的人。亲属关系结束时，亦同。

우에도또한같다.

2. 촉탁인또는그대리인의법정대리인인경우

3. 촉탁받은사항에관하여이해관계가있는경우

4. 촉탁받은사항에관한대리인이거나보조인인경우또는대리인이었거나보조인이었던경우

[전문개정 2009.2.6.]

제 22 조(서명시의기재사항)

공증인이직무상서명할때에는그직명(職名), 소속및사무소소재지를적어야한다.

[전문개정 2009.2.6.]

제 23 조(공증인의보조자)

① 공증인은보조자를두고그직무를보조하게할수있다.

② 제 1 항에따라보조자를두려는공증인은대통령령으로정하는바에따라제 77 조의 2 에따른대한공증인협회에신고하여야한다. 보조자를교체또는해고하거나보조자가사망한경우에도또한같다.

[전문개정 2009.2.6.]

제 24 조(서류등의반출금지, 보존)

①다음각호의서류및장부는재난을피하기위하여부득이한경우와법무부장관또는소속지방검찰청검사장의명령이나허가를받은경우가아니면사무소밖으로반출(搬出)할수없다. <개정 2013.5.28.>

1. 공증인이작성한증서의원본과그부속서류

2. 제 57 조제 4 항에따라공증인이보존하는사서증서의사본과그부속서류

3. 제 63 조제 3 항에따라공증인이보존하는정관(제 57 조의 2 제 7 항및제 66 조의 2 제 4 항에따라준용되는사서증서와법인의사록을포함한다)과그부속서류

4. 제 66 조의 8 제 1 항및제 2 항에따라지정공증인이보존하거나보관하는정보, 전자문서등과그부속서류

5. 그밖에법령에따라공증인이작성한장부

②제 1 항의서류등은마이크로필름이나그밖의전산정보처리조직에의하여보존할수있다.

③제 1 항의서류등을그대로보존하거나제 2 항에따라보존하는경우그보존방법, 보존장소, 보존기간, 폐기, 및그밖에필요한사항은법무부령으로정한다.

[전문개정 2009.2.6.]

제 4 장증서의작성

(개정 2009. 2. 6.)

제 25 조(증서를작성할수없는경우)

공증인은다음각호의어느하나에관하여는증서를

2. 公证员是委托人和他的代理人的法定代理人的。

3. 公证员与委托事项有利害关系。

4. 公证员是受申请事项的代理人或者辅佐人，或者曾经是代理人或者辅佐人。

（全文于 2009 年 2 月 6 日修订）

第二十二条（署名时的记载事项）

公证员履行职务签名时应该记载其职称、所属和事务所的地点。

（全文于 2009 年 2 月 6 日修订）

第二十三条（公证员的书记员）

（一）公证员可以设立书记员辅助其履行职务。

（二）根据第一项想要设立书记员的公证员根据大总统令第七十七条第二款的规定，向大韩公证员协会申告。书记员选拔、解职及死亡时亦同。

（全文于 2009 年 2 月 6 日修订）

第二十四条（禁止携出文件和文件保存）

（一）除躲避事变等不得已情况外，未经司法部长和所属地方检察厅检察长命令或允许，不得将下列文件和簿册携出事务所。（2013 年 5 月 28 日修订）

1. 公证员出具的公证书的原件和附属资料；

2. 根据第五十七条第四项公证员保存的私署证书的手抄本和附属资料；

3. 根据第六十三条第三项公证员保存的章程（包括根据第五十七条第二款第七项和第六十六条第二款第四项准用的私署证书和法人登记录）和附属资料；

4. 根据第六十六条第八款第一项和第二项指定公证员保存或者保管的信息、电子文件等和附属资料；

5. 公证员依法制作的其他簿册。

（二）第一项的材料等可以用影像或其他电子信息处理系统保存。

（三）第一项的材料径行保存或以第二项规定之方式保存的，其保存方法、保存场所、保存时间、报废时间和其他必需事项由司法部法令规定。

（全文于 2009 年 2 月 6 日修订）

第四章 公证书的出具

（2009 年 2 月 6 日修订）

第二十五条（不得出具公证书的事项）

公证员就下列任一情形，不得出具公证书。

작성할수없다 .

1. 법령을위반한사항

2. 무효인법률행위

3. 무능력으로인하여취소할수있는법률행위

[전문개정 2009.2.6.]

제 26 조 (사용언어)

① 공증인이작성하는증서에는국어를사용하여야한다 . 다만 , 촉탁인의요구가있는경우에는외국어를병기 (併記) 할수있다 .

② 제 1 항단서의경우국어와병기한외국어의내용이서로다른경우에는국어로작성한내용이우선하는것으로한다 .

[전문개정 2009.2.6.]

제 27 조 (촉탁인의확인)

① 공증인이증서를작성하기위하여는촉탁인의성명과얼굴을알아야한다 .

② 공증인이촉탁인의성명이나얼굴을모르면다음각호의어느하나에해당하는방법으로촉탁인이맞다는것을증명하게하여야한다 . 다만 , 촉탁인이외국인인경우에는여권이나대한민국에주재하는그촉탁인의본국영사가발행한증명서로써그촉탁인임을증명할수있다 .

1. 주민등록증이나그밖에권한있는행정기관이발행한사진이첨부된증명서를제출하게하는방법

2. 공증인이성명과얼굴을아는증인 2 명에게그촉탁인임이확실하다는것을증명하게하는방법

3. 그밖에제 1 호및제 2 호의방법에준하는확실한방법

③급박한사유로공증인이증서를작성할때에는증서를작성한후 3 일이내에증서의작성에관한규정에따라제 2 항의절차를밟을수있다 .

④제 3 항의절차를밟았을경우에는그증서가급박한사유로작성된것이아니라는이유로그효력을상실하지아니한다 .

[전문개정 2009.2.6.]

제 28 조 (통역인의사용)

촉탁인이국어를해득 (解得) 하지못하는경우또는듣지못하거나말하지못하는등말로의사소통이불가능한사람으로서문자도해득하지못하는경우에공증인이증서를작성하려면통역인을사용하여야한다 .

[전문개정 2009.2.6.]

제 29 조 (참여인의참여)

① 촉탁인이시각장애인이거나문자를해득하지못하는경우에공증인이증서를작성할때에는참여인을참여하게하여야한다 .

1. 与法律相违背的事项；

2. 无行为能力人的行为；

3. 因无行为能力可撤销的法律行为。

（全文于 2009 年 2 月 6 日修订）

第二十六条（使用语言）

（一）公证员在出具公证书时应该使用国语。但经公证员要求可同时使用外语。

（二）在根据第一项规定书写的情况下，国语和外国语内容不一致时，应该以国语制作的内容为准。

（全文于 2009 年 2 月 6 日修订）

第二十七条（确认委托人）

（一）公证员为了出具公证书应该知晓委托人的姓名并与其认识。

（二）公证员如果不知道委托人的姓名或者与其不认识，应该用以下任何一种方法来确认证明委托人的身份。但委托人是外国人时可通过护照，委托人在大韩民国居住时可通过本国领事出具的证明，证明其身份。

1. 身份证或者有权机关制作的其他带有照片的盖章证书；

2. 应公证员要求，提供两名知道委托人姓名、与其相识的证人证明其身份；

3. 与第一项和第二项类似的其他用于确认申请人身份的方法。

（三）公证员在紧急情况下出具的公证书，可以作成后三日内，依照出具公证书的有关规定，履行前款手续。

（四）根据第三项规定出具的证书，不因是在紧急情况下制作的而丧失其效力。

（全文于 2009 年 2 月 6 日修订）

第二十八条（翻译在场）

委托人语言不通或是聋哑人、文盲时，公证员出具公证书时必须有翻译在场。

（全文于 2009 年 2 月 6 日修订）

第二十九条（见证人在场）

（一）委托人是盲人或文盲时，公证员在出具公证书时必须要有见证人在场。

② 촉탁인이참여인의참여를청구한경우에는제 1 항을준용한다 .

[전문개정 2009.2.6.]

제 30 조（대리촉탁）

대리인에의하여촉탁되었을경우그대리인에게는제 27 조부터제 29 조까지의규정을준용한다 .

[전문개정 2009.2.6.]

제 31 조（대리권의증명）

① 대리인의촉탁으로공증인이증서를작성할경우에는대리권을증명할증서를제출하게하여야한다 .

② 제 1 항의증서가인증을받지아니한사서증서일경우에는그증서외에권한있는행정기관이작성한인감증명서또는서명에관한증명서를제출하게하여증서가진정한것임을증명하게하여야한다 .

③ 증서의작성에관한규정에따라대리또는그방식의결함을추후보완한경우에는그증서는결함이있었다는이유로효력이

[전문개정 2009.2.6.]

제 32 조（허락・동의가필요한법률행위의공증）

① 제 3 자의허락이나동의가필요한법률행위에관하여공증인이증서를작성할때에는그허락이나동의가있었음을증명할증서를제출하게하여야한다 .

② 제 1 항의경우에는제 31 조제 2 항및제 3 항을준용한다 .

[전문개정 2009.2.6.]

제 33 조（통역인・참여인의선정과자격）

① 통역인과참여인은촉탁인이나그대리인이선정하여야한다 .

② 참여인은통역인을겸할수있다 .

③ 다음각호의어느하나에해당하는사람은참여인이될수없다 . 다만 , 제 29 조제 2 항에따라촉탁인이참여인의참여를청구한경우에는그러하지아니하다 .

1. 미성년자

2. 시각장애인이거나문자를해득하지못하는사람

3. 서명할수없는사람

4. 촉탁사항에관하여이해관계가있는사람

5. 촉탁사항에관하여대리인또는보조인이거나대리인또는보조인이었던사람

6. 공증인의친족 , 피고용인또는동거인

7. 공증인의보조자

[전문개정 2009.2.6.]

제 34 조（증서의내용）

공증인은증서를작성할때그가들은진술 , 목격한

（二）委托人要求见证人在场时，适用第一项的规定。

（全文于 2009 年 2 月 6 日修订）

第三十条（代理委托）

公证员在接受当事人的代理人提出的申请时，前三条的规定适用于该代理人。

（全文于 2009 年 2 月 6 日修订）

第三十一条（代理权的证明）

（一）由代理人提出委托，公证员出具公证书的，应向公证员提供有代理权的证明。

（二）根据第一项提出的私署证书在没有得到认证的情况下，为了证明其证书属实，除了证书本身之外，公证员须让该代理人提交官方机关制作的关于印鉴或者签名的证书。

（三）根据证书制作的相关规定，补正其代理和代理方式的瑕疵后，证书效力不受影响。

（全文于 2009 年 2 月 6 日修订）

第三十二条（需要许可、同意的法律行为的公证）

（一）与需要第三者许可或者同意的法律行为相关的公证书制作时，需要提供第三人许可或者同意的证明材料。

（二）第一项规定的情况适用本法第三十一条第二项和第三项的准用规则。

（全文于 2009 年 2 月 6 日修订）

第三十三条（翻译、见证人的选定和资格）

（一）翻译和见证人应由委托人或代理人选定。

（二）见证人可以兼任翻译。

（三）符合下列任一情形的，不能成为见证人。但是，根据本法第二十九条第二项委托人要求见证人参与的除外。

1. 未成年人；

2. 视觉有障碍或者是不识字的人；

3. 不能签名的人；

4. 与委托的事项有利害关系的人；

5. 与委托事项有关的代理人和辅佐人或者曾经是代理人和辅佐人；

6. 公证员的亲属、雇员和同居者；

7. 公证员的书记员。

（全文于 2009 年 2 月 6 日修订）

第三十四条（公证书的内容）

公证员在出具公证书的时候，应该记载其听取的

사실, 그밖에실제로경험한사실과그경험한방법을적어야한다.

[전문개정 2009.2.6.]

제 35 조(기재사항)

공증인이작성하는증서에는그내용외에다음각호의사항을모두적어야한다.

1. 증서의번호
2. 촉탁인의주소·직업·성명및나이(법인인경우에는그명칭및사무소소재지)
3. 대리인에의하여촉탁되었을경우에는그사유, 대리권을증명할증서를제출하게한사실, 그대리인의주소·직업·성명및나이
4. 촉탁인이나그대리인의성명과얼굴을아는경우에는그사실
5. 제 3 자의허락이나동의가있었음을증명하는증서를제출하게하였을경우에는그사유와제 3 자의주소·직업·성명및나이(법인인경우에는그명칭및사무소소재지)
6. 제 27 조제 2 항에따른증명이있을경우에는그사유, 증인의주소·직업·성명·나이또는그확인의방법
7. 제 27 조제 3 항의경우에는그사유
8. 제 31 조제 2 항에따른증명이있었을경우에는그사유
9. 통역인이나참여인을참여하게하였을경우에는그사유와통역인또는참여인의주소·직업·성명및나이
10. 작성연월일과장소

[전문개정 2009.2.6.]

제 35 조의 2(부기)

① 공증인은공정증서에적힌양쪽당사자또는그대리인의촉탁을받아채무의전부변제사실이나계약의전부해소사실을증서의원본에부기(附記)할수있다.

② 제 1 항에따라원본에부기를할때에는그연월일을명확하게적고촉탁인또는그대리인과공증인이서명날인하여야한다.

③ 제 1 항의경우에는제 27 조부터제 33 조까지및제 36 조부터제 38 조까지의규정을준용한다.

[전문개정 2009.2.6.]

제 36 조(증서의작성방법)

① 공증인이증서를작성할때에는보통의쉬운용어를사용하고글자획을명확하게써야한다.

② 글자가연결되어야할자행(字行)에빈공간이있을때에는직선또는사선을그어그부분에다른글자가없음을표시하여야한다.

陈述，目击的事实，还有他实际经历的事实，并应记明实际考察的方法。

（全文于 2009 年 2 月 6 日修订）

第三十五条（公证书的记载事项）

公证员在出具公证书时，除了公证书的内容外，下列事项也应记录在册。

1. 公证书编号；
2. 委托人的住所、职业、姓名和年龄（法人的话要说明名称和事务所所在地）；
3. 由代理人委托时，事由、证明有代理权的证明事实、代理人的住所、职业、姓名和年龄；
4. 了解委托人或者代理人的姓名和并与其认识的事实；
5. 需要提供第三人允许或者同意的证明时，需要写明事由和第三人的住所、职业、姓名和年龄（法人的话，应该写明名称和事务所所在地）；
6. 根据第二十七条第二项有证明的情况下，证明的事由、证人的住所、职业、姓名和年龄以及确认的方法；
7. 本法第二十七条第三项的情况下的事由；
8. 本法第三十一条第二项下规定的有证明书时的事由；
9. 翻译或者见证人在场时间、事由和翻译和见证人的住所、职业、姓名和年龄；
10. 出具的年、月、日和场所。

（全文于 2009 年 2 月 6 日修订）

第三十五条第二款（附记）

（一）公证员在公证书上记录双方当事人和接受代理人的委托，财务全部偿还的事实或者解约的事实可以在公证书原本的基础上用附记记录。

（二）根据第一项在原本的基础上用附记记载的时候，应该明确写明年、月、日，委托人和代理人及公证员签字捺印。

（三）从本法第二十七条至第三十三条和第三十六条到第三十八条的规定，适用于第一项规定的情形。

（全文于 2009 年 2 月 6 日修订）

第三十六条（公证书的出具方法）

（一）出具公证书的时候应该使用通俗易懂的语言和正确的书写方式。

（二）行文时，文字应该连贯，有空格时应该用直线或者曲线标出，说明这部分没有其他文字。

[전문개정 2009.2.6.]

제 37 조 (글자의수정 · 삽입 · 삭제)

① 증서의글자는수정할수없다 .

② 증서에글자를삽입할때에는삽입한글자수와그위치를칸의밖이나끝부분여백에적고공증인 , 촉탁인또는그대리인과참여인이이에날인하여야한다 .

③ 증서의글자를삭제할때에는그글자를명확히읽을수있도록글자의모양은남겨두고삭제한글자수와그위치를칸의밖이나끝부분여백에적고공증인 , 촉탁인또는그대리인과참여인이이에날인하여야한다 .

④ 제 1 항부터제 3 항까지를위반한정정 (訂正) 은효력이없다 .

[전문개정 2009.2.6.]

제 38 조 (증서의작성절차)

① 공증인은그가작성한증서를모든참석자에게읽어주거나열람하게하여촉탁인또는그대리인의이의가없음을확인하고그취지를증서에적어야한다 .

② 통역인을참여시켰을경우에는제 1 항의절차외에통역인에게증서의취지를통역하게하고그취지를증서에적어야한다 .

③ 제 1 항과제 2 항에따라각각의취지를적으면공증인과참석자는각자증서에서명날인하여야한다 .

④ 참석자로서서명할수없는사람이있으면그사유를증서에적고공증인과참여인이날인하여야한다 .

⑤ 공증인은증서가여러장으로이루어지는경우에는각장에걸쳐직인으로간인 (間印) 하여야한다 .

[전문개정 2009.2.6.]

제 39 조 (서면의인용)

① 공증인이작성하는증서에다른서면을인용하고이를그증서에첨부하는경우에는공증인은그증서와첨부서면에걸쳐직인으로간인하여야한다 .

② 제 1 항의첨부서면에관하여는제 36 조부터제 38 조까지의규정을준용한다 .

③ 제 1 항과제 2 항에따른첨부서면은공증인이작성한증서의일부로본다 .

[전문개정 2009.2.6.]

제 40 조 (부속서류의연철)

①다음각호의부속서류는공증인이작성한증서에연철 (連綴) 하여야한다 . 다만 , 촉탁인이부속서류원본의반환을청구한경우에는원본대신그등본을연철할수있다 .

1. 대리권을증명하는증서
2. 권한이있는행정기관이발행한증명서
3. 제 3 자의허락또는동의를증명하는증서
4. 그밖의부속서류

（全文于 2009 年 2 月 6 日修订）

第三十七条（文字的修改、插入和删除）

（一）公证书中文字不能修改。

（二）在公证书中插入文字时，将该字数及位置记载于栏外或者结尾空白处，并由公证员、当事人或者其代理人以及见证人在该处盖章。

（三）自公证书删除文字时，为了使文字能够被清晰地读出，应该保持文字的原样，将删除的文字数和删除位置记载于栏外或者结尾空白处，并由公证员、当事人或者其代理人以及见证人在该处盖章。

（四）违反第一项至第三项规定的修改无效。

（全文 2009 年 2 月 6 日修订）

第三十八条（出具公证书的程序）

（一）公证员出具的公证书应该向所有的参与者读出或者使其阅读，来确认委托人和代理人无异议，并且将这一事实写入证书中。

（二）有翻译人参与的情况下除了第一项的程序外，应该让翻译人翻译公证书的内容，并将这一事实记录在公证书里。

（三）根据第一项和第二项进行记载时，公证员及列席者应该在公证书中签名盖章。

（四）作为列席者如果不能在公证书里签名的，应该在公证书里写明原因，并由公证员和见证人盖章。

（五）公证书有数页的时候，必须在每页的装订线处加盖骑缝章。

（全文于 2009 年 2 月 6 日修订）

第三十九条（书面引用）

（一）在公证员出具的公证书中引用其他文书的内容，在公证书中附上引用文书时，应该在公证书和其文书的装订线处加盖骑缝印。

（二）本法第三十六条至第三十八条的规定适用于第一项中书面引用的情形。

（三）根据第一项和第二项规定附上的书面引用，视为公证员出具的公证书的一部分。

（全文于 2009 年 2 月 6 日修订）

第四十条（附属材料的连缀）

（一）下列各项附属材料在公证员出具公证书时应该体现在公证书里。但是，如果委托人请求退回附属材料的原本的，可连缀其抄本以代替原本。

1. 证明代理权的公证书；
2. 官署证书；
3. 证明第三人同意或许可的证书；
4. 其他的附属材料。

②공증인은증서와그부속서류간및부속서류상호간에걸쳐직인으로간인하여야한다.

[전문개정 2009.2.6.]

제 41 조 (원본멸실의경우)

① 증서의원본이멸실 (滅失) 된경우공증인은이미발급한증서의정본 (正本) 또는등본을회수하여소속지방검찰청검사장의인가를받아멸실된증서를대신하여보존하여야한다.

② 제 1 항의증서에는소속지방검찰청검사장의인가를받아멸실된증서를대신하여보존한다는취지와인가연월일을적고공증인이서명날인하여야한다.

[전문개정 2009.2.6.]

제 42 조 (인지의첨부)

공증인은「인지세법」에따라인지세납부의대상이되는공정증서를작성한경우에는촉탁인에게증서의원본에인지를붙이도록하여야한다.

[전문개정 2009.2.6.]

제 43 조 (원본의열람)

① 촉탁인, 그승계인또는증서의취지에관하여법률상이해관계가있음을증명한자는증서원본의열람을청구할수있다.

② 제 1 항에따라공증인이증서의원본을열람하게하는경우에는제 27 조제 1 항・제 2 항및제 30 조를준용한다.< 개정 2012.1.17.>

③ 공증인이촉탁인의승계인에게증서원본을열람하게할경우에는승계인임을증명하는증서를제출하게하여야한다.

④ 검사는언제든지증서원본의열람을청구할수있다.

[전문개정 2009.2.6.]

제 43 조의 2(대리권의증명)

① 대리인의촉탁으로공증인이증서의원본을열람하게하는경우에는대리권을증명할증서를제출하게하여야한다.

② 공증인은제 1 항의증서가인증을받지아니한사서증서일경우에는그증서외에서명에관한증명서를제출하게하여증서가진정한것임을증명하게하여야한다.

[본조신설 2012.1.17.]

제 44 조 (증서원부)

공증인은증서원부를작성하여비치하여야한다.

[전문개정 2009.2.6.]

제 45 조 (증서원부의기입사항)

①증서원부에는증서를작성할때마다진행순서에따라다음각호의사항을모두적어야한다.

（二）公证员应该在公证书和附属材料间的相互装订处加盖骑缝章。

（全文于 2009 年 2 月 6 日修订）

第四十一条（原件灭失的情况）

（一）在公证书原件灭失的情况下，已经发给公证员的公证书正本和副本收回后，经所属地方检察厅检察长许可，可作为原件保留。

（二）第一项规定的经所属地方检察厅检察长认可的替代后的原件应写明这一替代原件保存的事实和认可的年月日，由公证员签名盖章。

（全文于 2009 年 2 月 6 日修订）

第四十二条（贴印花税票）

公证员制作根据《印花税法》应缴纳印花税的公证书时，公证员应该让委托人依据印花税法在公证书的原本上贴足印花。

（全文与 2009 年 2 月 6 日修订）

第四十三条（阅读原本）

（一）委托人，其继承人和能够证明与公证书的内容有法律上的利害关系的人可以申请阅览公证书原件。

（二）第一项规定的公证员允许阅览公证书原件的情况，适用本法第二十七条第一项、第二项和第三十条的规定。（于 2012 年 1 月 17 日修订）。

（三）在公证员允许委托人的继承人阅览公证书原件的情况下，继承人应该提供相关的身份证明。

（四）检察官在任何情况下都可以要求阅览公证书原本。

（全文于 2009 年 2 月 6 日修订）

第四十三条第二款（代理权的证明）

（一）代理人向公证员申请阅览公证书的，代理人需要提供代理权证明。

（二）当第一项中的证明是未经认证的私署证书时，公证员可以要求提交其他相关书面证明，以证实其真实性。

（本条于 2012 年 1 月 17 日修订）

第四十四条（公证书原簿）

公证员应该出具公证书原簿并且公开。

（全文于 2009 年 2 月 6 日修订）

第四十五条（公证书原簿的记入事项）

（一）根据每次公证书制作的顺序，公证书原簿中应记载以下所有事项：

1. 증서의번호와종류

2. 촉탁인의주소와성명 (법인인경우에는그명칭과사무소소재지)

3. 작성연월일

②제 1 항은증서를작성한사실을적을장부에관하여법령에특별한규정이있으면적용하지아니한다 .

[전문개정 2009.2.6.]

제 46 조 (증서정본의발급)

① 촉탁인또는그승계인은증서정본의발급을청구할수있다 .

② 제 1 항에따라공증인이증서정본을작성하는경우에는제 27 조제 1 항 · 제 2 항 , 제 30 조 , 제 31 조제 1 항 · 제 2 항및제 43 조제 3 항을준용한다 .

③ 촉탁인의승계인이증서정본의발급을청구하는경우에제출할증서에관하여는제 31 조제 2 항을준용한다 .

[전문개정 2009.2.6.]

제 47 조 (증서정본의기재사항)

①증서정본에는공증인이다음각호의사항을모두적고서명날인하여야한다 .

1. 증서의전문 (全文)

2. 정본이라는사실

3. 발급을청구한자의성명

4. 작성연월일과장소

②제 1 항에따르지아니하면증서정본으로서의효력이없다 .

[전문개정 2009.2.6.]

제 48 조 (초록정본)

① 여러개의사건을연달아적은증서나여러사람각자에대한관계가다른증서에관하여는유용한부분과증서의방식에관한부분만을발췌하여그정본을작성할수있다 .

② 제 1 항의정본에는증서의일부를발췌하여작성한초록 (抄錄) 정본이라는사실을적어야한다 .

[전문개정 2009.2.6.]

제 49 조 (정본발급사실의기재)

공증인은증서의정본을발급할때에는그증서원본의끝부분에촉탁인이나그승계인아무개에게정본을발급하였다는사실과그발급연월일을적고서명날인하여야한다 .

[전문개정 2009.2.6.]

제 50 조 (등본의발급)

① 촉탁인 , 그승계인또는증서의취지에관하여법률상이해관계가있음을증명한자는증서또는그부속서류의등본발급을청구할수있다 .

1. 公证书的编号和种类；

2. 委托人的住所和姓名（法人的话，名称和事务所所在地）；

3. 制作的年、月、日。

（二）第一项规定的公证书应记入内容，如法律有特别规定的则不适用。

（全文于 2009 年 2 月 6 日修订）

第四十六条（公证书正本的发给）

（一）委托人及其继承人可以要求发给公证书正本。

（二）第一项中规定的公证员出具公证书正本时，应适用本法第二十七条第一项、第二项，第三十条，第三十一条第一项、第二项和第四十三条第三项的规定。

（三）委托人的继承人要求发给公证书正本时，应根据本法第三十一条第二项的规定提交相关材料。

（全文于 2009 年 2 月 6 日修订）

第四十七条（公证书正本的记载事项）

（一）公证书正本中公证员应该记录下列事项并签名盖章。

1. 公证书全文；

2. 本件系正本；

3. 要求发给者的姓名；

4. 制作的年、月、日和场所。

（二）不按第一项的要求出具的证书正本，不具有公证书正本的效力。

（全文于 2009 年 2 月 6 日修订）

第四十八条（抄录正本）

（一）关于并列记载数个事件的公证书或者同数人有不同关联的公证书，可以摘录其有用部分及关于公证书方式的有关记载，作成正本。

（二）根据第一项制作的正本中应写明其摘录自原公证书的事实。

（全文于 2009 年 2 月 6 日修订）

第四十九条（正本发给事实的记载）

公证员发给公证书正本时，在公证书原件末尾应写明委托人或者继承人要求发给的事实，写明发给日期并签名盖章。

（全文于 2009 年 2 月 6 日修订）

第五十条（核证副本的发给）

（一）委托人、其继承人和能够证明与公证书内容有法律上利害关系者，都能要求发给公证书和附属材料。

② 제 1 항에따라공증인이증서의등본을작성하는경우에는제 27 조제 1 항 · 제 2 항 , 제 30 조 , 제 43 조제 3 항및제 43 조의 2 를준용한다 .< 개정 2012.1.17.>

[전문개정 2009.2.6.]

제 51 조 (등본의기재사항)

증서의등본에는공증인이다음각호의사항을모두적고서명날인하여야한다 .

1. 증서의전문
2. 등본이라는사실
3. 작성연월일과장소

[전문개정 2009.2.6.]

제 52 조 (초록등본)

① 증서의등본은증서의일부에관하여작성할수있다 .

② 제 1 항의등본에는증서의일부를발췌하여작성한초록등본이라는사실을적어야한다 .

[전문개정 2009.2.6.]

제 53 조 (부속서류의등본)

증서의부속서류의등본을작성하는경우에는제 51 조및제 52 조를준용한다 .

[전문개정 2009.2.6.]

제 54 조 (청구자의등본작성)

① 증서또는그부속서류의등본을청구하는자는이에적어야할사항을직접적고공증인에게서명날인만을청구할수있다 .

② 공증인이제 1 항의등본에서명날인하면그등본은공증인자신이작성한것과동일한효력이있다 .

[전문개정 2009.2.6.]

제 55 조 (정본 · 등본작성방법)

① 증서의정본 · 등본또는그부속서류의등본이여러장으로되어있으면공증인은각장에걸쳐직인으로간인하여야한다 .

② 증서의정본 · 등본또는그부속서류의등본을작성하는경우에는제 36 조및제 37 조를준용한다 .

[전문개정 2009.2.6.]

제 56 조 (유언서 · 거절증서작성의특칙)

공증인이유언서를작성할때에는제 17 조제 3 항본문을적용하지아니하고 , 공증인이거절증서를작성할때에는제 27 조부터제 31 조까지의규정을적용하지아니한다 .

[전문개정 2009.2.6.]

제 56 조의 2(어음 · 수표의공증등)

① 공증인은어음 · 수표에첨부하여강제집행을

（二）根据第一项公证员制作核证副本时，适用本法第二十七条第一项、第二项，第三十条，第四十三条第三项和第四十三条第二款的规定。（于 2012 年 1 月 17 日修订）

（全文于 2009 年 2 月 6 日修订）

第五十一条（核证副本的记载事项）

公证书核证副本中公证员应该记载下列事项并签名盖章。

1. 公证书的正文；
2. 核证副本字样；
3. 制作的年、月、日和场所。

（全文于 2009 年 2 月 6 日修订）

第五十二条（摘录抄本）

（一）就证书抄本的一部分可作成摘录抄本。

（二）第一项中的摘录抄本中应该写明是截取公证书中的一部分制作的摘录抄本的事实。

（全文于 2009 年 2 月 6 日修订）

第五十三条（附属材料的抄本）

公证书附属材料的抄本的制作适用本法第五十一条和第五十二条的规定。

（全文于 2009 年 2 月 6 日修订）

第五十四条（请求者自作抄本）

（一）请求交付公证书或者其附属文件的抄本者，可自行抄录应记载事项，而只要求公证员在其抄本上签名盖章。

（二）根据第一项制作的抄本经公证员签字盖章后，具有与公证员制作之抄本相同的效力。

（全文于 2009 年 2 月 6 日修订）

第五十五条（出具公证书正本和抄本的方法）

（一）公证书的正本、抄本和附属材料的抄本如果有数页的话，公证员应该在每页装订处加盖骑缝章。

（二）公证书的正本抄本和附属材料的抄本的制作应该适用第三十六条和第三十七条的规定。

（全文于 2009 年 2 月 6 日修订）

第五十六条（出具遗嘱书、拒绝证书的特别规定）

公证员公证遗嘱时不适用本法第十七条第三项的规定，出具拒绝证书时不适用本法第二十七条至第三十一条的规定。

（全文于 2009 年 2 月 6 日修订）

第五十六条第二款（票据、支票的公证等）

（一）公证员可以针对票据和支票上强制执行的

인낙(認諾)한다는취지를적은공정증서를작성할수 있다.

② 제 1 항에따른증서는어음・수표의발행인과 수취인, 양도인과양수인또는그대리인의촉탁이있을 때에만작성할수있다.

③ 공증인이제 1 항에따른증서를작성할때에는 어음・수표의원본을붙여증서의정본을작성하고, 그 어음・수표의사본을붙여증서의원본및등본을작성한 후, 증서의정본은어음・수표상의채권자에게내주고, 그등본은어음・수표상의채무자에게내주며, 그원본 은공증인이보존한다.

④ 제 1 항에따른증서는「민사집행법」제 56 조 에도불구하고그어음또는수표에공증된발행인, 배서 인(背書人)및공증된환어음을공증인수(公證引受) 한지급인에대하여는집행권원으로본다.

⑤ 제 4 항에따라집행권원으로보는증서에대한 집행문(執行文)은공증된어음・수표의수취인이나 공증배서(公證背書)된양수인에게만부여한다.

⑥ 제 1 항의경우에는제 25 조부터제 35 조까지, 제 35 조의 2, 제 36 조부터제 38 조까지, 제 40 조 부터제 43 조까지및제 43 조의 2 를준용한다.<개정 2012.1.17.>

[전문개정 2009.2.6.]

제 56 조의 3(건물・토지・특정동산의인도등 에관한법률행위의공증등)

① 공증인은건물이나토지또는대통령령으로정 하는동산의인도또는반환을목적으로하는청구에대하 여강제집행을승낙하는취지를기재한공정증서를작성 할수있다. 다만, 임차건물의인도또는반환에관한공 정증서는임대인과임차인사이의임대차관계종료를원 인으로임차건물을인도또는반환하기전 6 개월이내에 작성되는경우로서그증서에임차인에대한금원지급에 대하여도강제집행을승낙하는취지의합의내용이포함 되어있는경우에만작성할수있다.

② 제 1 항에따른공정증서작성을촉탁할때에는 어느한당사자가다른당사자를대리하거나어느한대리 인이당사자쌍방을대리하지못한다.

③ 제 1 항에따른공정증서는「민사집행법」제 56 조에도불구하고강제집행의집행권원으로본다.

④ 제 3 항에따라집행권원으로보는증서에대한 집행문은그증서를보존하는공증인이그공증인의사무 소가있는곳을관할하는지방법원단독판사의허가를받 아부여한다. 이경우지방법원단독판사는허가여부를 결정하기위하여필요하면당사자본인이나그대리인을 심문할수있다.

[본조신설 2013.5.28.]

承诺为内容制成法定公证书。

（二）根据第一项的规定，只有在票据、支票的发行人和收取人，让渡人和受让人和他的代理人有委托的时候公证员才可以进行公证。

（三）公证员根据第一项的规定在出具公证书的时候，附上票据、支票的原件。出具的公证书正本附上票据、支票的抄本，再加上原件制作核准副本，制作好之后将公证书的正本发给票据、支票的债权人，而核证副本也会发给票据、支票的债务人，原件则由公证员保存。

（四）根据第一项的规定进行公证的文书不适用《民事执行法》第五十六条的规定，要求对票据和支票公证的发行人、背书人和接受票据的公证引受的支付人都有申请执行的权利。

（五）从第四项中规定的公证书执行权限来看，申请执行的权利是赋予票据和支票公证后的收取人或者公证背书受让人的。

（六）第一项规定的情况适用本法第二十五条至第三十五条，第三十五条第二款，第三十六条至第三十八条，第四十条至第四十三条和第四十三条第二款的规定。（于 2012 年 1 月 17 日修订）

（全文于 2009 年 2 月 6 日修订）

第五十六条第三款（建筑物、土地、特定动产的让渡等相关的法律行为的公证等）

（一）公证员可以对建筑物或者土地，根据大总统令规定的动产的让渡和变换的请求强制执行为内容的记载事项进行公证。但是，出租的建筑物的让渡和变换的公证的情况有所不同。由于出租人和承租人之间的租赁关系的存在，作为出租的建筑物的让渡和变化前的六个月内的公证事项，在公证书里面应该包含承租人的优先权和获得强制执行的内容，在有此合意的内容的情形下，才可以进行公证。

（二）在根据第一项规定接受委托进行的公证中，一方当事人不得为另一方当事人的代理人，或者同一代理人不得同时代理双方当事人。

（三）根据第一项出具的公证书不适用《民事执行法》第五十六条的规定，此公证书拥有强制执行效力。

（四）根据第三项制作的有执行力的公证书，经保存公证书的公证员所属事务所所在地管辖法院法官允许，赋予执行文。地方法院法官为决定是否允许，如有必要可审问当事人本人或其代理人。

（本条于 2013 年 5 月 28 日修订）

[종 전 제 56 조 의 3 은 제 56 조 의 4 로 이 동 <2013.5.28.>]

제 56 조의 4(집행문부여의제한)

① 공증인은공정증서를작성한날부터 7 일 (제 56 조의 3 에따른공정증서중건물이나토지의인도 또는반환에관한공정증서인경우에는 1 개월) 이 지나지아니하면집행문을부여할수없다 . < 개정 2013.5.28.>

② 공증인은제 35 조의 2 제 1 항에따른부기가 있으면집행문을부여할수없다 .

[전문개정 2009.2.6.]

[제 56 조의 3 에서이동 , 종전제 56 조의 4 는 제 56 조의 5 로이동 <2013.5.28.>]

제 56 조의 5(집행권원인공정증서의정본등의 송달)

① 제 56 조의 3 및 「민사집행법」 제 56 조제 4 호에따른집행권원인증서의정본또는등본이나그증서 에관한같은법제 39 조제 2 항 · 제 3 항의집행문및증 명서등본의송달은우편으로하거나대법원규칙으로정 하는방법으로한다 . 다만 , 제 46 조또는제 50 조에 따라증서의정본또는등본을발급받은자에대하여는 그증서의정본또는등본이송달된것으로본다 . < 개정 2013.5.28.>

② 우편에의한송달은신청을받아공증인이수행 한다 .

③ 제 2 항에따른송달에관하여는「민사소송법」 제 176 조제 2 항 , 제 178 조제 1 항 , 제 179 조부터 제 183 조까지 , 제 186 조및제 193 조를준용한다 .

[전문개정 2009.2.6.]

[제 56 조의 4 에서이동 <2013.5.28.>]

제 5 장사서증서의인증

(개정 2009. 2. 6.)

제 57 조 (인증방법)

① 사서증서의인증은촉탁인으로하여금공증인 앞에서사서증서에서명또는날인하게하거나사서증서 의서명또는날인을본인이나그대리인으로하여금확인 하게한후그사실을증서에적는방법으로한다 .

② 사서증서의등본에대한인증은사서증서와대 조하여그와일치함을인정한후그사실을적는방법으로 한다 .

③ 사서증서에글자의삽입 , 삭제 , 수정 , 난외 (欄

（2013 年 5 月 28 日第五十六条第三款移动到第五十六条第四款）

第五十六条第四款（执行文与否的限制）

（一）自制成之日起未满七日的公证书（对有关建筑物或土地让渡或转换的公证书，根据第五十六条第三款的规定，为一个月），不能赋予其执行文。（于 2013 年 5 月 28 日修订）

（二）根据本法第三十五条第二款第二项的规定有附记的话，公证员不能交付执行。

（全文于 2009 年 2 月 6 日修订）

（2013 年 5 月 28 日从本法第六条第三项移动，之后从第五十六条第四款移动到第五款）

第五十六条第五款（执行权利人公证书正本等的送达）

（一）根据本法第五十六条第三款和《民事执行法》第五十六条第四项的规定，执行权利人的证书正本和核证副本或者公证书相关的法的第三十九条第二项、第三项的执行通知和公证书核证副本的送达是用信件的形式送达或者是根据大法院规则规定的方式送达的。但是，根据本法第四十六条和第五十条的规定，对于公证书的正本和核证副本的发给者来说，这种正本和核证副本的发给就是意味着对其的送达。（2013 年 5 月 28 日修订）

（二）公证员应申请进行邮寄送达。

（三）根据第二项的规定进行的送达适用《民事诉讼法》第一百七十六条第二项，第一百七十八条第一项，第一百七十九条至第一百八十三条，第一百八十六条和第一百九十三条的规定。

（全文于 2009 年 2 月 6 日修订）

（2013 年 5 月 28 日，从本法第五十六条第四款处移动而来）

第五章　私署证书的认证

（2009 年 2 月 6 日修订）

第五十七条（认证的方法）

（一）私署证书的认证，是指公证员当面让当事人在该证书上签名盖章或者让当事人或其代理人对证书上的签名或者盖章予以确认，对于后一种情况，应在证书中记明。

（二）私署证书的核证副本的认证，是指将该副本与证书核对后，认为确实无误时，将该情况载入副本。

（三）自书公证书中文字有插入、删除、修改、

外）기재또는그밖에정정된부분이있거나파손되거나그밖에겉보기에현저히의심할만한사유가있을경우에는그상황을인증문에적어야한다.

④ 공증인은제 1 항및제 2 항에따라인증을부여한증서의사본과그부속서류를보존하여야한다.

[전문개정 2009.2.6.]

제 57 조의 2（선서인증）

① 공증인은사서증서에인증을부여할때촉탁인이공증인앞에서사서증서에적힌내용이진실함을선서하고이에서명또는날인하거나사서증서의서명또는날인을확인한경우에는그선서사실을증서에적어야한다.

② 공증인은「민사소송법」제 322 조각호의어느하나에해당하는사람에대하여는제 1 항의선서를시키지못한다.

③ 제 1 항의선서인증은대리인에의하여촉탁할수없다.

④ 공증인은선서에앞서촉탁인에게선서의취지를밝히고，증서에적힌내용이거짓이라는것을알면서선서하는경우에는과태료처분을받을수있다는뜻을알려주어야한다.< 신설 2013.5.28.>

⑤ 제 1 항에따른선서는촉탁인이자필로 "양심에따라이증서에적힌내용이진실함을선서하며，만일위내용이거짓이라면과태료처분을받기로맹세합니다" 라고적은선서서로하여야한다.< 개정 2013.5.28.>

⑥ 공증인은촉탁인으로하여금선서서를소리내어읽고기명날인또는서명하게하며，촉탁인이선서서를적을수없거나읽지못하는경우나기명날인또는서명하지못하는경우에는제 29 조에따른참여인으로하여금이를대신하게한다.< 개정 2013.5.28.>

⑦ 제 1 항의선서인증에관하여는제 63 조제 1 항・제 3 항및제 65 조제 1 항・제 3 항을준용한다.< 개정 2013.5.28.>

[본조신설 2009.2.6.]

제 58 조（증서에의기재）

인증을부여하여야할증서에는등부번호（登簿番號），인증의연월일및장소를적고공증인과참여인이서명날인한후증서와인증부（認證簿）의사이에간인하여야한다.

[전문개정 2009.2.6.]

제 59 조（사서증서에대한인증부여시의준용）

사서증서에인증을부여하는경우에는제 25 조부터제 33 조까지，제 36 조，제 37 조및제 38 조제 5 항을준용한다.

[전문개정 2009.2.6.]

栏外记载和其他修改或破损，或有其他外观上可疑之处的，应记载于公证书。

（四）根据第一项和第二项认证的公证书的正本和附属材料，应该由公证员保存。

（全文于 2009 年 2 月 6 日修订）

第五十七条第二款（宣誓认证）

（一）公证员在对私署证书进行公证的时候，委托人应该在公证员面前就私署文书内容的真实性宣誓，并签名盖章，私署证书在有签名和盖章确认的情况下，宣誓的事实也要写在公证书里。

（二）凡符合《民事诉讼法》第三百二十二条中任何一点者，公证员无须要求其按照第一项进行宣誓。

（三）在第一项规定的宣誓认证中，当事人不能委托代理人进行宣誓。

（四）在宣誓之前公证员应该向委托人说明宣誓的内容，告知委托人如果明知公证书内容虚假依然宣誓的，将处以罚款。（本文于 2013 年 5 月 28 日修订）

（五）就第一项中的宣誓，委托人应亲手书写如下，我以良心发誓，确保证书内容之真实，否则愿受罚款处罚。（本文于 2013 年 5 月 28 日修订）

（六）公证员应该让委托人自己读出宣誓书捺印盖章和签名，如委托人不会书写或阅读宣誓书，或不能签名或盖章的，应该根据本法第二十九条的规定由见证人替代其参加公证。（本文于 2013 年 5 月 28 修订）

（七）第一项中规定的宣誓认证相关内容适用本法第六十三条第一项、第三项和第六十五条第一项、第三项的规定。（于 2013 年 5 月 28 日修订）

（本条于 2009 年 2 月 6 日新设）

第五十八条（公证书的记载）

需要认证的公证书须记载登记编号、公证的年月日和场所，经公证员和见证人签名盖章后，在公证书和认证簿的装订处加盖骑缝章。

（全文于 2009 年 2 月 6 日修订）

第五十九条（关于私署证书认证时的准用规则）

私署证书公证时应该适用本法第二十五条至第三十三条，第三十六条，第三十七条和第三十八条第五项的规定。

（全文于 2009 年 2 月 6 日修订）

제 60 조（인증부）

공증인은인증부를작성하여비치하여야한다 .

［전문개정 2009.2.6.］

제 61 조（인증부의기재사항）

인증부에는인증을부여할때마다진행순서에따라다음각호의사항을모두적어야한다 .

1. 등부번호

2. 촉탁인의주소와성명（법인인경우에는그명칭과사무소소재지）

3. 사서증서의종류와서명날인한자

4. 인증의방법

5. 참여인의주소와성명

6. 인증연월일

［전문개정 2009.2.6.］

제 62 조삭제 (2009. 2. 6.)

제 63 조（정관인증의절차）

①「상법」제 292 조와그준용규정에따라정관의인증을촉탁하려면정관（전자문서로작성된정관은제외한다 . 이하같다）두통을제출하여야한다 .

②정관의인증은촉탁인또는그대리인으로하여금공증인앞에서제출된각정관에발기인이서명또는기명날인하였음을확인하게한후그사실을적는방법으로한다 .

③공증인은제 2 항의기재를한정관중한통은자신이보존하고다른한통은촉탁인또는그대리인에게돌려주어야한다 .

④제 2 항의경우에는제 57 조제 3 항과제 58 조부터제 61 조까지의규정을준용한다 .

［전문개정 2009.2.6.］

제 64 조（부속서류의연철）

①다음각호의부속서류는제 63 조제 3 항에따라공증인이보존하는정관에연철하여야한다 .

1. 대리권을증명하는증서

2. 권한이있는행정기관이발행한증명서

3. 제 3 자의허락또는동의를증명하는증서

4. 그밖의부속서류

②제 1 항의경우에는제 40 조제 2 항을준용한다 .

［전문개정 2009.2.6.］

제 65 조（보존정관등이멸실된경우）

① 제 63 조제 3 항에따라보존하는정관이멸실된경우에는공증인은촉탁인에게돌려준정관으로등본을작성하거나이미발급한정관의등본을회수하여소속지방검찰청검사장의인가를받아멸실된정관을대신하여보존하여야한다 .

② 제 57 조제 4 항에따라보존하는증서사본이멸

第六十条（认证簿）

公证员应该制作认证簿并且进行公开。

（本文于 2009 年 2 月 6 日修订）

第六十一条（认证簿的记载事项）

认证簿按进行公证的先后顺序登记，记录以下全部事项：

1. 登记编号；

2. 委托人的住所和姓名（法人的话，名称和事务所所在地）；

3. 私署证书的种类和签名盖章的人；

4. 认证的方法；

5. 见证人的住所和姓名；

6. 认证的年、月、日（全文于 2009 年 2 月 6 日修订）。

第六十二条（于 2009 年 2 月 6 日删除）

第六十三条（章程公证的程序）

（一）根据《商法》第二百九十二条和其准用规则，申请章程公证应提交两份章程（以电子形式制作的章程除外，以下同上）。

（二）章程认证是公证员当面要求委托人和代理人承认他们提交给公证员的章程上的签名和盖章，且确认后予以记录的公证行为。

（三）章程根据第二项规定公证后，其中一份由公证员自己保存，另一份交还委托人及其代理人。

（四）第二项所载情况适用本法第五十七条第三项和第五十八条至第六十一条的规定。

（全文于 2009 年 2 月 6 日修订）

第六十四条（附属材料的连缀）

（一）下列附属材料，应该根据本法第六十三条第三项的规定记录在由公证员保存的章程里面：

1. 证明代理权的证明；

2. 相关有权的行政机关发放的证明书；

3. 第三人的允许和同意的证明书；

4. 其他的附属材料。

（二）第一项所载情况适用第四十条第二项的规定。

（全文于 2009 年 2 月 6 日修订）

第六十五条（保存的章程等灭失后的处理）

（一）根据本法第六十三条第三项保存的章程如灭失的，公证员可根据返还给委托人的章程制作核准副本或回收已发放的核准副本，经所属地方检察厅检察长许可，上述副本可代替已灭失的章程进行保存。

（二）根据第五十七条第四项保存的公证书副本

실된경우에는공증인은촉탁인이소지하는증서에따른사본을작성하여소속지방검찰청검사장의인가를받아멸실된증서사본을대신하여보존하여야한다.

③ 제 1 항및제 2 항의경우에는제 41 조제 2 항을준용한다.

[전문개정 2009.2.6.]

제 66 조（공증인보존정관등에대한준용）

공증인이보존하는정관과그부속서류에관하여는제 43 조, 제 43 조의 2 및제 50 조부터제 55 조까지의규정을준용한다. < 개정 2012.1.17.>

[전문개정 2009.2.6.]

제 66 조의 2（법인의사록의인증）

① 법인등기를할때그신청서류에첨부되는법인총회등의의사록은공증인의인증을받아야한다. 다만, 자본금의총액이 10 억원미만인회사를「상법」제 295 조제 1 항에따라발기설립하는경우또는대통령령으로정하는공법인이나비영리법인의경우에는그러하지아니하다. < 개정 2009.5.28.>

② 제 1 항에따른인증을하는공증인은그총회등의결의의절차및내용이진실에부합（符合）하는지를확인하여야한다.< 개정 2009.2.6.>

③ 제 2 항에따른확인은공증인이해당법인의의결장소에참석하여결의의절차및내용을검사하거나해당의결을한자중그의결에필요한정족수이상의자또는그대리인의촉탁을받아의사록의내용이진실에부합하는지에관하여진술을듣고, 촉탁인또는그대리인으로하여금공증인앞에서의사록의서명또는기명날인을확인하게한후그사실을적는방법으로한다.< 개정 2009.2.6.>

④ 제 1 항에따른의사록을인증하는경우에는제 57 조제 3 항, 제 58 조부터제 61 조까지, 제 63 조제 1 항・제 3 항, 제 64 조, 제 65 조제 1 항・제 3 항및제 66 조를준용한다.< 개정 2009.2.6.>

[본조신설 1985.9.14.]

[제목개정 2009.2.6.]

제 5 장의 2 전자문서등에대한인증

（신설 2009. 2. 6.）

제 66 조의 3（지정공증인의지정등）

① 법무부장관은대통령령으로정하는시설을갖춘공증인을지정공증인으로지정하고고시할수있다.

② 제 1 항의지정을받으려는공증인은법무부령으로정하는바에따라법무부장관에게지정신청을하여

如灭失的，公证员可根据委托人持有的公证书制作抄本，经所属地方检察厅检察长许可，上述抄本可代替已灭失的副本进行保存。

（三）第一项和第二项所载情况应该适用本法第四十一条第二项的规定。

（全文于 2009 年 2 月 6 日修订）

第六十六条（与公证员保存章程相关的准用规定）

与公证员保存章程和其附属材料相关的事项适用第四十三条，第四十三条第二款和第五十条至第五十五条的规定。

（于 2012 年 1 月 17 日修订）

（全文于 2009 年 2 月 6 日修订）

第六十六条第二款（法人议事录的认证）

（一）法人登记时，其申请资料和法人大会议事录应经公证员认证。但根据《商法》第二百九十五条发起成立资本总额小于十亿元的公司，以及成立大总统令规定的公法人或非营利性法人的除外。（本文于 2013 年 5 月 28 日修订）

（二）进行第一项规定的公证时，公证员应确认大会决议的程序和大会内容的真实性。（本文于 2009 年 2 月 6 日修订）

（三）第二项规定的确认的内容有，公证员应该确认相当法律规定的参与的决议场所，决议的程序和参与决议的人中的能通过决议的所必须的法定人数和接受代理人的委托，听取关于议事录里面的内容的真实性的事实的陈述，委托人和代理人要在向公证员提交的议事录上签名和盖章，并对这一事实进行确认，并以这种方法进行公证。（本文于 2009 年 2 月 6 日修订）

（四）第一项规定的议事录认证的情况，应该适用第五十七条第三项，第五十八条至第六十一条，第六十三条第一项、第三项，第六十四条，第六十五条第一项、第三项和第六十六条的规定。

（于 2009 年 2 月 6 日修订）

（本条于 1985 年 9 月 14 日新增）

（2009 年 2 月 6 日更改标题）

第二节　关于电子文书等的认证

（于 2009 年 2 月 6 日新增）

第六十六条第三款（指定公证员的指定等）

（一）司法部长可以指定具备大总统令规定之设施的公证员为指定公证员。

（二）如欲获得第一项中规定的指定，公证员应根据司法部令之规定，向司法部长提出申请。

야한다 .

③ 지정공증인이취급하는전자문서등에대한공증사무에관하여는제 6 장을적용하지아니한다 .

④ 지정공증인의자격 · 지정절차등에관하여그밖에필요한사항은대통령령으로정한다 .

[본조신설 2009.2.6.]

제 66 조의 4(지정공증인의지정취소)

①법무부장관은지정공증인이다음각호의어느하나에해당하면지정공증인지정을취소할수있다 .

1. 스스로지정취소를원하는경우

2. 제 66 조의 3 제 1 항에따른시설을갖추지못하는경우

②지방검찰청검사장은소속지정공증인에게제 1 항각호의어느하나에해당하는사유가있으면지체없이법무부장관에게보고하여야한다 .

③법무부장관은제 1 항제 2 호의사유로지정공증인의지정을취소하려면청문을거쳐야한다 .

[본조신설 2009.2.6.]

제 66 조의 5(전자문서의인증)

①전자문서에대한인증은다음각호의어느하나에해당하는방법으로한다 . < 개정 2013.5.28.>

1. 촉탁인으로하여금대통령령으로정하는바에따라전자문서에전자서명을하게한후그사실을적은정보를전자문서에전자적방식으로첨부하는방법

2. 전자문서의전자서명을촉탁인이나그대리인으로하여금확인하게한후그사실을적은정보를전자문서에전자적방식으로첨부하는방법

②지정공증인은전자문서를인증할때에촉탁인이그앞에서전자문서의내용이진실함을선서하고이에전자서명을하거나전자서명을확인한경우에는그선서사실을적은정보를전자문서에전자적방식으로첨부하여야한다 .

③제 1 항에따른인증에관하여는제 25 조부터제 33 조까지의규정을준용한다 .

④제 2 항에따른선서인증에관하여는제 25 조부터제 29 조까지 , 제 32 조 , 제 33 조 , 제 57 조의 2 제 2 항부터제 4 항까지및제 6 항을준용한다 .< 개정 2013.5.28.>

[본조신설 2009.2.6.]

제 66 조의 6(전자화문서의인증)

① 지정공증인은전자화문서와전자화대상문서를대조하여서로일치하는경우에는전자화문서에대하여제 57 조제 2 항의인증을부여할수있다 .

（三）指定公证员在从事电子文书相关公证时，不适用第六章的规定。

（四）关于指定公证员的资格、指定的程序等相关事宜和其他必要事项均由大总统令规定。

（本条于 2009 年 2 月 6 日新增）

第六十六条第四款（指定公证员的指定的取消）

（一）指定公证员符合下列任一情形的，司法部长可取消其指定：

1. 公证员自愿取消指定；

2. 根据本法第六十六条第三款的规定不具备应有之设施。

（二）地方检察厅检察长如发现所属的指定公证员符合第一项中的任一情形时，应该立即向司法部长报告。

（三）司法部长如根据第一项第二点取消指定的，应公开进行。

（本条于 2009 年 2 月 6 日新增）

第六十六条第五款（电子文书的认证）

（一）关于电子文书的公证是由以下列举的任何一种方法进行认证的。（于 2013 年 5 月 28 日修订）

1. 是通过让委托人根据大总统令的规定在电子文书上进行电子签名后将这一事实记录，将信息以电子文件的形式记录下来的方法进行认证。

2. 是通过让电子文书申请公证的委托人或者其代理人在电子文书上签字并确认后，将这一事实进行记录，将信息以电子文件的形式记录下来的方法进行认证。

（二）指定公证员在公证电子文书的时候，让委托人对电子文件里的内容的真实性进行宣誓，对宣誓内容进行电子签名或确认电子签名。

（三）根据第一项的规定关于公证的事项适用于本法第二十五条至第三十三条的规定。

（四）根据第二项关于宣誓公证的规定适用于第二十五条至第二十九条，第三十二条，第三十三条，第五十七条第二款第二项至第四项和第六项的规定。

（于 2013 年 5 月 28 日修订）

（本条于 2009 年 2 月 6 日新增）

第六十六条第六款（电子化文书的认证）

（一）指定公证员，在对电子化文书和以电子化为对象的文书相对比，在其相互一致的情况下，关于电子化文书可以适用本法第五十七条第二项的规定进行认证。

② 전자화문서의인증에관하여는제 25 조부터제 33 조까지의규정을준용한다 .

[본조신설 2009.2.6.]

제 66 조의 7(지정공증인의전자서명)

지정공증인은제 66 조의 5 제 1 항・제 2 항및제 66 조의 6 제 1 항에따라전자문서등에인증을부여하는경우에는해당전자문서등에수록된정보및이에첨부한정보에대하여전자서명을하고 , 이를확인할수있는정보를해당전자문서등에전자적방식으로첨부하여야한다 .

[본조신설 2009.2.6.]

제 66 조의 8(인증한전자문서등의보존등)

① 제 66 조의 5 제 1 항・제 2 항및제 66 조의 6 제 1 항에따라전자문서등에인증을부여한지정공증인은인증한전자문서등에수록된정보와의동일성을확인할수있는정보를보존하여야한다 .

② 촉탁인은지정공증인에게제 66 조의 5 제 1 항・제 2 항및제 66 조의 6 제 1 항에따라인증을부여받은전자문서등과동일한정보를수록한전자문서등의보관을청구할수있다 .

[본조신설 2009.2.6.]

제 66 조의 9(인증정보의제공등)

①촉탁인 , 그승계인또는전자문서등의내용 , 그진위및존재여부등에관하여법률상이해관계가있음을증명한자는지정공증인에게다음각호의사항을청구할수있다 .

1. 자신이보유하고있는전자문서등에수록된정보와제 66 조의 8 제 1 항의전자문서등에수록된정보가동일하다는증명

2. 제 66 조의 8 제 2 항에따라보관하는전자문서등과동일한정보의제공

②제 1 항제 2 호에따른정보의제공은지정공증인이보관하는전자문서등의내용을증명하는서면을교부하는방법으로할수있다 .

③지정공증인은제 1 항에따라전자적방식으로증명또는정보제공을하는경우에는제 66 조의 7 의조치를하여야한다 .

[본조신설 2009.2.6.]

제 66 조의 10(위임규정)

촉탁인및지정공증인이사용하는전자서명 , 전자문서등의형식 , 전자문서등에대한인증의절차와그밖에필요한사항은법무부령으로정한다 .

[본조신설 2009.2.6.]

（二）关于电子化文书的公证事项适用于本法第二十五条至第三十三条的规定。

（本条于 2009 年 2 月 6 日新增）

第六十六条第七款（指定公证员的电子签名）

指定公证员可以，根据本法第六十六条第五款第一项、第二项和第六十六条第六款第一项的规定对电子文书进行认证，对适当的电子文书中收录的信息和相关的信息进行电子签名，并且经确认后，信息以电子文件的形式记录下来的方法进行认证。

（本条于 2009 年 2 月 6 日新增）

第六十六条第八款（公证的电子文书的保存等）

（一）根据本法第六十六条第五款第一项、第二项和第六十六条第六款第一项的规定对电子文书进行认证，公证员应当对公证过的电子文书中收录的信息及其统一性进行确认，并将确认的信息进行保存。

（二）根据本法第六十六条第五款第一项、第二项和第六十六条第六款第一项的规定委托人可以要求公证员对电子文书进行认证，对公证过的电子文书中收录的信息及其统一性进行确认，并且可以要求保存电子文书。

（本条于 2009 年 2 月 6 日新增）

第六十六条第九款（认证信息的提供等）

（一）委托人、继承人和能够证明其与电子文书内容、真伪、是否存在具有法律上利害关系者，可就下列事项请求公证。

1. 自己保有的电子文书所记录的信息和第六十六条第八款第一项的电子文书所记录的信息一致的证明。

2. 提供根据第六十六条第八款第二项规定保管的电子文书及与电子文书具有统一性的信息。

（二）第一项第二点规定的信息的提供，可以以指定公证员通过书面交付证明其所保管的电子文书的书面材料的方式进行。

（三）指定公证员应该根据第一项的规定以电子的方式提供证明和提供信息，具体根据第六十六条第七款的措施进行。

（本条于 2009 年 2 月 6 日新增）

第六十六条第十款（委任规定）

适用于委托人和指定公证员的电子签名、电子文书的形式，电子文书的认证程序和其他必要的事项均由司法部令规定。

（本条于 2009 年 2 月 6 日新增）

제 66 조의 11 (기술의개발 · 보급)

법무부장관은지정공증인이수행하는전자문서등의인증에필요한기술을개발하고보급하여야한다 .

[본조신설 2009.2.6.]

제 6 장대리 , 겸무및인계

(개정 2009. 2. 6.)

제 67 조 (공증직무대리의촉탁)

① 공증인이질병이나그밖의부득이한사유로직무를수행할수없으면다른공증인에게대리를촉탁할수있다 .

② 공증인이제 1 항에따라대리를촉탁하였을때에는지체없이그사유를소속지방검찰청검사장에게신고하여야한다 . 대리를해임하였을때에도또한같다 .

[전문개정 2009.2.6.]

제 68 조 (공증직무의대리명령)

① 제 67 조제 1 항의경우에공증인이대리를촉탁할수없을때에는소속지방검찰청검사장은그관할구역의다른공증인에게대리를명할수있다 .

② 공증인이그직무를수행할수있게되었을때에는소속지방검찰청검사장은제 1 항의명령을철회하여야한다 .

[전문개정 2009.2.6.]

제 69 조 (대리공증인의사무소)

① 대리공증인이제 67 조및제 68 조에따라그직무를수행하는사무소는피대리공증인 (被代理公證人) 의사무소로본다 .

② 대리공증인이직무상서명할때에는피대리공증인의성명 , 소속 , 사무소소재지와그의대리공증인이라는사실을적어야한다 .

③ 대리공증인에관하여는제 21 조를적용한다 .

[전문개정 2009.2.6.]

제 70 조 (사무소서류의봉인)

공증인의사망 , 면직또는사임으로인하여필요하다고인정할때에는소속지방검찰청검사장은그가지정한공무원에게지체없이사무소의서류를봉인 (封印) 하게하여야한다 .

[전문개정 2009.2.6.]

제 71 조 (겸무명령)

① 공증인이사망 , 면직또는사임한후즉시후임자가임명되지아니한경우에는소속지방검찰청검사장은그관할구역의다른공증인에게겸무 (兼務) 를명할수있다 .

第六十六条第十一款（技术的开发和普及）

司法部应普及并开发指定公证员执行电子文书认证所必需的技术。

（本条于 2009 年 2 月 6 日新增）

第六章　代理、兼任和交接

（于 2009 年 2 月 6 日修订）

第六十七条（公证员职务代理的委托）

（一）公证员因疾病或其他不得已事由不能履职的，可委托其他公证员代理其职务。

（二）公证员根据第一项委托其他公证员的，应立即将委托事由向所属地方检察厅检察长进行申告。解除代理的程序亦同。

（于 2009 年 2 月 6 日修订）

第六十八条（公证员职务的代理命令）

（一）公证员出现第六十七条第一项之情形而未能找到其他公证员代理其职务的，应由所属地方检察厅检察长在辖区内指定其他公证员进行代理。

（二）当公证员可以依法履行其职务时，所属地方检察厅检察长应该解除前款代理。

（全文于 2009 年 2 月 6 日修订）

第六十九条（代理公证员的事务所）

（一）第六十七条、第六十八条规定的代理公证员，在执行代理职务时，以被代理公证员的事务所为其事务所。

（二）代理公证员为职务上签名时，应写明被代理公证员的姓名、隶属、事务所所在地和他是代理公证员的事实。

（三）关于代理公证员的事项适用本法第二十一条的规定。

（全文于 2009 年 2 月 6 日修订）

第七十条（事务所材料的封存）

公证员死亡、免职或转属后，其所属地方检察厅检察长如认为必要时，应立即指派人员封存事务所的有关材料。

（全文于 2009 年 2 月 6 日修订）

第七十一条（兼职命令）

（一）公证员死亡、免职或转属后，如无继任者或来不及任命继任者的，所属地方检察厅检察长应命令其辖区内的其他公证员兼任其职位。

② 후임자가그직무를수행할수있게되었을때에는소속지방검찰청검사장은제 1 항의명령을철회하여야한다 .

[전문개정 2009.2.6.]

제 72 조 (서류의접수)

① 공증인이면직또는사임한경우에는후임자나겸무자는전임자의참여아래지체없이서류를접수하여야한다 .

② 전임자가사망이나그밖의사유로참여할수없는경우에는후임자또는겸무자는소속지방검찰청검사장이지정하는공무원의참여아래서류를인수하여야한다 .

③ 제 70 조에따른서류의봉인후에임명된후임자나겸무자는소속지방검찰청검사장이지정한공무원의참여아래봉인을풀고서류를인수하여야한다 .

[전문개정 2009.2.6.]

제 73 조 (겸무자서류인도시의준용)

겸무자가서류를다시다른공증인에게인도하는경우에는제 72 조를준용한다 .

[전문개정 2009.2.6.]

제 74 조 (겸무자또는후임자라는사실의기재)

① 겸무자가직무상서명하는경우에는겸무자라는사실을적어야한다 .

② 전임자나겸무자가작성한증서에의하여후임자가정본이나등본을작성하고이에서명할때에는후임자라는사실을적어야한다 .

[전문개정 2009.2.6.]

제 75 조 (서류의인계명령)

① 공증인이사망 , 면직또는사임한경우에정원이변경되었거나그밖의사유로후임자가필요하지아니하게된경우에는법무부장관은공증인이소속한지방검찰청관할구역의다른공증인에게서류의인계 (引繼) 를명하여야한다 .

② 제 1 항에따라서류의인계를명령받은공증인에관하여는제 72 조및제 74 조제 2 항을준용한다 .

[전문개정 2009.2.6.]

제 76 조 (공증인의정직에관한준용)

① 공증인의정직 (停職) 에관하여는제 70 조 , 제71조, 제72조제3항및제74조제1항을준용한다.

② 제 1 항의경우에겸무자의사무소는정직자의사무소로본다 .

[전문개정 2009.2.6.]

（二）有继任者可以履行其职务时，所属的地方检察厅检察长应撤回前款命令。

（全文于 2009 年 2 月 6 日修订）

第七十二条（材料的接收）

（一）公证员免职或转属的，应与其继任人或兼任人办理有关材料之移交；

（二）公证员因死亡或其他事由不能办理移交的，其继任人或兼任人应会同所属地方检察厅检察长指定之人员接收材料；

（三）依第七十条规定封存之材料，继任人或兼任人应会同所属地方检察厅检察长指定之人员解除封印，接收材料。

（全文于 2009 年 2 月 6 日修订）

第七十三条（兼任人移交材料时之准用）

前条之规定，于兼任人将有关材料移交其他公证员时，准用之。

（全文于 2009 年 2 月 6 日修订）

第七十四条（兼任者和继任者对事实的记载）

（一）兼任者为职务上签名时，应标明其为兼任者的事实。

（二）继任者根据前任或者兼任的公证员出具的公证书正本或者核准副本的，签名时应标明其为继任者的事实。

（全文于 2009 年 2 月 6 日修订）

第七十五条（材料的交接）

（一）公证员死亡、免职或转属，且因人员变动或其他事由而无继任者的，司法部长应命令将其材料移交其所属地方检察厅辖区内的其他公证员。

（二）与第一项规定的接到材料交接命令的公证员相关的事项应该适用于本法第七十二条和第七十四条第二项的规定。

（全文于 2009 年 2 月 6 日修订）

第七十六条（关于公证员停职的准用规则）

（一）公证员停职相关的事项适用本法第七十条，第七十一条，第七十二条第三项和第七十四条第一项的规定。

（二）兼任人依照第一项执行职务时，以停职者之事务所为事务所。

（全文于 2009 年 2 月 6 日修订）

제 77 조 (검사등의공증인직무수행시의준용)

검사나등기소장이제 8 조에따라공증인의직무를 수행하는경우에는제 72 조및제 73 조를준용한다 .

[전문개정 2009.2.6.]

第七十七条（检察官等执行公证员职务时的准用）

检察官或者法院登记所书记员根据第八条规定执行公证员职务的，适用本法第七十二条和第七十三条的规定。

（全文于 2009 年 2 月 6 日修订）

제 6 장의 2 대한공증인협회

(개정 2009. 2. 6.)

第二节（大韩公证员协会）

（于 2009 年 2 月 6 日修订）

제 77 조의 2(목적과설립)

① 적절하고통일된공증업무를위한지도 · 감독을 수행하고 , 공증제도의개선과발전을도모하며 , 공증인의품위를향상시키기위하여대한공증인협회를둔다 .

② 대한공증인협회는법인으로한다 .

③ 대한공증인협회는다음각호의사항을포함하는회칙을정하여법무부장관의인가를받아설립한다 . 회칙을변경하려는경우에도또한같다 .

1. 명칭과사무소의소재지
2. 회원의가입과탈퇴에관한사항
3. 총회 , 이사회 , 그밖의기관의구성 · 권한및회의에관한사항
4. 임원의선임 · 임기및직무에관한사항
5. 회원의권리와의무에관한사항
6. 회원의지도와감독에관한사항
7. 자산과회계에관한사항

[전문개정 2009.2.6.]

第七十七条第二款（目的和设立）

（一）为了对公正的和统一的公证业务进行指导和监督，谋求公证制度的改善和发展，提高公证员的品行设立了大韩公证员协会。

（二）大韩公证员协会为法人。

（三）大韩公证员协会以下列各条为其会章，并经司法部长同意设立。会章之变更亦须经司法部长同意。

1. 名称和事务所所在地；
2. 入会和退会相关事项；
3. 大会、理事会和其他内设机构之组成、权限和会议相关的事项；
4. 委员的选任、任期和职务相关的事项；
5. 会员的权利和义务的相关事项；
6. 会员指导和监督的相关事项；
7. 资产和协会账目相关事项。

（全文于 2009 年 2 月 6 日修订）

제 77 조의 3(입회의무)

① 공증인은대한공증인협회의회원으로가입하여야한다 .

② 인가공증인은공증담당변호사중에서대표자 1 명을선정하여대한공증인협회회원으로서의권리를 행사하고의무를수행한다 .

③ 인가공증인의공증담당변호사는대한공증인 협회의준회원이된다 .

[본조신설 2009.2.6.]

第七十七条第三款（入会义务）

（一）公证员应该加入大韩公证员协会成为会员。

（二）认可公证员的公证律师应该选举出一名代表加入大韩公证员协会行使权利和履行义务。

（三）认可公证员中的公证律师是大韩公证员协会的准会员。

（本条于 2009 年 2 月 6 日新增）

제 77 조의 4(임원)

①대한공증인협회에는다음각호의임원을둔다 .

1. 협회장 1 명
2. 부협회장 5 명이내
3. 상임이사 10 명이내
4. 이사 50 명이내
5. 감사 3 명이내

②임원은총회에서선임한다 .

[본조신설 2009.2.6.]

第七十七条第四款（人员）

（一）大韩公证员协会包括下列成员。

1. 会长一名；
2. 副会长五名以内；
3. 常任理事十名以内；
4. 理事五十名以内；
5. 监事三名以内。

（二）委员由协会大会选举产生。

（本条于 2009 年 2 月 6 日新增）

제 77 조의 5(총회)

① 대한공증인협회에총회를둔다 .

第七十七条第五款（大会）

（一）大韩公证员协会召开大会。

② 총회는대한공증인협회에서회칙에따라선출한대의원으로구성한다 .

③ 다음각호의사항은총회의결의를거쳐야한다 .

1. 회칙의개정 , 규칙의제정과개정
2. 임원과운영위원의선출과해임
3. 예산과결산
4. 그밖에회칙에서정하는사항

[본조신설 2009.2.6.]

제 77 조의 6(운영위원회)

① 대한공증인협회에회칙의규정에따라운영위원회를둔다 .

② 운영위원회는대한공증인협회의운영에관한중요사항을결의한다 .

[본조신설 2009.2.6.]

제 77 조의 7(자문과건의)

대한공증인협회는공공기관의자문에답하고 , 공증사무와관련된개선사항을공공기관에건의할수있다 .

[본조신설 2009.2.6.]

제 77 조의 8(회원연수등)

① 대한공증인협회는공증인의윤리의식을함양하고전문성과직무수행능력을향상시키기위하여회원 (준회원을포함한다) 및제 23 조제 1 항에따른보조자를상대로연수교육을하여야한다 .

② 연수교육의시간 , 방식 , 절차와그밖에필요한사항은대한공증인협회가정한다 .

③ 대한공증인협회의장은매년 1 월말일까지전년도에실시한연수교육상황과실적을법무부장관에게보고하여야한다 .

[본조신설 2009.2.6.]

제 77 조의 9(공증서류의통합보관)

① 대한공증인협회는법무부장관의허가를받아공증인을대신하여제 24 조제 1 항각호에따른서류등과제 66 조의 8 제 1 항・제 2 항에따른정보 , 전자문서등을통합보관할수있는시설을설치・운영할수있다 . 이경우그시설기준및허가절차등에관하여는법무부령으로정한다 .

② 제 1 항에따라대한공증인협회가통합보관하는서류등 , 정보및전자문서등은공증인이보존하거나보관하는것으로본다 .

③ 법무부장관은대한공증인협회가제 1 항에따른시설을갖추지못하는경우그허가를취소할수있다 . 이경우청문을거쳐야한다 .

④ 제 1 항에따른통합보관의절차 , 비용및그밖에필요한사항은대한공증인협회가정한다 .

（二）大会由根据大韩公证员协会会章选举的成员组成。

（三）下列事项是由大会决议的事项：

1. 会章的变更，规则的制定和变更；
2. 委员和运营委员的选举和解职；
3. 预算和决算；
4. 其他会章规定的事项。

（本条于 2009 年 2 月 6 日新增）

第七十七条第六款（运营委员会）

（一）大韩公证员协会根据协会规定设立运营委员会。

（二）运营委员会负责对大韩公证员协会运营有关的重要事项进行决议。

（本条于 2009 年 2 月 6 日新增）

第七十七条第七款（质询和建议）

大韩公证员协会对公共机关的质询进行回答，并就公证和相关事宜之改善向公共机关提出建议。

（本条于 2009 年 2 月 6 日新增）

第七十七条第八款（会员培训等）

（一）大韩公证员协会为了培养公证员的伦理性和提高职务能力的专门性应该对会员和根据本法第二十三条第二项规定的能力不足者进行培训教育。

（二）培训的时间、方式、步骤和其他必要事项由大韩公证员协会决定。

（三）大韩公证员协会会长应于每年一月底前，向司法部长报告上一年度的培训情况和实效。

（本条于 2009 年 2 月 6 日新增）

第七十七条第九款（公证材料的统一保管）

（一）大韩公证员协会经司法部长同意，可代替公证员建立并运行设施，用以统一保管第二十四条第一项规定的各种材料和第六十六条第八款第一项、第二项规定的信息、电子文书等。这种情况下，设备的标准和许可的程序等相关事项由司法部令规定。

（二）第一项中规定的由大韩公证员协会统一保管的材料等，信息和电子文件可以看作是由公证员保存或者保管的。

（三）大韩公证员协会如不具备第一项规定的增设设施的条件，司法部长可以取消许可。取消许可应公开进行。

（四）根据第一项同意保管的程序，费用和其他必需的事项是由大韩公证员协会决定的。

[본조신설 2009.2.6.]

제 77 조의 10(감독)

① 대한공증인협회는법무부장관의감독을받는다 .

② 대한공증인협회는총회의결의내용을지체없이법무부장관에게보고하여야한다 .

③ 법무부장관은제 2 항의결의내용이법령을위반한다고인정하면취소할수있다 .

[본조신설 2009.2.6.]

제 77 조의 11(위임규정)

대한공증인협회의조직 · 운영등에관하여그밖에필요한사항은대통령령으로정한다 .

[본조신설 2009.2.6.]

제 7 장감독과징계

(개정 2009. 2. 6.)

제 78 조 (감독기관)

① 공증인은법무부장관이감독한다 .

② 법무부장관은공증인에대한감독권의일부를지방검찰청검사장에게위임하거나대한공증인협회의장에게위탁할수있다 .

[전문개정 2009.2.6.]

제 79 조 (감독권의내용)

제 78 조제 1 항의감독권은다음각호의사항을포함한다 .

1. 공증인의부적절한직무수행에관하여주의를촉구하거나적절하게직무를취급하도록지시하는것

2. 직무내외를불문하고공증인의지위에적합하지아니한사항이있는경우에는이에관하여경고하는것 . 이경우경고하기전에그공증인에게변명의기회를주어야한다 .

[전문개정 2009.2.6.]

제 80 조 (서류의검열)

법무부장관은소속직원에게공증인이보존하거나보관하는서류등을검열하게할수있다 .

[전문개정 2009.2.6.]

제 81 조 (이의신청)

① 촉탁인이나이해관계인은공증인의사무취급에관하여소속지방검찰청검사장에게이의를신청할수있다 .

② 제 1 항의이의에대한지방검찰청검사장의처분에관하여는다시법무부장관에게이의를신청할수있다 .

③ 제 1 항및제 2 항에따른이의신청및처리절차

（本条于 2009 年 2 月 6 日新增）

第七十七条第十款（监督）

（一）大韩公证员协会接受司法部长的监督。

（二）大韩公证员协会大会的决议内容应该立即向司法部长报告。

（三）司法部长如果认为第二项中的决议内容违法的，可予以撤销。

（本条于 2009 年 2 月 6 日新增）

第七十七条第十一款（委任规定）

关于大韩公证员协会的组织、运营和其他必要相关事项由大总统令直接规定。

（本条于 2009 年 2 月 6 日新增）

第七章　领导和异议

（于 2009 年 2 月 6 日改定）

第七十八条（领导机关）

（一）公证员受司法部长监督。

（二）司法部长将对于公证员的监督权部分赋予地方检察厅检察长，部分赋予大韩公证员协会会长。

（全文于 2009 年 2 月 6 日修订）

第七十九条（监督权的内容）

根据第七十八条第一项的规定，监督权包含下列内容。

1. 纠正公证员不适当的职务行为，令其正当履职。

2. 无论职务内容，只要公证员作出不符其职务之事项，即可予以警告。在给予警告处分之前要给予公证员辩明的机会。

（全文于 2009 年 2 月 6 日修订）

第八十条（材料的检阅）

司法部长可以让下属职员对公证员保存或者保管的材料进行检阅。

（全文于 2009 年 2 月 6 日修订）

第八十一条（异议申请）

（一）委托人或者利害关系人可以就公证事务相关的问题，向所属的地方检察厅检察长提出异议申请。

（二）对地方检察厅检察长根据第一项作出之决定不满的，也可以再次向司法部长提出异议申请。

（三）与第一项、第二项规定的异议申请和处理程序相关的事项由司法部令规定。

등에관한사항은법무부령으로정한다 .

[전문개정 2009.2.6.]

제 82 조 (징계사유및보고)

①법무부장관은공증인이다음각호의어느하나에 해당하면제 85 조에따른공증인징계위원회에징계의 결을요구하여야한다 .

1. 이법및이법에따른명령을위반한경우

2. 감독권자의직무상명령또는그밖의직무상의 무를위반하거나품위를손상하는행위를한경우

3. 대한공증인협회의회칙을위반한경우

②지방검찰청검사장및대한공증인협회의장은공 증인에게징계사유가있다고인정되면지체없이법무부 장관에게보고하여야한다 .

③제 1 항에따른징계의결요구는징계사유가발생 한날부터 3 년이지나면하지못한다 .

[전문개정 2009.2.6.]

제 83 조 (징계의종류)

공증인에대한징계의종류는다음각호와같다 .

1. 해임 (인가공증인의경우에는인가취소)

2. 1 년이하의정직

3. 1 천만원이하의과태료

4. 견책

[전문개정 2009.2.6.]

제 84 조 (징계기관)

공증인에대한징계는제 85 조에따른공증인징계 위원회의의결에따라법무부장관이한다 .

[전문개정 2009.2.6.]

제 84 조의 2(인가공증인에대한징계)

인가공증인의공증담당변호사에게징계사유가있 는경우에는해당공증담당변호사뿐만아니라인가공증 인도징계할수있다 . 다만 , 인가공증인이그위반행위 를방지하기위하여해당업무에관하여상당한주의와감 독을게을리하지아니한경우에는그러하지아니하다 .

[본조신설 2009.2.6.]

제 85 조 (징계위원회)

① 공증인에대한징계사건을심의 · 의결하기위 하여법무부에공증인징계위원회 (이하 “징계위원회” 라한다) 를둔다 .

② 징계위원회는위원장 1 명과위원 6 명으로구 성하며 , 위원이부득이한사유로직무를수행할수없을 때에는그직무를대행하게하기위하여예비위원 6 명을 둔다 .

③ 위원장은법무부차관이된다 .

④ 위원및예비위원은다음각호의사람이되며 , 임기는 2 년으로한다 .

（全文于 2009 年 2 月 6 日修订）

第八十二条（惩戒事由和报告）

（一）对有下列情形之一的公证员，法务部应向第八十五条规定的公证员惩戒委员会要求作出惩戒决议：

1. 违反本法和依法作出的命令；

2. 违反上级的职务命令或其他职务义务，或有损害品行之行为；

3. 违反大韩公证员协会会规。

（二）地方检察厅的检察长和大韩公证员协会的会长认为公证员有惩戒事由的，应立即向司法部长报告。

（三）第一项规定的惩戒决议须于惩戒事由发生之日起三年内提起，否则无效。

（全文于 2009 年 2 月 6 日修订）

第八十三条（惩戒的种类）

对公证员的惩戒如下：

1. 免职（对认可公证员，则为解除认可）；

2. 一年以下的停职；

3. 一千万以下的罚款；

4. 谴责。

（全文于 2009 年 2 月 6 日修订）

第八十四条（惩戒机关）

对于公证员的惩戒，根据本法第八十五条规定的公证员惩戒委员会的决议，由司法部长官进行惩戒。

（全文于 2009 年 2 月 6 日修订）

第八十四条第二款（关于对认可公证员的惩戒）

认可公证员的公证律师出现惩戒事由时，不但可以惩戒公证律师，而且也可以惩罚认可公证员。但若认可公证员在公证律师执行相关业务时，为防止其出现违法行为尽到了合理的注意义务，并未怠于监督，则可不受惩罚。

（本条于 2009 年 2 月 6 日新增）

第八十五条（惩戒委员会）

（一）为了对公证员的惩戒事件进行审议、决议在司法部内设立了公证员惩戒委员会（以下称惩戒委员会）。

（二）惩戒委员会由一名委员长、六名委员组成，为了当委员因不得已的原因无法执行职务时，有人替代其执行职务，设立六名预备委员。

（三）委员长为司法部的次长。

（四）委员和预备委员从下列人员中产生，任期为两年：

1. 법무부의실장・국장또는검사중에서법무부장관이지명하는 3 명

2. 공증인, 법학교수및학식과경험이풍부한사람중에서법무부장관이위촉하는사람각 1 명

⑤위원장은징계위원회의업무를총괄하고회의를소집하며그의장이된다.

⑥위원장이부득이한사유로직무를수행할수없을때에는위원장이지정하는위원이그직무를대행하고, 위원이부득이한사유로직무를수행할수없을때에는위원장이지정하는예비위원이그직무를대행한다.

[전문개정 2009.2.6.]

제 85 조의 2(징계혐의자의출석・진술권등)

① 위원장은징계심의기일을정하고징계혐의자에게출석을명할수있다.

② 징계혐의자는징계심의기일에출석하여말또는서면으로자기에게유리한사실을진술하거나필요한증거를제출할수있다.

③ 징계위원회는징계심의기일에심의를시작하고징계혐의자에대하여징계사유가되는사실과그밖에필요한사실에대하여심문할수있다.

④ 징계혐의자는변호사또는변호사에준하는학식과경험이있는사람을특별변호인으로선임하여징계사건에대한진술과증거제출을하게할수있다.

⑤ 징계위원회는직권으로또는징계혐의자나특별변호인의청구를받아감정을명하거나증인을심문할수있으며관계행정기관이나그밖의기관에대하여사실조회또는서류의제출을요청할수있다.

⑥ 징계위원회는징계혐의자가위원장의출석명령을받고징계심의기일에출석하지아니할경우에는서면으로심의할수있다.

⑦ 위원장은출석한징계혐의자나선임된특별변호인에게징계사건에대한최종의견을진술할기회를주어야한다.

[본조신설 2009.2.6.]

제 85 조의 3(제척사유)

위원장과위원은자기또는자기의친족이나친족이었던사람에대한징계사건의심의에관여하지못한다.

[본조신설 2009.2.6.]

제 85 조의 4(징계의결)

징계위원회는징계사건의심의를마치면재적위원과반수의찬성으로징계를의결한다.

[본조신설 2009.2.6.]

제 85 조의 5(과태료의집행)

① 제 83 조제 3 호에따른과태료를내지아니할때

1. 司法部长自司法部的室长、局长和检察员中指定的三人；

2. 由司法部长官委任的公证员、法学教授和博学广历者各一名。

（五）委员长总领惩戒委员会的业务，召开会议，并成为委员会的议长。

（六）委员长因不得已的原因不能执行其职务时，由委员长指定的委员代替他执行职务，委员因不得已的原因不能执行其职务时，由委员长指定的预备委员代替他执行职务。

（全文于 2009 年 2 月 6 日修订）

第八十五条第二款（惩戒嫌疑人的出席和陈述权等）

（一）委员长在确定惩戒审议的日期后可以命令惩戒嫌疑人出席。

（二）惩戒嫌疑人在惩戒审议日当天出席，可以以口头和书面的方式做对自己有利的陈述或者提交必要的证明材料。

（三）惩戒委员会在惩戒审议日开始审议，针对惩戒嫌疑人的惩戒事由的事实和其他必要的事实进行询问。

（四）惩戒嫌疑人可以委托律师或者具有律师的学识和经验的人作为自己的特别辩护人，针对惩戒事件作出陈述和提交证据。

（五）惩戒委员会凭职权或者应惩戒嫌疑人或其特别辩护人的请求下达命令或者询问证人，对于相关的行政机关或者其他的机关进行事实询问并要求其提交材料。

（六）惩戒委员会对接到委员长出席命令而不能出席的惩戒嫌疑人，以书面的方式进行审查。

（七）委员长应该给出席的惩戒嫌疑人或其委托的特别辩护人，针对惩戒事件做最终陈述意见的机会。

（本条于 2009 年 2 月 6 日新增）

第八十五条第三款（回避事由）

委员长和委员不能参加针对自己或自己的亲属或者曾经的亲属的惩戒事件的审议。

（本条于 2009 年 2 月 6 日新增）

第八十五条第四款（惩戒决议）

惩戒委员会就惩戒事由完成审议后，经所有委员过半数同意，通过惩戒决议。

（本条于 2009 年 2 月 6 日新增）

第八十五条第五款（罚款的执行）

（一）没有上交第八十三条第三点规定的罚款的，

에는검사의명령으로집행한다.

② 제 1 항의집행에관하여는「비송사건절차법」제 249 조를준용한다.

③ 공증인이낸신원보증금은제 19 조제 3 항의경우외에는다른공과금및채권보다우선하여과태료에충당한다.

[본조신설 2009.2.6.]

제 85 조의 6(위임규정)

징계위원회의운영이나그밖에징계에필요한사항은대통령령으로정한다.

[본조신설 2009.2.6.]

제 85 조의 7(「형사소송법」등의준용)

서류의송달, 기일의지정이나변경및증인·감정인의선서와급여에관한사항에대하여는「형사소송법」과「형사소송비용등에관한법률」을준용한다.

[본조신설 2009.2.6.]

제 86 조(직무정지)

① 공증인이구속되거나구류의형을받으면석방될때까지그직무가정지된다.

② 법무부장관은제 84 조에따른징계절차가개시된공증인에대하여징계결정의결과정직또는해임(인가공증인의경우인가취소)에이르게될가능성이매우크고그대로두면공정하고적절한공증사무의수행이곤란하다고인정되면징계절차가끝날때까지공증인의직무를정지시킬수있다.

③ 징계위원회는제 2 항에따라직무가정지된날부터 3 개월내에해당공증인에대하여징계에관한의결을하여야한다. 다만, 징계위원회의결정으로 3 개월의범위에서그기간을연장할수있다.

④ 공증인의직무정지에관하여는공증인의정직에관한규정을준용한다.

[전문개정 2009.2.6.]

제 86 조의 2(직무정지의해제)

법무부장관은직무정지기간중인공증인에대한징계절차의진행상황에비추어정직또는해임(인가공증인의경우에는인가취소)에이르게될가능성이크지아니하고, 공정하고적절한공증사무수행이곤란하다고인정할사유가없어졌다고인정할만한상당한이유가있으면직권으로그직무정지를해제할수있다.

[본조신설 2009.2.6.]

제 86 조의 3(직무정지기간의합산)

직무정지명령을받은공증인이해당징계사건에서정직처분을받으면직무정지기간은그전부또는일부를정직기간에포함한다.

[본조신설 2009.2.6.]

可以根据检察官的命令执行。

（二）关于第一项中的执行情况适用《非讼事件程序法》第二百四十九条的规定。

（三）公证员交的身份保证金，除第十九条第三项规定的情况外，应优先于其他国家税收及债权充抵罚款。

（本条于 2009 年 2 月 6 日新增）

第八十五条第六款（委任规定）

惩戒委员会的运营和其他有关惩戒的必要事项由大总统令规定。

（本条于 2009 年 2 月 6 日新增）

第八十五条第七款（《刑事诉讼法》等的准用）

材料的送达、日期的指定或者变更、证人和鉴定人的选举和工资相关的事项适用《刑事诉讼法》和《刑事诉讼费用等相关法律》的规定。

（本条于 2009 年 2 月 6 日新增）

第八十六条（职务中止）

（一）公证员被拘留或者被判处刑罚的，直到刑满释放前中止一切职务。

（二）司法部长根据本法第八十四条的规定公开惩戒的程序，且就惩戒结果而言公证员极有可能被停职或解职，从而对公证和公证事务的执行造成困难的，经司法部长指示，在惩戒程序终结前中止公证员的职务行为。

（三）惩戒委员会根据第二项规定对公证员停职的，应于停职之日起三个月内就惩戒措施作出决议。但是惩戒委员会可以在三个月的权限范围内进行延长。

（四）关于公证员职务中止的相关事项适用公证员停职的规则。

（全文于 2009 年 2 月 6 日修订）

第八十六条第二款（职务停止的解除）

司法部长在公证员职务停止期间，根据公证员惩罚执行的情况，对再次停止或者免职（认可公证员的情况是取消认可）的可能性不大的情况下，在有值得确信的理由认为在再次行使固定和适当的公证事务会出现困难的事由消失时，可以根据职权解除停职。

（本条于 2009 年 2 月 6 日新增）

第八十六条第三款（职务停止期间的核算）

被处以停职的公证员在惩戒程序中已先行停职的，计算停职时间时应包括先行停职的时间。

（本条于 2009 年 2 月 6 日新增）

제 8 장벌칙
(신설 2009. 2. 6.)

제 87 조(벌칙)

공증인이아니면서공증인의표시또는기재를하거나이익을얻을목적으로공증사무를취급한다는표시또는기재를한자는 3 년이하의징역또는 2 천만원이하의벌금에처한다. 이경우징역과벌금은병과(併科)할수있다.

[전문개정 2009.2.6.]

제 88 조(벌칙)

임명공증인또는인가공증인의공증담당변호사가제 66 조의 2 제 2 항을위반한경우에는 500 만원이하의벌금에처한다.

[전문개정 2009.2.6.]

제 89 조(양벌규정)

인가공증인의공증담당변호사가그인가공증인의업무에관하여제 88 조의위반행위를하면그공증담당변호사를벌하는외에그인가공증인에게도해당조문의벌금형을과(科)한다. 다만, 인가공증인이그위반행위를방지하기위하여해당업무에관하여상당한주의와감독을게을리하지아니한경우에는그러하지아니하다.

[본조신설 2009.2.6.]

제 90 조(과태료)

① 제 57 조의 2 제 1 항또는제 66 조의 5 제 2 항에따라선서를할때사서증서또는전자문서의내용이거짓이라는것을알면서선서한사람에게는 300 만원이하의과태료를부과한다.

② 제 1 항에따른과태료는해당공증인이소속된지방검찰청의검사장이부과·징수한다.

③ 제 1 항에도불구하고그위반자가자신또는제 3 자에대한재판에서자신의사서증서또는전자문서에적힌거짓내용을정정하는진술을한경우에는과태료를감경하거나면제한다.

[본조신설 2013.5.28.]

부칙(제 11823 호, 2013. 5. 28.)

제 1 조(시행일)

이법은공포후 6 개월이경과한날부터시행한다.

제 2 조(선서인증의방식및과태료부과에관한적용례)

제 57 조의 2 제 4 항부터제 6 항까지및제 90 조의개정규정은이법시행후제 57 조의 2 의개정규정에따라선서인증을하는경우부터적용한다.

第八章　罚规
（于 2009 年 2 月 6 日新增）

第八十七条（罚规）

冒充公证员，以获利为目的使用公证员或公证事务的标识和记录的，处三年以下的有期徒刑或者两千万以下的罚款，或两者并处。

（全文于 2009 年 2 月 6 日修订）

第八十八条（罚规）

任命公证员和认可公证员的公证律师如违反第六十六条第二款第二项的规定，应处五百万元以下的罚款。

（全文于 2009 年 2 月 6 日修订）

第八十九条（双罚规定）

认可公证员的公证律师，认可公证员执行业务如果违反了第八十八条规定的话，除了要惩罚公证律师，认可公证员也要受到相应的处罚。但若认可公证员在公证律师执行相关业务时，为防止其出现违法行为尽到了合理的注意义务，并未怠于监督，则可不受惩罚。

（本条于 2009 年 2 月 6 日新增）

第九十条（罚款）

（一）根据本法第五十七条第二款第一项和第六十六条第五款第二项的规定，如明知私署证书或电子文书内容虚假而进行宣誓的，对宣誓人处以三百万元以下的罚款。

（二）第一项规定的罚款应该向公证员所属的地方检察厅的检察长上交。

（三）符合第一项的规定，但违规者自己和第三者对裁判中的自己的私署证书和电子文书写的虚假内容能够进行真实性的陈述的话，可以减轻或者免除处罚。

（本条于 2013 年 5 月 28 日新增）

分则（2013 年 5 月 28 日第 11823 号令）

第一条（实行日）

本法公布六个月后生效。

第二条（宣誓公证的方式和关于罚款的适用）

第五十七条第二款第四项至第六项和第九十条的规定，从本法实行后，宣誓公证的情况开始适用于第五十七条第二款的规定。

公证法施行令

공증인법시행령

[시행 2013.11.29.] [대통령령제 24850 호 , 2013.11.20., 일부개정]
법무부 (법무과) 02-2110-3178~9

제 1 조 (목적)

이영은「공증인법」에서위임된사항과그시행에필요한사항을규정함을목적으로한다 .

[전문개정 2010.2.4.]

제 1 조의 2(임명공증인임명절차)

①「공증인법」(이하 "법" 이라한다) 제 11 조에따라임명공증인으로임명받으려는사람은법무부령으로정하는임명신청서에다음각호의서류를첨부하여법무부장관에게제출하여야한다 .

1. 주민등록표등본또는초본
2. 이력서및경력증명서
3. 사무소의설치예정지를적은서류
4.「공무원채용신체검사규정」에따른신체검사서

②법무부장관은제 1 항에따른신청서의기재사항에흠이있거나첨부서류가미비되어있으면신청인에게보완을요구할수있다 .

③법무부장관은제 1 항에따른서류를심사할때에필요하다고인정하면사실및증거조사를하거나신청인에게관련자료의제출을요구할수있다 .

④법무부장관은법제 11 조에따라공증인을임명할때에는공증인임명대장에다음각호의사항을적고 , 공증인임명서를신청인에게발급하여야한다 .

1. 임명번호및임명연월일
2. 임명공증인의성명및주소
3. 사무소의소재지
4. 제 1 호부터제 3 호까지에서규정한사항외에필요한사항

⑤법무부장관은제 4 항에따라신청인에게공증인임명서를발급하면소속지방검찰청검사장과법제 77 조의 2 에따른대한공증인협회 (이하 "대한공증인협회" 라한다) 에통지하여야한다 .

[본조신설 2010.2.4.]

公证法施行令

2013 年 11 月 29 日起实行，大总统令第 24850 号，
2013 年 11 月 20 日部分公开
司法部法务科 (02–2110–3178–9)

第一条（目的）

本法令为规范《公证法》中委任事项和与其执行必须的事项而制定。

（全文于 2012 年 2 月 4 日修订的）

第一条第二款（任命公证员的任命程序）

（一）根据《公证法》（以下称法）第十一条的规定，如欲受任公证员者，必须根据司法部令的规定向司法部长提交任命申请书和下列各种附属材料：

1. 身份证的原件和复印件；
2. 简历和经历证明书；
3. 写有事务所设立所在地的证明材料；
4.《公务员聘用身体检查规定》规定的身体检查书。

（二）司法部长认为第一项规定的申请书的记载事项有错误或者附属材料不足的话，可以要求申请人补充材料。

（三）司法部长审查第一项规定的材料时，如认为必要，可就事实和公证书进行调查，要求申请人提供相关的资料。

（四）司法部长根据法第十一条任命公证员时，在任命书上应该写明以下事项，并应向申请人发出通知：

1. 任命编号和任命年、月、日；
2. 任命公证员的姓名和住所；
3. 事务所所在地；
4. 除第一点至第三点规定事项以外的其他事项。

（五）司法部长根据第四项的规定向申请人颁发公证员任命书的同时，应通知其所属的地方检察厅检察长和本法第七十七条第二项规定的大韩公证员协会。（以下称大韩公证员协会）。

（本条于 2010 年 2 月 4 日新增）

제 1 조의 3(인가공증인인가절차)

①법제 15 조의 2 에따라공증인가를받으려는자는법무부령으로정하는인가신청서에다음각호의서류를첨부하여법무부장관에게제출하여야한다 .

1. 정관또는규약

2. 공증담당변호사로지정될변호사의이력서및경력증명서

3. 공증담당변호사로지정될변호사의「공무원채용신체검사규정」에따른신체검사서

4. 사무소의설치지또는예정지를적은서류

②법무부장관은제 1 항에따른신청서의기재사항에흠이있거나첨부서류가미비되어있으면신청인에게보완을요구할수있다 .

③법무부장관은제 1 항에따른서류를심사할때에필요하다고인정하면사실및증거조사를하거나신청인에게관련자료의제출을요구할수있다 .

④법무부장관은법제 15 조의 2 에따라공증인가를할때에는공증인인가대장에다음각호의사항을적고 , 공증인가서를신청인에게발급하여야한다 .

1. 인가번호및인가연월일

2. 인가공증인의명칭

3. 사무소의소재지

4. 공증담당변호사의성명및주소

5. 제 1 호부터제 4 호까지에서규정한사항외에필요한사항

⑤법무부장관은제 4 항에따라신청인에게공증인가서를발급하면소속지방검찰청검사장과대한공증인협회에통지하여야한다 .

[본조신설 2010.2.4.]

제 2 조 (공증인의표시등)

①공증인은그사무소 (인가공증인의경우에는주사무소만을말한다 . 이하같다) 에다음각호의구분에따라간판을게시하여야한다 .

1. 임명공증인 : 임명공증인의성명을나타낼수있는공증인 ○○○사무소라고적은간판

2. 인가공증인 : 법제 15 조의 2 에따라공증인가를받았음을나타내는간판

②인가공증인의분사무소에는 "공증인가" 또는이와유사한표시를할수없다 .

[전문개정 2010.2.4.]

제 2 조의 2 삭제 (2010. 2. 4.)

제 2 조의 3[종전제 2 조의 3 은제 37 조의 3 으로이동 (2013. 11. 20.)]

제 2 조의 4 삭제 (1993. 12. 31.)

第一条第三款（认可公证员的认可程序）

（一）根据法第十五条第二款的规定，如欲受认可为认可公证员者，必须根据司法部令的规定向司法部长提交认可申请书和下列附属材料：

1. 章程和规约；

2. 作为指定的公证律师的律师的简历和经历证明书；

3. 作为公证律师指定的律师，根据《公务员聘用身体检查规定》所做的身体检查书；

4. 写明事务所的设立地和预设地的证明材料。

（二）司法部长根据第一项的规定认为申请书的记载事项有错误或者附属材料不全的，可以要求申请人补充材料。

（三）司法部长审查第一项规定的材料的，如认为必要，可就事实和公证书进行调查，可以要求申请人提供相关的资料。

（四）根据法第十五条第二款的规定，司法部在认可公证员时，在认可书上应该写明以下事项，并应该向申请人发出通知：

1. 认可的编号和认可的年、月、日；

2. 认可公证员的名称；

3. 事务所所在地；

4. 公证律师的姓名和住所；

5. 除第一点至第四点规定外的其他必要事项。

（五）司法部长根据第四项的规定向申请人颁发公证员认可书的同时，应同时通知其所属的地方检察厅检察长和法第七十七条第二款规定的大韩公证员协会。

（本条于 2010 年 2 月 4 日新增）

第二条（公证员的标识等）

（一）公证员的事务所（认可公证员的话，主事务所，下同）应该挂有遵守以下规定，具有区分度的牌子。

1. 任命公证员：出现任命公证员姓名的"公证员某某"事务所的广告牌；

2. 认可公证员：表明按照法第十五条第二款的规定经过公证认可的广告牌。

（二）认可公证员的本事务所内不能用使用任命公证员和其他类似的标识。

（全文于 2010 年 2 月 4 日修订）

第二条第二款删除（2010 年 2 月 4 日）

第二条第三款（第二条第三款于 2013 年 11 月 20 日移动到第三十七条第三款）

第二条第四款删除（1993 年 12 月 31 日）

제 3 조 (직인)

공증인은그사무소에법무부령이정하는직인 (職印) 을비치하여야한다 . < 개정 1993.12.31., 2010.2.4., 2011.12.30.>

[전문개정 1990.10.13.]

제 3 조의 2 삭제 (1990. 10. 13.)

제 4 조 (보조자채용등의신고)

① 법제 23 조제 2 항전단의규정에의하여공증인이보조자를두고자하는때에는보조자의자필이력서 , 가족관계등록부의기본증명서및신원진술서를갖추어대한공증인협회에신고하여야한다 . < 개정 2006.6.12., 2010.2.4.>

② 법제 23 조제 2 항후단의규정에의하여공증인이보조자를교체또는해고하거나보조자가사망한때에는지체없이그사실을대한공증인협회에신고하여야한다 .< 개정 2010.2.4.>

[전문개정 1999.6.29.]

제 5 조 (보조자의서약)

공증인은보조자에대하여직무상지득한비밀을누설하지아니하겠다는뜻의서약을시켜야한다 .

제 6 조삭제 <1999.6.29.>

제 7 조 (증서기타의용지등)

① 공증사무소에서작성하는증서기타서류의용지는「행정업무의효율적운영에관한규정」의표준규격에준하여야하고 , 그용지에는공증사무소의명칭을인쇄하여야한다 . < 개정 1991.6.19., 2011.12.21.>

② 공증사무소에서사용하는서류의양식 , 작성방법 , 편철순서기타공증사무처리에관하여필요한사항은법무부령으로정한다 .

[전문개정 1990.10.13.]

제 7 조의 2(작성자의표시)

인가공증인은공증에관한문서를작성할때소속 , 사무소의소재지및명칭을적고 , 법제 15 조의 3 에따라신고된공증담당변호사가공증담당변호사라고표시한뒤서명날인하여야한다 .

[전문개정 2010.2.4.]

제 8 조 (집무시간)

공증인의집무시간은공무원의근무시간에관한규정을준용한다 .

제 9 조 (사무소내의게시)

사무소내에는보기쉬운곳에법제 7 조에따른수수료 , 일당 , 여비 , 실비및보관료 (지정공증인의사무소로한정한다 . 이하같다) 의표준액과집무시간외

第三条（职务印章）

公证员应该根据司法部令的规定向所属的事务所提交自己的职务印章。

（1993 年 12 月 31 日，2010 年 2 月 4 日，2011 年 12 月 30 日修订）（全文于 1990 年 10 月 13 日修订）

第三条第二款删除（1990 年 10 月 13 日）

第四条（书记员的雇佣等的申告）

（一）欲根据法第二十三条第二项前段的规定招收书记员的，必须向大韩公证员协会提交书记员的自书简历、家庭关系记录簿的基本证明书和新人陈述书进行申告。（2006 年 6 月 12 日，2010 年 2 月 4 日修订）

（二）出现法第二十三条第二项后段规定的书记员解职或辞退或死亡的情形的，应该立即将这一事实向大韩公证员协会进行申告。（2010 年 2 月 4 日修订）

（全文于 1996 年 6 月 29 日修订）

第五条（书记员的签约）

公证员应该跟书记员签订不得外泄通过执行职务获知的秘密的协议。

第六条删除（1999 年 6 月 29 日）

第七条（公证书其他的用纸等）

（一）在公证事务所里，除出具公证书外，其他材料的用纸应该遵守《行政业务的有效运行的相关规定》的标准规则，这些用纸上应该要印刷上公证事务所的名称。（1991 年 6 月 19 日，2011 年 12 月 21 日修订）

（二）在公证事务所里使用的材料的样式、制作的方法、编辑的顺序等其他有关公证事务处理的必要事项均由司法部令规定。

（全文于 1990 年 10 月 13 日修订）

第七条第二款（制作人的标识）

认可公证员，在制作关于公证的文书时，应该写明所属、事务所所在地和名称，法第十五条第三款的规定进行申告的公证律师，在标识公证律师的标志之后应该签名和盖章。

（全文于 2010 年 2 月 4 日修订）

第八条（职务时间）

公证员工作时间适用有关公务员工作时间的准用规则。

第九条（事务所内的布告）

在事务所内显著处应该张贴布告，公示法第七条规定的手续费、日薪、差旅费、实际费用和保管费（地点限于指定公证员的事务所，以下亦同）的收费标准，

라도긴급한사유가있는경우에는법제 2 조에따른촉탁（이하“촉탁”이라한다）에응한다는뜻을게시하여야한다 . < 개정 2010.2.4.>

和在工作时间之外因紧急事由就法第二条规定之委托事项进行的操作。（2010 年 2 月 4 日修订）

제 9 조의 2 삭제 (1993. 12. 31.)

第九条第二款删除（1993 年 12 月 31 日）

제 9 조의 3 삭제 (2010. 2. 4.)

第九条第三款删除（2010 年 2 月 4 日）

제 10 조（사무취급의순서）

공증인은특별한사유가없는한촉탁을받은순서에의하여사무를취급하여야한다 .

第十条（处理事务的顺序）

公证员在无特别的事由的情况下，应该根据接受委托的顺序处理事务。

제 11 조（촉탁의거절의경우）

① 공증인이촉탁을거절한경우에촉탁을한자（이하“촉탁인”이라한다）의청구가있으면그이유서를교부하여야한다 . < 개정 2010.2.4.>

② 제 1 항의경우에는지체없이그사유를소속지방검찰청검사장과대한공증인협회의장에게보고하여야한다 .< 개정 2010.2.4.>

第十一条（拒绝委托的情况）

（一）公证员拒绝委托人的委托时，应委托人（以下称委托人）要求，应发给委托人拒绝的理由书。（2010 年 2 月 4 日修订）

（二）在第一项的情况下应该立即将事由向所属的地方检察厅的检察长和大韩公证员协会的会长报告。（2010 年 2 月 4 日修订）

제 12 조（증서의작성과인증에의심이있는경우의조치）

① 공증인이법률행위에관한증서를작성하거나인증을함에있어서당사자의능력기타법률행위의효력에영향을미칠사항에대하여의심이있는경우에는관계인에게그뜻을말하고필요한설명을요구하여야한다 .

② 공증인이법률행위가아닌사실에관하여증서를작성함에있어서그사실로인하여영향을받을권리관계에대하여의심이있는경우에도제 1 항과같다 .

第十二条（出具公证书或进行认证时存疑时的措施）

（一）公证员就法律行为出具公证书或进行认证时，如对直接影响当事人能力和其法律行为效力的事件存疑的，应要求相关人员进行说明，并可要求其签名。

（二）公证员在制作不是关于法律行为的事实相关的公证文书时，对因此受到相关影响的权利相关人有疑义时，参照第一项的规定处理。

제 13 조（본인에대한통지）

① 증인이대리인의촉탁에의하여증서를작성한경우에는증서를작성한날로부터 3 일내에다음각호의사항을본인에게통지하여야한다 . 다만 , 대리인이본인의고용인이거나동거인인경우에는예외로한다 . < 개정 2010.2.4.>

1. 증서의건명 · 번호및작성연월일
2. 공증인의성명및사무소
3. 대리인과상대방의성명및주소
4.「민사집행법」제 56 조제 4 호에규정된사항의기재유무

②공증인이제 1 항의통지를하였을때에는증서원부의비고란에통지의요지 · 통지의방법과연월일을기재하여야한다 .

第十三条（对于本人的通知）

（一）公证员应该在接受到代理人的委托时出具公证书，从证书制作之日起三日以内应该将下列事项通知本人。但是代理人是本人的共同所有人或者是共同居住的人除外。（2010 年 2 月 4 日修订）

1. 证书的名称、编号和制作年、月、日；
2. 公证员的姓名和事务所；
3. 代理人和相对方的姓名和住所；
4.《民事执行法》第五十六条第四号的规定的事项的记载。

（二）公证员在根据第一项的规定进行通知的时候，在证书原本的预告栏上写明通知的用纸、通知的方式和通知的年、月、日。

제 14 조（동시에수개의촉탁을한경우의증명서）

① 공증인이 1 인의촉탁인으로부터동시에수개의촉탁을받은경우에그촉탁인이법제 27 조제 2 항 , 제 56 조의 2 제 6 항 , 제 59 조 , 제 63 조제 4 항 , 제 66 조의 2 제 4 항 , 제 66 조의 5 제 3 항 · 제 4 항및제 66 조의 6 제 2 항에따라공증인에게제출하여야

第十四条（同时有多个委托的情况下的证明书）

（一）公证员从一人那里接受委托，同时还接受了数个委托的情况下，委托人根据法第二十七条第二项，第五十六条第二款第六项，第五十九条，第六十三条第四项，第六十六条第二款第四项，第六十六条第五款第三项、第四项和第六十六条第六款第二项的

하는행정기관이발행한증명서(이하“증명서”라한다)는 1 부로할수있다. < 개정 1986.12.31., 2010.2.4.>

② 제 1 항의경우에는 1 개의촉탁에관한서류에그증명서원본(원본제출이불가능한때에는그사본)을철하고기타의촉탁에관한서류에는그사유를기재한서면을작성하여철하여야한다.< 개정 1986.12.31.>

제 15 조(원본의환부청구)

촉탁인이법제 40 조제 1 항에기재된부속서류의원본의환부를청구할때에는공증인은원본에갈음하여그등본을작성하고원본환부의사유와등본작성일자를기재한후이에날인하여촉탁에관한서류에철하여야한다. < 개정 1986.12.31.>

제 16 조(증서정본재교부청구)

공증인은법률행위에관한증서의정본의재교부를청구하는자가있는경우에그정본을요구하는사유에대하여의심이있는경우에는청구자에대하여그사유를증명시켜야한다.

제 17 조(수수료등예납의영수증)

공증인이촉탁인에게법제 7 조에따른수수료, 일당, 여비, 실비및보관료의개략적산정금액을예납시킨때에는영수증을교부하여야한다. < 개정 2010.2.4.>

제 18 조(장부의비치등)

①공증사무소에는다음각호의장부를비치하여야한다. < 개정 1999.6.29.>

1. 증서원부·인증부·접수부·확정일자부및신탁표시부

2. 공정증서원본철·사서증서인증서사본철·정관인증서철및거절증서등본연철장

3. 신청서철·계산서철및면식부

4. 공증사무소규약철또는정관철·보조자신고철·공증업무처리현황보고서철및공증서류검열부

②제 1 항의장부의서식과편철순서는법무부령으로정한다.

[전문개정 1990.10.13.]

제 19 조(기입순서)

증서원부와인증부에는미리등부번호를인쇄하여두고청구의순서에따라기재하여야한다.

제 20 조(증서원부인증등)

① 증서원부와인증부는공증인또는대한공증인협회가조제(調製)한것을사용하되, 그기재전에법무부장관의인증을받아야한다. < 개정 2011.12.30.>

② 증서원부와인증부에는법무부장관이그매수

规定应该向公证员提交的行政机关发布的证明书，公证员可以以接到第一份证明书的时间为准。（1986 年 12 月 31 日、2010 年 2 月 4 日修订）

（二）根据第一项的规定一个相关委托的文件的证明书的原件（在原件不能提供的情况下可提供副本）装订，其他的与委托相关的材料的记载事由制作成书面形式并进行装订。（1986 年 12 月 31 日修订）

第十五条（原本的还本要求）

委托人在对根据法第四十条第一项的规定记载的附属资料的原本要求更换的时候，对原本进行复印并制作核准副本将原本更换的事由和核准副本的制作日期记载后进行盖章，并将委托相关的材料进行装订。（1986 年 12 月 31 日修订）

第十六条（证书正本的再交付要求）

公证员在有人对关于法律行为相关的证书正本要求再次交付的情况下，如果他对正本要求的事由有所怀疑的话，可以让请求人自己证明事由的正当性。

第十七条（手续费等的预纳金的发票）

公证员应该向委托人交付要求他们预先缴纳的根据法第七条的规定的手续费、日工资、差旅费、实际费用的保管费的大概金额的发票。（2010 年 2 月 4 日修订）

第十八条（账簿的公开等）

（一）在公证事务所内部应该公布以下规定的账簿内容：

1. 证书原本，认证簿，接受簿，确定日期簿和信托标识簿；

2. 公证书原本册，私署证书认证书手抄本册，章程认证册和拒绝认证证书的核准副本的连册；

3. 申请书册，决算册和面识簿；

4. 公证事务所规约册和规章册，辅助人申告册，公证业务处理现状报告书和公证材料审查簿。

（二）第一项中规定的账簿的形式和编辑顺序是由司法部令规定的。

（全文是 1990 年 10 月 13 日修订）

第十九条（计入的顺序）

证书原本和认证簿，应该预先印刷好核准副本的号码，并根据要求的顺序进行记录。

第二十条（公证原本的认证等）

（一）公证书的原本和认证簿不是由公证员和大韩公证员协会制作并使用的，记载之前应该受到司法部长的认证。（2011 年 12 月 30 日修订）

（二）司法部长在公证书原本和认证本的封面的

를표지의뒷면에기재하고기명하여직인을압날한후 직인으로간인(間印)하여야한다. 다만, 직인의 간인은천공(穿孔)방식으로갈음할수있다.< 개정 1990.10.13., 2011.12.30.>

③ 법제78조제2항에따라법무부장관은제1항및제2항에따른인증에관한업무를대한공증인협회의장에게위탁한다.< 신설 2011.12.30.>

[제목개정 2011.12.30.]

제21조(접수번호)

접수번호는매년새로이정하여야한다.

제22조(주민등록증등에의하지아니한증명)

공증인이인증부여의촉탁을받은경우에주민등록증이나기타본인임을증명하는서류에의하지아니하고 본인임을증명하였을때에는그사유를인증부비고란에 기재하여야한다. < 개정 1986.12.31.>

제23조(촉탁인이다수인경우의기재방법)

① 증서원부에촉탁인의성명을기재하여야할경우에촉탁인이 2인이상인때에는당사자쌍방각 1인만을기재하고그외의자에대하여는그인원수만을기재한다.

② 정관및의사록의인증에관하여인증부에촉탁인의성명과주소또는서명날인자의성명을기재할경우에그인원이 2인이상인때에도제1항과같다.< 개정 1986.12.31.>

③ 공증인이정관및의사록의인증을할때에는인증부의비고란에회사의명칭을기재하여야한다.< 개정 1986.12.31.>

제24조(서류의접수와목록)

① 법제72조·제73조·제75조및제76조의규정에의하여서류를접수한경우에는서류의목록을작성하고그끝에접수의사유및연월일을기재하고이에참여한공무원이있을때에는그공무원및접수자가서명·날인하여야한다.

② 공증인은제1항의규정에의하여작성한서류의목록의등본을지체없이소속지방검찰청검사장에게 제출하여야한다.

제25조(겸무명령에의한겸무자의겸무취급)

① 법제71조제1항의규정에의한겸무자는자기의사무소에서전임자의사무를취급할수있다.

② 제1항의경우에는지체없이그사유를법무부장관에게신고하여야한다.

제26조(대리자·후임자·겸무자의제시)

공증인의대리자·후임자또는법제71조의규정에의한겸무자는그직무를행하는사무소의보기쉬운곳

背面记载买受的内容后签名并盖章之后应该盖上职务印章。但是职务印章的间印可以以穿孔的方式进行。（1990年10月13日，2011年12月30日修订）

（三）根据法第七十八条第二项的规定司法部长根据第一项和第二项的规定将与公证相关的业务委托给大韩公证员协会会长。（2011年12月30日新增）

（标题是2011年12月30日修订的）

第二十一条（接受号码）

接受号码是每年都应该更新变化的。

第二十二条（不依靠身份证的证明）

公证员在接受认证有无的委托的情况下在不依赖公民身份证或者其他能证明本人的材料是证明本人的时候应该将其事由记录在认证本的预告栏上。（1986年12月31日修订）

第二十三条（委托人是多数人的情况的记载方法）

（一）在公证书原件上应该记录委托人的签名的时候，委托人是两人以上的情况下，当事人双方应该各记录其中一名，对于其他的人员来说，只记载人员数目就可以了。

（二）章程和议事录的相关的认证，要记载委托人的姓名和住所和签名盖章的人的姓名的记载的情况下，如果是人员在两名以上的情况下与第一项的规定相同。（1986年12月31日修订）

（三）公证员在公证章程和议事录的认证时应该在认证本的预告栏上记录下公司的名称。（1986年12月31日修订）

第二十四条（文件的接受和目录）

（一）根据法第七十二条、第七十三条、第七十五条和第七十六条的规定，在接受材料的时候，应该制作材料的目录，在目录的结尾处应该记载接收的事由和年、月、日，接受材料有公务员在场的情况下，公务员和接受者都应该签名和盖章。

（二）公证员根据第一项的规定制作的材料的目录的核准副本应该立即提交给所属的地方检察厅的检察长。

第二十五条（根据兼任命令的兼任者的兼任职务）

（一）根据法第七十一条第一项的规定，兼任者应该从事的是他们事务所的前任的职务。

（二）遇到第一项的情况应该立即将其事由向司法部长进行报告。

第二十六条（代理人、继任者和兼任者的公示）

公证员的代理人，继任者和根据法第七十一条的规定的兼任者，在其执行职务的事务所的显眼的地

에대리자, 후임자또는겸무자로서직무를수행한다는뜻을게시하여야한다. < 개정 2010.2.4.>

제 27 조 (후임자작성문서의번호)

후임자가작성하는문서의번호는전임자또는겸무자가작성한문서번호의순서에따라기재하여야한다.

제 28 조 (직무를집행할수없는경우의신고)

공증인이질병기타부득이한사유로인하여직무를집행할수없는경우에다른공증인에게그직무의대행을촉탁할수없을때에는지체없이그사유를소속지방검찰청검사장에게신고하여야한다. 공증인이그직무를다시집행할수있게된경우에도또한같다.

제 29 조 (성명 · 주소의변경, 면직 · 사망의신고)

① 공증인이그성명또는주소를변경하였거나면직된경우에는지체없이그사유를소속지방검찰청검사장에게신고하여야한다.

② 제 1 항의규정은공증인이사망한경우에그직계비속에대하여이를준용한다.

제 30 조 (법무부장관의지시)

공증인이공증사무를취급함에있어서의심이있을때에는법무부장관의지시를받아공증사무를처리하여야한다. < 개정 2010.2.4.>

[제목개정 2010.2.4.]

제 31 조 (법무부장관에대한서류의제출)

공증인이법무부장관에게서류를제출할경우에는소속지방검찰청검사장을거쳐야한다. 다만, 긴급한사유가있는경우에는예외로한다.

제 32 조 (공증인명부)

지방검찰청검사장은공증인명부를갖추어두고, 이에다음각호의사항을기재하여야한다. < 개정 2010.2.4.>

1. 임명공증인 : 공증인의성명, 주소, 생년월일및사무소의소재지

2. 인가공증인 : 명칭, 사무소의소재지, 공증담당변호사의성명, 주소및생년월일

제 33 조 (면직사유등의보고)

지방검찰청검사장은소속공증인이법제 13 조, 제 15 조제 1 항 · 제 3 항 (제 15 조의 4 제 3 항에서준용하는경우를포함한다), 제 15 조의 4 제 2 항또는제 15 조의 8 제 1 항에해당하는사유가있다고인정할때에는즉시이를법무부장관에게보고하여야한다. 공증인이성명또는주소를변경하거나사망한경우에도또한같다. < 개정 2010.2.4.>

方，公示他们作为代理人、继任者和兼任者执行职务的相关的信息。（2010 年 2 月 4 日修订）

第二十七条（继任者制作文书的编号）

继任者制作的文书的编号和前任者和兼任者制作的文书的编号应该按顺序进行记载。

第二十八条（不能履行职务时的申告）

公证员疾病或者因其他不得已的事由不能履行职务的时候，如果找不到其他可以代替的公证员代替履行职务的时候，应该立即将这一事由向其所属的地方检察厅的检察长进行申告。公证员如果可以再次执行职务的情况也是履行这一程序。

第二十九条（姓名、住所的变更，免职、死亡的申告）

（一）公证员在姓名和住所的变更或者是免职的情况下，应该立即将事由向所属的地方检察厅的检察长申告。

（二）根据第一项的规定公证员死亡的情况下适用于相关的职权非属的相关规定。

第三十条（司法部长的指示）

公证员在执行公证事务的时候有怀疑的情况下，应该接受司法部长的指示来处理公证事务。（2010 年 2 月 4 日修订）

（标题是 2010 年 2 月 4 日修订的）

第三十一条（应该向司法部长提交的材料）

公证员向司法部长官提交材料的时候应该知会所属的地方检察厅的检察长。但是，在有紧急情况的时候除外。

第三十二条（公证员任命名册）

地方检察厅检察长会制作公证员任命名册，记录以下所列各项事项。（2010 年 2 月 4 日修订）

1. 任命公证员：公证员的姓名，住所，出生年、月、日和事务所所在地；

2. 认可公证员：名称，事务所所在地，公证吕的姓名，住所和出生年、月、日。

第三十三条（免职事由等的报告）

地方检察厅的检察长，如果认为所属的公证员有法第十五条第一项、第三项（包含第十五条第四款第三项的准用情况），第十五条第四款第二项和第十五条第八款第一项的事由的情况下，应该立即将这一事实向司法部长报告。公证员的姓名和住所要变更的情况或者是死亡的情况下是相同的。（2010 年 2 月 4 日修订）

제 34 조 (재임명및재인가)

① 임기만료후재임명을원하는임명공증인은법제 15 조제 1 항의규정에의한임기만료 3 개월전에 , 법제 15 조의 8 제 1 항에따른유효기간만료후재인가를원하는인가공증인은유효기간만료 3 개월전에소속지방검찰청검사장을거쳐법무부장관에게서면으로재임명또는재인가를신청하여야한다 . < 개정 2010.2.4.>

② 제 1 항의신청이있는경우에는당해지방검찰청검사장은공증인의신청서에의견서를첨부하여법무부장관에게상신하여야한다 .

③ 법무부장관은제 1 항에따른공증인의재임명또는재인가를한경우소속지방검찰청검사장과대한공증인협회에통지하여야한다 .< 신설 2010.2.4.>

[전문개정 1982.3.8.]

[제목개정 2010.2.4.]

제 35 조 (임기또는유효기간만료후의집무)

제 34 조제 1 항의규정에의하여재임명또는재인가의신청을한공증인은그임기또는유효기간이만료되더라도재임명또는재인가여부가결정될때까지그직무를집행할수있다 . < 개정 1982.3.8., 2010.2.4.>

[제목개정 2010.2.4.]

제 36 조 (합동사무소)

2 인이상의임명공증인이사무의합리화또는품위의향상을도모하기위하여필요한경우에는합동사무소를설치할수있다 . < 개정 2010.2.4.>

제 37 조 (합동사무소의설치절차)

① 임명공증인이합동사무소를설치하고자할때에는규약을정하여법무부장관의인가를받아야한다 . 규약을변경하고자할때에도또한같다 . < 개정 2010.2.4.>

② 제 1 항의규약에는다음각호의사항을정하여야한다 .

1. 명칭
2. 사무소의소재지
3. 구성원에관한사항
4. 임원에관한사항
5. 수입에관한사항
6. 경비에관한사항
7. 가입 · 탈퇴에관한사항

제 37 조의 2(특정동산의범위)

법제 56 조의 3 제 1 항본문에서 "대통령령으로정하는동산" 이란「민법」제 99 조제 2 항의동산중다음각호의어느하나에해당하지아니하는것을말한다 .

1.「선박법」에따라등록된선박

第三十四条（再任命和再认可）

（一）任期满后，想要获得再次任命的任命公证员根据法第十五条第一项的规定的任期满之前的三个月前，法第十五条第八款第一项的规定在有效时间届满后想要获得再次认可的认可公证员在有效期间届满三个月之前，要向所属的地方检察厅检察长和司法部长提交书面的再任命和再认可的申请。（2010 年 2 月 4 日修订）

（二）在收到根据第一项的规定的申请的情况下，当值的地方检察厅的检察长应该制作好公证员申请书的意见书，并和申请书一块向司法部长报告。

（三）司法部长在根据第一项的规定对公证员再任命和再认可的情况下，应该通知所属的地方检察厅检察长和大韩公证员协会。（2010 年 2 月 4 日新增）

（全文 1982 年 3 月 8 日修订）

（标题是 2010 年 2 月 4 日修订的）

第三十五条（任期和有效时间期满后的职务）

根据第三十四条第一项的规定，申请再任命和再认可的公证员在任期或者是有效期间届满后，直到决定再任命或者再认可与否之前一直执行职务。

（1982 年 3 月 8 日，2010 年 2 月 4 日修订）

（标题是 2010 年 2 月 4 日修订的）

第三十六条（联合事务所）

为了提高两个以上任命公证员的事务的合力和行为，在必要的情况下，会设立联合事务所。（2010 年 2 月 4 日修订）

第三十七条（联合事务所的设立程序）

（一）任命公证员想要设立联合公证事务所的时候，应该要约定规约并且得到司法部长的认可。想要变更规约的时候也是如此。（2010 年 2 月 4 日修订）

（二）第一项中所提及的规约应该包含下列所列各项事项：

1. 名称；
2. 事务所所在地；
3. 与成员相关的事项；
4. 与高级管理人员相关的事项；
5. 关于加入的事项；
6. 与经费相关的事项；
7. 与加入、退出相关的事项。

第三十七条第二款（特定动产的范围）

法第五十六条第三款第一项正文中的"依据大总统令规定的动产"是指《民法》第九十九条第二项的动产中不属于以下列举的任何一项的动产：

1. 根据《船舶法》规定登记的船舶；

2.「건설기계관리법」에따라등록된건설기계

3.「자동차관리법」에따라등록된자동차

4.「항공법」에따라등록된항공기

5.「공장및광업재단저당법」에따라공장재단이나광업재단으로등기된기업재산

6. 그밖에다른법령에따라등기되거나등록된동산

[본조신설 2013.11.20.]

2. 根据《建设机器管理法》登记的建设机器；

3. 根据《车辆管理法》登记的车辆；

4. 根据《航空法》登记的航空器；

5. 根据《工程和矿业财团抵押法》的规定以工程财团或者矿业财团身份登记的企业财团；

6. 其他的根据其他法令规定登记活动登录的动产。

（本条是 2013 年 11 月 20 日新增的）

제 37 조의 3(의사록인증제외대상법인)

법제 66 조의 2 제 1 항단서에서 "대통령령이정하는공법인또는비영리법인" 이란「민법」제 32 조에따라주무관청의허가를받아설립된비영리법인또는공법인중다음의요건을모두갖춘법인으로서주무관청의추천을받아법무부장관이지정·고시하는법인을말한다.

1. 설립목적및수행사무가공익적일것

2. 주무관청의감독으로법인총회등의결의절차와내용의진실성에대한분쟁의소지가없을것

[전문개정 2010.2.4.]

[제 2 조의 3 에서이동 <2013.11.20.>]

第三十七条第三款（除了议事录认证之外的法人）

法第六十六条第二款第一项的规定根据大总统令规定的公法人和非营利性的法人是指根据《民法》第三十二条的规定得到主管机关的同意后设立的非营利性法人，还有作为公法人又同时具备以下的要件，作为法人得到主管机关的推荐并由司法部长指定的法人。

1. 设立的目标和执行的事务是公益性的；

2. 接受主管机关的领导，法人大会等的决议程序和内容的真实性没有可以争论的余地。

（全文是 2010 年 2 月 4 日修订的）

（本条是 2013 年 11 月 20 日从本法第二条第三款处移动过来的）

제 38 조(지정공증인의시설)

법제 66 조의 3 제 1 항에서 "대통령령으로정하는시설" 이란다음각호와같다.

1. 전자문서또는전자화문서에대한인증사무를처리하는데에적합한바닥면적 16 제곱미터이상의사무실

2. 전자문서또는전자화문서에대한인증이가능하도록이동식저장매체의지원이가능하고정보통신망에연결되어있는인증사무용컴퓨터및프린터등그사용에필요한주변기기

3. 스캐너등전자화문서를작성하는데에사용되는화상입력장치

4. 그밖에전자문서또는전자화문서에대한인증사무처리에필요하여법무부장관이고시한시설또는설비

[본조신설 2010.7.26.]

第三十八条（指定公证员的设施的）

法第六十六条第三款第一项中规定的根据大总统令规定的设施是指以下所列的几项：

1. 处理关于电子文书和电子化文书的认证事务的地方应该有适当的面积，至少要十六平方米以上的办公室；

2. 关于使电子文书和电子化文书的认证成为可能的移动式的储存媒体的支援，可以连接信息通信系统的认证事务用的电脑和打印机等在使用时所必须的周边机器；

3. 扫描仪等制作电子化文书的时候使用的影像输入装置；

4. 除此之外的处理关于电子文书和电子化文书的认证事务所必需的由司法部长指示的设施和设备。

（本条是 2010 年 7 月 26 日新增的）

제 38 조의 2(지정공증인의지정절차등)

① 법무부장관은법제 66 조의 3 제 2 항에따른공증인의지정신청을심사할때현장조사등필요한조사를하거나신청인에게관련자료의제출을요구할수있다.

② 법무부장관은법제 66 조의 3 제 1 항에따라지정공증인을지정한경우에는제 1 조의 2 제 4 항의공증인임명대장또는제 1 조의 3 제 4 항의공증인인가대장에지정번호및지정연월일을부기하여야한다.

③ 법무부장관은법제 66 조의 3 제 1 항에따라지정공증인을지정하면소속지방검찰청검사장과대한

第三十八条第二款（指定公证员的指定程序等）

（一）司法部长可以根据法第六十六条第三款第二项的规定在审查公证员的指定申请的时候进行现场调查等必要的调查或者要求申请人提交相关的资料。

（二）司法部长应该根据法第六十六条第三款第一项的规定在指定指定公证员的时候，根据第一条第二款第四项的公证员的任命通知和第一条第三款第四项的认可通知书上记载指定编号和指定的年、月、日。

（三）司法部长根据法第六十六条第三款第一项的规定在指定指定公证员的同时应该通知所属的地方

공증인협회에통지하여야한다.

④ 법제 66 조의 3 제 1 항에따른지정의유효기간은그공증인의임기로한다.

[본조신설 2010.7.26.]

제 38 조의 3(전자문서에대한전자서명)

법제 66 조의 5 제 1 항제 1 호에따른전자문서에대한인증은촉탁인으로하여금지정공증인앞에서전자문서에전자서명을하게하는방법으로한다.

[본조신설 2010.7.26.]

제 39 조 (대한공증인협회의설립인가신청등)

대한공증인협회는법제 77 조의 2 제 3 항에따라설립인가또는회칙변경인가를신청하려면신청서에다음각호의서류를첨부하여야한다.

1. 회칙
2. 회칙작성에관한회의록

[전문개정 2010.2.4.]

제 39 조의 2(총회)

① 대한공증인협회는총회를개최하려는경우에는그일시, 장소및의제를총회개최 1 주전까지법무부장관에게보고하여야한다.

② 대한공증인협회는법제 77 조의 10 제 2 항에따라총회의결의내용을보고할때에는그총회의의사록사본을첨부하여야한다.

[본조신설 2010.2.4.]

제 40 조삭제 (2010. 2. 4.)

제 41 조삭제 (2010. 2. 4.)

제 42 조 (대한공증인협회의건의등)

대한공증인협회는공증사무와공증제도에관하여법무부장관에게건의하거나그자문에응할수있다. <개정 2010.2.4.>

[본조신설 1999.6.29.]

[제목개정 2010.2.4.]

제 43 조 (공증인징계위원회의사무직원)

① 법제 85 조에따른공증인징계위원회 (이하 "징계위원회" 라한다) 의운영을위하여징계위원회에간사와서기각 1 명을둔다.

② 간사와서기는법무부소속공무원중에서법무부장관이임명한다.

③ 간사는위원장의명을받아징계에관한기록등서류의작성과보관에관한사무에종사하며, 서기는간사를보조한다.

[본조신설 2010.2.4.]

检察厅的检察长和大韩公证员协会。

（四）法第六十六条第三款第一项规定的指定的有效期间就是公证员的任期。

（本条是 2010 年 7 月 26 日新增的）

第三十八条第三款（关于电子文书的电子签名）

根据法第六十六条第五款第一项的规定关于电子文书的认证是公证员让委托人在指定公证员面前在电子文书上进行电子签名的方式进行公证的。

（本条是 2010 年 7 月 26 日新增的）

第三十九条（大韩公证员协会的成立的认可申请等）

大韩公证员协会根据法第七十七条第二款第三项的规定想要进行设立许可和会章变更的许可的申请的话，在申请书中应该包含以下几项所列的材料：

1. 会章；
2. 制作会章相关的会议录。

（全文是 2010 年 2 月 4 日修订的）

第三十九条第二款（大会）

（一）大韩公证员协会如果想要召开大会的话应该在开会之前的一周前把开会的日期、场所和议题报告给司法部长。

（二）大韩公证员协会根据法第七十七条第十款第二项的规定报告大会决议的内容时应该包含大会议事录的手写本。

（本条是 2010 年 2 月 4 日新增的）

第四十条删除（2010 年 2 月 4 日）

第四十一条删除（2010 年 2 月 4 日）

第四十二条（大韩公证员协会的建议等）

大韩公证员协会可以对公证事务和公证制度相关的事项向司法部长提供建议或者回答质询。（2010 年 2 月 4 日修订）

（本条是 1999 年 6 月 29 日新增的）

（标题在 2010 年 2 月 4 日修订）

第四十三条（公证员惩戒委员会的事务职员）

（一）根据法第八十五条的规定为了维持公证员惩戒委员会（以下称惩戒委员会）的正常运营，惩戒委员会设立干事和秘书各一名。

（二）干事和秘书是由司法部长在司法部中所有的公务员中任命的。

（三）干事是根据委员长的命令记录关于惩戒的一些事项等，从事材料的制作和保管相关的事务，秘书是负责辅佐干事的。

（本条是 2010 年 2 月 4 日新增的）

제 44 조 (예비심사)

① 징계위원회는징계사건의심의에필요하다고인정할때에는위원을지정하여심의기일전에예비심사를하게할수있다 .

② 제 1 항의예비심사에관하여법제 85 조의 2 제 2 항부터제 6 항까지의규정을준용한다 .

[본조신설 2010.2.4.]

제 45 조 (징계의양정)

징계위원회는공증인의직무성적 , 직무위반의정도 , 그밖의사정을고려하여징계여부 , 징계의종류및징계의정도를정하여야한다 .

[본조신설 2010.2.4.]

제 46 조 (간사의참여와심의기록의작성)

① 간사는징계사건의심의에참여하여심의기록을작성하고위원장과함께이에서명날인하여야한다 .

② 제 44 조에따른예비심사에참여한간사는심의기록을작성하고심사에관여한위원과함께이에서명날인하여야한다 .

[본조신설 2010.2.4.]

제 47 조 (징계결정서의작성)

① 징계위원회가징계를의결하였을때에는결정서를작성하여위원장과심의에관여한위원이이에서명날인하여야한다 .

② 징계에관한의결결과는징계혐의자에게송달하고 , 관할지방검찰청검사장과대한공증인협회의장에게통지하여야한다 .

[본조신설 2010.2.4.]

제 48 조 (징계심의의정지)

징계사건에관하여공소가제기된때에는그사건에대한재판이확정될때까지징계심의를정지하여야한다 .

[본조신설 2010.2.4.]

제 49 조 (징계위원회의면직의결절차)

법제 14 조제 2 항에따른의결절차에관하여는법제 85 조의 2, 제 85 조의 3, 제 85 조의 4, 제 85 조의 7, 이영제 44 조제 1 항 , 제 46 조및제 47 조를준용한다 .

[본조신설 2010.2.4.]

제 50 조 (민감정보및고유식별정보의처리)

①법무부장관 (법제 78 조제 2 항에따라법무부장관의권한을위임받거나위탁받은자를포함한다) 은다음각호의사무를수행하기위하여불가피한경우「개인정보보호법시행령」제 18 조제 2 호에따른범죄경력자료에해당하는정보 (이하이조에서 "범죄경력정보" 라한다) 나같은영제 19 조제 1 호부터제 4 호까

第四十四条（预备审查）

（一）惩戒委员会，在认为需要对惩戒事件进行审议的时候，指定委员，并在审议日之前责令指定的委员进行预备审查。

（二）关于第一项中规定的预备审查的情况适用于法第八十五条第二款第二项至第六项的规定。

（本条是 2010 年 2 月 4 日新增的）

第四十五条（惩戒的决定）

惩戒委员会应该根据公证员的职务性质，职务违反的程度，考虑之外的其他事由来决定惩戒与否，惩戒的种类及惩罚的程度。

（本条是 2010 年 2 月 4 日新增的）

第四十六条（干事的参与和审议记录的制作）

（一）干事参与惩戒事项的审议，并且制作审议记录，和委员长一起在审议记录上签名盖章。

（二）根据第四十四条的规定，参与预备审查的干事应该制作审议记录，并且与审查相关的委员一起在制作的审议记录上签名盖章。

（本条是 2010 年 2 月 4 日新增的）

第四十七条（惩戒决定书的制作）

（一）惩戒委员会在决议惩戒的时候会制作惩戒决定书，并且和委员长和审议相关的委员一起在惩戒决定书上签名和盖章。

（二）关于惩戒议决的结果应该向惩戒嫌疑人送达，通知有管辖权的地方检察厅检察长和大韩公证员协会的会长。

（本条是 2010 年 2 月 4 日新增的）

第四十八条（惩戒审议的中止）

惩戒事件在提起公诉时，直到对案件作出最终判决为止应该中止惩戒审议。

（本条是 2010 年 2 月 4 日新增的）

第四十九条（惩戒委员会的免职决议程序）

根据法第十四条第二项的规定，与决议程序相关的事项适用于法第八十五条第二款、第八十五条第三款、第八十五条第四款、第八十五条第七款，本令第四十四条第一项、第四十六条和第四十七条的规定。

（本条是 2010 年 2 月 4 日新增的）

第五十条（敏感信息和固有识别信息的处理）

（一）司法部长（包括根据法第七十八条第二项的规定司法部长接受委任的权限或者接受委托的人）为了执行以下事务在不可避免的情况下会处理包含（根据《个人信息保护法施行令》第十八条第二款规定的犯罪经历信息（以下称犯罪经历信息）或者相同的本令第十九条第一项至第四项规定的身份证号码、

지의규정에따른주민등록번호, 여권번호, 운전면허의 면허번호또는외국인등록번호(이하이조에서 “주민등록번호등” 이라한다)가포함된자료를처리할수있다.

1. 법제6조, 제8조, 제10조, 제11조, 제14조, 제15조, 제15조의2부터제15조의4까지, 제15조의7, 제15조의8 및제15조의10에따른 공증인의겸직허가, 공증사무의대행, 공증인의정원, 공증인의임명·면직·재임명·당연퇴직, 공증인가, 공증담당변호사의지정신고(지정변경의신고를포함한다)·당연퇴직, 재인가, 공증인가의취소및공증인·공증담당변호사의직무교육에관한사무

2. 법제17조에따른공증인사무소설치·이전의 인가에관한사무

3. 법제20조에따른서명과직인의인영신고·변경신고의보고에관한사무

4. 법제24조에따른서류및장부의반출·보존·폐기에관한사무

5. 법제66조의3 및제66조의4에따른지정공증인의지정및지정취소에관한사무

6. 법제75조에따른서류의인계명령에관한사무

7. 법제77조의2에따른대한공증인협회설립및 회칙변경의인가에관한사무

8. 법제77조의8에따른연수교육상황과실적의 보고에관한사무

9. 법제77조의9에따른공증서류의통합보관시설설치·운영의허가및허가취소에관한사무

10. 법제77조의10에따른대한공증인협회의 감독, 총회의결의내용보고및총회결의의취소에관한 사무

11. 법제78조에따른공증인의감독에관한사무

12. 법제80조에따른서류등의검열에관한사무

13. 법제81조제2항에따른이의신청에관한사무

14. 법제82조및제84조에따른공증인징계의 결의요구및징계에관한사무

15. 법제85조에따른공증인징계위원회의구성 및운영에관한사무

16. 법제86조및제86조의2에따른공증인의 직무정지및직무정지해제에관한사무

17. 제25조에따른겸무자의겸무취급사유의신고에관한사무

18. 제30조에따른공증사무의처리지시에관한 사무

护照号码、驾驶证的号码和外国人登录证号码（以下在本条中称身份证号码）的材料。

1. 根据该法第六条，第八条，第十条，第十一条，第十四条，第十五条，第十五条第二款至第十五条第四款，第十五条第七款，第十五条第八款和第十五条第十款的规定的关于公证员兼职许可、公证事务的代理、公证员的定员、公证员的任命、免职、再任命、当然退职、公证认可、公证律师的指定申告（包含指定变更的申告），当然退职、再认可、公证认可的取消和公证员公证律师的职务培训的事务；

2. 该法第十七条规定的公证员事务所的设施，和跟以前认可的事项相关的事务；

3. 该法第二十条规定的签名和职务印章的使用的申告，变更申告的相关的事项；

4. 该法第二十四条规定的资料和账簿的搬出、保存和废弃相关的事项；

5. 该法第六十六条第三款和第六十六条第四款的规定的指定公证员的指定和指定取消相关的事务；

6. 该法第七十五条的规定的材料的交接命令相关的事项；

7. 该法第七十七条第二款的规定关于大韩公证员协会的建立和会章变更许可事务；

8. 根据该法第七十七条第八款的规定的研修情况和实际情况报告相关的事务；

9. 根据该法第七十七条第九款规定的关于公证材料的统一保管设施设置，运营的允许和取消允许的事务；

10. 该法第七十七条第十款的规定关于大韩公证员协会的领导，大会的决议内容的报告和大会决议的取消相关的事务；

11. 该法第七十八条规定的关于公证员的监督相关的事务；

12. 该法第八十条规定的材料等的与检验相关的规定；

13. 该法第八十一条第二项规定的与异议申请相关的事务；

14. 该法第八十二条和第八十四条规定的关于公证员惩戒决议的要求和与惩戒相关的事务；

15. 该法第八十五条规定的关于公证员惩戒委员会的组成和与运营相关的事务；

16. 该法第八十六条和第八十六条第二款规定的关于公证员的停职和与解除停职相关的事务；

17. 与第二十五条规定的兼任者的兼职事务的履行事由的申告相关的事务；

18. 与第三十条规定的公证事务的处理的指示相关的事务；

19. 제 37 조에따른합동사무소의설치인가및규약의변경인가에관한사무

20. 제 37 조의 3 에따른의사록인증제외대상법인의지정 · 고시에관한사무

21. 제 1 호부터제 20 호까지에규정된사무를수행하기위하여필요한사무

②지방검찰청검사장은다음각호의사무를수행하기위하여불가피한경우범죄경력정보나주민등록번호등이포함된자료를처리할수있다 .

1. 법제 14 조제 3 항에따른임명공증인의면직사유와관련한보고에관한사무

2. 법제 15 조의 3 에따른공증담당변호사의지정및지정변경신고에관한사무

3. 법제 15 조의 7 제 3 항에따른공증인가의취소사유와관련한보고에관한사무

4. 법제 18 조및제 19 조에따른신원보증금의납부 · 환급에관한사무

5. 법제 20 조에따른서명과직인의인영신고 · 변경신고의보고에관한사무

6. 법제 24 조에따른서류및장부의반출 · 보존 · 폐기에관한사무

7. 법제 41 조에따른원본멸실과관련한인가에관한사무

8. 법제 65 조 (제 66 조의 2 제 4 항에서준용하는경우를포함한다) 에따른보존정관 , 증서사본및의사록의멸실과관련한인가에관한사무

9. 법제 66 조의 4 제 2 항에따른지정공증인지정취소의사유와관련한보고에관한사무

10. 법제 67 조에따른공증직무대리의촉탁및그대리의해임신고에관한사무

11. 법제 68 조에따른공증직무의대리명령및그명령의철회에관한사무

12. 법제 70 조에따른사무소서류의봉인에관한사무

13. 법제 71 조에따른겸무명령및그명령의철회에관한사무

14. 법제 72 조 (제 73 조 , 제 75 조부터제 77 조까지및제 86 조에서준용하는경우를포함한다) 에따른서류의인수 · 인도 · 인계에관한사무

15. 법제 81 조제 1 항에따른이의신청에관한사무

16. 법제 82 조제 2 항에따른공증인의징계사유와관련한보고에관한사무

17. 제 11 조에따른촉탁거절사유의보고에관한사무

18. 제 28 조에따른직무의대행촉탁불가능및직무집행재개의사유신고에관한사무

19. 제 29 조에따른성명 · 주소의변경 , 면

19. 与第三十七条规定的联合事务所的设置的许可和规约变更许可相关的事务；

20. 与第三十七条第三款规定的除了议事录的认证以外的其他认证对象的法人的指定相关的事务；

21. 为了执行第一项至第二十项的规定的事务所必须的事务。

（二）地方检察厅检察长在执行下列所列的事务的时候在不可避免的情况下可以处理包含犯罪经历信息或者身份证号码等的材料。

1. 该法第十四条第三项关于任命公证员的免职事由和相关联的报告的事务；

2. 该法第十五条第三款规定的与公证律师的指定和指定变更的申告相关的报告事务；

3. 该法第十五条第七款第三项与关于公证认可的取消事由相关联的报告事务；

4. 该法第十八条和第十九条规定的身份保证金的缴纳和返还的事务；

5. 该法第二十条规定的与签名和职务印章的使用申告、变更申告相关的报告事务；

6. 该法第二十四条规定的材料和账簿的发出、保存和废弃相关的事项；

7. 根据该法第四十一条的规定的原本的灭失和相关的认可的事务；

8. 根据该法第六十五条（包含第六十六条第二款第四项的准用的情况）的规定保存的章程，证书的抄本和议事录的灭失和相关的认可的事务；

9. 该法第六十六条第四款第二项规定的指定公证员指定的取消的事由和相关的报告的事务；

10. 该法第六十七条规定的与公证员职务的代理的委托和代理卸任申告相关的事务；

11. 该法第六十八条规定的与公证员职务的代理命令和命令撤回的相关的事项；

12. 该法第七十条规定的与事务所的材料的封存相关的事务；

13. 该法第七十一条规定的兼务命令和命令的撤回相关的事务；

14. 该法第七十二条（包含第七十三条，第七十五条至第七十七条和第八十六条准用的情况）规定的材料的接收、引渡、交接等相关的事务；

15. 该法第八十一条第一项规定异议申请的事务；

16. 该法第八十二条第二项规定的公证员的惩戒事由和相关的报告的事务；

17. 该法第十一条规定的拒绝委托的事由和与其有关的报告的事务；

18. 第二十八条规定的职务代理的委托的不能和职务执行的事由的申告的相关事项；

19. 第二十九条规定的与姓名、住所的变更、免

직 · 사망의신고에관한사무

20. 제 31 조에따른법무부장관에대한서류의제출에관한사무

21. 제 33 조에따른결격사유등의보고에관한사무

22. 제 34 조에따른임명공증인의재임명및인가공증인의재인가신청시의견서의상신에관한사무

23. 제 1 호부터제 22 호까지에규정된사무를수행하기위하여필요한사무

③대한공증인협회의장은다음각호의사무를수행하기위하여불가피한경우범죄경력정보나주민등록번호등이포함된자료를처리할수있다 .

1. 법제 23 조에따른공증인의보조자와관련한신고에관한사무

2. 법제 77 조의 2 에따른공증업무의지도 · 감독에관한사무

3. 법제 77 조의 7 에따른공공기관의자문및건의에관한사무

4. 법제 77 조의 8 에따른회원 (준회원을포함한다) 및공증인보조자의연수교육에관한사무

5. 법제 77 조의 9 에따른공증서류의통합보관시설설치 · 운영에관한사무

6. 법제 82 조제 2 항에따른공증인의징계사유와관련한보고에관한사무

7. 제 11 조에따른촉탁거절사유의보고에관한사무

8. 제 1 호부터제 7 호까지에규정된사무를수행하기위하여필요한사무

④공증인 (법제 8 조에따라공증인의직무를수행하는검사또는등기소장 , 법제 15 조의 3 에따른공증담당변호사를포함한다) 과법제 23 조의공증인보조자는법제 2 조에따른공증인의직무를수행하기위하여불가피한경우범죄경력정보나주민등록번호등이포함된자료를처리할수있다 .

⑤징계위원회및제 43 조제 1 항의간사와서기는법제 85 조의징계사건을심의 · 의결하기위하여불가피한경우범죄경력정보나주민등록번호등이포함된자료를처리할수있다 .

[본조신설 2013.11.20.]

부칙 (제 24850 호 , 2013. 11. 20.)

이영은 2013 년 11 월 29 일부터시행한다

职、死亡的申告相关的事务；

20. 第三十一条规定的关于向司法部长提交材料相关的事务；

21. 第三十三条规定的缺席事由等的关于报告的相关事务；

22. 第三十四条规定的任命公证员的再任命和认可公证员的再认可的申请时的意见书的相关的事务；

23. 为了执行从第一项至第二十二项规定的事务所必需的事务。

（三）大韩公证员协会会长为了执行下列所列的事务时在不可避免的情况下可以处理包含犯罪经历信息或者身份证号码等的材料。

1. 该法第二十三条规定的关于公证员的书记员和与申告相关的事务；

2. 该法第七十七条第二款规定的公证业务的指导，领导相关的事务；

3. 该法第七十七条第七款规定的公共机关的质询和建议相关的事务；

4. 该法第七十七条第八款规定的与会员（包含准会员）和公证员书记员的培训相关的事项；

5. 该法第七十七条第九款规定的公证材料的统一保管和设施设置，运营相关的事务；

6. 该法第八十二条第二项规定的公证员的惩戒事由和与报告相关的事务；

7. 第十一条规定的与拒绝委托的事由相关的报告的事务；

8. 为了执行从第一项至第八项规定的事务的必要的事务。

（四）公证员（包括该法第八条规定的执行公证员职务的检察和登记所书记员，该法第十五条第三款规定的公证律师）和根据该法第二十三条规定的公证员的书记员和该法第二条规定的公证员为了执行职务，在不可避免的情况下可以处理包含犯罪人经历信息或者公民身份证号码的材料。

（五）惩戒委员会和第四十三条第一项规定的干事和秘书为了处理根据该法第八十五条规定的惩戒事由的审议和决议在不可避免的情况下可以处理包含犯罪人经历信息或者公民身份证号码的材料。

（本条是 2013 年 11 月 20 日新增的）

分则（第 24850 号，2013 年 11 月 20 日）

本令从 2013 年 11 月 29 日开始实行。

公证员手续费规则

공증인수수료규칙

[시행 2010.2.7.]
[법무부령제 693 호 , 2010.2.5., 일부개정]
법무부 (법무과) 02-2110-3178~9

제 1 조 (목적)

이규칙은공증인법제 7 조제 5 항에의하여공증인의수수료・일당 , 여비및실비에관한사항을규정함을목적으로한다 . < 개정 1985.8.1., 2010.2.5.>

제 2 조 (법률행위에관한증서등의작성에대한수수료)

법률행위에관한증서에대한수수료와「공증인법」(이하 "법" 이라한다) 제 56 조의 2 에의하여어음및수표에강제집행할뜻을기재하는증서의작성에대한수수료는이규칙에다른규정이있는경우를제외하고는다음의구별에따른다 . < 개정 1974.8.26., 1979.6.15., 1985.8.1., 1991.10.7., 1993.2.24., 1996.12.31., 2010.2.5.>

법률행위의목적또는어음및수표의가액	수수료
200 만원까지	1 만 1 천원
500 만원까지	2 만 2 천원
1 천만원까지	3 만 3 천원
1 천 500 만원까지	4 만 4 천원
1 천 500 만원초과시	초과액의 2 천분의 3 을더하되 ,300 만원을초과하지못함

[전문개정 1971.2.12.]
[제목개정 2010.2.5.]

제 3 조 (법률행위에관한증서의장수등)

① 법률행위에관한증서작성의수수료는증서의장수가 4 장을초과할때에는그초과하는 1 장마다 500 원을더한다 . < 개정 1971.2.12., 1974.8.26., 1979.6.15., 1991.10.7., 1996.12.31., 2010.2.5.>

② 제 1 항의장수는 1 행 20 자 24 행을 1 장으로한다 . 다만 , 1 장에미달한것은이를 1 장으로본

公证员手续费规则

（2010.2.7 实行）
（司法部令第 693 号，2010.2.5 部分修订）
司法部（司法科）-02-2110-3187-9

第一条（目的）

本规则是为了规范公证法第 7 条第 5 项中规定的公证员的手续费、日工资、差旅费和实际费用相关的事项而制定的。（1985.8.1.，2010.2.5. 修订）

第二条（与法律行为相关的公证书的出具的手续费）

关于法律行为出具的公证书的手续费和根据《公证法》（以下称法）第五十六条第二款规定票据和发票的强制执行的事项进行记载的方式出具的公证书的手续费，除本规则之外的有其他规定的情况下，有以下的区别。（1974.8.26.，1979.6.15.，1985.8.1.，1991.10.7.，1993.2.24.，1996.12.31.，2010.2.5. 修订）

法律行为的目的和票据和收票的金额	手续费
少于 200 万	11000 元
少于 500 万	22000 元
少于 1000 万	33000 元
少于 1500 万	44000 元
超过 1500 万	超过的多收两千分之三，最多不超过 300 万

[全文于 1971.2.12. 修订]
[标题于 2010.2.5. 修订]

第三条（关于法律行为的公证书张数等）

① 关于法律行为的公证书在出具时的手续费是以不超过四张为标准的，当证书的张数超过四张的时候每超过一张多收 500 元。（1971.2.12.，1974.8.26.，1979.6.15.，1991.10.7.，1996.12.31.，2010.2.5. 修订）

② 第一项规定的张数是以一行 20 个字，24 行为一张的。但是不足一张的时候按一张计算。

다 .< 개정 1979.6.15., 2010.2.5.>

[제목개정 2010.2.5.]

제 4 조 (가액결정의표준시)

법률행위의목적의가액은증서작성에착수한때의 가액에의한다 .

제 5 조 (당사자쌍방의촉탁의경우)

당사자쌍방의촉탁에의하여증서를작성하는경우에있어서는법률행위의목적의가액은각급부의가액을합산한액에의하되 , 그수수료는당사자쌍방이분담한다 .

[전문개정 1971.2.12.]

제 6 조 (당사자일방의촉탁의경우)

당사자일방의촉탁에의하여증서를작성하는경우에는촉탁인이급부할가액을법률행위의목적의가액으로한다 . 다만 , 상대방의급부가금전을목적으로하는것인경우에는그액에의한다 .

제 7 조 (주된법률행위와부수된법률행위)

주된법률행위와함께이에부수된법률행위에관한증서를작성하는경우에는주된법률행위에의하여수수료를산정한다 .

제 8 조 (채권담보물의가액등)

채권의담보에관한증서를작성하는경우에는그담보목적물의가액과채권액중적은가액을법률행위의목적의가액으로한다 . < 개정 2010.2.5.>

[제목개정 2010.2.5.]

제 9 조 (지역권설정의가액)

지역권의설정을목적으로하는법률행위에관한증서를작성하는경우지역권설정으로인한요역지의가격증가액과승역지의가격감소액중많은가액을법률행위의목적의가액으로한다 .

[전문개정 2010.2.5.]

제 10 조 (정기에지급할채권의가액)

① 정기에지급할채권의가액은전기간에지급할총액에의한다 . 다만 , 그가액은동산의임대차에있어서는 1 년 , 부동산의임대차및상공업의수습을목적으로하지아니한고용계약에있어서는 5 년 , 기타의경우에있어서는 10 년분의급부의가액을초과할수없다 .

② 기간의정함이없는정기에지급할채권의가액은제 1 항단서에규정한기간내에지급할총가액에의한다 .< 개정 1979.6.15., 2010.2.5.>

③ 제 1 항및제 2 항의경우에있어서상대방의급부의목적이금전이아닌경우에는그가액은정기에지급할채권의가액과동일한것으로본다 .< 개정 1979.6.15.>

（1979.6.15，2010.2.5. 修订）

[标题是 2010.2.5. 修订的]

第四条（决定金额的标准）

法律行为的目标金额由着手出具公证书时的金额决定。

第五条（当事人双方委托的情况）

受当事人双方委托出具公证书的，法律行为的标的金额由各方给付的金额合计确定，手续费由当事人双方分担。

[全文于 1971.2.12. 修订]

第六条（当事人一方委托的情况）

接受当事人一方的委托出具公证书时，委托人给付的金额就是法律行为的标的金额。但是，在由相对方给付的是金钱为标的的情况，则是依据其金额决定的。

第七条（主法律行为和附属法律行为）

出具与主法律行为和附属法律行为相关的公证书时，手续费以主法律行为为准收取。

第八条（债权担保物的金额等）

出具有关债权担保物的公证书时，以担保物的金额和财产物的金额两者中的较少的金额作为法律行为的标的金额。（2010.2.5. 修订）

[标题于 2010.2.5. 修订]

第九条（地役权设定的金额）

就以设立地役权为目的的法律行为出具公证书的，需役地因设立地役权而增加的价格额和供役地相应减少的价格额中，较高者即该法律行为的标的金额。

[全文于 2010.2.5. 修订]

第十条（定期支付的债权的金额）

① 定期支付的债权的金额是根据总体上支付的总额所决定的。但是，其金额不得超过动产契约的一年的给付的金额，不动产契约和工商业中不以实习为目的的雇佣签约的 5 年给付的金额，其他情况的 10 年给付的金额。

② 未规定债权到期日的债权的金额根据第一项规定的时间内支付的总额为标准决定。（1979.6.15.，2010.2.5. 修订）

③ 在第一项和第二项的情况下，对方给付的目标金额不是金钱的话，可以看作其金额和定期给付的债权的金额是统一的。

（1979.6.15. 修订）

제 11 조 (당사자일방의가액의산정불능의경우)

당사자일방의급부의가액을산정할수없는경우에는그급부는상대방의급부와동일한가액인것으로본다 .

第十一条（当事人一方的金额不能算定的情况）

当事人一方给付的金额不能算定时，其给付的金额可以看作与跟对方给付的是相同的。

제 12 조 (부대적목적의경우)

과실 , 손해배상및비용이법률행위에부대되는목적인경우에는그가액은이를법률행위의목적의가액에산입하지아니한다 . < 개정 2010.2.5.>

第十二条（附带的标的的情况）

在过失，损害赔偿和费用成为法律行为的附带的标的的情况下，其金额是不算入法律行为标的金额里面的。<2010.2.5. 修订 >

제 13 조 (목적가액의산정불능의경우)

법률행위의목적의가액을산정할수없는경우에는그가액은 2 천만 100 원으로본다 . 다만 , 그최저가액이 2 천만 100 원을초과하거나그최고가액이이에미달한것이명백한경우에는그최저가액또는최고가액으로써법률행위의목적의가액으로한다 . < 개정 1971.2.12., 1974.8.26., 1979.6.15., 1985.8.1., 1991.10.7., 2006.12.14.>

第十三条（标的金额不能算定的情况）

在法律行为的标的金额不能算定的情况下，其金额以 20100 万元为标准。但是，最小金额若超过 20100 万元或在其最高额并未达到 20100 万元的情况的话，则以最低金额或者最高额作为法律行为的标的金额。

（1971.2.12.，1974.8.26.，1979.6.15.，1985.8.1.，1991.10.7.，2006.12.14. 修订）

제 13 조의 2 (집합건물의소유와관리에관한규약등)

① 「집합건물의소유및관리에관한법률」(이하” 집합건물법” 이라한다) 제 3 조제 3 항 , 제 4 조제 2 항 , 제 20 조제 4 항 , 제 21 조제 2 항의규정에의한규약의설정에관한증서작성의수수료는각각다음의구별에따른다 . < 개정 1991.10.7., 1996.12.31., 2010.2.5.>

전유부분의개수	수수료
10 개까지의부분 1 개마다	4 천 400 원
10 개를초과한 50 개까지의부분 1 개마다	2 천 300 원
50 개를초과한 100 개까지의부분 1 개마다	1 천 700 원
100 개를초과하는부분 1 개마다	1 천 100 원

第十三条第二款（集体建筑物的所有和管理相关的规定等）

① 根据《集体建筑物的所有和管理相关的法律》（以下称《集体建筑物法》）第三条第三项，第四条第二项，第二十条第四项，第二十一条第二项的规定，规约设定相关的公证书的出具的收费是有以下各种区分的。（1991.10.7.，1996.12.31.，2010.2.5. 修订）

占有部分的个数	手续费
少于 10 个的部分每 1 个	4400 元
超过 10 个少于 50 个的部分的每 1 个	2300 元
超过 50 个少于 100 个的部分的每 1 个	1700 元
超过 100 个的部分的每 1 个	1100 元

② 합건물법제 51 조제 1 항및제 2 항의규정에의한규약의설정에관한증서작성의수수료는각각다음의구별에따른다 .< 개정 1991.10.7., 1996.12.31.>

단지내건물의동수	수수료
5 동까지이부분 1 동마다	9 천원
5 동을초과하는부분 1 동마다	4 천원

②《集体建筑物法》第五十一条第一项和第二项规定的规约设定的相关的公证书的出具的手续费是有以下各种区别的。

（1991.10.7.，1996.12.31. 修订）

小区内建筑物的栋数	手续费
少于 5 栋的部分每栋	9000 元
超过 5 栋的部分每栋	4000 元

③제 1 항및제 2 항에규정하는것을제외한집합건물법에의하여설정하는규약에관하여증서를작성하는경우의수수료는제 1 항의예에의한다 .

④제 1 항내지제 3 항에기재된규약의변경에관한증서작성의수수료는그설정에관한수수료와같은금액으로한다 . 다만 , 규약의설정에관한증서를작성한공증인이그규약의변경에관한증서를작성하는경우그

③除按照第一项和第二项规定的之外，根据《集体建筑物法》的规定设定规约的相关公证书的出具的情况的手续费根据第一项的规定办理。

④ 第一项乃至第三项记载的规约的变更的相关的公证书的出具的手续费和其设定相关的手续费是相同的。但是，制作规约的设定的相关公证书的公证员，在出具规约变更的相关的公证书的情况下，其手续费

수수료는규약의설정에관한증서작성수수료의 10 분의 5 의금액(1 만 6 천원미만인경우에는 1 만 6 천원)으로한다 .< 개정 1991.10.7., 2010.2.5.>

⑤제 1 항내지제 3 항에기재한규약의폐지에관한증서작성의수수료는 1 만 6 천원으로한다 .< 개정 1991.10.7., 1996.12.31.>

[본조신설 1986.12.24.]

[제목개정 2010.2.5.]

제 14 조 (승인증서등의작성)

다음각호의사항에관한증서를작성하는경우의수수료와법제 35 조의 2 의부기수수료는제 2 조의구별에의하여각각그 10 분의 5 로한다 . < 개정 1986.12.24., 2010.2.5.>

1. 승인허가또는동의
2. 당사자쌍방이이행하지아니한계약의해제
3. 유언의전부또는일부의취소
4. 증서에작성된법률행위의보충또는변경

[제목개정 2010.2.5.]

제 15 조 (사실에관한증서)

① 법률행위가아닌사실에관한증서작성의수수료는이규칙에다른규정이있는경우를제외하고는그사실의실험및증서의작성에소요된 1 시간당 2 만 5 천원으로한다 . < 개정 1971.2.12., 1974.8.26., 1979.6.15., 1985.8.1., 1986.12.24., 1991.10.7., 1993.2.24., 1996.12.31., 2010.2.5.>

② 1 시간을초과하는경우에는그초과된 1 시간마다제 1 항의수수료에 5 천원을더한다 . 다만 , 1 시간에미달한경우에는이를 1 시간으로본다 .< 개정 1971.2.12., 1974.8.26., 1979.6.15., 1985.8.1., 1986.12.24., 1991.10.7., 1996.12.31., 2010.2.5.>

제 16 조 (집회의결의에관한증서)

제 15 조의규정은주주총회 , 기타집회의결의에관하여증서를작성하는경우에이를준용한다 . < 개정 1979.6.15.>

제 17 조 (관련된사실에관한증서)

법률행위와함께이와관련된사실에관하여증서를작성하는경우의수수료는제 15 조의예에의한다 . 다만 , 그액이법률행위만에관한증서작성의수수료의액보다적은경우에는그중많은액에의한다 . < 개정 2010.2.5.>

제 18 조 (여러사실의증서)

관련되지아니한여러개의사실에관하여증서를작성하는경우에는그수수료의액은각사실에관하여이를산정한다 . < 개정 2010.2.5.>

[제목개정 2010.2.5.]

是规约设定的相关的公证书的出具费的 5/10。(在不满 16000 元的情况下，以 16000 元对待)(1991.10.7.，2010.2.5. 修订)

⑤第一项乃至第三项记载的规约的废弃的相关的公证书的出具的手续费是 16000 元。(1991.10.7.，1996.12.31. 修订)

[本条于 1986.12.24. 新增]

[标题于 2010.2.5. 修订]

第十四条（承认公证书等的出具）

下列所列各项的事项相关的公证书的出具的情况的手续费和法第三十五条第二款的附加手续费是第二条规定的各项的 5/10。(1986.12.24.，2010.2.5. 修订)

1. 承认许可和同意；
2. 当事人双方不能履行的合同的解除；
3. 遗嘱的全部或者一部分的取消；
4. 已经出具好的公证书的法律行为的补充和变更。

[标题于 2010.2.5. 修订]

第十五条（关于事实的公证书）

① 不属于法律行为而是关于事实方面的事项的公证书的出具的手续费，除了本规定还有其他规定的情况下，除外的再现事实和证书的出具所用的时间每小时 25000 元。(1971.2.12.，1974.8.26.，1979.6.15.，1985.8.1.，1986.12.24.，1991.10.7.，1993.2.24.，1996.12.31.，2010.2.5. 修订)

② 在超过 1 小时的情况下，每超过 1 小时在第一项的手续费的基础上加 5000 元。不足 1 小时的以 1 小时计。(1971.2.12.，1974.8.26.，1979.6.15.，1985.8.1.，1986.12.24.，1991.10.7.，1996.12.31.，2010.2.5. 修订)

第十六条（与集会的决议相关的公证书）

第十五条规定的每周大会，以及其他的集会的决议的相关的公证书的出具的情况适用本法的规定。(1979.6.15. 修订)

第十七条（与相关联的事实相关的公证书）

法律行为和与其相关联的事实相关的事项的公证书的出具时的手续费是以第十五条的规定为依据的。但是，其金额与关于法律行为的相关的公证书的出具的手续费的金额相比较少的情况下，以其中较多的金额为准。(2010.2.5. 修订)

第十八条（多个事实的公证书）

对于相互没有关联的多个事实的相关的公证书的出具的情况其手续费的金额是依据各个事实的具体情况决定的。(2010.2.5. 修订)

[标题于 2010.2.5. 修订]

제 19 조 (위임장등)

① 위임장, 수취서또는거절증서를작성하는경우에는그수수료는 1 만원으로한다. < 개정 1971.2.12., 1974.8.26.,1979.6.15.,1986.12.24.,1991.10.., 1993.2.24., 1996.12.31., 2010.2.5.>

② 제 1 항의규정에있어서작성에소요된시간이 1 시간을초과하는경우에는초과하는 1 시간마다 3 천원을더한다. 다만, 1 시간에미달한경우에는이를 1 시간으로본다.< 개정 1971.2.12., 1974.8.26., 1979.6.15., 1986.12.24., 1996.12.31., 2010.2.5.>

③ 초청장을작성하는경우에는그수수료는피초청인 5 명까지 2 만 5 천원으로하고, 5 명을초과하는경우에는초과하는 1 명마다 2 천원을더한다.< 신설 1996.12.31.>

第十九条（委任状等）

① 委任状、受取书和拒绝证书的出具的情况其手续费是 10000 元。（1971.2.12.，1974.8.26.，1979.6.15.，1986.12.24.，1991.10.7.，1993.2.24.，1996.12.31.，2010.2.5. 修订）

② 在第一项有规定的情况下，出具所用的时间超过 1 小时的，每超过 1 小时增加 3000 元。但不满 1 小时的以 1 小时计算。（1971.2.12，1974.8.26，1979.6.15，1986.12.24，1996.12.31，2010.2.5. 修订）

③ 出具聘书的情况下，其手续费如果是不满 5 名的受聘者的话是 25000 元，超过 5 名时，每超过 1 人加收 2000 元。（1996.12.31. 新增）

제 19 조의 2 (주식회사의설립경과등조사 • 보고)

상법제 298 조제 3 항 · 제 299 조의 2 · 제 310 조제 3 항또는제 313 조제 2 항의규정에의하여주식회사의설립에관한사항을조사 · 보고하는경우에는그수수료는발행주식의액면총액 5 천만원까지는 100 만원으로하고, 5 천만원을초과하는경우에는그초과액의 2 천분의 3 을더하되, 300 만원을초과하지못한다.

[본조신설 1996.12.31.]

[제목개정 2010.2.5.]

第十九条第二款（股份公司的设立等的调查和报告）

根据《商法》第二百九十八条第三项，第二百九十九条第二款，第三百一十条第三项和第三百一十三条第二项的规定，就股份公司的设立相关事宜进行调查和报告的，公司发行股份总额不超过 5000 万元的话，其手续费是 100 万，超过 5000 元时另加其超过额的 3/2000，但是不能超过 300 万元。

[本条于 1996.12.31. 新增]

[标题于 2010.2.5. 修订]

제 20 조 (인증행위)

① 인증의수수료는증서작성의수수료의 10 분의 5 로하되, 50 만원을초과하지못한다. < 개정 1996.12.31., 2006.12.14., 2010.2.5.>

② 법제 57 조의 2 제 1 항의인증의경우에는제 1 항의수수료에 10 분의 5 를더하되, 75 만원을초과하지못한다.< 신설 2010.2.5.>

③ 외국어로적은사서증서의경우에는제 1 항의수수료의 2 배로하되, 100 만원을초과하지못한다. < 신설 2010.2.5.>

④ 집합건물법제 39 조에규정된의사록및같은법제 41 조에규정된서면에의한결의서의인증수수료는각각 1 만 2 천원으로한다.< 개정 1991.10.7., 1993.2.24., 2010.2.5.>

[전문개정 1986.12.24.]

第二十条（认证行为）

① 认证的手续费是出具公证书的手续费的 5/10，但是不超过 50 万元。（1996.12.31.，2006.12.14.，2010.2.5. 修订）

② 对法第五十七条第二款第一项规定的公证行为，在第一项规定的手续费上再加 5/10，但是不超过 75 万元。（2010.2.5. 新增）

③ 以外语书写公证书的，手续费是第一项规定的手续费的 2 倍，但是不超过 100 万元。（2010.2.5. 新增）

④《集体建筑物法》第三十九条规定的议事录和法第四十一条中规定的书面决议书的认证的手续费是 12000 元。

（1991.10.7.，1993.2.24.，2010.2.5. 修订）

[全文于 1986.12.24. 修订]

제 21 조 (상법상의정관등의인증)

① 상법의규정에의한정관인증의수수료는발행주식의액면총액 5 천만원까지는 8 만원으로하고, 5 천만원을초과할경우에는그초과액의 2 천분의 1 을더하되 100 만원을초과하지못한다. < 개정 1979.6.15., 1985.8.1., 1991.10.7., 1993.2.24.,

第二十一条（商法上的规章等的认证）

① 根据商法的规定认证章程的手续费，如果其发行股票的总额不超过 5000 万的话是 8 万元，如果超过 5000 万的话应该增加其超过的额的 1/2000，但是不能超过 100 万元。（1979.6.15.，1985.8.1.，1991.10.7.，1993.2.24.，1996.12.31.，2006.12.14. 修订）

1996.12.31., 2006.12.14.>

② 법인의등기절차에첨부되는의사록의인증의수수료는 3 만원으로한다 .< 개정 1974.8.26., 1979.6.15., 1991.10.7., 1993.2.24., 1996.12.31., 2006.12.14.>

[전문개정 1971.2.12.]

[제목개정 2010.2.5.]

제 21 조의 2 (위임장의인증)

위임장인증의수수료는 3 천원으로한다 .

[본조신설 2010.2.5.]

제 22 조 (사서증서의확정일자)

사서증서에확정일자를붙이는경우에는그수수료는 1 천원으로한다 . < 개정 1971.2.12., 1974.8.26., 1979.6.15., 1985.8.1., 1991.10.7., 2010.2.5.>

제 23 조 (집행문부여행위)

증서의정본에집행문을붙이는경우에는그수수료는 1 만원으로한다 . 다만 , 「민사집행법」 제 57 조에서준용하는같은법제 30 조제 2 항 , 제 31 조제 1 항 , 제 35 조제 1 항의경우에는 1 만원을더한다 . < 개정 1971.2.12., 1974.8.26., 1979.6.15., 1985.8.1., 1993.2.24., 2010.2.5.>

제 23 조의 2 (우편에의한송달의수수료)

① 법제 7 조제 2 항에따른통지또는송달에필요한실비는 「우편법」 에따른우편요금으로한다 .

② 법제 56 조의 4 에따른우편에의한송달의수수료는 4 천원으로한다 .

[전문개정 2010.2.5.]

제 24 조 (증서의정본등의교부)

① 증서의정본또는등본이나그부속서류의등본및정관또는그부속서류의등본의교부에관한수수료는 1 장에 500 원으로한다 . 다만 , 법제 54 조제 1 항 (법제 66 조에서준용하는경우를포함한다) 의경우에는 1 장에 200 원으로한다 . < 개정 1971.2.12., 1974.8.26., 1979.6.15., 1991.10.7., 1993.2.24., 1996.12.31., 2010.2.5.>

② 제 3 조제 2 항의규정은제 1 항의경우에이를준용한다 .< 개정 1979.6.15.>

[제목개정 2010.2.5.]

제 25 조 (증서원본등의열람)

증서의원본및그부속서류또는정관및그부속서류의열람에대한수수료는 1 회에 1 천원으로한다 . < 개 정 1971.2.12., 1974.8.26., 1979.6.15., 1993.2.24., 1996.12.31., 2006.12.14.>

[제목개정 2010.2.5.]

② 法人登记程序附属议事录的认证的手续费是3万元。(1974.8.26., 1979.6.15., 1991.10.7., 1993.2.24., 1996.12.31., 2006.12.14. 修订)

[全文于 1971.2.12. 修订]

[标题于 2010.2.5. 修订]

第二十一条第二款（委任状的认证）

认证委任状的手续费是 3000 元。

[本条于 2010.2.5. 新增]

第二十二条（私署公证书的确定日期）

在私署公证书上写下确定日期的，其手续费是 1000 元。(1971.2.12., 1974.8.26., 1979.6.15., 1985.8.1., 1991.10.7., 2010.2.5. 修订)

第二十三条（执行书赋予的行为）

在公证书的正本上附上执行书的，其手续费是1万元。但是根据《民事执行法》第五十七条准用的，和相同规定的法的第三十条第二项，第三十一条第一项，第三十五条第一项的规定情况要再加 1 万元。(1971.2.12., 1974.8.26., 1979.6.15., 1985.8.1., 1993.2.24., 2010.2.5. 修订)

第二十三条第二款（关于书信的送达的手续费）

① 法第七条第二项规定的通知和送达所必须的实际费用根据《书信法》规定的书信费用收取。

② 根据法第五十六条第四款规定的关于书信的送达的手续费是 4000 元。

[全文于 2010.2.5. 修订]

第二十四条（公证书的正本等的交付）

①公证书的正本和核准副本或者其附属材料的核准副本和规章及其附属材料的核准副本的交付的手续费是每张 500 元。但是，根据法第五十四条第一项 (包括法第六十六条中准用的情况) 规定的情况的话每张是 200 元。(1971.2.12., 1974.8.26., 1979.6.15., 1991.10.7., 1993.2.24., 1996.12.31., 2010.2.5. 修订)

②第三条第二项的规定适用于第一项规定的准用规则。(1979.6.15. 修订)

[标题于 2010.2.5. 修订]

第二十五条（公证书正本等的阅览）

公证书的正本和其附属材料和规章及其附属材料的预览的手续费是 1 次 1000 元。(1971.2.12., 1974.8.26., 1979.6.15., 1993.2.24., 1996.12.31., 2006.12.14. 修订)

[标题于 2010.2.5. 修订]

제 26 조（수수료의정함이없는사항）

수수료의정함이없는사항에대한수수료는그사항에가장유사한사항에대한수수료와동일한액으로한다.

제 27 조（특수한사정하에서의직무집행）

공증인이촉탁인의청구에따라토요일，공휴일또는야간에직무를집행하거나，병상에서직무를집행한경우의수수료는이규칙에서정한수수료에 10 분의 5 를더한금액으로한다.

[전문개정 2010.2.5.]

제 28 조（공증업무중지등의경우）

공증인이직무의집행에착수한후촉탁인의청구에의하여이를중지하거나，촉탁인，통역인또는참여인등의귀책사유로인하여이를완결하지못한때에는제 15 조의예에따라수수료를받는다. 다만，수수료는직무집행을완결한경우에받을수있는수수료액을초과하지못한다. < 개정 2010.2.5.>

[제목개정 2010.2.5.]

제 29 조（일당，여비등）

공증인이출장하여직무를행할때에는촉탁인은수수료외에다음각호의비용을부담하여야한다. < 개정 1974.8.26., 1979.6.15., 1985.8.1., 1993.2.24., 1996.12.31., 2006.12.14., 2010.2.5.>

1. 일당

4 시간이내에는 5 만원으로하고，4 시간을초과하는경우에는 10 만원으로한다.

2. 철도임또는선임

1 등여객운임. 다만，운임에등급이없는경우에는승차또는승선에요하는운임

3. 항공임또는자동차운임

실비액

4. 숙박비

실비액

[전문개정 1971.2.12.]

[제목개정 2010.2.5.]

제 30 조（수수료등의감액불가）

공증인은수수료，일당，여비및실비（이하 "수수료등" 이라한다）를임의로감액할수없다.

[전문개정 2010.2.5.]

제 31 조（촉탁인이여러사람인경우）

동일한사항에관하여여러사람이함께촉탁하는경우수수료등은각촉탁인이연대하여지급하여야한다.

[전문개정 2010.2.5.]

第二十六条（手续费无法确定的事项）

关于手续费无法确定的事项的手续费应该是参照与其最相类似的事项的收费，与其执行相同的手续费的金额。

第二十七条（特殊事由下的职务执行）

公证员在委托人的请求下在星期六、公休日和夜班的时间执行职务或者在其病假期间执行职务的情况下的手续费应该再加正常情况下费用的 5/10。

[全文于 2010.2.5. 修订]

第二十八条（公证业务中止等的情况）

公证员在着手进行执行职务之后，根据委托人的请求中止职务或者因为委托人，翻译或者见证人的一些归责事由不能完成规定的事务的时候根据第十五条的例子的规定收取手续费。但是，此时收取的手续费不能超过完全履行职务时收取的手续费的金额。（2010.2.5. 修订）

[标题于 2010.2.5. 修订]

第二十九条（日薪、差旅费等）

公证员在出差执行职务的时候，委托人除了要承担手续费还要负担以下各项所列的费用。（1974.8.26.，1979.6.15.，1985.8.1.，1993.2.24.，1996.12.31.，2006.12.14.，2010.2.5. 修订）

1. 日薪，4 个小时以内是 5 万元，超过 4 小时的情况是 10 万元；

2. 火车费和船费为一等乘客的费用，但是，如果无运费等级的情况下以一般乘车或乘船的费用为标准；

3. 航空费和汽车费，为实际费用额；

4. 住宿费，为实际费用。

[全文于 1971.2.12. 修订]

[标题于 2010.2.5. 修订]

第三十条（手续费等的不能减少金额）

公证员不能任意的减少手续费，日薪、差旅费和实际费用（以下称手续费等）的金额。

[全文于 2010.2.5. 修订]

第三十一条（委托人是多人的情况）

关于同一事项有很多人委托的情况，手续费等费用是应该由各个委托人分担并支付的。

[全文于 2010.2.5. 修订]

제 32 조 (공증력없는문서작성의수수료등)

공증인이작성한문서에공증의효력이인정되지아니하는경우에는공증인은수수료등을받을수없다 . 다만, 공증인의과실이없는경우에는그러하지아니하다 . < 개정 2010.2.5.>

제 33 조 (수수료등의청구)

공증인은촉탁받은사항에관하여그직무를완결하지아니하면제 28 조에서정한경우를제외하고는수수료등의지급을청구할수없다 . < 개정 2010.2.5.>

제 34 조 (수수료등의면제)

당사자본인이다음각호의어느하나에해당하는경우에는수수료 , 일당및여비의지급을면제한다 .

1.「국민기초생활보장법」제 2 조제 2 호에따른수급자

2.「한부모가족지원법」제 5 조에따른보호대상자

[전문개정 2010.2.5.]

제 35 조 (수수료등의예납등)

① 공증인은촉탁인으로하여금수수료등의개략적산정금액을예납하게할수있다 . < 개정 2010.2.5.>

② 제 1 항의경우에촉탁인은예납에갈음하여수수료등의개략적산정금액을공탁할수있다 .< 개정 1979.6.15., 1985.8.1., 2010.2.5.>

③ 공증인은촉탁인이제 1 항및제 2 항의규정에의하여수수료등의개략적산정금액을예납또는공탁하지아니할경우에는그촉탁을거부할수있다 .< 개정 1979.6.15., 2010.2.5.>

[제목개정 2010.2.5.]

제 36 조 (계산서의교부)

① 공증인은촉탁인이수수료등을지급한때에는계산서를교부하여야한다 . < 개정 2010.2.5.>

② 계산서에는각항목별로이규칙의관계규정을인용하여그계산의근거를명백하게적어야한다 .< 개정 1985.8.1., 2010.2.5.>

제 37 조 (수수료등의미지급의경우)

촉탁인이수수료등을지급하지아니하는경우에는공증인은촉탁받은사항에관한증서의정본 · 등본및집행문의교부를거절할수있다 . < 개정 2010.2.5.>

제 38 조 (특례)

법제 8 조에따라검사또는등기소장이공증사무를대행하는경우의수수료 , 일당및여비는수입인지로납부하게할수있다 .

[전문개정 2010.2.5.]

第三十二条（制作没有公证效力的文书的手续费等）

公证员对制作的文书的公证效力不予认证的时候，公证员得不到手续费等费用。但是，在公证员本身没有过错的情况下除外。（2010.2.5. 修订）

第三十三条（手续费等的请求）

公证员在对接受委托人委托的事项的时候，不能完整履行其职务的话，除了第二十八条中规定的情况下，不能要求委托人支付手续费。（2010.2.5. 修订）

第三十四条（手续费等的免除）

当事人本人有下列任一现象的，可以免除手续费、日薪和差旅费的支付。

1.《国民基本生活保障法》第二条第二号规定的供给者；

2.《单亲父母家庭支援法》第五条规定的保护人。

[全文于 2010.2.5. 修订]

第三十五条（手续费等的预交等）

①公证员可以要求委托人提交预交手续费等大致决定的金额。（2010.2.5. 修订）

②在第一项的情况下委托人代替预交的手续费的话，可以将大概算定的金额进行提存。（1979.6.15.，1985.8.1.，2010.2.5. 修订）

③公证员在委托人根据第一项和第二项的规定未预交收费等的大致商定的金额或者不进行提存时可以拒绝委托公证。（1979.6.15.，2010.2.5. 修订）

[标题于 2010.2.5. 修订]

第三十六条（清单的交付）

① 公证员在委托人支付手续费等的费用时应该交付费用清单。（2010.2.5. 修订）

② 清单上不同的项目适用于不同的相关规则的规定，在清单中还应该明白地写明计算的根据。（1985.8.1.，2010.2.5. 修订）

第三十七条（手续费等费用未支付的情况）

在委托人未支付手续费等相关费用的情况下，公证员可以拒绝交付与接受委托事项相关的公证书的正本和核准副本和执行书。（2010.2.5. 修订）

第三十八条（特例）

根据法第八条规定的检察员或者法院登记处书记员在执行公证事务的情况下的手续费、日薪和差旅费可以返还给受益人。

[全文于 2010.2.5. 修订]

부칙 (제 693 호 , 2010. 2. 5.)

제 1 조 (시행일)

이규칙은 2010 년 2 월 7 일부터시행한다 .

제 2 조 (경과조치)

이규칙시행전에촉탁한공증인의직무에관한수수료등은종전규정에따르다

分则（第 693 号，2010.2.5）

第一条（实行日）

本规则从 2010 年 2 月 7 日开始实行。

第二条（经过措施）

在本规则实施日前，接受委托的公证事务收取手续费等相关费用的，应根据之前的规定。

科威特

科威特国 1961 年第 4 号公证法法令

دولة الكويت
قانون رقم 4 لسنة 1961 بإصدار قانون التوثيق (4 1961)

عدد المواد: 19
تاريخ الطباعة: 04/05/2018

科威特国
1961 年第 4 号公证法法令（1961/4）

条款数量：19
打印日期：2018/05/04

فهرس الموضوعات

主题索引

10 - قانون التوثيق (1 - 19)

10.1 - قانون الإصدار (1 - 2)

المادة رقم 1

ينشأ بدائرة العدل مكتب للتوثيق يرأسه كاتب العدل ويساعده عدد من الموثقين. ويختص هذا المكتب بتوثيق المحررات الرسمية، وبالتصديق على التوقيعات وإثبات التاريخ في المحررات العرفية. ويصدق رئيس العدل على توقيع كاتب العدل ومساعديه في المحررات التي يختصون بها.

10. 公证法（1—19）

10.1 组织法（1—2）

第一条

公证机构由一名公证员领导，并有若干公证员协助其工作，公证机构专门负责公证官方文件和非官方文件的签名和日期。公证员应在其出具的文件上签字。公证员入职前应在司法部长的见证下宣誓将忠实履行职责。司法部设有由司法公证官领导的公证机构，并由若干公证员协助其工作，该公证机构专门负责公证官方文件、非官方文件的签名和日期。在公证员的职权范围内，公证员签名的文件意味着其已经公证过。

ينشأ بوزارة العدل مكتب للتوثيق يرأسه كاتب العدل ويساعده عدد من الموثقين، ويختص هذا المكتب بتوثيق المحررات الرسمية، وبالتصديق على التوقيعات، وإثبات التاريخ في المحررات العرفية. ويكتفى بتوقيعاتهم على كافة المحررات التي يختصون بها. ويؤدي كاتب العدل والموثقون قبل مباشرة أعمالهم يمينا أمام وزير العدل بأن يقوموا بأعمال وظائفهم بالصدق والأمانة.

公证员在入职前，应当在司法部长的见证下宣誓，保证诚实守信地履行职责。

10.2 - توثيق المحررات الرسمية

(2 - 12)

10.2 官方文件

（2—12）

المادة رقم 2

يقوم كاتب العدل بتوثيق المحررات التي يوجب القانون أن يطلب المتعاقدون توثيقها، وبإثباتها في الدفاتر المعدة لذلك وحفظ أصولها، وبإعطاء الصور التي يطلبها ذوو الشأن منها، وبوضع الصيغة التنفيذية على صورها الواجبة التنفيذ، وإثباتها في الفهارس الخاصة بها.

第二条

公证员应当按照公证法律要求当事人申请公证和核准的官方文件，并在正本上予以注明。公证员应当保存该文件的正本，为当事人提供副本，出具执行副本，并在专门的索引中加以标注。

المادة رقم 3

يختص كاتب العدل بتوثيق جميع المحررات الرسمية، عدا ما كان منها متعلقا بالوقف أو بالأحوال الشخصية. ويكون توثيق كتاب الوقف وما يدخل عليه من تغييرات أمام أحد قضاة المحكمة الكلية. ويوثق المحررات المتعلقة بالأحوال الشخصية بالنسبة إلى المسلمين أحد قضاة المحكمة الكلية. على أنه يجوز لرئيس دائرة العدل أن يفوض مأذونين في توثيق عقود الزواج والمصادقة عليها وإشهادات الطلاق. أما غير المسلمين فيوثقون محرراتهم المتعلقة بالأحوال الشخصية أمام كاتب العدل أو أمام جهات التوثيق الخاصة بهم.

第三条

公证员有权公证所有官方文件，但有关慈善捐助或个人状况的文件除外。

慈善捐助及其变更的公证应由一名合议庭的法官负责。

穆斯林的个人状况的公证由一名合议庭的法官负责，司法部长可以委派公证员公证结婚证书和离婚证书。

非穆斯林的个人状况的公证应在公证机构或其专属的公证机构处进行。

المادة رقم 4

لرئيس دائرة العدل إصدار قرارات بتفويض أئمة المساجد في القرى وممثلي الحكومة بالخارج في القيام بما يفوضون به من أعمال التوثيق في الجهات الكائنة بها. ويقوم كاتب العدل بالتصديق على توقيعات هؤلاء المفوضين.

第四条

司法部长应授权村庄清真寺的伊玛目和科威特政府的海外代表，在其所在机构执行委托给他们的公证工作。公证员应当公证前述受委托人的签名。

المادة رقم 5

يجب على الموثق أن يتحقق من شخصية ذوي الشأن بشهادة شاهدين بالغين عاقلين معروفين له، أو بالاطلاع على جواز سفرهم أو ورقة رسمية أخرى تقوم مقامهم. وعليه أن يثبت هذا الاطلاع في المحرر ذاته.

第五条

公证员应通过下列依据之一核实当事人的身份：两位认识当事人且理智健全的成年证人的证词，当事人的护照或其他正式文件。公证员在公证文件时应当注明上述情况。

المادة رقم 6

يجب على الموثق قبل إجراء التوثيق أن يتثبت - على قدر الإمكان - من أهلية المتعاقدين ورضائهم. فإذا اتضح له عدم توافر الأهلية أو الرضا أو إذا كان المحرر ظاهر البطلان

第六条

公证文件之前，公证员应当核实当事人的资格和真实意思。当事人不具备相应资格，文件违反当事人的真实意愿或文件明显无效的，公证员应拒绝公证，

رفض التوثيق وأعاد المحرر إلى ذوي الشأن مع إبداء أسباب الرفض كتابة

المادة 7 مكرر

لمن رفض توثيق محرره أن يتظلم إلى قاضي الأمور الوقتية بالمحكمة الكلية خلال خمسة عشر يوما من إبلاغه الرفض. وله أن يطعن في القرار الصادر من هذا القاضي طبقا للقواعد المنصوص عليها في المادتين 171 و 172 من قانون المرافعات المدنية والتجارية. ولا يحوز قرار القاضي أو حكم المحكمة في التظلم من رفض التوثيق قوة الشيء المقضي به في موضوع المحرر.

المادة 8 مكرر

لا تسلم صور المحررات التي تم توثيقها إلا لأصحاب الشأن. ويجوز تسليم صورة من المحرر للغير بأمر من قاضي الأمور الوقتية بالمحكمة الكلية.

المادة 9 مكرر

لا يجوز تسليم صورة تنفيذية ثانية من المحرر الموثق إلا بحكم من قاضي الأمور المستعجلة.

المادة 10 مكرر

لا يجوز أن تنقل من مكتب التوثيق أصول المحررات التي تم توثيقها ولا الدفاتر أو الوثائق المتعلقة بها. ويجوز للسلطات القضائية الاطلاع عليها في مكان حفظها. ولا يجوز ضم دفتر من دفاتر التوثيق إلى ملف دعوى منظورة.

المادة 11 مكرر

إذا أصدرت سلطة قضائية قرارا بضم أصل محرر موثق إلى ملف دعوى منظورة أمامها، وجب أن ينتقل القاضي إلى مكتب التوثيق لتحرير صورة مطابقة للأصل الرسمي، ويعمل بذيلها محضر يوقعه القاضي وكاتب العدل وكاتب المحكمة ثم يضم أصل المحرر إلى ملف النزاع وتقوم الصورة مقامه لحين رده.

المادة 12 مكرر

لا يجوز للموثق أن يباشر توثيق محرر يخصه شخصيا أو تربطه بأصحاب الشأن فيه صلة قرابة أو مصاهرة إلى الدرجة الرابعة

المادة 4 مكرر

مع عدم الإخلال بأية عقوبة أشد ينص عليها القانون يعاقب بالحبس مدة لا تزيد على سنتين وغرامة لا تجاوز مائتي دينار أو بإحدى هاتين العقوبتين، كل من حرر عقد زواج للغير أو وثق تصادقا عليه دون أن يكون من القضاة أو الموثقين المختصين أو المأذونين أو المفوضين في أعمال التوثيق طبقا للقانون.

将文件退回给当事人，并书面告之拒绝理由。

第七条

根据《民事和商业诉讼法》第一百七十一条和第一百七十二条之规定，公证员拒绝公证的，当事人可在收到拒绝通知的十五日内，向合议庭临时事务法官提出申诉。法官和法院对该申诉的判决不包括对文件内容本身的判断。

第八条

已公证的文件的副本只能交付当事人。

公证员可以按合议庭临时事务法官的命令，将副本交付第三人。

第九条

除非有紧急事务法官的裁决，经过公证的文件不得交付第二份执行副本。

第十条

不得从公证机构转移已公证的文件、文本或与之相关的文件正本。司法机关可以在文件保管地检查文件。任一公证文本不能纳入在待审案件的卷宗中。

第十一条

如果司法当局决定将公证文本原件归入待审案件卷宗，法官应到公证机构出具一份与原件一致的副本，在副本结尾附上记录，法官、公证员和法院书记应在副本上签名，方可将原件归入待审案件的卷宗。在返还正本以前，用副本代替正本。

第十二条

公证员不得公证专属其本人，或与其具有四代近亲、姻亲关系的当事人的文件。

第四条之二　未经主管法官、公证员或授权人批准，为他人订立婚约或出具公证文件的，在不违背法律规定的任何更严厉的处罚的情况下，应单处最高两年监禁或最高两百第纳尔罚款，或二者并罚。

10.3 - التصديق على التوقيعات وإثبات التاريخ
(10 - 19)

المادة رقم 13
يقوم كاتب العدل بالتصديق على توقيعات ذوي الشأن في المحررات العرفية بناء على طلبهم وبإثبات ذلك في السجلات الخاصة بذلك وبإعطاء الشهادات بحصول التصديق.

المادة رقم 14
يجب على الموثق قبل التوقيع من ذوي الشأن أن يستوثق منهم عن موضوع المحرر الذي يرغبون في التصديق على توقيعاتهم فيه.

المادة رقم 15
إذا كان المحرر المقدم للتصديق على توقيعات ذوي الشأن فيه بلغة أجنبية وجب أن يشتمل على ملخص باللغة العربية موقع عليه منه.

المادة رقم 16
تسري على التصديق على التوقيعات أحكام المواد الرابعة والخامسة والثامنة والثانية عشرة من هذا القانون.

المادة رقم 17
يقوم كاتب العدل بإثبات تاريخ المحررات العرفية التي تقدم إليه لهذا الغرض وذلك بوضع خاتم ذي تاريخ عليها بعد إثبات ذلك في السجلات الخاصة. وتعطى الشهادات بإثبات التاريخ من واقع هذه السجلات.

المادة رقم 18
يصدر قرار من رئيس دائرة العدل باللائحة التنفيذية تشمل بيان إجراءات التوثيق والتصديق على التوقيعات وإثبات التاريخ، وتنظم الدفاتر والفهارس والصور والشهادات، وتحدد الرسوم الواجب أداؤها.

المادة رقم 19
على رئيس دائرة العدل تنفيذ هذا القانون ويعمل به من تاريخ نشره في الجريدة الرسمية ويلغى كل نص يتعارض مع أحكامه

10.3 签名与日期公证
（10—19）

第十三条
公证员应按当事人的要求公证非官方文件中当事人的签名，并在该文件上注明经过公证，同时出具公证书。

第十四条
在当事人签名之前，公证员必须从当事人处核实其申请公证签名的文件的内容。

第十五条
当事人申请公证的文件包含外文的，应附有相应的阿拉伯语摘要。

第十六条
本法第四条、第五条、第八条和第十二条的规定适用于签名公证。

第十七条
对于需要公证日期的非官方文件，公证员应当在公证之后将其归入专门的档案，并在该文件上加盖带有日期的印章。
公证员公证的内容以档案中记载的日期为准。

第十八条
司法部长应按执行条例发布决定，决定内容包括对公证程序、签名公证、日期公证，文本、索引、照片和证书规范的说明，以及收费标准。

第十九条
本法自官方公报发布之日起生效。任何与本法规定不一致的法律条文均应予以废止。

吉尔吉斯斯坦

公证法

LAW OF THE KYRGYZ REPUBLIC
of May 30, 1998 No. 70
About notariate
(The last edition from 12-01-2018)
Accepted by General Court of Jogorku Kenesh of the Kyrgyz Republic on May 6, 1998

吉尔吉斯斯坦公证法
颁布于 1998 年 5 月 30 日，70 号文

（最新版于 2018 年 12 月 1 日颁布）
该法由吉尔吉斯斯坦共和国议会于 1998 年 5 月 6 日签署

Section 1. Organizational bases of activities of notariate

Chapter 1. General provisions

Article 1. Legislation on notariate

Article 2. Notariate

1. The notariate represents system of state bodies, officials and private notaries to whom the obligation is assigned to provide according to the Constitution of the Kyrgyz Republic, this Law and other regulatory legal acts of the Kyrgyz Republic protection of the rights and legitimate interests of citizens and legal entities by making by the notary of stipulated by the legislation notarial actions of the Kyrgyz Republic on behalf of the Kyrgyz Republic.

2. The private notary performs the functions delegated by the state specified in part one of this Article.

Article 3. Notarial actions

1. Notarial actions represent actions of the notary according to the certificate of the indisputable facts, the legal events having legal value, to witnessing of documents, giving to documents of executive force and legal reliability and other actions directed to the protection of the rights of

第一部分　公证活动的组织基础

第一章　总则

第一条　公证法律

第二条　公证员

1.“公证员”包括国家公证员和私营公证员。公证员应当依照《吉尔吉斯斯坦共和国宪法》，本法及吉尔吉斯斯坦共和国的其他法规履行职责，并依照法律规定代表吉尔吉斯斯坦共和国开展公证活动，保护公民和法人的合法权益。

2. 私营公证员参照本条第一部分的规定执行国家赋予的公证职能。

第三条　公证行为

1. 公证行为是公证员依照不可辩驳的事实和具有法律意义的事件，公证相关文件，并赋予该文件以执行力和公信力的行为。同时，公证行为还依照本法保护公民与法人组织的合法权益。

citizens and legal entities, their legitimate interests provided by this Law.

2. Notarial actions in the Kyrgyz Republic are made according to this Law by the state and private notaries.

3. In absence cases in the settlement of the notary the state powers on making of notarial actions by authorized state body are delegated to local government bodies according to the legislation on procedure for delegation to local government bodies of separate state powers.

4. Notarial actions in the territory of other states are made by the officials of consular establishments of the Kyrgyz Republic authorized on making of these actions.

5. The list of the notarial actions provided by this Law is not exhausted. By regulatory legal acts of the Kyrgyz Republic also other notarial actions can be provided.

Article 4. Notary

1. The citizen of the Kyrgyz Republic having the higher legal education, the years of service on legal specialty at least three years which passed six-months training at the state or private notary, passed the qualification examination having the license for the occupation right private notarial activities can be the private notary. The procedure for passing of training is determined by the Government of the Kyrgyz Republic.

2. The notary public is government employee. To occupation notarial activities do not allow persons:

- recognized as incapacitated or it is limited capable in the procedure established by the law;

- having criminal record for intentional crime irrespective of, it is removed or it is extinguished.

3. Persons who worked as the notary public at least 5 years obtain the license for the occupation right private notarial activities without passing qualification examination based on the decision of the qualification commission according to part two of article 12 of this Law.

4. When making notarial actions notaries have the equal rights and bear identical responsibility.

5. The documents processed by the state and private notaries have identical legal force.

6. Notaries have the right to create notarial chambers.

7. The rights and obligations of the notary are determined by this Law.

Article 4-1. Independence of the notary

1. The notary when implementing notarial activities is impartial, independent and is guided by the Constitution, other regulatory legal acts of the Kyrgyz Republic.

2. 吉尔吉斯斯坦共和国的国家公证员和私营公证员依照本法实施公证行为。

3. 缺少公证员时，国家授权机构应当依照向地方政府授权的法律程序，将组织公证活动的权力赋予地方政府机构。

4. 吉尔吉斯斯坦共和国政府授权的领事机构的官员有权在其他国家领土上组织实施公证活动。

5. 本法没有穷尽所有公证行为。吉尔吉斯斯坦共和国的规范性法案，也能列举其他公证行为。

第四条　公证员

1. 受过高等法律教育，具有三年以上法律专业的学习背景，在国家或私营公证机构接受过六个月的培训，并通过私营公证资格考试的吉尔吉斯斯坦共和国公民可以担任私营公证员。公证员培训的程序由吉尔吉斯斯坦共和国政府决定。

2. 公证员是政府的雇员。下列人员不能进行公证活动：

- 法律上规定的无民事行为能力人或限制民事行为能力人；

- 有故意犯罪记录的人，无论该记录是否被移除或撤销。

3. 依照本法第十二条第二款的规定，没有通过公证员资格考试的人员应当工作至少五年，才能取得私营公证员营业执照。

4. 参与公证活动时，公证员之间享有平等的权利，并承担同等的责任。

5. 国家公证员与私营公证员所出具的法律文件具有同等的法律效力。

6. 公证员有权设立公证机构。

7. 公证员的权利和义务由本法规定。

第四条第一款　公证员的独立性

1. 公证员依照《吉尔吉斯斯坦共和国宪法》和其他法律法规独立、公正地开展公证活动。

Article 5. Assistant notary

1. - Voided by the Law KR of March 4, 2010 No. 45.

第五条　助理公证员

根据吉尔吉斯斯坦共和国 2010 年 3 月 4 日第 45 号法令，本条规定已废止。

Article 6. Restrictions in activities of the notary

1. The notary has no right:

(1) be engaged in business activity and any other activities, except notarial, scientific and teaching;

(2) render intermediary services in case of the conclusion of agreements;

2. make notarial actions on the name and on its own behalf, addressed to and on behalf of the spouse (the spouse), their and relatives (parents, children, grandsons, brothers, sisters, the grandfather, the grandma);

3. make notarial actions addressed to and from employee name of this notary office, the workers consisting in employment relationships with the notary.

第六条　公证活动的限制条款

1. 公证员不得从事下列活动：

（1）商业活动及其他营利性活动，但公证、科学及教学活动除外；

（2）在缔结协议时，提供中介服务。

2. 为本人办理公证，或代表本人参加公证活动，为本人的配偶或亲属（父母，子女，孙子女，外孙子女，兄弟姐妹，祖父母，外祖父母）办理公证，或代表上述人员参与公证活动；

3. 为本公证机构雇员或与公证员有雇佣关系的人员办理公证事项。

Article 7. Observance of mystery of the made notarial actions

1. Notaries and other officials, representatives to make notarial actions, shall keep in secret data which became known to them in connection with making of notarial actions. The obligation of preserving mystery of the made notarial actions extends also to persons who knew of committed notarial actions in connection with execution of service duties by them including after the termination of the employment contract.

2. Data on committed notarial actions, and also the documents concerning them are issued only to physical persons and legal entities at the request of which or concerning which notarial actions were made.

3. Data and documents on committed notarial actions are issued upon the demand of court, prosecutor's office, investigation authorities and inquiry in connection with the criminal or civil cases which are in their production.

4. Provision of data and documents on committed notarial actions in any other cases is forbidden.

5. Data on the will are issued only after the death of the testator.

第七条　公证行为的保密职责

1. 公证员，从事公证工作的公务员和公证机构的代表应当保守在公证活动时知悉的秘密。其他知悉公证活动相关情况的人同样负有保密义务。公证员、从事公证活动的公务员和公证机构的代表在离职后依然负有上述保密义务。

2. 公证员只能向申请公证的自然人和法人，以及与公证活动有利害关系的人提供公证资料和相关文件。

3. 为满足法院、检察院和调查当局正在调查的刑事或民事案件的需要，公证员应向其提供公证资料和相关文件。

4. 禁止在其他任何情况下向外界提供有关犯罪的公证数据和文件。

5. 关于遗嘱的资料只能在立遗嘱人死亡后公布。

Article 8. Notarial clerical work

1. The notarial clerical work is performed by the notaries and other officials making notarial actions according to the rules approved by the Government of the Kyrgyz Republic.

2. Control of execution of rules of notarial clerical work by notaries and officials of executive bodies per-

第八条　公证文书

1. 公证员和其他公证机构工作人员依照吉尔吉斯斯坦共和国政府制定的法规出具公证文书。

2. 公证员与执行机构的工作人员负责公证文书工作，吉尔吉斯斯坦共和国的司法部负责监督公证文书。

forms the Ministry of Justice of the Kyrgyz Republic.

Article 8-1. Single electronic base of notarial documents of the Kyrgyz Republic

1. The single electronic base of notarial documents of the Kyrgyz Republic is complex of program technical means intended for automation of processes of collection, obtaining, search, transfer, processing, storage, use and provision of data on notarial activities and providing all types of information exchange. The procedure for maintaining single electronic base of notarial documents is determined by the Government of the Kyrgyz Republic.

第八条第一款　吉尔吉斯斯坦共和国自然人公证文件电子数据库

1. 吉尔吉斯斯坦共和国的自然人公证文件电子数据库是一种复杂的程序化技术工具，其目的是使公证活动中数据的收集、获取、检索、转移、处理、储存、使用和供应的过程自动化，并提供各种类型的信息共享服务。个人公证文件电子数据库的维护流程由吉尔吉斯斯坦共和国政府决定。

Article 9. Language of notarial clerical work

1. The notarial clerical work is conducted in the state or official language. If person who addressed for making of notarial action does not know language in which the notarial clerical work is conducted, texts of the processed documents shall be translated to it by the translator.

第九条　公证文书的语言

1. 公证文书工作应使用国家官方语言。从事公证工作的人不懂公证活动中使用的语言，应当由翻译人员为其翻译。

Article 10. Personal seal, stamps and forms of the private notary

1. The private notary has personal seal with the image of the State Emblem of the Kyrgyz Republic, specifying of license number, surname, name, middle name and name of the notarial district, stamps of certifying texts, personal forms. The seal of the private notary may contain also individual remedies.

第十条　私营公证员印章、邮票及表格

私营公证员持有带有吉尔吉斯斯坦共和国国徽图案的自然人印章，注明批准文号、姓氏、名字、中间名和公证区的名称、证明文件印章和自然人表格。私营公证员的印章也刻有自然人补救办法等信息。

Chapter 2. State regulation of notarial activities

第二章　国家公证条例

Article 11. License for the right of private notarial activities

1. The license for the occupation right private notarial activities (further - the license) is granted by the Ministry of Justice of the Kyrgyz Republic within a month after passing qualification examination based on the decision of the qualification commission for a period of 5 years. Action of the license is prolonged without passing qualification examination the next 5 years if during implementation of private notarial activities the license was not suspended on the basis provided by the paragraph the second parts one of article 13 of this Law.

第十一条　私营公证营业执照

1. “私营公证营业执照”（以下简称“执照”）由吉尔吉斯斯坦共和国司法部根据资格审查委员会的决定，在申请人通过资格考试后一个月内出具，有效期五年。依据本法第十三条第二款的规定，私营公证员在执业期间没有被吊销执照的，不需要通过资格考试，营业执照可以延期五年。

Article 12. Qualification commission

1. The qualification commission is formed under the Ministry of Justice of the Kyrgyz Republic with participation of representatives of notarial chamber.

2. The qualification commission considers applica-

第十二条　资格审查委员会

1. 资格审查委员会由吉尔吉斯斯坦共和国司法部的相关人员和公证机构的代表组成。

2. 资格审查委员会负责受理公民对私营公证营业

tions of persons applying for receipt of the license for the occupation right private notarial activities, holds qualification examination for the occupation right private notarial activities, considers the claims which arrived on actions of persons having the license for the occupation right private notarial activities with the subsequent adoption of the relevant decision.

3. Legal status of the qualification commission is determined by the Provision approved by the Government of the Kyrgyz Republic.

4. The qualification commission holds exam at persons wishing to be engaged in notarial activities.

5. Persons who did not pass qualification examination are allowed to its repeated delivery not earlier than in year after decision making by the qualification commission.

Article 13. Suspension of action and revocation of license

1. Suspension of action of the license for the right of notarial activities is performed based on the decision of the Ministry of Justice of the Kyrgyz Republic in cases:

- violations of procedure for making of the notarial actions and other regulatory legal acts regulating notarial activities;

- addresses of person having the license for the occupation right private notarial activities.

2. The procedure for suspension of action of the license for the right of notarial activities is determined by the Ministry of Justice of the Kyrgyz Republic.

3. The decision of the Ministry of Justice of the Kyrgyz Republic on suspension of action of the license can be appealed in court according to the procedure, established by the law, from the date of its obtaining.

4. The response of the notary of the license for the right of notarial activities can be made by the Ministry of Justice of the Kyrgyz Republic in cases:

- additions by the notary of the powers at own will;

- losses of nationality of the Kyrgyz Republic or departure out of limits of the Kyrgyz Republic on the permanent residence;

- entries into force of conviction of the court pronounced concerning the notary;

- removal concerning the notary of the judgment about legal incapacity or recognition incapacitated in the procedure established by the law;

- impossibility to fulfill duties of the notary for health reasons (in the presence of the medical certificate);

执照的自然人申请，组织私营公证资格考试，并在通过有关决定后审议由取得私营公证营业执照的人所提出的要求。

3. 资格审查委员会的法律地位由吉尔吉斯斯坦共和国政府颁布的法规决定。

4. 资格审查委员会面向希望从事公证活动的人组织资格考试。

5. 未通过资格考试的人员，可在资格委员会作出决定一年后再次提交申请。

第十三条　暂停执业与吊销执照

1. 在下列情况下，根据吉尔吉斯斯坦共和国司法部的决定，暂停公证员执业行为：

- 违反公证程序，或违反法规从事公证活动；

- 为开展公证活动，游说拥有营业执照的私营公证员。

2. 吉尔吉斯斯坦共和国司法部制定暂停执照的程序。

3. 当事人自收到吉尔吉斯斯坦共和国司法部暂停执照的决定之日起，可依照法律规定的程序，向法院提起上诉。

4. 关于公证员为进行公证活动取得营业执照的相关事项，可在下列情况下由吉尔吉斯斯坦共和国司法部答复：

- 公证员根据自己的意愿请求被赋予额外的职权；

- 丧失吉尔吉斯斯坦共和国国籍或被取消吉尔吉斯斯坦共和国永久居留的限制；

- 法院宣布的关于公证员的定罪生效判决；

- 依照法律规定，裁定取消或确认关于公证员丧失法律行为能力的判决；

- 由于健康原因不能履行公证员的职责（在有医疗证明的情况下）；

- violations by the notary of the requirements provided by Articles 6,7 these Laws;

- triple suspension of action of the license;

- single gross violation of the legislation.

5. In case of response at the notary of the license for the occupation right notarial activities for the bases provided by paragraphs the seventh - the ninth parts four of this Article, it cannot be allowed to passing qualification examination for receipt of the repeated license.

6. The decision on response at the notary of the license for the right of notarial activities can be appealed in court from the date of its obtaining in a month.

Article 14. Notarial district (territory of activities of the notary)

1. The notarial district (the territory of activities of the notary) is established according to administrative-territorial division in the Kyrgyz Republic. In the cities having district or other administrative division, the notarial district is all territory of the respective area.

2. The notary shall have the room for making of notarial actions within the notarial district.

3. The notarial district can be changed by the decision of the Ministry of Justice of the Kyrgyz Republic.

4. Each citizen for making of notarial action has the right to address any notary, except as specified, the stipulated in Article 34 presents of the Law.

5. Making by the notary of notarial action outside the notarial district, in the case provided by part six of this Article does not involve recognition of invalidity of this action.

The part six voided according to the Law of the Kyrgyz Republic of 03.07.2014 No. 111

6. The number of private notaries is not limited.

Article 15. Oath of the notary

- Voided by the Law KR of March 4, 2010 No. 45

Article 16. Offices of notary public

- Voided by the Law KR of March 4, 2010 No. 45

Article 17. Private notary office

- Voided by the Law KR of March 4, 2010 No. 45

Article 18. State register of private notaries

1. The register of private notaries conducts the Ministry of Justice of the Kyrgyz Republic.

- 公证员违反本法第六条、第七条的规定；

- 被暂停执照超过三次的；

- 曾严重违反法律。

5. 公证员有本条第四款第七项至第九项所规定的情形的，不得再次报考资格考试申请执照。

6. 对公证员为进行公证活动取得营业执照相关事项的决定，公证员可在获得营业执照一个月内向法院提出上诉。

第十四条　公证区（公证员的活动领域）

1. 公证区（公证员的活动区域）由吉尔吉斯斯坦共和国按照行政区域划分设立。在设区或下辖其他行政区划的城市，每个区或每个行政区域即一个公证区。

2. 公证员应当拥有在公证区内开展公证活动的办公场所。

3. 公证区的变更决定由吉尔吉斯斯坦共和国司法部决定。

4. 每位公民都有权向作出公证的公证员提出基于本法第三十四条规定的要求，但有特殊规定的除外。

5. 依照本条第六部分的规定，公证员在公证区以外实施的公证活动无效。

根据吉尔吉斯斯坦共和国 2014 年 3 月 7 日第 111 号法令，第十四条第六款已废止。

6. 私营公证员的数量没有限制。

第十五条　公证员宣誓

根据吉尔吉斯斯坦共和国 2010 年 3 月 4 日第 45 号法令，本条规定已废止。

第十六条　国家公证机构

根据吉尔吉斯斯坦共和国 2010 年 3 月 4 日第 45 号法令，本条规定已废止。

第十七条　私营公证机构

根据吉尔吉斯斯坦共和国 2010 年 3 月 4 日第 45 号法令，本条规定已废止。

第十八条　私营公证员登记

1. 私营公证员登记注册工作由吉尔吉斯斯坦共和国司法部负责。

2. The register shall contain name and legal address of private notaries, date of issue of the license, license number and sample of personal seal of the private notary made in accordance with the established procedure. Any changes fixed in the register shall be brought to the attention the Ministry of Justice of the Kyrgyz Republic within a month.

2. 登记簿上应当载明私营公证员的姓名、法定地址、执照签发日期、执照号和按照既定程序制作的私营公证员印章样本。任何事项的更改，应当在提交注册登记申请后一个月内向吉尔吉斯斯坦共和国司法部提出申请。

Article 19. Departmental notarial archive

1. In the Kyrgyz Republic the departmental notarial archive which is component of National Archive Fund and performing storage of notarial documents is established.

2. Questions of the organization of activities and competence of departmental notarial archive are determined by the regulations on the Public notarial Records Office approved by the Government of the Kyrgyz Republic.

The part three voided according to the Law of the Kyrgyz Republic of 05.18.2016 No. 64

The part four voided according to the Law of the Kyrgyz Republic of 03.04.2010 No. 45

The part five voided according to the Law of the Kyrgyz Republic of 05.18.2016 No. 64

第十九条　公证档案室

1. 公证档案室作为吉尔吉斯斯坦共和国国家档案基金的组成部分，负责公证文件的保存工作。

2. 公证档案室的组织、活动和权限等问题都由吉尔吉斯斯坦共和国政府颁布的《公证档案室条例》确定。

根据吉尔吉斯斯坦共和国2016年5月18日第64号法令，第十九条第三款已废止；

根据吉尔吉斯斯坦共和国2010年3月4日第45号法令，第十九条第四款已废止；

根据吉尔吉斯斯坦共和国2016年5月18日第64号法令，第十九条第五款已废止。

Chapter 3. Rights, obligations and responsibility of the notary

第三章　公证员的权利、义务与责任

Article 20. Rights of the notary

1. The notary has the right:

- make the notarial actions provided by this Law for the benefit of the physical persons and legal entities which addressed it, except as specified, when the place of making of notarial action is determined by the legislation of the Kyrgyz Republic or international treaties which came in the procedure established by the law into force which participant is the Kyrgyz Republic.

- constitute drafts of transactions, statements and other documents, to produce copies of documents and the statement from them, and also to make explanations concerning making of notarial actions;

- request physical persons and legal entities of the data and the documents necessary for making of notarial actions. Specified persons shall submit data and documents (including additional) no later than ten days from the moment of receipt of the requirement to them.

2. By the legislation of the Kyrgyz Republic also others can be presented to the notary of temper.

第二十条　公证员的权利

1. 公证员拥有如下权利：

为申请公证的自然人和法人的利益实施公证行为。除非有特殊规定，公证活动的地点由吉尔吉斯斯坦共和国法律或吉尔吉斯斯坦共和国参与缔结的国际条约确定。

- 起草交易、报表和其他文件，提供文件的副本及其说明，并就公证相关问题作出解释；

- 要求自然人和法人在收到要求之日起十天内向公证员提交公证所需的资料和文件（包括附加文件）。

2. 依照吉尔吉斯斯坦共和国的法律，公证员可酌情要求自然人和法人提交其他材料。

Article 21. Obligations of the notary

1. The notary shall:

- render physical persons and legal entities assistance in realization of their rights and protection of legitimate interests;

- explain to physical persons and legal entities of the right and obligation, to warn about consequences of the made notarial actions legal lack of information could not be used by it to the detriment;

- keep in secret data which became known to it in connection with implementation of its professional activity, including after the abdication or dismissal, except as specified, provided by the law;

- refuse making of notarial action in case of its discrepancy to the legislation of the Kyrgyz Republic or to the international treaties which came in the procedure established by the law into force which participant is the Kyrgyz Republic.

2. The notary carries out the obligations and compliance with this Law, other regulatory legal acts of the Kyrgyz Republic. The court can exempt the notary from obligations of preserving secret if against the notary criminal case in connection with making of notarial action is brought.

3. The notary in cases, stipulated by the legislation the Kyrgyz Republic, shall provide to tax authority the certificate necessary for calculation of tax on the property, of property value which is carrying over citizens according to the procedure of inheritance or donation.

Article 22. Responsibility of the notary

1. The notaries and other officials authorized on making of notarial actions in case of making of the actions contradicting the legislation of the Kyrgyz Republic bear responsibility in the procedure established by the law.

2. The notary who intentionally divulged data on committed notarial action or made the notarial action contradicting the legislation of the Kyrgyz Republic shall compensate by a court decision caused thereof damage. In other cases the loss is indemnified by the notary if it cannot be compensated in other procedure.

3. In case of non-presentation or untimely submission to tax authority of the data provided by part three of article 21 of this Law, the notary can be made judicially responsible according to the legislation of the Kyrgyz Republic.

Article 22-1. Insurance of the private notary

1. The private notary shall insure the civil responsi-

第二十一条　公证员的义务

1. 公证员有如下义务：

- 协助自然人和法人认识到他们的权利和应受保护的合法利益；

- 向自然人和法人说明权利和义务，警告其在未提交关键信息的情况下作出的公证行为可能产生的损害结果；

- 依照本法规定，除特殊情况外，公证员在任职期间、辞职后或被解雇后对于与公证活动有关的秘密资料，始终负有保密义务；

- 如果申请公证的行为违反了吉尔吉斯斯坦共和国法律或吉尔吉斯斯坦共和国依法参与缔结的国际条约的规定，公证员应拒绝公证。

2. 公证员履行义务并遵守本法与吉尔吉斯斯坦共和国的其他规范性法规。如果公证涉及刑事案件，法院可以免除公证员的保密义务。

3. 依照吉尔吉斯斯坦共和国法律的规定，公证员应当向税务机关提供证明财产应税税额的证明材料以及公民因继承或捐赠取得的财产的应税税额的证明材料。

第二十二条　公证员的责任

1. 公证员和被授权进行公证的公务员违反吉尔吉斯斯坦共和国法律的，应当承担相应的法律责任。

2. 公证员故意泄露公证资料或作出违反吉尔吉斯斯坦共和国法律的公证行为，应当由法院判决其补偿由此产生的损失。在其他程序中，若不能对当事人予以补偿，则由公证员赔偿其行为造成的损失。

3. 公证员违反本法第二十一条第三款的规定，没有向税务部门提供数据或未及时提交的，应承担相应的法律责任。

第二十二条第一款 私营公证员保险

1. 私营公证员应根据保险合同的条款，对公证行

bility according to the obligations arising owing to damnification as a result of making of notarial actions by the conclusion of the insurance contract. The notary has no right to carry out the obligations without the conclusion of the insurance contract.

为产生的损害承担相应的民事赔偿责任。如未订立保险合同，公证员无须承担责任。

2. The minimum insurance sum is determined in 500-fold size of settlement indicator established by the law.

2. 最低保险赔偿金额是法律规定的结算指标的五百倍。

Chapter 4. Financial provision of Activities of Notaries

第四章　公证活动的财务规定

Article 23. Payment of notarial actions and other services rendered by notaries

第二十三条　公证费用与公证员提供其他服务的费用

1. For making of notarial actions the notary and officials of local government bodies collect the state fee at the rates established by the Government of the Kyrgyz Republic.

1. 公证员和地方政府机构的官员按照吉尔吉斯斯坦共和国政府的规定收取公证费。

2. Services in preparation of draft documents and other services of private notaries are paid by the addressed persons by agreement and remain at the disposal of the private notary. Rates for services in preparation of draft documents and other paid services of notaries public are established by the Government of the Kyrgyz Republic.

2. 私营公证员和当事人协商确定起草文件和提供其他服务的费用。国家公证员起草文件和提供其他有偿服务的收费标准由吉尔吉斯斯坦共和国政府确定。

Part 3 voided according to the Law of the Kyrgyz Republic of 03.07.2014 No. 111

（根据吉尔吉斯斯坦共和国2014年3月7日第111号法令，第二十三条第三款已废止）

3. Notarial action is recognized committed after payment of the state fee or the amount according to rate.

3. 公证申请人支付确定数额的费用后，公证员确认受理公证申请。

4. Privileges on payment of the state fee for physical persons and legal entities, stipulated by the legislation about the state fee, extend to these persons when making notarial actions, designing documents, issue of copies and accomplishment of technical work both notaries public, and private notaries.

4.《国家公证费法》对自然人和法人缴纳国家公证费的规定，适用于国家公证员和私营公证员进行公证活动、设计文件、出具副本和完成相关技术工作时的情形。

5. In case of departure of the notary for making of notarial action out of the place of the work the interested physical persons and legal entities refund it the actual transportation expenses.

5. 公证员离开工作场所办理公证事项的公证申请人应当支付其实际支出的交通费用。

Article 24. Financing of notarial activities

第二十四条　公证活动经费

1. Source of financing of activities of the private notary are the means received by it for the making of notarial actions and rendering services of legal and technical nature, other receipts which are not contradicting the legislation of the Kyrgyz Republic.

1. 私营公证员的资金来源于公证活动和提供法律技术的收入以及其他不违反吉尔吉斯斯坦共和国的法律规定的收入。

2. The money received by the private notary after tax payment, other obligatory payments arrives in its property.

2. 扣除私营公证收取的相关费用的应纳税款后，剩余部分划拨入公证员的账户中。

3. Private notaries have the right to open settlement and other accounts, including currency, in any bank.

3. 私营公证员有权在任何银行开立结算账户和包括活期账户在内的其他类型账户。

4. The money which is on deposit accounts of private

4. 私营公证员存款账户上的存款不是他们的收入。

notaries is not their income.

Chapter 5. Control of activities of notaries

Article 25. Judicial control of making of notarial actions

1. Refusal in making of notarial action or the wrong making of notarial action are appealed judicially.

Article 26. Control of execution by notaries of professional obligations

1. Control of execution of professional obligations by notaries is exercised by the Ministry of Justice of the Kyrgyz Republic. Control of observance by notaries of the tax legislation is exercised by tax authorities according to the procedure and terms, stipulated by the legislation the Kyrgyz Republic.

2. Inspection of the organization of work of the notary is carried out once in four years. The first check of the organization of work of the notary who for the first time started implementation of notarial activities shall be carried out in year after its position assignment of the notary.

3. Notaries shall represent to the officials authorized on conducting checks, the data and the documents concerning settlings with physical persons and legal entities.

Article 27. The certificate officials of the wills and powers of attorney equated to notarially certified

1.Are equated to notarially certified documents:

- wills and powers of attorney of the citizens who are on treatment in hospitals, sanatoria and other medical institutions, certified by the chief or the chief physician of such organization;
- wills and powers of attorney of the military personnel, and at home stations of military units, connections, military-training organizations where there are no state and private notaries and other bodies making notarial actions
- also wills and powers of attorney of workers and employees, members of their families and members of families of the military personnel certified by the commander (chief) of this part, connection, organization or institution;
- wills and powers of attorney of persons who are in places of detention or being held in custody, certified by the chief of the relevant organizations;
- wills and powers of attorney of the full age capable citizens who are in organizations of social protection,

第五章　公证监督

第二十五条　公证行为的司法监督

1. 当事人有权对拒绝公证或错误公证提出上诉。

第二十六条　对公证员履行职业义务的监督

1. 对吉尔吉斯斯坦共和国司法部有权监督公证员履行职业义务的情况。税务当局依照吉尔吉斯斯坦共和国法律规定的程序和条款对公证员遵守税法的情况进行监督。

2. 司法部每四年对公证员的活动进行一次检查。对第一次开展公证活动的公证员，司法部应在其取得公证员资格的一年后进行第一次检查。

3. 公证员应当向被授权进行检查的官员提供自然人和法人居所地的数据和文件。

第二十七条　行政机构认定的遗嘱和授权委托书的效力等同于经过公证的文书效力

1. 下列遗嘱和授权委托书的效力等同于经公证的文书：

- 在医院、疗养院和其他医疗机构接受治疗的，并经该组织负责人或主任医师证明的公民设立的遗嘱和授权委托书；
- 军事人员，以及在没有国家和私营公证员及其他公证机构的军事单位、通讯部门、军事训练组织的驻地的相关人员设立的遗嘱和授权委托书；
- 通讯部门的工人、雇员及其家属，以及军事人员的家属设立的，经相关军事单位、通讯部门等单位的首长认可的遗嘱和授权委托书；
- 被拘留或被羁押的公民设立的，经有关组织负责人认可的遗嘱和授权委托书；
- 在社会保障组织中的，有完全行为能力的成年公民设立的，由管理该组织的机构或其他相关社会保

certified by administration of this organization or the head (his deputy) of relevant organ of social protection of the population.

障组织的负责人（或其副手）认可的遗嘱和授权委托书。

Section 2. Notarial actions and rules of their making

第二部分　公证行为

Chapter 6. The notarial actions made by notaries and authorized officers

第六章　公证员及被授权人员的公证行为

Article 28. The notarial actions made by private notaries

1. Private notaries make the following notarial actions:

1) is certified by transactions;

2) grant certificates on the property right to share in common property of spouses;

3) witness fidelity of copies of documents and their statements them;

4) witness authenticity of the signature on documents;

5) witness fidelity of the translation of documents from one language on another;

6) certify the fact of finding of the citizen in live;

7) certify the fact of finding of the citizen in certain place;

8) certify identity of the citizen with person represented in the photo;

9) certify time of production of documents;

10) is transferred by statements of physical persons and legal entities to other physical persons and legal entities;

11) is accepted in the deposit by sums of money and securities;

12) is made by executive texts;

13) is made by protests of bills of exchange;

14) is shown by checks to payment and certify non-payment of checks;

15) accept documents on storage;

16) is made by ship's protests;

17) is provided by proofs.

18) certify the agreement on voluntary conveyance of property and securities by inadequate person to the subject of legalization.

2. Notarial actions in case of realization of legalized personal and real estate can be performed only in case of payment term of the income tax.

第二十八条　私营公证员有权实施的公证行为

1. 私营公证员有权实施下列公证行为：

（1）为交易行为进行公证；

（2）出具夫妻共有财产的权属证书；

（3）公证文件副本和相关当事人陈述的真实性；

（4）公证文件签字的真实性；

（5）公证翻译文件的真实性；

（6）公证公民在某地生活的事实；

（7）公证公民在具体地点居留的事实；

（8）公证照片中所代表的人的身份；

（9）公证出示文件的时间；

（10）公证自然人或法人的陈述向其他自然人或法人转达的声明；

（11）公证存款金额与证券数量；

（12）公证制定执行文本；

（13）公证汇票拒付声明；

（14）公证支票支付和不支付支票的行为；

（15）保管文件；

（16）公证船舶海事声明书；

（17）公证提供的证据；

（18）公证不适格主体和合法主体间的财产与证券自愿转让协议。

2. 只有在自然人缴纳所得税之后，公证员方可公证合法财产和不动产。

3. By regulatory legal acts of the Kyrgyz Republic also other notarial actions can be provided.

Article 29. The notarial actions made by notaries public

1. Notaries public make notarial actions, the stipulated in Article 28 these Laws, and also impose and remove property acquisition bans, grant certificates on the right to inheritance, take measures to protection of heritable property and certify authenticity of the facsimile signature of person with limited opportunities of health. In the absence of the notary public or impossibility of making of the called notarial actions by him making of these notarial actions is entrusted by the decision of the Ministry of Justice of the Kyrgyz Republic to other notary public.

2. The certificate on the property right in case of the death of one of spouses is granted by the notary public whose competence includes execution of the succession law.

Article 30. The notarial actions made by officials of executive bodies

1. In case of absence in the settlement of the notary officials of executive bodies, representatives to make notarial actions, make the following notarial actions:

1) is certified by wills;

2) is certified by powers of attorney;

3) take measures to protection of heritable property;

4) witness fidelity of copies of documents and statements from them;

5) witness authenticity of the signature on documents.

2. By legal acts of the Kyrgyz Republic making and other notarial actions can be assigned to the officials specified in this Article.

Article 31. The notarial actions made by officials of consular establishments of the Kyrgyz Republic

1. Officials of consular establishments of the Kyrgyz Republic make the following notarial actions:

1) is certified by transactions, except agreements on alienation of the real estate which is in the territory of the Kyrgyz Republic;

2) take measures to protection of heritable property;

3) grant certificates on the right to inheritance;

4) grant certificates on the property right to share in common property of spouses;

5) witness fidelity of copies of documents and state-

3. 吉尔吉斯斯坦共和国法律规定的其他公证。

第二十九条　国家公证员有权实施的公证行为

1. 依照本法第二十八条的规定，国家公证员有权实施公证行为，强制执行或解除财产购置禁令，出具继承权权属证书，采取措施保护遗产，公证不完全健康的人的签名副本的真实性。公证员不在场或无法公证的，吉尔吉斯斯坦共和国司法部可以决定委托其他国家公证员公证。

2. 配偶一方死亡的，国家公证员有权出具财产权权属证书。公证员的职权包括继承法规定的相关事项。

第三十条　行政机关有权实施的公证行为

1. 缺少公证员时，行政机关有权实施下列公证活动：

（1）公证遗嘱；

（2）公证授权委托书；

（3）采取措施保护遗产；

（4）公证文件和陈述的副本的真实性；

（5）公证文件签字的真实性。

2. 依照吉尔吉斯斯坦共和国相关法案，在本条中提及的行政机关人员也可以实施其他公证行为。

第三十一条　吉尔吉斯斯坦共和国领事机构有权实施的公证行为

1. 吉尔吉斯斯坦共和国领事机构人员可以进行下列公证行为：

（1）公证交易行为，不包括在吉尔吉斯斯坦共和国境内签订的房地产转让协议；

（2）采取措施保护遗产；

（3）授予继承权权属证书；

（4）授予夫妻共有财产权属证书；

（5）公证文件和陈述副本的真实性；

ments from them;

6) witness authenticity of the signature on documents;

7) witness fidelity of the translation of documents from one language on another;

8) certify the fact of finding of the citizen in live;

9) certify the fact of finding of the citizen in certain place;

10) certify identity of the citizen with person represented in the photo;

11) certify time of production of documents;

12) is accepted in the deposit by sums of money and securities;

13) is made by executive texts;

14) accept documents on storage;

15) is provided by proofs;

16) is made by ship's protests.

2. By legal acts of the Kyrgyz Republic also other notarial actions made by officials of consular establishments of the Kyrgyz Republic can be provided.

Article 32. The notarial actions made in notarial archives

1. Registrars in departmental notarial archive issue duplicates and witness fidelity of copies and statements from documents which are stored in cases of these archives.

Article 33. Procedure for making of notarial actions

1. The procedure for making of notarial actions by notaries is established by this Law and other regulations of the Kyrgyz Republic.

2. The procedure for making of notarial actions by officials of consular establishments is established by regulatory legal acts of the Kyrgyz Republic.

3. The procedure for making of notarial actions by local government bodies, is established by the Instruction about procedure for making of notarial actions approved by the Government of the Kyrgyz Republic.

Chapter 7. Basic rules of making of notarial actions. Issue of duplicates of documents

Article 34. Place of making of notarial actions

1. Notarial actions are made by any notary, except as specified, presents of the Law provided by Articles 29,of 41,of 50,56-58,63,of 64,of 68,of 69,of 81,, and other cases when according to the legislation of the Kyrgyz Republic

（6）公证文件签字的真实性；

（7）公证翻译文件的真实性；

（8）公证某人在某地生活的事实；

（9）公证公民在具体地点居留的事实；

（10）公证照片中所代表的人的身份；

（11）公证出示文件的时间；

（12）公证存款金额与证券数量；

（13）公证制定执行文本；

（14）保管文件；

（15）公证提供的证据；

（16）公证船舶海事声明书。

2. 依照吉尔吉斯斯坦共和国相关法案，吉尔吉斯斯坦共和国领事机构官员也可以实施其他公证行为。

第三十二条　公证档案机关有权实施的公证行为

1. 公证档案机关的书记官负责出具文件副本和公证保存在档案中的文件与陈述副本的真实性。

第三十三条　公证行为的程序

1. 吉尔吉斯斯坦共和国的法律和其他法规规定了公证员进行公证的程序。

2. 吉尔吉斯斯坦共和国的监督法规规定了领事机构官员进行公证的程序。

3. 地方政府机构的公证程序依照吉尔吉斯斯坦共和国政府批准的公证程序的指示制定。

第七章　公证行为的基本规则，出具文件副本

第三十四条　公证场所

1. 任何公证员均可实施公证行为，但不包括本法第二十九条、第四十一条、第五十条、第五十六条至第五十八条、第六十三条、第六十四条、第六十八条、第六十九条、第八十一条所规定的情形，以及依照吉

notarial action be made by certain notary.

Article 35. Bases and terms of adjournment and suspension of making of notarial action

1. Making of notarial action can be postponed in case:

- need of reclamation of additional data from physical persons and legal entities;

- directions of documents for examination.

2. Making of notarial actions shall be postponed if according to the law it is necessary to request interested persons about lack of objections from them against making of these actions.

3. The term of adjournment of making of notarial action cannot exceed one month from the date of pronouncement of the resolution on adjournment of making of notarial action.

4. According to the statement of the interested person challenging in court the right or the fact for which certificate other interested person addressed making of notarial action it can be postponed for term no more than ten days. If during this term the interested person does not submit the document confirming the fact of receipt of his petition, notarial action shall be made.

5. In case of obtaining from court of the message on receipt of the statement of the interested person challenging the right or the fact about which certificate asks other interested person making of notarial action stops to permission of case by court.

6. By legal acts of the Kyrgyz Republic also other bases for adjournment and suspension of making of notarial actions can be established.

Article 36. Identification of the notarial action which addressed for making

1. When making notarial action the notary identifies the personality of the notarial action of the citizen, his representative or the representative of the legal entity which addressed for making.

2. Identification shall be made based on the passport or the identity certificate excluding any doubts concerning the identity of the citizen who addressed for making of notarial action.

尔吉斯斯坦共和国法律规定，由特定公证员实施公证行为的其他情况。

第三十五条　延迟和暂停公证

1. 下列情况下可以延期公证：

- 需要收集更多关于自然人或法人的信息；

- 审查文件的指引。

2. 依法有必要确认利害关系人对提起公证有无异议时，应当推迟进行公证。

3. 延期公证的期限，自作出中止公证的决议公布之日起算，最长不得超过一个月。

4. 利害关系人在法庭上提出对其他利害关系人要求公证的权利或事实的质疑，公证员可以延期公证，延期不得超过十天。在该期限内，利害关系人未提交确认相关事实或支持其主张的文件，公证员应当恢复公证。

5. 在收到来自法院的利害关系人质疑其他利害关系人要求公证的权利和事实的信息后，公证机构应停止相应案件的公证工作。

6. 依照吉尔吉斯斯坦共和国法律规定的其他可以延期和暂停公证的情形。

第三十六条　申请公证员的身份识别

1. 在进行公证时，公证员应当确认申请公证的公民及其代理人、法人的代表人的资格。

2. 公证员应当依照护照和其他身份证明文件核实公民身份，不得存在有关身份确认的任何疑虑。

Article 37. Check of capacity to act of citizens and legal capacities of the legal entities participating in transactions

1. In case of the certificate of transactions capacity to act of citizens becomes clear and legal capacity of the legal entities participating in transactions is checked. In case of transaction by the representative also its powers are checked.

第三十七条 核实公民的行为能力和法人参与交易的行为能力

在有交易证明书的情况下，公民的行为能力得以确认，法人参与交易的法律行为能力应当受到检查。在法人代表进行交易的情况下，也应当对其权力进行检查。

Article 38. Procedure for the signature of notarially certified transaction, the statement and other documents

1. Contents of notarially certified transaction, and also statement and other documents shall be read aloud to participants. The documents processed in notarial procedure are signed in the presence of the notary.

2. If the citizen owing to physical defects, disease or for any other reasons cannot personally undersign, according to its order, at its presence and in the presence of the notary other citizen with indication of the reasons owing to which the document could not be signed with own hand by the citizen who addressed for making of notarial action can sign the transaction, the statement or other document.

3. If the citizen owing to physical defects has no opportunity to append the sign manual and does not wish to trust signing of the transaction, statement or other document from his name to the third party, it can sign the necessary document with use of the facsimile signature which authenticity makes sure according to this Law.

第三十八条 对交易证明书和文件上的签字进行公证的程序

1. 经公证的交易内容，声明和其他文件，应当向当事人公开宣读。公证程序中处理的文件需在公证员在场的情况下签字。

2. 如果公民因身体缺陷、疾病或其他原因，不能依指示在本人和公证员在场的情况下亲自签字，其他公民可以在说明该文件不能由申请人亲自签署的原因后，代为在交易证明书、陈述或其他文件上签字。

3. 公民因身体缺陷无法亲笔签名，也不希望委托第三方签署交易证明书、陈述或者其他文件的，可以依照本法规定使用能够确保真实性的摹真签章签署必要的文件。

Article 39. Requirements to the documents submitted for making of notarial actions

1. The notaries and other persons making notarial actions do not take for making notarial actions the documents having erasures or additions, the crossed-out words and other not stipulated corrections, and also the documents performed by pencil.

2. The text of notarially certified transaction shall be written clearly and accurately, the numbers relating to contents of the document and time frames are specified at least once by words, and names of legal entities - without reducings, with indication of addresses of their bodies, surnames, names and middle names of citizens, the address of their residence shall be written completely.

3. In the document which amount exceeds one leaf sheets shall be stitched, numbered and under seal.

第三十九条 提交公证文件的要求

1. 公证员和其他开展公证工作的人员在公证时，不得接受有擦除或增添痕迹、有划去的字句和其他不合规定的更正痕迹的文件，也不得接受用铅笔书写的文件。

2. 经过公证的交易文本应当清楚、准确，与文件内容和时限有关的数字至少用文字注明一次。法人的名称应当完整，并注明其登记注册地、办公地址、法人代表的姓名和中间名。

3. 页数超过一页的文件，须装订、编号和盖章。

Article 40. Making of certifying texts and issue of certificates

1. Certifying texts are made in case of the certificate of transactions, witnessing of fidelity of copies of documents and statements from them, authenticity of the signature on documents, fidelity of the translation of documents from one language on another, in case of the certificate of time of production of documents on the relevant documents.

2. In confirmation of inheritance right, the property right, the certificate of the facts of finding of the citizen in live and in certain place, identity of the citizen with person represented on photos, acceptances on document storage, authenticity of the facsimile signature of person with limited opportunities of health appropriate certificates are granted.

第四十条　制作和出具公证书

1. 公证员公证交易证明书，文件和声明副本的真实性，签字的真实性，翻译文件的真实性和生产日期证明书的真实性时，应当出具核证文本。

2. 公证员可以对确认继承权与财产权，证实某公民尚在人世的事实或在某地出现的事实证明，确认照片中出现的公民的身份，文件的储存和接收及有限健康的人的传真签名的真实性等事项出具公证书。

Article 41. Restrictions of the right of making of notarial actions

1. The notary has no right to make notarial actions on the name and on its own behalf, addressed to and on behalf of the spouse (the spouse), their and relatives (parents, children, grandsons, brothers, sisters, the grandfather, the grandma).

第四十一条　公证行为的权利限制

公证员不得以本人的名义或代表本人实施公证行为，不得以本人配偶及其亲属（父母、子女、孙子女、兄弟、姐妹、祖父母、外祖父母）的名义或代表他们实施公证行为。

Article 42. Refusal in making of notarial action

1. The notary refuses making of notarial action if:

- making of such action contradicts the law;
- action is subject to making by other notary;
- the incapacitated citizen or the representative who does not have necessary powers requested making of notarial action;
- the transaction made on behalf of the legal entity contradicts the purposes specified in its charter or provision;
- the transaction does not conform to requirements of the law;
- the documents submitted for making of notarial action do not conform to requirements of the legislation.

2. The notary at the request of person to whom it is refused making of notarial action shall state causes of failure in writing and explain procedure for its appeal. In these cases the notary no later than three working days issues the decree on refusal in making of notarial action.

第四十二条　拒绝公证

1. 在下列情形下，公证员应当拒绝进行公证：

- 违反法律的行为；
- 已经由其他公证员公证过的行为；
- 无行为能力的公民或无权代理人要求进行的公证；
- 法人代表提交的交易文本与法人章程的目的相矛盾；
- 交易文本不符合法律规定；
- 为申请公证提交的文件不符合法律规定。

2. 公证员应当向申请人书面说明拒绝公证的理由，并释明对应的上诉程序。公证员应当在三个工作日作出拒绝公证的决定。

Article 43. Appeal of notarial actions or refusal in their making

1. The interested person considering wrong committed notarial action or refusal in making of the notarial

第四十三条　对公证行为或拒绝公证决定的上诉

1. 认为公证行为错误或拒绝公证的决定不合理的利害关系人，有权上诉。

action having the right to take a legal action.

2. The dispute on the right which arose between interested persons based on committed notarial action is considered by court according to the procedure of claim production.

Article 44. Registration of notarial actions

1. All notarial actions made by the notary are registered in the register.

2. The notary shall issue statements from the register according to the written application of the organizations and persons specified in parts two, third, fourth and fifth article 7 of this Law.

Article 45. Forms of registers of registration of notarial actions, notarial certificates, certifying texts

1. Forms of registers of registration of notarial actions, notarial certificates, certifying texts on transactions and the witnessed documents are established by the Government of the Kyrgyz Republic.

Article 46. Issue of duplicates of notarially certified documents

1. In case of loss of documents which copies are stored in cases at the notary, according to written applications of citizens, legal representatives of legal entities, from name or at the request of which notarial actions were made duplicates of the lost documents are issued.

2. Issue of duplicates of documents is made with observance of requirements Articles 7of and 44 presents of the Law.

Chapter 8. Certificate of transactions

Article 47. The transactions certified in notarial procedure

1. The notary certifies transactions for which the legislation of the Kyrgyz Republic establishes obligatory notarial form. At the request of the parties the notary can certify and other transactions.

Article 48. Explanation to the parties of sense and value of the draft of the transaction

1. The notary shall explain to the parties sense and value of the draft of the transaction provided by them and to check whether there corresponds its content to actual intents of the parties and whether contradicts requirements of the law.

2. 利害关系人因既成公证行为产生的权利纠纷，由法院根据利害关系人的申请按法定程序解决。

第四十四条　公证登记

1. 公证员所作的所有公证行为均需在注册登记簿上登记。

2. 公证员应当依照本法第二部分、第三部分、第四部分和第五部分第七条规定的组织和人员的书面申请，依照登记簿的登记发布声明。

第四十五条　公证登记表、公证书、核证文本

关于交易和见证文件的公证登记表、公证书和核证文本，都由吉尔吉斯斯坦共和国政府制作。

第四十六条　出具经过公证的文件和副本

1. 公民和法人遗失公证文件的，若该文件副本保存在公证机构，公证员可以根据公民和法人代表的书面申请向其出具公证文件的副本。

2. 出具文件副本应符合本法第七条和第四十四条的规定。

第八章　交易证明书

第四十七条　经公证程序公证的交易

公证员依照吉尔吉斯斯坦共和国法律规定的强制公证形式对交易进行公证。根据当事人的要求，公证员也可以对其他类型的交易进行公证。

第四十八条　应当事人要求解释交易文件草案的法律意义

公证员应当向当事人解释其所提供的交易文件草案的法律意义，并核实草案内容符合与当事人实际意图和法律要求。

Article 49. The certificate of agreements of alienation in about pledge of the property which is subject to registration

1. Agreements of alienation and on pledge of the property which is subject to registration can be certified on condition of submission of the documents confirming the property right on the alienated or pledged property.

Article 50. Certificate of agreements on alienation of the apartment house and other structures

1. The certificate of agreements on alienation of the apartment house, apartment, giving, garden house, garage, and also other structures is made by the notary in the location of the specified property.

Article 51. Certificate of wills

1. The notary certifies the wills of capable citizens constituted according to requirements of the legislation of the Kyrgyz Republic and personally provided by them to the notary. The certificate of wills through representatives is not allowed.

2. In case of the certificate of wills from testators production of evidence, the pases confirming their rights the bequeathed property is not required.

Article 52. Procedure for change and cancellation of wills

1. The notary in case of receipt of the statement for cancellation of the will, and equally in the receipt of the new will canceling or changing the will constituted earlier does about it mark in the will copy which is stored at the notary and in the alphabetic book of accounting of wills. The statement for cancellation of the will shall be notarially certified.

Article 53. Certificate of powers of attorney

1. The notary certifies powers of attorney on behalf of one or several persons, addressed to one or several persons.

2. The power of attorney issued according to the procedure of retrust is subject to the notarial certificate after submission of the main power of attorney in which the retrust right, or after production of evidence of the fact that the representative under the main power of attorney is forced to it by force of circumstances for protection of interests issued the power of attorney is stipulated. The power of attorney issued according to the procedure of retrust shall not comprise more rights, than it is provided under the main power of attorney. Effective period of the power

第四十九条　已登记的质押财产转让协议证明

公证员可以在提交确认让与质押财产权文件的前提下予以公证已登记的质押财产的转让。

第五十条　公寓楼及其他建筑物的转让协议证明书

公寓楼、附属建筑、花园房、车库及其他建筑物的转让协议证明书由上述不动产所在地的公证员出具。

第五十一条　遗嘱证明书

1. 根据吉尔吉斯斯坦共和国的法律规定，公证员根据有完全民事行为能力的公民亲自提交的遗嘱进行公证。法律不允许通过代理人提交遗嘱以申请公证。

2. 立遗嘱人能够出示证据证明该遗嘱的有效性的，无须出具确认遗赠财产权利的证据。

第五十二条　变更和撤销遗嘱程序

公证员如收到撤销遗嘱的申请书，以及撤销或变更较早订立遗嘱的新遗嘱时，须在存放于公证员处的遗嘱副本和按字母排序的遗嘱登记簿上作出标记。撤销遗嘱的申请书须经公证。

第五十三条　授权委托书的公证

1. 公证员可以公证授权委托书，包括委托一人或数人的授权委托书和代理一人或数人的授权委托书，并邮寄给对应的委托人。

2. 按照再委托程序发出的授权委托书，须在提交主委托书后，或在出示证据证明主委托书所指的代理人因利益保障问题而被迫向其发出授权书后，进行公证。按照再委托程序发出的授权委托书不应包含比主委托书所规定的权利更多的权利。再委托的授权委托书的有效期不得超过所主委托书的有效期。

of attorney issued according to the procedure of retrust cannot exceed effective period of the power of attorney based on which it is issued.

Article 54. Number of copies of notarial documents

1. Number of copies of documents in which contents of the transaction certified in notarial procedure are stated shall be at least two, one of which remains in cases of notary office.

Chapter 9. Taking measures to protection of heritable property. Issue of certificates on the right to inheritance

Article 55. The notice of heirs on the opened inheritance

1. The notary who received the message on the opened inheritance shall inform on it those heirs, the residence or works of which is known to it.

2. The notary can also make challenge of heirs by the room of the public notice or the message on it in mass media.

Article 56. Receipt of statements for inheritance acceptance or about refusal of it

1. The notary in the place of opening of inheritance according to the legislation of the Kyrgyz Republic adopts statements for inheritance acceptance or for refusal of it. The statement for inheritance acceptance or for refusal of it shall be made in writing.

Article 57. Adoption of claims from creditors of the testator

1. The notary in the place of opening of inheritance according to the legislation of the Kyrgyz Republic accepts claims from creditors of the testator. Complaint shall be made in writing.

Article 58. Protection of heritable property

1. The notary in the place of opening of inheritance according to citizens, legal entities or on the initiative takes measures to protection of heritable property, when necessary for the benefit of heirs, legatees, creditors or the state.

Article 59. The order about taking measures to protection of heritable property

1. If the property of the testator or his part is not in the place of opening of inheritance, the notary in the place of opening of inheritance sends to the notary and if in this settlement there is no notary, then to the official of relevant

第五十四条　公证文件及其副本的数量

公证员应当为记载经过公证的交易内容的文件制作至少两份副本，其中一份交公证机构保管。

第九章　采取措施保护遗产，出具继承权权属证书

第五十五条　公开遗产的继承人通知

1. 公证员收到关于公开遗产的信息后，应当将其住所或工作情况等信息告知法定继承人。

2. 公证员还可以通过公共告知室或大众媒体向继承人提出质疑。

第五十六条　收到接受或拒绝继承的声明

依照吉尔吉斯斯坦共和国的法律规定，遗产所在地的公证员有权受理接受或拒绝继承的声明。接受或者拒绝继承的声明应当以书面形式提出。

第五十七条　受理立遗嘱人债权人的请求

依照吉尔吉斯斯坦共和国的法律规定，遗产所在地的公证员有权受理立遗嘱人债权人对债权的申请。该申请应当以书面形式提出。

第五十八条　遗产的保护

遗产所在地的公证员为了公民、法人或者主张继承权的自然人，也为了继承人、受遗赠人、债权人或者国家的利益，应当采取措施保护遗产。

第五十九条　采取措施保护遗产的命令

1. 如立遗嘱人或其部分财产不在遗产所在地，遗产所在地的公证员应当将相关材料送交有管辖权的公证员，遗产所在地的公证员可以向遗产所在地有权公证的行政机关官员发出采取保护措施的请求。

organ of the executive authority making notarial action in the location of heritable property the order about taking measures to its protection.

2. The notary or official of relevant organ of the executive authority who took measures to protection of heritable property report to the notary public in the place of opening of inheritance about acceptance of the specified measures.

2. 采取措施保护遗产的相关行政机关的官员或公证员，应当向遗产所在地的公证员报告采取特殊措施的情况。

Article 60. The inventory of heritable property and its transfer on storage

第六十条 遗产的保管及转移

1. The notary public makes the inventory of this property for protection of heritable property and gives him to storage to heirs or other persons.

1. 公证员为保护遗产而进行清点，并将其交给继承人或其他适格当事人保管。

2. If as a part of inheritance there is property requiring management and also in case of presentation of the claim by creditors of the successor before inheritance acceptance by heirs the notary public appoints the keeper of heritable property. In the area where there is no notary public, the relevant organ of the executive authority appoints in the specified cases over heritable property of the guardian.

2. 如果遗产的一部分需要管理，且继承人的债权人在继承人接受继承之前提出债权请求权，公证员应当指定遗产的管理人。在没有公证员的地区，相关行政机关在特定情况下可以指定遗产的监护人。

3. The keeper, the guardian and other persons to whom the heritable property is transferred to storage are warned about responsibility for waste, alienation or concealment of heritable property and for the losses caused by heirs.

3. 将遗产转移保管的管理人、监护人和其他适格当事人应当对浪费、非法转移或隐藏遗产给继承人造成的损失承担责任。

Article 61. Remuneration for storage of heritable property

第六十一条 遗产的保管费用

1. The keeper, the guardian and other persons to whom the heritable property is transferred to storage if they are not heirs, have the right to earn reward for storage of heritable property from heirs.

1. 遗产的管理人、监护人和其他负责保管遗产的人，如果不是继承人，有权要求继承人支付保管遗产的费用。

2. To specified persons necessary expenses are also refunded but to storage and management of heritable property, less actually received benefit from use of this property.

2. 因使用遗产所得的收益大于保管费用的，保管和管理遗产的特定人员应当退还相应的保管收益。

Article 62. The termination of measures to protection of heritable property

第六十二条 停止保护遗产的措施

1. Protection of heritable property continues before inheritance acceptance by heirs and if it is not accepted them - that before the expiration for the inheritance acceptance established by the legislation of the Kyrgyz Republic.

1. 在继承人接受遗产之前，若继承人明确表示不接受遗产，则在吉尔吉斯斯坦共和国法律规定的期限届满之前，对遗产的保护将继续进行。

2. The notary in the place of opening of inheritance shall notify previously heirs on the termination of measures to protection of heritable property and if the property on inheritance right passes to the state - the relevant state body.

2. 遗产所在地的公证员应当提前通知继承人在遗产保护期限届满后将停止采取保护措施，遗产所有权将转移给国家或相关的国家机构。

Article 63. Payment of expenses at the expense of heritable property

1. The notary in the place of opening of inheritance before inheritance acceptance by heirs and if it is not accepted, then before issue to the state of the certificate on the right to inheritance, gives the order about payment for the account of heritable property of the following expenses:

1) on care of the testator during his disease, and also on its funeral and on arrangement of the place of burial;

2) on protection of heritable property and on management of it, and also on the publication of the message on challenge of heirs.

2. By legal acts of the Kyrgyz Republic also other cases of payment of expenses at the expense of heritable property can be established.

Article 64. Place and terms of issue of the certificate on the right to inheritance

1. According to the written application of heirs the notary but to the place of opening of inheritance grants the certificate on the right to inheritance.

2. Issue of the certificate on the right to inheritance is made in the terms established by legal acts of the Kyrgyz Republic.

Article 65. Procedure for issue of the certificate on the right to inheritance

1. The certificate on the right to inheritance is granted to the heirs who accepted inheritance according to regulations of the civil legislation of the Kyrgyz Republic.

2. The heir who passed term for inheritance acceptance can be included in the certificate on the right to inheritance with the consent of all other heirs who accepted inheritance. This consent shall be declared in writing before issue of the certificate on the right to inheritance.

3. The certificate on the right to inheritance is granted to all heirs together or to everyone depending on their desire.

4. The notary reports about issue of the certificate on the right to inheritance addressed to the minor or incapacitated heir to guardianship and custody bodies at the place of residence of the heir for protection of its valuable interests.

5. Upon transition of property on inheritance right to the state the certificate on the right to inheritance is issued to the relevant state body.

Article 66. Conditions of issue of the certificate on the right to inheritance on the law

1. The notary in case of issue of the certificate on

第六十三条　遗产保管费用的支付

1. 在继承人接受遗产之前，如果继承人明确表示不接受遗产，那么遗产所在地的公证员应在出具遗产权属证书之前，责令继承人向遗产账户支付下列费用：

1）立遗嘱人患病期间的看护费和丧葬费用；

2）保护和管理遗产，以及发布对继承人质疑的信息所产生的费用；

2. 吉尔吉斯斯坦共和国的法律规定的其他费用。

第六十四条　出具继承权权属证书的地点和条件

1. 根据继承人的书面申请，公证员可在遗产所在地授予继承权权属证书。

2. 公证员根据吉尔吉斯斯坦共和国法律规定的条款出具继承权权属证书。

第六十五条　继承权权属证书的出具程序

1. 依照吉尔吉斯斯坦共和国民事法律的规定，公证员应当向继承人出具继承权权属证书。

2. 符合接受继承条件的继承人，需经接受继承的其他继承人一致同意，才可取得继承权权属证书。在出具继承权权属证书之前，继承人应以书面形式宣告新的继承人。

3. 公证员根据所有继承人的意愿统一出具，或向每人出具一份继承权权属证书。

4. 公证员为了保护未成年或无行为能力的继承人的利益，应向继承人居所地的监护人和监护机构出具继承权权属证书。

5. 遗产转移给国家所有时，公证员应当向有关国家机关出具继承权权属证书。

第六十六条　法律上关于继承权权属证书的出具条件

1. 公证员在出具继承权权属证书时，应当根据

the right to inheritance under the law by reclamation of the corresponding proofs checks the fact of death of the testator, time and the place of opening of inheritance, availability of the relations which are the basis for calling to inheritance under the law of persons who submitted the application for issue of the certificate on the right to inheritance, structure and the location of heritable property.

法律的规定复核相应的证据，核查立遗嘱人死亡的事实、继承开始的时间和地点，主张继承权的人和立遗嘱人是否具有法律要求的人身关系，以及确认遗产的内容和地点。

2. If one or several legal heirs are deprived of opportunity to produce the evidence of the relations which are the basis for calling to inheritance, they can be included in the certificate on the right to inheritance with the consent of all other heirs who accepted inheritance and produced such evidence.

2. 如果一个或几个合法继承人被剥夺了提出继承权相关证据的机会，那么他们可以在接受继承并已出示所需证据的所有其他继承人的同意下被列入继承权权属证书中。

Article 67. Conditions of issue of the certificate on the pas right inheritance according to the will

第六十七条　根据遗嘱出具继承权证书的条件

1. The notary in case of issue of the certificate on the right to inheritance according to the will by reclamation of the corresponding proofs checks the fact of death of the testator, will availability, time and the place of opening of inheritance, structure and the location of heritable property.

1. 公证员在出具继承权权属证书时，应当根据遗嘱复核相关的证据，核查立遗嘱人死亡的事实、时间和地点和遗嘱有效性，以及遗产的组成和地点。

2. The notary finds out also the group of people, having the right to obligatory share in inheritance.

2. 公证员还应当查明哪些人有权利取得遗产份额。

Chapter 10. Issue of certificates on the property right to share in common property. Imposing and removal of prohibition of property acquisition

第十章　共有财产产权证书的出具，财产取得禁令的强制执行和解除

Article 68. Issue of the certificate on the property right to share in common property

第六十八条　共有财产产权证书的出具

1. The notary according to the joint written statement of spouses or owners (joint or equity property) grants the certificate on the property right to share in common property.

1. 公证员根据配偶或共有人（共同或权益财产）的联合书面声明，出具共同财产所有权证书。

2. The certificate on the property right to real estate is granted by the notary in the location of this property.

2. 不动产权属证书由该不动产所在地的公证机构出具。

Article 69. Issue of the certificate on the property right to share in common property according to the statement of the surviving spouse

第六十九条　根据未亡配偶的陈述出具共有财产权证书

1. In case of the death of one of spouses the certificate on the property right to share in common property of spouses is granted by the notary public in the place of opening of inheritance according to the written application of the surviving spouse with the notice of the heirs who accepted inheritance.

1. 在配偶一方死亡的情况下，遗产所在地的公证员根据未亡配偶的书面申请，在通知已接受继承的继承人后，出具夫妻共同财产产权证书。

2. The certificate on the property right to share in common property of spouses is granted to the surviving spouse on half of the common property acquired during scrap.

2. 夫妻共有财产的一半在婚姻存续期间取得的，公证员应为未亡配偶出具共有财产权属证书。

3. The share of the died spouse in common property also can be determined by the written application of the heirs who accepted inheritance and with the consent of the surviving spouse in the certificate on the property right.

3. 在拥有遗产权属证书的未亡配偶的同意下，已接受继承的继承人通过提交书面申请，可以继承已死亡配偶在共同财产中的份额。

Article 70. Imposing and removal of prohibition of property acquisition

第七十条 财产取得禁令的强制执行和解除

1. Imposing and removal of prohibition of property acquisition is performed on conditions and according to the procedure, established by legal acts of the Kyrgyz Republic.

1. 公证员应当依照吉尔吉斯斯坦共和国法律规定的条件和程序强制执行和解除财产取得禁令。

Chapter 11. Witnessing of fidelity of copies of documents and statements from them, authenticity of the sign and facsimile signature and fidelity of the translation

第十一章 公证文件声明副本、签名和传真签名以及译文的真实性

Article 71. Witnessing of fidelity of copies of documents and statements from them

第七十一条 公证文件和声明副本的真实性

1. The notary witnesses fidelity of copies of documents and statements from them issued by legal entities, and also citizens provided that these documents do not contradict legal acts of the Kyrgyz Republic.

1. 公证员可以公证法人和公民出具的文件和声明副本的真实性，并证明这些文件不违反吉尔吉斯斯坦共和国的法律法规。

2. Fidelity of the statement can be attested only when the document of which the statement is made contain solutions of several the separate, not connected among themselves questions. The statement shall reproduce the complete text of part of the document on certain question.

2. 声明的真实性只有在文件中包含几个独立的、没有相关性的解决方案时才能被公证。同时，声明中应当附有关于某些具体问题的文件全文。

Article 72. Witnessing of fidelity of the copy of the document issued by the citizen

第七十二条 公证公民签署文件副本的真实性

1. Fidelity of the copy of the document issued by the citizen is witnessed by the notary when authenticity of the signature of the citizen on the document is certified by the notary or the official of the organization for place of employment, study or the citizen's residence.

当文件上的公民签名真实性经公证员或公民工作地、学习地或住所地的公证机构工作人员公证后，则公民签署的文件副本的真实性得以被公证。

Article 73. Witnessing of fidelity of the copy from the copy of the document

第七十三条 公证文件副本的真实性

1. Fidelity of the copy from the copy of the document is witnessed by the notary under condition if fidelity of the copy is notarized or the copy of the document is issued by the legal entity from whom the authentic document proceeds. In the latter case the copy of the document shall be made on the form of this legal entity, is under seal and to have mark that the authentic document is at the legal entity.

公证员在文件副本的真实性已被公证或经认证法人已出具文件副本的情况下，可以证明文件副本复印件的真实性。在后一种情况下，文件的副本应当以法人章程规定的形式制作，并盖章注明鉴定文书在法人处保存。

Article 74. Witnessing of authenticity of the signature on the document

第七十四条 公证文件上签名的真实性

1. The notary witnesses authenticity of the sign manual on the document which contents do not contradict legal

1. 文件内容不违反吉尔吉斯斯坦共和国的法律法规的，公证员可以公证文件签名的真实性。

acts of the Kyrgyz Republic.

2. The notary, witnessing authenticity of the sign manual, does not certify the facts stated in the document, and only confirms that the signature is made by certain person.

2. 公证员公证亲笔签名的真实性时，不附带证明文件中所述事实的真实性，只确认该签字是由具体行为人签署的。

Article 74-1. Witnessing of authenticity of the facsimile signature of person with limited opportunities of health

第七十四条第一款　对有限健康的人的摹真签章真实性的见证

1. The facsimile signature (facsimile) - specially made stamp (cliche) replacing the sign manual of persons with limited opportunities of health which owing to the state of health have no physical capacity independently to make the sign manual (sight violation, lack of extremity, incoordination of movements, paralysis).

1. 摹真签章（摹真）——特别是（老旧的）特制印章，可以替代有限健康的人的亲笔签名。这些人由于健康状况（如视力障碍、肢体不足、运动不协调、瘫痪等），没有独立签名的能力。

2. Person with limited opportunities of health provides to the notary the stamp (cliche) made by means of technical means, undersigns it in the presence of the notary then the notary certifies the specimen signature and grants to person with limited opportunities of health the certificate on authenticity of this facsimile.

2. 有限健康的自然人通过技术手段将特制印章交给公证员，并在公证员在场的情况下签名。接着，公证员就可以见证该签字样本并出具摹真签章的公证书。

3. The certified facsimile completely is equated on the legal value to the sign manual.

3. 经公证的摹真签章与亲笔签名具有同等的法律效力。

4. In case of loss of the facsimile and production of new stamp its repeated notarial certificate is required.

4. 若摹真签章不慎丢失，公证员需要重新公证新的签章。

Article 75. Witnessing of fidelity of the translation

第七十五条　公证译文的真实性

1. The notary witnesses fidelity of the translation from one language on another if the notary knows the corresponding languages.

1. 如果公证员通晓相应的语言，那么该公证员可以公证译文的真实性。

2. If the notary does not know the corresponding languages, the translation can be made by the translator whose authenticity of the signature is witnessed by the notary.

2. 公证员不通晓相应语言的，可以由签名真实性经过公证的译者进行翻译。

Chapter 12. Certificate of the facts

第十二章　事实公证

Article 76. The certificate of the fact of finding of the citizen in live

第七十六条　对公民所在地事实的公证

1. The notary certifies the fact of finding of the citizen in live.

1. 公证员可以公证公民所在地的事实。

2. The certificate of the fact of stay in live the minor is made at the request of his legal representatives (parents, adoptive parents, guardians, custodians), and also the organizations on which care there is minor.

2. 公证员依照未成年人法定代理人（父母、养父母、监护人和保管人）和照顾未成年人的组织的要求，出具未成年人居住地证明。

Article 77. The certificate of the fact of finding of the citizen in certain place

第七十七条　对公民在某地停留的事实的公证

1. The notary at the request of the citizen certifies the fact of stay it in certain place.

1. 公证员依据公民的请求，公证某人在某一地停留的事实。

2. The certificate of the fact of stay in certain place of

2. 公证员依照未成年人法定代理人（父母、养父

the minor is made but request of his legal representatives (parents, adoptive parents, guardians, custodians), and also the organizations on which care there is minor.

母、监护人和保管人）和照顾未成年人的组织的要求，出具未成年人在某地停留的事实。

Article 78. The certificate of identity of the identity of the citizen with person represented in the photo

1. The notary certifies identity of the identity of the citizen with person represented in the photo provided by this citizen.

第七十八条　公证照片中的人的身份

公证员可以公证公民提供的照片中的人的身份。

Article 79. Certificate of time of production of documents

1. The notary certifies time of presentation of the document to it.

第七十九条　对出示文件时间的公证

公证员可以公证公民出示的文件时间。

Chapter 13. Transfer of statements of physical persons and legal entities. Acceptance in the deposit of sums of money and securities

第十三章　自然人和法人声明的转呈、接收存款中的数额与证券数额的公证

Article 80. Transfer of statements

1. The notary reports petitions from citizens, legal entities to other citizens, legal entities personally on receipt or sends by mail with the return notification. Statements can be transferred also with use of the telefax, computer networks and other technical means. The expenses connected with use of technical means for transfer of statements are paid by person at the request of whom notarial action is made.

2. At the request of person who submitted the application to it the certificate on transfer of the statement is granted.

第八十条　转呈声明书

1. 公证员将收到的公民、法人提交的申请书转呈给其他公民、法人，并附上退回通知。声明还可以使用传真、计算机网络和其他技术手段传送。转呈声明使用技术所产生的相关费用由申请公证的人承担。

2. 应当向提出转呈声明书请求的自然人出具证明文书。

Article 81. Acceptance in the deposit of sums of money and securities

1. The notary in the cases provided by the civil legislation of the Kyrgyz Republic accepts from the debtor in the deposit sums of money and securities for transfer to their creditor.

2. The notary informs the creditor on receipt of sums of money and securities and according to its requirement issues it receivable sums of money and securities.

3. Acceptance in the deposit of sums of money and securities is made by the notary in the place of obligation fulfillment.

第八十一条　接收账户中的存款与证券

1. 公证员依照吉尔吉斯斯坦共和国民事法律的规定，根据债权人的请求，将债务人存款和证券转移给债权人。

2. 公证员根据债权人的请求，在收到存款和证券之后，告知其应收款项金额和证券的数额。

3. 接收存款和证券的工作由义务履行地的公证员负责。

Article 82. Return of sums of money and securities to person who introduced them in the deposit

1. Return of sums of money and securities to person who introduced them in the deposit is allowed only from

第八十二条　将存款及证券转交给所有人

只有在提供存款和证券的人的书面同意下，或在法院作出决定的情况下，才可以将存款和证券返还给

written consent of person for benefit of which the contribution, or by a court decision is made.

所有权人。

Chapter 14. Making of executive texts

Article 83. Collection of sums of money or reclamation of property from the debtor

1. For collection of sums of money or reclamation of property from the debtor the notary makes executive texts on the documents establishing debt and on notarially certified documents.

2. For collection of sums of money by the address of collection on pledged property the notary makes executive text on all documents establishing debt including on the pledge agreement.

Article 84. The list of documents according to which debt collection is made in indisputable procedure

1. The list of documents according to which debt collection is made in indisputable procedure for pas the basis of executive texts is established by the Government of the Kyrgyz Republic.

Article 85. Conditions of making of executive text

1. The executive text is made:

1) if the submitted documents confirm indisputability of debt or other responsibility of the debtor to the claimant;

2) if from the date of emergence of right of action there passed no more than three years.

2. If for the requirement according to which the executive text is issued the legislation of the Kyrgyz Republic establishes other prescriptive limit, the executive text is issued within this term.

Article 86. Content of executive text

1. The executive text made by the address of collection on pledged property shall contain the following:

1) surname, initials, position of the notary making executive text;

2) name and address of the claimant;

3) name and address of the debtor and pledger;

4) designation of term for which collection is made;

5) the size of the amount which is subject to collection including penalty fee, percent if those are due;

6) name of subject of pledge and its address, name (name) of the owner (pledger) and his address;

7) date (number, month, year and register died) agreements of pledge;

8) the size of the amount of the state fee paid by the

第十四章　执行文本的制作

第八十三条　向债务人收取款项或收回财产

1. 为了向债务人收取款项或收回财产，公证员需要对确定债务的文件和经公证的文件制作执行文书。

2. 通过质押财产托收收取款项时，公证员需要对包括质押协议在内的所有确定债权的文件制作执行文本。

第八十四条　按无可争辩的程序收取债务所依据的文件清单

吉尔吉斯斯坦共和国政府依照收取债务的文件清单，通过法定程序制作执行文本。

第八十五条　执行文本的出具条件

1. 有下列情形的，可以出具执行文本：

（1）若提交的文件确认债务人对债权人的债务或其他责任是无可争议的；

（2）诉讼权利产生之日起三年内申请出具执行文本。

2. 公证员出具执行文本应符合吉尔吉斯斯坦共和国法律的规定和其他限制性规定。

第八十六条　执行文本的内容

1. 质押财产托收的执行文本应当包括下列内容：

（1）公证员的姓名、首字母、公证员出具执行文本的地点；

（2）债权人的姓名和住址；

（3）债务人和担保人的姓名和住址；

（4）指定收取款项的履行期限；

（5）应收取的资产金额，包括罚款费用和滞纳金；

（6）质押人的姓名及住址、业主姓名（姓名）及住址；

（7）质押协议签订的日期（数量、月、年、注销登记截止日期）；

（8）应由债权人和债务人支付的国家公证费用

claimant and which is subject to payment by the debtor;

9) date (year, month, number) making of executive text;

10) number at which the executive text is registered in the register;

11) the signature of the notary who made executive text;

12) notary's seal.

Article 87. Procedure for collection on executive text

1. Collection on executive text is made according to the procedure, established by the civil procedural legislation of the Kyrgyz Republic for execution of judgments.

Article 88. Terms of presentation of executive text

1. The executive text can be shown to forced execution within three years from the date of its making if the legislation of the Kyrgyz Republic does not establish other terms.

2. Recovery of the passed term is made for presentation of executive text according to the civil procedural legislation of the Kyrgyz Republic.

Chapter 15. Making of protests of bills of exchange, presentation of checks to payment and the certificate of non-payment of checks

Article 89. Protest of the bill of exchange

1. The protest of the bill of exchange in non-payment, the non-acceptance and not dating of the acceptance is made by the notary according to legal acts of the Kyrgyz Republic for the translated and promissory note.

Article 90. Presentation of the check to payment and the certificate of non-payment of checks

1. The notary in the location of the payer accepts for presentation to payment the check provided after ten days if the check is drawn for the territories of the Kyrgyz Republic; provided after twenty days if the check is drawn to pas of the territory of state members of the Commonwealth of Independent States; provided after seventy days if the check is drawn for the territories of any other state, from the date of issue of the check, but no later than 12 hours following after that the term of day.

2. In case of check non-payment the notary certifies check non-payment by text on the check and notes about it in the register. Along with text on the check the notification is sent to the issuer about non-payment of its check by bank and making of text of pas the check.

3. At the request of the payee the notary in case of non-payment of the check makes executive text.

金额；

（9）出具执行文本的日期（年、月、编号）；

（10）执行文本在登记册中登记的编号；

（11）出具执行文本的公证员的签名；

（12）公证员盖章。

第八十七条　执行文本的收集程序

公证员依照《吉尔吉斯斯坦共和国民事诉讼法》规定的执行判决程序收集执行文本。

第八十八条　依据执行文本申请强制执行

1. 吉尔吉斯斯坦共和国法律没有其他规定的，当事人可在执行文本作成之日起三年内申请强制执行。

2. 依照《吉尔吉斯斯坦共和国民事诉讼法》的规定，当事人可申请恢复过期的执行文本的效力。

第十五章　汇票拒付、支票付款提示及不付款证明书的出示

第八十九条　汇票的拒付

对于汇票的拒付、拒绝承兑行为和不接受承兑日期的抗兑行为，公证员依照吉尔吉斯斯坦共和国法律法规对经过翻译的汇票进行公证。

第九十条　支票付款提示和不付款证明书

1. 如果支票是在吉尔吉斯斯坦共和国领土内开出的，那么付款人所在地的公证员应当在支票开出后十天内接受该支票的付款提示；如果是在独联体成员国的领土内开出的，那么应当在二十天内接受；如果支票是在其他国家的领土内开出的，那么应当在七十天后接受；上述期限的起算日是支票开出之日，但最多不应当迟于该日期后的十二小时内。

2. 若有支票被拒付，公证员应当在支票上用文字注明该支票被拒付，并在登记簿上登记，连同支票上的文本一起，通知开票人有关银行拒付支票的情况，以及支票正文的制作情况。

3. 应收款人的要求，公证员可以在支票被拒付的情况下出具执行文本。

Chapter 16. Acceptance on document storage

Article 91. Acceptance on document storage

1. The notary accepts documents but inventories on storage. One copy of the inventory remains at the notary, other copy is issued to person who checked documents.

Part 2 voided according to the Law of the Kyrgyz Republic of 03.07.2014 No. 111

2. To person who checked documents the certificate is granted.

Article 92. Return accepted on document storage

1. The documents accepted on storage return to checked them or legally authorized person upon presentation of the certificate and the inventory or by a court decision.

Chapter 17. Making of ship's protests

Article 93. Statement for the ship's protest

1. The notary accepts for the purpose of providing proofs for protection of the rights and legitimate rights of interests of the shipowner the statement of the ship master for the incident taking place during swimming or the parking of the vessel which can be the basis for presentation to the shipowner of property requirements.

2. The statement for the ship's protest shall contain the description of circumstances of incident and the measures taken by the captain for ensuring safety of the property entrusted to it.

3. In confirmation of the circumstances stated in the application for the ship's protest the ship master according to the legislation of the Kyrgyz Republic regulating merchant shipping along with the statement or in time no later than seven days from the moment of calling port or from the moment of incident if it took place in port, shall provide to the notary on review the logbook and the statement certified by the captain from the logbook.

Article 94. Terms of the statement for the ship's protest

1. The statement for the ship's protest according to the legislation of the Kyrgyz Republic regulating merchant shipping moves within twenty four hours from the moment of receipt of the vessel to port. If the incident causing the necessity of the statement of the ship's protest happened in port, the protest shall be declared within twenty four hours from the moment of incident.

第十六章　接收、保管文件

第九十一条　接收、保管文件

1. 公证员接收当事人提交的文件后应妥善保管，并在公证机构留存一份文件清单，另一份则发给核对文件的人。

第二部分依照吉尔吉斯斯坦共和国 2014 年 3 月 7 日第 111 号法令已废止

2. 应当向核对文件的人员出具资格证书。

第九十二条　返还已接收保管的文件

1. 依法储存的文件，应当在授予证书或法院裁决时，归还给核对者或合法授权的人。

第十七章　海事声明公证

第九十三条　海事声明书

1. 为提供保护船主合法权益的证据，公证员应接受船长对航行或船舶停泊期间发生的事故所作的陈述。该陈述可作为船主提出财产请求的依据。

2. 海事声明书应当包含对事故发生情况的描述，以及船长为确保委托给他的财产的安全所采取的措施。

3. 为确认海事声明书中所述的情况，船长应当依照吉尔吉斯斯坦共和国关于规范商船的法律规定，在不迟于停靠港口之日起七天内，或自事件发生之日起七天内（如果事故发生在港口），向公证员提供航海日志，第一款中船主对事故的陈述和船长核证航海日志后作出的陈述。

第九十四条　海事声明书条款

1. 依照吉尔吉斯斯坦共和国规范商船的法律，船只的海事声明应当在船只靠港后 24 小时内移送。如果海事声明书所述的事件发生在港口，该声明应当在事故发生之时起 24 小时内宣告。

2. If it appears impossible to declare protest at the scheduled time, the reasons of it shall be specified in the statement for the ship's protest,

Article 95. Creation of the act of the ship's protest

1. The notary based on the statement of the captain, data of the logbook, and also poll of the captain and whenever possible at least two witnesses from among command structure of the vessel and two witnesses from crew draws up the statement of the ship's protest and assures him the signature and official stamp. The copy of the act of the ship's protest is issued to the captain or the authorized person.

Chapter 18. Providing proofs

Article 96. Providing the proofs necessary in case of case in courts or administrative authorities

1. At the request of interested persons the notary provides the proofs necessary in case of case in court or administrative authority if reasons to believe are had that production of evidence will become impossible or difficult subsequently.

2. The notary does not provide proofs on case which at the time of the address of interested persons to the notary is in production of court or administrative authority.

Article 97. Actions of the notary for providing proofs

1. According to the procedure of providing proofs the notary interrogates witnesses, examines written and physical evidences, appoints examination.

2. In case of accomplishment of legal proceedings on providing proofs the notary is guided by the relevant standards of the civil procedural legislation of the Kyrgyz Republic.

3. The notary informs on time and the place of providing proofs of the party and interested persons, however their absence is not obstacle for accomplishment of actions for providing proofs.

4. Providing proofs without notice of one of the parties and interested persons is made only in cases, being urgent or when it is impossible to determine who will participate in case subsequently.

5. In case of absence of the witness or the expert in challenge the notary reports about it in national court at the place of residence of the witness or expert for taking measures, provided by legal acts of the Kyrgyz Republic.

2. 如果发生了不可抗力导致海事声明的宣告无法完成，应当在海事声明书中说明原因。

第九十五条　海事声明书的产生

公证员根据船长的陈述、航海日志的数据和船长的民意调查，如有可能，还可邀请至少两名来自船只管理层的见证人和两名船员见证人起草海事声明书，见证人应向公证员保证签字和官方盖章的真实性。海事声明的副本应当交予船长或经授权的人。

第十八章　提供证据

第九十六条　向法院或行政机关提供必要的证据

1. 依照利害关系人的请求，公证员有理由相信利害关系人日后将不可能提出证据，或提出证据很困难，应当提供证据，以便法院或行政当局审理案件。

2. 在向公证员告知利害关系人的地址并且该案件是由法院或行政当局管辖时，公证员不提供有关案件的证据。

第九十七条　公证员举证行为

1. 按照举证程序，公证员可以询问证人，审查书证和物证，并指定审查。

2. 公证员提供证据应当符合《吉尔吉斯斯坦共和国民事诉讼法》的规定。

3. 公证员应当及时通知当事人和利害关系人提供证据的时间和地点，当事人或利害关系人缺席并不妨碍举证程序的进行。

4. 只有在出现紧急情况或无法确定谁将继续参与诉讼的情况下，公证员可以在不通知一方利害关系人的情况下进行举证质证。

5. 吉尔吉斯斯坦共和国法律规定，在证人或专家缺席被质疑的情况下，公证员应当向证人或专家居住地的国家法院报告采取措施的情况。

6. The notary warns the witness and the expert about responsibility for making obviously false evidence or the conclusion and for refusal or evasion from making the indication or the conclusion.

Chapter 19. Application by the notary of regulations of foreign law. International agreements

Article 98. Application of regulations of foreign law

1. The notary according to the legislation of the Kyrgyz Republic, international treaties applies regulations of foreign law.

2. The notary accepts the documents constituted according to requirements of international treaties and also makes certifying texts in shape, stipulated by the legislation other states if it does not contradict international treaties of the Kyrgyz Republic.

Article 99. Protection of heritable property and issue of the certificate on the right to inheritance

1. The actions connected with protection of the property which is in the territory of the Kyrgyz Republic which remained after the death of the foreign citizen, or the property which is due to the foreign citizen after the death of the citizen of the Kyrgyz Republic and also with issue of the certificate on the right to inheritance concerning such property are performed according to the legislation of the Kyrgyz Republic.

Article 100. Acceptance by the notary of the documents constituted abroad

1. The documents constituted abroad with participation of officials of competent authorities of other states or from them outgoing are accepted by the notary on condition of their legalization by body of the Ministry of Foreign Affairs of the Kyrgyz Republic.

2. Without legalization such documents are accepted by the notary when it is stipulated by the legislation the Kyrgyz Republic and international treaties of the Kyrgyz Republic.

Article 101. Relations of the notary with judicial authorities of other states

1. The procedure for relations of the notary with judicial authorities of other states is determined by the legislation of the Kyrgyz Republic and international treaties of the Kyrgyz Republic.

6. 公证员应当告诫证人和专家提供明显虚假证据或作虚假陈述，拒绝或逃避作出提示和给出结论所需承担的法律责任。

第十九章　公证员对外国法与国际公约的适用

第九十八条　外国法的适用

1. 公证员依照吉尔吉斯斯坦共和国的法律和国际条约，适用外国法的规定。

2. 公证员应当根据国际条约的要求，在不违背吉尔吉斯斯坦共和国订立或参与的国际条约和其他国家法律的情况下，接受和制定认证文本。

第九十九条　保护遗产和出具继承权证书

公证员应当依照吉尔吉斯斯坦共和国法律的规定，保护外国公民死亡后遗留在吉尔吉斯斯坦共和国境内的财产，或吉尔吉斯斯坦共和国公民死亡后，外国公民有权继承的财产，以及出具上述财产的继承权权属证书。

第一百条　公证员接收来自国外的文件

1. 公证员应当接受吉尔吉斯斯坦共和国外交部认可的，由其他国家政府官员参与起草或制作的文件。

2. 外国文件没有被合法化的，公证员应当依照吉尔吉斯斯坦共和国法律和吉尔吉斯斯坦共和国加入的国际条约的规定接收这些文件。

第一百零一条　公证员与其他国家司法机关的关系

公证员与其他国家司法当局的关系由吉尔吉斯斯坦共和国法律和吉尔吉斯斯坦共和国加入的国际条约决定。

Article 102. Providing the proofs which are required for business management in bodies of other states

1. The notary provides the proofs which are required for business management in bodies of other states.

Article 103. International treaty

1. If the international treaty which came in the procedure established by the law into force which participant is the Kyrgyz Republic determines other rules about notarial actions, than those which are provided by regulatory legal acts of the Kyrgyz Republic, when making notarial actions rules of the international treaty are applied.

2. If the international treaty which came in the procedure established by the law into force which participant is the Kyrgyz Republic refers to competence of the notary making notarial, actions, not stipulated by the legislation the Kyrgyz Republic, the notary makes this notarial action according to the procedure, established by the Government of the Kyrgyz Republic.

Section 3. Final provisions

Article 104. Entry into force of this Law

1. This Law becomes effective from the date of official publication.

2. Recognize invalid:

- The law of the Kyrgyz SSR "About the state notariate" (Sheets of the Supreme Council of the Kyrgyz SSR, 1974, appendix to No. 13);

- The resolution of the Supreme Council of the Kyrgyz SSR "About enforcement of the Law of the Kyrgyz SSR "About the state notariate" (Sheets of the Supreme Council of the Kyrgyz SSR, 1974, No. 13, the Art. 76)."

President of the Kyrgyz Republic

A. Akayev

3.Disclaimer! This text was translated by AI translator and is not a valid juridical document. No warranty. No claim.

第一百零二条　提供其他国家的机构在商业管理方面所需的证明

公证员可以为其他国家的机构提供在商业管理方面所需的证明。

第一百零三条　国际条约

1. 吉尔吉斯斯坦共和国订立的或参与的，且已经生效的国际条约规定其法律效力高于吉尔吉斯斯坦共和国法律的，公证员在开展公证活动时应当适用上述国际条约。

2. 吉尔吉斯斯坦共和国订立的或参与的，且已经生效的国际条约规定了公证员开展公证活动的行为能力的事项，而吉尔吉斯斯坦共和国法律没有相关规定时，公证员开展公证活动时应当适用吉尔吉斯斯坦共和国的法律。

第三部分　最终条款

第一百零四条　本法的生效条件

1. 本法自正式公布之日起生效。

2. 下列法律确认无效：

- 吉尔吉斯苏维埃社会主义共和国"关于国家公证员"的法律（吉尔吉斯苏维埃社会主义共和国最高委员会名单，1974 年，第 13 号附录）；

- 吉尔吉斯斯坦苏维埃社会主义共和国最高委员会"关于执行吉尔吉斯斯坦苏维埃社会主义共和国法律和国家公证员"的决议（吉尔吉斯斯坦苏维埃社会主义共和国最高委员会名单，1974 年，第 13 号，第 76 条）。

吉尔吉斯斯坦共和国总统：a. 阿卡耶夫

3. 免责声明！本法的英文文本系由人工智能翻译的，吉尔吉斯斯坦共和国政府不保证翻译的准确性，本法英译本不具有法律效力。

老挝

老挝人民民主共和国公证机构法

LAO PEOPLE'S DEMOCRATIC REPUBLIC
PEACE INDEPENDENCE DEMOCRACY UNITY PROSPERITY
President's Office No. 20
DECREE of the PRESIDENT of the LAO PEOPLE'S DEMOCRATIC REPUBLIC

On the Promulgation of the Law on Notary Offices Pursuant to Chapter 5, Article 53, point 1 of the Constitution of the Lao People's Democratic Republic; and

Pursuant to Resolution No. 04/PSA, dated 8 January 1992, of the 7th Session of the second Legislature of the People Supreme Assembly regarding the adoption of the Law on Notary Offices.

The President of the Lao People's Democratic Republic

Article 1. The Law on Notary Offices is hereby promulgated.

Article 2. This decree shall enter into force on the date it is signed.

Vientiane, 6 April 1992 President of the Lao People's Democratic Republic

Kaysone PHOMVIHANH

老挝人民民主共和国
和平 独立 民主 统一 繁荣

总统办公室第二十号文件

根据《老挝人民民主共和国宪法》第五章第一节第五十三条的规定；

根据第二届最高人民议会第七次例会于1992年1月8日通过的第04号决议。

老挝人民民主共和国主席关于宣布施行公证机构法的老挝人民民主共和国主席令：

第一条 公证机构法特此颁布。

第二条 主席令于签署当日开始生效。

万象1992年4月6日 老挝人民民主共和国主席

凯山·丰威汉

LAO PEOPLE'S DEMOCRATIC REPUBLIC
PEACE INDEPENDENCE DEMOCRACY UNITY PROSPERITY
People's Supreme Assembly
LAW ON NOTARY OFFICES

老挝人民民主共和国
和平 独立 民主 统一 繁荣

最高人民议会
公证机构法

Chapter 1
General Principles

Article 1: The Status and Role of Notary Offices

The notary offices are State organisations at local levels, and are under the Ministry of Justice.

The notary offices have the duty to certify the correctness and factual existence of contracts and various documents as provided in the laws, in order to protect the legitimate rights and interests of individuals and legal entities, to contribute to the education and training of all citizens to be aware of, to respect and to implement the laws, and to increase justice and social order.

Article 2: Management and Supervision of Notary Offices

The Ministry of Justice uniformly manages and supervises the activities of notary offices throughout the country.

Article 3: Activities of Notary Offices

In undertaking their activities, notary offices must perform in accordance with the laws of the Lao People's Democratic Republic.

Article 4: Maintaining Confidentiality in Notary Activities

Notary officers and other officers who are responsible for notary activities must maintain1 confidentiality for individuals and legal entities who request certification, as well as regarding other matters of which such persons have knowledge when performing their activities.

Documents certified by notary officers shall be given only to the individuals and legal entities concerned. In the event that there is a request by the People's Courts, the Office of the Public Prosecutor or the Investigation Organisation4, [the notary office] may deliver only such documents which relate to a case that relates to legal proceedings being carried out by such agencies.

Notary officers or other officers in charge of notary activities who disclose confidential information received in [the performance of] notary activities shall be liable in accordance with the laws.

Article 5: Language Used in Notary Activities

All activities of the notary offices shall be in the Lao language. In the event that there are documents [written] in foreign languages or a person involved in the notary activities does not know the Lao language, there must be a

第一章 总则

第一条 公证机构的地位和职能

公证机构是由国家设立的，隶属于司法部的地方级机构。

公证机构依法办理各类协议和文件的公证事项以维护自然人及法人的正当权益，提高公民自愿遵守法律的意识，规范公证活动。

第二条 公证机构的管理与指导

司法部统一管理和指导全国公证机构的一切活动。

第三条 公证活动

在公证活动中，公证机构要严格遵守老挝人民民主共和国的相关法律。

第四条 公证事务的保密性

公证员及其与公证活动相关的其他工作人员，对其在公证活动中所接触到的当事人的秘密，负有保守秘密的义务。

公证员应当仅向当事人交付相关的公证文书。如人民法院、检察机关或侦查机关要求提供相关文书，公证机构将只交付与该机关法律程序相关的文件。

公证员及其他与公证活动相关的工作人员，如若对其接触的公证活动有泄密行为，依法承担法律责任。

第五条 公证活动用语

一切公证活动均需使用老挝语。在公证活动中，如有不懂老挝语的外国人或外语文件，需配备翻译或将文件翻译为老挝语。

translation into the Lao language by a translator.

Article 6: Assistance [Provided by] Notary Officers

Notary officers and other officers in charge of notary activities must assist individuals and legal entities that request certification of documents and explain [to them] the rights and obligations that may arise from such certification.

第六条 公证员的协助工作

公证员及其他与公证活动相关的工作人员，需协助前来申请公证的当事人，告知其在公证活动中的权利和义务。

Chapter 2
The Establishment and Composition of Notary Offices

第二章 公证机构的设立和构成

Article 7: Establishment of Notary Offices

A notary office is established within the justice division at each province or prefecture.

In foreign countries, Lao embassies or consulates are responsible for notary activities, except for contracts relating to fixed assets located in the Lao PDR.

第七条 公证机构的设立

公证机构设立于各省、市司法部门。

驻外使领馆负责海外本国公民的公证事务，涉及老挝境内不动产协议的相关公证事项除外。

Article 8: Composition of Notary Office Personnel

Each notary office comprises a director, deputy director(s), notary officers and some assistants based upon the actual volume of work.

第八条 公证机构的人事构成

每一个公证机构设有主任一名、副主任一名或多名，依实际工作需要设公证员及相关公证助理人员若干。

Article 9. Qualifications of Notary Officers

Notary officers are civil servants.

Lao citizens who are to be appointed as notary officers must meet the following conditions:

1. [Be] 25 years of age or older;

2. Have high level legal education, or its equivalent, and have had at least two years' experience relating to justice or legal work; or have intermediate level legal education, or its equivalent, and have had practical experience relating to the work above-mentioned for at least three years;

3. Have ethics of justice and revolutionary ethics, and be honest in the preservation of justice.

第九条 公证员的资格条件

公证员为国家公务员。

委任为公证员的老挝公民须符合下列条件：

1. 年龄在二十五周岁以上；

2. 具有高等法学教育背景或同等水平，且具有两年及其以上司法或法律工作经验；具有中等法学教育背景或同等水平，且具有上述法律实务工作经验三年以上；

3. 公道正派，品行较好，具备优良的职业道德。

Article 10: Appointment and Dismissal of Notary Officers

Notary officers are appointed and dismissed by the Minister of Justice.

第十条 公证员的任职和罢免

公证员由司法部长任命和罢免。

Chapter 3
Activities of Notary Offices

第三章 公证活动

Article 11: Activities of Notary Offices

Notary offices perform the following activities:

1. Certifying the correctness of various contracts, such as: sale- purchase contracts, loans, assignments, wills,

第十一条 公证活动

公证机构办理下列公证活动：

1. 各类合同的准确性公证，如买卖合同、借贷合同、转让合同、遗嘱等；

and others5;

2. Using methods to protect property relating to inheritance;

3. Certifying the right to inherit;

4. Certifying property rights as matrimonial property or initial assets6 of husband and wife;

5. Certifying copies of documents;

6. Certifying signatures;

7. Certifying the correctness of translation of language;

8. Certifying the identity of a person compared with a photograph;

9. Certifying the date and time of document submission;

10. Certifying letters or various documents as provided by the laws;

11. Receiving and preserving documents relating to the activities of notary officers;

12. Signing documents in the presence of contractual parties.

If a document or matter relates to a notary officer's spouse or close kin, the notary officer cannot certify [such document or matter].

Article 12. Obligations of Notary Officers and Other Officers in Charge of Notary Activities

Regarding the certification of documents, notary officers must first review the correctness of the documents and events in detail and depth, before certifying [them].

Article 13. Activities of Notary Offices and Collection of Fees Relating to Notary Activities

The activities of notary offices and the collection of fees relating to notary activities are prescribed in specific regulations relating to notary offices in compliance with State financial regulations.

Chapter 4
Final Provisions

Article 14: Budget of Notary Offices

The budget of notary offices is subject to the State budget.

Article 15: Seals of Notary Offices

Each notary office has its own seal consisting of a circle, at the outer top edge of which "Lao People's Democratic Republic" is written. At the bottom of [the circle], [the name of] the province or prefecture is written. And

2. 依法维护遗产继承的公证；

3. 遗产继承权公证；

4. 婚前财产和夫妻共有财产的公证；

5. 档案公证；

6. 签名公证；

7. 译文与原文相符的公证；

8. 身份公证；

9. 文书提交日期公证；

10. 法律规定的各类文书的公证；

11. 与公证活动相关的文书接收、保存公证；

12. 协议双方当面签署文件的公证。

与公证员及其配偶、亲属相关的文书和事件的公证，公证员不能参与公证。

第十二条　公证员及与其他公证活动相关工作人员的责任和义务

在进行公证活动前，公证员需仔细检查文书及相关事项的准确性，再进行公证。

第十三条　公证活动和公证费的收取

公证机构的公证活动以及公证费的收取严格按照国家财政法的规定。

第四章　附则

第十四条　公证机构的预算

公证机构的预算列入国家财政预算。

第十五条　公证机构的印章

各公证机构有专门的印章，印章为圆形，在印章圆形外侧上方刻有“老挝人民民主共和国”，下方写有省或市的名字，圆形内侧写有“省、市级公证机构”。

within [the circle], “Notary Office of the [relevant] province or prefecture” is written.

This law was adopted by the unanimous decision of the full session of the People’s Supreme Assembly in Session No. 7 of the second legislature of the People’s Supreme Assembly on 30 December 1991 at 15. 45 hours.

President of the People’s Supreme Assembly
Nouhak PHOUMSAVANH

本法律于 1991 年 12 月 30 日 15 时 45 分在第二届最高人民议会第七次全体会议上一致通过。

最高人民议会主席
努哈·普沙万

马来西亚

1959 年公证法

Notaries Public
LAWS OF MALAYSIA
REPRINT
Act 115
NOTARIES PUBLIC
ACT 1959
Incorporating all amendments up to 1 January 2006

PUBLISHED BY
THE COMMISSIONER OF LAW REVISION, MALAYSIA UNDER THE AUTHORITY OF THE REVISION OF LAWS ACT 1968
IN COLLABORATION WITH
PERCETAKAN NASIONAL MALAYSIA BHD

2006
NOTARIES PUBLIC ACT 1959
First enacted： 1959
(OrdinanceNo. 41 of 1959)
Revised: 1973
(Act 115 w.e.f. 1 August 1973)

PREVIOUS REPRINTS
First Reprint: 1995
Second Reprint: 2000

LAWS OF MALAYSIA
Act 115

NOTARIES PUBLIC ACT 1959
ARRANGEMENT OF SECTIONS

马来西亚公证法

再版
第 115 号法案号法令
1959 年公证法

整合截至 2006 年 1 月 1 日的所有修正案

由马来西亚法律修订专员
基于 1968 年《法律修订法》授权

与马来西亚国家印刷有限公司
联合公布

2006 年
1959 年《公证法》
第一次颁布：1959 年
（1959 年第 41 号条例）
修订：1973 年
（第 115 号法令，自 1973 年 8 月 1 日起生效）

此前再版版本
第一次再版 1995 年
第二次再版 2000 年

马来西亚法律
第 115 号法令

1959 年《公证法》
条款安排

Section

1. Short title
2. Interpretation
3. Appointment of notaries public
4. Privileges of notaries public
5. Misconduct of notaries public
6. Penalty for exercise of functions of notary public by unauthorizedpersons
7. Rules
8. Saving
9. Repeal and transitional provisions

条款

1. 简称
2. 解释
3. 公证员的任命
4. 公证员的特权
5. 公证员的不当行为
6. 未经授权者行使公证员职能的处罚
7. 规则
8. 保留
9. 废止及过渡性规定

LAWS OF MALAYSIA
Act 115
NOTARIES PUBLIC ACT 1959

马来西亚法律
第 115 号法令
1959 年《公证法》

An Act relating to notaries public.

[Peninsular Malaysia—1 October 1959, Ord. 41 of 1959;

Sabah and Sarawak—18 March 1965,L.N. 98/1965]

与公证员有关的法案

[马来西亚半岛——1959 年 10 月 1 日第 41 号条例；

沙巴和砂拉越——1969 年 3 月 18 日，L.N. 98/1965]

Short title

1. This Act may be cited as the Notaries Public Act 1959.

简称

1. 本法可引述为《1959 年公证法》。

Interpretation

2. In this Act, unless the context otherwise requires—

"Bar Council" means the central council of the Malaysian Barestablished under section 47 of the Legal Profession Act 1976[Act 166];

"notary public" means a person who has been appointed as anotary public under section 3 but does not include any personwhose appointment has been revoked under section 5;

"place of practice" means the territory or part thereof withinwhich a person is appointed to practise as a notary public undersection 3;

"prescribed" means prescribed by or under this Act;

"State Attorney General" means the State Attorney General,Sabah, or the State Attorney General, Sarawak, as the case mayrequire.

3. (1) Subject to subsection (3), the Attorney General may, from time to time, appoint fit and proper persons to be notaries public to practise within Peninsular Malaysia or Sabah or Sarawak or such part of those territories for

解释

2. 本法中，除上下文另有要求外——

"出庭律师理事会"是指根据《1976 年法律职业法》（第 166 号法令）第 47 条建立的马来西亚出庭律师中央理事会。

"公证员"是指按照第 3 条被任命为公证员者，但不包括按照第 5 条已被撤销任命者。

"执业地"是指按照第 3 条，被任命为公证员者执业的地区或部分。

"规定"是指经由本法规定或在本法中有所规定。

"州检察长"视情况，可指代沙巴州检察长或砂拉越州检察长。

3.（1）在遵守第（3）款的前提下，总检察长可随时任命合适人选担任公证员，在马来西亚半岛、沙巴州或砂拉越州全境或部分地区执业，其任期于任命时确定。

such period as may be specified in the appointment.

(1A) Notwithstanding any other law to the contrary, where any person has been appointed to be a notary public before the coming into force of this subsection and no period is specified in that appointment, the appointment shall cease to have effect upon the expiry of the period of two years from the date of coming into force of this subsection.

（1A）无论其他法律中是否存在相反的规定，凡遇在本款生效前被任命为公证员，同时任命时未明确任期的，其任命应于本款生效之日起两年后到期。

(1B) Nothing in subsection (1A) shall be construed as preventing the reappointment under subsection (1) of any person whose appointment has ceased to have effect by virtue of subsection (1A), and every such reappointment shall be deemed to be a new appointment.

（1B）对其任命因第（1A）款而终止者而言，第（1A）款中不存在任何可解释为禁止其被重新任命的内容，凡遇此类重新任命均应视为新任命。

No person shall be appointed to be a notary public unless he is a practising advocate or a pleader licensed under the Pleaders and Petition Writers Enactment of the State of Terengganu [Tr. 59 of 1356] and who was so licensed before 1 January 1956:

凡任命为公证员者，须为根据丁加奴州《辩护人和状师法》[1356 年第 59 条] 获得执照的执业辩护律师或辩护人，并须于 1956 年 1 月前获得上述执照。

Provided that in any place in which a suitable advocate is not available for appointment, the Attorney General may, in his discretion, appoint a public officer to be a notary public, and any fees received by a public officer so appointed in respect of his functions as a notary public shall be paid into the Consolidated Fund.

如某地无适格律师可供任命，总检察长可根据其自由裁量权，任命一位公职人员为公证员，如此任命的公职人员就履行其公证员职能收取的所有费用均应交至统一基金。

(3)The Attorney General shall not make any appointment under this section without consulting the Bar Council or, in relation to Sabah or Sarawak, without consulting the State Attorney General.

（3）未经与出庭律师理事会协商，或涉及沙巴州或砂拉越州时未经与州检察长协商，总检察长不得根据本条规定作出任命。

(4)In making any appointment under this section the Attorney General shall have regard to the number of notaries public already practising in the place where the applicant proposes to practise and to the convenience of the inhabitants of such place, but, subject as aforesaid, the Attorney General shall have absolute discretion in making or refusing to make any such appointment and there shall be no appeal from his decision.

（4）在根据本条作出任命时，总检察长应考虑申请人申请执业地已有执业公证员的数量，并考虑当地居民的便利程度，但如前所述，总检察长就作出或拒绝此类任命具有绝对的裁量权，不得就其决定提起上诉。

(5) If it shall appear to the Attorney General or, where the placeof practice is in Sabah or Sarawak, to the State Attorney General,that any notary public is about to be absent from his place ofpractice for a period exceeding one month, the Attorney Generalor the State Attorney General, may appoint any person, being apractising advocate, to be a notary public temporarily during theabsence of that notary public.

（5）总检察长如遇公证员将离开其执业地达一个月以上的，或当执业地位于沙巴州或砂拉越州时，州检察长如遇上述情况的，总检察长或州检察长可任命具备执业辩护律师身份者在公证员离开期间担任临时公证员。

(6) No temporary appointment of a notary public shall haveeffect for a longer period than twelve months and any suchappointment shall lapse on the death or on the return to his placeof practice of the notary public on

（6）临时公证员的任命不得超过 12 个月，且此类任命会因原公证员死亡或返回执业地而失效。

account of whose departure theappointment was made.

(7)Everyappointment under

subsection (1) or (5) and the lapseof every temporary appointment under subsection (6) shall bepublished in the Gazette.

（7）凡根据第（1）款或第（5）款作出任命，以及根据第（6）款而使临时任命失效的，均应在公报上进行公布。

Privileges of notaries public

公证员的特权

4. (1) Every notary public shall have and may exercise within hisplace of practice all the powers and functions which are ordinarilyexercised by notaries public in England*:

4.（1）所有公证员在其执业地均应享有在英格兰公证员通常所能行使的所有权力和职能。

Provided that, except for the purposes of and to the extentnecessary to give effect to subsection (2), such powers shall notinclude power to administer any oath or affirmation in connectionwith any affidavit or statutory declaration which is executed forthe purpose of being used in any court or place within Malaysia,or to take or attest any such affidavit or statutory declaration.

但公证员的此类权力中，不包括提取或证实为用于马来西亚境内法庭或地点而签署的宣誓书或法定声明，亦不包括实施与上述宣誓书或法定声明相关的宣誓或确认，除非是为实现第（2）款之目的，在使第（2）款生效的必要限度内行使。

(2) Without prejudice to the generality of the powers and functionsconferred by subsection (1), a notary public may—

（2）在不损害第（1）款中赋予的权力和职能的广泛性的前提下，公证员可以——

(a) administer any oath or affirmation in connection with any affidavit or statutory declaration which is executed—

（a）实施与下列宣誓书或法定声明有关的宣誓或确认：

(i) for the purpose of confirming or proving the due execution of any document;

(ii) by any master or member of the crew of anyvessel in respect of any matter concerning thatvessel; or

(iii) for the purpose of being used in any court or place outside Malaysia and may take or attest any such affidavit or statutory declaration; and

(b)have and exercise such other powers and functions as may be prescribed.

（i）宣誓书或法定声明为确认或证明任一文件之妥善签立而签署；

（ii）宣誓书或法定声明由任一船只的船长或船员成员就该船只相关事宜而签署；或者

（iii）宣誓书或法定声明为用于马来西亚境外的法庭或地点而签署，且公证员可提取或证实上述宣誓书或法定声明。同时

（b）按照规定拥有并行使其他此类权力或职能。

Misconduct of notaries public

公证员的不当行为

5. If it shall appear to the Attorney General or in the case of a temporary appointment in Sabah or Sarawak, to the State Attorney General, that any person being a notary public—

5. 身为公证员者，总检察长发现，或当公证员临时受任于沙巴州或砂拉越州时，州检察长发现——

(a) has been struck off the roll of advocates or ceased to be licensed as a pleader in the State of Terengganu, as the case may be; or

（a）公证员视具体情况，已自辩护律师名册中除名，或不再持有丁加奴州辩护人执照；或者

(b) has exercised any of the functions of a notary public outside his place of practice,the Attorney General or the State Attorney General, as the case may be, shall, by order under his hand, revoke the appointment of that

（b）公证员在其执业地之外行使公证员职能，则视具体情况，由总检察长或州检察长以其自身名义发布命令，撤销对该人的任命，并将该命令通过公报发布。

person and shall cause the order to be published in theGazette.

Penalty for exercise of functions of notary public by unauthorized persons

6. Any person who exercises, within Malaysia, any of the functions of a notary public otherwise than in accordance with this Act shall be guilty of an offence and shall on conviction before a Sessions Court in Semenanjung Malaysia or the Court of a Magistrate of the First ClassT in Sabah and Sarawak be liable to a fine not exceeding five hundred ringgit.

Rules

7. (1) The Rules Committee in respect of Peninsular Malaysia and the Chief Judge of the High Court in Sabah and Sarawak after consultation with the State Attorney General concerned in respect of Sabah and Sarawak may make rules—

(a) for the guidance and control of persons entitled to exercise the functions of a notary public under this Act;

(b) to fix the fees payable to notaries public;

(c) to fix the fees payable by any person on appointment asa notary public:

Provided that no such rule shall require any fee tobe paid in respect of any appointment as a notarypublic deemed to have been made by virtue of subsection 8(1); and

(d) prescribing the powers and functions of notaries public.

(2) All rules made under this section shall be published in theFederal Gazette or the Sabah or the Sarawak State Gazette, as thecase may be.

Saving

8. (1) Any person who immediately before the commencement ofthis Act was lawfully entitled to practise as a notary public withinPeninsular Malaysia or any part thereof (other than a person entitledto practise as a notary public in the State of Johore by virtue ofsection 4 of the Notaries Public Ordinance 1947 [Ord. 47 of 1947])shall be deemed to have been appointed a notary public in accordancewith this Act to practise as a notary public within PeninsularMalaysia or (if he was entitled to practise only within a part ofPeninsular Malaysia) within such part as the case may be.

未经授权者行使公证员职能的处罚

6. 凡在马来西亚境内不遵守本法，行使公证员的任何职能的，皆构成违法行为，一经马来西亚半岛的法院或沙巴州及砂拉越州的一等治安法官法庭定罪，将承担最高 500 林吉特的罚款。

规则

7.（1）规则委员会可于马来西亚半岛范围内，沙巴州和砂拉越州高等法院首席法官经与相关的州检察长协商，可于沙巴州和砂拉越州范围内，就下列事宜制定规则：

（a）指导和控制按照本法被授予行使公证员职能的人；

（b）确定向公证员支付的费用标准；

（c）确定被任命为公证员者需支付的费用标准；

假如任何有关委任为公证员的费用的支付的规则没有明确的规定，则可适用第 8 条第（1）款；同时

（d）规定公证员的权力和职能。

（2）所有依据本条制定的规则均应视情况公布于联邦公报或沙巴州或砂拉越州的州公报。

保留

8.（1）恰于本法实施前被合法授权在马来西亚半岛或其部分地区作为公证员执业者（根据《1947 年公证员条例》[1947 年第 47 号法令] 第 4 条授权在柔佛州执业的公证员除外），根据具体情况，视为已根据本法被任命为可在马来西亚半岛境内或其部分地区（如其原授权执业范围仅限于马来西亚半岛部分地区）执业的公证员。

(2) (Omitted).

(3) The name of every person who has been deemed to havebeen appointed a notary public by virtue of subsection (1) shall,within three months of the coming into force of this Act, or suchlonger period as the Attorney General may in any particular casepermit, be published in the Gazette; and such publication shall beconclusive evidence of the right of every such person to practiceas a notary public under this section.

Repeal and transitional provisions

9. (1) The Notaries Public Ordinance 1947 is repealed.

(2) Notwithstanding the repeal of the said Ordinance any rules made thereunder and in force immediately before the commencement of this Act shall, so far as they are not inconsistent with this Act, be deemed to have been made under this Act, and shall continue in force untilrevoked or repealed by rules made under this Act, and shall, unless the context otherwise requires, apply and have effect throughout Peninsular Malaysia.

（2）（已删除）

（3）所有根据第（1）款被视为已受任公证员者，其姓名应于本法生效之日起 3 个月内，或如遇特殊情形，在总检察长可准许的更长时限内，公布于公报；此类公布是证明此类人根据本条有权作为公证员执业的确凿证据。

废止及过渡性条文

9.（1）《1947 年公证员条例》已废止。

（2）尽管上述条例已废止，但恰于本法实施前根据该条例制定并生效的规则，如不和本法冲突的，视为根据本法制定，非经根据本法制定的规则撤销或废止则一直有效，同时，除上下文另有要求外，适用并生效于马来西亚半岛全境。

蒙古

公证法（修订本）

НОТАРИАТЫН ТУХАЙ /Шинэчилсэн найруулга/

НЭГДҮГЭЭР БҮЛЭГ
НИЙТЛЭГ ҮНДЭСЛЭЛ

1 дүгээр зүйл.Хуулийн зорилт

1.1.Энэ хуулийн зорилт нь нотариатын үйл ажиллагааны зарчим, нотариатчийн эрх зүйн байдлыг тогтоож, нотариатын үйлдэл хийх замаар иргэн, хуулийн этгээдийн эрх, хууль ёсны ашиг сонирхлыг хангахтай холбогдсон харилцааг зохицуулахад оршино.

2 дугаар зүйл.Нотариатын тухай хууль тогтоомж

2.1.Нотариатын тухай хууль тогтоомж нь Монгол Улсын Үндсэн хууль[1], Иргэний хууль[2], энэ хууль болон эдгээртэй нийцүүлэн гаргасан хууль тогтоомжийн бусад актаас бүрдэнэ.

2.2.Монгол Улсын олон улсын гэрээнд энэ хуульд зааснаас өөрөөр заасан бол олон улсын гэрээний заалтыг дагаж мөрдөнө.

2.3.Нотариатчаар гэрчлүүлэхтэй холбогдсон харилцааг зөвхөн хуулиар тогтоох бөгөөд хуульд тусгайлан зааснаас бусад тохиолдолд төрийн байгууллага, албан тушаалтан баримт бичгийг нотариатчаар гэрчлүүлэх шийдвэр гаргаж болохгүй.

3 дугаар зүйл.Нотариатын зарчим

3.1. Нотариатч дараахь зарчмыг баримтлана:

3.1.1. хууль дээдлэх;

3.1.2. хараат бус, бие даасан байх;

3.1.3. тэгш эрхийг хангах;

公证法（修订本）

第一章　基本原则

第一条　法律宗旨

1. 本法的宗旨在于规定公证活动的原则、公证员的法律地位；对公证事务中公民、法人的权利、合法权益等关系进行调节。

第二条　公证制度的相关法律法规

2.1. 公证制度的相关法律法规由《蒙古国宪法》[1]、民法[2]、本法和与之相关的其他法规文件组成。

2.2. 蒙古国加入的国际条约有与本法规定不同的，则遵从国际条约的规定。

2.3. 公证员所涉及的公证对象只能由法律规定，且在法律专门规定之外的其他情形下，国家机关、公职人员不得作出需由公证员对文件予以公证的决定。

第三条　公证原则

3.1. 公证员遵循下列原则：

3.1.1. 崇尚法律；

3.1.2. 非隶属、地位独立；

3.1.3. 保障平等权利；

3.1.4. шударга ёсыг сахих;

3.1.5. үйлчлүүлэгчийн нууцыг хадгалах;

3.1.6. ёс зүйн дүрмийг чанд баримтлан ажиллах.

4 дүгээр зүйл.Нотариатч, түүний чиг үүрэг

4.1. Нотариатчийн үйл ажиллагааг нотариатч болон энэ хуулийн 16.2, 16.3-т заасан нотариатчийн үүрэг гүйцэтгэгч эрхлэн явуулна.

4.2. Нотариатчийн чиг үүргийг тусгай зөвшөөрлийн үндсэн дээр эрхлэн гүйцэтгэж, нотариатын үйлчилгээний хөлс, орлогоор санхүүжин ажиллаж байгаа иргэнийг нотариатч гэнэ.

4.3. Нотариатч нь төрийн нэрийн өмнөөс хөндлөнгийн гэрчийн үүрэг гүйцэтгэж, эд хөрөнгийн болон түүнтэй холбоотой эд хөрөнгийн бус харилцаанд оролцож байгаа этгээдэд эрх зүйн зөвлөгөө өгөх үндсэн чиг үүргийг хэрэгжүүлнэ.

4.4. Нотариатч дор дурдсан тодорхой чиг үүргийг хэрэгжүүлнэ:

4.4.1. нотариатчаар гэрчлүүлснээр хүчин төгөлдөр, үл маргах шинжтэй болох үйлдэл, баримт бичгийг гэрчлэх;

4.4.2. үйлчлүүлэгч хүсвэл нотариатчаар гэрчлүүлэхээр хуульд заасанаас бусад үйлдэл, баримт бичгийг үл маргах шинжтэй болгох зорилгоор гэрчлэх;

4.4.3. гарын үсгийн үнэн зөвийг гэрчлэх;

4.4.4. хууль зүйн агуулга бүхий үйлдэл, баримт бичгийг хуульд заасан тохиолдолд болон шүүх, төрийн бусад байгууллагын хүсэлтээр гэрчлэх;

4.4.5. хуульд заасан бусад.

4.5. Нотариатч гэрчилсэн үйлдэл, баримт бичигт холбогдох нотлох баримтыг хадгалах бөгөөд тэдгээрийн хуулбарыг болон хуульд заасны дагуу баримт бичгийн эхийг шаардлагатай этгээдэд олгоно.

5 дугаар зүйл.Нотариатчийн ажлын байр

5.1. Нотариатч тогтоосон тойрогтоо үйл ажиллагаа эрхлэн явуулах ажлын байртай байх бөгөөд хуульд өөрөөр заагаагүй бол нотариатч нотариатын үйлдлийг зөвхөн ажлын байрандаа хийнэ.

5.2. Эрүүл мэндийн болон хүндэтгэн үзэх бусад шалтгаанаар үйлчлүүлэгч нотариатчийн ажлын байранд ирэх боломжгүй бол нотариатч түүний хүсэлтээр байгаа газарт нь очиж нотариатын үйлдэл хийж болно.

6 дугаар зүйл.Нотариатчид тавих шаардлага

6.1.Дараахь шаардлагыг хангасан Монгол Улсын

3.1.4. 信守正义；

3.1.5. 保守服务对象的秘密；

3.1.6. 严格持守道德规范。

第四条　公证员及其职责

4.1. 公证员的业务活动，由公证员和本法第 16.2 款、第 16.3 款规定的代理公证员主持进行。

4.2. 公证员是在特许的基础上履行公证员职责，以公证服务的酬劳、收入为经费开展工作的公民。

4.3. 公证员以国家的名义，履行中立证明的义务；对涉及财产的和与其相关的非财产关系的对象，履行提供法律建议的基本职责。

4.4. 公证员实施下面的具体职责：

4.4.1. 对经公证员公证后即可充分有效、不发生争端的行为，文件予以公证；

4.4.2. 若当事人要求，由公证员对法律规定以外其他行为、文件公证的，则以不产生争端为目的予以公证；

4.4.3. 对签名的真实有效性公证；

4.4.4. 对具有法律意义的行为、文件，在法律规定和法院、其他国家机关要求的情况下予以公证；

4.4.5. 其他法律规定。

4.5. 公证员应保存公证的行为、文件相关的证据，并可将其复印件和法律规定的文件原件提供给必要的对象。

第五条　公证员的工作场所

5.1. 公证员在指定区域的工作场所从事业务活动，且在法律未作其他规定的情况下，公证员只在其工作场所内进行公证活动。

5.2. 当事人如因健康和应当重视的其他原因不能前来公证员的工作场所的，公证员可应其要求前往其所在地点进行公证。

第六条　对于公证员的要求

6.1. 满足下列要求的蒙古国公民有权从事公证业务：

иргэн нотариатын үйл ажиллагаа эрхлэх эрхтэй:

6.1.1. мэргэшлийн шалгалтад тэнцсэн;

6.1.2. ял шийтгэлгүй;

6.1.3. нотариатын үйлдэл хийх ажлын байртай.

6.2. Нотариатч багшлах, эрдэм шинжилгээний ажил эрхлэхээс өөр ажил, албан тушаал хавсран гүйцэтгэхийг хориглоно.

6.3. Нотариатч өөрийн орны болон олон улсын нотариатын байгууллагын сонгуульт ажил, албан тушаал эрхэлж болно.

7 дугаар зүйл.Нотариатын тойрог

7.1.Нотариатч тогтоосон тойрогт үйл ажиллагаагаа явуулах бөгөөд тойрог сольж ажиллахыг хориглоно.

7.2.Нотариатын тойрог, түүнд ажиллах нотариатчийн тоог энэ хуулийн 8.1-д заасан Монголын Нотариатчдын Танхимын саналыг харгалзан хууль зүйн асуудал эрхэлсэн Засгийн газрын гишүүн тогтооно.

7.3.Үл хөдлөх эд хөрөнгийг бусдад шилжүүлэхтэй холбогдсон аливаа хэлцэл болон өвлөх эрхтэй холбогдсон баримт бичгийг зөвхөн тухайн эд хөрөнгө байгаа тойргийн нотариатч гэрчилнэ.

7.4.Нотариатч тойрог шилжих тохиолдолд мэргэшлийн шалгалт дахин өгөх бөгөөд уг шалгалтад тэнцсэн нотариатч тухайн тойрогт сул орон тоо гартал дараалал хүлээнэ.

8 дугаар зүйл.Нотариатын байгууллагын бүтэц, зохион байгуулалт

8.1.Нотариатчдыг эгнээндээ нэгтгэсэн, тэдний мэргэжлийн үйл ажиллагааг энэ хууль болон өөрийн дүрэмд заасны дагуу уялдуулан зохицуулах, эрх ашгийг нь хамгаалах зорилготой Монголын Нотариатчдын танхим /цаашид “Танхим” гэх/ ажиллана.

8.2.Нотариатын байгууллага нь Танхимын бүх гишүүдийн хурал, Танхим, түүний Удирдах зөвлөл, танхимын аймгийн болон нийслэл дэх дүүргийн тойргийн салбараас бүрдэх бөгөөд тэдгээрийн эрх хэмжээг Танхимын дүрмээр тогтооно.

8.3.Танхимын ерөнхийлөгч Танхимын өдөр тутмын үйл ажиллагааг удирдах бөгөөд түүний бүрэн эрхийн хугацаа 4 жил байна. Танхимын ерөнхийлөгчийг нэг удаа улируулан сонгож болох бөгөөд түүний эрх хэмжээг Танхимын дүрмээр тогтооно.

8.4.Танхимын дэргэд Сахилгын болон Хяналтын

6.1.1. 业务考试合格；

6.1.2. 未受刑事处罚；

6.1.3. 具备公证业务的场所。

6.2. 禁止公证员兼任教师、学术研究以外的其他工作、公职。

6.3. 公证员可以从事本国和国际公证机构推选的工作、公职。

第七条　公证区域

7.1. 公证员应在指定的区域开展业务，禁止变更区域进行工作。

7.2. 公证区域及其公证员的人数在兼顾本法第8.1 款规定的蒙古国公证员联合会的意见的情况下，由主持司法工作的政府委员决定。

7.3. 与不动产转移相关的一切协议和与继承权相关的文件只能由该财产所在地的公证员公证。

7.4. 若遇有公证员转换区域的情形，则应重新进行业务考试。且考试合格的该公证员应在该区域空出编制前依顺序等候。

第八条　蒙古国公证员联合会的结构、组织

8.1. 蒙古国公证员联合会（以下简称“联合会”），以将公证员统一到自己的队伍中，并依照本法和自身章程的规定对其业务活动给予协调兼顾，维护其权益为宗旨开展工作。

8.2. 联合会由联合会全体委员会议、联合会及其理事会、联合会在省和首都区的区域分支组成，其权限由联合会章程规定。

8.3. 联合会的主席领导联合会的日常工作，其任期为四年。联合会主席可连选连任一届，其权限由联合会章程规定。

8.4. 联合会下属有纪律和监督委员会，其权限由

зөвлөл ажиллах бөгөөд тэдгээрийн эрх хэмжээг Танхимын дүрмээр тогтооно.

8.5.Танхимын бүх гишүүдийн хурал Танхимын дүрмийг батлах, түүнд нэмэлт, өөрчлөлт оруулах бүрэн эрхийг хэрэгжүүлнэ.

8.6.Танхим нь нийт нутаг дэвсгэрийн хэмжээнд нотариатын үйл ажиллагаатай холбогдсон бүртгэл, мэдээллийн нэгдсэн цахим санг бүрдүүлж ажиллах бөгөөд хуульд заасан төр, байгууллага, хувь хүний нууцтай холбоотойгоос бусад мэдээ, мэдээлэл, тайлан, тоо баримтыг улсын бүртгэлийн асуудал эрхэлсэн төрийн захиргааны байгууллагатай үнэ төлбөргүй солилцож, харилцан мэдээлнэ.

联合会章程规定。

8.5. 联合会全体委员会议享有批准联合会章程并对其进行补充、修改的权力。

8.6. 联合会应承担全国涉及公证业务的登记、信息综合电子库的工作，并与国家负责统计工作的行政机关无偿地开展除法律规定的涉及国家、个人秘密以外的其他信息、报告、数据的交换和公报工作。

ХОЁРДУГААР БҮЛЭГ НОТАРИАТЫН ҮЙЛДЭЛ ХИЙХ ХЭЛ, ТАМГА, БАТАЛГААНЫ ТЭМДЭГ, БАРИМТ, ҮЙЛЧИЛГЭЭНИЙ ХӨЛС, ЗАРДАЛ

第二章 公证的语言、印章、担保印章、凭据、服务报酬、费用

9 дүгээр зүйл.Нотариатын үйлдэл хийх хэл

9.1.Нотариатын үйлдэл хийх, баримт бичиг, нотариатын үйлдэл хийсэн тухай тэмдэглэл үйлдэх албан ёсны хэл нь монгол хэл байна.

9.2.Хилийн чанадад ажиллаж байгаа Монгол Улсын дипломат төлөөлөгчийн газар нь нотариатын үйлдэл, баримт бичгийг монгол хэлээр үйлдэх бөгөөд үйлчлүүлэгчийн хүсэлтээр холбогдох баримт бичгийг орчуулан өгч болно.

第九条 公证的语言

9.1. 进行公证活动，制作文件、公证活动的笔录等的正式语言为蒙古语。

9.2. 在境外工作的蒙古国外交代表处的公证活动，制作文件应以蒙古语进行，应当事人的要求可对相关文件予以翻译。

10 дугаар зүйл.Нотариатчийн тамга, баталгааны тэмдэг

10.1.Нотариатч тогтоосон загварын дагуу үйлдсэн тамга, баталгааны тэмдэг, хэвлэмэл хуудас хэрэглэнэ.

10.2.Нотариатч ажиллаагүй сумын Засаг даргын Тамгын газрын дарга нотариатчийн үүргийг хавсран гүйцэтгэхдээ тухайн сумын Засаг даргын Тамгын газрын тамга, тэмдгийг хэрэглэнэ.

10.3.Хилийн чанадад ажиллаж байгаа Монгол Улсын дипломат төлөөлөгчийн газрын эрх бүхий албан тушаалтан нь нотариатчийн үүргийг хавсран гүйцэтгэхдээ тухайн дипломат төлөөлөгчийн газрын тамга, тэмдгийг хэрэглэнэ.

第十条 公证员的印章、担保印章

10.1. 公证员使用依照规定的模式制作的印章、担保印章、印刷单据。

10.2. 没有公证员的县的县长办公室主任兼任公证员的，使用该县县长办公室印章、证书。

10.3. 境外工作的蒙古国外交代表处有权的公职人员兼任公证员的，使用该外交代表处的印章、证书。

11 дүгээр зүйл.Нотариатын баримт

11.1.Нотариатч болон энэ хуульд заасан эрх бүхий албан тушаалтны хийсэн нотариатын үйлдсэн буюу гэрчилсэн бусад баримт бичиг, түүний хуулбар, лавлагааг нотариатын баримт гэнэ.

第十一条 公证凭证

11.1. 公证员和本法规定的其他有权的公职人员进行公证活动所制作的或公证的其他文件，及其复印件、副本称为公证凭证。

11.2.Энэ хуульд заасны дагуу үйлдэж олгосон нотариатын баримт нотлох баримтын эх сурвалж болох бөгөөд хуульд заасан тохиолдолд нотариатын баримтыг гүйцэтгэх баримт бичигт тооцно.

11.2. 依照本法制作授予的公证文书是证据原始件，且在法律规定的情形下属于公证凭证。

12 дугаар зүйл.Нотариатын үйлчилгээний хөлс, зардал

第十二条　公证服务的报酬、费用

12.1.Нотариатын үйлчилгээ төлбөртэй байна.

12.1. 公证服务系有偿服务。

12.2.Нотариатч хуульд заасан нотариатын үйлдэл хийх, хууль зүйн зөвлөгөө өгөх, баримт бичиг боловсруулах, нотариатын үйлдлийн талаар лавлагаа гаргахад үйлчилгээний хөлс авах бөгөөд үйлчлүүлэгчийн хүсэлтээр ажлын байрнаасаа өөр газар очиж үйлчилсэн бол үйлчилгээний хөлс болон тээврийн зардлыг үйлчлүүлэгчээс авна.

12.2. 公证员进行法律规定的公证事务，提供法律咨询、制作文书，作出公证应收取服务报酬。若有应当事人的要求前往工作场所以外的处所服务的，则向当事人收取服务报酬和交通费用。

12.3.Танхимын саналыг үндэслэн хууль зүйн асуудал эрхэлсэн Засгийн газрын гишүүн энэ хуулийн 12.2-т заасан нотариатын үйлчилгээний хөлс болон тээврийн зардлын хэмжээг батална.

12.3. 负责司法事务的政府委员根据联合会的意见对本法第 12.2 款规定的公证服务报酬和交通费用的数额予以批准。

12.4.Энэ хуулийн 16.2, 16.3-т заасан албан тушаалтан нотариатын үйлчилгээний хөлсийг Улсын тэмдэгтийн хураамжийн тухай хуульд[3] заасны дагуу авна.

12.4. 本法第 16.2. 款、第 16.3. 款规定的公职人员依照国家印花税法[3]的规定对公证服务报酬予以征收。

12.5.Нотариатч энэ хуульд заасНаас бусад үйлчилгээний хөлс, зардал болон шагнал, урамшуулал авахыг хориглоно.

12.5. 禁止公证员收取本法规定以外的其他报酬、费用、奖励、激励等。

12.6.Нотариатч үйлчлүүлэгчийн хүсэлтээр нотариатын үйлчилгээг цуцлах тохиолдолд үйлчилгээний хөлс болон тээврийн зардлыг буцаан олгохгүй.

12.6. 公证员在遇有应当事人的要求撤销公证的，已收取的服务报酬和交通费用不予返还。

12.7.Нотариатч энэ хуулийн 12.3-т заасан үйлчилгээний хөлс болон тээврийн зардлын хэмжээг баталсан шийдвэрийг үйлчлүүлэгчид харагдахуйц газар байрлуулна.

12.7. 公证员应将关于本法第 12.3 款规定的服务报酬和交通费用数额的批文放置于当事人可见的位置。

ГУРАВДУГААР БҮЛЭГ
ЗАСГИЙН ГАЗРЫН ГИШҮҮНИЙ БҮРЭН ЭРХ

第三章　政府委员的权力

13 дугаар зүйл.Хууль зүйн асуудал эрхэлсэн Засгийн газрын гишүүний бүрэн эрх

第十三条　负责司法的政府委员的权力

13.1.Хууль зүйн асуудал эрхэлсэн засгийн газрын гишүүн нотариатын талаар дараахь бүрэн эрхийг хэрэгжүүлнэ:

13.1. 负责司法的政府委员在公证方面实施以下权力：

13.1.1.нотариатчийн үйл ажиллагаанд баримтлах дүрэм, журам, заавар, аргачлал батлах;

13.1.1. 批准公证业务应当遵守的章程、程序、指令、措施；

13.1.2.нотариатын тухай хууль тогтоомжийн биелэлтийг зохион байгуулах;

13.1.2. 组织公证法规的落实；

13.1.3.нотариатчийн ёс зүйн дүрмийн хэрэгжилтэд

13.1.3. 对公证员道德规范的情况进行监督；

хяналт тавих;

13.1.4.нотариатчийн мэргэшлийн шалгалтыг зохион байгуулах;

13.1.5.нотариатын үйл ажиллагаа эрхлэх тусгай зөвшөөрөл олгох, түдгэлзүүлэх, хүчингүй болгох;

13.1.6.нотариатчдын нэгдсэн бүртгэл хөтлөх;

13.1.7.нотариатчийг бэлтгэх, сургах, давтан сургах ажлыг зохион байгуулах;

13.1.8.нотариатчдын үйл ажиллагаанд судалгаа, дүгнэлт хийх;

13.1.9.хуульд заасан бусад.

13.2.Энэ хуулийн 13.1-д заасан бүрэн эрхэд хамаарах зарим асуудлыг Танхимаар гэрээний үндсэн дээр шилжүүлэн гүйцэтгүүлж болно.

13.1.4. 组织公证员技能考试；

13.1.5. 授予从事公证业务的专门许可，以及授权的中止、撤销；

13.1.6. 主持公证员的统一登记；

13.1.7. 组织公证员的培养、培训、进修工作；

13.1.8. 对公证员的业务活动进行调研、评价；

13.1.9. 法律规定的其他事项。

13.2. 本法第 13.1. 款规定的与权力执行相关的事项，可在协商的基础上移交联合会执行。

ДӨРӨВДҮГЭЭР БҮЛЭГ МЭРГЭШЛИЙН ШАЛГАЛТ, НОТАРИАТЫН ҮЙЛ АЖИЛЛАГАА ЭРХЛЭХ ТУСГАЙ ЗӨВШӨӨРӨЛ

第四章 技能考试、从事公证业务的专门许可

14 дүгээр зүйл.Мэргэшлийн шалгалт

14.1.Нотариатын үйл ажиллагаа эрхлэх тусгай зөвшөөрлийг энэ хуульд заасан журмын дагуу зохион байгуулсан мэргэшлийн шалгалтад тэнцсэн тохиолдолд олгоно.

14.2.Мэргэшлийн шалгалтад хуульчийн сонгон шалгаруулалтад тэнцсэн иргэн оролцоно. /Энэ хэсгийг 2013 оны 12 дугаар сарын 12-ны өдрийн хуулиар хүчингүй болсонд тооцсон/

第十四条 技能考试

14.1. 从事公证业务的专门许可，应在依照本法规定的程序组织的技能考试中合格的情况下授予。

14.2. 通过专业选拔考试合格的公民方可参加（该款按照 2013 年 12 月 12 日的法律予以废止）。

15 дугаар зүйл.Мэргэшлийн хороо

15.1.Нотариатчийн мэргэшил, ур чадварын түвшинд дүгнэлт гаргах, мэргэшлийн шалгалт явуулах чиг үүрэг бүхий Мэргэшлийн хороо хууль зүйн асуудал эрхэлсэн төрийн захиргааны төв байгууллагын дэргэд ажиллана.

15.2.Мэргэшлийн хороо долоон гишүүний бүрэлдэхүүнтэй байх бөгөөд даргыг нь гишүүдийн олонхийн саналаар тэдгээрийн дотроос сонгоно.

15.3.Мэргэшлийн хорооны бүрэлдэхүүнд шүүх, хууль зүйн асуудал эрхэлсэн төрийн захиргааны төв байгууллага, Танхимаас тус бүр хоёр, эрдмийн зэрэг цолтой хуульч нэг хүний төлөөлөл байна.

15.4.Мэргэшлийн хорооны гишүүн хууль зүйн ухааны магистр болон түүнээс дээш эрдмийн зэрэг, цолтой байна.

15.5.Мэргэшлийн хорооны гишүүний бүрэн эрхийн хугацаа 4 жил байна.

15.6.Мэргэшлийн хорооны бүрэлдэхүүн, ажиллах

第十五条 技能委员会

15.1. 对公证员业务技能的水准作出评价、具有开展技能考试职能的技能委员会隶属于国家中央司法行政机关。

15.2. 技能委员会由七名成员组成，主任以成员多数的选举意见在他们中间产生。

15.3. 技能委员会成员由法院、国家中央司法行政机关、联合会各二人，具有专业职称的律师一人组成。

15.4. 技能委员会成员应是法学硕士或以上学历、专业等级、职称的人。

15.5. 技能委员会成员任期为四年。

15.6. 技能委员会成员、工作程序由负责司法的

журмыг хууль зүйн асуудал эрхэлсэн Засгийн газрын гишүүн батална.

15.7.Мэргэшлийн шалгалтыг нотариатын тойрог, нотариатчийн орон тоо, хэрэгцээг харгалзан улсын хэмжээнд гурван жил тутам явуулах бөгөөд нотариатч ажиллаагүй тухайн тойрогт мэргэшлийн шалгалт явуулах эсэхийг хууль зүйн асуудал эрхэлсэн Засгийн газрын гишүүн тухай бүр шийдвэрлэнэ.

15.8.Мэргэшлийн шалгалт эхлэхээс 45-аас доошгүй хоногийн өмнө энэ тухай өдөр тутмын хэвлэл мэдээллийн хэрэгслээр нийтэд мэдээлнэ.

16 дугаар зүйл. Нотариатын үйл ажиллагаа эрхлэх тусгай зөвшөөрөл олгох

16.1.Энэ хуулийн 6.1-д заасан шаардлагыг хангасан иргэнд Мэргэшлийн хорооны саналыг үндэслэн хууль зүйн асуудал эрхэлсэн Засгийн газрын гишүүн нотариатын үйл ажиллагаа эрхлэх тусгай зөвшөөрөл олгоно.

16.2.Нотариатч ажиллаагүй суманд хууль зүйн асуудал эрхэлсэн Засгийн газрын гишүүнээс эрх авсан сумын Засаг даргын Тамгын газрын дарга нотариатчийн үүргийг хавсран гүйцэтгэнэ.

16.3.Хилийн чанадад ажиллаж байгаа дипломат төлөөлөгчийн газарт хууль зүйн асуудал эрхэлсэн Засгийн газрын гишүүнээс эрх авсан албан тушаалтан нотариатчийн үүргийг хавсран гүйцэтгэнэ.

16.4.Энэ хуулийн 16.2, 16.3-т заасан нотариатчийн үүргийг хавсран гүйцэтгэж байгаа албан тушаалтанд энэ хуульд заасан нотариатчийн эрх, үүрэг, холбогдох бусад зүйл, заалт нэгэн адил хамаарна.

17 дугаар зүйл.Нотариатын үйл ажиллагаа эрхлэх тусгай зөвшөөрлийг түдгэлзүүлэх

17.1.Хууль зүйн асуудал эрхэлсэн Засгийн газрын гишүүн нотариатын үйл ажиллагаа эрхлэх тусгай зөвшөөрлийг дараахь үндэслэлээр түдгэлзүүлж болно:

17.1.1.энэ хуульд заасан нотариатын үйлдэл хийх журмыг зөрчсөн нь тогтоогдсон бол 3 сар хүртэл хугацаагаар;

17.1.2.нотариатч эрүүгийн хариуцлагад татагдсан тохиолдолд эрх бүхий байгууллагын саналыг үндэслэн эцсийн шийдвэр гартал;

17.1.3.энэ хуулийн 21.2, 21.3, 22.1, 24.1-д заасныг зөрчсөн бол 6 сар хүртэл хугацаагаар;

17.1.4.нотариатч төрийн албан тушаалд томилогдсон, сонгогдсон тохиолдолд тухайн шийдвэрийг нь үндэслэн.

政府委员批准。

15.7. 技能考试根据公证辖区、公证员编制、需求情况在全国范围每三年举行一次。是否在没有公证员的辖区进行考试，由负责司法的政府委员临时决定。

15.8. 在举行技能考试前不少于四十五天，应通过日常媒体向公众公告考试安排。

第十六条　公证业务专门许可的授予

16.1. 满足本法第 6.1. 款条件的公民，依据技能委员会的意见、由负责司法的政府委员授予其从事公证业务的专门许可。

16.2. 在没有公证员的县，由负责司法的政府委员授权的县长办公室主任代理公证员。

16.3. 在境外工作的外交代表机构，由负责司法的政府委员授权的公职人员代理公证员。

16.4. 本法第 16.2. 款、第 16.3. 款规定的兼职公证员的公职人员，本法规定的公证员权益、职责，相关的其他条款、规定同样对其适用。

第十七条　公证业务专门许可的中止

17.1. 负责司法的政府委员可根据下列理由中止从事公证业务的专门许可：

17.1.1. 违反本法规定的公证活动程序的，中止业务三个月；

17.1.2. 遇有公证员被追究刑事责任的，根据相关权力机关的意见，作出最终处理；

17.1.3. 违反本法第 21.2. 款、第 21.3. 款、第 22.1. 款、第 24.1. 款规定的，中止业务六个月。

17.1.4. 遇有公证员被任命或当选国家公职的，可根据相关决定中止业务。

17.2.Энэ хуулийн 17.1-д заасан түдгэлзүүлэх үндэслэл арилсан тохиолдолд хууль зүйн асуудал эрхэлсэн Засгийн газрын гишүүн нотариатын үйл ажиллагаа эрхлэх тусгай зөвшөөрлийг сэргээнэ.

18 дугаар зүйл.Нотариатын үйл ажиллагаа эрхлэх тусгай зөвшөөрлийг хүчингүй болгох

18.1.Хууль зүйн асуудал эрхэлсэн Засгийн газрын гишүүн дараахь үндэслэлээр нотариатын үйл ажиллагаа эрхлэх тусгай зөвшөөрлийг хүчингүй болгоно:

18.1.1. нотариатч эрүүл мэндийн болон хүндэтгэн үзэх бусад шалтгаанаар үүрэгт ажлаа гүйцэтгэх боломжгүй болсон бол өөрийнх нь хүсэлт, эсхүл эмнэлгийн дүгнэлт, холбогдох байгууллагын тодорхойлолтыг үндэслэн;

18.1.2.нотариатын үйл ажиллагаа эрхлэх тусгай зөвшөөрлийг хуурамч баримт бичиг бүрдүүлэн авсан нь тогтоогдсон;

18.1.3.нотариатч гэмт хэрэг үйлдсэн гэм буруутай нь нотлогдож, шүүхийн шийтгэх тогтоол хүчин төгөлдөр болсон;

18.1.4.нотариатч эрх зүйн чадамжгүй болсон;

18.1.5.нотариатын үйл ажиллагаа эрхлэх тусгай зөвшөөрлийг түдгэлзүүлсэн хугацаанд зөрчлийг арилгах талаар тавьсан шаардлагыг биелүүлээгүй;

18.1.6.нотариатчийн ёс зүйн хэм хэмжээг ноцтой зөрчсөн.

18.2.Нотариатын үйл ажиллагаа эрхлэх тусгай зөвшөөрөл хүчингүй болсон тохиолдолд нотариатч тамга, баталгааны тэмдэг, баримт бичгээ Танхимд хүлээлгэн өгнө.

18.3.Энэ хуулийн 18.2-т заасныг зөрчсөн бол тамга, баталгааны тэмдэг, баримт бичиг хүчингүй болсныг нийтэд мэдээлнэ.

19 дүгээр зүйл.Нотариатчийн үйл ажиллагаа дуусгавар болох

19.1.Дараахь тохиолдолд нотариатчийн үйл ажиллагаа дуусгавар болсонд тооцно:

19.1.1.нас барсан;

19.1.2.Монгол Улсын харьяатаас гарсан.

19.2.Нотариатч Монгол Улсын харьяатаас гарсан тухайгаа хууль зүйн асуудал эрхэлсэн Засгийн газрын гишүүнд мэдэгдэнэ.

17.2. 本法第 17.1. 款规定的中止的事由消除后，负责司法的政府委员应恢复对其公证业务的许可。

第十八条 公证业务专门许可的撤销

18.1. 负责司法的政府委员，根据下列理由撤销从事公证业务的专门许可：

18.1.1. 公证员由于健康和应当重视的其他原因已不可能履行职责的，根据其本人请求、医疗结论或相关机关的说明处理；

18.1.2. 公证业务专门许可系伪造文件的；

18.1.3. 公证员涉嫌犯罪法院判决生效的；

18.1.4. 公证员已不具备行为能力；

18.1.5. 在中止从事公证业务专门许可期间，中止业务的事由未消除的；

18.1.6. 严重违反公证员道德标准的；

18.2. 从事公证业务专门许可被撤销后，公证员应将印章、担保印章、文件交还联合会。

18.3. 如有违反本法第 18.2. 款规定的，应向公众宣告其印章、担保印章已作废。

第十九条 公证员业务的终止

19.1. 在下列情形下，公证员业务终止：

19.1.1. 去世；

19.1.2. 丧失蒙古国国籍。

19.2. 公证员应将终止蒙古国国籍的事项告知负责司法的政府委员。

ТАВДУГААР БҮЛЭГ НОТАРИАТЧИЙН ТАНГАРАГ, ЭРХ, ҮҮРЭГ, БАТАЛГАА

20 дугаар зүйл.Нотариатчийн тангараг

20.1.Нотариатч анх үйл ажиллагаагаа эхлэхийн өмнө тангараг өргөх бөгөөд тангараг өргөх ёслолын журмыг хууль зүйн асуудал эрхэлсэн Засгийн газрын гишүүн батална.

21 дүгээр зүйл.Нотариатчийн эрх, үүрэг

21.1.Нотариатч дараахь эрх эдэлнэ:

21.1.1.нотариатын үйлдэл хийлгэж байгаа этгээд /цаашид "үйлчлүүлэгч" гэх/-ийн хувийн байдлыг тогтоох;

21.1.2.нотариатын үйлдэл хийхэд зайлшгүй шаардлагатай баримт бичиг, түүний хуулбар, шаардлагатай мэдээллийг иргэн, хуулийн этгээдээс шаардан авах;

21.1.3.шаардлагатай гэж үзвэл холбогдох этгээдийг дуудан ирүүлэх;

21.1.4.хуульд заасан бусад.

21.2.Нотариатч дараахь үүрэг хүлээнэ:

21.2.1.үйлчлүүлэгчид эрх, үүргийг нь тайлбарлан, тухайн үйлдлийг өөрийн хүсэл зоригийн дагуу хэрэгжүүлж байгаа эсэхийг тодруулан, эрх зүйн үр дагавар, хууль зүйн ач холбогдлыг тайлбарлаж зөвлөгөө өгөх;

21.2.2.нотариатчийн ёс зүйн дүрмийг чанд сахиж, мэргэжлийн нууцыг хадгалах;

21.2.3.гишүүний татвараа төлөх;

21.2.4.хариуцлагын даатгалд даатгуулах;

21.2.5.нотариатын үйлдэлд холбогдох баримт бичгийн үнэн, зөв эсэхийг хянаж нягтлах;

21.2.6.нотариатын үйлдэлд холбогдох баримт бичиг, түүний хуулбар, шаардлагатай мэдээллийг хуулийн байгууллагын шаардсаны дагуу гаргаж өгөх;

21.2.7.нотариатын үйлдэл хийх эрхээ гагцхүү өөрөө хэрэгжүүлж, тамга, баталгааны тэмдгийг бусдад шилжүүлэхгүй байх;

21.2.8.гэрчлүүлэхээр ирүүлсэн баримт бичгийн жинхэнэ эх мөн эсэх нь эргэлзээтэй байвал уг баримт бичгийг олгосон байгууллагаас лавлагаа болон хуулбарыг авах, тодорхойлолт гаргуулах, зайлшгүй шаардлагатай гэж үзвэл магадлан шинжлүүлэх;

21.2.9.нотариатын үйлдэл хийх явцад үйлчлүүлэгч хууль зөрчсөн болох нь илэрвэл зохих арга хэмжээ

第五章 公证员宣誓、权益、职责、保障

第二十条 公证员宣誓

20.1. 公证员在开始从事业务前应进行宣誓，宣誓仪式的程序由负责司法的政府委员批准。

第二十一条 公证员的权利、义务

21.1. 公证员享有下列权利：

21.1.1. 确定申请公证的对象（以下称“当事人”）的个人身份；

21.1.2. 要求公民、法人提供公证活动必需的文件及其复印件、必要的信息；

21.1.3. 认为必要时传唤相关人员；

21.1.4. 法律规定的其他事项。

21.2. 公证员承担下列义务：

21.2.1. 向当事人说明其权利、义务，说明所进行的公证行为是否在按照其意愿实行，并对公证的效力、法律意义给予说明、建议；

21.2.2. 严格遵守公证员道德规范、保守业务秘密；

21.2.3. 缴纳委员税赋；

21.2.4. 参加责任保险；

21.2.5. 认真核查与公证活动相关的文件是否真实、正确；

21.2.6. 应司法机关的要求，提供与公证活动相关的文件及其复印件、必要的信息；

21.2.7. 由其本人行使公证活动的职权，不得将印章、担保印章移交他人；

21.2.8. 若对送交公证的文件是否确为正式原件存有疑虑，则可向提供该文件的机构要求查询或获取复印件、出具说明，认为必要的可进行鉴定；

21.2.9. 在公证过程中，如发现当事人的违法行为，应向相关机关报告并采取相应的措施；

авахуулахаар холбогдох байгууллагад мэдэгдэх;

21.2.10.хуульд заасан бусад.

21.3.Нотариатчийн үйл ажиллагаанд дараахь зүйлийг хориглоно:

21.3.1.хуурамч баримт бичгийг гэрчлэх;

21.3.2.баримт бичгийн хуулбарыг эх хувьтай нь тулгахгүйгээр гэрчлэх;

21.3.3.нотариатын үйлдэл хийж болохгүй нөхцөл байдлыг нуун дарагдуулж нотариатын үйлдэл хийх;

21.3.4.нотариатын үйлдэл хийх явцдаа олж мэдсэн үйлчлүүлэгчийн нууцыг задруулах;

21.3.5.нотариатын үйлдэл хийх, эрх зүйн зөвлөгөө өгөхөөс үндэслэлгүйгээр татгалзах.

22 дугаар зүйл.Нотариатын мэргэжлийн нууц

22.1.Нотариатч төр, байгууллага, хувь хүний нууцад хамаарах асуудлаар нотариатын үйлдэл хийж байгаа бол тэдгээрийн нууцыг холбогдох хууль тогтоомжид заасны дагуу хамгаална.

22.2.Нотариатын үйл ажиллагаа дуусгавар болсон ч нууцыг хадгалах үүрэг хэвээр хадгалагдана.

22.3.Албан үүргээ гүйцэтгэх явцдаа нотариатын үйлдлийн нууцыг мэдсэн бусад этгээдэд энэ хуулийн 22.1, 22.2 дахь хэсэг нэгэн адил хамаарна.

23 дугаар зүйл.Нотариатчийн хараат бус, бие даасан байдлын баталгаа

23.1.Нотариатын үйлдэл хийхэд дарамт шахалт үзүүлэх, хөндлөнгөөс оролцох, саад учруулах, нотариатын үйлдэл хийхийг хууль бусаар шаардахыг хориглоно.

24 дүгээр зүйл. Нотариатчийн хариуцлагын даатгал

24.1.Нотариатч нь нотариатын үйлдлийг буруу хийсэн, үйлчлүүлэгчийн хувийн байдлыг буруу тогтоосон зэрэг бусад буруутай үйлдлийн улмаас үйлчлүүлэгчид хохирол учруулсан тохиолдолд түүнийг нөхөн төлөх зорилгоор хариуцлагын албан журмын даатгалд даатгуулна. /Энэ хэсэгт 2011 оны 10 дугаар сарын 6-ны өдрийн хуулиар өөрчлөлт оруулсан/

24.2.Нотариатч даатгалын байгууллагаа өөрөө сонгоно.

24.3.Энэ хуулийн 24.1-д заасан даатгалын нөхөн төлбөрийн хэмжээ нь нийслэлд нэг сарын хөдөлмөрийн хөлсний доод хэмжээг хоёр зуу дахин нэмэгдүүлсэнээс доошгүй, орон нутагт нэг сарын хөдөлмөрийн хөлсний доод хэмжээг нэг зуу дахин

21.2.10. 法律规定的其他事项。

21.3. 公证活动中禁止下列事项：

21.3.1. 公证伪造的文件；

21.3.2. 不将文件复印件与原件核对而公证；

21.3.3. 隐瞒不可以公证的状况而进行公证；

21.3.4. 泄露在公证活动中知悉的当事人的秘密；

21.3.5. 无正当理由放弃公证、提供权益建议。

第二十二条　公证业务秘密

22.1. 如果公证员的公证活动中涉及国家机关、个人秘密，那么应当依照相关法律法规保守秘密。

22.2. 公证活动结束后，公证员仍应履行保守秘密的义务。

22.3. 本法第 22.1. 款、第 22.2. 款同样适用于在履行公职的过程中知悉公证活动秘密的其他人员。

第二十三条　公证员的管辖区域、独立性保障

23.1. 在进行公证活动时禁止施加压力、外部干预、设置障碍，以及要求其进行非法公证。

第二十四条　公证员责任保险

24.1. 因为公证员错误的公证活动、错误地确定当事人的个人状况等错误行为而给当事人造成损失的，以补偿该损失为目的，公证员参加责任义务保险。（本款依 2011 年 10 月 6 日的法律进行了修订）

24.2. 公证员自行选择保险机构。

24.3. 本法第 24.1 款规定的保险补偿数额，首都为不低于一个月劳动报酬最低标准的 200 倍，其他地方为不低于一个月劳动报酬最低标准的 100 倍。

нэмэгдүүлснээс доошгүй байна.

ЗУРГАДУГААР БҮЛЭГ НОТАРИАТЫН ҮЙЛДЭЛ, НОТАРИАТЫН БҮРТГЭЛ, ХУГАЦАА

25 дугаар зүйл.Нотариатын үйлдлийн төрөл

25.1.Нотариатын үйлдэл дараахь төрөлтэй байна:

25.1.1.гэрээ, хэлцэл гэрчлэх;

25.1.2.гэрээслэл гэрчлэх;

25.1.3.итгэмжлэл гэрчлэх;

25.1.4.өвлөх эрхийн гэрчилгээ олгох;

25.1.5.өвлөгдөх эд хөрөнгийг хамгаалах;

25.1.6.хуулийн этгээд үүсгэн байгуулах баримт бичиг гэрчлэх;

25.1.7.эд хөрөнгийн эрхийн бүртгэлтэй холбогдох баримт бичиг гэрчлэх;

25.1.8.гэр бүлийн гишүүдийн дундаа хамтран болон дундаа хэсгээр өмчлөх эд хөрөнгөөс ногдох хэсгээ өмчлөх эрх гэрчлэх;

25.1.9.баримт бичгийн хуулбарыг гэрчлэх;

25.1.10.баримт бичигт зурсан гарын үсгийн үнэн зөвийг гэрчлэх;

25.1.11.нотариатын мэдэгдэх хуудас бичих.

25.2.аавал гэрчлүүлэх нотариатын үйлдлийг зөвхөн хуулиар тогтоох бөгөөд үүнээс бусад үйлдлийг үйлчлүүлэгчийн хүсэлтээр гэрчилнэ.

26 дугаар зүйл.Нотариатын бүртгэл

26.1.Нотариатч баримт бичиг, үйл явдлыг гэрчлэхдээ нотариатын бүртгэл хөтөлж түүнд нотариатчийн хийсэн нотариатын үйлдлийг он, сар өдрийн дарааллаар нь үнэн зөв, засваргүй, гаргацтай, тодорхой бичнэ.

26.2.Нотариатын бүртгэлийн дэвтэрт үйлчлүүлэгчийн овог, эцэг /эх/-ийн нэр, өөрийн нэр, иргэний үнэмлэхний болон регистрийн дугаар, оршин суугаа газрын хаяг, хэрэв нотариатын үйлдэл хийхэд тэмдэглэл хөтөлсөн бол энэ тухай тус тус тэмдэглэнэ.

26.3.Үйлчлүүлэгч, нотариатын үйлдэл хийхэд оролцсон гэрч, бусад оролцогч нотариатын бүртгэлийн дэвтэрт гарын үсэг зурна.

26.4.Нотариатын үйлдэл хийсэн баримт бичигт дарсан баталгааны тэмдгийн дардас дээрх дугаар нь тухайн бүртгэлийн дугаартай ижил байна.

26.5.Нотариатын бүртгэлийг уусдаггүй нэг өнгийн бэхээр хөтөлнө.

第六章 公证业务、公证登记、期限

第二十五条 公证业务类型

25.1. 公证业务具有下列类型：

25.1.1. 合同协议公证；

25.1.2. 遗嘱公证；

25.1.3. 授权委托公证；

25.1.4. 继承权公证；

25.1.5. 遗产保护公证；

25.1.6. 法人设立文件公证；

25.1.7. 产权登记文件公证；

25.1.8. 继承人间继承遗产份额公证；

25.1.9. 文件复印件公证；

25.1.10. 文件签名真实、准确性公证；

25.1.11. 起草公证可执行债权文书。

25.2. 必须公证的公证业务由法律规定，其他业务则应当事人的申请公证。

第二十六条 公证登记

26.1. 公证员在对文件、事物公证时需制作登记表，其中应将公证员所作公证活动按照年、月、日的顺序真实、准确、无涂改、清晰、明确地予以登记。

26.2. 公证登记表中应载明当事人的姓、父（母）的名字、本人名字、公民身份证和登记号、住宅地址。如在公证活动中做了笔录，对此也要分别记录。

26.3. 当事人、见证人及其他参与公证活动的均应在公证登记册上签名。

26.4. 公证活动文件上加盖的担保印章的号码应与相应的登记号相同。

26.5. 公证登记应使用不会消失的同色墨汁制作。

27 дугаар зүйл.Үйлчлүүлэгчийн хувийн байдлыг тогтоох

27.1.Нотариатч үйлчлүүлэгчийн хувийн байдлыг тогтоохдоо түүний иргэний баримт бичиг, хуулийн этгээд бол улсын бүртгэлийн гэрчилгээ, дүрмийг үндэслэх бөгөөд итгэмжлэл, төлөөлөл нь зохих ёсоор бүрдсэн эрх зүйн чадамжтай эсэхийг шалгаж, шаардлагатай бол эрх бүхий байгууллагын тодорхойлолт, эсхүл тухайн хүнийг таних хоёр гэрчээр тодорхойлуулан тогтоож болно.

27.2.Үйлчлүүлэгчийн эрүүл мэндийн байдал нь илтэд муудах зэрэг зайлшгүй нөхцөл байдлын улмаас нотариатын үйлдлийг яаралтай хийхэд хүрвэл үйлчлүүлэгчийн хувийн байдлыг тусгайлан тодруулахгүйгээр нотариатын үйлдэл хийсний дараа тодруулж болно.

28 дугаар зүйл.Үйлчлүүлэгчийн эрх, үүрэг

28.1.Үйлчлүүлэгч дараахь эрх эдэлнэ:

28.1.1.энэ хуулийн 7.3-т зааснаас бусад тохиолдолд нотариатчийг өөрөө чөлөөтэй сонгох;

28.1.2.нотариатчийн хууль бус үйлдлийн талаар Танхимд, эсхүл хууль зүйн асуудал эрхэлсэн Засгийн газрын гишүүнд гомдол гаргах;

28.1.3.нотариатчийн буруутай үйлдлийн улмаас хохирол учирвал нөхөн төлүүлэх;

28.1.4.хуульд заасан бусад эрх.

28.2.Үйлчлүүлэгч дараахь үүрэг хүлээнэ:

28.2.1.нотариатын үйлдэл хийлгэх баримт бичгийг үнэн зөв бүрдүүлж өгөх;

28.2.2.нотариатчийн шаардсан асуудлаар амаар буюу бичгээр тайлбар өгөх.

28.2.3.Үйлчлүүлэгчийн буруутай үйл ажиллагаанаас учирсан хохирлыг нотариатч хариуцахгүй.

29 дүгээр зүйл.Нотариатын үйлдэл хийх хугацаа

29.1.Энэ хуулийн 30, 31 дүгээр зүйлд зааснаас бусад тохиолдолд нотариатын үйлдлийг тухай бүрт нь хийнэ.

30 дугаар зүйл.Нотариатын үйлдэл хийхийг хойшлуулах, түдгэлзүүлэх

30.1.Үйлчлүүлэгч согтууруулах ундаа, мансууруулах бодис хэрэглэсэн, эсхүл өөрийн үйлдэлд хяналт тавих чадваргүй байгаа бол энэ нөхцөл байдлыг арилах хүртэл нотариатын үйлдэл хийхийг хойшлуулна.

30.2.Иргэн, хуулийн этгээдээс баримт бичиг,

第二十七条　当事人个人身份的确定

27.1. 公证员在确定当事人的个人身份时应以其公民身份证件，法人则以国家登记证件、章程为依据，并对其代理人、代表是否具有相应的权限（法律）能力进行查验。必要时由相应权力机关的说明，或由两名与之相识的人作为证明人进行说明后加以确定。

27.2. 由于当事人的身体健康状况明显恶化等不可避免的情形而需尽快进行公证活动的，可在公证活动进行后查清其个人身份。

第二十八条　当事人的权利、义务

28.1. 当事人享有下列权利：

28.1.1. 除本法第 7.3 款规定以外的其他情形下，可自行选择公证员；

28.1.2. 就公证员的非法行为向联合会、负责司法的政府委员申诉；

28.1.3. 如因公证员的行为过错而遭受损失的，可要求其赔偿；

28.1.4. 法律规定的其他权利。

28.2. 当事人承担下列义务：

28.2.1. 提供完整、真实、准确的公证活动文件；

28.2.2. 对于公证员提问进行口头或书面的说明；

28.2.3. 因当事人错误行为而造成的损失，公证员不予负责。

第二十九条　公证活动的期限

29.1. 除本法第 30 条、第 31 条规定的情形下，公证活动应当立即进行。

第三十条　公证活动的推延、中止

30.1. 当事人有使用致醉、迷幻物品的或不能控制自己行为的，则公证活动推延至此类状况消除为止。

30.2. 若出现公民、法人的文件及其复印件，或

түүний хуулбар, шаардлагатай мэдээллийг нэмж гаргуулах буюу тэдгээрийг шинжлүүлэх шаардлага гарсан тохиолдолд нотариатын үйлдэл хийхийг тодорхой хугацаагаар хойшлуулж болно.

30.3.Нотариатчаар гэрчлүүлж байгаа баримт бичиг буюу эрхийн талаар шүүхэд нэхэмжлэл гаргасан тухай өөр этгээдээс өргөдөл ирүүлсэн тохиолдолд уг асуудлаар нотариатын үйлдэл хийхийг 3-7 хүртэл хоногийн хугацаагаар хойшлуулах бөгөөд энэ хугацаанд нэхэмжлэл гаргасан нь тогтоогдвол шүүхийн шийдвэр гартал нотариатын үйлдэл хийхийг түдгэлзүүлнэ.

31 дүгээр зүйл.Нотариатын үйлдэл хийхээс татгалзах

31.1.Нотариатч дараахь тохиолдолд нотариатын үйлдэл хийхээс татгалзана:

31.1.1.үйлчлүүлэгчийн баримт бичиг нь хууль тогтоомж, Монгол Улсын олон улсын гэрээнд харшилж байвал;

31.1.2.өөртэй нь болон түүний гэр бүлийн гишүүнтэй нь холбоотой асуудал байвал;

31.1.3.өөрийнх нь байнгын үйлчлүүлэгчийн хувийн нууцтай холбоотой асуудлаар бусад этгээд нотариатын үйлдэл хийлгэхийг хүсвэл;

31.1.4.үйлчлүүлэгч нь эрх зүйн чадамжгүй, эсхүл төлөөлөх эрхгүй байвал;

31.1.5.хэрэг хянан шийдвэрлэх ажиллагаанд өөрөө итгэмжлэгдсэн төлөөлөгчөөр оролцвол уг хэрэгт холбогдох баримт бичгийг;

31.1.6.хуульд заасан бусад.

31.2.Нотариатч энэ хуулийн 31.1-д зааснаас бусад үндэслэлээр нотариатын үйлдэл хийхээс татгалзах эрхгүй.

31.3.Энэ хуулийн 31.1-д заасныг зөрчиж хийсэн нотариатын үйлдлийг шүүх нотариатчийн болон сонирхогч этгээдийн хүсэлтээр хүчингүйд тооцно.

32 дугаар зүйл.Орчуулагч /хэлмэрч/-ийг оролцуулах

32.1.Үйлчлүүлэгч нь хэлгүй, дүлий, эсхүл монгол хэл мэдэхгүй бол нотариатын үйлдэл хийх, баримт бичиг үйлдэхдээ тэдгээрийн хууль ёсны төлөөлөгч / асран хамгаалагч, харгалзан дэмжигч/ болон орчуулагч /хэлмэрч/-ийг оролцуулна. Үйлчлүүлэгч нь орчуулагч / хэлмэрч/-ийг өөрөө сонгоно.

32.2.Орчуулагч /хэлмэрч/ нь зориуд худал орчуулах буюу хэлмэрчилвэл хууль тогтоомжид заасны

者必要的信息需要补交、需要查验的，则公证活动可以在确定的期限内推延。

30.3. 公证员公证的文件或权利，诉至法院的，则可因该问题而推延公证活动三天至七天。其间，案件被正式受理的，应在法院作出生效裁判前中止公证活动。

第三十一条　放弃公证

31.1. 公证员在下列情况下放弃公证：

31.1.1. 当事人的文件与蒙古国法规、蒙古国参加的国际条约冲突的；

31.1.2. 与其（公证员本人）或家庭成员有关联的；

31.1.3. 当事人申请公证的事项与其他当事人个人秘密相关的；

31.1.4. 当事人无行为能力或无权代表的；

31.1.5. 如以代理人身份参加公证活动的，须提交与代理授权权限相关的材料；

31.1.6. 法律的其他规定。

31.2. 公证员除第 31.1 款规定外，无权以其他理由放弃公证。

31.3. 对违反本法第 31.1 款规定而作出的公证，法院应公证员和利害关系人的要求裁定其无效。

第三十二条　翻译（口译）人员

32.1. 当事人为聋哑或不懂蒙古语的，进行公证活动、制作文件时，应邀请其法定代理人（监护人、扶养人）和翻译（口译）人员参加。当事人自行选择翻译（口译）人员。

32.2. 翻译（口译）人员故意虚假翻译或口译的，则依法承担责任。

дагуу хариуцлага хүлээнэ.

32.3.Хоёр ба түүнээс дээш талууд нотариатын үйлдэл хийлгэж байгаа тохиолдолд нэг тал нь нөгөө талдаа орчуулагч /хэлмэрч/-ийн үүрэг гүйцэтгэхийг хориглоно.

32.4.Үйлчлүүлэгч гарын үсгээ өөрийн мэддэг хэл дээр зурж болно.

33 дугаар зүйл.Гэрч оролцуулах

33.1.Үйлчлүүлэгч нь хараагүй, хэлгүй, дүлий, бичиг үсэг мэддэггүй, түүнчлэн эрх зүйн чадамжгүй этгээд байвал нотариатын үйлдэл хийх, баримт бичиг үйлдэхдээ тэдгээрийн хууль ёсны төлөөлөгч /асран хамгаалагч, харгалзан дэмжигч/ болон нотариатч шаардлагатай гэж үзвэл гэрчийг оролцуулна. Энэ тохиолдолд дараахь этгээдийг гэрчээр оролцуулахыг хориглоно:

33.1.1.насанд хүрээгүй;

33.1.2.эрх зүйн чадамжгүй;

33.1.3.бичиг үсэг мэддэггүй;

33.1.4.монгол хэл мэддэггүй;

33.1.5.тухайн нотариатчийн байнгын үйлчлүүлэгч.

33.2.Үйлчлүүлэгч хүсвэл нотариатын үйлдэл хийхэд гэрч оролцуулж болно.

34 дүгээр зүйл.Нотариатын үйлдэл хийсэн тухай тэмдэглэл, түүний агуулга

34.1.Энэ хуулийн 32, 33 дугаар зүйлд заасан үйлчлүүлэгч, түүнчлэн бусад оролцогч оролцож байгаа бол нотариатын үйлдэл хийхэд тэмдэглэл хөтөлнө.

34.2.Энэ хуулийн 34.1-д заасан тэмдэглэлд дараахь зүйлийг тусгана:

34.2.1.үйлчлүүлэгч, түүний хууль ёсны төлөөлөгчийн овог, эцэг /эх/-ийн нэр, өөрийн нэр;

34.2.2.нотариатын үйлдэл хийхэд оролцсон гэрч, орчуулагч /хэлмэрч/ зэрэг бусад оролцогчийн овог, эцэг /эх/-ийн нэр, өөрийн нэр, нас, мэргэжил, оршин суугаа газрын хаяг, тэдгээрийн тайлбар, түүнчлэн гэрч, орчуулагч /хэлмэрч/-ийг оролцуулсан үндэслэл;

34.2.3.холбогдох баримт бичгийг танилцуулсан арга хэлбэр, үйл ажиллагааны үр дүн, дэс дараалал;

34.2.4.нотариатчийн албан тушаал, овог, эцэг /эх/-ийн нэр, өөрийн нэр;

34.2.5.баримт бичгийг үйлдсэн он, сар, өдөр, цаг, минут.

35 дугаар зүйл.Тэмдэглэл үйлдэх журам

35.1.Тэмдэглэл нь гаргацтай, утга агуулгын хувьд

32.3. 在遇有两个或以上当事人同时进行公证活动时，不得由一方为另一方承担翻译（口译）任务。

32.4. 当事人可以自己通晓的语言签字。

第三十三条　见证人

33.1. 当事人如是盲人、聋哑人、文盲以及无行为能力人，在进行公证活动、制作文件时可要求其法定代理人（监护人、扶养人）和公证员认为必要的见证人参加。下列人员不得作为见证人参与公证活动：

33.1.1. 未成年人；

33.1.2. 无行为能力人；

33.1.3. 文盲；

33.1.4. 不懂蒙古语的人；

33.1.5. 该公证员的其他当事人。

33.2. 如果需要，见证人可以参与公证。

第三十四条　公证活动笔录及其内容

34.1. 若是本法第 32 条、第 33 条规定的当事人及其他人员参加的，则在进行公证活动时制作笔录。

34.2. 本法第 34.1 款规定的笔录应包含下列事项：

34.2.1. 当事人、其法定代理人的姓、父（母）名、本人名字；

34.2.2. 参加公证活动的见证人，翻译（口译）人员等其他参加者的姓、父（母）名、本人名字、年龄、专业、住址，以及见证人、翻译（口译）人员参加的原因；

34.2.3. 阐释相关文件的方式、行为结果、顺序；

34.2.4. 公证员的姓、父（母）名、本人名字；

34.2.5. 制作文件的年、月、日、时、分。

第三十五条　笔录制作的程序

35.1. 笔录应字迹清晰、内容明了，无字词修改，

ойлгомжтой, үг үсгийн засваргүй, энэ зүйлийн 35.6-д зааснаас бусад тохиолдолд оруулгагүй байна.

35.2.Нотариатч тэмдэглэл үйлдсэний дараа үйлчлүүлэгч болон бусад оролцогчид уншиж сонсгоно.

35.3.Тэмдэглэлд үйлчлүүлэгч болон нотариатын үйлдэл хийхэд оролцсон гэрч, орчуулагч /хэлмэрч/ зэрэг бусад оролцогч гарын үсэг зурж, нотариатч тамга, баталгааны тэмдгээ дарж баталгаажуулна.

35.4.Гарын үсэг зурж чаддаггүй хүмүүс оролцож байгаа, эсхүл энэ хуулийн 27.2-т заасан нөхцөл байдал үүссэн бол энэ тухай тайлбар бичнэ.

35.5.Тэмдэглэл хоёр буюу түүнээс дээш хуудастай бол хуудсыг дугаарлан хуудас бүрт үйлчлүүлэгч болон бусад оролцогч гарын үсэг зурж баталгаажуулна.

35.6.Үйлчлүүлэгч хүсвэл утга агуулгыг нь өөрчлөхгүйгээр тэмдэглэлд нэмэлт, өөрчлөлт оруулж болох бөгөөд энэ тохиолдолд үйлчлүүлэгч болон нотариатын үйлдэл хийхэд оролцсон гэрч, орчуулагч /хэлмэрч/ зэрэг бусад оролцогч гарын үсэг зурж, нотариатч тамга, баталгааны тэмдгээ дарж баталгаажуулна.

35.7.Энэ хуулийн 35.6-д заасныг зөрчиж хийсэн нэмэлт, өөрчлөлтийг хүчингүйд тооцно.

36 дугаар зүйл.Үрэгдүүлсэн материал нөхөн бүрдүүлэх

36.1.Нотариатч өөрт үлдсэн материалыг үрэгдүүлсэн тохиолдолд үйлчлүүлэгчид өгсөн хувиас хуулбар хийж авах бөгөөд хуулбар дээр энэ тухай тэмдэглэл хийж, баримт бичиг хадгалах журмын дагуу хадгална.

37 дугаар зүйл.Үндсэн материал шалгах

37.1.Нотариатч нь үйлчлүүлэгч, түүний эрх залгамжлагч болон итгэмжлэгдсэн төлөөлөгчийн хүсэлтээр баримт бичиг гэрчлэхдээ тэдгээрт холбогдох бусад үндсэн материалыг шалгаж болно.

37.2.Тухайн иргэн, хуулийн этгээдэд холбогдолгүй асуудлаар үндсэн материалыг шалгахыг хориглоно.

38 дугаар зүйл.Баримт бичгийн хуулбар хийх

38.1.Үйлчлүүлэгч нь гэрчлүүлсэн баримт бичгээ үрэгдүүлбэл нотариатч үлдсэн хувиас хуулбар хийж өгнө.

39 дүгээр зүйл.Баримт бичгийг хадгалах

39.1.Нотариатч нь нотариатын үйлдэл хийх үндэслэл болгосон материалыг, гэрчилсэн баримт бичгийн хамт, олгосон дугаарын дагуу үдэж хадгална.

除本法第 35.6 款的规定外，不增补事项。

35.2. 公证员制作笔录后应向当事人和其他参与人宣读。

35.3. 笔录应有当事人和参与公证活动的见证人、翻译（口译）人员等签名，并由公证员加盖印章、标记印章后生效。

35.4. 若有不能签名者参与的，或者有本法第 27.2 款规定的情况发生的，则就此作出说明。

35.5. 笔录有两页或两页以上的应写明页码，每页均有当事人和其他参与人签名，以为有效。

35.6. 如当事人要求，可不改变内容地对笔记进行增补修改，且当事人和参与公证活动的见证人、翻译（口译）人员等其他人员应签名，公证员加盖印章、担保印章，以为有效。

35.7. 违反本法第 35.6 款规定进行的增补、修改视为无效。

第三十六条　灭失材料的补救与保存

36.1. 公证员留存的材料如有灭失，可将交付当事人的文本复制，并在复印件上对此作出记载后、依留存文件的程序保存。

第三十七条　基础材料检查

37.1. 公证员应当事人、继承人和委托代表的要求，就文件公证时，可对与此相关的基础文件进行检查。

37.2. 禁止以与该公民、法人无关的问题，检查基础材料。

第三十八条　制作文件复印件

38.1. 当事人如将其持有的公证文书遗失，公证员应以留存文本为准为其制作复印件。

第三十九条　文件的保存

39.1. 公证员应将公证活动依据的文件与已公证的文件一同，编码装订保存。

39.2.Шаардлагатай гэж үзвэл нотариатч гэрчилж байгаа баримт бичигтэй холбоотой зүйлийг гэрэл зураг, бусад бололцоотой аргаар бэхжүүлэн авч хадгална.

39.3.Нотариатч энэ хуулийн 39.1-д заасны дагуу дугаарлан үдсэн материалыг зохих журмын дагуу архивт шилжүүлэн хадгалуулна.

ДОЛДУГААР БҮЛЭГ
НОТАРИАТЫН ТОДОРХОЙ ҮЙЛДЭЛ ХИЙХ ЖУРАМ

40 дүгээр зүйл.Гэрээслэл гэрчлэх

40.1.Нотариатч гэрээслэлийг гэрчлэхдээ дараахь баримт бичгийг үндэслэнэ:

40.1.1.гэрээслэл үйлдэх үед гэрээслэгч нь өөрийн үйлдлийг бүрэн ойлгох оюун ухааны хувьд эрүүл гэдгийг нотолсон мэргэжлийн эмчийн магадлагаа;

40.1.2.гэрээслэж байгаа хөдлөх болон үл хөдлөх эд хөрөнгө, эрх нь гэрээслэгчийн өмч болохыг нотолсон баримт.

40.2.Нотариатч гэрээслэлийг гэрчилж, түүнд гэрээслэгч өөрөө гарын үсэг зурна.

40.3.Гэрээслэгч өвчтэй, эсхүл хүндэтгэн үзэх бусад шалтгаанаар гэрээслэлд өөрөө гарын үсэг зурж чадахгүй бол түүний хүсэлтийг үндэслэн хөндлөнгийн этгээдээр гарын үсэг зуруулж болох бөгөөд энэ тохиолдолд үйлчлүүлэгчийн дээрх шалтгааныг тодорхойлсон тэмдэглэлийг гэрчийг оролцуулан үйлдэнэ.

40.4.Гэрээслэгч Иргэний хуулийн 525.1-д заасны дагуу гэрээслэлээ өөрчилсөн буюу цуцалсан бол энэ тухай мэдээллийг 30 хоногийн дотор өөрчилсөн гэрээслэл, цуцалсан баримт бичгийн хамт уг гэрээслэлийг гэрчилсэн нотариатч, эсхүл Танхимд ирүүлнэ.

40.5.Нотариатч энэ хуулийн 40.4-т заасан баримт бичгийг хүлээн авмагц анхны гэрээслэл болон гэрээслэлийн бүртгэлийн дэвтэрт өөрчилсөн буюу цуцалсан тухай тэмдэглэл хийж, хувийг хавсаргана. Гэрээслэлийг анх гэрчилсэн нотариатч байхгүй тохиолдолд Танхимын ерөнхийлөгч энэ зүйлд заасан ажиллагааг гүйцэтгэнэ.

40.6.Гэрээслэл биелүүлэх тухай баримт бичгийг гэрээслэлд заавал хавсаргана.

40.7.Нотариатч гэрээслэлийн хувь тус бүрт тамга, баталгааны тэмдгээ дарж гэрчлүүлсэн он, сар, өдрийг бичиж, гарын үсэг зуран нэг хувийг гэрээслэгчид

39.2. 公证员在必要时，可使用拍照及其他可能的方法固定保存与公证相关的文件、物品。

39.3. 公证员应当将依照本法第 39.1 款规定编码装订的文件，依照相应的程序移交档案部门保存。

第七章　公证的程序

第四十条　遗嘱公证

40.1. 公证员在遗嘱公证时，应核实以下情况：

40.1.1. 订立遗嘱时遗嘱订立人对自身的行为充分理解，其智力健全并得到专业医生结论的证实；

40.1.2. 核实列入遗嘱的动产和不动产的权利属于遗嘱订立人。

40.2. 公证员为遗嘱公证，并由遗嘱订立人本人签字。

40.3. 遗嘱订立人因病或其他应当重视的原因不能在遗嘱上签名的，根据其意愿可由第三人签字。在此情况下，应在公证书中记录遗嘱订立人无法亲自签名的原因并附相关证据。

40.4. 遗嘱订立人如依照《民法》第 525.1 款的规定修订或撤销遗嘱的，则在三十天内将修订的遗嘱、撤销的文件送交为该遗嘱公证的公证员或联合会。

40.5. 公证员在收到本法第 40.4 款规定的文件后，应立即在初始遗嘱和遗嘱登记册上对有关遗嘱进行修订或废除的记录，并加入附件。若为初始遗嘱公证的公证员不在场，则由联合会主席完成本条规定的行为。

40.6. 必须将执行遗嘱的文件附入遗嘱。

40.7. 公证员须在每一份遗嘱附件上加盖印章、担保印章，注明公证的年、月、日，签名，并将一份交予遗嘱订立人，余者交予联合会。

гардуулж, үлдэх хувийг Танхимд хадгалуулна.

40.8.Иргэний хуулийн 523.2-т заасан этгээд гэрээслэлийг гэрчилж болох бөгөөд энэ тохиолдолд нотариатчаар гэрчлүүлсний нэгэн адил үзнэ.

40.9.Иргэний хуулийн 523.2-т заасан этгээд гэрээслэлийг гэрчилсэн тохиолдолд өөрт үлдсэн хувийг Танхим, эсхүл энэ хуулийн 8.2-т заасан Танхимын салбарт хүлээлгэн өгөх бөгөөд уг гэрээслэлийг хүлээн авсан нотариатч гэрээслэлийг бүртгэлийн дэвтэрт бүртгэж, хүлээлгэн өгсөн этгээдээр гарын үсэг зуруулна.

41 дүгээр зүйл.Итгэмжлэл гэрчлэх

41.1.Итгэмжлэлд төлөөлүүлэгч болон төлөөлөгчийн овог, эцэг /эх/-ийн нэр, өөрийн нэр, хаяг, итгэмжлэл олгосон он, сар, өдөр, төлөөлүүлэгчээс төлөөлөгчид олгож байгаа бүрэн эрх болон хугацааг бичнэ. Хуулийн этгээдээс итгэмжлэл олгосон тохиолдолд Иргэний хуулийн 64.2.1, 64.2.2-т заасан шаардлага хангасан эсэхийг нягталж үзнэ.

41.2.Төлөөлөгчид эрх олгосон үйл ажиллагааг бусдаар гүйцэтгүүлэх, эсхүл итгэмжлэлийг гуравдагч этгээдэд шилжүүлэх бол энэ тухай итгэмжлэлд тусгайлан заах бөгөөд ийнхүү заагаагүй бол итгэмжлэгчийн ашиг сонирхлыг хамгаалах зайлшгүй шаардлагатайгаас бусад тохиолдолд шилжүүлсэн итгэмжлэлийг гэрчлэхийг хориглоно.

41.3.Нотариатч итгэмжлэл олгохдоо Иргэний хуулийн 62.6, 64.5-д заасан хугацааг баримтлах ба хугацаатай олгох итгэмжлэлд хугацааг тоо болон үсгээр бичнэ.

42 дугаар зүйл.Өвлөгдөх эд хөрөнгийг хамгаалах

42.1.Иргэний хуулийн 537 дугаар зүйлд заасны дагуу өв нээгдсэн газрын нотариатч өвлөгдөх эд хөрөнгийг хамгаалах арга хэмжээ авч болно.

42.2.Нотариатч өвлүүлэгч нь банкинд хадгаламжтай эсэхийг шалгаж, хадгаламж гэрээслэгдсэн бол энэ тухай өвлөгчид мэдэгдэнэ.

42.3.Өвлүүлэгчийн эд хөрөнгө, түүний зарим хэсэг нь өв нээгдсэн газраас өөр газар байгаа бол нотариатч түүнийг хамгаалах арга хэмжээ авна.

42.4.Нотариатч нь өвлөгдөх эд хөрөнгийг бүртгэж, хадгалагч томилох бөгөөд бүртгэл хийхэд хоёроос доошгүй гэрчийг байлцуулан өвлөгдөх эд хөрөнгө, түүний оршин байгаа газар, бүртгэл хийсэн он, сар, өдөр, оролцогч, эд хөрөнгө хадгалахаар хүлээж авсан этгээдийн овог, эцэг /эх/-ийн нэр, өөрийн нэр,

40.8.《民法》第 523.2 款规定的人员可以为遗嘱公证，且与公证员公证同样适用本法的规定。

40.9.《民法》第 523.2 款规定的人员为遗嘱公证时，其留存的附件应送交联合会，或本法第 8.2 款规定的联合会部门。受理该遗嘱的公证员，应将遗嘱登记在登记册，并要送交人员签字。

第四十一条　授权委托公证

41.1. 授权委托书应写明委托者和受委托者的姓、父（母）名、本人名字、地址、授予委托的年、月、日，委托者授予被委托者的权力范围及期限。若是法人授予的委托，则应核查其是否满足《民法》第 64.2.1 款和第 64.2.2 款的要求。

41.2. 受托人的代理行为由他人完成，或者转委托的，应就此在授权委托书中专门约定；若未作约定，则除为保护委托者利益的必要情形以外，禁止为转委托公证。

41.3. 公证员在公证委托时，应遵守《民法》第 62.6 款、第 64.5 款规定的期限，在公证的授权委托书上用数字和文字写明其期限。

第四十二条　遗产保护

42.1. 依照《民法》第 537 条的规定，遗产所在地的公证员，可采取保护遗产的措施。

42.2. 公证员应查明被继承人是否有银行存款，若存款另有遗嘱，则应将此告知继承人。

42.3. 被继承人的部分财产处于财产发现地以外的其他地方的，公证员应对其采取保护措施。

42.4. 公证员应对遗产进行登记，委派保管员。在登记时应有不少于两名见证人在场，并记录遗产所在地、登记时间、参与者、财产保管者的姓、父（母）名、本人名字、注册号码、地址等。登记单应制作不少于三份，并由参与人员签字。

регистрийн дугаар, хаяг зэргийг тэмдэглэж, бүртгэлийг гурваас доошгүй хувь үйлдэж оролцогчдоор гарын үсэг зуруулна.

42.5.Өвлөгдөх эд хөрөнгийг хамгаалах боломжгүй бол нотариатч энэ тухай акт үйлдэж сонирхогч талуудад мэдэгдэнэ.

42.6.Өвлөгч нь өв хүлээн авахаас татгалзсан тохиолдолд нотариатч эд хөрөнгийг хамгаалах арга хэмжээг дуусгавар болгох тухай бусад өвлөгчид мэдэгдэх бөгөөд бусад өвлөгчид өв хүлээн авахаас татгалзвал өвлөгдөх хөрөнгийг төрийн зохих байгууллагын өмчлөлд шилжүүлж гэрчилгээ олгоно.

43 дугаар зүйл.Өвлөх эрхийн гэрчилгээ олгох

43.1.Өв нээгдсэн газрын нотариатч өвлөгчийн бичгээр гаргасан хүсэлтийг үндэслэн Иргэний хуульд заасны дагуу өвлөх эрхийн гэрчилгээ олгоно.

43.2.Хууль ёсны өвлөгчид өвлөх эрхийн гэрчилгээ олгохдоо дараахь баримт бичгийг үндэслэнэ:

43.2.1.хууль ёсны өвлөгч болохыг нотлох баримт бичиг;

43.2.2.өвлүүлэгчийн нас барсны гэрчилгээ, сураггүй алга болсонд тооцсон болон нас барсан гэж зарласан бол энэ тухай шүүхийн шийдвэр;

43.2.3.өвлөгдөх эд хөрөнгийн оршин байгаа газар, бүрэлдэхүүн, тоо хэмжээ, тэдгээр нь өвлүүлэгчийн өмч болохыг нотлох баримт бичиг;

43.2.4.хууль ёсны өвлөгчөөр тогтоосон шүүхийн шийдвэр;

43.2.5.өвлөгчийн бичгээр гаргасан хүсэлт, түүний оршин суугаа баг, хорооны Засаг даргын тодорхойлолт.

43.3.Өвлөгч нь Иргэний хуулийн 528.5-д заасны дагуу өв хүлээн авахаас татгалзвал нотариатч хүсэлтийг нь гэрчилж түүнд ногдох хэсгийг хууль ёсны бусад өвлөгчид санал болгож зөвшөөрвөл өвлөх эрхийн гэрчилгээ олгоно.

43.4.Өвлөх эрхийн гэрчилгээнд өвлөгдөх эд хөрөнгө, ногдох хэсгийг тодорхой заах бөгөөд түүнийг тогтоохдоо Иргэний хуулийн 522, 531, 533 дугаар зүйлийг баримтална.

43.5.Өвлөгч нь насанд хүрээгүй буюу эрх зүйн чадамжгүй бол өвлөх эрхийн гэрчилгээг болон хууль ёсны төлөөлөгч /эцэг /эх/, асран хамгаалагч, харгалзан дэмжигч/-д нь олгож, энэ тухай тусгайлан тэмдэглэл үйлдэнэ.

43.6.Өвлөгдөх эд хөрөнгө барьцаанд байгаа нөхцөлд өвлөх эрхийн гэрчилгээг уг эд хөрөнгийг

42.5. 如遗产不可能被保护，公证员应就此制作文件予以公告。

42.6. 如继承人放弃接受遗产的，公证员应将财产保护措施结束告知其他继承人。如果其他继承人亦放弃接受遗产的，那么遗产移交国家相应机关所有，并出具公证书。

第四十三条　继承权公证

43.1. 遗产发现地公证员根据继承人的书面申请，依照民法规定授予其继承权公证书。

43.2. 授予合法继承人继承权公证书以下列文件为依据：

43.2.1. 证实合法继承人的文件；

43.2.2. 被继承者去世的证明，或宣告失踪和宣告死亡的法院裁定；

43.2.3. 遗产所在地、构成、数量，证明其属于被继承人的文件；

43.2.4. 法院作出的确定申请人为合法继承人的裁定；

43.2.5. 继承人书面提出的申请，其居住地乡镇、社区政府负责人的说明。

43.3. 继承人依照《民法》第 528.5 款的规定放弃接受遗产的，公证员为其申请公证。并将其应得部分向其他合法继承人提议得到其同意后授予其继承权公证书。

43.4. 继承权公证书应当载明遗产及其分配份额，对此的确定应遵循《民法》第 522 条、第 531 条、第 533 条的规定。

43.5. 继承者未成年人、无行为能力人的，则继承权公证书授予其法定代理人（父亲、母亲、监护人、扶养人），就此制作专门笔录。

43.6. 遗产为抵押状态的，继承权公证书经该财产抵押权人同意后方可授予继承人。

барьцаалсан байгууллагын зөвшөөрлийг үндэслэн өвлөгчид олгоно.

43.7.Эрх бүхий байгууллага өвлөгдөх эд хөрөнгийг битүүмжилсэн бол уг өвлөгдөх эд хөрөнгийг битүүмжлэлээс чөлөөлөгдтөл өвлөх эрхийн гэрчилгээ олгохыг хориглоно.

43.7. 相关权力机关查封遗产的，在遗产被解封前禁止授予继承人公证书。

43.8.Өвлөх эрхийн гэрчилгээний загварыг хууль зүйн асуудал эрхэлсэн Засгийн газрын гишүүн батална.

43.8. 继承权公证书样式由负责司法的政府委员批准。

44 дүгээр зүйл.Гарын үсэг гэрчлэх

第四十四条　签字的公证

44.1.Нотариатч хуульд нийцсэн баримт бичигт зурсан гарын үсгийн үнэн зөвийг гэрчилнэ.

44.1. 公证员对合法文件上签字的真实性、准确性予以公证。

44.2.Нотариатч хуулийн этгээдийг төлөөлсөн эрх бүхий албан тушаалтны гарын үсгийг гэрчлэх бол тухайн байгууллагын тамга, тэмдэг дарагдсан эсэхийг нягтална.

44.2. 公证员对代表法人的有权代表人的签字予以公证，并核查是否加盖了该单位的印章。

44.3.Хэлгүй, дүлий, ярьж чаддаггүй буюу монгол хэл мэддэггүй хүний гарын үсгийн үнэн зөвийг гэрчлэхдээ үйлчлүүлэгчийн иргэний баримт бичгийг шалгаж гарын үсэг зурахад гэрч оролцуулах эсэхийг асууж тодруулах ба шаардлагатай гэж үзвэл гэрч оролцуулж тэмдэглэл хөтөлнө.

44.3. 对口吃、失聪、无语言能力或不懂蒙古语的人签字的真实性、准确性进行公证时，应查验当事人的公民证件，征询签字时是否要见证人参加。认为必要的，则邀请见证人参加，并制作笔录。

44.4.Үйлчлүүлэгч биечлэн ирж тухайн баримт бичиг болон нотариатын үйлдлийн бүртгэлийн дэвтэрт гарын үсгээ зурна.

44.4. 当事人应亲自在相关文件和公证活动登记册上签字。

45 дугаар зүйл.Нотариатчийн мэдэгдэх хуудас, түүний агуулга

第四十五条　可执行债权文书公证

45.1.Төлбөрийг нотолсон баримт бичгийг үндэслэн төлбөр төлөгчөөс мөнгө, эд хөрөнгийг гаргуулах болон үүргийн гүйцэтгэлийг Иргэний хэрэг шүүхэд хянан шийдвэрлэх тухай хуулийн 184.1-д заасан журмаар барьцааны зүйлээс гаргуулахаар талууд харилцан тохиролцож байгуулсан гэрээг гэрчлэхдээ нотариатч мэдэгдэх хуудас үйлдэнэ. /Энэ хэсэгт 2015 оны 7 дугаар сарын 2-ны өдрийн хуулиар өөрчлөлт оруулсан/

45.1. 在依据已证实的债权债务文件要求债务人偿还债务时，按照《民事诉讼法》第 184.1 款规定的程序，各有关方面一致同意从抵押物实现债权时，公证员应制作可执行债权文书。（本款依照 2015 年 7 月 2 日的法律修订）

45.2.Энэ хуулийн 45.1-д заасан мэдэгдэх хуудас үйлдэхдээ нотариатч дараахь нөхцөлийг харгалзана:

45.2. 制作本法第 45.1 款规定的可执行债权文书时应参考下列情况：

45.2.1.баримт бичиг нь төлбөр төлөгчөөс төлбөр авагчид төлбөр төлөх нь маргаангүй гэдгийг нотолж байгаа эсэх;

45.2.1. 债权人是否确认文书对债务人的债务履行不存异议；

45.2.2.нэхэмжлэл гаргах эрх үүссэнээс хойш гурван жилийн хугацаа өнгөрсөн эсэх.

45.2.2. 债务履行期限届满是否经过了三年。

45.3.Нотариатчийн мэдэгдэх хуудсанд дараахь зүйлийг заана:

45.3. 公证员作出的可执行债权文书载明下列事项：

45.3.1.мэдэгдэх хуудас олгож байгаа нотариатчийн овог, эцэг /эх/-ийн нэр, өөрийн нэр, харьяалах тойрог;

45.3.1. 作出可执行债权文书的公证员的姓、父（母）名、本人名字、所辖区域；

45.3.2.ямар баримт бичгийг үндэслэж мэдэгдэх хуудас үйлдэж байгаа;

45.3.3.төлбөр авагч, төлбөр төлөгчийн овог, эцэг /эх/-ийн нэр, өөрийн нэр, ажлын болон оршин суугаа газрын хаяг, аж ахуйн нэгж, байгууллагын оноосон нэр, үйл ажиллагаа явуулж байгаа газрын хаяг, банкин дахь харилцах дансны дугаар, улсын бүртгэлийн дугаар;

45.3.4.төлбөр гаргуулах хугацаа;

45.3.5.төлбөрийн хэмжээ, шаардлагын зүйл, хэрэв мэдэгдэх хуудас үйлдэхэд үндэс болгосон баримт бичигт заасан бол хүү, торгуулийн хэмжээ;

45.3.6.нотариатын үйлчилгээний хөлс, зардлын хэмжээ;

45.3.7.мэдэгдэх хуудас үйлдсэн он, сар, өдөр, дугаар.

45.4.Нотариатч мэдэгдэх хуудсыг хэвлэмэл хуудас дээр үйлдэж, тамга дарж, гарын үсэг зурна.

45.5.Нотариатчийн мэдэгдэх хуудсанд заасан төлбөрийг Шүүхийн шийдвэр гүйцэтгэх тухай хуульд[4] заасан журмын дагуу гаргуулна.

46 дугаар зүйл.Гэрээ, хэлцэл гэрчлэх

46.1.Нотариатч хуульд заасан дараахь гэрээ, хэлцлийг гэрчилнэ:

46.1.1.үл хөдлөх эд хөрөнгийг бусдад шилжүүлэх хэлцэл;

46.1.2.гэрлэгчдийн эд хөрөнгийн эрхтэй холбогдсон гэрээ;

46.1.3.орон сууц дангаар өмчлөх эрх үүсгэх хэлцэл;

46.1.4.өөрт бэлэн байгаа бүх эд хөрөнгө, түүний тодорхой хэсгийг бусдын өмчлөлд шилжүүлэх, хязгаартайгаар эзэмшүүлэх, ашиглуулах /узуфрукт/ гэрээ;

46.1.5.тэжээн тэтгэх гэрээ;

46.1.6.эрх шилжүүлэх гэрээ;

46.1.7.зээлийн гэрээ;

46.1.8.хувьцаа, бусад үнэт цаасыг бусдын өмчлөлд шилжүүлэх гэрээ.

46.2.Нотариатч гэрээ, хэлцлийг гэрчлэхдээ хуульд нийцсэн болон талуудын хүсэл зоригийн илэрхийлэл мөн эсэхийг дор дурдсаны дагуу нягтална:

46.2.1.талууд тэгш эрхийн үндсэн дээр гэрээ, хэлцэл байгуулсан эсэх;

46.2.2.бусдын дарамт, шахалт болон бусад хүчин зүйлсийн нөлөөлөлд автаагүй эсэх;

45.3.2. 作出可执行债权文书的文件依据；

45.3.3. 债权人、债务人的姓、父（母）名字、本人名字、工作和住址，企业、机关准确名称、开展业务的地址，银行账户号码、国家登记号码；

45.3.4. 执行期限；

45.3.5. 执行金额、要求等事项，如果据以作出可执行债权文书的合同中有约定利息的，从其约定；

45.3.6. 公证服务报酬、费用的数额；

45.3.7. 作出可执行债权文书的年、月、日。

45.4. 公证员可执行债权文书为印刷格式，加盖印章、签字。

45.5. 公证员可执行债权文书规定的费用按照法院裁定执行法[4]规定的程序收缴。

第四十六条　合同、协议的公证

46.1. 公证员为法律规定的下列合同、协议公证：

46.1.1. 不动产转移的协议；

46.1.2. 与婚姻财产权相关的合同；

46.1.3. 住宅单独所有的协议；

46.1.4. 个人现有的全部财产，将一部分移交他人所有或有限度的支配、利用合同；

46.1.5. 抚养合同；

46.1.6. 权利转移合同；

46.1.7. 借贷合同；

46.1.8. 股票、其他有价证券转交他人所有的合同。

46.2. 公证员对合同、协议进行公证时，依照下列情形确定其是否合法和各方真实意思表示：

46.2.1. 各方是不是在权利平等的基础上订立的合同、协议；

46.2.2. 是否受到他人胁迫、强制和其他因素的影响；

46.2.3.агуулга нь үйлчлүүлэгчийн хүсэл зоригийг бүрэн илэрхийлж чадсан эсэх;

46.2.4.үүсэх үр дагавар, үр дүнд бодитой хандаж чадсан эсэх.

46.3.Энэ хуулийн 46.2-т заасан нөхцөл байдлын аль нэг нь зөрчигдсөн бол нотариатч гэрээ, хэлцлийг гэрчлэхээс татгалзана.

46.4.Гэрээ, хэлцлийг төлөөлөгчөөр дамжуулан хийж байгаа бол төлөөлөгчийн бүрэн эрх, итгэмжлэл хуульд заасан шаардлага хангасан эсэхийг нягтална.

46.5.Хуулийн этгээдийн нэрийн өмнөөс хийж байгаа гэрээ, хэлцлийг гэрчлэхдээ түүнийг хуулийн дагуу төлөөлж байгаа этгээдийн эрх хэмжээ нь гэрээ, дүрэм, Төлөөлөн удирдах зөвлөлийн шийдвэрт тусгагдсан эсэхийг шалгана.

46.6.Нотариатч гэрээ, хэлцлийг гэрчлэхдээ түүний агуулга, гарах үр дагавар, үүргээ биелүүлээгүй нөхцөлд хүлээх хариуцлага зэргийг бүрэн гүйцэд ойлгосон эсэхийг талуудаас тодруулна.

46.7.Хөдлөх болон үл хөдлөх эд хөрөнгө, эрхийг бусдад шилжүүлэх гэрээ, хэлцлийг гэрчлэхдээ уг хөрөнгө, эрх нь тухайн этгээдийн хууль ёсны өмчлөл, эзэмшил, ашиглалтад байгаа эсэхийг нотлох эрхийн баримт бичгийг, хуулийн этгээдийн хувьд үүсгэн байгуулах гэрээ, дүрмийг үндэслэл болгоно.

46.8.Зохих байгууллагад бүртгүүлснээр хүчин төгөлдөр болох гэрээ, хэлцэлд нэмэлт, өөрчлөлт оруулсан, хугацааг сунгасан, цуцалсан, дуусгавар болгосныг гэрчлэхдээ гэрээний талуудын хүсэлтийг үндэслэн бие даасан нотариатын үйлдэл хийх бөгөөд ингэхдээ анхдагч гэрээг үндэслэж түүний хуулбарыг нотариатын баримтад хавсаргана.

46.9.Үл хөдлөх эд хөрөнгийн баримт бичигт нэмэлт, өөрчлөлт оруулах болон дундын өмчлөлд байгаа үл хөдлөх эд хөрөнгийг бусдын өмчлөл, эзэмшил, ашиглалтад шилжүүлэх гэрээ, хэлцлийг гэрчлэхдээ түүний улмаас эрх, хууль ёсны ашиг сонирхол нь шууд хөндөгдөж болох иргэн, аж ахуйн нэгж, байгууллагын зөвшөөрлийг үндэслэнэ.

46.10.Нотариатч гэрчилсэн гэрээ, хэлцлийн хувийг талуудад өгч, өөрт үлдэх хувьд холбогдох баримт бичгийг хавсаргаж, архивт хадгална.

47 дугаар зүйл.Эд хөрөнгийн эрхийн бүртгэлтэй холбогдох баримт бичиг гэрчлэх

47.1.Нотариатч эд хөрөнгө өмчлөх эрх, түүнтэй холбоотой эд хөрөнгийн бусад эрхтэй холбогдсон

46.2.3. 内容是否完整地表达了当事人的真实意思；

46.2.4. 对于可能产生的后果、结果是否已知晓。

46.3. 如有违反本法第 46.2 款规定情形的任何一项，公证员应放弃为合同、协议公证。

46.4. 合同、协议如果是通过代表签署的，那么应对代表的权限是否符合授权委托的相关规定进行核查。

46.5. 在对代表法人签署的合同、协议公证时，应对代理人的权限是否符合合同、章程、董事会决定中的规定进行核查。

46.6. 公证员对合同、协议公证时，应向有关各方对其内容、产生的后果、未能履行的法律责任予以阐释。

46.7. 在对动产和不动产及权利移交他人的合同、协议公证时，对该财产、权利是否为该当事人合法所有、支配、利用，应以能够证明其权利的文件、法人设立合同、章程为依据。

46.8. 在为有关机关登记合法有效的合同、协议进行补充、修改、延期、撤销公证时，根据合同各方的要求，可进行单独公证。为此应以最初的合同为依据，其复印件并入公证文件。

46.9. 在为不动产文件补充、修改和共有的不动产移交他人所有、支配、利用的合同、协议公证时，应以利益受到直接影响的公民、企业、机关的同意为依据。

46.10. 公证员应将公证的合同、协议的副本送交各方，将留存下来的副本连同相关文件归档保管。

第四十七条　财产权登记文件的公证

47.1. 公证员可为财产所有权及与之相关的其他财产权利文件公证。

баримт бичгийг гэрчилж болно.

47.2.Энэ хуулийн 47.1-д заасан баримт бичгийг гэрчлэхдээ тухайн баримт бичиг нь Эд хөрөнгө өмчлөх эрх, түүнтэй холбоотой эд хөрөнгийн бусад эрхийн улсын бүртгэлийн тухай хуульд[5] заасан шаардлагад нийцэж байгаа эсэхийг нягтална.

48 дугаар зүйл.Гэр бүлийн гишүүдийн дундаа хамтран өмчлөх эд хөрөнгөөс гишүүнд ногдох хэсгээ өмчлөх эрхийг гэрчлэх

48.1.Бичгээр байгуулсан гэрээг үндэслэн нотариатч гэрлэгчдийн эд хөрөнгийн эрхийг гэрчилж болох бөгөөд гэр бүлийн гишүүдийн хамтран өмчлөх дундын эд хөрөнгөөс гишүүний өөрт ногдох хэсгийг өмчлөх эрх нь тухайн өдөр гэрлэгчдийн дундын өмчлөлд байсан эд хөрөнгөд хамаарах бөгөөд уг эд хөрөнгийн шинж байдлыг гэрээнд тодорхой тусгана.

48.2.Нотариатч гэрлэгчдийн өөрт ногдох хэсгийн өмчлөх эрхийг гэрчлэхдээ гэрлэлтийн гэрчилгээ, гэрлэлт цуцалсан тухай шүүхийн шийдвэр, нас барсны гэрчилгээ, сураггүй алга болсонд тооцсон, эсхүл нас барсан гэж зарласан шүүхийн шийдвэр, гэрлэгчдийн дундаа үл хөдлөх, хөдлөх эд хөрөнгө өмчлөх эрхийг нотолсон баримт бичгийг үндэслэнэ.

48.3.Үл хөдлөх, хөдлөх эд хөрөнгө гэрлэгчдийн дундын хөрөнгийн бүрэлдэхүүнд байгаа эсэхийг гэрчлэхдээ уг эд хөрөнгийг зохих байгууллагад бүртгүүлсэн баримт бичиг, татвар, хураамж төлсөн баримт нотолгоог үндэслэл болгоно.

48.4.Банкны зээлээр орон сууц барьсан буюу их засвар хийсэн бол гэрлэгч тус бүрт ногдох хэсгийг өмчлөх эрхийг зээл олгогчийн лавлагааг үндэслэн гэрчилнэ.

48.5.Гэрлэгчдийн хэн нэг нь нас барсан бол тэдний дундын үл хөдлөх, хөдлөх эд хөрөнгөөс эхнэр буюу нөхрийн хүсэлтээр түүнд ногдох хэсгийн өмчлөх эрхийг энэ тухай өв залгамжлагчид мэдэгдэн тэмдэглэл хөтөлж, гарын үсэг зуруулсны дараа гэрчилнэ.

48.6.Энэ хуулийн 48.5-д заасан мэдэгдэлд эхнэр буюу нөхөрт олгох эд хөрөнгийн бүрэлдэхүүнийг заана.

48.7.Нас барагчийн эхнэр буюу нөхөр нь түүний насанд хүрээгүй хүүхэд болон эрх зүйн чадамжгүй өв залгамжлагчийн хууль ёсны төлөөлөгч биш бол энэ хуулийн 48.5-д заасан мэдэгдлийг тэдгээрийн хууль ёсны төлөөлөгч /эцэг, /эх/, асран хамгаалагч, харгалзан дэмжигч/-д өгнө.

47.2. 为本法第 47.1 款规定的文件公证时，应审查该文件是否符合财产所有权、与之相关的其他财产权利国家登记法[5]的规定。

第四十八条　家庭共有财产份额所有权公证

48.1. 以书面合同为依据、公证员可为夫妻的财产权公证。如果家庭共有财产份额的所有权与结婚当日共有财产有关，对此财产的状况应在合同中明确反映。

48.2. 公证员在为夫妻共有财产份额所有权公证时，应依据结婚证明、离婚法院判决，死亡证明、失踪文件，或法院宣告死亡的裁定，夫妻共有不动产、动产的文件进行公证。

48.3. 为不动产、动产是否为夫妻共有财产组成部分公证时，以该财产在相应机关登记的文件、完税凭证、收费凭据等为依据。

48.4. 以银行贷款兴建住宅或大范围装修的，夫妻份额的所有权，以借贷方的证明为依据。

48.5. 夫妻任何一方去世时，其共有的不动产、动产应妻子或丈夫的要求，将其份额的所有权通知其继承人，并制作笔录，签字后予以公证。

48.6. 本法第 48.5 款规定的通知应授予妻子或丈夫财产的份额。

48.7. 去世的妻子或丈夫不是其未成年子女或无行为能力继承人的法定代理人的，则应将本法第 48.5 款规定的通知送交法定代理人（父亲、母亲、监护人、扶养人）。

48.8.Мэдэгдлийг шуудангаар явуулж болох бөгөөд хэрэв өв залгамжлагч өөрөө биечлэн ирсэн бол нотариатч түүнд амаар мэдэгдэж, нас барагчийн эхнэр буюу нөхрийн өргөдөлтэй танилцуулан гарын үсэг зуруулна.

48.8. 通知可由邮局邮递。当遗产继承人亲自到场的，公证员可向其口头通知，阐释去世者妻子或丈夫的申请，由继承人签字。

49 дүгээр зүйл.Баримт бичгийн хуулбар гэрчлэх

第四十九条　文件复印件的公证

49.1.Баримт бичгийн бүрэн буюу хэсэгчилсэн хуулбарын агуулга нь хуульд харшлаагүй бол нотариатч хуулбарыг эх хувьтай нь тулган шалгасны үндсэн дээр гэрчилнэ.

49.1. 文件全文或部分内容的复印件与法律无抵触的，公证员在将复印件与原件核对的基础上公证。

49.2.Өөр өөр утга санаа агуулсан баримт бичгийн аль нэг хэсгийн хуулбарын үнэн зөвийг гэрчилж болох бөгөөд ийнхүү гэрчлэхдээ үндсэн агуулгыг илэрхийлсэн хэсгийг заавал хамт гэрчилнэ.

49.2. 可以为包含不同内容的复印件的某一部分内容的真实性、准确性公证，作此公证时须对表示基本内容的部分同时公证。

49.3.Анхны хуулбар урьд нь нотариатчаар гэрчлэгдсэн, эсхүл уг баримт бичгийг олгосон иргэн, хуулийн этгээд түүний үнэн зөвийг тодорхойлсон тохиолдолд баримт бичгийн хуулбарын хуулбарыг гэрчилнэ.

49.3. 初始复印件已经公证员公证的，或者提供该文件的公民、法人已证实其真实性、准确性的，可对文件复印件的复印件公证。

50 дугаар зүйл.Хуулийн этгээд үүсгэн байгуулах баримт бичиг гэрчлэх

第五十条　法人设立文件的公证

50.1.Нотариатч хуулийн этгээдийг үүсгэн байгуулсан баримт бичгийг гэрчлэхдээ үүсгэн байгуулагчийн иргэний үнэмлэх, эсхүл түүнтэй адилтгах баримт бичиг, хуулийн этгээдийг үүсгэн байгуулах шийдвэр зэргийг үндэслэл болгоно.

50.1. 公证员为法人设立文件公证时，以创立者的公民证件或其他有效的证件、设立法人的决定等为依据。

50.2.Нотариатч Иргэний хуулийн 33 дугаар зүйлд заасан хуулийн этгээдийг үүсгэн байгуулсан баримт бичгийг гэрчлэхдээ тухайн баримт бичиг нь Компанийн тухай[6], Нөхөрлөлийн тухай[7], Хоршооны тухай[8], Төрийн бус байгууллагын тухай хуульд[9] заасан шаардлагад нийцэж байгаа эсэхийг нягтална.

50.2. 公证员依《民法》第 33 条的规定为法人设立文件公证时，应审查其文件是否符合《公司法》[6]、《社团法》[7]、《合作社法》[8]、《非政府机构法》[9] 规定的要求。

НАЙМДУГААР БҮЛЭГ
БУСАД ЗҮЙЛ

第八章　其他事项

51 дүгээр зүйл.Нотариатын үйл ажиллагаанд тавих хяналт

第五十一条　对于公证活动的监督

51.1.Хууль зүйн асуудал эрхэлсэн төрийн захиргааны төв байгууллага болон Танхимын дэргэдэх Сахилгын зөвлөл /цаашид “Сахилгын зөвлөл” гэх/ нотариатчдын үйл ажиллагаанд хяналт тавина.

51.1. 负责司法的国家中央行政机关和联合会下属的纪律委员会对公证员的行为进行监督。

52 дугаар зүйл.Нотариатын баримт бичгийг шалгах

第五十二条　公证文件的检查

52.1.Хууль зүйн асуудал эрхэлсэн төрийн захиргааны төв байгууллага нотариатын баримт

52.1. 负责司法的国家中央行政机关对公证文件进行检查，必要时抽调相关专业人员参加。

бичигт шалгалт хийх бөгөөд шаардлагатай гэж үзвэл холбогдох мэргэжлийн хүмүүсийг татан оролцуулж болно.

53 дугаар зүйл.Нотариатчийн ёс зүйн дүрэм

53.1.Нотариатч нь нотариатчийн ёс зүйн дүрмийг үйл ажиллагаандаа мөрдлөг болгоно.

53.2.Нотариатчийн ёс зүйн дүрмийг хууль зүйн асуудал эрхэлсэн Засгийн газрын гишүүн батална.

53.3.Нотариатчийн ёс зүйн дүрмийг зөрчсөн нотариатчид сахилгын шийтгэл ногдуулна.

54 дүгээр зүйл.Сахилгын шийтгэл

54.1.Сахилгын зөвлөл нотариатчийн гаргасан зөрчлийн шинж байдлыг харгалзан сануулах арга хэмжээ авна.

54.2.Энэ хуулиар тогтоосон журам, нотариатчийн ёс зүйн хэм хэмжээг ноцтой зөрчсөн нь захиргааны болон эрүүгийн хариуцлага хүлээлгэхээргүй бол Сахилгын зөвлөл нотариатын үйл ажиллагаа эрхлэх тусгай зөвшөөрлийг хүчингүй болгох саналыг хууль зүйн асуудал эрхэлсэн Засгийн газрын гишүүнд гаргана.

54.3.Хууль зүйн асуудал эрхэлсэн Засгийн газрын гишүүн Сахилгын зөвлөлийн саналыг үндэслэн нотариатын үйл ажиллагаа эрхлэх тусгай зөвшөөрлийг хүчингүй болгоно.

54.4.Нотариатч Сахилгын зөвлөлийн шийдвэрийг эс зөвшөөрвөл хууль зүйн асуудал эрхэлсэн Засгийн газрын гишүүнд гомдол гаргаж болно.

54.5.Энэ хуулийн 16.2, 16.3-т заасан нотариатын үүрэг гүйцэтгэгч мөн хуулийн 54.1-д заасан зөрчил гаргасан бол холбогдох төрийн захиргааны байгууллага сахилгын шийтгэл ногдуулна.

МОНГОЛ УЛСЫН ИХ ХУРЛЫН ДАРГА
Д.ДЭМБ

ЭРЭЛ

[1] Монгол Улсын Үндсэн хууль- "Төрийн мэдээлэл" эмхтгэлийн 1992 оны 1 дугаарт нийтлэгдсэн.

[2] Иргэний хууль- "Төрийн мэдээлэл" эмхтгэлийн 2002 оны 7 дугаарт нийтлэгдсэн.

[3] Улсын тэмдэгтийн хураамжийн тухай хууль- "Төрийн мэдээлэл" эмхтгэлийн 2011 оны 1 дугаарт нийтлэгдсэн.

第五十三条　公证员的道德规范

53.1. 公证员在公证活动中应遵循公证员道德规范。

53.2. 公证员道德规范由负责司法的政府委员批准。

53.3. 对违反公证员道德规范的公证员处以纪律处分。

第五十四条　纪律处分

54.1. 纪律委员会根据公证员所犯过错的情形采取警示措施。

54.2. 严重违反本法规定的规则、公证员道德标准，尚不足以承担行政和刑事责任的，纪律委员会可向负责司法的政府委员提出撤销其从事公证业务的专门许可。

54.3. 负责司法的政府委员根据纪律委员会的意见，撤销公证员从事公证业务的专门许可。

54.4. 公证员如不服纪律委员会的决定，可向负责司法的政府委员申诉。

54.5. 本法第 16.2 款、第 16.3 款规定的代理公证员犯有本法第 54.1 款规定的过失的，相关国家行政机关对其处以纪律处分。

蒙古国国会主席
德·敦布日勒

注解：

[1]《蒙古国宪法》——《国家公报》汇编 1992 年第 1 期发布。

[2]《民法》——《国家公报》汇编 2002 年第 7 期发布。

[3]《蒙古国印花税法》——《国家公报》汇编 2011 年第 1 期发布。

[4] Шүүхийн шийдвэр гүйцэтгэх тухай хууль-"Төрийн мэдээлэл" эмхтгэлийн 2002 оны 8 дугаарт нийтлэгдсэн.

[5] Эд хөрөнгө өмчлөх эрх, түүнтэй холбоотой эд хөрөнгийн бусад эрхийн улсын бүртгэлийн тухай хууль-"Төрийн мэдээлэл" эмхтгэлийн 2003 оны 25 дугаарт нийтлэгдсэн.

[6] Компанийн тухай хууль- "Төрийн мэдээлэл" эмхтгэлийн 1999 оны 34 дугаарт нийтлэгдсэн.

[7] Нөхөрлөлийн тухай хууль- "Төрийн мэдээлэл" эмхтгэлийн 1995 оны 8-9 дугаарт нийтлэгдсэн.

[8] Хоршооны тухай хууль- "Төрийн мэдээлэл" эмхтгэлийн 1998 оны 2 дугаарт нийтлэгдсэн.

[9] Төрийн бус байгууллагын тухай хууль- "Төрийн мэдээлэл" эмхтгэлийн 1997 оны 3 дугаарт нийтлэгдсэн.

[4]《法院决定执行法》——《国家公报》汇编 2002 年第 8 期发布。

[5]《财产所有权及与之相关的其他财产权利的国家登记法》——《国家公报》汇编 2003 年第 25 期发布。

[6]《公司法》——《国家公报》汇编 1999 年第 34 期发布。

[7]《社团法》——《国家公报》汇编 1995 年第 8—9 期发布。

[8]《合作社法》——《国家公报》汇编 1998 年第 2 期发布。

[9]《非政府机构法》——《国家公报》汇编 1997 年第 3 期发布。

尼泊尔

公证法

Notary Public Act, 2063

Date of authentication publication:
2063/06/28/0 (14 December, 2006)

Act No. 9 of the Year of 2063 B.S.

An Act Made to Provide for Notary Public

Preamble: Whereas, it is expedient to make legal provisions regarding Notary public by confirm real person in preparing documents and putting signature on the document and to control fraud and fraudulent activities and to provide for simple and easy way in translating document and to maintain the interest of the general public,

Now, therefore be it enacted by the House of Representatives in the first year of the Declaration of House of Representative, 2063 (2006)

Chapter 1 Preliminary

1. Short Title and Commencement:

(1) This Act may be called "Notary Public Act, 2063".

(2) This Act shall come into force on such date as the Government of Nepal may appoint in Nepal Gazette by a Notification.

2. Definitions:

In this Act unless the subject or context otherwise requires:

(1) "Notary Public" means a person who holds certificate of Notary Public in pursuant to Section 14.

(2) "Council" means Nepal Notary Public Council as

公证法，2063

颁布日期：
2063/06/28/0（2006 年 12 月 4 日）

2006 年第 9 号法律

为公证机构制定的一项法律

序言：为了公证机构公证准备文件的真实当事人并在文件上签名、避免欺诈和欺诈活动，提供简单易用的翻译文件、维护公共利益，制定法律规范是有利的，

因此，现众议院在“众议院 2063 宣言”的第一年（2006）颁布本法律。

第一章 预备内容

1. 简称和生效时间：

（1）本法案称为《2063 年公证法》。

（2）本法案自尼泊尔政府在政府公报上公布之日起生效。

2. 定义：

在本法案中，除另有规定外：

（1）“公证员”是指依照本法第 14 条持有公证员执业证书的人。

（2）“理事会”是指依照本法第 3 条成立的公证

established pursuant to section 3.

(3) "Chairperson" means chairperson of the Council.

(4) "Member" means member of the Council and this expression also includes the Chairperson.

(5) "Secretary" means person appointed or designated pursuant to Section 7.

(6) "Certificate" means the certificate awarded to work as Notary Public pursuant to Section 14.

(7) "Document" means any document between two or more persons to transfer, to amend or to extend any kind of right or to create liability and this expression also includes a document which is to be used in foreign country or affidavit to be submitted in the court or office or any other document of similar nature.

(8) "Paper" means a paper issued from government or public office or private organization and this expression also includes the Document.

(9) "Certification" means the act of certification of a document by the Notary Public pursuant to Section 27.

(10) "Representative" means the following persons:

(a) Person having obtained authorized power of attorney pursuant to the prevailing law to certify documents, or

(b) Person authorized, to put signature on behalf of a firm, company or an autonomous body incorporated pursuant to Prevailing Law.

(11) "Law Practicener" means a person registered as a law preacticener pursuant to the Prevailing Law.

(12) "Prescribed" or "as prescribed" means 'prescribed' or 'as prescribed' in Rules framed under this Act.

Chapter 2 Establishment of council and Provision Regarding its Functions, Duties and Powers

3. Establishment of Council:

(1) A Council named as Nepal Notary Public Council has been established to manage the translation of the paper and certification of document in an easy and accessible manner.

(2) The office of the Council Shall be located in the Kathmandu valley.

4. The Council to be an Autonomous Body:

(1) The council shall be an autonomous corporate body with perpetual succession.

(2) There shall be a separate seal for the functioning of the Council.

(3) The Council may acquire, possesses and sell moveable and immoveable property as an individual.

员理事会。

（3）"主席"是指公证员理事会主席。

（4）"会员"是指公证员理事会的成员，包括主席。

（5）"秘书"是指依照本法第 7 条任命或指定的人。

（6）"证书"是指依照本法第 14 条规定授予的从事公证员职业的证书。

（7）"文件"是指两人或两人以上之间转让、修改、扩展关于权利或创设义务的任何文件，本表述还包括将在外国使用的文件或宣誓书提交给法庭或政府机关的书面陈述以及任何具有类似性质的其他文件。

（8）"文书"是指由政府、公共机构或私人组织出具的文书，本表述包括上述所指的"文件"。

（9）"认证"是指公证员依照本法第 27 条对文件进行认证的行为。

（10）"代表"是指以下人员：

（a）根据现行法律取得授权委托书对文件予以证明的人，或者

（b）取得授权，并依照现行法律规定代表企业、公司或自治团体签字的人。

（11）"法律执业者"是指根据现行法律注册登记为法律执业者的人。

（12）"规定"或"按照规定"是指本法规定或按照本法规定。

第二章　理事会的设立及其法定的职能、责任和权力

3. 理事会的设立：

（1）设立名称为尼泊尔公证员理事会，以简易方式进行文书的翻译和文件的认证。

（2）理事会的办公室应设置在加德满都。

4. 理事会是一个自治机构：

（1）理事会是一个永续存在的自治性公司。

（2）理事会的运营应当有分离独立使用的印章。

（3）理事会可以以自己的名义取得、拥有和出售动产和不动产。

(4) The council may file a case in its own name and a case may be filed against it, as an individual.

5. Composition of the Council:

(1) The composition of the Council shall be as following:

(a) Attorney General - Chairperson

(b) President, Nepal Bar Association - Member

(c) Secretary, Ministry of law, Justice and Parliamentary affairs - Member

(d) Secretary (Law) office of the Prime minister and Council of Ministers - Member

(e) Secretary, Nepal Law Commission - Member

(f) Secretary, Ministry of Land Reform and Management - Member

(g) Secretary, Ministry of Foreign Affairs - Member

(h) Registrar, the Supreme Court - Member

(2) The secretary as of Section 7 shall work as the secretary the Council.

(3) The procedure relating to the meetings of the council shall be as prescribed.

6. Functions, Duties and Powers of the Council:

In addition to the functions, duties and powers mentioned in other places of this Act, the Council shall have the following functions, duties and powers:

(1) To prepare (draft) and implement the policy regarding Notary Public.

(2) To distribute the Certificate of Notary public.

(3) To monitor the activities of the Notary Public that whether or not this Act or code of conduct made by the council is abided by.

(4) To form committee, as required and confer powers, duties and functions to such committee.

(5) To appoint the auditor, and

(6) To perform other functions as prescribed.

7. Secretary:

(1) There shall be a secretary to function as an administrative chief of the Council.

(2) The Council shall appoint, an individual who holds a graduate degree in law, to the post of secretary as prescribed.

(3) Until the period of the appointment of the secretary pursuant to Sub-section (2), the Government of Nepal may designate a Gazetted Officer of judicial service, in request of the Council, to work as the secretary of the Council.

（4）理事会可以以自己的名义提起诉讼，并可以以自己的名义独立应对诉讼。

5. 理事会的组成：

（1）理事会的组成应当包括如下：

（a）首席检察官——主席

（b）尼泊尔律师协会主席——会员

（c）法律、司法和议会事务部部长——会员

（d）总理的秘书（法律）办公室和部长理事会——会员

（e）尼泊尔法律委员会秘书——会员

（f）土地改革与管理部部长——会员

（g）外交部部长——会员

（h）最高法院司法常务官——会员

（2）理事会秘书由本法第 7 条规定的秘书担任。

（3）与理事会会议有关的程序应符合本法的规定。

6. 理事会的职能、责任和权力：

除本法其他章节提到的职能、责任和权力以外，理事会还具有以下职能、责任和权力：

（1）准备（起草）和实施有关公证员的政策。

（2）发放公证员证书。

（3）监督公证员的活动是否遵守本法或理事会制定的行为准则的规定。

（4）根据要求设立委员会并明确其权力、责任和职能。

（5）指定审计机构。

（6）本法规定的其他职能。

7. 秘书：

（1）理事会设秘书一名，担任行政长官。

（2）理事会应依本法规定委任具有法学硕士学位的人担任秘书。

（3）在根据第（2）款委任的秘书在任职期间结束前产生空缺的，尼泊尔政府可以根据理事会的要求，指定一名从事司法服务的公报官员担任理事会秘书。

(4) The tenure of office of the secretary shall be of four years.

(5) Notwithstanding anything contained in Sub-section (4), if the Secretary does not function honestly or he/she falls in bad conduct or his/her work is not satisfactory, then the Council may remove him/her at any time.

(6) Before removing the secretary from the post pursuant Sub-section (5), he/she shall be provided opportunity to submit clearance.

(7) The functions, powers, duties, remuneration and terms and conditions of service of the secretary shall be as prescribed.

8. Employees of the Council:

(1) The number of employees in the Council as per necessity.

(2) The appointment, terms of service remuneration and facility of the employees of the council shall be as prescribed.

9. Fund of the Council:

(1) There shall be a separate Fund of the Council.

(2) The following amounts shall be credited to the fund created under Sub- section (1):

(a) Money obtained from Government of Nepal.

(b) Money obtained from any individual or organization.

(c) Money obtained as fee from the person who receives certificate.

(d) Money received as the guarantee

(e) Money obtained from other sources.

(3) All the expenditures of the council shall be borne in from the Fund, mentioned Sub-section (1).

Provided that, the moneys mentioned in Clause (d) shall not be expended in the functions of the council.

(4) Operation of the Fund of the Council shall be done as prescribed.

(5) Audit of the Council shall be done as prescribed.

Chapter 3 Provisions Relating to the Certificate of the Notary Public

10. Practice of Notary Public is Prohibited without Certificate:

No one shall practice as a Notary Public without obtaining certificate pursuant to this Act.

11. Bar to Practice without Passing Examination:

(1) Out of the functions of the Notary Public, a per-

（4）秘书的任期为四年。

（5）尽管第（4）款规定了秘书的任期，如果秘书未能诚实履行其责任、有不正当行为或者其未能达到工作要求，理事会可以随时对其提出解聘。

（6）在根据第（5）款规定解除秘书职务之前，应给拟被解除职务的秘书自证清白的机会。

（7）秘书的职能、权力、责任、报酬、服务期限和条件应符合本法的规定。

8. 理事会的雇员：

（1）理事会的雇员人数根据实际需要确定。

（2）理事会雇员的任命、服务报酬条款、配备设施等应当符合本法的规定。

9. 理事会基金：

（1）理事会应当设立一个独立的基金。

（2）以下款项应计入第（1）款规定的基金：

（a）从尼泊尔政府获得的资金；

（b）从任何个人或组织获取的资金；

（c）向申请执业证书的人员收取的费用；

（d）保证金费用；

（e）通过其他渠道获取的资金。

（3）理事会所有的支出均由第（1）款规定的基金承担。

但（d）款所述款项（保证金费用）不得用于理事会的运营。

（4）理事会基金应依照规定使用。

（5）依照规定对理事会进行审计。

第三章　公证员执业证书的有关规定

10. 禁止未取得执业证书的人开展公证活动：

未依本法规定取得执业证书，任何人不得以公证员的身份实施公证。

11. 未通过考试禁止执业：

（1）想要取得翻译以及理事会规定的公证员职能

son who wants to get certificate for translation and other special function as prescribed by the Council shall have to pass the examination relating to the Notary public.

(2) The examination mentioned in Sub-section (1) may conducted by the Council itself or the council may cause to conduct such examination to any of the institution which provides training in relation to law and justice or which conducts examination of the law practitioner.

(3) The course content, types of examination and other provisions relating to examination pursuant Sub-section (1) shall be as prescribed.

12. Qualification of Notary public:

The following persons shall be eligible to be a Notary Public:

(1) A law parctitioner who has continuously practiced law for a period of Seven years.

(2) A person who has retired from at least Gazetted class two officer of the Nepal judicial service.

13. Disqualification of Notary Public:

The following persons shall be disqualified to be a Notary Public:

(1) Person who has not passed the examination conducted pursuant to Section 11.

(2) Person who is not qualified pursuant to Section 12.

(3) Person who has been punished as an offender by the court of law in the cases of Murder, Theft, Dacoit, Fraud, Fraudulence, Corruption, Rape, Consumption and trafficking of Narcotic Drug, trafficking in person or serious offence of similar nature.

(4) Person having not good character.

(5) Non-Nepali citizen

(6) Person having declared insolvent.

(7) Person not having in normal mental condition.

14. Provision relating to Certificate:

(1) Any Person interested to obtain a certificate of Notary Public shall apply to the Council in the prescribed form accompanied by the prescribed fees.

(2) If the Council receives application pursuant to Sub-section (1), it shall form a committee to verify such application and recommend accordingly as prescribed.

(3) If the committee formed pursuant to Sub-section (2) recommends to certificate and the recommendation seems reasonable upon verification, Council shall issue certificate in the prescribed form taking guarantee from the applicant as stated in Section 17.

以外的其他特殊资格，必须通过与公证员有关的考试。

（2）第（1）款所述考试可由理事会自行组织，理事会也可以安排任何提供法律或司法培训、法律职业资格考试的机构组织。

（3）与第（1）款所述考试有关的课程内容、考试类型和其他要求应符合规定。

12. 公证员资格：

以下人员可以获得公证员资格：

（1）连续执业满 7 年以上的法律职业者。

（2）从尼泊尔司法服务部门退休的二级以上官员。

13. 公证员资格的取消：

以下人员应当取消公证员资格：

（1）没有通过本法第 11 条规定的考试的人；

（2）不具备本法第 12 条规定的资格条件的人；

（3）因谋杀、盗窃、抢劫、诈骗、欺诈、腐败、强奸、毒品消费和运输、贩卖人口或具有类似性质的严重犯罪案件被法院作为罪犯受过处罚的人；

（4）品格低劣的人；

（5）非尼泊尔公民；

（6）被宣告破产的人；

（7）精神状态不正常的人。

14. 与执业证书有关的规定：

（1）任何想要获得公证员执业证书的人，需以规定的形式向理事会提出申请并缴纳规定的费用。

（2）如果理事会接受了第（1）款规定的申请，需成立委员会对该申请进行审核，并按照规定提出相应的建议。

（3）如果根据第（2）款成立的委员会建议授予执业证书并且该建议经审核是合理的，理事会应按照第 17 条规定的形式向申请人颁发执业证书并收取申请人的保证金。

(4) The working place of the Notary Public shall be as mentioned in the certificate.

（4）执业证书中应记载公证员的工作地点。

15. Description relating to Notary Public to be Sent:

(1) After distributing certificate pursuant to section 14, the Council shall send the descriptions of the Notary Public such as name, surname, address and other necessary description, to the Bar Association and the District Court where the Notary Public is going to work.

(2) After receiving description as stated in Sub-section (1) the concerned Bar Association and District Court shall make such description public.

15. 有关公证员的说明：

（1）在根据第 14 条颁发执业证书后，理事会应将包含公证员的姓名、住址和其他必要信息的说明送交公证员执业所在地的律师协会和地方法院。

（2）收到第（1）款所述的说明后，有关律师协会和地方法院应公开该说明。

16. Validity and Renewal of Certificate:

(1) The certificate issued pursuant to Section 14 shall be valid for Five years.

(2) A person who wants to renew certificate, shall apply before the Council along with prescribed fees, sixty days before expiry of the certificate.

(3) If an application is received pursuant to Sub-section (2), the Council may renew the certificate upon conducting inquiry as required.

(4) The other provisions regarding renewal of certificate shall be as prescribed.

16. 证书的有效期和续期：

（1）根据第 14 条颁发的执业证书有效期为 5 年。

（2）执业证书的续期，应当在证书有效期届满前 60 日内向理事会提出申请，并缴纳规定的费用。

（3）如收到第（2）款所述申请，理事会可根据需要进行调查以决定证书的续期。

（4）执业证书的续期应当符合其他有关规定的要求。

17. Guarantee to be Submitted:

(1) Person intending to obtain certificate shall submit Fifty Thousand rupees in cash or a bank guarantee equal to that amount, as a guarantee, from the bank as appointed by the Council.

(2) The guarantee amount mentioned in Sub-section (1), shall be used for the liability arised out of the prescribed work performed in the capacity of Notary Public.

(3) If the guarantee amount submitted by the Notary Public if is reduced to bear the liability as mentioned in Sub-section (2), then, equal to the reduced amount in cash or in the form or bank guarantee, shall be submitted to the Council with in 30 days.

(4) Other provisions regarding guarantee shall be as prescribed.

17. 提供保证金：

（1）拟取得执业证书的人，应当向理事会指定的银行存入 50000 卢比现金或者等值的银行保函作为保证金。

（2）第（1）款所述保证金应用于承担以公证员身份履行规定工作所产生的责任。

（3）如果公证员提供的保证金因为承担第（2）款所述责任减少，那么公证员应当在 30 日内以现金或银行保函的形式向理事会补足担保的金额。

（4）遵守其他规定中有关保证金的要求。

18. Cancellation of the Certificate:

(1) The certificate of the Notary Public shall be cancelled in following conditions:

(a) if declared guilty and punished by the court in the crime as stated in Clause (3) and (4) of Section 13,

(b) if case of his/her death,

(c) if the mental condition is not normal,

18. 执业证书的撤销：

（1）在下列情况下，公证员的执业证书应被撤销：

（a）因为第 13 条第（3）款和第（4）款所述罪行被法院宣告有罪并受到惩罚；

（b）公证员死亡；

（c）精神状况不正常；

(d) if certificate is not renewed,

(e) it law practitioner certificate is cancelled or if the name is removed from the registration of the law practitioner,

(f) if Notary public him/herself voluntary applies for the revocation of the certificate..

(2) If Notary Public commits misconduct or acts against this Act or Rules here under, the Council may cancel his/her certificate.

(3) Before cancelling a certificate pursuant to Sub-section (2), the Council shall provide fifteen days' time to the Notary Public to submit his/her clarification.

(4) If a certificate is cancelled pursuant to this Section, the Council shall inform the concerned District court and Bar Association immediately.

Chapter 4 Provisions relating to Functions and Duties of the Notary Public

19. Functions may be Performed by the Notary Public:

The Notary Public may, subject to the provisions of this Act, perform the following functions:

(1) Certification of any document;

(2) To translate a paper written in one language into another language, and

(3) To attest the copy of any original paper.

20. Activities not to be Performed by the Notary Public:

The Notary Public shall not perform the following activities:

(1) To do certification of the document which is not registered in the register-book of his/her office,

(2) To certify any document which itself is an original document,

(3) To do certification of document which is to be done by himself /herself,

(4) To do certification of the document which is concerned to his/her own transaction and interest,

(5) To do certification of the document which is concerned to his/her close relatives,

Explanation: For the purpose of this Clause "close relatives" shall mean relatives as prescribed,

(6) To disclose any known fact received in the course of certification of the documents, without the consent of the concerned person, except as provided in the law,

(7) To add and delete or amend or alter in the Docu-

(d)执业证书未续期；

(e)法律职业资格证书被取消或从法律职业者名册中除名；

(f)公证员自愿申请撤销执业证书。

(2)如果公证员实施不当行为或违反本法规定，理事会可以撤销其执业证书。

(3)在根据第（2）款的规定撤销证书之前，理事会应为公证员提供15天时间提交有关抗辩声明。

(4)如果根据本条规定取消公证员执业证书，理事会应当及时通知地方法院和律师协会。

第四章 关于公证员职能和责任的规定

19. 公证员可以履行的职能：

根据本法的规定，公证员可以履行下列职能：

(1)任何文件的公证；

(2)将以一种语言的文书翻译为另一种语言的文书，和

(3)任何原始文件副本的证明。

20. 公证员不得进行的活动：

公证员不得进行下列活动：

(1)对未在其办公室登记簿中登记的文件进行认证；

(2)对本身是原始文件的任何文件进行认证；

(3)对公证员自身出具的文件进行认证；

(4)对与其自身有利害关系的任何文件进行认证；

(5)对与其近亲属有关的文件进行认证；

解释：就本条而言，“近亲属”指法律规定范围内的亲属。

(6)在未经有关人员同意的情况下泄露在文件认证过程中获取的任何已知事实，法律另有规定的除外；

(7)添加、删除、修订或更改在公证机构安全保

ment or Paper which is laying safely with the Notary Public,

(8) To do certification of a document without fulfilling the procedure prescribed in Section 27,

(9) To do certification of any document unauthorisely or negligently,

(10) To take excess fees for certification or translation of document than fixed for it ,

(11) To translate doubtful paper,

(12) To translate differing the stated date, number or content of the document,

(13) To do the function of Notary Public beyond the jurisdiction,

(14) To do certification of document without presenting the person who has to make the document before himself/herself,

(15) To function against the Code of Conduct,

(16) To function in contravention of this Act or Rules made thereunder, and

(17) To do other work as prescribed.

21. Oath to be Taken:

The Notary Public shall have to take oath as prescribed before beginning the work.

22. Office to be Established:

(1) The Notary Public shall establish an office in his/her working place.

(2) The Office as stated in Sub-section (1) shall not be opened more than one places.

(3) Notary Public shall keep a sign-board outside the office stating name and license number on it and the certificate in the office which could be seen by all.

23. Register-Book to be Maintained:

(1) Notary Public shall maintain separate register books relating to the certification and translation of the documents.

(2) The matters to be stated in the register book pursuant to Sub-section (1) shall be as prescribed.

(3) Notary Public shall have to keep the document certification register safely among the register books, as stated in Sub-section (1), to the period of five years after the end of the last page of the record book.

24. Files to be Maintained:

(1) To safely keep the certified document or translated paper, Notary Public shall have to maintain a separate file in his/her office.

管下的文件或文书；

（8）未依照本法第 27 条规定的程序对文件进行认证；

（9）未经授权对文件进行认证或认证文件有重大过失；

（10）对文件的认证或翻译收取超额费用；

（11）翻译可疑文书；

（12）翻译的日期、编号或内容与文件不符；

（13）在管辖范围以外履行公证员的职能；

（14）未在当事人亲自在场的情况下制作并认证文件；

（15）违反公证员行为准则；

（16）违反本法或根据本法制定的其他规则，以及

（17）其他规定的行为。

21. 宣誓：

公证员在开始工作前应按照规定进行宣誓。

22. 办事处的设立：

（1）公证员应在其工作的地点设立办事处。

（2）第（1）款所述办事处只能对一个地方开放。

（3）公证员应在其办公室外设置一个所有人可见的标志牌，注明其姓名和执业证书编号，在办公室内他人可见的地方放置执业证书。

23. 登记簿的保存：

（1）公证员应当对有关文件的认证和翻译分别制作独立的登记簿。

（2）根据第（1）款制作的登记簿所列明的事项需符合有关规定。

（3）公证员应当按照第（1）款规定将有关文件的认证妥善记录在登记簿上，留存至登记簿最后一页记录完毕后 5 年。

24. 档案的留存：

（1）为安全保存经过认证的文件或翻译文书，公证员应当在其办事处留存一份独立的档案。

(2) In the file as stated in Sub-section (1) a copy should be kept stating the name, surname and address of the person who causes for the certification of the document and translation of the paper.

(3) The file maintained by the Notary Public pursuant to Sub-section (1) shall be submitted to the Council by the Notary Public if he/she gives up such work and by his/her successor if he/she dies or becomes mentally abnormal.

25. Report to be Submitted:

(1) The Notary Public shall prepare an annual report of his/her activities and submit if to the in the concerned District court and Council every year within last day of Baishakha.

(2) The Notary Public, conducting certification of document relating to the transfer of immoveable property shall have to send the details to the concerned Land Revenue Office, every month.

(3) The matters to be included in the report pursuant to Sub-section (1) shall be as prescribed.

26. To be Regarded as official Misconduct:

Any act, committed by the Notary Public pursuant to Section 20, shall be considered official misconduct.

Chapter 5 Provisions relating to Certification of the Document and Translation of the Paper

27. Procedure relating to Certification of:

(1) A person, who wants certification of document, shall have to apply to the Notary Public as prescribed.

(2) While applying pursuant to Sub-section (1), the applicant shall present two witnesses who know him/her before the Notary Public. While presenting witness in that way document which shows the identity of witness should be submitted.

(3) when an application pursuant to Sub-section (1) is received, Notary Public shall have to confirm whether the person who put signature on the document is real or not.

(4) While confirming a person pursuant to Sub-section (3), a Notary Public may ask for additional paper, inquire with applicant and his/her witness or take written statement of the applicant on the matter.

(5) If the Notary Public is going to certify a document which is to be submitted to an office or Court, then, the Notary Public may cause to take oath of the applicant as prescribed.

(6) If the Notary Public knows the applicant per-

（2）在第（1）款所述档案中应保留一份包含进行文件认证和文书翻译人员姓名、住址的副本。

（3）公证员终止公证工作后，其根据第（1）款留存的档案应提交给理事会；如果公证员死亡或精神状况不正常，由其继承人提交给理事会。

25. 提交报告：

（1）公证员应当对其公证活动编制年度报告，并在每年 Baishakha（印度历的 2 月）最后一天之前提交给相应的地区法院和理事会。

（2）公证员对有关不动产转让的文件进行认证，应当按月向有关的地方税务部门报送详细的信息。

（3）根据第（1）款列入报告的有关事项应符合有关规定。

26. 视为渎职行为的情形：

公证员实施的任何本法第 20 条规定的行为应当被认为是渎职行为。

第五章　有关文件公证和文书翻译的规定

27. 公证的程序：

（1）想要对文件进行公证的人应当按规定向公证员提出申请。

（2）申请人在根据第（1）款进行申请时，应当向公证员提供 2 名与其熟悉的证人。通过此种方式提供证人的同时，应当提供能够证明证人身份的文件。

（3）公证员收到根据第（1）款提出的申请时，必须确认在文件上的签名是否真实。

（4）公证员根据第（3）款确认申请人的身份时，可以要求提供其他文书，对申请人及其证人进行询问或要求申请人就此事项提交书面陈述。

（5）公证员对提交办事处或法庭的文件进行公证，应当依照规定进行宣誓。

（6）如果公证员亲自了解申请人，或根据第（2）

sonally or if the applicant is confirm on the basis of paper asked pursuant to Sub-section (2) or examination of the witness presented by the applicant then, the Notary Public may do certification by causing to put, signature and thumb impression of the applicant on the document as prescribed.

款要求提供文书的申请人经过确认，或对申请人提供的证人进行审查后，公证员可以依规定通过签名、捺印等方式进行公证。

(7) Other provisions relating to certification of the document shall be as prescribed.

（7）其他相关规定中有关文件公证的要求。

28. Procedure relating to Translation of Paper:

28. 有关文书翻译的程序：

(1) A person, who wants to translate paper shall have to apply to the Notary Public for translation of the paper as prescribed.

（1）想要对文书进行翻译的人员应按规定向公证员提出申请。

(2) If an application is received pursuant to Sub-section (1), then, the Notary Public shall have to confirm whether such paper is authentic or not.

（2）如果公证员接受了第（1）款所述的申请，公证员应当确认该文书是否真实。

(3) If there is any doubt in relation to the authenticity of the paper, then, the Notary public may investigate or verify such paper or may inquire to the office or institution which has issued the paper.

（3）如果对文书的真实性有任何疑问，公证员可以调查或核实该文书，或向制作文书的办事处或机构进行询问。

(4) If the paper seems authentic by the inquiry pursuant to Sub-section (1), then, the Notary public shall have to translate the paper and have to verify such paper as prescribed.

（4）如果根据第（1）款的调查表明该文书是真实的，公证员应翻译该文书并按规定进行核验。

(5) Other provisions relating to translation of the paper shall be as prescribed.

（5）其他相关规定中对于文书翻译的要求。

29. Procedure relating to Attestation:

29. 与证明有关的程序：

Procedures to be followed by the Notary Public, in the course of attestation of a copy of the original paper, shall be as prescribed.

公证员对原始文书的副本进行证明的程序应当符合相关规定。

30. Fees to be taken by the Notary Public:

30. 公证员收取的费用：

Fees to be taken by the Notary Public for certification of the document or translation of paper shall be as prescribed.

公证员对文书证明和文件翻译收取的费用应当符合相关规定。

Chapter 6 Provisions relating to Supervision, Inquiry and Suspension

第六章　监督、调查和暂停职务有关的规定

31. May do Supervision and Monitoring:

31. 可以进行的指导和监督：

(1) The Council may supervise or monitor the activities and functions of the Notary Public or may ask for paper, information or clearance from the Notary Public in relation to his/her functions and activities.

（1）理事会可以指导或监督公证员的活动和职责，或要求公证员提供与其职责和活动有关的文书、资料或许可证明。

(2) The paper, information or clearance asked by the Council pursuant to Sub-section (1), shall be given in the time, to the Council by the Notary Public to the council in time.

（2）第（1）款所述理事会要求的文书、资料或许可证明，公证员应当及时提交给理事会。

32. Complain, Inquiry and Suspension:

(1) Anyone who knows the misconduct of any Notary Public, may complain to the Council, within two years from the date of cause of action.

(2) If a complaint is filed pursuant to Sub-section (1) or any misconduct of the Notary Public reveals in the course of supervision or monitoring pursuant to Section 31 or by any other source, then, the Council may ask the concerned Notary Public for clarification or information in the prescribed time frame or may ask him/her to appear before itself for recording statement.

(3) If it seems appropriate to suspend the Notary Public on the basis of the statement recorded or information collected or clarification received pursuant to Sub-section (2), the Council may suspend such Notary Public.

(4) The period of suspension pursuant to Sub-section (3) shall not exceed more than two months and within that period the Council shall have to complete the function relating to complain.

(5) The other provisions relating to investigation of the complain shall be as prescribed.

Chapter 7 Provision relating to Penalties and Compensation

33. Penalty:

(1) A person, who practice as a Notary Public without obtaining Certificate pursuant this Act, shall be punished with an imprisonment for a period of three years or fined up to One Hundred Fifty Thousand Rupees or with both.

(2) A Notary Public who, commits misconduct shall be punished with the imprisonment for up to Four years or a fine up to of Two Hundred Thousand Rupees or with both.

(3) If the content written in the document brought for certification is proved false, the person preparing such document shall be punished with imprisonment for a period up to four years or a fine up to Two Hundred Thousand Rupees or with both.

(4) If the oath taken by a person pursuant to Sub-section (5) proved false, such person shall be punished with the imprisonment up to three months or a fine up to Fifteen Thousand Rupees or with both.

(5) If a person who becomes a witness the certification of the document, confirms wrong person or gives wrong description or statement or makes wrong written statement shall be punished with imprisonment for a peri-

32. 投诉、调查和暂停职务：

（1）任何人知悉公证员实施的不当行为，可以在该行为发生之日起 2 年内向理事会投诉。

（2）如果任何人根据第（1）款进行投诉，或理事会在根据第 31 条进行指导和监督的过程中或通过其他任何来源发现公证员存在任何不当行为，理事会可以要求公证员在规定的时间内进行解释或说明，或要求其出席作出声明并记录。

（3）根据第（2）款规定的记录的声明、收集到的信息或收到的解释说明，如果认为暂停公证员的职务是恰当的，理事会可以要求该公证员停职。

（4）根据第（3）款规定的停职期间不得超过 2 个月，在此期间，理事会应当依职权处理完有关投诉的一切事项。

（5）其他相关规定中有关投诉调查的要求。

第七章　与处罚和赔偿有关的规定

33. 处罚：

（1）未根据本法取得执业证书而以公证员身份执业的人，处 3 年有期徒刑，并处或单处最高 150000 卢比的罚款。

（2）公证员实施不当行为，处 4 年以下有期徒刑，并处或单处最高 200000 卢比的罚款。

（3）如果认证文件中的内容被证明是虚假的，那么准备该文件的人应当处 4 年以下有期徒刑，并处或单处最高 200000 卢比的罚款。

（4）根据第（5）款进行虚假宣誓的人，处 3 个月以下有期徒刑，并处或单处最高 15000 卢比的罚款。

（5）作为公证文件中的证人如果被证明是虚假的或作出了错误的描述或书面陈述，处 6 个月以下有期徒刑，并处或单处最高 25000 卢比的罚款，或二者并罚。

od up to six months or be fined up to Twenty-Five Thousand Rupees or with both.

(6) If a person who causes for certification of a document fraud with, fraudlelent or deceptively accompaning with the Notary Public such person shall be punished with the imprisonment up to one year or a fine up to Fifty Thousand Rupees or with both.

（6）如果某人实施文件认证欺诈或公证员与其串通，将被处以 1 年以下有期徒刑或最高 50000 卢比的罚款，或二者并罚。

(7) If a person, who translates or causes for translation changes the date, numerical or content, such person shall be punished with imprisonment up to three Months or fined not exceeding Fifteen Thousand Rupees or with both.

（7）在翻译文件中非法篡改日期、数字或内容的人，处 3 个月以下有期徒刑，并处或单处最高 15000 卢比的罚款。

(8) If, a person who commits any act against this Act or Rule framed thereunder, except as provided in this Section, shall be punished with the imprisonment up to Three Months or a fine up to Fifteen Thousand Rupees or with both.

（8）任何违反本法或根据本法制定的规则的行为，除本节另有规定外，处 3 个月以下有期徒刑，并处或单处最高 15000 卢比的罚款。

34. Compensation:

34. 赔偿：

(1) If a person who suffers harm or losses due to the misconduct of the Notary Public, the aggrieved person may file suit for compensation in the concerning District Court within two years from the date of occurrence of the misconduct.

（1）因公证员的不当行为而遭受伤害或损失的，受害人可以在不当行为发生之日起 2 年内向有关地方法院提起诉讼。

(2) Notwithstanding anything contained in Sub-section (1), the person signing in the document or his/her representative, shall be equally liable for the harm or loss caused by the misconduct of the Notary Public in the following conditions:

（2）在下列情况下，即使前款有所规定，文件签署人或其代表应当对公证员的不当行为造成的伤害或损失承担同等责任：

(a) If the misconduct is occurred while doing function of the person who puts signature on the document, and

（a）如果文件签署人在履行其职能时发生不当行为；

(b) If the person has consented, knowingly that the Notary Public is committing a misconduct.

（b）知悉并同意公证员从事不当行为。

Chapter 8 Miscellaneous

第八章　其他规定

35. To be Considered as a Post of Public Responsibility:

35. 被视为公共责任的岗位：

The Notary Public shall be considered as the post of public responsibility.

公证员职业应当被视为承担公共责任的岗位。

36. Seal of the Notary Public and it's Use:

36. 公证员的印章及其使用：

(1) The Seal of the Notary Public shall be as prescribed.

（1）公证员的印章应符合规定。

(2) The seal of Notary Public pursuant to Sub-section (1) shall not be used in other functions except in the function of the Notary Public.

（2）根据第（1）款的规定，公证员的印章不得用于公证员职能以外的其他职能。

37. To Frame and implement the Code of Conduct:

The council shall frame and implement a code of conduct which is to be abided by the Notary Public.

38. Record of the Notary Public to be Maintained:

The Council shall maintain the record of the Notary Public as prescribed.

39. Special Provisions regarding Translation:

(1) Notwithstanding anything contained in this Act, the institution established pursuant to the prevailing law with a power to translate the papers, at the time of the commencement of this Act, may translate the papers with approval of the Council.

(2) The institution which has obtained approval pursuant to Sub-section (1), shall follow the procedures as stated in Section 28 while translating paper.

(3) If the institution, which has obtained approval pursuant to Sub-section (1), translates any paper against this Act, the chief of the institution shall be liable for penalty pursuant to Section 33.

40. No bar to File a case pursuant to Prevailing Law:

The Notary public, person who causes certification of document or who translates a paper causes for at the against this Act and that Act is punishable under any other law, in that case this Act shall not bar to file a case pursuant to such other law.

41. Delegation of Powers:

If an act committed by the Notary Public or a person who causes for certification of a document or translation of a paper against this Act is punishable under any prevailing law, this Act shall not be deemed to a bar to file a case against them.

42. Government of Nepal to be the Plaintiff:

(1) The Government of Nepal shall be the plaintiff in the cases under this Act.

(2) A case under this Act shall be regarded as included in the schedule-1 of Government cases Act, 2049.

43. Liaison with Government of Nepal:

The Ministry of Law & Justice shall liaison the council with Government of Nepal.

44. Power to Frame Rules:

The Council may frame necessary Rules to implement the objectives of this Act.

37. 制定并实施行为准则：

理事会应当制定并实施公证员的行为准则。

38. 公证员记录的保存：

理事会应按照规定保存公证员的记录。

39. 有关翻译的特殊规定：

（1）即使本法有所规定，根据现行法律设立的有权翻译文件的机构，在本法生效时，经理事会批准可以翻译文件。

（2）根据第（1）款获得批准的机构，在翻译文书时应当参照适用第 28 条所述的程序。

（3）如果根据第（1）款获得批准的机构在任何文书的翻译活动中违反本法的规定，机构的主管人员应当根据第 33 条接受处罚。

40. 根据现行法律规定不得提起诉讼：

公证员、违反本法规定进行文件公证或文书翻译案的人，如果其行为本法和可根据其他法律进行处罚，在这种情况下，本法的规定不妨碍依据其他法律的规定提起诉讼。

41. 授权：

公证员或违反本法规定进行文件公证或文书翻译的人，根据其他任何现行法律规定应当受到处罚，本法的规定不应当被视为向其提起诉讼的限制。

42. 尼泊尔政府作为原告：

（1）本法规定下形成的诉讼，尼泊尔政府应当列为原告。

（2）本法规定下的案件应当纳入政府案件法案 2049 的附表 1 中。

43. 尼泊尔政府的联络员：

司法部是理事会与尼泊尔政府之间的联络员。

44. 制定规则的权力：

理事会可以制定为实现本法目标的必要规则。

公证员条例 2063

Notary Public Rules, 2063

In exercising the power conferred by Section 44 of the Notary Public Act, 2063, the Notary Public Council has framed the following Rules:

1. Short Title and Commencement:

(1) These rules may be called the "Notary Public Rules, 2063".

(2) These Rules shall come into force immediately.

2. Definitions:

In these Rules, unless the subject and context otherwise require:

(1) "Act" means the Notary Public Act, 2063.

(2) "Document to be used in a foreign country" means the document or paper necessary as per law of a particular country for the sake of any work and action in a foreign country.

Chapter-One Provision Relating to Meeting and Function of the Council

3. Meeting of the Council:

(1) Meeting of the Council shall be held as required.

(2) Meeting of the Council shall be held at the venue and time as decided by the chairperson.

(3) At least three days before the holding a meeting, the Secretary of the Council shall notify all the members about the meeting stating agenda, venue and time of the meeting. If a meeting is to be held all of sudden for any reasons such a meeting may be held giving notice of reasonable time.

(4) Meeting shall be chaired by the chairperson of the Council and in his/her absence it shall be chaired by the president of Nepal Bar Association.

(5) The quorum of meeting shall be deemed constituted if at least five members are present.

(6) In the meeting of the Council decision of the majority shall be prevailed and in case of a tie the chairperson of the meeting shall use casting vote.

(7) The decision of the meeting of the Council shall be recorded in a separate minute-book and it shall be veri-

公证员条例 2063

为行使《公证法 2063》第 44 条授予的权力，公证员理事会制定了下列规则：

1. 简称和生效时间：

（1）本条例简称为《公证员条例 2063》。

（2）本条例颁布之日起立即生效。

2. 定义：

在这些规则中，除另有规定外：

（1）“法案”系指《公证法 2063》。

（2）“在外国使用的文件”系指为了在外国进行任何工作或行动而根据特定国家的法律所必备的文件或文书。

第一章　有关理事会会议和职能的规定

3. 理事会会议：

（1）理事会会议应当按规定举行。

（2）理事会会议应当在主席决定的地点和时间举行。

（3）理事会秘书应当至少在会议召开前 3 天将会议议程、地点和时间通知所有成员。如果由于任何原因临时召开会议，会议的通知应当提供合理的时间。

（4）会议应当由理事会主席主持，理事会主席不主持，会议由尼泊尔律师协会主席主持。

（5）至少有 5 名成员出席视为满足会议出席的法定人数。

（6）理事会会议的决议以多数票通过作出，如果出现赞成票和反对票相等的情况，理事会主席应当行使一票决定权。

（7）理事会会议的决议应记录在一份单独的会议记录簿中，并由会议主持人核实。

fied by the person who chairs the meeting.

(8) The allowance to be obtained by the members for participation in the meeting of Council shall be as fixed by the Council.

4. Functions of the Council:

In addition to the functions provided in the Act, the Council shall have the following functions:

(1) To approve the budget of the Council.

(2) To make arrangements to protect and promote the property of the Council.

(3) To provide direction to the Secretary in relation to the functions and actions of the Council.

(4) To perform other functions to be performed by Council.

Chapter-Two Provisions Relating to Secretary

5. Provisions relating to Appointment of Secretary:

(1) To appoint the Secretary of the Council pursuant to Sub-section (2) of Section 7, the Council shall have to call application publicly from the persons who are qualified pursuant to the Act, providing thirty days' time and stating remuneration, terms and conditions of the service.

(2) After verifying the application received pursuant to Sub-rule (1), the applicants who seemed qualified shall be taken written examination based on the curriculum as designed by the Council.

(3) At least three examinees who obtain highest marks in the examination held pursuant to Sub-rule (2) shall be selected for interview.

(4) A person who secures highest score in written examination held pursuant to Sub-rule (2) and interview held pursuant to Sub-rule (3) shall be selected by the Council to appoint for the post of secretary and other two persons in the order of their merit shall be listed as alternative candidates by the Council.

(5) The notice of selection pursuant to Sub-rule (4) shall be published publicly by the Council.

(6) The person who has been selected pursuant to Sub-rule (4) shall have to be appeared before the Council within fifteen days along with the appointment letter from the date of notice published pursuant to Sub-rule.

(7) If such person does not appear in that period, the Council may appoint secretary from the alternative list based on the merit.

(8) If the post of the secretary filled pursuant to Sub-

（8）成员参加理事会会议的津贴由理事会确定。

4. 理事会的职能：

除了公证法中规定的职能，理事会还具有下列职能：

（1）批准理事会的预算。

（2）对理事会财产的保值增值作出安排。

（3）关于理事会的职能和行动向秘书提供指导。

（4）履行理事会的其他职能。

第二章　有关秘书的规定

5. 有关委任秘书的规定：

（1）根据第 7 条第（2）款委任理事会秘书，理事会应当公开依据公证法规定符合资格人员的申请通知，提供 30 日的申请期限并说明服务的报酬、期限和条件。

（2）在核实根据第（1）款规则收到的申请后，通过资格复核的申请人进入根据理事会设置的课程安排的笔试。

（3）根据第（2）款规定的笔试成绩，至少选择分数前 3 名的申请人进入面试。

（4）在根据第（2）款和第（3）款进行的笔试和面试中获得第 1 名的申请人由理事会委任为秘书，其他 2 名申请人根据其能力列为后备人员。

（5）理事会应当根据第（4）款的结果公开发布选任通知。

（6）根据第（4）款被选任的申请人应当在前款规定的通知发布之日起 15 日内携带委任书到理事会就职。

（7）如果前款规定的申请人未在规定期限内办理就职，理事会可根据能力条件从后备人选名单中委任秘书。

（8）如果根据第（6）款任命的秘书职位在公告

rule (6) vacates in any way within six months from the date of publication of result, in such case one shall be appointed from among the candidates listed in alternative list based on the merit.

之日起 6 个月内发生空缺，在这种情况下，应当根据能力条件从后备人选名单中选择 1 人委任。

(9) If the post of the secretary is vacated after the period referred to in Sub-rule (7) such post shall be fulfilled following the procedure as mentioned in this Rule.

（9）如果秘书职位在第（7）款所述的期限后发生空缺，那么应当根据本条规定的程序填补秘书的职位。

(10) If no application is received within the period as referred to in Sub- rule (1), the Council shall call it again for applications providing Seven days period and if no applications is received on such call or if the applicants are not found fit, then the Council may appoint the secretary through negotiation.

（10）如果在第（1）款所述的期限内没有收到申请，理事会应当另行提供 7 日的期限延长申请通知，如果仍未收到申请或没有符合资格的人选，理事会可以通过协商委任秘书。

(11) Remuneration of the secretary shall be fixed by the Council and shall not be less than the basic pay scale of non-technical Second class Gazetted Officer of Nepal Civil Service.

（11）秘书的薪酬由理事会确定，且不得少于尼泊尔民事服务非技术类二级公报官员的基本薪酬。

(12) The Secretary shall enjoy leave and other facilities as determined by the Council.

（12）秘书根据理事会的规定享受休假和使用设备。

(13) Notwithstanding anything contained in this Rule, Council may provide additional facility to the officer who is designated pursuant to Sub-section (3) of Section 7 of the Act.

（13）尽管本条例有所规定，理事会可以向《公证法》第 7 条第（3）款指定的官员提供额外便利。

6. Functions, Duties and Powers of Secretary:

6. 秘书的职能、责任和权力：

In addition to the provision of the Act, there shall be the following functions, duties and powers of the secretary:

除了《公证法》的规定外，秘书还具有以下职能、责任和权力：

(1) To implement or cause to implement the decisions and directions of the Council.

（1）实施或者具体落实理事会的决定和指示。

(2) To perform necessary functions to conduct smoothly the functions and proceedings of the committee formed by the Council.

（2）为理事会组成的委员会职能和程序的顺利实施履行必要的职能。

(3) To perform functions relating to personnel administration and office management of the Council.

（3）履行与理事会人事管理和办公室管理有关的职能。

(4) To cause to maintain the Account of the Council up-dated.

（4）持续更新理事会的账目。

(5) To maintain the record of Notary Public safe and up-dated.

（5）对公证员记录的安全保管和持续更新。

(6) To prepare the budget of the Council and submit it before the Council for approval.

（6）编制理事会预算并提交理事会审批。

(7) To prepare proposal and programme relating to the functions to be performed by the Council and to present it before the Council for approval.

（7）编制有关理事会履行职能的议案和方案，并将其提交理事会审批。

(8) To do other functions as prescribed by the Council.

（8）履行理事会规定的其他职能。

Chapter-Three Provisions Relating to Examination, Certificate and Seal of the Notary Public

7. Examination and Curricular of the Notary Public:

(1) Examination of Notary Public to be conducted pursuant to Section 11 of the Act, shall be conducted or cause to be conducted by the Council at least once in a year.

(2) While conducting or causing to be conducted the examination pursuant to Sub-rule (1), it shall be conducted pursuant to the terms and procedure as specified by the Council.

(3) Examination to be conducted pursuant to Sub-rule (2) shall be conducted in written form. The weightage of score of the written examination shall be as determined by the Council.

(4) For the sake of conducting examination pursuant to Sub-rule (1), the Council may form a three-member committee in the convenorship of any of its member including an expert of the related subject.

(5) Other functions and procedure relating to meeting of the committee formed pursuant to Sub-rule (4) shall be as determined by the Council.

8. To Publish Notice for an Examination:

(1) To conduct an examination pursuant to Rule 7, the Council shall publish a thirty days public notice stating venue and date of the examination therein.

(2) A candidate who intends to appear in the examination as referred to in Sub-section (1) shall submit an application in a format as referred to in Scheduled-1 along with One Thousand Rupees as an examination fees.

9. To Apply:

(1) Except to obtain a certificate pursuant to Section 11 of the Act, a person who is interested to practice as a Notary Public shall apply before the Council in a format as referred to in Schedule-1 to obtain certificate.

(2) While submitting application pursuant to Sub-section (1), one shall pay Five Hundred Rupees as fees.

10. Formation of Recommendation Committee:

(1) For the purpose of Sub-section (2) of Section 14 of the Act, there shall be a committee in the Council having following members:

(a) Member of the Council as designated by the Council - Coordinator

(b) A first class Gazatted officer of Nepal Judicial

第三章 有关公证员考试、执业证书和印章的规定

7. 公证员的考试和课程：

（1）《公证法》第11条规定的公证员考试应当由理事会组织或授权组织，至少每年举行一次。

（2）根据第（1）款组织的考试应按照理事会具体规定的条款和程序进行。

（3）根据第（2）款举行的考试应当以书面形式进行。笔试成绩的权重由理事会决定。

（4）为举行第（1）款规定的考试，理事会可以成立一个由3人组成的委员会，委员会成员来自于理事会成员，包括有关领域的专家。

（5）根据第（4）款组成的委员会，其职能和程序由理事会决定。

8. 发布考试通知：

（1）根据第7条举行的考试，理事会应当提前30日发布通知，通知中说明考试的地点和日期。

（2）有意参加第（1）款所述考试的考生，应当填写提交附表1的表格并缴纳1000卢比的考试费。

9. 申请：

（1）除了根据《公证法》第11条的要求取得执业证书外，打算以公证员身份执业的，应当按照附表1的表格向理事会提出申请。

（2）在根据第（1）款提交申请时，应当缴纳500卢比的费用。

10. 推荐委员会的成立：

（1）为《公证法》第14条第（2）款之目的，理事会应设立一个委员会，成员构成如下：

（a）理事会指定的委员会成员担任协调员；

（b）理事会指定一名尼泊尔司法服务一级公报官

Service prescribed by the Council - Member

(c) Representative of Nepal Association - Member

(2) The secretary shall function as member-secretary of the committee formed pursuant to Sub-rule (1).

(3) Procedures relation to the meeting of the Committee formed pursuant to Sub-section (1) shall be as determined by the Council.

(4) Meeting allowance of the members of the recommendation committee shall be as fixed by the Council.

11. Format of License of Notary Public:

Format of a certificate of Notary Public shall be as referred to in Schedule-1.

12. Certificate Fee:

A person who is qualified to obtain certificate of a Notary Public shall pay Five Thousand Rupees as a certificate fee.

13. Renewal of Certificate:

(1) A Notary Public shall make an application to the Council along with Five Thousand Rupees as a fee to renew the certificate pursuant to Section 16 of Act.

(2) If an application is received pursuant to Sub-section (1), the Council may renew the certificate upon making investigation whether the Notary Public has committed official misconduct and upon examining additional evidence as per-necessity if it deems it appropriate.

(3) The validity of renewal made pursuant to Sub-rule (2) shall be Five years.

14. Provision Relating to Deposit:

(1) When a Notary Public pays the deposit as prescribed in Section 17 of the Act in cash then the Council shall receive and deposit it in a separate account.

(2) Notary Public who submits a Bank-guarantee shall submit such a Bank guarantee as per the terms set out by the Council.

(3) While fixing terms and conditions pursuant to Sub-rule (2), there shall be a condition inter alia that it shall be paid immediately at the time of demand of the Council. The validity period of Bank guarantee shall be Six years.

(4) The deposit which is deposited pursuant to Section 17 of the Act shall be used only for the purpose of compensation if it is to be paid in the case of official misconduct of the Notary Public.

(5) A person, who is entitled for compensation pursuant to Sub-rule (4), shall apply before the Council within

员担任成员；

（c）尼泊尔协会代表担任会员。

（2）秘书应当担任根据第（1）款组建的委员会的秘书。

（3）根据第（1）款组建的委员会的有关会议程序，由理事会决定。

（4）委员会成员的会议津贴由理事会确定。

11. 公证员执照的样式：

公证员证书的样式参见附表 1。

12. 证书费用：

有资格取得公证员证书的人，为获得执业证书应当缴纳 5000 卢比的证书费用。

13. 证书的续期：

（1）公证员根据《公证法》第 16 条进行证书续期，应当向理事会提交申请，并缴纳 5000 卢比费用。

（2）收到根据第（1）款提出的申请，理事会可以在调查公证员是否存在官方认定的不当行为的情况下对证书进行续期，并在认为合适时根据需要审查其他证据。

（3）根据第（2）款进行续期后的有效期为 5 年。

14. 有关保证金的规定：

（1）公证员以现金支付《公证法》第 17 条规定的保证金，理事会应接受并将其存入一个单独的账户中。

（2）提交银行担保的公证员应当根据理事会规定的条款提供银行担保。

（3）在根据第（2）款确定条款和条件的同时，除其他规定外，应理事会的要求应当立即支付。银行担保的有效期限是 6 年。

（4）根据《公证法》第 17 条存入的保证金，如果在公证员存在官方认定的不当行为的情况下进行的支付，仅用于赔偿目的。

（5）根据第（4）款有权获得赔偿的人，应当在最终决定或指令交付赔偿之日起 6 个月内向理事会提

Six months from the date of the final decision or order delivered for compensation.

(6) After receiving an application pursuant to Sub-rule (4), the Council shall pay the compensation amount to the extent of the deposited amount.

(7) Deposit amount pursuant to the Act and these Rules shall be paid back to the Notary Public by the Council on following conditions:

(a) If the Notary Public dies or

(b) If the Notary Public does not renew the license or files application to cancel the license voluntarily.

(8) Notwithstanding anything contained in Sub-rule (7), if any claim for compensation against the Notary Public is pending before his/her death, or renewal of certificate or cancellation of his/her certificate, in such a case, the deposit amount shall be paid back if the final decision relating to the claim does not decides for compensation.

(9) While paying back the deposit amount of a deceased Notary Public on the basis of Clause (a) of Sub-rule (7) it shall be paid to the close relative as referred to in Rule 26.

15. Oath:

(1) A person, who has obtained certificate and intends to practice in a district upon establishing an office of a Notary Public, shall have to take oath before that district judge of the same district in the format as referred to in Schedule-3.

(2) The document of an oath pursuant to Sub-rule (1) shall be send by the concerned District Court to the Council and such document shall be kept by the Council on the record of concerned Notary Public.

16. Seal of the Notary Public:

(1) The format of the Seal of a Notary Public shall be as referred to in Schedule-4.

(2) The Council shall cause to prepare the Seal as referred to in Sub- rule (1).

(3) A person who has obtained the certificate of a Notary Public who intends to obtain a Seal pursuant to Sub-rule (1) shall apply to the Council and if an application is so received, the Council shall make available such a Seal upon collecting the cost as it has been fixed.

(4) A Notary Public, who has taken a Seal pursuant to this Rule, shall inform to the Council if it lost or it becomes useless and the Council shall make available another Seal upon collecting cost therefor.

(5) If, the Notary Public does not want to practice as

出申请。

（6）在收到根据第（4）款提出的申请后，理事会应当在存续的保证金范围内支付赔偿金额。

（7）出现下列情况之一，公证法和本条例规定的保证金应由理事会如数退还给公证员：

（a）公证员死亡；

（b）公证员执业证书没有续期或提交申请自愿注销执业资格。

（8）尽管第（7）款有所规定，如果在公证员死亡或对执业证书进行续期或注销其执业资格之前存在任何向其提出的损害赔偿请求，在这种情况下，如果与损害赔偿请求有关的最终判决并未获得支持，保证金应当如数退还给公证员。

（9）在根据第（7）款第（a）项将保证金退还已故公证员时，应当退还给其本条例第 26 条规定的近亲属。

15. 宣誓：

（1）任何取得执业证书并打算在某一设立公证机构的地区执业的，应以附表 3 载明的内容向该地区的法官宣誓。

（2）第（1）款规定的宣誓文件应当由有关地方法院送交理事会，并且该文件应由理事会保存在有关公证员的记录中。

16. 公证员的印章：

（1）公证员印章的样式应当参照附表 4 的规定。

（2）理事会应当制作第（1）款所述的印章。

（3）根据第（1）款取得公证员证书并希望取得印章的，应当向理事会提出申请；申请被接收的，理事会收取制作印章的规定成本费用后向申请人提供印章。

（4）根据本条例取得印章的公证员，如果印章丢失或失效应当通知理事会，理事会可以收取相关成本费用并提供新的印章。

（5）如果公证员不想再以公证员身份继续执业，

a Notary Public, he/she shall return the Seal to the Council.

应当向理事会交还印章。

Chapter-Four Provision Relating to Certification of Document, Translation of Paper and Verification of Copy of an Original Document

第四章　与文件公证，文书翻译和原始文件副本核查有关的规定

17. Procedure to Certification of Document:

(1) Whosoever is interested for certification of a document shall apply in the format as referred to in Schedule-5 along with the following documents:

(a) Copy of citizenship certificate or passport.

(b) If there is no citizenship certificate or passport then applicant's identity card having recent photograph, signature, address, age, surname and name or letter sticking photograph and stating above details certified by Village Development Committee or concerning ward office of municipality where applicant resides or any identity card which may satisfy the Notary Public and in the case of a foreigner a paper showing identity certified by the concerned embassy.

(c) Relationship verification paper, if so required.

(d) If someone wants to certify in the capacity of an agent power of attorney or letter of authority for certification and two copies of documents intended to be certified.

(2) Notary Public shall register the application received pursuant to Sub-rule (1) in the document certification Register.

(3) Before certifying the document, Notary Public shall read out the statement of the document to be heard and communicate the meaning to applicant who signs on document and shall keep the paper (memo) so prepared in the file.

(4) Notary Public shall cause to sign the witness of the applicant in the document to be certified or in a paper as referred to in Sub-rule or in a separate paper.

(5) If the document produced for certification is to be submitted in any court or office or it is an affidavit, in such a case, Notary Public shall cause for an oath pursuant to Schedule-6 of the applicant who puts signature on the document.

(6) After an oath pursuant to Sub-rule (5), Notary Public shall sign and put seal at the end of the document along with the statement as referred to in Schedule-7.

(7) While certifying documents except as stated in Sub-Rule (5), the Notary Public shall sign at the end of the document or in a separate paper writing the statement

17. 文件公证的程序：

（1）文件的公证，当事人应当按照附表 5 规定的格式提出申请，并提交下列文件：

（a）公民身份证明或护照的复印件；

（b）如果没有公民身份证明或护照，那么申请人可以提供有最近照片、签名、地址、年龄、姓氏和名字或证件照片的身份证，并说明上述信息经乡村发展委员会或申请人居住地市政府办公室证明，或可以满足公证员要求的任何身份证；如果是外国人，需提交有关大使馆能够证明其身份的文书。

（c）关系核查文书（如需要）；

（d）如果对委托书或授权书进行公证，那么需要提交两份待公证文书的复印件。

（2）公证员应当在文件公证登记簿中登记根据第（1）款收到的申请。

（3）在公证文件之前，公证员应宣读要核查的文件的陈述，并将其含义传达给在文件上签字的申请人，同时将准备的文件（备忘录）保存在档案中。

（4）公证员应当让申请人的证人在待公证的文件中或在条款提及的文书中或在单独的一页签名。

（5）如果公证的文件将要提交任何法院或办公室，或者作为宣誓书，在这种情况下，公证员应当要求在文件上签名的申请人根据附表 6 进行宣誓。

（6）在根据第（5）款进行宣誓后，公证员应当在文件的最后签名和盖章，并附加附表 7 提及的声明。

（7）在公证文件时，除了第（5）款规定的要求以外，公证员应在文件末尾签名，或在单独另一页中书面陈述文件中所载事项是真实的。如果进行虚假证

that the matter written in the document is true and if it is proved false he or she shall be responsible pursuant to the law and shall cause to put signature of the applicant pursuant to Schedule-8.

明，公证员应当依法承担责任。申请人应当根据附表8的要求在文件上签名。

(8) While writing name and surname by the Notary Public pursuant to Sub-rule (5) or (6), he/she shall have to write the name and surname as stated in the certificate.

（8）公证员根据第（5）款和第（6）款所签的姓名应当与其执业证书所载的姓名相一致。

(9) If the document produced for certification is relating to lease, rent, transfer of title, sale and purchase and sale deed of immovable property, Notary Public shall confirm whether or not that immoveable property is under the title of the person who put signature on the deed as well as verifying whether or not that property is already leased or freezed in any way by any office and also verify land ownership certificate, receipt of revenue and other necessary matters.

（9）如果公证的文件涉及不动产的租赁、出租、所有权转让、买卖和销售契约，公证员应当确认该不动产是否属于在契约上签名的人所有，以及核查该等财产是否已经由任何办公室以任何方式出租或冻结，并核查土地所有权证书、完税证明和其他必要事项。

(10) While certifying the statement of the document relating to the transfer of immoveable property, Notary Public shall certify more than two copies of the document as stated in prevailing law and in other condition at least two copies shall be certified.

（10）公证员在公证有关不动产转让的文件声明时，应当根据现行法律规定核查两份以上文件副本，其他条件下也应当至少核查两份副本。

(11) The Notary Public shall mention the serial number of certification on the certified document as it appears in the Register-Book of the office.

（11）公证员应在录入公证机构登记簿时在公证文件上注明系列编号。

18. Procedure to Translate Paper:

18. 翻译文书的程序：

(1) Whosoever is interested to translate a paper shall have to apply in a format as referred to in Schedule-9 before the Notary Public along with true copy, copy thereof and other paper which shows his/her identity.

（1）文书的翻译，应当按照附表9规定的格式向公证员提出申请，并提交真实的文书、文书的复印件和证明其身份的其他文书。

(2) Application received pursuant to Sub-rule (1) shall be registered in the Translation Register by the Notary Public.

（2）根据第（1）款收到的申请，公证员应当在翻译登记簿中进行登记。

(3) The Notary Public may translate the paper if there is reasonable ground to believe that the paper is true and authentic.

（3）在有合理理由相信文书是真实准确的前提下，公证员可以对文书进行翻译。

(4) Notary Public shall put registration number in each translated document as referred to in Sub-rule (2).

（4）根据第（2）款的规定，公证员在翻译登记簿进行登记时应当对每一份翻译文书标注登记号码。

(5) Notary Public shall put signature on translated document or paper as referred to in Schedule-10.

（5）公证员应当根据附表10的要求在翻译的文件或文书上签字。

19. Procedure of Verification (Attestation):

19. 核查（证明）程序：

(1) Whosever wants to verify (attested) any paper shall have to apply in the format as referred to in Schedule-11 before the Notary Public along with true copy, one additional copy along with the copies required for verification and paper which shows his/her identity.

（1）对任何文书进行核查（证明），应当按照附表11规定的格式向公证员提出申请，并提交真实的文件副本、核查所需要的复印件和证明申请人身份的文书。

(2) Application received pursuant to Sub-rule (1)

（2）根据第（1）款收到的申请，公证员应当在

shall be registered in a separate Register-Book by the Notary Public.

(3) Confirming whether or not the paper to be verified is true if necessary, the Notary Public may make a paper (memo) from the applicant stating that "the copy is as good as the original copy."

(4) If the paper submitted pursuant to Sub-rule (1) is found authentic upon an inquiry pursuant to Sub-Rule (3), the Notary Public may verify such copy of the paper as referred to in Schedule-12.

(5) A verified copy pursuant to this Rule shall be kept safely in the office by the Notary Public up to a period of Five years.

20. Fee of a Notary Public:

(1) Notary Public may charge following remunerations for the following functions:

(a) For certification of document not exceeding Five Hundred Rupees per document.

(b) For translation:

i Document in a format such as citizenship certificate, land ownership registration certificate, birth, death and marriage registration certificates not exceeding One Hundred Fifty Rupees per paper.

ii Legal document, decision or order of a court, statute of corporate body or other similar paper not exceeding Five Hundred Rupees per page.

iii Paper except otherwise provided in Sub-clauses (i) and (ii), recommendation letter of local body and other similar paper not exceeding Two Hundred Rupees.

(c) Verification of the copy of a document not exceeding Fifty Rupees per paper.

(2) Upon receiving remuneration by the Notary Public pursuant to Sub-rule (1), receipt therefor shall be given to the concerned person and the record thereof shall be updated in register book accordingly.

Chapter-5 Miscellaneous

21. Matters to be Shown in Register Book:

(1) In the Register-Book relating certification of the document, Notary Public shall put page number and Seal stating the following matters:

(a) Date of submission of application for the certification document.

(b) Name of the person, surname, age, address, photograph and thumb impressions of both thumbs who put signature on document.

单独的登记簿中进行登记。

（3）为了确认文件的真实性，如有必要，公证员可以要求申请人出具一份文书（备忘录），说明待核查文书的复印件与原件是一致的。

（4）如果根据第（1）款提交的文书经根据第（3）款进行的询证被证实为真实的，公证员可以根据附表12的规定核查文书的副本。

（5）根据本条规定核查的文书副本应当由公证员妥善保管于公证机构，保存期限不得少于5年。

20. 公证员的费用：

（1）公证员可以就以下职能行为收取报酬：

（a）文件公证每份文件不得超过500卢比。

（b）翻译：

（i）公民身份证、土地所有权登记证、出生证明、死亡证明、结婚登记证明等文书，每份不得超过150卢比。

（ii）法院的法律文书、决定、裁定，公司的内部规则或者其他类似文书，每页不超过500卢比。

（iii）除第（i）项和第（ii）项规定的文书外，地方机构的推荐文书或其他类似文书不得超过200卢比。

（c）对文件副本进行核查每份不得超过50卢比。

（2）公证员收到当事人根据第（1）款支付的报酬，应当出具发票，并且在登记簿上做相应的更新记录。

第五章　其他事项

21. 记载于登记簿的事项：

（1）公证员应当在与文件公证有关的登记簿中记载下列事项，并标注页码和加盖印章：

（a）提交文件公证申请的时间；

（b）文件签名人的姓名、年龄、地址、照片和双手拇指手印；

(c) Name of witness, surname, age, address, signature and thumb impressions of both hands.

(d) Fee received for certification.

(e) Date of certification of document.

(2) In the Translation Register-Book, the Notary Public shall put page number and seal on every page and state the following matters:

(a) The date of application submitted to translate the document.

(b) Name, surname, age and address of the person who request for translation of the document or paper.

(c) Page number and subject of the translated document.

(d) Fee for translation.

(e) Date of translation done for applicant.

(3) In the Verification Register-Book, the Notary shall put page number and seal on every page upon stating the following matters:

(a) Name, surname, address and age of the person who has requested for verification of the documents.

(b) Page number and subject of verified document.

(c) Fee for verification.

(d) Date of document verification.

(4) After mentioning matters in the Record Book to be maintained pursuant to Sub-rules (1), (2) and (3), Notary Public shall put his/her full signature on the top and bottom of all pages of the Register Book.

22. File to be Submitted:

(1) If a Notary Public is not in a position to continue his/her profession he/she him/herself or in a case of his/her death, his/her heir shall submit the files as referred to in Sub-section (3) of Section 24 of the Act, to the Council.

(2) The Council, upon examining whether the file received pursuant to Sub-rule (1) is to be kept safely or not, may destroy it after Five years from the date of its arrival, if not necessary to keep it safely.

23. Matters to be Stated in the Report:

(1) Notary Public shall state the following matters in the report to be submitted pursuant to Section 25 of the Act:

(a) Name and surname of Notary Public.

(b) Certificate number.

(c) Validity date of certificate.

(d) Name, surname, age and address of the person requested for translation and certification of document or verification of papers.

（c）证人的姓名、年龄、地址、签名和双手拇指手印；

（d）公证收取的费用；

（e）文件公证的时间。

（2）公证员应当在翻译登记簿中的每一页标注页码和加盖印章，并记载下列事项：

（a）提交文件翻译申请的时间；

（b）申请翻译文件或文书当事人的姓名、年龄和地址；

（c）翻译文件的页码和主题；

（d）翻译费用；

（e）翻译完成时间。

（3）公证员应当在核查登记簿的每一页标注页码和加盖公章，并记载下列事项：

（a）申请对文件进行核查当事人的姓名、地址和年龄；

（b）核查文件的页码和主题；

（c）核查费用；

（d）核查文件的时间。

（4）根据第（1）款、第（2）款和第（3）款保存的登记簿，在记载事项完成后，公证员应当在登记簿每一页的页眉和页脚处签署其全名。

22. 提交的文件：

（1）如果公证员无法继续执业或者公证员死亡，公证员本人或者其继承人应当根据《公证法》第24条第（3）款的规定，向理事会提交有关文件。

（2）理事会在检查根据第（1）款收到的文件是否需要被妥善保管后，如果没有必要继续妥善保管，可以自收到之日起5年后予以销毁。

23. 报告中应载明的事项：

（1）公证员应当在根据《公证法》第25条提交的报告中记载下列事项：

（a）公证员的姓名；

（b）执业证书编号；

（c）证书的有效日期；

（d）申请翻译和公证文件或核查文书当事人的姓名、年龄和地址；

(e) Subject, nature and number of certified document, translated paper or verified paper.

(f) Fee received by Notary Public.

(2) The Notary Public, who does certification of document relating to transfer of title of immovable property, shall state the subject of title transfer, measurement of immoveable property and amount stated in the document in addition to the details mentioned in monthly report to be submitted pursuant to Sub-rule (1).

（e）公证文件、翻译文书或核查文书的主题、性质和编号；

（f）公证员收取的费用。

（2）对不动产所有权转让文件进行公证的公证员，除了在根据第（1）款提交的月度报告中提及的细节外，还应说明所有权转让的对象、不动产的计量方式和文件中载明的金额。

24. Descriptions to be Mentioned in the Record of Notary Public:

The Council shall mention the name, surname, address (permanent, professional), age and contact telephone number, copy of the certificate of academic qualification, copy of law practitioners license, date of expiry of the certificate of Notary Public, date of renewal of the certificate of Notary Public and other necessary descriptions of the Notary Public in the record of every Notary Public.

24. 公证员档案中应记载的内容：

理事会应在每一个公证员的档案中记载公证员的姓名、地址（永久居住地、办公地址）、年龄、电话号码、学历证明复印件、法律从业资格证书复印件、公证员执业证书到期日、公证员执业证书续期日以及其他必要的信息。

25. Provision Relating to Inquiry of complains:

(1) The Council may form a three-member inquiry committee, if so required, in the convenorship of any of its member to inquire the complaint received pursuant to Section 32 of the Act.

(2) The committee formed pursuant to Sub-rule (1) may ask or inquire or demand other evidence from the concerned Notary Public.

(3) If the Council or the committee, in relation to an inquiry pursuant to the Act or these Rules, orders to submit clarification or information, the concerned Notary Public shall submit clarification or information along with evidence and proof to the Council within the time-frame given by the Council or Committee.

(4) The committee formed pursuant to Sub-rule (1), upon completing inquiry and investigation pursuant to Sub-rule (2), shall submit its report to the Council along with its opinion.

(5) After submission of the report pursuant to Sub-rule (4) by the Committee formed pursuant to Sub-rule (1), the Council shall decide, upon considering the report and proof and evidence, whether the Notary Public has committed official misconduct or not.

(6) While making decision pursuant to Sub-rule (5), if it is found that Notary Public has committed official misconduct, the Council shall cancel his/her certificate pursuant to Section 18 of the Act.

(7) While making decision pursuant to Sub-rule (5),

25. 有关投诉调查的规定：

（1）根据需要，理事会可以成立一个由3人组成的调查委员会，在其任一成员召集下调查根据《公证法》第32条收到的投诉。

（2）根据第（1）款成立的委员会可以向相关公证员进行询问或调查，或者要求相关公证员提供其他证据。

（3）如果理事会或委员会要求就根据公证法或本规条例提起的调查命令提交有关说明或信息，相关公证员应当在理事会或委员会规定的时间内提交相应的说明或信息，并提交相应的证据或证明。

（4）根据第（1）款成立的委员会，再根据第（2）款的规定进行询证和调查后，应当向理事会提交报告附带其具体意见。

（5）根据第（1）款成立的委员会在根据第（4）款提交报告后，理事会应当在考虑报告内容和有关证据的基础上，决定公证员是否存在官方认定的不当行为。

（6）根据第（5）款作出的决定，如果发现公证员存在官方认定的不当行为，理事会应当依据《公证法》第18条的规定注销其公证员资格。

（7）根据第（5）款作出的决定，如果发现公证

if it is found that no official misconduct has been committed, suspension shall be ipso facto cancelled from the date of such decision.

员不存在官方认定的不当行为，对其停职措施应当自决定作出之日起取消。

26. Close Relation:

For the purpose of Clause (5) of section 20 of Act, close relatives shall mean father, mother, husband, wife son, daughter, grandson, granddaughter, elder sister, younger sister, elder brother, younger brother, nephew nice, daughter and son of sister, grandfather, grandmother of Notary Public and other relatives as determined by the Council.

26. 密切联系

本着《公证法》第 20 条第（5）款之目的，近亲属指公证员的父亲、母亲、丈夫、妻子、儿子、女儿、孙子、孙女、姐姐、妹妹、哥哥、弟弟、侄子、外甥（女）、祖父、祖母以及理事会认定的其他近亲属。

Schedule-1
(Related to Rule 9)

To the Chairperson,
Nepal Notary Public Council,
Kathmandu

Subject: Application for the certificate of Notary Public

Sir,

Whereas, continuously practicing as a legal practitioner since _______/ retired from the post of Nepal judicial service, I am desirous to work as a_______in the capacity of Notary Public and I have passed the examination of Notary Public and therefore, I am applying to obtain the certificate of Notary Public enclosing necessary papers and fees.

Name and Surname:
Permanent Address:
District and place to work as a Notary Public:
Contact address and telephone number, if any:
Copy of the certificate of academic qualification:
Copy of the license of a law practitioner:
Copy of the citizenship certificate:
For retired officer any evidence which clearly shows his/her retirement:
Two copies of photograph:
Name and Surname to be written as a Notary Public:
Specimen of full signature:
Date:

Signature of applicant

附表 1
（关于第 9 条）

致加德满都尼泊尔公证委员会主席：

主题：公证员执业证书申请

敬启者：

鉴于，本人自 ______/ 从尼泊尔司法服务机构退休之日起持续从事法律职业，本人希望以公证员的身份作为 ______ 工作，本人已经通过公证员考试。因此，本人申请公证员执业证书，并提交必要的文书和缴纳必要的费用。

姓名：
永久居住地：
以公证员身份工作的地区和地点：
联系地址和电话号码（如有）：
学历证书复印件：
法律从业资格证书复印件：
公民身份证复印件：
对于退休的官员，证明其退休的证据：

两张照片：
公证员的姓名：
完整签名样本：
日期：

申请人签字

Schedule-2
(Related to Rule 11)

Nepal Notary Public Council

Certificate No.
Notary public Certificate
Pursuant to a decision made by the Council on __________ this certificate is conferred on Mr./Ms./Mrs. __________ son/daughter of __________ permanent resident of __________

附表 2
（关于第 11 条）

尼泊尔公证员理事会

证书编号：
公证员证书
根据理事会于 ______ 作出的决定，本证书授予 ______ 先生 / 女士，______ 的儿子 / 女儿，永久居住地为 _______，_______ 城市 / 乡村 _______ 号 _______ 发展委员会 _____

Ward no. ____________ of municipality metropolitan city/sub-metropolitan city/village __________ Development committee __________ district after having been enrolled his/her name as a/an ____________ under the Notary Public Act, 2006 to do __________

Secretary Chairperson
Seal of the Council
Date of Issue (A.D.)

Schedule-3
(Related to Rule 15)

Format of Oath Taken by Notary Public

I ________ Notary Public certificate no. __________, Notary Public of __________ district__________swear in the name of God/I solemnly affirm that while practicing as a Notary Public, I shall practice subject to the Notary Public Act, 2063 and Rules thereunder and other prevailing laws to the extent possible of my knowledge, wisdom, rational and qualification without any bias, anger, reservation, prejudice and partiality against anyone and with honesty and impartiality.

Signature of District Judge
Name and Surname:
Date:

Signature of Notary Public
Name, Surname:
Certificate No.:
Signature:
Date:

Schedule-4
(Related to Rule 16)

Seal of Notary Public

Schedule-5
(Related to Sub-rule (1) of Rule 17)

Format of Application for Certification of Document

To the Notary Public
District ____________
Subject: In Relation to Certification of Document

I, hereby, apply for certification of following documents along with the fees to be paid as per Rule:

(a) Documents
1.
2.

(b) Papers which show that the documents are related to the applicant
1.
2.
3.

________区；根据2006年公证法注册他/她的姓名作为____ __________，从事__________。

秘书长 主席
理事会印章
颁发日期（公元）

附表3
（关于第15条）

公证员宣誓的格式

本人__________，公证员证书编号______________，________________地区的公证员以上帝的名义/本人庄严声明，在作为公证员执业期间，将根据公证法2063和公证条例及其他现行法律开展公证活动，尽我所能的知识、智慧、理性和资质，没有任何偏见、愤怒和保留，不偏袒任何人，保证诚实和公正。

地区法官签字
姓名：
日期：

公证员签字
姓名：
证书编号：
签名：
日期：

附表4
（关于第16条）

公证员的印章

附表5
[关于第17条第（1）款]

文件公证申请的格式

致_____地区公证员：

主题：关于文件公证

本人特此申请以下文件的公证并根据公证条例支付有关费用：

（a）文件
1.
2.

（b）与申请人有关的文书
1.
2.
3.

Applicant's name, surname:
Address:
Signature:
Date:

Schedule-6
(Related to Sub-rule (5) of Rule 17)

Format of Oath to be Administered by the Notary Public

I ________aged________years, a resident of___________ _________grandson/granddaughter of _____________ son/ daughter of_____________, in presence of Notary Public Mr./ Ms./Mrs ____________ (Certificate no.) do swear in the name of God/Solemnly affirm and declare that the content of this document is true and correct. I shall personally be liable under law in force, if the content is found otherwise.

Signature:
Date:

Schedule-7
(Related to Sub-rule (6) of Rule 17)
Form of Verification of Document for Administering Oath by the Notary Public

The applicant Mr. /Ms. /Mrs. ________ is personally known to me or on verification of the submitted documents and on interview of his or her witness (Name, surname, age and address of the witness) it has been found that his/her personal details are found to be true and correct. I, hereby, verify that he/she has taken oath in my presence and has signed in this document in presence of the said witness on ___________ date.

Signature:
Name:
Date:
Certificate number of the Notary Public:
Date of expiry of certificate:
Seal of the Notary Public

Schedule-8
(Related to Sub-rule (7) of Rule 17)
Form of Verification of Document by Administering Oath

The applicant Mr. /Ms. /Mrs. ________ is personally known to me or on verification of the submitted documents and on interview of his or her witness (Name, surname, age and address of the witness) it has been found that his/her personal details are found to be true and correct. I, hereby, verify that he/ she has signed in this document in presence of the said witness on _______ date.

Signature:
Name:

申请人的姓名：
地址：
签名：
日期：

附表 6
[关于第 17 条第（5）款]

公证员主持的宣誓格式

本人__________，年龄______，居住于__________，__________的孙子／孙女，__________的儿子／女儿，在公证员__________先生／女士（证书编号：）的见证下以上帝的名义／庄严地确认并声明本文件的内容真实无误。如果存在任何错误内容，本人将根据现行法律承担责任。

签名：
日期：

附表 7
[关于第 17 条第（6）款]
公证员主持的核查文件的宣誓格式

本人经核查提交的文件及与申请人__________先生／女士的证人（见证人的姓名、年龄及地址）了解申请人的情况，申请人的个人信息是真实准确的。本人特此确认，申请人已在本人面前进行宣誓，并且于_____日，在证人在场的情况下在文件上进行签名。

签名：
姓名：
日期：
公证员执业证书编号：
证书有效期：
公证员印章

附表 8
[关于第 17 条第（7）款]
核查文件宣誓的格式

本人经核查提交的文件及与申请人___________先生／女士的证人（见证人的姓名、年龄及地址）了解申请人的情况，申请人的个人信息是真实准确的。本人特此确认，申请人已在本人面前进行宣誓，并且于_______日，在证人在场的情况下，在文件上进行签名。

签名：
姓名：

Date:
Certificate number of the Notary Public:
Date of expiry of certificate:
Seal of the Notary Public:

Schedule-9
(Related to Sub-rule (1) of Rule 18)
Form of Application for Translation

To the Notary Public
______________ District
Subject: In Relation to Translation

I am applying enclosing the fees to be paid as per Rule to translate the following documents or papers from ________ language to __________ language.

(a) Documents
1.
2.
3.
(b) Papers which show that papers are related to the applicant
1.
2.
3.

Name and surname of applicant
Address:
Signature:
Date:

Schedule-10
(Related to Sub-rule (5) of Rule 18)
Format of Translation Copy of Document

"The translation copy is true and verified."
Signature:
Name/Surname:
Date:
Certificate number of the Notary Public:
Date of expiry of certificate:
Seal of the Notary Public:

Schedule-11
(Related to Sub-rule (1) of Rule 19)
Form of Application for Verification of Copy of Document

To,
The Notary Public,
________________ District
Subject: In Relation to verification of document.

I am applying enclosing the fees to be paid as per Rule for verification of the following papers or documents:

(a) Papers
1.
2.
3.
4.

日期：
公证员执业证书编号：
证书有效期：
公证员印章

附件 9
[关于第 18 条第（1）款]
翻译申请的格式

致 ______ 地区公证员：

主题：关于翻译

本人根据公证条例支付有关费用申请将下列文件由 ________ 语言翻译为 ________ 语言。

（a）文件
1.
2.
3.
（b）与申请人有关的文书
1.
2.
3.

申请人的姓名：
地址：
签名：
日期：

附表 10
[关于第 18 条第（5）款]
翻译文件副本的格式

"翻译文件副本是真实的且已经过核查。"
签名：
姓名：
日期：
公证员执业证书编号：
证书有效期：
公证员印章

附表 11
[关于第 19 条第（1）款]
申请核查文件副本的格式

致 ______ 地区公证员：

主题：关于核查文件

本人根据公证条例支付有关费用申请核查下列文书或文件：

（a）文书
1.
2.
3.
4.

5.

(b) Papers which shows that the papers are related to the applicant

(c) Rs.__________ fee to be paid is along with it.

Name and surname of applicant:

Address:

Signature:

Date:

Schedule-12

(Related to Sub-rule (4) of Rule 19)

Form of Verification of Copy of Document

Verification of true copy of original

Name:

Surname:

Signature:

Date:

Certificate number of the Notary Public:

Date of expiry of certificate:

Seal of the Notary Public:

5.

（b）与申请人有关的文书

（c）支付的费用

申请人的姓名：

地址：

签名：

日期：

附表 12

[关于第 19 条第（4）款]

核查文件副本的格式

核查原件的真实副本

姓名：

签名：

日期：

公证员执业证书编号：

证书有效期：

公证员印章

阿曼

公证法

تانون الكعاب بالمدد

اسل الأول
تعريفات

مادة (١) : يكون للكلمات والعبارات التاية المعانى المبيغة قرين كل مذبا :
الوزارة : وزارة العدل .
الوزير: وزير العدل.

الغمل الثانى
تعيين الكتاب بالعدل واختصاصهم الكانى

مادج (٢): الكاب بالعدل هو مدير دائرته وإذا تعدد الكتاب بالعدل فى دائرة واحدة تولى أقدمهم إدارة الدائرة .

مادة (٣): يشترط فى الكاب بالعدل - فضلا عن الشروط العامة لدطوف المنصوص عليها فى قانون اخدمة الدنجة - أن يكون حاصلا على مؤهل جامعى فى الشريعة أو القانون من إحدى الجامعات أو الكليات المعترن بما وألا تكون قد صدرت ضده أحكام جزائية أو تاديبية لأسباب ماسة بالذمة أو الشرف ولو كان قد رد إليه اعتبارم .

مادة >،: يؤدى الكاب بالعدل قبل مباشرته مهام وظيفته اليمين الآتية أقم بالله العظيم أن أودى عملى بالصدق والشرف والأمال وأن أحافظ على أسرار وظيفتى وأن أحترم القوانين وذلك أمام الوزير أو من يغوبه> ٠

مادة (٠): يخصص لكل دائرة من دوائر الكتاب بالعدل حاتم رسى ذختم به المعاملات يشلمه مدير الدائرة ويكون مفع الوؤسم .

الغمل الثالث
الاختمامات وسورات

مادة (٦): يتولى الكاتب بالعدل تحرير العفرد التى يختص بتحريرها وغيرها ضاحررات ، والتصديق على

公证法

第一章　定义

第一条　下列词语和表达具有以下含义：

部：司法部。
部长：司法部长。

第二章　公证员的任命及其职权范围

第二条　公证员是其所在部门的管理者，如果一个部门的公证员超过一个人，那么由该部门最早入职的人任部门管理者。

第三条　除了《公务员法》规定的一般雇用条件之外，公证员还须获得大学或者被认可的学院的法学学位，并且没有因诽谤或作风原因而受过刑事或纪律处罚，即使已经对其恢复名誉。

第四条　公证员在履职之前，应当在部长或部长委托人面前作以下宣誓：“我向伟大的真主发誓，我将以忠诚、庄重和诚信来履行我的工作，保守我的工作中的秘密并遵守法律。”

第五条　各公证机构配备业务印章，交由公证机构主任保管。

第三章　职权范围和职业禁止

第六条　公证员应编写属于其职权范围内的合同与其他文件，按照本法的规定公证合同的签署和非官

التوقيعات ، وإثبات تاريخ المحررات العرفية، على الحفو
المفصوص عليه في هذا القانون ، وإجراء أي معاملة أخرى
يغمي القانون على اختصاصه بها .

مادة (٧): يحرر الكاتب بالعدل العقود والمحررات التي
يوجب القانون أو يطلب ذوو الشأن تحريرها ويتور إثباتها
في السجلات المعدة لذلك دون كشط أو محو أو إضافة أو
فواصل وعدو حدوث مهو أو خطأ أو قيام ذا يدعو إلى التصحيح
أو الإضافة فيتم ذلك بالمداد الأحمر وبحضور ذوى الشأن
ويوقع الكاتب العدل على التصحيح .

وعليه حفظ أصول ما حرره وإعطاء المرور التي يطلبها
ذوو الشأن وإثبات ذلك في القراس الخاصة .

وعلى الكاتب بالعدل أن يقرأ أخرر على ذوى الشأن أمام
شاهدين راشدين عاقلين ويثبت ذلك في أخرر المطلوب
تحريره .

مادة (٨): يصادق الكاتب بالعدل على توقعات ذوى
الشأن في المحررات العرفية بناء على طلبهم ويثبت
التصديق في الجالات والغراس الخاصة بذلك .

ويجب على الكاتب بالعدل قبل التعديق على توقيع
ذوى الشأن أن يتحقق من إلمامهم بموضوع المحرر الذي يرغبون
في السديق على توقعاتهم فيه ، وبعد توقيع ذوى الشأن
في المحرر والسجل يحرر الكاتب بالدلل محضرا

بذلك في ذيل المحرر ويوقعه الشهود والموقعون على
المحرر ثم يدلم المحرر إلى

صاحب الشأن بعد توقعه الاستلام في مجل
التصديقات. ويجوز إعطاء شهادات من واقع سجلات
التصديقات لمن يديها من ذوى الشأن ، ولا يجوز إعطاؤها لغير
ذوى الشأن إلا بأمر من المحكمة .

يجب على الكاتب بالعدل قبل تحرير العقود :
أو المحررات ، أو التعديق على توقعجات ذوى الشان
في المحررات العرفية أن يتثبت من شخصية ذوى الشان
الوثائق الرسمية المثبتة كخعيتهم وتمدد ترعن ذلك فله أن
يطلب منهم معرفين أثفين ، كما يجب عليه أن يتبنت من
أهلية أطراف المحرر وصفاتهم .

وإذا اتفح للكاتب العدل عدم توافر الأهلية أو الصفة أو
كان الوضوع مخالفا للنظام العام أو اكاونين الارية فيتعين
عليه رفض تحرير العقد أو المحرر المطلوب أو التعديق
على توقيعات ذوى الشان فيه مبه• بيان أسباب الرفض •

ويجب على الكاب العدل إذا أصر ذوو العلاقة على
طلبهم أن يعرف الأمر إلى المحكمة القدائية أيى تقع دائرته
ضمن نطاق اختصاصها التى لها أن تقرم أو أن تلزمه بإجراء
المطلوب .

(: إذا كان الكاب العدل يجهل لغة ذوى العلاقة أو أحدهم
أو كان بينهم أصم أو أبكم وتعذر عليه بجب ذلك أمانثغاف
إدرا أو إفهامهم مضمون الوثيقة فعلى الكاب العدل أن يفهمهم
و يتلقى تصرإحاتهم وذلك بواسطة مترجم أو خبير بعد
تحليفهم يمين أغلى أن يقوم واجبه بمدق وشرف وأمانة وعلى
الكاب العدل أن يدون ذلك بالوثيقة ويوقع على ذلك المترجم

方文件的日期，开展法律规定的其职权范围内的其他业务。

第七条 公证员应编写应法律要求或申请人要求其编写的合同，并确认在拟定完成的文本中没有涂改、擦除、添加，在出现纰漏或错误进行修正或添加时，应用红色字体完成，且此过程要在申请人面前进行，公证员应在修正的地方签名。

公证员应当保存其编写的文件正本，申请人如有要求可交给其文件副本，并在相关文件中记录。

公证员应在申请人及两位成年、理智的见证人面前宣读所编写的内容，并且记录在所编写的文件上。

第八条 公证员应根据申请人要求对非官方合同的申请人签署进行公证，并对此文本和相关索引进行公证。

在申请人签署文件和文本后，公证员在进行签署公证之前，应核实确认申请人已知晓文件的内容，在申请人签署文件之后，公证员应在文本末尾处签名，并由见证人在记录上签名，然后在申请人在签收记录上签名之后，将公证书交给申请人。

公证书可以提供给申请人请求的有关人，除法院命令外，不得将其提供给除申请人之外的第三方。

第九条 在编写合同或其他文件，或公证非官方文件中申请人在签署之前，公证员应通过身份证明核实申请人的身份。如果申请人不能提供身份证明，那么公证员应要求其提供两名介绍人，同样公证员还应核实文件申请人的资质。

如果公证员发现提交人没有资质或性质不符，或者该合同主体违反公共秩序或现行法律，必须拒绝编写合同或所提文件或公证申请人的签署，并说明拒绝的原因。

如果申请人坚持要将事情提交至公证机构辖区范围内的初级法院，那么由法院来决定批准或采取必要的措施。

第十条 如果公证员不能理解申请人的语言，或其中有聋哑人，因此无法表达其意愿或使之理解文件的内容，公证员应当通过翻译或专家接受陈述，专家应当诚实、庄重和守信地完成工作进行宣誓。公证员必须在文件中记录这些内容，翻译、专家、申请人、两名见证人和公证员应当在文件上签名。应根据部长

روجأ ردقي نأو لدح!ا بتاكلاو ناداهكاو ةقالعلاوذو ريجلاوأ
نم رارق اهب ردمي ىتلا دعاوقلل اقفو ريبخلا وأ مجرتملا
. مهل اهئاداب ناشلا ىوذ فلكيو ناشلا اذه ىف ريزولا

وأ دوهشلا وأ ةقالعلا ىوذ دحأ ناك اذإ :(١ ١) **ةدام**
ذخأي نأ لدعلاب بناكلا ىلعف عينوتلا لهجي نيفرعملا
. ررغا ىف كلد تبثيو مهابإ ةمصب

ةقرو ض رثكأ ىلع تبتك دق ةقيثولا تناك اذإ :
ددع افورحو امقر ركذيو ، امهيقرت لدعلاب بذاكلا ىلع نيعت
ةفرو لك ةياهن ىف عقويو ةرئادلا متاز عفيو ةقيثولا قاروأ
. دجو نإ ريجلا وأ محرتلاو دوهشلاو ةقالعلا ىوذ عم

ةيفرعلا تاررخما خيرات لدعلاب بتاكلا تبثي :
ررحيو كلذل ةدعملا سراهغلاو تالجلا ىن ةعباتتم ماقرأب
هجاردإ مقرو هميدقت خرات هيف تبثي ررحنا ىلع أرضحم
نأشلا بمحاص ىل١ مهلي مث لدعلاب بناكلا هعقويو لجلا ىف
خيراكا تابثال ةدعملا تالبلا عقاو نم تاداهش ءاطعإ زوجيو
نأشلا ىوذ ريغل اهؤاطعإ زوجي الو نأشلا ىوذ نم اهبلطي نمل
- ةمكحما نم رمأب الإ

ناشلا ىوذ بلط ىلع ءانب لدعلاب بناكلا ررحي :
ردمي ىذلا تاءارجإلا قفو قاللعلا تاداهشإ , جاوزلا قئاثو
تالبلا ديدحتب ارارق ريزولا ردصي . ريزولا نم رارق اهب
نايبو اهكسمي نأ.لدعلاب بناكلا ىدع بجي ىتلا سراهغلاو
قئاثولا كلذكو ايروص وأ ةيمألا قئاثولا ظغح ةيغيك
• ةلسا ءارجإ دفع لدعلاب باكلا اهيلإ دغشا ىتلا قاروألاو
: ىتأي ام لدعلاب باكلا ىلع رظحي :

دوقع ىأ ىف تاعيقوتلا ىلع قيدصتلاوأ ريرحت - أ
اهيلع قيدميا وأ امريرحت نأ ىلع نيناوقلا صغت تاررحموأ
. ىرخأ ةؤج صاصتخا نم

ررحم ىأ ىف تاعجفوتلا ىلع قيدصتلا وأ ريرحت - ب
وأ مرييغت وأ هلقن وأ راقع ىلع ىفيع قح ءاشنإب قلعتم
. هلاوز وأ هليدعت

ررحم ىأ ىف تاعيقوتلا ىلع قيدصتلا وأ ريرحت-ج
ةهجلا ةقفاوم نودب ةيراحت ةسؤم نهر وأ ةبه وأ حد نمغتي
.ةقيثولاو ةقفاوملا ةروص ظغح لدعلاب بناكلا ,ىلعو ةمتخلا

وأ هعورف وأ هلوصأ دحأل وأ هل نوكي ءارجإ ىأ ةرخاب - د
مهفم ىأ لوبف وأ ةيصخشب ةعقغم هيف اهيدلاو وأ هتجوز
.لجفك وأ ريبخ وأ مجرف وأ فرد• وأ دهاشك

اذإ ريعلا ىلإ نأشلا ىوذ صخت تامولعم ةيأ ءاشفإ - د
. هتفيظو بس اهيلع عاط١ وأ لصح دق ناك

قئاثو وأ سراهف وأ تالجس ةيأ هترئاد نم لقني نأ - و
زرجي الو هترئاد جراخ ىلإ هتدهع ىف نوكت ةيمسر قاروأ وأ
هذه ىفو ةمكغا نم رارفب الإ ةروظنم ىرعد فلم ىلإامس ىأ أف•
.ةمكغا ريئر نمو هس ةعقوم اهنع ةقدمم ةروص ذ فحي ةلاحلا

ىعن امم ةلماعم ةيأ ءارجال هرقم جراخ لقتني نأ —— ز
ىف ايباتك كلذ ناشلا ووذ بلط اذإ الإ نوناذلا اذه ىف هيلع
. ريزولا اهددحي ىتلا تاءارجإلل اقفوو تالاحلا

تابثإ روتي وأ تاعيقوتلا ىلع قداعي وأ ررحي نأ - ح

决议发布的规则评估翻译或专家的酬劳，并由申请人承担支付。

第十一条　如果申请人、见证人或介绍人不会签名，公证员必须让其捺印，并在文件中说明。

第十二条　如果文件写在多张纸上，公证员应给文件编号，用数字标明文件页码，并加盖公证机构的印章。在每页文件末尾，应有公证员、申请人、见证人、翻译人员或专家（如果有）的签字。

第十三条　公证员应当在文件和索引中以连号编排非官方文件的日期，并编写文件备忘录，备忘录中应确认提交日期和入档编号，公证员在上面签字然后交给申请人。公证书只能提供给提出请求的申请人，除法院命令外，不得将其提供给除申请人之外的第三方。

第十四条　公证员应当根据申请人的要求，按照部长决议发布的程序出具结婚和离婚证明。

第十五条　部长应发布决定，规定公证员必须持有的文件和索引，说明如何保存原始文件或其复印件，以及公证员在进行业务时所需要的文件和书面材料。

第十六条　禁止公证员进行以下行为：

（A）超越法律规定的范围公证合同或文件。

（B）编写或公证任何与不动产物权的创建、转让、变更、修改或撤销相关的文件。

（C）在未经有关方面同意的情况下编写或公证任何包括企业的转让、捐赠或抵押的文件，公证员应保存同意函和文件的副本。

（D）公证员、其长辈、晚辈、妻子或父母在公证行为中有任何个人利益或收受见证人、介绍人、翻译、专家、担保人的好处。

（E）向第三方披露由其职业便利而获得的或看到的专属申请人的信息。

（F）将所在部门的在其职责保管下的任何记录、索引、文件或官方材料转交给外界。除法院的决定外，任何需要被纳入待审案件卷宗的文件，如要被纳入卷宗，在这种情况下，应出具由他和法院院长签署的公证文本。

（G）除非申请人在案件中按照部长规定的程序提出书面申请，否则不可到工作场所之外从事本法规定的任何业务。

（H）在任何交易中，只有在支付完规定的费用

اكاريخ ، فى أية معاملة إلا بعد استيفاء الرسوم المقررة

اسل الرابع

سام عاما

ماده (١٧): يجب أن تكشب جميع انحررات التى يحررها
الكاتب بالعا، ل باللغة العربية ، أما انحررات المكشوبة
بفجر اللغة العربية فلا يجوز للكاتب بالعدل أن يصادق
عليها ما لم يتم ترجمتها إلى اللغة العربية بواسطة مكتب
الترجمة القانونية وعندئذ يتم التصديق على امخرر
وعلج١٠ الترجمة معا.

ماده (١٨): يصدر وزير العدل قرارا بتحديد الرسوم على
تحرير العقود وغيرها ٠٠:، انحررات أو التصديق على
التوقيعات فيها أو إثبات تاريخها ، وكذلك قواعد تقدير
أجور المترجمين و الخبراء ، وذلك بالاتفاق مع وزارة المالية .

ماده (١٩): تعفى من الرسوم جميع المعاملات التى يجريها
الكاتب بالعدل بناء على طلب الجهات الرسمية فى الدولة

后才能在业务中编写或公证合同或证明日期。

第四章 总则

第十七条 公证员编写的所有文件必须用阿拉伯文撰写，用阿拉伯语以外文字编写的文件，除非法律翻译办公室翻译成阿拉伯文，否则公证员不能对其进行公证。届时，应将文件原件和翻译件一起公证。

第十八条 部长应与财政部协调作出决定，以规定合同和其他文件的编写费用，及公证合同的签署费用，并评定翻译人员和专家的报酬标准。

第十九条 公证员应国家要求进行的所有业务，应予以免费。

巴基斯坦

巴基斯坦 1961 年公证条例

THE NOTARIES ORDINANCE, 1961

(XIX of 1961)

CONTENTS

TEXT

THE NOTARIES ORDINANCE, 1961

(XIX of 1961)

[14th June, 1961]

An Ordinance to provide for and to regulate the pro-

巴基斯坦 1961 年公证条例

（1961 年第 19 号文件）

目录

正文

1961 年公证条例

（1961 年第 19 号文件）

[1961 年 6 月 14 日]

本条例提供和规范巴基斯坦公证员执业的有关

fession of notaries in Pakistan

WHEREAS it is expedient to provide for and to regulate the profession of notaries in Pakistan;

NOW, THEREFORE, in pursuance of the Proclamation of the seventh day of October, 1958, and in exercise of all powers enabling him in that behalf the President is pleased to make and promulgate the following Ordinance:

1. Short title, extent and commencement

(1) This Ordinance may be called the Notaries Ordinance, 1961.

(2) It extends to the whole of Pakistan.

(3) It shall come into force on such date as the Provincial Government may, be notification in the official Gazette, appoint.

2. Definitions

In this Ordinance, unless the context otherwise requires

(a) "instrument" includes every document by which any right or liability is, or purports to be, created, transferred, modified, limited, extended, suspended, extinguished or recorded;

(b) "Legal practitioner" means a legal practitioner as defined in the Legal Practitioners and Bar Councils Act, 1973 (XXXV of 1973) ;

(c) "notary" means a person appointed as such under this Ordinance:

(d) "prescribed" means prescribed by rules made under this Ordinance;

(e) "Register" means a Register of Notaries to be maintained under section 4.

3. Power to appoint notaries

The [* * *] Provincial Government, for the whole or any part of the Province, may appoint as notaries any legal practitioners or other persons who possess such qualifications as may be prescribed.

4. Registers

(1) The [* * *] Provincial Government shall maintain, in such form as may be prescribed, a Register of the notaries appointed by that Government and entitled to practise as such under this Ordinance.

(2) Every such Register shall include the following particulars about the notary whose name is entered therein, namely:

(a) his full name, date of birth, residential and profes-

行为。

为了在巴基斯坦提供公证服务的便利和规范公证职业的活动，

总统现根据 1958 年 10 月 7 日的公告，并为了行使其被授予的所有权力，制定和颁布以下条例：

1. 简称、适用范围和生效时间

（1）本条例可简称为《1961 年公证条例》。

（2）本条例适用于整个巴基斯坦地区。

（3）本条例自省政府在官方公报上发布之日起生效。

2. 定义

在本条例中，除文意另有所指：

（a）"文书"包括任何创设、转让、修改、限制、延长、暂停、终止或记载权利或责任的文件；

（b）"法律执业者"按照 1973 年法律执业者与律师委员会法案（1973 年第 35 号法案）中的法律从业者的定义；

（c）"公证员"指根据本条例被委任为公证员的人员：

（d）"规定"指根据本条例的有关规则所作出的规定；

（e）"登记簿"指根据本条例第 4 条进行保存的公证员登记簿。

3. 委任公证员的权力

[* * *] 省政府，对于该省的全部或任何部分，可以委任任何法律执业者或根据规定具备该等资格的其他人员为公证员。

4. 登记簿

（1）[* * *] 省政府应以规定的形式保存经该政府委任并有权根据本条例从事公证活动的公证员的登记簿。

（2）登记簿应当记载有关公证员的下列信息：

（a）其全名、出生日期、住所及工作地址；

sional address;

(b) the date on which his name is entered in the Register;

(c) his qualification; and

(d) any other particulars which may be prescribed.

5. Entry of names in the Register and issue or renewal of certificates of practice

(1) Every notary who intends to practise as such shall, on payment to the Provincial Government of the prescribed fee, if any, be entitled

(a) to have his name entered in the Register maintained by that Government under section 4, and

(b) to a certificate authorizing him to practise for a period of three years from the date on which the certificate is issued to him.

(2) Every such notary who wishes to continue to practise after the expiry of the period of three years referred to in clause (b) of sub-section (1) shall, at such time before the expiry of the said period as may be prescribed, submit to the Provincial Government an application for renewal of his certificate of practice accompanied by the prescribed fee.

(3) On receipt of an application under sub-section (2) from a notary, the Provincial Government may, if, after such inquiry as it may deem fit, it is satisfied that the conduct of the notary during the preceding three years has been unobjectionable, renew the certificate of practice for a period of three years.

(4) A person who has been in practice as a notary for a continues period of six years shall not be appointed as a notary unless a period of not less than three years has elapsed since the expiry of the period for which his certificate of practice was renewed.]

6. Annual publication of lists of notaries

The [* * *] Provincial Government shall, not later than the end of January each year, publish in the Official Gazette a list of notaries appointed by that Government and in practice at the beginning of that year together with such details pertaining to them as may be prescribed.

7. Seal of notaries

Every notary shall have and use, as occasion may arise, a seal of such form and design as may be prescribed.

8. Functions of notaries

(1) A notary may do all or any of the following acts by virtue of his office, namely:

（b）其名字被录入登记簿的日期；

（c）其从业资格；以及

（d）其他特别规定的任何要求。

5. 在登记簿上登记姓名和执业证书的颁发或续期

（1）但凡意图获得公证员执业证书的，都应当向省政府缴纳规定的费用：

（a）将其姓名载入该政府根据本条例第 4 条保存的登记簿；

（b）获得的职业证书有效期为 3 年，自获得颁发证书之日起算。

（2）任何公证员想要在第（1）款（b）项所述的 3 年有效期满后继续执业，应当在规定期限届满之前向省政府提交执业证书续期申请，并支付规定的费用。

（3）省政府在收到公证员根据第（2）款提出的申请后，经过调查对公证员过去 3 年的行为没有异议并符合规定要求的，可以对其执业证书续期 3 年。

（4）除非自其执业证书延期的期限届满不超过 3 年未申请续期，否则任何一名已连续执业满 6 年的公证员不得继续申请续期。

6. 公证员名单的年度公布

[* * *] 省政府应于每年 1 月底之前，在官方公报上公布该政府于本年年初委任并执业的公证员名单，以及规定的与公证员有关的详细资料。

7. 公证员印章

每一位公证员均有权拥有并使用（视情况而定）规定形式及设计的印章。

8. 公证员的职能

（1）公证员可基于其职务从事下列全部或部分行为，即：

(a) verify, authenticate, certify or attest the execution of any instrument;

(b) present any promissory note, hundi or bill of exchange for acceptance or payment or demand better security;

(c) note or protest the dishonour by non-acceptance or non-payment of any promissory note, hundi or bill of exchange or protest for better security or prepare acts of honour under the Negotiable Instruments Act, 1881(XXVI of 1881) , or serve notice of such note or protest;

(d) note and draw up ship's protest, boat's protest or protest relating to demurrage and other commercial matters;

(e) administer oath to, or take affidavit from, any person;

(f) prepare bottomry and respondantia bonds, charter parties and other mercantile documents;

(g) prepare, attest or authenticate any instrument intended to take effect in any country or place outside Pakistan in such form and language as may conform to the law of the place where such deed is intended to operate;

(h) translate, and verify the translation of, any document from one language into another;

(i) any other act which may be prescribed.

(2) No act specified in sub-section (1) shall be deemed to be a notarial act except when it is done by a notary under his signature and Official seal.

9. Bar of practice without certificate

Subject to the provisions of this section, no person shall practise as a notary or do any notarial act under the official seal of a notary unless he holds a certificate of practice in force issued to him under section 5:

Provided that nothing in this sub-section shall apply to the presentation of any promissory note, hundi or bill of exchange for acceptance or payment by the clerk of a notary acting on behalf of such notary.

10. Removal of names from Register

The Provincial Government may, by order, remove from the Register maintained by it under section 4 the name of the notary if he

(a) makes a request to that effect; or

(b) has not paid any prescribed fee required to be paid by him; or

(c) is an undischarged insolvent; or

(d) has been found, upon inquiry in the prescribed manner, to be guilty of such professional or other miscon-

（a）核验、认证、授权、证明任何文书的执行；

（b）就本票、信贷证券或汇票提示承兑、付款或要求更多保障；

（c）根据《1881 年可转让票据法》，就本票、信贷证券、汇票的拒绝承兑或拒付等拒绝兑现行为进行签注或制作拒绝证书，或出具拒绝证书以要求更多保障，或送达上述签注或拒绝证书的通知；

（d）提示并起草海事声明、船舶声明或与滞期费及其他商业安排有关的声明；

（e）主持宣誓或接受宣誓书；

（f）起草押船借贷合同、货船抵押债券、租船合同以及其他商业文件；

（g）准备、证明或认证符合契约所在地法律的形式和语言的文书，使其在巴基斯坦境外的任何国家或地方生效；

（h）翻译或核验文件的翻译；

（i）可以规定的任何其他行为。

（2）第（1）款规定的任何行为只有在公证员附加其签名及公章时才能够被视为公证行为。

9. 未取得证书的执业禁止

根据本条的规定，除非获得根据本条例第 5 条向其颁发的有效执业证书，任何人不得从事公证行为或者利用公证员的公章从事任何公证活动：

但本款不适用于公证员助理代表公证员提示承兑或提示支付本票、信贷证券、汇票的情形。

10. 从登记簿上除名

如果公证员存在下列情形之一，省政府可以根据指示从其根据本条例第 4 条保存的登记簿中对公证员进行除名：

（a）提出有效的除名要求；

（b）未支付任何需由其支付的规定费用；

（c）因为未清偿债务而发生破产；

（d）通过规定的方式进行调查后，政府认为其犯有不再适合担任公证员的罪行或其他不当行为。

duct as, in the opinion of the Government, renders him unfit to practise as a notary.

11. Construction of references to notaries public in other laws

Subject to the provisions of section 16, any reference to a notary public in any other law shall be construed as a reference to a notary entitled to practise under this Ordinance.

11. 其他法律中引用的公证员的解释

在符合本条例第 16 条规定的前提下，任何其他法律对“公证员”概念的引用都应当解释为有资格根据本条例执业的公证员。

12. Penalty for falsely representing to be a notary, etc.

Any person who

(a) falsely represents that he is a notary without being appointed as such, or

(b) practises as a notary or does any notarial act in contravention of section 9, shall be punishable with imprisonment for a term which may extend to three months, or with fine, or with both.

12. 对虚假公证等行为的处罚

任何人不得有下列行为之一：

（a）在其没有被授予公证资格的情况下不当地对外表示其为公证员，或者

（b）违反本条例第 9 条以公证员的身份行事或从事任何公证活动，处以 3 个月以下的监禁或罚款，或二者并行。

13. Cognizance of offences

(1) No court shall take cognizance of any offence committed by a notary in the exercise or purported exercise of his functions under this Ordinance save upon complaint in writing made by an officer authorized by the [* * *] Provincial Government by general or special order in this behalf.

(2) No magistrate other than a magistrate of the first class shall try an offence punishable under this Ordinance.

13. 犯罪行为的认定

（1）除非由 [* * *] 省政府授权的官员以书面形式通过一般或特别指令，否则任何法院不得将公证员行使或准备行使本条例规定的职能认定为犯罪。

（2）除一等地方法官外，任何地方法官不得审判根据本条例规定应予惩罚的罪行。

14. Reciprocal arrangements for recognition of notarial acts done by foreign notaries

If the Federal Government is satisfied that by the law or practice of any country or place outside Pakistan, the notarial acts done by notaries within Pakistan are recognised for all or any limited purposes in that country or place, the Federal Government may, by notification in the official Gazette, declare that the notarial acts lawfully done by notaries within such country or place shall be recognised within Pakistan for all purposes or, as the case may be, for such limited purposes as may be specified in the notification.

14. 关于承认外国公证员公证行为的互惠安排

如果联邦政府认为根据巴基斯坦境外任何国家或地区的法律或惯例，巴基斯坦公证员作出的公证行为在该国家或地区能够被全部或部分承认，联邦政府可以通过官方公报通知声明，就公证员在该国家或地区合法作出的公证行为，应当在巴基斯坦境内承认其所有目的或在公报中可以载明承认的有限目的范围。

15. Power to make rules

(1) The Provincial Government may, by notification in the official Gazette, make rules to carry out the purposes of this Ordinance.

(2) In particular, and without prejudice to the generality of the foregoing power, such rules may provide for all or any of the following matters, namely:

15. 制定规则的权力

（1）省政府可以通过官方公报，制定规则以落实本条例的目的。

（2）在适用于个例，且不损害前述权力的广泛性的前提下，此类规则可就下列全部或部分事项进行规定：

(a) the qualifications of a notary, the form and manner in which applications for appointment as a notary may be made and the disposal of such applications;

(b) the certificates, testimonials or proofs as to character, integrity, ability and competence which any person applying for appointment as a notary may be required to furnish;

(c) the fees payable for appointment as a notary and for the issue and renewal of a certificate of practice, and exemption, whether wholly or in part, from such fees in specified classes of cases;

(d) the fees payable to a notary for doing any notarial act;

(e) the form of Registers and the particulars to be entered therein;

(f) the form and design of the seal of a notary;

(g) the manner in which inquiries into allegations or professional or other misconduct of notaries may be made;

(h) the acts which a notary may do in addition to those specified in section 8 and the manner in which a notary may perform his functions.

16. Saving of Act XXVI of 1881

Nothing in this Ordinance affects the provisions of the Negotiable Instruments Act, 1881(XXVI of 1881) , or any appointment made in pursuance of section 138 of that Act or the powers of any person so appointed.

16-A Delegation

The Provincial Government may, by notification in the official Gazette, direct that all or any of the powers exercisable by it under this Ordinance or the rules made thereunder, shall in such circumstances, within such area, and under such conditions, if any, as may be specified in the notification, be exercisable also by an officer or authority subordinate to it.

（a）公证员的资格、委任申请的形式和方式，以及对申请的处理；

（b）任何申请成为公证员的人都需要提供可能关系其品格、诚信、能力和胜任资格的证书、鉴定书或证明；

（c）任命为公证员、颁发执业证明和执业证明续期需缴纳的费用，以及在特定类别的案件中对于前述费用的全部或部分免除；

（d）公证员从事任何公证行为的费用；

（e）登记簿的形式及其中记载的详情；

（f）公证员印章的形式及设计；

（g）针对公证员犯有职业或其他不当行为的指控进行调查可采取的方式；

（h）除本条例第 8 条载明的行为外，公证员可以采取的行动和履行职责的方式。

16. 对 1881 年第 26 号文件的保留

本条例中的任何内容均不会影响《1881 年可流通票据法案》（1881 年第 26 号）的规定或根据该法令第 138 条作出的任何委任或委任任何人的权力。

16-A 授权

通过官方公报，省政府可以指示其根据本条例或据本条例制定的规则可以行使的全部或部分权力，通知中在载明的具体情况、行使的区域和条件下，也可以由省政府下属的官员或权力机关行使。

菲律宾

2004 年公证执业规则

2004 Rules on Notarial Practice

RULE I
IMPLEMENTATION

SECTION 1. Title.

- These Rules shall be known as the 2004 Rules on Notarial Practice.

SEC. 2. Purposes.

- These Rules shall be applied and construed to advance the following purposes:

(a) to promote, serve, and protect public interest;

(b) to simplify, clarify, and modernize the rules governing notaries public; and

(c) to foster ethical conduct among notaries public.

SEC. 3. Interpretation.

- Unless the context of these Rules otherwise indicates, words in the singular include the plural, and words in the plural include the singular.

RULE II
DEFINITIONS

SECTION1. Acknowledgment.

- "Acknowledgment" refers to an act in which an individual on a single occasion:

(a) appears in person before the notary public and presents an integrally complete instrument or document;

(b) is attested to be personally known to the notary public or identified by the notary public through competent evidence of identity as defined by these Rules; and

(c) represents to the notary public that the signature

《2004 年公证执业规则》

规则一　实施

第 1 条　名称

本规则被称为《2004 年公证执业规则》。

第 2 条　目的

本规则应以促进以下目的的方式适用和解释：

（a）为了促进、服务于以及保护公共利益；

（b）为了简化、澄清以及使公证员规则现代化；以及

（c）为了在公证员之间培养道德行为。

第 3 条　解释

除非本规则上下文中另有说明，单数形式的名词包括复数，而复数形式的名词包括单数。

规则二　定义

第 1 条　承认

"承认"是指在某一单独场合中，个人作出的下列行为：

（a）亲临公证员现场，提交完整的文书或文件；

（b）被证实该个人为公证员所熟识，或可通过本规则规定的有效证据使公证员识别其身份；

（c）向公证员表示在文书或者文件上签名是其为

on the instrument or document was voluntarily affixed by him for the purposes stated in the instrument or document, declares that he has executed the instrument or document as his free and voluntary act and deed, and,if he acts in a particular representative capacity,that he has the authority to sign in that capacity.

了实现文书或者文件的宗旨而自愿进行的署名。声明其已经作为自由并且自愿的行为或者行动执行了该文书或者文件。而且，如果是在特定代表权限范围内所为行为，那么其已经获得了该代表权限范围内签名的授权。

SEC. 2. Affirmation or Oath.

- The term “Affirmation” or “Oath” refers to an act in which an individual on a single occasion:

(a) appears in person before the notary public;

(b) is personally known to the notary public or identified by the notary public through competent evidence of identity as defined by these Rules; and

(c) avows under penalty of law to the whole truth of the contents of the instrument or document.

第 2 条　声明或宣誓

“声明”或“宣誓”是指在某一单独场合中，个人作出的下列行为：

（a）亲临公证员现场；

（b）为公证员个人所熟识，或可通过本规则规定的有效证据使公证员识别其身份；

（c）公开宣称就文书或文件内容的真实性承担法律责任。

SEC. 3. Commission.

- “Commission” refers to the grant of authority to perform notarial acts and to the written evidence of the authority.

第 3 条　任命 / 委任状

“任命 / 委任状”是指授予实施公正行为之职权以及证明该职权的书面凭证。

SEC. 4. Copy Certification.

- “Copy Certification” refers to a notarial act in which a notary public:

(a) is presented with an instrument or document that is neither a vital record, a public record, nor publicly recordable;

(b) copies or supervises the copying of the instrument or document;

(c) compares the instrument or document with the copy; and

(d) determines that the copy is accurate and complete.

第 4 条　副本核实

“副本核实”是指公证员的下列公证行为：

（a）文书或文件提交至公证员，该文书或文件既非重要记录、公共记录，也无公开记录可查；

（b）复制该文书或文件，或监督其复制；

（c）与文书或者文件的复制件进行比较，同时将文书或文件与其副本进行比较；并

（d）确认该副本准确、完整。

SEC. 5. Notarial Register.

- “Notarial Register” refers to a permanently bound book with numbered pages containing a chronological record of notarial acts performed by a notary public.

第 5 条　公证登记簿

“公证登记簿”是指编有页码，按照时间顺序记录公证员所实施的公证行为的永久装订本。

SEC. 6. Jurat.

- “Jurat” refers to an act in which an individual on a single occasion:

(a) appears in person before the notary public and presents an instrument or document;

(b) is personally known to the notary public or identified by the notary public through competent evidence of identity as defined by these Rules;

(c) signs the instrument or document in the presence of the notary; and

第 6 条　宣誓证明

“宣誓证明”是指在某一单独场合中，个人作出的下列行为：

（a）亲临公证员现场，提交文书或文件；

（b）为公证员个人所熟识，或可通过本规则规定的有效证据使公证员识别其身份；

（c）在公证员见证下签署文书或者文件；并

(d) takes an oath or affirmation before the notary public as to such instrument or document.

（d）在公证员面前就该文书或文件进行宣誓或声明。

SEC. 7. Notarial Act and Notarization.

- "Notarial Act" and "Notarization" refer to any act that a notary public is empowered to perform under these Rules.

第 7 条　公证行为及公证

"公证行为"和"公证"是指根据本规则，公证员被授权实施的所有行为。

SEC. 8. Notarial Certificate.

- "Notarial Certificate" refers to the part of, or attachment to, a notarized instrument or document that is completed by the notary public, bears the notary's signature and seal, and states the facts attested to by the notary public in a particular notarization as provided for by these Rules.

第 8 条　公证（证）书

"公证（证）书"是指经公证的文书或文件的一部分或其附件，其由公证员完成，载有公证员的签名和印章，载明了本规则规定的特定公证行为中经公证员证实的事实。

SEC. 9. Notary Public and Notary.

- "Notary Public" and "Notary" refer to any person commissioned to perform official acts under these Rules.

第 9 条　公证人和公证员

"公证人"和"公证员"是指根据本规则被任命实施职务行为的人。

SEC. 10. Principal.

- "Principal" refers to a person appearing before the notary public whose act is the subject of notarization.

第 10 条　当事人

"当事人"是指亲临公证员现场，其行为接受公证的人。

SEC. 11. Regular Place of Work or Business.

- The term "regular place of work or business" refers to a stationary office in the city or province wherein the notary public renders legal and notarial services.

第 11 条　通常工作地或营业地

"通常工作地或营业地"是指公证员于某市或某省提供法律或公证服务的固定办公室。

SEC. 12. Competent Evidence of Identity.

- The phrase "competent evidence of identity" refers to the identification of an individual based on:

(a) at least one current identification document issued by an official agency bearing the photograph and signature of the individual; or

(b) the oath or affirmation of one credible witness not privy to the instrument, document or transaction who is personally known to the notary public and who personally knows the individual, or of two credible witnesses neither of whom is privy to the instrument, document or transaction who each personally knows the individual and shows to the notary public documentary identification.

第 12 条　有关身份的有效证据

"有关身份的有效证据"是指用于识别个人身份的下列证据：

（a）至少一份近期由官方机构出具的带有个人照片和签名的身份证明文件；或者

（b）宣誓或声明，由一名公证员个人熟识且与相关个人相熟，并与相关文书、文件或交易无利害关系的可信证人出具，或由两名熟识相关个人，向公证员出示了其公开身份证明文件，与相关文书、文件或交易无利害关系的可信证人出具。

SEC. 13. Official Seal or Seal.

- "Official seal" or "Seal" refers to a device for affixing a mark, image or impression on all papers officially signed by the notary public conforming the requisites prescribed by these Rules.

第 13 条　公章或者印章

"公章"或"印章"是指符合本规则规定要素，用于在公证员正式签署的文件上加盖记号、图像或印记的设备。

SEC. 14. Signature Witnessing.

-The term "signature witnessing" refers to a notarial

第 14 条　署名见证

"署名见证"是指在某一单独场合中，个人作出

act in which an individual on a single occasion:

(a) appears in person before the notary public and presents an instrument or document;

(b) is personally known to the notary public or identified by the notary public through competent evidence of identity as defined by these Rules; and

(c) signs the instrument or document in the presence of the notary public.

SEC. 15. Court.

- "Court" refers to the Supreme Court of the Philippines.

SEC. 16. Petitioner. -

"Petitioner" refers to a person who applies for a notarial commission.

SEC. 17. Office of the Court Administrator.

- "Office of the Court Administrator" refers to the Office of the Court Administrator of the Supreme Court.

SEC. 18. Executive Judge.

- "Executive Judge" refers to the Executive Judge of the Regional Trial Court of a city or province who issues a notarial commission.

SEC. 19. Vendor –

"Vendor" under these Rules refers to a seller of a notarial seal and shall include a wholesaler or retailer.

SEC. 20. Manufacturer.

- "Manufacturer" under these Rules refers to one who produces a notarial seal and shall include an engraver and seal maker.

RULE III
COMMISSIONING OF NOTARY PUBLIC

SECTION 1. Qualifications.

- A notarial commission may be issued by an Executive Judge to any qualified person who submits a petition in accordance with these Rules.

To be eligible for commissioning as notary public, the petitioner:

(1) must be a citizen of the Philippines;

(2) must be over twenty-one (21) years of age;

(3) must be a resident in the Philippines for at least one (1) year and maintains a regular place of work or business in the city or province where the commission is to be issued;

的下列公证行为：

（a）亲临公证员现场，提交文书或文件；

（b）为公证员个人所熟知，或通过本规则规定的有效证据向公证员证明其身份；并

（c）在公证员在场的情况下签署文书或者文件。

第 15 条　法院

"法院"是指菲律宾最高法院。

第 16 条　申请人

"申请人"是指申请公证员任命的人。

第 17 条　法院行政长官办公室

"法院行政长官办公室"是指最高法院行政长官的办公室。

第 18 条　行政法官

"行政法官"是指某市或某省地区法院签发公证员委任状的行政法官。

第 19 条　供应商

本规则中的"供应商"指的是公证印章的销售商，含批发商和零售商。

第 20 条　生产商

本规则中的"生产商"指的是公证印章的制造商，含雕刻师和铸印人。

规则三　公证员之任命

第 1 条　资格

根据本规则，行政法官可向具备相应资格的申请者颁发公证员委任状。

符合受任为公证员条件者应：

（1）必须是菲律宾公民；

（2）必须年满 21 周岁；

（3）必须在菲律宾居住满 1 年，并且在受任命的市或者省有通常工作地或营业地；

(4) must be a member of the Philippine Bar in good standing with clearances from the Office of the Bar Confidant of the Supreme Court and the Integrated Bar of the Philippines; and

(5) must not have been convicted in the first instance of any crime involving moral turpitude.

SEC. 2. Form of the Petition and Supporting Documents.

- Every petition for a notarial commission shall be in writing, verified, and shall include the following:

(a) a statement containing the petitioner's personal qualifications, including the petitioner's date of birth, residence, telephone number, professional tax receipt, roll of attorney's number and IBP membership number; ,

(b) certification of good moral character of the petitioner by at least two (2) executive officers of the local chapter of the Integrated Bar of the Philippines where he is applying for commission;

(c) proof of payment for the filing of the petition as required by these Rules; and

(d) three (3) passport-size color photographs with light background taken within thirty (30) days of the application. The photograph should not be retouched. The petitioner shall sign his name at the bottom part of the photographs.

SEC. 3. Application Fee.

- Every petitioner for a notarial commission shall pay the application fee as prescribed in the Rules of Court.

SEC. 4.Summary Hearing on the Petition.

- The Executive Judge shall conduct a summary hearing on the petition and shall grant the same if:

(a) the petition is sufficient in form and substance;

(b) the petitioner proves the allegations contained in the petition; and

(c) the petitioner establishes to the satisfaction of the Executive Judge that he has read and fully understood these Rules.

The Executive Judge shall forthwith issue a commission and a Certificate of Authorization to Purchase a Notarial Seal in favor of the petitioner.

SEC. 5. Notice of Summary Hearing.

- (a) The notice of summary hearing shall be published in a newspaper of general circulation in the city or province where the hearing shall be conducted and posted in a conspicuous place in the offices of the Executive

（4）必须是资格完备的菲律宾律师协会成员，具备最高法院律师协会之友办公室和菲律宾统一律师协会出具的许可证；且

（5）不得因违反公德而初审被判有罪。

第 2 条　申请书与支持材料的格式

公证员委任申请应采用书面形式，经过证实，并包括以下内容：

（a）含有申请人个人申请资质信息的声明，包括申请者的生日、住址、电话号码、职业完税收据、律师名单编号和菲律宾统一律师协会会员号；

（b）至少两位菲律宾统一律师协会在申请人申请委任地分会的行政官员就申请人品格良好出具的证明；

（c）按照本规则已支付提交申请所需费用的证明；

（d）3 张在申请日前 30 天内拍摄，浅色背景，护照尺寸的彩色照片。该照片不得修饰。申请人应在照片的底部签上自己的姓名。

第 3 条　申请费

每一位申请公证员委任的人都应缴纳按照《法院规则》规定的申请费用。

第 4 条　关于申请的简易听证

行政法官应当就申请主持简易听证，并在满足下列条件时同等批准：

（a）该申请书就形式和实质而言都是充分的；

（b）申请人证明了其申请书中的陈述；

（c）申请者使行政法官足以确信其已阅读并完全理解了本规则。

行政法官应立即颁发委任状以及购买公证印章授权的证明以支持申请人。

第 5 条　简易听证的通知

（a）简易听证的通知应公布于举办听证的市或省的主流报纸，并张贴于行政法官办公室和法院书记员办公室的显著处。公布费用由申请人承担。通知中可包含多个申请人。

Judge and of the Clerk of Court. The cost of the publication shall be borne by the petitioner. The notice may include more than one petitioner.

(b) The notice shall be substantially in the following form;

NOTICE OF HEARING

Notice is hereby given that a summary hearing on the petition for notarial commission of (name of petitioner) shall be held on (date) at (place) at (time). Any person who has any cause or reason to object to the grant of the petition may file a verified written opposition thereto, received by the undersigned before the date of the summary hearing.

____

Executive Judge

SEC. 6. Opposition to Petition.

- Any person who has any cause or reason to object to the grant of the petition may file a verified written opposition thereto. The opposition must be received by the Executive Judge before the date of the summary hearing.

SEC. 7. Form of Notarial Commission.

- The commissioning of a notary public shall be in a formal order signed by the Executive Judge substantially in the following form:

REPUBLIC OF THE PHILIPPINES
REGIONAL TRIAL COURT OF ____________

This is to certify that (name of notary public) of (regular place of work or business) in (city or province) was on this (date) day of (month) two thousand and (year) commissioned by the undersigned as a notary public, within and for the said jurisdiction, for a term ending the thirty-first day of December (year)

____

Executive Judge

SEC. 8. Period Of Validity of Certificate of Authorization to Purchase a Notarial Seal.

- The Certificate of Authorization to Purchase a Notarial Seal shall be valid for a period of three (3) months from date of issue, unless extended by the Executive Judge.

A mark, image or impression of the seal that may be

（b）该通知应大致采用以下格式：

听证通知

特此通知，关于（申请人的名字）申请公证员委任的听证会将于（日期）（时间）在（地点）举行。任何有反对批准该申请的原因和理由的人可前去提交经证实的书面反对意见，署名其下者已于听证会举办日期前收悉其反对意见。

____

行政法官

第 6 条　针对申请的反对意见

凡就批准申请有反对原因或理由的人，均可提交经证实的书面反对意见。反对意见应由行政法官于简易听证会举办日之前收悉。

第 7 条　公证员委任状的格式

委任公证员，应以行政法官签名的正式命令形式进行，并大致采用以下格式：

菲律宾共和国
____________区域审判法院

兹证明（某市或某省）（通常工作地或营业地）的（公证员姓名），于 20（ ）年（ ）月（ ）日就前述辖区内，被署名其下者任命为公证员，任期至（某年）12 月 31 日。

____

行政法官

第 8 条　购买公证员印章的授权证书的有效期

如未经行政法官延展其有效期，购买公证员印章的授权证书自颁发之日起，于 3 个月内有效。

根据授权证书所购买的印章的标记、图像或者印

purchased by the notary public pursuant to the Certificate shall be presented to the Executive Judge for approval prior to use.

记应提交给行政法官，由行政法官批准使用。

SEC. 9. Form of Certificate of Authorization to Purchase a Notarial Seal.

-The Certificate of Authorization to Purchase a Notarial Seal shall substantially be in the following form:

第 9 条 购买公证员印章的授权证书的格式

购买公证印章的授权证书应大致采用以下格式：

REPUBLIC OF THE PHILIPPINES
REGIONAL TRIAL COURT OF____________
CERTIFICATE OF AUTHORIZATION TO PURCHASE A NOTARIAL SEAL

This is to authorize (name of notary public) of (city or province) who was commissioned by the undersigned as a notary public, within and for the said jurisdiction, for a term ending, the thirty-first of December (year) to purchase a notarial seal.

Issued this (day) of (month) (year).

____

Executive Judge

菲律宾共和国
______________区域审判法院
购买公证员印章的授权证书

（某市或某省）的（公证员姓名）经署名其下者任命，就前述辖区充当公证员，任期结束于（某年）12 月 31 日，特此授权其购买公证员印章。

（年月日）颁发

____

行政法官

SEC. 10. Official Seal of Notary Public.

- Every person commissioned as notary public shall have only one official seal of office in accordance with these Rules.

第 10 条 公证员的公章

根据本规则，凡任命为公证员者都应只有一个公章。

SEC. 11. Jurisdiction and Term.

- A person commissioned as notary public may perform notarial acts in any place within the territorial jurisdiction of the commissioning court for a period of two (2) years commencing the first day of January of the year in which the commissioning is made, unless earlier revoked or the notary public has resigned under these Rules and the Rules of Court.

第 11 条 辖区与任期

除根据本规则和《法院规则》提前撤销公证员任命或公证员自行辞职外，受任公证员者自其受任之年 1 月 1 日起的两年内，可在任命法院辖区内任何地点实施公证行为。

SEC. 12. Register of Notaries Public.

- The Executive Judge shall keep and maintain a Register of Notaries Public in his jurisdiction which shall contain, among others, the dates of issuance or revocation or suspension of notarial commissions, and the resignation or death of notaries public. The Executive Judge shall furnish the Office of the Court Administrator information and data recorded in the register of notaries public. The Office of the Court Administrator shall keep a permanent, complete and updated database of such records.

第 12 条 公证员登记

行政法官应当保存和维护一份其辖区内公证员的登记簿。该登记簿除其他信息外，应当包含公证员任命的颁发、撤销或中止日期，以及公证员的辞职或死亡日期。行政法官应当向法院行政长官办公室提供公证员登记簿中记录的信息和数据。法院管理办公室就此类数据应当保持一份永久、完整、不断更新数据的数据库。

SEC. 13. Renewal of Commission.

- A notary public may file a written application with

第 13 条 委任的续期

公证员可在委任到期前 45 日之内向行政法官提

the Executive Judge for the renewal of his commission within forty-five (45) days before the expiration thereof. A mark, image or impression of the seal of the notary public shall be attached to the application.

Failure to file said application will result in the deletion of the name of the notary public in the register of notaries public.

The notary public thus removed from the Register of Notaries Public may only be reinstated therein after he is issued a new commission in accordance with these Rules.

SEC. 14. Action on Application for Renewal of Commission.

- The Executive Judge shall, upon payment of the application fee mentioned in Section 3 above of this Rule, act on an application for the renewal of a commission within thirty (30) days from receipt thereof. If the application is denied, the Executive Judge shall state the reasons therefor.

RULE IV
POWERS AND LIMITATIONS OF NOTARIES PUBLIC

SECTION 1. Powers.

–(a) A notary public is empowered to perform the following notarial acts:

(1) acknowledgments;

(2) oaths and affirmations;

(3) jurats;

(4) signature witnessings;

(5) copy certifications; and

(6) any other act authorized by these Rules.

(b) A notary public is authorized to certify the affixing of a signature by thumb or other mark on an instrument or document presented for notarization if:

(1)the thumb or other mark is affixed in the presence of the notary public and of two (2) disinterested and unaffected witnesses to the instrument or document;

(2) both witnesses sign their own names in addition to the thumb or other mark;

(3) the notary public writes below the thumb or other mark: "Thumb or Other Mark affixed by (name of signatory by mark) in the presence of (names and addresses of witnesses) and undersigned notary public"; and

(4) the notary public notarizes the signature by thumb or other mark through an acknowledgment, jurat, or signature witnessing.

(c) A notary public is authorized to sign on behalf of

交委任续期的书面申请。申请中应附上公证员印章的标记、图像或者印模。

未提交上述申请的，将导致公证员自公证员登记簿中除名。

从公证登记簿上除名的公证员只有在按照本规则获得新的委任后才能重新载入登记簿。

第 14 条　委任续期申请的处理

在支付本规则第 3 条提到的申请费用后，行政法官应当在收到之日起 30 日内处理公证员委任续期的申请。如果申请被拒绝，行政法官应说明其原因。

规则四　公证员的权力和限制

第 1 条　权力

（a）公证员根据授权实施以下公证行为：

（1）确认；

（2）宣誓与声明；

（3）宣誓证明；

（4）签名见证；

（5）副本核实；以及

（6）本规则授权的任何其他行为。

（b）满足下列条件时，就向其提交进行公证的文书或文件，公证员有权证实其上以拇指指印或其他方式进行的签名；

（1）拇指指印或其他标记在公证员以及两位无利害关系证人的见证下盖在文书或者文件之上；

（2）除拇指指印或其他标记外，两位证人也均进行了署名；

（3）公证员在拇指指印或其他标记下面书写："该拇指指印或其他标记是由（以记号签名者）在（见证人的名字和地址）和签字公证员的见证下加盖的"；同时

（4）公证员应通过确认、宣誓证明或签名见证，对该拇指指印或其他记号之签名进行公证。

（c）满足下列条件时，公证员有权代表因身体原

a person who is physically unable to sign or make a mark on an instrument or document if:

(1) the notary public is directed by the person unable to sign or make a mark to sign on his behalf;

(2) the signature of the notary public is affixed in the presence of two disinterested and unaffected witnesses to the instrument or document;

(3) both witnesses sign their own names ;

(4) the notary public writes below his signature: "Signature affixed by notary in presence of (names and addresses of person and two \2]witnesses)"; and

(5) the notary public notarizes his signature by acknowledgment or jurat.

因不能在法律文书或者文件上签字或盖章的人签字：

（1）公证员受不能签字或做标记以代替签字者的指示，代表其签字；

（2）公证员的签字在两位无利害关系证人的见证下盖在文书或者文件之上；

（3）两位见证人都签下了他们自己的名字；

（4）公证员要在他的签名下写明："公证员签名是在（委托人及两位见证人的名字和住址）见证之下进行的"；同时

（5）公证员通过确认或宣誓证明，对其签名进行公证。

SEC. 2. Prohibitions.

- (a) A notary public shall not perform a notarial act outside his regular place of work or business; provided, however, that on certain exceptional occasions or situations, a notarial act may be performed at the request of the parties in the following sites located within his territorial jurisdiction:

(1) public offices, convention halls, and similar places where oaths of office may be administered;

(2) public function areas in hotels and similar places for the signing of instruments or documents requiring notarization;

(3) hospitals and other medical institutions where a party to an instrument or document is confined for treatment; and

(4) any place where a party to an instrument or document requiring notarization is under detention.

(b) A person shall not perform a notarial act if the person involved as signatory to the instrument or document -

(1) is not in the notary's presence personally at the time of the notarization; and

(2) is not personally known to the notary public or otherwise identified by the notary public through competent evidence of identity as defined by these Rules.

第 2 条　禁令

（a）公证员不能在其通常工作地或营业地以外实施公证行为；

然而，如遇某些例外场合或情形，可应当事方申请在其辖区内的下列地点实施公证行为：

（1）公共机构，会议厅及可能进行就职宣誓的类似地点；

（2）酒店或其他类似地点中，用于签署需公证文书或文件的公共职能区域；

（3）文书或文件的一方当事人为接受治疗而无法离开的医院或其他医疗机构；

（4）待公证文书或文件的一方当事人受押的场所。

（b）文书或文件签署方出现下列情形的，不得实施公证行为：

（1）在公证时未亲自现身于公证员面前；同时

（2）不为公证员所熟识，或无法通过本规则规定的有效证据向公证员证实其身份。

SEC. 3. Disqualifications.

- A notary public is disqualified from performing a notarial act if he:

(a) is a party to the instrument or document that is to be notarized;

(b) will receive, as a direct or indirect result, any commission, fee, advantage, right, title, interest, cash, property, or other consideration, except as provided by

第 3 条　取消资格

如公证员有下列行为，取消公证员实施公证行为的资格：

（a）公证员是待公证法律文书或者文件的一方当事人；

（b）公证员将直接或者间接收受本规则或者法律规定外的任何佣金、费用、好处、权利、所有权、利益、现金、财产或其他报酬的；或者

these Rules and by law; or

(c) is a spouse, common-law partner, ancestor, descendant, or relative by affinity or consanguinity of the principal within the fourth civil degree.

SEC. 4. Refusal to Notarize.

- A notary public shall not perform any notarial act described in these Rules for any person requesting such an act even if he tenders the appropriate fee specified by these Rules if:

(a) the notary knows or has good reason to believe that the notarial act or transaction is unlawful or immoral;

(b) the signatory shows a demeanor which engenders in the mind of the notary public reasonable doubt as to the former's knowledge of the consequences of the transaction requiring a notarial act; and

(c) in the notary's judgment, the signatory is not acting of his or her own free will.

SEC. 5. False or Incomplete Certificate.

- A notary public shall not:

(a) execute a certificate containing information known or believed by the notary to be false.

(b) affix an official signature or seal on a notarial certificate that is incomplete.

SEC. 6. Improper Instruments or Documents.

- A notary public shall not notarize:

(a) a blank or incomplete instrument or document; or

(b) an instrument or document without appropriate notarial certification.

RULE V
FEES OF NOTARY PUBLIC

SECTION 1. Imposition and Waiver of Fees.

- For performing a notarial act, a notary public may charge the maximum fee as prescribed by the Supreme Court unless he waives the fee in whole or in part.

SEC. 2. Travel Fees and Expenses.

- A notary public may charge travel fees and expenses separate and apart from the notarial fees prescribed in the preceding section when traveling to perform a notarial act if the notary public and the person requesting the notarial actagree prior to the travel.

SEC. 3. Prohibited Fees.

- No fee or compensation of any kind, except those expressly prescribed and allowed herein, shall be collected

（c）公证员是当事人的配偶、事实伴侣、长辈、后代或四亲等内之姻亲或血亲。

第 4 条　拒绝公证

如遇下列情形，公证员不得应当事人请求实施任何公证行为，即使当事人已按照本规则规定支付了合理的费用：

（a）公证员知悉或者有合理的理由相信该公证行为或者事务是违法的或者违反道德的；

（b）签字人之举止，令公证员对其先前能否理解待公证事务之后果产生合理怀疑的；以及

（c）据公证员判断，签字人并非基于其自由意志行事。

第 5 条　虚假或者不完整的证书

公证员不能：

（a）签署包含公证员已知或相信为虚假信息的证书；

（b）在不完整的公证书上签署其正式签名或者加盖公章。

第 6 条　不完备的法律文书或者文件

公证员不能就下列材料进行公证：

（a）空白或者不完整的法律文书或者文件；或者

（b）未经合理公证认证的法律文书或者文件。

规则五　公证费用

第 1 条　费用的征收和免除

实施公证行为，公证员可按照最高法院规定收取最高费用，公证员全部或者部分免除费用的除外。

第 2 条　差旅费及开支

如果公证员和要求公证的当事人在出差前达成协议，公证员可在前文条款规定的公证费之外单独收取差旅费及开支。

第 3 条　禁止的费用

除了明确规定并允许收取的费用以外，提供公证服务不得收取或收受任何费用、报酬。

or received for any notarial service.

SEC. 4. Payment or Refund of Fees.

- A notary public shall not require payment of any fees specified herein prior to the performance of a notarial act unless otherwise agreed upon.

Any travel fees and expenses paid to a notary public prior to the performance of a notarial act are not subject to refund if the notary public had already traveled but failed to complete in whole or in part the notarial act for reasons beyond his control and without negligence on his part.

第 4 条 费用的支付或者退还

除另有约定，公证员在实施公证行为前不得要求支付本规则中列明的各项费用。

若公证员已经出差，但由于其不可控制的原因而未能完成全部或部分公证行为，且其不存在过失的，则在实施公证行为前向公证员支付的差旅费和开支不予退还。

SEC. 5. Notice of Fees.

- A notary public who charges a fee for notarial services shall issue a receipt registered with the Bureau of Internal Revenue and keep a journal of notarial fees. He shall enter in the journal all fees charged for services rendered.

A notary public shall post in a conspicuous place in his office a complete schedule of chargeable notarial fees.

第 5 条 费用告示

收取公证服务费的公证员应当出具国税局登记的发票，同时记录一份公证费用日志，其就提供服务收取的全部费用均应记入日志。

公证员应当在其办公室显著位置张贴其完整的公证费用价目表。

RULE VI
NOTARIAL REGISTER

规则六 公证登记簿

SECTION 1. Form of Notarial Register.

- (a) A notary public shall keep, maintain, protect and provide for lawful inspection as provided in these Rules, a chronological official notarial register of notarial acts consisting of a permanently bound book with numbered pages.

The register shall be kept in books to be furnished by the Solicitor General to any notary public upon request and upon payment of the cost thereof. The register shall be duly paged, and on the first page, the Solicitor General shall certify the number of pages of which the book consists.

For purposes of this provision, a Memorandum of Agreement or Understanding may be entered into by the Office of the Solicitor General and the Office of the Court Administrator.

(b) A notary/ public shall keep only one active notarial register at any given time.

第 1 条 公证登记簿的形式

（a）公证员应当按照本规则规定，记录、维护、保护一份公证登记簿，并在依法检查时予以提供，该登记簿需按时间顺序记录，并采用编制了页码的永久装订本形式。

公证登记簿应用书册的形式保存，书册由副总检察长应公证员的要求，经支付其费用后提供给公证员。登记簿应当被适当地标记页码，在第一页，副总检察长应当证实全册页数。

为实现本规定之目的，副总检察长办公室和法院行政长官办公室可以缔结协议备忘录或谅解备忘录。

（b）就任一给定时间段，公证员应只记录一本有效的公证登记簿。

SEC. 2. Entries in the Notarial Register.

- (a) For every notarial act, the notary shall record in the notarial register at the time of notarization the following:

(1) the entry number and page number;

(2) the date and time of day of the notarial act;

(3) the type of notarial act;

第 2 条 公证登记簿的条目

（a）对所有公证行为，公证员都应在公证时将下列内容记入登记簿：

（1）条目编号和页码；

（2）公证行为的日期和时间；

（3）公证行为的种类；

(4) the title or description of the instrument, document or proceeding;

(5) the name and address of each principal;

(6) the competent evidence of identity as defined by these Rules if the signatory is not personally known to the notary;

(7) the name and address of each credible witness swearing to or affirming the person's identity;

(8) the fee charged for the notarial act;

(9) the address where the notarization was performed if not in the notary's regular place of work or business; and

(10) any other circumstance the notary public may deem of significance or relevance.

(b) A notary public shall record in the notarial register the reasons and circumstances for not completing a notarial act.

(c) A notary public shall record in the notarial register the circumstances of any request to inspect or copy an entry in the notarial register, including the requester's name, address, signature, thumbmark or other recognized identifier, and evidence of identity. The reasons for refusal to allow inspection or copying of a journal entry shall also be recorded.

(d) When the instrument or document is a contract, the notary public shall keep an original copy thereof as part of his records and enter in said records a brief description of the substance thereof and shall give to each entry a consecutive number, beginning with number one in each calendar year. He shall also retain a duplicate original copy for the Clerk of Court.

(e) The notary public shall give to each instrument or document executed, sworn to, or acknowledged before him a number corresponding to the one in his register, and shall also state on the instrument or document the page/s of his register on which the same is recorded. No blank line shall be left between entries.

(f) In case of a protest of anydraft, bill of exchange or promissory note, the notary public shall make a full and true record of all proceedings in relation thereto and shall note therein whether the demand for the sum of money was made, by whom, when, and where; whether he presented such draft, bill or note; whether notices were given, to whom and in what manner; where the same was made, when and to whom and where directed; and of every other fact touching the same.

(g) At the end of each week, the notary public shall certify in his notarial register the number of instruments or

（4）法律文书、文件或者程序的标题或者描述；

（5）每一位当事人的姓名和住址；

（6）如果签署方不为公证员所熟知，需记入本规则规定的证明身份的有效证据；

（7）每一位宣誓或者声明当事人身份的可信证人的名字和住址；

（8）公证行为所收取的费用；

（9）如在公证员通常工作地或营业地以外的地点实施公证的，该地点的地址；

（10）公证员认为有意义或者有关联的其他任何情况。

（b）公证员应当在公证登记簿上记录未能完成公证行为的原因和情况。

（c）公证员应当在公证登记簿上记录任何要求查阅或者复制公证登记簿条目的情形，包括申请人的名字、住址、签名、拇指指印或者其他辨认标记，以及身份证据。如拒绝其查阅或者复印日记账条目，原因也应被予以记录。

（d）法律文书或者文件是合同的，公证员应当保存其一份原始副本作为其记录的一部分，同时在前述的记录当中加入其内容的简要描述，并应当给所有条目进行连续编号，每一日历年从 1 开始编号。他也应当保留一份副本给法院书记员。

（e）公证员应为所有在其面前签署、宣誓或确认的法律文书或文件进行编号，标号与其在登记簿上的编号相对应，同时在法律文书或者文件上也应载明其登记簿上相同内容所在的页码。条目之间不能留有空白行。

（f）在制作汇票或者本票拒绝证书时，公证员应当就所有的相关过程作出一份充分、真实的记录，同时应当记录是否有提出金额的要求，由谁于何时何地提出；是否其就此类汇票或本票进行了提示；是否发送的通知，向谁以何种方式发送；相同的通知在哪里作出、什么时候、向谁、在哪里实施；类似的所有其他因素。

（g）每周末，公证员应当在其公证登记簿上确认在其面前签署、宣誓、确认或制作拒绝证书的法律文

documents executed, sworn to, acknowledged, or protested before him; or if none, this certificate shall show this fact.

(h) A certified copy of each month's entries and a duplicate original copy of any instrument acknowledged before the notary public shall, within the first ten (10) days of the month following, be forwarded to the Clerk of Court and shall be under the responsibility of such officer. If there is no entry to certify for the month, the notary shall forward a statement to this effect in lieu of certified copies herein required.

SEC. 3. Signatures and Thumbmarks.

- At the time of notarization, the notary's notarial register shall be signed or a thumb or other mark affixed by each:

(a) principal;

(b) credible witness swearing or affirming to the identity of a principal; and

(c) witness to a signature by thumb or other mark, or to a signing by the notary public on behalf of a person physically unable to sign.

SEC. 4. Inspection, Copying and Disposal.

- (a) In the notary's presence, any person may inspect an entry in the notarial register, during regular business hours, provided;

(1) the person's identity is personally known to the notary public or proven through competent evidence of identity as defined in these Rules;

(2) the person affixes a signature and thumb or other mark or other recognized identifier, in the notarial .register in a separate, dated entry;

(3) the person specifies the month, year, type of instrument or document, and name of the principal in the notarial act oracts sought; and

(4) the person is shown only the entry or entries specified by him.

(b) The notarial register may be examined by a law enforcement officer in the course of an official investigation or by virtue of a court order.

(c) If the notary public has a reasonable ground to believe that a person has a criminal intent or wrongful motive in requesting information from the notarial register, the notary shall deny access to any entry or entries therein.

SEC. 5. Loss, Destruction or Damage of Notarial Register.

- (a) In case the notarial register is stolen, lost, de-

书或者文件的数量；如果没有，那么证书应显示该事实。

（h）每月条目的经核实副本和在公证员面前确认的法律文书的副本原件，应于下个月的前 10 日内，提交至法院书记员处并由其负责。如当月无条目可供核实的，公证员应当提交一份具有同等效力的声明以替代此处所要求的经核实副本。

第 3 条　签字和拇指指印

在公证期间，公证员的公证登记簿应当有下列人员的签字、拇指指印或者其他标记：

（a）当事人；

（b）宣誓或者声明当事人身份的可信证人；

（c）用拇指指印或其他标记替代签名时的见证人，或公证员代表因身体原因不能签字者签名时的见证人。

第 4 条　查阅、复制与处理

（a）如满足下列条件，在公证员在场的情况下，任何人都可以按照规定在常规的工作时间内，要求查阅公证登记簿上的条目：

（1）该人为公证员个人所熟识，或者通过本规则规定的有效证据证明了身份；

（2）于公证登记簿上单列条目，载明日期，由该人在公证登记簿上签名并留下拇指指印或其他标记或其他可识别的标记；

（3）该人就其所查找的公证活动，指明月份、年份、法律文书或文件的类型、当事人的姓名；且

（4）仅向该人展示其指明的条目。

（b）执法人员可于正式调查时，或凭借法院命令，查阅公证登记簿。

（c）如果公证员有合理的理由相信当事人从公证登记簿上获取信息带有犯罪意图或者不正当动机，公证员可拒绝其查看任何其中的条目。

第 5 条　公证登记簿的丢失、毁坏或损坏

（a）公证登记簿被盗、丢失、毁坏、损坏或因其

stroyed, damaged, or otherwise rendered unusable or illegible as a record of notarial acts, the notary public shall, within ten (10) days after informing the appropriate law enforcement agency in the case of theft or vandalism, notify the Executive Judge by any means providing a proper receipt or acknowledgment, including registered mail and also provide a copy or number of any pertinent police report.

他原因致使其不能作为公证行为记录使用或辨识的，公证员应于 10 日内，在通知相应的执法机构后（如涉及盗窃或恶意破坏），以包括挂号信在内的可提供回执或确认的任何方式通知行政法官，并提供相关警方报告的副本或编号。

(b) Upon revocation or expiration of a notarial commission, or death of the notary public, the notarial register and notarial records shall immediately be delivered to the office of the Executive Judge.

（b）在公证委任被撤销或者期满，或者公证员死亡的情况下，公证登记簿以及公证记录应当立即交付行政法官办公室。

SEC. 6. Issuance of Certified True Copies.

- The notary public shall supply a certified true copy of the notarial record, or any part thereof, to any person applying for such copy upon payment of the legal fees.

第 6 条　经核实为真实的副本的签发

凡申请获取经核实为真实的公证记录副本或其中一部分的，经支付法定费用后，公证员应向其提供相应的副本。

RULE VII
SIGNATURE AND SEAL OF NOTARY PUBLIC

规则七　公证员的签名以及印章

SECTION 1. Official Signature.

- In notarizing a paper instrument or document, a notary public shall:

(a) sign by hand on the notarial certificate only the name indicated and as appearing on the notary's commission;

(b) not sign using a facsimile stamp or printing device; and

(c) affix his official signature only at the time the notarial act is performed.

第 1 条　官方签名

公证纸质的法律文书或者文件时，公证员应当：

（a）在公证书上手签自己的名字，该签名应与公证员委任书上的一致；

（b）不能通过传真图章或打印设备签名；同时

（c）只能于实施公证行为时进行官方签名。

SEC. 2. Official Seal.

- (a) Every person commissioned as notary public shall have a seal of office, to be procured at his own expense, which shall not be possessed or owned by any other person.

It shall be of metal, circular in shape, two inches in diameter, and shall have the name of the city or province and the word "Philippines" and his own name on the margin and the roll of attorney's number on the face thereof, with the words "notary public" across the center.

A mark, image or impression of such seal shall be made directly on the paper or parchment on which the writing appears.

(b) The official seal shall be affixed only at the time the notarial act is performed and shall be clearly impressed by the notary public on every page of the instrument or

第 2 条　公章

（a）所有受任公证员者都应当有一枚公章，公章由其自费获取，且该公章不得由他人持有或所有。

公章应当是金属材质、圆形，直径为两英寸，印章的边缘应当有城市名或省名以及“菲律宾”字样与公证员自己的姓名，在其表面有律师编号，在公章的中心刻有“公证员”的字样。

此类印章之标记、图像或者印记都应直接加盖于载有文字的纸张或羊皮纸上。

（b）只能于实施公证行为时加盖公章，且应由公证员清晰加盖于经公证的法律文书或文件的每一页上。

document notarized.

(c) When not in use, the official seal shall be kept safe and secure and shall be accessible only to the notary public or the person duly authorized by him.

(d) Within five (5) days after the official seal of a notary public is stolen, lost, damaged or other otherwise rendered unserviceable in affixing a legible image, the notary public, after informing the appropriate law enforcement agency, shall notify the Executive Judge in writing, providing proper receipt or acknowledgment, including registered mail, and in the event of a crime committed, provide a copy or entry number of the appropriate police record.

Upon receipt of such notice, if found in order by the Executive Judge, the latter shall order the notary public to cause notice of such loss or damage to be published, once a week for three (3) consecutive weeks, in a newspaper of general circulation in the city or province where the notary public is commissioned.

Thereafter, the Executive Judge shall issue to the notary public a new Certificate of Authorization to Purchase a Notarial Seal.

(e) Within five (5) days after the death or resignation of the notary public, or the revocation or expiration of a notarial commission, the official seal shall be surrendered to the Executive Judge and shall be destroyed or defaced in public during office hours.

In the event that the missing, lost or damaged seal is later found or surrendered, it shall be delivered by the notary public to the Executive Judge to be disposed of in accordance with this section.

Failure to effect such surrender shall constitute contempt of court.

In the event of death of the notary public, the person in possession of the official seal shall have the duty to surrender it to the Executive Judge.

SEC. 3. Seal Image.

- The notary public shall affix a single, clear, legible, permanent, and photographically reproducible mark, image or impression of the official seal beside his signature on the notarial certificate of a paper instrument or document.

SEC. 4. Obtaining and Providing Seal.

- (a) A vendor or manufacturer of notarial seals may not sell said product without a written authorization from the Executive Judge.

(b) Upon written application and after payment of the

（c）当公章不被使用的时候，应妥善保管，只有公证员以及经其正式授权的人才能使用。

（d）公证员的公章被盗、丢失、损坏或者因其他原因无法加盖清晰图样的，公证员应于5日内，在通知相应的执法机构之后，以包括挂号信在内的可提供回执或确认的方式书面通知行政法官，如涉及犯罪的，还应提供相关警方记录的副本或条目编号。

收到上述通知后，行政法官应命令公证员将丢失或者损害的通知连续3周，每周在公证员被委任的市或者省的主流报纸予以公布一次。

此后，行政法官应当给公证员颁发一份用以购买公章的新授权证书。

（e）在公证员死亡、辞职或者公证委任被撤销或期满后5日内，公章应当交给行政法官，并在办公时间内公开销毁。

如失踪、遗失或受损的印章其后又被发现或交还，该印章应当由公证员移送给行政法官，由行政法官按照本条规定处置。

拒绝交出公章构成藐视法庭。

在公证员死亡之后，占有该公章的人有义务将公章移送给行政法官。

第3条　印章图像

公证员应于纸质法律文书或文件的公证书上，在其签名旁加盖独立、清晰、易于辨识、永久、可通过影像复制的公章标记、图像或者印记。

第4条　获取以及提供印章

（a）无行政法官书面授权的，公证员印章的供应商或者制造商不得销售该产品。

（b）在提交书面申请并支付完申请费用之后，行

application fee, the Executive Judge may issue an authorization to sell to a vendor or manufacturer of notarial seals after verification and investigation of the latter's qualifications. The Executive Judge shall charge an authorization fee in the amount of Php 4,000 for the vendor and Php 8,000 for the manufacturer. If a manufacturer is also a vendor, he shall only pay the manufacturer's authorization fee.

政法官经过验证和调查公证印章的供应商和经销商的资质，可向其出具销售许可。行政法官应当向供应商收取 4000 菲律宾比索的许可费，向制造商收取 8000 菲律宾比索的许可费。如果制造商同时也是供应商，则只需要支付制造商的许可费。

(c) The authorization shall be in effect for a period of four (4) years from the date of its issuance and may be renewed by the Executive Judge for a similar period upon payment of the authorization fee mentioned in the preceding paragraph.

（c）授权书自出具之日起 4 年内有效，同时经支付前述段落提到的授权费用后，可由行政法官按类似任期时长进行续期。

(d) A vendor or manufacturer shall not sell a seal to a buyer except upon submission of a certified copy of the commission and the Certificate of Authorization to Purchase a Notarial Seal issued by the Executive Judge. A notary public obtaining a new seal as a result of change of name shall present to the vendor or manufacturer a certified copy of the Confirmation of the Change of Name issued by the Executive Judge.

（d）非经提交经核实的委任状副本和行政法官颁发的授权购买公章证书，供应商或制造商不得向买方销售印章。由于更名需要获得新印章的公证员应当向供应商或者制造商提供一份由行政法官所颁发的经核实的更名确认书副本。

(e) Only one seal may be sold by a vendor or manufacturer for each Certificate of Authorization to Purchase a Notarial Seal,

（e）就每份授权购买公章的证书，供应商或者制造商只能销售一枚印章。

(f) After the sale, the vendor or manufacturer shall affix a mark, image or impression of the seal to the Certificate of Authorization to Purchase a Notarial Seal and submit the completed Certificate to the Executive Judge. Copies of the Certificate of Authorization to Purchase a Notarial Seal and the buyer's commission shall be kept in the files of the vendor or manufacturer for four (4) years after the sale.

（f）在销售完成后，供应商或者经销商应在授权购买公章的证书上加盖印章的标记、图像或者印记，并且将完成后的证书交给行政法官。授权购买公章的证书副本和购买者的委任状副本应当在销售之后，由供应商或者经销商保存 4 年。

(g) A notary public obtaining a new seal as a result of change of name shall present to the vendor a certified copy of the order confirming the change of name issued by the Executive Judge.

（g）由于更名需要获得新公章的公证员应当向供应商或者制造商提供一份由行政法官颁发的确认更名命令的经证实副本。

RULE VIII
NOTARIAL CERTIFICATES

规则八　公证（证）书

SECTION 1. Form of Notarial Certificate.

- The notarial form used for any notarial instrument or document shall conform to all the requisites prescribed herein, the Rules of Court and all other provisions of issuances by the Supreme Court and in applicable laws.

第 1 条　公证书的形式

用于任何公证法律文书或者文件的公证形式都应当符合本规则规定的所有要素，符合《法院规则》和其他所有由最高法院发布的规定，并符合现行法律的规定。

SEC. 2. Contents of the Concluding Part of the Notarial Certificate.

- The notarial certificate shall include the following:

第 2 条　公证书结论部分的内容

公证书应当包括以下几个方面：

(a) the name of the notary public as exactly indicated in the commission;

(b) the serial number of the commission of the notary public;

(c) the words "Notary Public" and the province or city where the notary public is commissioned, the expiration date of the commission, the office address of the notary public; and

(d) the roll of attorney's number, the professional tax receipt number and the place and date of issuance thereof, and the IBP membership number.

（a）委任状上明确载明的公证员姓名；

（b）公证员委任状的序列号；

（c）"公证员"字样、公证员被委任的城市或者省、委任期满的日期、公证员的办公地址；以及

（d）律师名单编号、职业完税收据的编号以及出具此公证书的地点和日期和菲律宾统一律师协会会员号。

RULE IX
CERTIFICATE OF AUTHORITY OF NOTARIES PUBLIC

规则九　公证员的授权证书

SECTION 1. Certificate of Authority for a Notarial Act.

- A certificate of authority evidencing the authenticity of the official seal and signature of a notary public shall be issued by the Executive Judge upon request in substantially the following form:

CERTIFICATE OF AUTHORITY FOR A NOTARIAL ACT

I, (name, title, jurisdiction of the Executive Judge), certify that (name of notary public), the person named in the seal and signature on the attached document, is a Notary Public in and for the (City/Municipality/Province) of the Republic of the Philippines and authorized to act as such at the time of the document's notarization.

IN WITNESS WHEREOF, I have affixed below my signature and seal of this office this (date) day of (month) (year).

____

(official signature)
(seal of Executive Judge)

第 1 条　对公证行为的授权证书

一份证明公章和公证员签名真实性的授权证书应由行政法官大致按照以下格式颁发：

公证行为的授权证书

我，（姓名，头衔，行政法官的辖区），证实（公证员的姓名），即所附文件上的印章和签名中指明的人，是菲律宾共和国（某市 / 某自治市 / 某省）的公证员，被授权于文件所附公证书载明的期限内从事公证。

为就此进行证明，我已于今日（年月日）将我的职位签名和职位印章附于其下。

____

（官方签名）
（行政法官印章）

RULE X
CHANGES OF STATUS OF NOTARY PUBLIC

规则十　公证员的情况变更

SECTION 1. Change of Name and Address.

Within ten (10) days after the change of name of the notary public by court order or by marriage, or after ceasing to maintain the regular place of work or business, the notary public shall submit a signed and dated notice of such fact to the Executive Judge.

The notary public shall not notarize until:

第 1 条　姓名和住址的变更

在公证员由于法院令或者婚姻，或者在中止维持固定的工作或者商业地点之后的 10 日之内，公证员应当向行政法官提交一份签署好名字和日期的有关该事实的通知。

公证员不得进行公证，直到：

(a) he receives from the Executive Judge a confirmation of the new name of the notary public and/or change of regular place of work or business; and

(b) a new seal bearing the new name has been obtained.

The foregoing notwithstanding, until the aforementioned steps have been completed, the notary public may continue to use the former name or regular place of work or business in performing notarial acts for three (3) months from the date of the change, which may be extended once for valid and just cause by the Executive Judge for another period not exceeding three (3) months.

（a）公证员收到行政法官所颁发的新的公证员名字和 / 或固定的工作或商业地点的授权证书的确认书；

（b）获得刻有新名字的公章。

尽管前面已经提到，直到前述步骤完成，公证员可以继续使用先前的名字或固定的工作或商业地，从变更之日起实施 3 个月公证行为，并且可延长 1 次有效期，但经行政法官同意的延期不能超过 3 个月。

SEC. 2. Resignation.

- A notary public may resign his commission by personally submitting a written, dated and signed formal notice to the Executive Judge together with his notarial seal, notarial register and records. Effective from the date indicated in the notice, he shall immediately cease to perform notarial acts. In the event of his incapacity to personally appear, the submission of the notice may be performed by his duly authorized representative.

第 2 条　辞职

公证员可以通过个人提交一份书面的、签好日期和姓名的正式的通知给行政法官，并且附上他的公章、公证登记簿和公证记录的方式辞职。从通知上显示的有效期开始，他应当立即停止实施公证行为。如果他不能亲自办理，通知的提交可由经正式授权代表履行之。

SEC. 3. Publication of Resignation.

- The Executive Judge shall immediately order the Clerk of Court to post in a conspicuous place in the offices of the Executive Judge and of the Clerk of Court the names of notaries public who have resigned their notarial commissions and the effective dates of their resignation.

第 3 条　辞职的公布

行政法官应当立即命令法院书记员在行政法官办公室和法院书记员办公室显眼的地方张贴辞职的公证员的姓名及其辞职的生效期。

RULE XI
REVOCATION OF COMMISSION AND DISCIPLINARY SANCTIONS

规则十一　撤销委任和纪律处分

SECTION 1. Revocation and Administrative Sanctions.

- (a) The Executive Judge shall revoke a notarial commission for any ground on which an application for a commission may be denied.

(b) In addition, the Executive Judge may revoke the commission of, or impose appropriate administrative sanctions upon, any notary public who:

(1) fails to keep a notarial register;

(2) fails to make the proper entry or entries in his notarial register concerning his notarial acts;

(3) fails to send the copy of the entries to the Executive Judge within the first ten (10) days of the month following;

第 1 条　撤销和行政处分

（a）如公证员出现可导致委任申请被拒的理由的，行政法官可撤销其任命。

（b）此外，行政法官对有下列行为之公证员可以撤销委任或者处以适当的行政处罚：

（1）没有记录公证登记簿的；

（2）未能就其公证行为在其公证登记簿上编制正确的条目；

（3）未能在下一月份的前 10 天内将条目副本送交行政法官；

(4) fails to affix to acknowledgments the date of expiration of his commission;

(5) fails to submit his notarial register, when filled, to the Executive Judge;

(6) fails to make his report, within a reasonable time, to the Executive Judge concerning the performance of his duties, as may be required by the judge;

(7) fails to require the presence of a principal at the time of the notarial act;

(8) fails to identify a principal on the basis of personal knowledge or competent evidence;

(9) executes a false or incomplete certificate under Section 5, Rule IV;

(10) knowingly performs or fails to perform any other act prohibited or mandated by these Rules; and

(11) commits any other dereliction or act which in the judgment of the Executive Judge constitutes good cause for revocation of commission or imposition of administrative sanction.

(c) Upon verified complaint by an interested, affected or aggrieved person, the notary public shall be required to file a verified answer to the complaint.

If the answer of the notary public is not satisfactory, the Executive Judge shall conduct a summary hearing. If the allegations of the complaint are not proven, the complaint shall be dismissed. If the charges are duly established, the Executive Judge shall impose the appropriate administrative sanctions. In either case, the aggrieved party may appeal the decision to the Supreme Court for review. Pending the appeal, an order imposing disciplinary sanctions shall be immediately executory, unless otherwise ordered by the Supreme Court.

(d) The Executive Judge may motu proprio initiate administrative proceedings against a notary public, subject to the procedures prescribed in paragraph (c) above and impose the appropriate administrative sanctions on the grounds mentioned in the preceding paragraphs (a) and (b).

SEC. 2. Supervision and Monitoring of Notaries Public.

- The Executive Judge shall at all times exercise supervision over notaries public and shall closely monitor their activities.

SEC. 3. Publication of Revocations and Administrative Sanctions.

- The Executive Judge shall immediately order the Clerk of Court to post in a conspicuous place in the offices

（4）未能在出具确认书时加盖其委任期满之日；

（5）如有填写登记簿的，未能将其公证登记簿提交给行政法官；

（6）未能按照行政法官的要求，在合理的时间内，就其履行职责的表现向行政法官提交报告；

（7）未能在实施公证行为时，要求当事人在场；

（8）未能根据个人熟识或有效证据识别当事人的身份；

（9）签署了规则四第 5 条规定的虚假或不完整的证书；

（10）故意实施其他法律禁止的行为，或故意不履行本规则所要求实施的行为；以及

（11）有其他的玩忽职守行为使行政法官有正当理由撤销委任或者实施行政处罚的。

（c）一旦被有利害关系、受影响或者权利受到侵害者投诉，且该投诉是经过核实的，公证员应对该投诉作出经核实的回答。

如果公证员的答复不令人满意，那么行政法官应当组织一场简易程序听证。如果投诉的指控无法证明，那么该投诉将会被驳回。如果指控正式确立，行政法官将会依法给予其相应的行政处罚。在任何情况下，受害方可上诉该决定至最高法院进行审查。上诉期间，施加纪律处分的命令暂不生效，最高法院另有命令的除外。

（d）行政法官可按照（c）款规定之步骤，自行发起对公证员的行政程序，并可基于（a）款和（b）款提及的理由，对其施加合适的行政处罚。

第 2 条　公证监督和监控

行政法官应当随时监督公证员，并且应当密切地监控其活动。

第 3 条　撤销委任以及行政处罚的公布

行政法官应当立即命令法院书记员在将被行政处罚的或者被撤销委任的公证员的名字贴示于行政法官

of the Executive Judge and of the Clerk of Court the names of notaries public who have been administratively sanctioned or whose notarial commissions have been revoked.

办公室和法院书记员办公室的显著处。

SEC. 4. Death of Notary Public.

- If a notary public dies before fulfilling the obligations in Section 4(c), Rule VI and Section 2(e), Rule VII, the Executive Judge, upon being notified of such death, shall forthwith cause compliance with the provisions of these sections.

第 4 条　公证员死亡

如果公证员在履行规则六第 4 节（c）款，规则七第 2 条（e）款义务之前死亡的，行政法官得到死亡通知后，应当立即促使这些条款的规定得到遵守。

RULE XII
SPECIAL PROVISIONS

规则十二　特别条款

SECTION 1. Punishable Acts.

- The Executive Judge shall cause the prosecution of any person who:

(a) knowingly acts or otherwise impersonates a notary public;

(b) knowingly obtains, conceals, defaces, or destroys the seal, notarial register, or official records of a notary public; and

(c) knowingly solicits, coerces, or in any way influences a notary public to commit official misconduct.

第 1 条　可罚行为

行政法官应对以下人进行起诉：

（a）故意冒充公证员；

（b）故意获取、隐藏、损伤或损毁公章、公证登记簿或者公证员官方记录的；

（c）故意唆使、强迫或者以任何方式影响公证员去实施职务不当行为。

SEC 2. Reports to the Supreme Court.

- The Executive Judge concerned shall submit semestral reports to the Supreme Court on discipline and prosecution of notaries public.

第 2 条　向最高法院报告

相关行政法官应当每半年就公证员纪律和诉讼事项向最高法院提交报告。

RULE XIII
REPEALING AND EFFECTIVITY PROVISIONS

规则十三　废止和有效性的规定

SECTION 1. Repeal.

- All rules and parts of rules, including issuances of the Supreme Court inconsistent herewith, are hereby repealed or accordingly modified.

第 1 条　废止

所有规则及其组成部分，包括由最高法院颁布的，与本规则不一致之处特此废止或进行相应的修正。

SEC. 2. Effective Date.

- These Rules shall take effect on the first day of August 2004, and shall be published in a newspaper of general circulation in the Philippines which provides sufficiently wide circulation.

第 2 条　生效日期

本规则于 2004 年 8 月 1 日起生效，并应公布于菲律宾国内发行范围足够广泛的主流报纸。

Promulgated this 6th day of July, 2004.

(Sgd.) Davide, Jr. C.J., Puno, Vitug, Panganiban, Quisumbing, Ynarez-Santiago, Sandoval-Gutierrez, Carpio, Austria-Martinez, Corona, Carpio-Morales, Callejo, Sr., Azcuna and Tinga, JJ.

2004 年 7 月 6 日发布

（签署人）Davide, Jr. C.J., Puno, Vitug, Panganiban, Quisumbing, Ynarez-Santiago, Sandoval-Gutierrez, Carpio, Austria-Martinez, Corona, Carpio-Morales, Callejo, Sr., Azcuna and Tinga, JJ.

新加坡

公证法（1997 年修订版）

Notaries Public Act
(CHAPTER 208)

Legislative History
NOTARIES PUBLIC ACT
(CHAPTER 208)
(Original Enactment: M Ordinance 41 of 1959)
REVISED EDITION 1997
(20th December 1997)
An Act relating to notaries public.
[18th March 1965]

Short title

1. This Act may be cited as the Notaries Public Act.

Interpretation

2. In this Act, unless the context otherwise requires—
"notary public" means a person who has been ap-

公证法
（第 208 章）

立法的历史
公证法
（第 208 章）
（原法案：马来西亚 1959 年第 41 号条例）
1997 年修订版
（1997 年 12 月 20 日）
有关公证员的法律
（1965 年 3 月 18 日）

简称

1. 本法可引述为《公证法》。

解释

2. 在本法当中，除非上下文另有规定，否则
"公证员" 是指按照第 3 条委任为公证员的人，

pointed as a notary public under section 3 but does not include any person whose appointment has been revoked under section 5;

"Senate" means the Senate of the Singapore Academy of Law constituted under the Singapore Academy of Law Act (Cap. 294A).

[34/95]

但是不包括按照第 5 条委任被撤销的人；

"评议会"是指新加坡法律学会下属的新加坡法律学会评议会。

Act（Cap. 294A）.

[34/95]

Appointment of notaries public

3.

—(1) The Senate may, from time to time, appoint fit and proper persons to be notaries public for a period not exceeding 12 months.

[18/83; 34/95]

(2) No person shall be appointed as a notary public unless he is a practising advocate and solicitor in Singapore and has so practised for not less than 7 years.

(3) The Senate shall not make any appointment under this section without consulting the Council of the Law Society of Singapore constituted under the Legal Profession Act

(Cap. 161).

[18/83; 34/95]

(4) In making any appointment under this section, the Senate shall have regard to the number of notaries public already practising in the place where the applicant proposes to practise and to the convenience of the inhabitants of that place, but, subject to this, the Senate shall have absolute discretion in making or refusing to make any such appointment and there shall be no appeal from its decision.

[34/95]

(5) If it appears to the Senate that any notary public is about to be absent from Singapore for a period exceeding one month, the Senate may appoint any person, being a practising advocate and solicitor in Singapore, to be a notary public temporarily during the absence of that notary public from Singapore.

(6) No temporary appointment of a notary public shall have effect for a period longer than 12 months and any such appointment shall lapse on the death or on the return to Singapore of the notary public on account of whose departure from Singapore the appointment was made.

(7) Every appointment under subsection (1) or subsection (5) and the lapse of every temporary appointment under subsection (6) shall be published in the Gazette.

公证员的委任

3.

（1）评议会可随时任命适当人选担任公证员，任期不超过 12 个月。

[18/83；34/95]

（2）任何人不得被任命为公证员，除非他是一位在新加坡有实践经验的辩护律师或初级律师，并且其执业经验不少于 7 年。

（3）评议会在没有咨询根据《法律职业法》建立的新加坡法律协会理事会的情况下，不能按照该条规定作出任何任命。

（Cap. 161）.

[18/83；34/95]

（4）在根据本条作出任何任命时，评议会应考虑申请人提出从业的地方已有的从业公证员数量，和当地居民的便利程度。评议会在据此作出或者拒绝任何委任方面享有绝对的自由裁量权，并享有不被上诉的权利。

[34/95]

（5）如果任何公证员将要离开新加坡超过 1 个月，评议会可以委任任何在新加坡有从业经验的辩护律师或初级律师作为该公证员离开新加坡期间的临时公证员。

（6）临时公证员委任的效力不超过 12 个月，任何临时委任都因死亡而失效或者因离开新加坡的被委任公证员回到新加坡而失效。

（7）所有第（1）款或者第（5）款下的任命以及第（6）款下的临时任命的失效都应在公报上公告。

Privileges of notaries public

4.

—(1) Every notary public shall have and may exercise within Singapore all the powers and functions which are ordinarily exercised by notaries public in England.

[18/83]

(2) Except for the purposes of and to the extent necessary to give effect to subsection (3), powers under subsection (1) shall not include power to administer any oath or affirmation in connection with any affidavit or statutory declaration which is executed for the purpose of being used in any court or place within Singapore or to take or attest any such affidavit or statutory declaration.

(3) Without prejudice to the generality of the powers and functions conferred by subsection (1), a notary public may —

(a) administer any oath or affirmation in connection with any affidavit or statutory declaration which is executed—

(i) for the purpose of confirming or proving the due execution of any document;

(ii) by any master or member of the crew of any vessel in respect of any matter concerning the vessel; or

(iii) for the purpose of being used in any court or place outside Singapore;

(b) take or attest any affidavit or statutory declaration referred to in paragraph (a); and

(c) have and exercise such other powers and functions as may be prescribed.

Misconduct of notaries public

5. If it appears to the Senate that any person being a notary public —

(a) has become a bankrupt or has made an arrangement with his creditors;

(b) has been struck off the roll of advocates and solicitors of Singapore; or

(c) has been found to be guilty of such professional or other misconduct as, in the opinion of the Senate, renders him unfit to practise as a notary public, the Senate shall by order revoke the appointment of the person and shall cause the order to be published in the Gazette.

[18/83; 34/95]

公证员的特权

4.

（1）每一位公证员在新加坡都应当具有并且能够行使通常在英国公证员能够行使的所有权力和职责。

[18/83]

（2）除为实现第（3）款的目的，并采取令第（3）款生效所必须的程度外，在第（1）款中的权力不应当包括执行任何与被要求在新加坡法院或地区行使，或证明的宣誓书或者法定声明有关的宣誓或者声明的权力。

（3）在不损害第（1）款中一般性的权利和职责的情况下，公证员可以：

（a）实施与下列宣誓书或法定声明有关的宣誓或声明——

（i）为确认或证实文件执行到期（而签署的宣誓书或法定声明）；

（ii）由任何船只的船长或船员成员就该船只相关事宜（而签署的宣誓书或法定声明）；或

（iii）为用于新加坡境外的法院或者其他地方（而签署的宣誓书或法定声明）。

（b）采取或者证实任何在（a）款当中涉及的宣誓书或者法定声明；同时

（c）按照规定享有并且履行这些权力和职责。

公证员的不当行为

5. 评议会认为，任何作为公证员的人：

（a）已经破产或与其债权人作出安排；

（b）已经从新加坡的辩护律师和初级律师名册中除名；或者

（c）已经发现其存在失职行为或者有其他不当的行为，按照评议会的意见，其不再适合作为公证员，评议会应该命令撤销该人的委任并将该命令在公报上公布。

[18/83；34/95]

Revocation of appointment of notary public under special circumstances

6. The Senate may, by notification in the Gazette, revoke the appointment of a notary public if the notary public requests that his appointment be revoked.

[18/83; 34/95]

Penalty for exercise of functions of notary public by unauthorised persons

7. Any person who exercises within Singapore any of the functions of a notary public otherwise than in accordance with the provisions of this Act shall be guilty of an offence and shall be liable on conviction before a District Judge to a fine not exceeding $10,000.

[20/2007 wef 01/06/2007]

Rules

8.

—(1) The Chief Justice, after consultation with the Senate, may make rules —

(a) for the guidance and control of persons entitled to exercise the functions of a notary public under this Act;

(b) to fix the fees payable to notaries public;

(c) to fix the fees payable to the Singapore Academy of Law by any person on appointment as a notary public, and on renewal of such appointment; and

(d) prescribing the powers and functions of notaries public.

[34/95]

(2) All rules made under this section shall be published in the Gazette, and shall come into force on the date of such publication or on such later date as may be specified in the rules.

LEGISLATIVE HISTORY
NOTARIES PUBLIC ACT
(CHAPTER 208)

This Legislative History is provided for the convenience of users of the Notaries Public Act. It is not part of the Act.

1. Malaysian Ordinance 41 of 1959—Notaries Public Ordinance 1959

Date of First Reading: 24 June 1959

(Bill published on 26 May 1959. No Bill number

在特殊情况下公证员委任的撤销

6. 如果公证员申请撤销其委任，评议会可以通过在公报上公告的方式，撤销该公证员的委任。

[18/83 ；34/95]

对未经授权的人行使公证员职责的处罚

7. 在新加坡境内违反本法规定，行使公证员职能者，构成违法行为，经地区法院法官定罪后，将承担最高 1 万美元罚款的责任。

[20/2007 wef 01/06/2007]

规则

8.

（1）首席法官，在与评议会磋商后，可就下列事项订立规则：

（a）指导和控制依据本法有权履行公证员职责的人员；

（b）确定支付给公证员的费用；

（c）确定被委任公证员向新加坡法律学会支付的费用，以及该委任续期的费用；同时

（d）规定公证员的权力和职责。

[34/95]

（2）根据本条订立的所有规则应会在公报上刊登，并在公布之日生效或在规则指定的更晚的日期生效。

立法史
公证法
（第 208 章）

该立法史出于《公证法》使用者便利而提供，并非法案组成部分。

1. 马来西亚 1959 年第 41 号条例——1959 年《公证员条例》

初审日期：1959 年 6 月 24 日

（法案在 1959 年 5 月 26 日出版。并没有给出法

given)

Date of Second and Third Readings: 25 June 1959

Date of commencement: 1 October 1959

2. Malaysian Ordinance 7 of 1961—Notaries Public (Amendment) Act 1961

Date of First Reading: 30 November 1960

(Bill published on 8 December 1960. No Bill number given)

Date of Second and Third Readings: 9 March 1961

Date of commencement: 1 June 1961

3. L.N. 98/1965—Modification of Laws (Notaries Public) (Extension and Modification) Order 1965

(This Order was made under the Malaysia Act)

Date of commencement: 18 March 1965

4. 1970 Revised Edition—Notaries Public Act (Chapter 11)

Date of operation: 1 March 1971

5. Act 18 of 1983—Notaries Public (Amendment) Act 1983

Date of First Reading: 30 August 1983

(Bill No. 12/1983 published on 7 September 1983)

Date of Second and Third Readings: 20 December 1983

Date of commencement: 20 January 1984

6. 1985 Revised Edition—Notaries Public Act

Date of operation: 30 March 1987

7. Act 34 of 1995—Singapore Academy of Law (Amendment) Act 1995

(Consequential amendments made by)

Date of First Reading: 7 August 1995

(Bill No. 27/1995 published on 8 August 1995)

Date of Second and Third Readings: 27 September 1995

Date of commencement: 1 January 1996

(section 11 — Consequential amendments to Notaries Public Act)

8. 1997 Revised Edition—Notaries Public Act

Date of operation: 20 December 1997

9. Act 20 of 2007—Legal Profession (Amendment) Act 2007

(Consequential amendments made by)

Date of First Reading: 9 March 2007

(Bill No. 10/2007 published on 10 March 2007)

Date of Second and Third Readings: 12 April 2007

Date of commencement: 1 June 2007

(Item (1) of the Schedule — Amendment of Notaries Public Act)

案的编号）

二审及三审日期：1959 年 6 月 25 日

生效日期：1959 年 10 月 1 日

2. 马来西亚 1961 年第 7 号条例——1961 年《公证员（修正案）法》

初审日期：1960 年 11 月 30 日

（法案在 1960 年 12 月 8 日出版，没有给出法案的编号）

二审及三审日期：1961 年 3 月 9 日

生效日期：1961 年 6 月 1 日

3. L.N. 98/1965——《诸法修正》(公证员)(扩展和修改)1965 年命令

（该命令是根据马来西亚法作出的）

生效日期：1965 年 3 月 18 日

4. 1970 年修订版——《公证法》(第 11 章)

实行日期：1971 年 3 月 1 日

5. 1983 年第 18 号法案——1983 年《公证员（修正案）法》

初审日期：1983 年 8 月 30 日

（1983 年第 12 号法案在 1983 年 9 月 7 日出版）

二审及三审日期：1983 年 12 月 20 日

生效日期：1984 年 1 月 20 日

6. 1985 年修订版——《公证法》

实行日期：1987 年 3 月 30 日

7. 1995 年第 34 号法案——由 1995 年《新加坡法律学会（修正案）法》修订

初审日期：1995 年 8 月 7 日

（1995 年第 27 号法案于 1995 年 8 月 8 日出版）

二审及三审日期：1995 年 9 月 27 日

生效日期：1996 年 1 月 1 日

（第 11 条——对《公证法》的修正案）

8. 1997 年修订版——《公证法》

实行日期：1997 年 12 月 20 日

9. 2007 年第 20 号法案——由 2007 年《法律职业（修正案）法》修订

初审日期：2007 年 3 月 9 日

（2007 年第 10 号法案于 2007 年 3 月 10 日出版）

二审及三审日期：2007 年 4 月 12 日

生效日期：2007 年 6 月 1 日

（计划表项目 1——《公证法》修正案）

公证员规则（1999 年修订版）

NotariesPublic Rules

1 Citation
2 Definitions
3 Fees
4 Duration of appointment
5 Application procedure
6 Register of notaries public
7 Instrument of appointment
8 (Deleted)
9 Register of documents administered

FIRST SCHEDULE
SECOND SCHEDULE

公证员规则

1. 引述
2. 定义
3. 费用
4. 委任期限
5. 申请程序
6. 公证员注册
7. 委任文书
8.（已删除）
9. 文件管理登记

第一计划表
第二计划表

Legislative History
NOTARIES PUBLIC ACT
(CHAPTER 208, SECTION 8)
NOTARIES PUBLIC RULES
R 1
REVISED EDITION 1999
(1st January 1999)
[1st January 1996]

立法的历史
公证法案
（第 208 章，第 8 条）
公证员规则
R1
1999 年修订版
（1999 年 1 月 1 日）
[1996 年 1 月 1 日]

Citation

1. These Rules may be cited as the Notaries Public Rules.

Definitions

2. In these Rules —

”Academy” means the Singapore Academy of Law constituted under the Singapore Academy of Law Act (Cap. 294A);

“affidavit” includes affirmation, statutory or other declaration;

“folio” means 100 words, each figure being counted as one word;

引述

1. 本规则可引述为《公证员规则》。

定义

2. 在本规则中

“学会”指的是按照《新加坡法律学会法》组建的新加坡法律学会（Cap. 294A）；

“宣誓书”包括证词，法定或其他的声明；

“单位字数”是指 100 字，每个数字被算作 1 个字；

"oath" includes affirmation and declaration;
"Secretary" means the Secretary to the Senate;
"Senate" means the Senate of the Academy;
"swear" includes affirm and declare.

Fees

3. The fees payable to the Academy for appointment or reappointment of notaries public, and the fees payable to a notary public, shall be as set out in the First Schedule.

[S 460/2008 wef 15/09/2008]

Duration of appointment

4. Notaries public shall be appointed for a period of one year and may be reappointed for each subsequent year as the Senate may, in its discretion, decide.

Application procedure

5.

(1) Applications for reappointment as notaries public shall be lodged with the Secretary 2 clear months before the expiry of each preceding period of appointment.

(2) An applicant shall lodge with the Secretary an application for his appointment or reappointment as a notary public, setting forth —

(a) his date of admission to the roll of the Supreme Court and the number of years that he has been in practice;

(b) whether he is or has ever been an undischarged bankrupt or has made an arrangement with his creditors;

(c) whether he has ever been convicted of any offence;

(d) whether he has ever been found guilty of any professional misconduct; or

(e) whether he is or has been the subject of disciplinary proceedings under Part VII of the Legal Profession Act (Cap. 161); and, if so, the date and nature of the complaint, whether the complaint resulted in the appointment of a Disciplinary Committee, and if so, the result of its inquiry.

Register of notaries public

6. The particulars of every notary public appointed by the Senate shall be registered with the Senate in a register maintained by the Secretary in such form as the Senate may determine.

"宣誓"包括确认和声明；
"秘书"是指评议会秘书；
"评议会"指学会的评议会；
"发誓"包括确认及声明。

费用

3. 因任命或重新任命为公证员而支付给学会的费用标准，以及向公证员支付的费用标准，应于第一计划表中列明。

[S 460/2008 wef 15/09/2008]

委任期限

4. 公证员的任命期为 1 年。评议会可在其自由裁量权范围内决定能否在下一年连任。

申请程序

5.

（1）申请公证员的连任应当在前述的委任期限届满前 2 个月内向评议会提出。

（2）申请人应向评议会申请公证员任命或重新任命，申请中阐明：

（a）他进入最高法院名单的日期，以及他已经从业的年数；

（b）他是否为或者曾经是一位未清偿债务的破产者或曾与其债权人达成和解协议；

（c）他是否曾被判犯有任何罪行；

（d）他是否曾被发现有任何失职行为；或者

（e）他是否正在或曾经接受过《法律职业法》（Cap. 161）第 7 条规定的纪律程序；如果是的话，被投诉日期和性质，投诉是否导致组成了纪律委员会；如果是的话，委员会调查的结果。

公证员的注册

6. 每一位由评议会任命的公证员的详情都应该以评议会确定的格式，向评议会登记在由秘书维护的登记簿当中。

Instrument of appointment

7.

(1) Every notary public shall upon appointment or reappointment receive a certificate of appointment.

(2) Every notary public shall exercise his appointment or reappointment in accordance with the conditions stated in the certificate of appointment.

(3) Every notary public shall upon appointment or reappointment receive a notary's stamp from the Academy specifying the expiry date of the appointment or reappointment.

(4) Every notary public shall stamp the expiry date of his appointment or reappointment on every document administered in exercise of his appointment or reappointment.

8. [Deleted by S 460/2008 wef 15/09/2008]

Register of documents administered

9. Every notary public shall —

(a) keep a register of documents administered in exercise of his appointment;

(b) furnish such information as the Secretary may require; and

(c) make the register available for inspection by the Secretary upon request.

委任文书

7.

（1）所有公证员，一经委任或再次委任，均应收到任命证书。

（2）所有公证员均应按照任命证书中载明的条件行使其委任或者再次委任（的职能）。

（3）所有公证员，一经委任或再次委任，均应收到来自学会颁发的公证员印章，载明委任或者再次委任的截止日期。

（4）所有公证员在行使其委任或再次委任（的职能）时，在其实施的所有文书上均应盖章表明其委任或再次委任的截止日期。

8.（已由 S 460/2008 wef 于 15/09/2008 删除）

文件管理登记

9. 所有公证员均应：

（a）就行使其任命所实施的文书造簿登记；

（b）应秘书的要求提供上述信息；并

（c）确保应要求可向秘书提供登记簿以供检查。

斯里兰卡

公证员条例

NOTARIES
[Cap. 110

CHAPTER 110
NOTARIES

AN ORDINANCE TO AMEND THE LAW RELATING TO NOTARIES AND TO MAKE FURTHER PROVISION FOR THE PROPER QUALIFICATION OF NOTARIES AND FOR THE MORE EFFICIENT AND FAITHFUL DISCHARGE OF THE DUTIES APPERTAINING TO THE OFFICE OF A NOTARY AND CONSOLIDATE THE LAW RELATIVE THERETO.

[27th March, 1907.]

(Ordinances Nos. 1 of 1907, 27 of 1909,18 of 1910,31 of 1917,22 of 1919,24 of 1927,10 of 1934,10 of 1936,7 of 1943,59 of 1943,51 of 1944,48 of 1947,Act No. 6 of 1951,Laws Nos. 24 of 1973,20 of 1976.)

1. Short title.

This Ordinance may be cited for all purposes as the Notaries Ordinance.

2. Appointment of notary by warrant of the Minister.

Every appointment to the office of notary shall be by warrant granted by the Minister, and shall specify the area within which, and the language or languages in which, the person appointed is authorized to practise.

3.Attorneys-at-law, qualified for admission as notaries [§3, Law 20 of 1976.]

Every attorney-at-law who has passed the prescribed

公证员条例
[第 110 章]

第 110 章
公证员条例

本条例对公证员的相关法律作出修订并就公证员适格资格，以及就更有效及更忠诚地履行公证机构和相关法律所要求的责任作进一步的规定。

[1907 年 3 月 27 日]

（1907 年 1 号、1909 年 27 号、1910 年 18 号、1917 年 31 号、1919 年 22 号、1927 年 24 号、1934 年 10 号、1936 年 10 号、1943 年 7 号、1943 年 59 号、1944 年 51 号、1947 年 48 号等条例、1951 年第 6 号法令、1973 年第 24 号、1976 年第 20 号等立法）

1. 简称

本条例可作为《公证员条例》为所有目的而引用。

2. 通过部长的令状任命公证员

每一个公证机构的任命均应由部长授予令状，并写明被指定人员授权执业的区域和语言。

3. 律师可以成为合格的公证员 [1976 年第 20 号法令第 3 条]

每名律师在其成为律师之前或之后通过规定的转

examination in conveyancing either before or after his admission as such attorney-at-law or has been admitted without examination in virtue of a legal qualification in the United Kingdom or elsewhere, requiring a pass in conveyancing shall be entitled, on application, to a warrant authorizing him to practise as a notary in the language in which he has passed the examination in conveyancing within the judicial zone in which he resides.

易审查，或在英国或其他地方凭合法资格未经审查被录取为律师，在申请时需要通过转易审查，以授予他在其所居住的司法辖区内以其通过转易审查的语言作为公证员执业。

4. Qualifications of other persons for notarial appointment. [§2, Law 24 of 1973]

(1) The Minister may appoint as notaries persons other than attorneys-at-law;

Provided that such persons—

(a) are of good character and repute;

(b) are of the age of twenty years;

(c) have been articled clerks, licensed as hereinafter provided, of an attorney-at-law and have duly served as such for two years; and

(d) have passed an examination prescribed by the Minister and are reported to be duly qualified by the Registrar- General.

(2)Every notary appointed under subsection (I) on or after the first day of May, 1951, shall be entitled to practise within the judicial zone in which he resides.

4A. Notaries practising in Judicial division deemed to practise in judicial zone. [§4, Law 20 of 1976]

Every warrant issued to a notary under the provisions of section 3* or section 4*, authorizing him to practise as a notary in any judicial division in which he resides, shall be deemed to authorize him to practise as a notary in the judicial zone in which he resides.

* This is a reference to sections 3 and 4 prior to their amendment by Law No. 20 of 1976 and Law No. 24 of 1973.

4. 其他人被任命为公证员的资格 [1973 年第 24 号法令第 2 条]

（1）部长可以任命律师以外的其他人员成为公证员；

但该人必须——

（a）具有良好的人品和声誉；

（b）年满 20 岁；

（c）已成为实习律师，按以下规定持有律师执照，并已履职两年；以及

（d）已通过部长规定的审查，并报总登记处正式批准。

（2）在 1951 年 5 月 1 日之后根据第（1）款任命的每名公证员，均有权在其居住的司法辖区内执业。

4A. 公证员在司法部门从业应被视为在司法辖区从业。[1976 年第 20 号法令第 4 条]

根据第 3* 条或第 4* 条的规定向公证员发出的每一份任命令状，授权他在居住地的任何司法部门中作为公证员执业，应被视为授权其在居住的司法辖区作为公证员执业。

* 是指在 1976 年第 20 号法令和 1973 年第 24 号法令修订之前的第 3 节和第 4 节。

5. Condition to be fulfilled before notary authorized to practise in one language can practise in another language.

A notary, who is authorized by warrant to practise in any particular language, shall be entitled, on passing such examination in any other language as may be prescribed by the Minister, to a warrant authorizing him to practise in that other language.

5. 公证员经授权以一种语言执业，满足条件后，可以用另一种语言执业

经令状授权以某种特定语言执业的公证员，在通过部长规定的其他语言执业的审查后，将授予他以该另一种语言执业的令状。

6.Number of articled clerks how determined.

The number of articled clerks to be licensed for and in each district shall be limited and determined by an Or-

6. 如何确定实习律师的数量

每个地区实习律师许可的数量应受限制，并由部长不定时发布的命令确定。

der to be issued from time to time by the Minister.

7.Admission of articled clerks and notaries.

The admission of persons to be articled clerks and notaries shall be subject to the regulations in the First Schedule, which shall be in force until revoked, amended, or altered by regulations made under section 8.

8.The Minister may make regulations for admission of articled clerks and notaries.

The Minister may from time to time revoke, amend, or alter such regulations, or may make new regulations. All regulations so made, and any revocation, amendment, or alteration of a regulation, shall be published in the Gazette.

9. Notary bound to have his office within his jurisdiction.

Every notary shall be bound to have his office within the area specified in his warrant; and any notary infringing this provision shall be liable to have his warrant withdrawn by the Minister.

10.Number and situation of notary's offices.

(1) No notary shall have more than two offices.

(a) No notary who is an attorney-at- law shall, for the purposes of his profession as a notary, have any office at any place other than—

(i)his residence; or

(ii)an office maintained and used by him for the purposes of his profession as an attorney-at-law.

(b) Where any notary who is an attorney- at-law has two offices for the purposes of his profession as a notary, one of such offices shall be at his residence:

Provided, however, that any such notary may, if authorized in that behalf in writing under the hand of the Registrar-General, have both such offices at places described in paragraph (a) (ii) of this subsection.

11. Minister's power to change the zone within which a notary is authurized, to practise. [§5, Law 20 of 1976]

The Minister may on application made in that behalf grant to a notary, having a warrant authorizing him to practise within a judicial zone, a fresh warrant authorizing him to practise within another judicial zone.

12. Notary to make declaration and give security.

(1) Every person to whom a warrant has been granted to practise as a notary shall before commencing to practise—

7. 录取实习律师和公证员

录取实习律师和公证员，应遵守附表 1 的规定，该规定在被根据第 8 条订立的规章撤销、修订或变更前一直有效。

8. 部长可以制定关于录取实习律师和公证员的规章

部长可能会不定时撤销、修正或更改此类规章，或者可能制定新的规章。据此制定的所有规章，以及对规章的任何撤销、修正或变更，均应在公报上公布。

9. 公证员必须在其管辖范围内设立办公室

每位公证员都必须在其授权所指明的范围内设立办公室；任何违反本规定的公证员对部长撤销其授权承担责任。

10. 公证机构的数量和情况

公证员不得设两个以上的办公室。

（a）从事律师的公证员，出于公证员履职的目的，不得在以下任何地方设立办公室：

（i）其住所；或者

（ii）作为律师用于维持律师业务的办公室。

（b）从事律师的公证员有两个办公室可用于公证员履职，其中一个办公室应在其住所：

但是，如果公证员经总登记处书面形式授权，那么可以在第（a）款第（ii）项所述的地方设立两个办公室。

11. 部长有权改变公证员授权执业的区域 [1976 年第 20 号法令第 5 条]

部长可以根据公证员在这方面的申请，授权他在一个司法辖区内执业，也可授予他在另一个司法辖区内执业的新令状。

12. 公证员制作申报单并给予担保

（1）作为公证员获得授权执业的令状，在开始执业前应该：

a. make and sign before the High Court Judge having jurisdiction over the area specified in the warrant a declaration in the form C in the Second Schedule;

b. execute a bond in favour of the Republic in the amount of two thousand rupees, conditioned for the due and faithful discharge of his duties as a notary, which amount shall be secured either by the hypothecation of immovable property or by the deposit of movable property (such immovable or movable property being property belonging to himself or some other person), or by the guarantee of the Insurance Corporation*; and file in the High Court holden in such zone an attested copy of his warrant.

(2) Every bond referred to in paragraph (b) of subsection (1) shall be signed in the presence of the High Court Judge having jurisdiction over the area specified in the warrant of the notary:

Provided that the guarantee of the Insurance Corporation* may be signed on behalf of the Corporation in the registered office of the Corporation.

* The reference to "an approved guarantee company" is replaced by a reference to the Insurance Corporation consequent to the amendment to section 2 (d) of the Public Officers' Security Ordinance by Act No. 4 of 1968.

13. Penalty for practising as notary without warrant, &c.

If any person shall practise or act as or exercise the office or functions of a notary without having obtained such warrant as aforesaid, or without having made and signed such declaration and given such bond and security as aforesaid, or without having filed an attested copy of his warrant, every such person shall be guilty of an offence, and liable on conviction thereof to a fine not exceeding two thousand rupees, or to simple or rigorous imprisonment for any period not exceeding three years, or to such fine as well as such imprisonment.

14. Discharge of Insurance Corporation.

(1) Any person who has given security on behalf of a notary by the hypothecation of immovable property or by the deposit of movable property, or the Insurance Corporation bound as surety to a notary, may apply to the High Court Judge having jurisdiction over the area specified in such notary's warrant to be discharged from any liability incurred by such person or such Corporation under section 12.

(2) The High Court Judge to whom any person or such Corporation applies under subsection (I) for a dis-

a. 在令状所列明区域拥有管辖权的高等法院法官处制作并签署附表 2 中表格 C 的申报单；

b. 设立共和国为受益人的保证，该金额应通过不动产的抵押或动产的存放来保障（此类不动产或动产是属于本人或其他人的财产），或由保险公司担保 *；并向高等法院提交其持有的在该区域执业许可证明文件的副本。

（2）第（1）款（b）段所提述的每项保证，应在公证员令状所列明区域内具有管辖权的高等法院法官在场的情况下签署：

但保险公司 * 的担保可在保险公司登记的办公处由保险公司代表签署。

* 所涉及的"认可的担保公司"被 1968 年第 4 号法令修正案第 2(d)条的公职人员担保条例中的"保险公司"所取代。

13. 没有资格而作为公证员执业的惩罚

如果任何人在未获得前述资格，或未经前述制作或签署此类申报单并给予此类保证或担保，或未提交令状的证明副本时，执业、担任或运营公证机构或行使公证员职能，均为犯罪。一经定罪，可处以不超过 2000 卢比的罚款，或被判处不超过三年的任意期限的轻微或严重的监禁，或处以罚款和监禁。

14. 保险公司的免责

（1）任何代表公证员通过不动产抵押或存放动产而提供担保的人，或者担任公证员担保人的保险公司，可向该公证员令状所列明区域的高等法院法官提出申请免除该人或该公司根据第 12 条所应承担的任何法律责任。

（2）该人或该公司根据第（1）款申请免除该人或该公司的法律责任，如其满足已向公证员发出六个

charge of such person's or such Corporation's liability may, if he is satisfied that such person or such Corporation has given six weeks' notice to the notary of his or its intention to make such application and that such person or such Corporation has good cause for claiming such discharge, endorse on the bond an order discharging such person or such Corporation from any liability in respect of any act of the notary done after the date of the order.

星期的通知，告知其意欲提出此类申请，并且该人或该公司有充分理由要求免责，则高等法院法官将在保证上签署一项命令，在该命令的签署日后免除该人或该公司对公证员的任何行为应承担的责任。

15. Omitted.

16. *When notary to furnish fresh security.

*Section 15 is omitted consequent to the amendment to section 2 (d) of the Public Officers'(Security) Ordinance by Act No . 4 of 1968.

(1) If at any time the security given by or on behalf of any notary shall perish or is lost or if any person who has given security by the hypothecation of immovable property or by the deposit of movable property or the Insurance Corporation bound as surety is discharged under section 14 (2) from liability, the notary shall execute a fresh bond in accordance with the provisions of section 12.

(2) If in any case to which subsection (I) applies any notary shall practise or act as a notary without having executed a fresh bond as provided in that subsection, he shall be guilty of an offence and liable on conviction thereof to the punishment provided in section 13.

15. 已省略。

16. * 公证员提供新的担保

*1968 年第 4 号法令修正案第 2（d）条的公职人员（担保）条例省略了第 15 条。

（1）如果任何公证员或公证员的代表提供的担保在任何时候灭失或遗失，或者通过不动产的抵押或动产的存放提供担保的人、保险公司担任担保人时根据第 14 条第（2）款被免除责任，公证员应按照第 12 条的规定提供新的担保。

（2）任何公证员在没有执行第（1）款所规定提供新的担保的情况下执业或担任公证员，即属犯罪，一经定罪，即按第 13 条处罚。

17. Enrolling of notaries in the High Court.

Upon a notary making and signing the declaration and giving the security required by section 12 the High Court Judge shall, without fee or reward, enroll his name and the date of his admission as a notary in a roll or book to be provided and kept for that purpose in the High Court holden in the relevant zone, and shall file the said declaration and bond, together with an attested copy of such warrant, of record in the said court.

17. 公证员在高等法院的登记

在公证员制作并签署声明，以及提供第 12 条所要求的担保后，高等法院法官应免费或作为奖励，将其姓名和作为公证员被录取的日期记载在登记册或薄中，保存在高等法院管辖相关区域内，其应向高等法院提交前述申报单和保证以及令状的证明副本一并保存。

18. List of notaries to be posted in the courts.[§6, Law 20 of 1976]

+ (1) A list of all persons authorized to act as notaries within any zone shall be kept at all times posted in some conspicuous place at the High Court holden in the zone for general information.

+ The reference to Magistrates' Courts in subsections (3) and (4) of this section is omitted and replaced by reference to Primary Courts, as the civil jurisdiction of Magistrates' Courts was taken over by Primary Courts.

(2) The Registrar of the court shall from time to time,

18. 在法院公示公证员名单 [1976 年第 20 号法令第 6 条]

（1）授权在某区域内担任公证员的人员名单，应始终公示在该区高等法院的显眼位置，以供一般参考。

本条第（3）款、第（4）款中的地方治安法院将被撤销并由初级法院所代替，这是由于初级法院接管了地方治安法院的民事裁判权。

（2）法院登记官应根据需要，剔除已逝的，或被

as occasion may require, correct the said list by striking therefrom the names of any notaries who have died or been struck off the roll of notaries, or have left the said zone, or ceased to practise as notaries therein.

开除名录的，或已离开前述区域的，或停止执业的公证员，不定时修正前述的名单。

(3) The Registrar shall on the thirtieth day of June and the thirty-first day of December in each year forward to the Registrar-General a copy of such list corrected up to date, and to each of the several District Courts, Family Courts and Primary Courts within the zone a corrected list of notaries entitled to practise within the jurisdiction of such District Courts, Family Courts and Primary Courts respectively.

（3）登记官应在每年的6月30日及12月31日向登记总署提交最新更正名单的副本，以及向地区内每个有管辖权的地区法院、家事法院和初级法院提交相应的执业公证员更正名单。

(4) Each District Judge, Judge of the Family Court and Judge of the Primary Court shall cause the list so received by him to be affixed to some conspicuous place on the wall of his court.

（4）每名地区法院法官，家事法院法官及初级法院法官均应将他所收到的名单公示在法院墙上的显眼位置。

19.Suspension of notary from office.[§7, Law 20 of 1976]

(1) Where a notary has been indicted before the High Court, the Minister may, on the application of the Attorney-General, suspend him from the office of notary pending his trial. If the notary shall be acquitted, or shall not be brought to trial within six months after his suspension, the same shall cease to be in force and shall be deemed to be removed.

(2) Where a notary, who is an attorney-at- law, has been suspended from his office as attorney-at-law, he shall during the period of the suspension be disqualified from discharging the duties of a notary.

19. 公证员在公证机构暂停执业[1976年第20号法令第7条]

（1）如果公证员在高等法院受到起诉，部长可应总检察长的申请，在审判前让他于公证机构暂停执业。如果公证员在暂停执业后六个月内被宣告无罪，或者未被审判，那么将自动恢复执业。

（2）从事律师的公证员作为律师被其所在事务所停职，则在停职期间丧失履行公证员职责的资格。

20. Cancellation of notary's warrant.

If any notary shall be lawfully convicted of any offence which, in the opinion of the Minister, renders him unfit to be entrusted with any responsible office, or if any such person, being an attorney-at-law, shall be duly removed from the office of attorney-at-law, every such person shall become disqualified for the office of notary, and the warrant granted to him shall be cancelled.

20. 取消公证员资格的令状

任何公证员如果被合法地定罪，部长认为不宜委托其负责任何公证机构，或者作为律师被其所在的事务所合理开除，都将被公证机构取消公证员资格，并取消授予他的令状。

21. Inquiry into notary's misconduct or incapacity.

(1) It shall be the duty of the High Court Judge within whose jurisdiction a notary resides, upon being satisfied, after due inquiry, that such notary -

(a) has been guilty of any offence, whether in his capacity of notary or otherwise, which in the opinion of the High Court Judge renders him unfit to be entrusted with the duties of a notary; or

21. 对公证员的不当行为或失去履职能力的调查

（1）在公证员所居住的、具有管辖权的高等法院法官经正当调查后确认该公证员：

（a）犯有罪行，不论是以公证员职权或其他方式，高等法院法官认为不宜委托其公证员的职责；或者

(b) has grossly misconducted himself in the discharge of the duties of his office; or

(c) has so conducted himself by repeated breaches of any of the rules made by or under this Ordinance that he ought not to be any longer entrusted with the performance of the said duties; or

(d)has been convicted three times or oftener for a violation or disregard of or neglect to observe the provisions of rule (26) in section 31; or

(e)has proved himself by reason of incompetence, age, physical or mental infirmity, or otherwise, incapable of discharging the duties of his office with advantage to the public,to report the same in writing to the Minister with the evidence taken at the inquiry.

(2) Where the report is to the effect that the notary has been guilty of any such offence or misconduct as is mentioned in clauses (a), (b), (c), or (d) of the last preceding subsection, the Minister may cancel the warrant of such notary, or may suspend him from office for such period as may appear just. Where the report is to the effect that the notary is incapable of discharging his duties with advantage to the public, the Minister may cancel his warrant or may require him to resign his office within a specified time, and in default of such resignation may cancel his warrant.

(3) For the purposes of such inquiry the High Court Judge shall have power to require the attendance before himself of the notary and of any witnesses, and the production of any document that the High Court Judge may deem material, and to examine such witnesses on oath or affirmation, and to examine such notary without oath or affirmation.

(4) Any person required to attend and be examined or to produce a document as aforesaid, who shall without reasonable cause fail to comply with such requirement, shall be guilty of an offence, and liable on conviction to a fine not exceeding one hundred rupees.

(5) No statement made by the notary at the inquiry shall be used in any criminal prosecution instituted against him.

22. Resignation of office.

(1) If a notary applies to the Registrar-General in writing to resign from and to cease to act in the office of notary, the Registrar-General shall forthwith forward the application to the Minister who may accept such resignation as from the date desired by the notary.

（b）在履行其职务时有严重不当行为；或者

（c）屡次违反本条例或根据本条例订立的任何规则，则他不应再受委托履行前述职务；或者

（d）因违反、无视或忽视遵守第31条第（26）款的规定而被定罪3次或更多；或者

（e）已证明其因无行为能力、年龄、身体或精神不健全或其他原因而无法为公众利益履行职务，则要以书面形式报告给部长，并在调查中提供证据。

（2）凡报告显示公证员犯了第（1）款第（a）项、第（b）项、第（c）项或第（d）项所述的任何罪名或不当行为，部长可以取消该公证员的资格，或者可以让其在一段合理的时间内暂停执业。如果报告显示该公证员无法为公众利益履行职责，部长可以取消其资格或者可以要求其在规定的时间内辞职，如拒绝辞职则取消其资格。

（3）为进行此种调查，高等法院法官有权要求公证员和任何证人出庭，并提交高等法院法官认为可能重要的文件，并审查这些证人的宣誓或证词，以及在没有宣誓或证词的情况下审查这些公证员。

（4）任何人如按前述所规定被要求出席、审查或出示前述文件，无正当理由而不履行这些要求时即属犯罪，一经定罪，可处不超过100卢比的罚款。

（5）公证员在调查中作出的陈述，不得用于对他提出的任何刑事控告中。

22. 从公证机构辞职

（1）如果公证员以书面形式向总登记处申请辞职并停止在公证机构任职，那么总登记处应在公证员意欲辞职之日将申请转交给可能接受辞职的部长。

(2) When a notary has resigned under this section his warrant shall be deemed to be cancelled for the purposes of sections 23, 24, 25 and 26.

(3) Notwithstanding such resignation a notary shall continue to remain subject to the provisions of this Ordinance and all rules contained therein or made thereunder in respect of all things done or omitted by him in the exercise of his functions as notary prior to the resignation.

（2）公证员根据本条辞职时，按照第 23 条、第 24 条、第 25 条及第 26 条，他的资格将被视为已取消。

（3）尽管已提出辞职，公证员在辞职前履职时所作出或遗漏的事务仍然应继续受本条例的条款规制。

23.*Certificate of cancellation or suspension of warrant to be transmuted to and posted in the local courts.[§8, Law 20 of 1976]

*See the footnote to section 18.

(1) Whenever a notary's warrant has been cancelled or a notary has been suspended from office, notice thereof shall be given in the Gazette, and a certificate that such warrant has been cancelled or notary suspended shall be transmitted, by the Secretary to the Ministry, to the Registrar-General and to the High Court Judge and several District Judges, Judges of the Family Courts and Judges of the Primary Courts within whose jurisdiction such notary shall have been authorized to act.

(2)The High Court Judge of the court in which the name of such notary is enrolled shall in the case of the cancellation of the notary's warrant cause his name to be immediately struck off the roll of notaries, and in the case of the notary's suspension from office, shall note the fact in the roll opposite his name.

(3) A copy of such certificate, with a translation in the Tamil and English languages subjoined thereto, shall be kept posted in some conspicuous place at every such High Court, District Court. Family Court and Primary Court for such period as the court may direct.

23.* 取消或暂停资格的文书将被转交当地法院并公布 [1976 年第 20 号法令第 8 条]

* 见第 18 节的脚注。

（1）当公证员的资格被取消或公证员被停职时，应在公报上公告，而取消或暂停令状的文书应由秘书转交给政府部门、总登记处、高等法院法官和对公证员被授权执业有管辖权的若干地区法官、家事法院法官和初级法院法官。

（2）如果公证员名字被登记在册，在取消公证员资格时，高等法院法官应立即将其名字从公证员登记册中删除，如果是公证员于公证机构暂停执业的，应在登记册其名称的对应处注明事实。

（3）该证明书的副本应加上泰米尔语和英语译文，在每个高等法院、地方法院的显眼位置公示。家事法院和初级法院的公布时间，法院将会作出指示。

24. Penalty on notary practising after notice of suspension, &c.

If any person shall act as or exercise the office or functions of a notary after having received notice of any such suspension as aforesaid, and before the same shall have been removed, or after having been convicted of any offence disqualifying him for the said office, or after having been removed from the office of attorney-at-law as hereinbefore mentioned, or after having received notice that the warrant granted to him has been cancelled or withdrawn as aforesaid, he shall be guilty of an offence, and be liable on conviction thereof to a fine not exceeding one thousand rupees, or to imprisonment, simple or rigorous, for any period not exceeding three years, or to such fine as

24. 公证员暂停执业后执业的处罚

任何人在收到前述暂停执业通知、开除通知，或在被判定犯有违法行为之后被取消公证资格，或如前述被律师事务所开除、或如前述收到取消执业资格的通知后，仍继续执业、担任或运营公证机构或行使公证员职能，则将被定罪，一经定罪，应承担责任，可处以不超过 1000 卢比的罚款，或处以不超过 3 年轻微或严重的监禁，或罚款和监禁并罚。

well as such imprisonment.

25. Minister may revoke cancellation of warrant.

(1) In any case in which a notary's warrant shall have been withdrawn or cancelled under the provisions of this Ordinance, the Minister may make an order revoking such withdrawal or cancellation, and issue a fresh warrant authorizing him to practise within the area in which he was practising immediately preceding such withdrawal or cancellation or within some other area.

(2)* Notice of revocation. [§9. Law 20 of 1976]

*See the footnote to section 18.

Notice of such order shall be given in the Gazette, and a copy thereof shall be transmitted, by the Secretary to the Ministry, to the High Court Judge having jurisdiction over the area specified in the fresh warrant issued under subsection (1) of this section, and to the several District Judges, Judges of the Family Courts and the Judges of the Primary Courts having jurisdiction within the said area and to the Registrar-General.

26.Restoration to. or insertion in, the roll of notaries ol the notary's name. &c.

(1) Upon receipt of a notice transmitted under section 25 (2) by a High Court Judge, he shall, if the notary's fresh warrant is produced before him, restore to, or insert in, the roll of notaries such notary's name.

(2) The High Court Judge restoring to, or inserting in, the roll of notaries the name of a notary shall require fresh security to be provided by such notary in terms of section 12.

(3) Every notary, whose name has been restored to, or inserted in, the roll of notaries under subsection (I) of this section and who has furnished fresh security in terms of section 12 shall be entitled to execute the office of a notary in conformity with the authority given to him by his fresh warrant.

27.Certificatesto be granted yearly to notaries by Registrar of the High Court.

(1) It shall be the duty of every Registrar of the High Court holden in every zone, on the application of any person entitled to practise as a notary within the jurisdiction of such court, to issue to him a certificate that such person is a notary and duly authorized to practise as such therein.

(2) All such certificates shall be applied for and granted on or before the first day of March in every year,

25. 部长可以撤销取消执业资格

（1）如果根据本条例条款取消公证员的资格的，部长可以作出撤销此类取消的命令，并发出新的令状，授权他在取消资格前的区域内或在其他区域立即执业。

（2）* 撤销通知。[1976 年第 20 号法令第 9 条]

* 见第 18 节的脚注。

该命令在公报上公告，其副本应由秘书转交给政府部门，转交给对根据本条第（1）款签发的新令状中列明范围有管辖权的高等法院法官，转交给在所列范围内有管辖权的若干地区法官、家事法庭法官和初级法院法官，以及转交给总登记处。

26. 在公证员名册中恢复或插入公证员姓名

（1）高等法院法官收到根据第 25 条第（2）款转交的通知后，如在他面前出示了公证员的新令状，他应在公证员名册中恢复或插入该公证员姓名。

（2）高等法院法官在公证员名册中恢复或插入该公证员姓名，该公证员应根据第 12 条提供新的担保。

（3）已根据本条第（1）款在公证员名册中恢复或插入姓名，并已根据第 12 条提供了新的担保的公证员，有权行使与新令状一致的公证员职权。

27. 高等法院登记官每年向公证员授予证明书

（1）每个区内高等法院的每一位登记官均有责任，按照该法院的管辖范围内被授权执业公证员的申请，出具其是公证员并正式授权其在此执业的证明书。

（2）证明书应于每年 3 月 1 日或之前申请及授予，并且有效期为 1 年，不得延长：

and shall be in force for one year and no longer:

Provided, however, that if such certificate shall not be applied for within the time limited, and it shall be shown to the satisfaction of the High Court Judge that the delay was due to accident, misfortune or other unavoidable cause, the High Court Judge may direct the Registrar to issue the required certificate notwithstanding such delay as aforesaid.

如果不能在规定的时限内申请证明书，但是高等法院法官认为该迟延是由于意外、灾难或其他不可避免的原因造成的，尽管存在前述迟延，高等法院法官仍然可以指示登记官出具必要的证明书。

(3) Such certificate shall be in the form D in the Second Schedule, and shall bear a stamp duty of ten rupees:

Provided that it shall be lawful for the Minister to authorize the issue of any such certificate on unstamped paper in any case in which the circumstances of any zone or place appear to him to render such a proceeding necessary or advisable.

（3）证明书须采用附表 2 中表格 D，并且须承担 10 卢比的印花税：

如果由于所在地区或场所致使必须或建议让部长在未盖章的纸上出具此类证明书的，也属于合法形式。

28.Notaries applying for certificates to make declaration.

(1) For the purpose of obtaining such certificate a declaration in writing, signed by such notary, containing the following particulars:—

(a)his name and place or places of residence;

(b3) the exact situation of his office or of each of his offices;

(c)the area in which he is authorized to practise;

(d) whether at any time since the date of the last declaration, if any, made by him under this section, the security given by or on behalf of him has perished or been lost, or any person who has given security by the hypothecation of immovable property or by the deposit of movable property, or the Insurance Corporation has been discharged under section 14 (2) from liability.

shall be delivered to the said Registrar, who shall, as soon as conveniently may be after the delivery of such declaration (unless he shall see cause and have reason to believe that the party applying for such certificate is not upon the roll of notaries or not authorized to practise as such in such zone or has not furnished security as required by this Ordinance), deliver to the said notary such certificate as aforesaid.

(2) Where a notary, who is an attorney-at- law, specifies in the declaration referred to in subsection (1), more than one residence, he shall in addition set out in that declaration which one of those residences he intends to use or uses as an office,

(3) If any person shall make any false statement in any such declaration, he shall be guilty of an offence, and be liable on conviction to a fine not exceeding five hun-

28. 公证员制作申报单申请证明书

（1）为取得该证明书，公证员要签署载有下列详情的书面申报单：

（a）姓名，地址或居住地；

（b3）其办公室或每个办公室的确切地址；

（c）授权执业的地区；

（d）自他根据本条作出的最后一次申报书（如有的话）之日起的任何时间，由他或代表他所作出的担保是否已经灭失或遗失，或通过不动产的抵押或动产的存放来提供担保，或保险公司已根据第 14 条第（2）款免除责任的情况。

申报单应提交给前述登记官，登记官应在申报单提交后尽快将前述证明书发给公证员（除非登记官有理由认为申请证明书的申请人不在公证员名册内，或未授权在该区域内执业，或未按本条例的要求提供担保）。

（2）从事律师的公证员拥有一个以上的住所，须在第（1）款所列的申报单中指明他拟使用的住所或拟用作办公室的住所。

（3）任何人如在申报单中作出虚假陈述，即属犯罪，一经定罪，可处不超过 500 卢比的罚款。

dred rupees.

29. Relief on refusal by Registrar

(1) On refusal by Registrar to grant any certificate, application to be made to the High Court.

In case the said Registrar shall decline to issue any such certificate to any notary as aforesaid, the notary may apply to the High Court holden in such zone, which is hereby authorized to make such order in the matter as shall be just.

(2)* Appeal to Court of Appeal.

Any party who is aggrieved by any order made under subsection (1) of this section, or by the refusal of a High Court Judge to direct the issue of a certificate in any case referred to in the proviso to section 27(2), may appeal against such order or refusal to the Court of Appeal.

* Subsection (3) is omitted as under the existing law there is no special procedure for appeals from an interlocutory order of the High Court.

30. Penalty on notaries practising without certificate.

If any person shall act as a notary without having obtained such certificate as aforesaid, he shall for or in respect of every deed executed or acknowledged before him as such notary, whilst he shall have been without such certificate, be guilty of an offence and be liable to a fine not exceeding fifty rupees.

31. Rules to be observed by notaries.

It is and shall be the duty of every Rules to be notary strictly to observe and act in observed by conformity with the following rules, that is notaries.to say:—

(1) Notary not to divulge secrets without permission.

He shall not divulge the secrets confided to him or of which he becomes possessed in the execution of his office, unless with the express permission of his employer or when required to do so by law.

(2) Attestation of documents drawn by any other person.

He shall not authenticate or attest a deed or instrument drawn in Sri Lanka by any other person, unless there shall be endorsed thereon a certificate signed by a notary certifying that such deed or instrument has been drawn by himself.

(3) When may the signature of a party or witness to a deed be taken.

He shall not require, permit, or suffer any party or any witness to any deed or instrument executed or to be

29. 登记官拒绝公证的救济

（1）如果登记官拒绝授予证明书，申请人可向高等法院提出申诉。

如果前述登记官拒绝向前述申请人出具证明书，申请人可向该区域的高等法院提出申诉，就此事项作出公正的指令。

（2）* 申请人向上诉法院提起上诉。

如果对根据本条第（1）款作出的指令感到不满，或因高等法院法官拒绝按照第 27 条第（2）款规定指示出具证明书，申请人可以针对该指令或拒绝出具决定向上诉法院提起上诉。

* 根据现行法律，第（3）款被省略，上诉不需要高等法院中间指令的特别程序。

30. 公证员无证执业的处罚

任何人在未取得前述证明书的情况下担任公证员，其作为公证员执行或承认的某个行为，即属犯罪，并可处以不超过 50 卢比的罚款。

31. 公证员应遵守的规则

公证员应严格遵守每一条规则并按照下列规则行动。例如：

（1）公证员未经许可不得泄露秘密。

公证员除非得到申请人的明确许可或法律要求，否则不得泄露其所掌握的秘密或执行职务时所掌握的秘密。

（2）公证任何人提交的文件。

公证员不得在斯里兰卡对任何人提出的契约或文书进行认证或证明，除非证明书上有公证员的背书，证明该契约或文书是由公证员作出的。

（3）当事人或证人签署契约的时间。

除非契约或文书的全部内容已最终确定，公证员不得要求、许可或让任何一方或证人在他面前在已生

executed before him to sign his name or make his mark to or acknowledge any such deed or instrument or any duplicate or other part thereof or any draft or copy thereof intended to be preserved in his protocol, or to sign his name or make his mark upon any paper or other material intended to be afterwards used for any such purpose, until the whole of such deed or instrument shall have been written or engrossed thereon.

(4) Material on which deeds may be written.

He shall not authenticate or attest any deed or instrument written on paper which is not of a reasonably durable description suitable for the purpose of such document, nor shall he attest any deed or instrument written on ola.

(5) Deeds to be written on undivided sheet or sheets signed by the Registrar of Lands.

He shall not authenticate or attest any deed or instrument which is written on more than one entire or undivided sheet or piece of paper, parchment, or other material, unless—

(a)each of the sheets or pieces used has been previously produced before the Registrar of Lands for the district in which the notary resides, and has been marked or signed or initialled by such registrar in order to prevent the sheets being used for any other purpose; or

(b)the parties executing the same and the notary shall sign every sheet or piece in which any part of the deed or instrument is written.

(6) Insufficiently stamped instrument not to be executed.

He shall not require, permit, or suffer any person to execute or acknowledge before him any deed or instrument which is insufficiently stamped.

(7) Stamps to be cancelled at the time of execution of deed.

He shall at the time of the execution or acknowledgment before him of every deed or instrument which is not stamped with an impressed stamp cancel the stamps thereon by writing or marking in ink on or across each stamp his name or initials, together with the true date of his so writing or marking, and shall write upon each stamp with ink the number of the deed or instrument to which such stamp is affixed.

(8) Two witnesses essential for every deed.

He shall not authenticate or attest any deed or instrument to which at least two witnesses have not subscribed their signatures in letters.

(9) Party executing the deed should be known to no-

效或即将生效的契约或文书上签署名字或符号，或在意欲保留在协议书中的契约、文书、副本、议定书中，或在任何之后将用于此用途的纸张或材料上签署名字或符号。

（4）可以书写契约的材质。

公证员不得认证或公证任何书写于不耐久和不适合该文件目的材质上的契约或文书，也不得公证任何书写在欧拉上的契约或文书。

（5）书写在未被分割的纸张上的契约或由国家登记官签署的纸上的契约。

公证员不得认证或公证书写在一张以上的整张或未被分割纸张或碎纸、羊皮纸或其他材料上的契据或文书，除非：

（a）所使用的每张纸张或碎片均是预先在公证员所在地区的土地登记处制作，并已由登记官做记号或签字或草签，以防止该纸张被用于任何其他目的；或者

（b）各方已经达成一致意见并且公证员须签署每张写着契约或文书内容的纸张或碎片。

（6）不能执行印章不完整的文件。

公证员不得要求、许可或容忍任何人在他面前执行或承认印章不完整的契约或文书。

（7）在执行契约时取消印章。

通过在每个印章上用墨水书写、标记其姓名、缩写对未盖章的契约或文书进行执行或认可，在执行或承认印章不符合法律规定的契约或文书时，公证员应通过书写或标记的实际日期取消印章，并且应在每个印章上用墨水书写印章中所附的契约或文书的编号。

（8）每份契约必须有两名证人。

公证员不得认证或公证不满足至少两名证人在其中签字的条件的契约或文书。

（9）一方执行契约时应为公证员所知或有两名证

tary or to two attesting witnesses.

He shall not authenticate or attest any deed or instrument unless the person executing the same be known to him or to at least two of the attesting witnesses thereto; and in the latter case, he shall satisfy himself, before accepting them as witnesses, that they are persons of good repute and that they are well acquainted with the executant and know his proper name, occupation, and residence, and the witnesses shall sign a declaration at the foot of the deed or instrument that they are well acquainted with the executant and know his proper name, occupation, and residence.

人见证。

公证员不得认证或公证任何契据或文书，除非执行该契约或文书的人为其所知或至少有两名见证人在场见证；在后一种情况下，在接受见证人之前，公证员应当确保他们是有良好声誉的人，并且他们知悉执行人并且知道其姓名、职业和居住地，见证人应在契约或文书下签署一份表明他们知悉执行人并知道其姓名、职业和居住地的声明。

(10) Where both person executing deed and attesting witnesses unknown to notary deed not to be executed.

He shall not authenticate or attest any deed or instrument in any case in which both the person executing the same and the attesting witnesses thereto are unknown to him.

（10）当公证员不知悉契约执行人和见证人时不能执行契约。

如果在公证员不知悉执行人和见证人时，不得认证或公证任何契约或文书。

(11) When deed to be read over and explained.

He shall not authenticate or attest any deed or instrument in any case in which the person executing or acknowledging the same shall be or profess to be unable to read the same, or in which such person shall require him to read over the same, unless and until he shall have read over and explained the same, or caused the same to be explained, in the presence and hearing of such person and, except in the case of wills and codicils, in the presence of the attesting witnesses.

（11）宣读并解释契约。

当执行或认可契约或文书的人不能阅读或自称不能阅读，或该人需要公证员宣读时，公证员不能认证或公证任何契约或文件，除非公证员宣读并解释，且执行人和见证人在场听到并理解，但遗嘱及其附件除外。

(12) when may deed be attested.

He shall not authenticate or attest any deed or instrument unless the person executing the same and the witnesses shall have signed the same in his presence and in the presence of one another, and unless he shall have signed the same in the presence of the executant and of the attesting witnesses.

（12）契约可能会被认证的时间。

公证员不得认证或公证任何契约或文书，除非执行人和见证人均在场并在公证员面前签署契约，且公证员也在执行人和见证人在场的情况下签署了契约。

(13) What deeds may not be attested by notary.

He shall not authenticate or attest any deed or instrument to which he is a party.

（13）公证员不得认证的契约。

公证员不得认证或公证有其参与的任何契约或文书。

(14) Full names of parties and witnesses to be ascertained.

He shall before any party or witness signs any deed or instrument ascertain the full name of such party or witness, and if the signature of such party or witness differs from the name given by such party or witness, the notary shall, in his attestation of such deed or instrument, describe such party or witness by such name and by the name written in the signature.

（14）查明当事人和见证人的全名。

公证员应在当事人或见证人签署契约或文书之前，查明其全名，如果当事人或见证人的签名与当事人或见证人自称的名字不同，公证员应在其认证的契约或文书中注明当事人或见证人自称的名字和所签的名字。

(15) Duty of notary in regard to deed signed with a

（15）公证员在以符号签署契约时的职责。

mark.

If any deed or instrument executed or acknowledged before him be signed by any of the parties or witnesses thereto with a mark, or with a signature in a language other than that in which the notary is authorized to practise, he shall write over such mark or signature in his own handwriting and at the time of execution the words "This is the mark (or signature, as the case may be) of A. B." (here insert the name of the person signing with the mark or signature); and in the case of a mark he shall besides require such person to affix to the deed or instrument the impression of his left thumb and shall write over such impression at the time and in the manner aforesaid the words "This is the left thumb impression of A. B." (here insert the name of the person whose thumb impression it is).

如果当事人或见证人在公证员面前以符号签署要执行或承认的契约，或者是用公证员授权执业之外的其他语言签名的，公证员应该亲自手写该符号或签名，并且在执行时写下“这是A.B.的符号（或签名，视情况而定）”（此处插入写下符号或签名之人的名字）；在有符号的情况下，他还应要求此人在契约或文书上加盖左拇指指印，并按前述时间和方式在手印上写“这是A.B.的左拇指指印”（此处插入手印所属人的名字）。

(16) Deeds affecting immovable property.

(a) He shall not authenticate or attest any deed or instrument other than a will or codicil affecting land or other immovable property, unless the deed or instrument embodies therein or in a schedule annexed thereto a description of the said land or other properly showing its boundaries (which shall include whenever practicable the names of the lands adjoining it and of their owners), its probable extent and situation (with respect to the town or village, pattu, korale, administrative district, and province), and its name and assessment number, if any;

(b) if such property consist of a share of a land or other property, the deed shall state whether it is a divided or undivided share, and the fractional part which it is of the whole. If it be a divided share, such share shall be clearly and accurately defined by its particular boundaries and extent; if it be an undivided share, the boundaries and extent shall be stated of the land of which it is a share:

Provided, however, that this rule shall not apply to any agreement to transfer, to mortgage, or to lease any such property.

(17) Registers in the land registry to be searched before executing deed affecting land.

(a) Before any deed or instrument (other than a will or codicil) affecting any interest in land or other immovable property is drawn by him, he shall search or cause to be searched the registers in the land registry to ascertain the state of the title in regard to such land and whether any prior deed affecting any interest in such land has been registered;

(b)If any such prior deed has been registered, he shall write in ink at the head of the deed the number of the

（16）对不动产有影响的契约。

（a）公证员不得认证或公证除遗嘱或遗嘱附件以外的、对土地或其他不动产有影响的契约或文书，除非该契约或文书中或其附表中附有对前述土地或其他财产的范围描述（在可行的情况下应包括相邻土地的名字和所有者的名字），其大致面积和情况的表述（相关的城镇或村庄、农作物、植物、行政区和省），如果有的话还应附有其名称和评估号码；

（b）若该财产包括一份土地或其他财产，则契约应说明它的份额是可分割的还是不分割的，以及它于整体中所占的份额。如果是可分割的份额，那么应清楚准确地界定该份额的范围和面积；如果是不可分割的份额，应用份额表明土地的范围和面积。

但是，本规则不适用此类财产的转让、抵押或租赁协议。

（17）在执行对土地有影响的契约前应检查土地登记处的登记情况。

（a）在发出对土地或其他不动产权益有影响的契约或文书（除遗嘱或遗嘱附件以外）之前，公证员须在土地登记处检查或安排检查登记册，以查明该土地的所有权状况，以及先前已有登记是否对该土地权益有影响；

（b）如果先前已有登记的契约，公证员应在契约的顶部用墨水写上登记册编号和先前已登记契约的

register volume and the page of the folio in which the registration of such prior deed has been entered:

Provided that if the parties to the transaction authorize the notary in writing to dispense with the search, the search shall not be compulsory, but he shall before the deed or instrument is tendered for registration write at the head thereof the reference to the previous registration, if any.

(18) Date of execution of deed to be inserted.

He shall correctly insert in letters in every deed or instrument executed before him the day, month, and year on which and the place where the same is executed, and shall sign the same.

(19) Erasures, interpolations, &c., not to be made after execution of deed.

He shall not make any erasure, alteration, or interpolation in any deed or instrument after the same has been signed by the executing party or parties.

(20) Attestation.

He shall without delay duly attest every deed or instrument which shall be executed or acknowledged before him, and shall sign and seal such attestation. In such attestation he shall state—

(a)that the said deed or instrument was signed by the party and the witnesses thereto in his presence and in the presence of one another;

(b)whether the person executing or acknowledging the said deed or instrument or the attesting witnesses thereto (and in the latter case he shall specify which of the said witnesses) were known to him;

(c)the day, month, and year on which and the place where the said deed or instrument was executed or acknowledged, and the full names of the attesting witnesses and their residences;

(d)whether the same was read over by the person executing the same, or read and explained by him, the said notary, to the said person in the presence of the attesting witnesses;

(e)whether any money was paid or not in his presence as the consideration or part of the consideration of the deed or instrument, and if paid, the actual amount in local currency of such payment;

(f)the number and value of the adhesive stamps affixed to or the value of the impressed stamps on such deed or instrument and the duplicate thereof;

(g)specifically the erasures , alterations, and interpolations which have been made in such deed or instrument,

页码。

但如果交易当事人以书面形式授权公证员免除检查，那么检查不是强制性的，但公证员应在契约或文书提交登记之前，在其顶部写下之前登记的相关内容（如果有的话）。

（18）插入执行契约的日期。

公证员应在每份执行的契约或文书中正确地插入其执行的年、月、日以及执行地点，并在其中签字。

（19）不得在契约执行后对公证书进行删除、添写等。

在执行方或当事人签署契约或文书后，不得对公证书进行任何涂改。

（20）公证。

公证员应毫不拖延地正式公证每一份应由其执行或承认的契约或文书，并应签署和盖章。在公证中，公证员应说明：

（a）前述契约或文书是由当事人和见证人在其面前及彼此在场的情况下签署的；

（b）公证员是否知悉执行或承认前述契约或文书的当事人或见证人（而在后一种情况下，公证员须将前述见证人列明）；

（c）前述契约或文书执行或承认的年、月、日，以及见证人全名和住址；

（d）执行人是否阅读了契约，或者由公证员向在场的人宣读并解释；

（e）是否已支付了公证费用，如果已支付，那么应写明按当地货币计算的该款项实际金额；

（f）加盖的印章数目及效力，或者加盖于契约或文书和其副本上印章的效力；

（g）是否在按前述条款宣读契约或文书之前作出了特定的删除、更改和添写，是否对其中的签名、序

and whether they were made before the same was read over as aforesaid, and the erasures, alterations, and interpolations, if any, made in the signatures thereto, in its serial number, and in the writing on the stamp affixed thereto.

列号和附加的印章进行了删除、更改和添写，如果有的话，在签名、序列号及加盖的印章上体现。

(21) Form of attestation.

Every such attestation shall be substantially in the form E in the Second Schedule, and shall be legibly signed by him in the language in which the deed or instrument is written, and also with his usual signature if the language or form of that signature be different from that in which such deed or instrument is written. Every erasure, alteration, or interpolation in the attestation shall be authenticated by the notary With the initial letters of his name.

（21）公证的形式。

公证书应采用附表 2 中表 E 的形式，并应由公证员按契约或文书所用语言签署易读的签名，如果签名的语言或形式不同于契约或文书，那么签署其常用签名。公证书中的每次删除、更改或添写均应写下公证员名字的首字母以证明为真。

(22) Deed not to be attested outside notary's jurisdiction or in language other than that in which he is authorized to practise.

He shall not authenticate or attest any deed or instrument in any area other than that in which he is authorized to practise, nor in any language other than that in which he is authorized to practise nor authenticate or attest any deed or instrument drawn in any language other than that in which he is authorized to practise.

（22）不得公证在公证员的管辖范围或其授权执业语言之外的契约。

除了在被授权执业的区域之外，公证员不得公证或认证任何契约或文书，也不得公证或认证任何使用其授权执业言语之外书写的契约或文书。

(23) Deeds to be numbered.

He shall number with consecutive integral numbers the documents executed or acknowledged before him, including wills and codicils, according to the order in which they are executed or acknowledged before him. If he shall change his area, as provided by section 11 of this Ordinance, and if the new area be in a different zone from the old area, he shall number consecutively the documents attested by him in the new area, commencing with number " 1 ".

（23）对契约编号。

公证员应将其执行或承认的文件按照执行或承认的顺序进行连续的编号，包括遗嘱和遗嘱的附件。如果公证员按照本条例第 11 条的规定更改了执业区域，并且新区域与旧区域位于不同的地方，那么公证员在新区域应将公证的文件从“1”开始连续编号。

(24) Protocol to be preserved by notary.

He shall carefully preserve as his protocol a draft or copy of every deed or instrument executed or acknowledged before him, to which shall be attached his signature and those of the party and witnesses to the original deed or instrument, and he shall keep a register thereof with a convenient index for the purpose of easy reference; and every such register shall be substantially in the form F in the Second Schedule, but in the case of wills and codicils only the number and date of the instrument shall be inserted in the register.

（24）公证员须保存议定书。

公证员应仔细保存每份其执行或承认的契约或文书的议定书或副本，附上公证员的签名，以及契约或文书原件上当事人和见证人的签名，并应保存有方便索引的登记册，以便参考；每份登记册须采用附表 2 中表 F 的形式，但就遗嘱和遗嘱的附件而言，只须在登记册插入该文书的编号及日期。

(25)Deeds executed before more than one notary.

Where any deed or instrument is executed or acknowledged before more than one notary—

(a)the notary who first attests such deed or instrument

（25）在不止一个公证员处公证的契约。

如果契约或文书在不止一个公证员处公证——

（a）首次公证该契约或文书的公证员须遵从第

shall comply with all the requirements of rule (20), and every other notary attesting such deed or instrument shall comply with the requirements of paragraphs (a) to (e) of the aforesaid rule and the provisions of paragraph (g) in respect of erasures, alterations and interpolations made in the signatures attested by him or in his serial number;

（20）款的所有要求，而其他公证该契约或文书的公证员须遵从前述第（a）项至第（e）项的要求，和第（g）项关于删除、更改和添写其公证的签名或其序列号的规定；

(b) every notary attesting the deed or instrument shall number such deed or instrument in accordance with the provisions of rule (23);

（b）每一位公证契约或文书的公证员均须按照第（23）款的规定对该契约或文书进行编号；

(c) the notary who first attests such deed or instrument shall preserve as his protocol the draft or copy referred to in rule (24), and shall comply with the requirements of that rule, and every other notary attesting such deed or instrument shall supply himself with a certified copy of the deed or instrument, which shall be deemed to be his protocol for the purposes of that rule; and

（c）首次公证该契约或文书的公证员须按第（24）款所述保存议定书或副本，并须符合该条的要求，而其他每位公证该契据或文书的公证员须提供其持有的经公证的契约或文书副本，并将该副本视为根据第（24）款要求而作的议定书；并且

(d) every notary attesting such deed shall, in addition, as far as possible, comply with the other provisions of section 31.

（d）每位公证该契约的公证员，应尽可能地遵守第 31 条其他条款的规定。

(26) Duplicates of deeds to be transmitted to Registrar of Lands.

（26）将契约的副本转交土地登记处。

(a) He shall deliver or transmit to the Registrar of Lands of the district in which he resides the following documents, so that they shall reach the registrar on or before the fifteenth day of every month, namely, the duplicate of every deed or instrument (except wills and codicils) executed or acknowledged before or attested by him during the preceding month, together with a list in duplicate, signed by him, of all such deeds or instruments, which list shall be substantially in the form F in the Second Schedule:

（a）公证员应在每月 15 日或之前将下列文件送交或转交其所在地区的土地登记处的登记官处，即包括公证员在上个月执行、承认、公证的每份契约或文书的副本（遗嘱和遗嘱的附件除外），以及由其签署的所有此类契约或文书的清单一式两份，该清单应采用附表 2 中表格 F 的形式。

Provided, however, that in the case of wills and codicils only the number and date of the document shall be inserted in such list;

但是，如果是遗嘱和遗嘱的附件，那么只须在该清单中插入文件的编号和日期。

(b) if no deed or instrument has been executed before any notary in any month, the notary shall, unless he is absent from Sri Lanka, furnish a nil list for that month on or before the fifteenth day of the following month;

（b）如果公证员在某月没有执行任何的契约或文书，除非他不在斯里兰卡，否则公证员应在下个月的第 15 日或之前提供该月的零公证列表。

(c) (i)where any deed or instrument which is to be executed or acknowledged by two or more parties is signed during any month by one or more, as the case may be, of such parties, the notary shall, notwithstanding that the deed or instrument has not been signed by all such-parties, include such deed or instrument in the list required to be delivered or transmitted under paragraph (a), and shall, if called upon so to do by written notice served on him personally or by registered post and signed by the Registrar of Lands of the district in which the notary resides, produce

（c）（i）在一个月或多个月内，被执行或承认的契约或文书由两方或多方当事人签署的，和尽管所有当事人还未签署契约或文书，但视情况此契约或文书属于需要按第（a）项送交或转交、要求亲自送达书面通知或以挂号邮递方式、要有公证员所在地区土地登记处签字的清单内，则在通知书所列明的日期或之前，应向登记官办公室提交该契约或文书的副本以供检查。

the duplicate of such deed or instrument for inspection at the office of the registrar on or before such date as may be specified in the notice;

(ii) where any such deed or instrument is not signed by all the parties thereto before the expiry of a period of three months from the date on which it is first signed by one of such parties, the notary shall, if called upon so to do by written notice served on him personally or by registered post and signed by the Registrar of Lands of the district in which the notary resides, deliver or transmit to the registrar the duplicate of such deed or instrument; and where any such duplicate has been so delivered or transmitted, the notary shall, at any time during the period of two years succeeding the date of such delivery or transmission, be entitled on demand to the return of the duplicate for the purpose of the completion of the deed or instrument.

（ii）如果该契约或文书在其中一方当事人首次签署之日起3个月期满之前未由所有当事方签署，那么公证员将亲自送达书面通知或以挂号邮递方式送达并且由公证员所在地区土地登记处签字，将该契约或文书的副本送交或转交给登记官；该副本已被送交或转交后，公证员有权在送交或转交之日后的2年内，为完成契约或文书而要求返还副本。

(27) Weekly list of work done to be transmitted to Registrar of Lands.

（27）向土地登记处转交每周所做工作的清单。

He shall deliver or transmit to the Registrar of Lands of the district within which he resides, so as to reach the registrar on or before every Wednesday, a list of the work done by him as notary in the week ending the previous Saturday. Every such list shall be substantially in the form G in the Second Schedule:

公证员应将其作为公证员在刚结束的上周六内所做工作的清单于每个星期三或之前送交或转交至其所在地区的土地登记机关的登记官处。每份清单应采用附表2中表格G的形式。

Provided that in the case of a will or codicil the names of the person or persons executing or acknowledging the instrument shall not be inserted.

但如果是遗嘱或遗嘱的附件，那么不得插入执行或承认该文书人的姓名。

(28) Transmission to the Registrar of land of deeds executed before different notaries.

（28）向土地登记处转交在不同公证员处执行的契约。

Where any deed or instrument other than a will or codicil shall be executed or acknowledged by two or more parties before more than one notary, the duplicate of such deed or instrument shall be delivered or transmitted by the notary who first attests such deed or instrument to the Registrar of Lands of the district in which he resides; and it shall not be necessary for the other notary or notaries employed in the execution of such deed or instrument to deliver or transmit any duplicate thereof to such registrar.

除遗嘱或遗嘱的附件外，应由两方或多方当事人在多于一名公证员处执行或承认契约或文书，则该契约或文书的副本应由首次证明该契约或文书的公证员送交或转交给他所在地区的土地登记处；其他公证员或者在执行该契据或文书时聘用的公证员，则无须将副本送交或转交给登记官。

(29) (Transmission to the Registrar of Lands of deeds affecting lands situated outside district in which notary resides. [§10, Law 20 of 1976.])

（29）向土地登记处转交对公证员所在地区以外土地有影响的契约。[1976年第20号法令第10条]

If a deed or instrument other than a will or codicil affects a land situated in a district other than that in which the notary before whom it is signed, and by whom it is attested, ‘shall reside, such notary, or in case such deed or instrument is attested by two or more notaries, then the notary upon whom is cast the duty of transmitting to the

除遗嘱或遗嘱的附件外，公证员签署或公证了对其所在地区之外土地有影响的契约或文书，对该公证员或该契约或文书应有2名或2名以上的公证员公证，而后公证员有义务在下一个月的第15日或之前将该契约或文书的副本转交给土地登记处（要按前述方式转交），并且将其公证的副本，以及由其签署的

Registrar of Lands the duplicate of such deed or instrument, shall on or before the fifteenth day of the month next following that in which the same was executed (besides transmitting the duplicate in manner aforesaid) deliver or transmit to the Registrar of Lands of the district in which such land shall be situated a copy thereof certified by him as correct, together with a list in duplicate in the form F in the Second Schedule, signed by him, of all such deeds or instruments as relate to lands in such last- mentioned district.

(30) Procedure in regard to deed executed by an attorney.

If he attest any deed or instrument executed before him by means of an attorney, he shall preserve a true copy of the power of attorney with his protocol, and shall forward a like copy with the duplicate to the Registrar of Lands.

(31) Notice of intention to change office or to 'discontinue practice to be given to High Court Judge.

He shall give one month's notice to the High Court Judge in the judicial zone in which he is authorized to practise, and also to the Registrar- General, of his intention to change his office or to discontinue his practice, and shall affix a written notice to that effect, signed by him, on the outside door or wall of the High Court holden in the zone,

(32) Notice on change of office.

Whenever he shall change his office he shall without delay give notice of such change to the Registrar of Lands of the district and the High Court Judge in the judicial zone and the Government Agent of the administrative district in which his new office is situated.

(33) Title deed of immovable property to be obtained wherever possible.

When a deed transferring any immovable property is executed or acknowledged before a notary, he shall use his best endeavours to obtain the title deed, if any, of such property, and make an endorsement thereon stating the number and date of the deed executed before him and the nature of the transaction and attach his signature thereto,

(34) Notary bound to furnish Registrar- General with explanation whenever called upon.

He shall, in regard to any irregularity, error, or omission discovered or alleged to have been discovered in the discharge of his duties as notary, and which appears to the Registrar- General to be a violation of the law, give an explanation in writing when required by the Registrar-General or by the Registrar of Lands under the order of the

所有关于前述地区土地的此类契约或文件副本清单按照附表 2 中表格 F 的形式，送交或交付给土地所在地区的土地登记处。

（30）关于律师执行契约的程序。

如果公证员公证通过律师在其面前执行的契约或文书，公证员应在其议定书中保存一份授权书的真实副本，并将该契约副本和授权书副本提交给土地登记处。

（31）向高等法院发出意欲更换职务或停止执业的通知。

公证员应提前一个月向授权其执业的司法区高等法院法官和总登记处发出其意欲更换职务或停止执业的通知，并且应在高等法院门外或墙上张贴由其签署的书面通知。

（32）更换职务的通知。

每当更换职务时，公证员应将更换职务事宜通知该地区土地登记处和该司法区高等法院法官，以及新职务所在地区的行政区政府代理人。

（33）尽可能地取得不动产的所有权证书。

在公证员面前执行或承认转让不动产的契约时，公证员应尽最大努力取得该财产的所有权证书（如有的话），在上面背书，写明在其面前执行契约的序号和日期、交易的性质，并附上签名。

（34）公证员必须在需要时向总登记处提供说明。

公证员在履行职务时发现或声称发现存在违规行为、错误或遗漏，并且总登记处可能会认为是违法时，基于总登记处要求或总登记处对土地登记处的命令要求，公证员应以书面形式作出说明。但自此类违规行为、错误或遗漏发生之日起满 24 个月后，不再需要提供该种说明。

Registrar-General, but such explanation shall in no case be called for after the expiry of twenty- four months from the date of the commission of such irregularity or error, or of such omission.

(35) Name to be affixed at entrance to office.

He shall cause his name, with the addition " Notary Public", to be painted or affixed in legible characters in the Sinhala language and the language in which he is authorized to practise in a conspicuous place at or near the entrance to his office or place of business, or, if he has more than one office or place of business, at the entrance to each such place.

(36) Additional rules applicable to notary who is not an attorney-at-law.

It shall be the duty of every notary, not being an attorney-at-law, strictly to observe and act in conformity with the following additional rules, that is to say:—

(a)Notary to hold office at approved place.

He shall live and hold office at such places as he may elect, subject to the approval of the Minister.

(b)* Records to be kept at notary's office.[§10, Law 20 of 1976]

He shall keep his records at his office or if he has more than one office, at such office as may be approved of by the Registrar-General and shall at all reasonable times permit the Registrar-General, the Government Agent of the administrative district, High Court Judge, District Judge, Judge of the Family Court, or Judge of the Primary Court within the zone, within which such notary resides to inspect such records at such office.

*See the footnote to section 18.

(c) When notary bound to be present in office.

He shall, unless prevented by sickness or other good cause, be present between the hours of 10 a.m. and 1 p.m. on Mondays and Thursdays, or, if such day be a public holiday, on the following day, at the office in which he keeps his records. The taking of instructions for or signature to a deed or instrument shall not be a good cause for absence from office, unless the person whose instructions or signature is to be taken is believed to be on the point of death.

(d) Notary to produce records when required.

He shall at all reasonable times, when required by any of the officers named in the rule (b), produce before him at the nearest land registry, kachcheri, court, resthouse, or other public place such records as may be specified in a notice to be served on such notary. The notice shall be deemed duly served if left at his residence or office.

（35）在办公室入口处张贴姓名。

公证员应在其名字旁冠以“公证员”，并用清晰易读的僧伽罗语和授权职业的语言印刷或张贴铭牌在其办公室显眼的地方或入口处或办公地点，如果公证员有两个办公室或办公地点，那么在每个办公室入口处均应印刷或张贴铭牌。

（36）适用于非律师公证员的附加规则。

每个非律师公证员都必须严格遵守以下附加规则，即：

（a）公证员在批准的地方任职。

公证员应按照部长的批准，在其所选择的地方居住和任职。

（b）* 将记录保存在公证机构。[1976 年第 20 号法令第 10 条]

公证员应将记录保存在其办公室或者经总登记处批准的一个以上的办公室内，并且允许总登记处、行政区政府代理人、高等法院法官、地区法官、家事法院法官或区域内初级法院法官，在合理的时间内于公证员所在的该办公室检查此类记录。

* 见第 18 节的脚注。

（c）公证员必须在办公室出勤。

除非因疾病或其他正当理由，公证员应在星期一和星期四上午 10 点至下午 1 点之间出勤，如果当天是公众假期，那么第二天公证员应到办公室对此进行记录。除非本应进行指导或签名的人正好死亡，否则对契约或文书进行指导或签字不能成为缺勤的正当原因。

（d）公证员在有要求时提交记录。

当第（b）项中所列官员有要求时，公证员应在合理时间内于最近的土地登记处、会场、法院、休息室或其他公共场所，提交通知中列明的记录。通知留置在公证员的住所或办公室，应视为已送达。

32. Provisions as to application of rules in section 31 in special cases.

(1) The provisions of rules (20), (23), (24), (25), and (26) set out in section 31, and of rule (16) as to the statement of the boundaries, shall not apply to any of the following deeds or instruments:—

(i) a power of attorney for use out of Sri Lanka;

(ii) a deed solely affecting property not situated in Sri Lanka;

(iii) a transfer of stock of any Government;

* See the footnote to section 18.

(iv) a transfer of stock, shares, or debentures of any company or corporation not having its registered office in Sri Lanka;

(v) a notice of protest by a ship's officer but not an extended protest.

(2) In the case of any deed or instrument which is to be executed by two or more parties, both or all of whom, as the case may be, do not sign the deed or instrument at the same time and place—

(i) the deed or instrument shall, for the purposes of the application of rules (6), (7), (23) and (25) set out in section 31, be deemed to be executed or acknowledged at the time when it is first signed by a party, or by two or more parties at the same time and place;

(ii) the deed or instrument shall, for the purposes of the application of rules(18) and (20) set out in section 31, be deemed to be executed or acknowledged whenever it is signed by a party, or by two or more parties at the same time and place; and

(iii) the provisions of rule (19) set out in section 31, shall apply after the deed or instrument is first signed by a party, or by two or more parties at the same time and place.

33. Instruments not to be invalid for non-compliance with section 31 in any matter of form.

No instrument shall be deemed to be invalid by reason only of the failure of any notary to observe any provision of any rule set out in section 31 in respect of any matter of form:

Provided that nothing hereinbefore contained shall be deemed to give validity to any instrument which may be invalid by reason of non-compliance with the provisions of any other written law.

34. Penalty for beaches of rules in section31.

(1) If any notary acts in violation of or disregards or

32. 在特殊情况下适用第 31 条规则的规定

（1）第 31 条第（20）款、第（23）款、第（24）款、第（25）款及第（26）款的规定，以及第（16）款关于范围的规定，不适用下列契约或文书：

（i）在斯里兰卡境外使用的授权书；

（ii）仅影响斯里兰卡境外财产的契约；

（iii）任何政府的股票转让；

* 见第 18 节的脚注。

（iv）转让任何公司或在斯里兰卡没有注册过办公室公司的股票、股份或债券；

（v）船舶官员的声明通知，延长的声明除外。

（2）若契约或文书由两方或多方当事人执行，则视情况而定，并不需要双方或全部当事人在同一时间及地点签署该契约或文书——

（i）就第 31 条第（6）款、第（7）款、第（23）款及第（25）款的适用而言，契约或文书应在一方当事人已经先签名时或者，双方或多方在同一时间及地点签名时，视为已被执行或承认；

（ii）就第 31 条第（18）款和第（20）款的适用而言，契据或文书应在一方签名时或者，双方或多方在同一时间及地点签名时，视为已被执行或承认；

（iii）应在契约或文书由一方当事人率先签名后或者，双方或多方在同一时间及地点签名后适用第 31 条第（19）款的规定。

33. 文书不因为未遵守第 31 条的规定而无效

任何文书均不得仅因为公证员未遵守第 31 条的规定而被视为无效：

但是，因为不遵守其他明文的规定而可能无效的文书，前述的任何内容不得视为对其赋予有效性。

34. 对违反第 31 条的处罚

（1）如果任何公证员违反、无视、忽视遵守对其

neglects to observe any of rules set out in section 31 or any rule made, approved and published in accordance with the provisions of section 36, binding upon him, he shall be guilty of an offence, and shall, on conviction after summary trial before a Magistrate, be liable to a fine not exceeding two hundred rupees, in addition to any civil liability he may incur thereby:

Provided, however, that where any notary acts in violation of or disregards or neglects to observe the provisions of rule (26) set out in section 31 the Registrar-General may, by a written notice served on him personally or sent by registered post, call upon such notary to comply with the requirements of the said rule within such further time as he may specify for such purpose, and any notary who fails to comply with the terms of such notice shall be guilty of an offence and shall, on conviction after summary trial before a Magistrate, be liable to a fine not exceeding five hundred rupees.

(2) If any notary has been convicted under the proviso to subsection (1) of this section for non-compliance with the terms of a notice calling upon him to comply with the requirements of rule (26) set out in section 31 relating to the delivery of certain documents to the Registrar of Lands of the district in which the notary resides, and the notary fails within a week of such conviction to deliver the documents specified in the notice to that registrar, the Minister may, on application made in that behalf by the Registrar-General, suspend the notary from his office as notary for such period as the Minister may deem fit.

35. Power to compound offences.

(1) In any case where the Registrar- General has reasonable grounds for believing that any notary has committed any offence referred to in section 28 (3), section 30, section 34, section 37 or section 41, the Registrar-General may, if he thinks fit, instead of instituting criminal proceedings against such notary, accept from him such sum of money as he may consider proper in composition of the offence; and where the Registrar-General has accepted any sum of money from any notary in composition of any alleged offence—

(i) criminal proceedings shall not be taken, or if already taken shall not be continued in respect of such offence; and

(ii) such composition shall not have the effect of discharging any person who has given security on behalf of a notary by the hypothecation of immovable property or

有约束力的第 31 条或者依第 36 条制定、批准和公布的规定，即属犯罪，经地方治安官简易判决后，可处以不超过 200 卢比的罚款，并承担可能因此导致的民事责任。

但是，如果任何公证员违反、无视、忽视遵守第 31 条第（26）款的规定，总登记处可通过亲自送达书面通知或以挂号邮递方式送达，通知公证员在之后遵守前述规定的要求。未按通知要求遵守规定的公证员即属犯罪，经地方治安官简易判决后，可处以不超过 500 卢比的罚款。

（2）如公证员因未按通知要求遵守第 31 条第（26）款中向所在的土地登记处送交特定文件的规定，已经根据本条第（1）款被定罪，且公证员在被定罪后一周内未能将通知中所列文件送交给登记官，部长可根据总登记处的申请，在部长认为合适的期间内暂停公证员的职务。

35. 对犯罪进行和解的权力

（1）对犯第 28 条第（3）款、第 30 条、第 34 条、第 37 条或第 41 条的公证员，总登记处有合理的理由相信他，在合适的情况下，可不对其提起刑事诉讼，而是接受其因构成犯罪所缴纳的罚金；如果总登记处已接受公证员因构成犯罪缴纳的罚金则——

（i）不得就该罪提起刑事诉讼，若已经提起刑事诉讼则不再继续；以及

（ii）该和解不包括解除第 12 条中代表公证员提供不动产抵押或存放动产的担保，或者保险公司作为担保人所承担责任的效力。

by the deposit of movable property, or the Insurance Corporation bound as surety from any liability incurred under section 12.

(2) All moneys received by the Registrar- General in composition of any offence shall be paid into the Treasury.

（2）总登记处收到公证员的因构成犯罪缴纳的罚金，均应存入国库。

36. Power to make rules.

(1) The Minister may make rules for the conduct of notaries, not being attorneys- at-law, in the discharge of their notarial duties.

(2) No rule made under subsection (1) of this section shall have effect until that rule has been approved by Parliament, and until the rule has been published in the Gazette.

(3) Every rule made, approved and published in accordance with the preceding provisions of this section shall be as valid and effectual as if it were herein enacted.

36. 制定规则的权力

（1）部长可以对非律师公证员就履行公证员职责制定行为规则。

（2）根据本条第（1）款订立的规则，只有通过议会批准，并在公报上公布后才能生效。

（3）按照本条前述规定所制定、批准和公布的每项规则，与本法同等效力。

37. Notary to use diligence in registering deeds.

Whenever a notary has received instructions to register, and a sufficient sum to meet the necessary expense of registering, any deed drawn or attested by him, and shall in such case fail to use due diligence in effecting such registration, he shall be guilty of an offence, and liable on conviction to a fine not exceeding one thousand rupees, in addition to any civil liability which he may incur by reason of his default.

37. 公证员在登记契约时应尽的勤勉义务

当公证员收到登记官的指示，并且已有足够的金额来支付登记所需的费用，却未能尽勤勉义务，没有登记已经由他认证或公证的契据时，即属犯罪，一经定罪可处不超过1000卢比的罚款，并承担可能因此导致的民事责任。

38. Notary to try to ascertain true consideration.

(1) It shall be the duty of every notary to endeavour to ascertain the true and full consideration for the execution of any deed, and to insert and set forth the same in such deed.

(2) Any notary who shall knowingly and wilfully insert or set forth in or upon any such deed any other than the full and true consideration or money directly or indirectly paid or secured, or agreed to be paid or secured for the same, or the actual value of the same, or shall abet the doing thereof, respectively, shall be guilty of an offence, and liable to a fine not exceeding one thousand rupees for every such offence, in addition to any civil liability which he may incur thereby.

38. 公证员查明对价的真实性

（1）每名公证员均有义务尽力查明所执行契据对价的真实性及全面性，并在该契据中插入和提出。

（2）除了对价的真实性及全面性，直接或间接支付提供担保的，同意为契约支付提供担保的，或在契约的真实价值外，公证员明知并故意在契约中插入或提出的其他行为，或者公证员怂恿进行此类行为，即属犯罪，每项罪行可处以不超过1000卢比的罚款。

39. Penalty on notary acting fraudulently.

If any notary—

(a) shall attest any fraudulent deed, knowing the same to be fraudulent; or

(b) shall knowingly and wilfully, with intent to prejudice or defraud any person, insert in any deed or instru-

39. 对公证员欺诈行为的处罚

任何公证员如果——

（a）明知契约是欺诈性的，还公证该欺诈性契约；或者

（b）明知且故意，意图损害或欺诈任何人，在契据或文书中插入不应插入的话语、字母、数字、事情

ment whatsoever any word, letter, figure, matter, or thing which ought not to have been inserted therein, or omit to insert therein any word, letter, figure, matter, or thing which ought to have been inserted therein; or

(c) shall attest any deed without the person whose signature or mark he attested and the attesting witnesses having appeared personally before him at the time when such deed was executed or acknowledged; or

(d) shall knowingly and wilfully make any false statement in the attestation to any deed executed or acknowledged before him; or

(e) shall wilfully, maliciously, or fraudulently misstate or misrepresent to any party thereto the contents or effect of any deed executed or acknowledged before him; or .

(f) shall by any other wilful act, either of commission or omission, commit or attempt to commit any fraud in the execution of his office; or

(g) shall wilfully, maliciously, or fraudulently deface, mutilate, injure, destroy, or make away with any deed or any draft, minute, or copy of any deed which had been in his charge or custody, or which he was bound to preserve,

every such notary shall in any of such cases be guilty of an offence, and shall be liable on conviction thereof to imprisonment, simple or rigorous, for any period not exceeding five years.

40. Fees of notaries

(1)The several fees specified in the Third Schedule shall and may be lawfully demanded and taken by notaries for the performance of the duties of their office as therein expressed:

Provided that—

(a)it shall be competent to any notary or client to agree to a higher or lower fee than that prescribed in the Third Schedule;

(b) such agreement, unless reduced to writing and signed by the parties, shall not be enforceable in a court of law.

(2)* [§11, Law 20 of 1976]

A correct copy of the Third Schedule in the Sinhala, Tamil and English languages of the fees chargeable by notaries shall be at all times posted in some conspicuous place at the High Court holden in every zone and at every District Court, Family Court and Primary Court, and at every Land Registry and kachcheri, and by every notary in each of his offices.

* See the footnote to section 18.

或物件，或省略应该插入的话语、字母、数字、事情或物件；或者

（c）公证没有见证人签名或符号的契约以及见证人在该契约执行或承认时没有亲自出现在公证员面前；或者

（d）明知且故意在执行或承认契约的公证中作出虚假陈述；或者

（e）故意、恶意或欺诈性地作出错误陈述或向任何一方歪曲其所执行或承认契约的内容或效力；或者

（f）其他故意行为，无论是作为还是不作为，在履行职务时犯下或试图犯下的任何欺诈行为；或者

（g）故意、恶意或欺骗性地污损、毁伤、伤害、毁坏、废除契约或者他负责、保管或有义务保护的契约草案、记录、副本。

在这些情况中的每个公证员均属犯罪，一经定罪，可处以轻微或严重的监禁，但不得超过5年。

40. 公证的费用

（1）附表3所列明的若干费用应该并可以由公证员合法提出并接受，因为公证员按里面所述履行了职责：

但是——

（a）任何公证员或申请人均有权同意高于或低于附表3所规定的费用；

（b）除非双方书写并签署了此种协议，否则不得在法院强制执行。

（2）*[1976年第20号法令第11条]

附表3公证员以僧伽罗语、泰米尔语和英语书写的收费标准应一直张贴在高等法院管辖的每一区显眼的地方，和地区法院、家事法院、初级法院，以及每一个土地登记处、会场，还有每个公证员的办公室。

* 见第18节的脚注。

(3)Any notary, if required by the client, shall give a written receipt for money paid to him as fees.

（3）如果申请人有要求，公证员应提供书面收据，载明收费情况。

41. Delivery to registrar of documents of notary dying, &c.

(1) If any person being removed from or ceasing to act in the office of notary, or, in case of the death of any such notary, if any of his heirs, executors, or administrators, or any other persons, into whose possession the same shall have come—

(a) shall wilfully lose or injure or destroy, or shall without just and lawful cause wilfully neglect or refuse to deliver over, as soon as conveniently may be, to the Registrar of Lands of the district in which such notary was resident, any drafts, minutes, or copies of any deeds executed or acknowledged before such notary, or any instruction book, register, index, deed, or document whatever possessed by such notary in right of his said office; or

(b) shall wilfully neglect or refuse to deliver over to the Registrar of Lands of the district the seal of office of such notary to be defaced and returned,

every such person shall be guilty of an offence, and shall on conviction thereof be liable to simple or rigorous imprisonment for any period not exceeding twelve calendar months, or to a fine not exceeding two hundred rupees, or to both.

(2) Where two or more notaries carry on a notarial business in partnership which has been notified to the Registrar-General, and one of the partners dies or retires from the business, the continuing partner may retain during the continuance of the business the documents specified in paragraph (a) of subsection (I). But a list of the documents shall be furnished to the Registrar-General by the continuing partner, who shall be responsible for their safe custody and for their delivery to the Registrar-General

(3) Where a notary who is an attorney-at- law has engaged for the purposes of his business an assistant who is also a notary and such assistant practises as a notary under such an engagement for the purposes of the business of the said notary who is an attorney-at-law, and the terms of such engagement have been notified by the parties to the Registrar-General, upon such assistant dying or leaving the service of his principal, the Registrar-General may (subject to the terms of the engagement) empower the said principal to retain the documents specified in paragraph (a)

41. 公证员死亡时文件送交登记官

（1）如果公证员被调走或停止在公证机构任职或去世，其继承人、遗嘱执行人或其他人在管理公证员财产时——

（a）故意遗失或破坏或毁坏，或在没有公正合法理由的情况下故意忽视或拒绝尽快将草案、会议记录、在该公证员处执行或承认的契约副本、指示书、登记册、索引、契约、文件，以及在该公证员办公室内的所有文件送交该公证员所在地区的土地登记处；或者

（b）故意忽视或拒绝向该区的土地登记处交付该公证员损毁或退回的印章。

有上述行为的人员均属犯罪，一经定罪，可处以不超过 12 个月轻微或严重的监禁，或不超过 200 卢比的罚款，或两者并罚。

（2）如果 2 名或 2 名以上公证员以合伙形式经营公证业务并已通知总登记处，其中一名合伙人死亡或退出业务时，继续经营的合伙人可在业务存续期间保留第（1）款第（a）项列明的文件。但是继续经营的合伙人应向总登记处提供文件清单，负责安全保管清单，并送交总登记处。

（3）律师公证员为其业务目的聘用了公证员助理，并且，出于前述从事公证员的业务目的，该助理受聘作为公证员执业。当事人已将该聘用通知了总登记处，在该助理死亡或不再服务于雇主后，总登记处可以（根据雇佣条款的规定）授权前述雇主保留第（1）款第（a）项所列明的文件，因此就本条例而言，所有此类文件须当作是在该雇主处执行或承认的文件，或在雇主的职权内产生的文件。但是，雇主应向总登记处提供文件清单，负责安全保管清单，并送交总登记处。

of subsection (1), and all such documents shall thereupon, for the purposes of this Ordinance, be deemed to be documents executed or acknowledged before such principal, or possessed by him in right of his office. But a list of the said documents shall be furnished to the Registrar-General by the principal who shall be responsible for their safe custody and for their delivery to the Registrar-General.

[§12, Law 20 of 1976.]

(4)Where the Registrar-General is satisfied that any notary has purchased the goodwill of the notarial business of another notary who carried on business in a place in the area within which the purchaser is authorised to practise, but who has since died or who has ceased to act in the office of notary otherwise than by reason of the cancellation or suspension of his warrant, the Registrar-General may empower the heirs, executors, or administrators of the deceased notary, or the notary so ceasing to act, to transfer to the notary so purchasing the goodwill of the said business the documents specified in paragraph (a) of subsection (1) (not being wills or codicils, or drafts, minutes, or copies of the same), or if such documents have been already delivered to the Registrar-General, may himself transfer the said documents as aforesaid, and the said documents shall thereupon, for all the purposes of this Ordinance, be deemed to be documents executed or acknowledged before the notary purchasing the goodwill or possessed by him in right of his office. But a list of the said documents shall be furnished to the Registrar-General by such notary, who shall be responsible for their safe custody and for their delivery to the Registrar-General.

(5) It shall be lawful to the Registrar- General to extend the application of the provisions of subsections (3) and (4) of this section—

(a) to any case in which an assistant has died or left the service of his principal within five years prior to the 27th day of October, 1917, notwithstanding that no notice of the terms of the engagement of such assistant has been given to the Registrar-General; or

(b) to any case in which any notary has died, or has ceased to act in the office of notary within the said period otherwise than by reason of the cancellation or suspension of his warrant:

Provided that the Registrar-General is satisfied that such a course has been assented to by all persons interested.

[1976 年第 20 号法令第 1 条]

（4）如总登记处认可公证员购买了在其授权执业范围内另一公证员的公证业务商誉，卖方公证员因为死亡或者因为取消或中止其令状之外等原因而停止在公证机构任职，则总登记处可授权已故公证员的继承人、遗嘱执行人、管理员或停止任职的公证员向买方公证员转移前述第（1）款第（a）项所列明的购买商誉业务文件（不是遗嘱及其附件、草案、会议记录或者该文件的副本），如果此类文件已经送交总登记处，或已由卖方自行转移前述文件，那么就本条例而言，此类文件须当作是在购买商誉的公证员处执行或承认的文件，或在其职权内产生的文件。但是，该公证员应向总登记处提供文件清单，负责安全保管清单，并送交总登记处。

（5）总登记处应合法延长本条第（3）款及第（4）款的申请时间——

（a）虽然没有向总登记处发出关于该助理的雇佣条款通知，但是助理去世或不再服务于雇主的案件是在 1917 年 10 月 27 日之前的 5 年内的情况；或者

（b）因取消或终止令状之外的原因，公证员在前述期间内去世或停止在公证机构任职的情况。

但总登记处要在所有利益相关者同意的情况下延长。

42. Notary to deliver to the registrar lists of duplicate deeds filed.

Whenever the duplicate of any deed shall be transmitted to the registrar by any notary under any rule in section 31 of this Ordinance, or whenever any document shall be delivered up to any registrar under section 41, such notary or other person transmitting or delivering the same shall tender to the registrar two lists thereof, and the said registrar shall, after ascertaining the correctness thereof, sign the said lists, and return one of them to the said notary or other party, and file the remaining list, and securely keep and preserve the same and the documents specified therein with the other records of his office:

Provided, however, that any document, other than a draft or copy of a will or codicil, which is delivered to the registrar under the last preceding section, may be destroyed by him at any time after the expiry of a period of two years from the date on which the document was delivered to him, if, after inspection duly made, he is satisfied that the duplicate of that document is preserved in the records of his office.

42. 公证员向登记员送交契约副本清单以归档

公证员应根据本条例第 31 条将契约副本转交登记官，或根据第 41 条将文件送交登记官，公证员或其他人在转交或送交文件时应向登记官提供两份清单。该登记官在查明其正确性后，应在前述清单上签字，将其中一份归还给公证员或另一方，并将余下的一份清单归档，妥善保管，同时在其办公室保留前述所列文件和其他记录。

但是，根据前一节送交给登记官的除草案、遗嘱及其附件的副本之外的文件，如经登记官正式检查并认可，且将该文件副本保留在其办公室的记录中，则登记官可以自收到转交文件之日起两年期满后的任何时间销毁该文件。

43. Interpretation.

In this Ordinance, unless the subject or context otherwise requires—

"High Court Judge "shall mean a Judge of the High Court; '

"Registrar-General "includes a Deputy Registrar-General.

[§§ 2 & 3, Law 23 of 1978.]

43. 说明

在本条例中，除非主题或上下文另有规定——

“高等法院法官” 指高等法院中的法官；

“总登记处” 包括总登记处代理机构。

[1978 年第 23 号法令第 2 条和第 3 条]

FIRST SCHEDULE

A

REGULATIONS FOR THE ADMISSION OF ARTICLED CLERKS UNDER

[Section 7]

1. Every person intending to be an articled clerk with a view to qualifying himself for the office of a notary shall be required to sit for a competitive examination. At every such examination the Registrar-General may reserve—

(a) not less than fifty per centum of the number of vacancies, for notaries' clerks who, at a date to be fixed by the Registrar-General from time to time in respect of each such examination, have been so employed for a continuous period of not less than five years; and

(b) the first four places out of the aforesaid fifty per centum for notaries' clerks with not less than 15 years (continuous or non-continuous) service at the aforesaid date;

附表一

A

关于录取实习律师的规定

[第 7 节]

1. 每个打算成为实习律师以期有资格成为公证员的人都需要参加竞聘考试。在每次考试时，总登记处可保留——

（a）职位空缺数目不少于 50%，实习律师自总登记处确定举行不定时的考试之日起，已经工作不少于 5 年；并且

（b）在前述 50% 中的前 4 名公证员文员应工作不少于 15 年（连续或非连续）。

if the notaries' clerks referred to in the aforesaid provisions of this regulation' obtain qualifying marks at the examination.

2. Every application by a candidate to sit for the examination referred to in regulation 1 shall—

(a) be sent to the Registrar-General;

(b) be susbstantiatly in form A 1 set out in the Second Schedule;

(c) be accompanied by at least two certificates of character, one of which shall be not more than three months old;

(d) be accompanied by the birth certificate of the candidate or such other authentic proof of age as may be, acceptable to the Registrar-General; and

(e) in the case of a notary' s clerk, be accompanied by a certificate or certificates from the notary or notaries under whom he is employed or has been employed in proof of his eligibility under regulation 1.

3. Every application shall be made in the language in which the candidate proposes to practise, and shall be in his own handwriting.

4. No person shall be permitted to sit for the examination unless he has reached the age of eighteen years on the date of the commencement of the examination.

5. The examination shall be conducted by the Commissioner of Examinations, who shall send a report to the Registrar-General, setting out the results of the examination in order of merit.

6. (1) On the receipt of the report referred to in regulation 5 from the Commissioner of Examinations, the Registrar-General shall make inquiries, regarding the character, repute and suitability of such number of the candidates named in the report as he may deem necessary.

The Registrar-General shall, after due consideration of the results of the examination and the information obtained in consequence of the Inquiries made under paragraph (1), select the required number of candidates to be articled clerks, and shall inform by registered letter each candidate so selected that he has been selected to be an articled clerk on the results of the examination, and that he is required within three months from the date of the letter, to nominate in writing the attorney-al-law with whom he proposes to enter into articles of agreement.

Every candidate who has within the time specified furnished the written nomination required under paragraph (2) shall be issued a licence for the purpose of entering into articles of agreement with the attorney-at- law named by him.

7. Every candidate to whom a licence has been issued shall, within six months of the date of the issue of such licence—

(a) enter into articles of agreement with the attorney-at-law named in the licence and commence apprenticeship; and

(b) send a copy of such articles of agreement to the Registrar-General.

8. No person shall be an articled clerk unless he has obtained a licence from the Registrar-General.

9. Every articled clerk shall serve his articles for a term of not less than two years.

[§ 3, Law 24 of 1973]

本规定前述条款中提到的人员同时在考试中取得合格分数。

2. 候选人申请参加规定 1 所述的考试，须——

（a）送交总登记处；

（b）采用附表 2 中的 A1 表格；

（c）至少附有 2 份人品证明书，其中 1 份证明书应在 3 个月内作出；

（d）附有候选人的出生证明书或总登记处可接受的其他可靠的年龄证明；以及

（e）如果是公证员的文员，须附有证明书，或者有公证员证明，或者有正在聘用他或聘用过他的公证员证明其有规定 1 的资格。

3. 每份申请均应以候选人意欲执业的语言制作，并亲笔书写。

4. 除非在考试开始之日已满 18 岁，否则不允许参加考试。

5. 考试由考试专员管理，其应按照分数由高到低列出考试结果，向总登记处发送报告。

6.（1）总登记处在收到规定 5 中由考试专员提交的报告后，在其认为必要时须就报告中所列候选人的人品、声誉及适当性进行调查。

总登记处在适当考虑考试结果和根据第（1）款调查所获信息后，应选择所需数量的候选人成为实习律师，并通过挂号信告知被选上的候选人其已根据考试结果被遴选为实习律师。并且告知其需要在信件发出之日起 3 个月内以书面形式指明他希望予以签约的律师。

应向根据第（2）段列明时间内提供书面指明的候选人出具证书，以便他与所指明的律师订立合约。

7. 已出具证书的候选人，须在出具该证书后 6 个月内——

（a）与该证书所指明的律师订立合约，并开始学徒训练；并且

（b）将该合约的副本送交总登记处。

8. 除非获得总登记处的证书，否则任何人不得成为实习律师。

9. 每名实习律师的合约履行期应不少于 2 年。

[1973 年第 24 号法令第 3 条]

10. If the attorney-at-law under whom the articled clerk is serving is not a notary practising in the language in which the clerk proposes to practise, he shall serve for one year as a clerk of such attorney-at-law, and for one subsequent year as a clerk in the office of a notary practising in the language in which he intends to practise and shall, in such a case, obtain a fresh licence from the Registrar-General and enter into fresh articles of agreement with the notary named in such licence. A copy of such articles of agreement shall be sent to the Registrar-General.

10. 如果实习律师所履职的律师公证员不是以实习律师所意欲的语言进行执业的，那么他应担任该律师1年的文员之后的1年应在使用其所意欲的语言执业的公证员办公室担任文员。在这种情况下，应从总登记处获得新的证书，并与证书中指明的公证员签订新的合约。该合约的副本应送交总登记处。

[§ 3, Law 24 of 1973.]

[1973年第24号法令第3条]

11. In the event of the attorney-at-law to whom any person is articled dying or discontinuing to practise in the zone in which he practised when such articles were entered into, or for any other good and sufficient reason, the Registrar-General may permit such articled clerk to transfer his articles to some other attorney-al-law, in which case the time during which he shall have served under his original articles shall be reckoned as part of the term of his apprenticeship, notwithstanding such transfer.

11. 如果律师在签订合约时死亡或者不能继续在所执业的区域执业，或者有其他正当且充分的理由时，总登记处可以允许该实习律师将他的合约转至其他律师处。虽然有这种转移，但是在这种情况下，其学徒期限由原合约继续计算。

12. In proof of service under regulations 9 and 10, the clerk shall, on or before the thirty-first day of March, the thirtieth day of June, the thirtieth day of September, and the thirty-first day of December, in each year, forward to the Registrar-General a certificate in form B in the Second Schedule to this Ordinance from the attorney-at-law or notary under whom he is serving.

12. 规定9和规定10中的服务证明，应在每年3月31日、6月30日、9月30日和12月31日当日或之前，向总登记处提交其向所服务的律师或公证员以本条例附表2表格B的形式出具的证明书。

13. Any articled clerk failing to furnish the certificate referred to in regulation 12 shall not be allowed, unless he explains such failure to the satisfaction of the Registrar-General, to count the period during which he shall have so failed as pan of the period of his apprenticeship.

13. 不能提供规定12证明书的实习律师，除非总登记处有理由采信其解释，否则不得将其未能证明的期间计为其学徒期。

14. For the purposes of these regulations, the expression “ notary’ s clerk “ means a clerk employed by a notary for the purposes of his professional work as a notary.

14. 就本规定而言，“公证员文员”一词是指公证员为其专业工作而聘用的文员。

REGULATIONS FOR THE ADMISSION OF NOTARIES UNDER

关于录取公证员的规定

[Section 7]

[第7节]

1. Every articled clerk who has served his articles for a term of not less than two years and is desirous of qualifying as a notary shall be required to sit for the final examination for notaries, for which he shall make a written application to the Registrar-General. Such application shall be substantially in form A2 in the Second Schedule to this Ordinance, and shall be supported by the documents mentioned in paragraph 9 of that form.

1. 凡履行合约的期限不少于2年，并希望获得公证员资格的实习律师，必须向总登记处提出书面申请以参加公证员的最终考试。该申请须采用本条例附表2中表格A2，并提供该表格第9段所述文件。

2. Every articled clerk who intends to make the application referred to in regulation I shall cause the notice of his intended application in Sinhala and in the language in which he intends to practise, to be affixed in some conspicuous part of the High Court holden in the Judicial /one in which he resides and to be published at least once in the Gazette and in a local newspaper in the language in which he intends to practise. Such notice shall be published at least one month before the date of the application to the Registrar-General.

2. 意欲提出规定1所述申请的实习律师，应用僧伽罗语和其意欲执业的语言将其要提交的申请张贴在其所居住的高等法院的显眼位置予以公示，并且至少在公报和当地报纸上用其意欲执业的语言公布一次。应在向总登记处提出申请之日前至少1个月完成上述公示、公布。

3. No articled clerk shall be eligible to sit for the examination referred to in regulation 1 after the expiry of two years from the date of the completion of his articles:

Provided that in any particular case the Minister may exempt an articled clerk from the operation of this regulation.

4. The Registrar-General shall, on the receipt of the application referred to in regulation 1, transmit such application, if it is in order, to the Council of Legal Education for the purpose of holding the examination mentioned in that regulation. The Council of Legal Education shall hold the examination and send a report to the Registrar-General setting out the results of the examination.

5. On the receipt of the report referred to in regulation 4, the Registrar-General shall, if he considers the applicant duly qualified, make a recommendation to the Minister that the applicant is fit to be appointed a notary public.

3. 实习律师自完成合约之日起2年后不再有资格参加规定1所述的考试。

但在特殊情况下，部长可以豁免对实习律师执行本规定。

4. 总登记处在收到规定1所述申请后，应按顺序送交法律教育委员会以便举行该规定的考试。法律教育委员会应举行考试并向总登记处发送报告，并列明考试结果。

5. 在收到规定4所述报告后，总登记处如认为申请人具有适当资格，则应向部长推荐任命该申请人为公证员。

SECOND SCHEDULE

Form Al

APPLICATION FOR PERMISSION TO SIT FOR THE COMPETITIVE EXAMINATION FOR THE SELECTION OF ARTICLED CLERKS

[Regulation 2, First Schedule-A.]

Date: ______________

The Registrar-General,

Colombo.

Sir,

I intend to become an articled clerk with a view to qualifying myself for the office of notary and hereby apply for admission to the competitive examination to be held on __________ for the selection of articled clerks.

2. My full name is: ______________

3. My place of residence is.: __________ in the district of __________

4. I shall be not less than 18 years of age on the date of the commencement of the examination. My birth certificate (or other authentic proofofage being __________) is attached marked (A).

5. I intend to serve as an articled clerk under Mr. ________ Attorney-at-Law of the Supreme Court.

6. The zone and the language in which I propose to practise are _________ (zone) and _________ (language), respectively.

7. (a) I attach the originals of two testimonials of character and suitability given to me by _______ of _______ and _______ of _________ marked (B)and (C).

*(b) I have served as a Notary' s clerk under the under-mentioned notary/notaries/during the period/periods noted against his/their names.

+Under notary ________________ of ___________ during the period from ______________ to ___________

*(c) I attach certificate/certificates from the notary/notaries referred to above in proof of my employment as clerk to a notary during the period/periods referred to above.

附表二

表 A1

申请参加遴选实习律师的竞聘考试

[附表一 A 的规定 2]

日期：________________

总登记处，

科伦坡。

先生，

我意欲成为一名实习律师，以有资格就职于公证机构，特此申请参加于________举行的遴选实习律师的竞聘考试。

2. 我的全名是：________________

3. 我的居住地是：位于________区的______________

4. 在考试开始之日，我已年满18周岁。我的出生证明（或是其他真实的年龄证明文件，即________________）已标为附件（A）。

5. 我意欲在最高法院法官________先生麾下担任实习律师。

6. 我意欲执业的区域和语言分别是________（区域）________________（语言）。

7. (a) 我附上由________的________和________的________给我写的两份人品和适格性的推荐信原件，并标为（B）和（C）。

*（b）我在某期间内于下述的公证员麾下担任公证员的文员。

+自________到________期间于________的公证员________下任职。

*（c）我将附上由前述公证员开具的证明书，证明我在前述期间被雇为公证员文员。

8.I request that I may be granted permission to sit for the competitive examination for the selection of articled clerks.

____

Signature of Applicant.

Postal address: .__________________

*Strike out inapplicable words.

* Repeat as often as may be necessary.

8. 我请求获准参加遴选实习律师的竞聘考试。

____

申请人签名。

邮寄地址：__________________

在不适用时可删除标 * 的条款。

必要时应再次提供标 + 的材料。

Form A2

APPLICATION FOR PERMISSION TO SIT FOR THE NOTARIAL FINAL EXAMINATION AND FOR ADMISSION AS A NOTARY PUBLIC

[Regulation I, First Schedule-B.]

Date: ______________

The Registrar-General,

Colombo.

Sir,

I hereby apply for permission to sit for the Notarial Final Examination and for eventual admission as a Notary.

2. My full name is: __________________

3.My place of residence is _________ in the district of __________________

4.I intend to practise in the __________________ zone.

5.I have attained the age of twenty years.

[E § 4, Law 24 of 1973.]

6.I served my articles under Mr. _______Attorney-at-Law of the Supreme Court, and Mr. _________Notary Public, the date of entering into articles being ________ and the date of completion being __________________

7.I propose to draw, authenticate or attest deeds in the __________________language.

8.The nature of the security I intend to offer is as follows:—

9. I attach—

(a)the licence granted to me by the Registrar-General to be an articled clerk marked (A);

(b)proof that the notice referred to in regulation 2 was affixed in some conspicuous part of the High Court holden in the zone marked (B);

(c)a copy of, or an extract from, the Gazette, and the local newspaper in which the notice referred to in regulation 2 was published marked (C);

(d)a certificate from the attorney-at-law and the notary (if any), to whom I had been apprenticed that I have duly served my term of articles and that in the opinion of such attorney-at-law and notary, I am a fit and proper person to be appointed a notary marked (D); and

(e)my birth certificate or such other authentic evidence of age to prove I have attained the age of twenty years marked (E).

[§ 4, Law 24 of 1973.]

表 A2

申请参加公证员最终考试以及公证员的录取

[附表一 B 的规定 I]

日期：______________

总登记处，

科伦坡。

先生，

我在此申请参加公证员最终考试以及公证员的最后录取。

2. 我的全名是：__________________

3. 我的居住地是：位于 _________ 区的 ._________

4. 我意欲在 _________ 区域执业。

5. 我已经满 20 周岁。

[1973 年第 24 号法令的 E 第 4 条]

6. 我在最高法院法官 ________ 先生和公证员 ________ 先生麾下履行了合约，起始日为 ________ 终止日为 ________

7. 我意欲以 _________ 语言起草、鉴定、公证契约。

8. 我意欲提供的担保种类如下：——

9. 我将附上——

（a）总登记处授予我成为实习律师的证书，标为（A）；

（b）规定 2 中所述通知已张贴在高等法院显眼位置的证据，标为（B）；

（c）按规定 2 于公报及本地报纸中所发布通知的副本或摘录，标为（C）；

（d）来自律师和公证员（如有）的证明书，以证明我已按条约担任学徒，并且该律师和公证员认为我适合被任命为公证员，标为（D）；以及

（e）我的出生证明或其他真实的年龄证明，以证明我已满 20 周岁，标为（E）。

[1973 年第 24 号法令第 4 条]

____

Signature of Applicant.

Postal address: ____________________

Form B

CERTIFICATE BY ATTORNEY-AT-LAW OR NOTARY

[Regulation 12 First Schedule -A.]

1, __________Attorney-at-Law of the Supreme Court of the Republic of Sri Lanka (or Notary Public, as the case may be), certify that the articled clerk named in the schedule hereto annexed has during the quarter ended __________ well and truly served me as clerk, and diligently discharged his duties as such and pursued his studies for the notarial profession.

(Signature) ____________________

Date

Schedule referred to

Name of Articled Clerk	Address	Date of Articles	Zone in which Clerk intends to practise	Zone in which Clerk intends to practise

Form C

DECLARATION TO BE MADE BEFORE JUDGE OF HIGH COURT

[Section 12(1).]

I, A. B., do sincerely promise and declare that I will truly and faithfully and to the best of my ability execute the office of a notary in pursuance of and in conformity with the authority given to me by warrant of the Minister bearing date the ____________ day of ____________ .

Form D

CERTIFICATE BY REGISTRAR, HIGH COURT

[Section 27.]

1, A. B; Registrar of the High Court holden in the zone of ____________ do hereby certify that C. D., of ___________ hath this day delivered and left with me the declaration in writing signed by him required by the Notaries Ordinance, and I further certify that the said C. D. is duly enrolled as a notary and authorized to practise as such in the __________language in the judicial zone of _________ within the district of _________

In witness whereof I have this _________ day of__________, at ___________ set my hand on this stamped certificate.

____

申请人签名。

邮寄地址：____________________

表格 B

律师或公证员出具的证明书

[附表一 A 的规定 12]

1，斯里兰卡共和国最高法院法官（或公证员，视具体情况而定）__________，证明附表所述文员在__________季度结束时确实作为我的文员履职，并且勤勉地履行其职责，为成为公证员不断努力。

（签字）____________________

日期

前述附表

实习律师的姓名	地址	合约的日期	该文员意欲执业的区域	该文员意欲执业的语言

表格 C

给高等法院法官的申报单

[第 12 条第（1）款]

我，A.B.，真诚地承诺并宣布，我将尽我所能真诚和忠实地履行公证员职责，以致力于符合部长通过令状授予的权力，部长签署的授权令状起效于_____月_______日。

表格 D

高等法院登记官授予的证明书

[第 27 条]

1，我 A.B，是___________区域高等法院的登记官，在此证明______________的 C.D 于今天递交了《公证员条例》所要求签署的书面声明，并且我证明 C.D 已被正式登记为公证员并被授权以__________语言在__________地区的__________司法区内执业。

为证明我所言，我于______月_____日，在__________地方在这张盖印证明书上按上手印。

(Signed) A. B., Registrar.

Form E

FORM OF ATTESTATION

[Section 31(21).]

I, A. B: Notary Public, do hereby certify and attest that the foregoing instrument having been read over by (or, read and explained by me, the said notary, to) the said Wahalafantrige Juanis Fernanda, who has signed this deed as Juanis (or with a mark, as the case may he), and who is known to me (if the case be so), in the presence of (insert the names of the witnesses in full, with their residence' ; or, if the name of witness differs from the signature, describe him as above by both the name and the name given in the signature), the subscribing witnesses hereto, both of whom is known to me (if the case he so), the same was signed by the said Wahalatantrige Juanis Fernando and also by the said witnesses in my presence and in the presence of one another, all being present at the same time, on the ___________day of ___________at ___________________.

And I further certify and attest that in line ___ of page____ the word or letter "______" was erased, and in line ______. of page ______ the word or letter "_______" was altered to the word or letter "_________" and in line _____ of page _____ the word or letter "________" was interpolated before the foregoing instrument was read over as aforesaid by me, the said notary, to the said Wahalafantrige Juanis Fernanda that on page _______ the letter "_______" was erased in the signature of _____ by him. and on page ______ the figure "______" on the serial number of the deed was altered by me to " _____- ______" , and on page ______ the date "______" on the stamp of the value of _________ and bearing vendor' s number was altered by me to "_______" , and that Rs ______ - ______ the consideration (or part consideration, or no consideration, as the case may he), was paid in my presence, and that the original of this instrument bears ______stamps of the value of Rs ______and the duplicate______ stamps of the value of Rs ______________

Notary Public.

Seal;

Date of attestation

（签名）登记官 A. B.。

表格 E

公证的形式

[第 31 条第（21）款]

我，A.B：公证员，特此证明并公证上述文书已经前述的 Wahalafantrige Juanis Fernanda 宣读并在契约上签署 Juanis 字样（或符号，视情况而定），以及在我也知道的见证人在场的情况下（插入见证人的全名和住址；如果见证人的名字与签名不同，要在前面说明他的姓名和签名），前述由 Wahalatantrige Juanis Fernando 签署的契约在我在场和他们彼此在场时于_____月_____日__________于_________地方签署。

我将进一步证明并公证在_____页_____行的"_____"单词或字母被删除，并且在_____页_____行的"_____"单词或字母被改为"_____"单词或字母，以及_____页_____行的"_____"单词或字母被添写。前述文书由我，即前述公证员阅读之前，Wahalafantrige Juanis Fernanda 在_____页被删除的"_____"字母处签上_____签名。在_____页的契约序列号_____数字被我改为"_____-_____"。并且在_____页标志上_____的价值的_____日期以及卖主的序号被我改为"__________"，并且_____-_____卢比的对价（或部分对价，或没有对价，视情况而定），是我在场时支付的，文书的原件有......卢比价值的.......标志，并且副本也有_____卢比价值的_____标志。

公证员。

盖章；

公证日期

Form F

REGISTER AND MONTHLY LIST OF DEEDS

[Section 31(24), (26) and(27)]

1	2	3	4		5	6	7	8
No	Date	Nature of Instrument	Name of Parties		District of Registration	Name of Land affected by Deed, first land only, if more than one	Consideration	Stamps on Duplicate
			Grantor	Grantee				

表格 F

登记官和每月契约清单

[第 31 条第（24）款、第（26）款和第（27）款]

1	2	3	4		5	6	7	8
序号	日期	文书的性质	当事人姓名		登记的地区	契约涉及的土地名称，如果涉及超过一份土地，仅限第一份土地	对价	副本上的印章
			出让人	受让人				

Form G

WEEKLY LIST

[Section 31 (27).]

1 Date and Place of Execution	2 No. of Deed	3 Nature of Deed	4 Names of Parties

THIRD SCHEDULE

TABLE OF NOTARIES' FEES

[Section 40.]

1.For drawing, engrossing, and attesting any deed of transfer of property, movable or immovable, and any mortgage or bond in common form, wherein the value or consideration is expressed, or any lease in common form without special covenants, wherein the rent value or consideration is expressed:Where such value or consideration (or in the case of a lease the rent comprised during the whole term)—

				Rs. c.
Does not exceed Rs. 75				1 0
Exceeds Rs. 75 and does not exceed Rs. 200				2 0
Do.	2 0	do.	350	3 0
Do.	350	do.	500	3 75
Do.	500	do.	750	4 50
Do.	750	do.	1000	5 25
Do.	1000	do.	1500	6 75
Do.	1500	do.	2000	8 25
Do.	2000	do.	3000	9 75
Do.	3000	do.	4000	12 00
Do.	4000	do.	5000	13 50
Do.	5000	do.	10000	15 00

Rs. 10,000 and upwards an additional 50 cents on every Rs. 1,000 of consideration:

Provided that where the term of lease exceeds five years, the fees payable on a lease in common form shall not exceed such as would be payable on a lease for five years.

2.For drawing, engrossing and attesting any deed of transfer, mortgage, or lease, or any bond, which is not in common form but contains various covenants, recitals, or conditions, or which includes the description of several parcels of lands, whether the consideration is therein expressed or not, and all agreements, deeds, powers of attorney, or other instruments, including last wills and other testamentary dispositions: for every such document, per folio of 120 words

. . . . Rs.c. 3 50

In cases where deed is sent to another notary for attestation, the above charges to hold for drawing and

表格 G

每周清单

[第 31 条第(27)款]

1 执行的日期和地点	2 契约编号	3 契约性质	4 当事人姓名

附表三

公证员费用价目表

[第 40 条]

1. 起草、正式写成、公证任何转移财产的契约，无论是动产或不动产、一般形式的抵押或债券，按标的价值或对价；如果是一般形式、没有特别约定的租赁，那么按租金所代表的价值或对价：该种价值或对价（或者是在租赁时整个期间所包含的租金）——

				卢比
不超过 75 卢比				1 0
超过 75 卢比 但不超过 200 卢比				2 0
Do.	200	do.	350	3 0
Do.	350	do.	500	3 75
Do.	500	do.	750	4 50
Do.	750	do.	1000	5 25
Do.	1000	do.	1500	6 75
Do.	1500	do.	2000	8 25
Do.	2000	do.	3000	9 75
Do.	3000	do.	4000	12 00
Do.	4000	do.	5000	13 50
Do.	5000	do.	10000	15 00

10000 卢比及以上时标的每增加 1000 卢比，公证费增加 50 分。

但是租赁期超过 5 年时，一般形式租赁的公证费不超过 5 年租赁期的公证费。

2. 起草、正式写成、公证任何不是一般形式的转移财产、抵押、租赁或债券，其中包含着各种契约、列举、条件或者含有对几块土地的描述，无论其是否有代表对价，所有的协议、契约、授权书或其他文书，包括遗嘱和其他遗嘱性的安排：此类文件每张对开的纸按每 120 个单词

……3 50 卢比收费

如果契约被送到另外一位公证员处公证，那么上述费用适用于起草和正式写成。

engrossing.

3.For attesting, in duplicate, any deed or instrument, not drawn by the notary himself, a sum equal to half the cost of drawing the deed, provided that the minimum fee shall be Rs. 1.50, and the maximum Rs. 10.50.

4.For examining, at the request of any party, the title of any property to be transferred, demised, or mortgaged, if there is only one deed

. . . . Rs.c. 2 50

If there are more deeds than one, then for each additional deed

. . . . Rs.c. 1 0

5.For preparing abstract of the title at the request of any party, for each deed abstracted

. . . . Rs.c. 1 0

6.For registering, at the request of any party, any deed in the office of the Registrar of Lands, half of the charges allowed for drawing, engrossing, and attesting such deed:

Provided that the maximum charge shall not exceed

. . . . Rs.c.5 0

7.For noting each bill of exchange or promissory note, including the copying of it in the book of registry or protest book and presentment

. . . . Rs.c.1 25

For protesting ditto

. . . . Rs.c.7 50

For every duplicate protest

. . . . Rs.c.2 50

8.For every act of honour on acceptance of payment supra protest

. . . . Rs.c.5 0

For every duplicate of such protest

. . . . Rs.c.2 50

9.For copy of a bill paid in part, and of receipt

. . . . Rs.c.1 50

10.For noting protest of ship or vessel, including the copying of it in the book of registry or protest book

. . . . Rs.c.7 50

11.For drawing, engrossing, attesting, and recording protest of ship or vessel, for every folio of 120 words or less

. . . . Rs.c.3 50

12.For every notarial copy or extract of deeds where parties require same (excepting the attestation),—

For every folio of 120 words

. . . . Rs.c.0 50

Fee for attesting same

. . . . Rs.c.2 50

13.For every duplicate deed engrossed, attested, and transmitted to the Registrar of Lands, half of the charges allowed for drawing, engrossing, and attesting such deed.

14.For preparing certificate of the Minister in charge of the subject of Foreign Affairs or other officer to any document intended to be sent abroad

. . . . Rs.c.2 50

15.For attendance, either at the notary' s office between

3. 对不是由公证员亲自起草的契约或文书进行一式两份的公证，其费用是起草契约费用的一半，但最低为 1.50 卢比，最高为 10.50 卢比。

4. 应任何一方当事人请求，审查任何财产权益的转移、终止、抵押契约，只有一份契约时，

……2 50 卢比

如果不止一份契约，那么每份契约另增加

……1 0 卢比

5. 应任何一方当事人请求准备权益摘要，则每份摘要的契约

……1 0 卢比

6. 应任何一方当事人请求在土地登记处登记契约，允许收取一半费用用于起草、正式写成和公证该契约：

但是最多不得收取超过

……5 0 卢比

7. 对注解每张汇票或本票，包括注解在登记册、声明册和陈述中的副本

……1 25 卢比

声明类似文书

……7 50 卢比

每份声明的副本

……2 50 卢比

8. 为了接受前述声明的付款进行的每个承兑行为

……5 0 卢比

该声明的每份副本

……5 0 卢比

9. 支付了部分的账单副本及其收据

……1 50 卢比

10. 注解船舶或船只声明，包括注解其在登记处的册子或声明册中的副本

……7 50 卢比

11. 起草、正式写成、认证和记录船舶或船只的声明，每张对开的纸上有 120 个单词或更少时

……3 50 卢比

12. 每份公证契约副本或契约摘要的同一性公证（认证除外）——

每张对开的纸上有 120 个单词时

……0 50 卢比

同一性公证的费用

……2 50 卢比

13. 每份正式写成、认证、交给土地登记处的契约副本，允许收取一般的费用用于起草、正式写成和认证该契约。

14. 筹备外交事务主管部长的公证书或其他官员打算送往国外的文件

……2 50 卢比

15. 公证员下午 5 点到早上 9 点在公证员办公室或其他

the hours of 5 p.m. and 9 a.m. or elsewhere, for any purpose, for every hour or part of an hour

. . . . Rs.c.2 50

16.For attendance at the registrar's office for the purpose of ascertaining the existence of instrument on one land

. . . . Rs.c.2 50

17.For each additional land in the same deed

. . . . Rs.c.0 50

18.For writing an application for that purpose

. . . . Rs.c.0 50

19.For attendance at any place other than the notary' s house or office, a charge of Re. 1 per mile going and 50 cents on return, or for any distance under a mile, shall be allowed as travelling expenses.

地点加班，无论为何目的，每小时或其中一小时

……2 50 卢比

16. 在登记处办公室查明某地是否存在某设备

……2 50 卢比

17. 在同一份契约中的每增加一块土地

……0 50 卢比

18. 写一份申请书

……0 50 卢比

19. 在公证员住所或办公室外外出办理公证时，去程每公里 1 卢比，回程 50 分。路程少于 1 公里时，仍应支付旅费。

NOTARIES (Amendment)
A LAW TO AMEND THE NOTARIES ORDINANCE.

[Chapter 105 Volume V page 56.]BE it enacted by the National State Assembly of the Republic of Sri Lanka as follows:

[31st August, 1976]

1. Short title

This law may be cited as the Notaries(Amendment) Law, No.24 of 1973.

2. Amendment of section 4 of Chapter 107.

Section 4 of the Notaries Ordinance, herein-after referred to as the "principal enactment". Is hereby amended by the substitution, for subsection (1) of that section, of the following subsection:-

"(1) the Minister may appoint as notories persons other than proctors of the Supreme Court:

Provided that such persons-

(a) are of good character and repute;

(b) are of the age of twenty years;

(c) have been articled clerks, licensed as hereinafter provided, of a proctor of the Supreme Court and have duly served as such for two years; and

(d) have passed an examination prescribed by the Minister and are reported to be duly qualified by the Registrar-General."

公证员条例（修正案）
修正公证员条例的法律

[第 105 章第 V 卷第 56 页] 斯里兰卡共和国国民议会颁布如下：

[1976 年 8 月 31 日]

1. 简称

本法可作为 1973 年第 24 号《公证员条例（修正案）》被引用。

2. 第 107 章第 4 节的修正案

《公证员条例》第 4 条，在此称为“主要规定”，经修订，由本段第（1）款对该条进行替换：

“（1）除了最高法院的监察员，部长可以任命公证员：

但该人员必须——

（a）具有良好的人品和声誉；

（b）年满 20 周岁；

（c）已成为实习律师，持有下述证书，作为最高法院的监察员并已认真履职 2 年；并且

（d）已通过部长规定的审查，并报送总登记处正式批准。”

NOTARIES (Amendment) LAW
A LAW TO AMEND THE NOTARIES ORDINANCE.

BE it enacted by the National State Assembly of the Republic of Sri Lanka as follows:

[31st August, 1976]

1. Short title

This law may be cited as the Notaries(Amendment) Law, No.20 of 1976.

2. Substitution of new expressions in the Notaries Ordinance

In the Notaries Ordinance, hereinafter referred to as the "principal enactment" there shall be substituted.

(a) for the expression "district", other than where such expression, is used with reference to an administrative district or a district of a Registrar of Lands, the expression "zone";

(b) for the expression "District Court", the expression "High Court";

(c) for the expression "District Judge", the expression "High court Judge";

(d) for the expression "division", the expression "zone";

(e) for the expression "judicial division", the expression "judicial zone";

(f) for the expression "judicial district", the expression "judicial zone";

(g) for the expression "a proctor", the expression "an attorney-at-law", for the expression "proctor", the expression "attorney-at-law", and for the expression "proctors", the expression "attorneys-at-law"; and

(h) for the expression "secretary", the expression "Registrar".

公证员条例（修正案）
修正公证员条例的法律

斯里兰卡共和国国民议会颁布如下：

[1976年8月31日]

1. 简称

本法可作为1976年第20号《公证员条例（修正案）》被引用。

2. 替换《公证员条例》中的词语

对《公证员条例》，以下简称为“主要规定”中的词语应予以替换。

（a）就“行政区”一词而言，除了用于提到行政区或行政区土地登记处外，替换为“地区”；

（b）“地方法院”替换为“高等法院”；

（c）“地方法院法官”替换“高等法院法官”；

（d）“部门”替换为“地区”；

（e）“司法部门”替换为“司法区”；

（f）“司法行政区”替换为“司法区”；

（g）“一位监察员”替换为“一位律师”，“监察员”替换为“律师”，“监察员们”替换为“律师们”；

（h）“秘书”替换为“登记官”。

PARLIAMENT OF THE DEMOCRATIC SOCIALIST REPUBLIC OF SRI LANKA
NOTARIES (AMENDMENT) ACT, NO. 47 OF 2011
[Certified on 24th November, 2011]

Printed on the Order of Government

Published as a Supplement to Part II of the Gazette of the Democratic Socialist Republic of Sri Lanka of Novem-

斯里兰卡民主社会主义共和国国民议会
公证员法案（修正案），2011年第47号
[2011年11月24日通过]

载于政府令状

于2011年11月25日作为对第二部分的增补于斯里兰卡民主社会主义共和国公报上公布

ber 25, 2011

PRINTED AT THE DEPARTMENT OF GOVERNMENT PRINTING, SRI LANKA

由斯里兰卡政府印刷部门印刷

TO BE PURCHASED AT THE GOVERNMENT PUBLICATIONS BUREAU, COLOMBO 5

购买于科伦坡 5 号的政府出版局

Notaries (Amendment) Act, No. 47 of 2011
[Certified on 24th November, 2011]
L.D.—O. 17/2011.
AN ACT TO AMEND THE NOTARIES ORDINANCE

公证员法案（修正案），2011 年第 47 号
［于 2011 年 11 月 24 日通过］
L.D.—O. 17/2011.
修正公证员条例的法案

BE it enacted by the Parliament of the Democratic Socialist Republic of Sri Lanka as follows:—

斯里兰卡民主社会主义共和国国民议会颁布如下：

1. Short title.

This Act may be cited as the Notaries (Amendment) Act, No. 47 of 2011.

1. 简称

本法可作为 2011 年第 47 号《公证员法案（修正案）》引用。

2. Amendment of section 31 of Chapter 107.

Section 31 of the Notaries Ordinance (Chapter 107) (hereinafter referred to as the "principal enactment") is hereby amended by the repeal of paragraph (a) of subsection (16) thereof and substitution therefor of the following paragraph:—

"(16) (a) He shall not authenticate or attest any deed or instrument, other than a will or codicil, affecting land or other immovable property, unless the deed or instrument embodies therin or in a Schedule annexed therto an accurate and clear description of the said land or other property affected thereby, showing its boundaries, extent, situation specifying the district, pattu, korale, Divisional Secretary's Division, local authority division and the Grama Niladari Division, and the village within the District in which the land is situated and in case the land is situated in any municipality, town or development area, declared under section 2 of the Municipal Councils Ordinance (Chapter 252) section 2 of the Urban Councils' Ordinance (Chapter 255) and section 2 of the Pradeshiya Sabha Act, No. 15 of 1987 respectively, the assessment number and the name, if any, of the street, in which it is situated.".

2. 第 107 章第 31 条的修正案

《公证员条例》（第 107 章）第 31 条（以下简称"主要规定"）现予修订，废除第（16）款第（a）项，并以下文取而代之：

"（16）（a）公证员不得认证或公证除遗嘱或遗嘱附件以外的、对土地或其他不动产有影响的契约或文书，除非该文书内或附表内对前述受影响的土地或其他财产进行了准确清楚的描述，包括它的范围、区域、农作物、植物、分区秘书部门、地方当局部门、格拉玛尼拉迪部门、该土地所在区域的村庄等。如果该土地位于自治区、乡镇或发展区内，分别根据《城市委员会条例》（第 255 章）的《市政委员会条例》（第 252 章）第 2 条，以及 1987 年第 15 号《区域会议法案》第 2 条公布评估编号及其所在街道的名称（如有的话）。"

3. Amendment of section 31 of the principal enactment.

Section 31 of the principal enactment is hereby

3. 对主要规定第 31 条的修正案

对主要规定第 31 条第（26）款现予以修订如下：

amended in subsection (26) as follows:—

(1) by the renumbering of paragraph (a) of that subsection as sub-paragraph (i) of paragraph (a) thereof;

(2) by the insertion immediately after the re-numbered sub-paragraph (i) of paragraph (a) of the following:—

"(ii) a certified copy of the list prepared under sub-paragraph (i) above shall be sent to the Commissioner or Secretary of the respective local authority, within whose area of authority the land described in the Schedule is situated;".

4. Replacement of Form F of the Second Schedule.

Second Schedule to the principal enactment is hereby amended in Form "F" thereof, by the substitution for the heading to column 6 of the aforesaid form, of the heading "Name of each local authority affected by each property in the Deed".

5.Sinhala text to prevail in case of inconsistency.

In the event of any inconsistency between the Sinhala and Tamil texts of this Act, the Sinhala text shall prevail.

（1）将该款第（a）项重新编号为第（a）项第（i）节；

（2）在重新编号的第（a）项第（i）节之后紧接插入：

"（ii）根据上文第（i）节编制的公证清单副本，应送交附表所述土地所在地有管辖权的地方当局专员或秘书；"。

4. 更换附表 2 表格 F

对主要规定的附表 2 表格 F 作出修订，将上述表格第 6 栏的标题改为"契约中每项财产所影响的每个地方当局的名称"。

5. 出现不一致时，以僧伽罗语为准

如果本法案的僧伽罗语和泰米尔语文本间出现不一致时，以僧伽罗语的文本为准。

塔吉克斯坦

塔吉克斯坦共和国公证法

LAW OF THE REPUBLIC OF TAJIKISTAN
of April 16, 2012 No. 810
About the state notariate

(In edition of the Laws of the Republic of Tajikistan of 13.06.2013 No. 970, 30.05.2017 No. 1438)

This Law regulates legal, organizational, social and economic basis of the state notariate, task and the principles of notarial activities in the Republic of Tajikistan,

and also the relations in the field of implementation of activities of the state notariate.

塔吉克斯坦共和国
公证法
2012 年 4 月 16 日 第 810 号

（本法载于 2013 年 6 月 13 日第 970 号、2017 年 5 月 30 日第 1438 号塔吉克斯坦共和国法）

本法规定了塔吉克斯坦共和国公证活动的法律依据，组织基础、社会基础和经济基础，公证活动的任务和原则，以及公证活动与执行领域的关系。

Section I. Legal and organizational basis of the state notariate

Chapter 1. General provisions

Article 1. Basic concepts

In this Law the following basic concepts are used:

-the state notariate - the structure of state body providing protection of the rights and legitimate interests of physical, legal entities and the state by making of notarial actions;

- the notary public (the main notary public, the senior notaries public, notaries public, the senior notaries public are registrars, the state notariusyarkhivariusa) - the official authorized based on this Law to make notarial actions on behalf of the Republic of Tajikistan, according to requirements, stipulated by the legislation the Republic of Tajikistan;

- notarial activities - the legal activities performed by notaries public and other officials, representatives to make notarial actions according to the procedure, established by

第一节　公证的法律依据和组织基础

第一章　总则

第一条　基本概念

在本法中使用以下基本概念：

公证机构：公证机构是通过开展公证活动保护公民、法人和国家的合法权益的国家机关。

公证员（首席公证员，高级公证员和一般公证员）：公证员是由本法授权，依照塔吉克斯坦共和国法律规定的要求，代表塔吉克斯坦共和国开展公证活动的官员。

公证活动：公证活动是公证员、其他官员和代表依照本法规定的程序进行的活动。

this Law;

- notarial actions - the actions of the notary public and authorized persons having legal value according to the certificate of the indisputable facts, legal events, certificates of documents, to giving to documents of legal reliability and accomplishment of other actions, stipulated by the legislation the Republic of Tajikistan;

- authorized body - the state body determined by the Government of the Republic of Tajikistan, the purpose which tasks and powers in the field of management of notarial activities are determined according to this Law and other regulatory legal acts;

- authorized persons - the officials having the right to make notarial actions according to provisions of this Law;

- the register of registration of notarial actions - data set about the committed notarial actions entered in notarial registers in single established procedure;

- certifying text - text which is made by the notary public in certain document, confirming the certificate of this action.

Article2. Persons making notarial actions

The following persons have the right to make notarial actions according to this Law:

- the notaries public performing notarial actions in offices of notary public (notaries public);

- chairmen of jamias of settlements and villages;

- authorized persons of diplomatic representations and consular establishments of the Republic of Tajikistan;

- other persons, representatives to make notarial actions according to this Law.

Article 3. Legislation of the Republic of Tajikistan on the state notariate

The legislation of the Republic of Tajikistan on the state notariate is based on the Constitution of the Republic of Tajikistan and consists of this Law, other regulatory legal acts of the Republic of Tajikistan, and also the international legal acts recognized by Tajikistan.

Article 4. Notarial activities

1. Notarial activities include making of notarial actions, record keeping, storage of notarial documents, and other actions provided by this Law.

2. Notarial activities are not business activity and its purpose profit earning is not.

3. Notarial certification of documents guarantees their evidentiary force and public recognition.

公证行为：公证行为是公证员和依法被授权人依据塔吉克斯坦共和国法律的规定，通过出具公证书和其他行为，赋予无可争议的事实、法律活动、证书、文件法律效力的行为。

被授权机构：被授权机构是塔吉克斯坦共和国政府指定的国家机构，目的是使公证活动符合本法、其他法律法规、规章的规定。

被授权人：被授权人是依照本法的规定有权实施公证行为的官员。

公证行为登记簿：公证行为登记簿用于记录在单一确定的程序中被认可的公证行为数据。

公证文本：公证文本是公证员制作的，具有公证效力的文本。

第二条　公证行为人

以下人员有权依照本法作出公证行为：

在公证机构中参与公证活动的公证员。

居委会和村委会主任。

塔吉克斯坦共和国外交代表和临时机构的被授权人。

其他依据本法有权作出公证行为的人。

第三条　塔吉克斯坦共和国关于公证机构的法律

塔吉克斯坦共和国关于公证机构的法律以塔吉克斯坦共和国宪法为基础，由本法和其他法律法规及塔吉克斯坦共和国承认的国际法律文件组成。

第四条　公证活动

1. 公证活动包括实施公证行为、保存记录、保管公证文件以及本法规定的其他活动。

2. 公证活动不是商业活动，具有非营利性。

3. 经公证的文件具有证明力，且被公众所承认。

4. Notarial actions on behalf of the Republic of Tajikistan in the territory of other states are made by authorized persons of diplomatic representations and consular establishments of the Republic of Tajikistan.

5. Physical persons and legal entities, irrespective of them organizationally - legal form, shall submit to the notary public of the data and the documents necessary for making of notarial action no later than ten days from the moment of their request.

Article 5. Control of notarial activities

1. Control of the notarial activities connected with observance of notarial clerical work in offices of notary public is performed by authorized body.

2. Check of activities of notaries public is performed based on the plan approved by authorized body and also based on claims and statements of physical persons and legal entities and representations of law enforcement agencies. Check based on claims and statements of physical persons and legal entities, and representations of law enforcement agencies, is performed within the specific claim and representation.

3. Activities check for the first time of the appointed notary public to this position is performed based on the plan approved by authorized body after one year of its activities.

4. Activities of notaries public can be performed before the termination of term of the employment contract (contract).

5. In case of detection of shortcomings of activities of the notary public, at the request of the head of authorized body repeated inspection can be carried out.

6. Check of notarial activities in the sphere of counteraction of legalization (washing) of income gained in the criminal way, and to financing of terrorism is carried out together with representatives of authorized body on counteraction of legalization (washing) of income gained in the criminal way and terrorism financing.

Article 6. Notary public tasks

Tasks of the notary public are ensuring protection of the rights and legitimate interests of physical persons and legal entities, also interests of the state by making of notarial actions on behalf of the Republic of Tajikistan.

Article 7. Principles of notarial activities

Notarial activities are performed on the basis of the principles of legality, independence, the mystery of mak-

4. 塔吉克斯坦共和国外交代表和领事机构的被授权人员代表塔吉克斯坦共和国在其他国家领土内实施的公证行为。

5. 自然人和法人，无论其组织形式如何，均应当在提出公证申请后十日内向公证员提交必要的数据和文件，以便进行公证活动。

第五条　对公证活动的监督

1. 由被授权机构监督公证工作中与公证文书规则相关的公证活动。

2. 公证活动的检查依照被授权机构核准的计划、自然人和法人以及执法机构的请求和陈述在具体范围内进行。

3. 被授权机构应当依照经过核准的计划，检查公证员就职后第一次参与的公证活动。

4. 公证员的公证活动应当在其雇佣合同期限内进行。

5. 对于有瑕疵的公证活动，被授权机构负责人可以要求复查。

6. 被授权机构和反洗钱及打击资助恐怖主义的国家机关的代表一起，共同检查可能涉及洗钱和资助恐怖主义的公证活动。

第六条　公证员的任务

公证员的任务是代表塔吉克斯坦共和国参与公证活动，保护自然人和法人的权利、合法利益以及国家利益。

第七条　公证活动的原则

公证活动应当遵守合法性原则、独立性原则和保密性原则。

ing of notarial actions.

Article 8. Legality in implementation of notarial activities

1. Notaries public or authorized persons when making notarial actions are guided by the Constitution of the Republic of Tajikistan, this Law, other regulatory legal acts of the Republic of Tajikistan, and also the international legal acts recognized by Tajikistan.

2. Notaries public and (or) authorized persons shall refuse making of notarial action according to requirements of part 1 of article 47 of this Law.

Article 9. Independence when making notarial actions

1. In the activities notaries public and authorized persons when making notarial actions are independent and submit only to the law.

2. Pressure upon notaries public and authorized persons in case of execution of the obligations assigned to them is forbidden also persons who made such actions are made responsible according to the procedure, stipulated by the legislation the Republic of Tajikistan.

Article 10. Mystery of notarial action

1. The mystery of the notarial actions made for them is guaranteed to physical persons and legal entities. Notaries public and authorized persons shall observe the mystery of the made notarial actions. Providing mystery of notarial actions is obligatory also for persons which stopped the activities as the notary public and the trainee.

2. Data (documents) on committed notarial actions, copies of the original or the duplicate of the documents which are stored in cases of office of notary public are issued only to physical persons and legal entities, from name, addressed to or at the request of which this document was processed, or to persons authorized by it.

3. Data (documents) on committed notarial actions are issued also:

- upon the demand of court on available for them in production of criminal, administrative, civil, family or economic cases;

- to bodies of prosecutor's office, the investigation and inquiry in connection with being in their production by criminal cases according to the procedure established by the legislation of the Republic of Tajikistan;

- to authorized body on counteraction of legalization (washing) of income gained in the criminal way and to

第八条　公证活动的合法性

1. 公证员或被授权人员在实施公证行为时应当遵守塔吉克斯坦共和国宪法、本法、其他法律以及塔吉克斯坦共和国承认的国际法律文件的规定。

2. 公证员和（或）被授权人员应当依照本法第四十七条第一款的规定拒绝公证。

第九条　公证活动的独立性

1. 公证员和被授权人依法独立行使公证职权。

2. 任何人都不得对依法履行职责的公证员和被授权人施加压力，否则将依照塔吉克斯坦共和国法律的规定追究法律责任。

第十条　公证活动的保密性

1. 为自然人和法人实施的公证行为都必须保密，且由公证员和被授权人对公证行为的保密性进行监督。具有公证员或公证实习生身份，但目前停止公证活动的人员，应当对先前参与的公证活动保密。

2. 存放在公证机构的公证数据（文件）的原件和复印件的副本只能发给应其要求该文件（数据）被处理过或者获得授权的自然人和法人。

3. 有以下情形之一的，公证机构可以提交应当保密的公证数据（文件）：

依照法院的要求，为解决刑事、行政、民事、婚姻家庭或经济案件提供必要的公证数据（文件）。

依照塔吉克斯坦共和国法律规定的程序，为检察院各机构调查刑事案件的事实提供必要的公证数据（文件）。

依照塔吉克斯坦共和国法律的规定，为反洗钱和打击资助恐怖主义的国家机关提供必要的公证数据

financing of terrorism in cases stipulated by the legislation the Republic of Tajikistan;

- to the legal executive concerning enforcement proceeding.

4. Withdrawal of seal of the notary public and the register of record of notarial actions, except as specified, stipulated by the legislation the Republic of Tajikistan, is forbidden.

5. The authentic notarial documents and registers of records of notarial actions withdrawn according to the legislation of the Republic of Tajikistan from offices of notary public return it.

6. The notaries public of the data having no right to disclose before opening of inheritance proceeding from the text of the will. Certificates of the will, the duplicate and copies of the will are issued to interested persons only after the death of the testator in case of presentation of the death certificate if the legislation of the Republic of Tajikistan does not provide other.

7. Rules about observance of mystery of notarial actions also extend to persons who knew of the mystery of making of notarial actions in connection with accomplishment of service duties by them.

8. Person disclosing the mystery of committed notarial actions is made responsible according to the procedure, established by the legislation of the Republic of Tajikistan.

Article 11. Language of notarial clerical work

1. The clerical work of notarial activities is performed in state language.

2. If persons who addressed for making of notarial action do not know state language, the text of the relevant documents is translated to them by the notary public, authorized persons or the professional translator.

3. The text of the certified notarial documents is constituted in state language and at the request of addressed or if necessary, it can be constituted with the translation into other language.

4. The clerical work of notarial activities in diplomatic representations and consular establishments of the Republic of Tajikistan abroad is performed in language of clerical work of activities of these bodies.

Article 12. Place of making of notarial action

1. Notarial actions except as specified, provided by this Law, are made in buildings of offices of notary public. The authorized body can determine other place for making of notarial actions.

（文件）。

依照执行部门的要求，提供必要的公证数据（文件）。

4. 除塔吉克斯坦共和国法律规定的情况外，不得撤销公证机构的印章效力、删除公证行为的记录。

5. 依照塔吉克斯坦共和国法律的规定，可以从公证机构撤回公证书和公证行为记录登记册。

6. 公证员无权在继承开始前披露遗嘱文本的内容。除塔吉克斯坦共和国法律另有规定外，遗嘱原本、副本和复印件只能在立遗嘱者死亡后发给利害关系人。

7. 公证行为的保密性规定也适用于因履行职责而知晓公证行为秘密的人。

8. 泄露公证活动秘密的，应当按照塔吉克斯坦共和国法律的规定承担相应的法律责任。

第十一条　公证文书的工作用语

1. 公证活动的文书应当使用本国语言。

2. 如果办理公证手续的人不懂本国语言，相关文件的文本应由公证员、被授权人或者专业的翻译人员为其翻译。

3. 公证书的文本以本国语言制作。依照当事人要求或在必要时，可以将公证书翻译成其他语言。

4. 在国外的塔吉克斯坦共和国外交代表和领事机构的公证文书工作应当使用本机构的工作语言。

第十二条　实施公证行为的地点

1. 除本法规定外，公证行为均应当在公证机构的办公楼内实施。但被授权机构可以选定其他实施公证行为的地点。

2. In cases when person owing to disease, disability or on other reasonable excuses cannot be in office of notary public, at its request notarial actions can be made in the location of this person.

3. The place of making of notarial actions by authorized persons of diplomatic representations and consular establishments of the Republic of Tajikistan is established by the legislation of the Republic of Tajikistan regulating activities of diplomatic representations and consular establishments of the Republic of Tajikistan.

4. Physical persons and legal entities have the right to address for making of notarial actions in any notary public of office of notary public of the corresponding territory or authorized persons, except as specified, if this Law provides certain place of making of notarial actions.

Article 13. Office of notary public

1. The office of notary public in the Republic of Tajikistan is established and liquidated by authorized body in the cities and areas. In the big cities and the cities having several areas in the territory in the territory of each district of the city or one of its parts separate offices of notary public can be founded.

2. In the capital of the Republic of Tajikistan - the city of Dushanbe the Main office of notary public of the Republic of Tajikistan is established. In the center of the Gorno-Badakhshan Autonomous Region and other regional centers one of offices of notary public is established as regional office of notary public. The main office of notary public of the Republic of Tajikistan and offices of notary public of the Gorno-Badakhshan Autonomous Region, areas, along with making of notarial actions, also perform methodical management of offices of notary public of administrative and territorial units. The authorized body can assign to the Main office of notary public, office of notary public of the Gorno-Badakhshan Autonomous Region, areas, making of the most difficult notarial actions.

3. Offices of notary public are not legal entities, and enter into structure of authorized body.

4. The number of employees of offices of notary public affirms authorized body within the established salary fund.

5. Technical employees of offices of notary public of the Republic of Tajikistan perform the activities according to the procedure, established by authorized body.

Article 14. Territoriality of making of notarial actions

1. The territory of making of notarial actions is administrative and territorial units in the territory of which

2. 由于疾病、残疾或者其他正当理由无法在公证机构参与公证活动的当事人，应其要求可以在当事人所在地进行公证。

3. 塔吉克斯坦共和国的外交代表和领事机构的被授权人进行公证行为的地点由关于塔吉克斯坦共和国外交代表和领事机构活动的法律规定。

4. 自然人和法人有权向相应地区任意公证机构的公证员或被授权人申请公证，但本法已指明公证地的除外。

第十三条　公证机构

1. 塔吉克斯坦共和国的公证机构由各城市和地区的指定授权机构设立和撤销。在大城市，下辖几个区域的城市，城市下辖区或下辖区的一部分地区均可以单独设立公证机构。

2. 在塔吉克斯坦共和国的首都杜尚别市设立塔吉克斯坦共和国首要公证机构。在戈尔诺 - 巴达赫尚自治区的中心和其他地区的中心设立的公证机构中的一个作为总公证机构的区域办事处。塔吉克斯坦共和国的首要公证机构和戈尔诺 - 巴达赫尚自治区公证机构除实施公证行为外，还负责行政区域内的公证机构的行政管理。授权机构可以将最难处理的公证工作移交给首要公证机构、戈尔诺 - 巴达赫尚自治区的公证机构和区域办事处办理。

3. 公证机构是编入授权机构组织结构中的非法人机构。

4. 授权机构根据公证机构的雇员数量确定薪资总额。

5. 塔吉克斯坦共和国公证机构的技术人员按照授权机构确定的程序开展活动。

第十四条　公证行为的地域性

1. 实施公证行为的地点是在其境内设有公证机构的行政区域。

there is office of notary public.

2. The territory of making of the notarial actions connected with real estate is determined according to division of administrative and territorial units of the Republic of Tajikistan.

3. The notary public has no right to make the notarial action connected with real estate outside the established territory of the founded office of notary public, except as specified, when he fulfills duties of other notary public according to the procedure, provided by this Law.

Article 15. Archives of offices of notary public

1. For the purpose of ensuring safety and centralized storage of notarial documents which are component of National Archive Fund of the Republic of Tajikistan under the Main office of notary public of the Republic of Tajikistan and offices of notary public of the Gornobadakhshansky autonomous region, areas with the authorized body - establishes archives of offices of notary public. The term of temporary storage of notarial documents in archives of offices of notary public constitutes three years. After the specified term, offices of notary public hand over notarial documents for storage in archives of offices of notary public under the Main office of notary public of the Republic of Tajikistan and in archives of offices of notary public of the Gorno-Badakhshan Autonomous Region and areas.

2. Archives of offices of notary public perform storage of notarial documents of offices of notary public of the Republic of Tajikistan.

3. The procedure for activities of archives of offices of notary public is determined by authorized body in coordination with the Head archival department under the Government of the Republic of Tajikistan.

4. Archives of offices of notary public have seal with the name, the image of the State Emblem of the Republic of Tajikistan and seal, the state notariusaarchivarius with indication of position, surname, name and the notary-registrar's middle name.

Article 16. Management of office of notary public and archives of offices of notary public

The main office of notary public of the Republic of Tajikistan the main notary public, offices of notary public of the Gorno-Badakhshan Autonomous Region, areas, others state notarial kontoramistarshy notaries public, notaries public and archives of offices of notary public - the senior notaries public - registrars based on this Law and the job description directs.

2. 依照塔吉克斯坦共和国行政区域的划分，确定与不动产有关的公证行为的地点。

3. 公证员按照本法规定的程序履行其他公证员的职责时，除另有规定外，无权实施与位于公证机构所在的区域以外的不动产有关的公证行为。

第十五条　公证机构档案馆

1. 为了确保集中存放在塔吉克斯坦共和国档案馆和塔吉克斯坦首要公证机构、戈尔诺 - 巴达赫尚自治区公证机构的公证文件的安全，各区域与授权机构合作建立区域公证机构档案馆。公证机构档案馆临时存放公证文件的期限为三年，在规定期限届满之后，公证机构将公证文件交给塔吉克斯坦共和国首要公证机构和戈尔诺 - 巴达赫尚自治区公证机构下属的档案馆保存。

2. 公证机构档案馆保管塔吉克斯坦共和国公证机构的公证文件。

3. 公证机构档案馆的工作程序由授权机构与塔吉克斯坦共和国政府总档案管理部门协调确定。

4. 公证机构档案馆的印章刻有其名称和塔吉克斯坦共和国国徽的图像，国家公证机构档案馆的印章上刻有级别、负责人的姓氏、名字和中间名。

第十六条　公证机构和公证机构档案馆的管理

塔吉克斯坦共和国首要公证机构的首席公证员，戈尔诺 - 巴达赫尚自治区公证机构和其他地区公证机构的高级公证员以及公证机构档案馆的登记员基于本法和工作指南开展工作。

Article 17. Position assignment and dismissal of the notary public

1. The notary public is appointed to position and dismissed according to the procedure, established by this Law and the legislation of the Republic of Tajikistan the head of authorized body.

2. The bases for dismissal of the notary public, except the bases, stipulated by the legislation the Republic of Tajikistan, are:

- cancellation of three and more notarial actions by court resolutions because of the notary public within one year;
- loss or transfer to other persons of seal of notary office with the image of the Coat of arms of the Republic of Tajikistan or seal with indication of surname, name and the notary public middle name;
- loss or transfer of the form to other persons with the established degree of protection intended for making of notarial actions;
- termination of citizenship of the Republic of Tajikistan or acquisition of nationality of other state.

Article 18. Suspension of operations of the notary public

Activities of the notary public for implementation of notarial actions stop on the following bases:

- with the assistance of notaries public in elections as the candidate of representative body of the Republic of Tajikistan;
- in case of pronouncement by court of the resolution on temporary discharge from the notary public position;
- in other cases, stipulated by the legislation the Republic of Tajikistan

Article 19. Clerical work and the reporting in offices of notary public

1. The clerical work in offices of notary public of the Republic of Tajikistan is conducted according to the procedure, established by the Instruction on clerical work in offices of notary public of the Republic of Tajikistan. The instruction on clerical work affirms as offices of notary public of the Republic of Tajikistan authorized body.

2. Offices of notary public in accordance with the established procedure hand over the statistic report about the activities to authorized body.

Article 20. Seal, stamp, forms of office of notary public

The office of notary public has seal with the image

第十七条　公证员的职务分配和解雇

1. 依照本法和塔吉克斯坦共和国法律规定的程序，由授权机构负责人指定公证员的职位或将其解雇。

2. 除塔吉克斯坦共和国法律规定的事由外，解除公证员职务的事由如下：

法院在一年内判决撤销公证员作出的三个或三个以上公证行为；

将印有塔吉克斯坦共和国国徽或印有公证员的姓氏、名字和中间名的印章的公证文件遗失或者泄露给他人；

故意将需要保密的公证文件遗失或泄露给他人；

丧失塔吉克斯坦共和国公民身份或者取得他国国籍。

第十八条　暂停公证员的职务活动

有下列情形的，暂停公证员的职务活动：

公证员作为候选人，在其他公证员的协助下，参与塔吉克斯坦共和国立法机构的选举；

法院宣布暂时解除公证员职务；

塔吉克斯坦共和国法律规定的其他情况。

第十九条　公证机构的文书工作和报告

1. 塔吉克斯坦共和国公证机构的文书工作依据塔吉克斯坦共和国公证机构文书工作指南进行。塔吉克斯坦共和国授权机构对公证机构的文书工作的确认作出指示。

2. 公证机构依照法定程序将有关活动的统计报告移交给被授权机构。

第二十条　公证机构的印章、印花税票、表格

公证机构拥有刻有塔吉克斯坦共和国国徽和国名

of the State Emblem of the Republic of Tajikistan with the name, the corresponding seals, forms and stamps.

的印章、相应的表格和印花税票。

Chapter 2. Financing of offices of notary public, collection of the state fee for making of notarial actions and additional legal service

第二章　公证机构的资金来源、公证费和附加法律服务的费用

Article 21. Financing of offices of notary public

Offices of notary public are financed by the republican budget, and also means which arrived in accordance with the established procedure due to additional legal paid services.

第二十一条　公证机构的资金来源

公证机构的资金来源于共和国的财政预算，同时也有一部分资金来源于对符合法律规定的附加法律服务的收费。

Article 22. Collection of the state fee and additional legal paid services for making of notarial actions

1. For making of notarial actions at physical persons and legal entities the state fee according to the Law of the Republic of Tajikistan “About the state fee” is collected.

2. Notaries public and authorized persons make notarial actions only after payment by physical persons and legal entities of the state fee and provision of the certifying document about the payment of the state fee and other payments established by the law. In the certified notarial document the notary public specifies the amount of the collected state tax and other payments according to the procedure, established by the legislation of the Republic of Tajikistan.

3. For rendering the additional legal paid services connected with making of notarial actions, notaries public levy payment from physical persons and legal entities. Procedure and amount of payment of additional: the paid services rendered by notaries public it is determined by the Government of the Republic of Tajikistan.

4. Calculation for rendering additional legal paid services is made by payment of means by physical persons and legal entities and provision of the certifying document about payment of additional legal paid services.

5. In case of departure of the notary public for making of notarial action out of the limits of notary office interested physical persons or legal entities refund it the actual transportation expenses.

6. Authorized persons of diplomatic representations and consular establishments of the Republic of Tajikistan for making of notarial actions collect consular fees according to the legislation of the Republic of Tajikistan.

第二十二条　公证费和附加法律服务的费用

1. 公证机构依照塔吉克斯坦共和国的收费标准对为自然人和法人实施的公证行为收取公证费。

2. 公证员和被授权人只有在自然人和法人支付公证费后才实施公证行为，并且应提供支付公证费和法律规定的其他款项的证明文件。在公证书中，公证员应当依照塔吉克斯坦共和国法律规定的程序，列明收取的公证费和其他支付款项的数额。

3. 公证员提供与公证行为有关的附加有偿法律服务，应当向自然人和法人收取额外的费用。额外费用支付的程序和数额以及有偿服务的提供由塔吉克斯坦共和国政府确定。

4. 公证员应当向自然人和法人提供附加的有偿法律服务的费用的计算方法和证明文件。

5. 若公证员在超出其公证机构管辖范围的地点进行公证，受益的自然人和法人应当支付公证员实际花费的交通费用。

6. 塔吉克斯坦共和国的外交代表和领事机构的授权人员依照塔吉克斯坦共和国法律的规定对实施的公证行为收取领事费。

Article 23. Salary of work of the notary public

The salary of the notary public is determined accord-

第二十三条　公证员的工资

公证员的工资依照《塔吉克斯坦共和国公共服务

ing to the procedure, established by the Law of the Republic of Tajikistan "About public service". Also remuneration according to the procedure, established by the Government of the Republic of Tajikistan is paid for rendering additional paid legal services to physical persons and legal entities, the notary public.

法》规定的程序确定。此外，依照塔吉克斯坦政府规定的程序，公证员向自然人和法人提供附加有偿法律服务的，也可获得报酬。

Chapter 3. Notary public, its rights and obligation

第三章　公证员的权利和义务

Article 24. Notary public

1. Person who has only citizenship of the Republic of Tajikistan, the higher legal education is appointed to position of the notary public, knows state language, has professional length of service at least three years, passed training in office of notary public and passed qualification examination.

2. Cannot be appointed to position of the notary public:

- persons recognized in accordance with the established procedure incapacitated or with special disability;

- persons who are earlier condemned for making of intentional crime;

- persons whose activities are stopped for non-execution of service duties or making of the discrediting act.

3. In case of position assignment of the notary public the requirements provided by the Laws of the Republic of Tajikistan "About public service" to "About fight against corruption"" are taken into account.

4. When making notarial action of the right and obligation of all notaries public are equal and the documents certified by them have identical legal force.

第二十四条　公证员

1. 担任公证员应当符合下列条件：具有塔吉克斯坦共和国国籍、从高等法学专业毕业、通晓本国语言、至少有三年的法律工作经验、通过公证机构的培训以及通过职业资格考试。

2. 有下列情形之一的，不得担任公证员：

依照法定程序被认定为无民事行为能力或有特殊残疾；

有故意犯罪记录；

因不履行服务职责或作出失信行为被停止职务的人。

3. 公证员职务的分配应当依照塔吉克斯坦共和国《关于公共服务与反腐败法案》的相关规定

4. 公证员的权利和义务是对等的，经公证员公证的文件具有同等的法律效力。

Article 25. Training in the state notariate

1. Persons appointed to the notary public position for the first time or after break in notarial activities more than three years, pass training in office of notary public During from three to six months. The procedure and duration of training are determined by authorized body.

2. After training term person takes qualification examination. If person on reasonable excuse could not pass qualification examination, the term of training is prolonged for term no more than three months.

3. With person who did not pass qualification examination, employment relationships stop.

第二十五条　国家公证培训

1. 首次担任公证员或者中断公证活动三年以上的人员，需要接受三至六个月的公证职务培训，培训的程序和时间由被授权机构决定。

2. 接受培训的人员应当参加职业资格考试。有正当理由不能通过职业资格考试的，培训期限最多延长三个月。

3. 没有通过职业资格考试的人员，雇佣关系即告终止。

Article 26. Qualification commission

1. The qualification commission under authorized body is created for the purpose of acceptance of qualification examinations.

第二十六条　资格认定委员会

1. 资格认定委员会是授权机构为认定职业资格考试的结果而设立的组织。

2. The procedure for creation of the qualification commission, structure, activities and its powers are established by authorized body.

3. Persons who did not pass qualification examination are allowed to its repeated delivery not earlier than in year after decision making by the qualification commission.

4. The head of authorized body can appeal the decision of the qualification commission within one month from the date of receipt of its copy.

2. 被授权机构确定设立资格认定委员会的程序，资格认定委员会的结构、活动及权力。

3. 未通过资格认定的人员，不得在资格认定委员会作出决定后一年内重复提交认定。

4. 授权机构负责人可在收到资格认定结果副本后一个月内提出复议。

Article 27. Notary public rights

The notary public has the right:

- make the notarial actions provided by this Law and other regulatory legal acts of the Republic of Tajikistan for the benefit of the physical persons and legal entities which addressed it;
- constitute drafts of transactions, statements and other documents;
- produce copies of documents and statements from them;
- give consultations concerning making of notarial actions;
- request from the documents and data necessary for making of notarial actions at physical persons and legal entities;
- have other rights established by this Law and other regulatory legal acts of the Republic of Tajikistan.

第二十七条　公证员的权利

公证员拥有以下权利：

依照本法和塔吉克斯坦共和国其他法律的规定，为维护自然人和法人的利益实施以下公证行为；

起草和解协议、声明和其他文件；

向自然人和法人出示文件和声明的副本；

提供公证法律咨询；

按要求提供自然人和法人进行公证时必要的文件和资料；

拥有本法和塔吉克斯坦共和国其他法律规定的其他权利。

Article 28. Notary public obligations

1. The notary public shall:

- make notarial actions according to requirements of this Law and other regulatory legal acts of the Republic of Tajikistan regulating notarial activities;
- warn physical persons and legal entities about consequence in law of the made notarial actions ignorance of consequence in law was not used to the detriment of their interests;
- keep in secret data which became known to it in connection with implementation of professional activity by it;
- refuse making of notarial action in case of its contradiction to the legislation of the Republic of Tajikistan;
- observe the mode of reception of citizens and representatives of legal entities;
- represent according to claims to the activities to authorized body of the data on committed notarial action, and in necessary cases, personal explanations, including concerning non-compliance with professional ethics, and

第二十八条　公证员的义务

1. 公证员需履行以下义务：

依照本法和塔吉克斯坦共和国关于公证活动的其他法律规范参与公证活动；

对不了解公证行为法律后果的自然人和法人，在不损害其利益的情形下，警告其相应的法律后果；

保存知晓的公证活动相关的秘密数据；

拒绝作出违反塔吉克斯坦共和国法律规定的公证行为；

依法接待公民和法定代表人；

公证员应当向授权机构说明其进行的公证行为，必要时，说明不遵守职业道德规范的事由，并且执行授权机构负责人和公证机构关于工作安排的命令；

also carry out orders and orders of the head of authorized body and offices of notary public on the organization of work;

- inform authorized body on counteraction of legalization (washing) of income gained in the criminal way and financing of terrorism on all suspicious transactions and transactions and transactions on the amount equivalent of 500 000 somoni and above or in foreign currency on the amount equivalent of 500 000 somoni and above;

- fulfill the requirements provided by the Law of the Republic of Tajikistan "About public service".

2. The notary public making notarial actions bears responsibility for the harm to physical persons and legal entities done to them according to provisions of the legislation of the Republic of Tajikistan.

Article 29. Notary public seal

1. The notary public has seal with the image of the State Emblem of the Republic of Tajikistan, complete specifying of the name of office of notary public, position, surname, name and notary public middle name.

2. The seal is made according to the standard and single sample, at the request of authorized body.

3. The impress of a seal and the specimen signature of the notary public are stored in authorized body.

4. The notary public during suspension of the activities shall hand over according to article 18 of this Law the seal for temporary storage to the authorized person of authorized body.

5. In case of release of the notary public from position, he shall hand over without delay the seal to the authorized person of authorized body. In case of evasion of the notary public from delivery of seal, he is made responsible according to the legislation of the Republic of Tajikistan.

Article 30. Restrictions in activities of the notary public

1. The notary public cannot perform other functions, be chosen in representative; bodies to be member of political parties, to be engaged in business activity, except for scientific, creative and pedagogical activities.

2. The notary public has no right to make notarial actions which result for it has property or other personal interest.

3. The notary public having no right to make notarial actions on the name and on its own behalf, addressed to and on behalf of close relatives - the wife (husband), chil-

通知授权机构可能或确实涉嫌洗钱和资助恐怖主义的交易，交易金额相当于五十万索莫尼以上的交易以及交易金额相当于五十万索莫尼以上的外币的交易；

遵守《塔吉克斯坦共和国公共服务法》的规定。

2. 依照塔吉克斯坦共和国法律规定，公证员因公证行为对自然人和法人造成损害的，应当承担责任。

第二十九条　公证员印章

1. 公证员的印章刻有塔吉克斯坦共和国国徽、公证机构的全称、公证员的职务、姓氏、名字和中间名。

2. 应授权机构的要求，印章按标准和同一样品制作。

3. 印章的压印和公证员的签字样本都应当由被授权机构保管。

4. 依照本法第十八条的规定，公证员在暂停职务期间应当将印章移交给授权机构的负责人临时保管。

5. 被解除职务的公证员，应当立即将印章交给授权机构的负责人，否则将依照塔吉克斯坦共和国的法律追究其责任。

第三十条　对公证员活动的限制规定

1. 公证员不能担任议会议员、成为党政机关成员、从事商业活动等其他职能，但不包括科学、创造性和教学活动。

2. 公证员不得办理涉及自身财产或者其他个人利益的公证行为。

3. 公证员不得以自己的名义或公证机构其他雇员的名义为近亲属——妻子（丈夫）、子女、父母、兄弟、姐妹和妻子（丈夫）的父母、兄弟、姐妹、子女、媒人、

dren, parents, brothers, sisters, and also parents, brothers, sisters and children of the wife (husband), matchmakers, brides, zyaty, and also jointly living with person, the representative to perform the state functions or to persons equated to him and conducting general economy, and also addressed to and from employee name of the relevant office of notary public.

4. The notarial actions provided by parts 2 and 3 of this Article are made by the notary public of other office of notary public, according to the procedure, established by this Law.

Article 31. Oath of the notary public

1. Person appointed to the notary public position for the first time takes the oath of the following content: "I, (surname, name and middle name) solemnly swear that I will carry out the notary public obligations according to the law, conscience, to protect the rights and legitimate interests of physical persons and legal entities, interests of the state, to keep secret of notarial actions, I will always protect worthy rank of the notary.".

2. The notary public is signed under the text of the oath which is stored in the personal record of the notary public.

3. Persons who did not take the oath cannot perform functions of the notary public.

4. The procedure for adoption of the oath is established by authorized body.

Section II. Notarial actions and procedure for their making

Chapter 4. The notarial actions made by notaries public and authorized persons

Article 32. The notarial actions made by notaries public

1. Notaries public make the following notarial actions:

- certify transactions (agreements, wills, powers of attorney, obligations and other transactions);
- accept and announce confidential wills;
- certify powers of the testamentary executor;
- take measures to protection of heritable property;
- grant certificates on the right to inheritance;
- grant certificates on the property right to share in joint property of spouses;
- witness fidelity of copies of documents and state-

未婚妻以及共同生活的人、其他涉及一般经济问题的公证员办理公证行为。

4. 本条第二款、第三款规定的公证行为，由其他公证机构的公证员依照本法规定的程序进行。

第三十一条 公证员的宣誓

1. 首次任职的公证员宣誓内容如下："本人（姓氏、名字、中间名）郑重宣誓，将依法履行公证员的义务，富有正义感，维护自然人和法人的权利和合法权益，维护国家利益，对公证行为保密，永远维护作为公证员的尊严。"

2. 公证员在宣誓书上签字，宣誓书存放于公证员的个人档案中。

3. 未宣誓者不得担任公证员之职务。

4. 宣誓程序由授权机构制定。

第二节 公证程序

第四章 公证员和授权人员的公证行为

第三十二条 公证员实施的公证行为

1. 公证员可以实施以下公证行为：

公证交易（协议、遗嘱、授权委托书、证券和其他交易）；

接受并宣布秘密遗嘱；

证明遗嘱执行人的权力；

采取措施保护遗产；

出具继承权证书；

出具配偶共同财产的财产权利证明；

见证文件的副本和陈述的真实性；

ments from them;

- impose and remove bans on alienation of real estate;
- witness authenticity of signatures on documents;
- certify fidelity of the translation of documents from one language on another;
- certify the fact of finding of person in live or in certain place;
- certify identity of person with person represented on picture;
- certify time of production of documents;
- transfer statements of physical persons and legal entities to other physical persons and legal entities;
- accept sums of money and securities in the deposit;
- make executive texts;
- make protests of bills of exchange;
- show checks to payment and certify non-payment of checks;
- accept documents for storage;
- provide proofs;
- grant certificates on the property right;
- make ship's protests;
- certify the consent of the spouse or the spouse to transaction requiring the notarial certificate.

2. By the legislation of the Republic of Tajikistan on notaries public making of other notarial actions can be assigned.

Article 33. The notarial actions made by chairmen of jamias of settlements and villages

1. Chairmen of jamias of settlements and villages make the following notarial actions:

- certify wills;
- certify powers of attorney, except for powers of attorney on control and the order of vehicles, real estate;
- witness fidelity of copies of documents and statements from them.

2. Chairmen of jamias of settlements and villages have no right to certify documents, held for use outside the Republic of Tajikistan.

Article 34. The notarial actions made by authorized persons of diplomatic representations and consular establishments of the Republic of Tajikistan

1. Authorized persons of diplomatic representations and consular establishments of the Republic of Tajikistan make the following notarial actions:

- certify transactions (agreements, wills, powers of

设立和解除禁止转让不动产规定；

公证文件上签名的真实性；

证明文件从一种语言翻译到另一种语言的真实性；

证明某人活着或在某地找到某人的事实；

证明图片上人的身份；

证明文件的制作时间；

将自然人和法人的陈述转达给其他自然人和法人；

承兑存款中的金额和有价证券；

制定执行文本；

制作拒兑汇票的证明书；

证明已付款的支票和未付款支票；

提存；

提供证据；

出具产权证书；

制作海事声明；

证明配偶同意或配偶需要公证书的一笔交易。

2. 依照塔吉克斯坦共和国法律规定可以实施的其他公证行为。

第三十三条　居委会和村委会主任实施的公证行为

1. 居委会和村委会主任可以实施以下公证行为：

证明遗嘱的效力；

证明授权委托书的效力，但控制权委托书和关于车辆、房产的指令除外；

公证文件副本和声明的真实性。

2. 居委会和村委会主任无权证明在塔吉克斯坦共和国境外使用的文件的效力。

第三十四条　塔吉克斯坦共和国外交代表和领事机构的授权人员实施的公证行为

1. 塔吉克斯坦共和国外交代表和领事机构的授权人员可以实施下列公证活动：

证明在塔吉克斯坦共和国境内除房地产协议外的

attorney and others), except agreements on real estate, being in the territory of the Republic of Tajikistan;

- at the request of the notary public take measures to protection and management of heritable property;

- grant certificates on the property right to share in joint property of spouses;

- grant certificates on the right to inheritance;

- witness authenticity of signatures on documents;

- witness fidelity of copies of documents and statements from them;

- certify the fact of finding of person in live or in certain place;

- certify time of production of documents;

- accept sums of money and securities in the deposit;

- make executive texts;

- accept documents for storage;

- provide proofs;

- make ship's protests.

2. Other notarial actions made by authorized persons of diplomatic and consular establishments of the Republic of Tajikistan can be provided by the legislation of the Republic of Tajikistan.

Article 35. The certificate of the wills and powers of attorney equated to notarially certified documents

1. Are equated to notarially certified documents:

- wills and powers of attorney of the military personnel at home stations of military units, military schools and other military structures where there is no office of notary public and authorized persons making notarial actions, also wills and powers of attorney of the workers living there, employees, members of their families and the members of families of the military personnel certified by commanders (chiefs) of these military units, institutions;

- the will and the power of attorney of persons which are in places of detention, certified by chiefs of these organizations;

- the will and the power of attorney of the persons which are during swimming in courts, or swimming under the flag of the Republic of Tajikistan, certified by captains of these courts;

- wills and powers of attorney of persons which are in prospecting expeditions, certified by chiefs of these expeditions;

- other documents certified according to the procedure, stipulated by the legislation the Republic of Tajikistan.

交易（协议、遗嘱、授权委托书和其他文件）；

依照公证员的要求采取措施保护和管理遗产；

出具配偶共同财产的财产权利证明；

出具继承权证书；

公证文件签名的真实性；

公证文件副本和陈述的真实性；

证明某人存活或在某地找到某人的事实；

证明文件的制作时间；

承兑存款中的金额和有价证券；

制定执行文本；

提存；

提供证据；

制作海事声明。

2. 依照塔吉克斯坦共和国法律规定，可以进行的其他公证行为。

第三十五条　遗嘱和授权委托书的证明等同于公证书

1. 下列文件的效力等同于公证书：

本国军事单位、军校、其他军队组织的军人的遗嘱和授权委托书，包括居住在营地里的工人、雇员和他们的家庭成员以及军属的遗嘱和授权委托书在没有公证机构和授权人员协助办理公证的情况下，由这些军事单位、组织的指挥官（首长）证明；

被拘留人员的遗嘱和授权委托书由该看守组织的负责人证明；

在庭院中游泳丧生的人，或在塔吉克斯坦共和国领土内因游泳丧生的人，其遗嘱和授权委托书由该区域的管理人证明；

探险队队员的遗嘱和授权委托书由该探险队的队长证明；

其他文件的证明依照塔吉克斯坦共和国法律规定的程序进行。

2. The certified wills provided by this Article shall be signed by the testator in the presence of one witness who also shall sign the will.

2. 本条规定的遗嘱证明应当由立遗嘱人在一名见证人的见证下签名，该见证人也要签名。

Article 36. Transfer of one copy of the will certified by authorized persons to the notary public

1. The authorized persons specified in Articles 33, of 34, and 35 these Laws shall within ten days from the date of the certificate of the will if on reasonable excuses it is impossible to send to this time, in case of opportunity, urgently to send one copy of the certified will for storage to office of notary public at the place of residence of the testator.

2. In case of lack of the permanent residence of the testator in the territory of the Republic of Tajikistan or if its residence is unknown, the will goes to office of notary public which is determined by authorized body.

3. The notary public shall check the certified will which arrived to him on storage, and in case of establishment of its discrepancy to the legislation of the Republic of Tajikistan, in writing report about it to the testator and the authorized person which certified the will for the purpose of its correct certificate.

4. Bears responsibility according to the legislation of the Republic of Tajikistan for damage caused to the heir (heirs) in connection with untimely transfer of the certified will, the authorized person.

第三十六条　将被授权人证明的一份遗嘱复印件移交给公证员

1. 除有正当理由外，本法第三十三条、第三十四条和第三十五条规定的被授权人员，应当自作出遗嘱证明之日起十日内，尽快将遗嘱证明的一份复印件移交立遗嘱人所在地的公证机构存放。

2. 若立遗嘱人在塔吉克斯坦共和国境内没有永久居住地，或者其居住地不明，遗嘱证明的复印件将由授权机构送往指定的公证机构。

3. 公证员需要检查移交其存放的遗嘱证明，若不符合塔吉克斯坦共和国法律的规定，公证员应当以书面形式通知立遗嘱人和遗嘱证明授权人员，要求其移交符合规定的遗嘱证明。

4. 依照塔吉克斯坦共和国法律的规定，被授权人员应当承担因未及时转交遗嘱而对继承人（继承人们）造成损害产生的法律责任。

Chapter 5. Basic rules of making of notarial actions

第五章　公证行为的基本规则

Article 37. Rules of making of notarial actions

Rules of making of notarial actions are established by this Law, other regulatory legal acts of the Republic of Tajikistan, the Instruction on procedure for making of notarial actions by notaries public of offices of notary public of the Republic of Tajikistan approved by authorized body.

第三十七条　公证行为的规则

依照本法、塔吉克斯坦共和国其他法律法规、公证行为的程序规定制定公证行为的规则。

Article 38. Terms of making of notarial actions, term and bases of adjournment and suspension of notarial actions

1. Notarial actions are made in day of presentation of all of documents necessary for this purpose and payment of the state fee. For making of difficult notarial actions this term can be prolonged up to five days.

2. Making of notarial actions can be postponed in need of reclamation of additional data and documents or the direction of documents for examination and emergence in the notary public of doubts concerning capacity to act of

第三十八条　公证的期限、休庭期和暂停公证的期限

1. 公证员应当在申请人提交所需文件和支付公证费的当天开始公证工作。如果公证事项较为复杂，该期限可以延长至五日。

2. 申请人需要补充资料和文件，或者公证员在检查文件时对一项交易中当事人的行为能力存疑，公证员可以推迟办理公证事项。

the parties of the transaction.

3. The term of adjournment of making of notarial actions from the date of pronouncement of the resolution on adjournment cannot be more than one month, except as specified, depending on receipt of documents and result of examination.

4. Making of notarial actions in case of dispute over protection of the violated right to the appeal of physical persons and legal entities to court, on the basis of the statement of the concerned party, can be postponed until ten days. If during this term the message on adoption of the statement to production of court does not arrive, notarial actions are made. In case of obtaining from court of the message on receipt of the statement of the interested person challenging the right or fact about the certificate of which asks other interested person, making of notarial actions stops before consideration of the case by court.

5. Other bases for adjournment and suspension of making of notarial actions can be established by the legislation of the Republic of Tajikistan.

Article 39. Making of notarial actions and identification of the notarial actions of persons which addressed for making

1. When making notarial actions the notary public identifies the personality of person, his representative and the representative of the legal entity who addressed for making of notarial actions.

2. Notarial actions are made by the notary public addressed to and (or) on behalf of person with its direct personal participation or its legal representative, addressed to or on behalf of the legal entity with direct participation of their authorized officers or their representative.

3. Identification shall be made based on the passport and other documents identifying the personality and testimonial of its residence, excluding any doubts concerning determination of the identity of addressed.

Article 40. Check of capacity to act of physical persons and legal capacities of the legal entities participating in transactions

1. In case of the certificate of transactions, first of all capacity to act of physical persons and legal capacity of legal entities is checked.

2. When checking legal capacity of the legal entities participating the party in the transaction, notaries public shall request from constituent documents, including, the certificate, the extract from the Unified State Register of

3. 除法律另有规定外，办理公证事项的休庭期限自公布休庭决议之日起算，最长不得超过一个月。若文件的送达和检查结果延误，则在必要的情况下可以适当延长期限。

4. 因保护被侵犯的自然人和法人向法庭提出上诉的权利而出现争议的，在利害关系人声明后，公证员可以推迟十日办理公证事项。在推迟期间内，若收到法院提供的声明，则应当进行公证。若收到法院提出的关于质疑利害关系人的权利和事实的声明，则在法院审理此案之前停止进行公证。

5. 依照塔吉克斯坦共和国法律的规定，其他可以休庭和暂停办理公证事项的理由。

第三十九条　申请人的身份证明

1. 公证前，公证员应当验明申请人及其代理人或法定代表人的身份。

2. 公证员向（或）代表直接参与人或其法定代理人，向（或）代表法人的授权机构代表实施公证行为。

3. 公证员应当依照护照和其他身份证明文件核实申请人的身份和经常居住地，排除关于其身份的怀疑。

第四十条　检查自然人的行为能力和参与交易的法人的法律地位

1. 公证员公证一项交易前，首先应当确认自然人和法人的民事权利能力和民事行为能力。

2. 公证员在检查参与交易的法人的民事权利能力时，应当要求当事人提交证书、营业执照、分支机构和代表机构的营业执照等文件，并检查交易是否符合相关文件的要求。

Legal Entities, their branches and representations and to check compliance of this action to requirements of constituent documents.

3. The notarial actions made on behalf of legal entities, their branches and representations shall not contradict the legislation of the Republic of Tajikistan, their charter or provision.

4. Powers of the representative are confirmed by the power of attorney issued on his name.

5. Notaries public do not require the power of attorney on transaction from heads of legal entities to whom the charter or provision confer powers. In these cases only the document certifying their official capacity is required.

6. If the elected collegiate organ manages the legal entity, the document on election of officials and on distribution of obligations between them shall be requested the head of this legal entity.

Article 41. Check of authenticity of signatures, procedure for signing of notarially certified documents

1. In case of the certificate of transactions and making of other notarial actions authenticity of signatures of the parties signing transactions and the other persons addressing for making of notarial actions is verified.

2. Transactions, other notarially certified documents and other documents shall be signed in the presence of the notary public by physical person, his representative, the representative of the legal entity. Along with the signature, also the surname, name and middle name by signatory personally can be written down. The notary public shall before signing of the document, provide acquaintance of participants of the transaction with the text of notarially certified document. At the request of the parties the text of the document can be read to them about what it will be stipulated in the text of the certified transaction.

3. If person owing to physical defects of disease, illiteracy or for other reasons cannot personally undersign on the document at his desire, at its presence and in the presence of the notary public the document can sign other favourites it person. With indication of the reasons owing to which the document could not be signed with own hand by person who addressed for making of notarial action. Also, at the request of addressed, the text of the certified document will be read to it aloud about what the mark in the text of the document will be made.

4. If deaf, mute or deaf-and-dumb person addressed for making of notarial action, is illiterate, when making

3. 公证员代表法人及其分支机构和作为他人代理人参与的公证活动不得违反塔吉克斯坦共和国法律和法人的章程规定。

4. 代理人的代理权由授权委托书确认。

5. 法定代表人的权力由公司章程或规定赋予，无须交易授权委托书。法定代表人只需向公证员提交法定代表人的身份证明。

6. 合议机关管理法人的，由合议机关负责人向公证员提交关于选举管理者和分配义务的文件。

第四十一条　检查签名的真实性，公证文件签署程序

1. 已有交易公证书，需要办理其他公证事项的，公证员应当核实公证书上交易双方签名的真实性和办理该交易公证的公证员身份。

2. 交易中涉及的公证文件应当在公证员的见证下，由自然人、代理人、法定代表人亲自签写全名（姓氏、名字、中间名）。在文件签署前，公证员应当向与交易参与者相熟的人提供公证文件的文本。依照当事人的请求，可以向他们宣读该文件，以便当事人了解经公证的交易文本的内容。

3. 当事人因身体缺陷、疾病、文盲或其他原因不能按自己的意愿亲自签署文件，在和公证员的共同见证下，该文件可以由其他与其亲近的人签署。公证员应当说明申请人不能亲自签署的原因。此外，依照请求，公证员可大声宣读该公证书，以便申请人了解公证书的内容。

4. 失聪者、失语者或聋哑人同时是文盲的，上述三种人申请公证时，需要有能与之交流的人代其签

notarial action there shall be person. Chosen as this person or the signer who can have a talk with it and confirm with the signature that contents of the transaction, the statement or other document certified by the notary correspond to desire of the deaf, mute or deaf-and-dumb person participating in notarial action.

字，并确认签署的公证内容符合参与公证活动的上述三类人的意愿。

Article 42. Reclamation of data and documents necessary for making of notarial action

1. The notaries public and authorized persons making the notarial actions having the right to request physical persons and legal entities of the data and the documents necessary for making of notarial action.

2. The data and documents necessary for making of notarial action shall be submitted in time, established by this Law.

3. Non-presentation of data and documents by physical persons and legal entities upon the demand of the notary public and authorized persons in time, established this by the Law, can be the basis for adjournment, suspension or refusal in notarial actions.

第四十二条 提交公证所需的资料和文件

1. 公证员和被授权人员在办理公证事项时有权要求自然人和法人提供公证所需的资料和文件。

2. 公证所需的资料和文件应当依照本法的规定及时提交。

3. 自然人和法人未依照本法的要求及时提交公证员和被授权人员办理公证事项所需的数据和文件的，可以作为休庭期、暂停或拒绝公证的依据。

Article 43. Requirements to the documents submitted for making of notarial actions

1. For making of notarial actions the following documents are not accepted:

- the documents having erasures or corrections, additions, the crossed-out words, documents completed with pencil and other, not stipulated corrections;

- the documents made in contradiction with statutory rules of clerical work of legal entities from which the document proceeds;

- documents, owing to damages and other reasons the having parts of the text or details of the document (date of creation or acceptance, the signature of the official or seal) which cannot be read;

- the documents contradicting requirements of the legislation of the Republic of Tajikistan.

2. Documents which amount makes more than one leaf shall be strung together, numbered and sealed by the authorized signature and corresponding.

第四十三条 办理公证事项需要提交的文件

1. 公证员办理公证事项时不得接受以下文件：

文字有删改的文件、全是由铅笔填写的文件或其他没有按规定更正的文件；

制作的文书违反法人的文书工作规则；

文件因受损坏或其他原因，无法识别文本的部分或文件的细节（创建或接受日期、官方的签字或印章）；

与塔吉克斯坦共和国法律规定相抵触的文件。

2. 数量超过一页的文件需要装订并编号，在授权签字后一一对应地密封起来。

Article 44. Requirements to notarially certified documents

1. Texts of notarially certified transactions, copies of the certified documents and statements from them and other notarial documents shall be written clearly and accurately, the numbers and terms relating to contents of the

第四十四条 公证文件的要求

1. 经公证的合同、文件和陈述副本以及其他公证文件应清楚、准确地书写。与经公证的交易内容有关的编号和术语应当在复印件中被至少指明一次，法人的名称，自然人的姓、名、中间名应当完整，并且注

certified transactions shall be designated at least once by copy-book, and names of legal entities, surnames, names and middle names of persons are specified completely and with indication of their addresses.

2. In case of detection in notarially certified document of errors of technical (arithmetic) nature, the notary public has the right, without changing sense and contents of the document, in the absence of dispute and prohibitions, based on the statement of the interested person to correct the made mistake.

3. Corrections are made based on pronouncement of the relevant resolution.

Article 45. Issue of certificates and making of certifying texts

1. In confirmation of the right to inheritance, the property right, the property right to share in joint property of spouses, the certificate of the fact of finding of person in live or in certain place, identity of person with person represented on picture, acceptances on document storage and transfers of statements appropriate certificates are granted.

2. In case of the certificate of transactions, witnessing of fidelity of copies of documents and statements from them, authenticity of the signature, imposing of prohibition on alienation of real estate, fidelity of the translation of documents from one language on another, certificates of executive texts, time of production of documents, on the relevant documents are made certifying texts in the forms approved by authorized body with sealing of the notary public.

3. In confirmation of making of the ship's protest and making of protest of bills of exchange and non-payment of checks acts are drawn up.

4. During the providing proofs and the announcement of the confidential will the protocol is constituted.

Article 46. Registration of notarial actions

1. All notarial actions are registered in the register of registration of notarial actions. The separate sequence number is assigned to each committed notarial action. Number at which notarial action is registered in the register is specified in the documents issued by the notary public.

2. Notarial action is considered committed after complete payment of the state fee and from the moment of registration in the register.

3. Forms of registers for registration of notarial actions and certifying texts are established by authorized

明他们的地址。

2. 如果在检查已公证的文件时发现技术（计算）类错误，公证员有权在不改变文件的意义和内容并且没有争议和禁令的情况下，以利害关系人的陈述为基础改正。

3. 依照有关决议的声明作出更正。

第四十五条　公证书的出具和制作

1. 对于继承权、财产权、夫妻共同财产权的确认，证明某人存活或在某处发现某人、图像上某人的身份、文件提存以及陈述的转达等公证事项，应当向当事人出具公证书。

2. 如果是公证交易、文件副本及其陈述的真实性、签名的真实性、禁止转让不动产的约定和解除、文件从一种语言翻译到另一种语言的真实性、制定执行文本、公证文件的制作时间以及其他相关文件，应当依照授权机构核准和公证员盖章的形式出具公证书。

3. 在公证海事声明、对汇票作出拒兑证明书以及公证未付款的机票时应当先草拟证书。

4. 在秘密遗嘱提供证据和宣告期间，应当先拟好草案。

第四十六条　公证登记

1. 公证活动应当在公证登记簿上登记。提交的公证行为应当单独按顺序编号，编号应当由公证员在文件中列明。

2. 公证行为自所有费用缴纳完毕并且在登记册上登记后生效。

3. 公证活动和公证文本在登记册登记的形式由授权机构确定。

body.

Article 47. Refusal in making of notarial action

1. The notary public refuses making of notarial action if:

- making of such action contradicts the law and interests of the state;

- action is subject to making by other office of notary public;

- requested making of notarial action incapacitated person, or the representative who does not have appropriate authority;

- the transaction made on behalf of the legal entity contradicts the purposes specified in its charter;

- the transaction is provided by persons which are not registered as the individual entrepreneur and the legal entity;

- the documents submitted for making of notarial action do not conform to requirements of the legislation of the Republic of Tajikistan.

2. The notary public, at the request of the addressed person to whom it is refused making of notarial actions shall report causes of failure in writing and explains procedure for its appeal. In these cases, the notary public no later than seven days from the date of the request for making of notarial action makes the decision on refusal in making of notarial action.

Article 48. Appeal of notarial actions or refusal in their making and procedure for the dispute resolution about the right based on committed notarial action

1. The interested person who considers committed notarial action or refusal in making of notarial action wrong, having the right to address in ores in the location of office of notary public.

2. The disputes on the right based on committed notarial action which arose between the interested Streets are considered judicially.

Chapter 6. Rules of making of separate types of notarial actions

Article 49. Notarially certified transactions

1. Notaries public and authorized persons certify transactions for which the legislation establishes obligatory notarial form of making of these actions.

2. At the request of physical persons and legal entities, notaries public can certify and other transactions for

第四十七条　拒绝公证

1. 有以下情形之一的，公证员应当拒绝公证：

该公证违背法律和国家利益；

该公证事项应当由其他公证机构办理；

申请人没有行为能力，或者其代理人没有代理权；

代表法人进行的交易与其公司章程的目的相违背；

交易由未登记为个体企业家和法定代表人的人作出；

为办理公证事项所提交的文件不符合塔吉克斯坦共和国法律的要求。

2. 公证员应当在当事人提出公证申请之日起七日内，作出拒绝公证的决定。申请人申请说明理由的，公证员应当以书面形式告知拒绝原因并说明上诉程序。

第四十八条　对公证、被拒绝公证的上诉和申请公证的权利基础的争议的解决程序

1. 申请公证或被拒绝公证的利害关系人，有权在公证员的公证机构所在地申诉。

2. 利害关系双方因申请公证的权利基础的争议应当被公平解决。

第六章　不同类型的公证活动的规则

第四十九条　交易公证

1. 公证员和被授权人员依照法律规定的强制性交易公证形式进行公证。

2. 应自然人和法人的要求，公证员可以公证塔吉克斯坦共和国法律没有规定强制公证的其他交易。

which the legislation of the Republic of Tajikistan does not establish the obligatory notarial certificate.

Article 50. Certificate of transactions of property acquisition

1. Notaries public certify transactions about the property acquisition, being property of physical persons and legal entities, and also belonging to legal entities by the right of economic maintaining or operational management according to the procedure established by the legislation of the Republic of Tajikistan.

2. The certificate of the transaction connected with alienation of real estate is made in the location of real estate.

3. If property, the property right or other right to property requires state registration, the transaction about alienation of this property makes sure of cases only in case of representation to the notary public of the document confirming state registration of the right to this property.

4. The agreements on property acquisition which are not certified in notarial procedure as the title document cannot be the basis for the notarial certificate of transactions of property acquisition.

5. Transactions about alienation of real estate from which taxes are levied to belonging to the citizen of the Republic of Tajikistan, foreign citizen, stateless persons or the foreign or international legal entity who is not taking the permanent location in the Republic of Tajikistan make sure only after representation to the notary public of the document confirming payment of the corresponding tax.

6. Agreements on alienation of apartment houses and rooms make sure with observance of requirements of the legislation of the Republic of Tajikistan.

7. Real estate which arrest or prohibition of alienation is imposed cannot be subject of the transaction.

Article 51. Certificate of the pledge agreement

1. If the property, the right to property or other property right requires state registration, the pledge agreement of property, the right to property or other property right make sure only by provision to the notary public of the title document having the corresponding state registration.

2. The pledge agreement of real estate is performed in the location of real estate. In case of the certificate of the pledge agreement of real estate general rules, the stipulated in Article 50 these Laws are applied.

第五十条　财产取得交易公证

1. 公证员依照塔吉克斯坦共和国法律规定的程序为财产取得的交易、自然人和法人的财产以及属于法人的经济维持、经营管理的相关权利进行公证。

2. 与不动产转让有关的交易公证在房地产所在地进行。

3. 如果财产、财产权和其他权利需要登记，那么关于该财产的转让交易公证应当确保只有在向公证员出示该财产的权利登记确认文件后进行。

4. 未经公证程序证明的财产取得产权证书，不能作为公证财产取得交易公证的依据。

5. 对属于塔吉克斯坦共和国的纳税公民、外国公民、无国籍人或者在塔吉克斯坦共和国无永久住所地的外国或国际法人的不动产转让交易的公证只有在其向公证员出示支付相应税款的证明文件后才能进行。

6. 公寓楼和楼内单元的转让协议应当遵守塔吉克斯坦共和国法律的要求。

7. 禁止转让的不动产不能作为交易标的物。

第五十一条　质押协议证明

1. 如果财产、财产权或其他权利需要登记，只有在向公证员提供相应的产权登记证明文件后才能进行财产质押协议、财产权或其他权利的公证。

2. 不动产的质押协议应当在不动产所在地进行。如果是不动产常规的质押协议证明，那么适用本法第五十条的规定。

Article 52. Certificate, change and cancellation of the will

1. The notary public and authorized persons certify the will with observance of requirements of the legislation of the Republic of Tajikistan. Also the notary public and authorized persons certify cancellation and change of wills.

2. The certificate of wills by means of the representative and on behalf of two and more persons is not allowed.

3. In case of the certificate of the will the notary public and authorized persons do not demand from the testator of representation of the fact of accessory to it the documents of title confirming its property right to the bequeathed property.

4. The will constituted by the notary public and the authorized person according to the testator in the presence of the witness makes sure after signing by her testator and witness.

5. Change or cancellation of the will is performed according to the procedure, provided by the civil legislation of the Republic of Tajikistan.

Article 53. Certificate of powers of attorney

1. The notary public and authorized persons certify the power of attorney on behalf of one or several persons addressed to one person or several persons according to the procedure, stipulated by the legislation the Republic of Tajikistan.

2. The certificate of the power of attorney according to the procedure of repeated retrust is not allowed.

3. The power of attorney issued according to the procedure of retrust to other person can be notarially certified only on submission of the main power of attorney in which the retrust right is stipulated. The power of attorney issued according to the procedure of retrust shall not comprise more rights, than it is provided under the main power of attorney. Effective period of the power of attorney issued according to the procedure of retrust cannot exceed effective period of the power of attorney based on which it is issued.

4. In case of the certificate of powers of attorney for the order and real estate administration and the transactions requiring the notarial certificate or registration in the procedure established by the legislation of the Republic of Tajikistan for the real estate which is joint property of spouses. The notary public shall receive notarially certified written consent of other spouse.

第五十二条　遗嘱的公证、变更和撤销

1. 公证员和被授权人依照塔吉克斯坦共和国法律的要求为遗嘱及遗嘱的撤销和变更事项进行公证。

2. 不允许公证员以代表的名义或代表两人以上对遗嘱进行公证。

3. 在遗嘱公证中，公证员和被授权人不需要立遗嘱者提供其受遗赠财产的财产权利附属证明文件。

4. 遗嘱是由公证员和被授权人依照立遗嘱者的意愿，在见证人的见证下制定的，并且应当让立遗嘱者和见证者签字确认。

5. 遗嘱的变更或撤销应当遵循塔吉克斯坦共和国民法规定的程序。

第五十三条　授权委托书

1. 公证员和被授权人依照塔吉克斯坦共和国法律的规定，可代表一人或数人向一人或数人对授权委托书进行公证。

2. 不允许重复出具授权委托书。

3. 依照恢复程序重新对其他人发出的授权委托书，只有在提交规定了后续权利的主要授权委托书后才能申请公证。依照恢复程序发出的授权委托书包含的权利不能超出主要授权委托书规定的范围。依照恢复程序发出的授权委托书的有效期不得超过原出具授权委托书的有效期。

4. 依照塔吉克斯坦共和国法律规定的程序，不动产的管理和订单及交易的授权委托书需要公证或登记作为配偶的共同财产的，公证员应当获得另一配偶的书面公证同意书。

Article 54. Number of copies of documents in which the text of the transaction is stated

Number of copies of the documents certified in notarial procedure is determined depending on the number of the parties participating in the transaction. And also one of them remains in cases of office of notary public.

第五十四条　经双方认可的交易公证书的副本数量

在公证程序中，应当根据参与交易的当事人的数量决定公证书的副本数量，且其中一份副本应当保留在公证机构。

Chapter 7. Protection of heritable property

第七章　可继承财产的保护

Article 55. Protection of heritable property

1. Notaries public in the place of opening of inheritance based on the statement of the heir or heirs, the testamentary executor, self-government institutions of settlements and villages, guardianship and custody bodies or other physical persons and legal entities take measures for protection of the heritable property necessary for the benefit of the state, the heir, heirs or creditors.

2. If the property of the testator or his part is not in the place of opening of inheritance, the notary public in the place of opening of inheritance sends to office of notary public in the location of heritable property the order about taking measures to its protection.

3. The notary public in the location of heritable property who took measures for protection of heritable property reports to office of notary public in the place of opening of inheritance about acceptance of the specified measures.

第五十五条　可继承财产的保护

1. 公证员应当依照继承人或遗嘱指定管理人的陈述公开遗产所在地。定居点和村庄的自治机构、监护人和监护机构或其他自然人和法人应当采取措施保护与国家、继承人和债权人利益相关的可继承财产。

2. 如果立遗嘱人的全部财产或部分财产不在公开的遗产所在地，公开的遗产所在地的公证员应当通知可继承财产所在地的公证机构对其采取保护措施。

3. 遗产所在地的公证员应采取措施保护遗产，并向公开的遗产所在地的公证机构报告保护情况。

Article 56. The notice of heirs on the opened inheritance

1. The notary public who received the message about opened inheritance, shall inform on it those heirs, the residence or works of which are known to it.

2. The notary public can also call heirs by the public announcement or the message on it in seal, at desire and at the expense of interested persons. These operations are performed in the terms established by the legislation of the Republic of Tajikistan for inheritance acceptance.

第五十六条　继承人继承遗产的公告

1. 公证员收到公开遗产的信息，应当到继承人的居住地和工作地通知其继承人。

2. 公证员也可以通过公告或者揭露密封信息的方式通知继承人，尽管这可能会损害利害关系人要求保密的权利。这些行动应当依照塔吉克斯坦共和国法律规定的继承接受条款进行。

Article 57. Production of the inventory of heritable property and appointment of his keeper or guardian

1. The notary public makes the inventory of this property for protection of heritable property and gives him to storage to heirs or other persons. The belongings list is made according to provisions of the legislation of the Republic of Tajikistan with participation of persons and at least two witnesses interested in protection of heritable property about what the relevant statement is drawn up.

2. The notary public makes the inventory of all prop-

第五十七条　制作遗产的详细目录并委任遗产的保管人或管理人

1. 为保护遗产，公证员应当制作详细的财产目录，并且交由遗产的继承人或其他人保存。财产清单应当依照塔吉克斯坦共和国法律的规定，由至少两名对保护遗产有利害关系的见证人参与起草。

2. 公证员应清点所有室内财产并制作详细目录。

erty which is in the building.

3. The property exception of the inventory is performed only judicially.

4. In cases if heirs and other persons do not show heritable property for creation of the inventory, destroyed heritable property or for other reasons the inventory of heritable property or acceptance of necessary measures is considered impossible, the notary public about it draws up the relevant statement.

5. The inventory of heritable property is made according to the procedure, established by the Instruction of clerical work in offices of notary public of the Republic of Tajikistan.

6. If as a part of inheritance there is property requiring management and also in case of presentation of the claim by creditors of the testator before inheritance acceptance by heirs, the notary public appoints the keeper of property.

7. The keeper and other persons to whom (entrusted) heritable property is transferred to storage are warned about criminal liability for assignment or waste of heritable property and about liability for the caused losses.

Article 58. Trust management of heritable property

1. Trust management of heritable property is exercised in cases if as a part of inheritance there is heritable property concerning which they need not only protection, but also management (the company property complex, share in the authorized (share) capital of economic society, securities, exclusive rights and another).

2. Trust management of heritable property is established by the notary public in the place of opening of inheritance according to the statement of persons specified regarding 1 article 55 of this Law, except as specified, if the constituent rights belong to the testamentary executor. On trust management of heritable property the notary public grants to the trustee the certificate.

3. In case of default of agreement between heirs about appointment of the trustee, the trustee is appointed judicially.

Article 59. The order about organization of trust management of heritable property

1. If the heritable property is in different places, the notary public in the place of opening of inheritance directs the order about organization of property trust management according to the procedure, the stipulated in Article 55 these Laws.

3. 没有纳入财产清单上的财产只能通过司法判决来执行。

4. 如果继承人和其他人因为毁坏遗产或其他原因而没有出示该遗产用于制作详细目录，那么认为该人无法获得财产或者接受必要措施，公证员可以就此制作相关声明。

5. 遗产详细目录应当依照塔吉克斯坦共和国公证机构的文书工作程序制作。

6. 遗产的部分财产需要管理或者在遗产被继承人接受之前，立遗嘱人的债权人提出偿还要求的，公证员应当任命财产管理人。

7. 公证员在委托管理人和其他受委托人管理遗产时，应当向其告知故意损坏或遗失遗产应承担的刑事责任。

第五十八条 遗产的信托管理

1. 当遗产的一部分需要保护和管理时，应当在遗产上设立信托，例如公司的财产综合体，在经济社团的授权（股份）资本中的股份、证券、专有权和其他。

2. 遗产的信托管理由公证员依照本法第五十五条第一款规定的人员在遗产的公开地设立的，但部分权利属于遗嘱执行人的除外。在遗产的信托管理中，公证员应当向受托人出具公证书。

3. 如果继承人就委派受托人一事无法达成合意，应当由司法判决指定受托人。

第五十九条 遗产信托的组织规则

1. 如果遗产在不同的地方，那么由公开继承所在地的公证员依照第五十五条规定的程序确定遗产信托的规则。

2. The notary public within one month reports about organization of trust management of heritable property to the notary public in the place of opening of inheritance.

2. 公证员应当在一个月内向公开遗产所在地的公证员报告遗产信托的情况。

Article 60. Transfer of heritable property to trust management

第六十条　转移遗产至信托管理部门

1. The property which is part of inheritance requiring management is transferred by the notary public based on the trust management agreement to person specified in the message on organization of trust management of heritable property or to certain notary public.

1. 遗产中的部分财产需要特别管理的，应当由公证员按照信托协议将托管权转交给遗产信托协议中约定的人或者特定的公证员。

2. Heirs, and also the other persons who are beneficiaries according to the trust management agreement of heritable property cannot be the trustee.

2. 继承人和其他从信托协议中获益的人不能担任受托人。

3. The trust management agreement shall be signed according to requirements of the civil legislation of the Republic of Tajikistan and this Law.

3. 遗产信托协议的制定过程和协议内容应当符合塔吉克斯坦共和国民法和本法的规定。

4. Essential terms of the contract of trust management of heritable property are the detailed description of the property delivered in trust management. Specifying about the beneficiary terms of submission of reports by the trustee person receiving property in case of the termination of management, the size and form of remuneration of the managing order of the heir or heirs for the benefit of whom trust management, payment terms of implementation of trust management and the basis of the termination of trust management is exercised.

4. 对受托财产的详细描述是遗产信托协议的核心条款。信托终止时，受托人应当在提交的报告中详细说明受托财产的受益情况、遗产继承人的受益情况、信托管理的酬劳和终止信托的原因。

Article 61. Payment of remuneration for implementation of trust management of heritable property

第六十一条　遗产信托应当支付的报酬

Payment of remuneration for implementation of trust management of heritable property to the trustee is performed in the amount of, determined by the agreement between the heir (heirs) and the trustee if the legislation of the Republic of Tajikistan does not provide other.

塔吉克斯坦共和国法律没有规定受托人酬劳的，遗产信托由继承人与托管人约定。

Article 62. Termination of trust management of heritable property

第六十二条　遗产信托的终止

1. Trust management of heritable property continues before inheritance acceptance by the heir or heirs and if the inheritance was not accepted them, before the expiration of the inheritance acceptance established by the legislation of the Republic of Tajikistan.

1. 受托人在继承人接受遗产之前管理遗产，继承人没有继承遗产的，在塔吉克斯坦共和国法律规定的接受继承的期限届满之前依然由受托人管理遗产信托。

2. The notary public shall notify heirs on the termination of trust management of heritable property and if the property passes to the state, the relevant state body.

2. 遗产信托终止时，公证员应当通知继承人，遗产转移至国家机关保管的，由相应的国家机关通知继承人。

Article 63. Termination of measures for protection of heritable property

1. Protection of heritable property continues before inheritance acceptance by all heirs and if it was not accepted before the expiration of the inheritance acceptance established by the legislation of the Republic of Tajikistan.

2. The notary public shall notify previously on the termination of measures for protection of heritable property of heirs, and in cases of their absence, the relevant state body.

Article 64. Issue of sums of money from heritable property

1. Person who incurred expenses on care of the sick testator to his death to protection and management of inheritance, also on funeral of the testator in case of absence of the heir to which it will be transferred inheritance or the testamentary executor, has the right to address the notary public in the place of opening of inheritance for covering of the expenses at the expense of heritable property. In this case addressed shall bring to the notary public the written proof confirming its expenses.

2. If the notary public considers acceptable requirements imposed by person before inheritance acceptance by heirs and if it was not accepted before issue to the state of the certificate on the right to inheritance, about issue of the following means from heritable property can give instructions:

- on covering of costs on care of the testator during his disease, and also on funeral;

- on content of persons which are dependent on the testator;

- on covering of expenses on protection of heritable property and on management of it.

3. In case of absence as a part of heritable property of sums of money, the notary public gives the assignment about issue of things which cost shall not exceed the amount of actually made expenses. At the same time such assignment is not given concerning heritable real estate and vehicles.

Chapter 8. Acceptance and announcement of the confidential will

Article 65. Acceptance and announcement of the confidential will

1. The notary public accepts the confidential will according to the procedure, established by the civil legisla-

第六十三条　终止遗产保护的措施

1. 公证员应当在全部继承人接受遗产前对遗产实施保护措施，继承人没有接受遗产的，公证员的保护措施应当持续至塔吉克斯坦共和国法律规定的接受继承的期限届满之日。

2. 公证员应当在终止对遗产的保护措施之前通知继承人，没有继承人的，应当通知相关国家机关。

第六十四条　从遗产中发放资金

1. 没有继承人时，遗嘱执行人有权要求公开遗产所在地的公证员从遗产中支付立遗嘱人生病期间的护理费、丧葬费以及管理遗产等所产生的费用，遗嘱执行人应当向公证员提交书面的开支证明。

2. 公证员在继承人接受遗产且在继承权公证书没有发布给国家之前，下列费用从遗产中支付：

立遗嘱人生病期间的护理费以及丧葬费；

维持立遗嘱人扶养的人的基本生活所需；

保管遗产所产生的费用。

3. 遗产不足以支付上述费用的，公证员可以出卖遗产。但遗产中的不动产和车辆禁止转让。

第八章　秘密遗嘱的宣告和接受

第六十五条　秘密遗嘱的宣告和接受

1. 公证员依照塔吉克斯坦民法规定的程序接受秘密遗嘱。

tion of the Republic of Tajikistan.

2. In case of presentation by interested persons of the death certificate of the testator, the notary public of office of notary public where the confidential will is stored, starts stage of the announcement of the confidential will.

3. The notary public according to the procedure, established by the legislation of the Republic of Tajikistan, in the established day and time of the announcement of the confidential will, at discretion invites two persons as witnesses from among the heirs who expressed desire to take part in case of the announcement of the confidential will and confirmed the related relations with the testator based on the document. In case of absence of witnesses from among legal heirs or refusal by them from participation in case of the announcement of the confidential will, the notary public has the right to invite other witnesses.

4. The protocol of the announcement of the confidential will contains the following data:

- date and place of creation of the protocol;
- receipt date of the data on opening of inheritance;
- date of opening of inheritance;
- surname, name, middle name, birth date and death, last residence of the testator;
- surname, name, middle name of the witnesses and other persons participating in case of the announcement of the confidential will;
- the address of office of notary public where the confidential will will be announced;
- record about condition of envelope in which there is envelope of the confidential will and condition of envelope in which there is confidential will.

5. The protocol of the announcement of the confidential will is signed by the notary public and witnesses and on it the notary public seal is set.

6. The original of the protocol is stored in cases of office of notary public, other copy is issued to persons specified in the confidential will, to persons who refused inheritance, also to the testamentary executor according to the procedure established by this Law.

Article 66. Certificate of power of the testamentary executor

1. Based on the written application of the testamentary executor (assignment) the notary public in the place of opening of inheritance according to the procedure, established by the civil legislation of the Republic of Tajikistan, will certify its power proceeding from contents of the will.

2. 利害关系人出示立遗嘱人的死亡证明书后，存放秘密遗嘱的公证机构的公证员即开始筹划宣告秘密遗嘱的工作。

3. 公证员依照塔吉克斯坦共和国法律规定的程序，在宣告秘密遗嘱的法定日期和时间内，酌情邀请有参加该秘密遗嘱宣告会意愿，且与立遗嘱人有亲属关系的两名继承人担任见证人。受邀的继承人缺席或拒绝参加该秘密遗嘱宣告会的，公证员有权邀请其他见证人。

4. 秘密遗嘱草案应包含以下内容：

制作草案的日期和地点；

接收公开遗产的资料的日期；

公开遗产的日期；

立遗嘱人的姓、名、中间名、出生和死亡日期，最后居住地；

见证人和其他参与秘密遗嘱宣告会的人的姓、名、中间名；

秘密遗嘱宣告地的公证机构地址；

对封存秘密遗嘱的信封的情况的相关记录。

5. 秘密遗嘱的宣告草案应当由公证员和见证人签名并加盖公证员的印章。

6. 该草案的原件应当存放在公证机构，其他复印件应当提交给秘密遗嘱中确定的继承人，拒绝继承遗产的继承人以及依照本法规定确定的遗嘱执行人。

第六十六条　遗嘱执行人的权力证明

1. 公开遗产所在地的公证员依照塔吉克斯坦共和国民法规定的程序，根据遗嘱执行人的书面申请，证明其依照遗嘱内容具有执行权。

2. Power of the testamentary executor the notary public make sure if:

- in heritable case there is not cancelled will according to which execution of the will is assigned to the applicant;

- in heritable case there are no data on release of the applicant by court from execution of the will;

- the consent of the applicant be testamentary executor shall be expressed in the text of the will or the statement attached to the will or it in the time established by the civil legislation of the Republic of Tajikistan, started execution of the obligations assigned to it.

2. 公证员应当确保遗嘱执行人具有下列权力：

在遗产案件中，被指派给申请人的遗嘱执行没有被取消；

在遗产案件中，没有关于法院释放遗嘱执行申请人的数据；

应当在遗嘱或遗嘱附属声明中表明同意申请人成为遗嘱执行人，或者该申请人在塔吉克斯坦共和国民法规定的时间内开始履行指派给执行人的义务。

Chapter 9. Issue of the certificate on the right to inheritance

第九章　遗产权利证书的出具

Article 67. Place and terms of issue of the certificate on the right to inheritance

1. According to the written application of heirs the notary public in the place of opening of inheritance grants the certificate on the right to inheritance.

2. Issue of the certificate on the right to inheritance is made in terms and according to the procedure, established by the civil legislation of the Republic of Tajikistan.

第六十七条　出具遗产权利证书的地点和条款

1. 公开遗产所在地的公证员依照继承人的书面申请授予其遗产权利证书。

2. 依照塔吉克斯坦共和国民法规定的程序和条款出具遗产权利证书。

Article 68. Opening of inheritance

1. Can be the basis of opening of heritable case:

- statement for inheritance acceptance or for refusal of it;

- statement for issue of the certificate on the right to inheritance;

- statement of the surviving spouse for the property right to share in joint property of spouses;

- the statement for taking measures for protection of heritable property or management of it, and also other statements which arrived concerning heritable property.

2. The specified documents are stored in heritable case of office of notary public on the place of opening of inheritance. In heritable case also other documents, stipulated by the legislation the Republic of Tajikistan join. The procedure for the production connected with heritable case is determined according to the Instruction on clerical work in offices of notary public of the Republic of Tajikistan.

第六十八条　遗产的公开

1. 下列文件可以作为公开遗产的依据：

接受或拒绝遗产的声明；

遗产权利证书出具的声明；

配偶中在世的一方对夫妻共同财产权利的声明；

采取措施保护遗产或管理遗产的声明，以及其他有关遗产的声明。

2. 指定文件存放在公开遗产所在地的公证机构。塔吉克斯坦共和国法律中也加入了遗产案例和其他文件。与遗产相关的案例的出示程序由塔吉克斯坦共和国公证机构的文书工作决定。

Article 69. Procedure for issue of the certificate on the right to inheritance under the law

1. The certificate on the right to inheritance under the law is granted to the heirs who accepted inheritance

第六十九条　依法出具遗产权利证书的程序

1. 公证员应当依照塔吉克斯坦共和国法律规定的程序给接受遗产的继承人出具遗产权利证书。

according to the procedure, established by the legislation of the Republic of Tajikistan.

2. The certificate on the right to inheritance under the law is granted to all heirs together or to each heir separately at will. The heirs who did not accept inheritance in the time established by the law can be included in the certificate on the right to inheritance under the law with the consent of other heirs who accepted inheritance. This consent shall be expressed in writing before issue of the certificate on the right to inheritance under the law.

3. The notary public reports in guardianship and custody bodies at the place of residence of the heir for its protection and protection of valuable interests of the minor heir about issue of the certificate on the right to inheritance under the law addressed to the minor guardian or the custodian or the incapacitated heir.

4. Upon transition of heritable property to the state by right on inheritance, the certificate on the right to inheritance under the law is granted to the relevant state body.

Article 70. Conditions of issue of the certificate on the right to inheritance on the law

1. The notary public in case of issue of the certificate on the right to inheritance under the law, by reclamation at heirs of the relevant documents, checks the fact of death of the testator, time and the place of opening of inheritance. Availability of the related relations with the testator which are the basis for calling to inheritance under the law of persons who submitted the application for issue of the certificate on the right to inheritance and structure of heritable property on which the certificate on the right to inheritance is granted.

2. If one or several legal heirs are deprived of opportunity to submit the documents which are the basis for calling to inheritance under the law they can be included in the certificate on the right to inheritance with the consent of all other heirs who accepted inheritance and submitted the documents which are the basis for calling to inheritance under the law.

Article 71. Conditions of issue of the certificate on the right to inheritance on the will

The notary public in case of issue of the certificate on the right to inheritance according to the will, checks the fact of death of the testator, will availability by reclamation at heirs of the relevant documents, the copy of the protocol on announcement of the closed will with mark regarding cancellation or changes, time and the place of opening of

2. 公证员可以同时向所有继承人出具遗产权利证书，也可以向每个继承人分别出具遗产权利证书。在其他接受遗产继承人的书面同意下，没有在法律规定的时间内接受遗产的继承人可以被列入遗产权利证书中。

3. 公证员应当向保护继承人和保护未成年继承人利益所在地的监护抚养机构报告关于依法给未成年继承人的监护人或抚养人或无民事行为能力的继承人出具遗产权利证书的情况。

4. 在通过遗产权利证书将遗产转让给国家时，公证员应当向相关国家机关出具遗产权利证书。

第七十条　依法出具遗产权利证书的条件

1. 公证员依法出具遗产权利证书时，应当要求继承人出具相关文件，核实立遗嘱人死亡的事实，公开遗产的时间和地点。遗产权利证书的申请人应当与立遗嘱人有亲属关系，才可参与继承、获得遗产权利证书，且有权安排遗产。

2. 如果一个或多个合法继承人丧失提交参与继承所需文件的机会，在其他接受遗产并且提交了参与邀请继承所需的文件的继承人的一致同意后，可以被列入遗产权利证书中。

第七十一条　依照遗嘱出具遗产权利证书的条件

公证员依照遗嘱出具遗产权利证书时，应当核实立遗嘱人死亡的事实、继承人提交的遗嘱相关文件的有效性、带有撤销或变更标注的遗嘱关闭声明协议副本、公开遗产的时间和地点、遗产的构成、有权分配遗产的人。

inheritance, structure of heritable property, the group of people having the right to obligatory share in inheritance.

Article 72. Conditions of issue of the certificate on the right to inheritance on the property which is subject to state registration

1. If real estate (its part) is part of heritable property, the notary public requires the title document on accessory of real estate to the testator, the document certifying state registration of the right to property, the certificate of technical inventory count, and also the reference of body of the arrest registering state registration about absence and prohibitions concerning real estate.

2. In case of inclusion in the certificate on the right to inheritance of other property which is subject to state registration (the vehicle, the motorcycle, the motor boat, etc.), the notary public checks documents on accessory of this property to the testator.

第七十二条　遗产中包括经国家登记的财产时出具遗产权利证书的条件

1. 遗产包括不动产或不动产的一部分时，公证员应当要求立遗嘱人提供配套的不动产产权证书、证明财产权的国家登记文件、财产估值的证明以及国家登记机关作出的与不动产相关的缺席登记和禁止性扣留的证明。

2. 如果遗产权利证书包含其他国家登记的财产（车辆、摩托车、机动船等），公证员应当检查立遗嘱人的财产附属文件。

Chapter 10. Issue of the certificate on the property right

第十章　财产权利证书的出具

Article 73. Procedure for issue of the certificate on the property right

The certificate on the property right to the real estate acquired according to the procedure, established by the legislation of the Republic of Tajikistan is issued by the notary public of office of notary public in the location of property.

第七十三条　出具财产权利证书的程序

依照塔吉克斯坦共和国法律规定的程序，由财产所在地的公证机构的公证员出具不动产的财产权利公证书。

Article 74. Conditions of issue of the certificate on the property right

For issue of the certificate on the property right to property documents, stipulated by the legislation the Republic of Tajikistan are submitted.

第七十四条　出具财产权利证书的条件

公证员应当依照塔吉克斯坦共和国法律的规定，出具财产权利证书。

Article 75. Issue of the certificate on the property right according to the joint statement of spouses

The notary public based on the joint statement of spouses issues to one of them or both spouses the certificate on the property right to the one second share in joint property which is considered their common property. The certificate on the property right can be granted to spouses both in the time spent in scrap, and within three years from the date of annulment of marriage.

第七十五条　依照夫妻共同声明出具财产权利证书

公证员根据夫妻共同声明，向配偶中的一方或双方出具共同财产的二分之一份额的财产权利证书。该财产权利证书可以在离婚期间内向配偶双方出具，也可以在婚姻宣告无效之日起三年内出具。

Article 76. Issue of the certificate on the property right in case of the death of one of spouses

1. In case of the death of one of spouses, the cer-

第七十六条　配偶一方死亡时，财产权利证书的出具

1. 配偶一方死亡的，公开遗产所在地的公证员依

tificate on the property right to share in joint property of spouses is granted according to the statement of the surviving spouse by the notary public in the place of opening of inheritance with the preliminary notice of other heirs.

照在世配偶的声明授予其分享夫妻共同财产的财产权利证书，并且向其他继承人发出预告通知。

2. In case of issue of the certificate on the property right to share in joint property of spouses (if the marriage agreement does not provide other), the relevant document confirming marriage of the applicant with the testator, the relevant document confirming accessory of property to the died spouse or the died spouse is submitted.

2. 结婚协议没有其他约定的，公证员向未亡配偶出具财产权利证书，证明在世配偶有权取得夫妻共同财产时，申请人应当提交申请人与立遗嘱人的婚姻关系相关证明文件和确认财产属于死去的配偶或为死去的配偶所有的证明文件。

Chapter 11. Imposing of prohibitions on alienation of real estate

第十一章　强制施行不动产转让的禁令

Article 77. Imposing of prohibitions on alienation of real estate

Imposing of prohibition of alienation of real estate is performed on basis and according to the procedure, established by the legislation of the Republic of Tajikistan.

第七十七条　强制施行不动产转让的禁令

依照塔吉克斯坦共和国法律规定的程序并以此为基础强制施行不动产转让的禁令。

Article 78. Removal of prohibitions

After receipt of the notice of physical persons and legal entities on repayment of the loan or data on termination of the contract on pledge, also data on termination of the contract on the perpetual maintenance with dependence the notary public removes prohibition on alienation of real estate.

第七十八条　解除禁令

在收到自然人和法人偿还贷款的通知或者终止抵押合同的资料以及终止永久性维护合同的资料之后，公证员可以解除转让不动产的禁令。

Chapter 12. Witnessing of fidelity of copies of documents and statements from them, authenticity of the signature and fidelity of the translation

第十二章　鉴定文件及其声明的副本的真实性以及签字和翻译的真实性

Article 79. Witnessing of fidelity of copies of documents and statements from them

1. The notary public and authorized persons witness fidelity of copies of documents, and statements from them issued by legal entities under condition if these documents do not contradict the legislation of the Republic of Tajikistan, have legal value and witnessing of fidelity of copies and statements from them it is not forbidden by the legislation of the Republic of Tajikistan. Witnessing of fidelity of passport copies, the military ID, official ID, or other document confirming membership in public organization and political party is forbidden.

2. The notary public does not witness fidelity of copies of documents and statements from them having erasures, corrections, or the additions, the crossed-out words and other not stipulated corrections, documents which text

第七十九条　鉴定文件及其声明的副本的真实性

1. 公证员和被授权人有权鉴定文件副本的真实性和法人在不违反塔吉克斯坦共和国法律的条件下发布的具有法律意义的声明原本和副本的真实性。公证员不得鉴定护照的副本、军人的身份证、官员的身份证或其他确认公共组织和政党成员资格的文件的真实性。

2. 公证员不能鉴定有删改的文件、有划线词和其他没有按规定更改的文件、文本无法阅读的文件、有其他损坏的文件以及用铅笔书写并且没有按规定更正的文件的真实性。

cannot be read, in connection with damage having other, not stipulated corrections also of the documents completed with pencil.

3. The notary public witnesses fidelity of copies of the documents constituted in foreign languages only in case of representation of their notarially certified translation.

4. Fidelity of copies of the document submitted by person is witnessed if authenticity of the signature of person in it it is certified in notarial procedure.

5. Fidelity of statements from documents makes sure only if the document from which the statement is taken is related to several single questions which are not connected among themselves, except as specified, when the legislation of the Republic of Tajikistan does not provide other. The statement shall contain the complete text of part of the document of rather certain question.

Article 80. Witnessing of fidelity of the copy from the copy of the document

Fidelity of the copy made of the copy of the document can be certified by the notary public under condition if fidelity of the copy is certified in notarial procedure or the copy of the document is issued by the legal entity from whom the authentic document proceeds. In this case the copy of the document shall be made on the official form of this legal entity, is under seal and to have mark that the authentic document is stored in documents of clerical work of the legal entity. Also it shall be certified by the sign and seal of the head of the legal entity.

Article 81. Witnessing of authenticity of the signature

1. The notary public witnesses authenticity of the signature on the document which contents do not contradict the legislation of the Republic of Tajikistan and does not represent contents of the transaction.

2. On the transaction only authenticity of the signature of person made instead of other person who cannot sign with own hand owing to physical defects, disease, illiteracy or for other reasons is witnessed.

3. The notary public witnessing authenticity of the signature does not certify authenticity of the facts stated in the document, and only confirms that the signature is made the corresponding face.

Article 82. Witnessing of fidelity of the translation from one language on another

1. The notary public witnesses fidelity of the trans-

3. 公证员只能通过已经公证的翻译文本鉴定外文文件的真实性。

4. 文件副本的签名经鉴定具有真实性，该文件副本具有真实性。

5. 塔吉克斯坦共和国法律没有其他规定的，只要该文件的声明与几个彼此间没有联系的单独问题有关，则可以鉴定为真实。该声明应当附上文件中的某些问题的部分全文。

第八十条　见证文件副本的复印件的真实性

如果副本的真实性经公证程序证明或者该文件的副本是由法人经官方的文件程序发布的，那么公证员可以证明文件的副本的复印件的真实性。在此种情况下，文件的副本应当由法人通过官方的形式制作，加盖印章并且拥有法人文书工作中存放文件的官方标志且需要经由法人的领导签字盖章证明。

第八十一条　鉴定签名的真实性

1. 公证员鉴定文件签名的真实性时，文件内容不得违反塔吉克斯坦共和国法律，也不涉及具体交易。

2. 在交易中，只有当签字人由于身体缺陷、疾病、文盲或其他原因无法亲手签字的，可以鉴定代签的真实性。

3. 公证员只公证签名的真实性，不证明文件中阐述事实的真实性，且只确认签名的表面真实性。

第八十二条　鉴定从一种语言翻译到另一种语言的真实性

1. 由了解相应语言的公证员鉴定从一种语言翻译

lation of the document from one language on another if knows the corresponding language.

2. If the notary public does not know the corresponding language, the translation of the document can be made by the translator whose authenticity of the signature is witnessed by the notary public.

至另一种语言的文件的真实性。

2. 如果公证员不了解相应的语言，那么该文件可以由翻译人员翻译，且由公证员鉴定签字的真实性。

Article 83. Issue of duplicates of notarially certified documents

1. In case of loss or spoil (impossibility of reading and another) notarially certified documents which one copy is stored in offices of notary public or in archives of offices of notary public their duplicates are issued on demand (statement) of physical person or legal entity or their legal representatives. The main notary public or his deputy, the senior notaries public in offices of notary public where one notary public works, the notary public, and in archive of office of notary public the senior notary public - the registrar.

2. The duplicate of powers of attorney is not issued.

3. The duplicate of wills is issued to the heirs specified in the will and to the testamentary executor after the death of the testator in case of presentation of the certificate on his death.

第八十三条　出具已公证的文件副本

1. 如果已公证的文件丢失或损毁（不可能再使用及类似后果），首要公证机构公证员或其助理、高级公证员以及公证机构档案馆的登记员按自然人、法人或者他们的法定代理（表）人的要求出具存放在公证机构或公证机构档案馆的副本的复印件。

2. 禁止出具授权委托书的复印件。

3. 立遗嘱人死亡后，公证员应当将遗嘱副本发给继承人和遗嘱执行人，以证明遗嘱人死亡的事实。

Chapter 13. Providing proofs

Article 84. Providing proofs

1. At the request of interested persons the notary public provides the proofs necessary in - case of initiation of proceedings in judicial or other authorities if reasons to believe are had that production of evidence in consequence will become impossible or difficult.

2. The notary public does not provide the proof when they at the time of the address of interested persons are under consideration of court, bodies of pretrial investigation and inquiry.

Article 85. Actions for providing proofs

1. For the purpose of providing proofs, the notary public in necessary cases interviews witnesses, performs survey of written and physical evidences, appoints the corresponding examination.

2. In case of accomplishment of actions for providing proofs, the notary public is guided by regulations of the procedural legislation of the Republic of Tajikistan.

3. The notary public informs on time and the place of providing proofs other party and interested persons, how-

第十三章　提供证据

第八十四条　提供证据

1. 如果有理由相信利害关系人不可能或难以提供证据，经利害关系人请求，公证员应当在司法部门或其他当局提起诉讼时提供必要的证据。

2. 在法院调查阶段和审判前侦查阶段调查利害关系人的信息时，公证员不提供证据。

第八十五条　提供证据

1. 为了提供证据，公证员在必要的情况下应当会见询问目击证人、调查书证和物证，并指定相应的审查。

2. 公证员应当依照塔吉克斯坦共和国的法律规定和程序规定提供证据。

3. 公证员应当通知其他当事人和利害关系人提供证据的时间和地点，但他们的缺席不会妨碍提供证据。

ever their absence is not obstacle for making of actions for providing proofs.

4. Providing proofs without notice of one of the parties and interested persons is performed only in immediate cases or if it is impossible to determine persons who will participate in this or that case subsequently.

4. 仅在紧急情况或无法确定随后参与案件的人员的情况下，公证员提供证据时可以不通知当事人和利害关系人。

Chapter 14. Certificate of the facts, transfer of the statement of physical persons and legal entities to other physical persons and legal entities

第十四章 事实公证、向其他自然人和法人转达自然人和法人的陈述

Article 86. The certificate of the fact of finding of person in live

1. The notary public certifies the fact of finding of person in live.

2. The certificate of the fact of stay in live the minor is made at the request of his legal representative (parents, adoptive parents, the guardian or the custodian), also organizations and other organizations in which care there is minor.

3. In case of the certificate of this fact the notary public grants to interested persons certificates.

第八十六条 公证某人存活的事实

1. 公证员可以公证某人存活的事实。

2. 只有经未成年人的法定代理人（父母、养父母、监护人或抚养人）和其他照顾未成年人的组织的申请，公证员方可公证未成年人存活的事实。

3. 在事实得到证明后，公证员应当向利害关系人出具公证书。

Article 87. The certificate of the fact of finding of person in certain place

1. The notary public at the request of person certifies the fact of stay it in certain place.

2. The certificate of the fact of stay in certain place of the minor is made at the request of his parents or persons replacing them, the guardian or the custodian, also organizations and other organizations in which care there is minor.

3. In case of the certificate of this fact the notary public grants to interested persons certificates.

第八十七条 公证在某地发现某人的事实

1. 公证员在当事人的申请下，公证其在某处停留的事实。

2. 只有经未成年人的法定代理人（父母、养父母、监护人或抚养人）和其他照顾未成年人的组织的申请，公证员方可公证未成年人在某处停留的事实。

3. 在事实得到证明后，公证员应当向利害关系人出具公证书。

Article 88. The certificate of identity of person with person represented on picture

1. The notary public certifies identity of person with person represented on picture and for confirmation of this fact grants to interested persons certificates.

2. The certificate of the fact of identity of the minor with person represented on picture is made at the request of his parents or persons replacing them, the guardian or the custodian, also organizations and other organizations in which care there is minor.

第八十八条 为图片上的人的身份进行公证

1. 公证员公证图片上人的身份，在确认事实后向利害关系人出具公证书。

2. 只有经图片上的未成年人的法定代理人（父母、养父母、监护人或抚养人）和其他照顾未成年人的组织的申请，公证员方可公证此未成年人的身份。。

Article 89. Certificates of time of presentation of the document

The notary public certifies time of presentation of

第八十九条 公证文件提交的时间

公证员公证文件提交的时间时，应当在文件首页

the document to it. About it entry in the document with indication of surname, name, middle name of person who showed the document is made.

指导文件制作者签署姓、名和中间名。

Article 90. Transfer of the statement of physical persons and legal entities to other physical persons and legal entities

1. The notary public transfers the statement of physical persons and legal entities to other physical persons and legal entities. The statement is transferred personally on receipt or sent by mail with the return notification.

2. The expenses connected with transfer of the statement pay physical persons or legal entities at the request of which this notarial action is made.

3. The certificate on transfer of the statement by the notary public is granted only at the request of the physical persons or legal entities which addressed for making of notarial action.

第九十条　将自然人和法人的声明转达给其他自然人和法人

1. 公证员向其他自然人和法人转达自然人和法人的声明时，应当在收到申请后亲自转达或通过发送带有回复通知的邮件转达。

2. 转达声明产生的费用由申请人支付。

3. 申请人申请的，公证员方可向其出具转达声明公证书。

Chapter 15. Acceptance in the deposit of sums of money and (or) securities

第十五章　接受资金和（或）有价证券的提存

Article 91. Acceptance in the deposit of sums of money and (or) securities

1. The notary public in the cases provided by the civil legislation of the Republic of Tajikistan accepts from the debtor in the deposit of office of notary public sums of money and (or) securities for transfer to their creditor.

2. About receipt of sums of money and (or) securities, the notary public informs the creditor and according to its requirement issues it this sum of money and (or) securities.

3. Acceptance in the deposit of sums of money and (or) securities is made by the notary public of office of notary public in the place of obligation fulfillment and (or) the place of opening of inheritance.

第九十一条　接受资金和（或）有价证券的提存

1. 在塔吉克斯坦共和国民法案件中，公证员有权接收债务人在公证机构提存资金和（或）有价证券以转移给债权人。

2. 接收资金和（或）有价证券后，公证员应当通知债权人并按债权人的要求给付资金和（或）有价证券。

3. 公证员应当在公证员履行义务的公证机构或者公开遗产所在地的公证机构接受提存资金和（或）有价证券。

Article 92. Return of sum of money and (or) securities

Return of sum of money and (or) securities to person who introduced them in the deposit is allowed only from the written consent to that of person (creditor) for benefit of which the sum of money and (or) securities or on court resolution were granted.

第九十二条　退还资金和（或）有价证券

只有经过债权人的书面同意，或者法院判决书的准许，公证员方可将资金和（或）有价证券退还给提存人。

Chapter 16. Making of executive texts

第十六章　执行文本的制作

Article 93. Making of executive texts

1. The notary public for collection of sum of money

第九十三条　执行文本的制作

1. 公证员依照确定债务的执行文本中规定的义务

and (or) reclamation from the debtor of property according to indisputable obligations makes executive texts on the documents establishing debt.

2. The list of documents according to which debt collection is made in indisputable procedure based on executive texts is established by the Government of the Republic of Tajikistan.

Article 94. Conditions of making of executive text

1. The executive text is made if:

- the submitted documents confirm indisputability of debt or other responsibility of the debtor to the creditor;

- from the date of emergence of right of action did not pass three years.

2. If for the requirement according to which the executive text is made the legislation of the Republic of Tajikistan establishes other term of limitation period, the executive text is made within it, term.

Article 95. Content of executive text

The executive text shall bear:

- surname, name and middle name of the notary public making executive text;

- surname, name, middle name and the creditor's address (for physical person);

- full name, the address and the settlement account of the creditor (for the legal entity):

- surname, name, middle name and the debtor's address (for physical person);

- full name, the address and the settlement account of the debtor (for the legal entity);

- specifying of term for which collection is made;

- designation of the amounts which are subject to collection or the objects which are subject to reclamation including penalty fee, percent from profit if those are due;

- designation of the amount of the state tax paid by the creditor, or which is subject to collection from the debtor;

- date (day, month, year) of making of executive text;

- number at which the executive text is registered in the register;

- the sign and seal of the notary public who made executive text.

Article 96. Procedure for collection on executive text

Collection on executive text is made according to the procedure, established by the Law of the Republic of

收集资金和（或者）收回债务人的财产。

2. 债务收集的文件清单是在以塔吉克斯坦共和国政府制定的执行文本为基础且通过无可争辩的程序制作的。

第九十四条　制作执行文本的条件

1. 公证员可以在下列情况下制作执行文本：

提交的文件中确认了无可争辩的债务或者债务人对债权人的其他责任；

自执行权利产生之日起三年内。

2. 依照执行文本的制作要求，如果塔吉克斯坦共和国法律规定了其他时效期限，那么执行文本应当在该期限内制作。

第九十五条　执行文本的内容

执行文本应当具有以下内容：

制作执行文本的公证员的姓、名和中间名；

债权人是自然人的，应当列明债权人的姓、名和中间名及地址；

债权人是法人的，应当列明债权人的全称、地址和资金账户；

债务人是自然人的，应当列明债务人的姓、名和中间名及地址；

债务人是法人的，应当列明债务人的全称、地址和资金账户；

指定收取的款项；

指定需要收取的款项或需要收回的物品，包括罚款，若到期，则收取利润的百分比；

指定债权人支付或者从债务人处收取的税额；

制作执行文本的日期（年、月、日）；

执行文本在登记册中登记的编号；

制作执行文本的公证员的签名和盖章。

第九十六条　执行文本的收取程序

执行文本的收取依照塔吉克斯坦共和国法律关于"强制执行程序"规定的程序进行。

Tajikistan "About enforcement proceeding".

Article 97. Term of presentation of executive text

1. The executive text can be shown by the claimant to forced execution within three years from the date of its making if the legislation of the Republic of Tajikistan does not provide other term.

2. Recovery of the passed term is made for presentation of executive text according to the procedure, established by the legislation of the Republic of Tajikistan.

第九十七条　执行文本提交的期限

1. 如果塔吉克斯坦共和国法律没有其他条款的规定，那么申请人可以在执行文本作出之日起三年内申请强制执行。

2. 依照塔吉克斯坦共和国法律规定的程序，可以通过恢复已过期限的方式来提交执行文本。

Chapter 17. Making of other notarial actions

第十七章　作出其他公证行为

Article 98. Statement for the ship's protest

1. For the purpose of providing the proof for protection of the rights and legitimate interests of the shipowner, the notary public adopts the written application of the ship master about the incident taking place during swimming or parking of the vessel which can be the presentation basis to the shipowner of property requirements.

2. The application for the ship's protest shall be submitted in the port of the Republic of Tajikistan to office of notary public or consular establishments within 36 hours. If the application cannot be submitted at the scheduled time, the reasons are specified in the statement for the ship's protest.

3. In confirmation of the circumstances stated in the application for the ship's protest, the logbook shall be shown to the notary public during the specified term on review and the statement certified by the captain from the logbook is provided.

第九十八条　海事声明报告

1. 为了保护船东的合法利益，公证员可以采纳船长对于船舶航行或停泊时发生的事件的书面申请作为提交船东的财产要求的基础。

2. 船长海事声明报告的申请书当在 36 小时内提交给塔吉克斯坦共和国港口所在地的公证机构或领事机构。如果该申请书不能在规定的时间内提交，应当在海事声明报告中详细说明原因。

3. 为了确认海事声明中阐述的情况，申请人应当在规定的期限内向公证员提交航海日志以供检查，并且提供船长在航海日志中核实的声明。

Article 99. Creation of the act of the ship's protest

The notary public based on the statement of the ship master, data of the logbook, and also poll of the captain and whenever possible at least two witnesses from among faces of command structure of the vessel and two witnesses from structure of crew draws up the statement of the ship's protest. The copy of the act is issued to the captain or the authorized person.

第九十九条　制作海事声明报告

公证员依照船长的陈述、航海日志的数据，以及船长的民意调查起草海事声明报告，并且在有可能的情况下，至少有两名管理层的见证人和两名全体船员的代表参与起草。海事声明报告的副本应当发给船长或被授权人。

Article 100. Protest of bills of exchange

The notary public makes protest of bills of exchange in non-payment, the non-acceptance and not dating of the acceptance according to the legislation of the Republic of Tajikistan on the translated and promissory note.

第一百条　汇票的拒付证明

公证员依照塔吉克斯坦共和国关于承兑和汇票的法律规定，对不支付、不承兑以及不在承兑日期内的汇票作出拒付证明。

Article 101. Presentation of the check to payment and the certificate of non-payment of the check

1. The notary public accepts the checks shown for payment provided by the payee because of the expiration established by the legislation of the Republic of Tajikistan.

2. The check for payment is shown in bank in the location of the payer.

3. In case of check non-payment, the notary public certifies this proof by making of the corresponding certifying text on the check.

4. At the request of the payee the notary public, in case of check non-payment, makes executive text.

第一百零一条 提供支票支付和未付款支票的证明

1. 在塔吉克斯坦共和国法律规定的期限届满时，公证员可以接受收款人提供的需被承兑的支票。

2. 支票由付款人所在地的银行支付。

3. 公证员通过在支票上制作相应的证明文本证明支票未付款。

4. 公证员依照收款人的要求，对未支付的支票制作执行文本。

Article 102. Acceptance on document storage and their return

1. The notary public accepts from physical persons and legal entities on storage documents according to the inventory about what to person who checked them the certificate and copy of the inventory is granted.

2. The documents accepted on storage return to the physical legal entities or the authorized person who checked them on presentation of the certificate and copy of the inventory, or on court resolution.

第一百零二条 保管和归还文件

1. 公证员依照自然人和法人提供的文件的详细清单保管文件，并授予核对该文件的人员公证书和详细清单的副本。

2. 接受存放的文件应当归还给自然人和法人，或对所出示的证书和详细清单副本进行核对的人，以及在法院判决后的被授权人。

Section III. Application of precepts of law of other states and international legal acts

第三节 其他国家法律法规和国际法律文件的适用

Chapter 18. Procedure for application of precepts of law of other states and international legal acts

第十八章 其他国家法律法规和国际法律文件的适用程序

Article 103. Notarial actions for foreign citizens and stateless persons, foreign legal entities

Foreign citizens, stateless persons and foreign legal entities have the right on an equal basis with citizens and legal entities of the Republic of Tajikistan to address to offices of notary public of the Republic of Tajikistan, and also to other bodies making notarial actions according to the procedure, established by the legislation of the Republic of Tajikistan.

第一百零三条 为外国公民和无国籍人、外国法人办理公证事项

外国公民、无国籍人和外国法人和塔吉克斯坦共和国的公民和法人享有平等的权利，可以依照塔吉克斯坦共和国法律规定的程序向塔吉克斯坦共和国的公证机构或其他机构提出公证申请。

Article 104. Application of regulations of foreign law

1. The notary public according to the legislation of the Republic of Tajikistan and the international legal acts recognized by Tajikistan applies regulations of foreign law.

2. The notary public accepts the documents constituted according to the international legal acts and also makes certifying texts in shape, stipulated by the legislation other

第一百零四条 外国法律法规的适用

1. 公证员依照塔吉克斯坦共和国法律和塔吉克斯坦共和国承认的国际法律文件适用国外法律法规。

2. 公证员接受不违反塔吉克斯坦共和国承认的国际法律文件，依照国际法律文件和类似的公证文本、其他国家法律的规定制定的文件。

states if it does not contradict the international legal acts recognized by Tajikistan.

Article 105. Protection of heritable property and issue of the certificate on the right to inheritance

The actions connected with protection of the property which is in the territory of the Republic of Tajikistan which remained after the death of the foreign citizen or protection of property to which the citizen after the death of the citizen of the Republic of Tajikistan has the right foreign. And also the actions connected with issue of the certificate on the right to inheritance concerning such property are performed according to the legislation of the Republic of Tajikistan and the international legal acts recognized by Tajikistan.

Article 106. Acceptance by the notary public of the documents processed in foreign state

1. The documents processed in foreign state with participation of foreign officials, competent authorities of other states or proceeding from them are accepted by the notary public according to regulations of the international legal acts.

2. Documents are accepted by the notary public when the procedure for their acceptance is stipulated by the legislation the Republic of Tajikistan and the international legal acts recognized by Tajikistan.

Article 107. The notary public relations with judicial authorities of other states

1. Orders of judicial authorities of other states about rendering legal assistance it is performed according to the legislation of the Republic of Tajikistan and the international legal acts recognized by Tajikistan.

2. The notary public performs the messages of judicial authorities of other states delivered to him in accordance with the established procedure about rendering legal assistance, except as specified, if execution of the order:

- execution of the order contradicts sovereignty of the Republic of Tajikistan or threatens its safety;

- execution of the order is not referred to competence of the notary public;

- execution of the order contradicts the legislation of the Republic of Tajikistan.

3. The notary public according to the procedure, the established legislation of the Republic of Tajikistan and the international legal acts recognized by Tajikistan having the right to address judicial authorities of other states with

第一百零五条　遗产的保护和遗产权利证书的出具

公证员应当保护外国公民死亡后位于塔吉克斯坦共和国领土内的财产以及塔吉克斯坦共和国公民去世后有权享有的外国财产，依照塔吉克斯坦共和国的法律和塔吉克斯坦共和国承认的国际法律文件，出具和此类财产有关的遗产权利证书。

第一百零六条　公证员接受在外国制作的文件

1. 公证员应当依照国际法律文件的规定接受外国官员或主管机关参与制作的文件。

2. 如果塔吉克斯坦共和国的法律和塔吉克斯坦共和国承认的国际法律文件规定了接受相应文件的程序，公证员应当接受这些文件。

第一百零七条　与其他国家司法机关的关系

1. 其他国家的司法机关可以依照塔吉克斯坦共和国的法律和塔吉克斯坦承认的国际法律文件的规定提供法律援助。

2. 除非有下列情形，公证员按照法定程序向当事人传达其他国家司法机关提供法律援助的信息：

接受法律援助将损害塔吉克斯坦共和国的主权或威胁塔吉克斯坦共和国的安全；

公证员无权接受法律援助；

接受法律援助与塔吉克斯坦共和国的法律相抵触。

3. 依照塔吉克斯坦共和国法律规定的程序和塔吉克斯坦共和国承认的国际法律文件，公证员有权向其他国家的司法机关申请法律援助。

orders about rendering legal assistance.

Article 108. Providing the proofs necessary for business management in relevant organs of other states

1. Notaries public provide the proofs necessary for business management in relevant organs of other states.

2. Actions for providing proofs are performed according to the procedure, established by the legislation of the Republic of Tajikistan.

Article 109. Application of the international legal acts

1. When making notarial actions, notaries public apply regulations of the legislation of the Republic of Tajikistan and the international legal acts recognized by Tajikistan.

2. If the international legal acts recognized by Tajikistan about notarial activities provide other procedure unlike the procedure established by legal acts of the Republic of Tajikistan regulations of the international legal acts recognized by Tajikistan are applied.

Chapter 19. Final provisions

Article 110. Responsibility for violation of requirements of this Law

Physical persons and legal entities are made for violation of requirements of this Law responsible according to the legislation of the Republic of Tajikistan.

Article 111. About recognition voided the Law of the Republic

Tajikistan "About the state notariate"

Article 112. Procedure for enforcement of this Law

Enact this Law after its official publication.

President of the Republic of Tajikistan

EmomaliiRahmon

RESOLUTION OF MAJLISI NAMOYANDAGON OF MAJLISI OLI OF THE REPUBLIC OF TAJIKISTAN

of February 29, 2012 No. 702

About adoption of law of the Republic of Tajikistan

第一百零八条　为其他国家有关机构的交易管理提供必要的证据

1. 公证员可以为其他国家有关机构的交易管理提供必要的证据。

2. 公证员应当依照塔吉克斯坦共和国法律规定的程序提供证据。

第一百零九条　国际法律文件的适用

1. 公证员在进行公证活动时，适用塔吉克斯坦共和国法律规定和塔吉克斯坦共和国承认的国际法律文件。

2. 若塔吉克斯坦共和国承认的关于公证活动的国际法律文件与塔吉克斯坦共和国法律相冲突，应当适用塔吉克斯坦共和国承认的国际法律文件。

第十九章　最后条款

第一百一十条　违反本法规定的责任

依照塔吉克斯坦共和国的法律，自然人和法人违反本法规定的，应当承担法律责任。

第一百一十一条　关于承认无效的共和国法

塔吉克斯坦"关于国家公证"的法律。

第一百一十二条　本法的执行程序

本法在正式公布后开始实行。

塔吉克斯坦共和国总统

埃莫马利·拉赫蒙

塔吉克斯坦共和国马吉里西·纳莫扬达贡的决议

2012 年 2 月 29 日第 702 号

关于通过塔吉克斯坦共和国"关于国家公证"的

"About the state notariate"

The Majlisi namoyandagon of MadzhlispOlya of the Republic of Tajikistan decides:

1. Adopt the Law of the Republic of Tajikistan "About the state notariate".

Chairman of Majlisi namoyandagon of Majlisi Oli of the Republic of Tajikistan

Sh. Zukhurov

法律

塔吉克斯坦共和国马日利普 · 奥利亚议会决定：

1. 通过塔吉克斯坦共和国"关于国家公证"的法律。

塔吉克斯坦共和国 Majlisi namoyandagon of Majlisi Oli 主席

Sh. Zukhurov

RESOLUTION OF MAJLISI MILLI OF MAJLISI OLI OF THE REPUBLIC OF TAJIKISTAN of March 29, 2012 No. 283

About the Law of the Republic of Tajikistan "About the state notariate"

Having considered the Law of the Republic of Tajikistan "About the state notariate", the Majlisi milli of Majlisi Oli of the Republic of Tajikistan decides:

Approve the Law of the Republic of Tajikistan "About the state notariate".

Chairman of Majlisi milli of Majlisi Oli of the Republic of Tajikistan

M. Ubaydulloyev

塔吉克斯坦共和国马吉里西 · 米利的决议

2012 年 3 月 29 日第 283 号

关于塔吉克斯坦共和国"关于国家公证"的法律

塔吉克斯坦共和国 Majlisi Milli of Majlisi Oli 审议了"关于国家公证"的塔吉克斯坦共和国法律后，决定：

批准塔吉克斯坦共和国"关于国家公证"的法律。

塔吉克斯坦共和国 Majlisi milli of Majlisi Oli 主席

M. Ubaydulloyev

土耳其

公证法

PART ONE
General Clauses

Notary profession

Article 1 – Notary Public is a public service. Notary Publics document operations for assuring security and preventing disagreements and execute other duties given by laws.

Foundation process of notary public's offices and their competences

Article 2 – In every place where a court of first instance or an individual civil court of peace has been established, a notary public's office is founded to be authorized to execute the notary public operations of this court according to its field of jurisdiction.

(Additional second clause: 2/3/2005-5309/art. 1)

However if the field of jurisdiction of the court of first instance covers more than one district, then notary public's offices can be established in other districts.

In so far, if there is more than one notary public office in municipality borders of one county, every notary public's office is authorized to execute all notary public operations in the municipality borders of the county and this without being restricted by the field of jurisdiction of the court of first instance.

(Additional fourth clause: 14/7/2004-5219/art. 8)

The operations of the first, second and third class notary public's offices situated in a district where the court of first instance has been erected continue. In these places, we can also establish more than one notary public's office. The notary public's offices whose operations continue in a district without a court of first instance or which is under

第一部分
通则

公证职业

第一条 公证是一项公共服务。公证员通过办理公证事务确保安全、避免分歧，并履行法律规定的其他义务。

公证机构的设立过程及其权限

第二条 在设立初审法院或者个人民事法院的地区设立公证机构，该公证机构有权在法院的管辖范围内进行公证活动。

（补充第 2 款：2005 年 3 月 2 日 -5309/ 第 1 条）

但若初审法院的管辖范围超过一个地区，则可以在初审法院管辖范围内的其他地区设立公证机构。

到目前为止，若在一个州的市边界内有一个以上的公证机构，则每个公证机构都有权在该市的边界内进行所有的公证业务且不受管辖范围的限制。

（补充第 4 款：2004 年 7 月 14 日 -5219/ 第 8 条）

在已设立初审法院的地区，一级、二级、三级公证机构继续运作，并且可以设立若干个公证机构。在没有设立初审法院的地区继续运作的公证机构和在初审法院统一管辖范围内重新设立的不在同一市边界内的公证机构，不受本法第一百零九条规定的约束。

the same field of jurisdiction recently reestablished but is not situated in the same municipality borders are not subject to the provisions of article 109.[1]

Foundation process of more than one notary public's office and closure of the notary public's office

Article 3 – The Ministry of Justice can establish more than one notary public's office in the places where arising business overload exists.

The Ministry of Justice uses its authority written here in above by taking into account in one hand the total of the gross income of the notary public's offices situated in one place and in the other hand the evolutions and developments in the business life.

Upon condition that they are dismantled, it can close more than one of the actual notary public's offices.

The Ministry of Justice takes the opinion of the Notaries Union of Turkey before it uses its authority about establishing or closing more than one notary public's office.

(Last additional clause: 14/7/2004-5219/art. 8).

If the first, second and third class notary public's offices situated in the district in which the court of first instance had been erected is dismantled, it can be closed by the Ministry of Justice upon the proposition of the Notaries Union of Turkey.

Classification of notary public's offices

Article 4 – The notary public's offices are divided into four classes.

The first, second and third class notary public's offices are classified by the Ministry of Justice who takes the opinion of the Notaries Union of Turkey.

This classification is based upon the population of the field of jurisdiction, the business overload and the notary public's income. Generally, the notary public's offices related to the same court are considered in the same class.

In every four year, the Ministry of Justice examines the notary public's offices' situation and announces its reclassification in the Official Journal.

The new notaries established during the four year mentioned in the above clause are classified without delay in accordance with the second clause and their estimated gross incomes and are announced in the Official Journal.

The provision of the article 31 concerning the right to relegation to the fourth class notary is reserved. In so

多个公证机构的设立过程和公证机构的撤销

第三条 司法部可以在业务负担过重的地区设立多个公证机构。

司法部利用本法规定的权力设立公证机构时，应当考虑设在同一地区内公证机构的收入总额和商业活动的演变和发展。

在需要撤销公证机构的情况下，司法部有权撤销一个以上现存的公证机构。

司法部在行使设立或撤销一个以上公证机构的权力之前，应当先听取土耳其公证员联合会的意见。

（最后一项补充条款：2004 年 7 月 14 日 -5219/ 第 8 条）

若设在初审法院所在地区的一级、二级和三级公证机构失去作用，司法部可以依照土耳其公证员联合会的提议撤销该公证机构。

公证机构的分级

第四条 公证机构分为四级。

司法部在听取土耳其公证员联合会的意见下将公证机构分为一级、二级、三级。

依照管辖区域的人口数量、业务负担和公证员的收入分级。一般认为，由同一法院管辖的公证机构属于同一级。

司法部每四年对公证机构的情况进行审查，并在《公报》中宣布公证机构的重新分级情况。

上述条款所述四年期间设立的新公证机构，司法部应当按照第二条及评估的总收入尽快予以分级，并在《公报》上公布。

保留第三十一条关于降级到四级公证机构的权利的规定。并在每年四月初确定并公布将会被提升到三

far, those who will be promoted to the third class notary public's offices are determined and announced at the beginning of April of each year.

Until the new classification is announced, the practice is done according to the old classification.

Notary public's office's class and the minimum service time

Article 4/a – (Added with article 1 of the Law 3588 dated 16/1/1989.)

The notary publics are divided into three classes. The service of third class of those who's gone into notary public by being appointed for the very first time as a third class notary public begin at its business start date.

The minimum service time of the first and/or third class notary public is four years. In the end of this time, the promotion of notary public's class depend upon the presence of positive convictions in the last good character document composed by the Justice inspector.

The promotion of notary public's class does not affect notary's class.

The notary who gives services in a notary public's office whose class has been promoted starts to execute the upper-class services in the same notary public's office beginning from the expiration of his service time if the notary public has not completed his service time related to his previous class and from the composition of the next positive character document if the latest character document formerly composed by Justice inspector indicates that the concerned does not possess the competences necessary to promote to the upper class.

PART TWO
Conditions of acceptance to the notary public

Article 5 – To be a notary public, it is imperative to complete the notary public internship in accordance with the provisions of this chapter and to receive the notary public certificate.

Exceptional cases

Article 6 – (Changed first clause: 14/04/2004 – 5134/art. 1)

Those who are appointed to the juridical or military magistrature or those who having been graduated from the law school are appointed to the administrative magistrature

级公证机构的名单。

在公布新的分级之前，公证机构依照旧的分级完成工作。

公证机构的等级和最低服务时间

第四 /a 条 （加入 1989 年 1 月 16 日第 3588 号法令第 1 条）

公证员分为三级。初次进入公证员行业的被任命为三级公证员，并从其执业之日起履行三级公证员的职责。

一级和（或）三级公证员的最低服务时间为四年。在这段期间结束时，公证员等级的提升取决于司法监察员作出的良好品格评定文件中是否存在正面评判。

公证员等级提升不影响公证机构的等级。

在被提升级别的公证机构服务的公证员，则开始执行其上一层级的服务。若该公证员之前等级相关的服务期限未届满，则从该公证员的服务期限届满之日起开始执行上一层级的服务；若最新的品格评定文件是正面的评判，则无论该公证员原等级的服务期限是否届满，都开始执行上一层级的服务。此外，由司法监察员评定相关人员不具备晋升到上一层级的资格。

第二部分
成为公证员的条件

第五条 成为公证员，必须按照本章的规定完成公证实习并取得公证员职业资格证书。

例外情况

第六条（修改后的第 1 款：2004 年 4 月 14 日 - 5134/第 1 条）

军事法官、从法学院毕业的法官或依照《律师法》取得律师资格的律师不受公证员必要实习和考试的限制。

or have been qualified as lawyer and those in accordance with the Advocacy Code have been accepted to the advocacy by being exempted from the imperative of internship and advocacy examinations are not subject to the notary public internship.

If those people, having enclosed the documents exposed at the paragraphs (a), (b) and (c) of the article 9, submit a petition to the Ministry of Justice, and if the examination process done with the additional documents that Ministry considers necessary reveals that there is no obstacle for them to became notary public, then the concerned is given the certificate indicated at the clause 3 of the article 17 and is registered to the notary public's office record indicated at the article 18.

若申请人向司法部提交的申请书附上第九条（a）款、（b）款和（c）款所披露的文件，司法部审查该申请书及文件后认为申请人不存在成为公证员的障碍因素，则向相关人员提供第十七条第三款所示的公证书，并且登记在第十八条所示的公证记录上。

Conditions of internship

Article 7 – For being accepted to the notary public internship, one must:

1.Be citizen of Turkish Republic,

2. (Changed with 13/6/2000-4579/art. 1)

Be over 21, but less than 40,

3. Be graduated from one of the Turkish law schools or, having been graduated from a foreign law school, pass successful examinations in lessons considered shortcoming by the Turkish law schools programs,

4. (Repealed. 13/6/2000 – 4579/art. 1)

5. Not have been condemned for a crime involving moral turpitude or a guilt that requires solitary confinement or not have been received one or more years in jail for intent crime,

6.Not have been lost the quality to become a judge, prosecutor, officer or lawyer in consequence of a verdict or a discipline decision,

7.Not have been known by its environment for his attitudes and behaviors incompatibles with notary public profession,

8.Not have been associated with a business incompatible with notary public and notary public internship,

9. Not have been limited by a court verdict,

10.Have retaken his/her rights after bankruptcy, (fraudulent or blamable insolvents are not accepted even if their rights are returned.)

11.Remove the debtor warrant, if decided,

12. Not be physically or mentally disable so that he could make his notary public duties as required and consistently,

实习条件

第七条 要获得公证员实习资格，必须符合以下条件：

1. 土耳其共和国公民；

2.（更改为 2000 年 6 月 13 日 -4579/ 第 1 条）

年龄为二十一周岁以上四十周岁以下，

3. 毕业于土耳其任何一所法学院或外国法学院，或成功通过土耳其法学院项目中的课程考试；

4.（废除。2000 年 6 月 13 日 -4579/ 第 1 条）；

5. 未因犯有道德恶劣罪或需要单独监禁的罪行而受到刑事处罚，或未因意图犯罪而被判处一年或多年监禁；

6. 没有因判决或处分、决定丧失成为法官、检察官、政府公务员或律师的资格；

7. 未因其态度和行为与公证员职业不相容而被外界所知；

8. 未与公证员和公证员实习不相容的业务有关联；

9. 未因法院判决而被限制权利；

10. 在破产后恢复其权利（但有欺诈性质或有过失的破产者恢复权利的不予接受）；

11. 被决定取消债务人的担保；

12. 不得有身体或精神上的残疾，能够按照要求一贯地履行公证职责；

13.Have his domicile in the place of internship.

Those who have been received five years of jail or solitary confinement or those who have conclusively condemned for debit, embezzlement, bribery, corruption, thievery, cheating, forgery, breach of trust and fraudulent bankruptcy are not accepted for notary public internship, even if they are amnestied.

If the internship applicant is under prosecution for a crime requiring one of the written inflictions of the paragraph 5 of the first clause, it can be decided to hold the decision about the internship demand until the prosecution's decision. If a public trial has been opened against the applicant for a crime which could require his prohibition from the public duties, it is imperative to not implement the demand of internship and to wait the trial result.

In so far, whatever the prosecution's decision, in the cases where the internship demand must be declined, the demand is immediately decided without waiting the result.

13. 住所在实习地。

被判五年监禁或单独监禁的人，或因借款、侵占、贿赂、贪污、盗窃、欺骗、伪造、背信和欺诈破产而被定罪的人，即使获得赦免，也不得参加公证员实习。

如果实习申请人因第一款第五项所列罪行之一而受到起诉，可以在检方作出决定之前，将有关其实习的决定搁置。若对申请人的罪行进行公开审判，且可能需要禁止他担任公职，则禁止其参与实习，等待审判结果。

对于申请人的实习请求必须被拒绝的情况，无论检方作出何种决定，都应当立即作出拒绝决定，而无须等待审判结果。

Works that are incompatible with internship

与公证员实习不相容的工作

Article 8 – The provisions of the first and second clauses of the article 50 of this Law and the provision concerning the prohibition of commerce inscribed in the third clause of the same article are applied to the interns.

第八条 本法第五十条第一款和第二款的规定以及同一条第三款关于禁止从事商业活动的规定适用于实习生。

Internship application

实习申请

Article 9 – The application for internship is made via a petition submitted to the notary public chamber to which all notary public's offices in the place of internship are related. Following pieces are attached to the petition:

a)Two authenticated copies of the documents enumerated in the seventh article concerning the conditions of internship,

b)A declaration concerning the presence or absence of obstacles cited in the paragraphs 5, 8, 10 and 11 of the seventh article,

c)A presentation note that will be composed by a member of the said notary public chamber concerning the moral conditions of the applicant for internship,

d)Domicile address suitable for notification,

One copy of those pieces are certified by the president of the chamber and then sent to the Notaries Union of Turkey. Other copies or originals are kept in the file at the chamber.

If the declaration given by the applicant appears incorrect, a prosecution is opened against him/her for

第九条 实习申请应当通过向实习所在地的公证机构递交。申请书应附有下列内容：

（a）两份已公证的关于第七条所列实习条件的文件副本；

（b）关于是否存在第七条第五款、第八款、第十款和第十一款所述障碍的声明；

（c）由实习地公证机构的一名成员就实习申请人的道德情况撰写的一份陈述说明；

（d）适宜接受通知的住所地址。

其中一份申请书经办公室主任核证后送交土耳其公证员联合会。其他副本或原件保存在办公室的档案中。

若申请人有虚假申报的嫌疑，则对他 / 她向政府部门作出虚假申报的罪行提起诉讼。

committing the crime of making a false declaration to the public authorities.

Internship notice

Article 10 – In ten days following the decision of internship, the demand of application for internship is announced together with the documents indicated in the article here in above for fifteen days in a suitable place of the municipality or of the justice department building of the said place.

Under the condition of showing clear proofs and facts, all persons have the right to make objection to the chamber for not proceeding to the registration for a while.

Report

Article 11– Before the announcement of the demand, the president of the chamber employs one of the chamber's notary public's offices for investigating and doing a report on the moral conditions of the demander and the compatibility of his/her works with the notary public internship.

The decision of acceptance, of rejection or of waiting until the prosecution's decision

Article 12 – In a one-month period following the end of the objection delay, the chamber board who takes into consideration the written report mentioned in the article 11 makes a justifiable decision concerning whether the candidate is accepted or rejected to the list of interns or the prosecution's decision is waited.

In fifteen days following the notification, the members of the chamber board, the Republic prosecutor or the concerned can make an objection to the Notaries Union of Turkey against this decision.

If there is no decision within the period indicated in the first clause, then it is considered that the demand has been denied. In this case, the demander of internship can make an objection to the Notaries Union of Turkey in fifteen days following the end of the one-month period.

The decision of acceptance of the chamber board and the decision of the Board of the Notaries Union of Turkey upon the objection become absolutes after the approbation of the Ministry of Justice. The concerned or the Notaries Union of Turkey can make an objection to the Council of State against the Ministry of Justice's decision.

实习通知

第十条 准予实习的决定作出后十日内，将申请人的实习申请连同本法第十五条所列的文件，在适当地点或者申请人所在地的司法机关大楼内公布。

在有充分的证据和事实的情况下，所有人都有权提出异议，阻止实习登记事宜的推进。

报告

第十一条 在宣布之前，公证机构办公室的主任应委派该公证机构的一名公证员调查和报告申请者的道德状况，以及他/她的工作与公证员实习是否冲突。

接受、拒绝或等待检方结论的决定

第十二条 在异议延期结束后的一个月内，公证机构委员会就候选人是否被接受或拒绝列入实习生名单或等待检方结论这一问题，依照第十一条规定的书面报告，作出合理的决定。

在通知发出后十五天内，公证机构委员会成员、共和国检察官或有关人员可以向土耳其公证员联合会对这一决定提出异议。

若在第一款规定的期限内没有作出决定，则认为该项申请已被拒绝。在这种情况下，实习申请者可以在该期限结束后的十五日内向土耳其公证员联合会提出异议。

经司法部批准后，公证机构办公室委员会的决定和土耳其公证员联合会委员会的反对决定成为绝对决定。有关人员或土耳其公证员联合会可以向国务院提出对司法部决定的反对意见。

Beginning of internship

Article 13 – The notary public internship begins from the date of registration to the list.

Determination of the number of interns and of with which notary public's office the internship will be done

Article 14 – In each December, the Ministry of Justice who takes into account in the one hand the numbers of the opened or closed or to be opened or closed notary public's offices and in the other hand the opinion of the Notaries Union of Turkey determines the number of interns to accept for the next year and publishes this condition for one time until the end of year in the Official Journal or in the journals of the determined locals. Notaries Union of Turkey can make an objection to the Council of State against the Ministry of Justice's decision.

The notary public's office with which the internship will be done is indicated in the chamber board's decision taken in accordance with the article 12.

If the notary public's office is closed or the notary public quits his affairs for more than two months because of an obstacle, the chamber board decides immediately that the intern completes its internship with a different notary public. In so far, this provision is not applied to the intern having completed its sixth month.

Internship duration and intern's duties

Article 15 – The internship duration is one year.

The internship is made without interruption. The chamber board authorizes the completion of the days during which the intern is absent for justifiable reasons only if the intern makes an application within one month that follows the disappearance of the problem.

In case of justifiable reasons, the president of the chamber can give permission to the intern.

In the notary public's office, the intern is in charge of exercising the works indicated in this law and regulation.

Reports on internship

Article 16 – The notary public's office in which the intern does his/her internship composes quarterly reports that indicate the intern's moral conditions and professional qualities and addresses it to the chamber it is related.

The latest of those reports includes the conclusive judgment on the possibility of the intern to be a notary public or on the necessity to prolong the internship for six

开始实习

第十三条 公证员实习从登记至实习名单之日起开始。

实习人员的人数和实习所在公证机构的确定。

第十四条 司法部于每年十二月依据已开设或已关闭或即将开设或即将关闭的公证机构的数目和土耳其公证员联合会的意见，决定第二年接受的实习生人数，并在官方刊物上或者地方具有影响力的刊物上一次性公布吸纳实习人员的条件直至年底。土耳其公证员联合会可以向国务院提出对司法部的决定的反对意见。

公证机构办公室委员会依照本法第十二条决定实习生实习的公证机构。

若公证机构关闭，或公证员辞职两个月以上，公证机构办公室委员会则立即决定实习生跟随另一名公证员完成实习。到目前为止，这一规定不适用于已完成六个月实习任务的实习生。

实习期和实习生职责

第十五条 实习期为一年。

实习是不间断的。实习生因正当理由缺勤的，只有在请假事由消失后一个月内提出申请，并由公证机构办公室委员会授权，才能继续完成实习。

在有正当理由的情况下，公证机构办公室主任可以允许实习生请假。

在公证机构，实习生负责完成本法和条例所规定的工作。

实习报告

第十六条 实习生所在的公证机构应当编写季度报告，说明实习生的道德水平和专业素质，并向与之有关的公证机构办公室报告。

最新的报告应当包含关于实习生是否能够成为公证员或是否有必要延长实习期的结论。

months.

If the notary public's office with which the internship is made is to be changed in accordance with the latest clause of the article 14, the missing quarterly report is arrayed along the report that covers the first quarter with the new notary public. If the internship place is not changed according to the same clause of the article 14 and if the intern is appointed by proxy to a different notary public's office in pursuant of the article 33, 34 and 35 and if the internship place is changed during the last quarter of the internship, then the quarterly reports and, under the condition that notary public does not return to his/her post until the end of the internship, the final report are composed by the president of the chamber or his deputy by taking into account the oldest reports and by collecting the necessary information.

依照第十四条的最新条款变更实习生所在公证机构的，缺失的季度报告将与新公证员一起在第一季度的报告中列出。若实习地点没有依照第十四条变更，且实习生是依照第三十三条、第三十四条和第三十五条，通过委托书被指定到另一个公证机构的，或者实习地点在实习的最后一个季度发生变化，则在公证员未返回的情况下，实习生继续原职位直至实习结束，该实习生的最后报告由公证机构办公室主任或副主任依照最早的报告，并收集必要的资料后撰写。

The president of the notary public chamber addresses the intern's file in which he/she included his/her own opinion and which is accompanied with his domicile address to the Presidency of the Notaries Union of Turkey.

公证机构办公室主任对实习生的档案发表意见，并附上土耳其公证员联合会主席的致辞。

After including its own objections, if any, the Presidency of the Notaries Union of Turkey addresses the file to the Ministry of Justice.

土耳其公证员联合会主席在提出自己的反对意见（如有）后，向司法部提交该文件。

The decision of the Ministry of Justice

司法部的决定

Article 17 – In 15 days which follows the arrival of the file, the Ministry of Justice decides whether the purpose of the internship has been achieved.

第十七条 在档案到达后十五日内，由司法部决定实习目的是否已经达到。

If the purpose has not been reached, this decision can prolong the notary public internship duration for six months or can put an end to the internship.

若没有达到这一目的，可以决定将公证员的实习期延长六个月，或终止其实习。

If the purpose has been reached, the Ministry of Justice delivers a certificate of notary public to the intern. This certificate authorizes the right to be appointed to a third class notary public's office in service.

若达到这一目的，司法部将向实习生颁发公证员职业资格证书。此证书授予该实习生担任三级公证员的权利。

The concerned intern, the notary public's office in which the internship is done and the Notaries Union of Turkey can make an objection to the Council of State against the decisions of the Ministry of Justice, made in accordance with this article.

相关实习生、实习生所在的公证机构和土耳其公证员联合会可以对司法部依照本条作出的决定向国务院提出异议。

The registry of the notary public certificate holders

公证职业资格证书持有人登记

Article 18 – The notary public certificate holders are enlisted in pursuant of their certificate numbers to the registry taken in the Ministry of Justice.

第十八条 公证职业资格证书持有人依照其在司法部登记的证书号码登记。

If those whose record has been deleted from the reg-

若已将记录从登记簿中删除，则应当在第二十五

ister request it, their re-registration is done in accordance with their application date fixed in pursuant of the second clause of the article 25. Those who are in this situation and who apply in the same day are arranged in order in accordance with their certificate numbers. If, at the day of registration, there are those whose registrations are to be done in pursuant to the first clause, then, this type of registration has priority.

条第二款规定的申请日期重新登记。有此种情形并在同一天提出申请的，按照其证书编号按顺序排列。如果在登记之日有依照第一款进行登记的人，那么此类登记享有优先权。

Other points that show the situation of the concerned and that are indicated in the regulation are also inscribed in the register. In case of appointment to the notary public, of death, of permanent loss of appointment conditions to the notary public or of other situations shown in this law, the mode of the removal of the registration is indicated in the regulation.

规章中所列的其他有关情况也载入登记册。若任命的公证员死亡、永久丧失公证员资格或者出现本法规定的其他情况，则依照规章的规定取消登记。

The obligation of address notification

地址通知义务

Article 19 – The ones who hold notary public certificate and who are enlisted in the register mentioned in the article 18 have the obligation to notify to the Ministry of Justice any change in the address that they have notified to the notary public chamber in pursuant of the article 9 and so in 15 days which follows the day of change.

第十九条 持有公证员职业资格证书并被列入第十八条所述登记册的人，有义务在变更之日后的十五日内，向司法部通报其依照第九条收到的公证机构地址发生变化的通知。

Internship wages

实习工资

Article 20 – The notary public internship is gainful.

第二十条 公证员实习是带薪实习。

The internship wage is fixed by the Notaries Union of Turkey who takes the opinion of the Ministry of Justice and is paid from the Union's budget between the beginning of the internship and the delivery of the notary public certificate by the Ministry of Justice.

实习工资由接受司法部意见的土耳其公证员联合会确定，且从实习开始至获得司法部提供公证员职业资格证书的期间，实习工资由联邦预算支付。

In case of illness of the intern justified in accordance with the regulation, the wages are not cut during the permission which is utmost two months, including the permission mentioned in the article 15.

若实习生因病请假，则在最长两个月的许可期间（包括第十五条所规定的许可期间）内不削减工资。

In case of prolongation of the internship in accordance with the article 17, the intern receives no wages for this prolongation.

若依照第十七条延长实习时间，延长的实习期间没有工资。

Excluding the involuntarily loss of one of the internship qualities, if the intern quits the internship or is dismissed from the internship or the holder of notary public certificate rejects two times the Ministry of Justice's proposal regarding his/her appointment for notary public or refuses to begin the work to which he is appointed after his/her application to the announced notary public and then is considered resigned or quits the career by his/her

非自愿丧失实习资格以外，如果实习生退出实习、被开除实习、持有公证员职业资格证书却两次拒绝接受司法部关于任命其为公证员的提议或拒绝履行指定的公证工作，将被视为辞职。同时，未在最初被任命的公证机构服务两年便因个人原因离职的，由土耳其公证员联合会依照破产法中关于执行判决的规定收取支付给他/她的实习工资总额。土耳其公证员联合会的这一应收款项的时效是上述收款事由发生之日

own will without serving at least two years at the notary public's office that he/she is first appointed, then the total amount of the wages that are paid to him/her for internship is collected by the Notaries Union of Turkey together with the legal interest of the payment period in accordance with the provisions of the Execution And Bankruptcy Law regarding to the execution of the sentences. This receivable of the Notaries Union of Turkey is brought under prescription in one year beginning from the date of occurrence of the payment reasons mentioned above or, in any cases, in ten years beginning from the delivery of the notary public certificate.

起一年内，或在其他任何情况下从公证员职业资格证书交付之日起十年内。

Responsibility of the intern

Article 21 – The interns are responsible as the real officer of all the businesses which they made during the internship duration in pursuant of the provisions of this law and regulation.

实习生的责任

第二十一条 实习人员依照本法和规章的规定，对实习期间从事的所有业务负责。

PART THREE
Appointing notary public

CHAPTER ONE
Announcement and application procedure

第三部分
委任公证员

第一章 公告及申请程序

Announcement

Article 22 – Notary publics that are vacant, opened or upgraded from fourth to third class will be announced for one time in The Official Gazette and the gazette that will be issued in that place, in Ankara and in Istanbul and in places which will be designated by The Ministry of Justice.

The announcement of the Notary publics that will be vacant because of age restriction is obligatory before the notary public will be dependent on age restriction.

The previous gross income of the notary public that is vacant or upgraded to the third class and foreseeable gross income of newly opened notary public that will be designated by the Ministry of Justice according to the precedents and the necessary documents for application will take place in the announcement.

公告

第二十二条 政府公报和安卡拉、伊斯坦布尔以及司法部指定地区发布的公报将一次对四级到三级的公证员空缺、开放或升级的岗位情况进行公布。

公告因年龄限制而空缺的公证员岗位须予以注明，公证员的委任应当遵守年龄限制的规定。

应当公告公证员空缺的岗位、升级为三级公证员的先前总收入及新开设的公证员岗位的预期总收入与申请所需的文件。

Application procedure

Article 23 – (Changed clause 1 13.06.2000 – 4579/ art. 2)

the ones who submit their applications to the an-

应用程序

第二十三条（修改后的第 1 款 2000 年 6 月 13 日 - 4579/ 第 2 条）

申请空缺的公证员岗位，应当将符合第七条第一

nounced notary publics are obliged to attach the document showing they didn't lose the conditions mentioned in Article 7, paragraphs 1,5 and the following and the document showing the completion of military service or the document showing unsuitability for the military service to the petition that will be submitted to the office of the director of the public prosecutions place of their residence that will be sent to the Ministry of Justice or the Ministry.

项、第五项和下列规定所述条件的文件及已服完兵役的证明文件或不适合服兵役的证明文件附在提交给住所地公证机构办公室主管的申请书中，并由其送交司法部或政府部门。

The Ministry of Justice will not take the request of the people with the uncompleted documents into consideration within the given period.

司法部将不予考虑在规定期限内未填完文件的人的申请。

The above-mentioned provision of the paragraphs will not be applied to the ones lawing as the notary public on the application dates.

上述规定不适用于在申请之日以公证员身份涉诉的公证员。

Last section, Article 9 provision will be applied in this case.

第九条的规定将适用于上述情形。

CHAPTER TWO
Designation to the third class notary public

第二章　指定三级公证员

Designation upon announcement

通知后指定

Article 24 – according to the Article 22 only the ones who possess a notary public certificate will be designated to the announced third class notary public.

Following a month completion of the last announcement date and completion of the period by all means as stipulated by the paragraph 2, Article 23 Article the Ministry of Justice designates the one at the top of the register, as stipulated by the Article 18 as the notary public, under the condition not to possess any hindrance

第二十四条　依照本法第二十二条的规定，持有公证员职业资格证书的人员，方可被指定为三级公证员。

第二十三条第二项规定的最后公告日期届满后，司法部应当依照第十八条的规定，在无其他障碍的情况下指定登记册上的第一名为公证员。

Designation upon proposal

经提议指定

Article 25 – (Abolished. Article 17, law no 3588 16/11/1989)

第二十五条（已废除。第3588/11/1989号法令第17条）

Upon the refusal of the proposal

提议被拒绝

Article 26 – (Abolished. Article 17, law no 3588 of 16/11/1989)

第二十六条（已废除。1989年11月16日第3588号法令第17条）

CHAPTER THREE
Designation as the first class, second class and third class notary publics

第三章　指定一级、二级和三级公证员

Designation procedure

指定程序

Article 27 – (amendment: Article 2, law no 3588 of

第二十七条（修正案：1989年11月16日第3588

16.11.1989)

The Ministry of Justice will designate one of the applicants as the notary public; the first class ones among the first class notary publics, second class ones among the first or the second class notary publics and third class ones among the first, second or third class notary publics following the completion of an announcement within a month period according to the Article 22. A person who possesses a notary public certificate can be designated as a third class notary only if a third or a higher class application is not submitted. Regarding a second or third class notary public designation, a priority has been given to the designation request of the higher class notary publics. Designation request of a notary public failed to law as a notary public for two years will not be taken into account.

During the designation process, seniority serves as a basis for notary publics among the same class, and incase of equality of seniority; qualification degree compared to employment record shall be taken in consideration. Those who certify in regulation that they speak at least one of the languages like German, French, English or Italian among the notary publics who have the same seniority and qualification shall be preferred over other candidates and those who graduated from one of the foreign faculties of law in one of the languages mentioned-above shall be preferred over others and those who have a doctorate in law shall be preferred over all. In case of equality of conditions on the above-mentioned situation, those who graduated previously shall be preferred. The person to be appointed shall be fixed, based on drawing lots in case of equality mentioned-above.

CHAPTER FOUR
Joint Provisions

Designation by means of transfer

Article 28 – (Abolished. Article 17, law no 3588 of 16/11/1989)

Designation request of the notary publics who leave by means of closing down the notary public office or by resigning

Article 29 – (Amendment: Article 3, law no 3588 of 16/11/1989)

When the adjudicatory power annuls a designation possession to a vacant or a newly started notary public

号法令第 2 条）

司法部将指定其中一名申请人为公证员；第一级公证员为一级公证员，第一级或第二级公证员为二级公证员，依照第二十二条的规定，第一级、第二级或第三级公证员在一个月内完成公告的为三级公证员。持有公证员职业资格证书的人只有在未提交第三级或更高级别申请的情况下，才能被指定为三级公证员。关于二级或三级公证员的指定，优先考虑较高级别的公证员的指定请求。未获法律认可达两年之久的公证员的指定请求将不予考虑。

在指定过程中，资历是评价同一等级公证员的依据，在资历相同的情况下，学历相对于职业经历更应该被纳入考虑的范围。依照规章的规定，在具有相同资历和学历的公证员中，若该公证员能证明自己至少懂德语、法语、英语或意大利语等其中一种语言，则应当优先于其他候选人，而以上述一种语言毕业的外国法学院毕业生应当优先于其他语言的毕业生。具有法律博士学位的人应当优先于所有候选人。在上述条件相同的情况下，优先考虑较先毕业的人。在上述所有条件相同的情况下，则依照抽签确定。

第四章　联合规定

以调任方式指定

第二十八条（已废除。1989 年 11 月 16 日第 3588 号法令第 17 条）

因公证机构被撤销而离职或辞职的公证员的指定请求

第二十九条（修正案：1989 年 11 月 16 日第 3588 号法令第 3 条）

当通过判决取消对空缺或新开放的公证机构职位的指定占有时，失业的公证员将恢复其先前的职责，

office, the unemployed notary public returns to law his former duty, if another notary public is designated for his former duty the notary public will be designated primarily for the vacant position of his notary public class or for the new notary public office that is newly started. The service period of the above-mentioned notary public is counted as he serves in the new notary public.

如果指定另一名公证员担任其原职务，那么该公证员将优先被指定担任其相应公证级别的空缺职位或新开放的公证员职位。上述公证员的服务期，按其在新公证员岗位的任职期间计算。

A notary public who quits his profession by means of resignation after fulfilling his/her two-years service period and submits his application upon announcement, and certifies his notary public competency; he shall be designated to a notary public of his/her class or a lower class on the date of his resignation as stipulated in the framework of principles within the first paragraph of Article 27.

公证员在满两年服务期后，以辞职方式离职，并在公告时提出申请且证明其作为公证员的能力；在第二十七条第一款规定的原则框架内，在辞职之日指定他 / 她为原级别的公证员或较低级别的公证员。

A notary public who quits his/her profession by means of resignation without fulfilling his/her two-years service period; shall be designated to a notary public of his/her class on date of his resignation by certifying his/her notary public competency and only if no other candidate is available as stipulated in the Article 24 and 27

公证员因辞职而未满两年服务期的，应当在辞职之日，通过证明其作为公证员的公证能力，并仅在第二十四条和第二十七条所规定的其他候选人不存在的情况下，被指定为其所在级别的公证员。

notary public who has resigned shall be designated to a lower class notary public upon his/her request as stipulated by the principles in first section of the article 27. In both cases, if there is more than one request the preference shall be given according to the second section of Article 27.

公证员辞职后，应当按照第二十七条第一款的规定，被指定为下一级公证员。在此种情况下，如果有不止一项的请求，那么应当依照第二十七条第二款的规定给予优先考虑。

a notary public who quits his profession by means of resignation can not submit his/her request for designation after completing the 6 months period of his resignation.

公证员通过辞职的方式离职，在辞职六个月内，不得提出指定申请。

a notary public who quits his profession twice by means of resignation can never be designated as a notary public again.

公证员如因辞职而两次离职，不能再被指定为公证员。

The deputy notary public who is designated before this law came into effect can not take advantage of the second and third section's provisions of the above-mentioned law. After resigning from the notary public office the above-mentioned ones can not be designated to a notary public office unless he/she possesses the qualifications and competencies mentioned in Article 7.

本法施行前指定的代理公证员，不得利用前述第二款、第三款的规定获益。上述公证员自从公证机构辞职后，必须具备第七条规定的资格和职权，方可被指定在一所公证机构任职。

To begin, to renounce and resign the duty

初任、放弃和辞职

Article 30 – notary public title is acquired by the notification of the designation decision. Notary public title of a notary public's designated or transferred to a notary public office in his/her class or in a higher class,

第三十条 公证员的头衔通过收到委任通知的方式取得。公证员的公证权利通过公证员的指定或者转到原等级或更高等级的公证机构的方式取得。

Article 31 – A person designated or transferred to a

第三十一条 被指定或调任到公证机构的公证

notary public office, have to commence his/her duty within a month period, following the appointment notification or transfer decision. Within this period, the appointed or transferred person failing to commence his/her duty without any justified reasons or in case he/she submits the designation or transfer request renouncement petition to the Ministry or the office of the director of the public prosecutions, following the appointment or transfer decision notification, this person shall be considered as a resigned person acting as a notary public.

员，必须在指定通知或调任决定后的一个月内开始履职。在此期间内，被指定或调任的公证员无任何正当理由却未能开始其职责，或他 / 她向司法部或公证办公室主任提交请求放弃指定或调任的申请，在作出指定或调任决定通知后，该人应当被视为已辞职的公证员。

(Article 17, Law no: 3588 of 16/11/1989 and last sentence of second paragraph abolished, Article 4 and third and fourth paragraphs of the same law amended as follows:)

（1989 年 11 月 16 日第 3588 号法令第 17 条和第 2 款的最后一句被废除，同一法律第 4 条和第 3 款、第 4 款修正如下）

The person who is designated as a notary public before the designation or transfer decision have not been notified to him/her, shall renounce from his/her request by submitting a petition to the Ministry or the office of the director of the public prosecutions. The designation request of a person who renounces three times as mentioned-above shall not be taken into consideration. If the above-mentioned person holds a notary public certificate his/her certificate shall be annulled. One of the present candidates shall be designated as a notary public in case a renunciation before the designation decision notification takes place without any further announcement according to the articles 24, 27 and 29.

在指定或调任决定的通知没有送达之前被指定为公证员的，应当向司法部或公证办公室主任提交申请书宣布放弃请求。对上述指定请求三次提出放弃的将不再予以考虑。上述人员持有公证员职业资格证书的，应当宣布其公证员职业资格证书无效。依照第二十四条、第二十七条、第二十九条的规定，在作出指定决定通知之前宣布放弃，若无其他情形，那么当前候选人中的一人应当被指定为公证员。

Period of starting the duty in a new notary public office for those who are already in the profession shall commence following the date of handover operation of the previous notary public office.

已在本行业任职的人员在新的公证机构任职的期间，自原公证员职务交接之日起开始计算。

(Last paragraph - Article 3, law no 4579 of 13.06.2000)

（上一款 -2000 年 6 月 13 日第 4579 号法令第 3 条）

Article 32 – The Ministry of Justice shall fix a month period to the notary public, who starts up a notary public office in a place that is not determined by the Ministry of Justice or moves his notary public office to the above-mentioned place, for moving his notary public office to the place determined by the Ministry of Justice. The notary public who fails to move his notary public office in the determined place shall be considered as resigned from his duty and his notary public office shall be moved to a determined place under the supervision of the Notary Public Association in Turkey.

第三十二条 司法部应当给予规定以外地区设立的公证机构，或将公证机构移至未规定地区的公证员一个月的期限，责令其将该公证机构移至司法部规定的地点。公证员若不将公证机构移至指定地点，应当视为辞职，公证机构应当在土耳其公证员联合会的监督下移至规定的地点。

PART FOUR
Power to Notary Public and Warrant

The management by proxy of the dismantled notary public's office

Article 33 – Whatever the reason, if a first, second or third class notary public's office is dismantled, the Office is managed by proxy by the intern who is completed the six month of his/her internship in the said Office, if there is more than one intern in this position, then by the senior intern, if there is no intern in this position, by an intern which will be found and charged by the notary public chamber and in the absence of all these options, by the chief clerk or, if unavailable, by the most senior clerk of the Office

(Changed clause 2: 16.11.1989 – 3588/art. 5)

(Changed phrase 1: 2/3/2005 – 5309/ art. 3)

If there is no available clerk in the notary public's office, this duty is fulfilled, upon the notification of the Republic Attorney General, by an enforcement officer, an assistant enforcement officer or an adequate justice officer who are appointed by the justice commission. If the deputy reveals insufficient during the controls, he/she can be changed any time.

The officer who rules the notary public's office in accordance with the above clauses receives a wage fixed by the notary public chamber; this wage can not be less than his/her monthly wage or revenues and is paid from the notary public's income. By the way, this wage can not be more than half of the gross income of the notary public's office.

(Changed: 16.11.1989 – 3588/art. 5)

The notary public's office's dues, the deputy's wages and the other expenditures of the notary public's office including the travel allocation which is given for the deputy's personal operations will be separated from the monthly gross income of the notary public's office and the balance together with the detailed list of income-expense will be addressed by the deputy to the Notaries Union of Turkey ultimately until the fifteenth calendar day of the following month.

Proxy in case of temporarily separations

Article 34 – If the notary publics are temporarily separated because of arresting, of constrained work ceasing and of dismissal, their duties are performed in pursuant

第四部分
公证员及授权书的权力

代为管理被撤销的公证机构

第三十三条 无论何种理由，若第一级、第二级或第三级公证机构被撤销，则该公证机构将由在此处实习满六个月的实习生代为管理。若在这个职位上有超过一位的实习生，则由较为年长的实习生代为管理。若在这个职位上没有实习生，则由公证员办公室的首席办事员（如果没有）或者办公室最高级办事员进行管理。

（更改第 2 款：1989 年 11 月 16 日 -3588/ 第 5 条）

（更改短语 1：2005 年 3 月 2 日 -5309/ 第 3 条）

若公证机构没有可用的办事员，则由司法委员会任命的一名执行官员、助理执法人员或合适的司法官员应共和国总检察长的通知履行这一职责。如果代理人在管理过程中有任何不妥，那么应当更换代理人。

依照本法的规定，管理公证机构的官员领取公证机构规定的工资；该工资不得低于其月工资或月收入，且不能超过公证机构总收入的一半，该工资由公证员的收入支付。

（更改：1989 年 11 月 16 日 -3588/ 第 5 条）

公证机构的税费、代理人的工资和公证机构的其他支出，包括代理人个人业务的旅费分配，将与公证机构的月总收入分开，余额连同收入——费用明细表由代理人在下个月的第十五个工作日前提交给土耳其公证员联合会。

暂时离职情况下的代理

第三十四条 若公证员因被逮捕、被迫停止工作和解雇而暂时离职，则应当依照第三十三条的规定履行其职责。

of the article 33.

In this case, excepting the case of temporarily dismissal, the notary public office's dues and the deputy's wage are separated and one half of the remained gross income is attributed to the notary public; the other half is withheld until the conclusive decision of the investigation and the prosecution and it's so in order to offset the debit or otherwise to restore to the notary public. In case of temporarily dismissal, notary public's office's dues and the deputy's wage are separated and the remained gross income is send to the Notaries Union of Turkey.

If the temporarily competent assistant notary public ceases to work because of the reasons mentioned in the first clause, a deputy is chosen according to the procedure indicated in the article 32. The deputy receives all the incomes.

Proxy in case of obstacle

Article 35 – The notary publics who left their businesses because of illness and justified reasons are substituted by the person who has the primary authority to sign in the said notary public's office.

If there is no person with authority to sign, the businesses are done by the intern having completed six months of his/her internship in the said notary public's office, if there is no intern in this situation, by the chief clerk or senior clerk of notary public and if there is no person to whom the attorney could be presented then by an another intern having the qualities mentioned here in above and who is considered adequate by the notary public chamber.

(Changed clause three: 2/3/2005 – 5309/art. 4)

If there is no available person, this duty is fulfilled, upon the application of the notary public to the Republic Attorney General, by an enforcement officer, an assistant enforcement officer or an adequate justice officer considered sufficient who are appointed by the justice commission in return of a wage appreciated in accordance of the third clause of the article 33.

If the temporary notary public assistants have the obstacles indicated in the first clause, then the last clause of the article 34 is applied.

Power

Article 36 – Notary public can give power of attorney to his intern having completed three months of his/her internship, to his chief clerk or to his another clerk in order

在此种情况下，除暂时解雇的情况外，公证机构的税费和代理人的工资分开，剩余总收入的一半归公证员；另一半则保留至调查和起诉的确切决定作出后，目的在于抵消债务或以其他方式归还给公证员。在暂时解雇的情况下，公证机构的税费和代理人的工资分开，剩余的总收入上交给土耳其公证员联合会。

若公证员的临时主管助理因第一款所述的理由而停止工作，则依照第三十二条规定的程序选择一名代理人。该代理人能得到临时主管助理的所有收入。

有履职障碍情况下的代理

第三十五条　公证员因疾病和正当理由离职的，由所在公证机构有签字权的人代理其职务。

若不存在有权力签字的人，则公证员业务由在该公证机构已完成六个月实习的实习生完成。若没有实习生，则由公证员的首席办事员或高级办事员完成，若无人能胜任代理，则由另一名具有上述资质且被公证员办公室认为适当的实习生代理。

（更改第 3 款：2005 年 3 月 2 日 -5309/ 第 4 条）

若无合适人选，则就公证员向共和国检察长提出的申请，由司法委员会任命的一名执法人员、助理执法人员或被认为具有足够资格的司法官员履行这一职责，并领取因第三十三条第三款而提高的工资。

若临时公证员助理有第一款所指的阻却事由，则适用第三十四条最后一款。

权力

第三十六条　公证员可以向实习期满三个月的实习生、首席办事员或者其他办事员出具委托书，以便接受帮助。

to receive help.

In case of more than one power of attorney, the priority order of these powers of attorney is indicated in the licenses.

The modalities in which the power of attorney can be granted are specified in the regulation.

当存在一份以上授权书的情况下，授权书的优先顺序应当在授权书中注明。

授权书的授予方式在该规章中作具体规定。

PART FIVE
Notary Public Oath, Guarantee, Samples of Signature and Seal

Notary Public Oath

Article 37 – Before they start to work, those who are first appointed to the notary public take an oath on their hearts and honors at the court of first instance or at the individual civil court of peace to which they are related; the oath indicates that they will execute this confided duty in a right manner and with no partiality. One of the three copied records is addressed to the Ministry of Justice. Another copy is addressed to the Republic General Attorney and the last one is held in the file at the notary public's office.

Guarantee

Article 38 – In two months which follows their beginning to work, those who enter in the notary public profession must guarantee 5 % of the annual gross income of the notary public's office. The guarantee can only be cash.

The guarantees of the notary public's offices that will be opened are paid according to the gross income estimated at the notary public advertisement.

Also, until the end of the February of the concerned year, the notary public's offices guarantee 1 % of the real gross income of the previous year.

The amount of the guarantee is paid into a national bank of which more than half of its capital belongs to the State. Those banks are shown in the regulation.

The guarantee is a counterbalance for the damages caused by the notary public's offices and hence for the fines assessed to them. Those moneys can not be transferred (assignment of claim) or discharged (hypothec) to someone else. According to the article 49, a part in withheld during the cession; the execution reveals possible from the rest.

In order to make him/her fulfill his/her obligations, the Ministry of Justice gives an adequate time, one month at best, to the notary public who does not pay the guar-

第五部分
公证员宣誓、担保、签名和盖章的样本

公证员宣誓

第三十七条 初次被任命为公证员的人，在初审法院或与之有关系的治安民事法院宣誓时，应当真心实意地宣誓；宣誓表明他们将以正确的方式、不带偏见地履行公证员的职责。三份复印件中有一份提交给司法部，另一份提交给共和国总检察长，最后一份在公证机构存档。

担保

第三十八条 在开始工作后的两个月内，进入公证机构的人必须用现金担保公证机构年收入的百分之五。

将要开设的公证机构的担保按公证员预估的总收入支付。

此外，直到每年度的二月底，公证机构担保前一年实际总收入的百分之一。

依照规定，担保金应当支付给国家持股超过一半的银行。

担保是对公证机构造成的损害以及被征收罚款的抵消。该款项不能转移给其他人（分配索赔）或被解除（抵押权）。依照本法第四十九条的规定，在转让期间被保留的一部分款项，可以从其剩余部分中执行。

为确保公证员履行义务，司法部给没有在固定时间内支付担保或不支付所有款项的公证员最多一个月的宽限时间，在此期限内未完成担保的公证员即被视

antee in the fixed time or who does not pay all sums. The notary public who does not complete his/her guarantee is considered resigned.

Samples of signature and seal

Article 39 – The notary publics are charged with the responsibility to send to the local governorship the three samples of their notarial seal and signature in 15 days which follows the date of their beginning to work.

Also, one sample of the signatures of the ones to whom a power of attorney is presented is sent to the local governorship in 15 days which follows the preparation of the said power of attorney.

PART SIX
Notary Public Office

Office quality and renting

Article 40 – notary public office shall be accepted as government office. Notary public shall make the renting contract on behalf of the office.

Notary public is responsible for all expenses of notary public office.

Document and books supply and destruction

Article 41 – according to the procedures mentioned in regulations, document and books and other office supplies and supply used in organs of Notaries Union of Turkey and destruction of document and papers shall be subject to the stipulations regarding government offices.

Personnel

Article 42 – Notary public office personnel consist of considerable amount of clerks and employees working under the service of the notary public.

In notaries public offices where there are at least two clerks, one shall works as head clerk.

Head clerk

Article 43 – head clerk is the personnel chief in the notary public office.

Head clerk is as well as responsible as notary public from documents, books and registered moveable property.

为辞职。

签名和盖章样本

第三十九条 公证员有责任在开始工作后十五日内将公证印章和签名的三份样本送交当地政府。

在准备本法规定的授权书后的十五日内，将授权委托书中的人的签名样本送交当地行政长官。

第六部分
公证机构

办公室的条件与租赁

第四十条 公证机构为政府机关。公证员应当代表公证机构订立租赁合同。

公证员负责公证机构的一切费用。

文件和书籍的提供和销毁

第四十一条 依照规章中规定的程序，土耳其公证员联合会使用的文件、书籍和其他办公用品、供给品，以及销毁文件和纸张，都应当遵守关于政府办公室的规定。

人员

第四十二条 公证机构人员由一定数量的办事员和雇员组成。

公证机构至少有两名办事员的，其中一人担任主管办事员。

主管办事员

第四十三条 主管办事员是公证机构的人事主任。

主管办事员与公证员一样，对文件、账簿和已登记的动产负责。

Conditions required for being a head clerk

Article 44 – Conditions required for being a head clerk are as follows:

possess conditions stipulated in government official law, not being discharged by a penal or disciplinary decision, complete candidacy period of six months, authentication of competency by the notary public

Candidate, whose competency has not been authenticated yet, shall work for another six months. If the candidate fails, he/she shall not work any longer in that Notary public office.

Those who completed courses opened by Notaries Union of Turkey or Chambers shall be a candidate in Notary public office before anyone else.

Contract obligation

Article 45 – notary publics hire candidates at least for a year contract. Notary public has the right to notice of report owing to incompetence of the candidate, unless written explicitly following the completion of candidacy period. In case candidacy period extends, the same stipulation shall be applied.

Within the notice of report period if the contract is not annulled or candidacy is not extended, the contract shall continue as clerk contract following the completion of the period.

Notary clerk and candidate contract shall be prepared as four copies and first copy shall be sent to notary chamber, second copy shall be sent to regional labor directorship within 15 days following the date it is prepared. The third copy shall be kept with notary public and the last shall belong to the clerk or candidate.

Authenticated copies of documents showing the candidate possess the conditions mentioned in Public Officials Law shall be attached to the copy sent to the Chamber.

Notary public shall notify the chamber within 15 days following the situation appears like; the clerk candidate contract became a clerk contract or the contract terminates for any reasons according to the second paragraph.

Notary publics who act contrary to the above-mentioned paragraphs, if found faulty, shall at least receive a condemnation for the first time.

The above-mentioned stipulation shall be applied for those who act contrary to the article 44.

In case discharge decision is final for notary clerk and candidate, clerk and candidacy contract shall be annulled

担任主管办事员所需的条件

第四十四条 担任主管办事员的条件如下：

具备政府官方法律规定的条件，未受过刑事处罚或纪律处分。主管办事员试用期为六个月，六个月后由公证员对其进行职业资格认证。

尚未通过职业资格认证的候选人应当再工作六个月。若通过失败，他/她将不再在该公证机构工作。

完成由土耳其公证员联合会或公证员办公室开设的课程的人，应当优先于其他人在公证机构担任公职。

合同义务

第四十五条 公证员雇用候选人至少应当签订一年的合同。除非在候选人任期结束后有明确的书面通知，公证员拥有因候选人不称职而报告通知的权利。候选期延长，也适用同样的规定。

在报告期限内，若合同未被废止或候选期未被延长，该合同则在该期间结束后继续作为办事员雇佣合同。

公证员和候选人签订的合同一式四份，第一份送交公证机构，第二份自编制之日起十五日内送交当地劳动局，第三份应当由公证员保管，最后一份应当交由办事员或候选人保管。

具有《公职人员法》所述条件的候选人的证明文件副本应当附上合同副本一并送交给公证员办公室。

公证员应当在以下情况出现后十五日内通知公证员办公室。即依照第二款的规定，办事员候选人合同转变为办事员合同或者因其他原因终止合同。

作出违反上述规定行为的公证员，若有过错应当受到处罚。

违反第四十四条规定的，适用上述规定。

当公证办事员和候选人的解雇决定为最终决定时，办事员和候选人合同应当在最后决定之日自动废

automatically on the date of the final decision. Clerk and candidate can not demand any indemnity for his reason.

Duties fail to be executed by the employees

Article 46 – employee shall not be employed as clerks.

Annual leave of absence or special leave

Article 47 – notary publics shall give the leave of absence to the clerks and employees who work in the notary public office at least a year as follows:

A) Those who work from 1 to 5 years (5 years included) shall have 15 days

B) Those who work from 5 to 15 years (15 years included) shall have 20 days

C) Those who work for more than 15 years shall have 1 month leave of absence.

Those who shall have their leave of absence away from the notary public office shall have a supplementary leave of absence up to 7 days, to compensate for period in arrivals and departures.

The competency period of clerks shall be taken into consideration in calculating service period of a year, mentioned in the first paragraph.

The notary public shall give to clerk and employees a leave of absence at most for ten days in a year including the departures and arrivals, under the condition of having a justified excuse. If those-above mentioned leave of absences exceeds ten days in total, the exceeding amount shall be deducted from the annual leave of absence.

Clerk and employees shall have their total salary within the period they are on leave, as stipulated in the above-mentioned paragraph.

Collective labor contracts and service agreements shall increase the above-mentioned periods shall be increased. Annual paid leave right shall not be abandoned.

Application of labor legislation stipulations

Article 48 – any relation arising from service agreement between clerk and employers with the notary public is subject to the labor legislation unless stipulated otherwise in this law.

Notary public office transfer

Article 49 – Whatever the reason, if a notary public office became vacant, the relevant notary public or the person authorized to sign shall notify the situation in writing

止。因其自身原因解雇的，办事员和候选人不能要求任何赔偿。

雇员不得履行的职责

第四十六条　雇员不得担任办事员。

年假或特别休假

第四十七条　公证员应当给予在公证机构工作至少一年的办事员和工作人员下列内容的休假：

A）工作一至五年（包括五年）的人应当有十五日的休假时间。

B）工作五至十五年（包括十五年）的人应当有二十日的休假时间。

C）工作超过十五年的，有一个月的休假时间。

请假离开公证机构去远方休假的，最多延长休假七日，以补偿到达和离开的时间。

在计算第一项所述一年的服务期时，应当考虑办事员胜任其职责的期限。

公证员应当在有正当理由的情况下，在一年中给予办事员和雇员最多十日的休假，包括离开和到达的时间。上述缺勤总天数超过十日的，应当从年假中扣除超出的天数。

办事员和雇员在前项规定的休假期间内可以领取全勤工资。

集体劳动合同和劳务协议应当增加上述期限。带薪休假权不得放弃。

劳动法的适用

第四十八条　办事员、用人单位与公证员之间的服务协议关系，除本法另有规定外，适用劳动法。

公证机构调任

第四十九条　公证机构岗位空缺的，无论出于何种原因，有关公证员或者被授权签名的人应当书面通知检察长办公室。检察长办公室应当将情况通知司法

to the office of the public prosecutors. The office of the public prosecutor shall notify the situation to the Ministry of Justice or notary chamber, if notary public died; to his/her rightful inheritors and shall examine his/her calculations and operations within two months at most and shall transfer document, book, paper and trusts to a representative along with a minutes, shell send the report to be prepared with a copy of the minutes to the Ministry of Justice. If the notary public has no connection, the Ministry of Justice shall make the notary public or to his/her rightful inheritors to return the guarantee. If the If the notary public has connection, compensated amount shall be deducted, and measures shall be taken according to the examination results of legally authorized bodies.

部或公证机构办公室；若公证员死亡，应当告知其合法继承人且在最多两个月内审查其工作的情况，并应当将文件、簿册和信托文件连同一份记录一并转交给代理人，将事先准备好的报告连同记录的副本送交给司法部。如果与该公证员没有联系的，司法部应当向其他公证员或者其合法继承人返还担保。如果与该公证员有联系的，应当扣除补偿金额，并依照法定机构的审查结果采取措施。

office of the public prosecutors or and notary public or present inheritors shall determine an item belonging to notary public in notary public office and shall be used by the representative, in return for a fee specified by notary chamber, until the new notary public takes over the duty

检察院、公证员、继承人应当在公证机构中确定属于公证员的项目，由代理人使用，以换取公证机构办公室规定的费用，直至新公证员接管职务为止。

Stipulation of first paragraph regarding, document, book, paper and trust transfer to the representative shall also be applied for notary public office transfer from; notary public to notary public, representative to notary public and from one representative to another.

关于第一款的规定，文件、簿册和信托文件转移给代理人的应当也适用于转移给公证机构的情形；包括公证员转移给公证员、代理人转移给公证员及从一个代理人转移给另一个代理人等。

If the parties shall not reach an agreement on the amount to be paid for the transfer of present items and installments from the previous to the last notary public within the notary public office, the notary chamber shall fix this amount.

若申请人在公证机构未对转让当前项目和上一个公证员就先前部分的总付款金额达成协议，则由公证机构办公室决定。

Notaries Union of Turkey shall pay the transportation fee, fixed according to the charges law, to the public prosecutor who is present in transfer of notary public office and justice officials assigned for help by the above-mentioned prosecutor. In so far, whatever the transfer period takes, transportation fee shall not be given for more than five days.

土耳其公证员联合会应当依照费用标准向调任到公证机构的检察官和受指派来帮助上述检察官的司法官员支付交通费用。无论调任期间多长，所支付的交通费不得超过五日的交通费。

PART SEVEN
The Obligations and Rights of Notary Publics

第七部分
公证员的义务和权利

CHAPTER ONE
The Obligations of Notary Publics

第一章　公证员的义务

Works that are incompatible with notary public position and are prohibited for notary publics

与公证员职位不相适应的工作和禁止公证员从事的工作

Article 50 – Any service or duty is compatible with

第五十条　任何服务或义务都与公证员职位相匹

notary public position; excluding the duties given by the juridical authorities, presidency or membership to the scientific or charity foundations, arbitration or testamentary executorships.

(Second clause repealed: 18/06/1997 – 4276/art. 25)

It is prohibited to the notary publics to gamble on the stock exchange, to trade in the meaning indicated at the clause 1 of the article 28 in the State Personal Law, to guarantee, to dump anyhow from the fees belonging to them, to use agents, to commit an act of publicity or competition and, by no means to conclude among them verbal or written accords regarding the notarial fees.

配；不包括司法局、院长或科学慈善基金的成员、仲裁或遗嘱执行人赋予的职责。

（第 2 款废除：1997 年 6 月 18 日 -4276/ 第 25 条）

禁止公证员在证券交易所投机，禁止依照《国家个人法》第二十八条第一款的含义进行交易、担保，不得以任何方式减免自身的支出，不得使用代理人，不得进行宣传或竞争行为，不得就公证费达成口头或书面协议。

Working hours of the notary publics

Article 51 – The daily work of the notary public's office starts together with the other local state departments. At the annual ordinary general assembly, the notary public chambers fix the daily work and leave hours of the member notary public which will be applied for one year and addressed them to the Notaries Union of Turkey and the Ministry of Justice. In so far, the working hours of the notary publics can only count one more hour than that of the other local state departments. Notary public's office can not accept any work except working hours. The provisions of the article 52 are reserved.

公证员的工作时间

第五十一条 公证机构的日常工作与其他当地国家部门共同开展。在年度总结大会上，公证员办公室确定公证员成员的日常工作内容和休假时间，申请时间为一年，并向土耳其公证员联合会和司法部提出申请。到目前为止，公证员的工作时间只能比其他地方政府部门多计算一小时。公证机构除在工作时间外，不得接受任何工作。第五十二条的规定已保留。

Prohibition of work for notary publics during holiday and exceptional cases

Article 52 – During the resting days or the resting hours of the working days, the notary publics are only authorized to arrange and confirm testaments or other notarial operations of whose delay risks to produce damage. It is imperative to show on the document the reason why the resting days and hours was worked and to register this operation on the first number after the rest of the daybook.

禁止公证员在假日和例外情况下工作

第五十二条 在休息日或工作日休息时间内，公证员只有权安排和确认其延迟可能造成损害的关于遗嘱或其他公证业务。且必须在工作日志中记录休息日和休息时间内工作的原因，并在日志本登记该业务。

Obligation for conformity to the ordering provisions

Article 53 – The notary publics can not make an operation contrary to the ordering provisions of the laws. This provision is also applied to the scope of the operations of which the signature confirmation has done.

遵守法律裁定条款的义务

第五十三条 公证员不得违反法律的规定执行业务。本规定同样适用于签字确认相关的业务范围。

Professional secrecy

Article 54 – Excepting the cases that law orders, the notary public and the notary public's office's clerks can not

职业保密条款

第五十四条 除法律规定的情形外，公证员和公证机构办事员不得泄露因职务原因而获悉的秘密。

reveal the secrets that they have learned because of their duties.

The secrecy of the documents and registers

Article 55 – The notary public's office's documents and registers can be examined by a court, an examining magistrature and the Attorney general of the Republic or by the persons that state departments authorized to conduct in the notary public's office an investigation of which the subject is also indicated.

The documents and registers cannot be taken out of the office unless the decision of the court or the examining magistrate.

If the court or the examining magistrate decides to keep the document in the file until the end of the trial, an authentic copy is prepared and is sent to the notary public in order to be held instead of the original document.

If the place where the notary public does not provide the opportunity to examine and the document must be addressed to another place, then the copy that will be certified by the tribunal court situated at the place of notary public is held in the same manner.

The copies demanded by the persons who have the inquiry authorization and by the Republic prosecutors are not subject to any notary public's office's fee. Only a typing fee is taken from the copies that are addressed to other official authorities.

Age restriction

Article 56 – When the notary publics complete the age of 65, they are subject to the age restriction. Concerning the calculation of the age, the provisions of the Law on Pension Fund of the Republic of Turkey are relatively applied.

CHAPTER TWO
Permission and Illness

The leave of notary publics

Article 57 – For the ones who have a service time from six months to 10 years (including ten years), the annual leave of the notary publics is 30 days; for those who have a greater service time, the annual leave is 40 days. Those times cover the departure and return times. The annual leave is given by the Ministry of Justice.

文件和登记册的保密条款

第五十五条 公证机构的文件和登记册可以由共和国的法院、地方预审法官和总检察长审查，也可以由国家主管部门授权在公证机构调查的人员进行审查。

除非法院或地方预审法官作出决定，否则不得将文件和登记册带出办公室。

如果法院或预审法官决定将文件保存在档案中直至审判结束，那么应编写一份真实副本送交公证员，以代替原始文件。

如果有的文件公证员没有机会检查，且该文件必须寄往另一个地方，那么将由设在公证员所在地的法院法庭核证该文件的副本，并以同样的方式持有。

被授权调查的人取得共和国检察官所要求的副本无须向公证机构支付任何费用。对寄给其他官方机关的副本中只收取打字费。

年龄限制

第五十六条 公证员年满六十五岁时，即受年龄限制。关于年龄的计算，适用《土耳其共和国养老金法》的规定。

第二章 请假许可与疾病

公证员的离开

第五十七条 服务时间为六个月至十年（包括十年）的公证员的年假为三十日；服务时间较长的，年假为四十日。年假时间涵盖了出发和返回的时间。年假由司法部规定。

The permission of the two successive years can be given together. In this case, the unused permissions of the past years are disqualified.

连续两年的假期申请可以一并批准。但两年以前未使用的假期则被取消。

Under the condition of justified obstacle, the notary publics can receive from the Republic prosecutor of his place a leave of absence which should not pass ten days including the departure and return times. If the total of those leaves passes 20 days, the surplus is deducted from the annual leave.

在有正当理由的情况下，公证员可从其所在地的共和国检察官那里得到请假许可，请假不得超过十日，包括离开和返回的时间。若该假期的总数超过二十日，超过的部分将从年假中扣除。

In so far, the notary public who must work in the organs of the Notaries Union of Turkey or who must leave his/her work because of the duties given by the Notaries Union of Turkey or the Ministry of Justice is considered on leave for the necessary time upon condition to inform the Republic prosecutor. Those leaves can by no means be deducted from the annual leave.

迄今为止，必须在土耳其公证员联合会各机构工作的公证员，或由于土耳其公证员联合会或司法部赋予的职责而必须离开工作地的公证员，在通知共和国检察官的情况下被视为必要的休假时间，该休假时间不得从年假中扣除。

The leaves granted in accordance with the provision of the third and fourth clause are immediately reported to the Ministry of Justice.

依照第三款和第四款的规定给予的假期应当立即向司法部报告。

Exceeding leave credit

超过休假信用时间

Article 58 – Those who exceed their leave credit 15 days without any justified obstacle are considered resigned. Those who exceed their leave credit with an inferior period or who leave their duties without permission are subject to a disciplinary penalty. In so far, the highest penalty for the first time is the censure.

第五十八条 在没有任何正当理由的情况下休假超过十五日的人被视为辞职。短期超过休假信用时间或未经许可擅自离开岗位的，将受到纪律处分。第一次最高的处罚是警告。

Operation to be done in case of illness of the notary publics

若公证员患病需进行手术

Article 59 – The notary publics who are sick are considered on leave under the following conditions in accordance with their service time and the report granted by the doctors of the Government or the State hospital through the Republic Attorney General:

1. The ones who have a five year (including five years) service time have a leave until three months,
2. The ones who have a service time until ten years (including ten years) have a leave until six months,
3. The ones who have a service time greater than ten years have a leave until one year.

第五十九条 生病的公证员依照其服务时间和政府或国家医院的医生出具的并由共和国总检察长批准的报告，在下列条件下休假：

1. 服务时间满五年（包括五年）的人有三个月的假期，
2. 服务时间满十年（包括十年）的人有六个月的假期，
3. 服务时间超过十年的人有一年的假期。

The leaves of notary publics whose continuing illness is certified via an official health association report can be prolonged twice. The duties of those notary publics who are not healed in the end of this time are terminated by the Ministry of Justice.

通过官方卫生协会报告证明未痊愈的公证员的休假可以延长两次。该期间结束后仍未痊愈的公证员的职务由司法部终止。

PART EIGHT
Duties of Notary Public

FIRST CHAPTER
General

Duties of notary public in general

Article 60 – Duties of notary public are as follows:

1. Arrange all kinds of legal procedures which are not given legally to any other office, instance or person (are not entitled by law)

2. arrange all kinds of legal procedures of undetermined instances that are stipulated formally by the laws and as stipulated by the said law,

3. make real property sale promise agreement

4. confirm signature, seal or any sign or date above the paper that is written outside as stipulated by this law,

5. give a copy of the original or copy or the document that is brought to the notary public office as stipulated by this law,

6. translate the documents from one language to another or from one writing to another,

7. make a formal complaint against someone, send notification and send notarized minutes,

8. enter the necessary registered legal procedures in an official register,

9. Execute other duties as stipulated by this law and by the other laws.

CHAPTER TWO
Particularly

Article 61 – Notary publics fix situation or form and value of a place or a thing and identity and expression of concerned parties and upon invitation to attend lottery and election and meetings of private institutions to certify the situation.

Safe keeping

Article 62 – notary publics guard the things entrusted to him for keeping or for giving to another person in accordance with the below mentioned decision.

One copy of the minutes is given to the person that trust the thing and the person that the trust belongs to is notified by the other copy.

第八部分
公证员的职责

第一章　一般规定

公证员的一般职责

第六十条　公证员的职责如下：

1. 组织进行法律规定的其他机关、实体或个人（法律未授权）无权参与的法律程序；

2. 组织进行其他法律、本法未作规定的争议的法律程序；

3. 订立房地产销售承诺协议；

4. 依照本法的规定公证在纸上的签名、印章或者在纸上写明的签名、日期的真实性；

5. 向公证机构提供本法规定的原件、副本或者复印件；

6. 把文件从一种语言翻译到另一种语言，或者从一种文字翻译到另一种文字；

7. 对某人提出正式控告，发送通知和登记公证记录；

8. 在官方登记册中登记必要的法律程序；

9. 执行本法和其他法律规定的其他职责。

第二章　特别规定

第六十一条　公证员可以公证地点或事物的情况、形式和价值，以及有关各方的身份和表现，还可以应邀参加抽奖、选举和私人机构的会议以公证有关情况。

安全保管

第六十二条　公证员保管委托给其保管或者依照本法规定给予他人的物品。

记录的副本发给委托人，另一份副本通知给受托人。

Entrust the trust

Article 63 – trusts are kept by the notary public accordingly.

Upon the request of the related person, the trust shall be put in a safe and be kept in a national bank after it is sealed by the notary public in the presence of the related person. The trust shall be kept in an iron case or in a secure box unless a bank is available.

Money trust

Article 64 – if the trust is money, notary public trust the money at latest the following day in the mane of the notary public office trust current account in the bank showing the name, surname and the address of the holder of the right.

Receipt is used for collecting and paying the trust money. Receipts of payment are two copies whereas payment invoice is only one copy. The person that trusts the thing gets the first copy of the receipts of payment.

The money shall be paid to the holder of the right by the bank in return of a check given by the notary public office.

Article 65 – Notary public shall notify the bank when the expenses related to the trust money are paid. In this case the time limit shall become invalid.

in case the trust is not taken in a year following the completion of the entrust period or in case expenditures and expenses are not paid, the notary public shall notify the person that entrust to pay expenditures and expenses, unless notification is available he shall notify his lawful successors, if any the person that trust is paid in favor of him.

If the related person fails to pay expenditures and expenses to the notary public within a month period following the notification, the notary public shall sell the trust in the municipality auction if not available he shall sell the trust in a suitable place and determines the condition by keeping the minutes. Notary public office expenses and total sales expenses, due trust until the day shall be subtracted by the sales total and the remaining shall be trust in the bank.

Trust transfer to the treasury

Article 66 – if the trust is worthless or fails to cover the sales cost, as stipulated by the first section of the Article 65 the notification fails, the trust shall be transferred to

保管信托财产

第六十三条　由公证员保管信托财产。

应相关人士要求，公证员应当安全地存管信托财产，即由公证员在相关人士的见证下，加盖印章后存放于国家银行。除非可保存于银行中，否则，信托财产应存放于保险箱。

货币信托

第六十四条　如果信托财产为货币形态，公证员最迟于收到款项的第二日，以公证机构的名义将该笔资金存入银行信托账户，并载明权利持有人的姓名和地址。

收据用于收取和支付信托资金。支付收据一式两份，而支付发票仅一份。委托该资金的申请人将获得支付收据的第一联。

在出示公证机构给出的支票后，银行应当将该资金支付给权利持有人。

第六十五条　公证员因从事与托管资金有关的业务而需支付费用时，应当通知银行。在此种情形中，时效失效。

若在委托期满后一年内未能取得信托财产或者未支付相关开支，公证员应当通知委托支付相关开支的人，若无法通知到该人，则应当通知其法定继承人、信托财产受益人。

若有关人员未能在通知作出后一个月内向公证员支付相关费用的，公证员应当在市拍卖会中出售该信托财产，如果不存在市拍卖会，那么应当在适当的地点出售该信托财产，并以记录的方式标明出售条件。公证机构因信托财产产生的花费应当从销售总额中扣除并且剩余款项应存入银行信托账户。

向财政部转交信托财产

第六十六条　如果信托财产无价值或者不足以支付第六十五条第一款中规定的销售成本，且未能作出通知的，应当递交至财政部。

the Treasury.

The money trusted to the bank by the notary public as a trust or upon the exercise of last paragraph provision of the article 65 shall be transferred to the Treasury, after the completion of the time limit.

公证员以信托方式委托给银行的款项或者在执行第六十五条最后一款规定后委托给银行的款项，应当在期限届满后交至财政部。

Right ownership regarding trusts

Article 67 – the trusts which be given to the other persons not mentioned in the minutes depends on the consent of the parties or decisions of the court.

信托财产的所有权

第六十七条 经当事人同意或由法院判决认可，可以将信托财产所有权转移至记录中未提及的其他人。

Book approval

Article 68 – notary publics keeps the necessary books according to the provisions of the Turkish Commercial Law and other laws and notary publics approve the above-mentioned books as required by the above-mentioned laws.

After the approval of the said book in the above-mentioned section, the notary public notifies instances as prescribed by the above-mentioned laws; of the sort, year, and page number of the approved book one by one or in a list with a registered letter.

Therefore, notary public charges the related person for letter fee as shown in the fee tariff and post expenses in cases where law obligates to notify one by one.

登记批准

第六十八条 公证员依照《土耳其商法》和其他法律的规定保管必要的登记簿册，并依照上述法律的要求批准上述登记。

上述部分所述的登记经批准后，公证员依照上述法律规定，逐个通知申请人批准登记的种类、年份和页数。

因此，公证员在法律规定必须逐个通知的情况下，按收费标准和邮寄费用的规定，向有关人员收取信函费。

Testament and duties regarding savings related to the death

Article 69 – notary publics keep open and secret testaments and they keep minutes regarding the above-mentioned testaments. They notify the situation in writing to the public registration office upon the death of persons trusted savings other than death, prepared by the notary publics, or testaments kept this way.

In case Public registration office certifies the death with a formal document or inform on death, notary publics entrust the approved copies of the testaments kept in their notary public office and covenant for title related to the death prepared by them to be sent to the office of the director of the public prosecutors.

与死亡有关的储蓄的遗嘱和义务

第六十九条 公证员保存公开和秘密的遗嘱及保存与上述遗嘱有关的记录。应当以书面形式将死者以外的死亡之人的信托储蓄或以该方式保存的遗嘱的情况通知给公共登记机构。

如果公共登记机构用正式文件或死亡通知证明死亡，公证员应当将保存在其公证机构中已核准副本的遗嘱和公证员准备的与死亡有关的所有权契据，送交给检察官办公室主管。

Notification procedures

Article 70 – any kind of document that will be used as notification will be notified to the relevant person according to the provisions of the Notification Law. Notifi-

通知程序

第七十条 任何用作通知的文件，将依照通知法的规定通知有关人员，公证机构的副本应当附在通知记录中。

cation minutes will be attached to the copy in the notary public office.

Distribution of monthly and yearly work schedules

Article 71 – Notary publics prepare a schedule at latest the 10th of each month, showing the quality and the number of the work that came in and came out from the notary public office and the fee, expenditure, duty and other tax costs and expenses that they took from the people within the previous month, and send it to the Notary Association in Turkey.

When the person gives notary public power of attorney, other than matters the as shown in the first section, the notary public who stands proxy for the person shows; the money that is paid to him and detained notary expenses and parts that he paid to the notary public and name and account number of the bank that he trusted the money detained, according to the Article 34, on the work schedule.

Each year until the end of March Notary publics organize a schedule of revenue, expenditure and amount of guarantee concerning the previous year and send it to the Ministry of Justice and Notaries Union of Turkey.

PART NINE
Aspects of Notary Operations

FIRST CHAPTER
General rules to comply for notary operations

Legal procedures and parties

Article 72 – Notaries certify legal procedures upon the request of concerned parties. Certification is done according to the related provisions and as shown in other laws and regulations. The person notified or not will be written on a copy that will be given to the relevant person and will be approved.

Related party is the one that requests the certification.

Notary publics are obliged to find out identity, address, skill and true intentions of the related parties.

If the person concerned is deaf, dumb or blind

Article 73 – (amended article with the title, Article 23, law no 5378 of 01.07.2005)

If the notary public understands that the person concerned is deaf, dumb or blind the operations shall be con-

每月和每年工作时间表的分配情况

第七十一条 公证员最迟在每月十号编制一份明细表，列明从公证机构受理和作出的工作质量和数量，以及前一个月内从申请人那里收取的费用、支出、关税和其他税费，并送交土耳其公证员协会。

申请人给予的公证授权委托书，除了载明第一节所列事项外，还应当载明办理申请人与其代理人的委托公证的公证员；并依照第三十四条的规定，在工作日程表上载明支付给申请人的钱、被扣留的公证费用和申请人向公证员支付的部分，以及信托被扣留款项的银行账号和名称。

每年三月底，由公证员编写一份有关前一年的收入、支出和担保金额的明细表，并将该表送交司法部和土耳其公证员联合会。

第九部分
公证业务方面

第一章　公证业务遵守的一般规则

法律程序和申请人

第七十二条 公证员依照申请人的请求，对法定程序进行公证。该公证应当依照有关规定和其他法律、法规的规定办理。已通知或未通知的人将被登记入一份副本中，该副本将交给相关人员，并将获得相应的批准。

相关申请人是申请公证的一方。

公证员有义务查明相关申请人的身份、地址、技能和真实意图。

如果相关人员是聋哑人或盲人

第七十三条 （经修订的第23条，2005年7月1日第5378号法令）

若公证员知道相关人员是聋哑人或盲人，则依照相关人员的请求，应当在两名见证人在场的情况下完

cluded with the presence of two witnesses upon the request of the person concerned. If the person concerned is deaf or dumb and can not communicate by writing the operations shall be concluded with the presence of two witnesses and a sworn translator.

成业务。若相关人员是聋哑人，不能以书面形式进行交流，则该业务应当在两名见证人和一名宣誓过的翻译人员在场的情况下进行。

If the person concerned can not speak Turkish

若相关人员不会说土耳其语

Article 74 – If the person concerned can not speak Turkish, the operations shall be concluded with the presence of a sworn translator.

第七十四条 若相关人员不会说土耳其语，应当在宣誓过的翻译员在场的情况下完成业务。

Using mark, seal or fingerprint replacing signature

使用标记、印章或指纹代替签名

Article 75 – if the person concerned and witness, translator, and expert can not sign or if they can not use a mark replacing signature, if any seal will be used, if not thumb print of left hand will be taken, if not any of the other fingers prints will taken and the printed finger will be written down.

(Amended section 2, Article 24, law no 5378 of 01.07.2005)

if a notary operation is signed or marked in any kind replacing the signature, upon the request of the person concerned or operation made on behalf of the person concerned excluding the blind persons who sign; the notary publics shall took the fingerprints of the person concerned, translator or expert in the notary public office as mentioned-above deem necessary regarding the quality of the operation, the state of the person signed or marked and his/her identity. If he uses the seal he shall also use the fingerprints. Notary publics took the witness, translator and expert oath in accordance with the Legal Proceedings Law.

第七十五条 若相关人员、见证人、翻译人员、鉴定人不能签名或者不能书写代替签名的标记的，有印章则使用印章，没有则用左手的拇指盖印，若没有（拇指）可以用其他手指盖印，并将盖印的手指记录下来。

（经修订的 2005 年 7 月 1 日第 5378 号法令第 24 条第 2 节）

依照相关人员的请求或代表相关人员（不包括签字的盲人）用签字或标记等任何形式代替签名的公证业务，公证员应当在上述被认为与业务质量、签字或标记的人的状况及其身份必要相关的公证机构提取相关人员、翻译人员或鉴定人员的指纹。相关人员应当同时使用印章和指纹。公证员依照《诉讼法》要求见证人、翻译人员和鉴定人宣誓。

Prohibition

禁止性规定

Article 76 – notary publics, witnesses, translators and experts can not participate in notary operations in cases as follows:

1. if he/she is personally involved or the person concerned is acting on behalf of him/her,
2. if they are married before, even though there isn't any matrimonial bond between the concerned parties,
3. If there is any affinity, blood relationship in third degree, ancestor, affinity in second degree (those degrees included) lineal consanguinity or collateral line, adoptive relationship between one of the involved party,
4. if the concerned party is the clerk or the employer of the notary public

第七十六条 在下列情况下，公证员、见证人和翻译人员及鉴定人员不得参加公证业务：

1. 若上述人员亲自参与或相关人员代表他 / 她参与；
2. 若上述人员与申请人之间有过婚姻关系；
3. 若上述人员与申请人有任何姻亲关系、三级血缘关系、直系亲缘关系、二级亲缘关系（包括）血缘关系或直系或旁系亲缘关系，以及与申请人一方之间的收养关系；
4. 若相关申请人是公证员的办事员或雇主；

5. If the concerned party is acting on behalf of the person as mentioned in the second, third and fourth point,

6. If the notary operation includes a deposition on one's own benefit or on the benefit of the person as mentioned in the second, third and fourth point.

5. 若相关申请人代表第二点、第三点和第四点所述的人；

6. 如第二点、第三点和第四点所述，公证业务包括为维护上述人员自身的利益或维护该申请人的利益所作的书面陈述。

First judge executing notary operations

Article 77 – in accordance with the article mentioned-above, if a notary public fails to execute notary operation and if there is no notary public available in that place, in accordance with the provisions of this law the first judge shall execute the notary operation, if the court of first instance is not present, judge of peace shall execute the notary operation.

执行公证业务的第一法官

第七十七条 依照前条规定，如果公证员不执行公证业务或没有公证员在场的，依照本法规定，第一法官应当执行公证业务，若无初审法院的，治安法官应当执行公证业务。

Other prohibition causes for witnesses:

Article 78 – The following persons can not be witnesses:

1. minors
2. incapacitated persons
3. according to the Legal Proceedings Law, persons who can not be heard as sworn witnesses
4. Clerk and employers of the notary public.

其他禁止作为见证人的原因

第七十八条 下列人员不得作为见证人：

1. 未成年人；
2. 无行为能力的人；
3. 依照《诉讼法》不能作为宣誓见证人被听取意见的人；
4. 公证员的办事员和雇主。

Documents required for operations by proxy

Article 79 – Those who wish to carry out notary procedures as deputy, parents, supervisors, substitute, representatives and heritors or on behalf of artificial persons such as companies or foundations are obliged to be able to present documents which, on the one hand, post their qualities and competences and, on the other hand, allow them to proceed to the desired operations. In addition to the paper of the original document, two other copies will be prepared without taxes or fees and will receive the descriptions of the operation as well as the date, the number and the place of delivery. One of these copies will be entrusted to concerned party and the other will be preserved by the body of notaries to be attached to the original document and the copies.

代理业务所需的文件

第七十九条 希望以代理身份进行公证程序的人，如父母、监护人、替补人员、代表和继承人或代表公司或基金会等的人，有义务提交表明他们的素质和能力及允许他们从事所希望的业务的文件。除原始文件外，还应当编写另外两份无须交税或收费的文件，将收到业务的详细说明、交付的日期、数量和地点记录进文件，并将其中一份交给申请人，另一份则附在原件和复印件上由公证机构保存。

Attachment of a photo

An article 80 – obligatory photo attachment procedure of the concerned person is shown in the regulation.

The notary public shall attach the photo person concerned to the relevant operation documents, if he considers

照片附件

第八十条 有关人员的必要照片附着程序载于本规章。

公证员应当依照业务的质量、有关人员的状况及其身份，或依照有关人员的要求（不包括第一节的范

it necessary for the quality of the operation, the state of the concerned person and his/her identity or upon the request of the concerned person excluding the extent of the first section.

围），将有关人员的照片附在相关业务文件上。

Protuberance, modification, termination, annulment and correction in notary operations

公证业务中的强调、修改、终止、废除和改正

Article 81 – regarding notary operations, protuberances without the signature of the concerned party and the approval of the notary public are not valid. Protrudes in handwritings are not acceptable.

第八十一条 在公证中，未经申请人签字、公证员批准的强调标注无效，即使手写亦无效。

After its completion, modification or termination and annulment or correction of a notary operation, under the condition of not changing the quality and the value of the previous work is possible through the execution of a new operation, same as the previous one.

一项公证业务完成后的修改或终止、废除或更正，在不改变先前工作的质量和价值的情况下，可通过执行一次新业务的方式来实现。

If the new operation is executed in other notary public office, this new notary public office shall send a copy of the new operation document to be attached to the previous operation document with a necessary explanation to the previous notary public office.

如果新业务在其他公证机构执行的，该新公证机构应当将新业务文件副本附在原业务文件上，并向原公证机构提供必要的说明。

Provisions of the notary operations

公证业务的规定

Article 82 – in accordance with the provisions of this law, certificated operations shall be official.

第八十二条 依照本法的规定，公证业务应当是正式的。

Legal operations executed by the notary publics in accordance with the second chapter of this part are valid until proven fraudulent.

公证员依照本部分第二章执行的公证业务在经证明属于欺诈之前是有效的。

In accordance with the third chapter of this part, signature authentication executed by the notary public is to certificate the authenticated signature belongs to the concerned person by means of the authentication of the signature and this operation shall not include the contents of the legal operations. The signature and the date are valid until proven fraudulent in those kinds of operations.

依照本部分第三章的规定，公证员进行的签名公证，是指通过对签名的鉴定，证明该签名属于申请人。签名和日期在这类业务中被证明属于欺诈之前都是有效的。

Notary operations excluding the provisions of the second and third section are valid until proven fraudulent.

除第二款和第三款规定的公证业务外，其他业务在被证明属于欺诈之前均有效。

Execution of the duty outside the notary public office

在公证机构以外履行职责

Article 83 – Notary publics execute notary operations in their notary public office. If the execution of the above-mentioned duty in the office causes delays or raises other kind of difficulties, the duty shall be executed outside the notary public office by showing the reason in the work documents.

第八十三条 公证员在公证机构执行公证业务。执行上述职务造成延期或者存在其他困难的，需要在公证机构以外执业的，应当在工作文件内说明理由并继续执行该业务。

The person authorized to sign shall have the same

被授权签字的人在进行业务时享有本法规定的

above-mentioned authority on the date of the operation.

权利。

SECOND CHAPTER
Regulation

第二章 行政法规

Form

形式

Article 84 – Notary publics execute the legal procedures by a minutes signed by other persons.

These minutes must have the following qualities:

1. Name and surname of the notary public and title of the notary public's office

2. Place and date of the procedures (in numbers and in writing)

3. (Amendment of 2/4/1998 – 4358/ Art. 3) ID card and address of the concerned party and if any of the translator, witness and expert and also tax ID card of the concerned party.

4. Minutes of concerned party regarding his/her true intentions

5. Participated parties signature and seal and signature of the notary public.

The original of the work document as prepared according to the aforementioned procedures is kept in the notary public's office and the copy of the document is given to the concerned party.

第八十四条 公证员执行法律程序时应当记录并签字。

该记录必须具备以下内容：

1. 公证员的名字、姓氏及公证机构的级别；

2. 执行程序的地点和日期（以数字和书面形式）；

3.（1998 年 4 月 2 日 -4358/ 第 3 条修订）相关申请人的身份证信息和地址，若有翻译员、见证人和鉴定人、申请人在场的，也应当记录他们的身份信息；

4. 关于申请人真实意图的记录；

5. 参与申请人的签字和公证员的盖章及签字。

按照上述程序编写的工作文件的原件保存在公证机构，将文件副本交给相关申请人。

Other registers in minutes

其他记录

Article 85 – in minutes there are registers regarding the acquaintance of the notary public with the concerned person, if not acquainted the source of the notary public's idea about the concerned persons personality. If the notary public can not reach a decision and execution of the operation is requested, means of proof shall be written to the minutes for identity proof and situation.

第八十五条 若无法知晓公证员与相关人员相识的方式，也应当在记录中登记公证员与相关人员的相识程度。公证员因此无法对被申请的业务作出决定并执行，应当将用于证明身份和情况的举证方法书写在笔录上。

Reading the minutes

阅读笔录

Article 86 – After writing down the declaration regarding the true intention of the person concerned the minutes is given to the person mentioned before.

The person concerned reads the minutes and if the contents are in accordance with his/her intentions he signs it after this matter is written.

第八十六条 在写下相关人员的真实意图后，应当将笔录交给本法规定的人阅读。

相关人员阅读记录，如果内容符合他 / 她的意思，那么他 / 她在阅读完毕后在笔录上签字。

If the person concerned is illiterate

如果相关人员是文盲

Article 87 – If the person concerned is illiterate, in the presence of the two witnesses the above-mentioned

第八十七条 如果相关人员是文盲，在有两名见证人在场的情况下，该相关人员向公证员陈述其意

person declares his/her intentions to the notary public. After the notary public writes down this declaration the minutes is read. The provisions of the other laws regarding the execution operation in the presence of the two witnesses are legally guaranteed.

Person concerned and witnesses sign this after declaring it is exactly written and this matter is written in the minutes.

Provision of the documents attached to the minutes

Article 88 – if the concerned person relates to a document in his/her declaration and this document is attached to the minutes then, this document becomes an integral part of the minutes. In accordance with the last section of the Article 84, during submission of the minutes copy; taking a copy of this document is upon the request on the person concerned.

Obligatory operations to be executed as arrangements

Article 89 – agreements and power of attorneys necessitates deed operations in terms of quality, and testament, conditional sale, real estate promise to sell, settlement deed, marriage contract, child adoption and acknowledgement, hereditary share agreement and other operations as prescribed by other laws arranged in accordance with the provisions of this chapter.

Validation Form

Article 90 – Under legal procedures notarization of the signature is carried out by a certificate of authenticity showing the signature belongs to the signing party.

Notarized signature of the original work document is given to the concerned party and a signed copy of the document is kept in the notary public's office.

Conditions of validation

Article 91 – validation is effective by signing in the presence of the notary public or accepting the signature belongs to the self by the person concerned.

Certificate of authenticity includes following matters

Article 92 – Certificate of authenticity must cover:

1. place and date of the operation (in figures and words),

2. (Changed: 2/4/1998 – 4358/art. 3) identity, address and tax identity number of the concerned person,

图。公证员把这份陈述记录下来后，当场宣读。由此遵循其他法律关于在两名见证人在场的情况下进行业务的规定。

相关人员和见证人在确认该记录完整且准确无误之后才签字。

笔录所附文件的提供

第八十八条 如果相关人员的陈述与一份文件有关，将该文件附在笔录之后，并且该文件成为笔录的组成部分。依照第八十四条最后一款，在提交笔录副本期间，根据相关人员的请求，可以提供本文件副本。

强制安排执行的业务

第八十九条 委托律师的协议和授权委托书关于契约的业务必须具有一定的质量，且必须执行遗嘱、有条件的买卖、房地产销售承诺、和解契约、婚姻合同、收养和确认子女、世袭股份协议以及其他依照本章规定安排的其他法定业务。

确认形式

第九十条 依照法定程序，签名公证应当由签字方申请人出具签名真实性证书。

原始工作文件经签名公证后，交给相关申请人，公证机构保存有签名的文件副本。

确认条件

第九十一条 在公证员面前签名或者由相关申请人核实属于本人的签名，具有确认效力。

有效力的公证书必须包含的内容

第九十二条 有效力的公证书必须包含以下内容：

1. 公证业务进行的地点和日期（以数字和文字表示）；

2.（修改：1998 年 4 月 2 日 -4358/ 第 3 条）相关人员的身份、地址及税务身份号码；

3. proof of identity , in case the notary public does not know the concerned person,

4. declaration if it is signed in presence or if it is signed outside and the concerned person accepts the signature belongs to him/her

5. the signature of the involved parties and the seal and the signature of the notary public.

3. 如果公证员不认识相关人员的，应包括身份证明；

4. 声明若是当场签名的，或者是在公证机构以外的地方签名的，相关人员应当核实属于他 / 她的签名；

5. 相关申请人的签名、印章和公证员的签名。

Seal, date, fingerprint and mark authentication

Article 93 – the provisions of this part is applied by comparison for notary authentication of the seal, date, fingerprint or marks replacing signatures.

印章、日期、指纹和标记鉴定

第九十三条 印章、日期、指纹和标记的公证鉴定，适用本部分的规定。

FOURTH CHAPTER
Giving copies

第四章 提供副本

Who can take copies?

Article 94 – copies of notary operations shall be only given to the concerned parties, legal representatives or agents or inheritors.

This copy shall be sent from the notary public office of another city by the hand of the notary public of the relevant place with the fee paid.

However, in accordance with the stipulations of the Turkish Civil Code; the copy of the testament shall not be given,unless opened, to persons other than the ones prepared the testament or the ones possess a special authority; the representative that carries the power of attorney authenticated by the notary public, in this regard.

谁能取得副本？

第九十四条 公证业务的副本，应当仅发给相关申请人、法定代表人、代理人或者继承人。

副本由相关地方的公证员亲自从另一个城市的公证机构寄出，并交纳费用。

但是，依照《土耳其民法典》的规定，遗嘱副本除非公开，否则不得提供给除遗嘱订立人或具有特别权力的人以外的人；在这方面，代理人持有的授权委托书由公证员认定。

Giving copies with the permission of the judge

Article 95 – Giving copies other than those mentioned-above depends upon the permission of the first judge or individual judge of peace.

According to the first section, if the documents to be given belong to the documents prepared in the consulates, the court of last residence in Turkey shall give the permission to the person that request the copy, in case the last residence is not determined, The Court of first instance shall give the permission

This permission is not subject to any expenditure or tax.

经法官允许提供副本

第九十五条 除上述规定以外，提供副本应当得到初审法官或个人治安法官的许可。

依照第一款，如果要提供的文件属于领事馆准备的文件，申请人在土耳其的最后居住地的法院应当准许其索取副本的请求，如果最后居住地无法确定，那么原讼法庭应当给予许可。

本项许可不受任何支出或税收方面的限制。

Giving a copy of a specified part

Article 96 – if the person concerned requests a copy of all or part of the documents he/she brought, the notary public shall write down all or a part of the requested doc-

提供特定部分的副本

第九十六条 如果相关人员要求提供其所带文件的全部或者部分副本的，公证员应当在保留文件原始形式的前提下，将所要求文件的全部或者部分誊写下

ument under the condition of protecting its original form and gives as man copies as the work owner requests.

来，并按照该文件所有人的要求提供副本。

Copy kept in the notary public office

Article 97 – one of the document copies is signed by the concerned person and shall be kept in the notary public office.

The copy kept shall be written in the copy to be given to the concerned person. By this way the returned copy shall be sealed and annotated.

存放于公证机构的副本

第九十七条 文件副本中的一份由相关人员签名，并保存在公证机构。

保存的副本应当在发给相关人员的副本中作相应的记录。通过这种方式退回的副本应当加盖印章并加注释。

Taking a copy by means of photocopying and by using similar methods

Article 98 – a copy can be taken by means of photocopying or by using similar methods. If there is any distortion on the original one, an explanation shall be made in certificate of authenticity

通过复印和类似方法获取副本

第九十八条 可以通过复印或使用类似方法取得副本。如果原件有失真的，应当在真实性公证书中作出注释。

A copy of the document in foreign language

Article 99 – if the requested copy of the document is in a foreign language, at first it is translated; then copy is taken in accordance with the provisions of this part and translation is attached to each copy and by this way put an annotation.

文件的外文副本

第九十九条 如果所要求提供的文件副本是外文的，那么首先应当翻译；然后按照本部分的规定复印，并在每一份副本上附上译文，且加上注释。

FIFTH CHAPTER
Other operations

第五章 其他业务

The extent of this chapter

Article 100 – notary operations excluding the first, the second and the fourth one is executed in accordance with the provisions of this chapter.

本章的范围

第一百条 除第一章、第二章、第四章以外的公证业务，依照本章的规定执行。

Minutes

Article 101 – the notary public minutes shall include following documents:

1. date and place of the minutes (in figures and words)
2. (Changed: 2/4/1998 – 4358/art. 3) identity, address and tax identity number of the concerned person,
3. proof of identity , in case the notary public does not know the concerned person,
4. subject of the minutes
5. the signature of the involved parties and the seal and the signature of the notary public.

Taking and giving entrust conditions are shown in the trust minutes.

记录

第一百零一条 公证记录应当包括下列文件：

1. 记录的日期和地点（以数字和文字表示）；
2. （修改：1998 年 4 月 2 日 -4358/ 第 3 条）有关人员的身份、地址及税务身份号码；
3. 如果公证员不认识相关人员的，那么需要身份证明；
4. 记录的主题；
5. 公证参与人的签名、印章和公证员的签名。

信托记录中显示了接受和给予委托的条件。

Operations recorded in minutes

Article 102 – the operations mentioned in the Article 61 and 62 of this law, are recorded in minutes.

Translation operation

Article 103 – notary public puts an annotation on the documents when translating from one language to another or one writing to another.

The identity and the address of the sworn translator must be included in this annotation and the notary public must write down the date, sign and seal the bottom of the document.

Translation outside the notary public office

Article 104 – if translation is not available in the notary public office where the person concerned is present, he/she can bring the document to a translation office in another place via the notary public office.

Commercial protest

Article 105 – non acceptance and nonpayment protest is in accordance with the provisions set out in the Turkish Commercial Law.

Official warning and written notice

Article 106 – in any kind of legal operations, official warning and written notice include as follows:

1. name, surname and address of the demandant and other party
2. subject of the warning and notice
3. signature of the demandant
4. notification annotation, sign and seal of the notary public, date (in figures and words)

The demandant can either write the official warning and written notice then take it to the notary public for notification or he/she can ask it from the notary public.

Approval of the book

Article 107 – notary publics approve the books as shown in the private law.

In cases where there is absence of consideration in private laws, total pages of the book are counted from the beginning until the end and each page is numbered and sealed regarding the book approval.

业务记录

第一百零二条 应当记录本法第六十一条和第六十二条所述的内容。

翻译业务

第一百零三条 公证员在从一种语言翻译到另一种语言，或一种文字翻译到另一种文字时，应当在文件上加上注释。

宣誓过的翻译人员的身份和地址必须包含于注释中，且公证员应当写下日期，并在文件的底部签名、盖章。

公证机构以外的翻译

第一百零四条 如果出具公证书的公证机构无法提供翻译，那么相关人员可以通过公证机构将文件送往其他翻译局。

商业拒付声明

第一百零五条 不接受和拒付声明适用《土耳其商法》的规定。

正式警告及书面通知

第一百零六条 在任何形式的法律业务中，正式警告和书面通知包括：

1. 申请者和其他申请人的名字、姓氏和地址；
2. 警告和通知的主题；
3. 申请者的签名；
4. 公证员的通知注释、签名、印章和日期（以数字和文字表示）。

申请者可以写正式警告和书面通知，然后将其交给公证员通知，或者也可以直接向公证员要求通知。

登记遵守

第一百零七条 公证员遵守私法中所列的登记要求。

在私法中没有考虑到的情况下，登记簿的总页数从开始到结尾计算且每一页都应有编号和盖章说明登记的批准。

Official registration

Article 108 – in officially registered operations; date and number of the operation, name and surname of the concerned parties and the quality of the operation are written below the sequence number in the register book.

正式登记

第一百零八条 在正式登记的业务中，业务的日期、数量，相关申请人的名字、姓氏和业务的质量，都应当登记在登记簿的对应序号下。

PART TEN
Revenues to be Distributed in Operations

第十部分
业务中的收入分配

Joint current accounts of the notary public offices

Article 109 – (Changed title of the tenth chapter with the title 16/11/1989 – 3588/art.6)

If there is more than one notary public office in the adjudication environment of the Court of first instance or if there is more than one adjudication environment of the Court of first instance in a municipal border of the city;

Under condition not to exceed %15 of any kind of fee and notary share amount gained from notary operations; the value of which is subject to charge and seal tax of each year is more than the amount resulted by multiplying indicator number 30.000 coefficient of officer salary as shown in Budget Law of the relevant year, the Notary Chamber Board shall deduct the fixed ratio then, the relevant notary public office shall trust the remaining amount in an (Joint current account of the notary public office) account in a national bank by within (5) days following the operation date at latest.

Joint current accounts of the notary public offices shall be trusted by the relevant chamber board therein, where the notary public offices are related to, before the beginning of the calendar year and this situation shall be notified to The Notaries Union of Turkey.

Notary publics can not avoid notary operations as shown in the above-mentioned section in any ways without legal reasons

公证机构共同往来账户

第一百零九条（更改后的第十章标题为1989年11月16日-3588/第6条）

在初审法院的审判区域中有一个以上的公证机构的，或者在本市的市级边界内有一个以上的初审法院的审判区域的；

在不超过从公证业务中获得的任何费用和公证份额总数的百分之十五的条件下，每年需缴纳费用和印章税的价值超过相关年度《预算法》规定的公务员薪金指标数30.000系数所产生的数额，公证员办公室委员会应当扣除相应年度的固定比率，相关公证机构最迟应当在五日内将剩余款项存入国家银行（公证机构共同往来账户）账户中。

公证机构的共同往来账户应当在日历年开始前，托管至公证机构的相关办公室委员会，并应当将托管情况通知土耳其公证员联合会。

公证员不得在没有正当理由的情况下以任何方式回避公证业务。

Joint current accounts in notary public office

Article 110 – (Repealed.16/11/1989 – 3588/art. 17)

公证机构共同往来账户

第一百一十条（废除1989年11月16日-3588/第17条）

Distribution of the revenue

Article 111 – (Changed clause 1. 16/11/1989 – 3588/art. 7)

According to the Article 109 money trusted in the joint account shall be paid equally every three months to

收入分配

第一百一十一条（修改后的第1条：1989年11月16日-3588/第7条）

依照第一百零九条的规定，共同账户所托管的款项，应当每三个月平均支付给负责此项职责的相关公

the relevant notary public or to the representative of the notary public therein, if any, charged with this duty. Payment conditions shall be fixed in annual statutory meetings.

Before the completion of the three months period as shown in the above-mentioned section, the share of the notary public; resigned for any kind of reasons and appointed notary public; transferred to another notary public office, shall be paid immediately to himself or to his inheritors without the completion of the period.

PART ELEVEN
Collecting Methods of Notary Fee, Tax, Charges and Duty

FIRST CHAPTER
NOTARY FEE

Fee tariff

Article 112 – notary operations fees calculated over charge and fees regarding; testament and deed of foundation preparation, writing, translation from one language to another or from one writing to another, comparison, official registration, entrust and operation exempt from charge, tax and duty mentioned in their law, and fees regarding authenticate the books and other charged operations as stipulated by law, amount of transportation fee of authorized representatives to sign with the notary publics shall be fixed in a tariff prepared by The Ministry of Justice after the decision of Notaries Union of Turkey.

In cases when notary operations have been executed via another notary public, the fee of the intermediary notary public shall be shown on the fee tariff.

(Changed last clause 16/11/1989-3588/art. 8)

All necessary changes in fees are made in March each year. Until the new tariff came into force the former tariff is valid.

Page count

Article 113 – page count fees are calculated according to the provisions of the charges law.

Paying expenses as advanced payments

Article 114 – notary expenses are collected as advance payments from the person concerned and deducted from the accrued amount. When the payment is not paid

证员或其中的公证员代表（如有）。支付条件应当在年度法定会议上确定。

在前款规定的三个月期间届满前，公证员的份额、因任何原因辞职的公证员、被指定的公证员、调任到另一公证机构的公证员，应当于期间届满前立即支付给相关人员或者其继承人。

第十一部分
公证费、税、手续费、关税的征收办法

第一章　公证费

收费标准

第一百一十二条　公证业务费用按手续费、其他费用计算；遗嘱、基础契约、书写、翻译，比较、正式登记、信托和免收的业务费用，以及法律规定的鉴定登记和其他收费业务、授权代表和公证员签名的交通费用等，在土耳其公证员联合会作出决定后，由司法部制定的收费标准确定。

由另一公证员执行公证业务的，应当在收费表上标明中介公证员的费用。

（修正后的最后一条：1989 年 11 月 16 日 -3588/第 8 条）

每年三月，政府会对收费作出必要的调整。在新收费标准生效之前，依照原先的收费标准执行。

页码计算

第一百一十三条　页码计算费用依照收费法的规定计算。

作为预付款支付费用

第一百一十四条　公证费由相关申请人预付的，应当从累计费用金额中扣除。未立即付款的，应当向申请人出具未加盖印章的收据，以换取预付款。

immediately, an unstamped receipt shall be given to the person concerned in return for advance payment.

Collecting final expenses

Article 115 – (Changed: 16/11/1989-3588/art.9)

The transcript of the final expenses shall be written on the original and copies of the operation documents in the notary public office and on the original copy of the document submitted to the person concerned. If the original copy is left at home then, the transcript of the final expenses shall be written on one of the copies submitted and two copies shall be prepared from the private receipts with sequence number issued by The Ministry of Finance and Customs. The transcript of expenses is separately shown as the original and the copies.

First page of the receipt shall be given to the person concerned who paid the expenses. The second page of the receipt shall be kept in the notary public office.

Apportionment of expenses

Article 116 – unless a legal prevision to the contrary or an agreement between the two parties exist, expenses of the operation shall be equally apportioned between the parties concerned.

Extra charges

Article 117 – (Changed clause 1: 16.11.1989-3588/ art. 10)

Within the limitation period regarding charges, if it is understood that, the notary public charged extra fee or charged extra notification fee; by multiplying relevant year of forty indicator number taken extra from each person with coefficient of officer salary as shown in Budget Law; any fees exceeding the equaled amount shall be returned to the person concerned by The Ministry of Justice and the said ministry shall inform The Union upon the notification to be sent to notary public for payment. If the person concerned is not paid within a month, despite the notary public charged the notification fee or the share of each person that is extra charged is same charged or less charged than the above-mentioned fee, it shall be sent to Notaries Union of Turkey. If the fee is not sent, The Union shall decide according to the stipulations regarding the execution of court order on the Execution and Bankruptcy Law.

收取最后费用

第一百一十五条（修改 1989 年 11 月 16 日 - 3588/第 9 条）

最后费用的记录应当登记在公证机构的业务文件原件和副本上，以及提交给相关人员的文件正本上。如果原件遗留在家中，那么最后费用的记录应当记录在所提交的其中一份副本上，同时准备两份由财政部和海关部出具的私人收据并标上序号。费用的记录分别以原件和副本列出。

收据的第一联应当发给支付费用的有关人员。收据的第二联应当保存在公证机构。

费用分摊

第一百一十六条　除非有相反的法律规定或双方之间有协议，否则业务费用应当在有关各方之间平均分摊。

额外费用

第一百一十七条（修改后的第 1 条：1989 年 11 月 16 日 - 3588/ 第 10 条）

在收费期限内，公证员收取额外费用或者收取额外通知费的，费用计算应当依照预算法规定的额外的人员薪金系数乘以相应的四十项指标数；超过同等数额的费用应当由司法部通知公证员退还给相关人员，且报告至土耳其公证员联合会。如果相关人员在一个月内未收到退款，即使公证员收取的通知费或每名额外收费的人的份额与上述费用相同或低于上述费用，也应当送交到土耳其公证员联合会。未缴纳费用的，由联合会依照执行法和破产法的规定作出决定。

Application of stipulations of the above-mentioned sections shall not hinder to award a disciplinary punishment.

前款规定的适用，不免除纪律处分。

SECOND CHAPTER
Collecting Methods of Charges, Tax and Duty

第二章　手续费、税及税的征收方法

Notary public share in return for receipt

公证员对票据业务的收费

Article 118 – prices of the charges, tax, and duty and paper holdings dues for notary operations and notary papers in accordance with the private laws (Changed expression: 30.12.2004-5281/art. 43-10-a) shall be collected in return for receipt.

第一百一十八条　公证业务和公证票据的手续费、税费和关税以及持有票据费依据私法的规定（变更表达：2004 年 12 月 30 日 -5281/ 第 43-10-a 条）收取，并出具收据。

Notary publics take a notary public share of three percent for charges, tax and duty they collect.

公证员收取百分之三的公证手续费、税费和关税。

This share is paid to the notary public in accordance with the stipulations regarding the payment of notary contribution.

该份额依照关于支付公证费的规定支付给公证员。

Payment of charges, tax and duty

缴纳的手续费、税费及关税

Article 119 – (Changed clause 1: 16/11/1989-3588/art. 11)

notary publics are obliged to notify the relevant tax office with a declaration on -prices of the charges, tax, and duty and paper holdings – that they collect in accordance with the Article 118 (Changed expression: 30.12.2004-5281/art.43-10-b) within the above-mentioned time period and pay it within the same time .

Declarations are prepared for two periods; first one starts from the 1st until the 15th and second one starts with the 16th until the end of the month. Declarations are submitted to the relevant offices following 7 working days of the 15thand last day of each month.

(Changed clause 3: 16/11/1989-3588/art. 11)

-collecting prices of the charges, tax, and duty and paper holdings –separate sums of declarations that belong to a relevant period (Changed expression: 30.12.2004-5281/art. 43-10-a), first and last daily fee number of the operations on the relevant dates must be written so as to show the total sum and must be prepared as three copies.

(Clause four: is repealed with 16/11/1989-3588/art. 17)

Notary public shall send the money that he/she is obliged to pay, via post office or bank post remittance to the relevant office within the period specified in the second section. In that case, remittance receipt shall be presented to the relevant office with the copies of the declaration.

第一百一十九条（修改后的第 1 款：1989 年 11 月 16 日 -3588/ 第 11 条）

公证员有义务通知有关税务机关，并在上述期间内，向有关税务机关申报其依照第一百一十八条收取的费用、税费和持有票据的费用（修改后的表述：2004 年 12 月 30 日 -5281/ 第 43-10-b 条）并在同一时间内缴纳税款。

申报分为两个阶段：第一阶段从第一天开始至第十五天，第二阶段从第十六天至月底止。申报应当在每月十五日和最后一天的七个工作日之后向有关办事处提交。

（更改第 3 款：1989 年 11 月 16 日 -3588/ 第 11 条）

收取手续费、税费和关税及持有票据的费用——属于相关时期的单独申报金额（更换表达：2004 年 12 月 30 日 -5281/ 第 43-10-a 条），必须在相关日期的第一次和最后一次业务的每日费用写上数目，以显示总金额，并必须准备三份副本。

（第 4 款：废除 1989 年 11 月 16 日 3588 号 / 第 17 条）

公证员应当在第二款规定的期限内，通过邮局或者银行汇款，将其必须支付的款项寄送到有关部门。且应当向有关部门提交汇款收据，并附上申报副本。

A copy and attached receipt copies of the two declaration copies that, the notary public shall submit to the relevant office, shall be kept in the said office. The other copy (covering costs shall be paid to the cashier) or (the receipt, covering the cost, sent by post office or bank post remittance shall be presented) annotations shall be returned to the notary public after it is signed and sealed. Notary public shall send this copy with the monthly work schedule, in accordance with the Article 71, to the Notaries Union of Turkey. Receipt for his payment from the relevant office shall be kept in his notary public office.

公证员向有关办事处提交的两份声明副本及其所附收据副本应当保存在该办事处。另一份应当在签字盖章后将其退回公证机构。公证员应当按照第七十一条的规定，将此副本连同每月工作时间表送交土耳其公证员联合会。公证员有关办事处付款的收据应当保存在公证机构。

The form and arrangement style of this declaration and application of this article shall be defined in the regulation that will be jointly prepared by the Ministry o Justice and the Ministry of Finance.

本条相关的申报、申请格式，由司法部和财政部共同制定的条例予以规定。

Additional charged payment

支付额外费用

Article 120 – if the notary publics fail to pay the prices of the charges, tax, and duty and paper holdings-to the relevant office within the period shown in Article 119 (Changed expression: 30.12.2004-5281/art. 43-10-c) or fail to transfer to the relevant office via post or bank within the specified period, they shall pay an additional charge of 10%, following first 30 days upon the completion of the last payment day and an extra additional charge of 2% subsequent each 30 days. This additional charged payment shall be paid to a national bank shown by the Notaries Union of Turkey; one of the 2 copies of the receipt shall be presented to the relevant office and prices of -the charges, tax, and duty and paper holdings – due (Changed expression: 30.12.2004-5281/art. 43-10-c) shall be paid. Unless the notary public can not present the receipt the collecting officer shall notify the state to the Notaries Union of Turkey.

第一百二十条 如果公证员未能在第一百一十九条规定的期限内向相关办事处支付手续费、税费和关税及持有票据的费用（修改后的表述：2004 年 12 月 30 日 -5281/ 第 43-10-c 条）或未能在规定期限内通过邮局或银行转账到有关办事处，那么应当在最后付款日结束后的第一个三十天之后再支付百分之十的额外费用，并在每三十天之后收取百分之二的额外费用。这笔额外的费用应当支付给土耳其公证员联合会指定的一家国家银行；两份收据副本中的一份应当提交给相关的办事处，且手续费、税费和关税及持有票据的费用也应当支付（更换表述：2004 年 12 月 30 日 -5281/ 第 43-10-c 条）。除非公证员不能出示收据，否则收费员应当将情况通知土耳其公证员联合会。

PART TWELVE
Responsibilities of the Notary Public’ s Offices

第十二部分
公证机构的职责

CHAPTER ONE
General Clauses

第一章 一般条款

Supervision and control authority

监督管理机构

Article 121 – The notary public’s offices are under the supervision and control of the Ministry of Justice and the Notaries Union of Turkey.

第一百二十一条 公证机构由司法部和土耳其公证员联合会监督和管理。

Inspection of the notary public's offices

Article 122 – The notary public's offices are under perpetual control of the Republic prosecutors and are inspected one time in a year at least. The notary public's offices next to the individual civil court of peace are subject to the inspections of the Republic Attorney General of the court of first instance to which those individual civil courts of peace are related.

(Changed clause 2: 16/11/1989 – 3588 / art. 12)

The notary public's offices are also inspected by the justice inspectors. The inspection is executed in accordance with the method and principles shown in the Regulation of the Inspection Board of the Ministry of Justice.

If necessary, the justice inspectors and the Republic prosecutors can take the documents, registries and volumes in the notary public's offices under protection in office.

(Additional clause: 16.11.1989-3588/art. 12)

The Notaries Union of Turkey executes its duty of supervision and control through a qualified union and the president or members of the board of directors of the Notary Public Chambers or the controlling committee that it will set up.

Constraining work ceasing

Article 123 – (Changed: 13.06.2000 – 4579 / art. 4)

In case of an act that constitutes a crime, the notary publics who are subject to an inquiry or a prosecution directed by the Justice inspector, Republic prosecutor, examining magistrate or the criminal court are, if considered necessary by the Ministry of Justice for the safety of the inquiry or prosecution, constrained to cease work until the conclusive decision of the said inquiry or prosecution.

If the notary public who was constrained to cease work during the inquiry or prosecution is condemned, in the end of the prosecution, with one of the crime cited in the second clause of the article 7, then, the constrained work ceasing continues until the conclusive decision.

The notary public who in accordance with the first clause was constrained to cease work during the inquiry or prosecution and who in the end of the prosecution is condemned for one of the crime showed in the second clause is constrained to cease work without waiting the conclusive decision. The provision of the second clause is also applied in this case.

检查公证机构

第一百二十二条　公证机构由共和国检察官永久管理，且至少在一年内接受一次检查。个人民事法院管辖区域内的公证机构须接受与之有关的一审法院的共和国总检察长的检查。

（修改后第 2 款：1989 年 11 月 16 日 -3588/ 第 12 条）

司法监察员也应当检查公证机构。检查依照司法部检查委员会条例所示的方法和原则进行。

若有必要，司法监察员和共和国检察官可以将公证机构的文件、档案和卷宗置于办事处的保护之下。

（增补条文：1989 年 11 月 16 日 -3588/ 第 12 条）

土耳其公证员联合会通过具有资格的工会和公证机构办公室委员会主任或成员或其将设立的管理委员会履行监督和管理职责。

被停止工作

第一百二十三条（更改：2000 年 6 月 13 日 –4579/ 第 4 条）

在构成犯罪的行为中，受到司法监察员、共和国检察官、地方预审法官或刑事法院指示的调查或起诉的公证员，若司法部认为为了调查或起诉的安全，则有必要停止该公证员的工作直至上述调查或起诉作出最后决定。

如果在调查或起诉期间被迫停止工作的公证员在起诉结束时被宣告有罪，且其中一项罪行符合第七条二款，那么受限制的工作将继续终止直至最后决定作出。

公证员如依照第一款在调查或起诉期间被迫停止工作，并在起诉结束时因第二款所列罪行之一而被定罪，则不得等待最后决定即停止工作。第二款也适用于此种情况。

The mode of prosecution

Article 124 – In cases during which an investigation appears necessary concerning the notary public, the Minister of Justice get the inquiry done by the justice inspectors or Republic prosecutors.

If a complaint is made to the Justice inspectorships or to the Republic Attorney General or if those authorities are aware of an illegal operation of the notary public, then they will proceed to the necessary inquiry and will send the document they prepared to the Ministry.

The third clause of the article 122 is also applied in case of inquiry.

One sample of the parts of the said document, prepared in accordance with the here in above mentioned clauses, which cover actions which do not constitute a crime but require a disciplinary prosecution is sent to the Disciplinary Committee of the Notaries Union of Turkey by the Ministry of Justice.

起诉方式

第一百二十四条 在有必要对公证员进行调查的情况下，司法部应当让司法监察员或共和国检察官进行调查。

如果有人向司法监察局或共和国总检察长举报，或者这些机关知晓公证员的非法业务，应当进行必要的调查，并将准备的文件送交司法部。

第一百二十二条第三款也适用于调查此类情况。

依照上述条款编写的所述文件中的一个样本，若涉及不构成犯罪但需要纪律处分的行为，司法部应当把该样本送交土耳其公证员联合会纪律委员会。

CHAPTER TWO
Disciplinary Penalties to be imposed upon the Notary Publics

第二章　对公证员的纪律处分

General points

Article 125 – In order to get a notary public service as required, the notary publics who act contrary to the seriousness and the honor of the profession or who fail to fulfill their duties or who fulfill their duties imperfectly or who commit actions that undermine the confidence necessary for their duties are punished with the penalties indicated in the following article in accordance with the quality of the situation and the degree of importance.

通用要点

第一百二十五条 为了得到公证业务，违反专业的严肃性和信用的公证员，或不履行职责的公证员，或履行职责有瑕疵的公证员，或泄漏机密信息的公证员，应当依照情况的严重性程度，处以下列条款所述的惩罚。

The disciplinary penalties

Article 126 – The disciplinary penalties to be imposed upon the notary publics are as follows:

A) Warning: Consists of a paper that indicates to the notary public to be more attentive.

B) Censure: Consists of a paper that indicated to the notary public that he/she is defective in his/her duty or action.

C) Fine: Is between 250 liras and 5000 liras.

D) Temporary dismissal: Consists of a dismissal which is between one month and six months. The notary public's quality is reserved.

E) Get out of business: To dismiss for the purpose of no reappointment.

纪律处分

第一百二十六条 对公证员的纪律处分如下：

（A）警告：由一份文件组成，警告公证员需更加审慎；

（B）谴责：在文件上载明公证员在履职或行为上有缺陷；

（C）罚款：二百五十里拉以上到五千里拉以下；

（D）暂停执业：期间为一个月至六个月，但保留其作为公证员的资格；

（E）停业：解雇且不再被复职。

The effect of the previous penalties

Article 127 – If the notary public is condemned two times by the article 157 and in other cases where the law orders, it is imperative to impose “the penalty to get out of business” to the notary public.

If a notary public, who has received a disciplinary penalty, commits in five years an action or behavior which requires the same disciplinary penalty, then the heavier penalty of the list indicated in the article 126 is imposed.

In so far, except the clause 2, the Disciplinary Committee freely appreciates the penalty without being tied by the order. Also, in case of second clause, a heavier penalty is still possible.

先前处罚的效力

第一百二十七条 依照第一百五十七条，如果公证员受到两次谴责，除法律规定的其他情况以外，必须对该公证员处以“停业处罚”。

如果受到纪律处分的公证员在五年内进行的行为或活动受到同样的纪律处分，那么对其行为依照第一百二十六条的规定加重处罚。

到目前为止，除第二款外，纪律委员会在不受命令约束的情况下自由行使处罚权力。此外，就第二款而言，仍有可能加重刑罚。

Right of Defense

Article 128 – At the disciplinary prosecutions concerning the notary publics, it is imperative to notify the imputed matter clearly and in written, to demand of the written defense and to give for this defense at least ten days.

辩护权

第一百二十八条 在对公证员的纪律处分中，必须以书面形式明确通知其被归责的事由，并要求其书面答辩，且给予至少十日的答辩时间。

Actions and behaviors before becoming a notary public and situation of those who have quitted the notary public’s offices

Article 129 – The actions and behaviors of a person before his notary public do not require a disciplinary prosecution if they do not require the penalty to get out of business.

The departure of the notary public from the notary public’s office cannot prevent the disciplinary prosecution proceeded upon his actions during his notary public service.

成为公证员前的行为和活动及离开公证机构后的行为和活动

第一百二十九条 一个人在成为公证员之前的行为和活动，如果不是被处以停业处罚，就不需要受到纪律处分。

公证员离开公证机构并不能阻碍其在担任公证员服务期间的行为受到纪律追诉。

Prosecution authority and prosecution’s decision

Article 130

– The disciplinary prosecution concerning the notary publics is performed by the Disciplinary Committee of the Notaries Union of Turkey.

Upon the complaints made concerning the president or members of the committee, the concerned can not assist to the committee’s works regarding this prosecution. For this reason, the missing memberships will be completed by their substitutes, in case of obstacle, by the most senior notary public without obstacle who is charged in the Board of the Notaries Union of Turkey.

Upon the arrival of the complaint, the committee will

检察机关与起诉的决定

第一百三十条

对公证员的纪律检查由土耳其公证员联合会纪律委员会进行。

在接到有关委员会主席或成员关于相关人员无法协助委员会进行这项检控工作的投诉后，该相关人员将被停止工作，空缺的职位将由土耳其公证员联合会委员会的最高级公证员替补。

在接到投诉后，委员会应当先决定该投诉或谴责

firstly decide whether the complaint or denouncement is worth to prosecute.

是否适当。

Operation to be done after the decision

决定后须进行的操作

Article 131 – If the Disciplinary Committee of the Notaries Union of Turkey decides whether the complaint or denouncement is worth to prosecute, it notifies this decision to the Republic prosecutor of the place where the notary public is working and to the complainant, if any.

第一百三十一条 若土耳其公证员联合会纪律委员会认为该控告或谴责值得起诉，则应当将起诉的决定通知公证员工作所在地的共和国检察官和申诉人（如有）。

The Republic prosecutor or the complainant can make an objection to this decision via a petition which is addressed directly or through the Notaries Union of Turkey to the Ministry of Justice in 15 days which follows the notification. The Notaries Union of Turkey immediately transfers all the received petitions to the Ministry of Justice. Upon objection, the Ministry examines the disciplinary record to be brought and makes a decision. This decision of the Ministry is definitive.

共和国检察官或申诉人可以直接或通过土耳其公证员联合会在通知后十五日内向司法部提出反对这一决定的请求。土耳其公证员联合会立即将收到的所有申请书转交司法部。如有异议，该部将审查提交的纪律记录并作出终局决定。

If the Committee has decided to prosecute the complaint or the denouncement, or the decision which indicated that there is no need for prosecution is undone by the Ministry of Justice, it is proceeded to the prosecution of the notary public who is complained about.

如果委员会决定起诉该控告或谴责，或司法部撤销表明没有必要起诉的决定，那么将对被控告的公证员进行起诉。

If the decisions that indicate that there is no ground for prosecution are rendered definitive, the reexamination of the same subject depends upon the availability of the new evidences and the fact that a three-year deadline is not exceeded starting from the date of the definitive decisions.

如果表明没有起诉理由的决定是最终确定的，那么对同一事件的重新审查取决于出现新的证据以及出现从最终决定之日起不超过三年最后期限的事实。

Prosecution method

起诉程序

Article 132 – After the decision to begin a prosecution, the Disciplinary Committee of the Notaries Union of Turkey designates one of his members for examining the affair.

第一百三十二条 在决定开始起诉后，土耳其公证员联合会纪律委员会指定其一名成员审查该事件。

This member collects evidences, takes the testimony on oath of whom he considers necessary and after demanding the pleadings, addresses the file together with a report to the Committee. It is imperative that this report be given in three months at maximum. However, if it is convinced that this is necessary, the Committee can prolong this time by two months.

该成员收集证据、宣誓过后进行作证（他认为有必要），并在要求答辩之后，必须将报告连同档案一起在三个月内提交给委员会。但是，若有必要，委员会可以将这一时限延长两个月。

The Committee must conclude the affair at the latest in two months which follows the entrusting the report.

委员会最迟必须在委托报告后的两个月内完成这一事务。

Trial

审判

Article 133 – Following the completion of the exam-

第一百三十三条 在检察官完成审查并向土耳其

ination made by the prosecuting member and his consigning of his report to the Disciplinary Committee of the Notaries Union of Turkey, if the notary public has demanded, the Committee decides that the examination be performed together with a trial. The trial is executed secretly.

公证员联合会纪律委员会提交报告之后，如果公证员提出要求，那么委员会将决定在执行审判的同时进行检查。

In spite of the invitation notification, if the notary public does not come or send a deputy to the trial, he continues to trial in contumacy. In so far, it is imperative to write on the notification that in case of no appearance the trial will be performed in contumacy.

虽然发出了邀请通知，但是如果公证员缺席或不派一名代表参加审判，他将因藐视法庭而被继续进行审判。到目前为止，必须在通知上写上如果没有出庭，审判将以藐视法庭处理。

The trial starts by the hearing of the report read by the member himself who made the first examination.

审判的开始是听取第一次被调查的成员宣读报告。

Presentation of the evidences, estimation and majority rule

证据、评判和多数规则的提出

Article 134 – The Disciplinary Committee of the Notaries Union of Turkey appreciates and designates in which manner the evidences will be shown and examined without being tied by demands, abandons and the previous decisions.

The decisions are made by the absolute majority.

第一百三十四条 土耳其公证员联合会纪律委员会鉴别并指定证据将以何种方式展示和审查，而不受要求、放弃和先前决定的约束。

该决定是由绝对多数作出的。

Hearing of witness and expert

听取见证人和鉴定人的意见

Article 135 – The calling of the witnesses or experts to the trial, or the hearing of them by a member, or to be contented with the reading of their written deposition is decided by the Disciplinary Committee of the Notaries Union of Turkey.

However, if the evidence of the examined matter depends uniquely upon a person's knowledge, this witness is heard in any case.

第一百三十五条 传唤见证人或鉴定人参加审判，或由其中一名成员听讯，或宣读他们的书面证词，由土耳其公证员联合会纪律委员会决定。

然而，如果被审查事项的证据完全取决于见证人的目睹情况，那么在任何情况下都会听取该见证人的证词。

Trial Record

审判记录

Article 136 – The trial record is composed by a member designated by another person. The records concerning the persons who were heard before or out of the trial must be read at trial.

第一百三十六条 审判记录由另一人指定的成员写成。审判前或审判结束听取的相关人员的记录必须在审判时宣读。

Execution of the rogatory letter

调查委托书的执行

Article 137 – The rogatory order is executed by the president of the notary public chamber which is the closest to the person to be heard or by a deputy designated by him.

第一百三十七条 调查令由距离被调查人最近的公证办公室主任或他指定的一名代理人执行。

Writ of summons for witnesses and experts

传召见证人及鉴定人的令状

Article 138 – The witnesses and experts are called in

第一百三十八条 依照《通知法》的规定传唤见

accordance with the provisions of the Law of Notification.

Concerning the one who does not appear in the court though duly called, or who keeps clear of testimony, expertise or swearing without a legal reason, it can be demanded from the court of first instance situated in the same place of the said person's domicile to impose him/her a fine between 20 liras and 200 liras, excluding the fees. Additionally, upon demand, penal court of peace of Ankara decides to bring the witnesses by force.

The witness who is punished in accordance with the provision of the hereinabove clause and who is recalled in order to not being brought by force and the expert who is recalled after being punished are punished again if they do not appear.

The justice of the peace decides both to fine or to bring by force in accordance with the record sample of the Disciplinary Committee.

Also, the member who in accordance with the article 132 was designated by the Disciplinary Committee of the Notaries Union of Turkey has the authority to request from the penal magistrate to bring by force the witness who did not appear.

证人和鉴定人。

对于虽被正式传唤但没有出庭，或在没有正当理由的情况下不提供证词、专门知识或宣誓的人，可以要求位于该人住所同一地点的初审法院对其处以二十里拉至二百里拉的罚款，但不包括其他费用。此外，应当要求安卡拉治安刑事法院以强制力传唤见证人。

依照上述条款的规定受到惩罚的见证人，以及在受到处罚后被召回的鉴定人，如果他们拒不出庭，将再次受到处罚。

治安法官依照纪律委员会的记录样本决定对其处以罚款或使用强制力。

此外，依照第一百三十二条被土耳其公证员联合会纪律委员会指定的成员有权要求刑事治安官以强制力传唤没有出庭的见证人。

Rejection and refusal of the President and members of the Disciplinary Committee of the Notaries Union of Turkey

土耳其公证员联合会纪律委员会主席和成员的剔除和拒绝

Article 139 – The President and the members of the Disciplinary Committee of the Notaries Union of Turkey can be rejected and refused because of the reasons indicated in the Code of Criminal Procedures.

The demand of rejection is examined with the participation of the members other than the one who the demand is about.

If the Committee can not convene about the rejection or the refusal, then the operation in pursuant of the clause 2 of the article 130 is performed.

第一百三十九条 土耳其公证员联合会纪律委员会主席和成员可因《刑事诉讼法》所述理由被排除和拒绝。

排除的要求是在所涉成员以外的成员参与下审查的。

如果委员会不能就排除或拒绝举行会议，那么依照第一百三十条第二款进行处理。

Decision and objection

决定和反对

Article 140 – One sample of the decision that the Disciplinary Committee of the Notaries Union of Turkey takes in the end of the examination with our without trial is notified to the concerned and to the Republic prosecutor situated in the place where the notary public is.

The concerned or the Republic prosecutor can make an objection to this decision via a petition which is addressed directly or through the Notaries Union of Turkey

第一百四十条 土耳其公证员联合会纪律委员会在审查结束时作出决定，并通知有关人员和位于公证员所在地的共和国检察官。

有关人员或共和国检察官可在收到通知后十五日内直接或通过土耳其公证员联合会向司法部提出反对这一决定的请求。

to the Ministry of Justice in 15 days which follows the notification.

Objection examination authority and approval of the decisions

Article 141 – The Disciplinary Committee of the Notaries Union of Turkey addresses the entire file by the end of the objection period to the Ministry of Justice; if it is objected to the Committee's decision, the objection petition is also addressed to the Ministry.

The decision becomes absolute with the approval of the Ministry of Justice.

The Ministry notifies the decisions to be taken in accordance with the clauses mentioned hereinabove to the concerned and the Notaries Union of Turkey and addresses the file to the Notaries Union of Turkey.

The concerned or the Notaries Union of Turkey can make an objection to the Council of State against the decision of the Ministry.

The Committee must agree with the decision to quash of the Ministry. Even after the decision on annulment, the provisions of the first and second clauses are applied. If, in spite of the annulment, the Committee takes an insistent decision based on the old decision, then the Ministry takes the necessary disciplinary decision ex officio. This decision is definitive. In so far, those who are showed in the forth clause can make an objection to the Council of State against the decision. The provision of the article 164 is reserved.

The Ministry can examine, if it considers necessary, the disciplinary records to be brought from the Notaries Union of Turkey.

反对审查机构和批准的决定

第一百四十一条 土耳其公证员联合会纪律委员会在反对期结束前向司法部提交全部档案；若反对委员会的决定，则一并向司法部提出反对请求。

经司法部批准，该项决定成为最终决定。

司法部将依照上述条款作出的决定通知有关人员和土耳其公证员联合会，并将档案送交土耳其公证员联合会。

相关人员或土耳其公证员联合会可就司法部的决定向国务院提出异议。

委员会必须同意撤销该司法部的决定。即使在作出废止决定之后，也适用第一款和第二款的规定。如果尽管废止了该决定，委员会仍依照先前的决定作出了一项坚持的决定，那么该司法部将依职权作出必要的纪律决定。且该决定是最终确定的。到目前为止，第四款所列的人可以反对国务院的决定。保留第一百六十四条的规定。

该司法部如认为必要，可审查土耳其公证员联合会提交的纪律记录。

The influence of the penalty inquiry and prosecutions upon the disciplinary penalties

Article 142 – The condemnation or acquittal of the notary public at the end of a prosecution does not represent an obstacle to impose him/her a disciplinary penalty.

However, the disciplinary prosecution concerning the notary public is kept waiting until the inquiry about the act that requires a disciplinary operation or decision reaches a definitive decision or a verdict.

刑罚调查与起诉对纪律处罚的影响

第一百四十二条 起诉结束时对公证员予以谴责或宣告无罪，并不影响对公证员处以纪律处分。

但是，对公证员的纪律起诉应当一直等到对需要采取纪律行动或作出决定的行为作出调查结果时，才能作出最后决定或裁决。

The application of disciplinary penalties

Article 143 – The disciplinary penalties are not applied until they become absolutes.

纪律处罚的适用

第一百四十三条 纪律处罚在成为绝对处罚之前不适用。

Witness and expert fees

Article 144 – In return of the time wasted and the effort made, an adequate payment can be provided to every witness and expert called by the Disciplinary Committee of the Notaries Union of Turkey. Travel fees and a daily wage are provided to the ones who have to travel because of the writ of summons.

Those fees are recovered from the party that is unjust. The fees which cannot be charged to anyone are in the responsibility of the Notaries Union of Turkey.

Execution of the disciplinary penalties, mode of payment of fines and various depenses

Article 145 – The penalties other than fine are executed by the Ministry of Justice.

The decisions of the Disciplinary Committee of the Notaries Union of Turkey that concern the payment of fines and fees are executed by the Notaries Union of Turkey in accordance with the provisions of the Execution and Bankruptcy Law that are clarify about the execution of the sentences. Those payments are income to the Notaries Union of Turkey.

Debt enforcement is executed by a lawyer to whom the President of the Union will give a proxy in accordance with general clauses.

CHAPTER THREE
Disciplinary penalties to impose upon notary public interns

Disciplinary penalties

Article 146 – The disciplinary penalties to impose upon the notary public interns are as follows:

A) Warning: Consists of a paper that indicates to the intern to be more attentive.

B) Censure: Consists of a paper that indicated to the intern that he/she is defective in his/her duty or action.

C) Wage cut: Consists of a cut which is no higher than the half of the intern's wage.

D) Get out of the internship: Consists to get the intern out of the internship in order to not get him back to the internship and to the notary public profession.

The provision of the article 127 is also relatively applied to the notary public intern.

见证人和鉴定人的费用

第一百四十四条 作为花费时间和精力的回报，可向土耳其公证员联合会纪律委员会传唤的每一名见证人和鉴定人提供足够的报酬。因传唤而必须远行的人，可获得旅费和每日工资。

上述费用由有过错的一方支付。不能向任何人收取的费用由土耳其公证员联合会负责。

执行纪律处罚、缴付罚款及各种开支的方式

第一百四十五条 罚款以外的处罚由司法部执行。

土耳其公证员联合会纪律委员会关于支付罚款和费用的决定，由土耳其公证员联合会依照《执行和破产法》阐明的执行条款的规定执行。执行收到资金作为土耳其公证员联合会的收入。

债务强制执行由一名律师执行，联邦总统将依照总则向该律师提供一份授权委托书。

第三章 对公证实习生施加纪律处分

纪律处分

第一百四十六条 对公证实习生的纪律处分形式如下：

（A）警告：向实习生表示需更加审慎；

（B）谴责：向实习生表明他/她在履职或行动上有缺陷；

（C）减薪：包括不高于实习生工资一半的减薪；

（D）离开实习：包括让实习生离开实习岗位，避免其回到实习和公证职业。

第一百二十七条的规定也适用于公证实习生。

Committee to impose the disciplinary penalty and objection

Article 147 – The disciplinary penalties concerning the notary public interns are also imposed by the Disciplinary Committee of the Notaries Union of Turkey.

The provisions regarding to the disciplinary acts and decision of the notary publics are also applied exactly to the interns. In so far, get out of the internship penalty of this section fulfills the get out of business penalty of the notary publics.

委员会施加纪律处分及异议

第一百四十七条 土耳其公证员联合会纪律委员会也对公证实习生进行纪律处分。

关于公证员的纪律行为和有关决定的规定也完全适用于实习生。到目前为止，从这一节的实习处罚中脱离的亦即脱离公证员业务的处罚。

CHAPTER FOUR
Disciplinary penalties to impose upon the notary public clerks and clerk candidates

Disciplinary penalties

Article 148 – The disciplinary penalties to impose upon the notary public clerks and the clerk candidates are as follows:

A) Warning: Consists of a paper that indicates to the notary public clerk and candidate to be more attentive.

B) Censure: Consists of a paper that indicated to the clerk or candidate that he/she is defective in his/her duty or action.

C) Wage cut: Consists of a cut which is no higher than the half of the clerk or candidate's wage.

D) Get out of the business: Consists to get the clerk or candidate out of the internship in order to not get him back to the internship and to the notary public profession.

The provision of the article 127 is also relatively applied to the notary public clerks and clerk candidates.

第四章 对公证办事员和办事员候选人施加的纪律处分

纪律处分

第一百四十八条 对公证办事员和办事员候选人的纪律处分形式如下：

（A）警告：向公证办事员、办事员候选人表示需更加审慎；

（B）谴责：向办事员或候选人表明他／她履职或行动有缺陷；

（C）减薪：包括不高于办事员或候选人工资一半的减薪；

（D）退出：包括让办事员或候选人退出实习，以免他回到实习和公证行业。

第一百二十七条的规定也适用于公证办事员、办事员候选人。

Authority to impose the disciplinary penalty

Article 149 – The notary public clerk or candidates receive disciplinary penalties from the notary public with whom they work.

Notary public must demand the pleadings of the clerk or candidate before taking the decision.

实施纪律处分的权力

第一百四十九条 公证办事员或候选人受到与其合作的公证员的纪律处分。

公证员在作出决定前，必须要求办事员或候选人提出答辩状。

Objection

Article 150 – Notary public notifies the decision made concerning any clerk or clerk candidate to the concerned one and the Republic Prosecutor.

Concerned clerk or candidate and the Republic Prosecutor can make an objection to the Disciplinary Committee of the Notaries Union of Turkey against this decision

异议

第一百五十条 公证员向相关人员和共和国检察官通报关于对相关的任何办事员或办事员候选人作出的决定。

有关办事员或候选人及共和国检察官可在十五日内向土耳其公证员联合会纪律委员会提出反对这项决定的申请。若无人反对，公证员将会在反对期结束时

in fifteen days. Even if there is no objection, notary public addresses the file concerning the decision to be examined to the Disciplinary Committee of the Notaries Union of Turkey at the end of the objection period. The decisions of the Committee are definitive.

The concerned ones' right to apply to the Council of State is reserved.

向土耳其公证员联合会纪律委员会提交关于待审查决定的档案。委员会的决定是最终确定的。

保留有关人员向国务院提出申请的权利。

CHAPTER FIVE
Offences to be Committed by Notary Public, Notary Public Assistants with Temporal Authority, Notary Public Deputies and Clerks and Clerk Candidates or Committed Against Them

第五章 由公证员、拥有临时权力的公证员助理、公证员代理人、办事员及办事员候选人所犯的罪行

Offences relating to duty

Article 151 – The offences that Notary Public, Notary Public Assistants with Temporal Authority, Notary Public Deputies and Clerks and Clerk Candidates have committed during their duty in the notary public's office or that Notary public who were in charge in the organs of the Notaries Union of Turkey have committed during or because of those duties are subject to be penalized in accordance with the provisions of the Turkish Criminal Law concerning the Civil servants and the quality of their acts.

If a person who is no notary public is elected to the General Secretarial of the Notaries Union of turkey or to the accountancy, the provision of the clause mentioned hereinabove is also applied to those persons.

与职责有关的罪行

第一百五十一条 公证员、有临时权力的公证员助理、公证员代理人、办事员和办事员候选人在公证机构任职期间所犯的罪行，或公证员在土耳其公证员联合会机构负责职务期间或因职责而犯下的罪行，应当依照《土耳其刑法》中关于对公务员及其行为的规定予以惩处。

有非公证员的人如果当选为土耳其公证员联合会总秘书或会计人员，上述条款的规定也适用于这些人。

Offences committed against the officers

Article 152 – The offences committed against the persons mentioned in the article hereinabove during or because of their duties are be penalized in accordance with the provisions of the Turkish Criminal Law concerning the offences committed against the Civil servants.

对公务员所犯的罪行

第一百五十二条 依照《土耳其刑法》关于对公务员所犯罪行的规定，对上述各条所述人员在职务期间或因其职务而犯下的罪行予以惩处。

Authorization for prosecution

Article 153 – The ability to prosecute the notary publics due to the offences they committed during or because of their duty depends upon the authorization granted by the Ministry of Justice.

授权起诉

第一百五十三条 由司法部授权起诉对公证员由于在工作期间或因其职责所犯的罪行。

The mode of prosecution

Article 154 – The file which is prepared by the Justice Inspectors or Republic Prosecutors is entrusted to the

起诉方式

第一百五十四条 司法监察员或共和国检察官将编写的档案交给司法部刑事事务局。如果在审查结束

GeneralDirectorate of Penal Affairs of the Ministry of Justice. If at the end of the examination, it is considered that there is need for prosecution, then the file is addressed to the Republic Attorney General of the Heavy Penal Court which is the closest to the Heavy Penal Court of the place where the offence is committed.

In five days, the Republic Prosecutor issues his/her indictment and addressed the file to the Heavy Penal Court who will decide whether the case is need of final inquiry.

In accordance with the Turkish Criminal Law, one sample of the indictment is notified to the notary public about who the prosecution is. Upon this notification and in the time indicated at the law, if the notary public demands the collection of some evidences or makes an acceptable will, those claims are taken into consideration. If necessary, the inquiry is deepened by the President.

The trials of the notary publics concerning whom the final inquiry decision is taken are executed in the Heavy Penal Court where the offence is committed.

Right to objection

Article 155 – In accordance with the general clauses, the Republic Prosecutor or the accused can make an objection against the decision made by the courts indicated in the article 154 and which decides that there is no need for arrest or release or the final inquiry.

This objection is examined by the Heavy Penal Court which is the closest to the one that made the objected decision, excluding the Heavy Penal Court where the offence is committed.

Red-handed case that requires heavy penalty

Article 156 – In case of red-handed activity which requires heavy penalty, the preparation and the first inquiry is executed in accordance with the general clauses.

Acting against prohibitions

Article 157 – The notary publics who act against the provisions of the clause 3 of the article 50 receive, for the first time, a heavy fine between 1 000 liras and 5 000 liras. In case of recurrence, the fine cannot be less than 3 000 liras.

He who intervenes in the hereinabove written act of the notary public receives a heavy fine between 500 liras and 2 000 liras.

If the mediator is a person who is considered as an

时，认为有必要起诉，那么将档案寄给距离犯罪发生地最近的重刑法院的共和国总检察长。

五日后，共和国检察官发出起诉书，并将案卷送交重刑法院，且由后者决定是否需要进行最后调查。

依照《土耳其刑法》，向公证员提供一份公诉书的副本。在提供后，并在法律规定的时间内，公证员需要收集某些证据或作出可接受的遗嘱的要求将得到考虑。如有必要，负责人将深入调查。

对被作出最后调查决定的公证员的审判在罪行发生的重刑法院进行。

异议权

第一百五十五条　依照总则，共和国检察官或被告可对法院依照第一百五十四条中作出的无须逮捕、释放或最后调查的决定提出异议。

由距离作出该决定的法院最近的重刑法院审查该反对意见，但犯罪地的重刑法院除外。

需要重罚的当场抓获的罪行

第一百五十六条　对需要从重处罚的现场抓获的罪行，依照总则准备和执行第一次调查。

违反禁令的行为

第一百五十七条　第一次违反第五十条第三款规定的公证员将被处以一千里拉以上五千里拉以下的罚款。如有再犯，罚款不得少于三千里拉。

凡公证员犯有涉及本法规定的行为，将被处以五百里拉以上二千里拉以下的罚款。

如果调解人是依照《土耳其刑法》而被认为是公

officer by the application of the Turkish Criminal Law or is a notary clerk or a clerk candidate, he/she is punished in accordance with the clause 1.

Those officers or various charged who are charged in public and private foundations which are part of the protocol arranged in pursuant to the paragraph 12 of the article 166 of this law but who act and behave against the essential of the said protocol and the notary publics who are a party to this crime are punished in accordance with the first clause of this article if their acts and behaviors do not require a heavier penalty.

Fraudulent acts of the notary publics

Article 158 – The notary publics, notary clerks and clerk candidates who arrange documents with an old date, reserve numbers in the daybook, commit fraudulent acts in the declarations which constitute the basis of the tax, stamp tax, contract or various fees or in the quittances which are attached to those declarations receive an imprisonment between three years and five years and a heavy fine between 1 000 liras and 3 000 liras.

Acts against the provisions of the tenth section

Article 159 – (Changed clauses I and II: 16.11.1989 – 3588/art. 13)

I – The notary publics who do not transfer in the indicated time limit the part of the income generated from the joint operations which should be transferred in the joint account in accordance with the first clause of the article 109 are, for the first time, punished as needed in paragraph (B) of the article 126 and the total amount of the fees and shares gained by the said criminal operation are re-collected and transferred to the joint current account of the Notary Publics.

II – a) Concerning the president and members of the Notary Chamber Board who do not execute the duties fixed in the first clause of the article 109, it is proceeded to the application of the articles 230 and 240 of the Turkish Criminal Law in accordance with the degree of culpability.

b) The notary public who acts against the last clause of the article 109 is punished in accordance with the clause (I),

III – The notary publics who are designated by the Chamber Board to pay the fees to the notary public in charge, to proceed a bank withdrawal in order to divide the account balance to the notary publics or to pay necessary

务员的人，或者是公证办事员、办事员候选人，那么应当依照第一款的规定对他 / 她进行处罚。

那些在公共和私人基金会中被指控的官员或其他被指控者，作出违反本法第一百六十六条第十二项规定的实质行为且不需要从重处罚的，依照本条第一款的规定处罚。

公证员的欺诈行为

第一百五十八条 公证员、公证办事员和办事员候选人整理以前的文件时，应当在工作日志上保留编号。在税收、印花税、合同或各种费用的申报中或与申报有关的收据中实施欺诈行为的，处以三年至五年的监禁，并处以一千里拉以上三千里拉以下的罚款。

违反第十节规定的行为

第一百五十九条 （修改后的第 1 款和第 2 款：1989 年 11 月 16 日 -3588/ 第 13 条）

Ⅰ. 未在规定时限内依照第一百零九条第一款的规定将部分应当转入共同账户的收入转入共同账户的公证员，第一次依照第一百二十六条（B）项的规定受到处罚，所述犯罪活动取得的费用和份额的总额将被没收并转入公证员的共同往来账户。

（Ⅱ-a）对于没有履行第一百零九条第一款规定的职责的公证员，依照罪责程度适用《土耳其刑法》第二百三十条和第二百四十条的规定。

（b）作出违反第一百零九条最后一款的行为的公证员应当依照第 I 款受到处罚。

Ⅲ. 公证员被办公室委员会指定向其他负责的公证员支付费用、进行银行提款以便将账户余额平均分给其他公证员或支付必要职务薪酬和履行与此有关的其他职责的，如有亏空现象将受到惩罚，如果其他法

obligations and to execute other duties relating to this are punished, in case of deficiency acts, with an imprisonment between one year and three years and a heavy fine between 500 liras and 2 000 liras if their acts do not require a heavier punishment by the other laws.

律不要求加重处罚的话，那么处以一年以上三年以下有期徒刑和五百里拉以上二千里拉以下的罚款。

Penal responsibility rising from observance and control

从规章的遵守和管理中产生的刑事责任

Article 160 – The notary who is not a party to the crimes committed by the clerks or clerk candidates working in the notary public's office is responsible in accordance with the provision of the article 230 of the Turkish Criminal Law if it is fixed that he did not accomplish his duty of observance and control on those persons.

第一百六十条 在公证机构工作的办事员或办事员候选人，如果确定其没有履行遵守规章和管理的义务，那么应当依照《土耳其刑法》第二百三十条的规定承担责任。

Exceptional cases

例外情况

Article 161 – The provisions of the articles 153 – 155 are not applied to the officers out of the notary public's offices.

第一百六十一条 第一百五十三条至一百五十五条的规定不适用于公证机构的官员。

CHAPTER SIX
Legal Responsibilities of the Notary Publics

第六章 公证员的法律责任

Article 162 – The notary publics are responsible against those who suffered damage for undone, erroneous or deficient works; even if they are executed by the interns, clerks and clerk candidates.

For the amount he paid in accordance with the first clause, the notary public can take recourse against the intern or notary personal that caused the undone, erroneous or deficient work

第一百六十二条 公证员（包括实习生、办事员和办事员候选人执行的工作）对因其执行未完成的、错误的或有缺陷的工作而遭受损害的人负有责任。

对于按照第一款支付的损害赔偿，公证员可以向造成未完成工作或工作有错误、有缺陷的实习生或其他公证员个人追偿。

PART THIRTEEN
Notaries Union of Turkey

第十三部分
土耳其公证员联合会

General clauses

一般条款

Article 163 – In order to ensure that the notary public profession be duly executed and developed, and that the coworkers have a union and solidarity between them, the Notaries Union of Turkey is established with a state-foundation quality and a juridical personality.

(Changed clause 2: 18.06.1997 – 4276/art. 26)

Union and its organs can not execute except their institutional aims.

In accordance with the protocol rules, Union attends the official ceremonies.

The Chamber Presidency and the chamber board membership duties are executed freely. The travel and re-

第一百六十三条 为了确保公证员的职业得到适当的执行和发展，并确保公证员之间有工会，土耳其公证员联合会的成立具有国家基础和法人资格。

（修正第 2 条：1997 年 6 月 18 日 -4276/ 第 26 条）

联合会及其机关不能执行除体制目标以外的目标。

依照协议规定，联合会应当出席官方典礼。

联合会主席的职位和联合会委员会成员的职责都是自主设置的。旅费和住宿费以及与这些职务有关的

siding fees as well as the other fees relating to those duties are paid by the Union's budget.

其他费用由联邦预算支付。

The Presidency, vice-presidency, general secretarial and accountancy duties of the Notaries Union of Turkey are gainful. The members who are not charged in the Presidency Council of the Notaries Union of Turkey as well as the president and members of the disciplinary committee receive attendance fees for the meetings they have attended.

土耳其公证员联合会的主席、副主席、总秘书和会计的职务是有收益的。在土耳其公证员联合会主席委员会中未被收取费用的成员和纪律委员会主席及成员出席会议均需收取出席费。

The travel and residing fees as well as the necessary expenditures of those who are selected from outside Ankara are paid from the Union's budget. The quantities of those elements are determined by the Congress.

安卡拉以外的人的旅费和住宿费以及必要的开支由联合会预算支付。具体由国会决定。

Supervision and control by the Ministry of Justice, constrained work ceasing and dismissal of organs

司法部的监督和管理，强制停止工作和解散机构

Article 164 – (Changed: 14.02.1984 – 2980/art. 2)

The Ministry of Justice has the right to supervise and control the Notaries Union of Turkey and the Union's local organs' chambers. All activities as well as the calculus and operations of the Union and the chambers are controlled by the Justice Inspectors and Republic prosecutors. The control mode is shown in the regulation.

第一百六十四条（修正：1984 年 2 月 14 日 - 2980/第 2 条）

司法部有权监督和管理土耳其公证员联合会和该联合会地方机关的办公室。所有活动以及联合会和办公室的运作均由司法监察员和共和国检察官依照行政法规中规定的管理模式负责。

(Changed clause 2: 18.06.1997 – 4276/art. 27)

The dismissal and replacement of the presidents and boards of the central organs of the Notaries Union of Turkey as well as of the notary chambers who act contrary to their aims are decided, upon the demand of the Ministry of Justice or the local Republic Attorney General, by the local court of first instance through a basic method and the trial is achieved at last in three months.

（修正第 2 款：1997 年 6 月 17 日 -4276/ 第 27 条）

土耳其公证员联合会中央机构的主席和委员会以及与其宗旨背道而驰的公证机构的撤换，应司法部或地方共和国总检察长的要求，由地方初审法院通过基本程序作出决定，且审判需在三个月内完成。

In one month, new organs are elected for the ones who were dismissed. The elected ones complete the service time of the old ones.

在一个月内，为被解散的机构选出新的人员。选出的人应当完成前人的服务时间。

The central and local organs of the Union must comply with the disposition of the Ministry of Justice concerning the decisions and acts of the Union's organs. The provisions of the hereinabove clauses are applied to the Union's organs which, without any legal reason, do not execute or do take an insistent decision based on an old decision that contravenes in one hand the dispositions of the Ministry and in the other hand the decision of stay of execution or the material decision of the administrative tribunals or, in spite of the warning from the Ministry, do not execute the operations imposed by the Law.

联合会的中央和地方机构必须遵守司法部关于联合会各机构的决定和行为的处理办法。上述条款的规定适用于本联合会的机构，这些机构在没有合法理由的情况下，不得执行或依照一项旧的决定作出新决定，该旧的决定指的是一方面违反了该部的处理办法，另一方面违反了暂停执行的决定或行政法庭的重大决定，或者，尽管受到了司法部的警告，却仍不执行法律规定的业务。

The dismissed organ's members' penal responsibilities, as written in the law, are reserved. The dispositions

有关于被解散机构的成员负有刑事责任的法律规定被保留。依照上述条款导致这些机关被解雇的处分

that cause the dismissal of those organs in accordance with the hereinabove clause are null.

(By assembling the article 27 of the Law 4276 dated 18/6/1997 with the clause six an seven, this clause is rearranged as the sixth clause)

However, in case of urgency where the national security and the public order require the prevention of the perpetration or the continuation of a crime or the seizure, the governor can give the cease and desist order concerning the president and boards of the Union's central organs and chambers. The decision of cease and desist order is presented for the approval of the judge in charge in twenty hours. The judge declares his/her decision in forty eight hours; otherwise, this administrative decision is automatically repealed.

无效。

（将 1997 年 6 月 18 日第 4276 号法令第 27 条与第 6 款、第 7 款合并，将该款重新安排为第 6 款）

然而，在国家安全和公共秩序要求预防犯罪或持续犯罪或扣押的紧急情况下，地方长官可向有关的联邦中央机构、联合会主席和委员会下达终止和停止命令。终止和停止命令将在二十小时内提交主管法官批准。法官应当在四十八小时内宣布他 / 她的决定；否则，这一行政决定将自动失效。

Membership

Article 165 – The notary publics are the natural members of the Notaries Union of Turkey. The notary publics who are subject to an age limitation become the Union's honorary members.

The Board of Union can decide the honorary membership of the individuals who have contributed to the profession.

会员资格

第一百六十五条 公证员是土耳其公证员联合会的自然成员。受年龄限制的公证员成为联合会的名誉成员。

联合会委员会可决定授予为该职业作出贡献的个人荣誉会员资格。

The duties of the Notaries Union of Turkey

Article 166

– The duties of the Notaries Union of Turkey are as follows:

1. Ensuring that the coworkers have a union and solidarity between them,
2. Issuing books and journals, organizing conferences, attending international meetings and executing different necessary works in order to develop the profession,
3. Opening courses to educate notary clerks,
4. Automatically or upon demand, voicing its opinions to the competent authorities concerning the subjects that relate to the notary public profession,
5. Fixing and recommending the professional rules that must be followed,
6. In accordance with the time and quantity indicated in the regulation, lending moneys to the notary public and their clerks,
7. Taking measures in order to ensure that its members be homeowners, educate their children in good environment and take advantage of the different social services,

土耳其公证员联合会的职责

第一百六十六条

土耳其公证员联合会的职责如下：

1. 确保同事之间有联合会和团结；
2. 出版书籍和期刊、组织会议、出席国际会议和开展各种必要的工作；
3. 开设培训公证办事员的课程；
4. 主动或应要求就与公证职业有关的问题向主管当局反映意见；
5. 确定和建议必须遵守的职业规则；
6. 在按照规例所规定的时间，将规例规定数额的款项借给公证员及其办事员；
7. 采取措施，确保其成员是私房屋主，在良好的环境中教育其子女，并在不同的社会服务中受益；

8. Before the opening of the legal year, presenting report to the Ministry of Justice that concerns its own works and needs,

9. Taking common measures in order to protect and preserve the notary documents,

10. Command and exploit the movable and real estate as well as the money of the Union in accordance with the Union's aims,

11. Preparing one-type contract draft for the contracts to be done between notary publics and the clerks as well as servants,

12. Ensuring that the notary operations be done in accordance with this law and especially, contacting with the relevant official and private institutions in order to prevent competition between notary publics concerning the protest of a bill of exchange (check, policy and promissory note) or other different subjects and connecting, if necessary, the obtained results to a protocol with which the parties shall comply,

13. Defending the general interests of the Notary Publics as well as the moral, order and the tradition of the Notary profession,

14. Indicating the amount of the allocation that the Union will spend to the notary chambers as well as the payment mode; this will be done by taking into consideration the number of the members and the field of activity of the said notary chambers,

15. (Addition: 2/3/2005-5309/art. 5)

If there is more than one district in the municipality border of a county, determining in every four year the distribution principles of all-type joint accounts of the notary public's offices and presenting it to the Ministry of Justice for approval; this procedure takes into account the seniority and the class of the said notary public's offices.

16. Executing other duties that are specified by the Laws[2],

8. 在年终时，向司法部提交关于其自身工作和需要的报告；

9. 采取通行措施保存公证文件；

10. 依照联合会的宗旨管理和利用联合会的动产和不动产以及货币；

11. 拟备范本合约草案，供公证员与办事员及受雇人签订；

12. 确保按照本法进行公证业务，特别是与有关官方和私人机构的联系应当严格遵守法律规定，以防止公证员就汇票（支票、保险单和本票）业务或其他不同主题的业务与之进行竞争，并在必要时将所取得的结果制成申请人应遵守的条约；

13. 维护公证员的一般利益以及公证职业的道德、秩序和传统；

14. 说明联合会将向公证机构拨款的数额以及付款方式，这将考虑到该公证办公室的成员数目和活动领域；

15.（增补：2005 年 3 月 2 日 -5309/ 第 5 条）

如果一个市的边界内有一个以上数量的区，那么每四年确定公证机构所有类型共同账户的分配原则，并提交司法部批准；这一程序应当考虑到所述公证机构的资历和级别；

16. 执行法律规定的其他职责。

The organs of the Notaries Union of Turkey

Article 167 – The Notaries Union of Turkey executes its duties through its organs.

The organs of the Union are as follows:

1. The President of the Notaries Union of Turkey,
2. The Conference of Presidents of the Notaries Union of Turkey,
3. The Board of the Notaries Union of Turkey,
4. The Disciplinary Committee of the Notaries Union

土耳其公证员联合会的机构

第一百六十七条 土耳其公证员联合会通过其机构履行职责。

联合会的机构组成如下：

1. 土耳其公证员联合会主席；
2. 土耳其公证员联合会主席会议；
3. 土耳其公证员联合会委员会；
4. 土耳其公证员联合会纪律委员会；

of Turkey,

5. The congress of the Notaries Union of Turkey,

6. Notary chambers.

5. 土耳其公证员联合会大会；

6. 公证办公室。

The duties of the President of the Notaries Union of Turkey,

土耳其公证员联合会主席的职责

Article 168 – The duties of the Notaries Union of Turkey are as follows:

1. Representing the Notaries Union of Turkey before the courts and other authorities as well as the protocols,

2. Presiding the Conference of Presidents and the Board and executing their decisions,

3. In accordance with the authorization that will be granted by the article 172, proceeding in the mane of the Union to the disposal and acquisition, making commitment, receiving the donations and applying the budget,

4. Establishing relations with the foreign notaries unions as well as law institutions,

5. Executing other duties that are specified by the Laws.

第一百六十八条 土耳其公证员联合会主席的职责如下：

1. 在法院和其他机构中或在签订合约书时代表土耳其公证员联合会；

2. 主持主席和委员会会议并执行其决定；

3. 依照第一百七十二条给予的授权，在联合会的职权范围内进行处置和获取、作出承诺、接受捐款和申请预算；

4. 与外国公证员协会和法律机构建立关系；

5. 执行法律规定的其他职责。

The Conference of Presidents of the Notaries Union of Turkey

土耳其公证员联合会主席会议

Article 169 – The President of the Union, Vice President, Secretary General and the Accountant compose the Conference of Presidents.

The Conference of Presidents operates at the moments when the Board is not assembled and its operations are undertaken within the framework of the authorization granted by the Board.

The Secretary General and the Accountant can be a hired outsider.

If one of the members of the Union's Conference of Presidents leaves his/her duty before the end of his/her service time, a new member is elected in one month for the remaining service time.

At times when the President is absent or, whatever the reason, the Presidency is empty, the execution of the President's authorities and duties belongs to the Vice President and in the absence of the Vice President to the most senior professional member of the Union Board.

The Secretary General of the Union arranges the record relating to the meetings of the Board of the Union, manages internal works and the typesetting of the Union, gives the necessary directives to the Union's officer and controls the officer's works.

第一百六十九条 主席会议由联合会主席、副主席、秘书长和会计组成。

主席会议是在委员会尚未组成时运作，并在委员会授权的框架内开展业务的。

可以雇用机构以外的人担任秘书长和会计。

如果联合会主席会议的一名成员在任职时间结束前离职，那么将在一个月内选出一名新成员，接替其并完成其剩余时间的任职。

当主席缺席或不论出于什么原因缺席，主席的权力和职责由副主席执行，副主席缺席时，由联合会委员会中职位最高的成员执行。

联合会秘书长安排与联合会委员会会议有关的记录、管理联合会的内部工作和排版工作、向联合会的官员发出必要的指示，并管理该官员的工作。

The Union's Accountant is authorized to manage the Union's assets in accordance with the decision of the Union's Conference of Presidents, to take and give moneys and to execute every observance relating to the budget application. The Union's Accountant signs together with the Union's President all the arranged papers that concern the money actions.

依照联合会主席会议的决定，联合会的会计有权管理联合会的资产，收取和发放款项，并执行与所有预算申请有关的规定。联合会的会计与联合会主席一起签署所有与金钱行为有关的文件。

The Board of the Notaries Union of Turkey

土耳其公证员联合会委员会

Article 170 – The Board of the Notaries Union of Turkey is composed of seven members and is elected by the Congress of the Notaries Union of Turkey for four years. The Board has also four substitutes.

The same notary public can not be elected more than one of the memberships of the Union's Board, Union's Disciplinary Committee and the Chamber Board.

In its first assembly following its election, the Board elects with secret vote a President, a vice president and, in case of no appointment from outside, a secretary general and an accountant. The elected president is also the president of the Notaries Union of Turkey.

第一百七十条 土耳其公证员联合会委员会由七名成员组成，由土耳其公证员联合会大会选出，任期四年。同时，委员会还有四位替补人员。

同一公证员不得同时当选为联合会委员会、联合会纪律委员会和办公室委员会的成员。

在选举后的第一届大会上，委员会以不记名投票的方式选举一名主席、一名副主席。若没有外部任命，则选举一名秘书长和一名会计师。当选的主席同时也是土耳其公证员联合会的主席。

Election mode and period of the Board of the Notaries Union of Turkey

土耳其公证员联合会委员会的选举方式和任期

Article 171 – The Board is elected among the notary publics who have at least five year seniority in the profession.

Those about whom it has been decided to open a final inquiry because of a crime that represents an obstacle to the notary public profession or those who have been punished during last five years by the Disciplinary Committee with fine or temporary dismissal can not be elected to the Board memberships.

(Third clause repealed: 14/2/1984-2980/art. 6)

It is imperative to write on the voting paper at least one more name than the half of the total number of members to be elected. The voting papers that contain fewer names are null. If the voting paper contains more names than the number of members to be elected, the extra names are not taken into account starting from the end of the list.

The candidates are aligned in accordance with the number of votes they received. Those who have been elected as the members and then the substitutes are aligned in pursuant to this alignment. In case of equality of votes, the candidate who is professionally senior, and if the seniority level is equal, the one who is older gains priority.

第一百七十一条 委员会成员是从在该行业至少有五年资历的公证员中选出的。

那些因实施妨碍公证员职业的行为而被调查的人，或在过去五年中受到纪律委员会罚款或暂时被解雇的人，都不能当选为委员会成员。

（第 3 款废除：1984 年 2 月 14 日 -2980/ 第 6 条）

投票纸上所填写的名字数量至少为岗位总数的 1.5 倍。没有达到相应数量的投票无效。如果投票纸中的名字数量比岗位总数多，那么从名单末尾开始再不考虑额外的名字。

候选人依照所获得的票数排序。已经当选的作为成员，然后替补人员将依照这一排序依次候补。在票数相同的情况下，资历深的候选人优先，如果资历相等，年龄较大的候选人优先。替补人员被分配到他们所获得的多数选票所在地的地方议会。

The substitutes are called to the council in accordance with the place they hold regarding the votes they received.

The duties of the Board members who lost the election competency end automatically.

The member whose service time is fulfilled can be reelected to the Board. In so far, half of the member and substitutes is renewed. The members to leave in two years which follow the election are determined via drawing of lots.

The recently elected substitutes are aligned in accordance with their votes and are added below the old substitutes.

The Board member who leaves before the end of the election period is replaced by the substitute who has received the highest vote and a substitute is elected in the first congress to be held.

If a public trial is opened against one of the Board members because of a crime that represents an obstacle to the notary public profession, the said member can not attend to the Board activities until the end of the trial; he/she is replaced by a substitute.

丧失选举资格的委员会成员的职责自动结束。

委员会成员任期满的可继续连任。到目前为止，有一半的成员和替补人员得到了更新。成员在选举后两年内以抽签的方式决定是否离开。

最近选出的替补人员依照他们的选票进行排序，并增加在旧的替补人员之后。

在选举结束前离开的委员会成员将由获得最高票数的替补人员取代，并在即将举行的第一届大会上再次选出一名替补人员。

如果对委员会的一名成员所犯的对公证员职业构成障碍的罪行进行公开审判，那么该成员在审判结束之前不能参加委员会的活动；而由替补人员代替其参加。

The duties of the Board of the Notaries Union of Turkey

土耳其公证员联合会委员会的职责

Article 172 – The duties of the Board are as follows:

1. Through examining the budget offers of every chamber, arranging the budget of the Notaries Union of Turkey and presenting it to the approval of the Congress and executing it,
2. Presenting report to the Congress concerning its activities and executing the Congress' decisions,
3. Managing the estates of the Notaries Union of Turkey and granting authorization to the President concerning the disposal and acquisition activities,
4. Deciding about the resignation of the members of the Board,
5. Preparing the agenda of the Union's Congress,
6. Arranging and executing the personal affairs of the paid official of the Union,
7. Executing supervision and control upon the notary chambers and notary publics,
8. Selecting the delegates who will attend to the local and foreign congress,
9. Presenting professional report to the related authorities,
10. Without showing the competent authority, exe-

第一百七十二条 委员会的职责如下：

1. 通过审查各办公室的预算申请，确定土耳其公证员联合会的预算，并在提交国会批准后予以执行；
2. 向大会提交关于其活动和执行大会决定的报告；
3. 管理土耳其公证员联合会的财产，并授权主席进行相关的处置和获取活动；
4. 决定委员会成员辞职；
5. 准备联合会代表大会的议程；
6. 安排和执行联合会受薪官员的个人事务；
7. 对公证办公室和公证员实行监督管理；
8. 挑选出席当地和外国代表大会的代表；
9. 向有关部门提交专业报告；
10. 在不向主管机构表明的情况下，执行法律规

cuting the duties that are specified to the Notaries Union of Turkey by the Laws,

11. Executing other duties that are specified by the Laws.

定赋予土耳其公证员联合会的职责；

11. 执行法律规定的其他职责。

Board meetings of the Notaries Union of Turkey and quorum

土耳其公证员联合会委员会会议和法定人数

Article 173 – The Board of the Union holds a regular meeting one time in a month. Upon the demand of the President or one of the Board members, the Board can be convened for an extraordinary meeting in every time when urgency comes up.

At the end of each meeting, the date of the next meeting is fixed. The date of the meeting is notified to the members via a call letter.

The member who does not attend three consecutive meetings without any justified and documented obstacle is considered resigned.

The Board of the Union assembles with the absolute majority of the members and takes decision with the absolute majority of attendants. In so far, at least four members should ally for one vote so that the Board can decide. In case of equality of votes, the party of which the President forms a part is considered superior.

第一百七十三条 联合会委员会在一个月内举行一次定期会议。应委员会主席或其中一名成员的要求，可在每次紧急情况下召开一次特别会议。

在每次会议结束时，确定下一次会议的日期。会议的日期通过一封召集信通知各成员。

连续三次不参加会议且没有任何正当理由的成员被视为辞职。

联合会委员会以绝对多数成员组成，并以出席者的绝对多数作出决定。到目前为止，至少有四名成员应当投相同票，以便委员会能够作出决定。在票数相等的情况下，主席的决定被视为最终决定。

The Disciplinary Committee of the Notaries Union of Turkey

土耳其公证员联合会纪律委员会

Article 174 – The Disciplinary Committee of the Notaries Union of Turkey is composed of five congress' members who are elected through secret vote by the Congress. Furthermore, three substitutes are elected.

The Committee elects a president among its members in its first meetings which follows the election.

The members of the Disciplinary Committee of the Notaries Union of Turkey are elected for four years. Those whose service time has been achieved can be reelected.

The clauses 1, 2, 3, 4, 5, 6, 9 and 10 of the article 171 are also applied here relatively.

第一百七十四条 土耳其公证员联合会纪律委员会由五名代表大会成员组成，由代表大会以不记名投票方式选出。此外，还选出三名替补人员。

委员会在选举后的第一次会议上从其成员中选出一名主席。

土耳其公证员联合会纪律委员会成员任期四年。服务期满的成员可以连任。

第一百七十一条第一款、第二款、第三款、第四款、第五款、第六款、第九款和第十款也对其适用。

The duties and meetings of the Disciplinary Committee of the Notaries Union of Turkey

土耳其公证员联合会纪律委员会的职责和会议

Article 175 – The Disciplinary Committee of the Notaries Union of Turkey executes the affairs that are granted to it by this law and regulation.

The Committee is holds a regular meeting one time in a month. Upon the demand of the President of the Un-

第一百七十五条 土耳其公证员联合会纪律委员会执行本法和规章赋予的职责。

委员会每月举行一次例会。应联合会主席或纪律委员会成员的要求，委员会可在紧急情况下召开特别

ion or of the President or the members of the Disciplinary Committee, the Committee can be convened for an extraordinary meeting in every time when urgency comes up.

会议。

The clauses 2 and 3 of the article 173 are also applied to the Disciplinary Committee relatively.

第一百七十三条第二款和第三款也适用于纪律委员会。

The Disciplinary Committee assembles with the absolute majority of the members and the decisions are taken if only at least three members agree on one vote. In case of equality of votes, the party of which the President forms a part is considered superior.

纪律委员会由绝对多数成员组成，只有至少三名成员达成一致意见，才能作出决定。在票数相等的情况下，主席的决定被视为最终决定。

The Congress of the Notaries Union of Turkey

土耳其公证员联合会代表大会

Article 176 – The highest organ of the Notaries Union of Turkey is the Congress of the Union.

The Congress of the Union is composed of two notary publics and presidents of notary chambers that are elected by the general assembly of the notary chambers. The notary chambers which have more than 10 notary publics elect a deputy for every 10 notary publics that surpass 10. The President and members of the Board of the Notaries Union of Turkey cannot be elected as a deputy. However, though they cannot attend to the voting relating to the activity report of the Board, they are natural members of the congress.

If possible, the same number of substitutes are also elected.

The notary publics who do not have the capacity to be elected to the Chamber Board can not be elected as deputy.

The Congress of the Union is assembled in the first week of every June. The date, the place and the agenda of the meeting is declared by the President of the Notaries Union of Turkey at least thirty days ago in journals; furthermore, it is also notified to the notary chambers.

Upon the written demand of the Ministry of Justice and of the one tenth of the notary publics being members of the Union, the Congress of the Union is convened to an extraordinary meeting. If the Board of the Union considers it necessary, it can convene the congress to an extraordinary meeting. It is imperative that the demands of the extraordinary meeting include a subject that is appropriate to the duties written in this law.

第一百七十六条　土耳其公证员联合会的最高机关是该联合会的代表大会。

联合会大会由两个公证员和由公证办公室会员大会选出的公证办公室主席组成。有超过十个公证员的公证办公室需选出一名代表。土耳其公证员联合会委员会主席和成员不能当选为代表，且不能参加与委员会活动报告有关的表决，但他们是大会的自然成员。

如果可能的话，也选出同等数量的替补人员。

丧失被选入办公室委员会的资格的公证员不能当选为代表。

联合会大会在每年六月的第一个星期召开。会议的日期、地点和议程至少在三十日前由土耳其公证员联合会主席在期刊上宣布；此外，还应当通知公证机构办公室。

应司法部和十分之一的作为联合会成员的公证员的书面要求，联合会大会召开特别会议。如果联合会委员会认为有必要，那么可以召集代表大会召开一次特别会议。特别会议要求必须有一个与本法规定的义务相适应的议题。

Meeting and decision quorum of the Congress

大会法定人数

Article 177 – In order to get the Congress of the Union assembled, the majority of the delegates must be ready.

第一百七十七条　为了召开联合会大会，大多数代表必须做好准备。如果会议当天没有多数代表出席，

If there is no majority on the meeting day, the meeting is done with the present delegates on the next day. In so far, there can be no meeting nor interview if at least one quarter of the members does not attend.

那么推迟至第二天与出席代表举行会议。到目前为止，如果有四分之一的成员缺席，那么会议不能举行。

If the quorum written in the first clause is not attained, the meeting is left for another day that does not exceed one month. If one quarter of the members does not yet attend to this second meeting, the meeting is left to the one month dates until the said quorum is attained.

如未能达到第一款所规定的法定人数，会议将延迟不超过一个月。如果四分之一的成员仍未出席第二次会议，会议将再次延迟至一个月后举行，直至达到上述法定人数为止。

(Additional clause 3: 14.02.1984 – 2980 / art. 3)

It is imperative to attend the meeting regarding the election of the Congress of the Union and vote; those who do not attend or vote without any valuable reason are punished by the Disciplinary Committee of the Union.

（增补第3款：1984年2月14日-2980/第3条）

必须出席关于选举的联合会大会并投票；缺席会议或没有正当理由缺席投票的成员将受到联合会纪律委员会的惩罚。

The Conference of Presidents of the Congress of the Union is composed of a president, a deputy president and four clerks. The President and members of the Board of the Union can not be elected to the Disciplinary Committee of the Union.

联合会大会主席会议由一名主席、一名副主席和四名办事员组成。联合会委员会主席和成员不能当选为联合会纪律委员会成员。

The Congress of the Union decides with the absolute majority of the attendants. In so far, the decisions which are related to the topics that are shown in the paragraph 10 of the article 166 can be taken only by the absolute majority of the full members of the Congress of the Union. . In case of equality of votes, the party of which the President forms a part is considered superior.

联合会大会决议效力以出席者的绝对多数决定。到目前为止，与第一百六十六条第十项所列议题有关的决定只能由联合会大会全体成员的绝对多数作出。在票数相等的情况下，主席的决定视为最终决定。

The duties of the Congress

大会的职责

Article 178 – The duties of the Congress of the Union are as follows:

1. Examining and accepting the activity report of the Board and, if not approved, proceeding to a reelection,
2. Discussing the budget and approving,
3. By virtue of the agenda and upon the proposal of the members, discussing and deciding the other affairs that are among the duties of the Notaries Union of Turkey,
4. Electing the members of the Board and Disciplinary Committee of the Union,
5. Fixing the entre fees and the dues to be paid by the notary publics,
6. Fixing the amount and the payment mode of the wages of the President, Vice-President, Secretary General and the Accountant of the Union as well as the attendance fees that will be granted to the members of the Board and the Disciplinary Committee,
7. Executing other duties that are given by laws.

第一百七十八条 联合会大会的职责如下：

1. 审查和接受委员会的活动报告，如未获批准，则进行委员会成员改选；
2. 讨论预算及批准；
3. 依照议程和各成员的提议，讨论和决定属于土耳其公证员联合会职责范围内的其他事务；
4. 选举联合会委员会和纪律委员会成员；
5. 确定加入的费用和公证员应缴付的会费；
6. 确定委员会主席、副主席、秘书长和会计师的工资数额和支付方式，以及委员会成员和纪律委员会成员的出席费；
7. 执行法律赋予的其他职责。

Notary chambers

Article 179 – A notary chamber is established for every municipality border in which there are three or more notary public's offices.

The Ministry of Justice determines to which chamber will be related the notary publics situated in places where there is no notary chamber and can relate the notary publics situated in places where there are less than 10 notary publics to a different chamber, if necessary.

The obligation to subscribe to a chamber

Article 180 – The notary chambers are the regional organs of the Notaries Union of Turkey.

Every notary public has the obligation to subscribe to the notary chamber which is in his/her region.

The duties of the notary chambers

Article 181 – The duties of the notary chambers are as follows:

1. Taking the necessary measures for the development of the profession,
2. Upon the request of the one of the concerned parties, trying to resolve the disagreements between the notary publics and the clerks, clerk candidates and the servants regarding service applications,
3. Submitting its opinions to the Ministry of Justice concerning the determination of the place where the new notary publics will be opened as well as the change of place of an existing notary public,
4. Aiding to ensure that the internal order of the notary public's office is appropriate to the clauses of the regulation,
5. Taking the necessary measures during the cession and the reception of a notary public's office with regard to protect the rights of the heritors of the deceased notary publics,
6. Sending delegates to the Congress of the Union,
7. Executing the duties granted by the Notaries Union of Turkey,
8. Executing other duties that are given by laws.

Organization of the notary chambers

Article 182 – The notary chambers compose of:

1. The president of the notary chamber,
2. The board of the notary chamber,

公证办公室

第一百七十九条 在每一个有三个或三个以上公证机构的市边界设立公证办公室。

司法部可决定将位于没有公证办公室的地区的公证员与哪一个办公室联系起来，并可视需要将位于少于十个公证员的地区的公证员们与另一个办公室联系起来。

加入办公室

第一百八十条 公证办公室是土耳其公证员联合会的区域机关。

每个公证员都需加入他/她所在地区的公证办公室。

公证办公室的职责

第一百八十一条 公证办公室的职责如下：

1. 采取必要措施发展该行业；
2. 应有关方的请求，解决公证员与办事员、办事员候选人和雇员之间关于服务合同关系的分歧；
3. 就新公证员的执业地点的确定以及现有公证员的变更向司法部提出意见；
4. 协助确保公证机构的内部秩序与本规章的条款相适应；
5. 在转让和接收公证机构期间采取必要措施保护已故公证员的继承人的权利；
6. 派代表出席联合会大会；
7. 执行土耳其公证员联合会授予的职责；
8. 执行法律赋予的其他职责。

公证办公室的组成

第一百八十二条 公证办公室由下列人员组成：

1. 公证办公室主任；
2. 公证办公室委员会；

3. The general assembly of the notary chamber.

3. 公证办公室大会。

The duties of the president of the notary chamber

Article 183 – The duties of the President of the Notary Chamber are as follows:

1. By virtue of the competence that will be granted by the President of the Notaries Union of Turkey, representing the Union before whatever authorities,

2. Representing the Chamber before the Protocol,

3. Presiding the Board of the Notary Chamber and executing the decisions to be taken.

公证办公室主席的职责

第一百八十三条 公证办公室主席的职责如下：

1. 土耳其公证员联合会主席授予公证办公室主席在任何机构前代表联合会的权限；

2. 在签订协议时代表公证办公室；

3. 主持公证办公室委员会并执行决定。

Board of the Notary Chamber

Article 184 – The Board of the Notary Chamber consists of the president and two members of the notary chamber.

The president and the members are elected for two years with the majority of the votes that are cast by the general assembly. One substitute is elected for the chambers with more than three notary publics; two substitutes are elected for the chambers with more than 10 notary publics.

In order to be elected for the presidency or the regular and substitutes membership of the Board, it is imperative to not have a decision requiring the opening of a final inquiry regarding a crime that pose an obstacle to the notary public profession nor a punishment of temporary dismissal from the notary public profession in the five last years. If the president or one of the members is definitively punished by a temporary dismissal during the election period, then the said duty ends automatically.

In cases where the president is absent or the presidency is empty for any reason, the member of the chamber board who has the highest level of seniority in the profession uses the power and executes the duties of the president. The provisions of the clauses 9 and 10 of the article 171 are also relatively applied to the members of the chamber board.

公证办公室委员会

第一百八十四条 公证办公室委员会由主席和公证办公室两名成员组成。

主席和成员由大会以多数票选出，任期两年。由三名以上的公证员组成委员会并选出一名替补人员。十名以上的公证员组成的委员会应选出两名替补人员。

为了当选为主席团成员或委员会的正式成员和替补成员，要求不得有实施犯罪行为，或者存在有碍公证职责履行的情形，或者在过去五年中受到暂时开除公证员职位的惩罚。如果主席或其中一位成员确定在选举期间受到暂时解雇的处罚，那么上述职责自动结束。

在主席缺席或主席职位因任何原因而空缺的情况下，在该职业中具有最高资历的办公室委员会成员使用该权力并执行主席的职责。第一百七十一条第九款和第十款的规定也适用于委员会成员。

The duties of the Board of the Chamber Board

Article 185 – The duties of the board of the notary chamber are as follows:

1. Arranging the offer of the expense budget of the chamber and submitting it to the approval of the general assembly,

2. Reporting to the general assembly of the notary

办公室委员会的职责

第一百八十五条 公证办公室委员会的职责如下：

1. 安排委员会的费用预算，并提交大会批准；

2. 向公证办公室大会报告其工作并执行大会的

chamber regarding its works and executing the decisions of the general assembly,

3. Executing the duties that are given to the chamber without showing any competent authority,

4. Executing other duties that are given by the laws.

决定；

3. 在不告诉任何主管机构的情况下执行办公室交给的职责；

4. 执行法律赋予的其他职责。

General Assembly of the Notary Chamber

公证办公室大会

Article 186 – The general assembly of the notary chamber consists of notary publics who are registered to the chamber.

(Changed first phrase clause 2: 16.11.1989 – 3588/ art. 14)

The general assembly assembles in April of the every year. The place, the time and the agenda of thee meeting is notified to the members by the president of the notary chamber at least one month ago.

If the board considers it necessary, it can convene the general assembly for an extraordinary meeting.

The provision of the last clause of the article 176 is also applied to the general assembly.

第一百八十六条　公证办公室大会由在公证办公室登记的公证员组成。

（更改首段第2款：1989年11月16日-3588/第14条）

大会每年四月举行。会议的地点、时间和议程由公证办公室主席在至少一个月前通知各成员。

如果委员会认为有必要，可以召集一次特别会议。

第一百七十六条最后一款的规定也适用于大会。

The meeting of the general assembly of the notary chamber

公证办公室大会会议

Article 187 – To hold the meeting, the majority of the members should be ready. If the majority is not ensured at the day of the meeting, the meeting is held on the next day with the present members.

(Changed clause 2: 14.02.1984 – 2980/art. 4)

It is imperative to attend the meeting regarding the election of the Congress of the Union and vote; those who do not attend or vote without any valuable reason are punished by the Disciplinary Committee of the Union.

In order to proceed to the out of agenda election of the president or the members or to negotiate the offers of the members in accordance with the third clause of the article 188, it is necessary that the majority of the registered chamber members be ready.

The conference of presidents of the general assembly consists of a president and two clerks. In so far, the conference of presidents of the general assembly of the chambers that have less than (10) members consists of a president and a clerk.

(Changed last clause: 14.02.1984 – 2980/art. 4)

The provision of the last clause of the article 177 is also applied to the general assembly of the notary chamber.

第一百八十七条　举行会议时，多数成员应当做好准备。如果大多数成员在会议当天缺席，那么在第二天与出席成员举行会议。

（修正第2款：1984年2月14日-2980/第4条）

必须出席关于选举的会议并投票；缺席会议或无正当理由缺席投票的人将受到联合会纪律委员会的惩罚。

为了依照第一百八十八条第三项进行主席或成员的议程外选举或就成员的提议进行协商，有必要让大多数登记的办公室成员做好参会准备。

大会的主席会议由一名主席和两名办事员组成。到目前为止，大会的主席会议如果少于十名公证办公室成员，那么由一名主席和一名办事员组成。

（修改后的最后一款：1984年2月14日-2980/第4条）

第一百七十七条最后一款的规定也适用于公证办公室大会。

The duties of the General Assembly of the Notary Chamber

Article 188 – The duties of the general assembly of the notary chamber are as follows:

1. Examining and accepting the activity report of the Board and, if not approved, proceeding to a reelection,

2. Negotiating and approving the offer of the expense budget of the chamber,

3. Upon the agenda and the proposals of the members, negotiating and deciding other affairs included by the duties of the chamber,

4. Electing the chamber board,

5. Executing other duties that are given by the laws.

公证办公室大会的职责

第一百八十八条 公证办公室大会的职责如下：

1. 审查和接受委员会的活动报告，若未获批准，则进行委员会改选；

2. 协商并批准办公室费用预算的提议；

3. 依照各成员对议程的建议，协商并决定办公室职责所包括的其他事务；

4. 选举办公室委员会；

5. 执行法律赋予的其他职责。

The revenues of the Notaries Union of Turkey

Article 189 – The revenues of the Notaries Union of Turkey are as follows:

1. The entry fees that will be paid by every member,

2. The monthly dues that will be not less than the 1% of the monthly gross income,

3. The donations,

4. The revenue of the discharged notary publics' offices.

5. If the notary publics receive the temporary dismissal punishment, the revenues that will be collected,

6. The moneys to be send in accordance with the second clause of the article 117,

7. The interests of the trust moneys of a notary and the relevant different revenues,

8. Salary increases that will be paid in accordance with the article 120,

9. The moneys that will be collected in accordance with the paragraph (C) of the article 126, 146 and 148,

10. The revenues that will be brought by the publications and the real estates of the Union,

11. Other revenues that will be ensured through the affairs that the Notaries Union of Turkey will execute in accordance with the provisions of this law.

土耳其公证员联合会的收入

第一百八十九条 土耳其公证员联合会的收入如下：

1. 每个会员支付的会费；

2. 不低于月总收入百分之一的每月会费；

3. 捐款；

4. 解散公证机构的收入；

5. 因公证员受到处罚所收取的罚款；

6. 依照第一百一十七条第二款收到的款项；

7. 公证员信托财产的利润和相关的不同收入；

8. 依照第一百二十条收取的加薪；

9. 依照第一百二十六条、第一百四十六条和第一百四十八条（C）项收取的款项；

10. 联合会的出版物和不动产所带来的收入；

11. 土耳其公证员联合会依照本法规定执行的事务所带来的其他收入。

Notification mode

Article 190 – The notification of the Notaries Union of Turkey and the chambers are executed in accordance with the Notification Law.

通知方式

第一百九十条 土耳其公证员联合会和办公室的通知依照《通知法》执行。

PART FOURTEEN
Notary operations in foreign countries

Authorized body

Article 191 – the consulates carry out the notary operations in foreign countries.

Office

Article 192 – in accordance with the stipulations of this law, notary operations in foreign countries are carried out in the consulate building

Invalid stipulations

Article 193 – excluding Articles 41, 51, 53, 54, 55, 60, 61, 68 to 70, 72 to 76, 78 to 108, 113 to 116 and Articles in Chapter Fourteen shall not be applied for consulates.

Not receiving a notary public salary

Article 194 – person who laws as notary public in foreign countries shall not receive a salary for notary publics.

Signature and seal authentication

Article 195 – the consul shall authenticate the signature and seal; found under notary operations belonging to the authorized body of the country concerned, in accordance with the procedure in foreign countries.

PART FIFTEEN
Miscellaneous

Resigning from the duty

Article 196 – (Changed: 16/11/1989-3588/art. 15)

Excluding second section of the Article 7, if the notary public fails to possess one of the competence or conditions shown in the article or as a result of the inspections held; that he/she is found incompetent in profession, according to the last two subsequent certificate of good behavior prepared by justice inspectors and if the justice inspection come to the final decision on the third inspection, that he/she is incompetent in profession after six

第十四部分
国外公证业务

授权机构

第一百九十一条 领事馆执行与外国有关的公证业务。

办公室

第一百九十二条 依照本法的规定，外国的公证业务在领事馆大楼内进行。

不适用的规定

第一百九十三条 第四十一条、第五十一条、第五十三条、第五十四条、第五十五条、第六十条、第六十一条、第六十八条至第七十条、第七十二条至第七十六条、第七十八条至第一百零八条、第一百一十三条至第一百一十六条以及第十四章的所有条款不适用于领事馆。

不领取公证员工资

第一百九十四条 在外国担任公证员的，不得领取公证员工资。

签名和印章鉴定

第一百九十五条 领事应当按照外国的程序，在属于有关国家授权机构的公证业务中，对签名和印章进行鉴定。

第十五部分
其他

辞职

第一百九十六条（修正：1989 年 11 月 16 日 3588 号 / 第 15 条）

如果公证员不具备第七条所示的一项或多项条件，或由于检查结果认为其未能具备该资格或条件，那么他 / 她将被认定为不胜任该职业，依照前两次由司法检查人员准备的行为表现证明，如果经过第三次司法检查后，他 / 她在任职六个月后的表现仍被认为不称职，司法部将解除他 / 她的职务。

months service following last inspection, he/she shall be discharged from the duty by The Ministry of Justice.

Applying stipulations regarding notary public

Article 197 – stipulations regarding notary publics, save for the exceptions and above-mentioned matters provided for, are also applied for the representatives of the notary public and temporarily authorized notary public assistants assigned in accordance with this law.

(Changed second clause: 2/3/2005-5309/art. 6)

Regarding the intern notary public Article 146 and regarding the notary public's clerk Article 148 disciplinary action shall be applied.

Substitutes of the notary public shall not make a disposition of any kind that can affect the state of the notary public office and the entire financial status or condition of the notary public, excluding routine notary operations without any written consent of the notary public.

(Changed fifth clause: 2/3/2005-5309/art. 6)

the stipulations of this law regarding public appointment, Notaries Union of Turkey, collective insurance, illness and leave of absence shall not be applied for the execution manager, deputy execution manager and employees of Justice appointed as notary public and temporarily authorized conveyancing clerk.

Regulation

Article 198 – the regulation that determines the application of the Notary Public Law arranges the following matters:

1. determine and change the location of the notary public office
2. interior arrangement of the notary public office
3. working style of the notary public office
4. keeping books
5. protecting papers, documents and books
6. form and usage style of the seal that will be used in the notary public office
7. style of the notary public internship
8. duties of interns
9. intern book and erasing the registers from the book
10. signature authorization conditions for interns, head clerks and clerks
11. banks to trust notary public guarantee
12. duties of clerk and functionaries
13. Joint current account of notary publics and distri-

适用有关公证员的规定

第一百九十七条 关于公证员的规定，除上述例外事项和规定事项外，也适用于公证员代表和依照本法指定的临时授权的公证员助理。

（修改后的第2款：2005年3月2日-5309/第6条）

第一百四十六条关于见习公证员和第一百四十八条关于公证办事员的规定适用纪律处罚。

替代公证员不得作出任何可能影响公证机构及公证员的整体财务状况或公证员的地位的行为，但这不包括未经公证员书面同意，进行的常规公证业务。

（修改后的第5款：2005年3月2日-5309/第6条）

本法关于公职任命、土耳其公证员联合会、集体保险、疾病和请假的规定不适用于执行经理、副执行经理和被指定为公证员及办事员的人。

规章

第一百九十八条 《公证法》适用的规章主要涉及如下方面：

1. 决定并更改公证机构的位置；
2. 公证机构的内部安排；
3. 公证机构的工作作风；
4. 记账；
5. 保护证件、文件和账簿；
6. 公证机构将使用的印章的形式和使用方式；
7. 公证员实习方式；
8. 实习生的职责；
9. 实习登记和从登记簿划除登记者；
10. 实习生、主管办事员和办事员的签字授权条件；
11. 托管公证员担保的银行；
12. 办事员及工作人员的职责；
13. 公证员的共同往来账户和该账户中的费用和

bution of expenses and revenues in the said account.

14. Inspection ways for notary publics, contents in the report and certificate of good character, notification period for reports to be sent to the ministry of justice that is prepared by the public prosecutors.

15. lending money to the notary public and his/her employees

16. legal arrangement left to the regulation or other matters to be arranged in the regulation to assure the application of legal provisions.

Signature and seal authentication

Article 199 – the governor's office of the relevant place shall authenticate the sign and seal of the notary public at the bottom of the document to be used in a foreign country and in accordance with the operation in Turkey.

Operation formulas

Article 200 – formulas of the notary operations are prepared by the Notaries Union of Turkey Board with the decision of the Notary Chambers and Ministry of Finance and distributed by the Notaries Union of Turkey to all notary public offices after it is approved by The Ministry of Justice.

The formulas prepared in accordance with the first section shall be valid for four years following its approval date, and revision or remain in effect for same period at the end of this period, shall be decided on the last meeting of the Union before the completion of the period

Obligation for collective insurance

Article 201 – notary publics who are uncovered by the article 202 are obliged to be covered by the collective insurance. However disability, old-age and death insurances are obligatory and work accident, occupational disease and disease, maternity insurances are optional for the notary publics.

Regarding the notary publics covered by the collective insurance, Social Insurance Law no: 506 and law no: 228 of 5thJanuary, 1961, annex and appending stipulations of the above-mentioned laws are applied not contrary to the private stipulations in the said law.

Notary publics uncovered by the collective insurance

Article 202 – notaries who benefit from the temporary Article 15 of this law and temporary Article 2 of the

收入分配；

14. 公证员的检查方式、报告内容、品行良好的证书、检察官向司法部递交报告的通知期限；

15. 借钱给公证员和他 / 她的雇员；

16. 为确保法律规定的适用而保留给该规章或其他事项的法律安排。

签名和印章认证

第一百九十九条 有关地区的省长办公室应当依照在土耳其的业务办理方法，对拟在外国使用的文件底部的公证员的签名和印章进行认证。

业务准则

第二百条 公证业务的准则由土耳其公证员联合会委员会依照公证办公室和财政部的决定编写，并由土耳其公证员联合会经司法部批准后分发给所有公证机构。

依照第一节编写的准则自批准之日起四年内有效，并在此期间结束时予以修订或在最后一次会议中作出该准则继续有效的决定。

集体保险义务

第二百零一条 第二百零二条规定的未保险的公证员有义务参加集体保险。其中残疾险、养老保险和死亡保险是强制性的，工作事故、职业病和疾病、生育保险是选择性的。

对于集体保险所涵盖的公证员，适用一九六一年一月五日第五百零六号社会保险法和一九六一年一月五日第二百二十八号附加法，但上述法律的附加规定不得违反本法中关于私人的规定。

集体保险中未保险的公证员

第二百零二条 受益于本法暂行第十五条和一九三九年三月十九日第一千一百三十六号法令暂行第

advocacy code no: 1136 of 19th March, 1939 and who get paid retiring pension or old age pension by T.R retirement fund in accordance with the social insurance law no: 506 or who benefit from the funds in accordance with the previsions of temporary Article 20 of this law shall not be covered by the collective insurance.

二条的公证员，依照社会保险法第五百零六号领取由T.R 退休基金支付的退休养恤金或老年抚恤金。依照本法暂行第二十条规定的受益人，不包括在集体保险的覆盖范围内。

Type contract preparation and modification

Article 203 – type contract that serves as a basis for making a contact between The Notaries Union and The Social Security Organization shall be determined by the meetings held between The Ministry of Labor, Notaries Union of Turkey and Social Security Organization. Same procedure shall be applied for the modification of the type contracts.

Chambers to be established after this law came into effect, shall apply to the Social Security Organization for making collective insurance contract according to the type contrlaw following a month of their establishment. Notary publics, who are registered in the newly established chamber, shall be covered by the collective insurance of the new chamber without prejudice to the rights that they earned by the collective insurance of the previous chamber.

基础合同的准备和修改

第二百零三条 公证员联合会与社会保障组织的基础合同内容，由劳动部、土耳其公证员联合会和社会保障组织举行的会议商定。基础合同的修改应当采用相同的程序。

本法生效后，在办公室建立一个月后应当向社会保障组织申请按照基础合同订立集体保险合同。在新成立的办公室登记的公证员，应当在不损害他们先前所享有的集体保险权利的情况下，参加新办公室的集体保险。

Consequence of non payment of premium debt and notary public contribution

Article 204 – the notary public who fails to pay the collective insurance premium within the period shown in the collective contract is discharged from service until he/she pays the due premium debt in accordance with the stipulations in the contract

Notary chamber chairman shall notify the name of the notary public fails to pay his/her premium debt within the specified period to The Ministry of Justice immediately.

Consequence of non payment of premium debt is restricted to the premium debtor notary public personally and any stipulation regarding this consequence including other notary public or notary chamber involved in the same collective premium shall not take part in the contract.

(Additional clause: 16/11/1989-3588/art. 16)

notary publics who fail to pay his/her notary public contribution to The Notaries Union of Turkey, despite the notifications of The Union and specified period, he/she shall be discharged from service by The Ministry of Justice until he/she pays total due premium debt with the interest. In case of a discharge from service, after deducting notary

未缴付保险费的后果及公证员摊款

第二百零四条 公证员在集体合同规定的期限内不缴纳集体保险费的，应当暂停其职务，直至其依照合同的规定支付到期的保险费时才恢复职务。

公证办公室主席应当及时通知未在规定期限内向司法部支付所欠保险费的公证员。

不支付保险费债务的后果仅限于保险费债务人、公证员和任何有关的其他公证员，包括与该集体保险费有关的公证办公室。其法律后果为不得参加本合同。

（增补条款：1989 年 11 月 16 日 -3588/ 第 16 条）

虽然有联合会的通知和规定的期限，但是仍未向土耳其公证员联合会支付公证员分摊费的公证员，将被司法部解除职务直到他 / 她支付全部到期保险费及利息为止。如果被解除职务，那么在扣除公证员相关期间的分摊费和替代费后，由代付人使用公证净收入支付到期的分摊款债务。若有剩余，则给予公证机构。

public contribution and substitute fee of the relevant period, the net notary revenue shall be used by the substitute for paying due contribution debt and if any left, the sum shall be given to the notary public.

Counting previous duty, subject to retirement, of the notary public as length of service

Article 205 – in accordance with this law, a notary public covered by the collective insurance and during his/her insurance appointed or chosen for a duty or service subject to retirement, two third of the notary public period served as a basis for his/her coverage shall be added to his/her length of service and adapted, duty or service salary and his/her salary, serves as a basis for retirement deduction shall be increased.

Change of profession

Article 206 – persons put on an old age insurance salary before they are subject to collective insurance in accordance with this law and advocacy code, and if they resign from their notary public or lawyer profession; their insurance on their previous profession shall continue in their present profession. The relevant person shall be subject to the stipulations of collective insurance contract, following his/her new profession date.

The stipulation of the above-mentioned section shall be also applied for the ones who benefit from the temporary article 14 of this law and temporary article 14 of Advocacy Code and those who change the profession before the completion of minimum insured period and premium payment obligation.

Amending article of Charges Law

Article 207 – Article 72, no 492 of 2nd July, 1964 Charges Law shall be amended as:

Notary operations carried out by the consulates

Article 72- stipulations of this law on notary charges shall be applied for notary operations carried out by the consulates.

(This amendment embroidered in Article 72, no 492 of 2/7/1964 Charges Law)

Abolished law and stipulations

Article 208 – without prejudice to the transition stip-

将公证员先前的职务期间计算为服务期

第二百零五条 依照本法，集体保险所涵盖的公证员在其被指定或选择退休的期间内，三分之二的公证员期间作为其保险总额的基础，并计入在他/她的服务年限、职务或服务薪金中，以此作为退休扣除款中应当增加的基础。

职业变更

第二百零六条 依照本法和宣传守则，在参加集体保险之前领取养老保险工资的人，如果他们从公证员或律师职业中辞职，那么他们先前的职业保险应当在其目前从事的职业中继续承保。相关人员应当在其新职业中继续遵守集体保险合同的规定。

上述部分的规定，也适用于受益于本法暂行第十四条和宣传守则暂行第十四条的人，以及在完成最低保险期限和保险费支付义务之前变更职业的人。

修改《收费法》条款

第二百零七条 1964年7月2日第492号《收费法》第七十二条应当修改为：

领事馆办理的公证业务

第七十二条 领事馆办理公证业务，适用本法关于公证收费的规定。

（1964年7月2日《收费法》第492号第72条载有该项修正案）

被废除的法律和规定

第二百零八条 在不影响本法过渡条款的情况

ulations in temporary articles of this law, notary public law no: 3456 and its amending laws and Article 48 and 51 , no 492 of 2nd July, 1964 Charges Law are abolished.

下，废除《公证员法》(第3456号)及其修正法和1964年7月2日第492号《收费法》第四十八条和第五十一条。

Elections

选举

Supplementary article- (supplement: Article 5, no 2980 of 14/2/1984)

According to this law, Notaries Union of Turkey center organs and Notary Chambers board and chairman election operations carried out balloting shall be executed under the supervision of the adjudication according to the above-mentioned fundamental principles.

At least 15 days prior to the conference and general meeting that took place before the election, three copies of candidate notary public list for the election, meeting agenda, place, date, time and writing regarding matters on second meeting, in case there is no majority, shall be committed to the arbitrator, who is the district election board chairman of the relevant place. If there is more than one district election board someplace, appointed judge shall be appointed by the higher election board. Considering other subjects on the agenda, meeting dates shall be organized; so as to allow meetings shall came to a conclusion on a Saturday night and elections shall be held the following day, on Sunday between 9a.m. to 5 p.m.

The judge shall examine the relevant registers and documents in detail, if necessary and if any, provide what is necessary, and then authenticate candidate notaries list and other matters specified in the above-mentioned section. Authenticated list and other matters related to the meeting shall be announced for three days in a legal way by attaching the announcement on the related chamber or union.

During the announcement period, any objection about the list shall be examined by the judge and he shall settle at least in two days.

Final lists and other matters related to the meeting shall be authenticated then sent to the Notaries Union of Turkey and Notary Chamber.

The judge shall appoint ballot box board; consist of a chairman and two members among public officers and notary publics who are not candidates. He shall also appoint three substitute members. In case the ballot box board chairman is not available, eldest member shall law as the chairman.

Ballot box board is charged with execution, manage-

补充条款(补编：第5条，1984年2月14日第2980号)

依照本法，土耳其公证员联合会中心机构、公证办公室委员会成员和主席的选举活动在依照上述基本原则的监督下进行。

在选举前至少十五日举行大会，应当准备三份公证候选人名单副本、会议议程、地点、日期、时间和书面的第二次会议注意事项。如果大会没有多数人出席，应当由作为相关地区的地区选举委员会主席的仲裁员负责。如果某些地区的地区选举委员会超过一个，那么由较高级别的选举委员会任命负责的法官。考虑到协商议程上的其他议题，应当安排会议日期，以便会议能在周六晚上得出结论，选举则将在下一天即周日的上午九点到下午五点举行。

该负责的法官应当详细审查有关的登记册和文件，如有必要，应当提供必要的资料，然后对候选公证员名单和上述章节中规定的其他事项进行认证。经认证的名单和其他与会议有关的事项，应当以法定的方式公告三日，并将公告附在有关的办公室或联合会的文件上。

在公告期间，对名单的任何异议应当由负责的法官审查，并至少在两日内解决。

最后名单和与会议有关的其他事项应当经过认证，然后送交土耳其公证员联合会和公证办公室。

该负责法官应当指定选举委员会成员，由一名主席和两名非候选人的公职人员和公证员组成，并指定三名候补成员。若选举委员会主席不在场，则由最年长的人员担任主席。

选举委员会负责依法执行、管理选举和计票，并

ment of the elections in accordance with the law and vote classification and they shall execute those above-mentioned duties continuously until the election and classification ends.

Election tools and equipments shall be provided from the district election board and location of the ballot box shall be decided by the judge.

At the end of the election period, election results shall be registered in minutes and signed by the ballot box board chairman and members. Temporary election results shall be announced by attaching a copy of minutes in the election place. Votes and other documents shall be entrusted to the District Election Board Directorate to be kept for three months period with a copy of the minutes.

Operations carries out during the election and objections to elections results following minutes keeping, shall be examined in details by the judge in the same day and he shall make a decision. After the completion of objection period and just after making a decision judge shall announce the final results as specified in the above-mentioned stipulations and shall notify the results to the relevant notary chamber and notaries union of Turkey.

Voting shall be executed in the basis of balloting open classification. The notary public who is not listed shall not vote. Voting shall be executed after proving the identity of the voter by checking his ID issued by notary chamber, notaries union of turkey, or authorized body and signing the name across the list. Voting shall be executed as, writing on the papers sealed by District Election Board that is given separately for each election by the ballot box chairman and shall be put in to the sealed envelopes. Any votes written on other papers or put into unsealed envelopes shall not be valid.

If the judge cancels the elections as a result of corruption that affects the elections results or illegal application, he shall fix a Sunday for repeating the election for a period that shall be not less than a month and not more than two months, and notify the relevant chamber or notaries union of Turkey. Only the election is held on that fixed date and election operations shall be executed in accordance with this article and other stipulations of the law.

District Election Board chairman shall pay the judge and the ballot box board chairman and members on the fundamental principles specified in "Law on Fundamental Principles of The Elections and Electoral Roll". This fee and other electoral expenses shall be paid by The Notaries Union of Turkey budget.

应当持续执行上述职责，直至选举和计票结束。

选举工具和设备应当由地区选举委员会提供，投票箱的位置应当由负责的法官决定。

在选举结束时，选举结果须登记在笔录上，并由选举委员会主席及委员签字。临时选举结果应当附上选举地点的笔录副本。选票和其他文件应当委托地区选举委员会主管保存三个月，并附上笔录副本。

选举期间进行的操作和保留笔录后对选举结果的反对意见，应当在同一天由法官详细审查，并作出决定。异议期限届满，法官作出决定后，应当公布上述规定的最终结果，并将结果通知有关办公室和土耳其公证员联合会。

投票应当在公开的基础上进行。未列入名单的公证员不得投票。通过检查其由公证办公室、土耳其公证员联合会或授权机构颁发的身份卡并在名单上签名证明其作为投票人的身份后，才能进行投票。在地区选举委员会盖章的纸张上以书面形式进行投票。每一次选举的选票由投票箱主席分别提供，并应当放入密封的信封内。在其他纸张上所作的投票，或未放入密封的信封内，均属无效。

法官因腐败影响选举结果或者因非法申请而取消选举的，应当在一个月以上但不超过两个月的期间内，安排在某个星期日重新选举，并通知有关办公室或土耳其公证员联合会。选举只能在该固定日期举行，且选举活动应当符合本条和其他法律的规定。

地区选举委员会主席须按《选举及选举基本原则法》所规定的基本原则，向法官及选举委员会主席及委员支付酬金。该费用和其他选举费用应当由土耳其公证员联合会列入预算中。

Any offenses committed against ballot box board chairman and members during the elections, shall be punished as committing an offense against a public officer.

Those who fail to obey the precautionary measures taken by the judge and the ballot box board for the execution of elections in order and in health shall be punished by a disciplinary action according to this law depending on the aggravation of the action.

在选举期间，对选举委员会主席和委员所犯的任何罪行，应当以对公职人员犯罪的标准对该违法行为进行处罚。

不遵守法官和选举委员会为有序和健康地执行选举而采取的预防措施的，应当依照本法的规定，并按照行为的严重程度予以纪律处分。

Permission for going abroad

Supplementary article 2- (Additional Article 5 no: 2980 of 14/2/1984)

Participating international meetings and conferences to represent the union and chambers is subject to the permission of the Ministry of Justice.

出国许可

补充第2条（补充第5条，1984年2月14日第2980号）

参加代表联合会和办公室的国际会议须经司法部批准。

Temporary articles

Temporary article 1- the stipulation of the Article 3 of this law, shall be applied after The Notaries Union of Turkey Board begins to function.

Temporary article 2- three months after this article came into effect, without applying the stipulation on taking the decision of Notaries Union of Turkey, the Ministry of Justice shall classify notary publics according to the article 4 and shall announce the situation.

This classification shall be valid for a year following the establishment of Notaries Union of Turkey until a second classification is made.

Temporary article 3- in accordance with the article 9, no: 3456 abolished notary law the appointed conveyancing clerk still on duty on date this law came in to effect shall be qualified as (the notary public) after this law came into effect and they are subject to all rights and obligations regarding the notary publics of this law.

The appointment of the above-mentioned people to a higher class notary public shall only be possible in case there is no other candidate available that possess the qualifications mentioned in paragraph (3), Article 7.

Persons who possess certificate of competence as notary public or conveyancing clerk and still waiting for the appointment process to be definite before this law came into effect, shall be appointed in accordance with abolished law no: 3456. However, certificate of competence of the above-mentioned persons shall be still valid in accordance with article 12, paragraph 2, no: 3456 abolished notary law.

暂行条款

暂行第一条 本法第三条的规定，应当在土耳其公证员联合会委员会开始运行后适用。

暂行第二条 本条款生效三个月后，若未适用土耳其公证员联合会作出的决定中的规定，则司法部应当依照第四条对公证员进行分级并宣布分级情况。

此次分级在土耳其公证员联合会成立后一年内有效，直至进行第二次分级。

暂行第三条 依照已废除的第3456号《公证法》第九条规定的，在本法生效之日仍在职位上管理财产或其他权益让与法律事务的办事员，应当被定性为公证员，并在本法生效后，受本法所有关于公证员权利和义务的规定的约束。

仅在没有其他符合第七条第三款所述资格候选人的情况下，上述人员方可被委任为高级公证员。

凡持有公证员或办事员资格证书在本法生效前仍在等待委任程序确定的人，应当依照已废除的第3456号《公证法》进行委任。依照已废除的第3456号《公证法》第十二条第二款的规定，上述人员的资格证书仍然有效。

Those who are still waiting to be appointed on the date of this law came into effect shall be registered in holders of the notary public certificate that shall be kept in the ministry mentioned in the article 18 and shall be appointed upon announcement with respect to the Article 24.

Those who act as conveyancing clerk before this law came into effect, shall benefit from the social security fights provided by this law in accordance with the principles specified in Temporary articles 14, 15, 16 and 17.

Temporary article 4- those who work under contract as notary employees in the notary public office on the date of this law came into effect shall continue to law as a notary public personnel unless they possess the qualifications mentioned in article 44.

Those who resign from their duties, no matter what happens after this law came into effect shall be appointed again as notary public personnel, if they possess the qualifications mentioned in article 44.

Those who made service agreement with the notary public, mentioned in first paragraph, shall be arranged in accordance with the stipulations of this law within six months following the submittal date of the single type contract to the relevant Notary Camber prepared in accordance with the paragraph 11, article 166. Notary publics who fail to apply the stipulation of the above-mentioned paragraph, shall be subject to the paragraph 6, article 45.

Temporary article 5- tariff shown in the article 112, shall came into effect within six months following the establishment of Notaries Union of Turkey Board of Directors began to function.

Until the tariff shown in the first paragraph prepared, last tariff that is prepared in accordance with the abolished no: 3456 law and first paragraph, article 51 no: 492 of 2/7/1964 charges law shall be applied.

Temporary article 6- regulation specified in article 198 is prepared by the Notaries Union of Turkey and is authenticated and came into effect by The Ministry of Justice.

Until the regulation came into effect, operations shall be executed with respects to the abolished no: 3456 notary law and ministry circular principles.

Temporary article 7

- Notaries Union of Turkey shall be established upon the notification of The Ministry of Justice following a year this law came into effect.

Date of the establishment of notary chambers and delegates to be elected to participate the first meeting of the Union conference, conference meeting place and date

本法施行之日仍有待任命的，应当在本法第十八条所述部门保存的公证书持有人处登记，并依照第二十四条的规定宣告任命。

在本法施行前担任管理财产或其他权益让与法律事务的办事员的人员，依照临时条款第十四条、第十五条、第十六条和第十七条规定的原则，享受本法规定的社会保障待遇。

暂行第四条 本法施行之日，依照合同在公证机构从事公证工作的人员，除非具备第四十四条所述的资格（成为主管办事员），否则应当继续依法担任公证员。

具备第四十四条所述资格却辞职的上述人员，无论本法施行后发生什么，都应当被重新任命为公证员。

第一款所称与公证员订立的服务协议，应当自提交之日起六个月内依照本法的规定办理。公证员依照第一百六十六条第十一项编制相关公证办公室的单一典型合同，若未依照前款规定申请的，应当遵守第四十五条第六款的规定。

暂行第五条 第一百一十二条规定的收费标准，应当在土耳其公证员联合会委员会开始运行后六个月内生效。

在第一款规定的收费表编制完毕前，依照已废除的第 3456 号法和 1964 年 7 月 2 日第 492 号《收费法》第五十一条第一款编制的收费表仍可适用。

暂行第六条 第一百九十八条规定的条例由土耳其公证员联合会制定，并经司法部认证生效。

在该条例生效之前，应当依照已废除的第 3456 号法和司法部通告的原则执行业务。

暂行第七条

土耳其公证员联合会应当在本法生效一年后由司法部通知成立。

成立公证办公室的日期和参加联合会大会第一次会议的代表人选、会议地点和日期以及其他必要事项应当由司法部通知。

and other necessary matters took part in the notification of The Ministry of Justice.

Notary provident fund reserve shall pay the notification, announcement, stationery and print expenses regarding the establishment of Notaries Union of Turkey and meeting room rent held for the first conference completely in accordance with the Notary provident fund regulations. The above mentioned expenses shall not be subject to the Bidding, Underbidding and Procurement Law and visa of The Government Accounting Bureau.

依照公证公积金的规定，公证公积金的储备金应当用于支付关于设立土耳其公证员联合会的通知费用、公告费用、文具购买费用和印刷费用，以及举办第一次会议的会议室租金。上述费用不受投标、投低价标、采购法和国家会计局规定的约束。

Temporary article 8- within the duties assigned to Notaries Union of Turkey with this law, the ones which are executed by The Ministry of Justice and other Instances and Councils as stipulated by the abolished notary public law no: 3456, shall continue to be executed by the authorized instances and councils in accordance with the stipulations of the abolished law until authorized union organs shall take up the duty.

暂行第八条 在本法规定的土耳其公证员联合会的职责范围内，由司法部和其他机构、委员会依照已废除的第 3456 号法，与被授权的机构和委员会依照已废除的法律的规定继续执行，直至经授权的联合会机关履行该职责为止。

When the relevant body of the Notaries Union of Turkey, take up appointment, incomplete operations shall be completed in accordance with the stipulations of abolished law.

当土耳其公证员联合会有关机构接受任命时，未完成的业务应当依照已废除法律的规定完成。

Temporary article 9- tenth section stipulations of this law shall be applied following the Notaries Union of Turkey Board of Directors take up appointment.

暂行第九条 本法第十节的规定，在土耳其公证员联合会委员会主席接受任命后适用。

Fixing and announcement mentioned in the second paragraph, article 109 fixing and paying advance payment mentioned in, article 110 shall be completed within a month following the first of the month when the Notaries Union of Turkey Board of Directors takes up appointment and this duty shall continue until the end of the calendar year.

第一百零九条第二款中涉及的确定和公告事宜，第一百一十条涉及的确定和支付预缴款项事宜，应当自土耳其公证员联合会委员会主席接受任命的第一个月起并在一个月内完成，且该职责将持续到年终结束。

Temporary article 10- article 83 and 88 in class 8 related to the notary provident fund abolished no: 3456 notary law and notary provident fund regulations prepared in accordance with the Article 88, same law shall be in effect until the Notaries Union of Turkey Board of Directors takes up appointment. Any money sent to the Notaries Union of Turkey in accordance with the Article 33, 34, 117 of this law shall be registered to notary provident fund reserve until Notaries Union of Turkey Board of Directors take up appointment.

暂行第十条 已废除的第 3456 号《公证法》第八类中第八十三条、第八十八条关于公证公积金的规定和依照第八十八条制定的公证公积金条例，同样的法律在土耳其公证员联合会委员会主席接受任命之前应当有效。在土耳其公证员联合会的委员会主席接受任命之前，依照本法第三十三条、第三十四条、第一百一十七条向土耳其公证员联合会送出的任何款项应当登记在公证公积金准备金中。

Within 3 months following this law came into effect, under the condition of a written application to the notary provident fund and transfer expenses are paid on their behalf; notary publics and conveyancing clerks shall be paid in an amount of %50 of their payment due fund with

在本法施行之日起三个月内，以书面申请公证公积金为条件，代为支付转款费用；依照暂行条款第十二条的规定支付公证员和管理财产或其他权益让与法律事务的办事员应缴的到期款项总额的百分之五十，并将其从根据公证公积金最终资产负债表应付的应计

respect to the Temporary article 12, taking it out of accrue due according to the notary provident fund final balance sheet. Payment procedure shall be subject to article 83 and 88 of the no: 3456 notary law and notary provident fund regulations. However, notary provident fund Board of Directors shall consist of five people, two of which are the senior notary publics of Ankara, appointed by The Ministry of Justice in accordance with the fund regulations.

款项中扣除。付款程序适用第3456号《公证法》第八十三条、第八十八条和公证公积金条例的规定。公证公积金委员会理事应当由五人组成，其中两位是安卡拉的高级公证员，由司法部依照基金条例任命。

Temporary article 11- The Ministry of Justice shall make a fund accountant prepare a final account, showing notary provident fund passive and active, notary public and conveyancing clerk fund share and notary contribution in respect of those who are present, notary publics employee account, reserve and old age fund, within a month following the transfer period completion; mentioned in first paragraph of the Temporary article 10 and shall authenticate after the inspection of Ministry Inspection Council and shall transfer the passive and active to be fixed in accordance with the fund final account along with fund documents and books and registered moveable property attached to a list authenticated by the ministry to the Notaries Union of Turkey.

暂行第十一条 司法部应当让基金会计师编制一份决算，以显示公证公积金的消极和积极状况，并由公证员和管理财产或其他权益让与法律事务的办事员共同出资。依照暂行第十条第一款所述，在转账期结束后一个月内，对于现任的公证员、公证雇员账户、储备金和养老基金的公证分摊款，应当经政府检查委员会检查后认证，并根据基金的决算连同基金文件、账簿和附在土耳其公证员联合会经司法部认证的清单上的已登记动产确定。

Within a month mentioned-above there shall not be any payments made from the fund budget. Within this period, share of the person from the fund, shall be paid by Notaries Union of Turkey following the transfer.

在上述一个月内，不得从基金预算中支付任何款项。在此期间内，任何人员从基金中获得的份额，应当在调任后由土耳其公证员联合会支付。

Temporary article 12- regarding their share and contribution transferred to the Notaries Union of Turkey, according to the final account mentioned in Temporary article 11, notary public and conveyancing clerks payment conditions shall be decided in the extraordinary meeting, held on a month following the transfer of present fund to the Union by the Notaries Union of Turkey Conference according to the temporary article 11.

暂行第十二条 依照暂行第十一条所述的决算，公证员和管理财产或其他权益让与法律事务的办事员的份额和捐款转给土耳其公证员联合会，付款条件应当在土耳其公证员联合会公会将现有资金转入联合会一个月后举行的特别会议上决定。

Temporary article 13- the indemnity of notary publics that shall be calculated over their service until the transfer date as mentioned in Temporary article 11, in accordance with the Articles 70, 85 abolished no: 3456 Notary Law and Articles 18, 19 Notary Provident fund Regulation, for the ones who are on duty in notary public offices on the date of this law came into force, shall be paid to the right owners with respect to abolished laws by the Notaries Union of Turkey following the transfer of the present fund without searching the condition of 5 years service.

暂行第十三条 依照已废除的第3456号《公证法》第七十条、第八十五条和《公证公积金条例》第十八条、第十九条的规定，对公证员的补偿金应当从其服务期间计算至暂行第十一条所述的调任日期之前。对于本法生效之日在公证机构任职的，在本基金转移后，如未能查询到服务期满五年，土耳其公证员联合会应当依照已废除的法律支付给权利人。

When calculating the service years of the above-mentioned persons, the indemnity given by the Notary provi-

依照已废除的第3456号公证法，在计算上述人员的服务年限时，其先前的服务中由公积金支付的保

dent fund in their previous service in accordance with the abolished no: 3456 Notary Law shall mot be taken into consideration.

障金年限不计算在内。

Temporary article 14- the first type contract which serves as a basis for the contract to be made between Notary Chambers and Social Security Organization with respect to the Article 86 of The Social Security Organization law no: 506, shall be fixed between the Notaries Union of Turkey, Ministry of Labor and Social Security Organization within three months following the first meeting of Notaries Union of Turkey with respect to the article 7 of this law on the date of this law came into effect. Notaries Union of Turkey Board shall send the prepared type agreement to all the notary chambers within Turkey in a month period. Notary chambers of the notary publics, who are obliged to participate in the collective insurance, shall apply to the Social Security Organization within two months following the arrival of type contract to the notary chamber to make a collective insurance contract according to the type contract. The contract shall come into effect at least in three months following the application date of the notary chamber.

暂行第十四条 第一类合同作为公证办公室与社会保障组织就《社会保障公约》第八十六条订立合同的基础，应由土耳其公证员联合会、劳动部和社会保障组织在本法第七条生效之日举行的第一次土耳其公证员联合会大会后三个月内确定。土耳其公证员联合会委员会应当将准备好的协议在一个月内送交土耳其的所有公证办公室。公证办公室的公证员有义务参加集体保险的，应当在其后两个月内向社会保障组织提出申请，并将合同送交公证办公室，依照该合同订立集体保险合同。本合同在向公证办公室提出申请后三个月内生效。

(A) Notary publics who are already 50 years old now and were already 30 years old on the date they are covered in the collective insurance, and fail to fulfill the conditions mentioned in article 60 of The Social Insurance Law and cannot benefit from old age salary and;

（A）已年满五十岁且在集体保险投保之日已满三十岁的公证员，但未达到《社会保险法》第六十条所述条件的人不能享受养老金工资；

a) Those who certify that they are registered lawyers in the notary public or the bar inscribed card for at least 2000 days within ten years, before their insurance starts,

（a）在保险开始前的十年内，证明自己是在公证机构注册的律师或持有律师证至少二千天的人；

b) Those who pay at least 200 days insurance premium each year on average during their insurance,

（b）在其保险期间每年平均缴付二百天保险费的人；

c) Notary publics who are insured at least for five years,

（c）至少投保五年的公证员，

Shall benefit from old age salary in accordance with the article 61 of The Social Insurance Law; like the ones already completed their insurance period of 15 years.

依照《社会保险法》第六十一条领取养老金工资；与已完成十五年保险的人享受同等待遇。

The notary public period as mentioned in paragraph (a) shall be requested from the Ministry of Justice and advocacy period shall be requested from the relevant bar within at least two years, following the insurance beginning date of the notary public and shall be fixed with the documents to be submitted to the Social Security Organization.

（a）款所述公证员期间应当向司法部申请，辩护期应当由相关律师至少在两年内申请，在公证员保险生效后，应当与提交社会保障组织的文件一起确定。

If the bar fails to arrange those above-mentioned documents, insured notary publics have all the rights to request damages and losses from the chairman of the board

如果律师协会未能安排上述文件，被保险人有权向委员会主席和有关律师公会成员请求损害赔偿。

and members of the relevant bar.

If the document showing the advocacy period is counterfeit, those who prepared and those who are insured shall be obliged to pay the damages in %50 extra and with the legal interest to the Social Security Organization.

Penal prosecution shall be applied for those above-mentioned persons.

(B) Notary publics who are already 50 years old now and were already 30 years old on the date they are covered in the collective insurance, and fail to fulfill the conditions mentioned in article 60 of The Social Insurance Law and cannot benefit from old age salary and those who are old aged; shall benefit from old age salary in accordance with the article 61, The Social Insurance Law, like the ones who have already completed their insurance period of 15 years and with the sane conditions as in paragraph (A).

Temporary article 15

- those who have at least served 15 years at total that serves as a basis for retirement in T.R. Retirement Fund, on the date of this law came into effect;

(A) notary publics who are resigned from their duty or service, no matter what happens, which they pay retirement deduction on the date before this law came into effect, under the condition that they do not benefit from retirement or old age salary, shall owe notary public or actual advocacy period completely or the remaining period that will sum up to 25 years needed for retirement service until this law came into effect as follows:

(B) those who are resigned from their duty or service, no matter what happens, which they pay retirement deduction on the date or after this law came into effect, and who are appointed as notary publics shall continue to be insured by the T.R. Retirement Fund without exceeding the 30 years period in total.

The person concerned shall apply to the T.R. Retirement Fund in writing via notary chamber within three months following his/her participation in the collective insurance of the relevant notary chamber for being a debtor with respects to the paragraph (A). The previous deduction paid to the T.R. Retirement Fund by the person concerned following his/her length of service taking into account, minimum promotion period of the said duty or service and counting as promoting every two or three years; the owed amount shall be reduction due (notary share also included) of the complete notary public or actual advocacy period until this law go into effect. However the reduction and the notary share shall be calculated by taking into account the

如果证明辩护期的文件是伪造的，伪造文件者和被保险人有义务额外支付百分之五十的损害赔偿金，并向社会福利单位支付法定利息。

对上述人员适用刑事起诉。

（B）已年满五十岁和在集体保险投保之日已满三十岁，但未达到《社会保险法》第六十条所述条件的公证员，不能享受养老金和老龄人的福利；但如（A）项所述，他们已完成十五年的保险期，并具备健全的条件，因此应当依照《社会保险法》第六十一条的规定享受养老金。

暂行第十五条

从本法生效之日起，依据 T.R. 退休基金的规定，以至少服务十五年作为退休依据；

（A）无论发生什么情况而辞职的公证员，在本法生效之日支付的退休金应扣减，在未从退休金或养老金中受益的情况下，应当给予公证员全部的实际辩护期间或在本法生效前职业退休所需共计二十五年的剩余期间。具体如下：

（B）在本法生效之日起，无论发生什么情况而辞职的人，以及被任命为公证员的人，应继续由 T.R. 退休基金承保，但不超过三十年的期限。

相关人员应当在他 / 她参加有关公证办公室的集体保险后三个月内，以书面形式就（A）款向 T.R. 退休基金申请成为债务人。在考虑相关人员的服务期长短后，向 T.R. 退休基金支付先前的扣减额。上述职务或服务的晋升期，按每两三年晋升一次计算；在本法生效前，应当扣除（公证员份额也包括在内）公证员完整的实际辩护期的应扣减额。但是，扣减额和公证份额的计算应当参照生效的 T.R.《退休金法》。

effective T.R. Retirement Fund Law of the relevant date.

Period due and previous duty or service period subject to T.R. Retirement Fund shall not exceed 30 years in total. It is impossible to owe the exceeding part of the notary public period.

Amount Due shall be paid in total or in installments in 10 years according to the request of the person concerned, upon the notification of T.R. Retirement Fund. Those who took their deduction upon resignation from previous duty or service subject to T.R. Retirement Fund shall be obliged to pay it back completely to The Fund with its legal interest within the period to pay the due amount or to pay the first installment. Those who fail to pay within the period mentioned-above shall not take advantage of this stipulation.

Those who owe shall have a right to be paid for retirement salary which shall be calculated by adding the period due to previous duty or service period that serves as a basis for their retirement, following the date they pay the entire amount due. Total period shall be 25 years for having a right to take retirement salary.

Regarding the installment payment; those who die before paying the entire amount or old-aged notary publics with respect to law no: 3454 or right owner inheritors shall benefit from old age or widow and orphan salary within the following month of the death or old age. Each of the annual installments due shall be divided into twelve equal amounts and deducted from old age or widow and orphan salary of the relevant year and the remaining amount shall be paid to the right owners.

Regarding the installment payment; those who fail to pay an installment on time and those who fail to pay upon notification by T.R. Retirement Fund within a month shall be obligor no more and T.R. Retirement Fund Law stipulations shall be applied over the period calculated, by adding the period that corresponds to amount paid to previous duty or service period.

With respect to the above-mentioned paragraphs, persons or inheritors who benefit from retirement, old age or widow and orphan salary, shall be paid bonus from the last place of service or duty which is subject to retirement, over the real duty or service amount before the amount due.

Those who wish to take benefit from paragraph (B) shall apply to the T.R. Retirement Fund with a petition, within a month following the notification date of being appointed as notary public, and shall not be paid retirement

退休金的到期期限和先前的职务或服务期合计不得超过三十年。超过部分不予支持。

在收到 T.R. 退休金通知后，应当按照相关人员的要求，以全部或十年分期付款方式支付到期款项。对于在之前辞职并获取 T.R. 退休基金的人，有义务在规定的期限内将退休金全部退还并支付法定利息。所谓规定的期限指的是在支付应缴款项或支付第一笔分期付款期间内。没有在上述期限内付款的人不得依照本法的规定受益。

欠债的人有权领取退休工资，退休工资的计算方法是将以前的职务或服务期加起来，作为退休的依据。在退休当天他们应当支付所欠的全部到期款项。领取退休工资的权利期限为二十五年。

关于分期付款，在支付全部金额前死亡的人或依照第 3454 号法令规定的老年公证员以及从老年公证员、寡妇或孤儿死亡后一个月内的抚恤金中受益的继承权利所有人，每年所付款项应当等额分成十二笔，并从老年公证员、遗孀和孤儿的抚恤金中扣除，剩余金额应当支付给权利所有人。

关于分期付款，未按时支付的，在一个月内经 T.R. 退休基金通知仍未缴纳的，不再享有该基金保障权。T.R. 退休金法的规定应适用于适当的期间加上与先前的职务或服务期相对应的期间内。

依照前项规定，从退休者、老年人、遗孀和孤儿工资中受益的个人或者继承人，应当从亡者最后的服务或职务场所中领取奖金。但须以退休为限，在到期总额前，超过实际职责或服务的总额应当扣除。

任何人士如欲根据（B）款获益，须在获委任为公证员的通知日期起一个月内，通过申请书向 T.R. 退休金提出申请，但不得支领退休工资，亦不得扣减任何款项。凡根据（A）款第二节为受益人而从（B） salary or shall not have any deduction. Those who take benefit from paragraph (B) by favor of second section of paragraph (A), this period shall commence following the Fund notification date regarding the acceptance of loan request.

款中受益者，应当在基金接受贷款申请的通知日期之后开始计算该期限。

Those who wish to apply to take benefit from paragraph (B) shall be obliged to pay deduction to the Fund, within the beginning of month following the Fund notification regarding the acceptance of T.R. Retirement Fund. Reductions (notary share is included) shall be paid directly or via a bank indicated by the T.R. Retirement Fund to the Fund within first week of the month.

欲从（B）款中受益者必须在收到 T.R. 退休金的受领通知后的月初，向基金支付扣减额。退休基金、扣减额（包括公证份额）应当在一个月的第一周内直接或通过 T.R. 退休基金指定的银行支付给基金。

Deduction or notary share (organization share) shall be calculated over salary levels promoting in every two or three years according to the minimum promotion period starting from the last seniority he/she acquired from his/her previous duty or service that he/she paid the deduction to the T.R. Retirement Fund

扣减额或公证份额（组织份额）应当依照他 / 她从其以前的职务或服务中应当支付给 T.R. 退休基金的扣减额，并按每两到三年晋升一次的工资水平计算。

In accordance with the paragraph (B), those who completed their 30 years period for retirement and insured by the T.R. Retirement Fund; request in writing to be uncovered by the Fund, die or got old according to the law: 5434 or fail to pay within a month period given by the fund; shall be no longer insured by the Fund, following the beginning of the month above-mentioned situations came into existence. The above-mentioned persons or their inheritors shall be paid retirement, old age or widow and orphan salary over their total period. Stipulations on due amount shall be applied by comparison regarding the bonus of the above-mentioned people.

依照（B）款，完成三十年服务期退休并由 T.R. 退休基金投保的人，书面请求由基金提供保险、死亡抚恤金或养老金。依照第 5434 号法令的规定或在基金规定的一个月内未付款的，在上述情况下，自本月初起不再由基金投保。上述人员或者他们的继承人，应当领取全部期间的退休、老年、遗孀和孤儿工资。有关应付金额的规定，应参照上述人员的奖金标准适用。

With respect to the temporary article 16, people with due amount and retirement service total of 15 years or more shall take advantage of paragraph (B) of this article.

关于暂行的第十六条，凡服务满十五年及以上的人领取适当的款项和退休金应当适用本条第（B）款的规定。

Total period of those persons who take advantage of the stipulation of this article; in debt according to paragraph (A) or still insured by the T.R. Retirement Fund according to paragraph (B), shall be added to their last salary from their duty, subject to retirement or to their senior pay, shall be adapted as if promoted or to be promoted in every 2 or 3 years according to the minimum seniority period of this duty.

依照本条规定获益的人，依照（A）款规定的债务或者按（B）款的规定仍由退休基金担保的，应当增加从他们的职务获得的最后工资。对于退休基金或他们的资历工资应当依照职务的最低资历每两年或三年晋升一次。

Temporary article 16- on the date this law came into effect, those who are on duty or service subject to the T.R. Retirement Fund, the duty or service that they paid retirement deduction for the period that they passed in notary public office, the period that shall not exceed fifteen years along with due periods with respect to other laws under

暂行第十六条 自本法生效之日起，在职务或服务中受 T.R. 退休基金约束者，须按他们在公证机构的职务或服务期间支付退休金扣减额，该期间依照 1965 年 2 月 23 日第 545 号法第五条的规定不得超过十五年。上述到期人数应当予以登记，且应当依照到期之日所支付的总额比率和扣除的额度确定支付额。

the condition of due amount on condition that in accordance with the principles of Article 5, law no: 545 of 23rd February, 1965 added to law no: 5434, shall be added to retirement services. Due amount to be registered on behalf of the above-mentioned persons shall be fixed, according to the deducted deductions and amounts paid ratio on the date of the period due.

According to this law and temporary articles 3 and 4 of Advocacy Code no: 1136 of 23rd march, 1969 in case due requests are made together, due period shall not exceed 15 years in total with previous due period according to other laws.

依照本法和1969年3月23日第1136号《辩护法》暂行第三条和第四条的规定，如果一起提出申请，与此前其他法律规定的期限相比，到期期限不应超过十五年。

With respect to the above-mentioned paragraph, two third of the period added to service for retirement as due, shall be adapted to be evaluated in every 2 or 3 years according to minimum seniority period of the duty or service still assigned and by this way, salary as the basis for retirement deduction and duty or service salary shall be increased.

关于前项规定，退休后的三分之二期间应按最低年资调整，每两年或三年评估一次。对指定的职责或服务，以工资作为退休金扣减额的依据，并增加职务或服务工资。

Those who wish to take benefit from the stipulation of this article shall apply to the T.R. Retirement Fund with a letter within 3 months following the date this law came into effect.

凡欲从本条规定中受益者，应当自本法施行之日起三个月内，向T.R. 退休基金书面申请。

Temporary article 17- after this law came into effect, right owner inheritors or notary publics and notary clerks who have no salary in accordance with the stipulations of Social Security Law or T.R. Retirement Fund whom they are subject to, on date of their death or old age, whom are died or old aged shall be paid in total by The Notaries Union of Turkey budget as follows: in case a notary public dies 10000 New Turkish Liras, in case a notary public gets old 7500 New Turkish Liras, in case a notary clerk dies 5000 New Turkish Liras, in case a notary clerk gets old 3000 New Turkish Liras. Shares arising from death or old age situation between the date this law came into effect and Notaries Union of Turkey Board begin to function shall be paid after Union Board begin to function.

暂行第十七条 本法施行后，依照《社会保障法》或者T.R. 退休基金的规定，无工资的权利继承人、公证员和公证办事员，他们在死亡或年老后的退休基金，应当由土耳其公证员联合会全额支付，预算如下：如果公证员死亡，那么得到一万新土耳其里拉；如果公证员年老，那么得到七千五百新土耳其里拉；如果公证办事员死亡，那么得到五千新土耳其里拉；如果公证办事员年老，那么得到三千新土耳其里拉。从本法律生效之日至土耳其公证员联合会开始运行之日，因死亡或年老情况而引起的经济损失，应当在联合会委员会开始运行后支付。

Old age certification and persons or shares to be paid in case of death shall be applied in accordance with the insurance organization of the person died or got old, which is either Social Security Organization or T.R. Retirement Fund.

因退休或死亡应当支付的资金或者份额，由死亡或者养老保险机构办理，即社会保障组织或者T.R. 退休基金。

Payments to be made in respect of this law shall be exempt from any tax or charge.

依照本法支付的款项，免征任何税款或费用。

Temporary article 18- those who are graduated from school of political sciences or faculty and passed differentiation examination in faculty of law for the incomplete classes before this law cam into effect shall be accepted as

暂行第十八条 毕业于政治学院或为教职员工通过法学院的区分考试的，在适用本法的过程中，应当被视为法律系毕业生。

a graduate of faculty of law in the application of this law.

Temporary article 19- in accordance with article 27 of this law, notary publics who wishes to apply for a notary public of a higher class, not inspected before by justice inspectors in accordance with the Article 122, shall be chosen by justice inspectors regarding their competency to the higher class appointment. Justice inspectors shall evaluate professional competence as at least average to reach a final decision regarding their competency to the higher class appointment in the last two certificate of good character, prepared by the previous relevant inspector.

暂行第十九条 依照本法第二十七条，希望申请高级公证员的公证员，应当依照第一百二十二条的规定，经司法检查人员就其担任高级职务的能力作出评判。司法检查员应当客观地评价其专业能力，并在此前检查员出具的两份品格证书的基础上，作出关于他们是否胜任较高级别职务的最后决定。

Temporary article 20- before this law came into effect, appointment announcement of open or available notary public office approved by the minister shall be in accordance with the abolished no: 3456 notary public law.

暂行第二十条 本法施行前，经公证部批准的公证员或者可任公证员职务的聘任公告，应当依照已废止的第 3456 号公证法的规定办理。

EFFECTIVE ARTICLES

生效条款

Effective date

生效时间

Article 209 – this shall go into effect 3 month after its publication.

第二百零九条 本法自公布之日起三个月后施行。

Effective body

生效机构

Article 210 – the stipulation of this law shall be executed by the council of ministers

第二百一十条 本法的规定由部长会议执行。

Stipulations not embroidered to the law no: 1512 of 18/1/1972

1972 年 1 月 18 日第 1512 号法令没有作出的规定

Temporary article of law no: 2980 of 14/02/1984

暂行法律条款：1984 年 2 月 14 日第 2980 号

Temporary article

暂行条款

- Notaries Union of Turkey center organs and notary chamber board and chairmen and Notaries Union of Turkey Conference delegates shall be elected in 3 months following 1st December, 1983 without requiring election term and duty period come to an end.

土耳其公证员联合会中心机关、公证办公室委员会以及土耳其公证员联合会会议主席和代表应当在 1983 年 12 月 1 日之后的三个月内选出。不需要明确任职期限。

Temporary articles no: 3588 of the date

暂行条款第 3588 号

Temporary article 1- before this law go into effect, class of notary publics on duty shall be fixed by promoting every four years in service, under the condition their reserved rights shall be reserved. Remaining period shall be counted as passed in the last fixed class.

暂行第一条 本法施行前，公证员的职务等级应当每四年提升一次，并保留其权利。剩余期间应当按最后等级的时间计算。

Temporary article 2- in accordance with the last paragraph of Article 112 of Notary Law, necessary amendments shall be made in a month, following this law go

暂行第二条 依照《公证法》第一百一十二条最后一项的规定，在本法实施后一个月内对其作出必要的修改，并自 1991 年 3 月起施行最后一次修改。

into effect and shall be valid until March 1991 that the last amendment shall be made.

Temporary article 3 – appointments that shall be made for announced vacant notary publics before this law go into effect, shall be in accordance with the previous same stipulations.

暂行第三条 本法施行前已经公告聘任结果的公证员，应当依照此前的规定办理。

土库曼斯坦

公证法

Law of Turkmenistan about notariate and notarial activities

This Law determines the organizational and legal basis of notariate, and also procedure of notarial activities in Turkmenistan.

Section I. Organizational and legal basis of activities of notariate

Chapter I. General provisions

Article 1. Notariate in Turkmenistan

The notariate in Turkmenistan is the system consisting of bodies and authorized persons on which tasks of implementation of notarial activities for the certificate of the indisputable rights, and also facts having legal value and giving of legal reliability to them are assigned.

Article 2. Main objective of notariate

The main objective of notariate is ensuring protection of the rights and legitimate interests of physical persons and legal entities, and also state interests by making of notarial actions on behalf of Turkmenistan.

Article 3. Legislation of Turkmenistan on notariate and notarial activities

1. The legislation of Turkmenistan on notariate and notarial activities is based on the Constitution of Turkmenistan and consists of this Law and other regulatory legal acts of Turkmenistan which govern the relations connected with implementation of notarial activities.

2. If the international treaty of Turkmenistan estab-

土库曼斯坦公证法

本法规定了土库曼斯坦公证活动的组织和法律依据，以及公证活动的程序。

第一部分　公证活动的组织和法律依据

第一章　总则

第一条　土库曼斯坦公证

土库曼斯坦公证系由机构和经授权的个人组成，其任务是对无权属纠纷的证书以及具有法律价值和法律依赖性的事实进行公证。

第二条　公证的主要目的

公证的主要目的是确保对自然人和法人权利和合法利益的保护，并且通过公证活动代表土库曼斯坦确保国家利益。

第三条　土库曼斯坦公证和公证活动立法

1. 土库曼斯坦有关公证和公证活动的立法以土库曼斯坦宪法为基础，并包括本法和土库曼斯坦的其他监管法规，该等法律适用于一切与公证有关的活动。

2. 如果土库曼斯坦签订的国际条约确立了本法规

lishes other rules than provided by this Law, then rules of the international treaty are applied.

定范围以外的其他规则，那么适用国际条约中的规则。

Article 4. Notarial activities

Notarial activities are making by the notary public of the notarial actions provided by this Law and other regulatory legal acts of Turkmenistan.

第四条 公证活动

公证活动是指本法和土库曼斯坦其他监管法规规定的公证机构进行的活动。

Article 5. Basic principles of notarial activities

Notarial activities in Turkmenistan are based on the principles of legality, justice, independence and safety of mystery of making of notarial actions.

第五条 公证活动的基本原则

土库曼斯坦的公证活动以合法、公平、独立和保密为原则。

Article 6. Legality when implementing notarial activities

Notarial activities in Turkmenistan are performed according to the Constitution of Turkmenistan, this Law, other regulatory legal acts and international treaties of Turkmenistan.

第六条 公证活动的合法性

土克曼斯坦的公证活动应依据土库曼斯坦宪法、本法、其他规范性法律文件和土库曼斯坦签订的国际条约开展。

Article 7. Justice when implementing notarial activities

1. Notarial activities are performed on equal terms for all persons irrespective of nationality, race, floor, origin, property and official capacity, the residence, language, the relation to religion, political convictions, party accessory or lack of belonging to any batch.

2. Notaries public, authorized persons to whom tasks of implementation of the notarial activities having no right to make notarial actions which results are of valuable or other private interest to them are assigned.

第七条 公证活动的公平性

1. 对于所有人，无论其国籍、种族、出身、财产和官方身份，住所、语言、宗教信仰、政治立场、属于或不属于任何政党，公证活动均在平等的条件下进行。

2. 公证机构和经授权的个人在开展公证活动时无权从事对其自身具有价值或者其他私人利益的公证活动。

Article 8. Independence when implementing notarial activities

1. Persons performing notarial activities in case of execution of the obligations assigned to them are independent and submit only to the laws of Turkmenistan.

2. Illegal impact on persons performing notarial activities, in case of execution of the obligations assigned to them is not allowed and involves the responsibility established by the legislation of Turkmenistan.

第八条 公证活动的独立性

1. 公证员在履行法定义务而从事公证活动时是独立的，并且只能遵守土库曼斯坦的法律。

2. 公证员在履行法定义务和土库曼斯坦法律规定的责任时，不受非法因素影响。

Article 9. Preserving mystery of making of notarial actions

1. Safety of mystery of the notarial actions made concerning them is guaranteed to physical persons and legal entities.

2. Persons performing notarial activities provide preserving mystery of committed notarial action.

3. Ensuring preserving mystery of committed notarial

第九条 公证活动的保密性

1. 自然人和法人公证活动的有关信息保密。

2. 公证员对其所从事的公证活动保密。

3. 当公证员不再履职时亦需对其履职获得的信息

actions is the mandatory requirement for persons which stopped notarial activities.

The obligation of preserving mystery of committed notarial actions extends also to trainees and assistants to notaries public.

4. Data on committed notarial actions, copies or duplicates of the documents issued by the notary public are issued only to physical persons and legal entities, from name, addressed to, according to the order or concerning which these actions were made.

5. Data on notarial actions and documents are issued according to the written requirement of court, bodies of prosecutor's office, inquiry and investigation, for the cases which are in their production, and also the bodies authorized by this Law to exercise control of activities of the notary public.

6. Data on committed notarial actions are issued according to the written requirement of the state registrar performing state registration of the rights to real estate and the related transactions except for of documents which according to regulatory legal acts of Turkmenistan are submitted only to interested persons.

7. Data on the will during lifetime of the testator are issued to him, and after the death of the testator – to persons and bodies specified in parts of the fourth or sixth this Article and also the testator's heirs if other is not stipulated by the legislation Turkmenistan.

8. Data on issue certificates on the right to inheritance are granted to the relevant tax authorities.

9. Obligation observe the mystery of making of notarial actions extends to persons who knew of these actions in connection with accomplishment of service duties by them, and also on other persons participating in notarial actions.

10. Persons which divulged data on committed notarial actions bear responsibility according to the legislation of Turkmenistan.

Article 10. Right to making of notarial actions

1. The right to make notarial actions within the powers, and also in cases and limits set by this Law have:

1) the notary public of office of notary public (further – the notary public);

2) officials Gengesha;

3) officials of diplomatic representations and consular establishments of Turkmenistan abroad;

4) the officials having the right to make notarial ac-

保密。

从事公证活动的所有保密义务扩大适用于公证员的实习生和助手。

4. 根据公证活动的相关要求，公证活动的信息、公证员出具的文件的副本或复印件仅向自然人和法人公布。

5. 法院、检察机关因其办理案件需要，书面请求获取公证信息及本法授权机构从事公证活动需要时，得向其提供公证信息。

6. 履行国家不动产登记及相关交易登记权利的国家登记机构书面要求提供公证信息的，可向其提供公证信息。但根据土库曼斯坦监管法律行为仅向利害关系人提交文件的除外。

7. 除土库曼斯坦法律另有规定外，立遗嘱人在世时所立遗嘱，在其去世后向本条第 4 款或第 6 款规定的个人或机构、立遗嘱人的继承人公布。

8. 有关继承权的公证书的信息得授予相关税务机关。

9. 对公证活动的保密义务应扩展到在其履职过程中知道这些活动的人员，以及参与公证活动的其他人员。

10. 根据土库曼斯坦法律的规定，泄露所从事的公证活动信息的人员应承担相应的法律责任。

第十条　从事公证活动的权利

1. 享有在本法规定的事项和限制范围内从事公证活动的权力的人员包括：

（1）公证机构的公证员（以下简称“公证员”）；

（2）地方人民委员会官员；

（3）土库曼斯坦境外外交代表和领事机构官员；

（4）根据本法第 37 条第 1 款，有权从事公证活

tions according to part one of article 37 of this Law.

For the purposes of this Law the officials specified in Items 2 - Item 4 this part, hereinafter are referred to as further as authorized officers.

2. When making notarial actions notaries public according to this Law have the equal rights and fulfill identical duties.

3. The documents processed within powers by the persons specified in part one of this Article, having the right to make notarial actions have identical legal force.

Article 11. Procedure for making of notarial actions

1. Notarial actions are made according to the procedure, established by the legislation of Turkmenistan.

2. When making notarial actions by the notary public the notarial act – the written instrument (notarially certified document) constituted, certified or certified according to the procedure, established by the legislation of Turkmenistan is drawn up.

Article 12. Notarial clerical work

1. The notarial clerical work is performed according to the Rules of maintaining notarial clerical work approved by the Ministry adalat Turkmenistan in coordination with the Head archival department under the Cabinet of Ministers of Turkmenistan.

2. The documents connected with the notarial actions made by notaries public authorized officers are subject to delivery in archive according to the procedure, established by the legislation of Turkmenistan.

Article 13. Notariate unified information system

1. Unified information system of notariate the automated information system intended for complex automation of processes of collection, processing of data on notarial activities and providing all types of information exchange (exchange) is recognized (further – unified information system). In unified information system are subject to inclusion of the data on notarial actions, including in the form of electronic documents. Contents of these data are determined according to this Law.

2. Electronic documents can be certified by the digital signature according to the legislation of Turkmenistan.

3. The procedure for creation, content, functioning and use of unified information system, and also procedure for provision of the data containing in it are determined by the Ministry adalat Turkmenistan.

4. Protection of the data containing in unified infor-

动的官员。

为本法之目的，本部分第 2 项至第 4 项指明的官员在下文中称为授权官员。

2. 在从事公证活动时，公证员依照本法享有平等的权利，履行相同的职责。

3. 本条第 1 款规定的有权从事公证活动的人员在权力范围内处理的文件具有相同的法律效力。

第十一条　从事公证活动的程序

1. 公证活动根据土库曼斯坦法律规定的程序进行。

2. 公证机构在从事公证时，根据土库曼斯坦法律规定的结构、方式或程序制作公证文书。

第十二条　公证文书工作

1. 公证文书工作根据土库曼斯坦公证部与土库曼斯坦内阁档案部门部长协商批准的公证文书工作规则进行。

2. 与公证授权官员从事的公证活动有关的文件，按照土库曼斯坦法律规定的程序进行归档交付。

第十三条　公证统一信息系统

1. 公证统一信息系统是自动化的信息系统，旨在用于复杂的自动化收集程序，处理公证活动的资料并提供各种类型受认可的信息交换（交换）（以下简称“统一信息系统”）。统一信息系统中包含公证活动的资料，并包括电子文件形式的资料。这些资料的内容根据本法确定。

2. 根据土库曼斯坦法律的规定，电子文件可以通过数字签名的方式进行公证。

3. 统一信息系统的创建、内容、功能和使用程序，以及提供系统中资料的程序由土库曼斯坦公证部确定。

4. 根据土库曼斯坦法律的规定，依法保护统一信

mation system is performed according to the legislation of Turkmenistan.

5. Persons having access to the data containing in unified information system and the faces performing data processing of unified information system not open to the third parties and not spread the information containing in this information system, except as specified, established by the legislation of Turkmenistan.

Such persons bear the responsibility established by the legislation of Turkmenistan for disclosure or illegal use of the specified data.

6. Creation and functioning of unified information system are financed by means of the Government budget of Turkmenistan.

Article 14. Language of notarial clerical work

The notarial clerical work is conducted in state language of Turkmenistan, the documents issued by results of making of notarial actions are drawn up in state language of Turkmenistan.

Chapter II. Legal status of the notary public

Article 15. The notary public in Turkmenistan

1. The citizen of Turkmenistan having the higher legal education, who passed training at the notary public within six months and certification if other is not provided by this Law can become the notary public.

2. Persons having the outstanding or not removed criminal record, and also the faces recognized in accordance with the established procedure incapacitated cannot be the notary public or it is limited by capable. Persons concerning whom the criminal cases on not rehabilitating bases and also exempted from the notary public position for the violations of the law of Turkmenistan allowed by them when making notarial actions are stopped cannot be the notary public also.

3. In case of decision making about position assignment of the notary public it is necessary to proceed from compliance of position of the notary public of personal and professional qualities of the applicant for the notary public position, at the same time the work experience of the lawyer, law enforcement officer or legal services of other legal entities is considered.

4. Making of notarial actions with violation of requirements of the legislation of Turkmenistan on notariate and notarial activities attracts responsibility according to the legislation of Turkmenistan.

息系统中的资料。

5. 有权访问统一信息系统中包含的资料的人员和处理统一信息系统资料的人员禁止将该等信息系统中的信息向第三方公开、传播，但土库曼斯坦法律另有特别规定的除外。

上述人员承担土库曼斯坦法律规定的泄露或非法使用有关数据的责任。

6. 统一信息系统的建立和运作由土库曼斯坦政府财政预算提供资金。

第十四条　公证文书工作的语言

公证文书工作以土库曼斯坦的国家语言进行，公证文书应以土库曼斯坦国家语言编写。

第二章　公证员的法律地位

第十五条　土库曼斯坦的公证员

1. 受过高等法律教育、在 6 个月内通过公证机构组织的公证员培训并获结业证书的土库曼斯坦公民可以成为公证员，本法另有规定的除外。

2. 有尚未执行或未被清除犯罪记录的人，以及根据规定程序认定为无行为能力的人不能成为公证员或其担任公证员的资格受到限制。对于尚未执行的刑事案件的罪犯和享有从事公证活动违反土库曼斯坦法律豁免权已经终止的人员，亦不能成为公证员。

3. 在对公证员的职位安排进行决策时，有必要基于个人担任公证员职位的合规性和专业能力并考虑律师、执法人员和其他法律服务的工作经历。

4. 违反土库曼斯坦法律规定从事公证活动应依法承担法律责任。

5. The property harm done by the notary public as a result of making of notarial actions is compensated according to the legislation of Turkmenistan.

Article 16. Assistants and notary public trainees

1. The notary public can have assistants and trainees whose rights, obligations and working conditions are determined according to the labor law of Turkmenistan.

2. Citizens of Turkmenistan can only be the assistant to the notary public.

3. The assistant to the notary public works as a part of office of notary public.

4. The citizens of Turkmenistan having the higher legal education can be trainees of the notary public. Candidate screen for acceptance by trainees of the notary public is performed according to personal and professional qualities.

Trainees pass training at the notary public.

The trainee of the notary public is appointed by the order of the Minister adalat Turkmenistan. The salary of the trainee of the notary public is established according to the legislation of Turkmenistan.

The procedure for passing of training affirms the Minister adalat Turkmenistan.

5. The assistant and the trainee on specifying and under responsibility of the notary public carry out its orders, they cannot make notarial actions and their activities have auxiliary character.

6. The purpose of training is acquisition by the trainee of professional knowledge and practical skills on making of notarial actions and the organization of work of the notary public.

7. More than two trainees cannot pass training at one notary public at the same time.

8. Passing of training is performed according to the Single program of the professional training of trainees approved by the order of the Minister adalat Turkmenistan.

The single program of professional training of trainees is obligatory for all trainees and shall contain list of the actions directed to acquisition by the trainee of special theoretical knowledge, practical skills of making of notarial actions and the organization of work of the notary public including studying of professional and ethical standards of behavior of the notary public, visit of the seminar occupations organized for notaries public or especially for trainees.

9. Upon termination of training the notary public

5. 公证员因公证活动造成的财产损失应依据土库曼斯坦法律予以赔偿。

第十六条　助理和公证实习生

1. 公证员可以配备助理和实习生，助理和实习生的权利、义务和工作条件根据土库曼斯坦劳动法确定。

2. 公证员的助理只能是土库曼斯坦公民。

3. 公证员的助理作为公证机构的成员进行工作。

4. 具有高等法律教育的土库曼斯坦公民可以成为公证员的实习生。公证员实习生人选根据其个人素质和专业素养进行筛选。

实习生在公证机构通过培训。

公证员实习生根据土库曼斯坦公证部的指令选任。公证员实习生的工资根据土库曼斯坦的法律确定。

通过培训的程序由土库曼斯坦公证部确定。

5. 助理和实习生根据公证员的指导工作并承担其责任，助理和实习生不能从事公证活动，其活动仅具有辅助性质。

6. 培训的目的是使实习生获得从事公证活动的专业知识和执业技能以及了解公证机构。

7. 同一名公证员不能同时对两名以上的实习生进行培训。

8. 根据土库曼斯坦公证部指令的批准，实习生专业培训以单独计划开展。

所有实习生均有义务参加实习生专业培训单独计划，并应包含针对实习生应掌握的特殊理论知识、公证活动执业技能以及公证员工作安排的清单，包括学习公证员工作的专业标准和道德标准，参加公证员组织的（特别是为实习生组织的）研讨会。

9. 培训结束时，公证员会对实习生通过培训计划

prepares the conclusion in which accomplishment by the trainee of the program of training is stated. In case of complete development by the trainee of the program of training the term of passing of training by it can be reduced.

In case of incomplete development by the trainee of the program of training extra time, but is provided no more than three months to it.

Complete development of the Single program of professional training of trainees is the compulsory provision of passing of training.

The trainee is appointed to the notary public position after passing of certification in Certifying commission of the Ministry adalat Turkmenistan on the right of implementation of notarial activities.

Article 17. Certifying commission of the Ministry adalat Turkmenistan on the right of implementation of notarial activities

1. Person applying for receipt of the right of implementation of notarial activities undergoes certification in Certifying commission of the Ministry adalat Turkmenistan on the right of implementation of notarial activities.

2. Structure of Certifying commission of the Ministry adalat Turkmenistan on the right of implementation of notarial activities, procedure for its work, and equally in procedure for carrying out certification by Certifying commission of the Ministry adalat Turkmenistan on the right of implementation of notarial activities affirm the Minister adalat Turkmenistan.

3. Ensuring work of Certifying commission of the Ministry adalat Turkmenistan on the right of implementation of notarial activities is performed by this ministry.

Article 18. Notary public

1. The notary public is the government employee holding position according to the procedure, established by the legislation of Turkmenistan. The requirements specified in part one of article 15 of this Law extend to the notary public.

2. Position assignment and dismissal of the notary public are performed by the Minister adalat Turkmenistan.

3. Class ranks are appropriated to notaries public, consultants of offices of notary public according to the Provision approved by the Cabinet of Ministers of Turkmenistan according to the procedure, established for employees of bodies adalat Turkmenistan.

的收获进行总结。如果实习生通过培训计划获得了全面提高，可以缩短培训的期限。

如果实习生未能在培训计划的时间内获得全面提高，可增加培训时间，但提供的额外时间不能超过3个月。

完成实习生专业培训单独计划获得全面提高是通过培训的强制性要求。

实习生在获得土库曼斯坦公证部认证委员会颁发的有权执行公证活动的证书后，方可在公证机构安排职位。

第十七条　土库曼斯坦公证部关于从事公证活动权利的认证委员会

1. 申请获得从事公证活动权利的人员通过土库曼斯坦公证部认证委员会获得关于从事公证活动权利的证明。

2. 土库曼斯坦公证部关于从事公证活动权利的认证委员会的组织结构、工作流程以及进行认证的程序由土库曼斯坦公证部长确定。

3. 土库曼斯坦公证部关于从事公证活动权利的认证委员会具体履行公证部的认证工作。

第十八条　公证员

1. 公证员是根据土库曼斯坦法定程序而任职的政府职员。本法第十五条第1款规定的要求适用于公证员。

2. 公证员的委任和撤职由土库曼斯坦公证部部长执行。

3. 根据土库曼斯坦部长内阁批准的规定和土库曼斯坦公证部为机构雇员规定的程序确定公证员和公证机构顾问的比例。

Article 19. Notary public rights

1. The notary public has the right:

1) to make the notarial actions provided by this Law and other regulatory legal acts of Turkmenistan for the benefit of the physical persons and legal entities which addressed it;

2) to constitute drafts of transactions, statements and other documents;

3) to produce copies of documents and the statement from them;

4) to give the legal consultations connected with notarial actions;

5) to receive payment for giving legal consultations, production of statements from documents, rendering other legal and technical services connected with notarial actions;

6) to request from legal entities of the data and the documents necessary for making of notarial actions, with condition of nondisclosure of the data which are the secret protected by the legislation of Turkmenistan and also to involve experts;

7) to be engaged in pedagogical, scientific and creative activities.

第十九条　公证员的权利

1. 公证员享有以下权利：

（1）从事本法和土库曼斯坦其他法律规定的公证活动，以使有关自然人和法人受益；

（2）起草交易文件、声明文件和其他文件；

（3）制作文件副本及其声明；

（4）提供与公证活动有关的法律咨询；

（5）就提供法律咨询、制作文件声明、提供与公证活动有关的其他法律和技术服务收取费用；

（6）要求法人提供从事公证活动所必需的信息和文件，受法律保护或专家认定的秘密信息与文件除外；

（7）从事教学、科学和创造性活动。

Article 20. Notary public obligations

1. The notary public shall:

1) to fulfill the professional duties according to this Law and the taken Oath;

2) to observe professional ethics;

3) to make notarial actions according to requirements of this Law and other regulatory legal acts of Turkmenistan;

4) to give help to physical persons and legal entities in realization of their rights and protection of legitimate interests, to explain them their rights and obligations;

5) to warn the addressed persons about consequences of the made notarial actions;

6) to keep in secret data which became known to it in connection with implementation of notarial activities;

7) to represent according to claims to the actions to the relevant organs considering these claims, data on committed notarial action, other documents, personal explanations;

8) to represent to authorized state body on counteraction of legalization of income gained in the criminal way and terrorism financing necessary information according to the legislation of Turkmenistan;

第二十条　公证员的义务

1. 公证员应：

（1）依照本法及其誓言履行专业职责；

（2）遵守职业道德；

（3）根据本法和土库曼斯坦其他法律的规定从事公证活动；

（4）帮助自然人和法人实现其权利、保护其合法利益，向自然人和法人解释其权利和义务；

（5）向有关人员警示从事公证活动的效果；

（6）对其知悉与实施的公证活动有关的信息进行保密；

（7）应有关机构的请求，对公证活动中的信息、其他文件、个人解释等诉求进行代理；

（8）根据土库曼斯坦法律，向授权国家机构提供反洗钱和恐怖主义融资的必要信息；

9) to represent to the relevant tax authorities of the data on property which carries over citizens according to the procedure of inheritance, and necessary certificates of the cost of this property;

10) to refuse making of notarial actions in case of their discrepancy to the legislation of Turkmenistan;

11) to fulfill other duties, stipulated by the legislation Turkmenistan.

2. Submission of information on notarial actions to authorized state body on counteraction of legalization of the income received in the criminal way and terrorism financing according to the procedure, stipulated by the legislation Turkmenistan, is not disclosure of mystery of notarial actions.

（9）按照继承程序向有关税务机关提供公民转让财产的信息，和该等财产价值的必要证明；

（10）公证申请如果与土库曼斯坦法律不符，有权拒绝公证；

（11）履行土库曼斯坦法律规定的其他职责。

2. 根据土库曼斯坦法律规定的程序，向经授权国家机构提交关于洗钱和恐怖主义融资的信息时，不得披露需要保密的事项。

Article 21. Territory of activities of the notary public

1. The territory of activities of the notary public within administrative-territorial division of Turkmenistan is determined by the Ministry adalat Turkmenistan.

2. The territory of activities of the notary public is observed when making the notarial actions provided by Articles 25, 59-60, 67, 74, 79-85, 96, 104 and 118 of these Laws. In all other cases physical persons and legal entities for making of notarial actions have the right to address any notary public.

第二十一条　公证员的活动范围

1. 土库曼斯坦行政区划范围内的公证员活动范围由土库曼斯坦公证部确定。

2. 公证员应在其活动范围内从事本法第 25 条、第 59 条至第 60 条、第 67 条、第 74 条、第 79 条至第 85 条、第 96 条、第 104 条和第 118 条规定的公证活动。在其他情况下，自然人和法人有权申请任何公证员从事公证活动。

Article 22. Oath of the notary public and regulation of professional ethics of the notary public

1. Notaries public in a festive atmosphere take the Oath of the following content:

"I, (surname, name, middle name), solemnly swear that I will fulfill the notary public duties fairly and honesty, according to the legislation of Turkmenistan and conscience, to respect and protect the rights and legitimate interests of citizens and legal entities, state interests, to keep secret of notarial actions, always and everywhere to protect purity of high rank of the notary public and to be worthy its."

2. The notary public is signed under the text of the Oath and it is stored in the personal record of the notary public.

3. Person who did not take the Oath cannot fulfill the notary public duties.

4. In case of execution of the obligations the notary public shall observe requirements of the legislation of Turkmenistan and Norma of professional ethics of the notary public.

第二十二条　公证员的宣誓和职业道德规范

1. 公证员在正式场合宣誓如下：

"我，（姓名），庄严宣誓，根据土库曼斯坦法律和我的忠诚，公平公正地履行公证职责，尊重和保护公民和法人的权利和合法权益、国家利益，保守公证活动的秘密，随时随地维护公证员高度的纯洁性并且尊重这份职业。"

2. 公证员在誓言下签字并存放在其个人档案中。

3. 未进行宣誓的人不能履行公证职责。

4. 公证员在履行义务时应遵守土库曼斯坦法律的规定以及公证员职业道德的要求。

Professional ethics of the notary public – set of the regulations determining requirements imposed to the notary public in case of execution of professional obligations by him including in customer relations, colleagues, representatives of state bodies and other organizations.

5. The procedure for adoption of the Oath and Norma of professional ethics of the notary public affirm the Ministry adalat Turkmenistan.

Article 23. Seal, stamps and forms of the notary public

1. The notary public has seal with the image of the State Emblem of Turkmenistan, with indication of the name of office of notary public and number assigned to the notary public and also stamps and forms.

2. The seal, stamps and forms of notaries public are made on the single samples approved by the Ministry adalat Turkmenistan. Prints of seals and specimen signatures of notaries public are stored in the Ministry adalat Turkmenistan.

3. Forms are made by typographical method and are documents of the strict reporting.

4. Production of seals, stamps and forms of offices of notary public is made at the expense of means of the Government budget of Turkmenistan by request of the Ministry adalat Turkmenistan or its bodies on places.

5. The notary public who stopped notarial activities shall hand over seal, stamps and forms in the relevant territorial authority of the Ministry adalat Turkmenistan.

Article 24. The restrictions connected with accomplishment of obligations of the notary public

The notary public has no right:

1) to be engaged in business activity personally or through authorized representatives;

2) to be engaged in other paid activities, except teaching, scientific and creative activities;

3) to render intermediary services in case of the conclusion, change and agreement cancelation;

4) to promote satisfaction of material interests of physical persons or legal entities by unreasonable use of the office powers for the purpose of receipt of material benefits;

5) to receive benefit in the form of money, values, other property or services of property nature, other property rights with use of ex-officio full powers or the related opportunities by them;

6) to request from physical persons and legal entities

公证员职业道德——在公证员履行其职业义务（包括客户关系、同事、国家机构和其他组织代表）时，遵守法律对公证员的要求。

5. 宣誓和公证员职业道德要求的适用程序由土库曼斯坦公证部确定。

第二十三条　公证员的印章、标志和表格

1. 公证员的印章上带有土库曼斯坦国徽的形状，并注明公证员的办公室名称和指定的公证员号码、标志和表格。

2. 公证员的印章、标志和表格均根据土库曼斯坦公证部批准的单独的样本制作。公证员印章和签名的底样均保存在土库曼斯坦公证部。

3. 表格采用印刷方式制作，并需要严格填报的文件。

4. 公证机构印章、标志和表格制作的费用根据土库曼斯坦公证部或其地方部门的请求由土库曼斯坦政府财政预算负担。

5. 停止从事公证活动的公证员应向土库曼斯坦公证部在其从业地的相关机构上交印章、标志和表格。

第二十四条　与公证员履行职务有关的限制

公证员无权从事以下行为：

（1）亲自或通过授权从事商业活动；

（2）除教学、科学和创造性活动外，从事其他有偿活动；

（3）在签署、变更及解除协议的活动中提供中介服务；

（4）为了获得物质利益不合理地使用机构权力以帮助自然人或法人获取物质利益；

（5）通过行使权力或利用有关机会获取金钱、好处、其他具有财产性质的物品或服务以及其他财产权利等利益；

（6）要求自然人和法人提供与公证活动无关的文件。

the documents which are not relating to the made notarial actions.

Article 25. The restrictions connected with making of notarial actions

1. Notaries public, authorized officers have no right to make notarial actions on the name and on its own behalf, addressed to and on behalf of the spouse (spouse), his (her), their and close relatives, addressed to and from employee name of the relevant offices of notary public, Gengesha, diplomatic representations and consular establishments of Turkmenistan abroad, and also addressed to and on behalf of the relevant office of notary public, Gengesha, diplomatic representation and consular establishment of Turkmenistan abroad.

2. The officials specified in part one of article 37 of this Law, having no right to certify wills, powers of attorney and to witness authenticity of signatures on the statement on the name and on its own behalf, addressed to and on behalf of the spouse (spouse), his (her), their and close relatives, addressed to and from employee name of relevant organs.

3. Parents, (including adoptive parents), spouses, children (including adopted), the grandfather, the grandmother on the father's side and mothers, grandsons, full and not full brothers and sisters treat the close relatives specified in parts one and the second this Article.

4. In the cases specified in parts one and the second this Article, notarial actions are made by other notaries public, officials Gengesha.

5. If according to the legislation of Turkmenistan notarial actions shall be made by specific notaries public, the place of making of notarial actions is determined by the Ministry adalat Turkmenistan.

6. The notarial actions made with abuse of regulations, established by this article, are invalid.

Article 26. Responsibility of the notary public, authorized officer

1. The notary public, the authorized officer in case of making of illegal actions by them bear responsibility, stipulated by the legislation Turkmenistan.

2. In case of violation of obligations and regulations of professional ethics the notary public is made responsible by the Minister adalat Turkmenistan according to the legislation of Turkmenistan.

第二十五条　从事公证活动的限制

1. 公证员、授权官员无权以其名义对其本人、配偶和近亲属，以其相关公证机构雇员、地方人民委员会、外交代表和土库曼斯坦境外的领事机构的名义或代表相关公证机构、地方人民委员会、外交代表和土库曼斯坦境外的领事机构从事公证活动。

2. 本法第 37 条第 1 款规定的官员无权公证遗嘱、授权委托书。无权代表自身利益公证其本人在声明上的签名，无权公证涉及其配偶或近亲属或以相关机构雇员利益的遗嘱和授权委托书。

3. 本条第 1 款和第 2 款中规定的近亲属包括：父母（包括养父母）、配偶、子女（包括养子女）、祖父母、外祖父母、孙子女及兄弟姐妹。

4. 在本条第 1 款和第 2 款规定的情况下，公证活动由其他公证员和地方人民委员会官员作出。

5. 如果根据土库曼斯坦法律的规定，公证活动应由特殊的公证员作出，从事公证活动的地点由土库曼斯坦公证部决定。

6. 根据本法的规定，滥用法规从事的公证活动无效。

第二十六条　公证员和授权官员的责任

1. 根据土库曼斯坦法律的规定，公证员、授权官员采取非法行动时应承担责任。

2. 如违反公证员职业道德的义务和要求，土库曼斯坦公证部可以根据土库曼斯坦法律要求公证员承担责任。

Chapter III. Financing of notarial activities. Payment for notarial actions and services

Article 27. Financing of activities of offices of notary public

Offices of notary public are financed by means of the Government budget of Turkmenistan.

Article 28. Payment of notarial actions and services

1. For the notarial actions made by notaries public, officials Gengesha the state fee in the amount of, established by the legislation of Turkmenistan is collected. The amount of the state tax is determined as a percentage proceeding from basic size for calculation of the state fee established by the Cabinet of Ministers of Turkmenistan.

2. Notaries public, officials Gengesha in each notarially certified document specify the amount of the state tax.

3. The amount of payment for giving legal consultations, production of statements from documents, rendering other legal and technical services of the notary public, the official Gengesh connected with notarial actions is determined as a percentage proceeding from the basic size established according to the legislation of Turkmenistan for calculations of social and other payments.

Rates for giving legal consultations, production of statements from documents, rendering other legal and technical services connected with notarial actions, and procedure for their collection affirm the Ministry adalat Turkmenistan in coordination with the Ministry of Economics and developments of Turkmenistan.

4. For the notarial actions made at the request of the interested person out of office premises of office of notary public or Gengesh, the established state fee is collected in double size and, besides, interested persons shall pay actually made expenses connected with departure for making of these actions.

5. For making of notarial actions by officials of diplomatic representations and consular establishments of Turkmenistan the consular fee, and also the expenses connected with making of notarial actions according to the legislation of Turkmenistan is abroad levied.

Chapter IV. Control of notarial activities

Article 29. Control of activities of the notary public

1. Control of legality of the made notarial actions and observance of Rules of maintaining notarial clerical work

第三章 公证活动的资金支持，公证活动和服务的费用

第二十七条 公证机构活动的资金支持

公证机构的资金来源于土库曼斯坦的政府预算。

第二十八条 公证活动和服务的费用

1. 对于公证员作出的公证活动，地方人民委员会官员按照土库曼斯坦法律的规定收取法定费用。国家税费的数额是根据土库曼斯坦内阁部长确立的法定费用计算百分比标准确定的。

2. 公证员、地方人民委员会官员在每份经过公证的文件中均规定了国家税费的金额。

3. 提供法律咨询、提供文件声明、提供公证员的其他法律和技术服务的费用数额，由与公证活动有关的地方人民委员会官员根据土库曼斯坦法律确定收取费用的比例确定。

提供法律咨询、提供文件声明以及提供其他与公证活动有关的法律和技术服务的费率以及费用收取的程序由土库曼斯坦公证部和土库曼斯坦经济与发展部协商确定。

4. 应非公证机构或地方人民委员会以外的利害关系人的请求而从事的公证活动，应收取双倍的法定费用。此外，利害关系人应就该等公证活动的实际支出支付有关费用。

5. 对于土库曼斯坦外交代表和领事机构官员的公证活动，根据土库曼斯坦法律的规定，领事费用和与公证活动有关的费用在境外征收。

第四章 公证活动的控制

第二十九条 公证员活动的控制

1. 土库曼斯坦公证部负责控制公证活动的合法性和公证文书制作规则的制定。

is performed by the Ministry adalat Turkmenistan.

2. Control of observance by the notary public, the authorized officer of the tax legislation of Turkmenistan is performed by tax authorities of Turkmenistan.

3. Control of observance by the notary public of the legislation of Turkmenistan on counteraction of legalization of income gained in the criminal way, and financing of terrorism is performed by authorized state bodies.

4. Officials of the bodies controlling activities of the notary public, authorized officer have the right to acquaintance with the data and documents concerning execution by them of obligations, the made (committed) notarial actions, settlings with physical persons and legal entities, and also other necessary documents.

5. Officials of the bodies controlling activities of the notary public, authorized officer shall keep the mystery of making of notarial actions which became to the activities of the notary public, known during checks, the authorized officer. These persons bear responsibility according to the legislation of Turkmenistan for disclosure of secret and the caused damage.

Article 30. Powers of the Ministry adalat Turkmenistan on regulation of the relations connected with notariates notarial activities

Ministry adalat Turkmenistan:

1) performs management, coordination and control of activities for the organization and law enforcement in the sphere of legal servicing of the population by notaries public;

2) is approved by Regulations on procedure for making of notarial actions;

3) is approved by Regulations on procedure for making of notarial actions by officials Gengesh;

4) approves in coordination with the Head archival department under the Cabinet of Ministers of Turkmenistan Rules of maintaining notarial clerical work;

5) is approved by the Procedure for passing of training;

6) develops methodical managements and explanatory materials concerning notariate and notarial activities;

7) develops and approves the Register for registration of notarial actions and form of books of notarial clerical work, samples of notarial certificates, transactions, the witnessed documents and certifying texts, and also other notarial acts, forms;

8) within the competence performs regulation of no-

2. 土库曼斯坦税务机关负责控制公证员和授权官员是否遵守土库曼斯坦税收法律。

3. 获授权的国家机构负责控制公证员是否遵守土库曼斯坦法律有关反洗钱和反恐怖主义融资的规定。

4. 控制公证员和授权官员活动的有关机构的官员有权获得与其履职相关的公证活动中与自然人、法人往来的信息和文件，以及其他必要的文件。

5. 控制公证员和授权官员活动的有关机构的官员应对其在检查过程中知悉的有关公证员从事的公证活动进行保密。根据土库曼斯坦法律的规定，该等人员对秘密信息的泄露和造成的损害承担责任。

第三十条　土库曼斯坦公证部监管公证员公证活动的有关权力

土库曼斯坦公证部：

（1）在公证员提供法律服务的范围内，对组织和执法活动进行管理、协调和控制；

（2）通过法规批准监管从事公证活动的程序；

（3）通过法规批准监管地方人民委员会官员从事公证活动的程序；

（4）与土库曼斯坦内阁档案部门总部部长协调批准保存公证文书工作的规则；

（5）批准通过培训的程序；

（6）制定有序管理公证活动的有关规定和解释性材料；

（7）制定和批准公证活动登记簿以及公证文书的样式、公证书样本、交易、证明文件和证明文本以及其他公证活动文件的样式等；

（8）根据本法，在权限范围内对公证活动进行

tarial activities according to this Law;

9) for giving legal consultations, production of statements from documents, rendering other legal and technical services connected with notarial actions and procedure for their collection in accordance with the established procedure approves rates;

10) carries out certification of notaries public;

11) in accordance with the established procedure considers questions of involvement of notaries public to disciplinary responsibility;

12) publishes managements and methodical recommendations about questions of notarial activities;

13) performs compliance with law of Turkmenistan when making by notaries public of notarial actions;

14) performs other powers provided by this Law, other regulatory legal acts of Turkmenistan.

Chapter V. Offices of notary public

Article 31. Offices of notary public

1. Offices of notary public are organizational form of implementation by notaries public of notarial activities.

2. The ministry adalat Turkmenistan keeps the register of offices of notary public and determines procedure for their activities.

Article 32. Organization of work of offices of notary public

1. The ministry adalat Turkmenistan creates and liquidates offices of notary public, directs their activities.

The structure and number of employees of offices of notary public affirm in accordance with the established procedure the Minister adalat Turkmenistan.

2. In the city of Ashgabat and the cities which are the velayatsky centers, one of offices of notary public is established as the first office of notary public.

The first office of notary public along with making of notarial actions performs methodical management of offices of notary public of the corresponding administrative and territorial unit, coordinates activities of notaries public, promotes advanced training of notaries public, protects and represents the interests of notaries public in public authorities, participates in project development of regulatory legal acts concerning notariate and notarial activities, issues duplicates, copies of the notarial documents which are stored in notarial archive and statements from them.

Making of the most difficult notarial actions can be assigned to the first office of notary public by the Ministry

监管；

（9）提供法律咨询、提供文件声明、提供与公证活动有关的其他法律或技术服务，并按照规定的程序和费率收取费用；

（10）向公证员颁发证书；

（11）按照规定的程序审议与公证员纪律责任有关的问题；

（12）公布有关管理公证活动问题的建议；

（13）确保公证员在从事公证活动时遵守土库曼斯坦法律；

（14）行使本法和土库曼斯坦其他监管法律规定的其他权力。

第五章　公证机构

第三十一条　公证机构

1. 公证机构是公证员开展公证活动的组织形式。

2. 土库曼斯坦公证部负责保管公证机构登记簿并决定其公证活动的程序。

第三十二条　公证机构的工作安排

1. 土库曼斯坦公证部负责建立和撤销公证机构，并指导其活动。

公证机构雇员的构成和数量根据土库曼斯坦公证部规定的程序确定。

2. 在阿什喀巴得和其他省份的中心城市，其中一个公证机构作为第一公证机构而建立。

第一公证机构和公证活动的实施由相应的行政和管辖内的部门进行有序管理，协调公证员的活动，促进公证员的高级培训，保护和代表公证员在公证机构中的利益，参与有关公证活动的监管法规的制定，对有关问题的重申，从其处获取在公证档案中保存的公证文件的副本。

最为复杂的公证活动由土库曼斯坦公证部指定第一公证机构从事。

adalat Turkmenistan.

3. The office of notary public is legal entity, has the seal with the image of the State Emblem of Turkmenistan and the name, and also stamps and forms. The manager heads office of notary public.

4. Offices of notary public are provided with local executive bodies office placements on the territories of their arrangement.

Employees of office of notary public in case of transfer to other area in connection with service are provided with office premises local executive bodies.

5. Offices of notary public keep the statistical and financial reporting according to the procedure, established by the legislation of Turkmenistan, and submit the reports connected with making of notarial actions, collection of the state fee and other payments in the Ministry adalat Turkmenistan and the relevant state bodies.

3. 公证机构是法人，拥有带有土库曼斯坦国徽形象的印章、名称、标志和表格。管理人对公证机构进行领导。

4. 公证机构在其安排的管辖范围设有当地执行机构办公室。

公证机构的雇员如果转移到与其服务有关的其他地区，那么该等地区应在当地设执行机构。

5. 公证机构根据土库曼斯坦法律规定的程序保存统计和财务报告，并提交与公证活动有关的报告，以及收取土库曼斯坦公证部和相关国家机构要求的法定费用和其他收费。

Article 33. Notarial archive

1. The notarial archive is created for completing, accounting, use and storage during the terms established by the legislation of Turkmenistan of the documents formed as a result of notarial activities.

2. The notarial archive of office of notary public contains in the relevant or higher office of notary public. The notary public provides proper document storage of archive.

3. Upon termination of storage duration of documents they are given to storage to the Public Records Offices of Turkmenistan according to the procedure, established by the legislation of Turkmenistan.

第三十三条 公证档案

1. 建立公证档案的目的是对根据土库曼斯坦法律规定而从事的公证活动所形成的文件进行编撰、核对、使用和保存。

2. 公证机构的公证档案包括与之相关的或更高级别的公证机构的档案。公证员对档案中的文件进行适当的保存。

3. 文件保存期限届满后，根据土库曼斯坦法律规定的程序将其存放至土库曼斯坦的公共档案室。

Section II. Making of notarial actions

Chapter VI. Powers of notaries public and other officials on making of notarial actions

Article 34. The notarial actions made by notaries public

1. Notaries public make the following notarial actions:

1) is certified by transactions (agreements, wills, powers of attorney, marriage contracts and others);

2) take necessary measures to protection of inheritance;

3) grant certificates on the right to inheritance;

4) grant certificates on the right to share in common property;

第二部分 公证活动

第六章 公证员及其他从事公证活动官员的权力

第三十四条 公证员从事的公证活动

1. 公证员可以从事以下公证活动：

（1）对交易（协议、遗嘱、授权委托书、婚姻合同和其他）进行公证；

（2）采取必要措施保护遗产；

（3）出具继承权公证书；

（4）出具分享共同财产的权利公证书；

5) impose prohibition on alienation of the apartment house, apartment, country house and other real estate in the cases established by the law;

6) witness fidelity of copies of documents and statements from them;

7) witness authenticity of the signature on documents;

8) witness fidelity of the translation of documents from one language on another;

9) certify the fact of finding of person in live;

10) certify the fact of finding of person in certain place;

11) certify identity of person with person represented in the photo;

12) certify time of production of documents;

13) is transferred by statements of physical persons and legal entities to other physical persons and legal entities;

14) is accepted in the deposit by money and securities;

15) is made by executive texts;

16) is made by protests of bills of exchange;

17) is shown by checks to payment and certify non-payment of checks;

18) accept documents on storage;

19) is made by ship's protests;

20) is provided by proofs.

2. According to the legislation of Turkmenistan making of other notarial actions also can be assigned to notaries public.

Article 35. The notarial actions made by officials Gengesha

1. Officials Gengesha make the following notarial actions:

1) is certified by wills;

2) is certified by powers of attorney;

3) take necessary measures to protection of inheritance;

4) witness fidelity of copies of documents and statements from them;

5) witness authenticity of the signature on documents.

2. Officials Gengesha, retaining one copy of the original of wills, shall transfer immediately one copy of its original, certified by them, to storage to office of notary public on the permanent residence of the testator.

（5）在法律规定的情况下，禁止转让住房、公寓、乡村房屋及其他不动产；

（6）公证声明和文件副本的真实性；

（7）公证文件上签字的真实性；

（8）公证将文件从一种语言翻译为另一种语言的准确性；

（9）公证某人存活的事实；

（10）公证在某地找到某人的事实；

（11）公证图片中显示的人的身份；

（12）公证文件制作的时间；

（13）将自然人和法人的陈述转述给其他自然人和法人；

（14）通过货币和证券接受存款；

（15）制作行政文本；

（16）制作汇票拒绝证书；

（17）通过支票显示支付情况以及公证未支付的支票；

（18）接受保存的文件；

（19）制作海事报告；

（20）提供证据公证。

2. 根据土库曼斯坦法律从事其他可以指定公证员实施的公证活动。

第三十五条　地方人民委员会官员从事的公证活动

1. 地方人民委员会官员可以从事以下公证活动：

（1）遗嘱公证；

（2）出具委托书公证；

（3）采取必要措施保护遗产；

（4）公证声明及文件副本的真实性；

（5）公证文件签名的真实性。

2. 地方人民委员会官员保留一份遗嘱原件的副本，并应立即将其公证的遗嘱原件副本送交遗嘱订立人永久居住地的公证机构保存。

3. According to the legislation of Turkmenistan making and other notarial actions which are not provided by this article can be assigned to officials Gengesha.

Article 36. The notarial actions made by officials of diplomatic representations and consular establishments of Turkmenistan abroad

1. Officials of diplomatic representations and consular establishments of Turkmenistan abroad make the following notarial actions:

1) is certified by transactions (agreements, wills, powers of attorney and others), except transactions about alienation and pledge of the real estate which is in Turkmenistan;

2) take necessary measures to protection of inheritance;

3) grant certificates on the right to inheritance;

4) grant certificates on the right to share in common property of spouses (the former spouses);

5) witness fidelity of copies of documents and statements from them;

6) witness authenticity of the signature on documents;

7) witness fidelity of the translation of documents from one language on another;

8) certify the fact of finding of person in live;

9) certify the fact of finding of person in certain place;

10) certify identity of person with person represented in the photo;

11) certify time of production of documents;

12) is accepted in the deposit by money and securities;

13) is made by executive texts;

14) accept documents on storage;

15) is made by ship's protests;

16) is provided by proofs.

2. Officials of diplomatic representations and consular establishments of Turkmenistan abroad, retaining one copy of the original of wills, shall transfer immediately one copy of its original certified by them to storage to office of notary public on the permanent residence of the testator.

3. According to the legislation of Turkmenistan making of other notarial actions which are not provided by this article also can be abroad assigned to officials of diplomatic representations and consular establishments of

3. 根据土库曼斯坦法律的规定从事本条未规定的其他公证活动。

第三十六条　土库曼斯坦境外的外交代表和领事机构官员从事的公证活动

1. 土库曼斯坦境外的外交代表和领事机构官员可以从事以下公证活动：

（1）对交易（协议、遗嘱、授权委托书和其他）进行公证，有关土库曼斯坦房地产转让和抵押的交易除外；

（2）采取必要措施保护遗产；

（3）出具继承权公证书；

（4）出具与配偶（前配偶）分享共同财产的权利公证书；

（5）公证声明及文件副本的真实性；

（6）公证文件签字的真实性；

（7）公证将文件从一种语言翻译为另一种语言的准确性；

（8）公证某人存活的事实；

（9）公证在某地找到某人的事实；

（10）公证图片中显示的人的身份；

（11）公证文件制作的时间；

（12）通过货币和证券接受存款；

（13）制作行政文本；

（14）接受保存的文件；

（15）制作海事报告；

（16）提供证据公证。

2. 土库曼斯坦境外的外交代表和领事机构官员保留一份遗嘱原件的副本，并应立即将其公证的遗嘱原件副本送交遗嘱订立人永久居住地的公证机构保存。

3. 根据土库曼斯坦法律的规定从事本条未作出规定的其他公证活动。

Turkmenistan.

Article 37. The certificate officials of wills and powers of attorney, and also witnessing of authenticity of the signature on the statements equated to notarially certified

1. Are equated to notarially certified documents:

1) wills and powers of attorney, and also statements of persons which are on treatment in the hospitals, other organizations of the state health care system providing medical care in the stationary conditions or living in houses boarding schools for aged and disabled people, – certified and authenticity of signatures on which it is certified by chief physicians, their deputies for medical part or doctors on duty of these hospitals, other healthcare institutions providing medical care in stationary conditions and also directors and chief physicians of houses boarding schools for aged and disabled people;

2) wills and statements of persons which are during swimming on ocean ships or courts, performing swimming in internal waters, floating under National flag of Turkmenistan, – certified and authenticity of signatures on which it is certified by captains (commanders) of these courts;

3) wills and statements of persons which are in prospecting and other similar expeditions, – certified and authenticity of signatures on which it is certified by chiefs of these expeditions;

4) wills and powers of attorney, and also statements of the military personnel and other persons who are on treatment in military hospitals and other military medical institutions, – certified and authenticity of signatures on which it is certified by chiefs, their deputies for medical part, seniors and doctors on duty of these military hospitals and other military medical institutions;

5) wills and powers of attorney, and also statements of the military personnel, and equally in workers, members of their families and members of families of the military personnel in places of dislocation of military units, connections, military organizations and military schools in which there are no notaries public and authorized officers – certified and authenticity of signatures on which it is certified by commanders (chiefs) of these military units, connections, military organizations and rectors (managers) of military schools;

6) wills and powers of attorney, and also statements of persons which are in the special rehabilitation center,

第三十七条 遗嘱和授权委托书的公证及对声明上签名真实性的公证

1. 以下文件视为公证文件：

（1）遗嘱和授权委托书，以及在医院、其他固定条件下提供医疗服务的国家医疗保健系统的机构接受治疗的人员的陈述，或者居住在养老院或残疾人救助中心的人员的陈述——经由主任医师、医疗部门代表或该等医院、其他固定条件下提供医疗服务的医疗机构负责的医生，以及养老院或残疾人救助中心的负责人和主任医师签字证明；

（2）在航行的船舶上的人员作出的遗嘱和声明，该等航行应在国内水域并且悬挂土库曼斯坦国旗——经由该等船舶的船长（指挥官）签字证明；

（3）正在从事勘探和其他类似探险的人员的遗嘱和声明——经由该探险的负责人进行签字证明；

（4）军事人员的遗嘱、授权委托书及声明，以及在军事医院或其他军事医疗机构接受治疗的其他人员——经由负责人、医疗部门代表以及该等军事医院及其他军事医疗机构负责医生签字证明；

（5）军事人员的遗嘱、授权委托书及声明，军事机构的员工、家庭成员的遗嘱、授权委托书及声明，在没有公证员和授权官员的军事单位、组织、军事机构和军事学校的地方的军事人员的家庭成员的遗嘱、授权委托书及声明——经由该等军事单位、组织、军事机构指挥官（首长）和军事学校的校长（管理人员）签字证明；

（6）在特殊康复中心、临时拘留中心、审前拘留中心和矫正机构的人员的遗嘱、授权委托书及声

temporary detention center, the pre-trial detention center and correctional facilities, – certified and authenticity of signatures, on which certified by chiefs of these bodies.

2. In case of the certificate of the wills provided by part one of this Article witnesses can be allowed. In this case the will is signed by the testator and witnesses.

3. The officials specified in part one of this Article, retaining one copy of the original of the will, shall transfer immediately one copy of its original certified by them to storage to office of notary public on the permanent residence of the testator.

If the testator had no permanent residence in Turkmenistan or the residence of the testator is unknown, the will goes to the Ministry adalat Turkmenistan which determines office of notary public in which the will will be stored.

4. Captains (commanders) of ocean ships shall give one copy of the original of wills certified by them, to the harbor master of Turkmenistan or the official of diplomatic representation and consular establishment of Turkmenistan in the state in which the foreign port, for the subsequent direction them in office of notary public on the permanent residence of the testator is located.

5. The certificate of wills and powers of attorney, witnessing of authenticity of signatures on statements is made by officials with observance of requirements of this Law.

6. The notary public shall check legality of the will which arrived on storage and in case of establishment of discrepancy to its law to report about it to the testator and the official who certified the will.

Section III. Rules of making of notarial actions

Chapter VII. General rules of making of notarial actions

Article 38. Procedure for making of notarial actions

The procedure for making of notarial actions is established by this Law, other regulatory legal acts of Turkmenistan and the Regulations on procedure for making of notarial actions approved by the Ministry adalat Turkmenistan.

Article 39. Place of making of notarial actions

1. Notarial actions are made in office premises of office of notary public, and also Gengesha, except as specified, when according to the legislation of Turkmenistan

明——经由该等机构的负责人签字证明；

2. 如对本条第 1 款规定的遗嘱进行证明可以允许有见证人。在该等情况下，遗嘱由遗嘱订立人和见证人共同签字。

3. 本条第 1 款规定的官员保留一份遗嘱原件副本，并应立即将其证明的遗嘱原件副本送交遗嘱订立人永久居住地的公证机构保存。

如果遗嘱订立人在土库曼斯坦没有永久居住地或者遗嘱订立人的居住地不明，遗嘱将交给土库曼斯坦公证部，该部门决定保存遗嘱的公证机构。

4. 航行船舶的船长（指挥官）应向土库曼斯坦港务部门或外国港口所在国的土库曼斯坦外交代表和领事机构官员提交一份其证明的遗嘱原件副本，随后送交遗嘱订立人永久居住地的公证机构。

5. 遗嘱和授权委托书的公证以及对声明上签字真实性的公证应由符合本法资格条件的官员作出。

6. 公证机构应检查所保存的遗嘱的合法性，如果存在法律瑕疵，应将该情况下向遗嘱订立人和公证该遗嘱的官员报告。

第三部分　从事公证活动的规则

第七章　从事公证活动的一般规则

第三十八条　从事公证活动的程序

从事公证活动的程序由本法、土库曼斯坦的其他监管法律和土库曼斯坦公证部批准的有关公证活动程序的法规规定。

第三十九条　从事公证活动的场所

1. 公证活动应在公证机构和地方人民委员会作出，除非另有规定，根据土库曼斯坦法律的规定，公证活动应在特定的场所进行。

notarial action be made in specifically certain place.

2. If persons for the benefit of whom notarial actions are made cannot be to office room where notarial actions are made, they can be made out of office rooms specified in part one of this Article. If notarial action is made out of office premises of office of notary public or Gengesh, then in certifying text on the document and in the Register for registration of notarial actions the place of making of notarial action with indication of its address and time registers.

3. The place of making of notarial actions by officials of diplomatic representations and consular establishments of Turkmenistan is abroad determined by the legislation of Turkmenistan on diplomatic representations and consular establishments of Turkmenistan.

Article 40. Terms of making of notarial actions

1. Notarial action is made in day of presentation of all documents necessary for making of notarial action, with payment of the state fee.

2. Making of notarial action can be postponed due to the need of reclamation of additional data or documents from physical persons and legal entities or the direction of documents for examination.

3. The term for which making of notarial action is postponed in these cases shall not exceed one month, except as specified, connected with accomplishment of orders in the territory of foreign state.

4. Making of notarial actions can be postponed also at the request of the citizens wishing to take a legal action for contest of the right or the fact about which certificate asks other interested person. In this case the notary public has the right to postpone making of notarial action for the term of no more than twenty working days. If at the scheduled time the written message on receipt of the statement of the interested person is not received from court, the notary public makes notarial action.

5. In case of obtaining from court of the written message on receipt of the statement of the interested person challenging the right or the facts which certificates are asked by other interested person making of notarial action stops to permission of case by court.

6. By the legislation of Turkmenistan also other bases for adjournment and suspension of making of notarial actions can be established.

2. 如果因公证活动而受益的人员不能前往从事公证活动的场所，那么公证活动可以在本条第一部分规定的办公场所以外的地点进行。如果公证活动在公证机构或地方人民委员会以外的场所进行，那么在对文件的文本进行公证和在登记处对公证活动进行登记时，注明公证活动的地址和时间。

3. 土库曼斯坦境外外交代表和领事机构官员从事公证活动的场所由土库曼斯坦有关外交代表和领事机构的法律确定。

第四十条　公证活动的期限

1. 公证在其必要的所有文件均已提交之日作出，并且收取法定费用。

2. 如需自然人或法人提交额外的信息和文件或需对文件进行检查，可以推迟公证活动的期限。

3. 公证活动延长的期限不得超过 1 个月，但在外国境内进行的公证及另有规定的除外。

4. 公证活动也可以根据有利害关系的公民的要求推迟，或者在其他利害关系人的要求下推迟。在该等情况下，公证员有权在不超过 20 个工作日的期限内推迟公证活动。如果在规定的时间内未收到法院送交的利害关系人的书面声明，那么公证员将作出公证。

5. 如果收到法院送交的利害关系人的书面声明，该等书面声明对其他利害关系人申请的公证适格性提出质疑，那么法院应暂停对该公证的许可。

6. 可以根据土库曼斯坦法律对延期或中止公证活动规定其他条件。

Article 41. Identification addressed for making of notarial actions

1. When making notarial actions the notary public, the authorized officer identify the personality of person who addressed for making of notarial action, his representative or representative of the legal entity.

2. Identification shall be made based on the passport or other documents excluding any doubts concerning the identity of person who addressed for making of notarial action.

第四十一条　公证申请人的身份证明

1. 在从事公证活动时，公证员、授权官员应对公证申请人及其代表或法人申请人的代表的身份进行识别。

2. 身份证明应基于护照或其他文件，应排除公证申请人身份的任何疑问。

Article 42. Check of capacity to act of physical persons and legal capacities of the legal entities participating in transactions

1. In case of the certificate of transactions capacity to act of physical persons becomes clear and legal capacity of the legal entities participating in transactions is checked. In case of transaction by the representative its powers are checked.

2. In case of the certificate of the will the notary public shall specify in it about capacity to act of the testator.

第四十二条　对参与交易的自然人的行为能力和法人的法律能力的检查

1. 在对交易进行公证时，应检查参与交易的自然人的行为能力和法人的法律能力。在由代表进行交易的情况下，则应检查代表是否获得授权及授权范围。

2. 在对遗嘱进行公证时，公证员应在其中说明遗嘱订立人的行为能力。

Article 43. Procedure for signing of notarial documents

1. Notarially certified transactions, and also statements and other documents are signed in the presence of the notary public, the authorized officer.

2. In case of the certificate of transactions and making of other notarial actions in cases, stipulated by the legislation Turkmenistan, authenticity of signatures of participants of the transactions and other persons who addressed for making of notarial actions is verified.

3. The notary public cannot require corporal appearance of officials of legal entities if he has samples of their signatures, provided in accordance with the established procedure, and authenticity of signatures does not raise doubts.

4. Contents of notarially certified transaction, and also statements and other documents shall be read by the notary public, the authorized officer aloud to all participants or is read by persons who addressed for making of notarial action.

5. Person who cannot sign with own hand the document owing to illiteracy, physical defect or disease can entrust its signing to other person in the presence of the notary public, the authorized officer. The signature of the last shall be certified by the notary public, the authorized officer. At the same time in certifying text the reason ow-

第四十三条　签署公证文件的程序

1. 经过公证的交易、声明和其他文件均在公证员、授权官员在场的情况下签署。

2. 在符合土库曼斯坦法律规定的交易公证和其他公证时，应核实交易参与方及其他公证申请人签名的真实性。

3. 公证员如果已有按照规定的程序取得签名的样本并且未对签名的真实性提出质疑，那么可不要求法人的代表人到场。

4. 经过公证的交易、声明和其他文件的内容应由公证员、授权官员大声朗读给所有的交易参与者或者公证申请人。

5. 由于文盲、身体缺陷或疾病而无法亲自在文件上签字的人员可以在公证员、授权官员在场的情况下委托其他人员代为签字。前述签名应由公证员、授权官员进行证明。在证明文本内容的同时，应说明不能亲自签署文件的原因。

ing to which person could not sign the document with own hand shall be specified.

Article 44. Use audio and videos when making notarial actions

1. For fixing of making of notarial action at request and at the expense of the addressed persons or at the initiative of the notary public, the authorized officer also the video can be made audio and vedios.

2. In case of implementation audio-and videos at the initiative of the notary public, the authorized officer are warned about it the addressed persons.

3. About carrying out audio-and videos the mark in certifying text together with which it is stored in archive becomes.

Article 45. Reclamation of the data and documents necessary for making of notarial action

The notary public, the authorized officer has the right to request legal entities of the data and the documents necessary for making of notarial actions. The requested data and documents shall be submitted in a month, except as specified, the orders connected with accomplishment in the territory of foreign state.

Article 46. Involvement of specialists

1. In case making of notarial action requires special knowledge or skills (survey of documents, conducting audio-, video record, etc.), the notary public, the authorized officer on own initiative or at the initiative of the addressed person, can involve the expert to receipt of consultations and rendering technical or other assistance at the expense of person who addressed for making of notarial action.

2. During notarial production the specialist gives consultations in oral or written form without carrying out special researches of expert nature.

3. About involvement of the specialist the mark in the issued document becomes.

Article 47. Requirements to the documents shown for making of notarial actions

1. The notary public, the authorized officer do not take for making notarial actions the documents having the erasures added, the crossed-out words and other not stipulated corrections, and also the documents performed by pencil and documents which text cannot be read.

2. The text of notarially certified transactions shall be written or printed clearly and accurately, the numbers and terms relating to contents of the document are designated

第四十四条　在公证中的音频和视频

1. 在公证申请人要求并支付费用的情况下或公证员、授权官员认为有必要的情况下可以制作音频、视频。

2. 如果公证员、授权官员主动使用音频视频，应提示公证申请人。

3. 有关使用音频视频的记录应与证明文本一并保存在档案中。

第四十五条　收回从事公证活动必要的信息和文件

公证员、授权官员有权要求法人提供从事公证活动必要的信息和文件。有关的信息和文件应在 1 个月内提交，外国境内进行的公证及另有规定的除外。

第四十六条　专家的参与

1. 如果公证活动的实施需要特殊的知识或技能（文件调查、录音、录像等），公证员、授权官员可以主动或在公证申请人要求的情况下让专家参与公证并提供技术支持或其他协助，费用由公证申请人承担。

2. 在进行公证的过程中，专家以口头或书面的形式提供咨询，但不对专家意见进行专门研究。

3. 出具的文件中应注明专家参与的情况。

第四十七条　从事公证活动需要出示的文件的要求

1. 公证员、授权官员从事公证活动时不得采用涂改等法律未规定的方式更正文件，也不得使用铅笔书写的文件和文本无法阅读的文件。

2. 经过公证的交易文本应清晰准确地书写或印刷，与文件内容有关的数字或术语至少一次使用全称。如申请人的姓名、住所地——不能缺漏并注明其

at least once by words, and names of legal entities – without reducings, with indication of their location, and the surname, name and middle name of physical person, the address of its residence shall be written completely.

3. In the document which amount exceeds one leaf sheets shall be stitched, numbered and under seal.

Article 48. Making of certifying text, issue of certificates and pronouncement of resolutions

1. The certificate of transactions, witnessing of fidelity of copies of documents and statements from them, witnessing of fidelity of the translations of documents from one language on another, and also witnessing of authenticity of signatures on documents is performed by making of certifying texts about it on the relevant document with sealing.

2. In confirmation of inheritance right, the property right, the certificate of the facts of finding of person in live and in certain place, identity of person with person represented on photos, acceptances on document storage, certificates of time of production of documents appropriate certificates are granted.

3. In case of appointment of the managing director of heritable property and purpose of examination the relevant decrees are issued.

Article 49. Issue of the duplicate of the lost document, copies of documents and statements from them

1. According to the written application of physical persons and legal entities, in the relation or at the request of which were made notarial actions, or their representatives in case of loss of the document certified or issued by the notary public the authorized officer issues the duplicate of the lost document, the copy of the document or the statement from the document.

2. Offices of notary public issue duplicates of the wills which arrived on storage according to requirements of this Law.

3. Copies of the notarial documents which are stored in office of notary public of the statement from them are issued with observance of the rules provided by this Law.

Article 50. Issue of the statement from the register for registration of notarial actions

The notary public, the authorized officer issues the statement from the Register for registration of notarial actions according to the written application of physical persons or request of legal entities, in the relation or at the

所在地，自然人的姓名及住址应完整填写。

3. 如果文件超过一页纸那么应该装订并注明页码。

第四十八条　制作公证文本、颁发公证书和公布公证效力

1. 交易文件公证、文件副本真实性的公证及声明公证、文本从一种语言翻译为另一种语言准确性的公证以及文件签名真实性的公证，通过在密封的有关文件上出具公证书的方式实现。

2. 在公证继承权、产权，公证某人在世或在某地的事实，公证图片上展示的人员的身份，接受文件保存、公证文件制作时间时，应颁发合适的公证书。

3. 在委任遗产管理人和出于检查目的的情况下，应颁布相关法令。

第四十九条　出具丢失文件复印件、副本的声明

1. 根据与公证活动有关或公证申请人的书面申请，可由公证员、授权官员就丢失文件出具声明或出具该等文件的复印件、副本及其中的有关声明。

2. 公证机构根据本法规定出具公证机构保存的遗嘱的复印件。

3. 有关在公证机构保存文件副本的声明，应根据本法的规定予以出具。

第五十条　出具有关公证活动登记的声明

公证员、授权官员根据申请公证的自然人或法人出具有关公证活动登记的声明。

request of which notarial actions were made.

Article 51. Registration of notarial actions

All notarial actions made by notaries public, authorized officers are registered in the Register for registration of notarial actions (including in the electronic register of unified information system of notariate). Number at which notarial action is registered in the register is specified in the documents issued by these persons and in certifying texts.

第五十一条　公证活动的登记

公证员、授权官员实施的所有公证活动应在登记处的公证行为登记簿中登记（包括在公证统一信息系统的电子登记簿中）。公证活动在登记簿中记载的号码应在向申请人出具的文件和公证书中注明。

Article 52. Refusal in making of notarial actions

1. The notary public, the authorized officer refuses making of notarial action in these cases if:

1) action is subject to making by other notary public, authorized officer;

2) incapacitated person, the representative of physical person or legal entity who does not have appropriate authority addressed for making of notarial action;

3) such action contradicts other requirements of the legislation of Turkmenistan.

2. The notary public, the authorized officer does not take for making notarial actions documents if they do not conform to requirements of the legislation of Turkmenistan or contain the data discrediting honor and advantage of citizens.

3. The notary public, the authorized officer which refused to physical person or legal entity making of notarial action according to the written application of this physical person or legal entity shall state causes of failure in writing and explain procedure for its appeal. In these cases the refusal in making of notarial action not later than in five-day time from the date of the address is drawn up by the notary public, the authorized officer by pronouncement of the resolution on refusal in making of notarial action.

4. By the regulatory legal acts regulating activities of diplomatic representations and consular establishments of Turkmenistan also other bases for refusal in making of notarial actions by officials of diplomatic representations and consular establishments of Turkmenistan abroad can be established, and also other procedure for such refusal is established.

第五十二条　拒绝公证

1. 如出现下列情况，公证员、授权官员可以拒绝公证：

（1）应由其他公证员、授权官员进行公证的；

（2）无行为能力人申请公证或由不具备适格授权的自然人或法人的代表申请公证的；

（3）该公证活动与土库曼斯坦法律的其他规定相冲突的。

2. 公证员、授权官员发现公证申请不符合土库曼斯坦法律的规定或者包含有损公民名誉和利益的信息，不得公证。

3. 拒绝公证的公证员、授权官员应当书面说明拒绝的理由，并说明其申诉程序。在该等情况下，拒绝公证应在公证申请人申请公证之日起 5 日内以拒绝公证的决议的方式作出。

4. 规范土库曼斯坦外交代表和领事机构活动的监管法律，亦可对土库曼斯坦境外的外交代表和领事机构官员拒绝公证的依据以及拒绝的程序进行规定。

Article 53. Appeal of notarial actions or refusal in their making

1. The interested person considering wrong committed notarial action or refusal in making of the notarial action having the right to file a lawsuit about it the claim

第五十三条　对公证活动的申诉及对申诉的拒绝

1. 如利害关系人认为错误地从事了公证活动或在拒绝公证的情况下，其有权在公证员活动的管辖范围内提起诉讼。

on the territory of activities of the notary public.

2. The interested person considering wrong committed notarial action or refusal in making of the notarial action having the right to file a lawsuit about it the claim on the territory of activities of the notary public or in the location of Gengesh.

3. Claims to the notarial action which is illegally made by the official of diplomatic representation and consular establishment of Turkmenistan abroad or to refusal in its making are considered according to the procedure, established by the legislation of Turkmenistan.

4. Claims to the wrong certificate of wills and powers of attorney, to the wrong witnessing of authenticity of the signature on the statement or refusal in their certificate by the officials specified in Items 1, 3-6 parts one of article 37 of this Law are filed a lawsuit in the location of legal entities in whom they work.

5. Claims to the wrong certificate of the will or the wrong witnessing of authenticity of the signature on the statement or refusal in them the captain (commander) of the ocean ship or vessel performing swimming in the internal waters floating under National flag of Turkmenistan are filed a lawsuit in vessel place of registration.

6. Consideration of such claims is made by court according to the procedure, established by the civil procedural legislation of Turkmenistan.

7. Notaries public, authorized officers take part in cases on claims to notarial actions or refusal in their making.

Article 54. Procedure for the dispute resolution about the right based on committed notarial action

The dispute on the right based on committed notarial action is considered according to the legislation of Turkmenistan according to the procedure of claim production.

Article 55. The measures taken by notaries public, authorized officers in case of identification of violation of the law

1. The notary public, the authorized officer who when making notarial actions revealed violation of the law by citizens or certain officials, report about it to the corresponding prosecutor.

2. If authenticity of the submitted document raises doubts, the notary public, the authorized officer has the right to detain this document and to direct it to examination.

3. The notary public, the authorized officer shall represent to authorized state body on counteraction of legali-

2. 如利害关系人认为错误地从事了公证活动或在拒绝公证的情况下，其有权在公证员活动的管辖范围或地方人民委员会所在地提起诉讼。

3. 根据土库曼斯坦法律规定的程序，对土库曼斯坦境外的外交代表和领事机构官员非法公证的诉讼或对其拒绝公证的诉讼应予以受理。

4. 本法第 37 条第 1 款第 1 项、第 3 项至第 6 项规定的有关官员错误公证遗嘱和授权委托书、错误公证声明上签字的真实性，或拒绝公证，可以在其工作的机构所在地提起诉讼。

5. 悬挂土库曼斯坦国旗在航行的船舶或船只的船长（指挥官）错误公证遗嘱、错误公证声明上签字的真实性，或拒绝公证，可以在其船舶注册地提起诉讼。

6. 法院根据土库曼斯坦民事诉讼法规定的程序审理此类诉讼。

7. 公证员、授权官员应出庭参加与公证活动有关的或因其拒绝公证而被提起的诉讼。

第五十四条　公证活动权利的争议解决程序

有关公证活动权利的争议根据土库曼斯坦法律及相关诉讼的程序进行审理。

第五十五条　公证员、授权官员发现违法行为时采取的措施

1. 公证员、授权官员在进行公证活动时发现公民或某些官员的违法行为，应向有关检察官报告。

2. 如果申请人对提交的文件真实性存在质疑，公证员、授权官员有权扣留该文件并进行检查。

3. 公证员、授权官员应代表授权的国家机构根据土库曼斯坦法律规定的程序对反洗钱、恐怖主义融

zation of income gained in the criminal way, and terrorism financing information on the transactions and transactions which are causing suspicion of legalization of income gained in the criminal way, and the terrorism financing, and also subject to mandatory control, according to the procedure established by the legislation of Turkmenistan

资，以及可能导致洗钱或恐怖主义融资等采取强制监管的措施。

Article 56. Claims to the actions of the notary public which are not connected with making of notarial actions

Claims to the actions of the notary public which are not connected with making of notarial actions are considered by the Ministry adalat Turkmenistan.

第五十六条　对公证员与公证活动无关的行为的诉讼

对公证员与公证活动无关的行为提起的诉讼由土库曼斯坦公证部规定。

Chapter VIII. Features of the certificate of transactions

第八章　交易公证的特点

Article 57. The transactions certified in notarial procedure

1. The notary public, the authorized officer, within the powers determined by this Law certify transactions for which the legislation of Turkmenistan establishes obligatory notarial form of their conclusion. At the request of the parties also other transactions can be certified.

2. In case of the certificate of transactions within the powers determined by this Law except transactions about alienation and pledge of the real estate which is in Turkmenistan, officials of diplomatic representations and consular establishments of Turkmenistan abroad are guided by this Law.

第五十七条　通过公证程序证明的交易

1. 公证员、授权官员在本法规定的权力范围内对土库曼斯坦法律强制规定需公证的交易予以公证。在当事人提出申请的情况下，其他交易也可以予以公证。

2. 如果在本法规定的权力范围内对交易进行证明，除了有关在土库曼斯坦境内的房地产转让和抵押交易外，土库曼斯坦境外的外交代表和领事机构官员亦受本法约束。

Article 58. Explanation to the parties of sense and value of drafts of transactions

The notary public, authorized officer certifying transactions shall explain to the parties sense and value of the prepared drafts of transactions and to check whether there corresponds their content to actual intents of the parties and whether it contradicts requirements of the legislation of Turkmenistan.

第五十八条　交易文件公证效力与意义的解释

公证员、授权官员对交易进行公证，应当向当事人说明起草的公证文件的意义和效力，并检查其内容是否符合当事人的真实意思，是否与土库曼斯坦法律的要求相抵触。

Article 59. The certificate of transactions of alienation or pledge of the real and other estate which is subject to state registration

1. In case of the notarial certificate of transactions of alienation or of pledge of the real and other estate which is subject to state registration accessory of this property to person making alienation or pledge, and also lack of prohibition of alienation or arrest is checked.

Lack of prohibition of alienation or arrest is checked based on the reference issued by relevant organ.

第五十九条　国家登记的房地产和其他财产转让、抵押交易的公证

1. 在对国家登记的房地产和其他财产的转让、抵押交易进行公证时，应检查转让、抵押的人员的身份以及是否存在禁止转让或抵押的情形。

根据有关机关提供的相关资料检查是否存在禁止转让或抵押的情形。

2. In case of the certificate of agreements of alienation of real estate the notary public will request from documents of title on alienable property and determines powers of the owner by alienation of the rights belonging to it.

3. The certificate of agreements on alienation and of pledge of real estate is made in the location of the specified property.

4. The pledge agreement of property (the right to such property) on which the property right or other right are subject to state registration makes sure on condition of representation to the notary public of the document confirming state registration of property (the right to such property) addressed to the pledger.

5. The agreement on mortgage makes sure the notary public in the location of real estate.

6. In the presence of prohibition on property the transaction about its alienation can be certified only in case of the consent of the creditor and acquirer to transfer of debt on the acquirer.

Article 60. Certificate of agreements on construction of the apartment house

1. Agreements on provision to citizens of the parcels of land for construction of apartment houses on the right of private property make sure notaries public in the place of withdrawal of the parcel of land.

2. In case of the certificate of the agreements specified in part one of this Article, the notary public checks agreement compliance to requirements of the legislation of Turkmenistan regulating the right of citizens to construction of real estate on the right of private property.

Article 61. Witnesses of the transaction

1. At the request of the parties of the transaction or the testator when making notarial actions witnesses who also sign the document can participate.

2. Persons for benefit of whom notarial actions are made cannot witness.

Article 62. Certificate of wills

1. The notary public, the authorized officer the wills of capable persons constituted according to requirements of the Civil code of Turkmenistan and provided by them personally make sure. The certificate of wills through representatives is not allowed.

2. In case of the certificate of the will from the testator production of evidence, confirming its rights to the bequeathed property is not required.

2. 在对房地产转让协议进行公证时，公证员将要求提供有关可转让财产的文件，并且决定转让人的权力。

3. 对房地产转让或抵押协议的公证应在所涉房地产所在地作出。

4. 财产权利或其他应进行国家登记的财产权利（该等财产附属权利）的抵押协议，应确保向公证员出具抵押权人对财产（该等财产附属权利）已进行国家登记的确权文件。

5. 抵押贷款协议应确保由不动产所在地的公证员公证。

6. 如财产具有禁止情形，只有在债权人同意的情况下，向受让方转让债务的交易才能予以公证。

第六十条　房屋建设协议的公证

1. 向公民提供私宅建设的协议应确保由收回土地所在地的公证员公证。

2. 在对本条第 1 款规定的协议进行公证时，公证员应核查协议是否符合土库曼斯坦法律关于公民建设私宅的有关规定。

第六十一条　交易的见证人

1. 应交易当事人或遗嘱订立人的请求，在进行公证活动时，见证人亦可在其参与的文件上签字。

2. 公证活动的受益人不能担任见证人。

第六十二条　遗嘱的公证

1. 公证员、授权官员对完全行为能力人据土库曼斯坦《民法典》而起草并由其亲自确认的遗嘱进行公证。不允许公证代立的遗嘱。

2. 如果遗嘱订立人能提供遗产权利的证据，那么不需要再另行确认其对遗产的权利。

3. Person to whom the property is bequeathed at the request of the testator has the right to take part in case of creation of the will.

Article 63. Procedure for change and cancellation of wills

In case of obtaining by the notary public, authorized officer of the statement for cancellation of the made will, and equally in the receipt of the new will changing or canceling earlier made will about it the mark in the will copy which is stored at them and in the Register for registration of notarial actions becomes. The signature on the statement for change or cancellation of the will shall be notarially attested.

Article 64. Certificate of powers of attorney

1. Notaries public, authorized officers can certify the power of attorney on behalf of one or several persons addressed to one or several persons.

2. The power of attorney can be issued for the term of no more than three years.

3. If in the power of attorney term is not specified, it saves the power within one year from the date of the certificate of it the notary public, the authorized officer. The power of attorney in which date of the certificate by her notary public, the authorized officer is not specified is invalid.

4. The power of attorney issued according to the procedure of retrust can be notarially certified only after submission of the main power of attorney in which the retrust right is stipulated. The power of attorney issued according to the procedure of retrust shall not comprise more rights, than it is presented them under the main power of attorney. Effective period of the power of attorney issued according to the procedure of retrust shall not exceed effective period of the main power of attorney based on which it is issued.

5. In the power of attorney issued according to the procedure of retrust except general details, date and the place of the certificate of the main power of attorney shall be specified.

6. The powers of attorney certifying the right to control and the order of automobile and cargo vehicles, buses, minibuses can be drawn up by their owners only on the close relatives without the retrust right.

This regulation does not extend to persons having disability, the guardians (custodians) of persons which do not have opportunity to manage road transport for health reasons, who are in dependence under the agreement of

3. 应遗嘱订立人的要求，受遗赠人有权参与遗嘱的订立。

第六十三条　变更及撤销遗嘱的程序

如果公证员、授权官员收到撤销遗嘱的声明，及变更或撤销旧遗嘱的新遗嘱，对遗嘱副本进行标记后应于公证活动登记处的登记簿内进行保存。变更或撤销遗嘱声明上的签字应进行公证。

第六十四条　授权委托书的公证

1. 公证员、授权官员可以对一人或多人向其他一人或多人出具的授权委托书进行公证。

2. 授权委托书的授权期限不得超过 3 年。

3. 如果授权委托书中未确定授权期限，那么自公证员、授权官员出具公证书之日起 1 年内有效。未载明公证员、授权官员出具公证书日期的授权委托书无效。

4. 根据转委托程序出具的授权委托书只有在提交了规定转委托权利的主授权委托书后才能进行公证。根据转委托程序出具的授权委托书不能包含超出主授权委托书规定的权利。根据转委托程序出具的授权委托书的有效期不能超过其据以订立的主授权委托书的有效期。

5. 除了一般规定，根据转委托程序出具的授权委托书中应载明公证主授权委托书的时间和地点。

6. 公证汽车、火车、公交车、巴士控制权的授权委托书只能在其所有者不存在转委托权利的情况下出具。

该规定不适用于残疾人，由于健康原因而无法进行道路交通而依赖于永久监护人员的监护人（保管人），以及土库曼斯坦监管法律规定的其他人员。

the perpetual maintenance and other persons provided by regulatory legal acts of Turkmenistan.

Article 65. Number of copies of the certified transaction

The quantity of authentic copies of the certified transaction is determined by the number of the parties, but there cannot be less than two copies, one of which remains in notarial case.

Chapter IX. Taking measures to protection of inheritance

Article 66. Duty to inform about the opened inheritance

The companies, organizations, or studied the organization where the dead worked, law-enforcement bodies, the housing and operational organizations for the residence of the dead, and also person owners of apartment houses in which there lived the dead shall report to notaries public, officials Gengesha or diplomatic representations and consular establishments of Turkmenistan abroad about availability of the property which remained after the dead whose heirs are absent, and data on the residence known for it or works of expected heirs.

Article 67. Measures for protection of inheritance

1. The notary public, the authorized officer in the place of opening of inheritance according to physical persons or legal entities or on the initiative take measures to protection of inheritance, when necessary for the benefit of the state, heirs, refusal of receivers or creditors.

2. If the property of the testator or his part are not in the place of opening of inheritance, the notary public, the authorized officer in the place of opening of inheritance sends to the notary public, the authorized officer in the location of heritable property the order about taking measures to its protection.

Article 68. The notice of heirs on the opened inheritance

1. The notary public, the authorized officer, having received the message on the opened inheritance, shall inform on it heirs, the residence or works of which is known to them.

In the presence of the will containing testamentary refusal, the notary public, the authorized officer shall inform legatees, the residence or works of which is known to it, of opening of inheritance according to the will.

第六十五条　交易公证书的副本数量

交易公证书的副本的数量由当事人决定，但不得少于两份，其中一份保存在公证档案中。

第九章　采取措施保护遗产

第六十六条　关于遗产继承的通知义务

死者生前工作的公司、组织或研究机构，死者住所的住房和经营组织或死者生前居住的房屋的所有权人应向公证员、地方人民委员会官员或土库曼斯坦境外外交代表或领事机构的官员报告无继承人死者遗产的处理情况，以及其他居民所知悉的信息或潜在继承人的住所的信息。

第六十七条　遗产保护措施

1. 自然人或法人遗产继承地的公证员、授权官员在必要时为了国家、继承人、拒绝接受者或债权人的利益可主动采取措施保护遗产。

2. 如果遗嘱订立人的全部或部分财产不在遗产继承地，遗产继承地的公证员、授权官员应向遗产所在地的公证员、授权官员送达采取遗产保护措施的指令。

第六十八条　关于继承开始的通知

1. 公证员、授权官员在收到遗产继承开始的信息后，应通知其知悉住所或工作地点的继承人。

在遗嘱中包含拒绝继承的内容，公证员、授权官员应根据遗嘱的内容通知其知悉住所或工作地点的继承人继承开始的事宜。

2. The notary public, the authorized officer can also make challenge of heirs by the public announcement or the message on it in seal.

2. 公证员、授权官员亦可通过公告或封条的形式对继承人资格提出质疑。

Article 69. Production of the inventory of heritable property and appointment of his keeper or guardian

1. The notary public, the authorized officer makes the inventory of this property for protection of heritable property and gives him to storage to heirs or other persons or appoints the guardian.

2. If as a part of inheritance there is property requiring management and also in case of presentation of the claim by creditors to the testator before inheritance acceptance by heirs, the notary public, the authorized officer appoints the keeper of property. In the area where there is no notary public, Gengesh appoints the guardian over heritable property and is reported in the relevant office of notary public about the opened inheritance and measures taken on its protection.

3. The keeper, the guardian and other persons to whom the heritable property is transferred to storage are warned about responsibility for waste, concealment or alienation of heritable property, and also about responsibility for the caused losses.

4. In case of impossibility to take measures for protection of heritable property or to perform the inventory of heritable property the notary public, the authorized officer draws up the statement of refusal to show heritable property for the inventory.

第六十九条 制作遗产财产清单并指定管理人或保管人

1. 公证员、授权官员制作财产清单以保护遗产财产，并交由继承人、其他人员或指定的保管人保管。

2. 如果作为遗产一部分的财产需要管理，并且债权人在继承人继承遗产之前向遗嘱订立人主张权利的，公证员、授权官员可以指定财产管理人。在没有公证员的地区，地方人民委员会指定遗产的保管人，并应就继承开始及遗产保护措施向有关公证机构进行报告。

3. 应告知管理人、保管人以及遗产交由其保管的其他人员损耗、隐匿或转移遗产应承担的责任，以及如造成损失应承担的责任。

4. 如果无法采取措施保护遗产或对遗产列明清单，那么公证员、授权官员应起草无法出具遗产清单的说明。

Article 70. Remuneration for storage of heritable property

1. The keeper, the guardian and other persons to whom the heritable property is transferred to storage if they are not heirs, have the right to earn reward for storage of heritable property.

2. Necessary expenses on storage and management of heritable property, less actually received benefit from use of this property are also refunded to specified persons.

第七十条 保管遗产的报酬

1. 如果管理人、保管人以及遗产交由其保管的其他人员并非继承人，那么有权就其对遗产的保管获取报酬。

2. 储存及管理遗产所需要的必要开支扣除后，剩余部分应返还给有权的特定人员。

Article 71. Removal of security measures from heritable property

1. Protection of heritable property continues before inheritance acceptance by all heirs and if it is not accepted – before the expiration of the terms of inheritance acceptance established by the Civil code of Turkmenistan.

2. In cases of the termination of measures for protection of heritable property the notary public, the authorized

第七十一条 遗产安全措施的取消

1. 在所有继承人开始继承之前应对遗产进行持续保护，如果继承人未接受继承，那么应在土库曼斯坦《民法典》规定的遗产继承期限届满前对遗产进行持续保护。

2. 如果终止对遗产的保护措施，公证员、授权官员应事先通知其继承人，如果没有继承人，那么遗产

officer shall be notified previously about it heirs and if they is not available, – the body having the right to dispose of state-owned property.

应归国家所有。

Article 72. Issue of sums of money from heritable property

1. In necessary cases the notary public, the authorized officer before inheritance acceptance by heirs and if it is not accepted, then before issue to the state of the certificate on the right to inheritance, does the order about issue of heritable property of sums of money on:

1) covering of costs on care of the testator during his disease, and also on its funeral;

2) content of persons which were dependent on the testator;

3) satisfaction of claims on the salary and the claims equated to them;

4) covering of expenses on protection of heritable property and on management of it, and also on the publication of the notice on the opened inheritance.

2. In case of absence as a part of heritable property of sums of money the order about issue of things which cost shall not exceed the amounts of actually made expenses becomes.

第七十二条 从遗产中支付的款项

1. 在必要的情况下，公证员、授权官员在继承人继承遗产之前，或继承人放弃继承遗产并出具继承权放弃声明时，应从遗产中支付以下款项：

（1）遗嘱订立人在罹患疾病期间的护理费用及丧葬费；

（2）受遗嘱订立人扶养的人员的必要开支；

（3）索要工资及其同等索要事项的支出；

（4）保护、管理遗产的费用，及发布遗产继承通知的费用。

2. 如果某些支出并非管理遗产支出的一部分，扣除部分不应超过管理遗产实际支出的金额。

Chapter X. Issue of the certificate on the right to inheritance

第十章 继承权公证

Article 73. Adoption of the statements connected with the right to inheritance

The notary public, the official of diplomatic representation and consular establishment of Turkmenistan abroad in the place of opening of inheritance according to the legislation of Turkmenistan adopts statements in writing for inheritance acceptance, about issue of the certificate on the right to inheritance, about inheritance acceptance and issue of the certificate on the right to inheritance, about refusal of inheritance by the heir, about issue of the certificate on the right to share in common property of spouses (the former spouses) or about acceptances of necessary measures to protection of inheritance and other types of statements.

第七十三条 继承权有关声明的采纳

遗产继承地的公证员、土库曼斯坦境外的外交代表和领事机构官员采纳继承权证明的声明、放弃继承以及继承权证明的声明、继承人放弃继承、关于与配偶（前配偶）分享共同财产权利的证明的声明或关于接受必要措施保护遗产的书面声明或者其他类型声明的形式接受继承。

Article 74. Place and terms of issue of the certificate on the right to inheritance

1. According to the written application of heirs the notary public, the official of diplomatic representation and consular establishment of Turkmenistan abroad in the place of opening of inheritance grants the certificate on the

第七十四条 继承权公证的地点和期限

1. 遗产继承地的公证员、土库曼斯坦境外的外交代表及领事机构官员根据继承人的书面申请出具继承权证书。

right to inheritance.

2. Issue of the certificate on the right to inheritance is made in the terms provided by the Civil code of Turkmenistan.

Article 75. Procedure for issue of the certificate on the right to inheritance

1. Certificates on the right to inheritance are granted to the heirs who accepted inheritance according to the Civil code of Turkmenistan which submitted the application for issue of the certificate on the right to inheritance in the place of opening of inheritance or actually started ownership or property administration that demonstrates acceptance of inheritance by them.

2. The heirs who did not accept inheritance in time, established by the Civil code of Turkmenistan, can be included in the certificate on the right to inheritance with the consent of all other heirs who accepted inheritance. This consent shall be stated in writing before issue of the certificate on the right to inheritance.

3. The certificate on the right to inheritance is granted to all heirs together or to everyone depending on their desire.

4. About issue of the certificate on the right to inheritance addressed to sponsored or the ward of the minor or incapacitated heir it is reported to guardianship and custody bodies at the place of residence of the heir for protection of its valuable interest.

5. Upon transition of property on inheritance right to the state, the certificate on the right to inheritance is granted to authorized state body.

6. In the presence of prohibition on property acquisition the certificate on the right to inheritance can be granted in case of the consent of the creditor and the heir (heirs) on transfer of debt on the heir (heirs).

Article 76. Conditions of issue of the certificate on the right to inheritance to legal heirs

1. In case of issue of the certificate on the right to inheritance to legal heirs by reclamation from heirs of the corresponding proofs the fact of death of the testator, time and the place of opening of inheritance, availability of the related and other relations with the testator which are the basis for recognition by legal heirs of persons who submitted the application for issue of the certificate on the right to inheritance, structure and the location of heritable property on which the certificate to frame on inheritance is granted is checked.

2. 继承权公证书应在土库曼斯坦民法典规定的期限内作出。

第七十五条　继承权公证的程序

1. 继承权证明授予根据土库曼斯坦《民法典》提交继承地的继承权证明申请而接受继承的继承人，或者实际上对遗产拥有所有权或进行管理而证明其接受继承的人。

2. 根据土库曼斯坦《民法典》的规定，没有及时接受继承的继承人经接受继承的所有其他继承人同意可以被载入继承权公证内。该等同意应在继承权公证之前以书面形式作出。

3. 继承权证书基于继承人的意愿授予所有继承人或授予每一位继承人。

4. 有关向受扶养人、未成年或无行为能力继承人的监护人授予继承权公证书的事宜应向继承人住所地的保管及托管机构报告，以保护遗产利益。

5. 在继承权财产归国家所有的情况下，应授予有关国家机关继承权公证。

6. 如存在禁止取得财产的情形，在债权人和继承人（们）同意继承人（们）的情况下，可以授予其继承权公证。

第七十六条　向法定继承人授予继承权公证的条件

1. 如果通过从继承人获得相应证据（包括证明其法定继承人身份的遗嘱订立人死亡的事实、继承开始的时间和地点以及其他与遗嘱订立人有关的信息）而授予其继承权公证的，应检查授予的继承权公证上载明的遗产的构成及地点。

2. If one or several legal heirs are deprived of opportunity to produce the evidence of the related and other relations with the testator which are the basis for their recognition to legal heirs they can be included in certificates on the right to inheritance with the consent of all other heirs who accepted inheritance and produced the corresponding evidence.

2. 如果一个或几个法定继承人被剥夺了提供与遗嘱订立人有关的证据的机会（该等证据是承认其为法定继承人的基础），如果接受继承并提供相应证据的所有其他继承人一致同意，该等继承人可以被授予继承权公证。

Article 77. Conditions of issue of the certificate on the right to inheritance on the will

第七十七条　据遗嘱出具继承公证的条件

1. In case of issue of the certificate on the right to inheritance according to the will by reclamation of the corresponding proofs the fact of death of the testator, will availability, time and the place of opening of inheritance, structure and the location of heritable property on which the certificate on the right to inheritance is granted is checked, and also the circle of the heirs having the right to obligatory share in inheritance is established.

1. 如果通过获取相应证据（包括遗嘱订立人死亡的事实、遗嘱的可获得性、继承开始的时间和地点）的方式根据遗嘱出具继承权公证的，应检查拟授予的继承权公证上载明的遗产的构成及地点，并界定享有继承权的继承人的范围。

2. In the presence of testamentary refusal are invited refusal about receivers, content of testamentary refusal and their right to the share which is due from the heir (heirs) is explained to them.

2. 在遗嘱接收人放弃继承遗产的情况下，应向其告知放弃继承的后果及其可以从遗产中分享到的利益。

Article 78. Conditions of issue of the certificate on the right to inheritance concerning the property which is subject to state registration

第七十八条　出具关于国家登记的财产的继承权公证的条件

1. If the apartment house or other real estate are part of heritable property, the testator needs the title document on accessory of the apartment house or other real estate, the certificate of relevant organ of structure of property and its assessment and according to the procedure, established by the legislation of Turkmenistan, is specified state registration of the specified property. At the same time based on the reference issued by relevant organ lack of prohibition (arrest) on alienation of the apartment house or other real estate is checked.

1. 如果房屋或其他不动产是遗产的一部分，遗嘱订立人需要附加有关房屋或其他不动产的所有权证明，有关机构关于财产构成及其评估的证明应根据土库曼斯坦法律规定的程序进行特定财产的特定国家登记。同时，根据有关机关颁布的相关文件对房屋或其他不动产禁止转让的情形进行检查。

2. For inclusion in the certificate on the right to inheritance of other property which is subject to state registration (the car and another), documents on accessory of this property to the testator are checked.

2. 为出具国家登记的其他财产（汽车及其他）的继承权公证，应检查遗嘱订立人在该财产上附加的文件。

Chapter XI. Issue of the certificate on the property right. Imposing and removal of prohibition of property acquisition

第十一章　出具财产权利公证.实施或解除财产流转的禁令

Article 79. Issue of certificates according to the joint statement of spouses (the former spouses)

第七十九条　根据与配偶（前配偶）的联合声明进行公证

1. Notaries public, officials of diplomatic representa-

1. 公证员、土库曼斯坦境外的外交代表或领事机

tions and consular establishments of Turkmenistan abroad according to the joint written statement of spouses (the former spouses) issue to one of them or both spouses (the former spouses) of the certificate on the property right to share in the common property acquired during scrap.

2. The specified certificates on the property right to the apartment house, part of the house, the apartment, the country house, the garden house, garage or other real estate are issued by notaries public in the location of this property.

构官员根据与配偶（前配偶）的联合书面声明，向配偶其中一人或配偶（前配偶）两人出具在离婚时可以获得分享共同财产权利的公证。

2. 有关房屋、房屋的一部分、公寓、乡间别墅、花园洋房、车库或其他房地产的财产权的特定公证由该财产所在地的公证员进行公证。

Article 80. Issue of the certificate in case of the death of one of spouses

1. In case of the death of one of spouses the certificate on the right to share in common property of spouses is granted in the place of opening of inheritance according to the written application of the surviving spouse with the preliminary notice on it of the heirs who accepted inheritance.

2. The certificate on the right to share in common property of spouses can be granted addressed to the surviving spouse on half of the common property acquired during scrap.

3. The share of the died spouse in common property also can be determined by the written application of the heirs who accepted inheritance with the consent of the surviving spouse in the certificate on the right to share in common property of spouses.

第八十条　在一方配偶死亡的情况下出具的公证

1. 在一方配偶死亡的情况下，配偶有关分享共同财产权利的公证根据未亡配偶的书面申请在继承地授予，并在公证中附加接受继承的继承人的初步通知。

2. 有关配偶分享共同财产权利的公证可以授予在离婚时能够获得一半共同财产的未亡配偶。

3. 过世配偶在共同财产中可以分享的部分也可以在未亡配偶同意的情况下，根据接受继承的继承人的书面申请，在配偶共同财产分配公证中予以确定。

Article 81. Issue of the certificate on the right to share in common joint property

1. The notary public according to the joint written statement of persons having property in common joint property after preliminary determination of share of each of them, issues to person or persons who wished to receive share in common property, the certificate on the right to share in common joint property.

2. The certificate on the right to share in common joint property on the real estate which is in common joint property, specified in part one of this Article is issued by notaries public.

3. The certificate on the right to share in common joint property on real estate is granted in the place of its stay.

第八十一条　共有财产分享权利的公证

1. 公证员在事先确定共有财产权利人各自的份额后，根据共有财产权利人共同出具的书面声明向希望获得共有财产份额的人员出具享有共有财产部分权利的公证。

2. 本条第 1 款规定的共同财产中的房地产分配权公证由公证员作出。

3. 共有财产分配权的公证在不动产所在地进行。

Article 82. Issue of the certificate on the property right to real estate in case of liquidation of sole proprietor company

The notary public according to the written application

第八十二条　独资企业清算后的不动产权利公证

公证员根据清算后的独资公司的所有权人的书面

of the owner after liquidation of sole proprietor company grants the certificate on the property right to real estate of the liquidated sole proprietor company.

申请，授予清算后的独资企业不动产权利公证。

Article 83. Issue of the certificate on real estate acquisition from the public biddings

Based on the act of sale of real estate from the public biddings the notary public in the location of real estate grants to the buyer the certificate on real estate acquisition from open tenderings.

第八十三条　通过公开竞标取得的不动产的公证

以公开招投标方式销售房地产的，由房地产所在地的公证员向买方授予公开竞标取得不动产的公证。

Article 84. Conditions of issue of the certificate on the property right to real estate

1. The notary public in case of issue of the certificate on the property right requires the title document on accessory of real estate.

2. The notary public by reclamation of the reference issued by relevant organ shall check whether there are no prohibitions of alienation or arrest of real estate.

第八十四条　不动产财产权公证的条件

1. 公证员在作出财产权公证时，需要附加有关房地产所有权的文件。

2. 公证员据有关机关提供的相关文件公证时应检查是否具有禁止不动产转让的情形。

Article 85. Imposing of prohibitions

1. According to notices of credit institutes or legal entities on issue to physical persons of the loan for construction, capital repairs and purchase of the house (part of the house), apartments or on acquisition of other real or other estate which is subject to state registration, and also in case of the certificate of the pledge agreement of property (the right to such property) the notary public in the location of the specified property imposes ban of alienation of this property.

2. In case of the certificate of the pledge agreement of the real and other estate which is subject to state registration (the right to such property), the notary public in writing reports in registration authorities in the place of its stay about the certificate of such agreement and imposing of prohibitions.

第八十五条　实施禁止

1. 根据信贷机构或法人向自然人发出的有关建造、维修及购买房屋（房屋的一部分）、公寓的贷款的通知，或取得其他需进行国家登记的不动产或其他财产的通知，以及在对财产（附属于财产的权利）抵押协议进行公证时，所涉财产所在地的公证员实施对有关财产的转让禁止。

2. 对需进行国家登记的不动产或其他财产（附属于财产的权利）的抵押协议进行公证时，公证员应以书面形式报告该财产所在地的登记机关对该抵押协议的公证以及转让禁止。

Article 86. Removal of prohibitions

The notary public, having received the notice of credit institute or the legal entity on repayment of the loan or termination of the contract on pledge of property (the right to such property), removes the alienation ban imposed according to the procedure, established by part one of article 85 of this Law what he in writing reports in registration authorities of property about.

第八十六条　取消禁止

公证员在收到信贷机构或法人关于偿还贷款或终止财产（附属于财产的权利）抵押协议的通知后，取消根据本法第85条第1款规定的转让禁止程序，应以书面报告的形式报告登记机关。

Chapter XII. Witnessing of fidelity of copies of documents and statements from them, authenticity of the signature and fidelity of the translation

第十二章　文件副本、副本中声明的真实性、签名的真实性及翻译的真实性的公证

Article 87. Witnessing of fidelity of copies of docu-

第八十七条　文件副本、副本中声明真实性的

ments and statements from them

1. The notary public, the authorized officer in writing witnesses fidelity of copies of documents and statements from them issued by physical persons and legal entities provided that these documents and their content do not contradict the legislation of Turkmenistan and have legal value.

Witnessing of fidelity of passport copies, military IDs, documents on membership in batch, labor union and other public association, certificates of the deputy of Majlis of Turkmenistan, the Ombudsman or his deputy, members of the Central commission on elections and holding referenda in Turkmenistan, Hulk of maslakhata and Gengesha is forbidden.

Witnessing of fidelity of copies of acts of the supreme bodies of the government and the public administration of Turkmenistan concerning the personal rights and interests of citizens is made only in the first offices of notary public.

The officials Gengesha making notarial actions cannot witness fidelity of copies of documents on the termination of educational and professional educational institutions.

2. Fidelity of the statement can be attested only from such documents which contents concern single questions. The statement shall contain the complete text of the part of the document concerning one or several questions stated in the document.

Article 88. Witnessing of fidelity of copies from copies of documents

Fidelity of the copy from the copy of the document is witnessed by the notary public, the authorized officer under condition if fidelity of primary copy is notarized or the copy of the document is issued by the legal entity from whom the authentic document proceeds. In the latter case the copy of the document shall be made on the form of this legal entity, is under seal and to have mark that the original of the document is at the legal entity.

Article 89. Witnessing of authenticity of the signature on the document

1. The notary public, the authorized officer witnesses authenticity of the signature on the document which contents do not contradict the legislation of Turkmenistan and does not represent transaction statement.

2. The notary public, the authorized officer, witnessing authenticity of the signature, does not certify the events stated in the document, and only confirms that the

公证

1. 公证员、授权官员以书面形式证明自然人及法人出具的文件及文件中声明副本的真实性，前提是这些文件及其内容未与土库曼斯坦法律相冲突并且具有法律意义。

禁止对护照复印件、军队证件、在工会和其他公共组织的会员资格，土库曼斯坦议会代表、监察员及其助手、选任和举行土库曼斯坦全民投票委员会的中央委员会的成员，对马斯拉哈特和地方人民委员会等事项进行公证。

土库曼斯坦政府最高机构和公共行政部门关于公民个人权益的文件副本的真实性公证仅在第一公证机构进行。

地方人民委员会官员不能公证有关教育和专业教育机构终止的文件副本的真实性。

2. 仅对文件中涉及的单一问题声明的真实性进行公证；若该文件涉及一个或多个问题，公证文件应包含完整的文件。

第八十八条　文件副本复印件的真实性公证

如果原始副本的真实性经过公证或文件副本是由出具真实文件的法人出具的，文件副本复印件的真实性由公证员、授权官员予以公证。在后一种情况下，文件的副本应由该法人制作并加盖印章，同时注明文件的原件存于法人处。

第八十九条　文件签字的真实性公证

1. 公证员、授权官员对文件上签字的公证，其内容不应违反土库曼斯坦法律，并且不代表交易声明。

2. 公证员、授权官员公证签名的真实性，并不对文件上记载的内容予以公证，仅对签名由某人作出进行确认。

signature is made by certain person.

Article 90. Witnessing of fidelity of the translation

1. The notary public, the official of diplomatic representation and consular establishment of Turkmenistan abroad witnesses fidelity of the translation from one language on another if he knows the corresponding languages.

2. If the notary public, the official of diplomatic representation and consular establishment of Turkmenistan abroad does not know the corresponding languages, the translation can be made by the translator, at the same time authenticity of the signature of the translator is witnessed by the notary public, the official of diplomatic representation and consular establishment of Turkmenistan abroad.

第九十条　翻译真实性的公证

1. 公证员、土库曼斯坦境外的外交代表和领事机构官员如通晓相应的语言，可公证翻译的真实性。

2. 如果公证员、土库曼斯坦境外的外交代表和领事机构官员不通晓相应的语言，可以由翻译人员进行翻译，同时公证员、土库曼斯坦境外的外交代表和领事机构官员应证明翻译人员签名的真实性。

Chapter XIII. Certificate of the facts

第十三章　对事实的公证

Article 91. The certificate of the fact of finding of person in live

1. The notary public, the official of diplomatic representation and consular establishment of Turkmenistan abroad certifies the fact of finding of person in live. The certificate of the fact of stay in live minor or incapacitated person is made at the request of his legal representatives (parents, adoptive parents, the guardian, the custodian), and also organizations and the organizations on which care there is minor or incapacitated person.

2. In confirmation of the specified fact to interested persons the certificate is granted.

第九十一条　公民在世事实的证明

1. 公证员、土库曼斯坦境外的外交代表和领事机构官员对公民在世的事实进行公证。对未成年人或无行为能力人在现场的事实进行公证的，由其法定代表人（父母、养父母、监护人、托管人）或未成年人或无行为能力人所在的组织提出请求。

2. 向利害关系人确认特定事实应出示证件。

Article 92. The certificate of the fact of finding of person in certain place

1. The notary public, the official of diplomatic representation and consular establishment of Turkmenistan abroad according to the written application of person certifies the fact of its stay in certain place. The certificate of the fact of stay in certain place of the minor is made based on the statement of his legal representatives (parents, adoptive parents, the guardian, the custodian), and also organizations and the organizations on which care there is minor.

2. In confirmation of the specified fact to interested persons the certificate is granted.

第九十二条　对公民在某地的事实进行公证

1. 公证员、土库曼斯坦境外的外交代表和领事机构官员根据有关人员的书面申请公证某人在某地的事实。对未成年人在某地的事实的证明，由其法定代表人（父母、养父母、监护人、托管人），以及未成年人所在组织的申请作出。

2. 向利害关系人确认特定事实应出示证件。

Article 93. The certificate of identity of person with person represented in the photo

The notary public, the official of diplomatic representation and consular establishment of Turkmenistan abroad certifies identity of person with person represented

第九十三条　对图片中人员身份的公证

公证员、土库曼斯坦境外的外交代表和领事机构官员对某人提供的图片中某人员身份的公证通过授予身份公证的方式作出。

in the photo provided by this person in witness whereof to it the certificate is granted.

Article 94. Certificate of time of presentation of the document

1. According to the statement of interested persons the notary public, the official of diplomatic representation and consular establishment of Turkmenistan abroad certify time of presentation of the document to it. At the same time it is not witnessed on the events stated in the document, and the fact of presentation of the document in certain time (year, month, day, hour, minute) only proves to be true.

2. The certifying text about it becomes on the document with indication of surname, name, middle names of the shown his face.

3. If several documents are at the same time shown, then notarial action is made concerning each of them.

第九十四条　对文件制作时间的公证

1. 公证员、土库曼斯坦境外外交代表和领事机构官员根据利害关系人的申请对文件制作的时间进行公证。同时，该等证明并不对文件中记载的事件予以公证，仅公证文件于特定时间（年、月、日、时、分）制作。

2. 公证文书应在文件的封面注明姓名等信息。

3. 如果几份文件是同时制作的，那么就每一份文件进行公证。

Chapter XIV. Transfer of statements of physical persons and legal entities. Acceptance of money and securities in the deposit

第十四章　自然人和法人声明的传达 存款和有价证券的接受

Article 95. Transfer of statements

1. Transfer of statements of physical persons and legal entities to other physical persons and legal entities is performed by the notary public personally on receipt or by mail with the return notification. Statements can be transferred also with use of the telefax, computer networks and other technical means.

2. The notary public at the request of person who submitted the application grants to it the certificate on transfer of the statement.

第九十五条　声明的传达

1. 公证员个人以收据或邮件的方式通过发送通知将某一自然人或法人的声明传达给另一个自然人或法人。声明也可以通过电话传真、电脑网络及其他技术手段传达。

2. 公证员应提供申请人申请声明传达的证明。

Article 96. Acceptance in the deposit of money and securities for transfer to the creditor

1. The notary public, the official of diplomatic representation and consular establishment of Turkmenistan abroad in cases, stipulated by the legislation Turkmenistan, accepts from the debtor in the deposit money and securities for transfer to their creditor.

2. The creditor is informed on receipt of money and securities and according to its requirement receivable money or securities are issued to it.

3. Acceptance of money and securities in the deposit is made in the place of obligation fulfillment.

第九十六条　接受存款和证券并交付给债权人

1. 公证员、土库曼斯坦境外的外交代表及领事机构的官员在土库曼斯坦法律规定的情形下接收债务人向债权人交付的存款和证券。

2. 债权人将根据向其提示的通知接收款项和证券。

3. 存款和证券的接收应在义务履行地实现。

Article 97. Refund and securities to person which introduced them in the deposit

The refund and securities to person which introduced them in the deposit is allowed only from written consent of person for benefit of which the contribution, or by a court decision is made.

第九十七条 向存款人退款及退回证券

只有在受益人书面同意或通过法院判决，才能向存款人退款或退回证券。

Chapter XV. Making of executive texts

第十五章 执行文书的制作

Article 98. Collection of sums of money or reclamation of property from the debtor

1. For collection of sums of money or reclamation from the debtor of property notaries public, officials of diplomatic representations and consular establishments of Turkmenistan abroad make executive texts on the documents establishing debt.

2. The list of documents according to which debt collection is made in indisputable procedure based on executive texts is established by the Cabinet of Ministers of Turkmenistan.

第九十八条 向债务人收款或收回财产

1. 为向债务人收款或收回财产，公证员、土库曼斯坦境外的外交代表和领事机构官员在债权债务文件中制作执行文书。

2. 通过执行文书以非诉方式实现债权的文件清单，由土库曼斯坦内阁部长进行规定。

Article 99. Conditions for making of executive texts

1. The executive text is made in the following cases:

1) if the submitted documents confirm indisputability of debt or other responsibility of the debtor to the claimant;

2) if from the date of emergence of right of action there passed no more than three years, and in the relations between legal entities – no more than one year.

2. If for the requirement according to which the executive text is issued the legislation of Turkmenistan establishes other prescriptive limit, the executive text is issued within this term.

第九十九条 制作执行文书的条件

1. 以下情形需制作执行文书：

（1）提交的文件证明债务是确定的或者证明债务人对债权人的其他责任；

（2）债务履行期限届满之日起不超过 3 年，或法人之间的债权债务关系不超过 1 年。

2. 如果土库曼斯坦法律对据以出具执行文书的要求规定了其他限制，那么执行文书应在该限制内出具。

Article 100. Content of executive text

The executive text shall comprise:

1) position, surname, name and middle name of the official making executive text;

2) name and address of the claimant;

3) name and debtor's address;

4) designation of term for which collection is made;

5) designation of the amounts which are subject to collection or the objects which are subject to reclamation including penalty fee, percent if those are due;

6) designation of the amount of the state fee paid by the claimant or which is subject to collection from the debtor;

第一百条 执行文书的内容

执行文书应包含以下内容：

（1）制作执行文书的官员的职位和姓名；

（2）债权人的姓名和地址；

（3）债务人的姓名和地址；

（4）债权实现的期限；

（5）应收取的金额或需要收回的标的，包括一定比例的罚金（如果已到期）；

（6）应由申请人支付的或者应向债务人收取的国家公证费用的数额；

7) date (year, month, number) making of executive text;

8) number at which the executive text is registered in the Register for registration of notarial actions;

9) the signature of the official who made executive text, the notary public seal.

（7）制作执行文书的日期（年、月、日）；

（8）执行文书在公证活动登记簿中记载的编号；

（9）制作执行文书的官员的签名、公证员的印章。

Article 101. Procedure for collection on executive text

Collection on executive text is made according to the procedure, the established legislation of Turkmenistan on enforcement proceeding for execution of judgments.

第一百零一条　执行文书的执行程序

执行文书的执行是根据土库曼斯坦关于执行法院判决的强制程序进行的。

Article 102. Term of presentation of executive text

1. In case claimant or the debtor is the physical person, the executive text can be shown to forced execution within three years from the date of its making, and according to all other requirements – within one year if the legislation of Turkmenistan does not establish other terms.

2. Recovery of the passed term is made for presentation of executive text according to the civil procedural legislation of Turkmenistan.

第一百零二条　提交执行文书的期限

1. 如果申请人或债务人是自然人，执行文书可自其作出之日起 3 年内强制执行。其他有效期限在 1 年内，土库曼斯坦法律另有规定的除外。

2. 执行期限届满的执行文书可依据土库曼斯坦民事诉讼法的规定恢复效力。

Chapter XVI. Making of protest of the bill of exchange, presentation of checks to payment and the certificate of non-payment of checks

第十六章　汇票异议公证 采用支票付款及支票未支付的公证

Article 103. Protest of the bill of exchange

The protest of the bill of exchange in non-payment, the non-acceptance and not dating of the acceptance is made by the notary public according to the legislation of Turkmenistan on the bill of exchange.

第一百零三条　汇票异议公证

公证员根据土库曼斯坦有关汇票的法律作出未支付、未承兑及未规定承兑日期的异议公证。

Article 104. Adoption of checks for presentation to payment and the certificate of non-payment of checks

1. The notary public in the location of the payer accepts for presentation to payment the checks provided after ten days, and foreign cheques – after six months from the date of issue of the check, but no later than 12 hours following after that the term of day.

2. In case of check non-payment the notary public certifies check non-payment by text on the check in the established form and does mark about it in the Register for registration of notarial actions. Along with text on the check the notary public sends the notification to the issuer about non-payment of its check bank and making of text on the check.

3. In case of check non-payment the notary public at the request of the payee makes executive text.

第一百零四条　采用支票付款和支票未支付的公证

1. 自支票签发之日起 10 日后、外国支票签发之日起 6 个月后，付款人所在地的公证员可以对上述支票进行提示付款，但不得在有效期届满前最后 12 小时申请。

2. 如果支票未付款，公证员以规定的格式在支票上备注的方式对支票进行未付款公证，并且在公证活动登记簿中进行登记。除了支票上的文本，公证员还会向支票签发人发送有关银行未付款和在支票上备注的通知。

3. 如果支票未付款，公证员可应收款人的要求制作执行公证书。

Chapter XVII. Acceptance on document storage

Article 105. Acceptance on document storage

1. The notary public, the official of diplomatic representation and consular establishment of Turkmenistan abroad accepts on storage documents according to the inventory. One copy of the inventory remains at the notary public, other copy is issued to person who checked documents.

2. At the request of person the notary public, the official of diplomatic representation and consular establishment of Turkmenistan abroad can accept documents and securities without inventory if they are packed properly (packaging is sealed the notary public, it is signed by the notary public and person who handed over documents and securities). Packaging is sealed and signed by the notary public, the official of diplomatic representation and consular establishment of Turkmenistan abroad, and also signed by person which handed over documents. In such cases the notary public, the official of diplomatic representation and consular establishment of Turkmenistan abroad bears responsibility for safety of packaging.

3. To person who checked documents the certificate is granted.

Article 106. Return accepted on document storage

The documents accepted on storage return to person which checked them or authorized by it upon presentation of the certificate or the copy of their inventory issued by the notary public, or by a court decision.

Chapter XVIII. Making of ship's protests

Article 107. Statement for the ship's protest

1. The notary public, the official of diplomatic representation and consular establishment of Turkmenistan abroad accept for the purpose of providing proofs for protection of the rights and legitimate interests of shipowners the statement of the captain (commander) of the vessel for the incident taking place during swimming or the parking of the vessel which can be the basis for presentation of property requirements to the shipowner.

2. The statement for the ship's protest shall contain the description of circumstances of incident and the measures taken by the captain (commander) for ensuring safety of the property entrusted to it.

3. In confirmation of the circumstances stated in the application for the ship's protest the captain (commander)

第十七章　接受文件保存

第一百零五条　接受文件保存

1. 公证员、土库曼斯坦境外的外交代表和领事机构官员根据有关目录接受文件保存。保存清单的一份副本保存在公证员处，其他副本提供给检查该等文件的人员。

2. 如果有关文件和证券已妥善包装（包裹应该是密封的，并且应由公证员及提交该文件和证券的人员签字），应有关人员的请求，公证员、土库曼斯坦境外的外交代表和领事机构官员可以不依据有关清单接受文件和证券。包裹应该密封并且由公证员、土库曼斯坦境外的外交代表和领事机构官员签名，并且应由提交文件的人员签名。在该情况下，公证员、土库曼斯坦境外的外交代表和领事机构官员应承担妥善包装的责任。

3. 应向检查文件的人提供公证书。

第一百零六条　保存文件的返还

文件检查人员、经公证书授权、经公证员作出的保存清单授权或法院决定授权的人员，可以获得公证机构返还的保存文件。

第十八章　制作海事报告公证

第一百零七条　海事报告的声明

1. 公证员、土库曼斯坦境外的外交代表和领事机构官员，出于保护船舶所有人权利及合法利益而提供证据的目的，接受船长（指挥官）有关船舶在远航时发生事故或有关船舶停泊的声明，该公证可以作为船舶所有人提交财产请求的基础。

2. 海事报告声明应包含有关事故情形的描述，以及船长（指挥官）采取的确保有关财产安全的措施。

3. 船舶的船长（指挥官）应根据土库曼斯坦法律确认海事报告申请中记载的事项，并提交申请。自土

of the vessel according to the legislation of Turkmenistan along with filing of application or in time no more than seven calendar days from the moment of calling of the vessel the port of Turkmenistan or from the moment of incident if it took place in port, shall provide to the notary public, the official of diplomatic representation and consular establishment of Turkmenistan abroad on review the sudovy magazine and certified by the captain (commander)

Article 108. Procedure and submission due dates of the statement for the ship's protest

1. The application for the ship's protest in the port of Turkmenistan is submitted to the notary public according to the legislation of Turkmenistan, and in foreign port – to the official of diplomatic representation and consular establishment of Turkmenistan abroad or to the competent foreign official according to the procedure, established by the legislation of this state.

2. The application for the ship's protest is submitted if incident happened in seaport, - within twenty four hours from the moment of incident, and during navigation of the vessel - within twenty four hours from the moment of arrival of the vessel or the captain (commander) of the vessel in the first seaport after incident.

3. In case of impossibility of presentation of protest at the scheduled time the reasons of it shall be specified in the statement for the ship's protest.

Article 109. Creation of the act of the ship's protest

The notary public, the official of diplomatic representation and consular establishment of Turkmenistan abroad based on the statement of the captain (commander) of the vessel, data of the logbook, and also poll of the captain (commander) and, whenever possible, at least two witnesses from among faces of command structure of the vessel and two witnesses from crew draws up the statement of the ship's protest and assures him the sign and seal. One copy of the act is issued to the captain (commander) of the vessel or person authorized by it.

Chapter XIX. Providing proofs

Article 110. Providing the proofs necessary in case of case in court or other competent authority

1. At the request of interested persons the notary public, the official of diplomatic representation and consular establishment of Turkmenistan abroad provides the proofs

库曼斯坦港口召回船舶之日起或事故发生之日起（如果事故发生在海港）7 个自然日之内应向公证员、土库曼斯坦境外的外交代表和领事机构官员提交公证申请并由船长（指挥官）予以证明。

第一百零八条　海事报告声明的程序和提交的截止日期

1. 有关土库曼斯坦港口的海事报告公证应根据土库曼斯坦法律向公证员提交申请。如在外国港口，则根据该国法律规定的程序，向土库曼斯坦境外的外交代表和领事机构官员或有权外国官员提交申请。

2. 如果在港口发生事故那么应在事故发生之日起 24 小时内提交海事报告公证申请；如在船舶航行期间，自事故发生后船舶的船长（指挥官）到达第一个港口之日起 24 小时内提交海事报告公证申请。

3. 如果无法在规定的时间内提交报告公证申请，应在海事报告声明中说明理由。

第一百零九条　制作海事报告公证书

公证员、土库曼斯坦境外的外交代表和领事机构官员基于船舶船长（指挥官）的声明、船舶日志的记录，以及船长（指挥官）的调查，在可能的情况下，至少两名船舶指挥部的见证人及两名船员中的见证人起草海事报告公证书，并加注公证标志和印章。应向船舶的船长（指挥官）或其授权的人出具一份该公证的副本。

第十九章　提供证据

第一百一十条　向法庭或其他有权机关提供必要的证据

1. 如果认为以后不可能或很难提供证据，公证员、土库曼斯坦境外的外交代表和领事机构官员应利害关系人的申请，向法庭或其他有权机关提供必要的

necessary in case of case in court or other competent authority if reasons to believe are had that production of evidence will become impossible or difficult subsequently.

证据。

2. Proofs on cases which at the time of the address of interested persons to the notary public are in production of court or other competent authority are not provided.

2. 利害关系人在法庭或其他有权机关向公证员出示的证据，公证员不向法庭提供。

Article 111. Actions for providing proofs

第一百一十一条 提供证据的行为

1. According to the procedure of providing proofs the notary public, the official of diplomatic representation and consular establishment of Turkmenistan abroad interviews physical persons, examines documents and objects, if necessary appoints examination.

1. 根据提供证据的程序，公证员、土库曼斯坦境外的外交代表和领事机构官员对自然人进行访谈、检查文件和标的、在必要时进行相关检查。

2. In case of accomplishment of legal proceedings on providing proofs the notary public, the official of diplomatic representation and consular establishment of Turkmenistan abroad is guided by the relevant standards of the civil procedural legislation of Turkmenistan.

2. 为完成提供证据的法律程序，公证员、土库曼斯坦境外的外交代表和领事机构的官员应遵守土库曼斯坦民事诉讼法的有关规定。

3. The notary public, the official of diplomatic representation and consular establishment of Turkmenistan abroad informs on time and the place of providing proofs of the party and interested persons, however their absence is not obstacle for accomplishment of actions for providing proofs.

3. 公证员、土库曼斯坦境外的外交代表和领事机构官员按时通知当事人和利害关系人提供证据的时间和地点，但如果未能通知的，不影响提供证据这一职能的履行。

4. Providing proofs without notice of one of the parties and interested persons is made only in cases, being urgent or when it is impossible to determine who will participate in case subsequently.

4. 只有在情况紧急或者无法确定随后将参与案件的人员时，才可以不通知任何当事人或利害关系人就提供证据。

5. In case of absence of the witness or the expert in challenge the notary public, the official of diplomatic representation and consular establishment of Turkmenistan abroad reports about it in court at the place of residence of the witness or expert for taking measures, stipulated by the legislation Turkmenistan.

5. 如果见证人或专家未提出质疑，公证员、土库曼斯坦境外的外交代表和领事机构官员应向见证人或专家所在地的法庭报告已根据土库曼斯坦法律规定履行相应的程序。

Section IV. Application of this Law concerning foreign citizens, stateless persons and legal entities of foreign states. Application of rules of law of foreign states. International agreements

第四部分 本法对外国公民、无国籍人和外国法人的适用 外国法律法规的适用国际协议

Article 112. Application of this Law concerning foreign citizens and stateless persons, and also legal entities of foreign states

第一百一十二条 本法对外国公民、无国籍人和外国法人的适用

Foreign citizens, stateless persons, legal entities of foreign states have the rights to the address, equal with citizens and legal entities of Turkmenistan, in the territory

外国公民、无国籍人、外国法人享有与土库曼斯坦公民和法人相同的权利，根据本法和土库曼斯坦其他监管法律规定的程序，在土库曼斯坦领土范围内申

of Turkmenistan behind making of notarial actions to notaries public, authorized officers according to the procedure, established by this Law and other regulatory legal acts of Turkmenistan.

请公证。

Article 113. Application by the notary public of rules of law of other states and rules of international law

1. The notary public applies rules of law of foreign states and rule of international law according to regulatory legal acts and international treaties of Turkmenistan.

2. Notaries public accept the documents constituted according to requirements of the legislation of foreign states and also make certifying texts in shape, stipulated by the legislation foreign states if it does not contradict international treaties of Turkmenistan.

第一百一十三条　公证员对其他国家法律法规和国际法法规的适用

1. 公证员根据土库曼斯坦的监管法律和签订的国际条约适用其他国家法律法规和国际法法规。

2. 如果与土库曼斯坦签订的国际条约不存在冲突，公证员可以承认据外国法律而出具的文件，也可以按照外国法律规定的形式制作公证文书。

Article 114. Application of the legislation of Turkmenistan in case of protection of heritable property of the foreign citizen or stateless person and issue of the certificate on the right to inheritance on such property. The powers of attorney intended for accomplishment of actions outside Turkmenistan

1. The actions connected with protection of the property which is in the territory of Turkmenistan and remained after the death of the foreign citizen or the stateless person, or remained after the death of the citizen of Turkmenistan whose heir is the foreign citizen or the stateless person and also with appointment of the trustee inheritance and issue of the certificate on the right to inheritance on such property are made according to the legislation of Turkmenistan.

2. The power of attorney certified by the notary public, the authorized officer intended for making of actions outside Turkmenistan which is not containing specifying of term of its action is valid before its cancellation by person who issued the power of attorney.

第一百一十四条　土库曼斯坦法律对于保护外国公民或无国籍人遗产的适用，以及对该财产继承权的证明旨在实现土库曼斯坦境外活动的授权委托书

1. 与土库曼斯坦境内财产保护有关的活动，在外国公民或无国籍人死亡后仍然存续。在土库曼斯坦公民死后继承，其继承人是外国公民或无国籍人的，可以根据土库曼斯坦法律委托受托人继承并申请继承权公证。

2. 公证员、经授权在土库曼斯坦境外从事活动的官员公证的授权委托书，如未说明该授权的期限，在出具授权委托书的人员取消之前有效。

Article 115. Acceptance by the notary public of the documents constituted outside Turkmenistan

The documents constituted outside Turkmenistan by officials of competent authorities of other states and also the documents proceeding from them are accepted by notaries public on condition of their legalization by the Ministry of Foreign Affairs of Turkmenistan if other is not provided by this Law, other regulatory legal acts and international treaties of Turkmenistan.

第一百一十五条　公证员接受土库曼斯坦境外制作的文件

如果本法、其他监管规定和土库曼斯坦国际条约没有相反的规定，其他国家有权机关官员在土库曼斯坦境外制作的文件，以及公证员接受的文件经土库曼斯坦外国事务部门认可而具有法律效力。

Article 116. Interaction of the notary public with judicial authorities of foreign states

1. Notaries public perform the messages of judicial

第一百一十六条　公证员与外国司法机构的交流

1. 公证员根据有关从事公证活动提供法律援助规

authorities of foreign states delivered by it in accordance with the established procedure about rendering legal assistance in making of notarial actions, except as specified, if they:

1) contradict sovereignty of Turkmenistan or threaten its homeland security;

2) do not enter competence of the notary public;

3) contradict the legislation of Turkmenistan.

2. Execution of orders of judicial authorities of foreign states about rendering legal assistance in making of notarial actions is made by notaries public according to the legislation and international treaties of Turkmenistan.

3. The notary public has the right to address judicial authorities of foreign states with orders about the rendering legal assistance according to the procedure established by regulatory legal acts and international treaties of Turkmenistan.

定的程序协助外国司法机构送达有关文书，以下情形除外：

（1）与土库曼斯坦主权相抵触或威胁其国土安全；

（2）不具备公证员的资格；

（3）与土库曼斯坦法律相抵触。

2. 公证员根据土库曼斯坦法律和国际条约协助外国司法机构送达有关文书。

3. 公证员有权根据土库曼斯坦监管法律和国际条约规定的程序处理协助外国司法机构文书送达中的事宜。

Article 117. Providing the proofs necessary for business management in bodies of other states

The notary public provides the proofs necessary for business management in bodies of other states.

第一百一十七条　为其他国家管理企业提供必要的证明

公证员为其他国家管理企业提供必要的证明。

Article 118. International agreements

If the international treaty of Turkmenistan refers to competence of the notary public making of notarial actions, not stipulated by the legislation Turkmenistan, the notary public makes notarial actions according to the procedure established by the Ministry adalat Turkmenistan.

第一百一十八条　国际协议

如果土库曼斯坦法律未规定土库曼斯坦签订的国际条约中有关公证员从事公证活动的能力，公证员根据土库曼斯坦公证部规定的程序从事公证活动。

Section V. Final provisions

第五部分　最后条款

Article 119. Entry into force of this Law

1. This Law becomes effective since January 1, 2016.

2. Recognize invalid from the date of entry into force of this Law:

part VIII of the Law of Turkmenistan "O modification and amendments in some legal acts of Turkmenistan", accepted on July 2, 2009 (Sheets of Majlis of Turkmenistan, 2009, No. 3, the Art. 45).

3. Until reduction of the laws and other regulatory legal acts of Turkmenistan in compliance with this Law they act so far as do not contradict this Law.

第一百一十九条　本法的生效

1. 本法自 2016 年 1 月 1 日起生效。

2. 以下内容自本法生效之日起认定为无效：

2009 年 7 月 2 日生效的土库曼斯坦法律“部分土库曼斯坦法律的修改和修订”第八部分（2009 年土库曼斯坦议会清单第 3 号，第 45 条）。

3. 土库曼斯坦法律和其他监管规定在根据本法修订之前，不被认定为与本法相冲突。

President of Turkmenistan
Gurbanguly Berdimuhamedov

土库曼斯坦总统
Gurbanguly Berdimuhamedov

阿联酋

公证法

Federal Law no. 4 of 2013
Issued on 6/06/2013 AD Corresponding to 27 Rajab 1434 H
REGULATING THE PROFESSION OF NOTARY PUBLIC

Abrogating
Federal Law no. 22/1991 dated 16/12/1991 AD

We, Khalifa bin Zayed Al Nahyan President of the United Arab Emirates After perusal of the Constitution,

The Federal Law No. 1 of 1972 on the Law on the Competencies of the Ministries and Powers of the Ministers, and its amending laws,

The Federal Law No. 6 of 1978 on the Establishment of Federal Courts and Transfer of the Jurisdiction of the Local Judicial Authorities in some Emirates to them, and its amending laws,

The Federal Law No. 3 of 1983 on the Federal Judiciary, and its amending laws, The Penal Code promulgated by Federal Law No. 3 of 1987, and its amending laws, The Federal Law No. 22 of 1991 on the Notary Public, and its amending laws,

The Law of Evidence in Civil and Commercial Transactions promulgated by Federal Law No. 10 of 1992, and its amending laws, The Civil Procedure Law promulgated by Federal Law No. 11 of 1992, and its amending laws, The Criminal Procedure Law promulgated by Federal Law No. 35 of 1992, and its amending laws,

The Federal Decree. Law No. 11 of 2008 on Human Resources in the Federal Government, and its amending laws,

The Federal Law No. 6 of 2012 regulating the profes-

联邦法 2013 年 4 号
2013 年 6 月 6 日发布，
伊斯兰历 1434 年“问候月”7 月 27 日发布，
公证法

废除
1991 年 12 月 16 日第 22/1991 号联邦法

阿拉伯联合酋长国总统 Khalifa bin Zayed Al Nahyan，在遵照《宪法》后，

依据如下法令：1972 年第 1 号联邦法职权法及其修正法、1978 年关于设立联邦法院和将部分酋长国地方司法管辖权移交给联邦法院的第 6 号联邦法及其修正法、1983 年关于联邦司法部的第 3 号联邦法及其修正法、1987 年第 3 号联邦法颁布的《刑法》及其修正法、1991 年第 22 号联邦法中的公证法及其修正法、1992 年第 10 号联邦法颁布的《民商事交易证据法》及其修正法、1992 年第 11 号联邦法颁布的《民事诉讼法》及其修正法、1992 年第 35 号联邦法颁布的《刑事诉讼法》及其修正法、2008 年联邦第 11 号法令关于联邦政府人力资源的法律及其修正法、2012 年关于翻译员的第 6 号联邦法、司法部长的建议、内阁会议和联邦国民议会的批准以及联邦最高委员会的批准，颁布下列法律：

sion of translator, And according to the suggestion of the Minister of Justice, the approval of the Council of Ministers and the Federal National Council and the ratification of the Federal Supreme Council,

Issued the following Law:

Chapter 1 Definitions

第一章 定义

Article 1.

The following words and expressions shall have the meanings stated beside them, unless the context requires otherwise:

State: The United Arab Emirates

Ministry: Ministry of Justice

Minister: Minister of Labour

President of the Court: President of the competent Court of First Instance

Unit: Competent Administrative Unit of Notary Public at the Ministry

Board: Private Notaries Admission Board

Notary Public: Legal specialist assuming the tasks contained in this Law, including two types: public notary public and private notary public

Public Notary Public: Public employee appointed at the Ministry and specialized in the works stated in this Law

Private Notary Public: Whoever licensed to exercise the Notary Public works according to the provisions of this Law

Record: Manual or electronic record prepared for writing and recording transactions conducted by the Notary Public

Instrument: Every document or contract made, authenticated or notified to the concerned persons according to the provisions of this Law or any other Law

Redaction: Creating or writing the document directly by the Notary Public upon request of the concerned persons and authenticating the same at the record

Authentication: Manual or electronic ratification of the Notary Public on the signature or thumbprint of the concerned persons

Concerned Persons: Whoever requires the redaction of a document or the authentication of his signature there-

第一条

除文本中另有明确规定外，下列概念或表达为如下意思：

国家：阿拉伯联合酋长国。

政府部门：司法部。

部长：劳工部长。

法院院长：一审管辖法院的院长。

部门：司法部公证机构行政主管部门。

委员会：私营公证员资格委员会。

公证员：依照本法从事专门活动的法律专家，包括公职公证员和私营公证员两种类型。

公职公证员：接受政府任命并专门从事本法所述工作的公职人员。

私营公证员：依照本法规定取得公证许可证的人员。

记录：为公证员实施书写和记录交易行为而准备的纸质或电子记录。

文书：依据本法或其他法律的规定，对当事人进行认证或通知的所有文件或合同。

编写：公证员应当事人的要求，直接制作或书写文书，并检验记录的一致性。

鉴定：公证员对当事人的签名或印章以书写或电子方式进行认证。

公证当事人：根据本法的规定，要求公证员对文件进行编写或者对其签名进行认证，或者要求证明文

on or requires to prove the date of the instrument or any transaction made by the Notary Public under the provisions of this Law

Chapter 2
Competencies of the Notary Public

Article 2.

The Notary Public shall:

1.Write contracts and instruments.

2.Authenticate the signatures of the concerned persons.

3.Prove the date of common law documents as stipulated in this Law.

4. Tender the oath.

5.Write and authenticate sworn statements.

6.Notify the warnings and protests that he writes or authenticates the signatures thereof to the concerned persons upon their request according to the provisions of this Law.

7.Place the writ of execution on the instruments edited or authenticated by him according to the provisions of this Law.

8.Any other competencies assigned to him under another Law.

Section 1
Writing Contracts and Instruments

Article 3.

The Notary Public shall write the contracts and instruments required under the Law by the concerned persons to be written and proven in the record prepared for the same, keep the original copies thereof, give the copies required by the concerned persons and prove the same in the record.

Article 4.

1. The Notary Public shall, before writing the contracts and instruments, verify the identity of the concerned persons by perusing their identity cards, passports or the like or any other official document issued by the State.

2.The Notary Public shall verify the capacity, characteristics and satisfaction of the concerned persons before reading the contracts and instruments for them. He shall warn them as per the consequences of general powers of attorney and contracts' documents, particularly the joint liability companies and limited partnerships. He shall prove

书的日期或证明任何交易行为的人。

第二章　公证员职能

第二条

公证员应当：

1. 起草合同和文书。

2. 验证当事人的签名。

3. 依照本法规定，认证法律文书的日期。

4. 宣誓。

5. 起草和认证宣誓证词。

6. 依据本法规定，按照当事人的要求，对书面警告和抗议的文书作出提示或者认证相应文书的签名。

7. 将执行令状加入依据本法编写或认证的文书上。

8. 其他法律赋予公证员的权限。

第一节　合同和文书的书写

第三条

公证员应当根据法律的规定，在与当事人提供的原始文件或者证明记录保持一致的前提下，起草合同和文书，并将原始文件的复印件进行备案；按当事人要求提供副本，并证明副本与原件相一致。

第四条

1. 公证员在起草合同和文书之前，应当查验当事人的身份证、护照或国家签发的其他官方文件，以核实他们的身份。

2. 公证员在进行合同和文书业务之前，应核实当事人的行为能力、特征和偿付能力。公证员应根据一般授权书和合同文件发生的法律效力，特别是无限公司和有限合伙企业的文件的法律效力，对当事人进行警示。公证员须证明该文书系当事人在场时所写，且当事人了解其内容，并予以记录。

in the record that the reading has actually taken place in their presence and they were aware of the content thereof.

Article 5.

1.If one of the concerned persons was illiterate, the Notary Public shall take his thumbprint and prove the same in the record.

2.If one of the concerned persons suffers from a handicap that prevents him from signing or making a thumbprint, he shall nominate a person whose identity shall be verified by the Notary Public through his identity card, passport or the like, and shall assign him to sign on his behalf at the end of the instrument and prove the same in the record.

Article 6.

1. If the Notary Public does not know the language of the concerned persons, he shall hire a certified translator to translate all that he requires in the presence of the concerned persons. If he was unable to do so, he shall ask the concerned persons to bring a translator who shall take an oath before him and sign at the end of the instrument. This shall be proven in the record.

2.If one of the concerned persons suffers from a disability that prevents him from expressing his will in a natural manner, the Notary Public shall refer to a competent expert or assign any person he deems convenient upon the request of the concerned persons, to provide assistance. He shall put the assistant to oath and let him sign at the end of the document, while he proves the same in the record.

3.If one of the concerned persons suffers from a mental disability, the custodian appointed by the Court shall sign on his behalf.

4.The concerned persons shall bear the fees of the translator or the assistant.

Article 7.

The record in which the contracts and instruments shall be proved, shall be numbered with serial numbers according to the dates, without any deletion, erasure or addition. In case of omission, error, need for correction, deletion or addition, this shall be done manually or electronically in the presence and with the signature of the concerned persons and the Notary Public shall sign the correction.

第五条

1. 若当事人中有人不识字，则公证员应当采集其指印并予以记录。

2. 若当事人中有人残疾以致不能签署或按指印，则该当事人应当委托一人以自己的名义在文件末尾代为签署，公证员应当根据身份证、护照或类似的文件核实受托人身份，并予以记录。

第六条

1. 如公证员不知悉当事人语言，公证员应当聘请一名有资质的翻译人员在当事人在场的情况下翻译他所需的一切资料。如不能，公证员应要求当事人聘请一名翻译人员，翻译人员应在公证员面前宣誓，并在文书末端签字。以上予以记录。

2. 如当事人因为遭受残疾妨碍其以正常的方式表达自己的意愿，公证员应当事人的请求，推荐合适的专家或指派其认为便利的人提供援助。公证员应让提供帮助的人宣誓，让其在文件的末端签名，并予以记录。

3. 若当事人有精神上的残疾，则由法庭指定的监护人代其签字。

4. 当事人应承担翻译或帮助服务所产生的一切相关费用。

第七条

认证合同和文件的记录，应按照日期编号，不得删除、涂改或者增加。如有遗漏、错误、需要更正、删除或增补，则应在当事人在场的情况下以手动或电子方式进行，并由当事人签字，公证员应在文书的更正版本上签字。

Section 2
Authentication of Signatures

Article8.

The Notary Public shall authénticate the signatures of the concerned persons in the common law documents upon their request, prove the authentication in the record and give certificates according to this record.

Article 9.

1.The Notary Public shall, before the signing of the concerned persons, verify their identities, capacities, eligibility, satisfaction and awareness of the subject of the instrument to be authenticated. After the signature of the concerned person on the instrument and the record, the Notary Public shall write a report of the same at the end of the instrument signed and sealed by his seal. He shall then hand over the instrument to the concerned persons after signing an acknowledgment of receipt in the authentications' record.

2.Certificates shall be given from the authentications' record to the concerned persons requiring the same. No certificates shall be given to others without a written order from the President of the Court.

Section 3
Putting to Oath, Writing and Authenticating Sworn Statements

Article 10.

1.The public Notary Public shall put persons to oath, write and authenticate sworn statements and verify the identity, eligibility, capacities and satisfaction of the concerned persons before writing and authenticating sworn statements.

2.The private Notary Public may apply for putting to oath and authenticating sworn statements, according to the conditions and procedures prescribed by the implementing regulations of this Law.

3.The Notary Public shall prove the above mentioned two paragraphs in the record prepared for the same, keep the original versions of the statements and give a copy thereof to the concerned persons.

第二节 签名的认证

第八条

公证员应依据当事人的请求，对其在普通法文件中的签名进行认证，予以记录，并根据该记录出具证明。

第九条

1. 公证员应在当事人签字之前，核实他们的身份、行为能力、资质、偿付能力和对待认证文书的了解。经当事人在文书和记录上签字后，公证员应当在文书末尾加盖印章并制作报告。当事人在认证记录中签署确认收据后，公证员应当将该文书交回给当事人。

2. 依据认证记录，向需要证明的当事人出具证书。未经法院院长书面批准，不得向他人出具证书。

第三节 宣誓、起草和认证宣誓证词

第十条

1. 公职公证员应当要求相关人员宣誓，并起草和认证宣誓词；公职公证员在起草、认证宣誓证词之前，核实当事人的身份、资格、行为能力和偿付能力。

2. 私营公证员可以按照本法实施条例规定的条件和程序申请宣誓、认证宣誓。

3. 公证员应当对上述两款内容予以记录，保存宣誓词原件并将副本交给当事人。

Section 4
Proving the Date of Instruments

Article 11.

1.The Notary Public shall prove the date of the common law documents with serial numbers in the record prepared for the same, write a report at the end of the instrument proving the date of submittal and the number of listing, signed and sealed by the Notary Public and handed over to the concerned persons.

2.The dates' proof certificates may be given from the authentications' record to the concerned persons requiring the same. No certificates shall be given to others without a written order from the President of the Court.

第四节　文件日期的公证

第十一条

1. 公证员公证普通法文件的日期，用数字编号的形式予以记录，并在文书的结尾处编写报告，以证明呈交文件的日期及编号，并由公证员签字并盖章，最后移交给当事人。

2. 日期公证书可以从认证记录中按要求发给当事人。未经法院院长书面批准，不得向任何人颁发公证书。

Section 5
Placing the Writ of Execution

Article 12.

1.The Notary Public shall seal the instruments written or authenticated by him according to the provisions of this Law and including consolidated and due obligations of specified amounts, with the writ of execution at the request of the concerned persons. Only one copy shall be handed over to the concerned person who has interest in the implementation of the content thereof.

2.It shall not be allowed to hand over a second executive copy to the concerned person unless according to a written order from the President of the Court in case of loss of the first copy or incapacity of use thereof.

第五节　执行令状的颁发

第十二条

1. 公证员应当依照本法规定在写好的文书上加盖签章或者亲自认证，包括具体的合计数额和到期应付款数额，并依据当事人的请求办法执行令状。只有与执行令状的履行有利害关系的当事人才能获取文件副本。

2. 除非在第一份副本遗失或不能使用的情况下并有法院院长的书面批准，不得向当事人提供第二份文件副本。

Chapter 3
Duties and Prohibitions of the Notary Public

Article 13.

The Notary Public shall:

1. Hold a manual or electronic record for writing and recording transactions.

2. Keep numbered files according to the dates of the original versions of the instruments written or authenticated by him or of which the dates or any other transaction are proved by him.

3. Keep a copy of any documents or instruments he relied upon at the time of the transaction according to the provisions of this Law.

Article 14.

The Notary Public shall not:

第三章　公证员的义务与禁止性规定

第十三条

公证员应当：

1. 为书面和电子交易做好纸质或电子记录。

2. 依据公证员起草、认证的文书的原件日期或公证员认证该交易的日期，进行编号。

3. 按照本法的规定，交易时所依据的所有文件或文书都应当复印并存档备份。

第十四条

公证员不得有下列行为：

1. Authenticate the signatures of the employees working in the federal government, local government, public authorities or public institutions of any of either governments, on the certificates, documents or other papers signed by them due to their professions at their employers.

2. Write, authenticate signatures or prove the date of the instrument if the eligibility, capacity or satisfaction of the concerned person was not proved or if the subject of the instrument is apparently invalid, violating the legislations in force, the public order or morals or intended to commit an act of fraud, while stating the reasons of prohibition. The concerned persons may appeal within seven days from the date of being aware of the same before the President of the Court. The decision of the latter shall be final.

3. Write or authenticate any contracts or instruments related to the personal status of Muslims or the Waqf.

4. Write or authenticate any contracts or instruments related to the establishment of the right of ownership or any right in rem on a real estate, transfer, change or remove the same.

5. Write or authenticate a contract of sale, donation or mortgage of a commercial shop before publication of the same in a daily newspaper widely spread in the State, fourteen days at least before conducting the transaction.

6. Write or authenticate any contracts or instruments stipulated by the Law that the writing or authentication thereof shall be the competence of another authority.

7. Commence any action where he, one of his ascendants, descendants, spouse or their parents, has an apparent or hidden personal interest or accept any of them as translator or assistant.

8. Disclose any information related to the concerned persons, obtained or perused by him due to his work.

9. Give any copy of the official documents to other than the concerned persons without the written permission of the President of the Court.

10. Move any record, documents, instruments or other official papers held by him to outside the office. The Public Prosecution may peruse the same at the place thereof or request their annexation by a written permission from the President of the Court. None of them shall be annexed to the file of a reviewed lawsuit unless by a decision from the Court. In such event, a copy thereof certified by him and by the President of the Court shall be kept.

11. Take commerce as his profession.

12. Combine his job with any other public or private profession.

1. 公证员不得公证在联邦政府、地方政府、公共机构或其他公共机构的公职人员的签名，以及因职务行为为他们的雇主自己签署的证书、文件或其他文本。

2. 公证员不得在未经核实当事人的资格、行为能力、偿付能力或者在文书的目的明显是非法的、违反现行法律强制性规定、公共秩序、道德或意图实施欺诈行为的情况下，起草、签署、认证文书的日期，并应当向当事人说明禁止的理由。当事人可在知悉有关情况之日起 7 日内向法院提起上诉。经过上诉之后的裁决为终审裁决。

3. 公证员不得起草、认证与穆斯林或宗教的个人身份有关的合同或文书。

4. 公证员不得起草、认证关于物权或者不动产物权的产生、转移、变更和消灭的任何合同和文书。

5. 在国家广泛发行的日报上刊登买卖合同、赠与合同或商店抵押合同之前，公证员不得对这类合同进行起草或公证，且至少在交易行为发生的两周前进行刊登。

6. 公证员不得起草或认证，依照法律规定应当由另一机构职权范围内管辖的合同或文书。

7. 公证员不得为与其长辈、晚辈、配偶或父母，以及有明显或潜在利害关系的人办理公证或让他们担任翻译员或助理。

8. 公证员不得泄露因工作获取的与当事人有关的任何信息。

9. 公证员未经法院院长书面批准，不得将公证文书副本给当事人以外的任何人。

10. 公证员不得将其持有的纪录、文件、文书或其他正式文件带离办公区外。公诉机关可在文件所在地阅读该文件，或经法院院长书面批准获得其附件。除非法院作出裁决，否则不得将该文件附于已复审的诉讼卷宗中。此时，应保存一份经公证员和法院院长核证的文书副本。

11. 公证员不得经商。

12. 公证员职业不得公私兼营。

Article15.

The concerned persons or their agents shall appear before the Notary Public by themselves.

Chapter 4
Public Notary Public

Article16.

Whoever appointed as public notary public shall:

1. Be a citizen of the State.

2.Be holder of a degree in Law or Sharia'a from a recognized university in the State.

3.Not be convicted of a crime involving moral turpitude even if he has recovered his civil rights.

4. Pass the prescribed procedures and tests.

Article 17.

The public Notary Public shall not move outside his office to conduct any transaction stipulated by the Law, unless according to the controls specified by the implementing regulations of this Law.

Article 18.

The public Notary Public shall be appointed by a decision from the Minister. His workplace shall be specified in the Courts or at any other place as deemed by the Unit.

Article 19.

The accredited State's consuls or their representatives in diplomatic missions shall carry out the works of the public Notary Public outside the State, according to the controls promulgated by a Council of Ministers' decision upon the Minister's suggestion.

Article 20.

1. The Council of Ministers shall issue – upon the Minister's suggestion – a special Law for the human and financial resources of the public Notary Public, provided that the provisions regulating the profession of the public Notary Public remain in force until the issuance of this Law.

2.The public Notary Public shall be granted a nature. of.work allowance at 50% of the basic salary of the occupied position.

3.The Minister shall issue a decision for the accommodation of the public Notaries upon issuance of the Council of Ministers' decision set forth in paragraph 1 of this Article.

Article 21.

The provisions of the Human Resources Law in the

第十五条

当事人或者其代理人应亲自到公证机构办理相关事宜。

第四章　公职公证员

第十六条

担任公职公证员，应当符合下列条件：

1. 属于本国公民。

2. 持有国家认可的大学法学学位或伊斯兰教法学学位。

3. 没有涉及道德缺陷问题而被定罪，即使已经恢复公民权利也不例外。

4. 遵循规定的程序和通过考试。

第十七条

依照本法实施条例另有规定的除外，公职公证员不得在规定办公区域外实施本法规定的交易。

第十八条

公职公证员由部长任命。公职公证员的工作地点应位于法院或经部门认可的其他地点。

第十九条

经认可的国家领事或外交使团代表应当依据部长的意见所作出的部长会议决定中执行措施，在境外开展公职公证员的工作。

第二十条

1. 部长会议应根据部长的建议，颁布一部关于公职公证员人力和财政的特别法，但关于公职公证员职业的规定在该法颁布之前仍然有效。

2. 公职公证员有权获得基本工资的 50% 作为工作津贴。

3. 基于本条第 1 款规定的部长会议决议，部长应当发布解决公职公证员住房问题的方案。

第二十一条

本法第 20 条未作规定的事项，公职公证员应适

federal government and all laws and regulations related to the public profession's affairs, shall be applied on the public Notaries for all that is not stated in the said Law indicated in Article 20 hereof.

用联邦政府的《人力资源法》和与国家公职人员有关的所有法律和规章。

Chapter 5
Private Notary Public

第五章 私营公证员

Article 22.

1.A Board shall be formed by the Minister's decision under the name (Private Notary Public Admission Board) with not less than six members including the President and Vice. President, in addition to a Notary Public.

2.The Board shall hold its meetings upon convocation of its President to review the submitted applications. The meeting shall be considered valid in the presence of the majority of the members and its decisions shall be issued by the majority of the votes of the members present. In case of equality, the side for which the President voted shall prevail. The implementing regulations of this Law shall determine the Board's work system and competencies.

第二十二条

1. 私人公证委员会应依照部长的决议组成并命名为"私营公证员委员会"，该委员会成员应当不少于六人，除公证员外应当包括主席和副主席。

2. 私营公证员委员会应在主席召集下举行会议，审查所提交的申请。会议在全体成员过半数出席时方可举行，其决议通过应当以出席会议成员的过半数同意。在赞成和反对票数持平时，委员会主席有一票决定权。本法的实施条例应当规定委员会的工作制度和职权范围。

Article23.

The Board shall authorize the citizens who already worked for a period of not less than five years in judicial work or its equivalent in Public Prosecution professions, at Fatwa and Legislation Departments, State affairs, teaching Islamic Sharia or Law in a recognized university or higher education institutes or any other legal work considered equivalent to the work in the judiciary and Public Prosecution according to the implementing regulations of this Law, or the works of the public Notary Public, to carry out the works of private Notary Public as per the conditions set forth in paragraphs 2, 3 and 4 of Article 16 hereof, in addition to any other conditions and procedures specified by the implementing regulations of this Law.

第二十三条

被任命的私营公证员委员会的委员应当在司法机关或者相应的公诉部门至少工作过 5 年，或者在专家裁判委员会、立法部门、国家事务机关、在公认的大学教授伊斯兰教教规或法律，或者依据本法的实施条例规定在高等教育机构以及其他与裁判官或公诉人性质相同的法律职业岗位工作不少于 5 年的公民。私营公证员依照本法第 16 条第 2 项、第 3 项、第 4 项规定的条件以及本法实施条例规定的其他条件和程序，执行私营公证工作。

Article 24.

In exception to paragraph 12 of Article 14 hereof, the working lawyer may exercise the works of the private Notary Public if he has the experience set forth in Article 23 hereof and after the consent of the Board.

第二十四条

除第 14 条第 12 项外，执业律师满足本法第 23 条规定的条件，经委员会同意，可以取得私营公证员资格。

Article 25.

1. A table for the registration of the private Notary Public in the State shall be created at the Unit and the implementing regulations of this Law shall specify its statements and registration procedures.

2.The private Notary Public shall not be registered

第二十五条

1. 注册成立私营公证员登记表应当在部门里现场填写，本法实施条例应当规定其要求的声明和具体登记程序。

2. 私营公证员应缴纳规定的费用，并依据本法实

in the table unless he pays the prescribed fees and he concludes professional liability insurance at an insurance company licensed in the State, according to the controls specified in the implementing regulations of this Law.

施条例的明确规定在国家认可的保险公司购买了职业责任保险，否则不得登记注册。

Article 26.

The private Notary Public shall exercise his works through an office licensed for that purpose or through a law firm. The implementing regulations shall specify the conditions necessary for the establishment of these offices and the supervision thereof.

第二十六条

私营公证员执业活动应当通过获得营业执照的专门公证机构或者律师事务所。本法实施条例应当具体规定设立此类公证机构的条件和前述规定的其他条件。

Article 27.

The Board shall review the irregularities of the private Notary Public committed in violation to the provisions of this Law and its implementing regulations.

第二十七条

委员会应当对私营公证员违反本法及其实施条例的违法行为进行审查。

Article 28.

1.The Board shall notify the private Notary Public and the Manager of the office through which he works of any complaint submitted against the private Notary Public, to respond to it within fifteen days from the date of notification thereof. The complaint shall be submitted to the Board accompanied with the response of the private Notary Public to decide concerning its archiving or transfer to investigation.

2.The private Notary Public may appeal against the Board's decision within fifteen days from the date of notification thereof before a Grievance Committee formed by a decision from the Minister. The Committee shall decide concerning the appeal within fifteen days from the date of submittal thereof.

3.The concerned persons may appeal the decision issued for the rejection of the appeal or expiry of the period specified for the settlement thereof without issuance of a decision by the competent Court of Appeal, within fifteen days from the date of notification of the rejection of the appeal or expiry of the settlement period without issuing a decision, and its judgment shall be final.

第二十八条

1. 委员会应当将对私营公证员提出的投诉，通知私营公证员及其工作机构的负责人，私营公证员应当自收到通知之日起 15 日内作出回应。投诉文书应连同私营公证员的答复一并提交委员会，以便就其存档或者移交调查作出决定。

2. 私营公证员对委员会裁决不服的，可以自通知之日起 15 日内向依据部长决议成立的申诉委员会提出上诉。申诉委员会应在上诉文书提交之日起 15 日内就上诉内容作出裁定。

3. 当事人可对驳回上诉的裁定或者法定期限届满未作出裁决的事项向申诉委员会提出上诉，当事人的上诉应当在收到驳回通知或者法定期限届满未作出裁决之日起 15 日内提出，上诉法院的裁决为最终判决。

Article 29.

1.No disciplinary sanction shall be imposed on the private Notary Public unless after conducting a written investigation with him and hearing his statements.

2.The investigation with the private Notary Public shall be conducted with a Public Prosecution member with the position of at least Attorney General at the request of the President of the Board.

3.The Attorney General may archive the investiga-

第二十九条

1. 非经实施书面调查并听取陈述，不得对私营公证员实施纪律制裁。

2. 对私营公证员的调查人员应由至少有 1 名具有总检察长职位的公诉人参与并依据委员会主席的要求进行。

3. 总检察长可以直接进入调查程序或者将私营公

tion or refer the private Notary Public to the Disciplinary Board.

证员案件移交纪律委员会。

Article 30.

The private Notary Public shall be disciplined through a Disciplinary Board formed by a decision from the Minister as follows:

1.One of the Presidents of the Courts of Appeal as President and with the membership of two of the judges selected by the Minister.

2.The Disciplinary Board may assign one of the Court of Appeal employees to conduct Secretariat works.

第三十条

私营公证员的纪律处分决定应当通过由部长决议组成的纪律委员会作出：

1. 纪律委员会由上诉法院院长和部长选任 2 名法官组成。

2. 纪律委员会可指派上诉法庭的 1 名雇员担任工作组的秘书。

Article 31.

1.The disciplinary action shall be filed before the Disciplinary Board by one of the Public Prosecutors assigned by the Attorney General. It shall be submitted by a petition including the accusation and the evidence supporting the same.

2.The Public Prosecution shall assign the private Notary Public to appear before the Council ten days at least before the date specified for the session. It shall pursue the disciplinary action until settlement thereof.

3.The Disciplinary Board shall proceed with the disciplinary action in the absence of the Notary Public transferred to discipline, if he refuses to attend the Disciplinary Board sessions without giving an acceptable excuse.

第三十一条

1. 违规指控应由总检察长指派的 1 名检察官向纪律委员会提出，且应当以起诉书的形式提交，其中应当包括具体指控内容和支持指控的证据。

2. 公诉机关应当在指定询问日提前至少 10 日以上告知私营公证员到庭，直至程序结束之前公诉机关都可以对私营公证员施加纪律约束。

3. 公证员无正当理由拒不出席纪律委员会的，纪律委员会应当缺席审理。

Article 32.

The Disciplinary Board shall conduct itself the investigations it deems necessary, may appoint one of its members for the same and may suspend the private Notary Public from the commencement of the work until the end of the trial.

第三十二条

在必要情况下，纪律委员会应当自行实施调查，可为此任命 1 名调查员，并暂停私营公证员的工作直至审判结束。

Article 33.

The Disciplinary Board's sessions and deliberations shall be confidential and its decisions shall be issued by majority including the reasons thereof. The private Notary Public shall be notified of the decision within fifteen days from the date of issuance thereof.

第三十三条

纪律委员会的会议和讨论应保密，其作出的裁定及其理由应当由半数以上表决通过。自裁定结果作出之日起 15 日内通知私营公证员。

Article 34.

1.The private Notary Public who violates the duties and prohibitions set forth in this Law shall be subject to one of the following disciplinary sanctions:

a. Warning.

b. Suspension of the license for a period not exceeding six months.

c. Cancellation of the license.

第三十四条

1. 私营公证员违反本法规定的义务和禁令，应当给予下列纪律处分之一：

a. 警告；

b. 暂扣执照，时长不超过 6 个月；

c. 吊销执照；

d. Deletion of the registration.

2.The imposition of the penalties shall not prejudice civil or criminal accountability when necessary.

Article 35.

The private Notary Public may appeal the decision of the Disciplinary Board before the competent Court of Appeal within thirty days from the date of issuance thereof in case of his presence, and from the date of notification in case of his absence, and its judgment shall be final.

Chapter 6
Arrest, Inspection, Crimes and Penalties Procedures

Article 36.

The employees of the Unit specified by a decision from the Minister shall act as judicial officers as per the crimes occurred in violation to the provisions of this Law and the decisions issued in implementation thereof, within the jurisdiction of each.

Article 37.

The Notary Public shall not be arrested or investigated or his office inspected for matters related to the performance of his works, without the permission of the Public Prosecution.

Article38.

Shall be penalized by imprisonment for a period not less than six months and a fine between AED thirty thousand and one hundred thousand or either of these penalties, whoever exercises the works of the Notary Public without having the competence to do so, or discloses one of the secrets he perused due to his work.

Article39.

The Notary Public shall be penalized by imprisonment for a period not exceeding six months and a fine between AED thirty thousand and one hundred thousand, or by either penalties, if he violates any of the provisions set forth in this Law.

Article 40.

The imposition of the penalties set forth in this Law shall not prejudice any other more severe penalty stipulated in another Law.

d. 从登记册上除名。

2. 处分的实施不妨碍民事或刑事责任的追究。

第三十五条

私营公证员可在纪律委员会裁定发出之日起 30 日内（公证员出席时）或通知之日起 30 日内（公证员未出席时），向有管辖权的法院上诉，上诉法院作出的判决为终审判决。

第六章　逮捕、调查、定罪和处罚程序

第三十六条

依据部长决议所指定的工作人员应在各自的管辖范围内担任司法官员，对触犯本法和本法实施条例的犯罪行为在司法管辖权范围内进行审理。

第三十七条

未经公诉机关批准，不得逮捕或调查公证员，也不得检查公证员的办公场所。

第三十八条

对无证经营或者非法泄露因工作获取的秘密信息的公证员，处 6 个月以上有期徒刑，单处或并处 3 万，10 万以下的阿联酋迪拉姆罚金。

第三十九条

公证员违反本法规定的，处 6 个月以下有期徒刑，单处或并处 3 万以上，10 万以下的阿联酋迪拉姆罚金。

第四十条

本法规定的处罚，不妨碍其他法律规定的更严厉的处罚。

Chapter 7
General and Transitional Provisions

Article 41.

The Notary Public shall take oath before the President of the Court as follows: (I swear by Almighty God to perform my duties with honesty and confidence and to preserve the secrets of my job), minutes of the oath shall be prepared and deposited in his file.

Article42.

The Unit shall supervise the Notary Public's works that shall be subject to administrative and technical inspection by such Unit.

Article43.

All instruments made by the Notary Public shall be written in Arabic, as per those written in a foreign language, they shall be translated into Arabic through a legal certified translator. The instrument and its translation shall then be ratified.

Article44.

The concerned persons may obtain a copy of any paper of their instruments kept at the Notary Public files or registered in the record.

Article 45.

1.The Ministry shall approve the official seals of the Notary Public and the writ of execution seals of the transactions conducted by the Notary Public, according to the conditions and circumstances stated in this Law and its implementing regulations.

2.The writ of execution seal shall be as follows: "The competent authorities and entities shall take the initiative to implement this document and apply its content even if obligatorily, whenever it is required to do so."

Article46.

1. The contract or instrument shall not be written, the signatures authenticated, the date of instruments proved or any other transaction set forth in this Law unless after paying the prescribed fees.

2.The documents and instruments written or authenticated and containing subjects linked to each other shall be taken in consideration in the transaction requiring the highest fee and this fee shall be paid alone.

3.The private Notary Public shall collect the legally prescribed fees in the transactions conducted by him.

第七章　一般性条款和过渡条款

第四十一条

公证员应在法院院长前宣誓，誓词如下："我向上帝发誓，诚实地履行职责，恪守信任，保守秘密"，宣誓应当记录，并归入公证员档案。

第四十二条

公证机构应当对公证员的工作进行监督，进行日常行政管理和技术检查。

第四十三条

公证员制作的所有文书均应当以阿拉伯文书写，外语文书应当通过经法律认证的翻译人员将其翻译成阿拉伯文，所有文书都应当进行认证。

第四十四条

当事人可取得公证机构档案处备存或在登记簿上记录的任何文书复印件。

第四十五条

1. 司法部根据本法及其实施条例规定的条件和情形，批准公证机构的公章和交易的执行印章。

2. 执行印章应当注明："各主管部门和单位应当主动实施本文件的要求，并履行文件中规定的义务。"

第四十六条

1. 未支付规定费用，不得起草合同或文书，不得公证签名或日期，或公证本法规定的其他任何交易。

2. 起草或认证相互关联的文件或文书，应当考虑交易的执行所需要的最高费用，并应当单独支付这笔费用。

3. 私营公证员开展业务，应依照法律规定收取费用。

4.A decision shall be issued by the Council of Ministers, upon the Minister's suggestion, specifying the fees of the transactions conducted by the Notary Public and the fees of the private Notary Public.

4. 参照部长建议，由部长委员会颁布一项决议，具体规定公职公证员和私营公证员的收费标准。

Article 47.

The federal and local authorities shall be exempted from the fees on all the transactions conducted by the Notary Public at the request of such authorities.

第四十七条

公证员应联邦政府和地方政府的要求开展的业务，不收取上述费用。

Chapter 8
Final Provisions

第八章　附则

Article48.

The Heads of the local justice departments may issue decisions related to the Notary Public exercising the work within the jurisdiction of any of these departments, specifying the rules, procedures, competencies, methods of appointment and registration and all other affairs as stated in the provisions of this Law and its implementing regulations.

第四十八条

地方司法机关负责人可以在司法管辖权范围内发布与公证员职权有关的决议、规则细则、程序、资格、任命方式和注册登记以及本法及其实施条例规定的其他事项。

Article 49.

The Minister shall issue a Charter of the principles and ethics related to the profession of the Notary Public. Any violation to any of its provisions shall entail the imposition of the prescribed disciplinary sanctions.

第四十九条

部长应发布与公证员职业有关的原则和道德准则，任何违反其规定的行为均应受到惩罚。

Article 50.

1.The Federal Law No. 22 of 1991 on the Notary Public and its amending laws shall be cancelled, in addition to any provision violating or contradicting any provision of this Law.

2.The implementing regulations and the decisions in force upon issuance of this Law shall remain effective in a way not contradicting the provisions thereof, until the issuance of the implementing regulations and decisions.

第五十条

1. 1991 年关于公证的第 22 号联邦法及其修正法以及与本法规定不一致的其他任何法律规定，当时自动丧失效力。

2. 基于本法发布的实施条例和决定，在本法新的实施条例和决定发布前继续有效，但不得与本法的现行规定相抵触。

Article 51.

The Council of Ministers shall – upon the Minister's suggestion – issue the implementing regulations of this Law within six months from the date of publication thereof in the Official Gazette.

第五十一条

部长委员会应当根据部长的建议，自本法在《政府公报》公布之日起 6 个月内发布本法的实施条例。

Article 52.

This Law shall be published in the Official Gazette and shall enter into effect three months from the date of publication thereof.

第五十二条

本法应在《政府公报》上公布，并自公布之日起 3 个月后生效。

Promulgated by Us at the Presidential Palace in Abu Dhabi: On: 27 Rajab 1434 H

Corresponding to: June 6, 2013 AD

Khalifa bin Zayed Al Nahyan President of the United Arab Emirates

The Present Federal Law was published in the Official Gazette issue 551(bis) p. 9

在阿布扎比总统府颁布：伊斯兰历1434年“问候月”7月27日，对应日期：2013年6月6日。

阿拉伯联合酋长国总统哈利法·本·扎耶德·阿勒纳哈扬 签署

现行《联邦法》已在《政府公报》第551页第9段上公布。

乌兹别克斯坦

乌兹别克斯坦共和国公证法

LAW OF THE REPUBLIC OF UZBEKISTAN
of December 26, 1996 No. 343-I
About notariate
(The last edition from 18-04-2018)

乌兹别克斯坦共和国法律
1996 年 12 月 26 日第 343–I 号
关于公证
（最新版于 2018 年 4 月 18 日颁布）

Section I. Organizational bases of activities of notariate

第一节　公证活动的组织基础

Chapter 1. Basic provisions

第 1 章　基本规定

Article 1. Notariate in the Republic of Uzbekistan

The notariate in the Republic of Uzbekistan is the legal institution designed to provide protection of the rights and legitimate interests of physical persons and legal entities by making by notaries of the notarial actions and directly related actions of legal and technical nature provided by legal acts.

Notarial actions in the Republic of Uzbekistan are made according to this Law notaries of offices of notary public (further-notary office). The register of notary offices conducts the Ministry of Justice of the Republic of Uzbekistan.

Notarial actions in the territory of other states are made by consuls of the Republic of Uzbekistan.

第 1 条　乌兹别克斯坦共和国公证机构

乌兹别克斯坦共和国的公证机构是通过公证员的公证活动，以及与之直接相关的由法律规定的具有法律和技术性质的行为来实现保护自然人和法人合法权益之目的的法律机构。

在乌兹别克斯坦共和国，公证活动由公证员办公室（以下简称公证机构）的公证员依照本法进行。公证机构的登记部门是乌兹别克斯坦共和国司法部。

外国领土上的公证活动由乌兹别克斯坦共和国领事作出。

Article 2. The notary in the Republic of Uzbekistan

The notary the citizen of the Republic of Uzbekistan can be not younger than twenty five years, having higher legal education, length of service on legal specialty at least three years, including with passing of training at least two years in notary office, the passed qualification examination. The term of passing of training for the persons who

第 2 条　乌兹别克斯坦共和国公证员

乌兹别克斯坦共和国的公证员是年龄不低于 25 岁，具有高等法学教育水平，从事法律专业工作 3 年及以上（其中需在公证机构经过至少 2 年培训，并通过资格考试）的公民。对于已经从事法官工作至少 5 年或从事与公证活动管理和监督相关职位工作至少 3 年的人员，其培训的时间为 1 年及以上。

worked in judgeship at least five years or on positions, connected with management and control of notarial activities, at least three years constitutes one year.

Cannot be the notary:

-person recognized in accordance with the established procedure as incapacitated or is limited by capable;

-person having the outstanding or not removed criminal record for making of intentional crime;

-person whose powers as the notary, the lawyer, the investigator, the prosecutor, the judge or other employee of law enforcement agencies were stopped in accordance with the established procedure for making of the offenses incompatible with its professional activity.

The notary can have the assistant and the trainee.

To notaries according to the legislation the special ranks - class ranks are given.

Article 2-1. Assistant notary

The citizen of the Republic of Uzbekistan having legal education can be the assistant notary.

Persons specified in part two of article 2 of this Law cannot be the assistant notary.

Employment of the assistant notary is made by the Ministry of Justice of the Republic of Karakalpakstan, and also justice departments of areas and the city of Tashkent (further - justice departments).

The assistant notary at the request of the notary has the right to participate in making of notarial actions, to constitute drafts of transactions, statements and other documents, to produce copies and duplicates of documents, statements from them, and also to make explanations concerning making of notarial actions.

Article 2-2. Trainee of the notary

The citizen of the Republic of Uzbekistan having the higher legal education can be the trainee of the notary.

Persons specified in part two of article 2 of this Law cannot be the trainee of the notary.

Employment of the trainee of the notary is made by the Ministry of Justice of the Republic of Karakalpakstan, justice departments.

The training takes place in notary office. The trainee of the notary performs the activities under the leadership of the notary, carrying out its personal errands.

The procedure for the organization of activities of the trainee of the notary is determined by the Ministry of Justice of the Republic of Uzbekistan.

以下人员不能成为公证员：

按照法定的程序确认为无行为能力人或限制行为能力人；

有故意犯罪的犯罪记录未执行完毕或未销除的人；

因有与其职业活动不相容的犯罪行为，按照法定的程序被剥夺权力的公证员、律师、调查人员、检察官、法官或其他执法机构的人员。

公证员可以配备助理和实习生。

根据法律授予公证员特殊的级别。

第 2–1 条　助理公证员

具有法律教育背景的乌兹别克斯坦共和国公民可以成为助理公证员。

本法第 2 条第 2 款规定的人员不能成为助理公证员。

助理公证员由卡拉卡尔帕克斯坦共和国司法部以及塔什干市、地区的司法部门（以下简称司法部门）聘用。

助理公证员根据公证员的要求，有权参与公证活动，起草交易、声明和其他文件，出具这些文件、声明的副本和复印件，并对所作出的相关公证活动予以解释。

第 2–2 条　实习公证员

拥有高等法学教育水平的乌兹别克斯坦共和国公民可以成为实习公证员。

本法第 2 条第 2 款规定的人员不得成为实习公证员。

实习公证员由卡拉卡尔帕克斯坦共和国司法部（司法部门）雇用。

实习公证员在公证机构接受培训，在公证员领导下进行活动，履行职责。

组织实习公证员活动的程序由乌兹别克斯坦共和国司法部规定。

Article 3. Oath of the notary

The notary at meeting of the Highest qualification commission under the Ministry of Justice of the Republic of Uzbekistan takes the oath of the following content:

- "Solemnly I swear fairly and to honesty fulfill duties of the notary, to strictly observe the Constitution and the laws of the Republic of Uzbekistan".

Article 3-1. Qualification commissions

The qualification commissions under the Ministry of Justice of the Republic of Karakalpakstan, justice departments (further - the qualification commissions) are created for the purpose of acceptance of qualification examinations at persons which passed training.

The qualification commissions are formed by decisions of the Ministry of Justice of the Republic of Karakalpakstan, justice departments of equal number of notaries and other employees of judicial authorities.

For the solution of question of carrying out tender to destination to position of the notary, adoption of the oath of the notary, consideration of appeals on decisions of the qualification commissions, and also generalization and the analysis of practice of work of the qualification commissions the Highest qualification commission under the Ministry of Justice of the Republic of Uzbekistan (further-the Highest qualification commission) as a part of eleven people is formed.

Judges of the Constitutional court of the Republic of Uzbekistan of the Supreme Court of the Republic of Uzbekistan, notaries and other employees of judicial authorities, representatives of legal profession are part of the Highest qualification commission. The staff of the Highest qualification commission affirms the Minister of Justice of the Republic of Uzbekistan.

Regulations on the Highest qualification commission and the qualification commissions affirm the Ministry of Justice of the Republic of Uzbekistan.

Article 4. Qualification examinations

Persons which passed training take qualification examination of the qualification commission.

The appeal on the decision of the qualification commission is submitted in the Highest qualification commission in monthly term from the date of delivery to the interested person of the decision of the qualification commission.

Persons which did not pass qualification examination are allowed to its repeated delivery not earlier than in year

第 3 条　公证员宣誓

公证员在乌兹别克斯坦共和国司法部最高资格委员会会议宣誓如下：

“我郑重地宣誓，忠诚地履行公证员职责，严格遵守乌兹别克斯坦共和国宪法和法律。”

第 3–1 条　资格委员会

卡拉卡尔帕克斯坦共和国司法部（司法部门）下属的资格委员会（以下简称资格委员会）是为组织已经过培训的人员进行资格考试而设立的。

资格委员会根据卡拉卡尔帕克斯坦共和国司法部，同等数量的公证员和其他司法机关组成雇员的司法部门的决议组建。

乌兹别克斯坦共和国司法部最高资格委员会（以下简称最高资格委员会）是司法部下属的 11 个部门之一，其职权是任命公证员，接受公证誓言，审议对资格委员会决定的上诉，及对资格委员会工作进行汇总与分析。

最高资格委员会由乌兹别克斯坦共和国最高法院法官、乌兹别克斯坦共和国宪法法院法官、公证员、司法机构的其他官员、法律职业代表组成。最高资格委员会的工作人员的任命应由乌兹别克斯坦共和国司法部长批准。

关于最高资格委员会和资格委员会的规定应由乌兹别克斯坦共和国司法部批准。

第 4 条　资格考试

通过培训的人员参加资格委员会组织的资格考试。

对资格委员会的决定的申诉应自该决定送达利害关系人之日起 1 个月内提交给最高资格委员会。

未通过资格考试的人员在资格委员会的决定作出 1 年后可以重新参加资格考试。

after decision making by the qualification commission.

The person who passed qualification examination, but not working as the notary within three years is allowed to position of the notary only after repeated passing of qualification examination by it.

通过资格考试后的 3 年内未担任公证员的人，只有重新通过资格考试才允许担任公证员。

Article 5. Independence of the notary

The notary is independent in the activities and is guided in case of its implementation by the legislation of the Republic of Uzbekistan.

第 5 条　公证员的独立性

公证员根据乌兹别克斯坦共和国的法律独立进行公证活动。

Article 6. Mystery of notarial actions

The notary, to other officials making notarial actions and also persons who knew of the made notarial actions in connection with accomplishment of service duties by them is forbidden to disclose the become data known for it including after the termination of the employment contract.

第 6 条　公证活动的保密性

公证员、其他从事公证活动的官员因履职知悉公证活动信息的人，应对其知道的与公证有关的信息保密。即使其雇佣合约终止，仍负有保密义务。

Data (documents) on committed notarial actions can be issued only to persons, from name or at the request of which these actions are made.

公证活动形成的信息（文件）只能提供给公证申请人及其代表人。

References (data) on committed notarial actions are issued upon the demand of court, prosecutor's office, investigation authorities in connection with the cases which are in their production.

公证员根据法院、检察院、侦查机关与其在办案件有关的要求，可提供公证活动的参考资料（信息）。

References (data) on the committed notarial actions connected with counteraction of legalization of income gained from criminal activities and to terrorism financing are provided in specially authorized state body in cases and procedure, stipulated by the legislation.

通过法律规定的程序，可向国家特别授权的机构提供与打击洗钱和资助恐怖主义有关的公证活动的参考资料（信息）。

Certificates of the certificate of lease agreements of the real estate and the amount of the rent, of property value which is carrying over according to the procedure inheritance or donation of citizens are represented to body of the State Tax Service in cases, stipulated by the legislation.

根据法律的规定，将根据继承或捐赠程序计算出财产价值的房地产租赁协议和租金证明报国家税务机关备案。

Certificates of the will are issued only after the death of the testator. References (data) on lack of prohibition of alienation or arrest of the object which is subject of the transaction are provided to credit bureau on its request.

遗嘱公证书仅在遗嘱订立人死亡后出具。应信贷局的要求，可向其提供关于未禁止转让或抵押的交易标的参考资料（信息）。

Persons guilty of violation of mystery of the made notarial actions, bear responsibility according to the procedure, established by the law.

违反公证活动保密义务的人应依照法律规定的程序承担责任。

Article 7. Restrictions in activities of the notary, assistant and trainee of the notary

The notary, the assistant and the trainee of the notary has no right:

- be engaged in business and other activity, except scientific, creative and pedagogical;

第 7 条　公证员、助理公证员和实习公证员的活动限制

公证员、助理公证员和实习公证员无权从事以下活动：

从事除科学、创造性和教学外的商业和其他活动；

- render intermediary services in case of the conclusion of agreements.

Article 8. Notary office

Notary offices are created and liquidated by the Ministry of Justice of the Republic of Uzbekistan.

The notary office has no the status of the legal entity.

The name of notary office shall contain words "office of notary public", specifying on the respective area, the city and, if necessary, number of notary office.

The notary office shall be in limits of the respective notarial district.

In notary office access to the notary of citizens, the mystery of notarial actions, safety of documents, materials of notarial clerical work and notarial archive, condition for acceptance of payments shall be provided.

Article 9.

It is excluded

Article 10. Notarial clerical work and reporting

The notary office shall ensure safety of documents and materials of notarial clerical work, to process the notarial archiving.

Documents and materials of notarial clerical work after three years are subject to transfer to departmental notarial archives under the Ministry of Justice of the Republic of Karakalpakstan, justice departments. Duplicates of notarially certified documents and the statements from registers issued by departmental notarial archives under the Ministry of Justice of the Republic of Karakalpakstan, justice departments are equated to notarially certified and for their issue the payment according to the procedure, established by the legislation is levied.

Departmental notarial archives under the Ministry of Justice of the Republic of Karakalpakstan, justice departments have seal with the image of the State Emblem of the Republic of Uzbekistan.

Rules of notarial clerical work, terms and procedure for storage of notarial documents affirm the Ministry of Justice of the Republic of Uzbekistan.

The Ministry of Justice of the Republic of Karakalpakstan, justice department is recorded receipts of the state fee and submit to bodies of the State Tax Service for them the report.

Article 11. Language in which notarial actions are performed

In the Republic of Uzbekistan notarial actions are

在达成协议的情况下提供中介服务。

第 8 条　公证机构

公证机构由乌兹别克斯坦共和国司法部设立和撤销。

公证机构不具有法人地位。

公证机构的名称应当包含“公证员办公室”字样，列明相应的地区、城市，并在必要时列明公证机构的编号。

公证机构应当位于各自的公证管辖区域内。

公证机构应有可访问的公证人员，且应保守公证活动的秘密，保证文件、公证人员案件材料和公证档案，提供接受付款的条件。

第 9 条

已删除。

第 10 条　公证文书和报告

公证机构应当确保公证文书文件和资料的安全，及时归档。

公证文书文件和材料可以在 3 年后转交给卡拉卡尔帕克斯坦共和国司法部（司法部门）下属的公证档案部门。该公证档案部门发布的公证文件和登记簿的副本等同于经过公证的证明，并根据法律规定的程序收费。

卡拉卡尔帕克斯坦共和国司法部下属的公证档案部门中应有乌兹别克斯坦共和国国徽。

公证文书规则、公证文件存放条款和程序应由乌兹别克斯坦共和国司法部批准。

卡拉卡尔帕克斯坦共和国司法部（司法部门）的费用记入法定费用，并向国家税务局申报。

第 11 条　公证活动的语言

在乌兹别克斯坦共和国，公证活动以国家语言

performed in state language.

Upon the demand of citizens the text of the processed document is issued by the notary or person making notarial actions in Russian or, in the presence of opportunity, - in other acceptable language.

Article 12. Seal, stamps, forms of the notary

The notary has personal seal with the image of the State Emblem of the Republic of Uzbekistan, specifying of surname, initials, positions of the notary and the name of notary office, stamps of certifying texts, forms of notary office.

The notary's seal is made on the single sample approved by the Ministry of Justice of the Republic of Uzbekistan.

The impress of a seal of the notary and the specimen signature of the notary are stored in the Ministry of Justice of the Republic of Karakalpakstan, justice departments.

Article 13. Control of execution by notaries of professional obligations

Control of execution by notaries of the professional obligations is exercised the Ministry of Justice of the Republic of Karakalpakstan, justice department.

Chapter 2. Network of notary offices, position assignment and dismissal of the notary

Article 14. Network and states of notary offices

The network of notary offices, their states affirm as the Republic of Uzbekistan the Ministry of Justice of the Republic of Uzbekistan.

In notary offices where two and more notaries work, one of them is appointed the senior notary with assignment of obligation on control of administrative and organizational work in this notary office.

Article 15. Procedure for organization and abolition of position of the notary. Position assignment of the notary

The position of the notary is established and abolished by the Ministry of Justice of the Republic of Uzbekistan.

The quantity of positions of notaries in certain territory (in the notarial district) is determined by the Ministry of Justice of the Republic of Uzbekistan according to the procedure, established by the Cabinet of Ministers of the Republic of Uzbekistan.

Position assignment of the notary in the notarial district is made by the Ministry of Justice of the Republic

进行。

根据公民的要求，经审核的文件文本可由公证员或作出公证行为的人员用俄语出具公证书，或在可能的情况下以其他可接受的语言出具。

第 12 条　印章、印戳、公证表格

公证员持带有乌兹别克斯坦共和国国徽形象并注明姓名、首字母、公证员职位、公证机构名称的印章，公证文本的印戳，公证机构的表格。

公证员的印章是根据乌兹别克斯坦共和国司法部批准的统一样本制作的。

公证员印章和公证员签名的印记留存在卡拉卡尔帕克斯坦共和国司法部（司法部门）。

第 13 条　监管公证员履行职责

卡拉卡尔帕克斯坦共和国司法部负责监管公证员履行职责。

第 2 章　公证机构体系、任命和解雇公证员

第 14 条　公证机构的体系和要求

乌兹别克斯坦共和国司法部批准公证机构体系及要求。

有 2 个以上公证员工作的公证机构，其中 1 位公证员被任命为高级公证员，并在本公证机构负责监督行政和组织工作。

第 15 条　公证员的任命和解雇程序、公证员的职位分配

公证员由乌兹别克斯坦共和国司法部任命和解雇。

特定地区（公证区）的公证员职位数量由乌兹别克斯坦共和国司法部按照乌兹别克斯坦共和国内阁的命令确定。

卡拉卡尔帕克斯坦共和国司法部根据最高资格委员会所举行的考试，在通过资格考试的人员中进行公

of Karakalpakstan, justice departments on the basis of the competition held by the Highest qualification commission among the persons who passed qualification examination. The procedure for carrying out tender is determined by the Ministry of Justice of the Republic of Uzbekistan.

证区内的公证员职位分配。任命程序由乌兹别克斯坦共和国司法部确定。

The termination of the employment contract with the notary is made by the Ministry of Justice of the Republic of Karakalpakstan, justice departments according to the labor law.

卡拉卡尔帕克斯坦共和国司法部根据劳动法终止与公证员签订的雇佣合同。

Article 16. Territory of activities of the notary (notarial district)

第 16 条　公证员的活动范围（公证区）

The territory of activities of the notary (the notarial district) is established according to administrative-territorial division of the Republic of Uzbekistan.

公证员的活动范围（公证区）是根据乌兹别克斯坦共和国的行政领土划分而确定的。

The Ministry of Justice of the Republic of Karakalpakstan, justice department taking into account specific circumstances can assign making of notarial actions in certain notarial district to the notary performing activities in other notarial district. The workplace within this notarial district shall be provided to the notary.

卡拉卡尔帕克斯坦共和国司法部根据具体情况，可以将某公证区内的公证活动指派给其他公证区的公证员进行公证。公证区内的工作场所应提供给该公证员。

Each citizen or the legal entity for making of notarial action has the right to address any notary, except as specified, 82 and 93 presents of the Law provided by Articles 37, of 44, of 51, of 52, of 59, of 62, of 63, of 74.

公民和法人有权利向任何公证员申请公证，本法第 82 条和第 93 条，第 37 条，第 44 条，第 51 条，第 52 条，第 59 条，第 62 条，第 63 条，第 74 条另有规定的除外。

Making by the notary of notarial action outside the established territory of activities does not involve recognition of invalidity of this action.

公证员在既定的公证区之外作出公证行为的，不能径直认定该公证行为无效。

The notary has the right to leave the served territory for the certificate of the will in case of serious illness of the testator in case of absence in this territory of the notary.

在遗嘱人患有严重疾病的情况下，公证员有权因公证遗嘱而离开其服务的公证区。

Chapter 3. Rights, obligations and responsibility of the notary

第 3 章　公证员的权利、义务和责任

Article 17. Rights of the notary

第 17 条　公证员的权利

The notary has the right:

公证员有权：

- make the notarial actions provided by this Law for all persons who addressed it, except as specified, when the place of making of notarial action is determined by the legislation;

除另有规定外，在法律规定从事公证活动的地点，对本法规定的所有人进行公证活动；

- constitute drafts of transactions and statements, to produce copies of documents and the statement from them, and also to make explanations concerning making of notarial actions;

起草契约和声明，制作文件副本及其声明，并对公证活动作出解释；

- request physical persons and legal entities of the data and the documents necessary for making of notarial actions;

要求自然人和法人提供公证所需的资料和文件；

- request and receive the data and documents necessary for making of notarial actions, from state bodies, the companies, and the organizations;

- address on behalf of physical persons and legal entities to the relevant state bodies for implementation of state registration of the rights to property and documents, and also legalization of documents for their action abroad with receipt of the documents processed by these bodies.

Article 18. Obligations of the notary

The notary shall:

- render physical persons and legal entities assistance in implementation of their rights and protection of legitimate interests, to explain them their rights and obligations;

- explain to the parties sense and value of the drafts of transactions provided by them and to check whether there corresponds their content to actual intents of the parties and whether they contradict requirements of the law;

- warn physical persons and legal entities about consequences of the made notarial actions legal lack of information could not be used by it to the detriment;

- refuse making of notarial action in case of its discrepancy to the legislation;

- in case of detection when making notarial actions of violation of legality by citizens or officials to report about it for acceptance of need of measures to the relevant companies, organizations, or the prosecutor;

- at least once in three years to perform increase in the professional qualification according to the procedure, determined by the Ministry of Justice of the Republic of Uzbekistan;

- in cases, stipulated by the legislation to represent to body of the State Tax Service of the certificate of the certificate of lease agreements of real estate and the amount of the rent, about property value, the inheritance which is carrying over according to the procedure or donation citizens;

- issue upon the demand of court, prosecutor's office, investigation authorities of the reference (data) on the committed notarial actions connected with the cases which are in production of these bodies;

- provide at the request of credit bureaus of the reference (data) on lack of prohibition of alienation or arrest of the object which is subject of the transaction;

- provide references (data) about are committed the notarial actions connected with counteraction of legalization of income gained from criminal activities and to ter-

为进行公证活动而要求并接收国家机关、公司和组织提供必要的资料和文件；

代表自然人和法人向有关国家机关申请对财产、文件，及其在国外的合法文件（同这些国家机关的回执一起）进行权利的国家登记。

第 18 条　公证员的义务

公证员应：

协助自然人和法人行使他们的权利和保护其合法利益，释明其权利和义务；

向当事人解释他们提供的契约草稿的意义和效力，并检查内容是否与当事人的真实意思相符，以及是否违反法律的规定；

提示自然人和法人因未提交必要信息而作出的公证活动可能产生的损害后果；

在不合法的情况下拒绝公证；

发现公民或者官员违法从事公证活动时，应当向相关公司、组织或检察机关反映，并采取必要的措施。

根据乌兹别克斯坦共和国司法部确定的程序，在 3 年内至少提升 1 次专业资格；

根据法律的规定，向国家税务机关提供根据继承或捐赠程序计算出财产价值的房地产租赁协议和租金证明。

根据法院、检察院、侦查机关的要求提供与这些机构在办理案件时有关的公证活动的参考资料（信息）；

根据信贷局的要求，提供关于未禁止转让或抵押的交易标的参考资料（信息）；

根据法律规定的程序，向国家特别授权的机构提供与打击洗钱和资助恐怖主义有关的公证活动的参考资料（信息）。

rorism financing in specially authorized state body in cases and procedure, stipulated by the legislation.

Article 19. Responsibility of the notary

The notary bears responsibility for violation of the professional obligations according to the procedure, stipulated by the legislation.

The damage caused by the notary owing to violation of the professional obligations is compensated by the state according to the procedure, determined by the Cabinet of Ministers of the Republic of Uzbekistan.

Article 20.

It is excluded.

Chapter 4. Financial provision of activities of notaries

Article 21. Payment of the notarial actions and other actions made by notaries

For making of notarial actions the notary collects the state fee at the rates established by the legislation.

In case of departure of the notary for making of notarial action out of the place of the work the interested physical persons or legal entities refund it the actual transportation expenses.

For the additional actions of legal and technical nature made by notaries under the agreement with the physical persons or legal entities which addressed the notary the payment according to the procedure, established by the legislation is levied.

Article 22. Financing of notary offices

Notary offices are financed according to the procedure, established by the legislation.

Section II. Notarial actions and rules of their making

Chapter 5. Notarial actions

Article 23. The notarial actions made by notaries

Notaries make the following notarial actions:

1) is certified by transactions;

2) is certified by wills;

3) grant certificates on the property right to share in common property of spouses;

4) are imposed and remove property acquisition bans;

5) grant certificates on the right to inheritance;

6) take measures to protection of heritable property;

第 19 条　公证员的职责

公证员违反职责将按照法律规定的程序承担责任。

公证员违反职责造成的损害由国家按照乌兹别克斯坦共和国内阁规定的程序予以赔偿。

第 20 条

已删除。

第 4 章　对公证活动的财政支持

第 21 条　公证员公证活动和其他活动的收费

为进行公证活动，公证员按法律规定的费率收取法定费用。

公证员离开工作地点公证时，利害关系人和法人应支付其实际发生的交通费用。

根据法律规定的程序，公证员根据与自然人或法人签订的合同而作出的具有法律和技术性质的附加行为的，亦应收取相关费用。

第 22 条　公证机构的财务

公证机构根据法律规定的程序管理财务。

第二节　公证行为及其规则

第 5 章　公证行为

第 23 条　公证员的公证行为

公证员可作出以下公证行为：

（1）对交易行为进行公证；

（2）对遗嘱进行公证；

（3）出具配偶共有财产所有权公证书；

（4）施予和解除财产取得禁令；

（5）出具继承权公证书；

（6）采取遗产保护措施；

7) witness fidelity of copies of documents and statements from them;

8) witness fidelity of the translation of documents from one language on another;

9) witness authenticity of the signature on documents;

10) grant certificates on real estate acquisition from the public biddings;

11) certify the fact of finding of the citizen in live;

12) certify the fact of finding of the citizen in certain place;

13) certify identity of the citizen with person, represented in the photo;

14) certify time of production of documents;

15) is transferred by statements of physical persons and legal entities to other physical persons and legal entities;

16) is accepted in the deposit by sums of money and securities;

17) accept documents on storage;

18) is shown by checks to payment and certify non-payment of checks;

19) is made by executive texts;

20) is made by protests of bills of exchange;

21) is made by ship's protests;

22) is issued by duplicates of notarially certified documents and the statement from registers.

Notaries can make and other notarial actions provided by legal acts.

Article 24.

It is excluded

Article 25.

It is excluded

Article 26. The wills and powers of attorney equated to notarially certified

Are equated to notarially certified documents:

- wills of the citizens who are on treatment in hospitals, hospitals, other stationary medical institutions or living in nursing homes and the disabled people certified by chief physicians, their deputies for medical part or doctors on duty of these hospitals, hospitals and other medical institutions, and also chiefs of hospitals, directors or chief physicians of nursing homes and disabled people;

- the wills of the citizens who are during swimming in the courts going under the flag of the Republic of Uzbekistan, certified by captains of these courts;

（7）公证文件、副本及其声明的真实性；

（8）公证文件翻译的准确性；

（9）公证文件签名的真实性；

（10）对招投标获得的房地产出具公证书；

（11）公证公民存活的事实；

（12）公证公民在特定地点的事实；

（13）公证照片中公民的身份；

（14）公证文件制作的时间；

（15）为自然人或法人向其他自然人或法人移交声明；

（16）接受货币和有价证券的保管；

（17）接受文件寄存；

（18）公证支票已支付和未支付；

（19）制作执行文书；

（20）作出票据的抗辩；

（21）制作海事报告；

（22）出具公证文件副本和登记簿声明。

公证员可以作出法律规定的其他公证行为。

第 24 条

已删除。

第 25 条

已删除。

第 26 条　等同于经过公证的遗嘱和授权委托书

以下为等同于经过公证的文件：

医院、疗养院和其他医疗机构的主任医师及其副手、值班医生、医院院长证明的在上述医院、疗养院和其他医疗机构接受治疗的公民的遗嘱。老年人和残疾人中心的负责人和主任医师证明的在老年人和残疾人中心生活的老年人和残疾人的遗嘱；

公民在悬挂乌兹别克斯坦共和国国旗的法院订立的遗嘱，经法院院长证明；

- the wills of the citizens who are in prospecting or other similar expeditions, certified by chiefs of these expeditions;

- the will and power of attorney of the military personnel, and at home stations of military units where there are no notaries, also the will and the power of attorney of the civilians working in these parts, members of their families and the members of families of the military personnel certified by commanders of military units except powers of attorney on control and the order of automotor-vehicles;

- wills and powers of attorney of persons who are in places of detention or being held in custody, certified by chiefs of the relevant organizations, except powers of attorney on control and the order of automotor-vehicles.

- The certificate of wills and powers of attorney is made by the officials specified in this Article according to the procedure, determined by the Ministry of Justice of the Republic of Uzbekistan.

Article 27. Transfer of the wills certified by officials in notary office

The officials listed in article 26 of this Law shall transfer immediately in one copy the wills certified by them to storage to notary office on the permanent residence of the testator.

If the testator had no permanent residence in the Republic of Uzbekistan or if the residence of the testator is unknown, the will goes to the notary office determined by the Ministry of Justice of the Republic of Uzbekistan.

The notary shall check arrived on storage the will and in case of establishment of discrepancy to its law to report about it to the testator and the official who certified the will.

Article 28. The notarial actions made by consuls

Consuls of consular establishments of the Republic of Uzbekistan make the following notarial actions:

1) is certified by transactions (agreements, wills, powers of attorney, etc.), except agreements on alienation and pledge of the property provided by part two of article 44 of this Law and which is in the Republic of Uzbekistan;

2) certify the fact of finding of the citizen in live;

3) certify the fact of finding of the citizen in certain place;

4) certify identity of the citizen with person, represented in the photo;

5) certify time of production of documents;

6) take measures to protection of heritable property;

正在进行勘探或其他类似考察的公民的遗嘱，由该探险队的长官证明；

除意志受控制外，军事人员，在没有公证员的军事单位驻地工作的相关人员、军事人员家属的遗嘱和授权委托书，由部队指挥官证明；

除意志受控制外，被拘留或羁押的人的遗嘱和授权委托书，由相关组织负责人证明。

本条授权的官员根据乌兹别克斯坦共和国司法部确定的程序，制作遗嘱和授权委托书的公证书。

第 27 条　官员公证遗嘱的移送

本法第 26 条所列官员，应立即向遗嘱订立人永久居住地的公证机构送达一份由其公证的遗嘱的复印件。

如果遗嘱订立人在乌兹别克斯坦共和国没有永久居住地，或者遗嘱订立人的住所不详，遗嘱将被送往由乌兹别克斯坦共和国司法部确定的公证机构。

公证员应当检查遗嘱是否已被送达存放地，如果不符合法律的规定，应通知遗嘱订立人并向公证遗嘱的官员报告。

第 28 条　领事公证活动

乌兹别克斯坦共和国领事机构的领事可进行下列公证活动：

（1）对交易行为进行公证，（协议、遗嘱、授权委托书等），但本法第 44 条第 2 款所规定的在乌兹别克斯坦共和国境内签订的财产转让和质押协议除外；

（2）公证公民存活的事实；

（3）公证公民在特定地点的事实；

（4）公证照片中公民的身份；

（5）公证文件制作的时间；

（6）采取遗产保护措施；

7) grant certificates on the right to inheritance;

8) grant certificates on the property right to share in common property of spouses;

9) witness fidelity of copies of documents and statements from them;

10) witness authenticity of the signature on documents;

11) witness fidelity of the translation of documents from one language on another;

12) is accepted in the deposit by sums of money and securities;

13) accept documents on storage;

14) is made by executive texts;

15) is made by ship's protests.

Consuls of consular establishments of the Republic of Uzbekistan can make and other notarial actions provided by legal acts.

Article 29. Procedure for making of notarial actions

The procedure for making of notarial actions by notaries, other officials having the right to make notarial actions is established by this Law and other acts of the legislation.

Chapter 6. Rules of making of notarial actions

Article 30. Place of making of notarial actions

Notarial actions are made in premises of notary offices.

In some cases, when the citizen owing to disease, disability or for other reasons cannot be in notary office, notarial actions can be made in the location of this citizen.

By the legislation also other cases of making of notarial actions out of premises of notary offices can be provided.

Article 31. Terms of making and suspension of notarial action

Notarial actions are made after their payment in day of representation of all of documents necessary for this purpose.

Making of notarial action can be postponed in need of reclamation of additional data or the direction of documents for examination.

Making of notarial actions shall be postponed if by law it is necessary to request from interested persons about lack of objections at them against making of these actions.

The term for which making of notarial action is postponed cannot exceed one month. Upon the demand of

（7）出具继承权公证书；

（8）出具配偶共有财产所有权公证书；

（9）公证文件副本及其声明的真实性；

（10）公证文件签名的真实性；

（11）公证文件翻译的准确性；

（12）接受货币和有价证券的保管；

（13）接受文件寄存；

（14）制作执行文书；

（15）制作海事报告。

乌兹别克斯坦共和国领事机构的领事可以作出法律规定的其他公证活动。

第 29 条　公证活动的程序

本法和其他法律规定了公证员及其他有权作出公证行为的官员进行公证活动的程序。

第 6 章　公证活动的规则

第 30 条　作出公证行为的场所

公证行为在公证机构作出。

在某些情况下，由于疾病、残疾或其他原因导致公民不能前往公证机构时，可在公民所在地进行公证。

法律可规定在其他地点进行公证。

第 31 条　进行和暂停公证活动的条款

公证活动应在提交所有必需文件并支付公证费用的当天进行。

在需要收集更多的资料或查明文件时，公证活动可以推迟。

在依法有必要确认利害关系人对公证无异议时，应当推迟进行公证。

推迟公证的期限不得超过 1 个月。根据公证申请人的请求，向其签发推迟公证的决议。

person who addressed for making of notarial action, the resolution on adjournment of making of notarial action is issued to it.

According to the statement of the interested person wishing to take a legal action for contest of the right or the fact about which certificate asks other interested person making of notarial action it can be postponed for term no more than ten days. If in this time the message on receipt of the statement is not received from court, notarial action shall be made.

利害关系人对待公证权利或事实欲采取法律手段维权时，根据利害关系人的声明，公证可以推迟不超过 10 日。在此期限内，未收到来自法院的有关信息，则应当继续进行公证。

In case of obtaining from court of the message on receipt of the statement of the interested person challenging the right or the fact about which certificate asks other interested person making of notarial action stops to permission of case by court.

如果收到来自法院的该利害关系人已采取法律手段维权的信息，那么在法院准予公证之前暂停公证活动。

By the legislation also other bases for adjournment and suspension of making of notarial actions can be established.

法律规定的其他可以推迟和暂停公证的事由。

Article 32. Identification of the notarial action which addressed for making

第 32 条 查验公证申请人的身份

When making notarial actions the notaries and other officials making notarial actions identify the personality of the notarial actions which addressed for making.

进行公证活动时，公证员和其他公证人员应当查验公证申请人的身份。

Identification shall be made based on the passport or other documents excluding any doubts concerning the identity of person who addressed for making of notarial action.

应根据护照或其他身份证明文件进行身份查验，应排除对公证申请人身份的任何怀疑。

Article 33. Check of capacity to act of citizens and legal capacities of the legal entities participating in transactions

第 33 条 查验公民的行为能力和法人参与交易的法律行为能力

In case of the certificate of transactions capacity to act of citizens becomes clear in accordance with the established procedure and legal capacity of the legal entities participating in transactions is checked. In case of transaction by the representative also its powers are checked.

根据规定的程序，在有交易证明书的情况下，确认公民的行为能力与法人参与交易的法律行为能力。在以代表人进行交易时，应对其授权范围进行查验。

Article 34. Procedure for the signature of notarially certified transactions, and also statements and other documents

第 34 条 公证的交易、声明和其他文件的签署程序

Notarially certified transactions, and also statements and other documents are signed in the presence of the notary.

需公证的交易、声明和其他文件均需在公证员在场的情况下签署。

If the citizen owing to physical defects, disease or for any other reasons cannot undersign with own hand, according to its order, at its presence and in the presence of the notary other citizen with indication of the reasons

如果公民由于身体缺陷、疾病或其他原因不能亲自签署文件，可由其他公民根据该公民的授权和公证员都在场的情况下签署，并说明该交易、声明和其他文件不能由公证申请人亲自签署的原因。

owing to which the document could not be signed with own hand by the citizen who addressed for making of notarial action can sign the transaction, the statement or other document.

The notary can not require corporal appearance of officials of the companies, organizations and organizations if in cases of notary office there are data on check of powers, the specimen signature of these officials received in case of the personal address, and authenticity of their signature does not raise doubts.

在公证机构有数据查验授权范围、有官员签名样本并排除对签名真实性怀疑的情况下，公证员不得要求公司、机构和组织的官员到场。

Article 35. Requirements to the documents submitted for making of notarial actions

Notaries do not take for making notarial actions the documents having erasures or additions, the crossed-out words and other not stipulated corrections, and also the documents performed by pencil.

The text of notarially certified transactions shall be written clearly and accurately, the numbers relating to contents of the document and time frames are specified at least once by words, and names of legal entities - without reducings, with indication of addresses of their bodies. Surnames, names and middle names of citizens shall be written completely with indication of the place of their residence.

The document consisting more than of one leaf shall be stitched, sheets are numbered and under seal.

第 35 条　公证活动所需文件的要求

公证员作出公证行为时，不接受有删除、添加、划掉文字的文件、没有按规定更正的文件及用铅笔书写的文件。

经过公证的交易文本应清晰准确地书写，与文件内容相关的数字和时限至少一次使用全称，法人的名称（无缩写）需注明其机构所在地。自然人的姓名应完整列明，并且注明其住址。

数量超过 1 页的文件需要装订、编号、盖章后进行密封。

Article 36. Making of certifying texts and issue of certificates

In case of the certificate of transactions, witnessing of fidelity of copies of documents and statements from them, authenticity of the signature on documents, fidelity of the translation of documents from one language on another, in case of the certificate of time of production of documents on the relevant documents certifying texts are made.

In confirmation of inheritance right, the property right, the certificate of the facts of finding of the citizen in live and in the certain place, identity of the citizen with person represented in the photo, acceptances on document storage appropriate certificates are granted.

第 36 条　公证文书的制作和公证书的颁发

交易文件公证、文件副本及其声明真实性公证、签名的真实性公证、文件翻译的准确性公证，出具文件时间的公证，均需制作公证文书。

对于公证继承权、财产权、某人存活或在特定地点、图中某人的身份、接受文件保存，应颁发合适的公证书。

Article 37. Restrictions of the right of making of notarial actions

Notaries have no right to make notarial actions on the name and on its own behalf, addressed to and on behalf of the spouses, their and relatives (parents, children, grandsons, brothers and sisters), addressed to and on behalf of

第 37 条　对公证权的限制

公证员无权以其个人名义为其配偶、亲属（父母、子女、孙子女、兄弟、姐妹）、有监护关系的人、同样履行公职的人员进行公证。

persons, related owing to guardianship, guardianship, and also addressed to and from employee name of this notary office.

Article 38. Refusal in making of notarial action

The notary refuses making of notarial action if:

making of such action contradicts the law;

action is subject to making by other notary;

the incapacitated citizen or the representative who does not have necessary powers requested making of notarial action;

the transaction made on behalf of the legal entity contradicts the purposes specified in its charter or provision;

the transaction does not conform to requirements of the law;

the documents submitted for making of notarial action do not conform to requirements of the legislation.

In case of refusal in making of notarial action the notary not later than in three-day time from the date of the address issues the decree on refusal in making of notarial action.

The notary at the request of person to whom it is refused making of notarial action shall state causes of failure in writing and explain procedure for its appeal.

Article 39. Appeal of notarial action, the resolution on adjournment of notarial action or refusal in its making

The interested person considering wrong committed notarial action, the resolution on adjournment of notarial action or refusal in making of the notarial action having the right to file a lawsuit about it the claim in the location of notary office.

Article 40. Registration of notarial actions

The notarial actions made by notaries are registered in the register. Each notarial action is registered at separate number.

Notaries issue statements from registers for registration of notarial actions according to the written application of the physical persons or legal entities specified in parts two and third article 6 of this Law.

Article 41. Forms of registers for registration of notarial actions, notarial certificates, certifying texts

Forms of registers for registration of notarial actions, notarial certificates, certifying texts on transactions and the witnessed documents are established by the Ministry of

第 38 条　拒绝公证

公证员在以下情况拒绝公证：

该行为违背法律；

应由其他公证员公证；

申请公证的公民无行为能力或代理人无适格授权；

代表法人进行的交易与其章程或文件规定的目的相抵触；

该交易不符合法律规定；

为公证所提交的文件不符合法律要求。

公证员拒绝公证的，不得迟于申请之日起 3 日内作出拒绝公证的决定。

公证员拒绝公证，应向公证申请人书面说明原因，并说明申诉的程序。

第 39 条　对予以公证、推迟公证、拒绝公证决定的申诉

利害关系人认为予以公证、推迟公证、拒绝公证的决定有误的，有权在公证机构所在地对其提起诉讼。

第 40 条　公证的登记

公证员所作的公证行为应登记在公证行为登记簿上。每项公证行为以不同的编号登记。

公证员应当根据本法第 6 条第 2 款、第 3 款规定的自然人或法人的书面申请，为公证行为登记簿发布声明。

第 41 条　公证行为登记簿、公证书、证明文本的形式

交易和证据文件的公证行为登记簿、公证书、证明文本的形式由乌兹别克斯坦共和国司法部制定。

Justice of the Republic of Uzbekistan.

Article 42. Issue of duplicates of notarially certified documents

In case of loss of the documents certified or issued by the notary which copies are stored in cases of notary office, according to written applications of physical persons and legal entities or their legal representatives, from name or at the request of which notarial actions were made duplicates of the lost documents are issued.

Issue of duplicates is made with observance of requirements of articles 6 and 40 of this Law.

Chapter 7. Certificate of transactions

Article 43. The transactions certified in notarial procedure

Notaries certify transactions for which the legislation establishes obligatory notarial form. At the request of the parties the notary also other transactions can make sure.

Article 44. The certificate of transactions of alienation and pledge of the property which is subject to registration

Transactions about alienation and pledge of the property which is subject to registration can be certified on condition of submission of the documents confirming the property right on the alienated or pledged property. At the same time accessory to his alienating person or the pledger and lack of prohibition of alienation and arrest is checked. In the presence of prohibition the transaction about alienation of the specified property can be certified only in case of the consent of the creditor and acquirer to transfer of debt on the acquirer.

The certificate of transactions of alienation and pledge of the apartment house (part of the house), apartments, dachas, the garden house, garage, and also other room, construction or structure is made in the location of the specified property.

Article 45. Certificate of wills

Notaries certify the wills of capable citizens constituted according to requirements of the legislation and personally provided by them to the notary. The certificate of wills through representatives is not allowed.

In case of the certificate of the will from the testator production of evidence, confirming its right to the bequeathed property is not required.

第 42 条　出具经过公证的文件副本

如果公证员公证或签发的文件遗失，其存放在公证机构的文件副本，应根据自然人和法人或其法定代表人的书面申请或公证机构的要求，以公证机构的名义出具丢失文件的副本。

出具文件副本应遵守本法第 6 条和第 40 条的规定。

第 7 章　交易公证

第 43 条　经公证的交易

公证员根据法律规定的强制性公证形式对交易进行公证。应当事人的要求，公证员可以公证其他类型的交易。

第 44 条　需登记的财产转让和质押交易的公证

在提交确认转让或质押财产的财产权文件的前提下，需登记的财产转让和质押的交易可以进行公证。同时检查该财产没有禁止转让和质押的情况。存在禁止转让和抵押的情况时，只有债权人和收购方均同意将债务转移给收购方时，才能对该交易予以公证。

对公寓楼（或一部分）、套房、别墅、花园房、车库和其他房屋的转让协议公证由该财产所在地的公证员进行。

第 45 条　遗嘱公证

根据法律的规定，公证员根据完全民事行为能力公民亲自提供的遗嘱进行公证。通过代表人提交的遗嘱不予公证。

如果遗嘱订立人出示财产证明，那么无须确认其对遗赠财产的权利。

Article 46. Procedure for change and cancellation of wills

Notaries in case of receipt of the statement for cancellation of the made will, and equally in the receipt of the new will canceling or changing the made will do about it mark in copy of the will which is stored at the notary and in the register for registration of notarial actions. The signature on the statement for cancellation of the will shall be notarially attested.

Article 47. Certificate of powers of attorney

Notaries certify powers of attorney on behalf of one or several persons addressed to one or several persons.

The power of attorney issued according to the procedure of retrust is subject to the notarial certificate after submission of the main power of attorney in which the retrust right, or after production of evidence of the fact that the representative under the main power of attorney is forced to it by force of circumstances for protection of interests issued the power of attorney is stipulated.

The power of attorney issued according to the procedure of retrust shall not comprise more rights, than it is provided under the main power of attorney. Effective period of the power of attorney issued according to the procedure of retrust cannot exceed effective period of the main power of attorney based on which it is issued.

Article 48. Number of copies of the document in which contents of the transaction are stated

Number of copies of the document in which contents of the transaction certified in notarial procedure are stated is determined by persons who addressed for making of notarial action, but cannot exceed the number of the parties participating in the transaction. However the will and pledge agreements of property, alienation of the apartment house and other real estate are represented to the notary at least in duplicate, one of which remains in cases of notary office.

Chapter 8. Taking measures to protection of heritable property, issue of certificates on the right to inheritance

Article 49. The notice of heirs on the opened inheritance

The notary who received the message on the opened inheritance shall inform on it those heirs, the residence or works of which is known to it.

The notary can also make challenge of heirs by the

第 46 条　变更和撤销遗嘱的程序

公证员收到撤销遗嘱的申请书，或收到撤销、变更先前遗嘱的新遗嘱时，须在存放于公证员处的遗嘱副本上标记并在遗嘱登记簿上登记。撤销遗嘱申请书上的签名须经公证。

第 47 条　授权委托书的公证

公证员对一人或数人向另外一人或数人提供的授权委托书进行公证。

依照转委托程序出具的授权委托书，在提交原授权委托书后，或者出示主委托的代表人被强制转委托的证据后，才能进行公证。

根据转委托程序出具的授权委托书的代理权限不得超出主授权委托书中的代理权限的范围。根据转委托程序出具的授权委托书的有效期限不得超过主授权委托书的有效期限。

第 48 条　详述交易内容的文件副本的数量

公证程序所公证的详述交易内容的文件副本的数量由交易中申请公证的人数确定，但不能超过参与交易的当事人的数目。但是，财产、公寓和其他不动产的遗嘱和质押协议至少一式两份，其中一份保留在公证机构。

第 8 章　采取措施保护遗产，出具继承权公证书

第 49 条　继承开始时通知继承人

公证员收到继承开始的信息，应当通知其知悉住所或工作地点的继承人。

公证员也可以通过公共告知室或大众媒体通知继

room of the public notice or the message on it in mass media.

承人。

Article 50. Receipt of statements for inheritance acceptance or about refusal of it

The notary in the place of opening of inheritance according to the legislation adopts statements for inheritance acceptance or for refusal of it. The statement for inheritance acceptance or for refusal of it shall be made in writing.

第 50 条　收到接受或放弃继承的声明

根据法律的规定，继承发生地的公证员有权受理关于接受或放弃继承的声明。接受或者放弃继承的声明应当以书面形式作出。

Article 51. Adoption of claims from creditors of the testator

The notary in the place of opening of inheritance according to the legislation accepts claims from creditors of the testator. Claims shall be declared in writing.

第 51 条　受理遗嘱订立人的债权人的债权主张

根据法律的规定，继承发生地的公证员有权受理遗嘱订立人的债权人对债权的主张。该主张应以书面形式提出。

Article 52. Protection of heritable property

The notary in the place of opening of inheritance according to physical persons and legal entities or on the initiative takes measures to protection of heritable property, when necessary for the benefit of heirs, legatees, creditors or the state.

第 52 条　遗产的保护

为了继承人、遗产受赠人、债权人或国家的利益，继承发生地的公证员应根据自然人、法人、主张继承权的人的需要主动采取措施保护遗产。

Article 53. The order about taking measures to protection of heritable property

If the property of the testator or his part are not in the place of opening of inheritance, the notary in the place of opening of inheritance sends to the notary, in the location of heritable property of the order about taking measures to its protection.

The notary who took measures to protection of heritable property reports to notary office in the place of opening of inheritance about acceptance of the specified measures and sends the copy of the inventory of heritable property.

第 53 条　采取措施保护遗产的命令

遗嘱订立人的全部或部分遗产不在继承发生地的，继承发生地公证员应当指令遗产所在地公证员采取措施保护遗产。

采取措施保护遗产的遗产所在地的公证员应当向继承发生地公证员报告其接受采取特殊措施的指令并发送遗产清单的副本。

Article 54. The inventory of heritable property and its transfer on storage

Notaries make the inventory of this property for protection of heritable property and report it to storage to heirs or other persons.

If as a part of inheritance there is property requiring management and also in case of presentation of the claim by creditors of the testator before inheritance acceptance by heirs, the notary appoints the managing director of inheritance.

Managing directors of inheritance and other persons to whom the heritable property is transferred to storage are warned about responsibility for waste, alienation or concealment of heritable property and for the losses caused to heirs.

第 54 条　遗产清单及遗产转移

公证员为保护遗产制作遗产清单，并将其报送给继承人或其他人。

如果遗产的一部分需要管理，且继承人的债权人在继承人接受继承之前提出债权主张的，公证员应指定遗产管理人。

遗产管理人和遗产交由其保管的其他人应对遗产的遗失、非法转移或隐匿而导致继承人的损失承担责任。

Article 55. Remuneration for storage of heritable property

Managing directors of inheritance and other persons to whom the heritable property is transferred to storage if they are not heirs, have the right to earn reward for storage of heritable property from heirs. Necessary expenses on storage and management of heritable property, less actually received benefit from use of this property are also refunded to specified persons.

Article 56. The termination of measures to protection of heritable property

Protection of heritable property continues before inheritance acceptance by heirs and if it is not accepted them - before the expiration for the inheritance acceptance established by the law.

The notary in the place of opening of inheritance shall notify previously heirs on the termination of measures of protection of heritable property and if the property on inheritance right passes to the state - the relevant state body.

Article 57. Payment of expenses at the expense of heritable property

The notary before inheritance acceptance by heirs and if it is not accepted, then before issue to the state of the certificate on the right to inheritance, gives the order about payment for the account of heritable property of the following expenses:

on care of the testator during his disease, and also on its funeral and on arrangement of the place of burial;

on content of the citizens who were dependent on the testator;

on satisfaction of claims on the salary and the claims equated to them;

on protection of heritable property and on management of it, and also on the publication of the message on challenge of heirs.

By legal acts also other cases of payment of expenses at the expense of heritable property can be established.

Article 58. Place and terms of issue of certificates on the right to inheritance

According to the written application of heirs the notary in the place of opening of inheritance grants certificates on the right to inheritance.

Issue of certificates is made in the terms established by the legislation.

第 55 条　遗产的保管费用

如果遗产管理人和其他保管遗产的人不是继承人，那么其有权从继承人那里获得遗产保管费。如果遗产增值大于其保管费用，那么上述人员应当退还多余的费用。

第 56 条　终止遗产保护措施

在继承人接受遗产之前或继承人不接受遗产时，对遗产的保护将持续至法律规定的期限。

继承发生地的公证员应当提前通知继承人遗产的保护期限。如果期限届满，遗产所有权将转移给国家或相关的国家机构。

第 57 条　遗产保管费用的支付

在继承人接受遗产前或继承人放弃遗产，遗产所在地的公证员应在出具继承权公证书之前，发出从遗产账户中支付下列费用的指令：

对遗嘱订立人患病期间的照料，以及丧葬所产生的费用；

受遗嘱订立人扶养人员的必要开支；

索要工资或同等索要事项的支出；

保护、管理遗产及发布遗产继承通知所产生的费用。

法律可规定其他原因产生应从遗产账户中支付的费用。

第 58 条　继承权公证的作出地点和条件

根据继承人的书面申请，公证员可在继承发生地作出继承权公证。

应在法律规定的期限内作出继承权公证。

Article 59. Procedure for issue of the certificate on the right to inheritance

The certificate on the right to inheritance is granted to the heirs who accepted inheritance according to the legislation.

The certificate on the right to inheritance is granted to all heirs together or to everyone depending on their desire.

Notaries report about issue of the certificate on the right to inheritance addressed to minor or incapacitated heirs to guardianship and custody bodies at the place of residence of heirs for protection of their valuable interests.

Upon transition of property on inheritance right to the state or in the cases provided by the law to self-government institutions of citizens, the certificate on the right to inheritance is granted to the relevant state body or self-government institutions of citizens.

Article 60. Conditions of issue of the certificate on the right to inheritance on the law

The notary in case of issue of the certificate on the right to inheritance under the law by reclamation of the corresponding proofs checks the fact of death of the testator, time and the place of opening of inheritance, availability of the relations which are the basis for calling to inheritance under the law of persons who submitted the application for issue of the certificate on the right to inheritance, structure and the location of heritable property.

If one or several legal heirs are deprived of opportunity to produce the evidence of the relations which are the basis for calling to inheritance, they can be included in the certificate on the right to inheritance with the consent of all other heirs who accepted inheritance and produced such evidence.

Article 61. Conditions of issue of the certificate on the right to inheritance on the will

The notary in case of issue of the certificate on the right to inheritance according to the will by reclamation of the corresponding proofs checks the fact of death of the testator, will availability, time and the place of opening of inheritance, structure and the location of heritable property.

The notary finds out also the group of people, having the right to obligatory share in inheritance.

第 59 条　继承权公证的作出程序

根据法律的规定，向接受继承的继承人出具继承权公证。

继承权公证根据各继承人的意愿统一出具一份或分别出具。

若公证员向未成年或无行为能力的继承人出具继承权公证，则应向其居所地的监护人和监护机构出具继承权公证，以保护其利益。

在遗产继承权转移至国家或法律规定的公民自治机构的情况下，公证员应向有关的国家机构或公民自治机构出具继承权公证。

第 60 条　作出法定继承权公证的条件

公证员作出法定继承权公证时，应根据相关证据，对遗嘱订立人死亡的事实、继承发生的时间和地点、遗产的组成和所在地进行审查。继承权公证申请人与遗嘱订立人之间应存在有效的法律关系才可公证其有关继承、遗产份额和遗产所在地等事项。

如果一名或多名法定继承人被剥夺了提供与遗嘱订立人有关的证据的机会（该证据是承认其为法定继承人的基础），他们可在其他提供了相关证据的继承人都同意的情况下，获得继承权公证。

第 61 条　据遗嘱出具继承公证

公证员出具遗嘱继承权公证时，应根据相关证据，对遗嘱订立人死亡的事实、遗嘱有效性、继承发生的时间和地点、遗产的组成和所在地进行核实。

公证员还应当明确享有部分继承权的人的范围。

Chapter 9. Issue of certificates on the property right to share in common property of spouses. Imposing and removal of prohibition of property acquisition

第 9 章 出具夫妻共有财产权利公证。实施和解除财产流转禁令

Article 62. Issue of certificates on the property right to share in common property of spouses

The notary according to the written application of spouses issues to one of them or both spouses of the certificate on the property right to share in the common property acquired during scrap.

The certificate on the property right to the apartment house (part of the house), the apartment, the dacha, the garden house, garage, and also other room, construction or structure it is issued by the notary in the place of their stay.

第 62 条 出具夫妻共有财产权利公证

公证员根据配偶的书面申请，向夫妻一方或双方出具婚姻关系存续期间获得的共同财产权利公证。

公寓房屋（房屋的一部分）、公寓、别墅、花园洋房、车库以及其他房产、建筑或结构的产权公证由该财产所在地的公证员出具。

Article 63. Issue of the certificate on the property right to share in common property according to the statement of the surviving spouse

In case of the death of one of spouses the certificate on the property right to share in common property of spouses is granted by the notary in the place of opening of inheritance according to the written application of the surviving spouse with the notice of the heirs who accepted inheritance.

The certificate on the property right to share in common property of spouses can be granted to the surviving spouse on half of the common property acquired during scrap.

The share of the died spouse in common property also can be determined by the written application of the heirs who accepted inheritance and with the consent of the surviving spouse in the certificate on the property right.

第 63 条 根据未亡配偶的申请出具共有财产产权证书

在配偶一方死亡的情况下，由遗产所在地的公证员根据未亡配偶的书面申请，出具夫妻共有财产权利公证书，并通知已接受继承的继承人。

若有一半的共有财产取得于婚姻关系存续期间，可向未亡配偶出具共有财产权利公证书。

在拥有遗产权利公证书的未亡配偶同意的情况下，已接受继承的继承人通过提交书面申请，可以确定其在已故配偶在共同财产中所占的份额。

Article 64. Imposing and removal of prohibition of property acquisition

Imposing and removal of prohibition of property acquisition are performed on conditions and according to the procedure, established by legal acts.

第 64 条 实施或解除财产流转禁令

根据法律规定的程序进行财产流转禁令的实施和解除。

Chapter 10. Witnessing of fidelity of copies of documents and statements from them, authenticity of the signature and fidelity of the translation

第 10 章 文件副本、副本中声明的真实性、签名、翻译的真实性的公证

Article 65. Witnessing of fidelity of copies of documents and statements from them

Notaries witness fidelity of copies of documents and statements from them issued by physical persons and legal entities provided that these documents do not contradict

第 65 条 文件副本、副本中声明真实性的公证

公证员公证自然人和法人出具的文件副本及副本中声明的真实性，条件是这些文件不违反法律，且具有法律意义。

the law, have legal value and witnessing of fidelity of copies and statements from them it is not forbidden by the law.

Fidelity of the statement can be attested only when the document of which the statement is made contain solutions of several the separate, not connected among themselves questions. The statement shall reproduce the complete text of part of the document on certain question.

Fidelity of the copy of the document issued by the citizen is witnessed by the notary when authenticity of the signature of the citizen on the document is certified by the notary or the official of the company, organization, organization for place of employment, study or the citizen's residence.

Article 66. Witnessing of fidelity of the copy from the copy of the document

Fidelity of the copy from the copy of the document is witnessed by notaries under condition if fidelity of the copy is notarized or if the copy of the document is issued by the company, organization, the organization from which the authentic document proceeds. In the latter case the copy of the document shall be stated on the form of this legal entity, is under seal also with mark that the authentic document is in this company, the organization.

Article 67. Witnessing of authenticity of the signature on documents

The notary witnesses authenticity of the signature on documents which contents do not contradict the legislation.

The notary, witnessing authenticity of the signature, does not certify the facts stated in the document, and only confirms that the signature is made by certain person.

Article 68. Witnessing of fidelity of the translation

The notary witnesses fidelity of the translation from one language on another if the notary knows the corresponding languages.

If the notary does not know the corresponding languages, the translation can be made by the translator whose authenticity of the signature is witnessed by the notary.

Chapter 11. Certificate of the facts

Article 69. The certificate of the fact of finding of the citizen in live

The notary certifies the fact of finding of the citizen

仅对文件中涉及的单一问题声明的真实性进行公证。若该文件涉及一个或多个问题，公证文件应包含完整的文件。

当公民签署的文件的真实性由公证员或者公司、机构、雇佣地的组织、研究机构的官方代表或者公民的居住地所公证，公证员可以公证公民出具的文件副本的真实性。

第 66 条　文件副本复印件的真实性公证

若文件副本的真实性经过公证，或文件副本是由出具原始文件的公司、组织、机构出具的，则公证员可以公证该文件副本复印件的真实性。在后一种情况下，该文件的副本应由该法人制作并加盖印章，同时注明该公司、组织、机构留存有原始文件。

第 67 条　文件签名的真实性公证

公证员公证内容不违反法律法规的文件上签名的真实性。

公证员公证签名的真实性，并不对文件上记载的内容予以公证，仅对签名由某人作出进行确认。

第 68 条　翻译真实性的公证

若公证员通晓相应的语言，则可公证该翻译的真实性。

如果公证员不通晓相应的语言，翻译可以由翻译人员翻译，公证员对其签名真实性进行公证。

第 11 章　对事实的公证

第 69 条　公民在世事实的公证

根据公民的申请，并当其在场的情况下，公证员

in live at personal request of the citizen and at its presence.

The certificate of the fact of stay in live the minor is made at the request of his legal representatives (parents, adoptive parents, guardians, custodians), and also organizations and the organizations on which care there is minor.

可公证公民在世的事实。

根据未成年人法定代理人（父母、养父母、监护人、托管人）以及未成年人保护机构和组织的申请，对未成年人在世的事实予以公证。

Article 70. The certificate of the fact of finding of the citizen in certain place

The notary at the request of the citizen certifies the fact of stay it in certain place.

The certificate of the fact of stay in certain place of the minor is made at the request of his legal representatives (parents, adoptive parents, guardians, custodians), and also organizations and the organizations on which care there is minor.

第 70 条　对公民在某地的事实进行公证

根据公民的申请，公证员公证该公民在某地的事实。

根据未成年人法定代理人（父母、养父母、监护人、托管人）以及未成年人保护机构和组织的申请，对未成年人在某地的事实予以公证。

Article 71. The certificate of identity of the identity of the citizen with person represented in the photo

The notary certifies identity of the identity of the citizen with person represented in the photo provided by this citizen.

第 71 条　对图中人员的身份的公证

公证员可以对公民所提供图片中某人的身份进行公证。

Article 72. Certificate of time of production of documents

The notary certifies time of presentation of the document to it.

第 72 条　对文件制作时间的公证

公证员可以为公民出具文件的时间进行公证。

Chapter 12. Transfer of statements of physical persons and legal entities. Acceptance in the deposit of sums of money and securities

第 12 章　自然人和法人声明的传达、存款和有价证券的接受

Article 73. Transfer of statements

The notary reports statements of physical persons and legal entities to other physical persons and legal entities. Statements are transferred by mail with the return notification or personally to addressees on receipt. Statements can be transferred also with use of the telefax, computer networks and other technical means.

The expenses connected with use of technical means for transfer of statements are paid by person at the request of whom notarial action is made.

At the request of person who submitted the application to it the certificate on transfer of the statement is granted.

第 73 条　声明的传达

自然人和法人向其他自然人和法人传达声明的情形，应由公证员在收到申请后亲自传达，或以邮寄方式传达。声明也可通过传真、计算机网络或其他技术手段传达。

使用技术手段传达而发生的费用由公证申请人负担。

应提交申请者的要求，可向其提供声明传达公证书。

Article 74. Acceptance in the deposit of sums of money and securities

The notary in cases, stipulated by the legislation, accepts from the debtor in the deposit sums of money and

第 74 条　存款和有价证券的接受

根据法律的规定，公证员接受债务人的存款和有价证券并转交给债权人。

securities for transfer to their creditor.

The notary informs the creditor on receipt of sums of money and securities and according to its requirement issues it receivable sums of money and securities.

Acceptance in the deposit of sums of money and securities is made by the notary in the place of obligation fulfillment.

Article 75. Return of sums of money and securities to person who introduced them in the deposit

Return of sums of money and securities to person who introduced them in the deposit is allowed only from written consent of person for benefit of which the contribution, or by a court decision is made.

Chapter 13. Making of executive texts

Article 76. Collection of sums of money or reclamation of property from the debtor

For collection of sums of money or reclamation of property from the debtor the notary makes executive texts on the documents establishing debt.

Article 77. The list of documents according to which debt collection is made in indisputable procedure

The list of documents according to which debt collection is made in indisputable procedure based on executive texts is established by the Cabinet of Ministers of the Republic of Uzbekistan.

Article 78. Conditions of making of executive text

The executive text is made:

- if the submitted documents confirm indisputability of debt or other responsibility of the debtor to the claimant;

- if from the date of emergence of right of action there passed no more than three years.

If for the requirement according to which the executive text is issued the legislation establishes other prescriptive limit, the executive text is issued within this term.

Article 79. Content of executive text

The executive text shall bear:

surname and initials, position of the notary making executive text;

name and address of the claimant;

name and debtor's address;

designation of term for which collection is made;

公证员在收到存款和有价证券后，应及时通知债权人，并根据债权人的请求向其发放货币和有价证券。

接受货币和有价证券的保管由义务履行地的公证员负责。

第 75 条　将保管的货币和有价证券退还给支付人

公证员只有经受益人的书面同意或经法院裁决，才允许将其保管的货币和有价证券退还给支付人。

第 13 章　执行文书的制作

第 76 条　向债务人收款或收回财产

为了从债务人那里收款或收回财产，公证员就确立债权债务的文件制作执行文书。

第 77 条　以非诉方式实现债权的文件清单

通过执行文书以非诉方式实现债权的文件清单由乌兹别克斯坦共和国内阁成员制作。

第 78 条　制作执行文书的条件

执行文书可以在下列情况下出具：

提交的文件确认债务人对债权人有无可争议的债务或其他责任；

债务履行期届满之日起不超过 3 年。

如果法律对于出具执行文书的要求规定了其他限制，那么执行文书应在该限制内出具。

第 79 条　执行文书的内容

执行文书应包含以下内容：

作出执行文书的公证员的姓名、职位；

债权人的姓名和地址；

债务人的姓名和地址；

债权实现期限；

designation of the amounts which are subject to collection or the objects which are subject to reclamation including penalty fee, percent if those are due;

designation of the amount of the state fee or rate, paid by the claimant or subject to collection from the debtor;

date (year, month, number) making of executive text;

number at which the executive text is registered in the register;

the signature of the notary who made executive text;

notary's seal.

Article 80. Terms of presentation of executive text and procedure for collection on it

The executive text can be shown to forced execution within three years from the date of its making if the legislation does not establish other terms.

Recovery of the passed term for presentation of executive text, and also collection on it is made according to the legislation.

Chapter 14. Making of protest of the bill of exchange. Presentation of the check to payment and the certificate of non-payment of the check

Article 81. Protest of the bill of exchange

The protest of the bill of exchange in non-payment, the non-acceptance and not dating of the acceptance is made by the notary according to the legislation.

Article 82. Presentation of the check to payment and the certificate of non-payment of the check

The notary in the location of the payer accepts for presentation to payment the check in case and procedure, stipulated by the legislation.

In case of check non-payment the notary certifies check non-payment by text on the check and notes about it in the register.

Along with text on the check the notification is sent to the issuer about non-payment of its check by bank and making of text on the check.

At the request of the payee the notary in case of non-payment of the check makes executive text.

Chapter 15. Acceptance on document storage and their return

Article 83. Acceptance on document storage

The notary accepts on storage documents according

应收取的金额或需要回收的标的，包括一定比例的罚金（如果已到期）；

应由申请人支付或向债务人收取的国家公证费用数额；

制作执行文书的日期（年、月、日）；

执行文书在公证活动登记簿中的编号；

制作执行文本的公证员签名；

公证员的印章。

第 80 条　执行文书提交执行的期限及执行程序

如果法律没有规定其他规定，执行文书可以在其作出之日起 3 年内被强制执行。

执行期限届满的执行文书的提交与执行根据法律的规定恢复。

第 14 章　汇票异议公证。支票付款及未付款公证

第 81 条　汇票异议公证

公证员根据法律的规定对汇票作出未支付、未承兑及未规定承兑日期的异议公证。

第 82 条　支票付款及未付款公证

付款人所在地的公证员根据法律规定的情形和程序接受提示付款。

在支票被拒付的情况下，公证员应核对该支票上的文本和登记簿上的说明。

关于银行拒付该支票和在支票上备注的通知会连同支票上的文本发送给出票人。

根据收款人的要求，公证员在支票被拒付的情况下出具执行公证书。

第 15 章　接受与返还保存文件

第 83 条　接受文件保存

公证员根据清单接受文件保存。保存清单的一份

to the inventory. One copy of the inventory remains at the notary, other copy is issued to person who checked documents.

副本留在公证员处，其他副本提供给检查文件的人员。

At the request of person the notary can accept documents without inventory if they are packed properly. Packaging is fastened with notary's seal, signed by it and person which handed over documents. In such cases the notary bears responsibility for safety of packaging.

根据申请人的要求，公证员可以在没有清单的情况下接受已妥善包装的文件。包裹上需由公证员和交付文件的人签名，并加盖公证印章。在此情况下，公证员应对已包装好的文件的安全负责。

Checked documents the certificate is granted.

检查文件后发放保存公证书。

Article 84. Return accepted on document storage

The documents accepted on storage return to checked them or legally authorized person upon presentation of the certificate and the inventory or by a court decision.

第 84 条　返还保存的文件

保存的文件在交存人、被合法授权的人出示证书和清单、经法院裁决后，检查并归还。

Chapter 16. Making of ship's protests

第 16 章　出具海事报告公证

Article 85. Statement for the ship's protest

The notary for the purpose of providing proofs for protection of the rights and legitimate interests of the shipowner adopts the statement of the ship master for the incident taking place during swimming or the parking of the vessel which can be the basis for presentation to the shipowner of property requirements.

第 85 条　海事报告的声明

公证员接受船长对船舶在航行或停泊期间发生的事故所作的声明，这可作为船主主张财产权利的基础，是保护船主权利和合法权益的证据。

The statement for the ship's protest shall contain the description of circumstances of incidents and the measures taken by the captain for ensuring safety of the property entrusted to it.

海事报告声明应包含对事故发生情况的描述，以及船长为确保托付于他 / 她的财产的安全所采取的措施。

Confirmation of the circumstances stated in the application for the ship's protest the ship master along with the statement or in time no later than 7 days from the moment of calling port or from the moment of incident if it took place in port, shall provide to the notary on review the logbook and the statement certified by the captain from the logbook.

船长应在不迟于停靠港之日起 7 日内，或自事故发生之日起 7 日内（若事故发生在港口），向公证员提供航海日志及由船长对航海日志核实的声明，以确认海事报告声明书中所述的情况。

Article 86. Terms of the statement for the ship's protest

The application for the ship's protest is submitted within 24 hours from the moment of receipt of the vessel to port. If the incident causing the necessity of the statement of the ship's protest happened in port, the protest shall be declared within 24 hours from the moment of incident.

第 86 条　海事报告条款

该船的海事报告应在船舶靠港后 24 小时内提交。若港口发生纠纷需要提交海事报告的，则应在事发后 24 小时内提交。

If it appears impossible to declare protest at the scheduled time, the reasons of it shall be specified in the statement for the ship's protest.

如果因不可抗力导致在预定的时间内不能提交海事报告，那么应在海事报告中说明理由。

Article 87. Creation of the act of the ship's protest

The notary based on the statement of the captain, data

第 87 条　出具海事报告公证书

公证员根据船长的陈述、航海日志的数据和船长

of the logbook, and also poll of the captain and, whenever possible, at least two witnesses from among command structure and two witnesses from crew draws up the statement of the ship's protest and assures him the signature and official stamp. The copy of the act of the ship's protest is issued to the captain or the authorized person.

的民意调查起草海事报告公证书，在可能的情况下，应由不少于两名船舶指挥员和两名船员见证，并保证其签字和官方印章的真实性。海事报告公证书的副本应出具给船长或经授权的人。

Chapter 17. Application of regulations of foreign law. International treaties

第 17 章　适用域外法律、国际条约

Article 88. Application by the notary of regulations of foreign law

The notary according to the legislation of the Republic of Uzbekistan, international treaties applies regulations of foreign law.

The notary accepts the documents constituted according to requirements of international treaties and also makes certifying texts in shape, stipulated by the legislation other states if it does not contradict international treaties of the Republic of Uzbekistan.

第 88 条　公证中域外法律的适用

公证员根据乌兹别克斯坦共和国法律以及国际条约的规定，适用域外法律。

公证员应当依据国际条约的要求编制文件，并在不与乌兹别克斯坦共和国订立或参加的国际条约相抵触的情况下，按照其他国家法律规定的形式出具公证书。

Article 89. Protection of heritable property and issue of the certificate on the right to inheritance

The actions connected with protection of the property which is in the territory of the Republic of Uzbekistan which remained after the death of the foreign citizen, or the property which is due to the foreign citizen after the death of the citizen of the Republic of Uzbekistan and also with issue of the certificate on the right to inheritance concerning such property are performed according to the legislation of the Republic of Uzbekistan.

第 89 条　遗产保护和出具继承权公证书

外国公民死亡后留在乌兹别克斯坦境内的财产、乌兹别克斯坦共和国公民死亡后留给他国公民的财产的保护；以及继承权的转让和与该财产有关的继承权的转让，应按照乌兹别克斯坦共和国法律进行。

Article 90. The powers of attorney intended for action abroad

The power of attorney certified by the notary intended for action making abroad which is not containing instructions about the term of its action is valid before its cancellation person, issued the power of attorney.

第 90 条　拟在国外诉讼的授权委托

拟在国外诉讼的授权委托需经公证员公证并出具授权委托公证书，该委托书未载明授权行为期限的，在被注销前有效。

Article 91. Acceptance by the notary of the documents constituted abroad

The documents constituted abroad with participation of officials of competent authorities of other states and from them outgoing are accepted by the notary on condition of their legalization by body of the Ministry of Foreign Affairs of the Republic of Uzbekistan.

Without legalization such documents are accepted by the notary when it is stipulated by the legislation also international treaties of the Republic of Uzbekistan.

第 91 条　公证员对境外文书的认可

境外其他国家主管机构的官员和其他人员参与起草或由这些机构出具的文件，应由乌兹别克斯坦共和国外交部认可的公证员认可。

只有符合乌兹别克斯坦共和国法律和国际条约规范，公证员才可以接受未经认定的文件。

Article 92. Relations of the notary with judicial authorities of other states

The procedure for relations of the notary with judicial authorities of other states is determined by the legislation and international treaties of the Republic of Uzbekistan.

Article 93. International treaty

If the international treaty of the Republic of Uzbekistan determines other rules about notarial actions, than those which are provided by legal acts of the Republic of Uzbekistan, when making notarial actions rules of the international treaty are applied.

If the international treaty of the Republic of Uzbekistan refers to competence of the notary making of notarial action, not stipulated by the legislation the Republic of Uzbekistan, the notary makes this notarial action according to the procedure, established by the Ministry of Justice of the Republic of Uzbekistan.

President of the Republic of Uzbekistan
Islam Karimov

第 92 条　公证员与其他国家司法机关的关系

公证员与其他国家司法当局的关系由乌兹别克斯坦共和国的法律和所加入的国际条约确定。

第 93 条　国际条约

如果乌兹别克斯坦共和国签署的国际条约规定的公证活动规则不同于乌兹别克斯坦共和国公证法，那么开展公证活动时应当适用国际条约的规则。

如果乌兹别克斯坦共和国签署的国际条约将乌兹别克斯坦共和国法律未规定的公证活动纳入公证员的职权范围，那么公证员应按照乌兹别克斯坦共和国司法部规定的程序开展公证活动。

乌兹别克斯坦共和国总统
伊斯兰 · 卡里莫夫 签署

越南

公证法

LUẬT
CÔNG CHỨNG
Căn cứ Hiến pháp nước Cộng hòa xã hội chủ nghĩa Việt Nam;
Quốc hội ban hành Luật công chứng.

公证法

根据越南社会主义共和国宪法

国会颁布公证法

Chương I
NHỮNG QUY ĐỊNH CHUNG

Điều 1. Phạm vi điều chỉnh

Luật này quy định về công chứng viên, tổ chức hành nghề công chứng, việc hành nghề công chứng, thủ tục công chứng và quản lý nhà nước về công chứng.

Điều 2. Giải thích từ ngữ

Trong Luật này, các từ ngữ dưới đây được hiểu như sau:

1. Công chứng là việc công chứng viên của một tổ chức hành nghề công chứng chứng nhận tính xác thực, hợp pháp của hợp đồng, giao dịch dân sự khác bằng văn bản (sau đây gọi là hợp đồng, giao dịch), tính chính xác, hợp pháp, không trái đạo đức xã hội của bản dịch giấy tờ, văn bản từ tiếng Việt sang tiếng nước ngoài hoặc từ tiếng nước ngoài sang tiếng Việt (sau đây gọi là bản dịch) mà theo quy định của pháp luật phải công chứng hoặc cá nhân, tổ chức tự nguyện yêu cầu công chứng.

2. Công chứng viên là người có đủ tiêu chuẩn theo quy định của Luật này, được Bộ trưởng Bộ Tư pháp bổ nhiệm để hành nghề công chứng.

3. Người yêu cầu công chứng là cá nhân, tổ chức Việt Nam hoặc cá nhân, tổ chức nước ngoài có yêu cầu công chứng hợp đồng, giao dịch, bản dịch theo quy định của Luật này.

第一章　总规

第一条　调整范围

本法规定公证员、公证机构、公证行业工作、公证程序和国家公证管理。

第二条　术语解释

在本法中，各个术语作如下理解：

1. 公证是公证机构的公证员根据法律的规定，对书面形式的合同、其他民事交易（以下称为合同、交易）的真实性、合法性，对从越南语译成他国语言或从他国语言译成越南语的证件、文本译本（以下称为译本）的准确性、合法性和不违反公序良俗进行公证认证或应个人、组织自愿要求进行公证认证的行为。

2. 公证员是依本法规定，符合标准，由司法部部长任命从事公证行业的人。

3. 公证申请人是根据本法规定提供合同、交易、译本进行公证的越南籍组织、个人或外国组织、个人。

4. Văn bản công chứng là hợp đồng, giao dịch, bản dịch đã được công chứng viên chứng nhận theo quy định của Luật này.

5. Tổ chức hành nghề công chứng bao gồm Phòng công chứng và Văn phòng công chứng được tổ chức và hoạt động theo quy định của Luật này và các văn bản quy phạm pháp luật khác có liên quan.

Điều 3. Chức năng xã hội của công chứng viên

Công chứng viên cung cấp dịch vụ công do Nhà nước ủy nhiệm thực hiện nhằm bảo đảm an toàn pháp lý cho các bên tham gia hợp đồng, giao dịch; phòng ngừa tranh chấp; góp phần bảo vệ quyền, lợi ích hợp pháp của cá nhân, tổ chức; ổn định và phát triển kinh tế - xã hội.

Điều 4. Nguyên tắc hành nghề công chứng

1. Tuân thủ Hiến pháp và pháp luật.
2. Khách quan, trung thực.
3. Tuân theo quy tắc đạo đức hành nghề công chứng.
4. Chịu trách nhiệm trước pháp luật và người yêu cầu công chứng về văn bản công chứng.

Điều 5. Giá trị pháp lý của văn bản công chứng

1. Văn bản công chứng có hiệu lực kể từ ngày được công chứng viên ký và đóng dấu của tổ chức hành nghề công chứng.

2. Hợp đồng, giao dịch được công chứng có hiệu lực thi hành đối với các bên liên quan; trong trường hợp bên có nghĩa vụ không thực hiện nghĩa vụ của mình thì bên kia có quyền yêu cầu Tòa án giải quyết theo quy định của pháp luật, trừ trường hợp các bên tham gia hợp đồng, giao dịch có thỏa thuận khác.

3. Hợp đồng, giao dịch được công chứng có giá trị chứng cứ; những tình tiết, sự kiện trong hợp đồng, giao dịch được công chứng không phải chứng minh, trừ trường hợp bị Tòa án tuyên bố là vô hiệu.

4. Bản dịch được công chứng có giá trị sử dụng như giấy tờ, văn bản được dịch.

Điều 6. Tiếng nói và chữ viết dùng trong công chứng

Tiếng nói và chữ viết dùng trong công chứng là tiếng Việt.

Điều 7. Các hành vi bị nghiêm cấm

1. Nghiêm cấm công chứng viên, tổ chức hành nghề công chứng thực hiện các hành vi sau đây:

a) Tiết lộ thông tin về nội dung công chứng, trừ trường hợp được người yêu cầu công chứng đồng ý bằng văn bản hoặc pháp luật có quy định khác; sử dụng thông

4. 公证书是公证员根据本法规定对合同、交易、译本进行了公证的证明。

5. 公证机构包括根据本法和各相关法律规范文本规定，允许其组织和执业的公证办公室和公证机构。

第三条　公证员的社会职责

公证员保障给合同、交易各方安全，在合理合法的基础上，提供国家委任进行的服务，防止纠纷；参与保护个人、组织合法权利、利益，稳定和发展社会经济。

第四条　公证行业的原则

1. 遵守宪法和法律。
2. 客观、忠诚。
3. 遵守公证行业道德原则。
4. 公证书应对法律和公证申请人负责。

第五条　公证书的法律效力

1. 公证书自公证员签字和公证机构盖章之日起生效。

2. 经公证的合同、交易对各方有强制执行力；如有义务一方不履行其义务，则另一方有权根据法律规定请求法院执行，合同、交易各方另有约定的除外。

3. 经公证的合同、交易具有证明效力；合同、交易中的经公证情节、事件可作为证据，但被法院宣布无效的除外。

4. 证件、文本译本经公证有使用价值。

第六条　用于公证的口头语言和书面文字

用于公证的口头语言和书面文字为越南语。

第七条　严禁的行为

1. 严禁公证员、公证机构实施以下行为：

（a）透露公证内容信息，得到公证申请人书面同意或法律另有规定的除外；为了侵害个人、组织的合法权利、利益而使用公证内容的信息。

tin về nội dung công chứng để xâm hại quyền, lợi ích hợp pháp của cá nhân, tổ chức;

b) Thực hiện công chứng trong trường hợp mục đích và nội dung của hợp đồng, giao dịch, nội dung bản dịch vi phạm pháp luật, trái đạo đức xã hội; xúi giục, tạo điều kiện cho người tham gia hợp đồng, giao dịch thực hiện giao dịch giả tạo hoặc hành vi gian dối khác;

(b) 对目的或内容违法、违反社会道德的合同、交易、译本进行公证；促使、促成参与合同、交易者捏造交易事实或为其他虚假行为而进行公证。

c) Công chứng hợp đồng, giao dịch, bản dịch có liên quan đến tài sản, lợi ích của bản thân mình hoặc của những người thân thích là vợ hoặc chồng; cha mẹ đẻ, cha mẹ nuôi; cha mẹ đẻ, cha mẹ nuôi của vợ hoặc chồng; con đẻ, con nuôi, con dâu, con rể; ông, bà; anh chị em ruột, anh chị em ruột của vợ hoặc chồng; cháu là con của con đẻ, con nuôi;

(c) 公证申请人是公证员本人或公证员的下列近亲属：妻子或丈夫；生父母、养父母；妻子或丈夫的生父母、养父母；生子、养子；女婿、儿媳；叔伯、姑母；亲生兄弟姐妹、妻子或丈夫的亲生兄弟姐妹；生子、养子的子女。

d) Từ chối yêu cầu công chứng mà không có lý do chính đáng; sách nhiễu, gây khó khăn cho người yêu cầu công chứng;

(d) 无正当理由拒绝公证要求、向公证申请人索贿或人为制造障碍。

e) Nhận, đòi hỏi tiền hoặc lợi ích khác từ người yêu cầu công chứng ngoài phí công chứng, thù lao công chứng và chi phí khác đã được xác định, thỏa thuận; nhận, đòi hỏi tiền hoặc lợi ích khác từ người thứ ba để thực hiện hoặc không thực hiện việc công chứng gây thiệt hại cho người yêu cầu công chứng và cá nhân, tổ chức có liên quan;

(e) 在已确定、协商好的公证费、公证酬劳和其他费用之外，从公证申请人处接受、索取金钱或其他利益；以办理或不办理公证为手段，从第三方处接受、索取金钱或其他利益，给公证申请人或相关个人、组织造成损害的。

f) Ép buộc người khác sử dụng dịch vụ của mình; cấu kết, thông đồng với người yêu cầu công chứng và những người có liên quan làm sai lệch nội dung của văn bản công chứng, hồ sơ công chứng;

(f) 强迫他人使用其服务；勾结、伙同公证申请人和其他对公证文本、公证文档内容作假的相关人员。

g) Gây áp lực, đe dọa hoặc thực hiện hành vi vi phạm pháp luật, trái đạo đức xã hội để giành lợi thế cho mình hoặc cho tổ chức mình trong việc hành nghề công chứng;

(g) 为本人或本人所在执业机构之利益，故意施压、恐吓或进行违法、违反社会道德的行为。

h) Quảng cáo trên các phương tiện thông tin đại chúng về công chứng viên và tổ chức mình;

(h) 利用各种通讯工具为公证员本人或本人所在执业机构进行广告。

i) Tổ chức hành nghề công chứng mở chi nhánh, văn phòng đại diện, cơ sở, địa điểm giao dịch khác ngoài trụ sở của tổ chức hành nghề công chứng; thực hiện các hoạt động sản xuất, kinh doanh, dịch vụ ngoài phạm vi hoạt động đã đăng ký;

(i) 公证机构在工作机构办事处以外地点设立分支、办公室代表处、办事处、其他交易地点；在已登记的执业范围外，进行生产、经营、服务活动。

j) Công chứng viên đồng thời hành nghề tại hai tổ chức hành nghề công chứng trở lên hoặc kiêm nhiệm công việc thường xuyên khác;

(j) 公证员同时在两个以上的公证机构执业，或常常兼任别的工作。

k) Công chứng viên tham gia quản lý doanh nghiệp ngoài tổ chức hành nghề công chứng; thực hiện hoạt động môi giới, đại lý; tham gia chia lợi nhuận trong hợp đồng, giao dịch mà mình nhận công chứng;

(k) 公证员在公证机构之外参与经营管理；进行中介、代理活动；参与经本人公证的合同、交易的利润分配。

l) Vi phạm pháp luật, vi phạm quy tắc đạo đức hành nghề công chứng.

(l) 违反法律、违反公证行业的职业道德。

2. Nghiêm cấm cá nhân, tổ chức thực hiện các hành

2. 严禁个人、组织从事以下行为：

vi sau đây:

a) Giả mạo người yêu cầu công chứng;

b) Người yêu cầu công chứng cung cấp thông tin, tài liệu sai sự thật; sử dụng giấy tờ, văn bản giả mạo hoặc bị tẩy xóa, sửa chữa trái pháp luật để yêu cầu công chứng;

c) Người làm chứng, người phiên dịch có hành vi gian dối, không trung thực;

d) Cản trở hoạt động công chứng.

Chương II
CÔNG CHỨNG VIÊN

Điều 8. Tiêu chuẩn công chứng viên

Công dân Việt Nam thường trú tại Việt Nam, tuân thủ Hiến pháp và pháp luật, có phẩm chất đạo đức tốt và có đủ các tiêu chuẩn sau đây thì được xem xét, bổ nhiệm công chứng viên:

1. Có bằng cử nhân luật;

2. Có thời gian công tác pháp luật từ 05 năm trở lên tại các cơ quan, tổ chức sau khi đã có bằng cử nhân luật;

3. Tốt nghiệp khóa đào tạo nghề công chứng quy định tại Điều 9 của Luật này hoặc hoàn thành khóa bồi dưỡng nghề công chứng quy định tại khoản 2 Điều 10 của Luật này;

4. Đạt yêu cầu kiểm tra kết quả tập sự hành nghề công chứng;

5. Bảo đảm sức khỏe để hành nghề công chứng.

Điều 9. Đào tạo nghề công chứng

1. Người có bằng cử nhân luật được tham dự khóa đào tạo nghề công chứng tại cơ sở đào tạo nghề công chứng.

2. Thời gian đào tạo nghề công chứng là 12 tháng.

Người hoàn thành chương trình đào tạo nghề công chứng được cơ sở đào tạo nghề công chứng cấp giấy chứng nhận tốt nghiệp khóa đào tạo nghề công chứng.

3. Bộ trưởng Bộ Tư pháp quy định chi tiết về cơ sở đào tạo nghề công chứng, chương trình khung đào tạo nghề công chứng và việc công nhận tương đương đối với những người được đào tạo nghề công chứng ở nước ngoài.

Điều 10. Miễn đào tạo nghề công chứng

1. Những người sau đây được miễn đào tạo nghề công chứng:

a) Người đã có thời gian làm thẩm phán, kiểm sát viên, điều tra viên từ 05 năm trở lên;

b) Luật sư đã hành nghề từ 05 năm trở lên;

c) Giáo sư, phó giáo sư chuyên ngành luật, tiến sĩ

（a）假冒公证申请人。

（b）公证申请人提供错误的资料、信息；为进行公证，使用假冒的文本、证件或对文本证件违法进行销毁、篡改。

（c）证人、翻译者有失信、欺骗行为。

（d）阻碍公证执业。

第二章　公证员

第八条　公证员标准

常住越南的越南公民，遵守宪法和法律，品行良好并满足下列条件的可认定、任命为公证员：

1. 有法学本科学历；

2. 在机关、组织工作时间 5 年以上，并获得法学学士学位；

3. 毕业于本法第 9 条规定的公证业务培训班或完成本法第 10 条第 2 款规定的公证业务进修班；

4. 达到公证业实习结业结果要求的；

5. 身体健康，胜任公证职业。

第九条　公证业务培训

1. 有法学学士学位的人可以参加由公证业务培训办事处举办的公证业务培训班。

2. 公证业务培训班培训时间为 12 个月。

完成公证业务培训课程者可获得公证培训机构颁发的公证业务培训结业证书。

3. 有关公证业务培训机构、公证业务培训课程模式和在国外接受公证培训者的细节由司法部部长规定。

第十条　免公证业务培训

1. 以下人员得以免除公证业务培训：

（a）从事审判、检察、侦查工作 5 年以上者；

（b）已经执业 5 年以上的律师；

（c）法学专业的教授、副教授、法学博士；

luật;

d) Người đã là thẩm tra viên cao cấp ngành tòa án, kiểm tra viên cao cấp ngành kiểm sát; chuyên viên cao cấp, nghiên cứu viên cao cấp, giảng viên cao cấp trong lĩnh vực pháp luật.

2. Người được miễn đào tạo nghề công chứng quy định tại khoản 1 Điều này phải tham gia khóa bồi dưỡng kỹ năng hành nghề công chứng và quy tắc đạo đức hành nghề công chứng tại cơ sở đào tạo nghề công chứng trước khi đề nghị bổ nhiệm công chứng viên. Thời gian bồi dưỡng nghề công chứng là 03 tháng.

Người hoàn thành khóa bồi dưỡng được cấp giấy chứng nhận hoàn thành khóa bồi dưỡng nghề công chứng.

3. Bộ trưởng Bộ Tư pháp quy định chi tiết về khóa bồi dưỡng nghề công chứng quy định tại khoản 2 Điều này.

Điều 11. Tập sự hành nghề công chứng

1. Người có giấy chứng nhận tốt nghiệp khóa đào tạo nghề công chứng hoặc giấy chứng nhận bồi dưỡng nghề công chứng phải tập sự hành nghề tại một tổ chức hành nghề công chứng. Người tập sự có thể tự liên hệ với một tổ chức hành nghề công chứng đủ điều kiện nhận tập sự về việc tập sự tại tổ chức đó; trường hợp không tự liên hệ được thì đề nghị Sở Tư pháp ở địa phương nơi người đó muốn tập sự bố trí tập sự tại một tổ chức hành nghề công chứng đủ điều kiện nhận tập sự.

Người tập sự phải đăng ký tập sự tại Sở Tư pháp ở địa phương nơi có tổ chức hành nghề công chứng nhận tập sự.

Thời gian tập sự hành nghề công chứng là 12 tháng đối với người có giấy chứng nhận tốt nghiệp khóa đào tạo nghề công chứng và 06 tháng đối với người có giấy chứng nhận bồi dưỡng nghề công chứng. Thời gian tập sự hành nghề công chứng được tính từ ngày đăng ký tập sự.

2. Tổ chức hành nghề công chứng nhận tập sự phải có công chứng viên đáp ứng điều kiện hướng dẫn tập sự theo quy định tại khoản 3 Điều này và có cơ sở vật chất bảo đảm cho việc tập sự.

3. Tổ chức hành nghề công chứng phân công công chứng viên hướng dẫn người tập sự.

Công chứng viên hướng dẫn tập sự phải có ít nhất 02 năm kinh nghiệm hành nghề công chứng. Công chứng viên bị xử lý kỷ luật, xử phạt vi phạm hành chính trong hoạt động hành nghề công chứng thì sau 12 tháng kể từ ngày chấp hành xong quyết định kỷ luật, quyết định xử phạt vi phạm hành chính mới được hướng dẫn tập sự

（d）法院高级审判员、检察院高级检察员；法律领域的高级专员、高级研究员和高级讲师。

2. 提请任命公证员之前，本条第 1 款规定的可免除公证业务培训者，应参加由公证业务培训机构举办的公证业务技能进修班和道德规则班，参加培训的时间为 3 个月。

完成进修班的人可获得公证业务进修班的结业证书。

3. 本条第 2 款关于公证业务进修班的细节由司法部部长规定。

第十一条　公证业务实习

1. 取得公证业务培训班结业证书或公证业务进修班结业证书者，需在公证机构进行实习。实习者可自行联系有资质接受实习生的公证机构进行实习；如无法自行联系的，司法机构可向实习者意图实习的、有资质接受实习生的当地公证机构推荐实习。

实习者应当在接受实习的公证机构所在地的司法机关进行登记。

对获得公证业务培训结业证书者，公证实习时间为 12 个月，对获得公证业务进修班结业证书者，实习时间为 6 个月，公证业务实习时间从登记实习之日起算。

2. 接受实习生的公证机构应当根据本条第 3 款的规定配备公证员进行指导，并配备资金用作实习保障。

3. 公证机构应配备公证员指导实习生。

指导实习生的公证员至少要有 2 年以上执业经验。在从事公证职业中，公证员因技术错误被处罚，违反行政法规被处分，从处理决定执行完毕之日其 12 个月后才能指导公证业实习生。1 名公证员不得同时指导 2 名以上实习生。

hành nghề công chứng. Tại cùng một thời điểm, một công chứng viên không được hướng dẫn nhiều hơn hai người tập sự.

Công chứng viên hướng dẫn tập sự phải hướng dẫn và chịu trách nhiệm về các công việc do người tập sự thực hiện quy định tại khoản 4 Điều này.

4. Người tập sự hành nghề công chứng được hướng dẫn các kỹ năng hành nghề và thực hiện các công việc liên quan đến công chứng do công chứng viên hướng dẫn phân công và chịu trách nhiệm trước công chứng viên hướng dẫn về những công việc đó. Người tập sự không được ký văn bản công chứng.

5. Khi hết thời gian tập sự, người tập sự hành nghề công chứng phải có báo cáo bằng văn bản về kết quả tập sự có nhận xét của công chứng viên hướng dẫn và xác nhận của tổ chức hành nghề công chứng nhận tập sự gửi đến Sở Tư pháp nơi mình đã đăng ký tập sự; được đăng ký tham dự kiểm tra kết quả tập sự hành nghề công chứng. Người đạt yêu cầu kiểm tra kết quả tập sự hành nghề công chứng được cấp giấy chứng nhận kết quả kiểm tra tập sự hành nghề công chứng.

6. Bộ trưởng Bộ Tư pháp quy định chi tiết việc tập sự và kiểm tra kết quả tập sự hành nghề công chứng.

Điều 12. Bổ nhiệm công chứng viên

1. Người đáp ứng đủ tiêu chuẩn quy định tại Điều 8 của Luật này có quyền đề nghị Bộ trưởng Bộ Tư pháp bổ nhiệm công chứng viên. Hồ sơ đề nghị bổ nhiệm công chứng viên được gửi đến Sở Tư pháp nơi người đề nghị bổ nhiệm công chứng viên đã đăng ký tập sự hành nghề công chứng.

2. Hồ sơ đề nghị bổ nhiệm công chứng viên gồm:

a) Đơn đề nghị bổ nhiệm công chứng viên theo mẫu do Bộ trưởng Bộ Tư pháp quy định;

b) Phiếu lý lịch tư pháp;

c) Bản sao bằng cử nhân luật hoặc thạc sĩ, tiến sĩ luật;

d) Giấy tờ chứng minh về thời gian công tác pháp luật;

e) Bản sao giấy chứng nhận tốt nghiệp khóa đào tạo nghề công chứng. Đối với người được miễn đào tạo nghề công chứng thì phải có bản sao giấy chứng nhận hoàn thành khóa bồi dưỡng nghề công chứng và giấy tờ chứng minh là người được miễn đào tạo nghề công chứng quy định tại khoản 1 Điều 10 của Luật này;

f) Bản sao giấy chứng nhận kết quả kiểm tra tập sự hành nghề công chứng;

g) Giấy chứng nhận sức khỏe do cơ quan y tế có

实习生根据本条第 4 款处理各种工作时，指导实习生的公证员要对其进行指导并负责。

4. 未经公证员授权，实习生不得从事公证活动和进行各种与公证员分工和负责任有关的工作。实习生不得在公证书上签字。

5. 实习结束时，公证业务实习生需作出实习结果书面报告，由指导实习的公证员作出评价，并经接受实习的公证机构确认后递交给登记实习的司法机构后，即可登记参加公证业务实习结果检查。公证业务实习结果达到要求者可获得公证业实习结果检查合格证书。

6. 实习工作和公证业务实习结果检查的细节由司法部长规定。

第十二条　任命公证员

1. 符合本法第 8 条规定标准者有权向司法部部长申请推荐任命公证员。推荐任命公证员的材料应递交给登记实习的司法机构，由其任命。

2. 申请推荐任命公证员的材料包括：

（a）司法部部长规定的推荐任命公证员表样本；

（b）法律从业简历表；

（c）学士、硕士或博士毕业证复印件；

（d）法律从业时间的证明材料；

（e）公证业务培训班结业证复印件。对于免除公证业务培训的要有公证业务进修班结业证复印件和符合本法第 10 条第 1 款规定免除公证业务培训条件的证明材料；

（f）公证业务实习检查结果证书复印件；

（g）由有权限的卫生机构提供的健康证明。

thẩm quyền cấp.

3. Trong thời hạn 10 ngày làm việc kể từ ngày nhận đủ hồ sơ đề nghị bổ nhiệm công chứng viên quy định tại khoản 2 Điều này, Sở Tư pháp có văn bản đề nghị Bộ trưởng Bộ Tư pháp bổ nhiệm công chứng viên kèm theo hồ sơ đề nghị bổ nhiệm; trường hợp từ chối đề nghị thì phải thông báo bằng văn bản, trong đó nêu rõ lý do cho người nộp hồ sơ.

4. Trong thời hạn 30 ngày kể từ ngày nhận được văn bản và hồ sơ đề nghị bổ nhiệm công chứng viên của Sở Tư pháp, Bộ trưởng Bộ Tư pháp xem xét, quyết định bổ nhiệm công chứng viên; trường hợp từ chối bổ nhiệm phải thông báo bằng văn bản, trong đó nêu rõ lý do, gửi cho Sở Tư pháp và người đề nghị bổ nhiệm.

Điều 13. Những trường hợp không được bổ nhiệm công chứng viên

1. Người đang bị truy cứu trách nhiệm hình sự, đã bị kết tội bằng bản án đã có hiệu lực pháp luật của Tòa án về tội phạm do vô ý mà chưa được xóa án tích hoặc về tội phạm do cố ý.

2. Người đang bị áp dụng biện pháp xử lý hành chính theo quy định của pháp luật về xử lý vi phạm hành chính.

3. Người bị mất hoặc bị hạn chế năng lực hành vi dân sự.

4. Cán bộ bị kỷ luật bằng hình thức bãi nhiệm, công chức, viên chức bị kỷ luật bằng hình thức buộc thôi việc hoặc sỹ quan, quân nhân chuyên nghiệp, công nhân, viên chức trong cơ quan, đơn vị thuộc Quân đội nhân dân, sỹ quan, hạ sỹ quan, công nhân, viên chức trong đơn vị thuộc Công an nhân dân bị kỷ luật bằng hình thức tước danh hiệu quân nhân, danh hiệu Công an nhân dân hoặc đưa ra khỏi ngành.

5. Người bị thu hồi chứng chỉ hành nghề luật sư do bị xử lý kỷ luật bằng hình thức xóa tên khỏi danh sách của Đoàn luật sư, người bị tước quyền sử dụng chứng chỉ hành nghề luật sư mà chưa hết thời hạn 03 năm kể từ ngày quyết định thu hồi chứng chỉ hành nghề luật sư có hiệu lực hoặc kể từ ngày chấp hành xong quyết định tước quyền sử dụng chứng chỉ hành nghề luật sư.

Điều 14. Tạm đình chỉ hành nghề công chứng

1. Sở Tư pháp nơi công chứng viên đăng ký hành nghề quyết định tạm đình chỉ hành nghề của công chứng viên trong các trường hợp sau đây:

a) Công chứng viên đang bị truy cứu trách nhiệm hình sự;

b) Công chứng viên đang bị áp dụng biện pháp xử lý

3. 自本法第 2 款规定的推荐任命公证员材料提交齐全之日起 10 个工作日内，司法部长同意推荐的，应向司法机关递送推荐任命公证员的文本，并附上申请推荐任命公证员的材料；拒绝推荐的，应书面说明理由，通知申请人。

4. 从收到司法机构任命公证员的推荐档案和文本之日起 30 日内，司法机关部长检查、决定任命公证员；如果拒绝任命应作书面通报说明原因，并递给司法机关和推荐任命的人。

第十三条　不能任命公证员的情形

1. 正在被追究刑事责任的，非故意犯罪但已被法院作出具有法律效力的判决书还未销案的，故意犯罪的。

2. 根据法律的规定，因行政违法行为正在接受行政处罚的。

3. 失踪或被限制民事行为能力的人。

4. 以罢免的形式被处罚的干部，以辞退工作的形式被处罚的公职人员、普通职员或以剥夺军人名誉、公安名誉的形式被处罚的隶属于人民军队的士官、专职军人、工人、机关职员和隶属于人民公安单位中的士官、下级士官、工人、职员或被开除行业的人。

5. 被指证贿赂并从律师资格名册中除名的形式处罚的，被律师业剥夺使用指证权的，自指证贿赂的有效决定或律师业剥夺使用律师权之日起未满 3 年的。

第十四条　暂停公证执业

1. 遇下列情形，公证员执业登记地的司法机构暂停其公证员执业：

（a）公证员正在被追究刑事责任；

（b）公证员正在接受行政处罚。

hành chính.

2. Thời gian tạm đình chỉ hành nghề công chứng tối đa là 12 tháng.

3. Sở Tư pháp quyết định hủy bỏ quyết định tạm đình chỉ hành nghề công chứng trước thời hạn đối với công chứng viên trong các trường hợp sau đây:

a) Có quyết định đình chỉ điều tra, đình chỉ vụ án hoặc bản án đã có hiệu lực của Tòa án tuyên không có tội;

b) Không còn bị áp dụng biện pháp xử lý hành chính theo quy định của pháp luật về xử lý vi phạm hành chính.

4. Quyết định tạm đình chỉ và quyết định hủy bỏ quyết định tạm đình chỉ hành nghề công chứng phải được gửi cho công chứng viên, tổ chức hành nghề công chứng nơi công chứng viên làm việc, Ủy ban nhân dân tỉnh, thành phố trực thuộc trung ương (sau đây gọi là Ủy ban nhân dân cấp tỉnh) và Bộ Tư pháp.

Điều 15. Miễn nhiệm công chứng viên

1. Công chứng viên được miễn nhiệm theo nguyện vọng của cá nhân hoặc chuyển làm công việc khác.

Công chứng viên nộp đơn đề nghị miễn nhiệm tại Sở Tư pháp ở nơi mình đăng ký hành nghề. Trong thời hạn 15 ngày kể từ ngày nhận được đơn đề nghị miễn nhiệm của công chứng viên, Sở Tư pháp có văn bản đề nghị kèm theo đơn đề nghị miễn nhiệm của công chứng viên gửi Bộ trưởng Bộ Tư pháp.

2. Công chứng viên bị miễn nhiệm trong các trường hợp sau đây:

a) Không còn đủ tiêu chuẩn công chứng viên theo quy định tại Điều 8 của Luật này;

b) Bị mất hoặc bị hạn chế năng lực hành vi dân sự;

c) Kiêm nhiệm công việc thường xuyên khác;

d) Không hành nghề công chứng trong thời hạn 02 năm kể từ ngày được bổ nhiệm công chứng viên hoặc không hành nghề công chứng liên tục từ 12 tháng trở lên;

e) Hết thời hạn tạm đình chỉ hành nghề công chứng quy định tại khoản 2 Điều 14 của Luật này mà lý do tạm đình chỉ hành nghề công chứng vẫn còn;

f) Đã bị xử phạt vi phạm hành chính đến lần thứ hai trong hoạt động hành nghề công chứng mà còn tiếp tục vi phạm; bị xử lý kỷ luật bằng hình thức từ cảnh cáo trở lên đến lần thứ hai mà còn tiếp tục vi phạm hoặc bị kỷ luật buộc thôi việc;

g) Bị kết tội bằng bản án đã có hiệu lực pháp luật của Tòa án;

h) Thuộc các trường hợp không được bổ nhiệm công chứng viên quy định tại Điều 13 của Luật này tại thời điểm

2. 暂停公证执业时间最长为 12 个月。

3. 遇下列情形，司法机构撤销其暂停公证员公证执业的决定：

（a）法院判决宣告其无罪、暂停调查或暂停案件审理；

（b）根据法律的规定，行政违法行为不再采用行政处理措施。

4. 暂停公证执业决定和撤销暂停公证执业决定都应送达给公证员、公证员执业的公证机构、省人民委员会、直辖市（以下称为省级人民委员会）和司法部。

第十五条　免任公证员

1. 根据个人意愿或转行，公证员可以免任。

公证员提交免任申请给自己登记执业的司法机构，自收到公证员提交免任申请之日起 15 日内，司法机构有提议文本，附加公证员免任提议申请单呈交给司法部部长。

2. 公证员在下列情况中被免职：

（a）根据本法第 8 条的规定，达不到公证员标准的；

（b）失踪或民事行为能力被限制的；

（c）常兼任别的工作的；

（d）从任命公证员之日算起 2 年内没有从事公证行业或没有持续从事公证行业 12 个月以上的；

（e）在本法的第 14 条第 2 款规定暂停公证执业已过期，然而暂停公证执业的事由仍存在的；

（f）在公证执业活动中，违反行政法规已被处罚 2 次还继续违反；已被警告处罚 2 次以上，还继续违反或被开除的；

（g）已有法院作出的具有法律效力的判决书；

（h）在可以任命的时机，属本法第 13 条规定的各种场合不可以免任公证员。

được bổ nhiệm.

3. Sở Tư pháp có trách nhiệm rà soát, kiểm tra việc bảo đảm tiêu chuẩn hành nghề của công chứng viên tại địa phương mình.

Khi có căn cứ cho rằng công chứng viên thuộc trường hợp bị miễn nhiệm quy định tại khoản 2 Điều này, Sở Tư pháp có văn bản đề nghị miễn nhiệm công chứng viên kèm theo các tài liệu liên quan làm căn cứ cho việc đề nghị miễn nhiệm gửi Bộ trưởng Bộ Tư pháp.

4. Trong thời hạn 15 ngày kể từ ngày nhận được hồ sơ đề nghị miễn nhiệm công chứng viên, Bộ trưởng Bộ Tư pháp xem xét, quyết định việc miễn nhiệm công chứng viên.

Điều 16. Bổ nhiệm lại công chứng viên

1. Người được miễn nhiệm công chứng viên theo quy định tại khoản 1 Điều 15 của Luật này được xem xét bổ nhiệm lại công chứng viên khi có đề nghị bổ nhiệm lại.

2. Người bị miễn nhiệm công chứng viên theo quy định tại khoản 2 Điều 15 của Luật này được xem xét bổ nhiệm lại công chứng viên khi đáp ứng đủ tiêu chuẩn công chứng viên quy định tại Điều 8 của Luật này và lý do miễn nhiệm không còn, trừ trường hợp quy định tại khoản 3 Điều này.

3. Người bị miễn nhiệm công chứng viên do bị kết tội bằng bản án đã có hiệu lực pháp luật của Tòa án về tội phạm do cố ý, bị xử phạt vi phạm hành chính đến lần thứ hai trong hoạt động hành nghề công chứng mà còn tiếp tục vi phạm, bị xử lý kỷ luật bằng hình thức từ cảnh cáo trở lên đến lần thứ hai mà còn tiếp tục vi phạm hoặc bị kỷ luật buộc thôi việc thì không được bổ nhiệm lại công chứng viên.

4. Thủ tục bổ nhiệm lại công chứng viên được thực hiện theo quy định tại Điều 12 của Luật này. Hồ sơ đề nghị bổ nhiệm lại công chứng viên gồm:

a) Đơn đề nghị bổ nhiệm lại công chứng viên theo mẫu do Bộ trưởng Bộ Tư pháp quy định;

b) Phiếu lý lịch tư pháp;

c) Giấy chứng nhận sức khỏe do cơ quan y tế có thẩm quyền cấp;

d) Bản sao quyết định miễn nhiệm công chứng viên;

e) Bản sao các giấy tờ chứng minh lý do miễn nhiệm không còn, trừ trường hợp quy định tại khoản 1 Điều này.

Điều 17. Quyền và nghĩa vụ của công chứng viên

1. Công chứng viên có các quyền sau đây:

a) Được pháp luật bảo đảm quyền hành nghề công chứng;

3. 司法机构有义务出面、检查公证员在执业当地的工作是否符合行业标准。

有证据证明，公证员属本条第 2 款规定被免任，司法机构将公证员免任提议文本附加有关免任提议的材料依据递交给司法部部长。

4. 自收到公证员免任材料之日起 15 日内，司法部部长确认并决定免任公证员。

第十六条　公证员再任命

1. 根据本法第 15 条第 1 款的规定，当有再任命推荐，经确认后，公证员可以再任命。

2. 根据本法第 15 条第 2 款规定被免任的公证员，除了该条第 3 款规定的情况外，在本法第 8 条规定公证员达到应用标准和不存在免任理由时可以考虑公证员再任命。

3. 被免任的公证员有故意犯罪由法院的有效判决书宣判的，在公证活动中违反行政法规被处罚达 2 次继续违反的，以警告形式处罚达 2 次以上继续违反或被开除的不可以再任命为公证员。

4. 公证员再任命的程序根据本法第 12 条规定，再任命公证员的提议材料包括：

（a）根据司法部部长规定的公证员再任命推荐表样本；

（b）法律职业简历表；

（c）由具有权限的卫生机构出具的健康证明；

（d）免任公证员决定复印件；

（e）除该条第 1 款规定的情况外，复印各种不再免任理由的证明。

第十七条　公证员的权利和义务

1. 公证员有以下权利：

（a）公证业务权利得到法律保障；

b) Tham gia thành lập Văn phòng công chứng hoặc làm việc theo chế độ hợp đồng cho tổ chức hành nghề công chứng;

c) Được công chứng hợp đồng, giao dịch, bản dịch theo quy định của Luật này;

d) Đề nghị cá nhân, cơ quan, tổ chức có liên quan cung cấp thông tin, tài liệu để thực hiện việc công chứng;

e) Được từ chối công chứng hợp đồng, giao dịch, bản dịch vi phạm pháp luật, trái đạo đức xã hội;

f) Các quyền khác theo quy định của Luật này và các văn bản quy phạm pháp luật khác có liên quan.

2. Công chứng viên có các nghĩa vụ sau đây:

a) Tuân thủ các nguyên tắc hành nghề công chứng;

b) Hành nghề tại một tổ chức hành nghề công chứng;

c) Tôn trọng và bảo vệ quyền, lợi ích hợp pháp của người yêu cầu công chứng;

d) Giải thích cho người yêu cầu công chứng hiểu rõ quyền, nghĩa vụ và lợi ích hợp pháp của họ, ý nghĩa và hậu quả pháp lý của việc công chứng; trường hợp từ chối yêu cầu công chứng thì phải giải thích rõ lý do cho người yêu cầu công chứng;

e) Giữ bí mật về nội dung công chứng, trừ trường hợp được người yêu cầu công chứng đồng ý bằng văn bản hoặc pháp luật có quy định khác;

f) Tham gia bồi dưỡng nghiệp vụ công chứng hàng năm;

g) Chịu trách nhiệm trước pháp luật và trước người yêu cầu công chứng về văn bản công chứng của mình; chịu trách nhiệm trước pháp luật về hoạt động của Văn phòng công chứng mà mình là công chứng viên hợp danh;

h) Tham gia tổ chức xã hội - nghề nghiệp của công chứng viên;

i) Chịu sự quản lý của cơ quan nhà nước có thẩm quyền, của tổ chức hành nghề công chứng mà mình làm công chứng viên và tổ chức xã hội - nghề nghiệp của công chứng viên mà mình là thành viên;

j) Các nghĩa vụ khác theo quy định của Luật này và các văn bản quy phạm pháp luật khác có liên quan.

Chương III
TỔ CHỨC HÀNH NGHỀ CÔNG CHỨNG

Điều 18. Nguyên tắc thành lập tổ chức hành nghề công chứng

1. Việc thành lập tổ chức hành nghề công chứng phải tuân theo quy định của Luật này và phù hợp với Quy hoạch tổng thể phát triển tổ chức hành nghề công chứng

（b）参与公证机构成立或根据公证机构的合同制度执业；

（c）根据本法规定公证合同、交易、译本；

（d）为进行公证，推荐能提供信息、材料的有关个人、单位和组织；

（e）拒绝为违反法律、社会道德合同、交易和译本公证；

（f）根据本法规定的其他权利和其他相关法律规范公证文本。

2. 公证员有以下义务：

（a）遵守公证业务的各种原则。

（b）在一个公证机构执业。

（c）尊重、保护和要求公证员的合法权利和利益。

（d）向公证申请人解释清楚他们的合法权利、义务、利益和公证的法律后果；如果拒绝公证请求应向公证申请人说明理由。

（e）保守公证秘密，公证申请人以书面形式同意或有别的法律规定的情况除外。

（f）参加每年的公证业务进修。

（g）在法律和公证申请人面前，对自己公证的文本负责任；作为一名合格的公证员，在法律面前，要对公证业务的办理负责任。

（h）参加公证业的行业协会。

（i）鉴于公证员、公证行业协会成员的身份，接受有权限的国家机关和公证机构的管理。

（j）根据本法和其他相关法律规定的其他义务。

第三章　公证机构

第十八条　成立公证机构的原则

1. 成立公证机构应当遵守本法规定并符合由政府首脑批准的公证机构总体发展规划。

do Thủ tướng Chính phủ phê duyệt.

2. Phòng công chứng chỉ được thành lập mới tại những địa bàn chưa có điều kiện phát triển được Văn phòng công chứng.

3. Văn phòng công chứng thành lập tại các địa bàn có điều kiện kinh tế - xã hội khó khăn, đặc biệt khó khăn được hưởng chính sách ưu đãi theo quy định của Chính phủ.

Điều 19. Phòng công chứng

1. Phòng công chứng do Ủy ban nhân dân cấp tỉnh quyết định thành lập.

2. Phòng công chứng là đơn vị sự nghiệp công lập thuộc Sở Tư pháp, có trụ sở, con dấu và tài khoản riêng.

Người đại diện theo pháp luật của Phòng công chứng là Trưởng phòng. Trưởng phòng công chứng phải là công chứng viên, do Chủ tịch Ủy ban nhân dân cấp tỉnh bổ nhiệm, miễn nhiệm, cách chức.

3. Tên gọi của Phòng công chứng bao gồm cụm từ "Phòng công chứng" kèm theo số thứ tự thành lập và tên của tỉnh, thành phố trực thuộc trung ương nơi Phòng công chứng được thành lập.

4. Phòng công chứng sử dụng con dấu không có hình quốc huy. Phòng công chứng được khắc và sử dụng con dấu sau khi có quyết định thành lập. Thủ tục, hồ sơ xin khắc dấu, việc quản lý, sử dụng con dấu của Phòng công chứng được thực hiện theo quy định của pháp luật về con dấu.

Điều 20. Thành lập Phòng công chứng

1. Căn cứ vào nhu cầu công chứng tại địa phương, Sở Tư pháp chủ trì phối hợp với Sở Kế hoạch và Đầu tư, Sở Tài chính, Sở Nội vụ xây dựng đề án thành lập Phòng công chứng trình Ủy ban nhân dân cấp tỉnh xem xét, quyết định. Đề án nêu rõ sự cần thiết thành lập Phòng công chứng, dự kiến về tổ chức, tên gọi, nhân sự, địa điểm đặt trụ sở, các điều kiện vật chất và kế hoạch triển khai thực hiện.

2. Trong thời hạn 30 ngày kể từ ngày Ủy ban nhân dân cấp tỉnh ra quyết định thành lập Phòng công chứng, Sở Tư pháp phải đăng báo trung ương hoặc báo địa phương nơi có trụ sở của Phòng công chứng trong ba số liên tiếp về các nội dung sau đây:

a) Tên gọi, địa chỉ trụ sở của Phòng công chứng;

b) Số, ngày, tháng, năm ra quyết định thành lập và ngày bắt đầu hoạt động của Phòng công chứng.

3. Trong trường hợp Ủy ban nhân dân cấp tỉnh quyết định thay đổi tên gọi hoặc địa chỉ trụ sở của Phòng công

2. 成立新的公证办公室只能在一些还没有条件发展公证机构的地方。

3. 公证办公室成立在经济、社会条件困难，特别难享受到政府规定优待政策的地方。

第十九条　公证办公室

1. 公证办公室由省级人民委员会决定成立。

2. 公证办公室是属司法机构的公立事业单位，有办事处、公章和独立的财政。

根据法律的规定，公证机构的负责人是室长，室长是公证员，由省级人民委员会主席任命、免任、革职。

3. 公证办公室的命名包括“公证办公室”词组，附加成立顺序和省名，直辖市可以成立公证办公室。

4. 公证办公室使用没有国徽图样的公章，决定成立后公证办公室可以刻印和使用公章。刻印章的手续、材料，使用和管理公证办公室的印章可以根据法律对公章的规定进行。

第二十条　公证办公室成立

1. 根据地方的公证需求，司法机构的倡议要与计划投资机构、财政机构、内务建设机构提案成立公证机构配合，省级人民委员会确认决定。提案要清楚指出公证办公室成立事宜，事先考虑好机构、命名、人事、办事处地点、各种物质条件和业务展开的计划。

2. 自省级人民委员会决定成立公证办公室之日起30日内，司法机构应该登报公告以下内容：

（a）公证办公室的名称、办事处地址；

（b）决定成立公证办公室的编号、年月日和开始执业的日期。

3. 如果省级人民委员决定更换公证办公室办事地点或名称，司法机构应根据本条第2款的规定登报更

chứng thì Sở Tư pháp phải đăng báo những nội dung thay đổi đó theo quy định tại khoản 2 Điều này.

Điều 21. Chuyển đổi, giải thể Phòng công chứng

1. Trong trường hợp không cần thiết duy trì Phòng công chứng thì Sở Tư pháp lập đề án chuyển đổi Phòng công chứng thành Văn phòng công chứng trình Ủy ban nhân dân cấp tỉnh xem xét, quyết định.

Chính phủ quy định chi tiết việc chuyển đổi Phòng công chứng thành Văn phòng công chứng.

2. Trường hợp không có khả năng chuyển đổi Phòng công chứng thành Văn phòng công chứng thì Sở Tư pháp lập đề án giải thể Phòng công chứng trình Ủy ban nhân dân cấp tỉnh xem xét, quyết định.

Phòng công chứng chỉ được giải thể sau khi thanh toán xong các khoản nợ, làm xong thủ tục chấm dứt hợp đồng lao động đã ký với người lao động, thực hiện xong các yêu cầu công chứng đã tiếp nhận.

Trong thời hạn 15 ngày kể từ ngày Ủy ban nhân dân cấp tỉnh ra quyết định giải thể Phòng công chứng, Sở Tư pháp phải đăng báo trung ương hoặc báo địa phương nơi có trụ sở của Phòng công chứng trong ba số liên tiếp về việc giải thể Phòng công chứng.

Điều 22. Văn phòng công chứng

1. Văn phòng công chứng được tổ chức và hoạt động theo quy định của Luật này và các văn bản quy phạm pháp luật khác có liên quan đối với loại hình công ty hợp danh.

Văn phòng công chứng phải có từ hai công chứng viên hợp danh trở lên. Văn phòng công chứng không có thành viên góp vốn.

2. Người đại diện theo pháp luật của Văn phòng công chứng là Trưởng Văn phòng. Trưởng Văn phòng công chứng phải là công chứng viên hợp danh của Văn phòng công chứng và đã hành nghề công chứng từ 02 năm trở lên.

3. Tên gọi của Văn phòng công chứng phải bao gồm cụm từ "Văn phòng công chứng" kèm theo họ tên của Trưởng Văn phòng hoặc họ tên của một công chứng viên hợp danh khác của Văn phòng công chứng do các công chứng viên hợp danh thỏa thuận, không được trùng hoặc gây nhầm lẫn với tên của tổ chức hành nghề công chứng khác, không được vi phạm truyền thống lịch sử, văn hóa, đạo đức và thuần phong mỹ tục của dân tộc.

4. Văn phòng công chứng phải có trụ sở đáp ứng các điều kiện do Chính phủ quy định.

Văn phòng công chứng có con dấu và tài khoản riêng, hoạt động theo nguyên tắc tự chủ về tài chính bằng

改的内容。

第二十一条　公证办公室转换、解体

1. 如果公证办公室不需要再维续，司法机构提案把公证办公室改为公证机构，省级人民委员会确认、决定。

政府规定公证办公室转成公证机构的细节。

2. 没有能力将公证办公室转成公证机构的话，司法机构提案撤销公证办公室，省级人民委员会确认、决定。

公证办公室要清算完各种欠款，履行已和劳动者签订的劳动合同手续，处理完已经接受的各公证请求后，才可以撤销。

自省级人民委员会决定撤销公证办公室之日起15日内，司法机构应登报公告关于撤销公证办公室的事宜。

第二十二条　公证机构

1. 对于合格的公司类型，公证机构根据本法的规定和其他相关的法律规范文件组织和活动。

公证机构应该有2名以上的合格公证员，公证机构无融资成员。

2. 根据法律的规定，公证机构的负责人是办公室主任，公证机构办公室主任应该是公证执业2年以上并且是公证机构合格的公证员。

3. 公证机构的命名应当包括“公证机构”词汇，附加办公室主任全名或其他一个由公证机构的公证员商量的一个合格公证员的全名，不可以和其他公证机构的名称有重复或混淆，不可以违反历史、文化、道德和民族的公序良俗。

4. 公证机构应有满足由政府规定条件的办事处。

公证机构有独立的财政和公章，根据自主原则处理财政，以收取的公证费、公证酬劳和其他各种收入

nguồn thu từ phí công chứng, thù lao công chứng và các nguồn thu hợp pháp khác.

5. Văn phòng công chứng sử dụng con dấu không có hình quốc huy. Văn phòng công chứng được khắc và sử dụng con dấu sau khi có quyết định cho phép thành lập. Thủ tục, hồ sơ xin khắc dấu, việc quản lý, sử dụng con dấu của Văn phòng công chứng được thực hiện theo quy định của pháp luật về con dấu.

Điều 23. Thành lập và đăng ký hoạt động Văn phòng công chứng

1. Các công chứng viên thành lập Văn phòng công chứng phải có hồ sơ đề nghị thành lập Văn phòng công chứng gửi Ủy ban nhân dân cấp tỉnh xem xét, quyết định. Hồ sơ đề nghị thành lập Văn phòng công chứng gồm đơn đề nghị thành lập và đề án thành lập Văn phòng công chứng, trong đó nêu rõ sự cần thiết thành lập, dự kiến về tổ chức, tên gọi, nhân sự, địa điểm đặt trụ sở, các điều kiện vật chất và kế hoạch triển khai thực hiện; bản sao quyết định bổ nhiệm công chứng viên tham gia thành lập Văn phòng công chứng.

2. Trong thời hạn 20 ngày kể từ ngày nhận đủ hồ sơ đề nghị thành lập Văn phòng công chứng, Ủy ban nhân dân cấp tỉnh xem xét, quyết định cho phép thành lập Văn phòng công chứng; trường hợp từ chối phải thông báo bằng văn bản và nêu rõ lý do.

3. Trong thời hạn 90 ngày kể từ ngày nhận được quyết định cho phép thành lập, Văn phòng công chứng phải đăng ký hoạt động tại Sở Tư pháp ở địa phương nơi đã ra quyết định cho phép thành lập.

Nội dung đăng ký hoạt động của Văn phòng công chứng bao gồm tên gọi của Văn phòng công chứng, họ tên Trưởng Văn phòng công chứng, địa chỉ trụ sở của Văn phòng công chứng, danh sách công chứng viên hợp danh của Văn phòng công chứng và danh sách công chứng viên làm việc theo chế độ hợp đồng của Văn phòng công chứng (nếu có).

4. Hồ sơ đăng ký hoạt động của Văn phòng công chứng gồm đơn đăng ký hoạt động, giấy tờ chứng minh về trụ sở của Văn phòng công chứng phù hợp với nội dung đã nêu trong đề án thành lập và hồ sơ đăng ký hành nghề của các công chứng viên hợp danh, công chứng viên làm việc theo chế độ hợp đồng lao động tại Văn phòng công chứng (nếu có).

Trong thời hạn 10 ngày làm việc kể từ ngày nhận đủ hồ sơ đăng ký hoạt động, Sở Tư pháp cấp giấy đăng ký hoạt động của Văn phòng công chứng; trường hợp từ chối

作为收入来源。

5. 公证机构使用没有国徽图样的公章，决定成立后公证机构可以刻印和使用公章，刻印鉴的程序、材料使用和管理公证机构的印鉴根据法律关于公章的规定进行。

第二十三条　成立和登记办公室活动

1. 公证员成立公证机构应当有成立公证机构的提议材料并递送给省级人民委员会审查、决定，成立公证机构的提案材料包括成立公证机构的提议申请书和提案单，材料里应明确指出成立所需的，事先准备好组织、名称、人事、办事地点、各种物质条件和开展实现的计划，参加成立公证机构公证任命决定的复印件。

2. 自收到成立公证机构提议材料之日起 20 日内，省级人民委员审核、决定允许成立公证机构；如拒绝成立应书面通报并说明理由。

3. 自收到允许成立决定之日起 90 日内，公证机构应当在已决定允许成立的当地司法机构登记执业。

公证机构登记执业内容包括公证机构的名称、公证机构主任的全名、公证机构办事地点、公证机构合格公证员名单、合同制的公证机构合同公证员名单（如有）。

4. 公证机构登记执业的材料包括登记执业申请书、符合已在成立提案内容中指出的公证机构办事地点证明书、合格公证员的执业登记档案、在公证机构工作的合同公证员（如有）。

自收到齐全的登记执业文件之日起 10 个工作日内，司法机构颁发公证机构执业证书；如果拒绝应书面通知并说明理由。

phải thông báo bằng văn bản và nêu rõ lý do.

5. Văn phòng công chứng được hoạt động công chứng kể từ ngày Sở Tư pháp cấp giấy đăng ký hoạt động.

Điều 24. Thay đổi nội dung đăng ký hoạt động của Văn phòng công chứng

1. Khi thay đổi một trong các nội dung quy định tại khoản 3 Điều 23 của Luật này, Văn phòng công chứng phải đăng ký nội dung thay đổi tại Sở Tư pháp nơi Văn phòng công chứng đã đăng ký hoạt động.

Việc thay đổi trụ sở của Văn phòng công chứng sang huyện, quận, thị xã, thành phố khác trong phạm vi tỉnh, thành phố trực thuộc trung ương nơi đã ra quyết định cho phép thành lập phải được Ủy ban nhân dân cấp tỉnh xem xét, quyết định và phải phù hợp với Quy hoạch tổng thể phát triển tổ chức hành nghề công chứng.

2. Văn phòng công chứng thay đổi tên gọi, trụ sở hoặc Trưởng Văn phòng công chứng thì được Sở Tư pháp cấp lại giấy đăng ký hoạt động trong thời hạn 07 ngày làm việc kể từ ngày nhận đủ hồ sơ đề nghị; trường hợp từ chối phải thông báo bằng văn bản và nêu rõ lý do.

Điều 25. Cung cấp thông tin về nội dung đăng ký hoạt động của Văn phòng công chứng

Trong thời hạn 10 ngày làm việc kể từ ngày cấp hoặc cấp lại giấy đăng ký hoạt động của Văn phòng công chứng, Sở Tư pháp phải thông báo bằng văn bản cho cơ quan thuế, cơ quan thống kê, cơ quan công an cấp tỉnh, Ủy ban nhân dân huyện, quận, thị xã, thành phố thuộc tỉnh, Ủy ban nhân dân xã, phường, thị trấn nơi Văn phòng công chứng đặt trụ sở.

Điều 26. Đăng báo nội dung đăng ký hoạt động của Văn phòng công chứng

1. Trong thời hạn 30 ngày kể từ ngày được cấp giấy đăng ký hoạt động, Văn phòng công chứng phải đăng báo trung ương hoặc báo địa phương nơi đăng ký hoạt động trong ba số liên tiếp về những nội dung sau đây:

a) Tên gọi, địa chỉ trụ sở của Văn phòng công chứng;

b) Họ, tên, số quyết định bổ nhiệm của công chứng viên hành nghề tại Văn phòng công chứng;

c) Số, ngày, tháng, năm cấp giấy đăng ký hoạt động, nơi đăng ký hoạt động và ngày bắt đầu hoạt động.

2. Trong trường hợp được cấp lại giấy đăng ký hoạt động, Văn phòng công chứng phải thực hiện việc đăng báo về nội dung đăng ký hoạt động theo quy định tại khoản 1 Điều này.

5. 自司法机构颁发执业证书之日起公证机构可以执业。

第二十四条　公证机构变更登记执业内容

1. 当变更本法第23条第3款规定内容之一时，公证机构应该在登记执业证的司法机构变更登记内容。

在公证机构省内的县、郡、镇、其他城市变更公证机构地点的，直辖市已经决定允许成立的，还应当经省级人民委员审核、决定并且要符合公证机构的整体发展规划。

2. 公证机构变更名称、办事地点或主任的，自收到齐全提议资料之日起7个工作日内司法机构再颁发执业证书；如果拒绝应书面通报并说明理由。

第二十五条　提供公证机构登记执业信息

自颁发公证机构执业证书或再颁发之日起10个工作日内，司法机构应书面通知省级税务局、统计局、公安局，省内的县、郡、市的人民委员会，以及设公证机构办事点的社、坊、市镇的人民委员。

第二十六条　公证机构登报执业内容

1. 自颁发执业证书之日起30日内，公证机构应通报给中央或下列内容中3个数字连续的登记执业的地方：

（a）公证机构名称、办事地点；

（b）在公证机构执业的公证员的任命编号、全名；

（c）登记执业证的编号、年月日，登记执业的地点和开始执业的日期。

2. 如果得到再颁发的执业证书，公证机构应根据本条第1款的规定对执业内容进行告知。

Điều 27. Thay đổi thành viên hợp danh của Văn phòng công chứng

1. Công chứng viên hợp danh của Văn phòng công chứng có thể chấm dứt tư cách thành viên hợp danh theo nguyện vọng cá nhân hoặc trong các trường hợp khác do pháp luật quy định.

Văn phòng công chứng có quyền tiếp nhận công chứng viên hợp danh mới nếu công chứng viên đó được các công chứng viên hợp danh còn lại chấp thuận.

Việc chấm dứt tư cách công chứng viên hợp danh và tiếp nhận công chứng viên hợp danh mới được thực hiện theo quy định của Luật này và pháp luật về doanh nghiệp.

2. Trường hợp công chứng viên hợp danh của Văn phòng công chứng chết hoặc bị Tòa án tuyên bố là đã chết thì người thừa kế của công chứng viên hợp danh được hưởng phần giá trị tài sản tại Văn phòng công chứng sau khi đã trừ đi phần nợ thuộc trách nhiệm của công chứng viên đó. Người thừa kế có thể trở thành công chứng viên hợp danh của Văn phòng công chứng nếu là công chứng viên và được các công chứng viên hợp danh còn lại chấp thuận.

Điều 28. Hợp nhất, sáp nhập Văn phòng công chứng

1. Hai hoặc một số Văn phòng công chứng có trụ sở trong cùng một tỉnh, thành phố trực thuộc trung ương có thể hợp nhất thành một Văn phòng công chứng mới bằng cách chuyển toàn bộ tài sản, quyền, nghĩa vụ và lợi ích hợp pháp sang Văn phòng công chứng được hợp nhất, đồng thời chấm dứt hoạt động của các Văn phòng công chứng bị hợp nhất.

Một hoặc một số Văn phòng công chứng có thể sáp nhập vào một Văn phòng công chứng khác có trụ sở trong cùng một tỉnh, thành phố trực thuộc trung ương bằng cách chuyển toàn bộ tài sản, quyền, nghĩa vụ và lợi ích hợp pháp sang Văn phòng công chứng nhận sáp nhập, đồng thời chấm dứt hoạt động của Văn phòng công chứng bị sáp nhập.

2. Ủy ban nhân dân cấp tỉnh xem xét, quyết định cho phép hợp nhất, sáp nhập Văn phòng công chứng.

3. Chính phủ quy định chi tiết thủ tục hợp nhất, sáp nhập Văn phòng công chứng.

Điều 29. Chuyển nhượng Văn phòng công chứng

1. Văn phòng công chứng được chuyển nhượng cho các công chứng viên khác đáp ứng các điều kiện quy định tại khoản 2 Điều này. Văn phòng công chứng chỉ được chuyển nhượng khi đã hoạt động công chứng được ít nhất

第二十七条　变更公证机构的合格成员

1. 公证机构的合格公证员可以根据自愿或由法律规定的其他情况注销合格成员资格。

新公证员如果得到各合格公证员的一致同意，那么公证机构有权接受新的合格公证员。

注销合格公证员资格和接受新的合格公证员要依据《公证法》和《经营法》的规定。

2. 公证机构的合格公证员死亡或被法院宣布死亡，除去该公证员应该承担的债务，其继承人可以享受公证机构的财产。如果是继承者是公证员并得到各正式公证员的一致同意，该继承者可以成为公证机构的合格公证员。

第二十八条　公证机构合并、整合

1. 一个省、直辖市内有两个或若干公证机构办事处，可以合并成一个新的公证机构，把全部财产，合法权利、义务和利益转到合并的公证机构，同时注销被合并的公证机构。

一个或若干公证机构可以整合进一个省、直辖市内办事处的，把全部财产，合法权利、义务和利益转入整合的公证机构，同时注销被整合的公证机构。

2. 省级人民委员会确认、决定公证机构的合并和整合。

3. 政府规定公证机构合并、整合程序的细节。

第二十九条　公证机构的转让

1. 满足本法第 2 款规定条件的，公证机构可以转让给其他公证员。公证机构执业至少 2 年以上才可以转让。

là 02 năm.

Công chứng viên đã chuyển nhượng Văn phòng công chứng không được phép tham gia thành lập Văn phòng công chứng mới trong thời hạn 05 năm kể từ ngày chuyển nhượng.

2. Công chứng viên nhận chuyển nhượng Văn phòng công chứng phải đáp ứng các điều kiện sau đây:

a) Đã hành nghề công chứng từ 02 năm trở lên đối với người dự kiến sẽ tiếp quản vị trí Trưởng Văn phòng công chứng;

b) Cam kết hành nghề tại Văn phòng công chứng mà mình nhận chuyển nhượng;

c) Cam kết kế thừa quyền và nghĩa vụ của Văn phòng công chứng được chuyển nhượng.

3. Ủy ban nhân dân cấp tỉnh xem xét, quyết định cho phép chuyển nhượng Văn phòng công chứng.

4. Chính phủ quy định chi tiết trình tự, thủ tục chuyển nhượng Văn phòng công chứng.

Điều 30. Thu hồi quyết định cho phép thành lập

1. Văn phòng công chứng bị thu hồi quyết định cho phép thành lập trong những trường hợp sau đây:

a) Văn phòng công chứng không thực hiện đăng ký hoạt động theo quy định tại Điều 23 của Luật này;

b) Hết thời hạn 06 tháng kể từ ngày được cấp giấy đăng ký hoạt động mà Văn phòng công chứng chưa bắt đầu hoạt động;

c) Văn phòng công chứng không hoạt động liên tục từ 03 tháng trở lên, trừ trường hợp toàn bộ các công chứng viên hợp danh bị tạm đình chỉ hành nghề công chứng;

d) Văn phòng công chứng chỉ còn một công chứng viên hợp danh và không bổ sung được thành viên hợp danh mới trong thời hạn 06 tháng kể từ ngày thiếu công chứng viên hợp danh;

e) Toàn bộ công chứng viên hợp danh của Văn phòng công chứng bị miễn nhiệm chết hoặc bị Tòa án tuyên bố là đã chết;

f) Văn phòng công chứng không bảo đảm duy trì điều kiện hoạt động theo quy định của Luật này và các văn bản quy phạm pháp luật khác có liên quan.

2. Sở Tư pháp có trách nhiệm kiểm tra, rà soát và lập hồ sơ đề nghị Ủy ban nhân dân cấp tỉnh ra quyết định thu hồi quyết định cho phép thành lập Văn phòng công chứng.

Điều 31. Chấm dứt hoạt động Văn phòng công chứng

1. Văn phòng công chứng chấm dứt hoạt động trong các trường hợp sau đây:

自公证员转让公证机构之日起 5 年内，不得参加设立新的公证机构。

2. 公证员转让公证机构应满足以下条件：

（a）对于将要接管公证机构的主任须有 2 年以上的公证执业经验；

（b）承担、接手公证机构转让前的工作；

（c）承担公证机构转让前的权利和义务。

3. 省级人民委员会确认、决定许可转让公证机构。

4. 政府规定公证机构转让的顺序、过程细节。

第三十条　收回许可成立的决定

1. 在下列情况下收回许可公证机构成立的决定：

（a）根据本法第 23 条的规定公证机构不进行执业登记的；

（b）自颁发执业证书之日起 6 个月之内，公证机构没有开始执业的；

（c）公证机构连续 3 个月以上不执业的，全部合格公证员被暂停执业的情况除外；

（d）公证机构只有 1 名合格的公证员和自空缺合格公证员之日起 6 个月内，不补充新的合格公证员的；

（e）被免任的公证机构合格公证员全部死亡或被法院宣告死亡的；

（f）根据本法或其他相关法律规范的规定，公证机构不保证维持执业条件的。

2. 司法机构有责任检查、审核和建立提议档案，省级人民委员决定收回许可公证机构成立决定的。

第三十一条　取消公证机构执业

1. 下列情况取消公证机构执业：

a) Văn phòng công chứng tự chấm dứt hoạt động;

b) Văn phòng công chứng bị thu hồi quyết định cho phép thành lập theo quy định tại Điều 30 của Luật này;

c) Văn phòng công chứng bị hợp nhất, bị sáp nhập.

2. Trong trường hợp chấm dứt hoạt động theo quy định tại điểm a khoản 1 Điều này thì chậm nhất là 30 ngày trước thời điểm dự kiến chấm dứt hoạt động, Văn phòng công chứng phải có báo cáo bằng văn bản gửi Sở Tư pháp nơi đã đăng ký hoạt động. Trước thời điểm chấm dứt hoạt động, Văn phòng công chứng có nghĩa vụ nộp đủ số thuế còn nợ, thanh toán các khoản nợ khác, làm xong thủ tục chấm dứt hợp đồng lao động đã ký với công chứng viên, nhân viên của tổ chức mình, thực hiện các yêu cầu công chứng đã tiếp nhận. Trường hợp không thể thực hiện xong các yêu cầu công chứng đã tiếp nhận thì phải thỏa thuận với người yêu cầu công chứng về việc thực hiện các yêu cầu đó.

Trong trường hợp chấm dứt hoạt động theo quy định tại điểm c khoản 1 Điều này thì quyền, nghĩa vụ của Văn phòng công chứng do Văn phòng công chứng được hợp nhất hoặc Văn phòng công chứng nhận sáp nhập tiếp tục thực hiện.

Văn phòng công chứng có nghĩa vụ đăng báo trung ương hoặc báo địa phương nơi đã đăng ký hoạt động trong ba số liên tiếp về thời điểm dự kiến chấm dứt hoạt động.

Sở Tư pháp có trách nhiệm thu hồi giấy đăng ký hoạt động của Văn phòng công chứng, báo cáo Ủy ban nhân dân cấp tỉnh thu hồi quyết định cho phép thành lập và thông báo bằng văn bản về việc chấm dứt hoạt động của Văn phòng công chứng với các cơ quan quy định tại Điều 25 của Luật này.

3. Trong trường hợp Văn phòng công chứng chấm dứt hoạt động theo quy định tại điểm b khoản 1 Điều này thì trong thời hạn 07 ngày làm việc kể từ ngày có quyết định thu hồi quyết định cho phép thành lập, Sở Tư pháp có trách nhiệm thu hồi giấy đăng ký hoạt động của Văn phòng công chứng, thông báo bằng văn bản với các cơ quan quy định tại Điều 25 của Luật này, đồng thời đăng báo trung ương hoặc báo địa phương nơi Văn phòng công chứng đã đăng ký hoạt động trong ba số liên tiếp về việc chấm dứt hoạt động của Văn phòng công chứng đó.

Trong thời hạn 60 ngày kể từ ngày bị thu hồi quyết định cho phép thành lập, Văn phòng công chứng có nghĩa vụ nộp đủ số thuế còn nợ, thanh toán xong các khoản nợ khác, làm thủ tục chấm dứt hợp đồng lao động đã ký với công chứng viên, nhân viên của tổ chức mình; đối với yêu cầu công chứng đã tiếp nhận mà chưa công chứng thì phải

（a）公证机构自行取消执业；

（b）根据本法第 30 条的规定，被收回许可公证机构成立决定；

（c）公证机构被合并、整合的。

2. 预计取消执业活动之前，根据本条第 1 款的规定，在取消前的 30 日内，公证机构要有书面报告递给登记执业的司法机构。取消执业之前，公证机构有义务缴清欠款，结清其他各种款项，完成取消和公证员、机构职员签订的劳动合同的手续，处理已经接受的各种申请，无法处理公证员的各种要求的，要与之商量处理他们的要求。

根据本条第 1 款的规定取消执业公证机构的权利、义务，由合并、接收或整合的公证机构继续处理。

公证机构有义务向中央或执业的地方进行登记。

司法机构有责任收回公证机构的营业执照，报告省级人民委员会收回许可成立的决定和向本法的第 25 条规定的单位书面通知公证机构取消执业。

3. 从决定收回成立许可之日起 7 个工作日内，公证机构根据该条第 1 款的规定取消公证机构营业，司法机构有责任收回公证机构的营业执照，书面通告本法第 25 条规定的各单位，同时在公证机构登记执业的地方登报公告。

被收回成立许可决定之日起 60 日内，公证机构有义务缴纳未交清的欠款，清算完其他欠款，处理完已和公证员、该组织的职员签订的劳动合同手续，对于已经接收的公证申请但还未处理完的，应把公证材料还给公证申请人。上述时限结束后公证机构还没有完成财产处理义务的，或因公证机构的全部公证员死

trả lại hồ sơ yêu cầu công chứng cho người yêu cầu công chứng. Hết thời hạn này mà Văn phòng công chứng chưa hoàn thành xong các nghĩa vụ về tài sản hoặc trường hợp Văn phòng công chứng chấm dứt hoạt động do bị thu hồi quyết định cho phép thành lập vì toàn bộ công chứng viên hợp danh của Văn phòng công chứng chết hoặc bị Tòa án tuyên bố là đã chết thì tài sản của Văn phòng công chứng, của công chứng viên hợp danh được sử dụng để thanh toán các khoản nợ của Văn phòng công chứng theo quy định của pháp luật về dân sự.

亡或被法院宣告死亡，被收回设立许可决定与取消公证机构执业的，为了清算其他欠款，根据民事法律的规定，公证机构、合格公证员的财产将因此被使用。

Điều 32. Quyền của tổ chức hành nghề công chứng

1. Ký hợp đồng làm việc, hợp đồng lao động với công chứng viên quy định tại điểm a và điểm c khoản 1 Điều 34 của Luật này và các nhân viên làm việc cho tổ chức mình.

2. Thu phí công chứng, thù lao công chứng, chi phí khác.

3. Cung cấp dịch vụ công chứng ngoài ngày, giờ làm việc của cơ quan hành chính nhà nước để đáp ứng nhu cầu công chứng của nhân dân.

4. Được khai thác, sử dụng thông tin từ cơ sở dữ liệu công chứng quy định tại Điều 62 của Luật này.

5. Các quyền khác theo quy định của Luật này và các văn bản quy phạm pháp luật khác có liên quan.

第三十二条　公证机构的权利

1. 依照本法第 34 条第 1 款 a 项和 c 项之规定与公证员和在本机构工作的人员签订工作合同、劳动合同。

2. 收取公证费、公证酬劳和其他费用。

3. 为了满足人民的公证要求，在国家行政单位工作的时间、日期外提供公证服务。

4. 本法的第 62 条规定，可以从公证资料机构获取、使用信息。

5. 根据本法规定和其他有关法律规定的其他权利。

Điều 33. Nghĩa vụ của tổ chức hành nghề công chứng

1. Quản lý công chứng viên hành nghề tại tổ chức mình trong việc tuân thủ pháp luật và quy tắc đạo đức hành nghề công chứng.

2. Chấp hành quy định của pháp luật về lao động, thuế, tài chính, thống kê.

3. Thực hiện chế độ làm việc theo ngày, giờ làm việc của cơ quan hành chính nhà nước.

4. Niêm yết lịch làm việc, thủ tục công chứng, nội quy tiếp người yêu cầu công chứng, phí công chứng, thù lao công chứng và chi phí khác tại trụ sở của tổ chức mình.

5. Mua bảo hiểm trách nhiệm nghề nghiệp cho công chứng viên của tổ chức mình theo quy định tại Điều 37 của Luật này và bồi thường thiệt hại theo quy định tại Điều 38 của Luật này.

6. Tiếp nhận, tạo điều kiện thuận lợi và quản lý người tập sự hành nghề công chứng trong quá trình tập sự tại tổ chức mình.

7. Tạo điều kiện cho công chứng viên của tổ chức mình tham gia bồi dưỡng nghiệp vụ công chứng hằng

第三十三条　公证机构的义务

1. 遵守法律和公证职业道德，在本单位中管理公证员执业。

2. 执行劳动、税务、财产、统计的有关法律规定。

3. 根据国家行政单位的工作日、工作时间执行工作制度。

4. 制定工作日志、公证程序、接待公证申请人的规章，收取公证费、公证酬劳和在本公证机构的其他费用。

5. 根据本法第 37 条的规定，为在本单位执业的公证员购买执业责任保险，根据本法第 38 条的规定补偿遭受的损失。

6. 有实习生在本机构实习时，要接受、创造有利条件并管理公证业实习生。

7. 为本单位的公证员参加每年的公证业务进修创造条件。

năm.

8. Thực hiện yêu cầu của cơ quan nhà nước có thẩm quyền về việc báo cáo, kiểm tra, thanh tra, cung cấp thông tin về hợp đồng, giao dịch, bản dịch đã công chứng.

9. Lập sổ công chứng và lưu trữ hồ sơ công chứng.

10. Chia sẻ thông tin về nguồn gốc tài sản, tình trạng giao dịch của tài sản và các thông tin khác về biện pháp ngăn chặn được áp dụng đối với tài sản có liên quan đến hợp đồng, giao dịch do công chứng viên của tổ chức mình thực hiện công chứng để đưa vào cơ sở dữ liệu công chứng quy định tại Điều 62 của Luật này.

11. Các nghĩa vụ khác theo quy định của Luật này và các văn bản quy phạm pháp luật khác có liên quan.

Chương IV
HÀNH NGHỀ CÔNG CHỨNG

Điều 34. Hình thức hành nghề của công chứng viên

1. Các hình thức hành nghề của công chứng viên bao gồm:

a) Công chứng viên của các Phòng công chứng;

b) Công chứng viên hợp danh của Văn phòng công chứng;

c) Công chứng viên làm việc theo chế độ hợp đồng lao động tại Văn phòng công chứng.

2. Việc tuyển dụng, quản lý, sử dụng công chứng viên quy định tại điểm a khoản 1 Điều này được thực hiện theo quy định của pháp luật về viên chức.

Việc ký và thực hiện hợp đồng lao động với công chứng viên quy định tại điểm c khoản 1 Điều này được thực hiện theo quy định của Luật này và pháp luật về lao động.

Điều 35. Đăng ký hành nghề

1. Tổ chức hành nghề công chứng đăng ký hành nghề cho công chứng viên của tổ chức mình tại Sở Tư pháp nơi tổ chức hành nghề công chứng đăng ký hoạt động.

Văn phòng công chứng đăng ký hành nghề cho công chứng viên của mình khi thực hiện đăng ký hoạt động hoặc thay đổi nội dung đăng ký hoạt động của Văn phòng công chứng quy định tại Điều 23 và Điều 24 của Luật này.

Phòng công chứng đăng ký hành nghề cho công chứng viên của mình sau khi có quyết định thành lập Phòng công chứng hoặc khi bổ sung công chứng viên.

2. Sở Tư pháp thực hiện đăng ký hành nghề và cấp Thẻ công chứng viên cho công chứng viên của tổ chức hành nghề công chứng; trường hợp từ chối phải thông báo bằng văn bản và nêu rõ lý do cho tổ chức hành nghề công

8. 根据有权限的国家机关的要求，报告、检查、核查、提供已公证的合同、交易、译本的信息。

9. 建立公证编号和保管公证档案。

10. 本法第 62 条规定，为了方便全体公证机构，本单位公证员公证过的合同、交易有关的财产来源信息、财产交易状况和其他各种信息应当共享。

11. 本法规定和其他法律规定的其他义务。

第四章　公证执业

第三十四条　公证员的执业形式

1. 公证员的执业形式包括：

（a）各公证办公室的公证员；

（b）公证机构的合格公证员；

（c）在公证机构工作的合同制公证员。

2. 本条第 1 款 a 项规定聘用、管理、使用公证员可以根据官方法律的规定执行。

本条第 1 款 c 项规定与公证员签订和执行劳动合同可以根据本法和劳动法的规定执行。

第三十五条　执业登记

1. 公证机构在登记公证机构执业的当地司法机构，给本单位的公证员登记执业。

本法第 23 条、第 24 条规定，公证机构在进行登记执业或变更公证机构登记内容时，给本单位的公证员登记执业。

在公证办公室决定成立后或补充公证员时，公证办公室给本单位的公证员登记执业。

2. 司法机构进行执业登记并给公证机构的公证员提供工作证件；如果拒绝应书面告知机构和公证员并说明理由。

chứng và công chứng viên.

3. Khi công chứng viên không còn làm việc tại tổ chức hành nghề công chứng thì tổ chức hành nghề công chứng có trách nhiệm thông báo cho Sở Tư pháp để xóa đăng ký hành nghề của công chứng viên. Công chứng viên không được ký văn bản công chứng kể từ ngày chấm dứt tư cách thành viên hợp danh hoặc chấm dứt hợp đồng làm việc, hợp đồng lao động tại tổ chức hành nghề công chứng.

3. 公证员不在公证机构工作时，公证机构有义务将之通告给司法机构，注销公证员的执业登记。自公证员注销在公证机构合格公证员资格或劳动合同之日起，公证员不可签署公证文书。

Điều 36. Thẻ công chứng viên

1. Thẻ công chứng viên là căn cứ chứng minh tư cách hành nghề công chứng của công chứng viên. Công chứng viên phải mang theo Thẻ công chứng viên khi hành nghề công chứng.

2. Công chứng viên được cấp lại Thẻ công chứng viên trong trường hợp Thẻ đã được cấp bị mất, bị hỏng.

Thẻ công chứng viên bị thu hồi trong trường hợp công chứng viên bị miễn nhiệm hoặc bị xóa đăng ký hành nghề.

3. Bộ trưởng Bộ Tư pháp quy định chi tiết mẫu Thẻ công chứng viên, thủ tục đăng ký hành nghề, cấp, cấp lại và thu hồi Thẻ công chứng viên.

第三十六条　公证员工作证件

1. 公证员的工作证件是证明公证员执业资格的依据，公证员执业时应携带公证员工作证件。

2. 如果已经提供的公证员工作证件丢失、损坏，公证员可以补办公证员工作证。

如果公证员被免任或被撤销执业，公证员工作证应被收回。

3. 司法部部长规定公证员工作证模板、登记执业程序，办理、补办公证员证的细节。

Điều 37. Bảo hiểm trách nhiệm nghề nghiệp của công chứng viên

1. Bảo hiểm trách nhiệm nghề nghiệp của công chứng viên là loại hình bảo hiểm bắt buộc. Việc mua bảo hiểm trách nhiệm nghề nghiệp cho công chứng viên phải được duy trì trong suốt thời gian hoạt động của tổ chức hành nghề công chứng.

2. Tổ chức hành nghề công chứng có nghĩa vụ mua bảo hiểm trách nhiệm nghề nghiệp cho công chứng viên hành nghề tại tổ chức mình.

Chậm nhất là 10 ngày làm việc kể từ ngày mua bảo hiểm hoặc kể từ ngày thay đổi, gia hạn hợp đồng bảo hiểm, tổ chức hành nghề công chứng có trách nhiệm thông báo và gửi bản sao hợp đồng bảo hiểm, hợp đồng thay đổi, gia hạn hợp đồng bảo hiểm trách nhiệm nghề nghiệp của công chứng viên cho Sở Tư pháp.

3. Chính phủ quy định chi tiết điều kiện bảo hiểm, mức phí bảo hiểm, số tiền bảo hiểm tối thiểu đối với bảo hiểm trách nhiệm nghề nghiệp của công chứng viên.

第三十七条　公证员的执业责任保险

1. 公证员的执业责任保险是强制类型的保险，公证机构执业期间，应当一直保持给公证员购买执业责任保险。

2. 公证机构有义务给在本单位执业的公证员购买执业责任保险。

自购买保险之日或变更、延长保险合同之日起10个工作日内，公证机构应将和保留保险合同、变更合同、延长保险合同期限有关的事宜通告给司法机构。

3. 政府规定保险条件、保险费用比例、对于公证员执业责任保险的最低保险费细节。

Điều 38. Bồi thường, bồi hoàn trong hoạt động công chứng

1. Tổ chức hành nghề công chứng phải bồi thường thiệt hại cho người yêu cầu công chứng và cá nhân, tổ

第三十八条　公证执业中赔偿、退换

1. 在公证过程中，由本单位公证员、职员或与之合作的翻译者造成的损失，公证机构要对公证申请人

chức khác do lỗi mà công chứng viên, nhân viên hoặc người phiên dịch là cộng tác viên của tổ chức mình gây ra trong quá trình công chứng.

和个人、其他组织进行赔偿。

2. Công chứng viên, nhân viên hoặc người phiên dịch là cộng tác viên gây thiệt hại phải hoàn trả lại một khoản tiền cho tổ chức hành nghề công chứng đã chi trả khoản tiền bồi thường cho người bị thiệt hại theo quy định của pháp luật; trường hợp không hoàn trả thì tổ chức hành nghề công chứng có quyền yêu cầu Tòa án giải quyết.

2. 公证员、职员或翻译合作者造成的损失应全额付给已根据法律规定补偿给遭受损失者的公证机构；如果不完全付清公证机构有权向法院提起诉讼。

Điều 39. Tổ chức xã hội - nghề nghiệp của công chứng viên

第三十九条　公证员协会

1. Tổ chức xã hội - nghề nghiệp của công chứng viên là tổ chức tự quản được thành lập ở cấp trung ương và cấp tỉnh để đại diện và bảo vệ quyền, lợi ích hợp pháp của các công chứng viên; ban hành quy tắc đạo đức hành nghề công chứng; giám sát việc tuân thủ quy định của pháp luật về công chứng, quy tắc đạo đức hành nghề công chứng; tham gia cùng cơ quan nhà nước trong việc tổ chức đào tạo, bồi dưỡng, tập sự hành nghề công chứng; tham gia ý kiến với cơ quan có thẩm quyền trong việc bổ nhiệm, miễn nhiệm công chứng viên, thành lập, hợp nhất, sáp nhập, chuyển nhượng, chấm dứt hoạt động của tổ chức hành nghề công chứng và thực hiện các nhiệm vụ khác liên quan đến hoạt động công chứng theo quy định của Chính phủ.

1. 公证员协会是为了代表和保卫公证员的合法权利和利益，在中央和省级成立并自行管理的组织；公证员协会颁布行业道德规则，监督公证员遵守法律规则、公证行业道德规则，协助国家机关组织行业道德进修、实习工作；在有权限的单位管理的公证员任命、免任，行业组织的成立、合并、融合、转让、取消和执行与国家规定公证活动相关的其他义务时，公证员协会参与提议。

2. Chính phủ quy định chi tiết về việc thành lập, cơ cấu tổ chức và nhiệm vụ, quyền hạn của tổ chức xã hội - nghề nghiệp của công chứng viên.

2. 政府规定关于公证员协会的成立、组织机构、义务和权限的细节。

Chương V
THỦ TỤC CÔNG CHỨNG HỢP ĐỒNG, GIAO DỊCH, BẢN DỊCH

第五章　公证合同、交易、译本的程序

Mục 1. THỦ TỤC CHUNG VỀ CÔNG CHỨNG

目录一　公证总程序

Điều 40. Công chứng hợp đồng, giao dịch đã được soạn thảo sẵn

第四十条　合同、交易的公证

1. Hồ sơ yêu cầu công chứng được lập thành một bộ, gồm các giấy tờ sau đây:

1. 公证的档案应装订成一本，包括以下材料：

a) Phiếu yêu cầu công chứng, trong đó có thông tin về họ tên, địa chỉ người yêu cầu công chứng, nội dung cần công chứng, danh mục giấy tờ gửi kèm theo; tên tổ chức hành nghề công chứng, họ tên người tiếp nhận hồ sơ yêu cầu công chứng, thời điểm tiếp nhận hồ sơ;

（a）公证申请，其内容应包括公证申请人的全名、地址，申请公证的内容，附加证件名目；公证机构名称，接受申请公证材料的人的全名。

b) Dự thảo hợp đồng, giao dịch;

（b）合同、交易草案。

c) Bản sao giấy tờ tùy thân của người yêu cầu công

（c）公证员的公证员证复印件。

chứng;

d) Bản sao giấy chứng nhận quyền sở hữu, quyền sử dụng hoặc bản sao giấy tờ thay thế được pháp luật quy định đối với tài sản mà pháp luật quy định phải đăng ký quyền sở hữu, quyền sử dụng trong trường hợp hợp đồng, giao dịch liên quan đến tài sản đó;

e) Bản sao giấy tờ khác có liên quan đến hợp đồng, giao dịch mà pháp luật quy định phải có.

2. Bản sao quy định tại khoản 1 Điều này là bản chụp, bản in hoặc bản đánh máy có nội dung đầy đủ, chính xác như bản chính và không phải chứng thực.

3. Công chứng viên kiểm tra giấy tờ trong hồ sơ yêu cầu công chứng. Trường hợp hồ sơ yêu cầu công chứng đầy đủ, phù hợp với quy định của pháp luật thì thụ lý và ghi vào sổ công chứng.

4. Công chứng viên hướng dẫn người yêu cầu công chứng tuân thủ đúng các quy định về thủ tục công chứng và các quy định pháp luật có liên quan đến việc thực hiện hợp đồng, giao dịch; giải thích cho người yêu cầu công chứng hiểu rõ quyền, nghĩa vụ và lợi ích hợp pháp của họ, ý nghĩa và hậu quả pháp lý của việc tham gia hợp đồng, giao dịch.

5. Trong trường hợp có căn cứ cho rằng trong hồ sơ yêu cầu công chứng có vấn đề chưa rõ, việc giao kết hợp đồng, giao dịch có dấu hiệu bị đe dọa, cưỡng ép, có sự nghi ngờ về năng lực hành vi dân sự của người yêu cầu công chứng hoặc đối tượng của hợp đồng, giao dịch chưa được mô tả cụ thể thì công chứng viên đề nghị người yêu cầu công chứng làm rõ hoặc theo đề nghị của người yêu cầu công chứng, công chứng viên tiến hành xác minh hoặc yêu cầu giám định; trường hợp không làm rõ được thì có quyền từ chối công chứng.

6. Công chứng viên kiểm tra dự thảo hợp đồng, giao dịch; nếu trong dự thảo hợp đồng, giao dịch có điều khoản vi phạm pháp luật, trái đạo đức xã hội, đối tượng của hợp đồng, giao dịch không phù hợp với quy định của pháp luật thì công chứng viên phải chỉ rõ cho người yêu cầu công chứng để sửa chữa. Trường hợp người yêu cầu công chứng không sửa chữa thì công chứng viên có quyền từ chối công chứng.

7. Người yêu cầu công chứng tự đọc lại dự thảo hợp đồng, giao dịch hoặc công chứng viên đọc cho người yêu cầu công chứng nghe theo đề nghị của người yêu cầu công chứng.

8. Người yêu cầu công chứng đồng ý toàn bộ nội dung trong dự thảo hợp đồng, giao dịch thì ký vào từng trang của hợp đồng, giao dịch. Công chứng viên yêu cầu

（d）所有权证明、使用权证明材料复印件，或可证明法律规定的必须登记的所有权、使用权证件的与待公证财产、交易相关证件的复印件。

（e）复印与合同、交易有关的依法必备的其他材料。

2. 本条第 1 款规定的复印件须内容齐全、正确与原件核对一致。

3. 公证员应核查公证申请材料中的文件。申请公证的材料齐全，如果材料与法律规定相符应予受理并注明公证编号。

4. 公证员应引导公证申请人遵守公证程序规定和各种与合同、交易有关的法律规定；向公证申请人解释清楚他们的合法权利、义务和利益，签订合同、交易的义务和法律后果。

5. 有义务指出在申请公证的材料中有疑问，有被威胁、强迫嫌疑的合同、交易。公证员对公证申请人的民事行为能力有怀疑或合同、交易对象没有描述具体、清楚的，公证员应提醒公证申请人明确有关事宜或根据公证员的提醒进行明确，若没有明确则拒绝公证。

6. 公证员应审查申请公证的合同、交易，如果起草的合同、交易有条款违反法律、违背社会公序良俗或合同、交易对象不符合法律规定，公证员应当指明给公证申请人改正，如果公证申请人不改正，公证员有权拒绝公证。

7. 公证申请人自行阐述合同、交易案件或公证员听取其要求由公证员阐述给公证申请人。

8. 公证申请人同意合同、交易全部内容就在合同、交易中需要签字的每一处签字，为了和之前记录的合同、交易的签字、口头证明做对照，公证员要求

người yêu cầu công chứng xuất trình bản chính của các giấy tờ quy định tại khoản 1 Điều này để đối chiếu trước khi ghi lời chứng, ký vào từng trang của hợp đồng, giao dịch.

公证申请人陈列出本条第 1 款规定的材料。

Điều 41. Công chứng hợp đồng, giao dịch do công chứng viên soạn thảo theo đề nghị của người yêu cầu công chứng

第四十一条 由公证员根据公证申请人的请求起草公证合同、交易

1. Người yêu cầu công chứng nộp một bộ hồ sơ theo quy định tại các điểm a, c, d và đ khoản 1 và khoản 2 Điều 40 của Luật này và nêu nội dung, ý định giao kết hợp đồng, giao dịch.

1. 公证申请人根据本法第 40 条第 2 款 a、b、c、d 项规定递交完整材料并注明合同、交易的内容、履行约定。

2. Công chứng viên thực hiện các việc quy định tại các khoản 3, 4 và 5 Điều 40 của Luật này.

Trường hợp nội dung, ý định giao kết hợp đồng, giao dịch là xác thực, không vi phạm pháp luật, không trái đạo đức xã hội thì công chứng viên soạn thảo hợp đồng, giao dịch.

2. 公证员执行本法的第 40 条第 3 款、第 4 款、第 5 款规定。

如果履行合同、交易的内容意愿真实且不违反法律、不违背社会道德，公证员应起草合同、交易。

3. Người yêu cầu công chứng tự đọc dự thảo hợp đồng, giao dịch hoặc công chứng viên đọc cho người yêu cầu công chứng nghe. Trường hợp người yêu cầu công chứng đồng ý toàn bộ nội dung trong dự thảo hợp đồng, giao dịch thì ký vào từng trang của hợp đồng, giao dịch. Công chứng viên yêu cầu người yêu cầu công chứng xuất trình bản chính của các giấy tờ quy định tại khoản 1 Điều này để đối chiếu trước khi ghi lời chứng, ký vào từng trang của hợp đồng, giao dịch.

3. 公证申请人自行阐述合同、交易草案或公证员阐述给公证申请人听。如果公证申请人同意合同、交易里的全部内容，应当在合同、交易上逐页签字。为了与以前保存的交易、合同的口头证明、签字对照，公证员应要求公证申请人出示本条第 1 款规定的原件证明。

Điều 42. Phạm vi công chứng hợp đồng, giao dịch về bất động sản

第四十二条 不动产合同、交易的公证范围

Công chứng viên của tổ chức hành, nghề công chứng chỉ được công chứng hợp đồng, giao dịch về bất động sản trong phạm vi tỉnh, thành phố trực thuộc trung ương nơi tổ chức hành nghề công chứng đặt trụ sở, trừ trường hợp công chứng di chúc, văn bản từ chối nhận di sản là bất động sản và văn bản ủy quyền liên quan đến việc thực hiện các quyền đối với bất động sản.

公证业、组织的公证员只可以在中央直属的省、市设立的公证机构办事处公证不动产合同、交易，公证遗嘱以遗产是不动产为由放弃继承和与执行不动产相关的各种权利的委托权利文本除外。

Điều 43. Thời hạn công chứng

第四十三条 工作时间

1. Thời hạn công chứng được xác định kể từ ngày thụ lý hồ sơ yêu cầu công chứng đến ngày trả kết quả công chứng. Thời gian xác minh, giám định nội dung liên quan đến hợp đồng, giao dịch, niêm yết việc thụ lý công chứng văn bản thỏa thuận phân chia di sản, văn bản khai nhận di sản, dịch giấy tờ, văn bản không tính vào thời hạn công chứng.

1. 公证期间是自收到公证申请材料之日到公布公证结果之日。验证和核实与合同、交易有关内容的时间，起草遗产分割协议、遗产申报的时间，翻译证明、文本的时间不算入公证期限。

2. Thời hạn công chứng không quá 02 ngày làm việc; đối với hợp đồng, giao dịch có nội dung phức tạp thì thời

2. 公证期限不超过 2 个工作日；内容复杂的合同、交易，公证时间可以延长但不超过 10 个工作日。

hạn công chứng có thể kéo dài hơn nhưng không quá 10 ngày làm việc.

Điều 44. Địa điểm công chứng

1. Việc công chứng phải được thực hiện tại trụ sở của tổ chức hành nghề công chứng, trừ các trường hợp quy định tại khoản 2 Điều này.

2. Việc công chứng có thể được thực hiện ngoài trụ sở của tổ chức hành nghề công chứng trong trường hợp người yêu cầu công chứng là người già yếu, không thể đi lại được, người đang bị tạm giữ, tạm giam, đang thi hành án phạt tù hoặc có lý do chính đáng khác không thể đến trụ sở của tổ chức hành nghề công chứng.

Điều 45. Chữ viết trong văn bản công chứng

1. Chữ viết trong văn bản công chứng phải rõ ràng, dễ đọc, không được viết tắt hoặc viết bằng ký hiệu, không được viết xen dòng, viết đè dòng, không được tẩy xoá, không được để trống, trừ trường hợp pháp luật có quy định khác.

2. Thời điểm công chứng phải được ghi cả ngày, tháng, năm; có thể ghi giờ, phút nếu người yêu cầu công chứng đề nghị hoặc công chứng viên thấy cần thiết. Các con số phải được ghi cả bằng số và chữ, trừ trường hợp pháp luật có quy định khác.

Điều 46. Lời chứng của công chứng viên

1. Lời chứng của công chứng viên đối với hợp đồng, giao dịch phải ghi rõ thời điểm, địa điểm công chứng, họ, tên công chứng viên, tên tổ chức hành nghề công chứng; chứng nhận người tham gia hợp đồng, giao dịch hoàn toàn tự nguyện, có năng lực hành vi dân sự, mục đích, nội dung của hợp đồng, giao dịch không vi phạm pháp luật, không trái đạo đức xã hội, chữ ký hoặc dấu điểm chỉ trong hợp đồng, giao dịch đúng là chữ ký hoặc dấu điểm chỉ của người tham gia hợp đồng, giao dịch; trách nhiệm của công chứng viên đối với lời chứng; có chữ ký của công chứng viên và đóng dấu của tổ chức hành nghề công chứng.

2. Bộ trưởng Bộ Tư pháp quy định chi tiết mẫu lời chứng của công chứng viên đối với hợp đồng, giao dịch.

Điều 47. Người yêu cầu công chứng, người làm chứng, người phiên dịch

1. Người yêu cầu công chứng là cá nhân phải có năng lực hành vi dân sự.

Trường hợp người yêu cầu công chứng là tổ chức thì việc yêu cầu công chứng được thực hiện thông qua người đại diện theo pháp luật hoặc người đại diện theo ủy quyền của tổ chức đó.

第四十四条　公证地点

1. 公证应该在公证机构办事处进行，本条第 2 款规定的情况除外。

2. 公证申请人是老人，行动不方便者，正被拘留、羁押，执行刑罚或有其他正当理由不能到公证机构办事处的，公证员可以在公证机构办事处以外的地方进行。

第四十五条　公证文本中的书写文字

1. 公证文本中的书写应当清晰、易读，不可以简写或潦草，不可以插线、压线写，不可以删除、空格，法律有其他规定的情况除外。

2. 公证时间应注明年、月、日，如果公证申请人申请或公证员认为需要的，应注明时、分。数字应该用阿拉伯数字和文字写明，法律有其他规定的除外。

第四十六条　公证员的口头公证

1. 对于公证员合同、交易的口头公证应注明公证时间、地点，公证员全名，公证机构名称；证明签订合同、交易的当事方完全自愿、有民事行为能力，合同、交易的内容、目的不违反法律，不违反公序良俗，合同、交易中的签字或盖章只属签订合同、交易的人的签字或盖章；公证员对口头公证负责任；有公证员的签字和公证机构的盖章。

2. 司法部长规定公证员对合同、交易口头公证的细节。

第四十七条　公证申请人、证人、翻译者

1. 公证申请人是有民事行为能力的个人。

公证申请人是组织的话，公证可以通过法人或组织授权的代表申请公证。

Người yêu cầu công chứng phải xuất trình đủ giấy tờ cần thiết liên quan đến việc công chứng và chịu trách nhiệm về tính chính xác, tính hợp pháp của các giấy tờ đó.

2. Trường hợp người yêu cầu công chứng không đọc được, không nghe được, không ký, điểm chỉ được hoặc trong những trường hợp khác do pháp luật quy định thì việc công chứng phải có người làm chứng.

Người làm chứng phải là người từ đủ 18 tuổi trở lên, có năng lực hành vi dân sự đầy đủ và không có quyền, lợi ích hoặc nghĩa vụ liên quan đến việc công chứng.

Người làm chứng do người yêu cầu công chứng mời, nếu người yêu cầu công chứng không mời được thì công chứng viên chỉ định.

3. Trường hợp người yêu cầu công chứng không thông thạo tiếng Việt thì họ phải có người phiên dịch.

Người phiên dịch phải là người từ đủ 18 tuổi trở lên, có năng lực hành vi dân sự đầy đủ, thông thạo tiếng Việt và ngôn ngữ mà người yêu cầu công chứng sử dụng.

Người phiên dịch do người yêu cầu công chứng mời và phải chịu trách nhiệm trước pháp luật về việc phiên dịch của mình.

Điều 48. Ký, điểm chỉ trong văn bản công chứng

1. Người yêu cầu công chứng, người làm chứng, người phiên dịch phải ký vào hợp đồng, giao dịch trước mặt công chứng viên.

Trong trường hợp người có thẩm quyền giao kết hợp đồng của tổ chức tín dụng, doanh nghiệp khác đã đăng ký chữ ký mẫu tại tổ chức hành nghề công chứng thì người đó có thể ký trước vào hợp đồng; công chứng viên phải đối chiếu chữ ký của họ trong hợp đồng với chữ ký mẫu trước khi thực hiện việc công chứng.

2. Việc điểm chỉ được thay thế việc ký trong trường hợp người yêu cầu công chứng, người làm chứng, người phiên dịch không ký được do khuyết tật hoặc không biết ký. Khi điểm chỉ, người yêu cầu công chứng, người làm chứng, người phiên dịch sử dụng ngón trỏ phải; nếu không điểm chỉ được bằng ngón trỏ phải thì điểm chỉ bằng ngón trỏ trái; trường hợp không thể điểm chỉ bằng hai ngón trỏ đó thì điểm chỉ bằng ngón khác và phải ghi rõ việc điểm chỉ đó bằng ngón nào, của bàn tay nào.

3. Việc điểm chỉ cũng có thể thực hiện đồng thời với việc ký trong các trường hợp sau đây:

a) Công chứng di chúc;

b) Theo đề nghị của người yêu cầu công chứng;

c) Công chứng viên thấy cần thiết để bảo vệ quyền lợi cho người yêu cầu công chứng.

公证申请人应出示完整的与公证相关的所需证明材料，并对所有证明材料的真实性、合法性负责。

2. 公证申请人是聋哑人或文盲的，可以以按手印或法律规定的其他方式进行公证，但公证时应有见证人。

见证人应是年满 18 周岁以上，有完全的民事行为能力，且与公证事项没有利害冲突的人。

见证人由公证申请人邀请，如果公证申请人无法邀请那么由公证员指定。

3. 公证申请人不通晓越南语的，则应为其配备翻译。

翻译者应年满 18 周岁以上，有完全的民事行为能力，精通越南语和公证申请人的语言。

翻译者由公证申请人员雇佣，翻译者应对其翻译的内容负法律责任。

第四十八条　在公证文本中签字、捺印

1. 公证申请人、证人、翻译者都应在公证员的面前，在合同、交易的文本上签字。

公证申请人有权限交接组织信用、其他经营合同，而此前在公证机构登记过签字字样的，其可以提前在合同里签字；公证员在进行公证时，应当把合同里的签字和此前的签字字样进行对比。

2. 公证申请人、证人、翻译者由于残疾或不能写字的情况，捺印可以代替盖章。捺印时，公证申请人、见证人、翻译者使用右手食指捺印；如果不能使用右手食指那么使用左手食指；如果双手食指都不能捺印可以用其他手指捺印，但要注明捺印的具体手指。

3. 捺印也可以和下列几种情形一起进行：

（a）公证遗产；

（b）应公证申请人的要求；

（c）公证员认为有必要保护公证申请人的权利的。

Điều 49. Việc ghi trang, tờ trong văn bản công chứng

Văn bản công chứng có từ hai trang trở lên thì từng trang phải được đánh số thứ tự. Văn bản công chứng có từ hai tờ trở lên phải được đóng dấu giáp lai giữa các tờ.

第四十九条 公证文本中注明的纸张、页数

公证文本有 2 页以上的要逐页注明页码顺序。公证文本有 2 张以上的应在相邻的各页盖骑缝章。

Điều 50. Sửa lỗi kỹ thuật trong văn bản công chứng

1. Lỗi kỹ thuật là lỗi do sai sót trong khi ghi chép, đánh máy, in ấn trong văn bản công chứng mà việc sửa lỗi đó không làm ảnh hưởng đến quyền và nghĩa vụ của người tham gia hợp đồng, giao dịch.

2. Việc sửa lỗi kỹ thuật trong văn bản công chứng được thực hiện tại tổ chức hành nghề công chứng đã thực hiện việc công chứng đó. Trường hợp tổ chức hành nghề công chứng đã thực hiện việc công chứng chấm dứt hoạt động, chuyển đổi, chuyển nhượng hoặc giải thể thì tổ chức hành nghề công chứng đang lưu trữ hồ sơ công chứng thực hiện việc sửa lỗi kỹ thuật.

3. Công chứng viên thực hiện việc sửa lỗi kỹ thuật có trách nhiệm đối chiếu từng lỗi cần sửa với các giấy tờ trong hồ sơ công chứng, gạch chân chỗ cần sửa, sau đó ghi chữ, dấu hoặc con số đã được sửa vào bên lề kèm theo chữ ký của mình và đóng dấu của tổ chức hành nghề công chứng. Công chứng viên có trách nhiệm thông báo việc sửa lỗi kỹ thuật đó cho người tham gia hợp đồng, giao dịch.

第五十条 修改公证文本中的技术错误

1. 技术错误是公证文本中粘贴、打字、复制时造成的，修改这些错误不影响签订合同、交易当事人的权利和义务。

2. 修改在公证文本中的技术错误可以在原公证机构处进行。如果原公证机构已经取消公证营业、转换或解散，作技术修改的公证机构须保留正在进行修改技术错误的材料。

3. 公证员有义务与公证材料中的证明材料进行对照，逐个错误地修改，然后用文字、记号修改并在旁边附上自己的签字和公证机构的盖章，公证员有义务把出现技术错误的地方通报给签订合同、交易的当事人。

Điều 51. Công chứng việc sửa đổi, bổ sung, hủy bỏ hợp đồng, giao dịch

1. Việc công chứng sửa đổi, bổ sung, hủy bỏ hợp đồng, giao dịch đã được công chứng chỉ được thực hiện khi có sự thỏa thuận, cam kết bằng văn bản của tất cả những người đã tham gia hợp đồng, giao dịch đó.

2. Việc công chứng sửa đổi, bổ sung, hủy bỏ hợp đồng, giao dịch đã được công chứng được thực hiện tại tổ chức hành nghề công chứng đã thực hiện việc công chứng đó và do công chứng viên tiến hành. Trường hợp tổ chức hành nghề công chứng đã thực hiện việc công chứng chấm dứt hoạt động, chuyển đổi, chuyển nhượng hoặc giải thể thì công chứng viên của tổ chức hành nghề công chứng đang lưu trữ hồ sơ công chứng thực hiện việc sửa đổi, bổ sung, hủy bỏ hợp đồng, giao dịch.

3. Thủ tục công chứng việc sửa đổi, bổ sung, hủy bỏ hợp đồng, giao dịch đã được công chứng được thực hiện như thủ tục công chứng hợp đồng, giao dịch quy định tại Chương này.

第五十一条 公证员变更、补充、毁销合同、交易

1. 当有全部参与合同、交易的当事人有书面讨论、承诺时，公证员才可以变更、补充、毁销已经公证的合同、交易。

2. 公证变更、补充、毁销已经公证的合同、交易可以在原公证机构和由原公证员进行。如果原公证机构已进行取消公证营业、转换、转让或解散，那么进行新公证的公证机构的公证员须保留变更、补充、销毁合同、交易的材料。

3. 变更、补充、销毁已公证过的合同、交易的公证手续按照本章规定的公证合同、交易的程序进行。

Điều 52. Người có quyền đề nghị Tòa án tuyên bố văn bản công chứng vô hiệu

Công chứng viên, người yêu cầu công chứng, người

第五十二条 有权申请法院宣告公证文本无效的人

有充分证据显示公证已违反法规时，公证员、公

làm chứng, người phiên dịch, người có quyền lợi, nghĩa vụ liên quan, cơ quan nhà nước có thẩm quyền có quyền đề nghị Tòa án tuyên bố văn bản công chứng vô hiệu khi có căn cứ cho rằng việc công chứng có vi phạm pháp luật.

证申请人、见证人、翻译者、利害相关的人、有权限的国家机关有权向法院申请宣告公证文本无效。

Mục 2. THỦ TỤC CÔNG CHỨNG MỘT SỐ HỢP ĐỒNG, GIAO DỊCH, CÔNG CHỨNG BẢN DỊCH, NHẬN LƯU GIỮ DI CHÚC

目录二　公证合同、交易、公证译本、接收遗嘱保留的程序

Điều 53. Phạm vi áp dụng

Thủ tục công chứng hợp đồng thế chấp bất động sản, hợp đồng ủy quyền, di chúc, văn bản thỏa thuận phân chia di sản, văn bản khai nhận di sản, văn bản từ chối nhận di sản được thực hiện theo quy định của Mục này và các quy định của Mục 1 Chương này mà không trái với quy định của Mục này.

第五十三条　适用范围

公证不动产抵押合同、委托合同、遗嘱、遗产分配协议文本；申明接受遗产文本；放弃继承遗产文本可以根据本目录的规定和本章“目录一”不违背本目录规定的各种规则进行。

Điều 54. Công chứng hợp đồng thế chấp bất động sản

1. Việc công chứng hợp đồng thế chấp bất động sản phải được thực hiện tại tổ chức hành nghề công chứng có trụ sở tại tỉnh, thành phố trực thuộc trung ương nơi có bất động sản.

2. Trường hợp một bất động sản đã được thế chấp để bảo đảm thực hiện một nghĩa vụ và hợp đồng thế chấp đã được công chứng mà sau đó được tiếp tục thế chấp để bảo đảm cho một nghĩa vụ khác trong phạm vi pháp luật cho phép thì các hợp đồng thế chấp tiếp theo phải được công chứng tại tổ chức hành nghề công chứng đã công chứng hợp đồng thế chấp lần đầu. Trường hợp tổ chức hành nghề công chứng đã thực hiện việc công chứng chấm dứt hoạt động, chuyển đổi, chuyển nhượng hoặc giải thể thì công chứng viên của tổ chức hành nghề công chứng đang lưu trữ hồ sơ công chứng hợp đồng thế chấp tiếp theo đó.

第五十四条　公证不动产抵押合同

1. 公证不动产抵押合同要在省、直辖市设置的不动产公证机构办事处进行。

2. 在法律允许的范围内，一处不动产为担保一个合同已经进行了抵押，如果为了担保其他的合同又继续抵押，则后续的各种合同都要在公证第一次抵押合同的公证机构进行公证。如果原公证机构已经取消公证营业，转换、转让或解散，办理后续抵押合同公证的公证员须保留后续抵押合同的公证材料。

Điều 55. Công chứng hợp đồng ủy quyền

1. Khi công chứng các hợp đồng ủy quyền, công chứng viên có trách nhiệm kiểm tra kỹ hồ sơ, giải thích rõ quyền và nghĩa vụ của các bên và hậu quả pháp lý của việc ủy quyền đó cho các bên tham gia.

2. Trong trường hợp bên ủy quyền và bên được ủy quyền không thể cùng đến một tổ chức hành nghề công chứng thì bên ủy quyền yêu cầu tổ chức hành nghề công chứng nơi họ cư trú công chứng hợp đồng ủy quyền; bên được ủy quyền yêu cầu tổ chức hành nghề công chứng nơi họ cư trú công chứng tiếp vào bản gốc hợp đồng ủy quyền này, hoàn tất thủ tục công chứng hợp đồng ủy quyền.

第五十五条　委托合同公证

1. 在公证委托合同时，公证员有义务仔细检查公证申请材料，向当事人解释清楚各方的权利、义务及委托的法律后果。

2. 若委托方和被委托方不能一起到公证机构，公证员可以应委托方的要求先到其居住地公证委托合同；再应被委托方的要求到其居住地继续公证该委托合同的原件，则完全结束委托合同的公证手续。

Điều 56. Công chứng di chúc

1. Người lập di chúc phải tự mình yêu cầu công chứng di chúc, không ủy quyền cho người khác yêu cầu công chứng di chúc.

2. Trường hợp công chứng viên nghi ngờ người lập di chúc bị bệnh tâm thần hoặc mắc bệnh khác mà không thể nhận thức và làm chủ được hành vi của mình hoặc có căn cứ cho rằng việc lập di chúc có dấu hiệu bị lừa dối, đe dọa hoặc cưỡng ép thì công chứng viên đề nghị người lập di chúc làm rõ, trường hợp không làm rõ được thì có quyền từ chối công chứng di chúc đó.

Trường hợp tính mạng người lập di chúc bị đe dọa thì người yêu cầu công chứng không phải xuất trình đầy đủ giấy tờ quy định tại khoản 1 Điều 40 của Luật này nhưng phải ghi rõ trong văn bản công chứng.

3. Di chúc đã được công chứng nhưng sau đó người lập di chúc muốn sửa đổi, bổ sung, thay thế, hủy bỏ một phần hoặc toàn bộ di chúc thì có thể yêu cầu bất kỳ công chứng viên nào công chứng việc sửa đổi, bổ sung, thay thế hoặc hủy bỏ đó. Trường hợp di chúc trước đó đang được lưu giữ tại một tổ chức hành nghề công chứng thì người lập di chúc phải thông báo cho tổ chức hành nghề công chứng đang lưu giữ di chúc biết việc sửa đổi, bổ sung, thay thế, hủy bỏ di chúc đó.

Điều 57. Công chứng văn bản thỏa thuận phân chia di sản

1. Những người thừa kế theo pháp luật hoặc theo di chúc mà trong di chúc không xác định rõ phần di sản được hưởng của từng người thì có quyền yêu cầu công chứng văn bản thỏa thuận phân chia di sản.

Trong văn bản thỏa thuận phân chia di sản, người được hưởng di sản có thể tặng cho toàn bộ hoặc một phần di sản mà mình được hưởng cho người thừa kế khác.

2. Trường hợp di sản là quyền sử dụng đất hoặc tài sản pháp luật quy định phải đăng ký quyền sở hữu thì trong hồ sơ yêu cầu công chứng phải có giấy tờ chứng minh quyền sử dụng đất, quyền sở hữu tài sản của người để lại di sản đó.

Trường hợp thừa kế theo pháp luật, thì trong hồ sơ yêu cầu công chứng phải có giấy tờ chứng minh quan hệ giữa người để lại di sản và người được hưởng di sản theo quy định của pháp luật về thừa kế. Trường hợp thừa kế theo di chúc, trong hồ sơ yêu cầu công chứng phải có bản sao di chúc.

3. Công chứng viên phải kiểm tra để xác định người để lại di sản đúng là người có quyền sử dụng đất, quyền sở

第五十六条　遗嘱公证

1. 遗嘱订立人应当是申请公证遗嘱的申请人，不委托其他人申请公证遗嘱。

2. 公证员怀疑遗嘱订立人患有神经病或其他没有意识、行为不能自主的疾病；有证据证明遗嘱订立人是被欺骗、胁迫的，公证员就要提醒遗嘱订立人清楚地作出意思表示，若清楚地作出意思表示，公证员有权拒绝公证该遗嘱。

遗嘱订立人的生命被威胁，而公证申请人没有提供本法第 40 条第 1 款规定的全部证明材料，应在公证文本中予以注明。

3. 遗嘱已公证过，但遗嘱订立人以后想变更、补充、替代、销毁一部分或全部遗嘱，可以请求任何一个公证员公证变更、补充、替换或销毁原公证过的遗嘱。如果原遗嘱仍保管在原公证机构，那么遗嘱订立人须告知正在保管该遗嘱的原公证机构变更、补充、代替、销毁原遗嘱。

第五十七条　公证分配遗产的协议文本

1. 遗嘱中没有明确指出根据法律或作出遗产分配方案的，有权申请公证文本的人应协商好遗产分配方案。

在商议遗产分配的文本中，遗产继承人可以将其继承的全部或一部分遗产赠送给其他继承人。

2. 如果遗产是土地使用权或法律规定的应该登记所有权的财产，那么在申请公证的材料里就附上被继承人的土地使用权、财产所有权证明材料。

如果根据法律继承，在要求工作的材料里应有《继承法》规定的被继承人和继承人的关系证明材料。如果根据遗嘱继承，在申请公证的材料里应有遗嘱的复印件。

3. 为了确认被继承人是遗产的合法所有权人、公证申请人是适格可以继承遗产的人，公证员应该进行

hữu tài sản và những người yêu cầu công chứng đúng là người được hưởng di sản; nếu thấy chưa rõ hoặc có căn cứ cho rằng việc để lại di sản và hưởng di sản là không đúng pháp luật thì từ chối yêu cầu công chứng hoặc theo đề nghị của người yêu cầu công chứng, công chứng viên tiến hành xác minh hoặc yêu cầu giám định.

审核；如果无法查清或有证据证明遗产或遗产继承不符合法律的规定，公证员可以拒绝公证申请或根据公证申请人的提议，公证员进行明确或要求鉴定。

Tổ chức hành nghề công chứng có trách nhiệm niêm yết việc thụ lý công chứng văn bản thỏa thuận phân chia di sản trước khi thực hiện việc công chứng.

进行公证之前，公证机构有义务密封受理待公证的财产分配协商文本。

4. Văn bản thỏa thuận phân chia di sản đã được công chứng là một trong các căn cứ để cơ quan nhà nước có thẩm quyền đăng ký việc chuyển quyền sử dụng đất, quyền sở hữu tài sản cho người được hưởng di sản.

4. 已公证的财产分配协商文本是国家机关登记土地使用权流转、财产所有权给遗产继承人的合法依据之一。

Điều 58. Công chứng văn bản khai nhận di sản

第五十八条　公证申明接受遗产的文本

1. Người duy nhất được hưởng di sản theo pháp luật hoặc những người cùng được hưởng di sản theo pháp luật nhưng thỏa thuận không phân chia di sản đó có quyền yêu cầu công chứng văn bản khai nhận di sản.

1. 依法继承遗产的唯一人或依法分配遗产的若干人，但协商不能继承遗产的人有权要求公证申明遗产接受文本。

2. Việc công chứng văn bản khai nhận di sản được thực hiện theo quy định tại khoản 2 và khoản 3 Điều 57 của Luật này.

2. 公证申明遗产接受文本可以根据本法第 57 条第 2 款和第 3 款的程序进行。

3. Chính phủ quy định chi tiết thủ tục niêm yết việc thụ lý công chứng văn bản thỏa thuận phân chia di sản, văn bản khai nhận di sản.

3. 政府规定密封受理公证的遗产分配协商文本、申明遗产接受文本。

Điều 59. Công chứng văn bản từ chối nhận di sản

第五十九条　公证放弃继承遗产的文本

Người thừa kế có thể yêu cầu công chứng văn bản từ chối nhận di sản. Khi yêu cầu công chứng văn bản từ chối nhận di sản, người yêu cầu công chứng phải xuất trình bản sao di chúc trong trường hợp thừa kế theo di chúc hoặc giấy tờ chứng minh quan hệ giữa người để lại di sản và người yêu cầu công chứng theo pháp luật về thừa kế; giấy chứng tử hoặc giấy tờ khác chứng minh người để lại di sản đã chết.

继承人可以申请公证放弃继承遗产的文本。当申请公证放弃继承遗产文本时，公证申请人在根据遗嘱继承或根据《继承法》继承时，应提供被继承人和公证申请人之间的关系证明材料；被继承人死亡证明或其他证明其已经死亡的证明，并出示遗嘱复印件。

Điều 60. Nhận lưu giữ di chúc

第六十条　接受保管遗嘱

1. Người lập di chúc có thể yêu cầu tổ chức hành nghề công chứng nhận lưu giữ di chúc của mình. Khi nhận lưu giữ di chúc, công chứng viên phải niêm phong bản di chúc trước mặt người lập di chúc, ghi giấy nhận lưu giữ và giao cho người lập di chúc.

1. 遗嘱订立人可以申请公证机构保管自己的遗嘱。当接受保管遗嘱时，公证员应当在立遗嘱人面前密封文本，开据接受保管的凭据给遗嘱订立人。

2. Đối với di chúc đã được tổ chức hành nghề công chứng nhận lưu giữ nhưng sau đó tổ chức này chấm dứt hoạt động, chuyển đổi, chuyển nhượng hoặc giải thể thì trước khi chấm dứt hoạt động, chuyển đổi, chuyển nhượng hoặc giải thể, tổ chức hành nghề công chứng phải thỏa thuận với người lập di chúc về việc chuyển cho tổ chức

2. 公证遗嘱接受保管后，如果该组织取消营业，转换、转让或解散的，在取消营业、转换或解散之前应和遗嘱订立人协商由其他公证机构接受保管。如果没有协商或协商未达成一致意见，那么应将遗嘱和保管遗嘱的费用一并退还给遗嘱订立人。

hành nghề công chứng khác lưu giữ di chúc. Trường hợp không có thỏa thuận hoặc không thỏa thuận được thì di chúc và phí lưu giữ di chúc phải được trả lại cho người lập di chúc.

3. Việc công bố di chúc lưu giữ tại tổ chức hành nghề công chứng được thực hiện theo quy định của pháp luật về dân sự.

3. 公布保管在公证机构的遗嘱可以根据民事法规定进行。

Điều 61. Công chứng bản dịch

1. Việc dịch giấy tờ, văn bản từ tiếng Việt sang tiếng nước ngoài hoặc từ tiếng nước ngoài sang tiếng Việt để công chứng phải do người phiên dịch là cộng tác viên của tổ chức hành nghề công chứng thực hiện. Cộng tác viên phải là người tốt nghiệp đại học ngoại ngữ hoặc đại học khác mà thông thạo thứ tiếng nước ngoài đó. Cộng tác viên phải chịu trách nhiệm đối với tổ chức hành nghề công chứng về tính chính xác, phù hợp của nội dung bản dịch do mình thực hiện.

第六十一条　公证译本

1. 证件、文本为进行公证而从越南语译成其他国家的语言或从其他国家的语言译成越南语的，翻译应当由公证机构的合作者进行。合作者应当是外语大学或其他大学毕业并精通该外国语言的人。公证机构的合作者应对自己翻译的译本内容的准确性、相符性负责任。

2. Công chứng viên tiếp nhận bản chính giấy tờ, văn bản cần dịch, kiểm tra và giao cho người phiên dịch là cộng tác viên của tổ chức mình thực hiện. Người phiên dịch phải ký vào từng trang của bản dịch trước khi công chứng viên ghi lời chứng và ký vào từng trang của bản dịch.

2. 公证员接收需要翻译的证件、文本原件，检查并交给本公证机构合作的翻译者进行。在公证员记录口头公证和在译本的每页签字之前，翻译者应当在译本的每页签字。

Từng trang của bản dịch phải được đóng dấu chữ “Bản dịch” vào chỗ trống phía trên bên phải; bản dịch phải được đính kèm với bản sao của bản chính và được đóng dấu giáp lai.

译本逐页的右上角空白的地方应当盖有“译本”字样的印章；译本应钉在原文版本的复印件后面并盖章装订好。

3. Lời chứng của công chứng viên đối với bản dịch phải ghi rõ thời điểm, địa điểm công chứng, họ tên công chứng viên, tên tổ chức hành nghề công chứng; họ tên người phiên dịch; chứng nhận chữ ký trong bản dịch đúng là chữ ký của người phiên dịch; chứng nhận nội dung bản dịch là chính xác, không vi phạm pháp luật, không trái đạo đức xã hội; có chữ ký của công chứng viên và đóng dấu của tổ chức hành nghề công chứng.

3. 公证员对译本的口头公证应注明盖章的时间、地点、公证员的全名、公证机构、翻译者的全名，公证译本中应有正式翻译者的签字；公证翻译的内容应准确、不违反法律规定、不违背社会道德，由公证员签字并加盖公证机构的印章。

4. Công chứng viên không được nhận và công chứng bản dịch trong các trường hợp sau đây:

a) Công chứng viên biết hoặc phải biết bản chính được cấp sai thẩm quyền hoặc không hợp lệ; bản chính giả;

b) Giấy tờ, văn bản được yêu cầu dịch đã bị tẩy xoá, sửa chữa, thêm, bớt hoặc bị hư hỏng, cũ nát không thể xác định rõ nội dung;

c) Giấy tờ, văn bản được yêu cầu dịch thuộc bí mật nhà nước; giấy tờ, văn bản bị cấm phổ biến theo quy định của pháp luật.

4. 下列情况，公证员不可以接收和公证译本：

（a）公证员知道或应当知道正本的权限不合格或不合理，假的正本；

（b）要求翻译的证件、文本已被擦拭、涂改、添加、减少或被破坏，破旧不堪不能确定清楚内容；

（c）要求公证的证件、文本属于国家机密，根据法律规定被普遍禁止的证件、文本。

5. Bộ trưởng Bộ Tư pháp quy định chi tiết mẫu lời chứng của công chứng viên đối với bản dịch.

Chương VI
CƠ SỞ DỮ LIỆU CÔNG CHỨNG VÀ LƯU TRỮ HỒ SƠ CÔNG CHỨNG

Điều 62. Cơ sở dữ liệu công chứng

1. Cơ sở dữ liệu công chứng bao gồm các thông tin về nguồn gốc tài sản, tình trạng giao dịch của tài sản và các thông tin về biện pháp ngăn chặn được áp dụng đối với tài sản có liên quan đến hợp đồng, giao dịch đã được công chứng.

2. Ủy ban nhân dân cấp tỉnh có trách nhiệm xây dựng cơ sở dữ liệu công chứng của địa phương và ban hành quy chế khai thác, sử dụng cơ sở dữ liệu công chứng.

3. Bộ Tư pháp chủ trì phối hợp với Bộ Tài nguyên và Môi trường, Bộ Xây dựng và các bộ, ngành có liên quan chỉ đạo, hướng dẫn việc xây dựng và quản lý, khai thác cơ sở dữ liệu công chứng tại các địa phương.

Điều 63. Hồ sơ công chứng

1. Hồ sơ công chứng bao gồm phiếu yêu cầu công chứng, bản chính văn bản công chứng, bản sao các giấy tờ mà người yêu cầu công chứng đã nộp, các giấy tờ xác minh, giám định và giấy tờ liên quan khác.

2. Hồ sơ công chứng phải được đánh số theo thứ tự thời gian phù hợp với việc ghi trong sổ công chứng.

Điều 64. Chế độ lưu trữ hồ sơ công chứng

1. Tổ chức hành nghề công chứng phải bảo quản chặt chẽ, thực hiện biện pháp an toàn đối với hồ sơ công chứng.

2. Bản chính văn bản công chứng và các giấy tờ khác trong hồ sơ công chứng phải được lưu trữ ít nhất là 20 năm tại trụ sở của tổ chức hành nghề công chứng; trường hợp lưu trữ ngoài trụ sở thì phải có sự đồng ý bằng văn bản của Sở Tư pháp.

3. Trong trường hợp cơ quan nhà nước có thẩm quyền có yêu cầu bằng văn bản về việc cung cấp hồ sơ công chứng phục vụ cho việc giám sát, kiểm tra, thanh tra, điều tra, truy tố, xét xử, thi hành án liên quan đến việc đã công chứng thì tổ chức hành nghề công chứng có trách nhiệm cung cấp bản sao văn bản công chứng và các giấy tờ khác có liên quan. Việc đối chiếu bản sao văn bản công chứng với bản chính chỉ được thực hiện tại tổ chức hành nghề công chứng nơi đang lưu trữ hồ sơ công chứng.

4. Việc kê biên, khám xét trụ sở của tổ chức hành nghề công chứng phải thực hiện theo quy định của pháp

5. 司法部部长规定公证员对译本口头公证的模板细节。

第六章　公证基本资料和保管公证档案

第六十二条　公证的基本资料

1. 公证的基本资料包括财产来源的各种信息、财产交易状态和可以采用的与合同、交易的财产公证有关的各种信息。

2. 省级人民委员有义务建设地方公证材料库和颁布查阅、使用公证基本材料的规章制度。

3. 司法部牵头，联合资源环境部、建设部和其他各部，配合相关部门进行行业指导工作，引导在各地方建设、管理和查阅公证基本资料。

第六十三条　公证档案

1. 公证档案包括要求公证的申请，公证文书正本，公证申请人已经提交的各种证明文件的复印件，各种身份证件、其他相关的证件和鉴定报告等。

2. 公证档案应当按照时间顺序归档，记上与公证文书中备注数字相符的数字。

第六十四条　保管公证档案的制度

1. 公证机构对公证档案要进行严密、有安全措施的保管。

2. 公证文书正本和在公证档案中的其他证件最少应留存在公证机构办事处20年；如果保管在办事处以外，应当经司法机构书面同意。

3. 如果公证档案与国家机关在办案件相关，国家机关有权书面要求提供公证档案给监察、检察、侦查、调查、控诉、审判、执行部门。公证机构有义务提供公证文书和其他相关证件复印件。比对公证文本复印件和正本只可以在留存着公证档案的公证机构进行。

4. 公证档案的编撰、研究工作应根据法律的规定和司法机构代表的政见或地方公证协会组织代表进行。

luật và có sự chứng kiến của đại diện Sở Tư pháp hoặc đại diện tổ chức xã hội - nghề nghiệp của công chứng viên tại địa phương.

5. Trường hợp Phòng công chứng được chuyển đổi thành Văn phòng công chứng thì hồ sơ công chứng do Văn phòng công chứng được chuyển đổi quản lý.

Trường hợp Phòng công chứng bị giải thể thì hồ sơ công chứng phải được chuyển cho một Phòng công chứng khác hoặc một Văn phòng công chứng do Sở Tư pháp chỉ định.

Trường hợp Văn phòng công chứng chấm dứt hoạt động thì Văn phòng công chứng đó phải thỏa thuận với một Văn phòng công chứng khác về việc tiếp nhận hồ sơ công chứng; nếu không thỏa thuận được hoặc Văn phòng công chứng chấm dứt hoạt động do toàn bộ công chứng viên hợp danh chết hoặc bị Tòa án tuyên bố là đã chết thì Sở Tư pháp chỉ định một Phòng công chứng hoặc một Văn phòng công chứng khác tiếp nhận hồ sơ công chứng.

Điều 65. Cấp bản sao văn bản công chứng

1. Việc cấp bản sao văn bản công chứng được thực hiện trong các trường hợp sau đây:

a) Theo yêu cầu của cơ quan có thẩm quyền trong các trường hợp được quy định tại khoản 3 Điều 64 của Luật này;

b) Theo yêu cầu của các bên tham gia hợp đồng, giao dịch, người có quyền, nghĩa vụ liên quan đến hợp đồng, giao dịch đã được công chứng.

2. Việc cấp bản sao văn bản công chứng do tổ chức hành nghề công chứng đang lưu trữ bản chính văn bản công chứng đó thực hiện.

Chương VII
PHÍ CÔNG CHỨNG, THÙ LAO CÔNG CHỨNG VÀ CHI PHÍ KHÁC

Điều 66. Phí công chứng

1. Phí công chứng bao gồm phí công chứng hợp đồng, giao dịch, bản dịch, phí lưu giữ di chúc, phí cấp bản sao văn bản công chứng.

Người yêu cầu công chứng hợp đồng, giao dịch, bản dịch, lưu giữ di chúc, cấp bản sao văn bản công chứng phải nộp phí công chứng.

2. Mức thu, chế độ thu, nộp, sử dụng và quản lý phí công chứng được thực hiện theo quy định của pháp luật.

Điều 67. Thù lao công chứng

1. Người yêu cầu công chứng phải trả thù lao khi

5. 公证办公室可以转换成公证机构的话，则公证档案由公证机构接手管理。

如果公证办公室被解散，公证档案应当转给一个其他公证办公室或由司法机构指定的公证机构。

公证机构取消营业的话，则该公证机构应当和其他公证机构协商接收公证档案的事宜；如果协商不成或公证机构取消营业是由全部正式的公证员死亡或被法院宣告死亡的，那么司法机构就要指定一个公证办公室或一个其他公证机构接收公证档案。

第六十五条　提供公证文书复印件

1. 可在下列情形提供公证文书复印件：

（a）在本法第 64 条第 3 款规定的各种情况下，根据有权机关的要求而提供；

（b）根据签订合同、交易的各方，与已公证的合同、交易有利害关系的人的要求。

2. 由保管公证文书正本的公证机构提供公证文书的复印件。

第七章　公证费、公证酬劳和其他支出

第六十六条　公证费

1. 公证费包含合同、交易、译本费，遗嘱保管费，公证文书复印费。

申请公证合同、交易、译本，保管遗嘱，提供公证复印件的人需缴纳公证费。

2. 收费标准，收、交、使用和管理公证费制度要依据法律的规定进行。

第六十七条　公证酬劳

1. 公证申请人在要求公证机构进行起草合同、交

yêu cầu tổ chức hành nghề công chứng thực hiện việc soạn thảo hợp đồng, giao dịch, đánh máy, sao chụp, dịch giấy tờ, văn bản và các việc khác liên quan đến việc công chứng.

2. Ủy ban nhân dân cấp tỉnh ban hành mức trần thù lao công chứng áp dụng đối với các tổ chức hành nghề công chứng tại địa phương. Tổ chức hành nghề công chứng xác định mức thù lao đối với từng loại việc không vượt quá mức trần thù lao công chứng do Ủy ban nhân dân cấp tỉnh ban hành và niêm yết công khai các mức thù lao tại trụ sở của mình. Tổ chức hành nghề công chứng thu thù lao cao hơn mức trần thù lao và mức thù lao đã niêm yết thì bị xử lý theo quy định của pháp luật.

3. Tổ chức hành nghề công chứng có trách nhiệm giải thích rõ cho người yêu cầu công chứng về thù lao công chứng.

Điều 68. Chi phí khác

1. Trường hợp người yêu cầu công chứng đề nghị xác minh, giám định hoặc thực hiện công chứng ngoài trụ sở của tổ chức hành nghề công chứng thì người yêu cầu công chứng phải trả chi phí để thực hiện việc đó.

Mức chi phí do người yêu cầu công chứng và tổ chức hành nghề công chứng thỏa thuận. Tổ chức hành nghề công chứng không được thu chi phí cao hơn mức chi phí đã thỏa thuận.

2. Tổ chức hành nghề công chứng phải niêm yết rõ nguyên tắc tính chi phí khác và có trách nhiệm giải thích rõ cho người yêu cầu công chứng về các chi phí cụ thể đó.

Chương VIII
QUẢN LÝ NHÀ NƯỚC VỀ CÔNG CHỨNG

Điều 69. Trách nhiệm của Chính phủ, Bộ Tư pháp và các bộ, ngành có liên quan trong công tác quản lý nhà nước về công chứng

1. Chính phủ thống nhất quản lý nhà nước về công chứng.

2. Bộ Tư pháp chịu trách nhiệm trước Chính phủ, Thủ tướng Chính phủ trong việc thực hiện quản lý nhà nước về công chứng, có các nhiệm vụ, quyền hạn sau đây:

a) Ban hành hoặc trình cơ quan nhà nước có thẩm quyền ban hành văn bản quy phạm pháp luật về công chứng;

b) Xây dựng, trình Chính phủ ban hành chính sách phát triển nghề công chứng, trình Thủ tướng Chính phủ ban hành Quy hoạch tổng thể phát triển tổ chức hành nghề công chứng trong cả nước;

易、打字、复印图片，翻译证明、文本和其他与公证相关的事项时应支付公证酬劳。

2. 省级人民委员会向地方各公证机构颁布公证酬劳标准。公证机构对每件公证事项制定的酬劳标准不得超过省级人民委员会颁布的标准，并在其办事处公布酬劳标准。公证机构收取的酬劳高于酬劳标准和公布的酬劳标准的，根据法律规定处理。

3. 公证机构有义务向公证申请人解释清楚公证酬劳。

第六十八条　其他费用

1. 如果公证申请人申请验明、鉴定或在公证机构办事处以外的地方进行公证，那么公证申请人应当支付由此产生的额外费用。

支付标准由公证申请人和公证机构协商。公证机构不得收取超过商定的费用。

2. 公证机构应张贴公告其他费用的支付原则，有义务向公证申请人进行解释。

第八章　国家公证管理

第六十九条　政府、司法部和在管理工作中与之相关的各行、各部的责任

1. 政府统一管理国家公证。

2. 司法部在国家公证业管理工作中，先于政府、政府首长起牵头作用，有下列各项权利和义务：

（a）颁布或向有权颁布公证法律规范的国家机关提交立法建议；

（b）在全国内建设、督促政府颁布的公证行业发展政策，督促政府首脑颁布的公证行业组织总体发展规划；

c) Chủ trì, phối hợp với các bộ, ngành có liên quan hướng dẫn, triển khai, quản lý việc thực hiện Quy hoạch tổng thể phát triển tổ chức hành nghề công chứng trong cả nước;

d) Tuyên truyền, phổ biến pháp luật về công chứng, chính sách phát triển nghề công chứng;

e) Bổ nhiệm, bổ nhiệm lại, miễn nhiệm công chứng viên;

f) Phê duyệt Điều lệ của tổ chức xã hội - nghề nghiệp toàn quốc của công chứng viên sau khi thống nhất ý kiến với Bộ Nội vụ; đình chỉ thi hành và yêu cầu sửa đổi những văn bản, quy định của tổ chức xã hội - nghề nghiệp của công chứng viên trái với quy định của Hiến pháp, Luật này và các văn bản quy phạm pháp luật khác có liên quan;

g) Kiểm tra, thanh tra, xử lý vi phạm, giải quyết khiếu nại, tố cáo về hoạt động công chứng theo thẩm quyền;

h) Định kỳ hằng năm báo cáo Chính phủ về hoạt động công chứng;

i) Quản lý và thực hiện hợp tác quốc tế về hoạt động công chứng;

j) Các nhiệm vụ, quyền hạn khác theo quy định của Luật này và các văn bản quy phạm pháp luật khác có liên quan.

3. Bộ Ngoại giao có trách nhiệm phối hợp với Bộ Tư pháp trong việc hướng dẫn, kiểm tra, thanh tra việc thực hiện công chứng của cơ quan đại diện Việt Nam ở nước ngoài, tổ chức bồi dưỡng nghiệp vụ công chứng cho viên chức lãnh sự, viên chức ngoại giao được giao thực hiện công chứng; định kỳ hằng năm báo cáo Bộ Tư pháp về hoạt động công chứng của cơ quan đại diện Việt Nam ở nước ngoài để tổng hợp báo cáo Chính phủ.

4. Bộ, cơ quan ngang bộ trong phạm vi nhiệm vụ, quyền hạn của mình có trách nhiệm phối hợp với Bộ Tư pháp trong việc thực hiện quản lý nhà nước về công chứng.

Điều 70. Nhiệm vụ, quyền hạn của Ủy ban nhân dân cấp tỉnh và các Sở Tư pháp trong công tác quản lý nhà nước về công chứng

1. Ủy ban nhân dân cấp tỉnh thực hiện việc quản lý nhà nước về công chứng tại địa phương và có các nhiệm vụ, quyền hạn sau đây:

a) Tổ chức thi hành, tuyên truyền, phổ biến pháp luật về công chứng, chính sách phát triển nghề công chứng;

b) Thực hiện các biện pháp phát triển tổ chức hành nghề công chứng trên địa bàn phù hợp với Quy hoạch tổng thể phát triển tổ chức hành nghề công chứng đã được Thủ

（c）在全国督促、配合相关各部、各行引导、开展、管理公证机构总体发展规划的工作；

（d）宣传、普及公证法、公证业发展政策；

（e）任命、再任命、免任公证员；

（f）批准全国公证员与内务部达成一致意见后的协会条例；暂停施行和要求修改公证员与《宪法》《公证法》相冲突的协会规章、规定和其他相关的规范性文件；

（g）在权限范围内检查、清算、处理、解决投诉违反公证活动规定的控告；

（h）每年定期作公证活动的报告；

（i）管理和协调公证活动的国际合作；

（j）《公证法》和其他有关规范性文件规定的其他任务、权限。

3. 在引导、检查、清查驻外的越南代表机关的公证工作中，外交部有义务配合司法部，给正领事员、能进行公证的外交职员组织公证业务培训；为了综合政府报告，每年定期向司法部报告驻外越南代表机关的公证活动情况。

4. 在其任务、权限范围内，部委、机关相平行的部委有义务配合司法部进行国家公证管理。

第七十条　省级人民委员的任务、权限和在国家公证管理工作中的各司法机构

1. 省级人民委员在地方进行国家公证管理并享有下列的各项任务、权限：

（a）组织施行、宣传、普及公证法律、公证行业发展政策。

（b）在符合政府首脑批准的公证机构发展总体规划的范围内，施行公证机构的发展措施。

tướng Chính phủ phê duyệt;

c) Quyết định thành lập Phòng công chứng, bảo đảm cơ sở vật chất và phương tiện làm việc cho các Phòng công chứng; quyết định việc giải thể hoặc chuyển đổi Phòng công chứng theo quy định của Luật này;

d) Ban hành tiêu chí xét duyệt hồ sơ đề nghị thành lập Văn phòng công chứng; quyết định cho phép thành lập, thay đổi và thu hồi quyết định cho phép thành lập Văn phòng công chứng, cho phép chuyển nhượng, hợp nhất, sáp nhập Văn phòng công chứng;

e) Ban hành mức trần thù lao công chứng tại địa phương;

f)Kiểm tra, thanh tra, xử lý vi phạm và giải quyết khiếu nại, tố cáo về công chứng theo thẩm quyền; phối hợp với Bộ Tư pháp trong công tác kiểm tra, thanh tra về công chứng;

g) Báo cáo Bộ Tư pháp về việc thành lập, chuyển đổi, giải thể Phòng công chứng; cho phép thành lập, hợp nhất, sáp nhập, chuyển nhượng Văn phòng công chứng trên địa bàn. Định kỳ hằng năm báo cáo Bộ Tư pháp về hoạt động công chứng tại địa phương để tổng hợp báo cáo Chính phủ;

h) Các nhiệm vụ, quyền hạn khác theo quy định của Luật này và các văn bản quy phạm pháp luật khác có liên quan.

2. Sở Tư pháp chịu trách nhiệm giúp Ủy ban nhân dân cấp tỉnh thực hiện quản lý nhà nước về công chứng tại địa phương, thực hiện các nhiệm vụ, quyền hạn quy định tại Luật này và các văn bản quy phạm pháp luật khác có liên quan.

Chương IX
XỬ LÝ VI PHẠM VÀ GIẢI QUYẾT TRANH CHẤP

Điều 71. Xử lý vi phạm đối với công chứng viên

Công chứng viên vi phạm quy định của Luật này thì tùy theo tính chất, mức độ vi phạm mà bị xử lý kỷ luật, xử phạt vi phạm hành chính hoặc bị truy cứu trách nhiệm hình sự, nếu gây thiệt hại thì phải bồi thường theo quy định của pháp luật.

Điều 72. Xử lý vi phạm đối với tổ chức hành nghề công chứng

Tổ chức hành nghề công chứng vi phạm quy định của Luật này thì bị xử phạt vi phạm hành chính, nếu gây thiệt hại phải bồi thường theo quy định của pháp luật.

（c）决定成立公证办公室，给予公证办公室物质基础保证和工作便利；根据《公证法》规定决定解散或转让公证办公室。

（d）颁布提议成立公证机构的档案查阅指标；决定许可成立、替换和收回成立公证机构的决定，允许转让、合并、融合公证机构。

（e）颁布地方公证酬劳标准。

（f）在权限范围内检查、清算、处理、解决违反公证法规的投诉；在公证的检查、清查工作中，配合司法部的工作。

（g）向司法部报告公证办公室的成立、转让和解散工作；在权限范围许可成立、合并、融合、转让公证机构；为了综合政府报告，每年定期向司法部报告地方公证活动。

（h）公证法和其他相关法律规定的其他权限、任务。

2. 司法机构有义务帮助省级人民委员会在地方进行国家公证管理，施行本法规定的任务、权限和其他与之相关的法律规范。

第九章　违法处理和争议解决

第七十一条　公证员的违法处理

公证员违反本法规定的，要根据性质、违反程度处以纪律处罚、行政处罚或追究刑事责任。如果造成损害，根据法律的规定进行补偿。

第七十二条　公证行业组织的违法处理

公证行业组织违反本法规定的，处以行政处罚。如果造成损害，根据本法的规定进行赔偿。

Điều 73. Xử lý vi phạm đối với người có hành vi xâm phạm quyền, lợi ích hợp pháp của công chứng viên, tổ chức hành nghề công chứng

Người có chức vụ, quyền hạn mà có hành vi xâm phạm quyền, lợi ích hợp pháp của công chứng viên, tổ chức hành nghề công chứng hoặc cản trở công chứng viên, tổ chức hành nghề công chứng thực hiện quyền, nghĩa vụ thì tùy theo tính chất, mức độ vi phạm mà bị xử lý kỷ luật hoặc bị truy cứu trách nhiệm hình sự, nếu gây thiệt hại thì phải bồi thường theo quy định của pháp luật.

第七十三条　对侵犯公证员和公证机构权利、合法利益行为的违法处理

有职务、权限的人侵犯公证员、公证机构权利、合法利益或妨碍公证员、公证机构实现权利、义务的，根据其行为的性质、违法程度处以纪律处理或追究民事责任。如果造成损害，要根据法律的规定进行赔偿。

Điều 74. Xử lý vi phạm đối với cá nhân, tổ chức hành nghề công chứng bất hợp pháp

1. Cá nhân không đủ điều kiện hành nghề công chứng mà hành nghề công chứng dưới bất kỳ hình thức nào thì phải chấm dứt hành vi vi phạm, bị xử phạt vi phạm hành chính hoặc bị truy cứu trách nhiệm hình sự, nếu gây thiệt hại thì phải bồi thường theo quy định của pháp luật.

2. Tổ chức không đủ điều kiện hành nghề công chứng mà hành nghề công chứng dưới bất kỳ hình thức nào thì phải chấm dứt hành vi vi phạm, bị xử phạt vi phạm hành chính, nếu gây thiệt hại thì phải bồi thường theo quy định của pháp luật.

第七十四条　对个人、公证机构不合法行为的处理

1. 个人达不到公证行业条件而从事公证业务的，无论其从业形式均应取消，并处以行政处罚或追究刑事责任。如果造成损害，应根据本法的规定进行赔偿。

2. 组织达不到公证行业组织条件而从事公证组织业务的，无论其从业形式均应取消，并处以行政处罚。如果造成损害，应根据本法的规定进行赔偿。

Điều 75. Xử lý vi phạm đối với người yêu cầu công chứng

Người yêu cầu công chứng có hành vi cung cấp thông tin, tài liệu sai sự thật, sử dụng giấy tờ, văn bản giả mạo, sửa chữa, tẩy xóa giấy tờ, văn bản trái pháp luật hoặc có hành vi gian dối khác khi yêu cầu công chứng thì tùy theo tính chất, mức độ vi phạm mà bị xử phạt vi phạm hành chính hoặc bị truy cứu trách nhiệm hình sự, nếu gây thiệt hại thì phải bồi thường theo quy định của pháp luật.

第七十五条　对公证申请人违法行为的处理

公证申请人在申请公证时提供错误信息、材料，使用假冒的证明材料、文本，抹去违反法律的证明、文本或有其他虚假行为的，根据其行为性质、违法程度处以行政处罚或追究民事责任。如果造成损害的，应根据本法进行赔偿。

Điều 76. Giải quyết tranh chấp

Trong trường hợp giữa người yêu cầu công chứng và công chứng viên, tổ chức hành nghề công chứng có tranh chấp liên quan đến hoạt động hành nghề công chứng thì các bên có quyền khởi kiện vụ việc ra Tòa án để giải quyết tranh chấp đó.

第七十六条　争议解决

如果公证申请人和公证员、公证机构之间产生纠纷，影响公证活动的顺利进行，争议各方有权向法院提出诉讼解决争议。

Chương X
ĐIỀU KHOẢN THI HÀNH

第十章　执行条款

Điều 77. Việc chứng thực bản sao từ bản chính, chứng thực chữ ký trong giấy tờ, văn bản của công chứng viên

1. Công chứng viên được chứng thực bản sao từ bản chính, chứng thực chữ ký trong giấy tờ, văn bản.

第七十七条　核实来自正本的复印件，公证员在证明、文本中的签字

1. 公证员可以从正本核实复印件和证件、文本中的签字。

2. Việc chứng thực bản sao từ bản chính, chứng thực chữ ký trong giấy tờ, văn bản được thực hiện theo quy định của pháp luật về chứng thực.

Điều 78. Việc công chứng của cơ quan đại diện nước Cộng hòa xã hội chủ nghĩa Việt Nam ở nước ngoài

1. Cơ quan đại diện ngoại giao, cơ quan đại diện lãnh sự của nước Cộng hòa xã hội chủ nghĩa Việt Nam ở nước ngoài được công chứng di chúc, văn bản từ chối nhận di sản, văn bản ủy quyền và các hợp đồng, giao dịch khác theo quy định của Luật này và pháp luật về lãnh sự, ngoại giao, trừ hợp đồng mua bán, chuyển đổi, chuyển nhượng, tặng cho, cho thuê, thế chấp, góp vốn bằng bất động sản tại Việt Nam.

2. Viên chức lãnh sự, viên chức ngoại giao được giao thực hiện công chứng phải có bằng cử nhân luật hoặc được bồi dưỡng nghiệp vụ công chứng.

3. Viên chức lãnh sự, viên chức ngoại giao thực hiện công chứng theo thủ tục quy định tại Chương V của Luật này, có quyền quy định tại các điểm c, d và đ khoản 1 và nghĩa vụ quy định tại các điểm a, c, d và đ khoản 2 Điều 17 của Luật này.

Điều 79. Điều khoản chuyển tiếp

1. Trong thời hạn 24 tháng kể từ ngày Luật này có hiệu lực thi hành, Văn phòng công chứng do một công chứng viên thành lập theo quy định của Luật công chứng số 82/2006/QH11 phải chuyển đổi thành Văn phòng công chứng được tổ chức và hoạt động theo quy định tại Điều 22 của Luật này. Văn phòng công chứng do một công chứng viên thành lập không thực hiện xong việc chuyển đổi trong thời hạn này thì Ủy ban nhân dân cấp tỉnh thu hồi quyết định cho phép thành lập, Sở Tư pháp thu hồi giấy đăng ký hoạt động công chứng.

Bộ Tư pháp hướng dẫn thủ tục chuyển đổi Văn phòng công chứng quy định tại khoản này.

2. Văn phòng công chứng được thành lập trước ngày Luật này có hiệu lực thi hành được giữ nguyên tên gọi đã đăng ký. Trường hợp Văn phòng công chứng thay đổi một trong các nội dung quy định tại khoản 3 Điều 23 của Luật này kể từ ngày Luật này có hiệu lực thi hành thì phải đăng ký lại hoạt động; trường hợp thay đổi một trong các nội dung quy định tại khoản 2 Điều 24 của Luật này thì phải thay đổi tên gọi của Văn phòng công chứng phù hợp với quy định tại khoản 3 Điều 22 của Luật này.

3. Tổ chức hành nghề công chứng được thành lập trước ngày Luật này có hiệu lực thi hành có nghĩa vụ mua

2. 根据法律的规定从正本处核实复印件和证件、文本中的签字。

第七十八条　越南社会主义共和国驻外代表机关的公证

1. 越南社会主义共和国驻外的外交代表机关、领事代表机关可以公证关于领事、外交，买卖合同、转换、转让、赠与、出租、抵押、除处理在越南的不动产分期付款外的遗嘱、放弃继承遗产的文书、委托文书和根据本法规定的其他合同、交易。

2. 有法学学士学位证书或受过公证业务进修的领事职员、外交职员可以进行公证业务。

3. 领事职员、外交职员根据本法第 4 章规定的程序进行公证，享有本法第 17 条第 1 款的 c、d 和 e 项规定的权利，履行本法第 17 条第 2 款 a、c、d 和 e 项规定的义务。

第七十九条　转接条款

1. 从本法生效之日起的 24 个月之内，由一个公证员根据 QH11/2006/82 号公证法成立的公证机构必须转换成本法第 22 条规定组织和活动的公证机构。如果在此时限内没有完成转换，那么由省级人民委员会收回成立许可，司法机构收回公证营业执照。

司法部指导上款规定的公证机构转换程序。

2. 在本法生效前成立的公证机构可以保留已登记的名称。自本法生效之日起，如果公证机构变更本法第 23 条第 3 款规定的内容之一应当重新登记营业。如果变更本法第 24 条第 2 款规定的内容之一，应将公证机构的名称改成符合本法第 22 条第 3 款的规定。

3. 在本法生效之日前成立的公证机构有义务根据本法第 37 条的规定，在本法生效后的 90 日之内，给

bảo hiểm trách nhiệm nghề nghiệp cho công chứng viên theo quy định tại Điều 37 của Luật này trong thời hạn 90 ngày kể từ ngày Luật có hiệu lực thi hành.

公证员购买行业责任保险。

4. Quy tắc đạo đức hành nghề công chứng được ban hành kèm theo Thông tư số 11/2012/TT-BTP ngày 30 tháng 10 năm 2012 của Bộ Tư pháp tiếp tục được thực hiện cho đến khi tổ chức xã hội - nghề nghiệp của công chứng viên quy định tại Điều 39 của Luật này ban hành mới Quy tắc đạo đức hành nghề công chứng.

4. 司法部 2012 年 10 月 30 日 TT-BTP/2012/11 号颁布的附加通知中的《公证行业道德规则》可以继续执行至本法第 39 条规定的公证员社会行业组织颁布新的《公证行业道德规则》。

Điều 80. Hiệu lực thi hành

Luật này có hiệu lực thi hành từ ngày 01 tháng 01 năm 2015.

Luật công chứng số 82/2006/QH11 hết hiệu lực kể từ ngày Luật này có hiệu lực thi hành.

第八十条　生效时间

本法自 2015 年 1 月 1 日起生效。

从本法生效之日起，QH11/2006/82 号公证法废止。

Điều 81. Quy định chi tiết

Chính phủ quy định chi tiết các điều, khoản được giao trong Luật.

Luật này đã được Quốc hội nước Cộng hòa xã hội chủ nghĩa Việt Nam khóa XIII, kỳ họp thứ 7 thông qua ngày 20 tháng 6 năm 2014.

第八十一条　规定细节

政府规定的各条、款的实施细节可以归到法律中。

本法于 2014 年 6 月 20 日由越南社会主义共和国国会第十三次会议通过，第七次修改。

国会主席
阮生雄

也门

公证法

قانون التوثيق رقم 7 لسنة 2010 بشأن التوثيق

قرار جمهوري رقم (7) لسنة 2010م

بشأن قانون التوثيق رقم 7 لسنة 2010 بشأن التوثيق

صدر اليوم القانون رقم " 7 " لسنة 2010م بشأن التوثيق.

واحتوى القانون على 55 مادة موزعة على سبعة فصول.

وفيما يلي نص القانون..

قانون رقم (7) لسنة 2010م

بشأن التوثيـــق

باسم الشعب :

رئيس الجمهورية :

بعد الإطلاع على دستور الجمهورية اليمنية.

وبعد موافقة مجلس النواب (أصدرنا القانون الآتي نصه

الفصل الأول

التسمية والتعاريف

مادة (1) : يسمى هذا القانون: (قانون التوثيق).

مادة (2) : لأغراض تطبيق أحكام هذا القانون تكون للألفاظ والعبارات

التالية المعاني المحددة أمام كل منها ما لم يقتض سياق النص معنى آخر:

الجمهورية :

الجمهورية اليمنية.

الـــوزارة :

وزارة العدل

الوزيـــــر :

وزير العدل.

2010 年公证法第 7 号令

2010 年共和国第（7）号令

2010 年公证事务法第 7 号令

2010 年公证法第（7）号令于 2010 年 8 月 7 日颁布。

本法共 55 条，分为 7 章。

法律规定如下：

2010 年公证法第（7）号令

以人民的名义：

共和国总统：

根据也门共和国宪法，经众议院批准颁布本法。

第一章　名称与定义

第一条　本法名称为《公证法》。

第二条　为了本法规定的顺利施行，本法中使用的单词和短语除非文本的上下文明确规定有其他含义，否则应当以下列定义为准：

共和国：也门共和国。

部：司法部。

部长：司法部长。

公证员：在其职责范围内执行本法和其他现行法律条例明确规定的公证工作的人员。

书记员：根据本法和其他现行法律，负责起草与

الموثق:

الموظف الذي يتولى في حدود مهامه واختصاصاته القيام بأعمال التوثيق المبينة في هذا القانون والقوانين الأخرى النافذة واللائحة.

الأمــــــين:

الشخص المكلف بالقيام بتحرير العقود المتعلقة بالأحوال الشخصية أو البيع أو الشراء أو الوصايا ونحوها بموجب هذا القانون والقوانين الاخرى النافذة.

لجان القبول:

اللجان المختصة بقبول الأمناء والمشكلة وفقا لأحكام هذا القانون واللائحة.لجان التأديب: اللجان المختصة بتأديب الأمناء المشكلة وفقا لأحكام هذا القانون واللائحة.

التحرير: إنشاء المحرر مباشرة من قبل الموثق أو الأمين وفقاً لأحكام هذا القانون واللائحة.

التصديق: تأشير الموثق على صحة توقيع الأمين في المحررات المحررة من قبله أو على صحة توقيعات ذوي العلاقة في المحررات العرفية و على اعترافهم بمضمونها تمهيداً لتوثيقها.

التوثيق: تقييد وتدوين الموثق للمحررات في السجلات المعدة لها بعد التصديق عليها واستيفاء الرسوم المقررة وإثبات تاريخ ورقم القيدعلى المحرر وختمه بخاتم قلم التوثيق وفقاً لأحكام هذا القانون واللائحة.

ذوو العلاقة: كل متعاقد أو موقع على المحرر أو من يقوم مقامه بصفة قانونية.

جدول رسوم التوثيق:

جدول رسوم التوثيق المبين في المادة (51) من هذا القانون.

المحرر عديم القيمة المالية: الورقة التي تثبت حقاً ولا تنقل ملكية وهي غير قابلة للتملك بذاتها وإن كان مبلغاً محدداً كعقود التسهيلات والقروض والضمانات العقارية وضمانات المنقول والكفالات وجدولة المديونيات وسندات الدين .

المحرر ذوالقيمة المالية:

1- المحرر الناقل للملكية كعقود البيع.

2- الورقة المالية القابلة للتملك بذاتها ولها قيمة ذاتية وقوة في

التعامل وقابلة للتصرف بأي نوع من أنواع التصرفات وقابلة للتداول في

الأسواق المالية كأسهم الشركات.

اللائحة: اللائحة التنفيذية لهذا القانون.

الفصل الثاني
إنشاء مكاتب وأقلام التوثيق
وتحديد اختصاصاتها

مادة (3): أ- تنشأ في نطاق محاكم الاستئناف بأمانة العاصمة ومحافظات الجمهورية مكاتب للتوثيق تتبعها

个人状况、销售合同、买卖合同、遗嘱等有关文书的人员。

批准委员会：专门负责按照本法的规定批准任命专门书记员的委员会。

纪律委员会：按照本法的规定监管书记员行为纪律的委员会。

起草：根据本法的规定由公证员或书记员起草文件。

公证核准：公证员对书记员已起草好的文件中签名的真实性，或非官方文件中的当事人签名的真实性，以及当事人对准备公证的文件内容的知悉程序进行核准。

公证：公证员根据本法的规定，审查文件之后在官方文本中登记和编写公证书，按规定收取公证费，核实文件中的文件号和印鉴。

当事人：当事人、文件签署人或其法定代表人。

公证费用表：

本法第 51 条中规定的公证费用。

无财务价值的文件：虽然文件中有确切的价值，但是只证明权利而不涉及转让所有权，且本身也不具有所有权的文件，如信贷、借贷、不动产担保、动产担保、债务清单和债券。

有财务价值的文件：

1. 所有权转让文件，如销售合同。

2. 可持有的有价证券，具有内在价值，可以互换，可以做任何处置，可以在金融市场交易，比如公司股票。

条例：本法实施条例。

第二章　公证局和公证机构的建立及其职权范围

第三条　应在上诉法院的管辖范围内，在首都市政局和共和国各区县的市政局设立公证局及下属的公

أقلام للتوثيق في نطاق المحاكم الابتدائية وتمارس مهامها واختصاصاتها وفقاً لأحكام هذا القانون واللائحة، ويجوز بقرار من الوزير إنشاء أقلام توثيق متخصصة ويحدد قرار إنشائها اختصاصها النوعي والمكاني.

ب-تحدد اللائحة التقسيمات الإدارية لمكاتب وأقلام التوثيق ومهام واختصاصات تلك التقسيمات.

مادة (4) : تمارس مكاتب التوثيق المهام والاختصاصات التالية:

1- تنفيذ خطط الوزارة المتعلقة بتنظيم وتطوير أعمال مكاتب وأقلام التوثيق ورفع التقارير الدورية بشأنها.

2- الرقابة والتفتيش على أعمال الأمناء وأقلام التوثيق.

3- تنظيم وتطوير مهنة الأمناء.

4- إقامة دعوى المساءلة التأديبية ضد الأمين المخالف لمهامه وواجباته وفقاً للإجراءات المنصوص عليها في هذا القانون واللائحة.

5- استقبال ملفات ترشيح الأمناء المرفوعة للمكتب من أقلام التوثيق واستيفاء إجراءاتها القانونية.

6- أية مهام واختصاصات منصوص عليها في هذا القانون واللائحة.

مادة (5) : يتولى قلم التوثيق ممارسة المهام والاختصاصات الآتية:

أ-تلقي المحررات العرفية والتصديق على توقيع ذوي العلاقة فيها وتوثيقها.

ب-تحرير وتوثيق المحررات التي توجبها التشريعات النافذة أو يطلب ذوو العلاقة توثيقها.

ج--استيفاء الرسوم المقررة قانوناً على كل محرر حرره أو وثقه.

د-حفظ سجلات ودفاتر تحرير العقود المحررة أو الموثقة من قبله وصور الأوراق التي تثبت صفة ذوي العلاقة.

هـ-حفظ صور المحررات التي تم توثيقها.

و-إعداد فهارس للمحررات التي تم توثيقها.

ز-إثبات المحررات العرفية وتأريخها في السجلات المعدة لها.

ح-إثبات المحررات الرسمية في السجلات المعدة لذلك.

ط-إعطاء الشهادات بحصول التصديق على التوقيعات من واقع السجلات.

ي-التأشير على الدفاتر التجارية.

ك-تحرير الاحتجاجات بإثبات الامتناع من قبول أو وفاء الأوراق التجارية.

ل-تحرير وتوثيق صكوك الوصية.

م-أية مهام واختصاصات منصوص عليها في هذا القانون واللائحة.

مادة (6) : يعين مديرو مكاتب التوثيق ورؤساء أقلام التوثيق وموظفوها بقرار من الوزير وفقاً لأحكام هذا القانون

证机构，在初级法院的管辖范围内，依照本法的规定行使其职权。允许按照部长的决定建立专门的公证机构并确定其职权范围。

本法确定公证局（处）的行政划分，并明确各划分区域的工作任务和职权范围。

第四条　公证局履行下列职能：

（1）执行司法部制定的规范和发展公证工作的计划，并定期提交工作报告；

（2）监督、检查书记员和公证机构的工作；

（3）主导规范和发展书记员的职业；

（4）按照本法规定及执行条例，对书记员违反职责的行为提起纪律问责诉讼；

（5）接收公证机构推荐的书记员的档案，并完成其法律程序；

（6）本法规定的其他职能。

第五条　公证机构履行以下职能：

（1）接收非官方文件，核准当事人的签字并公证。

（2）起草和公证符合法律规定或当事人要求的文件。

（3）收取起草或公证文件的法定费用。

（4）保存起草或公证合同的档案和文本、证明当事人身份文件的复印件。

（5）保存公证文件的复印件。

（6）为已经公证的文件设置索引。

（7）在记录文本中公证非官方件及其日期。

（8）在记录文本中公证官方文件。

（9）为已公证的文件签字并出具公证书。

（10）公证商业文书。

（11）起草拒绝或同意履行商业文书的辩词。

（12）起草和公证遗嘱。

（13）本法规定的其他职能。

第六条　由部长根据本法的规定任命公证局、公证机构的领导和工作人员。

واللائحة.

مادة (7): تتولى الوزارة تنظيم وتطوير مكاتب وأقلام التوثيق والإشراف والرقابة والتفتيش على أعمالها وتأهيل وتدريب العاملين في هذه المكاتب، وتبين اللائحة الأحكام والإجراءات المنظمة لذلك.

مادة (8): يتولى موثقون معينون بقرار من الوزير مباشرة إجراءات التحرير والتوثيق في أقلام التوثيق وفقاً لأحكام هذا القانون واللائحة ويشترط في الموثق ما يلي :

1. أن يكون يمني الجنسية.

2. أن يكون كامل الأهلية خالياً من العاهات المؤثرة على مزاولة المهنة.

3. أن لا يقل عمره عن خمسة وعشرين عاماً.

4. أن يكون حائزاً للشهادة الجامعية في الشريعة والقانون أو في الحقوق من إحدى الجامعات المعترف بها في الجمهورية.

5. أن يكون حسن السمعة محمود السيرة والسلوك.

6. أن لا يكون قد صدر ضده حكم قضائي بات في جريمة مخلة بالشرف أو الأمانة, ما لم يكن قد رد إليه اعتباره.

7. أن لا يكون قد سبق فصله من وظيفة عامة بقرار تأديبي أو بحكم قضائي نهائي.

8. أن يجتاز بنجاح الاختبار المقرر للقبول وفقاً للأحكام والإجراءات التي تحددها اللائحة.

مادة (9) : مع مراعاة قانون الوقف يجب على الموثق عند ممارسة مهامه الالتزام بما يلي:

1- التحقق من شخصية ذوي العلاقة وأهليتهم ورضاهم وأن يذكر ذلك في الوثيقة مع ذكر الاسم الكامل لكل منهم ومهنته وعمره والشهود وتدوين التاريخ والمبالغ بالأرقام والحروف كاملة وتحدد اللائحة طريقة التحقق من هوية ذوي العلاقة وأهليتهم ورضاهم.

2- عدم توثيق أي محرر في التصرفات العقارية إلا بعد التأكد من ملكية المتصرف للعقار بأن يكون مسجلاً في السجل العقاري في المناطق التي يوجد بها مكاتب للسجل العقاري ما لم فأقلام التوثيق بالمحاكم هي المختصة.

3- عدم تحرير أو توثيق أي محرر يخالف الشريعة الإسلامية والقوانين النافذة.

4- التأكد من ذوي العلاقة عن موضوع المحرر الذي يرغبون توثيقه وقراءته عليهم مع ذكر ذلك فيه ثم التوقيع عليه مع ذوي العلاقة والشهود.

مادة (10): يحظر على قلم التوثيق تسليم المحررات التي تم توثيقها أو تحريرها أو صور منها لغير ذوي العلاقة ويجوز تسليم صورة طبق الأصل من المحرر لغير بقرار أو بأمر من المحكمة التي يقع بدائرتها القلم وتحدد اللائحة الحالات التي يجوز فيها تسليم صور المحررات لصاحب الشأن والإجراءات المنظمة لذلك.

مادة (11): لا يجوز للموثق أن يحرر أو يوثق محرراً

第七条 司法部应当规范和发展公证局和公证机构的公证活动，对其工作进行监督和检查，对其工作人员进行培训，解释公证工作的条例、规定和标准流程。

第八条 部长任命的公证员应当依照本法的规定，直接执行公证工作。公证员需满足以下条件：

（1）具有也门国籍；

（2）无影响从事公证工作的缺陷；

（3）年龄不低于 25 周岁；

（4）获得也门正规大学法律专业毕业证书；

（5）声誉良好、品行端正；

（6）没有因名誉问题构成犯罪而被判刑，除非已经恢复其名誉；

（7）没有因纪律处分或最终司法裁决而被开除公职；

（8）按照本法规定的规则和程序顺利通过入职考试。

第九条 依据《公益慈善捐赠法》，公证员在履行其职能时必须遵守以下规定：

（1）核实有关人员的身份、资格和意愿，并在文件中记录每个人的全名、职业、年龄、见证人，记录日期和金额的大写和小写。事先规定核实当事人的身份、资格和意愿的程序及方法。

（2）公证员只有在确认交易人享有所有权之后才可以对不动产交易进行公证，即当事人的不动产应当在公证机构所在地设置的不动产登记办公室完成登记，法院所在地的公证机构有权限公证。

（3）不得起草和公证任何违反伊斯兰教法或现行法律的文件。

（4）确保当事人知悉意欲公证的文件内容，应对其宣读和提醒，并与当事人和见证人一起在文件上签字。

第十条 公证机构不得将已经公证、编辑或复印的文件交付给第三方，与正本一致的文件副本可按公证机构所在辖区内的法院裁决或指令交付给第三方。条例应当说明可将副本交付给第三方的情形和程序。

第十一条 公证员不得对专属其本人或与其具有

يخصه شخصياً أو يخص من تربطه به صلة قرابة إلى الدرجة الرابعة.

الفصل الثالث شروط منح تراخيص مزاولة مهنة الأمين ومهامه وواجباته

مادة (12): يشترط فيمن يرخص له بمزاولة مهنة الأمين ما يلي:

أ- أن يكون يمني الجنسية.

ب- أن يكون كامل الأهلية خالياً من العاهات المؤثرة على مزاولة المهنة.

ج- أن لا يقل عمره عن خمسة وعشرين عاماً.

د- أن يكون ملماً بأحكام المعاملات الشرعية والأحوال الشخصية وقوانين الإثبات والرسوم والضرائب العقارية والسجل العقاري والمساحة وغيرها من القوانين الأخرى ذات العلاقة.

هـ- أن يكون عدلاً أميناً محمود السيرة والسلوك حسن السمعة ملتزماً بالشعائر الإسلامية.

ز- أن لا يكون قد صدر ضده حكم قضائي بات في جريمة مخلة بالشرف أو الأمانة ما لم يكن قد رُدّ إليه اعتباره.

ح- أن لا يكون قد فصل من وظيفة عامة بقرار إداري تأديبي أو بحكم قضائي نهائي.

ط- أن يكون مرشحاً من أهل المنطقة التي يرغب في مزاولة المهنة بها.

ي- أن يجتاز الامتحان المقرر لمزاولة المهنة.

مادة (13): مع مراعاة أحكام المادة (12) من هذا القانون تكون الأولوية في منح تراخيص مزاولة المهنة للحاصلين على مؤهلات جامعية في الشريعة والقانون أو الحقوق من جامعة معترف بها في الجمهورية وللقضاة المتقاعدين والعلماء المعتبرين في مناطقهم وفقاً لما تبينه اللائحة.

مادة (14):

أ- تشكل في نطاق كل محكمة استئناف لجنة لقبول الأمناء وتحدد اللائحة طريقة تشكيلها وتنظيم أعمالها والصلاحيات المخولة لها. ب- تبين اللائحة إجراءات قبول الأمناء.

مادة (15): يمنح الترخيص بمزاولة مهنة الأمين بقرار من الوزير.

مادة (16): تجدد تراخيص الأمناء كل ثلاث سنوات من قبل مكتب التوثيق حسب الشروط والإجراءات التي تحددها اللائحة.

مادة (17): يمارس الأمين المهام التالية:

أ- تحرير عقود الزواج وشهادات الطلاق والرجعة على النماذج الرسمية المعدة لذلك.

ب- تحرير الوكالات والتصرفات والمحررات الأخرى التي يوجبها هذا القانون والقوانين النافذة أو بناء على طلب ذوي المصلحة وفقاً لما تحدده اللائحة.

ج- أية مهام أو اختصاصات أخرى منصوص عليها في هذا

亲属关系的当事人的文件进行公证。

第三章　授予执业书记员的条件及其职责与义务

第十二条　担任执业书记员，应该具备下列条件：

（1）具有也门国籍；

（2）无影响从事书记员工作的缺陷；

（3）年龄不低于 25 周岁；

（4）熟悉交易和个人状况的法规以及公证法，不动产的税费、登记和面积等其他相关法律；

（5）公正可信、品行优良、遵守伊斯兰教法；

（6）没有因名誉问题构成犯罪而被判刑，除非已经恢复其名誉；

（7）没有因行政纪律处分或最终司法裁决而被开除公职；

（8）获得从事该行业人士的推荐；

（9）通过入职考试。

第十三条　根据本法第 12 条的规定，正如条例所述应当优先授予拥有伊斯兰教法大学、共和国正规大学法律专业文凭、在地方上受认可的退休法官和学者资格从事公证工作。

第十四条　（1）在每个上诉法院的范围内，应组成批准任命书记员委员会，条例应规定其组织方式、工作安排和权力范围。（2）条例应说明批准任命书记员的程序。

第十五条　书记员执业证书应由部长决定授予。

第十六条　书记员的执业证书应当按照规定的条件和程序由公证局每三年更新一次。

第十七条　书记员应履行下列职责：

（1）根据官方样本起草婚姻、离婚和复婚协议；

（2）根据条例规定，起草委托书、行为书等其他现行法律或有关利益方要求起草的文件；

（3）本法规定的其他职能或权限。

القانون واللائحة.

مادة (18): يجب على الأمين عند قيامه بمهامه الالتزام بما يلي:

أ- التحقق من شخصية ذوي العلاقة وأهليتهم ورضاهم وأن يذكر ذلك في الوثيقة مع ذكر الاسم الكامل لكل منهم والمهنة والعمر والشهود وتدوين التاريخ والمبالغ بالأرقام والحروف كاملة وتحدد اللائحة طريقة التحقق من هوية ذوي العلاقة وأهليتهم ورضاهم.

ب- عدم تحرير أي محرر في تصرف عقاري لم يسجل في السجل العقاري بالمناطق التي يوجد بها سجل عقاري مالم فأقلام التوثيق بالمحاكم هي المختصة .

ج- قراءة المحرر الذي حرره على ذوي العلاقة والشهود مع ذكر ذلك فيه ثم التوقيع معهم في ذيل المحرر.

د- حفظ أصول المحررات وصور العقود بدفاتر تحرير الأوراق التي تثبت صفة ذوي العلاقة وصور أولياتها المحررات التي حررها.

هـ- تقديم المحررات التي حررها إلى قلم التوثيق الواقع في دائرة عمله لتوثيقها قبل تسليمها لأصحاب الشأن وفي حالة رغبة ذوي العلاقة يقدم تلك المحررات إلى قلم التوثيق بأنفسهم لتوثيقها يجب على الأمين إثبات ذلك بمحضر موقع من ذوي العلاقة ويبلغ قلم التوثيق بنسخة منه.

و- تقديم دفاتر قيد المحررات التي تم تحريرها إلى قلم التوثيق كل ثلاثة أشهر للمراجعة والتأشير على قيودها.

مادة(19): يحظر على الأمين تسليم المحررات التي تم تحريرها أو صورها منها لغير ذوي العلاقة.

مادة(20): لا يجوز للأمين أن يحرر محررا إذا كان هذا المحرر يتعلق بحق له أو لزوجه أو أحد فروعه أو أصوله إلا برضا جميع من لهم علاقة بذلك ويستثنى من ذلك عقود الزواج فيجوز للأمين تحريرها إذا كان طرفا العقد أو أحدهما من أصوله أو فروعه.

مادة (21) لا يجوز للأمين تحرير عقود خارج نطاق اختصاصه المكاني المرخص له العمل فيه.

مادة(22) يمارس الأمين عمله في مكتب خاص به يضع عليه لوحة يبين فيها اسمه ونطاق اختصاصه ورقم وتاريخ الترخيص الصادر له بمزاولة المهنة وتستثنى من ذلك المناطق النائية .

مادة (23) يتقاضى الأمين أتعابه من ذوي العلاقة وفقا للأسس والمعايير التي تحددها اللائحة.

الفصل الرابع
إنشاء المحررات وتوثيقها.

مادة (24) يجب عند تحرير العقود والمحررات الأخرى وكافة التصرفات القانونية مراعاة أحكام القوانين النافذة المتعلقة بها.

第十八条 书记员在履行职责时应遵守以下规定：

（1）核实当事人的身份、资格和意愿，并在文件中填写所有当事人的全名、职业、年龄、见证人，用大小写的方式记录日期和号码；条例应明确核实当事人身份、资格和意愿的方法。

（2）不得起草未经登记注册的不动产交易文件，如所在地没有不动产登记机构，该项工作应在法院的公证机构完成。

（3）向当事人和证人宣读起草的文件，并与其一起在文件末尾处签名。

（4）保留起草的合同书以及证明当事人属性的文件副本以及其起草文件的初稿。

（5）在文件交付当事人之前，将起草好的文件提交公证机构公证；如当事人自愿提交公证机构公证，书记员必须制作有本人和当事人签名的记录以证实文件，并抄送公证机构。

（6）每3个月向公证机构提交已起草文件的记录本，以便审查和监督。

第十九条 严禁书记员将起草的文件及其副本交给当事人以外的人。

第二十条 书记员不得起草与本人、配偶或家庭成员、其他近亲属的权利有关的文件，除非所有与该文件有利害关系的人员都同意。如果婚姻合同双方或其中一方来自其家庭成员或近亲，那么不受此限。

第二十一条 书记员不得起草其执业范围以外的合同。

第二十二条 书记员应在专属办公室开展工作，并在该办公室设置牌匾，公示其姓名、职权范围以及执业许可证的编号和颁发日期，偏远地区不受此限。

第二十三条 书记员的费用应当由当事人根据条例规定的标准支付。

第四章 制作文件并认证

第二十四条 起草合同及其他文件和执行所有法律行为时，必须遵守现行相关法律的规定。

ةدام (25): ام ررحملا قيثوت وأ ريرحت يف طرتشي
يلي :
1. ةيمالسإلا ةعيرشلا ماكحأل افلاخم نوكي الأ
. ةذفانلا نيناوقلاو
2. ةغلب ًابوتكم ناك اذإو ةيبرعلا ةغللاب ًانودم نوكي نأ
مجرتم ةطساوب ةيبرعلاب ًامجرتم نوكي نأ بجو ةيبنجأ
.دمتعم
3. وأ ةفاضإ وأ بطش نودب حضاو طخب نوكي نأ
وأ هببس ىلإ شماهلا يف ريشُأ اذإ الإ ررحملا نتم يف رشح
ةقالعلا يوذو ةقيثولا ريرحتب ماق نم عيقوت عم هحيحصت
.ةيرهوج اوحن وأ ةفاضإلا تناك نإ

ةدام (26): وأ اهافرط نوكي يتلا تاررحملا ءاشنإ زوجي ال
مصألاك ةدارإلا ىلع ةرثؤملا ةصاخلا تاجايتحالا يوذ نم امهدحأ
.قثوملا لبق نم الإ مكبألا و

ةدام (27): 1 - مكبألا وأ مصألا تاحيرصت نوكت
عدت ال فقوم ذاختاب نوكت امك افرع ةلوادتملا ةراشإلاب
.دوصقملا ةقيقح ىلع هتلالدب الكش لاحلا فورظ
2-اذإ ناك قثوملا دنع هتباتك ررحملا هقيثوتو لهجي ةغل
املتعاقدين وأ أحدهم أو كان بينهم أصم أو أبكم وتعذر عليه
ببسب كلذ لاتعبير نع إرادته فعلى قثوملا نأ يتلقى
.دمتعم مجرتم وأ ريبخ ةطساوب مهتاريبعت
3-يقسم املترجم وأ الخبير لبق ءدبلا يف هلمع نأب
يقوم بترجمة التصريحات وأ التعبير نع إرادة املتعاقدين
.ةقيثولا يف كلذ ىلإ راشيو ةنامأو قدصب
4-يوقع املترجم وأ الخبير عم يوذ العالقة ىلع
الوثيقة التي قام بترجمة تصريحات املتعاقدين فيها وأ
.اهنأشب مهتدارإ نع ريبعتلاب كرتشا

ةدام (28): اذإ اتضح مدع رفاوت ةيلهألا وأ اضرلا ىدل
املتعاقدين وأ اذإ زواج ليكولا دودح هتلاكو وأ اذإ ناك ررحملا
املطلوب توثيقه ظاهر البطالن وجب ىلع قثوملا ضفر
توثيق ررحملا وإعادته ىلإ يوذ العالقة عم إبداء أسباب
الرفض كتابة وفقاً لإلجراءات التي تحددها الالئحة
.التنفيذية

ةدام (29): يحق ألي شخص رفض توثيق محرره أن
يتظلم لدى رئيس املحكمة االبتدائية الواقع بدائرتها قلم
التوثيق خالل (30) يوما من تاريخ إبالغه بالرفض وعلى
رئيس املحكمة الفصل في التظلم في مدة ال تزيد على (15)
.يوماً من تاريخ تقديم التظلم

ةدام (30): أ-يجب على ذوي العالقة تقديم املحررات
بأنفسهم أو من يمثلهم قانوناً أو بواسطة األمين الذي تولى
تحريرها بتفويض من صاحب الشأن وذلك لتوثيقها لدى
قلم التوثيق املختص وفقاً ألحكام هذا القانون والالئحة.
ب- تبين الالئحة التنفيذية اإلجراءات واملدد التي
.تقدم خاللها املحررات إلى قلم التوثيق لتوثيقها
ج -تفرض غرامة على كل من تجاوز املدة املحددة
لتقديم املحرر بنسبة ال تقل عن 5 باملائة وال تزيد
على 10باملائة من قيمة الرسم املقرر قانوناً على املحرر

第二十五条　起草或公证的文件需满足以下条件：

（1）不得违反伊斯兰教法和现行法律的规定；

（2）用阿拉伯语起草，外语书写的文件须由合格的翻译人员翻译成阿拉伯语；

（3）书写工整，不得涂改、添加、插入、编辑正文，如果是必要的添加或修改，应在页边标明修改原因，并附上起草文件的人和当事人的签名。

第二十六条　除公证员外，其他人不得起草双方当事人或其中一方是有表达障碍的特殊人士如聋哑人的合同。

第二十七条　（1）聋哑人通过通用的手语声明其立场，同时该声明陈述在任何情况下，其他人不允许质疑其真实意图；

（2）如果公证员在撰写和记录文件时不明晰当事人的语言或其中一方是无法正常陈述的聋哑人，那么公证员必须通过专家或合格的翻译人员了解其陈述；

（3）翻译人员或专家应在其工作开始前宣誓，忠实地翻译当事人陈述和表达的意愿，并应在文件中注明；

（4）翻译人员或专家应与当事人一起签署其参与翻译的当事人陈述或其参与表达意愿的任何文件。

第二十八条　如果当事人没有资格或意愿，或者代理人超出其代理范围，或者要求公证的文件是无效的，那么公证员必须拒绝公证此类文件，将其退还给当事人，并根据执行条例规定的程序书面说明拒绝原因。

第二十九条　文件被拒绝公证的任何人，有权在收到拒绝通知之日起 30 日内向公证机构所在地的初级法院院长提出申诉，法院院长应在收到申诉之日起 15 日内作出裁定。

第三十条　（1）当事人应当亲自或通过其法定代表人按照当事人授权起草文件的书记员的要求提交文件，以便按照本法的规定向公证主管部门进行公证；

（2）执行条例应规定文件提交公证机构进行公证的程序和时间；

（3）对超过规定期限提交文件的人，罚款金额应不低于法定费用的 5%，不高于 10%；有金融价值的文件，其罚款金额不超过 2 万里亚尔；无金融价值的

فيما يتعلق بالمحررات ذات القيمة المالية على أن لا تتجاوز الغرامة عشرين ألف ريال، وتكون الغرامة بالنسبة للمحررات عديمة القيمة المالية بما يساوي الرسم الثابت المقرر قانوناً على المحرر.

د- يستثنى من الغرامة المشار إليها في الفقرة (ج) من هذه المادة المحررات السابق إنشاؤها قبل صدور هذا القانون.

مادة (31): تكون للمحررات الموثقة من قبل الموثق حجية المحررات الرسمية ما لم يثبت تزويرها أو بطلانها بالطرق القانونية، أما المحررات الناقلة للملكية العقارية والرهن العقاري فلا تكتسب هذه الحجية إلا بين طرفيها فقط، أما حجيتها أمام الكافة فلا تكون إلا بعد تسجيلها في السجل العقاري.

الفصل الخامس
الرقابة والتفتيش على
الأمناء ومساءلتهم التأديبية

مادة (32): تتولى الوزارة ومكاتب أو أقلام التوثيق التفتيش الدوري والمفاجئ على أعمال الأمناء والإطلاع على سجلاتهم والتراخيص الصادرة لهم لمراقبة تنفيذهم أحكام هذا القانون والقوانين النافذة الأخرى وتبين اللائحة الإجراءات المنظمة لذلك.

مادة (33) أ- مع مراعاة أحكام المادة (37) من هذا القانون يتولى قلم التوثيق التحقيق مع الأمين في المخالفات التي يرتكبها وفيما يقدم ضده من شكاوى ويرفع رئيس قلم التوثيق أوراق التحقيق إلى مكتب التوثيق مشفوعةً برأيه إما بالحفظ أو باتخاذ إجراءات المساءلة التأديبية وفي الحالتين يتولى مكتب التوثيق فحص الأوراق ويصدر مدير المكتب قراراً مسبباً إما بالحفظ أو بالإحالة إلى لجنة التأديب لاتخاذ إجراءات المساءلة التأديبية.

ب- يباشر مكتب التوثيق الدعوى التأديبية بحق الأمين في المخالفات المنسوبة إليه أمام لجنة تأديب الأمناء وتحدد اللائحة إجراءات التحقيق والمساءلة التأديبية للأمين وله الحق في الدفاع عن نفسه بالطرق المتاحة قانوناً.

مادة (34) تشكل في نطاق محاكم الاستئناف بأمانة العاصمة ومحافظات الجمهورية لجان لتأديب الأمناء يرأس كل منها قاض وتحدد اللائحة كيفية تشكيلها ونظام عملها.

مادة (35): العقوبات التأديبية التي توقعها لجنة التأديب على الأمين هي:-

أ- الإنذار الكتابي.

ب- الغرامة التي لا تزيد على خمسين ألف ريال.

ج- التوقيف عن مزاولة المهنة مدة لا تقل عن شهر ولا تزيد على ستة أشهر.

د- سحب الترخيص.

مادة (36) القرارات التي تصدرها لجنة التأديب نهائية

文件，其罚款金额不超过其法定费用；

（4）在本法颁布之前制作的文件，不受本条第3款规定的罚款的约束。

第三十一条　公证员所公证的文件应具有官方文件的效力，除非通过法律手段证明其伪造或无效。不动产变更和抵押的文件仅在缔约双方之间有此效力，只有完成不动产登记后才具有普遍效力。

第五章　监督和检查书记员的纪律

第三十二条　司法部、公证局和公证机构应定期和不定期地检查书记员的工作，并审查他们的档案和发给他们的执业证书，以监督他们执行本法和其他法律规定的情况。条例应说明检查工作的程序。

第三十三条　（1）在符合本法第37条规定的前提下，公证机构应调查书记员涉嫌的违纪行为和针对他的投诉。公证机构主任应将调查文件提交给公证局，并对是否作出处分提出意见。公证局应对文件进行审查，公证局主任应将处罚与否的决定提交至纪律委员会，以便采取纪律问责。

（2）公证局应将对书记员的违纪起诉交给书记员纪律委员会处理。条例应规定书记员的纪律处分和问责程序，书记员有权依法为自己辩护。

第三十四条　在首都市政局和共和国各区县的上诉法院内，应成立书记员纪律委员会，对书记员实施纪律处分。由法官主持委员会工作，由条例规定其组织机构和工作制度。

第三十五条　纪律委员会对书记员的纪律处罚是：

（1）书面警告；

（2）不超过5万里亚尔的罚款；

（3）1个月以上，6个月以下的停职；

（4）吊销执业证书。

第三十六条　除吊销执业证书的处罚外，纪律委

دعب الإ اهذيفنت متي الف صيخرتلا بحس ةبوقع ادع
نإ اهئاغلإ وأ اهفيفخت يف قحلا هلو اهيلع ريزولا ةقداصم
نم نيرهش ىلع ديزت ال ةدم يف نيمألل و ًاغوسم كلذل دجو
بحس رارق يف نعطلا قح ريزولا ةقداصمب هغالبإ خيرات
ةنجل اهترئادب عقاولا فانئتسالا ةمكحم ماما صيخرتلا
رارقلا هردصم بيدأتلا.

ةدام **(37)** : يف ةلاح ةفلاخم نيمألا ماكحأل تارقفلا (د ، هـ
قيثوتلا ملق ىلوتي نوناقلا اذه نم (18) مقر ةداملا نم ((و ،
ًةباتك هراذنإ هصاصتخا قاطن يف نيمألا لمع عقاولا
نيمألا عم قيقحتلا ءارجإ متي ةفلاخملا راركت ةلاح يفو
ةلءاسملا تاءارجإ ذاختال قيثوتلا بتكم ىلإ رمألا عفريو
نوناقلا اذه ماكحأل ًاقفو ةيبيدأتلا.

سداسلا لصفلا
قيثوتلا موسر

ةدام **(38):** 1-يفرض رسم قيثوتلا ةبسنب سمخ داولا
يف ةئاملا (0.20بالمائة) ىلع تاررحملا تاذ ةميقلا ةيلاملا
مسرو تباث ةبسنلاب تاررحملل ةميدع ةميقلا ةيلاملا ذو كلذ
ًاقفو لودجل موسر قيثوتلا نيبملا يف ةداملا (51).

2-اذإ ناك ررحملا وذ ةميقلا ةيلاملا ريغ ردقم هيف ةميقلا
(نمثلا) فيتم اهريدقت ضرغل ليصحت موسرلا ددحتو
ةحئاللا ةيذيفنتلا سسألا تاءارجإلاو ةمزاللا كلذل.

ةدام**(39):**

1- لصحت ًامدقم عيمج موسر قيثوتلا ةنيبملا يف
لودج موسر قيثوتلا لبق ذاختا يأ ءارجإ بولطم متيو
اهديروتو اقفو نوناقل ليصحت لاومألا ةماعلا.

2-يحصل رسم يفاضإ بواقع (25بالمائة) نم ةميق
مسرلا نيبملا يف لودج موسر قيثوتلا كلذو حلاصل
قودنص معدلا يئاضقلا قبطتو ناشب ليصحت هديروتو
ماكحألا صوصنملا اهيلع يف نوناق موسرلا ةيئاضقلا.

3-صصخت ةبسن (50بالمائة) نم مسرلا يفاضإلا
لصحملا اقفو ةرقفلل (2) نم هذه ةداملا حلاصل معد ريوطتو
لامعأ قيثوتلا ةيمنتو تاردق نيقثوملا نيبتو ةحئاللا
ةيذيفنتلا ماكحألا تاءارجإلاو ةمظنملا كلذل.

ةدام **(40):** ىفعت نم دادس موسر قيثوتلا:

أ- تاءارجإ قيثوت تاررحملا ةرداصلا ةحلصمل ةلودلا
وأ يأ نم اهتزهجأ، وأ تائيهلا قفارملاو ةيمدخلا ةماعلا نوكتو
ةعضاخ موسرلل تاءارجإلا ةرداصلا نم ةلودلا وأ يأ نم اهتزهجأ
ةحلصمل ريغلا.

ب-ةيصولا فقولاو رذنلاو يف هوجو ربلا ناسحإلاو.

ةدام**(41):** زوجي قثوملل وأ نيمألا نأ لقتني ىلإ لحم
ىوذ ةقالعلا تلحريرحت وأ قيثوت ررحملا يف يتلاح ضرملا وأ
ةرورضلا لمحتيو مدقم بلطلا فيراصم لاقتنالا.

员会颁布的决定是最终决定。除非部长批准，否则吊销执业证书的决定不得执行。如果部长有法律根据，有权减轻或取消这一决定。书记员在收到部长批准吊销执业证书的决定后，2 个月内有权向颁布决定的纪律委员会所在地的上诉法院提起申诉。

第三十七条　书记员违反本法第 18 条第 4 款、第 5 款、第 6 款的规定，公证机构应在其职权范围对书记员作书面警告。如果其违规行为重复多次，应在对其进行调查核实的基础上提交至公证局，公证局根据本法规定采取纪律问责。

第六章　公证费

第三十八条　（1）公证费用应按照第 51 条规定的公证费用表，按照有财务价值文件的 0.20% 和无财务价值文件的固定费用收取。

（2）如果有财务价值的文件没有估价，应当为收取费用而进行估价，执行条例应规定估价依据及其必要程序。

第三十九条

（1）公证费用表中显示的所有文件费用应在采取任何公证行为之前提前收取，并应根据《公共资金收取法》的规定缴纳；

（2）为法律援助基金的利益，应加收公证费用表中显示的费用价值的 25% 的额外费用，《法律费用法》规定的条款适用于此项费用的收取和缴纳；

（3）按照本条第 2 款收取的额外费用的 50% 应用于支持和发展公证工作以及提高公证员的能力；执行条例应规定相关规定和程序。

第四十条　免缴公证费：

（1）公证国家机关或公共服务机构和设施的文件，此公证费由国家或机构来承担；

（2）用于公益慈善的遗嘱或捐赠。

第四十一条　在当事人患病或必要的情况下，公证员或书记员可应邀到当事人处进行起草或公证文件。由提出申请的当事人承担差旅费。

الفصل السابع
الأحكام الختامية

مادة (42): في حالة تعذر قيام الأمين بأداء مهامه وواجباته لمرض أو سفر أو لتوقيفه عن العمل يباشر مهامه واختصاصاته الأمين الأقرب إلى نطاق اختصاصه المكاني بتكليف يصدر من مكتب التوثيق بناء على عرض قلم التوثيق على أن لا تزيد مدة التكليف عن ستة أشهر.

مادة (43) 1- يحظر نقل السجلات والدفاتر أو الوثائق المحفوظة لدى أقلام التوثيق من مقر الإدارة إلا في حال انتقال المقر إلى موقع آخر، ويجوز إذا اقتضى الحال الاطلاع عليها في مكان حفظها تحت إشراف رئيس القلم والموظف المختص وفقا للإجراءات المنصوص عليها في اللائحة.

2- إذا أصدرت المحكمة قرارا بضم محرر موثق محفوظ لدى قلم التوثيق إلى دعوى منظورة أمامها، وجب على قلم التوثيق عمل نسخة مطابقة للمحرر المحفوظ يدون بذيلها محضرا ويوقعه قلم التوثيق وفقا للإجراءات المنصوص عليها في اللائحة وتضم النسخة إلى ملف النزاع وتقوم مقام الأصل في الاستدلال على موضوع النزاع أثناء نظر القضية فقط.

مادة (44): تعد الوزارة نماذج السجلات والدفاتر والأوراق والأختام ونظم التقنية المتعلقة بأعمال التوثيق والأمناء ويصدر بها قرار من الوزير.

مادة (45): أ- على ورثة الأمين في حالة وفاته تقديم جميع السجلات والمحررات التي كانت بحوزته قبل وفاته مع الختم إلى قلم التوثيق التابع له محل عمله لحفظها وذلك خلال شهرين من تاريخ الوفاة ويأخذ الورثة سندا بذلك ما لم تر المحكمة المختصة مصلحة بقاء ذلك لدى الوراث للأمين عدا الختم.

ب- في حالة استقالة الأمين أو صدور قرار تأديبي بسحب الترخيص منه وفقا لأحكام هذا القانون وجب عليه تقديم الختم والسجلات والمحررات التي كانت بحوزته إلى قلم التوثيق.

ج- تبين اللائحة التنفيذية الإجراءات المنظمة للأحكام الواردة في الفقرتين السابقتين.

مادة (46): أ- تتولى القنصليات الجمهورية مهام تحرير وتوثيق المحررات المتعلقة بمواطني الجمهورية في الخارج وفقا لأحكام هذا القانون ولائحته.

ب- تحصل الرسوم وفقا للإجراءات المحددة في القوانين النافذة.

مادة (47) تصادق الوزارة على المحررات الموثقة والأحكام المطلوبة للخارج وتبين اللائحة التنفيذية الأحكام والإجراءات المنظمة لذلك.

مادة (48): يمنح الموثقون والعاملون في مكاتب وأقلام التوثيق بدل توثيق يصدر بتحديده قرار من مجلس القضاء الأعلى بناء على عرض من الوزير.

مادة (49) يؤدي الموثق والأمين قبل مباشرة مهامه أمام

第七章　最后规定

第四十二条　如果书记员因疾病、旅行或停职而不能履行其职责和义务，应由公证局基于公证机构的申请委托最接近其职权范围的书记员代为履行其职责和义务，但委托期限不得超过6个月。

第四十三条　（1）除非驻地搬到另一地点，否则禁止将保存在公证机构的档案、文本或文件从驻地转移到另一地点。如有必要，可在公证机构主任和专门雇员的监督下，按照条例规定的程序在保存地点查看。

（2）如果法院决定将保存在公证机构的已公证文件提交到其待审案件中，那么公证机构必须根据条例规定的程序复制与原保存文件一致的副本，并在末尾处做记录和签名。副本被提交到待审案件卷宗中，仅在审理过程中具有替代正本的作用。

第四十四条　司法部应根据部长决议作出准备、公证与书记员工作有关的档案、文本、文件、印鉴和技术系统的样本。

第四十五条　（1）在书记员去世的情况下，其继承人应在其去世后2个月内向其任职的公证机构上交所有在他去世前保存的印章、档案和文件，除非主管法院认为这些东西留在继承人处更为有益，但印章必须上交；

（2）如果书记员辞职或根据本法规定吊销其执业证书，他必须将印章和档案以及他所管理的文件交给公证机构；

（3）执行条例规定了上述两款的组织程序。

第四十六条　（1）共和国领事馆应按照本法及其条例的规定，负责起草和公证与海外侨民有关的文件。

（2）公证费用应按照现行法律规定的程序收取。

第四十七条　司法部应批准已公证文件和对外申请规定。执行条例应规定有关程序。

第四十八条　根据部长的要求向公证局和公证机构的公证员和职员发放公证津贴，发放标准由最高法官委员会确定。

第四十九条　公证员和书记员在履职之前，应

رئيس المحكمة الابتدائية الواقع عمله في نطاق اختصاصها اليمين التالية: (أقسم بالله العظيم أن أقوم بمهامي وواجباتي بصدق وأمانة وإخلاص طبقاً لأحكام الشريعة الإسلامية والقوانين النافذة وأن أحافظ على الأسرار المتعلقة بعملي).

مادة (50) مع مراعاة ما نص عليه هذا القانون والأحكام العامة لموظفي المحاكم المنصوص عليها في قانون السلطة القضائية يخضع الموثقون في مكاتب أو المالية التوثيق للقانون العام لموظفي الجهاز الإداري للدولة.

مادة (51) يعتبر جدول رسوم التوثيق التالي جزءً من أحكام هذا القانون. جدول رسوم التوثيق// البيـــــان //نوع الرسم// المبلغ بالريال//

1-إنشاء المحرر من قبل الموثق

أ- المحرر عديم القيمة المالية //ثابت// 400// أربعمائة ريال

ب- المحرر ذو القيمة المالية// ثابت 800 ثمانمائة ريال

ج- عقد الزواج والطلاق أو المراجعة//ثابت//400أربعمائة ريال

د- الوكالة // ثابت 400أربعمائة ريال

2- توثيق المحـــــرر:

أ- المحرر عديم القيمة المالية ثابت 2.000 ألفا ريال

ب- المحرر ذو القيمة المالية نسبي(0.20بالمائة عشرين من المائة في المائة (خمس واحد في المائة)

ج- عقد الزواج أو الطلاق أو الرجعة ثابت400 أربعمائة ريال

د- الوكالة ثابت 400 أربعمائة ريال

هـ- محرر قسمة بين الورثة ثابت 2.000 ألفا ريال

3-صورة طبق الأصل لكل صفحة من المحرر ثابت80 ثمانون ريال

4-الاطلاع أو البحث (عن أي محرر)ثابت400 أربعمائة ريال

5- توجيه الاحتجاج ثابت 400 أربعمائة ريال

6-التأشير على دفتر تجاري ثابت 400 أربعمائة ريال

7- التصديق للخارج لأي محرر موثق أو حكم ثابت400 أربعمائة ريال

8- ترخيص مهنة الأمين ثابت 3.000 ثلاثة آلاف ريال

9- تجديد مهنة الأمين ثابت 2.000 ألفا ريال

10-طلب انتقال الموثق إلى محل ذوي العلاقة ثابت400 أربعمائة ريال

11-كل إجراء لم ينص عليه ثابت400 أربعمائة ريال

مادة (52): تصدر اللائحة التنفيذية لهذا القانون بقرار رئيس مجلس القضاء الأعلى بناء على عرض الوزير وبعد موافقة مجلس القضاء

مادة (53): يصدر الوزير كافة القرارات والتعليمات اللازمة لتنفيذ أحكام هذا القانون.

当在其工作所在地的初级法院院长面前作以下入职宣誓："我以伟大的真主发誓，我将按照伊斯兰教法和现行法律的规定诚实守信，忠诚尽责地履行我的工作和职责，保守我的工作秘密。"

第五十条 除了符合本法和其他法律中关于法律职员的一般规定外，公证员应当遵守国家行政机关职员的一般法律。

第五十一条 下列公证费用表应视为本法规定的组成部分。

1. 由公证员起草文件：

（1）无金融价值的文件固定收费 400 里亚尔；

（2）有金融价值的文件固定收费 800 里亚尔；

（3）结婚、离婚和复婚文件固定收费 400 里亚尔；

（4）委托书固定收费 400 里亚尔。

2. 公证文件：

（1）无金融价值的文件固定收费 2000 里亚尔；

（2）有金融价值的文件收费标准为文件价值的 0.20%；

（3）结婚、离婚和复婚公证固定收费 400 里亚尔；

（4）委托书固定收费 400 里亚尔；

（5）遗产分配固定收费 2000 里亚尔。

3. 与文件正本一致的副本每一页固定收费 80 里亚尔。

4. 查看任何文件固定收费 400 里亚尔。

5. 提取辩诉材料固定收费 400 里亚尔。

6. 签署商业文本固定收费 400 里亚尔。

7. 对外公证文件或裁决书固定收费 400 里亚尔。

8. 颁发书记员执业证固定收费 3000 里亚尔。

9. 更新书记员执业证固定收费 2000 里亚尔。

10. 申请公证员到当事人处办理业务固定收费 400 里亚尔。

11. 本法中没有规定的其他公证项目固定收费 400 里亚尔。

第五十二条 根据部长的要求，经最高司法委员会主席的批准与决定颁布本法的执行条例。

第五十三条 部长应颁布实施本法所需的所有决定和指示。

مادة (54) يلغى القرار الجمهوري بالقانون رقم (29) لسنة 1992م وتعديلاته بالقانون رقم (34) لسنة 1997م كما يلغى كل حكم أو نص يتعارض أو يخالف نصوص وأحكام هذا القانون.

مادة (55): يعمل بهذا القانون من تاريخ صدوره، وينشر في الجريدة الرسمية.

صدر برئاسة الجمهورية - بصنعاء
بتاريخ 26 شعبان 1431هـ
الموافق 7 أغسطس 2010 م
علي عبد الله صالح
رئيس الجمهورية

第五十四条 废止 1992 年第（29）号共和国法令，以 1997 年第（34）号法令替代。同时废止任何与本法条文和规定相抵触或相违背的规定或条文。

第五十五条 本法自官方公报上公布之日起生效。

共和国总统 阿里 · 阿卜杜拉 · 萨利赫
伊历 1431 年 8 月 26 日
公历 2010 年 8 月 7 日
于萨那颁布此法